THIRD EDITION

The Making of the West

PEOPLES AND CULTURES

THIRD EDITION

The Making of the West

PEOPLES AND CULTURES

Volume I: To 1740

Lynn Hunt
University of California, Los Angeles

Thomas R. Martin
College of the Holy Cross

Barbara H. Rosenwein
Loyola University Chicago

R. Po-chia Hsia
Pennsylvania State University

Bonnie G. Smith
Rutgers University

BEDFORD/ST. MARTIN'S

Boston ■ New York

For Bedford/St. Martin's

Executive Editor for History: Mary Dougherty
Director of Development for History: Jane Knetzger
Senior Developmental Editor: Heidi L. Hood
Senior Production Editor: Karen S. Baart
Senior Production Supervisor: Dennis Conroy
Executive Marketing Manager: Jenna Bookin Barry
Editorial Assistants: Lindsay DiGianvittorio and Katherine Flynn
Production Associate: Lindsay DiGianvittorio
Production Assistant: David Ayers
Copyeditor: Janet Renard
Text Design: Janis Owens, Books By Design, Inc.
Page Layout: Boynton Hue Studio
Photo Research: Gillian Speeth
Indexer: Leoni Z. McVey & Associates, Inc.
Cover Design: Donna Lee Dennison
Cover Art: Arrival of the Crusaders in Constantinople for the Battle between the French and the Turks 1147–1148 A.D. From Grandes Chroniques de France, illuminated by Jean Fouquet, Tours, c. 1455–1460. Bibliothèque Nationale de France.
Cartography: Mapping Specialists Limited
Composition: Aptara
Printing and Binding: R.R. Donnelley & Sons Company

President: Joan E. Feinberg
Editorial Director: Denise B. Wydra
Director of Marketing: Karen Melton Soeltz
Director of Editing, Design, and Production: Marcia Cohen
Managing Editor: Elizabeth M. Schaaf

Library of Congress Control Number: 2007927405

Manufactured in the United States of America.

2   3   4   5   6   12   11   10   09   08

For information, write: Bedford/St. Martin's, 75 Arlington Street, Boston, MA 02116 (617-399-4000)

ISBN-10: 0–312–45294–2   ISBN-13: 978–0–312–45294–0   (combined edition)
ISBN-10: 0–312–45295–0   ISBN-13: 978–0–312–45295–7   (Vol. I)
ISBN-10: 0–312–45296–9   ISBN-13: 978–0–312–45296–4   (Vol. II)
ISBN-10: 0–312–46508–4   ISBN-13: 978–0–312–46508–7   (Vol. A)
ISBN-10: 0–312–46509–2   ISBN-13: 978–0–312–46509–4   (Vol. B)
ISBN-10: 0–312–46510–6   ISBN-13: 978–0–312–46510–0   (Vol. C)
ISBN-10: 0–312–46663–3   ISBN-13: 978–0–312–46663–3   (high school edition)

Preface

WHEN A BOOK GOES INTO its third edition, authors feel affirmed but also encouraged to do even better. Instructors who have read and used our book confirmed that the new synthesis we offered in the first and second editions enabled them to bring the most current conceptualizations of the West into their classroom. From the start, our goal has been to create a text that demonstrates that the history of the West is the story of an ongoing process, not a finished result with only one fixed meaning. We wanted also to make clear that there is no one Western people or culture that has existed from the beginning until now. Instead, the history of the West includes many different peoples and cultures. To convey these ideas, we have written a sustained story of the West's development in a broad, global context that reveals the cross-cultural interactions fundamental to the shaping of Western politics, societies, cultures, and economies. Indeed, the first chapter opens with a section on the origins and contested meaning of *Western civilization*. In this conversation, we emphasize our theme of cultural borrowing between the peoples of Europe and their neighbors that has characterized Western civilization from the beginning. Continuing this approach in subsequent chapters, we have insisted on an expanded vision of the West that includes the United States and fully incorporates eastern Europe and Scandinavia. Through the depth and breadth embraced in our narrative, we have been able to offer sustained treatment of crucial topics such as Islam and provide a more thorough treatment of globalization than any competing text. Our aim has been to convey the relevance of Western history throughout the book as essential background to today's events, from debate over European Union membership to conflict in the Middle East. Instructors have found this synthesis essential for helping students understand the West in today's ever-globalizing world.

Equally valuable to instructors has been the way our book is organized with a chronological framework to help students understand how political, social, cultural, and economic histories have influenced each other over time. We know from our own teaching that introductory students need a solid chronological framework, one with enough familiar benchmarks to make the material easy to grasp. Each chapter treats all the main events, people, and themes of a period in which the West significantly changed; thus, students learn about political events and social and cultural developments as they unfolded. This chronological integration also accords with our belief that it is important, above all else, for students to see the interconnections among varieties of historical experience — between politics and cultures, between public events and private experiences, between wars and diplomacy and everyday life. Our chronological synthesis provides a unique benefit to students: it makes these relationships clear while highlighting the major changes of each age. For teachers, our chronological approach ensures a balanced account and provides the opportunity to present themes within their greater context. But perhaps best of all, this approach provides a text that reveals history as a process that is constantly alive, subject to pressures, and able to surprise us.

Despite gratifying praise from the many reviewers who helped shape this edition, we felt we could do even more to help students and instructors. First, we have further highlighted thematic coverage to help students discern major developments. The most extensive changes we made to this end appear in the Renaissance and Reformation chapters; we rewrote and reorganized the three chapters of the second edition to create a more meaningful two. Chapter 13 includes new coverage of Renaissance art and architecture and the Ottomans' influence on the West, while Chapter 14 offers new consideration of the European Reformation in the context of global exploration and the spread of print culture. We have worked to make key developments clearer in other chapters as well. We united and expanded the discussion of early Canaanites and Hebrews in Chapter 2, added extended coverage of the first and second crusades in Chapter 10, refocused a section on religious fervor and later crusades in Chapter 11, consolidated coverage of the scientific revolution in Chapter 15, and combined and strengthened a section on industrialization in Chapter 21.

A second way we have chosen to help students identify and absorb major developments is by adding and refining signposts to guide student reading. Most notably, we have added new chapter-opening focus questions. Posed at the end of the opening vignettes, these single questions encapsulate the essence of the era covered in the chapter and guide students toward the core message of the chapter. To further help students as they read, we have worked hard to ensure that chapter and section overviews outline the central points of each section in the clearest manner possible. In addition, we have condensed some material to better illuminate key ideas.

A third way we have made this book more useful is by adding a special feature called Seeing History. We know that today's students are attuned to visual sources of information, yet they do not always receive systematic instruction in how to "read" or think critically about such sources. Similarly, we know instructors often wish to use visual evidence as the basis of class discussion but do not have materials appropriate for introductory students readily at hand. We have crafted our Seeing History features to address these needs. Each single-page Seeing History feature contains a pair of images—such as paintings, sculpture, photographs, and artifacts—accompanied by background information and probing questions designed to guide students through the process of reading images as historical evidence and to help them explore different perspectives and significant historical developments.

Finally, as always, we have incorporated the latest scholarly findings throughout the book so that students and instructors alike have a text that they can confidently rely on. In the third edition, we have included new and updated discussions of topics such as the demography of the later Roman republic and its effect on social change, the social and political causes of the Great Famine of the early fourteenth century, the emergence of the plague in Europe, the development of new slave-trading routes in the seventeenth and eighteenth centuries, the refugee crisis following World War II, and the enlargement of the European Union, among others.

Aided by a fresh and welcoming design, new pedagogical aids, and new multimedia offerings that give students and instructors interactive tools for study and teaching, we believe we have created a new edition even more suited to today's Western civilization courses. In writing *The Making of the West: Peoples and Cultures*, we have aimed to communicate the vitality and excitement as well as the fundamental importance of history. Students should be enthused about history; we hope we have conveyed some of our own enthusiasm and love for the study of history in these pages.

Pedagogy and Features

We know from our own teaching that students need all the help they can get in absorbing and making sense of information, thinking analytically, and understanding that history itself is debated and constantly revised. With these goals in mind, we retained the class-tested learning and teaching aids that worked well in the first and second editions, but we have also done more to help students distill the central story of each age and give them more opportunities to develop their own historical skills.

The third edition incorporates more aids to help students sort out what is most important to learn while they read. *New chapter focus questions* guide them toward the central themes of the era and the most significant information they should take away from their reading. Boldface *key terms* have been updated to concentrate on likely test items and have been expanded to include people. To help students read and study, the key terms and people are defined in a *new running glossary* at the bottom of pages and collected in a comprehensive *glossary* at the end of the book.

The study tools introduced in the previous edition continue to help students check their understanding of the chapters and the periods they cover. *Review questions*, strategically placed at the end of each major section, help students recall and assimilate core points in digestible increments. The *Chapter Review section* provides a clear study plan with a table of important events, a list of key terms and people, section review questions repeated from within the chapter, and "Making Connections" questions that encourage students to analyze chapter material or make comparisons within or beyond the chapter. *Vivid chapter-opening anecdotes* with overviews and *chapter outlines*, *timelines*, and *conclusions* further reinforce the central developments covered in the reading.

But like a clear narrative synthesis, strong pedagogical support is not enough on its own to encourage active learning. To reflect the richness of the themes in the text and offer further opportunities for historical investigation, we include a rich assortment of *single-source documents* (two per chapter). Nothing can give students a more direct experience of the past than original voices, and we have endeavored to let those voices speak, whether it is Frederick Barbarossa replying to the Romans when they offer him the emperor's crown, Marie de Sévigné's description of the French court, or an ordinary person's account of the outbreak of the Russian Revolution.

Accompanying these primary-source features are our unique features that extend the narrative by revealing the process of interpretation, providing a solid introduction to historical argument and critical thinking, and capturing the excitement of historical investigation:

- NEW *Seeing History* features guide students through the process of reading images as historical evidence. Each of the ten features provides a pair of images with background information and questions that encourage visual analysis. Examples include comparisons of pagan and Christian sarcophagi, Persian and Arabic coins, Romanesque and Gothic naves, pre- and post–French Revolution attire, and Italian propaganda posters from World War I.

- *Contrasting Views* features provide three or four often conflicting primary-source accounts of a central event, person, or development, such as Julius Caesar, the First Crusade, Joan of Arc, Martin Luther, the English Civil War, and late-nineteenth-century migration.

- *New Sources, New Perspectives* features show students how historians continue to develop fresh insights using new kinds of evidence about the past, from tree rings to Holocaust museums.

- *Terms of History* features explain the meanings of some of the most important and contested terms in the history of the West and show how those meanings have developed — and changed — over time. For example, the discussion of *progress* shows how the term took root in the eighteenth century and has been contested in the twentieth.

- *Taking Measure* features introduce students to the intriguing stories revealed by quantitative analysis. Each feature highlights a chart, table, graph, or map of historical statistics that illuminates an important political, social, or cultural development.

The book's map program has been widely praised as the most comprehensive and inviting of any competing survey text. In each chapter, we offer three types of maps, each with a distinct role in conveying information to students. Four to five *full-size maps* show major developments, two to four *"spot" maps* — small maps positioned within the discussion right where students need them — aid students' understanding of crucial issues, and *"Mapping the West"* summary maps at the end of each chapter provide a snapshot of the West at the close of a transformative period and help students visualize the West's changing contours over time. For this edition, we have carefully considered each map, simplified where possible to better highlight essential information, and clarified and updated borders and labels where needed.

We have striven to integrate art as fully as possible into the narrative and to show its value for teaching and learning. ***Over 425 illustrations***, carefully chosen to reflect this edition's broad topical coverage and geographic inclusion, reinforce the text and show the varieties of visual sources from which historians build their narratives and interpretations. All artifacts, illustrations, paintings, and photographs are contemporaneous with the chapter; there are no anachronistic illustrations. Furthermore, along with the new Seeing History features, our substantive captions for the maps and art help students learn how to read visuals, and we have frequently included specific questions or suggestions for comparisons that might be developed. Specially designed visual exercises in the Online Study Guide supplement this approach. A new page design for the third edition supports our goal of intertwining the art and the narrative, and makes the new study tools readily accessible.

Supplements

As with previous editions, a well-integrated ancillary program supports *The Making of the West: Peoples and Cultures*. Each print and new media resource has been carefully revised to provide a host of practical teaching and learning aids. (Visit the online catalog at **bedfordstmartins.com/hunt/catalog** for ordering information and special packaging options.)

For Students

PRINT RESOURCES

Sources of THE MAKING OF THE WEST, Third Edition — Volumes I (to 1740) and II (since 1500) — by Katharine J. Lualdi, University of Southern Maine. This companion sourcebook provides written and visual sources to accompany each chapter of *The Making of the West*. Political, social, and cultural documents offer a variety of perspectives that complement the textbook and encourage students to make connections between narrative history and primary sources. Short chapter summaries and document headnotes contextualize the wide array of sources and perspectives represented, while discussion questions guide students' reading and promote historical thinking skills. The third edition features five or more written documents per chapter and one-third more visual sources. Available free when packaged with the text and now available in the e-book (see below).

NEW Trade Books. Titles published by sister companies Farrar, Straus and Giroux; Henry Holt and Company; Hill and Wang; Picador; and St. Martin's Press are available at a 50 percent discount when packaged with Bedford/St. Martin's textbooks. For more information, visit **bedfordstmartins.com/tradeup**.

NEW *The Bedford Glossary for European History*. This handy supplement for the survey course gives students historically contextualized definitions for hundreds of terms — from Abbasids to Zionism — that students will encounter in lectures, reading, and exams. Available free when packaged with the text.

Bedford Series in History and Culture. Over 100 titles in this highly praised series combine first-rate scholarship, historical narrative, and important primary documents for undergraduate courses. Each book is brief, inexpensive, and focused on a specific topic or period. Package discounts are available.

NEW MEDIA RESOURCES

NEW *The Making of the West e-Book with e-Sources*. This one-of-a-kind online resource integrates the text of *The Making of the West* with the written and visual sources of the companion sourcebook *Sources of THE MAKING OF THE WEST* and the self-testing and activities of the Online Study Guide into one easy-to-use e-book. With search functions stronger than in any competing text, this e-book is an ideal study and reference tool for students. Instructors can easily add their own documents, images, and other class material to customize the text.

Online Study Guide at bedfordstmartins.com/hunt. The popular Online Study Guide for *The Making of the West* is a free and uniquely personalized learning tool to help students master themes and information presented in the textbook and improve their historical skills. Assessment quizzes let students evaluate their comprehension and provide them with customized plans for further study through a variety of activities. Instructors can monitor students' progress through the online Quiz Gradebook or receive e-mail updates.

A Student's Online Guide to History Reference Sources at bedfordstmartins.com/hunt. This Web site provides links to history-related databases, indexes, and journals, plus contact information for state, provincial, local, and professional history organizations.

The Bedford Research Room at bedfordstmartins.com/hunt. The Research Room, drawn from Mike Palmquist's *The Bedford Researcher*, offers a wealth of resources — including interactive tutorials, research activities, student writing samples, and links to hundreds of other places online — to support students in courses across the disciplines. The site also offers instructors a library of helpful instructional tools.

The Bedford Bibliographer at bedfordstmartins.com/hunt. *The Bedford Bibliographer*, a simple but powerful Web-based tool, assists students with the process of collecting sources and generates bibliographies in four commonly used documentation styles.

Research and Documentation Online at bedfordstmartins.com/hunt. This Web site provides clear advice on how to integrate primary and secondary sources into research papers, how to cite sources correctly, and how to format in MLA, APA, Chicago, or CBE style.

The St. Martin's Tutorial on Avoiding Plagiarism at bedfordstmartins.com/hunt. This online tutorial reviews the consequences of plagiarism and explains what sources to acknowledge, how to keep good notes, how to organize research, and how to integrate sources appropriately. The tutorial includes exercises to help students practice integrating sources and recognize acceptable summaries.

For Instructors

PRINT RESOURCES

Instructor's Resource Manual. This helpful manual by Malia Formes (Western Kentucky University), Dakota Hamilton (Humboldt State University), and Paul A. Townend (University of North Carolina Wilmington) offers both first-time and experienced teachers a wealth of tools for structuring and customizing Western civilization history courses of different sizes. For each chapter in the textbook, the *Instructor's Resource Manual* includes an outline of chapter themes; a chapter summary; lecture and discussion topics; film and literature suggestions; writing and class-presentation assignments; research topic suggestions; and in-class exercises for working with maps, illustrations, and sources. The new edition includes model answers for the review questions in the book as well as a chapter-by-chapter guide to all the supplements available with *The Making of the West.*

Transparencies. A set of over 200 full-color acetate transparencies for *The Making of the West* includes all full-sized maps and many images from the text.

NEW MEDIA RESOURCES

NEW HistoryClass. Bedford/St. Martin's online learning space for history gives you the right tools and the rich content to create your course, your way. An interactive e-book and e-reader enable you to easily assign relevant textbook sections and primary documents. Access to the acclaimed content library, Make History, provides unlimited access to thousands of maps, images, documents, and Web links. The tried-and-true content of the Online Study Guide offers a range of activities to help students access their progress, study more effectively, and improve their critical thinking skills. Customize provided content and mix in your own with ease—everything in HistoryClass is integrated to work together in the same space.

Instructor's Resource CD-ROM. This disc provides PowerPoint presentations built around chapter outlines, maps, figures; selected images from the textbook, plus jpeg versions of all maps, figures, and selected images; and questions for instructor use with i>clicker, a personal response system.

Computerized Test Bank—by Malia Formes, Western Kentucky University; available on CD-ROM. This fully updated test bank offers over 80 exercises per chapter, including multiple-choice, identification, timelines, map labeling and analysis, source analysis, and full-length essay questions. Instructors can customize quizzes, edit both questions and answers, as well as export them to a variety of formats, including WebCT and Blackboard. The disc includes answer keys and essay outlines.

Book Companion Site at bedfordstmartins.com/hunt. The companion Web site gathers all the electronic resources for *The Making of the West,* including the Online Study Guide and related Quiz Gradebook, at a single Web address, providing convenient links to lecture, assignment, and research materials such as PowerPoint chapter outlines and the digital libraries at Make History.

NEW Make History at bedfordstmartins.com/hunt. Comprising the content of Bedford/St. Martin's five acclaimed online libraries—Map Central, the Bedford History Image Library, DocLinks, HistoryLinks, and PlaceLinks, Make History provides one-stop access to relevant digital content including maps, images, documents, and Web links. Students and instructors alike can search this free, easy-to-use database by keyword, topic, date, or specific chapter of *The Making of the West* and download the content they find. Instructors can also create entire collections of content and store them online for later use or post their collections to the Web to share with students.

Content for Course Management Systems. A variety of student and instructor resources developed for this textbook is ready for use in course management systems such as Blackboard, WebCT, and other platforms. This e-content includes nearly all of the offerings from the book's Online Study Guide as well as the book's test bank.

Videos and Multimedia. A wide assortment of videos and multimedia CD-ROMs on various topics in European history is available to qualified adopters.

Acknowledgments

In the vital process of revision, the authors have benefited from repeated critical readings by many talented scholars and teachers. Our sincere thanks go to the following instructors, whose comments often challenged us to rethink or justify our interpretations and who always provided a check on accuracy down to the smallest detail.

Abel Alves, *Ball State University*
Gene Barnett, *Calhoun Community College*
Giovanna Benadusi, *University of South Florida*

Marjorie K. Berman, *Red Rocks Community College*

Gregory Bruess, *University of Northern Iowa*

James M. Burns, *Clemson University*

Kevin W. Caldwell, *Blue Ridge Community College*

William R. Caraher, *University of North Dakota*

Joseph J. Casino, *Villanova University, St. Joseph's University*

Sara Chapman, *Oakland University*

Michael S. Cole, *Florida Gulf Coast University*

Robert Cole, *Utah State University*

Theodore F. Cook, *William Patterson University*

Jo Ann Hoeppner Moran Cruz, *Georgetown University*

Luanne Dagley, *Pellissippi State Technical Community College*

Frederick H. Dotolo III, *St. John Fisher College*

Mari Firkatian, *University of Hartford*

David D. Flaten, *Tompkins Cortland Community College*

Ellen Pratt Fout, *The Ohio State University*

Rebecca Friedman, *Florida International University*

Helen Grady, *Springside School, Philadelphia, Pennsylvania*

Padhraig S. Higgins, *Pennsylvania State University*

Ronald K. Huch, *Eastern Kentucky University*

Michael Innis-Jiménez, *William Paterson University*

Jason M. Kelly, *Indiana University–Purdue University Indianapolis*

Nathaniel Knight, *Seton Hall University*

Elizabeth A. Lehfeldt, *Cleveland State University*

Charles Levine, *Mesa Community College*

Keith P. Luria, *North Carolina State University*

Kathryn Lynass, *Arizona State University*

Michael Mackey, *Community College of Denver*

John McManamon, *Loyola University*

Anthony Makowski, *Delaware County Community College*

John W. Mauer, *Tri-County Technical College*

Lynn Wood Mollenauer, *University of North Carolina–Wilmington*

Michelle Anne Novak, *Houston Community College*

Jason M. Osborne, *Northern Kentucky University*

James A. Ross-Nazzal, *Houston Community College–Southeast College*

Daniel Sarefield, *The Ohio State University*

Nancy E. Shockley, *New Mexico State University*

Dionysios Skentzis, *College of DuPage*

Daniel Stephen, *University of Colorado at Boulder*

Charles R. Sullivan, *University of Dallas*

Emily Sohmer Tai, *Queensborough Community College of the City University of New York*

David Tengwall, *Anne Arundel Community College*

Andrew Thomas, *Purdue University*

Paul A. Townend, *University of North Carolina–Wilmington*

David Ulbrich, *Ball State University*

Karen T. Wagner, *Pikes Peak Community College*

William Welch Jr., *Troy University*

David K. White, *McHenry County College*

James Theron Wilson, *Ball State University*

Many colleagues, friends, and family members have made contributions to this work. They know how grateful we are. We also wish to acknowledge and thank the publishing team at Bedford/St. Martin's who did so much to bring this revised edition to completion: president Joan Feinberg, editorial director Denise Wydra, publisher for history Mary Dougherty, director of development for history Jane Knetzger, senior editor Heidi Hood, senior editor Louise Townsend, senior editor Sara Wise, freelance editors Betty Slack and Dale Anderson, editorial assistant and production associate Lindsay DiGianvittorio, executive marketing manager Jenna Bookin Barry, senior production editor Karen Baart, managing editor Elizabeth Schaaf, art researcher Gillian Speeth, text designer Janis Owens, page makeup artist Cia Boynton, cover designer Donna Dennison, and copyeditor Janet Renard.

Our students' questions and concerns have shaped much of this work, and we welcome all our readers' suggestions, queries, and criticisms. Please contact us at our respective institutions or via **history@bedfordstmartins.com**.

Brief Contents

Contents

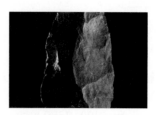

CHAPTER 3
The Greek Golden Age, c. 500–c. 400 B.C.E. 69

CHAPTER 4
From the Classical to the Hellenistic World, 400–30 B.C.E. 103

CHAPTER 7
The Transformation of the Roman Empire, 284–600 C.E.   *195*

CHAPTER 8
Islam, Byzantium, and the West, 600–750   *231*

CHAPTER 17
The Atlantic System and Its Consequences, 1690–1740 *519*

Maps and Figures

Maps

CHAPTER 14

CHAPTER 15

CHAPTER 16

CHAPTER 17

Figures

Special Features

Documents

Contrasting Views

New Sources, New Perspectives

Terms of History

Seeing History

Taking Measure

To the Student

This guide to your textbook introduces the unique features that will help you understand the fascinating story of Western Civilization.

The Roman Empire
44 B.C.E.–284 C.E.

Tools to help you focus on what is important

Read the **chapter outlines** to preview the topics and themes to come.

In 203 C.E., Vibia Perpetua, wealthy and twenty-two years old, sat in a Carthage jail, nursing her infant while awaiting execution; she had received the death sentence for refusing to sacrifice to the gods for the Roman emperor's health and safety. One morning the jailer dragged her off to the city's main square, where a crowd had gathered. Perpetua described in a journal what happened when the local governor tried to persuade her to save her life:

> My father came carrying my son, crying "Perform the sacrifice; take pity on your baby!" Then the governor said, "Think of your old father; show pity for your little child! Offer the sacrifice for the imperial family's welfare." "I refuse," I answered. "Are you a Christian?" asked the governor. "Yes." When my father would not stop trying to change my mind, the governor ordered him flung to the earth and whipped with a rod. I felt sorry for my father; it seemed they were beating me. I pitied his pathetic old age.

The brutality of Perpetua's punishment failed to break her: gored by a wild cow and

Perpetua ... ian faith requi ... of faithfulness

Augustus created a disguised monarchy—the *principate*—to end the violence, ingeniously masking his creation as a restoration of the republic. He retained the republic's name and its institutions for sharing power—the Senate, the consuls, the courts—while in reality making himself sole ruler. He concealed his monarchy by referring to himself not as a *rex* ("king") but only with the informal title *princeps* ("first man among social equals"), an honorary designation from the republic indicating general agreement about who was the leading individual of the time, or who was the most distinguished Roman senator. *Princeps* is therefore the position we call "emperor." Each new princeps was supposed to be designated only with the Senate's approval, but in practice each ruler chose his own successor, as in a monarchy. More than a thousand years would pass before republican government reappeared in Western civilization.

The challenge for Romans during the empire was to maintain political stability and prosperity. Augustus's political system brought peace for two hundred years, except for a struggle between generals for rule in 69 C.E. This **Pax Romana** (from

principate: Roman political system invented by Augustus as a disguised monarchy with the princeps ("first man") as emperor.

Pax Romana: The two centuries of relative peace and prosperity in the Roman Empire under the early principate begun by Augustus.

ened the principate and destabilized the empire. The emergence of Christianity created a new religion that would over centuries transform the Roman world, but this change also created tension because the growing presence of Christians made other Romans worry about punishment from the gods. In the third century C.E., a crisis developed when generals competing to rule reignited prolonged civil war. By the 280s C.E., Roman government teetered once more on the brink of disintegration.

FOCUS QUESTION: How did Augustus's "restored republic" successfully keep the Pax Romana for more than two centuries, and why did it fail in the third century?

Creating the Pax Romana

Inventing tradition takes time. Augustus created his new political system gradually; as his biographer expressed it, Augustus "made haste slowly." Augustus succeeded because he won the struggle for power, reinvented government, and built legitimacy and loyalty by communicating an image of himself as a dedicated leader. His professed respect for tradition and his reign's length established

Read the **focus questions** at the start of each chapter to think about the main ideas you should look for as you read.

Greek models. In works such as the Prima Porta statue, Augustus had himself portrayed as serene and dignified, not careworn and sick, as he often was. As with architecture, Augustus used sculpture to project a calm and competent image of himself as the "restorer of the republic" and founder of a new age for Rome.

REVIEW: How did the peace gained through Augustus's "restoration of the republic" affect Romans' lives?

Maintaining the Pax Romana

Augustus made political changes to promote stability and prosperity (and his personal glory)—above all by preventing civil war—but his new system lacked a way to block struggles for power when

Timeline:
- 30 Octavian conquers Egypt
- 27 Augustus inaugurates *principate*
- 30 Jesus crucified
- 64 Rome burns; Nero blames Christians
- 80s Domitian's campaigns against invaders

B.C.E. — 0 — 50 C.E. — 100 C.E.

- 69 Civil war during Year of the Four Emperors
- 70 Titus destroys Jewish temple
- 70–90 New Testament Gospels

Consult the **running glossary** for definitions of the bolded **Key Terms and People.**

Preview chapter events and keep track of time with **chapter timelines.**

Use the **review questions** at the end of each major section to check your understanding of key concepts.

Special features introduce the way historians work and help you learn to think critically about the past.

Numerous **individual primary-source documents** offer direct experiences of the past and the opportunity to consider sources historians use.

Contrasting Views provide three or four often conflicting eyewitness accounts of a central event, person, or development to foster critical thinking skills.

New Sources, New Perspectives show how new evidence leads historians to fresh insights—and sometimes new interpretations.

Seeing History pairs two visuals with background information and probing questions to encourage analysis of images as historical evidence.

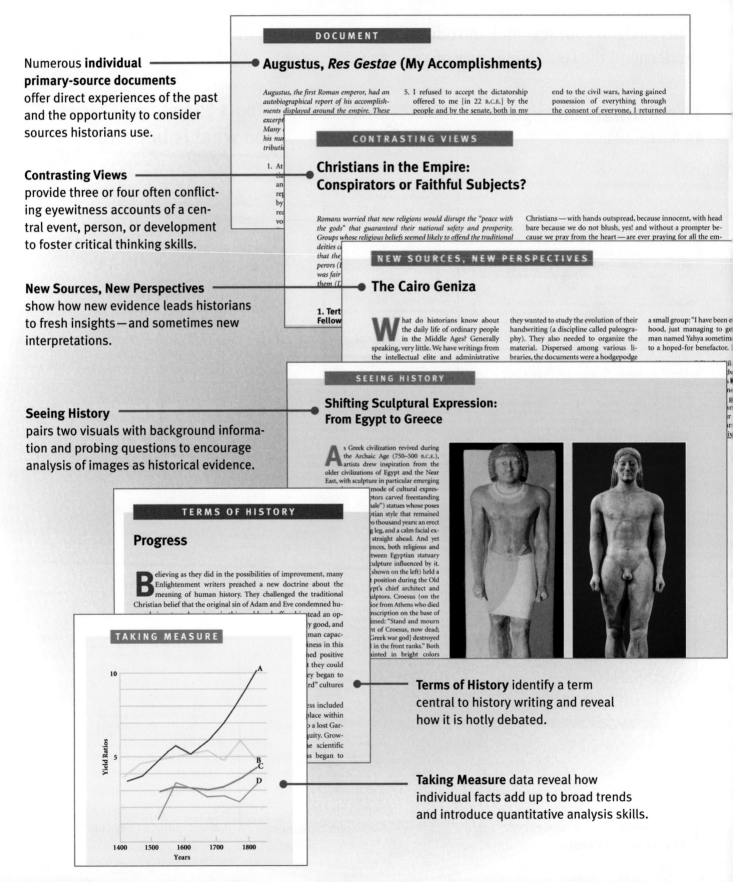

DOCUMENT

Augustus, *Res Gestae* (My Accomplishments)

Augustus, the first Roman emperor, had an autobiographical report of his accomplishments displayed around the empire. These excerpt... Many ... his nu... tributi...

1. At ...
an ...
rep ...
by ...
rea ...
vo ...

5. I refused to accept the dictatorship offered to me [in 22 B.C.E.] by the people and by the senate, both in my

end to the civil wars, having gained possession of everything through the consent of everyone, I returned

CONTRASTING VIEWS

Christians in the Empire: Conspirators or Faithful Subjects?

Romans worried that new religions would disrupt the "peace with the gods" that guaranteed their national safety and prosperity. Groups whose religious beliefs seemed likely to offend the traditional deities ... that the ... perors (... was fair ... them (...

1. Tert...
Fellow...

Christians—with hands outspread, because innocent, with head bare because we do not blush, yes! and without a prompter because we pray from the heart—are ever praying for all the em-

NEW SOURCES, NEW PERSPECTIVES

The Cairo Geniza

What do historians know about the daily life of ordinary people in the Middle Ages? Generally speaking, very little. We have writings from the intellectual elite and administrative

they wanted to study the evolution of their handwriting (a discipline called paleography). They also needed to organize the material. Dispersed among various libraries, the documents were a hodgepodge

a small group: "I have been e... hood, just managing to ge... man named Yahya sometim... to a hoped-for benefactor. ...

SEEING HISTORY

Shifting Sculptural Expression: From Egypt to Greece

As Greek civilization revived during the Archaic Age (750–500 B.C.E.), artists drew inspiration from the older civilizations of Egypt and the Near East, with sculpture in particular emerging ... mode of cultural expres-... tors carved freestanding ... hale") statues whose poses ... tian style that remained ... o thousand years: an erect ... g leg, and a calm facial ex-... straight ahead. And yet ... ences, both religious and ... tween Egyptian statuary ... culpture influenced by it. ... shown on the left) held a ... t position during the Old ... ypt's chief architect and ... ulptors. Croesus (on the ... ior from Athens who died ... nscription on the base of ... imed: "Stand and mourn ... t of Croesus, now dead; ... Greek war god] destroyed ... l in the front ranks." Both ... inted in bright colors

Terms of History identify a term central to history writing and reveal how it is hotly debated.

TERMS OF HISTORY

Progress

Believing as they did in the possibilities of improvement, many Enlightenment writers preached a new doctrine about the meaning of human history. They challenged the traditional Christian belief that the original sin of Adam and Eve condemned hu... ... ... tead an op-... y good, and ... man capac-... iness in this ... ed positive ... t they could ... ey began to ... rd" cultures

...ss included ... place within ... o a lost Gar-... quity. Grow-... e scientific ... s began to

Taking Measure data reveal how individual facts add up to broad trends and introduce quantitative analysis skills.

TAKING MEASURE

Yield Ratios vs. Years (1400–1800), with curves labeled A, B, C, D

Art and maps extend the chapter, and help you analyze images and put events in geographical context.

MAP 12.1 Europe in the Time of Frederick II, r. 1212–1250
King of Sicily and Germany and emperor as well, Frederick ruled over territory that encircled—and threatened—the papacy. Excommunicated several times, Frederick spent much of his career fighting the pope's forces. In the process he made so many concessions to the German princes that the emperor thenceforth had little power in Germany. Meanwhile, rulers of smaller states, such as England, France, and Castile-León, were increasing their power and authority.

Full-size maps show major historical developments and carry informative captions.

"Spot" maps offer geographical details right where you need them.

Lombard Italy, Early Eighth Century

Mapping the West summary maps provide a snapshot of the West at the close of each chapter.

Major Religions in the West, c. 1150
The broad washes of color on this map tell a striking story: by 1150, there were three major religions, each corresponding to a broad region. To the west, north of the Mediterranean Sea, Catholic Christianity held sway; to the east, the Greek Orthodox Church was ascendant; all along the southern Mediterranean, Islam triumphed. Only a few places defied this logic: one was a tiny outpost of Catholic crusaders who ruled over a largely Muslim population. What this map does not show, however, are the details: Jewish communities in many cities, lively varieties of Islamic beliefs within the Muslim world, communities of Coptic Christians in Egypt, and scattered groups of heretics in Catholic lands.

The Murder of Thomas Becket
Almost immediately after King Henry II's knights murdered Archbishop Thomas Becket in his church at Canterbury, Becket was viewed as a martyr. In this early depiction of the event, one of the murderers knocks off Becket's cap, while another hits the arm of Becket's supporter, who holds the bishop's cross-staff. (British Library, London, UK/The Bridgeman Art Library.)

■ For more help analyzing this image, see the visual activity for this chapter in the Online Study Guide at bedfordstmartins.com/hunt.

Web references direct you to visual activities designed to help you analyze images.

Tools to help you remember the chapter's main points and do further research

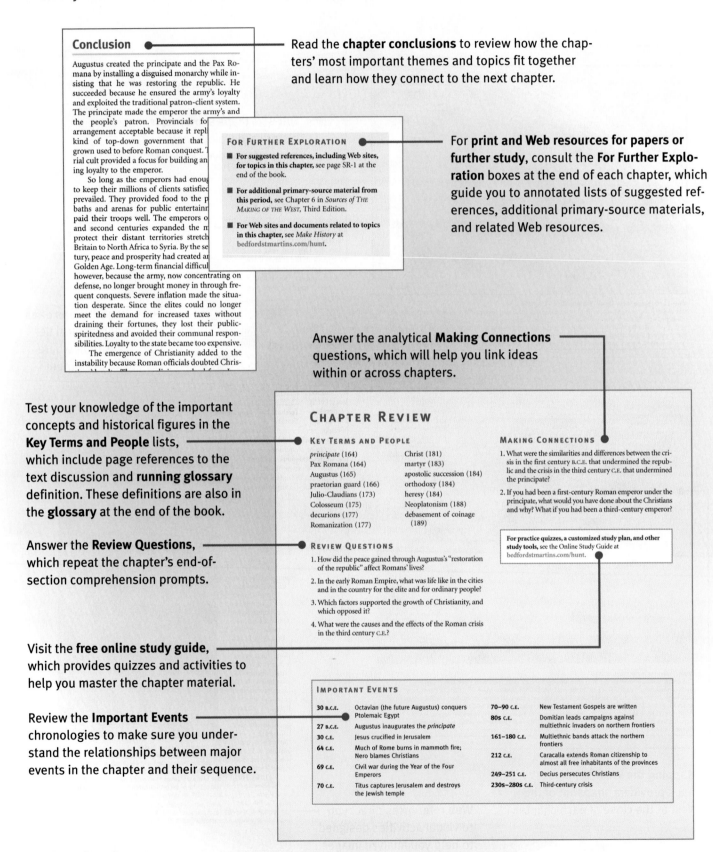

Conclusion

Augustus created the principate and the Pax Romana by installing a disguised monarchy while insisting that he was restoring the republic. He succeeded because he ensured the army's loyalty and exploited the traditional patron-client system. The principate made the emperor the army's and the people's patron. Provincials fo[und this] arrangement acceptable because it repli[cated the] kind of top-down government that [they had] grown used to before Roman conquest. T[he impe-] rial cult provided a focus for building an[d renew-] ing loyalty to the emperor.

So long as the emperors had enoug[h money] to keep their millions of clients satisfie[d, peace] prevailed. They provided food to the p[oor and] baths and arenas for public entertainm[ent, and] paid their troops well. The emperors o[f the first] and second centuries expanded the m[ilitary to] protect their distant territories stretch[ing from] Britain to North Africa to Syria. By the se[cond cen-] tury, peace and prosperity had created a[n imperial] Golden Age. Long-term financial difficul[ties arose,] however, because the army, now concentrating on defense, no longer brought money in through frequent conquests. Severe inflation made the situation desperate. Since the elites could no longer meet the demand for increased taxes without draining their fortunes, they lost their public-spiritedness and avoided their communal responsibilities. Loyalty to the state became too expensive.

The emergence of Christianity added to the instability because Roman officials doubted Chris[tians' loyalty. The new religion evoked fierce...]

Read the **chapter conclusions** to review how the chapters' most important themes and topics fit together and learn how they connect to the next chapter.

FOR FURTHER EXPLORATION

■ **For suggested references, including Web sites, for topics in this chapter,** see page SR-1 at the end of the book.

■ **For additional primary-source material from this period,** see Chapter 6 in *Sources of THE MAKING OF THE WEST*, Third Edition.

■ **For Web sites and documents related to topics in this chapter,** see *Make History* at bedfordstmartins.com/hunt.

For **print and Web resources for papers or further study,** consult the **For Further Exploration** boxes at the end of each chapter, which guide you to annotated lists of suggested references, additional primary-source materials, and related Web resources.

Answer the analytical **Making Connections** questions, which will help you link ideas within or across chapters.

Test your knowledge of the important concepts and historical figures in the **Key Terms and People** lists, which include page references to the text discussion and **running glossary** definition. These definitions are also in the **glossary** at the end of the book.

CHAPTER REVIEW

KEY TERMS AND PEOPLE

principate (164)
Pax Romana (164)
Augustus (165)
praetorian guard (166)
Julio-Claudians (173)
Colosseum (175)
decurions (177)
Romanization (177)

Christ (181)
martyr (183)
apostolic succession (184)
orthodoxy (184)
heresy (184)
Neoplatonism (188)
debasement of coinage (189)

MAKING CONNECTIONS

1. What were the similarities and differences between the crisis in the first century B.C.E. that undermined the republic and the crisis in the third century C.E. that undermined the principate?

2. If you had been a first-century Roman emperor under the principate, what would you have done about the Christians and why? What if you had been a third-century emperor?

For practice quizzes, a customized study plan, and other study tools, see the Online Study Guide at bedfordstmartins.com/hunt.

Answer the **Review Questions,** which repeat the chapter's end-of-section comprehension prompts.

REVIEW QUESTIONS

1. How did the peace gained through Augustus's "restoration of the republic" affect Romans' lives?

2. In the early Roman Empire, what was life like in the cities and in the country for the elite and for ordinary people?

3. Which factors supported the growth of Christianity, and which opposed it?

4. What were the causes and the effects of the Roman crisis in the third century C.E.?

Visit the **free online study guide,** which provides quizzes and activities to help you master the chapter material.

Review the **Important Events** chronologies to make sure you understand the relationships between major events in the chapter and their sequence.

IMPORTANT EVENTS

30 B.C.E.	Octavian (the future Augustus) conquers Ptolemaic Egypt	**70–90 C.E.**	New Testament Gospels are written
27 B.C.E.	Augustus inaugurates the *principate*	**80s C.E.**	Domitian leads campaigns against multiethnic invaders on northern frontiers
30 C.E.	Jesus crucified in Jerusalem	**161–180 C.E.**	Multiethnic bands attack the northern frontiers
64 C.E.	Much of Rome burns in mammoth fire; Nero blames Christians	**212 C.E.**	Caracalla extends Roman citizenship to almost all free inhabitants of the provinces
69 C.E.	Civil war during the Year of the Four Emperors	**249–251 C.E.**	Decius persecutes Christians
70 C.E.	Titus captures Jerusalem and destroys the Jewish temple	**230s–280s C.E.**	Third-century crisis

How to Read Primary Sources

In each chapter of this textbook you will find many primary sources to broaden your understanding of the development of the West. Primary sources refer to firsthand, contemporary accounts or direct evidence about a particular topic. For example, speeches, letters, diaries, song lyrics, and newspaper articles are all primary sources that historians use to construct accounts of the past. Nonwritten materials such as maps, paintings, artifacts, and even architecture and music can also be primary sources. Both types of historical documents in this textbook — written and visual — provide a glimpse into the lives of the men and women who influenced or were influenced by the course of Western history.

To guide your interpretation of any source, you should begin by asking several basic questions, listed below, as starting points for observing, analyzing, and interpreting the past. Your answers should prompt further questions of your own.

1. **Who is the author?** Who wrote or created the material? What was his or her authority? (Personal? institutional?) Did the author have specialized knowledge or experience? If you are reading a written document, how would you describe the author's tone of voice? (Formal, personal, angry?)

2. **Who is the audience?** Who were the intended readers, listeners, or viewers? How does the intended audience affect the ways that the author presents ideas?

3. **What are the main ideas?** What are the main points that the author is trying to convey? Can you detect any underlying assumptions of values or attitudes? How does the form or medium affect the meaning of this document?

4. **In what context was the document created?** From when and where does the document originate? What was the interval between the initial problem or event and this document, which responded to it? Through what form or medium was the document communicated? (For example, a newspaper, a government record, an illustration.) What contemporary events or conditions might have affected the creation of the document?

5. **What's missing?** What's missing or cannot be learned from this source, and what might this omission reveal? Are there other sources that might fill in the gaps?

Now consider these questions as you read "Columbus Describes His First Voyage (1493)," the document on the next page. Compare your answers to the sample observations provided.

DOCUMENT

Columbus Describes His First Voyage (1493)

In this famous letter to Raphael Sanchez, treasurer to his patrons, Ferdinand and Isabella, Columbus recounts his initial journey to the Bahamas, Cuba, and Hispaniola (today Haiti and the Dominican Republic), and tells of his achievements. This passage reflects the first contact between native Americans and Europeans; already the themes of trade, subjugation, gold, and conversion emerge in Columbus's own words.

Indians would give whatever the seller required; . . . Thus they bartered, like idiots, cotton and gold for fragments of bows, glasses, bottles, and jars; which I forbad as being unjust, and myself gave them many beautiful and acceptable articles which I had brought with me, taking nothing from them in return; I did this in order that I might the more easily conciliate them, that they might be led to become Christians, and be inclined to entertain a regard for the King and Queen, our Princes and all Spaniards, and that I might induce them to take an interest in seeking out, and collecting, and delivering to us such things as they possessed in abundance, but which we greatly needed. They practise no kind of idolatry, but have a firm belief that all strength and power, and indeed all good things, are in heaven, and that I had descended from thence with these ships and sailors, and under this impression was I received after they had thrown aside their fears. Nor are they slow or stupid, but of very clear understanding; and those men who have crossed to the neighbouring islands give an admirable description of everything they observed; but they never saw any people clothed, nor any ships like ours. On my arrival at that sea, I had taken some Indians by force from the first island that I came to, in order that they might learn our language, and communicate to us what they know respecting the country; which plan succeeded excellently, and was a great advantage to us, for in a short time, either by gestures and signs, or by words, we were enabled to understand each other. These men are still travelling with me, and although they have been with us now a long time, they continue to entertain the idea that I have descended from heaven.

Source: Christopher Columbus, *Four Voyages to the New World.* Translated by R. H. Major (New York: Corinth Books, 1961), 8–9.

1. **Who is the author?** The title and headnote that precede each document contain information about the authorship and date of its creation. In this case, the Italian explorer Christopher Columbus is the author. His letter describes events in which he was both an eyewitness and a participant.

2. **Who is the audience?** Columbus sent the letter to Raphael Sanchez, treasurer to Ferdinand and Isabella — someone who Columbus knew would be keenly interested in the fate of his patrons' investment. Because the letter was also a public document written to a crown official, Columbus would have expected a wider audience beyond Sanchez. How might his letter have differed had it been written to a friend?

3. **What are the main ideas?** In this segment, Columbus describes his encounter with the native people. He speaks of his desire to establish good relations by treating them fairly, and he offers his impressions of their intelligence and naiveté — characteristics he implies will prove useful to Europeans. He also expresses an interest in converting them to Christianity and making them loyal subjects of the crown.

4. **In what context was the document created?** Columbus wrote the letter in 1493, within six months of his first voyage. He would have been eager to announce the success of his endeavor.

5. **What's missing?** Columbus's letter provides just one view of the encounter. We do not have a corresponding account from the native Americans' perspective nor from anyone else travelling with Columbus. With no corroboration evidence, how reliable is this description?

Note: You can use these same questions to analyze visual images. Start by determining who created the image — whether it's a painting, photograph, sculpture, map, or artifact — and when it was made. Then consider the audience for whom the artist might have intended the work and how viewers might have reacted. Consult the text for information about the time period, and look for visual cues such as color, artistic style, and use of space to determine the central idea of the work. As you read, consult the captions in this book to help you evaluate the images and to ask more questions of your own.

Authors' Note

The B.C.E./C.E. Dating System

"When were you born?" "What year is it?" We customarily answer questions like these with a number, such as "1987" or "2004." Our replies are usually automatic, taking for granted the numerous assumptions Westerners make about how dates indicate chronology. But to what do numbers such as 1987 and 2004 actually refer? In this book the numbers used to specify dates follow a recent revision of the system most common in the Western secular world. This system reckons the dates of solar years by counting backward and forward from the traditional date of the birth of Jesus Christ, over two thousand years ago.

Using this method, numbers followed by the abbreviation B.C.E., standing for "before the common era" (or, as some would say, "before the Christian era"), indicate the number of years counting backward from the assumed date of the birth of Jesus Christ. B.C.E. therefore indicates the same chronology marked by the traditional abbreviation B.C. ("before Christ"). The larger the number following B.C.E. (or B.C.), the earlier in history is the year to which it refers. The date 431 B.C.E., for example, refers to a year 431 years before the birth of Jesus and therefore comes earlier in time than the dates 430 B.C.E., 429 B.C.E., and so on. The same calculation applies to numbering other time intervals calculated on the decimal system: those of ten years (a decade), of one hundred years (a century), and of one thousand years (a millennium). For example, the decade of the 440s B.C.E. (449 B.C.E. to 440 B.C.E.) is earlier than the decade of the 430s B.C.E. (439 B.C.E. to 430 B.C.E.). "Fifth century B.C.E." refers to the fifth period of 100 years reckoning backward from the birth of Jesus and covers the years 500 B.C.E. to 401 B.C.E. It is earlier in history than the fourth century B.C.E. (400 B.C.E. to 301 B.C.E.), which followed the fifth century B.C.E. Because this system has no year "zero," the first century B.C.E. covers the years 100 B.C.E. to 1 B.C.E. Dating millennia works similarly: the second millennium B.C.E. refers to the years 2000 B.C.E. to 1001 B.C.E., the third millennium to the years 3000 B.C.E. to 2001 B.C.E., and so on.

To indicate years counted forward from the traditional date of Jesus' birth, numbers are followed by the abbreviation C.E., standing for "of the common era" (or "of the Christian era"). C.E. therefore indicates the same chronology marked by the traditional abbreviation A.D., which stands for the Latin phrase *anno Domini* ("in the year of the Lord"). A.D. properly comes before the date being marked. The date A.D. 1492, for example, translates as "in the year of the Lord 1492," meaning 1492 years after the birth of Jesus. Under the B.C.E./C.E. system, this date would be written as 1492 C.E. For dating centuries, the term "first century C.E." refers to the period from 1 C.E. to 100 C.E. (which is the same period as A.D. 1 to A.D. 100). For dates C.E., the smaller the number, the earlier the date in history. The fourth century C.E. (301 C.E. to 400 C.E.) comes before the fifth century C.E. (401 C.E. to 500 C.E.). The year 312 C.E. is a date in the early fourth century C.E., while 395 C.E. is a date late in the same century. When numbers are given without either B.C.E. or C.E., they are presumed to be dates C.E. For example, the term *eighteenth century* with no abbreviation accompanying it refers to the years 1701 C.E. to 1800 C.E.

No standard system of numbering years, such as B.C.E./C.E., existed in antiquity. Different people in different places identified years with varying names and numbers. Consequently, it was difficult to match up the years in any particular local system with those in a different system. Each city of ancient Greece, for example, had its own method for keeping track of the years. The ancient Greek historian Thucydides, therefore, faced a problem in presenting a chronology for the famous Peloponnesian War between Athens and Sparta, which began (by our reckoning) in 431 B.C.E. To try to explain to as many of his readers as possible the date the war had begun, he described its first year by three different local systems: "the year when Chrysis was in the forty-eighth year of her priesthood at Argos, and Aenesias was overseer at Sparta, and Pythodorus was magistrate at Athens."

A Catholic monk named Dionysius, who lived in Rome in the sixth century C.E., invented the system of reckoning dates forward from the birth of Jesus. Calling himself *Exiguus* (Latin for "the little" or "the small") as a mark of humility, he placed Jesus' birth 754 years after the foundation of ancient Rome. Others then and now believe his date for Jesus's birth was in fact several years too late. Many scholars today calculate that Jesus was born in what would be 4 B.C.E. according to Dionysius's system, although a date a year or so earlier also seems possible.

Counting backward from the supposed date of Jesus' birth to indicate dates earlier than that event represented a natural complement to reckoning forward for dates after it. The English historian and theologian Bede in the early eighth century was the first to use both forward and backward reckoning from the birth of Jesus in a historical work, and this system gradually gained wider acceptance because it provided a basis for standardizing the many local calendars used in the Western Christian world. Nevertheless, B.C. and A.D. were not used regularly until the end of the eighteenth century. B.C.E. and C.E. became common in the late twentieth century.

The system of numbering years from the birth of Jesus is far from the only one in use today. The Jewish calendar of years, for example, counts forward from the date given to the creation of the world, which would be calculated as 3761 B.C.E. under the B.C.E./C.E. system. Under this system, years are designated A.M., an abbreviation of the Latin *anno mundi*, "in the year of the world." The Islamic calendar counts forward from the date of the prophet Muhammad's flight from Mecca, called the *Hijra*, in what is the year 622 C.E. The abbreviation A.H. (standing for the Latin phrase *anno Hegirae*, "in the year of the Hijra") indicates dates calculated by this system. Anthropology commonly reckons distant dates as "before the present" (abbreviated B.P.).

History is often defined as the study of change over time; hence the importance of dates for the historian. But just as historians argue over which dates are most significant, they disagree over which dating system to follow. Their debate reveals perhaps the most enduring fact about history — its vitality.

Elevation

Feet	Meters
Over 13,120	Over 4,001
6,561–13,120	2,001–4,000
1,641–6,560	501–2,000
661–1640	201–500
0–660	0–200
Below sea level	Below sea level

⊛ National capital
• Major city

0   150   300 miles
0   150   300 kilometers

NORWAY
Bergen
Oslo
SWEDEN
Stockholm
Göteborg

North Sea

Baltic Sea

NORTHERN IRELAND
SCOTLAND
Glasgow
Edinburgh
Belfast
DENMARK
Aarhus
Copenhagen
Kaliningrad
Gdańsk

IRELAND
Dublin
UNITED KINGDOM
Liverpool
WALES
Birmingham
ENGLAND
Thames R.
London
Cork

NETHERLANDS
Amsterdam
Rotterdam
Antwerp
Brussels
BELGIUM
Elbe R.
Berlin
POLAND
Vistula

English Channel

ATLANTIC OCEAN

Seine R.
Paris
Luxembourg
LUXEMBOURG
GERMANY
Frankfurt
Rhine R.
Prague
CZECH REP.
Brno
Cracow
Oder R.

FRANCE
Loire R.
LIECHTENSTEIN
Zürich
Bern
SWITZERLAND
Munich
Vaduz
A L P S
Innsbruck
Vienna
Bratislava
AUSTRIA
Graz
Danube R.
Budapest
HUNGARY
SLOVAKIA

Bay of Biscay

Lyon
Rhône R.
Milan
Po R.
SLOVENIA
Ljubljana
Zagreb
CROATIA
Belgrade

Oporto
PYRENEES
ANDORRA
Ebro R.
Andorra la Vella
Marseille
MONACO
A P E N N I N E S
San Marino
SAN MARINO
Adriatic Sea
Split
BOSNIA AND HERZEGOVINA
Sarajevo
Podgorica

PORTUGAL
Madrid
SPAIN
Barcelona
Corsica
Rome
ITALY
MONTENEGRO
Tirana
ALBANIA

Lisbon
Seville
Sardinia
Naples
Tyrrhenian Sea

Gibraltar (Br.)
BALEARIC IS.
Palermo
Sicily
Ionian Sea

Algiers
Tunis

Rabat
Valletta
MALTA

MOROCCO
TUNISIA
Mediterranean

ALGERIA
Tripoli

LIBYA

80°N

Greenland
(Den.)

Alaska

ICELAND

60°N

UNI
KINGI

CANADA

IRELA

40°N

FRAN

UNITED STATES

PORTUGA

S

ATLANTIC
OCEAN

Azores
(Port.)

MOROC

Canary Is.
(Sp.)

20°N

Western Sahara
(Mor.)

Hawaii

MEXICO

BAHAMAS

DOMINICAN
REPUBLIC

HAITI

Puerto Rico (U.S.)

CUBA

ST. KITTS AND NEVIS

MAURITANI

JAMAICA

Guadeloupe (Fr.)

ANTIGUA AND BARBUDA
DOMINICA

CAPE
VERDE

BELIZE

Martinique (Fr.)

ST. VINCENT AND THE GRENADINES

SENEGAL

GUATEMALA

HONDURAS

ST. LUCIA

BARBADOS

GAMBIA

MA

EL SALVADOR

NICARAGUA

GRENADA

GUINEA-BISSAU

TRINIDAD AND TOBAGO

GUINEA

COSTA RICA

GUYANA

SURINAME

SIERRA LEONE

PANAMA

VENEZUELA

French Guiana (Fr.)

LIBERIA

COLOMBIA

CÔTE D'IVOIR

PACIFIC OCEAN

0°

Equator

Galápagos Is.
(Ec.)

ECUADOR

BURKINA FAS

GHA

SAMOA

PERU

BRAZIL

TONGA

20°S

BOLIVIA

PARAGUAY

Easter I.
(Chile)

CHILE

ATLANTIC
OCEAN

URUGUAY

0   1,500   3,000 miles

0   1,500   3,000 kilometers

ARGENTINA

40°S

Falkland Is.
(U.K.)

60°S

80°S

160°W   140°W   120°W   100°W   80°W   60°W   40°W   20°W

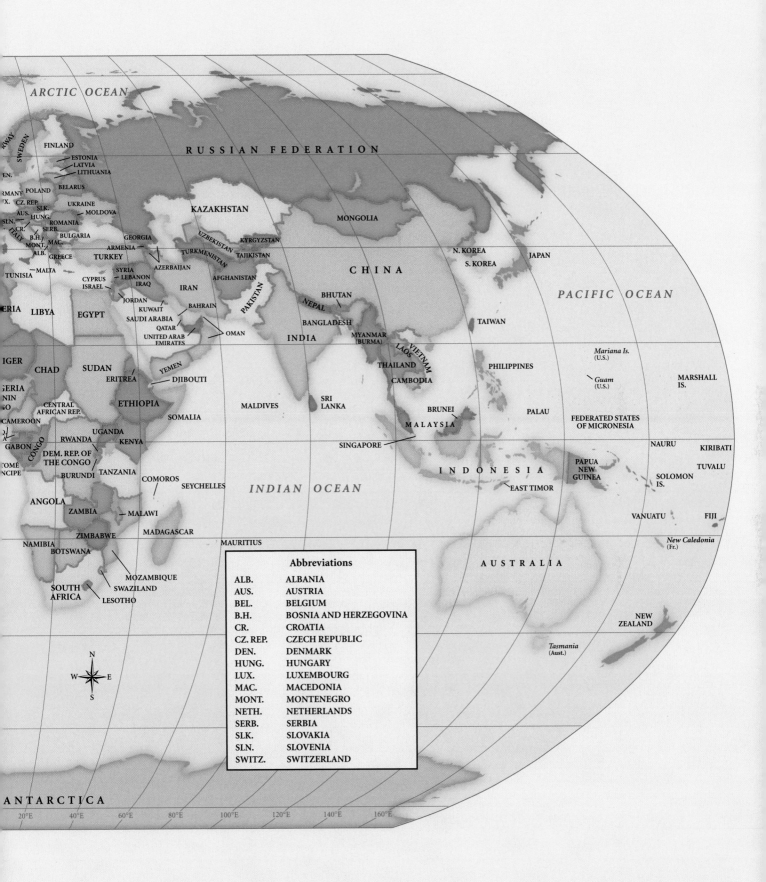

ARCTIC OCEAN

SWEDEN
FINLAND
RWAY
ESTONIA
LATVIA
EN.
LITHUANIA
RMANY POLAND BELARUS
X. CZ. REP.
SLK. UKRAINE
AUS. HUNG. MOLDOVA
SLN. ROMANIA
CR. SERB.
ITALY B.H. BULGARIA
MONT. MAC.
ALB. GREECE TURKEY
TUNISIA MALTA
CYPRUS SYRIA
ISRAEL LEBANON
IRAQ
JORDAN
KUWAIT
SAUDI ARABIA
QATAR
UNITED ARAB
EMIRATES

RUSSIAN FEDERATION

KAZAKHSTAN
MONGOLIA

UZBEKISTAN KYRGYZSTAN
TURKMENISTAN TAJIKISTAN
ARMENIA
AZERBAIJAN AFGHANISTAN
IRAN
PAKISTAN
BAHRAIN
OMAN

N. KOREA
S. KOREA
JAPAN

CHINA

PACIFIC OCEAN

ERIA LIBYA EGYPT
IGER CHAD SUDAN
GERIA ERITREA
NIN CENTRAL YEMEN
O AFRICAN REP. DJIBOUTI
CAMEROON ETHIOPIA
UGANDA SOMALIA
GABON RWANDA KENYA
OMÉ CONGO DEM. REP. OF
NCIPE THE CONGO
BURUNDI TANZANIA
COMOROS SEYCHELLES
ANGOLA
ZAMBIA MALAWI
ZIMBABWE MADAGASCAR
NAMIBIA MAURITIUS
BOTSWANA
SOUTH MOZAMBIQUE
AFRICA SWAZILAND
LESOTHO

NEPAL BHUTAN
BANGLADESH
INDIA MYANMAR
(BURMA)
LAOS VIETNAM
THAILAND
CAMBODIA
MALDIVES SRI
LANKA
BRUNEI
MALAYSIA
SINGAPORE
INDONESIA
EAST TIMOR

TAIWAN

PHILIPPINES

Mariana Is.
(U.S.)
Guam
(U.S.)

MARSHALL
IS.

PALAU
FEDERATED STATES
OF MICRONESIA

NAURU KIRIBATI
PAPUA
NEW TUVALU
GUINEA
SOLOMON
IS.
VANUATU FIJI
New Caledonia
(Fr.)

INDIAN OCEAN

AUSTRALIA

NEW
ZEALAND

Tasmania
(Aust.)

Abbreviations	
ALB.	ALBANIA
AUS.	AUSTRIA
BEL.	BELGIUM
B.H.	BOSNIA AND HERZEGOVINA
CR.	CROATIA
CZ. REP.	CZECH REPUBLIC
DEN.	DENMARK
HUNG.	HUNGARY
LUX.	LUXEMBOURG
MAC.	MACEDONIA
MONT.	MONTENEGRO
NETH.	NETHERLANDS
SERB.	SERBIA
SLK.	SLOVAKIA
SLN.	SLOVENIA
SWITZ.	SWITZERLAND

N
W E
S

ANTARCTICA

20°E   40°E   60°E   80°E   100°E   120°E   140°E   160°E

About the Authors

LYNN HUNT, Eugen Weber Professor of Modern European History at the University of California, Los Angeles, received her B.A. from Carleton College and her M.A. and Ph.D. from Stanford University. She is the author of *Revolution and Urban Politics in Provincial France* (1978); *Politics, Culture, and Class in the French Revolution* (1984); *The Family Romance of the French Revolution* (1992); and *Inventing Human Rights* (2007). She is also the coauthor of *Telling the Truth about History* (1994); coauthor of *Liberty, Equality, Fraternity: Exploring the French Revolution* (2001, with CD-ROM); editor of *The New Cultural History* (1989); editor and translator of *The French Revolution and Human Rights* (1996); and coeditor of *Histories: French Constructions of the Past* (1995), *Beyond the Cultural Turn* (1999), and *Human Rights and Revolutions* (2000). She has been awarded fellowships by the Guggenheim Foundation and the National Endowment for the Humanities and is a fellow of the American Academy of Arts and Sciences. She served as president of the American Historical Association in 2002.

THOMAS R. MARTIN, Jeremiah O'Connor Professor in Classics at the College of the Holy Cross, earned his B.A. at Princeton University and his M.A. and Ph.D. at Harvard University. He is the author of *Sovereignty and Coinage in Classical Greece* (1985) and *Ancient Greece* (1996, 2000) and is one of the originators of *Perseus: Interactive Sources and Studies on Ancient Greece* (1992, 1996, and www.perseus.tufts.edu), which, among other awards, was named the EDUCOM Best Software in Social Sciences (History) in 1992. He serves on the editorial board of STOA (www.stoa.org) and as codirector of its DEMOS project (online resources on ancient Athenian democracy). A recipient of fellowships from the National Endowment for the Humanities and the American Council of Learned Societies, he is currently conducting research on the comparative historiography of ancient Greece and ancient China.

BARBARA H. ROSENWEIN, professor of history at Loyola University Chicago, earned her B.A., M.A., and Ph.D. at the University of Chicago. She is the author of *Rhinoceros Bound: Cluny in the Tenth Century* (1982); *To Be the Neighbor of Saint Peter: The Social Meaning of Cluny's Property, 909–1049* (1989); *Negotiating Space: Power, Restraint, and Privileges of Immunity in Early Medieval Europe* (1999); *A Short History of the Middle Ages* (2001); *Emotional Communities in the Early Middle Ages* (2006); and *Reading the Middle Ages: Sources from Europe, Byzantium, and the Islamic World* (2006). She is the editor of *Anger's Past: The Social Uses of an Emotion in the Middle Ages* (1998) and coeditor of *Debating the Middle Ages: Issues and Readings* (1998) and *Monks and Nuns, Saints and Outcasts: Religion in Medieval Society* (2000). A recipient of Guggenheim and National Endowment for the Humanities fellowships, she is currently working on a general history of emotions in the West.

R. PO-CHIA HSIA, Edwin Erle Sparks Professor of History at Pennsylvania State University, received his B.A. from Swarthmore College and his M.A. and Ph.D. from Yale University. He is the author of *Society and Religion in Münster, 1535–1618* (1984); *The Myth of Ritual Murder: Jews and Magic in Reformation Germany* (1988); *Social Discipline in the Reformation: Central Europe 1550–1750* (1989); *Trent 1475: Stories of a Ritual Murder Trial* (1992); *The World of the Catholic Renewal* (1997); and *Noble Patronage and Jesuit Missions: Maria Theresa von Fugger-Wellenburg (1690–1762) and Jesuit Missionaries to China and Vietnam* (2006). He has edited or coedited *In and Out of the Ghetto: Jewish-Gentile Relations in Late Medieval and Early Modern Germany* (1995); *The German People and the Reformation* (1998); *Calvinism and Religious Toleration in the Dutch Golden Age* (2002); *A Companion to the Reformation World* (Blackwell Companion Series, 2004); *Cultural Translation in Early Modern Europe* (2007); and *Cambridge History of*

Christianity, Volume 6, *Reform and Expansion, 1500–1660* (2007). An academician at the Academia Sinica, Taiwan, he has also been awarded fellowships by the Woodrow Wilson International Society of Scholars, the National Endowment for the Humanities, the Guggenheim Foundation, the Davis Center of Princeton University, the Mellon Foundation, the American Council of Learned Societies, and the American Academy in Berlin. Currently he is working on the cultural contacts between Europe and Asia between the sixteenth and eighteenth centuries.

BONNIE G. SMITH, Board of Governors Professor of History at Rutgers University, earned her B.A. at Smith College and her Ph.D. at the University of Rochester. She is the author of *Ladies of the Leisure Class* (1981); *Confessions of a Concierge: Madame Lucie's History of Twentieth-Century France* (1985); *Changing Lives: Women in European History Since 1700* (1989); *The Gender of History: Men, Women, and Historical Practice* (1998); *Imperialism* (2000); and *Europe in the Contemporary World: 1900 to the Present* (2007). She is also the coauthor and translator of *What Is Property?* (1994); editor of *Global Feminisms since 1945* (2000) and *Women's History in Global Perspective* (3 vols. 2004–2005); coeditor of *History and the Texture of Modern Life: Selected Writings of Lucy Maynard Salmon, Gendering Disability* (2004); and general editor of *Oxford Encyclopedia of Women in World History* (4 vols. 2007). She has received fellowships from the Guggenheim Foundation, the National Endowment for the Humanities, the National Humanities Center, the Davis Center of Princeton University, and the American Council of Learned Societies. Currently she is studying the globalization of European culture since the seventeenth century.

THIRD EDITION

The Making of the West

PEOPLES AND CULTURES

Prologue:
The Beginnings
of Human Society
TO C. 4000 B.C.E.

I n 1997, archaeologists working in the East African nation of Ethiopia discovered fossilized skulls that dated from at least 160,000 years ago. These bones are the oldest remains ever found from the species *Homo sapiens* ("wise human being")—people whose brains and appearances were similar (though not identical) to ours. This new information excited scientists because it supported the "out of Africa" theory about human origins, which claims that *Homo sapiens* first appeared in Africa perhaps as early as 200,000 years ago and then spread from that continent all over the world.

The innovations that early human beings made in technology, trade, religion, and social organization formed the basis of our modern way of life. They also led to the emergence of war. Just as with the discovery of the skull, researchers keep uncovering new information that changes our knowledge about the past and therefore our thinking about how the past relates to the present. This process of discovery always involves questioning and debate. When we study history, therefore, we have to expect disagreements, especially about how to understand past events, what those events meant then, and what they mean today. Recent discoveries of human remains in Asia, for example, have reignited debate over the "out of Africa" theory, bringing back the once-discarded idea that human beings arose independently in different parts of the earth.

Scientists studying fossilized bones and those studying human mitochondrial DNA (the type inherited from the mother) have shown that it took millions of years for the earliest human species to emerge. According to the "out of Africa" theory, human beings exactly like us

Stone Age Handaxe
Archaeologists regard stone cutting tools like this one, called a handaxe, as the first great invention. Stone Age peoples made handaxes for hundreds of thousands of years, probably using hammers made from bone or wood to chip off flakes from the stone to create knifelike edges for cutting and scraping. This sharp tool would have been especially useful for butchering animals, such as the hippopotamuses that African hunter-gatherers killed for meat. Shown here at its full size (about seven and three-quarter inches top to bottom), this handaxe was, like all others, shaped to fit the human palm; users probably wrapped the tool in a piece of hide to protect their hands from cuts. (© *The Trustees of The British Museum.*)

(*Homo sapiens sapiens, meaning* "wise, wise human being") first developed in sub-Saharan Africa more than fifty thousand years ago. Starting about forty-five thousand years ago, those human beings began moving out of Africa, first into the Near East[1] and then into Europe and Asia.

This migration took place in the period commonly called the Stone Age, during which human beings made their most durable tools from stones, before they learned to work metals. Human society began in the Stone Age, which archaeologists divide into two parts to mark the greatest turning point in human history, the invention of agriculture and the domestication of animals and the enormous changes in human society that these innovations brought. The first, older part, the **Paleolithic** ("Old Stone") **Age**, dates from about 200,000 B.C.E. to about 10,000 B.C.E. The second, newer part, the **Neolithic** ("New Stone") **Age**, dates from about 10,000 B.C.E. to about 4000 B.C.E.

Archaeology—the study of physical evidence from the past—is our only source of information about the Stone Age; there are no documents to inform us about the lives of early human beings because people did not invent writing until about 4000–3000 B.C.E. Historians sometimes label the

---

[1] The term *Near East*, like *Middle East*, has undergone several changes in meaning over time. Both terms reflect the geographical point of view of Europeans. Today, the term *Middle East*, more commonly employed in politics and journalism than in history, usually refers to the area encompassing the Arabic-speaking countries of the eastern Mediterranean region as well as Israel, Iran, Turkey, Cyprus, and much of North Africa. Ancient historians, by contrast, generally use the term *ancient Near East* to designate Anatolia (often called Asia Minor, today occupied by the Asian portion of Turkey), Cyprus, the lands around the eastern end of the Mediterranean, the Arabian peninsula, Mesopotamia (the lands north of the Persian Gulf, today Iraq and Iran), and Egypt. In this book we will observe the common usage of the term *Near East* to mean the lands of southwestern Asia and Egypt.

Paleolithic Age: The "Old Stone" Age, dating from about 200,000 to 10,000 B.C.E.

Neolithic Age: The "New Stone" Age, dating from about 10,000 to 4000 B.C.E.

---

time before the invention of writing *prehistory*, because *history* traditionally means having written sources about the past. Historians also usually do not apply the word *civilization* to human society in the Stone Age because people then had not yet begun to live in cities or form **political states** (people living in a defined territory and organized under a central political authority), important characteristics that historians look for when defining civilization. (The first cities and political states emerged about the same time as writing, as we will see in Chapter 1.)

It was in the Neolithic Age that, instead of only hunting and gathering food in the wild, people learned how to produce their own food by raising crops and domesticating animals. These technological innovations produced lasting changes in human society, especially in strengthening social hierarchy, supporting gender inequality, and encouraging war for conquest. Historians continue to debate what was positive and what was negative in the consequences, intentional and unintentional, that this turning point produced for human society.

FOCUS QUESTION: What were the most significant changes in humans' lives during the Stone Age?

The Paleolithic Age, 200,000–10,000 B.C.E.

Human society began during the Paleolithic Age and was organized to suit a mobile way of life because human beings in this early period roamed around in small groups to hunt and gather food in the wild. The most notable feature of early Pa-

---

political states: People living in a defined territory with boundaries and organized under a system of government with powerful officials, leaders, and judges.

■ 50,000–45,000 *Homo sapiens sapiens* migrate from Africa into southwest Asia and Europe

■ 10,000–8000 Neolithic Revolution in the Fertile Crescent and the Sahara Desert

200,000 B.C.E.	50,000 B.C.E.	10,000 B.C.E.	0

■ 200,000–160,000 Beginning of Paleolithic Age

■ 8000 Walled settlement at Jericho

■ 7000–5500 Farming community thrives at Çatalhöyük

leolithic society was that the group probably made important decisions in common, with all adult men and women having a more or less equal say. Over time, however, Paleolithic peoples created a more complex social organization as they developed trade to acquire goods from long distances, technology such as fire for heat and cooking, religious beliefs to express their understanding of death, and a hierarchical ranking of people in society to denote differences in status.

The Life of Hunter-Gatherers

The characteristics of human society in the Paleolithic period originally reflected the conditions of life for **hunter-gatherers**, the term historians use for people who roamed all their lives, hunting wild animals and foraging. They never settled permanently in one place. Although they knew a great deal about how to survive in the natural environment, they had not yet learned to produce their own food by growing crops and raising animals. Instead, they hunted wild game for meat; fished in lakes and rivers; collected shellfish along the shore; and gathered wild grains, fruits, and nuts.

Archaeology reveals that a change in weather patterns apparently motivated hunter-gatherers of the *Homo sapiens sapiens* type to begin wandering out of Africa around 50,000–45,000 B.C.E. Long periods without rain drove game animals into southwest Asia and then Europe to find water, and at least some of the mobile human populations who hunted them in African lands followed this moving food into new continents. There is no evidence to explain why some hunter-gatherers left Africa in the Paleolithic period while others stayed behind.

When these *Homo sapiens sapiens* hunter-gatherers reached Europe and Asia, they met there earlier types of human beings who had already migrated out of Africa, such as the heavy-browed, squat-bodied Neanderthal type (named after the Neander valley in Germany, where their fossil remains were first found; their body type is often used to represent "cave men" in popular art). Eventually *Homo sapiens sapiens* replaced all earlier types of people around the globe, walking across then-existent land bridges to reach the Americas and Australia.

Archaeological excavations of hunter-gatherers' campsites tell us about their lives on the move, showing that over time they invented new forms of tools, weapons, and jewelry and began burying their dead with special care. Anthropologists have also reconstructed the lives of ancient hunter-gatherers from comparative study of the few groups who lived on as hunter-gatherers into modern times, such as the !Kung San of southern Africa's Kalahari Desert, the Aborigines in Australia, and the Coahuiltecans in the American Southwest. These two categories of evidence suggest that Paleolithic hunter-gatherers banded together in groups numbering around twenty or thirty to hunt and gather food that they shared with each other. Their average life expectancy was about twenty-five to thirty years. Since they had not learned to domesticate animals or to make wheels for carts, they walked everywhere. Because women of childbearing age had to carry and nurse their babies, it was difficult for them to roam long distances. They and the younger children therefore gathered plants, fruits, and nuts close to camp and caught small animals such as frogs and rabbits. The plant food that they gathered provided the majority of the group's diet. Men did most of the hunting of large animals, which frequently took them far from camp to kill prey at close range with rocks and spears; butchered hippopotamus bones found near the skulls in Ethiopia show that early humans hunted these dangerous animals. Women probably participated in hunts when the group used nets to catch wild animals.

Each band of Paleolithic hunter-gatherers moved around searching for food, usually ranging over an area that averaged roughly sixty miles across in any one direction. They tended not to intrude on other bands' areas, but there were no set boundaries or central settlements to identify a band's territory. To judge from the battles observed between surviving tribes of hunter-gatherers, when bands fought with each other, the conflict was more skirmish than total battle, and there was as much display as serious fighting; for ancient hunter-gatherers, there was nothing to take from another group that one's own group did not already possess, except other people. Hunter-gatherers' constant walking, bending, and lifting kept them in fine physical shape for hunting and the occasional battle, but they counted on their knowledge as much as their strength. Most important, they planned ahead for cooperative hunts at favorite spots, such as river crossings or lakes with shallow banks, where experience taught they were likely to find herds of large animals fording the stream and drinking water.

---

hunter-gatherers: Human beings who roam to hunt and gather food in the wild and do not live in permanent, settled communities.

Homo sapiens sapiens: The scientific name (in Latin) of the type of early human being identical to people today; it means "wise, wise human being."

A Paleolithic Shelter
This is a reconstruction of a hut that Paleolithic people built around fifteen thousand years ago from the bones of giant mammoths in what is now Ukraine, in east-central Europe. Animal hides would have been used to cover the structure, like a tent on poles. It was big enough for a small group to huddle inside to survive cold weather. *(RIA Novosti.)*

Paleolithic hunter-gatherers also used their knowledge to establish camps year after year in particularly good spots for gathering wild plants. They took shelter from the weather in caves or temporary dwellings made from branches and animal skins. On occasion, they built sturdier shelters, such as the dome-like hut found in Ukraine that was constructed from the bones of mammoths. Nevertheless, they never built permanent homes; they had to roam to survive.

Hunter-gatherers probably lived originally in egalitarian societies, meaning that all adults enjoyed a general equality in making decisions for the group. This cooperation reflected the fact that men and women both worked hard to provide food for the group, even if they tended to divide this labor by gender, with men doing more hunting and women more gathering. At some point, however, differences in social status began to emerge. Most likely, age was the first basis of social status: older people of both genders won prestige and probably positions of leadership from the wisdom gained from long experience of life in an era when most people died of illness or accidents before they were thirty years old. Women past childbearing age, who were therefore free to help out in multiple ways, and strong and clever men who hunted dangerous animals also likely held higher status.

Technology, Trade, Religion, and Hierarchy

Paleolithic people made changes in their lives that turned out to be important for the later development of civilization. In technology, learning how to create ever sharper edges and points in stone or bone or wood created better cutting tools and weapons for hunting, digging out roots, and making clothes from animal skins, thereby increasing the chances for survival. The discovery of how to make fire was especially important because Paleolithic people had to endure the cold of extended ice ages, when the northern European glaciers moved much farther south than usual. The coldest part of the most recent ice age started about twenty thousand years ago and created a harsh climate in much of Europe for nearly ten thousand years. Hunter-gatherers' knowledge of how to control fire led to the invention of cooking. This was a crucial innovation because it turned indigestible wild plants, such as grains, into edible and nutritious food.

Long-distance trade also began in the Stone Age. When hunter-gatherers encountered other bands, they exchanged things they had made, such as blades and jewelry, as well as natural objects such as flint or seashells. Trade could move valuable objects great distances from their original region: for example, ocean shells worn as jewelry made their way inland, far from the sea, through repeated swaps from one group to another.

Archaeological discoveries suggest that Paleolithic hunter-gatherers developed religious beliefs, a crucial factor in the evolution of human society; ancient peoples always saw religion as necessary for living a successful and just life. Colorful late Paleolithic cave paintings found in Spain and France hint at hunter-gatherers' religious ideas as well as display their artistic ability. Using strong, dark lines and earthy colors, Paleolithic artists painted on the walls of caves that were set aside as special places, not used as day-to-day shelters. The paintings, which primarily depict large animals, suggest that these powerful beasts played a significant role in the religion of Paleolithic hunter-gatherers. Still, there remains a great deal we cannot yet understand about their beliefs, such as the meaning of the dots, rectangles, and hands that they often drew beside their paintings of animals.

Stone Age burial sites provide evidence of religious beliefs. The early skulls found in Ethiopia have missing jaws and marks in the bone, indications that these early people cut away the flesh from dead persons' heads as part of a careful burial process (and not for cannibalism, as some have said). Another indication of belief is the care with which later Paleolithic bands buried their dead, decorating the corpses with red paint, flowers, and seashells. This elaborate procedure suggests that Stone Age people wondered about the mystery of death and perhaps had ideas about an afterlife.

Important evidence for early religious beliefs also comes from the discovery of specially shaped female figurines at late Paleolithic sites all over Europe. Modern archaeologists called these statuettes of women with extra-large breasts, abdomens, buttocks, and thighs Venus figurines, after the Roman goddess of sexual love (see the Venus of Willendorf, shown here). The oversized features of these sculptures suggest that the people who made them had a special set of beliefs and rituals regarding fertility and birth.

Burials reveal more than religious beliefs; they also show that, by late Paleolithic times, hunter-gatherer society had begun to mark significant differences in status among people. Those who were buried with valuable items such as weapons, tools, animal figurines, ivory beads, and bracelets must have had special social standing. These object-rich burials reveal that late Paleolithic groups had begun organizing their society according to a **hierarchy**, a ranking system identifying certain people as more important and more dominant than others. This is the earliest evidence for social

differentiation, the marking of certain people as wealthier, more respected, or more powerful than others in their society.

Despite their varied knowledge and technological skill, prehistoric hunter-gatherers lived precarious lives that were dominated by the relentless search for something to eat. Survival was a risky business. The groups that survived were those that

hierarchy: The system of ranking people in society according to their importance and dominance.

Prehistoric Venus Figurine
This limestone statuette, four and a half inches high, was found at Willendorf, in Austria. Carved in the later Paleolithic period and originally colored red, it probably was meant to have symbolic power expressing the importance of women's fertility. The emphasis on the woman's breasts and pubic area have led scholars to call such statuettes Venus figurines, after the Roman goddess of love and sex; archaeologists have uncovered many of them all across Europe. Since no written records exist to explain the significance of such figurines' hairstyle, obesity, and pronounced sexual characteristics, we can only speculate about the complex meanings that early peoples attributed to them. How would you explain this figurine's appearance? *(© SuperStock.)*

Bison Painting in the Cave at Lascaux
Stone Age people painted these bison on the rock walls of a large cave at Lascaux in central France about 15,000 B.C.E., to judge from radiocarbon dating of charcoal found on the floor. Using black, red, yellow, and white pigments, the artists made the deep cave into an art gallery by filling it with pictures of large mammals such as these European buffaloes, horses, deer, bears, and wooly rhinoceroses. Some scholars have suggested that the scenes symbolized the importance of hunting to the people who painted them, but this guess seems wrong because the bones from butchered animals found in the cave are 90 percent reindeer, while no reindeer pictures exist in the cave. *(© Caves of Lascaux, Dordogne, France/The Bridgeman Art Library.)*

■ **For more help analyzing this image,** see the visual activity for this prologue in the Online Study Guide at **bedfordstmartins.com/hunt.**

learned to cooperate in finding food and shelter; to profit from innovations such as fire, tools, and trade; and to teach their children the knowledge, beliefs, and social traditions that had helped them endure in a harsh world.

> **REVIEW:** What were the most important activities, skills, and beliefs that helped Paleolithic hunter-gatherers survive?

The Neolithic Age, 10,000–4000 B.C.E.

By around 10,000 to 8000 B.C.E., people in the Near East had opened the way to a different kind of society by learning to produce their food and build permanent settlements that housed larger populations than the twenty- to thirty-member bands of hunter-gatherers. In this new society, dominance by men replaced the general equality in status and decision making between men and women that likely existed in earlier times. In addition, war became a prominent part of human life.

The invention of agriculture and permanent settlements in the Neolithic Age occurred over a long time, but, once established, they changed forever the way human beings lived; eventually, these changes would make civilization possible. Daily life as we know it today still depends on agriculture and the domestication of animals, developments that began about 10,000–8000 B.C.E., at the beginning of the Neolithic period. These radical innovations in the way humans acquired food caused such fundamental changes in our way of life that they are called the **Neolithic Revolution**.

The Neolithic Revolution

Revolutionary change took place in human history in the Neolithic Age when hunter-gatherers learned to sow and harvest crops and to raise animals for food. Exactly how they gained this knowledge remains mysterious. Recent archaeological research, however, indicates that it took thousands of years for people to develop agriculture. The process began in the part of the Near East that we call the Fertile Crescent because, unlike most regions of the earth, its hillier regions hap-

pened to have the right combination of soil, water, temperature, and wild mammals for the invention of farming and the domestication of animals. The Fertile Crescent stretches in an arc, or crescent, along the foothills and lowlands that run northward from modern Israel across southeastern Turkey and Syria and then turn in a southeasterly direction down to the plain of the lower stretches of the Tigris and Euphrates rivers in what is now southern Iraq (Map 1).

The slow process of trial and error through which former hunter-gatherers developed agriculture had complex origins. Recent archaeological excavations at Göbelki Tepe ("stomach-shaped little hill"), a site in southeastern Turkey, have revealed stone-lined rooms in the earth decorated with stone pillars eight feet tall or more that are carved to depict animals, from boars and bears to birds and snakes. Free-standing sculptures of animals seem to have been placed atop the rooms' walls. Radiocarbon dating suggests these rooms were built around 9300 B.C.E., which would make them contemporary with the first attested agriculture or perhaps even earlier. Some scholars speculate that hunter-gatherers built these monuments for religious purposes and that the large amount of time they spent together in one place to create such elaborate structures and art led them to develop agriculture as a new way to feed themselves.

Only further archaeological research can reveal whether Stone Age religious activity had the unintentional consequence of generating agriculture. What seems certain is that climate change contributed significantly to the Neolithic Revolution. About ten to twelve thousand years ago, the long-term weather pattern in the Fertile Crescent became milder and rainier than it had been during the ice age that had just ended. This change promoted the growth of abundant fields of wild cereal grains. Similarly, recent archaeological research reveals that increased rain in the Sahara Desert, in central Africa, created there lush grasslands called savannahs that attracted hunter-gatherer nomads from the southern part of the continent; in a slow process of change, these people built settlements, domesticated cattle instead of only hunting wild animals, and created intricate pottery suited to their new way of life.

The hunter-gatherers living in the Fertile Crescent began to gather more and more of their food from the now easily available wild grains. This regular supply of food in turn promoted human fertility, which led to a growth in population, a process that might have already begun as a result

---

Neolithic Revolution: The invention of agriculture, the domestication of animals, and the consequent changes in human society that occurred about 10,000–8,000 B.C.E. in the Near East.

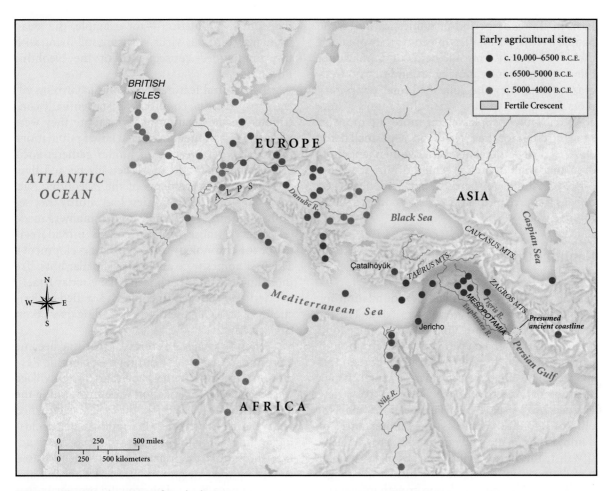

MAP 1　The Development of Agriculture
From around 10,000 to 8000 B.C.E., people learned to plant seeds to grow nourishing plants and to domesticate animals in the Fertile Crescent, the foothills of the semicircle of mountains that curved up and around from the eastern end of the Mediterranean down to Mesopotamia, where reliable rainfall and moderate temperatures prevailed. At about the same time, domestication of animals took place in the grasslands then flourishing in the Sahara region of Africa. The invention of irrigation in the Fertile Crescent allowed farmers to grow lush crops in the region's arid plains, providing resources that eventually spurred the emergence of the first large cities by about 4000 B.C.E.

of the milder climate. The more children that were born, the greater the need to exploit the food supply efficiently. Over centuries, people learned to plant part of the seeds from one crop of grain to produce another crop. Since Neolithic women did most of the gathering of plant food, they had the greatest knowledge of plant life and therefore probably played the major role in the invention of agriculture and the fashioning of tools needed to turn grains into food, such as grinding stones for making flour. At this early stage in the development of agriculture, women and children did most of the agricultural labor, using hand tools to grow and harvest crops, while men continued to hunt.

During the early Neolithic period, people also learned to breed and herd animals that they could

eat, a development that helped replace the meat previously acquired by hunting large mammals, many of which had by now been hunted to extinction. Fortunately for the people in the Fertile Crescent, their region was home to surviving large mammals that could be domesticated. Unlike African animals such as the zebra or the hippopotamus, the wild sheep, goats, and cattle of the Fertile Crescent could, over the span of generations, be turned into animals accustomed to live closely and interdependently with human beings. The sheep was the first animal to be domesticated as a source of meat, beginning about 8500 B.C.E. (The dog had been domesticated much earlier but was not usually eaten.) By about 7000 B.C.E., domesticated animals had become common throughout the Near

East. In this early period of domestication, some people lived as pastoralists, meaning they obtained their food mainly from the herds of animals that they kept, frequently moving around to find fresh grazing land. They also cultivated small temporary plots from time to time when they found a suitable area. Other people, relying more and more on growing crops for their livelihood, kept small herds close to their settlements. Men, women, and children alike could therefore tend the animals. These earliest domesticated herds seem to have been used only as a source of meat, not for products such as milk or wool.

Neolithic Origins of Modern Life and War

The Neolithic Revolution laid the foundation for civilization and our modern way of life. The remarkable new knowledge of how to produce food and the consequent division and specialization of labor emerged through innovative human responses to the link between environmental change and population growth (see "New Sources, New Perspectives," page P-12). Furthermore, the Neolithic Revolution reveals the importance of **demography** — the study of the size, growth, density, distribution, and vital statistics of the human population — in understanding historical change.

Agriculture and population growth influenced each other during the Neolithic Age. First, to be able to raise crops on a permanent basis, people had to stop roaming and settle in one place with adequate land and water. Farming communities thus sprang up in the Fertile Crescent starting around 10,000 B.C.E., sharing the region with pastoralists. Parents began to have more children because agriculture required a great deal of labor and because the ready availability of food from the fields and herds could support a larger population. At the same time, living in close quarters with domesticated animals, which might well be penned right next to or even inside the house, exposed people in these settlements to new epidemic diseases transmitted from animals to humans. Hunter-gatherers had largely escaped this danger because they had no groups of animals around them every day, although they could sometimes become infected by eating diseased wild animals. Since many viruses that afflict people today originated in domesticated animals before moving into

the human population — for example, the avian influenza (bird flu) virus — we are still living with this unintended consequence of the Neolithic Revolution.

Two central features of Neolithic farming villages helped create conditions that eventually contributed to the creation of civilization: they were permanent, and they supported larger populations than were characteristic of hunter-gatherer society. Much bigger and more densely packed than the temporary settlements of the Paleolithic Age, early farming communities had sturdy houses built from mud bricks and used containers made of pottery (whose broken remains provide evidence for chronology and cultural development). The first homes were apparently circular huts, like those known from Jericho (in what is today Israel). Around two thousand people had settled in Jericho by 8000 B.C.E., their huts sprawling over about twelve acres.

Jericho's remains also reveal that war became a prominent part of life during the Neolithic Revolution. The most remarkable part of the village was the massive fortification wall surrounding the community. Ten feet thick, the wall was crowned with a stone tower thirty feet in diameter enclosing an internal flight of stairs; this massive structure shows that the inhabitants of Jericho feared attacks by their neighbors (see Jericho's wall and tower, on page P-11). The growing prosperity that the Neolithic Revolution had brought evidently also spurred war for conquest and acquisition.

Neolithic people from the Fertile Crescent opened the way for civilization to develop in other regions by gradually spreading their knowledge of agriculture abroad. Farmers looking for more land migrated westward from the Near East and brought the new technology of farming into areas where it was not previously known. Although recent scholarship argues that human beings in other areas, especially Asia, independently developed agriculture and the domestication of animals, migrants from the Near East were the ones who spread this knowledge across Europe by 4000 B.C.E.

Daily Life in the Neolithic Village of Çatalhöyük

An archaeological site northwest of the Fertile Crescent, in present-day Turkey, provides vital evidence for the vast changes in human life brought on by this spread of knowledge during the Neolithic Age, especially how agriculture's greater efficiency in providing food led to the division and specialization of labor. At this site, on a plain near

---

demography: The study of the size, growth, density, distribution, and vital statistics of the human population.

Tower in the Stone Wall of Neolithic Jericho
The circular mass in the center of this photograph is the base of a tower in the stone wall that the people of Jericho (today in Israel) built to protect their community around 8000–7000 B.C.E. This is one of the earliest defensive walls ever discovered: most of the people in this era still lived in unwalled collections of mud huts, but the inhabitants of Jericho had reached a more complex level of social organization that allowed them to collaborate on major building projects. The agricultural fields that lay outside the walls supplied the overwhelming majority of Jericho's economy, while the wall surrounding their settlement provided security for the residents' homes and storehouses and thus protected their improving standard of living. *(Photo: Zev Radovan.)*

a river, a large mound rises from the countryside. Known to us only by its modern Turkish name, Çatalhöyük (meaning "Fork Mound"), the site reveals what daily life was like in a Neolithic farming community. By 7000 to 6500 B.C.E., the farmers of Çatalhöyük had erected a settlement of mud-brick houses sharing common walls. They constructed their dwellings in the rectangular shape still used for most homes today, with one striking difference: they had no doors in their outer walls. Instead, they entered their homes by climbing down a ladder through a hole in the flat roof. Since this hole also served as a vent for smoke from the family fire, getting into a house at Çatalhöyük could be a grimy experience. But the absence of exterior doors also meant that the walls of the community's outermost houses served as the village's fortification wall to defend it against attacks.

The people of Çatalhöyük fed themselves by growing wheat, barley, and vegetables such as field peas; they diverted water from the nearby river into their fields to increase their harvests. They also kept domesticated cattle to provide their main supply

of meat and, by this time, hides and milk. They continued to hunt, too, as we can tell from the hunting scenes they drew on the walls of some of their buildings, recalling the cave paintings of much earlier times. Unlike hunter-gatherers, however, these villagers no longer had to depend on the hit-or-miss luck of the hunt or risk being killed by wild animals to acquire meat and leather. At its height, the village's population reached perhaps six thousand people.

The diversity of occupations practiced at Çatalhöyük reveals a significant change from earlier times, anticipating the division of labor characteristic of the later cities of the first fully developed civilizations. Since the community could produce enough food to support itself without everyone having to work in the fields or herd cattle, some people could develop crafts as full-time occupations. Just as others in the community produced food for them, craft specialists produced goods for those who produced the food. Craft specialists continued to fashion tools, containers, and ornaments in the traditional way—from wood,

Daily Bread, Damaged Bones, and Cracked Teeth

The invention of agriculture helped people produce a more predictable and plentiful supply of food, which in turn allowed the population to expand. This change came at a price. Recent scientific research in biological anthropology and osteological archaeology (the study of ancient bones and teeth) has uncovered dramatic evidence of the physical stress endured by some of the individuals working in early agriculture. Excavators at Tell Abu Hureyra in Syria have found bones and teeth from people living around 6000 B.C.E. that reveal the pain that the new technology could cause. The big toes of these ancient people especially show proof of extreme and prolonged dorsiflexion—bending the front of the foot up toward the shin. Dorsiflexion made the ends of the toe bones become flatter and broader than normal through the constant pressure of being bent in the same position for long periods of time.

What activity could the people have been pursuing so doggedly that it deformed their bones? The only posture that creates such severe bending of the foot is kneeling for extended periods. Osteologists confirmed that kneeling was common in this population by finding several cases of arthritic changes in knee joints and lower spines in skeletons at the site.

But why were the people kneeling for so long? Other bone evidence offered the first clue to solving this mystery. The skeletons showed strongly developed attachment points for the deltoid muscle on the humerus (the bone in the upper arm) and prominent growth in the lower arm bones. These characteristics mean that the people had especially strong deltoids for pushing their shoulders back and forth and powerful biceps for rotating

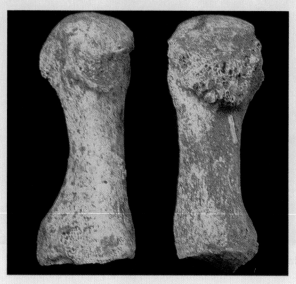

Bones from Tell Abu Hureyra, Syria
These big toes from a middle-aged man reveal severe arthritic changes to the joint. Osteologists interpret this damage as evidence of extreme and prolonged dorsiflexion, or bending of the foot. *(The Natural History Museum, London.)*

their forearms. Whatever they were doing made them use their shoulders and arms vigorously.

The skeletons' teeth provided the next clue. Everyone except the very youngest individuals had deeply worn and often fractured teeth. This damage indicated that they regularly chewed

bone, hide, and stone—but they now also worked with the material of the future: metal. So far, archaeologists are certain only that metalworkers at Çatalhöyük knew how to fashion lead into pendants and to hammer naturally occurring lumps of copper into beads and tubes for jewelry. But traces of slag, the scum that floats on molten metal, have been found on the site, suggesting that the workers may have begun to develop the technique of smelting metal from ore. This tricky process—the basis of true metallurgy and an essential technology of civilization—required temperatures of seven hundred degrees centigrade and took centuries for metalworkers to perfect. Other workers

at Çatalhöyük specialized in weaving textiles, and the scraps of cloth discovered there are the oldest examples of this craft ever found. Like other early technological innovations, metallurgy and the production of cloth apparently also developed independently in other places.

Trade—another central aspect of human existence that became increasingly prominent in the Neolithic Age—also figured in the economy of this early farming community. The trading contacts the Neolithic villagers made with other settlements increased the level of economic interconnection among far-flung communities that had begun in the Paleolithic period. Trade allowed the people of

Sculpture from Giza, Egypt
In this statuette, a woman grinds grain into flour. The sculptor shows her rubbing her severely flexed left foot with the toes of her right foot, probably trying to ease the throbbing resulting from hours of kneeling. *(Courtesy of the Oriental Institute of the University of Chicago.)*

food full of rock dust, which probably resulted from grain being ground in rock bowls.

The final clue came from art. Later paintings and sculptures from the region show people, usually women, kneeling down to grind grain into flour by pushing and rotating a stone roller back and forth on heavy grinding stones tilted away from them. This posture is exactly what would cause deformation of the big toes and arthritis in the knees and lower back. People grinding grain this way would have to push off hard from their toes with every stroke down the stone, and vigorously use the muscles of their shoulders and forearms to apply pressure to the roller. In addition, the flour would pick up tiny particles from the wearing down of the stones used to grind it; bread made from it would have a sandy consistency hard on teeth. That Neolithic people worked so constantly and so hard at processing the grain they grew, no matter the toll on their bones and their teeth, shows how vital this supply of food had become to them.

At this Syrian site, everyone's bones — men's, women's, and even children's — show the same signs of the kneeling and grinding activity. Evidently the production of flour for bread was so crucial that no gender division of this labor was possible or desirable, as it seems to have become in later times. Regardless of who used it, this new technology that provided essential food for the community took its toll in individual pain and hardship.

QUESTIONS TO CONSIDER

1. What other new technologies that have increased productivity and bettered human life have also involved new pains and stresses?
2. How do you decide what price — financial, physical, emotional — is worth paying for new technology? Who will make those decisions?

FURTHER READING

Hillman, G. "Traditional Husbandry and Processing of Archaic Cereals in Recent Times: The Operations, Products, and Equipment Which Might Feature in Sumerian Texts." *Bulletin on Sumerian Agriculture* 1 (1984): 114–52.

Molleson, Theya. "Seed Preparation in the Mesolithic: The Osteological Evidence." *Antiquity* 63 (1989): 358.

Moore, A. M. T. "The Excavation of Tell Abu Hureyra in Syria: A Preliminary Report." *Proceedings of the Prehistoric Society* 41 (1975): 50–71.

Çatalhöyük to acquire goods from far away, such as shells from the Mediterranean Sea to wear as ornaments and a special flint from far to the east to shape into ceremonial daggers. The villagers acquired these prized materials by offering obsidian in exchange, a local volcanic glass whose glossy luster and capacity to hold a sharp edge made it valuable.

Religion was a central feature of life in the community, as seen from the shrines and burial sites uncovered by archaeologists. The villagers outfitted their shrines with paintings and sculptures of bulls' heads and female breasts, perhaps as symbols of male and female elements in their re-ligion. Like the hunter-gatherers before them, they sculpted figurines depicting amply endowed women, who perhaps represented goddesses of birth, although some figurines recently found with skeletal designs suggest they were also related to ideas about death. The villagers had a deep interest in the mystery of death, demonstrated by the skulls displayed in the shrines and wall paintings of vultures devouring headless corpses. They buried their dead, some holding skulls decorated with painted plaster, under the floors of their houses. Perhaps they believed their dead ancestors had power and therefore wanted to keep them close by. A remarkable wall painting also suggests

Model of a House at Çatalhöyük
Archaeologists built this model of a house to show how Neolithic villagers lived in Çatalhöyük (today in central Turkey) from around 6500 to 5500 B.C.E. The wall paintings and bull-head sculpture had religious meaning, perhaps linked to the graves that the residents dug under the floor for their dead. The main entrance to the house was through the ceiling, as the houses were built right next to each other without streets in between, only some space for dumping refuse; the roofs served as walkways. Why do you think the villagers chose this arrangement for their settlement? *(Çatalhöyük Research Project.)*

that the people of Çatalhöyük regarded the volcano looming over their settlement as an angry god whom they needed to please. As it turned out, Çatalhöyük never recovered from a volcanic eruption that overwhelmed the settlement about fourteen hundred years after its foundation.

The people of Çatalhöyük had a clear social hierarchy, another example of the lasting changes that occurred in the Neolithic Age. The villagers developed a hierarchical society because they needed leaders to plan and regulate irrigation, trade, the exchange of food and goods between farmers and crafts producers, and the defense of the community against enemies. These leaders held more authority than had been required to

maintain peace and order in Paleolithic hunter-gatherer bands because their responsibilities were more complicated. Furthermore, households that were successful in farming, herding, crafts production, and trade generated surpluses in wealth that set them apart from those whose efforts proved less fortunate.

Gender Inequality in the Neolithic Age

The social equality between men and women that had existed in hunter-gatherer bands dwindled away during the Neolithic Age. By about 4000 B.C.E., when the first political states had begun to emerge in the Near East, **patriarchy** was the rule. (Political states also emerged at various other distant places around the world, including India, China, and the Americas—whether through independent development or some process of mutual influence we cannot yet say.) The reasons for the appearance of patriarchy remain uncertain, but they perhaps involved gradual changes in agriculture and herding over many centuries. After about 4000 B.C.E., plows pulled by large animals were used to cultivate land that was difficult to sow. Men apparently operated this new technology of plowing, probably because it required much more physical strength than digging with sticks and hoes, as women had done with hand tools in the earliest period of agriculture. Men also looked after the larger herds that had become more common in settled communities; people were now keeping cattle as sources of milk and raising sheep for wool. The herding of a community's large groups of animals tended to take place at a distance from the home settlement because the animals continually needed new grazing land. As with hunting in hunter-gatherer populations, men, free from having to nurse children, took on this task, which required ranging a long way from home.

Women probably became more tied to the central settlement because they had to bear and raise more children as agriculture became more intensive and therefore required more and more labor than had food gathering or the earliest forms of farming. Women also took responsibility for the new labor-intensive tasks needed to process the secondary products of larger herds. For example, they now turned milk into cheese and yogurt and made cloth by spinning and weaving wool. Men's predominant role in agriculture and herding in the late Neolithic period, combined with women's lessened mobility and increasingly home-based tasks, apparently led to women's loss of equality with men in these early times of human society.

REVIEW: What were the consequences of the Neolithic Revolution for people's lives?

Conclusion

Permanent homes, more reliable food supplies from agriculture and domesticated animals, specialized occupations, hierarchical societies in which men hold the most power, and war have characterized Western history from the Neolithic period forward. For this reason, the broad outlines of the life of Neolithic villagers might seem unremarkable to us today. But the Neolithic way of life in built environments surrounded by cultivated fields and herds would have seemed astounding, we can guess, to Paleolithic hunter-gatherers such as the roaming African hippopotamus hunters who now rank as the earliest known *Homo sapiens.* The Neolithic Revolution was the most important change in the early history of human beings; it literally overturned the ways in which people interacted with the natural environment and with one another. Now that farmers and herders could produce a surplus of food to support other people, specialists in art, architecture, crafts, religion, and politics could emerge. Hand in hand with these developments came a new division of labor by gender that saw men begin to take over agriculture and herding while women took up new tasks at home, leading to a loss of gender equality. At the same time, war between newly prosperous communities became common. These changes altered the course of human history and spurred the development of civilization as we know it today.

FOR FURTHER EXPLORATION

- **For suggested references, including Web sites, for topics in this chapter,** see page SR-1 at the end of the book.

- **For Web sites and documents related to topics in this chapter,** see *Make History* at bedfordstmartins.com/hunt.

---

patriarchy: Dominance by men in society and politics.

CHAPTER REVIEW

KEY TERMS AND PEOPLE

Paleolithic Age (P-4)

Neolithic Age (P-4)

political states (P-4)

hunter-gatherers (P-5)

Homo sapiens sapiens
(P-5)

hierarchy (P-7)

Neolithic Revolution (P-8)

demography (P-10)

patriarchy (P-15)

REVIEW QUESTIONS

1. What were the most important activities, skills, and beliefs that helped Paleolithic hunter-gatherers survive?

2. What were the consequences of the Neolithic Revolution for people's lives?

MAKING CONNECTIONS

1. Explain whether you think human life was more stressful in the Paleolithic period or the Neolithic period.

2. What do you think were the most important differences and similarities between Stone Age life and modern life? Why?

> **For Practice quizzes, a customized study plan, and other study tools,** see the Online Study Guide at bedfordstmartins.com/hunt.

IMPORTANT EVENTS

200,000–160,000 B.C.E.	Beginning of the Paleolithic ("Old Stone") Age	8000 B.C.E.	Walled settlement at Jericho (in modern Israel)
50,000–45,000 B.C.E.	*Homo sapiens sapiens* migrate from Africa into southwest Asia and Europe	7000–5500 B.C.E.	Farming community thrives at Çatalhöyük (in modern Turkey)
10,000–8000 B.C.E.	The Neolithic ("New Stone") Revolution in the Fertile Crescent and the Sahara Desert		

Early Western Civilization
4000–1000 B.C.E.

A ncient Egyptian kings believed that the gods judged them after death to decide their fate in the afterlife. In *Instructions for Merikare*, for example, written sometime around 2100–2000 B.C.E., Merikare's father, the king, warns his son to rule with justice because even a king would face a day of judgment to determine whether his choices had been good or evil: "Make secure your place in the cemetery by being upright, by doing justice, upon which people's hearts rely. . . . When a man is buried and mourned, his deeds are piled up next to him as treasure." Being judged pure of heart led to an eternal reward; if the dead king reached the judges "without doing evil," he would be transformed so that he would "abide [in the afterlife] like a god, roaming [free] like the lords of time." A central part of the justice demanded of an Egyptian king was to keep the country unified under a strong central authority and combat disorder. It was the development of centralized authority that brought the most striking changes to the lives of people as civilization emerged following the Neolithic Age.

The gods provided the Egyptians with a model of central authority. Eventually ordinary Egyptians came to believe that they, like the kings, could win eternal rewards by living justly and worshipping the gods with prayers and rituals. An illustrated guidebook containing instructions for mummies on how to travel safely in the underworld, commonly called the *Book of the Dead*, explained that on the day of judgment the jackal-headed god Anubis would weigh the dead person's heart on a scale against the goddess Maat (literally "What Is Right") and her feather of Truth, with the bird-headed god Thoth carefully

Weighing of the Heart on Judgment Day
This painting on papyrus (paper made from a river reed) from about 1275 B.C.E. illustrates a main concern of ancient Egyptian religious belief: the day of judgment when the gods decided a person's fate after death. Here, a man named Any is having his heart (in the left balance) weighed against the feather of Truth of the goddess Maat. The feather stands for "What Is Right." The jackal-headed god Anubis works the scales, while the bird-headed god Thoth records the result. The standing male figure on the left symbolizes Any's destiny, and the seated figures above are the jury of gods. The painting formed part of Any's copy of the *Book of the Dead*, a collection of instructions and magic spells to help the dead person in the afterlife, on the assumption that the verdict would be positive and bestow a blessed eternal life.
(British Museum, London, UK / Bridgeman Art Library.)

writing down the result (see the illustration on page 2). Pictures in the *Book of the Dead* also show the Swallower of the Damned—a hybrid monster featuring a crocodile's head, a lion's body, and a hippopotamus's hind end—who crouched behind Thoth ready to eat the heart of anyone who failed the test of purity. These stories, like many others in Egyptian mythology, taught that living a just life was the most important human goal because it was the key to winning the gods' help for a blessed existence after death.

The earliest Western civilizations arose in Mesopotamia, Egypt, Anatolia, Crete and other Aegean islands, and Greece. Each of these civilizations believed in the need for a centralized authority, but the forms of that authority differed. In Egypt, a single, central authority united the country; in other civilizations, smaller independent states competed with each other. Each civilization believed that religion and justice were basic building blocks for organizing human society. All believed that many gods existed; other religious beliefs and practices could differ, however. For example, the Greeks, unlike the Egyptians, believed that most people could expect only a gloomy, shadowlike existence following their deaths.

International trade and wars to win territory and glory were constants in all these civilizations. Trade and war brought the peoples of these civilizations into frequent contact with other populations far away; they exchanged not only goods and technologies but also ideas. This sort of cultural diversity has always characterized Western civilization. The question arises, then, of what historians mean by the concept *Western civilization*. What defines it in particular, as compared to other civilizations?

> **FOCUS QUESTION:** What changes did Western civilization bring to human life?

The Controversial Concept of Western Civilization

The meaning of the concept *Western civilization* begins with geography. The study of civilization in "the West" focuses on the peoples living on the continent of Europe and around the Mediterranean Sea on the continents of Africa and Asia. Chronologically, the story of Western civilization begins with the history of Sumer in Mesopotamia and of Egypt in Africa and extends to the present day. Defining *Western civilization* with greater depth is a difficult challenge because it involves three passionately debated topics: the concept of civilization in general, the vagueness of the idea of the West geographically, and—most controversial of all—the nature and the value of the West's ideas and ways of life.

Defining Western Civilization

To define Western civilization, we begin by defining **civilization** in general (see "Terms of History," page 6). Historians traditionally define it as a way of life in political states with a central authority based on cities and a more complex level of human activity and interaction than in earlier times. A village became a city by growing in population to house tens of thousands of people in a dense settlement with large buildings and by becoming a political center. The first civilizations are also identified by having diverse economies generating surplus resources, strong social hierarchies, a sense of local identity, and some knowledge of writing. As these political states acquired larger surpluses,

---

civilization: A way of life that includes political states based on cities with dense populations, large buildings constructed for communal activities, diverse economies, a sense of local identity, and some knowledge of writing.

■ 4000–1000 Bronze Age

■ 3050 Egypt united

4000 B.C.E.	3500 B.C.E.	3000 B.C.E.	2500 B.C.E.

■ 4000–3000 Writing, first cities

■ 2687–2190 Old Kingdom

they built armies and fought ever more frequent and intense wars.

We generally use *civilization* and related terms such as *civilized behavior* as if everyone agreed that the development of civilization brought progress and afforded people greater opportunities for prosperity and more complex interactions with one another, but some commentators deny that civilization represents a better and more just way of life than the way the earliest human beings lived. They argue that people were healthier, more equal in power, and more peaceful before they created cities and political states. Such comparisons are hard to evaluate because there is so little evidence about early human life (see the Prologue). If there truly was less war then, it might be simply because so many fewer people existed and they were spread so much farther apart — but it also probably matters that they lacked the surpluses to support extensive warfare. In any case, human beings all over the world chose to develop civilization, and no peoples have ever decided to reject it in favor of a simpler life.

The assumption that civilizations are defined by geography and their particular ideas and practices (their culture) began in ancient times. The Greeks invented the geographic notion of the West. Building on ideas they probably learned from their Near Eastern neighbors, they created the term *Europe* to indicate the West (where the sun sets), as distinct from the East (where the sun rises). The Greeks, like modern historians, were not sure exactly where to draw the boundaries of the West because its geographical meaning was then, and remains now, vague. The boundaries shift depending on what period is being described, and the word *Western* in *Western civilization* sometimes refers to peoples and places beyond Europe, and sometimes not. For example, the region that is today Turkey was certainly part of Western civilization at the time of the Roman Empire; yet in the opening years of the twenty-first century, Europeans and Turks alike are debating what changes in Turkish life and politics it would take — and what the financial and cultural costs would be — for Turkey to be judged Western enough to join the European Union.

Because it is difficult to identify precisely what set of ideas and customs makes up the culture of a particular civilization, the most controversial questions about Western (or any) civilization are, What are its particular ideas and practices? and Are those ideas and practices different from and superior to those of others? For example, Mesopotamian religion and Egyptian religion were both forms of **polytheism**. The Sumerians, who built the world's first cities, believed that the deities were unpredictable and often harsh to humans, and that people had to ward off divine anger by serving the gods obediently, building them temples, worshipping them, and bringing them gifts. The Egyptians also believed that they had to respect the gods to find happiness, but they thought that their gods lovingly provided them with life's delights and that, if their king fulfilled his duties, Maat would bless them with justice. As we will see in Chapters 2 and 3, the Hebrews made **monotheism** (belief in one god) a distinctive feature in Western civilization.

The Greeks inherited from their neighbors in the Near East the idea that regional differences meant that one people's culture was better than another's. Merikare's father, for instance, sternly warned him, "[Beware of the] miserable Asiatic [Near Easterner], wretched because of where he's from, a place with no water, no wood. . . . He doesn't live in one place, hunger propels his legs. . . . He doesn't announce the day of battle, he's like a thief darting around a crowd." The Greeks also

---

polytheism: The worship of multiple gods.

monotheism: The belief in only one god, as in Judaism, Christianity, and Islam.

TERMS OF HISTORY

Civilization

Our word *civilization* comes from the ancient Roman word *civilis*, which meant "suitable for a private citizen" and "behaving like an ordinary, unpretentious person." Today, the word *civilization* often expresses the judgment that being civilized means achieving a superior way of life. Consider, for example, these definitions from *The Random House Webster's College Dictionary* (1997), p. 240:

> *civilization*: **1.** an advanced state of human society, in which a high level of culture, science, and government has been reached. **2.** those people or nations that have reached such a state. **3.** any type of culture, society, etc. of a specific place, time, or group: *Greek civilization*. **4.** the act or process of civilizing or being civilized. **5.** cultural and intellectual refinement. **6.** cities or populated areas in general, as opposed to unpopulated or wilderness areas. **7.** modern comforts and conveniences, as made possible by science and technology.

All these definitions imply that *civilization* means an "advanced" or "refined" way of life compared to a "savage" or "rude" way. Ancient peoples often drew this sort of comparison between themselves and those whom they saw as crude. Much later, this notion of superiority became prominent in European thought after voyagers to the Americas reported on what they saw as the barbarous life of the peoples they called Indians. Because these Europeans saw Native American life as lacking discipline, government, and, above all, Christianity, it seemed to them to be "uncivilized." Today, this sense of comparative superiority in the word *civilization* has become so accepted that it can even be used in nonhuman contexts, such as in the following startling comparison: "some communities of ants are more advanced in civilization than others."[1]

Sometimes *civilization* is used without much definitional content at all, as in the *Random House* dictionary's third definition. Can the word have any deep meaning if it can be used to mean "any type of culture, society, etc. of a specific place, time, or group"? This empty definition reveals that studying civilization still presents daunting challenges to students of history today. It should be their task to make *civilization* a word with intellectual content and a reality with meaning for improving human life, as those who first used the word thought that it was.

[1] Sir John Lubbock, *On the Origin and Metamorphoses of Insects,* 2nd ed. (London, 1874), p. 13.

technology, for example, led to the creation of ever better tools and weapons, but it also turned out to be another factor prompting more visible differences in social status: people constructed status for themselves in part by acquiring metal objects. Some contemporary scientists claim that this development was inevitable because human beings are by nature "status-protecting organisms."

It would be misleading, however, to define Western civilization by a simple list of characteristics: we have to find the nature and value of Western civilization by studying its history. As we shall see, Western civilization evolved to a large extent through cultural interaction provoked by international trade and war. Contact with unfamiliar ways and technologies spurred people to learn from one another and to adapt for themselves the inventions and beliefs of others. Western civilization therefore developed in a mixing of different cultures. In the long run, the story of Western civilization expanded to include not only cultural and political interaction among the West's diverse peoples themselves but also between them and the peoples of the rest of the globe. It is clearly a mistake to understand the word *Western* to mean "fenced off in the West from the rest of the world."

Locating Early Western Civilization

The first step in defining Western civilization and studying its history is locating where it began. If we accept the traditional definition of *civilization* in general, then civilization in the West locates its deepest foundations in two places: (1) Mesopotamia, where the people of Sumer had developed separate cities and political states by 4000–3000 B.C.E., and (2) Egypt, in northeastern Africa, whose civilization emerged beginning around 3050 B.C.E., when a strong ruler made the country into a unified political state stretching along the Nile River. Both these societies waged frequent wars to protect their civilization, to demonstrate their superiority over outsiders, and to seize resources through conquest.

The story of Western civilization next spreads beyond Mesopotamia and Egypt. By around 2000–1900 B.C.E., civilization had also appeared in Anatolia (today Turkey), the island of Crete and other islands in the eastern Mediterranean Sea, and Greece. All these peoples learned from the older civilizations of Mesopotamia and Egypt, shared the sense that nothing in life was more important than religion, and waged war for defense and conquest. Comparably complex societies also emerged in India, China, and the Americas in different eras starting around 2500 B.C.E.; however, these societies pursued independent paths of de-

contributed to Western civilization new and unique ideas about the kind of central authority human beings should create to govern themselves and about the importance of reason for human thought.

In every known civilization people have insisted on establishing social hierarchies. The invention of increasingly sophisticated metallurgical

velopment. Their direct connections to the West began only much later.

If studying the history of Western civilization is the best way to seek its definition, we must then trace the commercial, military, and intellectual interactions of its diverse peoples and regions. We begin with the Mesopotamians, the Egyptians, the Minoans on Crete and the Aegean islands, and the Mycenaeans in Greece. The fragility of what we traditionally call civilization will become apparent when we come to the mysterious era of widespread violence that lasted from about 1200 to 1000 B.C.E. and nearly put an early end to civilization in the West.

REVIEW: What are the challenges of defining Western civilization?

Mesopotamia, Home of the First Civilization, 4000–1000 B.C.E.

The Neolithic Revolution (see the Prologue, pages P-8–P-10) created the economic basis of civilization by providing enough surplus agricultural resources to allow many people to work full-time at occupations other than farming and by encouraging permanent settlements that could grow into cities. These changes in the physical conditions of life generated changes in society. The first place where farming villages gradually became cities was Mesopotamia, where climate change had promoted agriculture and domestication of animals in the Fertile Crescent. Sumer, the name for southern Mesopotamia, developed the first cities. By 4000–3000 B.C.E., the Sumerians had built large urban communities, each controlling its surrounding territory as a separate political state. Studies have revealed the interlocking physical and social conditions of the first civilization: cities at the center of society, successful agriculture on arid plains made possible by complex irrigation, religion as the guide to life, a social hierarchy with kings at the top and slaves at the bottom, the invention of writing to keep track of economic transactions and record people's stories and beliefs, and war to demonstrate cultural superiority and gain land and riches.

The riches for which people now fought had a new component: metal. Items made of metal had become central to wealth and power after craft workers invented the technology of metallurgy about 4000 B.C.E. Historians label the period from about 4000 to 1000 B.C.E. the Bronze Age because at this time bronze, an alloy of copper and tin, was the most important metal for weapons and tools; iron was not yet in common use. Owning metal objects strengthened visible status divisions in society between men and women and rich and poor. Long-distance commerce increased to satisfy people's desire for resources and goods not available in their homelands and stimulated the invention of the alphabet to supplement earlier forms of writing. Rulers created systems of law to regulate the complex economic and social activities of civilization, instruct their subjects to be obedient to their rulers, and show the gods that they were fulfilling the divine command to maintain order by dispensing justice.

Cities and Society, 4000–2350 B.C.E.

The first cities, and thus the first civilization, emerged in Sumer when its inhabitants figured out how to raise crops on the fertile but dry plains between and around the Tigris and Euphrates rivers (Map 1.1). This flat region was spacious enough for the growth of cities, but it was not ideal for agriculture: little rain fell, temperatures soared to 120 degrees Fahrenheit, and devastating floods occurred unpredictably. First Sumerians and then other Mesopotamians turned this marginal environment into rich farmland by diverting water from the Tigris and Euphrates rivers to irrigate the plains. A system of irrigation canals that required constant maintenance helped limit flooding. The need to organize workers to maintain the canals promoted the growth of centralized authority in Mesopotamian city-states, which led to the emergence of kings as rulers. In this way, civilization created monarchy as a political system.

Food surpluses produced by Mesopotamian farmers spurred population growth, increased the number of crafts producers, and led to the emergence of cities. Each city controlled agricultural land outside its fortification walls and built large temples inside them. Historians call this arrangement—an urban center exercising political and economic control over the countryside around it—a **city-state**. Mesopotamia became a land of separate and independent city-states, each with its own central authority.

The Cities of Sumer. We do not know the origins of the Sumerians; they spoke a language whose background remains obscure. By around 3000

---

city-state: An urban center exercising political and economic control over the surrounding countryside.

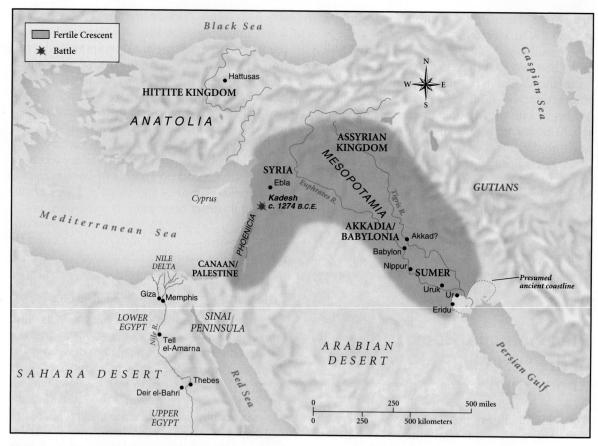

MAP 1.1 The Ancient Near East, 4000–3000 B.C.E.
The diverse region we call the ancient Near East encompassed many different landscapes, climates, peoples, and languages. Kings ruled its independent city-states, the centers of the world's first civilizations, beginning around 4000–3000 B.C.E. Trade by land and sea for natural resources, especially metals, and wars of conquest kept the peoples of the region in constant contact and conflict with one another.
■ How did geography facilitate—or hinder—the development of civilization in the Near East?

B.C.E. the Sumerians had established twelve independent city-states—including Uruk, Eridu, and Ur—which remained fiercely separate communities warring over land and natural resources. By around 2500 B.C.E., each of the Sumerian cities had expanded to twenty thousand residents or more.

These first city-states had similar layouts. Irrigated fields filled the outer perimeter of their territories, with villages housing agricultural workers closer to the urban center. A fortress wall surrounded the city itself. Outside the city's gates, bustling centers of trade developed, either at a harbor on the river or in a marketplace along the overland routes leading to the city. Inside the city, the most prominent buildings were the **ziggurats** (see the ziggurat of Ur in Sumer at right), temples of a stair-step design that soared up to ten stories high.

ziggurats (ZIH guh rats): Mesopotamian temples of massive size built on a stair-step design.

Cities were crowded, though some space was left open for parks. Urban dwellers lived in mud-brick houses constructed around an open court. Most houses had only one or two rooms, but the wealthy constructed two-story dwellings that had a dozen or more rooms. Rich and poor alike could become ill from the water supply, which was often contaminated by sewage because no system of waste disposal existed. Pigs and dogs scavenged in the streets and areas where garbage was dumped before it could be cleared away.

Agriculture and trade made Sumerian city-states prosperous. They bartered grain, vegetable oil, woolens, and leather with one another and with foreign regions, from which they acquired natural resources not found in Sumer, such as metals, timber, and precious stones. Sumerian traders traveled as far east as India, sailing for weeks to reach that distant land, where the Indus civilization's large cities emerged about five

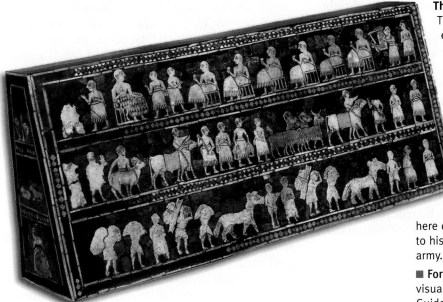

The "Standard of Ur" of Sumer

This wooden box, about twenty inches long and eight inches high, was found in a large grave in the Royal Cemetery at Ur dating to about 2600–2400 B.C.E. Its pictures, inlaid in white shell, red limestone, and blue lapis lazuli on all sides of the box, have made this mysterious object famous because they provide some of our earliest visual evidence for Sumerian life. This side shows animals being led to a banquet scene, where a musician playing a lyre entertains men in their characteristic woolen fleeces or fringed skirts. The large figure at the left is probably the king, here celebrating his role as the gods' representative to his subjects. The other side shows a Sumerian army. *(© Copyright The Trustees of the British Museum.)*

■ **For more help analyzing this image,** see the visual activity for this chapter in the Online Study Guide at bedfordstmartins.com/hunt.

hundred years after Sumer's. Technological innovation further strengthened the early Mesopotamian economy, especially beginning around 3000 B.C.E., when Sumerians invented the wheel in a form sturdy enough to be used on carts for transport.

Religious officials predominated in the early Sumerian economy because they controlled large farms and gangs of laborers, whose work for the gods supported the ziggurats and their related activities. Priests and priestesses supervised a large amount of property and economic activity. By around 2600 B.C.E., however, kings dominated the economy because their leadership in Mesopotamia's

frequent wars won them control of their territories' resources; some private households also amassed significant wealth by working large fields.

Kings in Sumer.   Kings and their royal families were the highest-ranking people in the Sumerian social hierarchy. A king formed a council of older men as his advisers and praised the gods as his rulers and the guarantors of his power. This claim to divinely justified power gave priests and priestesses political influence. Although a Sumerian queen was respected as the wife of the king and the mother of the royal children, the king held supreme power in the patriarchal city-states of

The Ziggurat of Ur in Sumer

King Ur-Nammu and his son Shulgi built this massive temple as an architectural marvel for their city of Ur (in what is today southern Iraq) in the early twenty-first century B.C.E. Its three massive terraces, one above another and connected by stairways, were constructed with a mud-brick core covered by a skin of baked brick, glued together with tar. The ziggurat's walls were more than seven feet thick to sustain its enormous weight. Its original height is uncertain, but the first terrace alone soared some forty-five feet above the ground. The enormous bulk of the Great Pyramid in Egypt, however, dwarfed it (see page 19). *(Hirmer Fotoarchiv.)*

Mesopotamia. Still, women had more legal rights under Sumerian law than they would in later Mesopotamian societies; only Egypt would give women greater legal standing than Sumer did.

The king's supreme responsibility was to ensure justice, which meant pleasing the gods, developing law, keeping order among the people, and fighting wars against other city-states both for defense and for conquest. In return, the king extracted surpluses from the working population as taxes to support his family, court, palace, army, and officials. If the surpluses came in regularly, the king mostly left the people alone to live their daily lives, although from time to time he relieved the poor of their debts as part of his divine mission to fight injustice.

To demonstrate their status atop the social hierarchy, Sumerian kings and their families lived in luxurious palaces that rivaled the scale of the great temples. The palace served as the city-state's administrative center and the storehouse for the ruler's enormous wealth. Members of the royal family dedicated a significant portion of the community's economic surplus to displaying their superior status. Archaeological excavation of the immense royal cemetery in Ur, for example, has revealed the dazzling extent of the rulers' riches — spectacular possessions crafted in gold, silver, and precious stones. These graves also yielded grislier evidence of the exalted status of the king and queen: the bodies of the servants sacrificed to serve their royal masters after death. The spectacle of wealth and power that characterized Sumerian kingship reveals the enormous gap between the upper and lower ranks of Sumerian society.

Slaves in Sumer. Just as it created monarchy, civilization also created slavery. Scholars dispute precisely how and why people began enslaving other people, but a greatly increased rigidity in social hierarchy was slavery's foundation. Slaves were those confined to the bottom. No single description of Mesopotamian slavery covers all its diverse forms or its social and legal consequences. Both the gods (through their temple officials) and private individuals could own slaves. People lost their freedom by being captured in war, by being born to slaves, by voluntarily selling themselves or their children to escape starvation, or by being sold by their creditors to satisfy debts. Foreigners enslaved as captives in war or in raids were considered inferior to citizens who fell into slavery to pay off debts. Children whose parents dedicated them as servants to the gods counted as slaves, but they could rise to prominent positions in the temple administrations.

In general, slaves depended almost totally on other people. They usually worked without pay and lacked nearly all rights. Although slaves frequently married each other and had families and sometimes formed relationships with free persons, masters could sell their slaves at will. Slave owners could buy, sell, demand sex from, beat, or even kill their slaves with impunity. Sumerians, like later Mesopotamians, apparently accepted slavery as a fact of nature, and there is no evidence of any sentiment for abolishing it.

Slaves worked as household servants, craft producers, and farm laborers, but historians dispute their economic significance compared with that of free workers. Most labor for the city-state seems to have been performed by free persons who paid their taxes through work rather than with money (which consisted of measured amounts of food or precious metal; coins were not invented until around 700 B.C.E. in Anatolia). Under certain conditions slaves could gain their freedom: masters' wills could liberate them, or they could purchase their freedom with earnings they could sometimes accumulate.

The Invention of Writing. Writing was also a creation of civilization. Beginning around 3500 B.C.E., the Sumerians invented writing to do accounting because economic transactions had increased in complexity as their populations expanded. Before writing, people drew small pictures on clay tablets to represent objects. At first, these pictographs symbolized concrete objects only, such as a cow. Over several centuries of development, nonpictorial symbols and marks were added to the pictographs to stand for the sounds of spoken language. The final version of Sumerian writing was not an alphabet, in which a symbol represents the sound of a single letter, but a mixed system of phonetic symbols and pictographs that represented the sounds of entire syllables or entire words.

Archaeologists call the Sumerians' fully developed script **cuneiform** (from *cuneus*, Latin for "wedge") because the writers used wedge-shaped marks pressed into clay tablets to record spoken language (Figure 1.1). Other Mesopotamian peoples subsequently adopted cuneiform to write their own languages. For a long time, only a few professionally trained men and women, known as scribes, mastered the new technology of writing. Schools sprang up to teach aspiring scribes, who

---

cuneiform (kyoo NEE uh form): The earliest form of writing, invented in Mesopotamia and done with wedge-shaped characters.

could then find jobs as accountants. Kings, priests, and wealthy landowners employed scribes to record who had paid their taxes and who still owed.

Writing soon created a new way to hand down stories and beliefs previously preserved only in memory and speech. The scribal schools extended their curriculum to cover nature lore, mathematics, and foreign languages. Written literature provided a powerful new tool for passing on a culture's traditions to later generations. Enheduanna, an Akkadian woman of the twenty-third century B.C.E., composed the world's oldest written poetry whose author is known. She was a priestess, prophetess, and princess, the daughter of King Sargon of the city of Akkad. Her poetry, written in Sumerian, praised the awesome power of the life-giving goddess of love, Inanna (also known as Ishtar): "the great gods scattered from you like fluttering bats, unable to face your intimidating gaze . . . knowing and wise queen of all the lands, who makes all creatures and people multiply." Later princesses, who wrote love songs, lullabies, songs of mourning, and prayers, continued the Mesopotamian tradition of royal women as authors and composers.

Mesopotamian Myths and Religion.

Writing developed into a crucial technology of perpetuating civilization because it provided a new way to record the traditions that helped hold communities together, especially myths (stories about the gods and the origins of civilization that people believed to be true) and religion (people's beliefs and communal practices in worshipping the gods). Mesopotamians believed that the gods had created the universe as a hierarchy demanding obedience from inferiors to superiors. They also believed that the gods controlled all areas affecting human existence, from war to fertility to the weather. The more critical a divinity's power over people's well-being, the more important the god. Each city-state honored a particular major deity as its special protector.

Mesopotamians viewed the gods as absolute masters to whom they owed total devotion, just as ordinary people owed complete obedience to their rulers. They believed that their deities looked like human beings and had human emotions, especially anger and an arbitrary will. Myths empha-

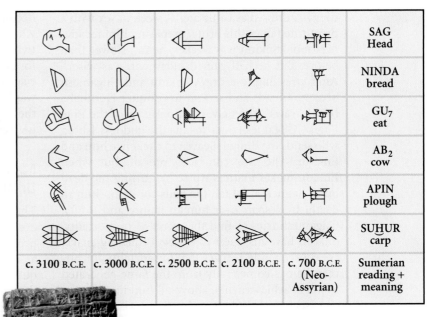

c. 3100 B.C.E.	c. 3000 B.C.E.	c. 2500 B.C.E.	c. 2100 B.C.E.	c. 700 B.C.E. (Neo-Assyrian)	Sumerian reading + meaning
					SAG Head
					NINDA bread
					GU₇ eat
					AB₂ cow
					APIN plough
					SUHUR carp

FIGURE 1.1 Cuneiform Writing
The earliest known form of writing developed in different locations in Mesopotamia in the 3000s B.C.E. when people began linking meaning and sound to signs such as these. The scribes who mastered the system used sticks or reeds to press dense rows of small wedge-shaped marks into damp clay tablets or chisels to engrave them on stone. Cuneiform was used for at least fifteen Near Eastern languages and continued to be written for three thousand years. Written about 1900 B.C.E., this cuneiform text records a merchant's complaint that a shipment of copper contained less metal than he had expected. His letter, impressed on a clay tablet several inches long, was enclosed in an outer clay shell, which was then marked with the sender's private seal. This envelope (photo at left) protected the inner text from tampering or breakage. *(© Copyright The Trustees of the British Museum.)*

sized the gods' awesome but unpredictable power and the limits of human control over what the gods might do to them. Mesopotamian divinities such as Enlil, god of the sky, and Ishtar (also called Inanna), goddess of love and war, would punish human beings who offended them by causing disasters like floods and famine.

The long poem *Epic of Gilgamesh* addresses the questions of the nature of civilization in a world ruled by divine central authority and the price that civilization demands from human beings. It tells the adventures of the hero Gilgamesh, who as king of the city of Uruk forces the city's young men to construct a temple and a fortification wall, and compels its young women to sleep with him. When the distressed inhabitants implore Anu, lord of the gods, to grant them a rival to Gilgamesh, Anu calls on Aruru, the mother of the gods, to create a wild man, Enkidu, "hairy all over . . . dressed as cattle are." A week of sex with a prostitute tames this brute, preparing him for civilization: "Enkidu was weaker; he ran slower than before. But he had gained judgment, was wiser." After wrestling to a draw, Enkidu and Gilgamesh become friends and set out to conquer Humbaba (or Huwawa), the ugly, giant monster of the Pine Forest. Gilgamesh later insults the goddess Ishtar, who sends the Bull of Heaven to challenge him and Enkidu. The two comrades prevail, but when Enkidu makes matters worse by hurling the dead bull's haunch at Ishtar, the gods condemn him to death. In despair over human failure and frailty, Gilgamesh tries to find the secret of immortality, only to have his quest foiled by a thieving snake. He subsequently realizes that immortality for human beings comes only from the fame generated by their achievements, above all building a great city such as Uruk, which encompasses "three square miles and its open ground." Only memory and gods live forever, he finds.

A late version of the *Epic of Gilgamesh* includes a description of a huge flood that covers the earth, recalling the devastating inundations that often struck Mesopotamia. When the gods send the flood, they warn one man, Utnapishtim, of the impending disaster, telling him to build a boat. He loads his vessel with his relatives, artisans, possessions, domesticated and wild animals, and "everything there was." After a week of torrential rains, he and his passengers disembark to repopulate and rebuild the earth. This story shows that ancient Mesopotamians realized their civilization might be flawed—after all, it angered the gods enough to want to destroy it. Their flood story foreshadows the biblical account of the flood and Noah's ark. The themes of Mesopotamian mythology, which lived on in poetry and song, also powerfully influenced the mythology of distant peoples, most notably the Greeks.

Religion lay at the heart of Mesopotamian civilization because people believed that the divinely created hierarchy of the universe determined the conditions of their lives. As a result, the priest or priestess of a city's chief deity enjoyed high status. The most important duty of Mesopotamian priests was to discover the will of the gods by divination. To perform this function, they studied natural signs by tracking the patterns of the stars, interpreting dreams, and cutting open animals to examine their organs for deformities signaling trouble ahead. These inspections helped the people

decide when and how to please their fickle gods, whether by giving them gifts or by celebrating festivals in their honor. During the New Year holiday, for example, the reenactment of the mythical marriage of the goddess Inanna and the god Dumuzi was believed to ensure successful reproduction by the city's humans, animals, and plants for the coming year.

Metals, the Akkadian Empire, and the Ur III Dynasty, c. 2350–c. 2000 B.C.E.

The growth of agriculture and trade promoted ever stronger city-states in Mesopotamia. Their prosperity led them into competition and conflict, as rulers led armies on brutal campaigns to conquer their neighbors and win glory and wealth. Although agricultural production remained the greatest source of wealth, the desire to acquire riches in metals pushed the kings of the Akkadians, a Mesopotamian people from the city-state of Akkad, to wage war to create the world's first **empire** (a political state in which one or more formerly independent territories or peoples are ruled by a single sovereign power).

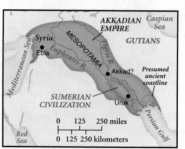

The Akkadian Empire, 2350–2200 B.C.E.

Early metallurgy presents a clear example of a recurrent theme in history since the Neolithic Revolution: technological change leading to changes in social customs and standards. In the case of metal, craftsmen invented ways to smelt ore and to make metal alloys at high temperatures. Pure copper, which had been available for some time, easily lost its shape and edge; bronze, by contrast, a copper-tin alloy hard enough to hold a razor edge, enabled smiths to produce durable and deadly swords, daggers, and spearheads. This new technology of metallurgy led kings and the social elite of the Akkadian empire to seek new and more expensive luxury goods in metal, improved tools for agriculture and construction, and, above all, bronze weapons of war.

The desire to accumulate wealth and to possess status symbols stimulated demand for metals and for the skilled workers who could create lavishly adorned weapons and exquisitely crafted jewelry. Rich men, especially, paid metalworkers to make them bronze swords and daggers decorated with expensive inlays, as on costly guns today. Such

empire: A political state in which one or more formerly independent territories or peoples are ruled by a single sovereign power.

weapons increased visible social differences between men and women because they marked the status of the masculine roles of hunter and warrior.

Mesopotamian monarchs' craving for metals spawned the development of empires. Ambition pushed rulers to acquire metals by conquest rather than by trade, and they started wars to capture territory containing ore mines. The first empire began around 2350 B.C.E., when Sargon, king of Akkad, launched invasions far to the north and south of his homeland in mid-Mesopotamia. In violent campaigns he overtook Sumer and the regions all the way westward to the Mediterranean Sea. Since Akkadians expressed their ideas about their own history in poetry and believed that the gods determined their fate, it was fitting that a poet of around 2000 B.C.E. credited Sargon's success to the favor of the god Enlil: "to Sargon the king of Akkad, from below to above, Enlil had given him lordship and kingship."

Sargon's grandson Naram-Sin continued the family tradition of conquering distant places. By around 2250 B.C.E., he had severely damaged Ebla, a large city whose site has only recently been discovered in modern Syria, more than five hundred miles from his home base in Mesopotamia. Archaeologists have unearthed many cuneiform tablets at Ebla, some of them in more than one language. These discoveries suggest that Ebla thrived as an early center for learning as well as a trading station.

The process of building an empire by force had the unintended consequence of spreading Mesopotamian literature and art throughout the Near East. The Akkadians, like many other peoples of the Near East, spoke a Semitic language unrelated to Sumerian, but in conquering Sumer they took over most of the characteristics of that region's religion, literature, and culture. The other peoples whom the Akkadians overran were then exposed to Sumerian beliefs and traditions, which they in turn adapted to suit their own purposes. In this way, war promoted cultural interaction.

Violence ended the Akkadian Empire. The traditional explanation for the empire's fall has been that the Gutians, a neighboring hill people, overthrew the Akkadian dynasty around 2200 B.C.E. by swooping down from, in the words of a poet, "their land that rejects outside control, with the intelligence of human beings but with the form and stumbling words of a dog." Research has revealed, however, that civil war is a more likely explanation for the Akkadian Empire's demise. A newly resurgent Sumerian dynasty called Ur III (2112–2004 B.C.E.) then seized power in Sumer and presided over a flourishing of Sumerian literature.

The Ur III rulers created a centralized economy, published the earliest preserved law code, and justified their rule by proclaiming their king to be divine. The best-preserved ziggurat was built in their era. Royal hymns, a new literary form, glorified the king; one example reads: "Your commands, like the word of a god, cannot be reversed; your words, like rain pouring down from heaven, are without number."

The development of civilization based on the centralized authority of kings did not bring stability to Mesopotamia. The Ur III kings could not protect their dynasty from monarchy's fatal weakness—its tendency to inspire powerful and ambitious internal rivals to conspire to overthrow the ruling dynasty and take power themselves. When civil war weakened the regime, Amorite marauders from nearby saw their opportunity to conduct damaging raids. The Ur III dynasty collapsed after only a century of rule.

Assyrian, Babylonian, and Canaanite Achievements, 2000–1000 B.C.E.

Assyrian innovations in commerce, Babylonian achievements in law, and the Canaanite invention of the alphabet are important landmarks in the history of Western civilization. New kingdoms emerged in Assyria and Babylonia in the second millennium B.C.E. following the fall of the Akkadian Empire and the Sumerian Ur III dynasty. Their accomplishments are especially remarkable because they occurred while Mesopotamia was experiencing prolonged economic troubles caused by climate change and agricultural pollution. By around 2000 B.C.E. the region's intensive irrigation had the unintended consequence of increasing the salt level of the soil so much that crop yields declined. When an extended period of decreased rainfall, especially in southern Mesopotamia, made the situation worse, the resulting economic stress generated political instability that lasted for centuries. In Canaan (ancient Palestine) on the eastern Mediterranean coast, a lively maritime trade with many diverse regions and the export of timber from inland fostered the growth of independent city-states.

The Kingdom of Assyria, 1900 B.C.E.

The Assyrians and Long-Distance Commerce.
The Assyrians inhabited northern Mesopotamia, just east of Anatolia. They took advantage of their geography to build an independent kingdom that

allowed long-distance trade conducted by private entrepreneurs. The city-states of Anatolia were rich sources of wood, copper, silver, and gold for many Mesopotamian states. By acting as intermediaries in this trade between Anatolia and Mesopotamia, the Assyrians became the leading merchants of the Near East. They produced woolen textiles for export to Anatolia in exchange for its raw materials, which they in turn sold to the rest of Mesopotamia.

Centralized state monopolies in which the king's officials managed international trade and redistributed goods according to their notions of who needed what had previously dominated the economies of Mesopotamian city-states. This kind of **redistributive economy** never disappeared in Mesopotamia, but by 1900 B.C.E. the Assyrian kings were allowing individuals to transact large commercial deals on their own initiative. This system allowed private entrepreneurs to maximize profits as a reward for taking risks in business. Private Assyrian investors provided funds to traders to purchase an export cargo of cloth. The traders then formed donkey caravans to travel hundreds of miles to Anatolia, where, if they survived the dangerous journey, they could make huge profits to be split with their investors. Royal regulators settled complaints of trader fraud and losses in transit.

Hammurabi of Babylon and Written Law. Mesopotamians established well-publicized laws, an important part of Western civilization. The growth of private commerce and property ownership in Mesopotamia created a pressing need to guarantee fairness and reliability in contracts and other business agreements. Mesopotamians believed that the king had a sacred duty to make divine justice known to his subjects by rendering judgments in all sorts of cases, from commercial disputes to crime. Once written down, the record of the king's decisions amounted to what historians today call a law code. King **Hammurabi** (r. c. 1792–c. 1750 B.C.E.) of Babylon, a great city on the Euphrates River in what is today Iraq, became the most famous lawgiver in Mesopotamia (see Document, "Hammurabi's Laws for Physicians," page 15). In making his laws, he drew on earlier Mesopotamian legal traditions, such as the laws of the earlier Sumerian Ur III dynasty.

In his code, Hammurabi proclaimed that his goals as ruler were to support "the principles of truth and equity" and to protect the less powerful members of society from exploitation. He gave a new emphasis to relieving the burdens of the poor as a necessary part of royal justice. The code legally divided society into three categories: free persons, commoners, and slaves. We do not know what made the first two categories different, but they reflect a social hierarchy in which some people were assigned a higher value than others. An attacker who caused a pregnant woman of the free class to miscarry, for example, paid twice the fine levied for the same offense against a commoner. In the case of physical injury between social equals, the code specified "an eye for an eye" (an expression still used today). But a member of the free class who killed a commoner was not executed, only fined.

Most of Hammurabi's laws concerned the king's interests as a property owner who leased many tracts of land to tenants in return for rent or services. The laws imposed severe penalties for offenses against property, including mutilation or a gruesome death for crimes ranging from theft to wrongful sales and careless construction. Women had only limited legal rights in this patriarchal society, but they could make business contracts and appear in court. A wife could divorce her husband for cruelty; a husband could divorce his wife for any reason. The law protected the wife's interests, however, by requiring a husband to restore his wife's property to her in the case of divorce.

Hammurabi's laws publicized an ideal of justice, but they did not necessarily reflect everyday reality. Indeed, Babylonian documents show that legal penalties were often less severe than the code specified. The people themselves assembled in courts to determine most cases by their own judgments. Why, then, did Hammurabi have his laws written down? He announces his reasons at the beginning and end of his code: to show Shamash, the Babylonian sun god and god of justice, that he had fulfilled the moral responsibility imposed on him as a divinely installed monarch — to ensure justice and the moral and material welfare of his people: "So that the powerful may not oppress the powerless, to provide justice for the orphan and the widow . . . let the victim of injustice see the law which applies to him, let his heart be put at ease." The king's responsibility for his society's welfare corresponded to the strictly hierarchical and religious vision of society accepted by all Mesopotamian peoples.

City Life and Learning. Hammurabi's laws offer glimpses into the daily life of Bronze Age Mesopotamian city dwellers. For example, crimes of burglary and assault apparently plagued urban

---

redistributive economy: A system in which state officials control the production and distribution of goods.

Hammurabi (ha muh RAH bee): King of Babylonia in the eighteenth century B.C.E., famous for his law code.

Hammurabi's Laws for Physicians

In Hammurabi's collection of 282 laws, the following decisions set the fees for successful operations and the punishment for physicians' errors. The prescription of mutilation of a surgeon as the punishment for mutilation of a patient from the highest social class (law number 218) squares with the legal principle of equivalent punishment ("an eye for an eye") that pervades Hammurabi's collection.

215. If a physician performed a major operation on a freeman with a bronze scalpel and has saved the freeman's life, or he opened up the eye-socket of a freeman with a bronze scalpel and has saved the freeman's eye, he shall receive ten shekels[1] of silver.

216. If it was a commoner, he shall receive five shekels of silver.

217. If it was a freeman's slave, the owner of the slave shall give two shekels of silver to the physician.

218. If a physician performed a major operation on a freeman with a bronze scalpel and has caused the freeman's death, or he opened up the eye-socket of a freeman and has destroyed the freeman's eye, they shall cut off his hand.

219. If a physician performed a major operation on a commoner's slave with a bronze scalpel and has caused his death, he shall make good slave for slave.

220. If he opened up [the slave's] eye-socket with a bronze scalpel and has destroyed his eye, he shall pay half his value in silver.

Source: Adapted from James B. Pritchard, *Ancient Near Eastern Texts Relating to the Old Testament*, 3rd ed. with supplement (Princeton, NJ: Princeton University Press, 1969), 175.

---

[1]A shekel is a measurement of weight (about three-tenths of an ounce), not a coin. A hired laborer earned about one shekel per week. The average price of a slave was about twenty shekels.

residents. Marriages were arranged by the bride's father and the groom and sealed with a legal contract. The detailed laws on surgery make clear that doctors practiced in the cities. Because people believed that angry gods or evil spirits caused serious diseases, Mesopotamian medicine included magic as well as treatment with potions and diet. A doctor might prescribe an incantation as part of his therapy. Magicians or exorcists offered medical treatment that depended primarily on spells and on interpreting signs, such as the patient's dreams or hallucinations.

Archaeological evidence supplements the information on urban life found in Hammurabi's code. City dwellers evidently enjoyed alcoholic drinks in a friendly setting because cities had many taverns and wine shops, often run by women proprietors. Contaminated drinking water caused many illnesses because sewage disposal was rudimentary. Relief from the odors and crowding of the streets could be found in the city's open spaces. The oldest known map in the world, an inscribed clay tablet showing the outlines of the Babylonian city of Nippur about 1500 B.C.E., indicates a substantial area set aside as a city park.

Bringing people together in cities evidently helped promote intellectual developments; Mesopotamian achievements in mathematics and astronomy had a profound effect that endures to this day. Creating maps, for example, required sophisticated techniques of measurement and knowledge of spatial relationships. Mathematicians devised algebra to solve complex problems, and they could derive the roots of numbers. They invented place-value notation, which makes a numeral's position in a number indicate ones, tens, hundreds, and so on. The system of reckoning based on sixty, still used in the division of hours and minutes and degrees of a circle, also comes from Mesopotamia. Mesopotamian expertise in recording the paths of the stars and planets probably arose from the desire to make predictions about the future, in accordance with the astrological belief that the movement of celestial bodies directly affects human life. The charts and tables compiled by Mesopotamian stargazers laid the foundation for later advances in astronomy.

Canaanites, Commerce, and the Alphabet.   The Canaanites expanded their population by absorbing merchants from many lands. Some scholars believe that the political structure of the Canaanite communities provided an antecedent for the city-states of Greece. The interaction in their cities of traders and travelers from many different cultures encouraged innovation in the recording of business transactions. This multilingual business environment produced an overwhelmingly important writing technology about 1600 B.C.E.: the alphabet. In this new system of writing, a simplified picture—a letter—stood for only one sound in the language, a dramatic change from complicated scripts such as cuneiform. The alphabet developed in the Canaanite cities later became the basis for the Greek and Roman alphabets and, hence, of modern Western alphabets. The Canaanite alphabet therefore ranks as one of the most important legacies contributing to the foundation of Western civilization.

> **REVIEW:** How did life change for people in Mesopotamia when they began to live in cities?

Egypt, the First Unified Country, 3050–1000 B.C.E.

The other earliest Western civilization arose in Egypt, in northeastern Africa. The Egyptians built a wealthy, profoundly religious, and strongly centralized civilization ruled by kings. Unlike the Mesopotamian city-states, Egypt became a unified country, the world's first large-scale state, whose prosperity and stability depended on the king's success in maintaining strong central authority over the entire country and defeating enemies. Egypt was located close enough to Mesopotamia to learn from its peoples but was geographically protected enough to develop its own distinct culture, which Egyptians believed was superior to any other. Like the Mesopotamians, the Egyptians believed that a just society was hierarchical and that justice should be dispensed top-down by the rulers to the rest of the people. The Egyptian rulers' belief in the immortality of their souls and the possibility of a happy afterlife motivated them to construct the most imposing tombs in history, the pyramids. Egyptian architecture, art, and religious ideas influenced later Mediterranean peoples, especially the Greeks.

From Egyptian Unification to the Old Kingdom, 3050–2190 B.C.E.

When climate change dried up the grasslands of the Sahara region of Africa about 5000–4000 B.C.E., people slowly migrated from there to the northeast corner of the continent, settling along the Nile River. They had formed a large political state by about 3050 B.C.E., when King Narmer (also called Menes)[1] united the previously separate territories

of Upper (southern) Egypt and Lower (northern) Egypt. (*Upper* and *Lower* refer to the direction of the Nile River, which begins south of Egypt and flows northward to the Mediterranean.) The Egyptian ruler therefore referred to himself as King of the Two Lands. By around 2687 B.C.E., the monarchs had forged a strong, centralized state, called the Old Kingdom by historians, which lasted until around 2190 B.C.E. (Map 1.2). Unlike their Mesopotamian counterparts, who ruled independent states in a divided land, Egyptian kings built only a few large cities in their united country. The first capital of the united country, Memphis (south of modern Cairo), grew into a metropolis packed with mammoth structures.

Narmer's unification created a state based on the narrow strip of fertile land on either side of the Nile, a ribbon of green fields zigzagging along the river's course for seven hundred miles southward from the Mediterranean Sea. The great desert flanking the fields on both sides protected Egypt from invasion, except through the northern Nile delta and from Nubia in the south. Under normal weather conditions, the Nile overflowed its channel for several weeks each year, when melting snow from the mountains of central Africa swelled its waters. This annual flood enriched the soil with nutrients from the river's silt and diluted harmful mineral salts. Unlike the random and catastrophic floods of the Mesopotamian rivers, the flooding of the Nile was predictable and beneficial. Trouble came only if dry weather in the mountains kept the flood from occurring. The surpluses that Egypt's multitude of farmers usually produced made the country prosperous. Date palms, vegetables, grass for pasturing animals, and grain grew in abundance. From their ample supplies of grain, the Egyptians made bread and beer, a staple beverage. Other sources of Egyptian wealth were the metal ores found in its deserts, the seaborne commerce conducted in its ports, and the goods exchanged with its African neighbors.

Egypt's diverse population included people whose skin color ranged from light to dark. Many ancient Egyptians would be regarded as black by modern racial classification, a distinction ancient people did not observe. The modern controversy over whether Egyptians were people of color is therefore anachronistic; if asked, ancient Egyptians

---

[1] Representing ancient Egyptian names and dates presents serious problems. Since the Egyptians did not include vowel sounds in their writing, we are not sure how to spell their names. The spelling of names here is taken from *The Oxford Encyclopedia of Ancient Egypt*, edited by Donald B. Redford (2001), with alternate names given in cases where they might be more familiar. Dates are approximate and similarly controversial; the scattered evidence for

Egyptian chronology embroils scholars in "a world of uncertainty and acrimonious debate" (Redford, *The Oxford Encyclopedia*, vol. 1, p. xi; for an explanation of the problems, see the article titled "Chronology and Periodization," vol. 1, pp. 264–68). The dates appearing in this book are compiled with as much consistency as possible from articles in *The Oxford Encyclopedia* and in the "Egyptian King List" given at the back of each of its volumes.

would presumably have answered that they identified themselves by geography, language, religion, and traditions. Like many ancient groups, the Egyptians called themselves simply The People. Later peoples, especially the Greeks, admired Egyptian civilization for its great antiquity and religion.

Although early Egyptians absorbed knowledge from both the Mesopotamians and their southern African neighbors, the Nubians, they developed their own scripts rather than using cuneiform. To write formal and official texts they used an ornate pictographic script known as **hieroglyphs** (Figure 1.2, page 18). They also developed other scripts for everyday purposes.

Nubian society perhaps deeply influenced early Egypt. A Nubian social elite lived in dwellings much grander than the small huts housing most of the population. Egyptians interacted with Nubians while trading for raw materials such as gold, ivory, and animal skins, and some scholars argue that Nubia's hierarchical political and social organization influenced the development of Egypt's politically centralized Old Kingdom. Eventually, however, Egypt's greater power led it to dominate its southern neighbor.

Religion and the Old Kingdom's Central Authority.

Although the Egyptians created a new path for civilization by creating a unified country under a central authority, keeping the country unified and stable turned out to be difficult. When the kings were strong, as during the Old Kingdom, the country was peaceful and rich, with flourishing international trade, especially along the eastern Mediterranean coast. However, when regional governors became rebellious and the king was weak, political instability resulted.

The king's power and success depended on his fulfilling his religious obligations. Like the Mesopotamians, Egyptians centered their lives on religion. They worshipped a great variety of gods, who were often shown in paintings and sculptures as creatures with both human and animal features, such as the head of a jackal or a bird atop a human body. This style of representing deities did not mean that people worshipped animals, but rather that they believed the gods each had a particular animal through which they revealed themselves to human beings. At the most basic level, Egyptian gods were associated with powerful natural objects, emotions, qualities, and technologies—examples are Re, the sun god; Isis, the

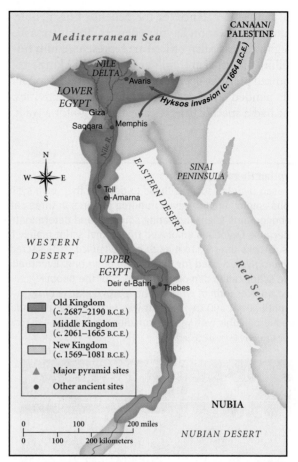

MAP 1.2 Ancient Egypt
Arid deserts closely embraced the Nile River, which provided Egyptians with water to irrigate their fields and a highway for traveling north to the Mediterranean Sea and south to Nubia. The only easy land route into and out of Egypt lay through the northern Sinai peninsula into the coastal area of the eastern Mediterranean; Egyptian kings always fought to control this region to secure the safety of their land.

goddess of love and fertility; and Thoth, the god of wisdom and the inventor of writing.

Egyptians regarded their king as a divinity in human form, identified with the hawk-headed god Horus. In the Egyptian view, the king's rule was divine because he helped generate maat, the supernatural force that brought order and harmony to human beings if they maintained a stable hierarchy. The goddess **Maat** embodied this force, which was the source of justice in a world that would, the Egyptians believed, fall into violent disorder if the king did not rule properly. To rule according to maat, the king made law, kept the forces

---

hieroglyphs: The ancient Egyptian pictographic script for writing official texts.

Maat (MAH aht): The Egyptian goddess ("What Is Right") embodying truth, justice, and cosmic order.

of nature in balance for the benefit of his people, and waged war on Egypt's enemies. To buttress his legitimacy as ruler, official art represented him fulfilling his ritual and military duties. The king's required piety (proper religious belief and behavior) demanded strict regulation of his daily activities: he had a specific time to take a bath, go for a walk, or make love to his wife. Most important, he had to ensure the country's fertility and prosperity. Thus, the king was supposed to guarantee a proper flooding of the Nile by performing his duties justly and in accordance with traditional order. A failure of the flood gravely weakened the king's authority and encouraged rebellions.

FIGURE 1.2 Egyptian Hieroglyphs

Ancient Egyptians used pictures such as these to develop their own system of writing around 3000 B.C.E. Egyptian hieroglyphs employ around seven hundred pictures in three categories: ideograms (signs indicating things or ideas), phonograms (signs indicating sounds), and determinatives (signs clarifying the meaning of the other signs). Because Egyptians employed this formal script mainly for religious inscriptions on buildings and sacred objects, Greeks referred to it as *ta hieroglyphica* ("the sacred carved letters"), from which comes the modern word *hieroglyphic*, used for this system of writing. Eventually, Egyptians also developed the handwritten cursive script called demotic (Greek for "of the people"), a much simpler and quicker form of writing. The hieroglyphic writing system continued until about 400 C.E., when it was replaced by the Coptic alphabet. Compare hieroglyphic writing with cuneiform (see page 11). *(Victor R. Boswell, Jr. © National Geographic Image Collection.)*

Hieroglyph	Meaning	Sound value
	vulture	glottal stop
	flowering reed	consonantal I
	forearm and hand	ayin
	quail chick	W
	foot	B
	stool	P
	horned viper	F
	owl	M
	water	N
	mouth	R
	reed shelter	H
	twisted flax	slightly guttural
	placenta (?)	H as in "loch"
	animal's belly	slightly softer than h
	door bolt	S
	folded cloth	S
	pool	SH
	hill	Q
	basket with handle	K
	jar stand	G
	loaf	T

Pyramids and the Afterlife.   Successful Old Kingdom rulers used expensive building programs to demonstrate their piety and exhibit their status atop the social hierarchy. In the desert outside Memphis, the Old Kingdom rulers erected the most stunning manifestations of their status and their religion: their huge tombs. These tombs—the pyramids (see photograph below)—formed the centerpieces of elaborate groups of buildings for royal funerals and religious ceremonies. Although the pyramids were not the first monuments built from enormous worked stones (that honor goes to temples on the Mediterranean island of Malta), they rank as the grandest.

Old Kingdom rulers spent vast resources on these huge complexes to proclaim their divine status and protect their mummified bodies for existence in the afterlife. King Khufu (r. 2609–2584 B.C.E.; also known as Cheops) commissioned the hugest monument of all—the Great Pyramid at Giza. At about 480 feet high, it stands taller than a forty-story skyscraper. Covering more than thirteen acres and 760 feet long on each side, it required more than two million blocks of limestone, some of which weighed fifteen tons apiece. Its exterior blocks were quarried along the Nile and then floated to the site on barges. Free workers (not slaves) dragged them up ramps into position using rollers and sleds.

The Old Kingdom rulers' lavish preparations for death reflected their strong belief in an afterlife. A hieroglyphic text addressed to the god Atum expresses the hope that the ruler will have a secure afterlife: "O Atum, put your arms around King Neferkare Pepy II [r. c. 2300–2206 B.C.E.], around this construction work, around this pyramid. . . . May you guard lest anything happen to him evilly throughout the course of eternity." The royal family equipped their tombs with elaborate delights for their existence in the world of the dead. Gilded furniture, sparkling jewelry, exquisite objects of all kinds—the dead kings had all this and more placed beside their coffins, in which rested their mummies. Archaeologists have even uncovered two full-sized cedar ships buried next to the Great Pyramid, meant to carry King Khufu on his journey into eternity.

Hierarchy and Order in Egyptian Society.   Old Kingdom rulers organized Egyptian society in a tightly structured hierarchy to preserve their authority and therefore support what they regarded as the proper order. Egyptians believed that their ordered society was superior to any other, and they despised foreigners, such as the Near Easterners criticized by Merikare's father.

The king and queen topped the hierarchy. Brothers and sisters in the royal family could marry each other, perhaps because such matches were believed necessary to preserve the purity of the royal line and to imitate the marriages of the gods. The priests, royal administrators, provincial

The Pyramids at Giza in Egypt
The kings of the Egyptian Old Kingdom constructed massive stone pyramids for their tombs, the centerpieces of large complexes of temples and courtyards stretching down to the banks of the Nile or along a canal leading to the river. The inner burial chambers lay at the end of long, narrow tunnels snaking through the pyramids' interiors. The biggest pyramid shown here is the so-called Great Pyramid of King Khufu (aka Cheops), erected at Giza (in the desert outside what is today Cairo) in the twenty-sixth century B.C.E. and soaring almost 480 feet high, several times taller than the famous Parthenon temple in fifth-century B.C.E. Athens (see page 79). (© John Lawrence/SuperStock.)

governors, and commanders of the army ranked next in the hierarchy. Then came the free common people, most of whom worked in agriculture. Free workers had heavy obligations to the state. For example, in a system called corvée labor, the kings commanded commoners to work on the pyramids during slack times for agriculture. The state fed, housed, and clothed them while they performed this seasonal work, but their labor was a way of paying taxes. Rates of taxation reached 20 percent on the produce of free farmers. Slaves captured in foreign wars served the royal family and the priests in the Old Kingdom, but privately owned slaves working in free persons' homes or on their farms did not become numerous until after the Old Kingdom. The king hired mercenaries, many from Nubia, to form the majority of the army.

Egypt preserved more of the gender equality of earlier times than did its neighbors. Women generally enjoyed the same legal rights as free men. They could own land and slaves, inherit property, pursue lawsuits, transact business, and initiate divorces. Old Kingdom portrait statues show the equal status of wife and husband: each figure is the same size and sits on the same kind of chair. Men dominated public life, while women devoted themselves mainly to private life, managing their households and property. When their husbands went to war or were killed in battle, however, women often took on men's work. Women could therefore serve as priestesses, farm managers, or healers.

The formalism of Egypt's art illustrates how much the civilization valued order and predictability. Almost all Egyptian sculpture and painting comes from tombs or temples, testimony to its people's deep desire to maintain proper relations with the gods. Old Kingdom artists excelled in stonework, from carved ornamental jars to massive portrait statues of the kings. These statues represent the subject either standing stiffly with the left leg advanced or sitting on a chair or throne, stable and poised. The concern for decorum (suitable behavior) also appears in the Old Kingdom literature the Egyptians called instructions, known today as **wisdom literature**. These texts gave instructions for appropriate behavior by officials. In the *Instruction of Ptahhotep*, for example, the royal minister Ptahhotep instructs his son, who will succeed him in office, not to be arrogant or overconfident just because he is well educated and to seek advice from ignorant people as well as the wise.

wisdom literature: Texts giving instructions for proper behavior by officials.

The Middle and New Kingdoms in Egypt, 2061–1081 B.C.E.

The Old Kingdom began to disintegrate in the late third millennium B.C.E. The causes remain mysterious. One suggestion is that climate changes caused the annual Nile flood to shrink and the ensuing agricultural failure discredited the regime—people believed the kings had betrayed Maat. Economic hard times probably fueled rivalry for royal rule between ambitious families, and civil war between a northern and a southern dynasty then ripped apart the Kingdom of the Two Lands. This destruction of the Old Kingdom's unity allowed regional governors to increase their power. Some governors, who had supported the kings while times were good, seized independence for their regions. It was the troubles of this period that made Merikare's father's advice so pressing: famine and civil unrest during the so-called First Intermediate Period (2190–2061 B.C.E.) thwarted all attempts to reestablish political unity.

The Middle Kingdom.   The kings of what historians label the Middle Kingdom (2061–1665 B.C.E.) gradually restored the strong central authority their Old Kingdom predecessors had lost. They waged war to extend the boundaries of Egypt farther south, while to the north they expanded diplomatic and trade contacts in the eastern Mediterranean region and with the island of Crete.

Middle Kingdom literature reveals that the reclaimed national unity contributed to a deeply felt pride in the homeland. The Egyptian narrator of *The Story of Sinuhe*, for example, reports that he lived luxuriously during a forced stay in Syria but still longed to return: "Whichever deity you are who ordered my exile, have mercy and bring me home! Please allow me to see the land where my heart dwells! Nothing is more important than that my body be buried in the country where I was born!" For this lost soul, love for Egypt outranks even personal riches.

From Hyksos Rule to the New Kingdom.   The Middle Kingdom lost its unity during the Second Intermediate Period (1664–1570 B.C.E.), when the kings proved too weak to suppress foreigners who had migrated into Egypt and gradually set up independent communities. By 1664 B.C.E., diverse bands of a Semitic people originally from the eastern Mediterranean coast took advantage of the troubled times to become Egypt's rulers. The Egyptians called these foreigners Hyksos (literally, "rulers of the foreign countries"). Recent archaeological discoveries have emphasized the role of Hyksos settlers in transplanting elements of foreign culture to Egypt: their capital, Avaris, boasted wall paintings done in the Minoan style current on the island of Crete. Some historians think the Hyksos also introduced such innovations as bronze-making technology, new musical instruments, humpbacked cattle, and olive trees; they certainly promoted frequent contact with other Near Eastern states. They also strengthened Egypt's capacity to make war by expanding the use of chariots and more powerful bows.

After a long struggle with the Hyksos, the leaders of Thebes, in southern Egypt, reunited the kingdom; the resultant series of royal dynasties is called the New Kingdom (1569–1081 B.C.E.). The kings of this period, known as pharaohs, rebuilt central authority by restricting the power of regional governors and promoted a renewed sense of national identity. To prevent invasions, the pharaohs built on the Hyksos innovations in military technology to create a standing army, still employing many mercenaries, and a military elite to lead it. Recognizing that knowledge of the rest of the world was necessary for safety, they engaged in regular diplomacy with neighboring monarchs to increase their cosmopolitan contacts. In fact, the pharaohs regularly exchanged letters on matters of state with their "brother kings," as they called them, in Mesopotamia, Anatolia, and the eastern Mediterranean region.

Warrior Pharaohs.   The New Kingdom pharaohs sent their reorganized military into foreign wars to gain territory and show their superiority to foreigners. They waged many campaigns abroad and presented themselves in official propaganda and art as the incarnations of warrior gods. They invaded lands to the south to win access to gold and other precious materials, and they fought up and down the eastern Mediterranean coast to control that land route into Egypt. Their imperialism has today earned them the epithet *warrior pharaohs.*

Massive riches supported the power of the warrior pharaohs. Egyptian traders exchanged local fine goods, such as ivory, for foreign luxury goods, such as wine and olive oil transported in painted pottery from Greece. Egyptian royalty displayed their wealth most conspicuously in the enormous sums spent to build stone temples. Queen Hatshepsut (r. 1502–1482 B.C.E.), for example, built her massive mortuary temple at Deir el-Bahri, near Thebes, including a temple dedicated to the god Amun (or Amen), to buttress her claim to divine birth and the right to rule. After

her husband (who was also her half brother) died, Hatshepsut proclaimed herself "female king" as co-ruler with her young stepson. In this way, she shrewdly sidestepped Egyptian political ideology, which made no provision for a queen to reign in her own right. She often had herself represented in official art as a king, with a royal beard and male clothing.

Religious Tradition and Upheaval.   Egyptians believed that their many gods oversaw all aspects of life and death. Glorious temples honored the traditional gods, and by the time of the New Kingdom their cults (that is, worship traditions and rituals) enriched the religious life of the entire population. The principal festivals of the gods involved lavish public celebrations. A calendar based on the moon governed the dates of religious ceremonies. (The Egyptians also developed a calendar for administrative and fiscal purposes that had 365 days, divided into 12 months of 30 days each, with the extra 5 days added before the start of the next year. (Our modern calendar derives from it.)

The early New Kingdom pharaohs from Thebes promoted their state god Amun-Re until he overshadowed the other gods. This Theban cult incorporated and subordinated the

Hatshepsut as Pharaoh Offering Maat
This granite statue, eight and a half feet tall, portrayed Hatshepsut, ruler of Egypt in the early fifteenth century B.C.E., as pharaoh wearing a beard and male clothing. She is performing her royal duty of offering *maat* (the divine principle of order and justice) to the gods. Egyptian religion taught that the gods "lived on maat" and that the land's rulers were responsible for providing it. Hatshepsut had this statue, and many others, placed in a huge temple she built outside Thebes, in Upper Egypt. Compare her posture to that of the statue of a woman grinding grain on page P-13. Why do you think Hapshetsut is shown as calm and relaxed, despite having her toes severely flexed? (*The Metropolitan Museum of Art, Rogers Fund, 1929 (29.3.1) Photograph by Schecter Lee. Photograph © 1986 The Metropolitan Museum of Art.*)

Declaring Innocence on Judgment Day in Ancient Egypt

The Egyptian collection of spells known today as the Book of the Dead instructed the dead person how to make a declaration of innocence to the gods judging the person's fate on the day of judgment. The declaration listed evils that the person denied having committed; presumably the divine judges could tell whether the deceased was speaking truthfully. This selection of denials, each directed to a specific deity, reveals what Egyptians regarded as just and proper behavior.

Wide-of-Stride who comes from On: I have not done evil.

Flame-grasper who comes from Kheraha: I have not robbed.

Long-nosed who comes from Khmun: I have not coveted.

Shadow-eater who comes from the cave: I have not stolen.

Savage-faced who comes from Rostau: I have not killed people.

Lion-Twins who come from heaven: I have not trimmed the measure.

Flint-eyed who comes from Kehm: I have not cheated.

Fiery-one who comes backward: I have not stolen a god's property.

Bone-smasher who comes from Hnes: I have not told lies.

Flame-thrower who comes from Memphis: I have not seized food.

Cave-dweller who comes from the west: I have not sulked.

White-toothed who comes from Lakeland: I have not trespassed.

Blood-eater who comes from slaughterplace: I have not slain sacred cattle.

Entrail-eater who comes from the tribunal: I have not extorted.

Lord of Maat who comes from Maaty: I have not extorted.

Wanderer who comes from Bubastis: I have not spied.

Pale-one who comes from On: I have not prattled.

Villain who comes from Anjdty: I have contended only for my goods.

Fiend who comes from slaughterhouse: I have not committed adultery.

Examiner who comes from Min's temple: I have not defiled myself.

Chief of the nobles who comes from Imu: I have not caused fear.

Wrecker who comes from Huy: I have not trespassed.

Disturber who comes from the sanctuary: I have not been violent.

Child who comes from On: I have not been deaf to Maat.

Foreteller who comes from Wensi: I have not quarreled.

Bastet who comes from the shrine: I have not winked.

Backward-face who comes from the pit: I have not copulated with a boy.

Flame-footed who comes from the dusk: I have not been false.

Dark-one who comes from darkness: I have not reviled.

Source: Translation from Miriam Lichtheim, *Ancient Egyptian Literature* (Berkeley: University of California Press, 1978), vol. 2, 126–27.

other gods without denying either their existence or the continued importance of their priests. The pharaoh Akhenaten (r. 1372–1355 B.C.E.) went a step further, however: he proclaimed that official religion would concentrate on worshipping Aten, who represented the sun. Akhenaten made the king and the queen the only people with direct access to the cult of Aten; ordinary people had no part in it. Some scholars identify Akhenaten's religion as a form of monotheism, but its underlying purpose was to strengthen his rule.

To showcase the royal family and the concentration of power that he sought, Akhenaten built a new capital for his god at Tell el-Amarna (see Map 1.2). He tried to force his revised religion on the priests of the old cults, but they resisted. Historians have blamed Akhenaten's religious zeal for leading him to neglect the practical affairs of ruling the kingdom, weakening its defense, but recent research on international correspondence found at Tell el-Amarna has shown that the pharaoh used

diplomacy in an attempt to pit foreign enemies against each other to prevent them from becoming strong enough to threaten Egypt. His policy failed, however, when the Hittites defeated the Mitanni, Egypt's allies in eastern Syria. Akhenaten's religious reform also died with him. During the reign of his successor, Tutankhamun (r. 1355–1346 B.C.E.) — famous today through the discovery in 1922 of his rich, unlooted tomb — the cult of Amun-Re reclaimed its leading role. The crisis created by Akhenaten's attempted reform emphasizes the overwhelming importance of religious conservatism in Egyptian life and the control of religion by the ruling power.

Life and Belief in the New Kingdom. Despite the period's wars, ordinary Egyptians' daily lives still revolved around their labor and the annual flood of the Nile. During the months when the river stayed between its banks, they worked their fields, rising early in the morning to avoid the searing heat. When the flooding halted agricultural work, the king required them to labor on his building projects. They lived in workers' quarters erected next to the building sites. Although slaves became more common as household workers in the New Kingdom, free workers, performing labor instead of paying taxes in money, did most of the work on this period's mammoth royal construction projects. Written texts reveal that workers lightened their burden by singing songs and telling adventure stories. They labored extensively: the majority of temples remaining in Egypt today come from the New Kingdom.

Ordinary people worshipped many different deities, especially gods they hoped would protect them in their daily lives. They venerated Bes, for instance, a dwarf with the features of a lion, as a protector of the household. They carved his image on amulets, beds, headrests, and the handles of mirrors. By the time of the New Kingdom, ordinary people believed that they, too, could have a blessed afterlife and therefore put great effort into preparing for it. Those who could afford the cost arranged to have their tombs outfitted with all the goods needed for the journey to their new existence. Most important, they had their corpses mummified so that they could have a body in the afterlife. Making a mummy required removing the brain and internal organs, drying the body with mineral salts to the consistency of old leather, and wrapping it in linen soaked with ointments. Every mummy had to travel to the afterlife with a copy of the *Book of the Dead*, whose collection of magical instructions warded off dangers and coached the dead person through his or her trial before the gods. The text listed many denials of sins that the dead person had to be able to recite, including "I have not committed crimes against people; I have not mistreated cattle; I have not robbed the poor; I have not caused pain; I have not caused tears" (see Document, "Declaring Innocence on Judgment Day in Ancient Egypt," page 22).

Magic played a large role in the lives of Egyptians. They sought spells and charms, both written and oral, from professional magicians to promote their eternal salvation, ward off demons, smooth the rocky course of love, exact revenge on enemies, and find relief from disease and injury. Egyptian doctors knew many medicinal herbs

(knowledge that was passed on to later civilizations), and they could perform demanding surgeries, including opening the skull. Still, no doctor could cure severe infections; as in the past, sick people continued to rely on the help of supernatural forces through prayers and spells.

> **REVIEW:** How did religion guide peoples' lives in ancient Egypt?

The Hittites, Minoans, and Mycenaeans, 2200–1000 B.C.E.

The first civilizations in the central Mediterranean region emerged in Anatolia, dominated by the warlike Hittite kingdom (see Map 1.1); on the large island of Crete and nearby islands, home to Minoan civilization; and on the Greek mainland, where Mycenaean civilization grew rich from raiding and trade (Map 1.3). As early as 6000 B.C.E., people from Anatolia began migrating westward and

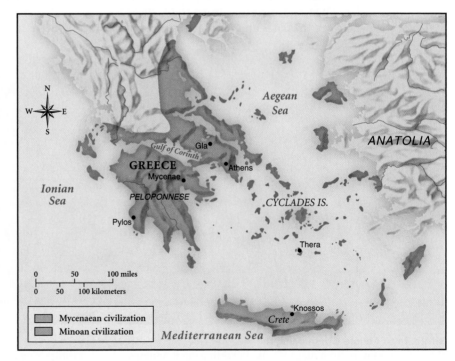

MAP 1.3 Greece and the Aegean Sea, 1500 B.C.E.
A closely packed jumble of mountains, islands, and seas defined the geography of Greece. The distances between settlements were mostly short, but rough terrain and seasonally stormy sailing made travel a chore. The distance from the mainland to the largest island in this region, Crete, where Minoan civilization arose, was sufficiently long to keep Cretans isolated from the turmoil of most of later Greek history.

southward to inhabit islands in the Mediterranean Sea. By around 2200 B.C.E., the rich civilization of the Minoans had emerged on the island of Crete and other islands in the Aegean Sea. The Anatolian peoples who stayed on the mainland also developed civilizations, of which the most aggressive and ambitious was the kingdom of the Hittites, who came into conflict with New Kingdom Egypt.

The peoples of all these civilizations enjoyed advanced technologies, elaborate architecture, striking art, a marked taste for luxury, and extensive trade contacts with Egypt and the Near East. The Hittites, like the Egyptians, created a unified state under a single central authority. The Minoans and the Mycenaeans, like the Mesopotamians, established separate states. All inhabited a dangerous world in which regional disruptions from around 1200 to 1000 B.C.E. ultimately overwhelmed their prosperous cultures. Nevertheless, their accomplishments paved the way for the later civilization of Greece, which would greatly influence the course of Western history.

The Hittites, 1750–1200 B.C.E.

By around 1750 B.C.E. the Hittites had made themselves the most powerful people of central Anatolia. They had migrated from the Caucasus area, between the Black and Caspian seas, and overcome indigenous peoples to set up their centralized kingdom. It flourished because they inhabited a fertile upland plateau in the peninsula's center, excelled in war and diplomacy, and controlled trade in their region and southward. The Hittites' military campaigns knifing southward threatened Egypt's possessions on the eastern Mediterranean coast.

Since the Hittites spoke an Indo-European language, they belonged to the linguistic family that eventually populated most of Europe. The original Indo-European speakers, who were pastoralists and raiders, had migrated as separate groups into Anatolia and Europe, including Greece, from somewhere in western Asia. Recent archaeological discoveries there of graves of women buried with weapons suggest that women in these groups originally occupied positions of leadership in war and peace alongside men; the prominence of Hittite queens in documents, royal letters, and foreign treaties perhaps sprang from that tradition.

As in other early civilizations, rule in the Hittite kingdom depended on religion. Hittite religion combined worship of the gods of Indo-European religion with worship of deities inherited from the original Anatolian population. The king served as high priest of the storm god, and Hittite belief demanded that he maintain a strict purity in his life as a demonstration of his justice and guardianship of social order. His drinking water, for example, always had to be strained. So strong was this insistence on purity that the king's water carrier was executed if so much as one hair was found in the water. Like Egyptian kings, Hittite rulers felt responsible for maintaining the gods' goodwill toward their subjects. King Mursili II (r. 1321–1295 B.C.E.), for example, issued a set of prayers begging the gods to end a plague: "What is this, o gods, that you have done? Our land is dying. . . . We have lost our wits, and we can do nothing right. O gods, whatever sin you behold, either let a prophet come forth to identify it . . . or let us see it in a dream!"

The kings conducted many religious ceremonies in

Hittite Royal Couple Worshipping the Weather God
This relief sculpture from Alaca Höyük, in north central Anatolia, shows a Hittite king and queen worshipping the weather god, as he was called, who is represented here by his sacred animal, the bull, standing on an altar. In Hittite mythology, the weather god was thought to ride over the mountains in a chariot pulled by bulls. He was a divine hero who overcame evil by slaying a great dragon. At first the monster defeated him, but the goddess Inaras tricked the dragon into getting drunk so that the weather god could kill him. What characteristics of bulls and dragons made them relevant for expressing religious ideas? *(Hirmer Fotoarchiv.)*

their capital, Hattusas, which grew into one of the most impressive cities of its era. Ringed by massive defensive walls and stone towers, it featured huge palaces aligned along straight, gravel-paved streets. Sculptures of animals, warriors, and, especially, the royal rulers decorated public spaces. Hittite kings maintained their rule by forging personal alliances—cemented by marriages and oaths of loyalty—with the noble families of the kingdom.

These rulers aggressively employed their troops to expand their power. In the periods during which ties between the kings and the nobles remained strong and the kingdom therefore preserved its unity, they launched extremely ambitious military campaigns. In 1595 B.C.E., for example, the royal army raided as far as Babylon, destroying that kingdom. Scholars no longer accept the once popular idea that the Hittites owed their success in war to a special knowledge of making weapons from iron, although their craftsmen did smelt iron, from which they made ceremonial implements. (Weapons made from iron did not become common in the Mediterranean world until well after 1200 B.C.E.—at the end of the Hittite kingdom.) Their army excelled in the use of chariots, and perhaps this skill gave them an edge.

The economic strength of the Hittite kingdom flowed from control over long-distance trade routes for essential raw materials, especially metals. The Hittites worked mightily to dominate the lucrative trade moving between the coast and inland northern Syria. The Egyptian New Kingdom pharaohs fiercely resisted Hittite expansion and power in this region. The Anatolian kingdom proved too strong, however, and in the bloody battle of Kadesh, around 1274 B.C.E., the Hittites checked the Egyptians in Syria, leading to a stalemate. Fear of Assyria eventually led the Hittite king to negotiate with his Egyptian rival, and the two war-weary kingdoms became allies sixteen years after the battle of Kadesh by agreeing to a treaty that is a landmark in the history of international diplomacy. Remarkably, both Egyptian and Hittite copies of the treaty survive. In it, the two monarchs pledged to be "at peace and brothers forever." The alliance lasted, and thirteen years later the Hittite king gave his daughter to his Egyptian "brother" as his wife.

The Minoans, 2200–1400 B.C.E.

Study of early Greek civilization traditionally begins with the people today known as Minoans, who inhabited the island of Crete and islands in the Aegean Sea by the late third millennium. The word *Minoan* was applied after the archaeologist Arthur Evans (1851–1941) searched the island for traces of King Minos, renowned in Greek myth as a fierce ruler who built the first great navy. Scholars today are not sure whether to count the Minoans as the earliest Greeks because they are uncertain whether the Minoan language, whose decipherment remains controversial, was related to Greek.

Minoans apparently had no written literature, only official records. They wrote these records in a script today called Linear A. If further research confirms a recent suggestion that Minoan was a member of the Indo-European family of languages (the ancestor of many languages, including Greek, Latin, and, much later, English), then Minoans can be seen as the earliest Greeks. Regardless of what the nature of the Minoans' language turns out to be, their interactions with the mainland deeply influenced Greek civilization.

By around 2200 B.C.E., Minoans on Crete and nearby islands had created what scholars call a **palace society**, in recognition of its sprawling, multichambered buildings that apparently housed both the rulers and their families and servants and the political, economic, and religious administration of the state. Minoan rulers combined the functions of ruler and priest, dominating both politics and religion. The palaces seem to have been largely independent, with no single one imposing unity. The general population clustered around the palaces in houses adjacent to one another; some of these settlements reached the size and density of small cities. On Crete, Knossos, which Evans thought had been Minos's headquarters, is the most famous such palace complex. Other, smaller settlements dotted outlying areas of the island, especially on the coast. The Minoans' excellent ports supported extensive international trade, above all with the Egyptians and the Hittites.

The most surprising feature of Minoan communities is that they did not build elaborate defensive walls. Palaces, towns, and even isolated country houses apparently saw no need to fortify themselves. The remains of the newer palaces—such as the one at Knossos, with its hundreds of rooms in five stories, indoor plumbing, and colorful scenes painted on the walls—have led some historians to the controversial conclusion that Minoans avoided war among themselves, despite their having no single central authority over their

---

palace society: Minoan and Mycenaean social and political organization centered on multichambered buildings housing the rulers and the administration of the state.

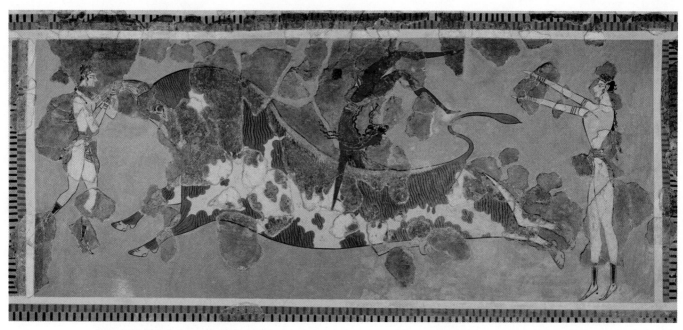

Wall Painting from Knossos, Crete
Minoan artists painted with vivid colors on plaster to enliven the walls of buildings. This painting from the palace at Knossos depicted an acrobatic performance in which a youth leaped in an aerial somersault over the back of a charging bull. Some scholars speculate this dangerous activity was a religious ritual instead of just a circus act; do you think this could be possible? Unfortunately, time and earthquakes have severely damaged most Minoan wall paintings, and the versions we see today are largely reconstructions painted around surviving fragments of the originals. *(©National Archaeological Museum, Athens, Greece / The Bridgeman Art Library.)*

independent settlements. Others object to this romantic vision of peaceful Minoans, arguing that the most powerful Minoans on Crete dominated some neighboring islands. Recent discoveries of tombs on Crete have revealed weapons caches, and a find of bones cut by knives has even raised the possibility of human sacrifice. The prominence of women in palace frescoes and the numerous figurines of buxom goddesses found on Minoan sites have also prompted speculation that Minoan society was female-dominated, but no texts have come to light to verify this. Minoan art certainly depicts women prominently and nobly, but the same is true of contemporary civilizations that men controlled. More archaeological research is needed to resolve the controversies concerning the nature of Minoan civilization.

The development of **Mediterranean polyculture**—the cultivation of olives, grapes, and grains in a single, interrelated agricultural system—profoundly increased the prosperity of Minoan society. This innovation made the most efficient use of a farmer's labor by combining crops that required intense work at different seasons. This system, which still dominates Mediterranean agriculture, had two major consequences. First, the combination of crops provided a healthy diet (the Mediterranean diet, as it is called in today's medical community), which in turn stimulated population growth. Second, agriculture became both more diversified and more specialized, increasing production of the valuable products olive oil and wine.

Agricultural surpluses spurred the growth of specialized crafts, just as they had in Mesopotamia and Egypt. To store and transport surplus food, Minoan artisans manufactured huge storage jars (the size of a modern refrigerator), in the process creating another specialized industry. Crafts workers, producing their sophisticated wares using time-consuming techniques, no longer had time to grow their own food or make the goods, such as clothes and lamps, they needed for everyday life. Instead, they exchanged the products they made for food and other goods. In this way, Minoan society experienced increasing economic interdependence.

The vast storage areas in Minoan palaces suggest that the rulers, like some Mesopotamian kings before them, controlled this interdependence through a redistributive economic system.

Mediterranean polyculture: The cultivation of olives, grapes, and grains in a single, interrelated agricultural system.

The Knossos palace, for example, held hundreds of gigantic jars capable of storing 240,000 gallons of olive oil and wine. Bowls, cups, and dippers crammed storerooms nearby. Palace officials would have decided how much each farmer or crafts producer had to contribute to the palace storehouse and how much of those contributions would then be redistributed to each person in the community for basic subsistence or as an extra reward. In this way, people gave the products of their labor to the local authority, which redistributed them as it saw fit.

The Mycenaeans, 1800–1000 B.C.E.

Ancestors of the Greeks had moved into the mainland region of Greece by perhaps 8000 B.C.E.; the first civilization definitely identified as Greek because of its Indo-European language arose in the early second millennium B.C.E., about the same time as the Hittite kingdom. These first Greeks are called Mycenaeans, a name derived from the hilltop site of Mycenae, famous for its rich graves, multichambered palace, and massive fortification walls. Located in the Peloponnese (the large peninsula forming southern Greece; see Map 1.3), Mycenae dominated its local area, but neither it nor any other settlement ever ruled all of Bronze Age Greece. Instead, the independent communities of Mycenaean civilization vied with one another in a fierce competition for natural resources and territory.

The nineteenth-century German millionaire Heinrich Schliemann was the first to discover treasure-filled graves at Mycenae. The burial objects revealed a warrior culture organized in independent settlements and ruled by aggressive kings. Constructed as stone-lined shafts, the graves contained entombed dead, who had taken hordes of valuables with them: golden jewelry, including heavy necklaces festooned with pendants, gold and silver vessels, bronze weapons decorated with scenes of wild animals inlaid in precious metals, and delicately painted pottery.

In his excitement at finding treasure, Schliemann proudly announced that he had found the grave of Agamemnon, the legendary king who commanded the Greek army against Troy, a city in northwestern Anatolia, in the Trojan War. Homer, Greece's first and most famous poet, immortalized this war in his epic poem *The Iliad*. Archaeologists now know the shaft graves date to around 1700–1600 B.C.E., long before the Trojan War could have taken place. Schliemann, who paid for his own excavation at Troy to prove to skeptics that the city had really existed, infuriated scholars with

his self-promotion. But his passion to confirm that Greek myth preserved a kernel of historical truth spurred him on to the work at Mycenae, which provided the most spectacular evidence for mainland Greece's earliest civilization.

Mycenaean Interaction with Minoan Crete.   Since the hilly terrain of Greece had little fertile land but many useful ports, settlements tended to spring up near the coast. Mycenaean rulers enriched themselves by dominating local farmers, conducting naval raids, and participating in seaborne trade. Palace records inscribed on clay tablets reveal that the Mycenaeans operated under a redistributive economy. On the tablets scribes made detailed lists of goods received and goods paid out, recording everything from chariots to livestock, landholdings, personnel, and perfumes, even broken equipment taken out of service. Like the Minoans, Mycenaeans apparently did not use writing to record the oral literature that scholars believe they created.

A special kind of burial chambers, called *tholos* tombs — spectacular underground domed chambers built in beehive shapes with closely fitted stones — shows that some Mycenaeans had become very rich by about 1500 B.C.E. The architectural details of the tholos tombs and the style of the burial goods placed in them testify to the far-flung expeditions for trade and war that Mycenaean rulers conducted throughout the eastern Mediterranean. Above all, however, they show a close connection with Minoan civilization because they display many motifs clearly inspired by Minoan designs.

Underwater archaeology has revealed the influence of international commerce during this period in promoting cultural interaction. Divers have discovered, for example, that a late-fourteenth-century B.C.E. shipwreck off Uluburun in Turkey carried such a mixed cargo and such varied personal possessions — from Canaan, Cyprus, Greece, Egypt, Babylon, and elsewhere in the Near East — that it is impossible to attach a single nationality to this tramp freighter.

The sea brought the Mycenaean and Minoan civilizations into close contact, but they remained different in significant ways. The Mycenaeans spoke Greek and made burnt offerings to the gods; the Minoans did neither. The Minoans extended their religious worship outside their centers, establishing sacred places in caves, on mountaintops, and in country villas, while the mainlanders concentrated the worship of their gods inside their walled communities. When the Mycenaeans started building palaces in the fourteenth century B.C.E., unlike the Minoans they designed them around *megarons* — rooms with

Decorated Dagger from Mycenae
The hilltop fortress and palace at Mycenae was the capital of Bronze Age Greece's most famous kingdom. The picture of a lion hunt inlaid in gold and silver on this sixteenth-century B.C.E. dagger expressed how wealthy Mycenaean men saw their roles in society: as courageous hunters and warriors overcoming the hostile forces of nature. The nine-inch blade was found in a circle of graves inside Mycenae's walls, where the highest-ranking people were buried with their treasures as evidence of their status. *(Nimatallah / Art Resource, NY.)*

prominent ceremonial hearths and thrones for the rulers. Some Mycenaean palaces had more than one megaron, which could soar two stories high with columns to support a roof above the second-floor balconies.

Documents found in the palace at Knossos reveal that by around 1400 B.C.E. the Mycenaeans had acquired dominance over Crete, possibly in a war over commerce in the Mediterranean. The documents were tablets written in **Linear B**, a pictographic script based on Minoan Linear A. The twentieth-century architect Michael Ventris proved that Linear B was used to write not Minoan, but a different language: Greek. Because the Linear B tablets date from before the final destruction of Knossos in about 1370 B.C.E., they show that the palace administration had been keeping its records in a foreign language for some time and therefore that Mycenaeans were controlling Crete well before the end of Minoan civilization. By the middle of the fourteenth century B.C.E., then, the Mycenaeans had displaced the Minoans as the Aegean region's preeminent civilization.

War in Mycenaean Society. By the time Mycenaeans took over Crete, war at home and abroad was the principal concern of well-off Mycenaean men, a tradition that they passed on to later Greek civilization. Contents of Bronze Age tombs in Greece reveal that no wealthy man went to his grave without his war equipment. Armor and weapons were so central to a Mycenaean man's identity that he could not do without them, even in death. Warriors rode into battle in expensive hardware—lightweight, two-wheeled chariots pulled by horses. These revolutionary vehicles, perhaps introduced by Indo-Europeans migrating

from Central Asia, first appeared in various Mediterranean and Near Eastern societies not long after 2000 B.C.E.; the first picture of such a chariot in the Aegean region occurs on a Mycenaean grave marker from about 1500 B.C.E. Wealthy people evidently desired this new form of transportation not only for war but also as proof of their social status.

The Mycenaeans seem to have spent more on war than on religion. In any case, they did not construct any giant religious buildings like Mesopotamia's ziggurats or Egypt's pyramids. Their most important deities were male gods concerned with war. The names of gods found in the Linear B tablets reveal that Mycenaeans passed down many divinities to the Greeks of later times.

The Period of Calamities, 1200–1000 B.C.E.

A state of political equilibrium, in which kings corresponded with one another and traders traveled all over the area, characterized the Mediterranean and Near Eastern world around 1300 B.C.E. Within a century, however, calamity had struck almost every major political state in the region, including Egypt, some kingdoms of Mesopotamia, and the Hittite and Mycenaean kingdoms. Neither the civilizations united under a single central authority nor the ones with separate and independent states survived. This period of international violence from about 1200 to 1000 B.C.E. remains one of the most fascinating and disturbing puzzles in the history of Western civilization.

The best clue to what happened comes from Egyptian and Hittite records. They document many foreign invasions in this period, especially from the sea. According to an inscription, in about 1190 B.C.E. a warrior pharaoh defeated a powerful coalition of seaborne invaders from the north, who had fought their way to the edge of Egypt. These

---

Linear B: The Mycenaeans' pictographic script for writing Greek.

Sea Peoples, as historians call them, comprised many different groups. Some had been mercenary soldiers in the armies of rulers whom they deserted; some were raiders by profession. Many may have been Greeks. The famous story of the Trojan War probably recalls this period of calamities because it portrays a seaborne Greek army attacking Troy and the surrounding region in Anatolia.

Apparently no single, unified group of Sea Peoples launched a tidal wave of violence. Rather, many different bands devastated the region. A chain reaction of attacks and flights in a recurring and expanding cycle put even more bands on the move. The turmoil reached far inland. The Babylonian kingdom collapsed, the Assyrians were confined to their homeland, and much of western Asia and Syria was devastated.

The reasons for these widespread calamities remain mysterious, but their consequences for the eastern Mediterranean region are clear. The once mighty Hittite kingdom fell around 1200 B.C.E., when raiders cut off its trade routes for raw materials. Invaders razed its capital city, Hattusas, which never revived. Egypt's New Kingdom repelled the Sea Peoples with a tremendous military effort, but the raiders destroyed the Egyptian long-distance trade network. Power struggles between the pharaohs and the leading priests undermined political stability. By the end of the New Kingdom, around 1081 B.C.E., Egypt had shrunk to its original territorial core along the Nile's banks. The calamities ruined Egypt's credit. For example, when an eleventh-century B.C.E. Theban temple official traveled to Phoenicia to buy cedar for a ceremonial boat, the city's ruler demanded cash in advance. Although the Egyptian monarchy hung on, power struggles between pharaohs and priests, made worse by frequent attacks from abroad, prevented the reestablishment of centralized authority. No Egyptian dynasty ever again became an aggressive international power.

In Greece, the troubles were homegrown. The Mycenaeans reached the zenith of their power around 1400–1250 B.C.E. The enormous domed tomb at Mycenae, called the Treasury of Atreus, testifies to the riches of this period. The tomb's elaborately decorated facade and soaring roof reveal the self-confidence of the Mycenaean warrior princes. The last phase of the extensive palace at Pylos on the west coast of the Peloponnese also dates from this time. It boasted glorious wall paintings, storerooms bursting with food, and a royal

bathroom with a built-in tub and intricate plumbing. But these prosperous Mycenaeans did not escape the widespread calamities that began around 1200 B.C.E. Linear B tablets record the disposition of troops to the coast to guard the palace at Pylos at this time. The palace inhabitants of eastern Greece constructed defensive walls so massive that the later Greeks thought giants had built them. These fortifications would have protected coastal palaces against seafaring attackers, who could have been either outsiders or Greeks. The wall around the inland palace at Gla in central Greece, however, which foreign raiders could not easily reach, confirms that, above all, Mycenaean communities had to defend themselves against other Mycenaean communities.

In Greece itself, then, the Sea Peoples apparently did relatively little damage. Rather, internal turmoil and major earthquakes destroyed Mycenaean civilization. Archaeology offers no evidence for the ancient tradition that Dorian Greeks invading from the north caused the destruction. Near-constant civil war by jealous local rulers overburdened the elaborate administrative balancing act necessary for the palaces' redistributive economies and hindered recovery from earthquake damage. The violence killed many Mycenaeans, and the disappearance of the palace-based redistributive economy put many others on the road to starvation. The calamity uprooted many of the remaining Greeks from their homes and forced them to wander abroad in search of new places to settle. Like people from the earliest times, they had to move to build a better life.

REVIEW: How did war determine the fates of the early civilizations of Anatolia, Crete, and Greece?

Conclusion

The best way to define Western civilization is to study its history, which begins in Mesopotamia and Egypt; these cultures in turn influenced the later civilization of Greece. Cities first arose in Mesopotamia around 4000 to 3000 B.C.E. Hierarchy had characterized society to some degree from the very beginning, but it, along with patriarchy, grew more pronounced once civilization and political states with centralized authority became widespread.

Trade and war were constants, both aiming in different ways at profit and glory. Indirectly, they often generated cultural interaction by putting

---

Sea Peoples: The diverse groups of raiders who devastated the eastern Mediterranean region in the period of calamities around 1200–1000 B.C.E.

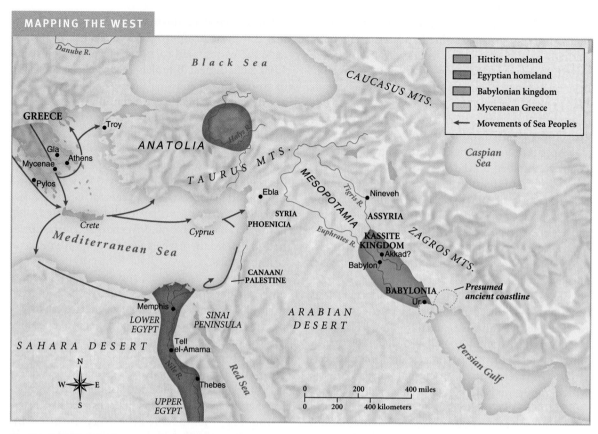

The Period of Calamities, 1200–1000 B.C.E.
Bands of wandering warriors and raiders set the eastern Mediterranean aflame at the end of the Bronze Age. This violence displaced many people and ended the power of the kingdoms of the Egyptians, the Hittites, and the Mycenaeans. Even some of the Near Eastern states well inland from the eastern Mediterranean coast felt the effects of this period of unrest, whose causes remain mysterious.

civilizations into close contact to learn from one another. Technological innovation was also a prominent characteristic of this long period. The invention of metallurgy, monumental architecture, mathematics, and alphabetic writing greatly affected people's lives. Religion was at the center of society, with the gods seen as demanding just and righteous conduct from everyone.

The Mediterranean Sea was a two-edged sword for the early civilizations that grew up around and near it: as a highway for transporting goods and ideas, it was a boon; as an artery for conveying attackers, it was a bane. Ironically, the raids of the Sea Peoples that smashed the prosperity of the eastern Mediterranean region around 1200–1000 B.C.E. also set in motion the forces that led to the next step in our story, the resurgence of Greece. Strife among Mycenaean rulers turned the regional unrest of those centuries into a local catastrophe; fighting each other for dominance, they so weakened their monarchies that they could not recover after natural disasters. To an outside observer, Greek society by around 1000 B.C.E. might

have seemed destined for irreversible economic and social decline, even oblivion. Chapter 2 shows how wrong this prediction would have been. After a difficult period of economic and population decline, Greeks invented a new form of social and political organization and breathed renewed life into their culture, inspired by their neighbors in the Near East and Egypt.

FOR FURTHER EXPLORATION

■ **For suggested references, including Web sites, for topics in this chapter,** see page SR-1 at the end of the book.

■ **For additional primary-source material from this period,** see Chapter 1 in *Sources of THE MAKING OF THE WEST,* Third Edition.

■ **For Web sites and documents related to topics in this chapter,** see *Make History* at bedfordstmartins.com/hunt.

CHAPTER REVIEW

KEY TERMS AND PEOPLE

civilization (4)

polytheism (5)

monotheism (5)

city-state (7)

ziggurats (8)

cuneiform (10)

empire (12)

redistributive
economy (14)

Hammurabi (14)

hieroglyphs (17)

Maat (17)

wisdom literature (20)

palace society (25)

Mediterranean
polyculture (26)

Linear B (28)

Sea Peoples (29)

MAKING CONNECTIONS

1. Compare and contrast the environmental factors affecting the emergence of the world's first civilizations in Mesopotamia and Egypt.

2. What were the advantages and disadvantages of living in a unified country under a single central authority compared to living in a region with separate city-states?

For practice quizzes, a customized study plan, and other study tools, see the Online Study Guide at bedfordstmartins.com/hunt.

REVIEW QUESTIONS

1. What are the challenges of defining Western civilization?

2. How did life change for people in Mesopotamia when they began to live in cities?

3. How did religion guide peoples' lives in ancient Egypt?

4. How did war determine the fates of the early civilizations of Anatolia, Crete, and Greece?

IMPORTANT EVENTS

4000–1000 B.C.E.	Bronze Age in southwestern Asia, Egypt, and Europe	2112–2004 B.C.E.	Ur III dynasty rules in Sumer
4000–3000 B.C.E.	Mesopotamians invent writing and establish first cities	2061–1665 B.C.E.	Middle Kingdom in Egypt
3050 B.C.E.	Narmer (Menes) unites Upper and Lower Egypt into one kingdom	1792–1750 B.C.E.	Hammurabi rules Babylon and issues his law code
2687–2190 B.C.E.	Old Kingdom in Egypt	1750 B.C.E.	Hittites establish their kingdom in Anatolia
2350 B.C.E.	Sargon establishes the world's first empire in Akkadia	1569–1081 B.C.E.	New Kingdom in Egypt
2300–2200 B.C.E.	Enheduanna, princess of Akkad, composes poetry	1400 B.C.E.	The Mycenaeans build their first palaces in Greece and take over Minoan Crete
2200 B.C.E.	Minoans build their first palaces	1274 B.C.E.	Battle of Kadesh in Syria between the Egyptians and the Hittites
		1200–1000 B.C.E.	Period of calamities ends many kingdoms

The Near East and the Emergence of Greece

1000–500 B.C.E.

The Greek poet Homer told violent stories recalling the period of calamities (1200–1000 B.C.E.) that had nearly destroyed Greek civilization. In his epic poem *The Iliad*, composed in the eighth century B.C.E., he narrated bloody tales of the Trojan War that were rich with legends born from mingled Greek and Near Eastern traditions, such as the story of the Greek hero Bellerophon. Driven from his home by a false charge of sexual assault, Bellerophon had to serve as "enforcer" for a king in Lycia (a region south of Troy), combating the king's most dangerous enemies. He had to fight—and kill—fierce tribesmen, Amazons, and even the king's own warriors, but his most famous contest pitted him against a monster. As Homer tells it, Bellerophon was ordered "to defeat the Chimera, an inhuman freak created by the gods, horrible with its lion's head, goat's body, and dragon's tail, breathing fire all the time." Riding on the winged horse Pegasus, Bellerophon triumphed by swooping down on the beast in an aerial attack. For his amazing heroics, the king gave Bellerophon his daughter in marriage and half his kingdom.

Homer's story provides evidence for the intercultural contact between the Near East and Greece that supported the revival of Greece after its civilization nearly disappeared. Both the Chimera and the horse-headed, hawk-bodied, lion-footed beast painted on the vase from Corinth shown in the chapter-opening illustration were creatures from Near Eastern myth taken over by Greeks. Greece's geography—countless ports on its long coastline and many islands—promoted contacts by sea through trade, travel, and war with its richer and stronger Near Eastern neighbors. In the centuries from 1000 to 500 B.C.E., these

Black-Figure Vase from Corinth
This vase was made in Corinth about 600 B.C.E., painted in the so-called black-figure style in which artists carved details into the dark-baked clay. In the late sixth century B.C.E., this style gave way to red-figure, in which artists painted details in black on a reddish background instead of engraving them; the result was finer detail (compare this vase painting with that on page 45). The animals and mythical creatures on the vase shown here follow Near Eastern models, which inspired Archaic Age Greek artists to put people and animals into their designs again after their absence during the Dark Age. Why do you think the artist depicted the animal at the lower right with two bodies but only one head? *(© Copyright The Trustees of the British Museum.)*

contacts, combined with the Greeks' value of competitive individual excellence, their sense of a communal identity, and their belief that people in general—and not just rulers—were responsible for instituting justice, helped Greeks reestablish the prosperity that they had lost and reinvent their civilization with a radically new concept of central authority: government without kings.

Despite the turmoil and economic distress that had destroyed so many Bronze Age communities by around 1000 B.C.E., people's desire for trade and cross-cultural contact endured and increased as conditions improved over the following centuries. The Near East, retaining monarchy as its traditional form of social and political organization, recovered more quickly than Greece. Near Eastern kings in this period extracted surpluses from subject populations to fund their palaces and their armies. They also continually sought new conquests to win glory, exploit the labor of conquered peoples, seize raw materials, and conduct long-distance trade.

By contrast, the wars and subsequent economic collapse of 1200–1000 B.C.E. had destroyed the political and social organization of Minoan and Mycenaean Greece, which developed in radically different forms thereafter. During Greece's slow recovery from poverty and depopulation from about 1000 to 750 B.C.E., Greeks sailed the Mediterranean Sea to maintain trade and cross-cultural contact with the older civilizations of the Near East. Their mythology, as in Homer, and their art, as on the Corinthian vase, reveal that they imported ideas as well as goods during this difficult era.

By the eighth century B.C.E., Greeks had begun to create their own kind of city-state, the *polis*, as a new form of political and social organization. The polis was a radical innovation because it made citizenship—not subjection to kings—the basis for society and politics, and included the poor as citizens. It gave legal—though not political—rights to women, but no rights to slaves. With the exception of occasional tyrannies, Greek city-states rejected central authority vested in a single ruler, instead governing themselves by having male citizens share political power. The extent of the power sharing varied, with small groups of upper-class men dominating in some places. In other places, however, the polis shared power among all free men, even the poor, eventually creating the world's first democracy. The Greeks' invention of democratic politics, limited though it might have been by modern standards, stands as a landmark in the history of Western civilization.

Religion and philosophy also changed profoundly in this period. Leaders and thinkers in the Near East and Greece gradually created new ways of belief and thought that slowly filtered down to the mass of people and greatly influenced the development of Western civilization. In religion, the Persians developed beliefs that saw human life as a struggle between good and evil, and the Hebrews embraced monotheism. In philosophy, the Greeks began to use reason and logic to replace mythological explanations of nature.

FOCUS QUESTION: How did the social and political organization that Greece developed differ from those of the Near East?

From Dark Age to Empire in the Near East, 1000–500 B.C.E.

The widespread violence in 1200–1000 B.C.E. had weakened or obliterated many communities and populations in the eastern Mediterranean. Historians have traditionally used the term *Dark Age* to refer to the era that followed, both because economic conditions were so gloomy for so many

■ 1000–750 Greek Dark Age

■ 800 Greek alphabet

■ 776 First Olympic Games

| 1000 B.C.E. | 900 B.C.E. | 800 B.C.E. |

■ 900–600 Neo-Assyrian Empire

■ 750 Greek polis begins to develop

people and because our knowledge of what happened is so limited. Though common, this term is controversial because recent archaeological research shows that, despite difficult conditions, people in this era were still actively pursuing trade and intercultural contacts. The Dark Age in the Near East lasted less than a century, while in Greece it lasted over two hundred years.

By 900 B.C.E., a powerful and centralized Assyrian kingdom had once again emerged in Mesopotamia. From this base, the Assyrians carved out a new empire even larger than the preceding one. The riches and power of this Neo-Assyrian Empire inspired first the Babylonians and then the Persians to build their own empires when Assyrian power collapsed. The traditional striving for empire remained constant in the Near East. The relatively powerless Hebrews, however, established a new path for civilization during this period by changing their religion. They developed monotheism and produced the Hebrew Bible, known to Christians as the Old Testament.

The New Empire of Assyria, 900–600 B.C.E.

When the Hittite kingdom fell around 1000 B.C.E., the Assyrians gained power by seizing supplies of metal and controlling trade routes in the eastern Mediterranean (Map 2.1). By 900 B.C.E., Assyrian armies punched westward all the way to the coast. In the eighth century B.C.E., the Neo-Assyrian kings conquered Babylon, in southern Mesopotamia, and they added Egypt to their empire in the seventh century.

Neo-Assyrian Militarism and Imperial Brutality.
A warrior culture pervaded Neo-Assyrian society. A military innovation made Assyrian armies unstoppable: foot soldiers, not cavalry, were the Assyrians' main strike force. These infantrymen excelled in using military technology such as siege

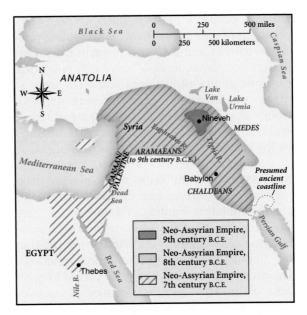

MAP 2.1 Expansion of the Neo-Assyrian Empire, c. 900–650 B.C.E.
Like their Akkadian, Assyrian, and Babylonian predecessors, the Neo-Assyrian kings dominated a vast region of the Near East to secure a supply of metals, access to trade routes on land and sea, and imperial glory. In so doing, they built the largest empire the world had yet seen. Also like their predecessors, they treated disobedient subjects harshly and intolerantly to try to prevent their diverse territories from rebelling.

towers and battering rams, while swift chariots carried archers. Campaigns against foreign lands brought in revenues supplementing the domestic economy, which centered on agriculture, animal husbandry, and long-distance trade. Neo-Assyrian kings kept order by brutal treatment of conquered peoples. Those allowed to stay in their homelands had to pay annual tributes to the Assyrians: these tributes included raw materials and luxury goods such as incense, wine, dyed linens, glasswork, and ivory. Worse was the fate of the large number of

657 Cypselus becomes tyrant

546–510 Peisistratus's rule

700 Spartans conquer Messenia

594 Solon's reforms

700 B.C.E.   **600 B.C.E.**   **500 B.C.E.**

700–500 Ionian philosophers invent rationalism

597, 586 Hebrew exile

508–500 Cleisthenes' reforms

630 Birth of Sappho

539 Cyrus captures Babylon; Hebrews return to Canaan

defeated people whom the kings routinely deported to Assyria for work on huge building projects—temples and palaces—in main cities. One unexpected consequence of this harsh policy was the undermining of the kings' native language: so many Arameans, for example, were deported from Canaan to Assyria that Aramaic had largely replaced Assyrian as the land's everyday language by the eighth century B.C.E.

Neo-Assyrian Life and Religion. When not making war, Neo-Assyrian men displayed their status and masculinity by hunting wild animals; the more dangerous the quarry, the better. The king hunted lions to demonstrate his vigor and power and thus his capacity to rule. Royal lion hunts provided a favorite subject for sculptors, who carved long relief sculptures that narrated a connected story. Although the Neo-Assyrian imperial administration preserved countless documents in its archives, literacy apparently mattered far less to the kingdom's men than did war, hunting, and practical technology. One king, for example, boasted that he invented new irrigation equipment and a novel method of metal casting. Only one Assyrian ruler ever proclaimed his scholarly accomplishments: "I have read complicated texts, whose versions in Sumerian are obscure and in Akkadian hard to understand. I do research on the cuneiform texts on stone from before the Flood." Women of the social elite probably had a chance to become literate, but they were excluded from the male dominions of war and hunting.

Public religion, which included deities adopted from Babylonia, reflected the prominence of war in Assyrian culture: even the cult of Ishtar, the goddess of love and fertility, glorified war-

fare. The Neo-Assyrians' passion for monumental architecture led them to build huge temples for the gods. The temples' staffs of priests and slaves grew so numerous that the revenues from temple lands were insufficient to support them; the kings had to supply extra funds from the spoils of conquest.

The Neo-Assyrian kings' harshness made even their own people, especially the social elite, dislike their rule. Rebellions were common throughout the history of the kingdom; a seventh-century B.C.E. revolt fatally weakened it. The Medes, an Iranian people, and the Chaldeans, a Semitic people who had driven the Assyrians from Babylonia, combined forces to invade the tottering kingdom. Recent research has disproved the long-standing assumption that the attackers destroyed the Assyrian capital at Nineveh in 612 B.C.E., but their invasion nevertheless ended the Neo-Assyrian kings' dreams of empire.

The Neo-Babylonian Empire, 600–539 B.C.E.

As leaders of the allies who overthrew the Neo-Assyrian Empire, the Chaldeans seized the lion's share of territory. Sprung from seminomadic herders along the Persian Gulf, by 600 B.C.E. they had established the Neo-Babylonian Empire, the most powerful in Babylonian history, if the shortest-lived: it fell to the Near East's next great empire, that of the Persians, in 539 B.C.E. The Chaldeans spent lavishly to turn Babylon into an architectural showplace, rebuilding the great temple of its chief god, Marduk, and constructing an elaborate city gate dedicated to the goddess Ishtar. Blue-glazed bricks and lions molded in yellow, red, and white decorated the gate's walls, which soared thirty-six feet high.

The Chaldeans adopted traditional Babylonian culture and preserved much Mesopotamian literature, such as the *Epic of Gilgamesh*. They also created many new works of prose and poetry, which the educated minority would often read aloud publicly for the enjoyment of the illiterate. Particularly popular were fables, proverbs, essays, and prophecies teaching morality and proper

Neo-Assyrian Guardian Creature
This human-headed, winged lion creature stood guard over a gate at the palace of a ninth-century B.C.E. Neo-Assyrian king. Carved from alabaster, the guardian stood ten feet tall, with a cap to signify its divine power. The sculptor gave it five legs so it would look natural when viewed either from the side or the front. The king reported in an inscription that he hosted 69,574 people at a party celebrating his new capital: "I feasted, wined, bathed, and honored them for ten days before sending them home in peace and joy." *(The Metropolitan Museum of Art. Gift of John D. Rockefeller Jr. 1932 (32.143.1.2) Photograph © 1981 The Metropolitan Museum of Art.)*

behavior. This so-called wisdom literature, a Near Eastern tradition going back at least to the Egyptian Old Kingdom, would greatly influence the later religious writings of the Hebrews.

The Chaldeans passed on their knowledge to others outside their region. Their advances in astronomy became so influential that the Greeks used the word *Chaldean* to mean "astronomer." The Chaldeans' primary motivation for observing the stars was the belief that the gods communicated their will to humans through natural phenomena, such as celestial movements and eclipses, abnormal births, patterns of smoke curling upward from a fire, and the trails of ants. The interpretation of these phenomena as messages from the gods exemplified the mixture of science and religion characteristic of ancient Near Eastern thought and proved influential on the Greeks.

The Persian Empire, 557–500 B.C.E.

Cyrus (r. 557–530 B.C.E.) founded the Persian Empire in what is today Iran through his skills as a general and a diplomat who respected others' religious beliefs. He continued the region's tradition

---

Cyrus: Founder of the Persian Empire.

of kings waging war to gain territory when he conquered Babylon in 539 B.C.E.; Cyrus capitalized on religious strife there by presenting himself as the restorer of traditional Babylonian religion, thereby winning local support. An ancient inscription has him proclaim: "Marduk, the great lord, caused Babylon's generous residents to adore me."

Cyrus's successors expanded Persian rule on the same principles of military strength and cultural tolerance. At its height, the Persian Empire extended from Anatolia (today Turkey), the eastern Mediterranean coast, and Egypt on the west to present-day Pakistan on the east (Map 2.2). Since Persian kings believed that they had a divine right to rule everyone in the world, they never stopped trying to expand their empire.

Persian Royal Magnificence and Decentralized Rule. The Persian monarchy's revenues produced wealth beyond imagination, and everything about the king emphasized his grandeur. His robes of purple outshone everyone else's; only he could step on the red carpets spread for him to walk on; his servants held their hands before their mouths in his presence so that he would not have to breathe the same air as they; he appeared larger than any other person in the sculpture adorning

The Great King of Persia
Like their Assyrian predecessors, the Persian kings decorated their palaces with large relief sculptures emphasizing royal dignity and success. This one from Persepolis shows officials and petitioners giving the king proper respect when entering his presence. To symbolize their elevated status, the king and his son, who stands behind the throne, are shown larger than everyone else. Do you think the way the sculptors portrayed the figures from the side is more or less artistic than the technique used by the Egyptian painters in the day of judgment painting on page 2? Why? *(Courtesy of the Oriental Institute of the University of Chicago.)*

■ **For more help analyzing this image,** see the visual activity for this chapter in the Online Study Guide at **bedfordstmartins.com/hunt**.

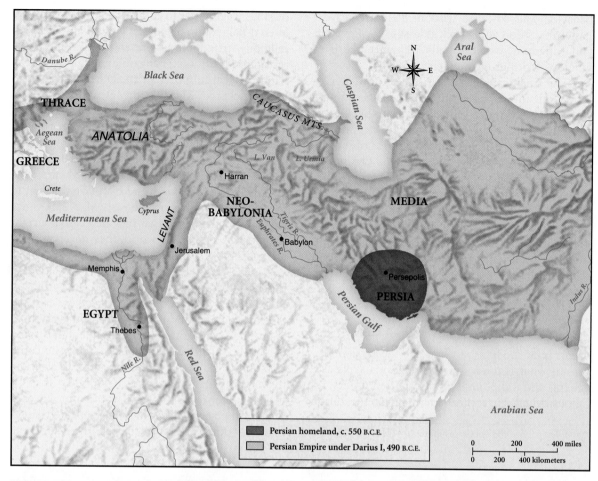

MAP 2.2 Expansion of the Persian Empire, c. 550–490 B.C.E.
Cyrus (r. c. 557–530 B.C.E.) initiated the Persian Empire, which his successors expanded to be even larger than the Neo-Assyrian Empire that it replaced. The Persian kings pressed hard outward from their inland center to gain coastal possessions for access to seaborne trade and naval bases. By late in the reign of Darius (r. 522–486 B.C.E.), the Persian Empire had expanded eastward as far as the western edge of India, while to the west it reached Thrace, the eastern edge of Europe. Unlike their imperial predecessors, the Persian kings won their subjects' loyalty with tolerance and religious freedom, although they treated rebels harshly.

his immense palace at Persepolis. To display his concern for his loyal subjects as well as the gargantuan scale of his resources, the king provided meals for fifteen thousand nobles, courtiers, and followers every day—although he himself ate hidden from his guests' view. Those who committed serious offenses against his laws or his dignity the king punished brutally, mutilating their bodies and executing their families. Contemporary Greeks, in awe of the Persian monarch's power and his lavish lifestyle, called him the Great King.

So long as his subjects—numbering in the millions and of many different ethnicities—remained peaceful, the king left them alone to live and worship as they pleased. The empire's smoothly functioning administrative structure sprang from Assyrian precedents: satraps (regional governors) ruled enormous territories with little interference from the kings. In this decentralized system, the governors' duties included keeping order, enrolling troops when needed, and sending revenues to the royal treasury.

Darius I (r. 522–486 B.C.E.) extended Persian power eastward to the Indus valley and westward to Thrace. Organizing this vast territory into provinces, he assigned each region taxes payable in the medium best suited to its local economy—precious metals, grain, horses, slaves. He also required each region to send soldiers to the royal army. A network of roads and a courier system for royal mail provided communication among the far-flung provincial centers. The Greek historian Herodotus reported that neither snow, rain, heat, nor darkness slowed the couriers from completing their routes as swiftly as possible, a feat transformed centuries later into the U.S. Postal Service motto.

Persian Religion. Ruling as absolute autocrats, the Persian kings believed themselves superior to everyone. They claimed not to be gods but rather to be the agents of Ahura Mazda, the supreme god of Persia. As Darius said in his autobiography, carved into a mountainside in three languages, "Ahura Mazda gave me kingship.... By the will of Ahura Mazda the provinces respected my laws."

Persian religion made Ahura Mazda the center of its devotion and took its doctrines from the teachings of the legendary prophet Zarathustra, who may have lived as long ago as 1200–1000 B.C.E. (The religion is called Zoroastrianism today from Zoroaster, the Greek name for this holy man.) Zarathustra proclaimed Ahura Mazda to be "the father of Truth" and "creator of Good Thought," who demanded purity from his worshippers and promised help to those who lived with truthfulness and justice. The most important doctrine of Zoroastrianism was **moral dualism**. This belief saw the world as the arena for an ongoing battle between the two opposing divine forces of good and evil. Ahura Mazda as the embodiment of good and light constantly struggled against the evil darkness represented by the Satan-like figure Ahriman. Human beings had to choose between the way of the truth and the way of the lie, between purity and impurity. Only those judged righteous after death made it across "the bridge of separation" to heaven and avoided falling from its narrow span into hell. Persian religion's emphasis on ethical behavior and on a supreme god had a lasting influence on others, especially the Hebrews.

The Hebrews, Origins to 539 B.C.E.

The Hebrews' development of a monotheistic religion makes them a principal building block in the foundations of Western civilization, even though they never rivaled the political and military power of the great empires in the Near East. Their religion, known as Judaism, developed over a long time. It reflected influences from the Hebrews' polytheistic neighbors in Canaan (ancient Palestine), but its initiation was the most important religious innovation in Western history.

Hebrew Origins and the Bible. The enduring legacy of the Hebrews to Western civilization

comes from the significance of the book that became their sacred scripture, the Hebrew Bible. This book deeply affected the formation of not only Judaism but also Christianity and, later, Islam. Unfortunately, no source provides definitive information on the historical background of the Hebrews or their religion. The Bible tells stories to explain God's moral plan for the universe, not to give a full account of Hebrew origins, and archaeology has not yielded a clear picture.

According to the Bible's account, the patriarch Abraham and his followers migrated from the Mesopotamian city of Ur to Canaan, perhaps around 1900 B.C.E. Once there, the Hebrews continued to live as semi-nomads, tending flocks of animals on the region's scanty grasslands and living in temporary tent settlements. They occasionally planted barley or wheat for a season or two and then moved on to new pastures. Traditionally believed to have been divided into twelve tribes, they never settled down or formed a political state in this period. Organized political and military power in the region remained in the hands of the Canaanites.

Abraham's son Isaac moved his pastoral people to various locations to try to avoid disputes with local Canaanites over grazing rights. Isaac's son Jacob, the story continues, moved to Egypt late in life when his son Joseph brought Jacob and other relatives there to escape famine in Canaan. Joseph had previously used his intelligence and charisma to rise to an important position in the Egyptian administration. The biblical story of the movement of a band of Hebrews to Egypt represents a crucial event in their early history, possibly reflecting a time when drought forced some Hebrews to migrate gradually from southwest Asia into the Nile delta of Egypt. They probably drifted in during the seventeenth or sixteenth century B.C.E. as part of the movement of peoples into Egypt at the time of Hyksos rule. By the thirteenth century B.C.E., the pharaohs had conscripted the Hebrew men into slave-labor gangs for farming and for construction work on large building projects.

According to the Book of Exodus, the Hebrew deity, Yahweh, instructed Moses to lead the Hebrews out of bondage in Egypt against the will of the king, perhaps around the mid-thirteenth century B.C.E. Yahweh sent ten plagues to compel the pharaoh to free the Hebrews, but the king still

Phoenicia and Canaan/Palestine

---

moral dualism: The belief that the world is the arena for an ongoing battle for control between divine forces of good and evil.

tried to recapture them during their flight. Yahweh therefore miraculously parted the sea to allow them to escape eastward; the water swirled back together and drowned the pharaoh's army as it tried to follow.

Covenant, Monotheism, and Hebrew Law. The biblical narrative then relates the crucial event in the history of the Hebrews: the formalizing of a covenant between them and their deity, who revealed himself to Moses on Mount Sinai in the desert northeast of Egypt. The covenant consisted of an agreement between the Hebrews and Yahweh that, in return for their promise to worship him exclusively as their only god and to live by his laws, Yahweh would make them his chosen people and lead them into a promised land of safety and prosperity. This binding agreement demanded human obedience to divine law and promised punishment for unrighteousness. Yahweh described himself to Moses as "compassionate and gracious, patient, ever constant and true . . . forgiving wickedness, rebellion, and sin, and not sweeping the guilty clean away; but one who punishes sons and grandsons to the third and fourth generation for their fathers' iniquity" (Exodus 34:6–7).

Because the earliest parts of the Hebrew Bible were probably composed about 950 B.C.E., more than three hundred years after the Hebrews' exodus from Egypt, the biblical account of the Hebrew covenant and laws deals with a distant, undocumented time. Like their neighbors in Canaan, the early Hebrews originally worshipped a variety of gods, including spirits believed to reside in natural objects such as trees and stones. Yahweh may have originally been the deity of the tribe of Midian, to which Moses's father-in-law belonged. The form of the covenant with Yahweh conformed to the ancient Near Eastern tradition of treaties between a superior and subordinates, but its content differed from that of other ancient Near Eastern religions because it made Yahweh the exclusive deity of his people. In the time of Moses, some Hebrews, despite their leaders' urging, continued to worship other local gods, such as Baal of Canaan.

The Hebrew Bible sets forth the religious and moral code the Hebrews had to follow. The **Torah** (the first five books of the Hebrew Bible, called the Pentateuch by Christians) recorded numerous laws for righteous living. Most famous are the Ten Commandments, which required Hebrews to worship Yahweh; honor their parents; refrain from work on the seventh day of the week (the Sabbath); and abstain from murder, adultery, theft, lying, and covetousness. Many of the Hebrews' laws shared the traditional form and content of earlier Mesopotamian laws, such as those of Hammurabi: if someone did a certain thing to another person, then a specified punishment was imposed on the perpetrator. For example, both Hammurabi's laws and Hebrew law covered the case of an ox that had gored a person; the owner was penalized only if he had been warned about his beast's tendency to gore and had done nothing to restrain it. Also like Hammurabi's laws, Hebrew law expressed an interest in the welfare of the poor as well as the rich. In addition, it secured protection for the lower classes and people without power, such as strangers, widows, and orphans.

Hebrew law and thus Hebrew justice differed significantly from Mesopotamian precedent, however, in applying the same rules and punishments to everyone, without regard to social rank. Hebrew law also eliminated vicarious punishment—a Mesopotamian tradition ordering, for example, that a rapist's wife be raped or that the son of a builder be killed if his father's negligent work caused the death of someone else's son. Hebrew women and children had certain legal protections, although their rights were less extensive than men's. For example, wives had less freedom to divorce their husbands than husbands had to divorce

Goddess Figurines from Judah
Many small statues of this type, called Astarte figurines after a goddess of Canaan, have been found in private houses in Judah dating from about 800 to 600 B.C.E. Hebrews evidently kept them as magical tokens to promote fertility and prosperity. The prophets fiercely condemned the worship of such figures as part of the development of Hebrew monotheism and the abandoning of polytheism. Compare the shape of these figurines to the body shape of the Venus figurine on page P-7. What do you think these shapes represented? *(Photo © Israel Museum, Jerusalem. Collection of the Israel Antiquities Authority.)*

Torah: The first five books of the Hebrew Bible, also referred to as the Pentateuch. It contains early Jewish law.

their wives, much as in the laws of Hammurabi. Crimes against property did not carry the death penalty, as they frequently did in other Near Eastern societies. Hebrew laws also protected slaves against flagrant mistreatment by their masters. Slaves who lost an eye or even a tooth from a beating were to be freed. Like free people, slaves enjoyed the right to rest on the Sabbath, the holy day of the seven-day Hebrew week.

The Hebrews who fled from Egypt with Moses made their way back to Canaan, joining their relatives who had remained there and somehow carving out separate territories for themselves. The twelve Hebrew tribes remained politically distinct under the direction of separate leaders, called judges, until the eleventh century, when their first monarchy emerged. Their monotheism gradually developed over the succeeding centuries.

The Consolidation of Hebrew Monotheism.

The Hebrews achieved their first national organization with the creation of a monarchy in the late eleventh century B.C.E. Saul became their first king, and his successors David (r. 1010–970 B.C.E.) and Solomon (r. c. 961–922 B.C.E.) brought the Hebrew kingdom to the height of its prosperity. The kingdom's wealth, based on international commerce conducted through its cities, was displayed above all in the great temple richly decorated with gold leaf that Solomon built in Jerusalem to be the house of Yahweh. This temple was the Hebrews' premier religious monument.

The Hebrews' unity and prosperity were short lived. After Solomon's death, the monarchy split into two kingdoms: Israel in the north and Judah in the south. The Assyrians destroyed Israel in 722 B.C.E. and deported its population to Assyria. In 597 B.C.E., the Babylonians conquered Judah and captured its capital, Jerusalem. In 586 B.C.E., they destroyed the temple to Yahweh and banished the Hebrew leaders, along with much of the population, to Babylon. The Hebrews always remembered the sorrow of this exile.

When the Persian king Cyrus overthrew the Babylonians in 539 B.C.E., he permitted the Hebrews to return to their part of Canaan, which was called Yehud, from the name of the southern Hebrew kingdom Judah. From this geographical term came the word *Jew*, a designation for the Hebrews after their Babylonian exile. Cyrus allowed them to rebuild their main temple in Jerusalem and to practice their religion. After returning from exile, the Jews were forever a people subject to the political domination of various Near Eastern powers, save for a period of independence during the second and first centuries B.C.E.

Solomon's Walls at Megiddo
Rulers in the Near East often fought to control the city of Megiddo because it controlled an important pass along a main north-south route near the eastern Mediterranean coast. The Hebrew king Solomon built strong fortification walls for it in the tenth century B.C.E., as recalled in the Hebrew Bible (1 Kings 9:15). A tunnel reaching hundreds of feet through rock to a spring hidden in a cave supplied water during a siege. Despite these defenses, the city later fell to the Egyptians and the Assyrians. *(Erich Lessing/Art Resource, NY.)*

Jewish prophets, both men and women, preached that their defeats were divine punishment for neglecting the Sinai covenant and mistreating their poor. Some prophets also predicted the coming end of the present world following a great crisis, a judgment by Yahweh, and salvation leading to a new and better world. This apocalypticism ("uncovering," or revelation, of the future), reminiscent of Babylonian prophetic wisdom literature, would greatly influence Christianity later. Yahweh would save the Hebrew nation, the prophets thundered, only if Jews strictly observed divine law.

Jewish leaders therefore developed complex religious laws to maintain ritual and ethical purity in all aspects of life. Marrying non-Jews was forbidden, as was working on the Sabbath. Fathers had legal power over the household, subject to intervention by the male elders of the community; women gained honor as mothers. Only men could initiate divorce proceedings. Ethics applied not only to obvious crimes but also to financial dealings; cheating in business transactions was condemned. Jews had to pay taxes and offerings to support and honor the sanctuary of Yahweh, and they had to forgive debts every seventh year.

The Jews' hardships had taught them that their religious traditions and laws gave them the strength to survive even when separated from their homeland. Gradually, they created the first undiluted monotheism by accepting their leaders' preaching that Yahweh was the only god and that they had to adhere to his divine will by obeying his laws. Jews retained their identity by following this religion, regardless of their personal fate or their geographical location. A remarkable outcome of these religious developments was that Jews who did not return to their homeland, instead choosing to remain in Babylon or Persia or Egypt, could maintain their Jewish identity by following Jewish law while living among foreigners. In this way, the **Diaspora** ("dispersion of population") came to characterize the history of the Jewish people.

Hebrew monotheism made the preservation and understanding of a sacred text, the Bible, the center of religious life. The chief priests compiled an authoritative scripture by adding to the Torah the books of the prophets, such as Isaiah, and other writings, including Psalms and wisdom literature. Making scripture the focus of religion proved the most crucial development for the history not only of Judaism but also of Christianity and Islam, because these later religions made their own sacred texts, the Christian Bible and the Qur'an, respectively, the centers of their belief and practice.

Although the ancient Hebrews never formed a militarily powerful nation, their monotheistic religion created a new path for Western civilization. Through the continuing vitality of Judaism and its impact on the doctrines of Christianity and Islam, the early Jews passed on ideas — chiefly monotheism and the notion of a covenant bestowing a divinely ordained destiny on a people if they obey divine will — whose effects have endured to this day. These religious concepts constitute one of the most significant legacies to Western civilization from the Near East in the period 1000–500 B.C.E.

> **REVIEW:** In what ways was religion important in the Near East from c. 1000 B.C.E. to c. 500 B.C.E.?

Diaspora (dee ASS por a): The dispersal of the Jewish population from their homeland.

Remaking Greek Civilization, 1000–750 B.C.E.

During the period of calamities of 1200–1000 B.C.E., the Greeks lost the distinguishing marks of civilization: they no longer had unified states, prosperous large settlements, or writing. Thus, during their Dark Age (c. 1000–750 B.C.E.), they had to remake their civilization. Trade, cultural interaction, and technological innovation led to recovery: contact with the Near East promoted intellectual, artistic, and economic revival, while the introduction of metallurgy for making iron made farming more efficient. As conditions improved, a social elite distinguished by wealth and the competitive pursuit of individual excellence proclaimed in Homeric poetry replaced the hierarchy of Mycenaean times. In the eighth century B.C.E., the creation of the Olympic Games and the emphasis on justice in the poetry of Hesiod promoted the communal values that fueled the remaking of Greek civilization and laid the foundation for a radically new form of political organization in which central authority was based on citizenship rather than subjection to kings.

The Greek Dark Age, 1000–750 B.C.E.

The fall of Mycenaean civilization brought to Greece the depressed economic conditions that so many people in other regions experienced during the worst years of their Dark Ages. One of the most startling indications of the severity of life in the Dark Age in Greece is that Greeks apparently lost their knowledge of writing when Mycenaean civilization fell. The Linear B script they had used to write Greek was difficult to master and probably known only by a few scribes, who used writing exclusively to track the flow of goods in and out of the palaces. When the Mycenaean states collapsed, the Greeks no longer needed scribes or writing. Oral transmission kept Greek cultural traditions alive.

Archaeology reveals that the Greeks, although spread across roughly the same geographical area as in Mycenaean times, cultivated much less land and had many fewer settlements in the early Dark Age (Map 2.3). No longer did powerful rulers sheltered in stone fortresses control redistributive economies providing a stable standard of living for their subjects. The number of ships carrying Greek adventurers, raiders, and traders dwindled. Large political states ceased to exist; people scratched out an existence as herders, shepherds, and subsistence

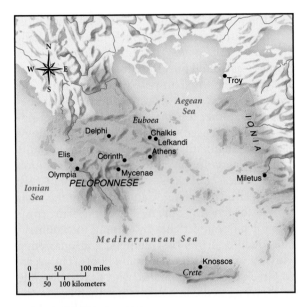

THE GREEK DARK AGE, 1000–750 B.C.E.

1000 B.C.E.	Almost all important Mycenaean sites except Athens destroyed by now
1000–900 B.C.E.	Greatest depopulation and economic loss
900–800 B.C.E.	Early revival of population and agriculture; beginning use of iron tools and weapons
800 B.C.E.	Greek trading contacts initiated with Al Mina in Syria
776 B.C.E.	First Olympic Games held
775 B.C.E.	Euboeans found trading post on island in the Bay of Naples
750 B.C.E.	Homeric poetry recorded in writing after Greeks learn to write again; Hesiod composes his poetry

MAP 2.3 Dark Age Greece

Recent archaeological research indicates that Greece was not as impoverished or as depopulated after the fall of the Mycenaean kingdoms as once assumed. The many small ports along Greece's jagged coastline and the short distances between its islands allowed seafaring trade and communication to continue. By island-hopping, boats could make it safely across the Aegean Sea and beyond, keeping the routes open to the Near East. Still, during the Dark Age, Greeks lived in significantly fewer and smaller population centers than in the Bronze Age. It took centuries for the region as a whole to revive.

farmers bunched in tiny settlements—as few as twenty people in many cases. The decimated population produced less food than before, causing its numbers to drop further. These two processes reinforced each other in a vicious circle, multiplying the negative effects of both.

The Greek agricultural economy remained complex despite the withering away of many traditional forms of agriculture. Since more Greeks than ever before made their living by herding animals, people became more mobile: they needed to move their herds to new pastures once the animals had overgrazed their current location. Lucky herders might find a new spot where they could grow a crop of grain if they stayed long enough. In this transient lifestyle, people built only simple huts and kept few possessions. Unlike their Bronze Age ancestors, Greeks in the Dark Age had no monumental architecture, and they even lost an old tradition in their everyday art: they stopped painting people and animals in their principal art form, ceramics.

Trade, Innovation, and Recovery in Greece. A geography that fostered seaborne trade allowed the Greeks to continue trading with the civilizations of the eastern Mediterranean even during the Dark Age. Trade promoted cultural interaction, and the Greeks learned to write again about 800 B.C.E. They adopted the alphabet from the Phoenicians, seafaring traders from Canaan. Greeks changed and added letters to achieve independent representation of vowel sounds so that they could express their language and record their literature, beginning with Homer's and Hesiod's poetry in the eighth century B.C.E. Near Eastern art inspired Greeks to resume depicting animals and people in their paintings (as on the Corinthian vase on page 32). Seaborne commerce encouraged elite Greeks to produce surpluses to trade for luxuries such as gold jewelry and gems from Egypt and Syria.

Most important, trade brought the new technology of iron metallurgy. The violence of the period of calamities had interrupted the traditional trading routes for tin, and without tin, metalworkers could not forge bronze weapons and tools. To make up for this loss, smiths in the eastern Mediterranean devised technology to smelt iron ore. Greeks then learned this skill through their eastern trade contacts and mined their own ore, which was common in Greece. Iron eventually replaced bronze in many uses, above all for agricultural tools, swords, and spear points. Bronze was still used for shields and armor, however, because it was easier to shape into thinner, curved pieces.

The iron tools' lower cost allowed more individuals to acquire them. Because iron is harder than bronze, implements kept their sharp edges longer. Better and more plentiful farming implements of iron helped increase food production, which

A Rich Woman's Model Granary from the Dark Age
This clay model of storage containers for grain was found in a woman's tomb in Athens from about 850 B.C.E. It apparently symbolizes the surpluses that the woman and her family were able to accumulate and indicates that she was wealthy by the standards of her time. The geometric designs painted on the pottery are characteristic of Greek art in this period, when human and animal figures were left out. By the Archaic Age, this had changed under Near Eastern influence. Contrast the lively animals painted some two hundred years later on the Corinthian vase illustrated at the opening of this chapter (page 32).
(American School of Classical Studies at Athens: Agora Excavations.)

supported a larger population. In this way, imported technology improved the people's chances for survival and thus helped Greece recover from the Dark Age's depopulation.

The Greek Social Elite and the Homeric Ideal.
With the Mycenaean rulers gone, leadership became more of an open competition in Dark Age Greece. Individuals who proved themselves excellent in action, words, charisma, and religious knowledge became the social elite. Competition defined Greek life, and excellence—*aretê* in Greek—was a competitive value. Men displayed aretê as warriors and persuasive public speakers; the highest aretê for women was savvy management of a well-organized household of children, slaves, and the family's storerooms. Members of the elite accumulated wealth by controlling agricultural land, which people of lower status worked for them as tenants or slaves.

The poems of **Homer**, Greece's first and most famous author, reflect the elite's ideals, especially the quest for aretê. The Greeks believed that Homer was a blind poet from Ionia (today Turkey's western coast) who composed the epic poems *The Iliad* and *The Odyssey*. Most modern scholars believe that Homer was the last in a long line of poets who, influenced by Near Eastern mythology, had been singing these stories for centuries, orally transmitting cultural values from one generation to the next. *The Iliad* tells the story of the Greek army in the Trojan War. Camped before the walls of Troy for ten years, the heroes of the army compete for glory and riches by raiding the countryside, dueling Troy's best fighters, and quarreling with one another over status and booty. The greatest Greek warrior is Achilles, who proves his aretê by choosing to die in battle rather than accept the gods' offer to return home safely but without glory. *The Odyssey* recounts the hero Odysseus's ten-year adventure sailing home after the fall of Troy and the struggle of his wife, Penelope, to protect their household from the schemes of rivals intent on seizing her family's status and wealth. Penelope proves her aretê by outwitting envious neighbors to preserve her family's prosperity for her husband's return.

Homer reveals that the white-hot emotions inflamed by an individual quest for excellence could provoke a disturbing level of inhumanity. As he prepares to duel Hector, the prince of Troy, Achilles brutally rejects the Trojan's proposal that the winner return the loser's corpse to his family and friends: "Do wolves and lambs agree to cooperate? No, they hate each other to the roots of their being." The victor, Achilles, mutilates Hector's body. When Hecuba, the queen of Troy, sees this outrage, she bitterly shouts, "I wish I could sink my teeth into his liver in his guts to eat it raw." The endings of Homer's poems suggest that the gods could help people achieve reconciliation after violent conflict, but the depth of human suffering makes it clear that excellence comes at a high price.

As in Homer, the real world of the Greek Dark Age had a small but wealthy social elite. On the island of Euboea, for example, archaeologists have discovered the tenth-century B.C.E. grave of a couple who took such enormous riches with them to the next world that the woman's body was covered in gold ornaments. They had done well in the competition for status and wealth; most people of the time were, by comparison, paupers, who had to

---

aretê (ah reh TAY): The Greek value of competitive individual excellence.

Homer: Greece's first and most famous author, who composed *The Iliad* and *The Odyssey*.

Athletic Competition
Greek vase painters loved to depict male athletes in action or training, perhaps in part because athletes were customers who would buy pottery with such scenes. As in this depiction of an Athenian foot race from around 530 B.C.E., the athletes were usually shown nude, which is how they competed, revealing their superb physical condition and strong musculature. Being in excellent shape was a man's ideal for several reasons: it was regarded as beautiful, it enabled him to strive for individual glory in athletic competitions, and it allowed him to fulfill his community responsibility by fighting as a well-conditioned soldier in the city-state's citizen militia. Why do you think the figure at the far left does not have a full beard? (See the caption on page 64 for a hint.) *(The Metropolitan Museum of Art, Rogers Fund, 1914 (14.130.12) Photograph © 1998 The Metropolitan Museum of Art.)*

scratch out a hard living. The poor could only dream of the heroic deeds and rich goods they heard about in Homer's poems.

The Values of the Olympic Games

Greece had recovered sufficiently by the eighth century B.C.E. to begin creating new forms of social and political organization. The most vivid evidence is the founding of the Olympic Games, traditionally dated to 776 B.C.E. This international religious festival showcased the competitive value of aretê.

Every four years, the games took place in a huge sanctuary dedicated to Zeus, the king of the gods, at Olympia, in the northwestern Peloponnese. Male athletes from elite families vied in sports, imitating the aretê needed for war: running, wrestling, jumping, and throwing. Horse and chariot racing were added to the program later, but the main event remained a two-hundred-yard sprint, the *stadion* (hence our word *stadium*). The athletes competed as individuals, not on national teams as in the modern Olympic Games. Winners

received a garland made from wild olive leaves to symbolize the prestige of victory.

The Olympics illustrate Greek notions of gender propriety: crowds of men flocked to the games, but women were barred on pain of death. Women had their own separate Olympic festival on a different date in honor of Hera, queen of the gods, in which only unmarried women could compete. They had separate games because most Greeks believed it was not proper for men and women to observe nonslave strangers of the opposite gender wearing no or little clothing. Eventually, professional athletes dominated the Olympics, earning their living from appearance fees and prizes at games held throughout the Greek world. The most famous winner was Milo, from Croton in Italy. Six-time Olympic wrestling champion, he stunned audiences with demonstrations of strength such as holding his breath until his veins expanded to snap a cord tied around his head.

Although the Olympics existed to glorify individual excellence, their organization reveals an important trend under way in Greek society: the games were open to any socially elite Greek male

Homer's Vision of Justice in the Polis

Homer's epics mainly tell tales of individual excellence from the heroic past of the Trojan War era, but he also hints at the development of communal values in the polis, which Greeks were creating at about the same time that he composed his works, around 750 B.C.E. We see this in one of the most striking passages in his Iliad, *which describes the pictures of a polis at war and a polis at peace that Hephaestus, the fire god, sculpted on a new shield for Achilles. Homer portrays the figures in the scenes as moving and talking, as if in a magical filmstrip. The picture of the polis at peace concerns finding a just resolution to a man's death. Homer doesn't tell us whether the death was accidental or criminal, or where the gold came from that would be the victorious arbitrator's reward for the best judgment, the one that would restore harmony to the community through justice.*

In the [polis at peace], weddings and celebrations were in full swing. Blazing torches lit the way for youthful brides being brought out from their homes and through the polis center. People sang the wedding song in loud, clear voices. The young men twirled in a lively dance to the music of flutes and lyres. The women lingered smilingly on their doorsteps, taking it all in with deep pleasure. Their husbands had gone off as a group to the polis's gathering place [agora], where a dispute was being conducted between two men over another's death and the payment of compensation. One of the two was proclaiming for all to hear that he would pay full compensation, while the other insisted that he would not accept any of it; both of them were declaring that arbitrators should settle the case. Each man had numerous supporters there yelling for him to prevail, and the heralds were trying hard to keep the crowd from rioting. The elders [i.e., the arbitrators] sat in a circle on sacred stone seats. The clear-voiced heralds handed them scepters, which each stepped forward with when it was his turn to say what he thought was a just resolution. A heap of gold lay in front of them as a reward for whichever elder pronounced the best decision.

Source: Homer, *The Iliad*, Book 18, lines 490–508. Translation by Thomas R. Martin.

---

good enough to compete and to any male spectator who could journey there. These rules represented beginning steps toward a concept of collective Greek identity. Remarkably for a land so often torn by war, once every four years an international truce of several weeks was declared so that competitors and fans from all Greek communities could safely travel to and from Olympia. By the mid-eighth century B.C.E., the Olympic Games channeled the competition for excellence—an individual, not a communal, value—into a new context of social cooperation and communal interest, essential preconditions for the creation of Greece's new political form, the city-state of citizens.

Homer, Hesiod, and Divine Justice in Greek Myth

Greeks' belief in divine justice inspired them to develop the communal and cooperative values that remade their civilization. This idea came not from scripture—Greeks had none—but from poetry that told myths about the gods and goddesses and their relationships to humans.

Homer's poems reveal that the gods had a plan for human existence; Zeus's will, for example, motivated the Trojan War's tragic events. Homer did not reveal, however, whether the divine plan was just. Bellerophon, the wronged hero whose brave efforts won him a princess bride and a kingdom, ended up losing everything. He became, in Homer's words, "hated by the gods and wandering the land alone, eating his heart out, a refugee fleeing from the haunts of men." The story gives no explanation for this tragedy and no reason to believe that justice underlay the divine plan (see Document, "Homer's Vision of Justice in the Polis," above).

Hesiod's poetry, by contrast, reveals how religious myths about justice contributed to the feeling of community that motivated the creation of Greece's new social and political organization. Hesiod's vivid stories, which originated in Near Eastern creation myths, show that existence, even for deities, entailed struggle, sorrow, and violence. The stories also reveal, however, that the divine order of the universe included a concern for justice that persisted in Hesiod's own time.

Hesiod's epic poem *Theogony* (Genealogy of the Gods) recounted the birth of the race of gods from the intercourse of primeval Chaos and Earth, the mother of Sky and numerous other offspring. Hesiod explained that when Sky began to imprison his siblings, Earth persuaded her fiercest son, Kronos, to overthrow him violently because "Sky first contrived to do shameful things." When Kronos later began to swallow his own children to avoid sharing power with them, his wife, Rhea (who was also his sister), had their son Zeus forcefully depose his father.

In his poem on conditions in his own world, *Works and Days*, Hesiod identified Zeus as the source of justice in human affairs and justice as a divine quality punishing evildoers: "For Zeus ordained that fishes and wild beasts and birds should eat each other, for they have no justice; but to human beings he has given justice, which is far the best." People, however, were responsible for instituting justice, and in Hesiod's time this meant the male social elite. They controlled their family members and household servants. Hesiod insisted that a leader should demonstrate aretê by employing persuasion instead of force: "When his people in their assembly get on the wrong track, he gently sets matters right, persuading them with soft words."

Hesiod complained that many elite leaders in his time fell short of this ideal, creating strife between themselves and the peasants—free proprietors of small farms owning a slave or two, oxen to work their fields, and a limited amount of goods acquired by trading the surplus of their crops. Hesiod warned that justice's divine origin should deter "bribe-devouring chiefs," who use "crooked judgements" to settle disputes among their followers and neighbors. The outrage that commoners felt at not receiving equal treatment served as a stimulus for the gradual movement toward a new form of social and political organization in Greece.

> **REVIEW:** What factors proved most important in the Greek recovery from the troubles of the Dark Age?

The Creation of the Greek Polis, 750–500 B.C.E.

The Greek Dark Age gave way to what historians call the Archaic Age (c. 750–500 B.C.E.). This new era saw the creation of the **polis**, the Greek city-state, an independent community of citizens inhabiting a city and the countryside around it. Greece's geography, dominated by mountains and islands, promoted the creation of hundreds of separate, independent city-states in its heartland in and around the Aegean Sea. From these original locations, Greeks dispersed widely around the

Mediterranean to settle hundreds more trading communities that often grew into new city-states. Individuals' drive for profit from trade, especially in raw materials, and free farmland probably started this process of founding new settlements.

Greeks made the idea of divine justice instituted by citizens the defining characteristic of their city-states. Thus, the Greek polis, as a community of citizens, differed from the Mesopotamian city-states, whose inhabitants were subjects of the king. Greek citizens usually governed themselves, though the political system itself varied. Surprisingly for the ancient world, poor citizens in Greek city-states enjoyed a rough legal and political equality with the rich. Not so surprisingly, women failed to attain equality with men, and slaves remained completely excluded from the benefits of the city-state's new emphasis on communal interests. This new direction in social and political organization was unprecedented in giving even a limited say to the poor, but it was never able to eliminate tension between the interests of the elite and those of ordinary people.

The Physical Environment of the Greek City-State

The ancient Greeks never constituted a nation in the modern political sense because their many city-states lacked a unifying organization. Greeks identified with one another culturally, however, because they spoke the same language and worshipped the same deities. Their homeland lay in and around the Aegean Sea, a section of the Mediterranean between modern Greece and Turkey dotted with large and small islands (Map 2.4).

The mountainous geography of Greece tended to isolate its communities and contributed to the city-states' feisty separateness. A single island could be home to multiple city-states; Lesbos, for example, had five. Because few city-states had enough farmland to support a large population, settlements numbering only several hundred to several thousand were the rule even after the population increase at the end of the Dark Age.

Only the sea offered practical long-distance travel in Greece. Greek rivers were little more than creeks, while land transport was slow and expensive because rudimentary dirt paths and dry riverbeds provided the only roads. The most plentiful resource was timber from the mountains for building houses and ships. Deposits of metal ore were scattered throughout Greek territory, as were clays suitable for pottery and sculpture. Various quarries of fine stone such as marble provided material for special buildings and works of art. The uneven distri-

---

polis: The Greek city-state, an independent community of citizens.

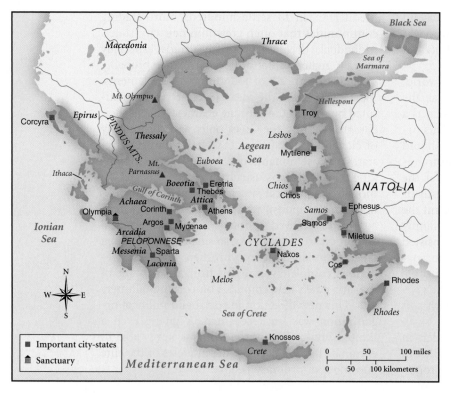

MAP 2.4 Archaic Greece, 750–500 B.C.E.
The Greek heartland lay in and around the Aegean Sea, in what is today the nation of Greece and the western edge of the nation of Turkey (ancient Anatolia). The "mainland," where Athens, Corinth, and Sparta are located, is the southernmost tip of the mountainous Balkan peninsula. The many islands of the Aegean area were home mainly to small city-states, with the exception of the large islands just off the western Anatolian coast, which were home to populous ones.

bution of these resources meant that some areas were considerably wealthier than others.

None of the mountains wrinkling the Greek landscape rose higher than ten thousand feet, but their steep slopes restricted agriculture. Only 20 to 30 percent of the total land area could be farmed. The scarcity of level terrain in most areas ruled out large-scale herds of cattle and horses; pigs, sheep, and goats were the common livestock. The domestic chicken had been introduced from the Near East by the seventh century B.C.E. The Mediterranean climate (intermittent heavy rain during a few months and hot, dry summers) limited a farmer's options, as did the fragility of the environment: grazing livestock, for example, could be so hard on plant life that winter downpours would wash away the limited topsoil. Because the amount of annual precipitation varied greatly, farming was a precarious business of boom and bust. Farmers grew more barley, the cereal staple of the Greek diet, than wheat, which people preferred but which was more expensive to cultivate. Wine grapes and olives were the other most important crops.

Trade and "Colonization," 800–580 B.C.E.

The polis emerged when Greeks were once again in frequent contact with Egypt and the Near East. The desire for trade and land that encouraged the Greeks to move around the Mediterranean brought them many opportunities for cross-cultural contacts. Greece's jagged coastline made sea travel practical: almost every community lay within forty miles of the Mediterranean Sea. But sailing meant dangers from pirates and, especially, storms; in fact, prevailing winds and fierce gales almost ruled out sea travel during winter. Sailors tried to hug the coast, hopping from island to island and putting in to shore at night, but sometimes the drive for profit required long, nonstop voyages over open waters. As Hesiod commented, merchants took to the sea "because an income means life to poor mortals, but it is a terrible fate to die among the waves."

The search for metals and other scarce resources drove traders far from home. *The Odyssey* describes the basic strategy of this commodity trading, when the goddess Athena appears disguised as a metal trader: "I am here...with my ship and crew on our way across the wine-dark sea to foreign lands in search of copper; I am carrying iron now." By 800 B.C.E., the Mediterranean swarmed with entrepreneurs of many nationalities. The Phoenicians established footholds as far west as Spain's Atlantic coast to gain access to inland mines there. Their North African settlement at Carthage (modern Tunis) would become one of the Mediterranean's most powerful cities in later times, dominating commerce west of Italy.

Greeks energetically joined this seaborne contest for profit as the scale of trade soared near the end of the Dark Age: archaeologists have found only two tenth-century B.C.E. Greek pots that were carried abroad, but eighth-century pottery has turned up at more than eighty foreign sites. By 750 B.C.E. (or earlier—the evidence is hard to date), Greeks had begun to settle far from their homeland, sometimes living in others' settlements, especially those of the Phoenicians in the western Mediterranean, and sometimes establishing trading posts of their own, as on an island in the Bay of Naples. Everywhere they traded with the local

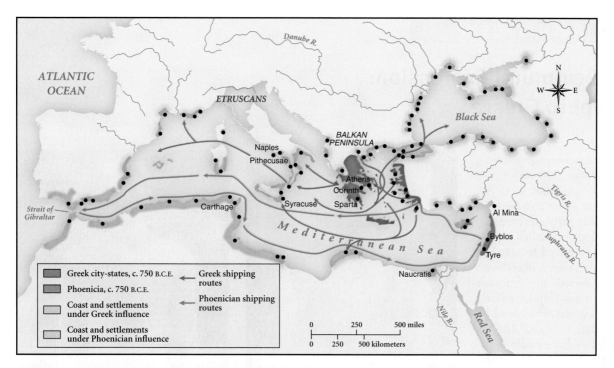

MAP 2.5 Phoenician and Greek Expansion, 750–500 B.C.E.
The Phoenicians were early explorers and settlers of the western Mediterranean; by 800 B.C.E. they had already founded the city of Carthage, which would become the main commercial power in the region. During the Archaic Age, groups of adventurous Greeks followed the Phoenicians' lead and settled all around the Mediterranean, hoping to improve their economic prospects by trade and farming. Sometimes they moved into previously established Phoenician settlements; sometimes they founded their own. Some Greek city-states established formal ties with new settlements or sent out their own expeditions to try to establish loyal colonies. ■ Where did Phoenicians predominantly settle, and where did Greeks?

populations, such as the Etruscans in central Italy, who imported large amounts of Greek goods, as the vases found in their tombs reveal. Greeks staying abroad for the long term would also cultivate vacant land, gradually building permanent communities. A shortage of arable territory in Greece drove some poor citizens abroad to find farmland of their own. Because apparently only males left home on trading and land-hunting expeditions, they had to find wives wherever they settled, either through peaceful negotiation or by kidnapping.

By about 580 B.C.E., Greeks had settled widely in Spain, present-day southern France, southern Italy and Sicily, North Africa, and along the Black Sea coast (Map 2.5). The settlements in southern Italy and Sicily, such as Naples and Syracuse, eventually became so large and powerful that this region was called Magna Graecia (literally, "Great Greece"), and its communities became rivals of Carthage for commercial dominance in the western Mediterranean.

Fewer Greeks settled in the eastern Mediterranean, perhaps because the monarchies there restricted foreign immigration. Still, a trading sta-

tion had sprung up in Syria by 800 B.C.E., and in the seventh century B.C.E. the Egyptians permitted Greek merchants to settle in a coastal town. These close contacts with eastern Mediterranean civilizations paid cultural as well as economic dividends. In addition to inspiring Greeks to reintroduce figures into their painting, Near Eastern art gave them models for statues: they began sculpting images that stood stiffly and stared straight ahead, imitating Egyptian statuary. (See "Seeing History," page 50.) When the improving economy of the later Archaic Age allowed Greeks again to afford monumental architecture in stone, their rectangular temples on platforms with columns reflected Egyptian architectural designs. Historians have traditionally called the settlement process of this era Greek colonization, but recent research questions this term's accuracy because the word *colonization* implies the process by which modern European governments officially installed colonies abroad. The evidence for these Greek settlements suggests rather that private entrepreneurship initiated most of them; official state involvement was minimal, at least in the beginning. Most com-

Shifting Sculptural Expression: From Egypt to Greece

As Greek civilization revived during the Archaic Age (750–500 B.C.E.), artists drew inspiration from the older civilizations of Egypt and the Near East, with sculpture in particular emerging as an important mode of cultural expression. Greek sculptors carved freestanding *kouros* ("young male") statues whose poses recalled the Egyptian style that remained unchanged for two thousand years: an erect posture, a striding leg, and a calm facial expression staring straight ahead. And yet important differences, both religious and stylistic, exist between Egyptian statuary and the Greek sculpture influenced by it.

Kaemheset (shown on the left) held a high government position during the Old Kingdom as Egypt's chief architect and supervisor of sculptors. Croesus (on the right) was a warrior from Athens who died in battle, as the inscription on the base of his statue proclaimed: "Stand and mourn at this monument of Croesus, now dead; raging Ares [the Greek war god] destroyed him as he battled in the front ranks." Both statues were painted in bright colors (traces of red survive on Croesus's statue); Kaemheset's lively decoration remains because it stood inside his closed tomb, while Croesus's stood outside. Croesus's statue differs from Kaemheset's in that it portrays him nude, even though warriors went into battle wearing armor. What do you think could have been the reasons for placing statues inside or outside tombs and for portraying their subjects clothed or nude?

Look more closely at the details of the figures—musculature, hair, hands, facial expression, stride. What stylistic similarities do you see? Art historians have argued that, despite the similarities, the *kouros* statues of Greece's Archaic period already show signs of the increasing naturalism and idealization of the human body that would characterize the later Greek classi-

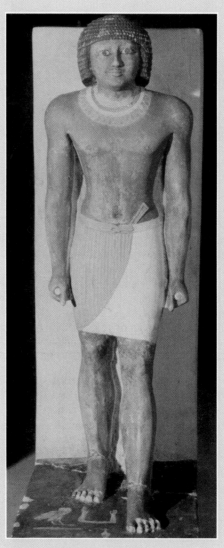

Limestone Statue of Kaemheset, Old Kingdom Egypt, c. 2400 B.C.E. *(Borromeo/Art Resource, NY.)*

Marble Statue of Croesus, Archaic Age Greece, c. 530–520 B.C.E. *(The Art Archive/ Archaeological Museum, Athens/Dagli Orti.)*

cal style (see page 87). What evidence do you see of that in the differences between the two sculptures? How do you account for the relatively static nature of Egyptian statuary, whose basic form changed very little over thousands of years? What historical factors might account for the dynamism of the Greek tradition?

monly, a Greek city-state in the homeland would establish ties with a settlement originally set up by its citizens privately and then claim it as its colony only after the community had grown into an economic success. Few instances are clearly recorded in which a Greek city-state officially sent out a group to establish a formally organized colony abroad. (See Document, "Cyrene Records Its Foundation as a Greek Colony," page 52.)

Citizenship and Freedom in the Greek City-State

The creation of the polis filled the political vacuum left by Mycenaean civilization's fall. The Greek city-state was unique because it was based on the concept of citizenship for all its free inhabitants, rejected monarchy as its central authority, and made justice the responsibility of the citizens. Moreover, except in tyrannies (in which one man seized control of the city-state), at least some degree of shared governance was common; this power sharing reached its purest form in democratic Greek city-states. Some historians argue that knowledge of the older cities on Cyprus and in Phoenicia influenced the Greeks in creating their new political systems; since monarchs dominated their subjects in those eastern states, however, this theory cannot explain the origin of citizenship in all Greek city-states and the sharing of power in many. The most famous ancient analyst of Greek politics and society, the philosopher Aristotle (384–322 B.C.E.), insisted that the forces of nature had created the city-state: "Humans are beings who by nature live in a city-state." Anyone who existed outside such a community, Aristotle remarked, must be either a simple fool or superhuman. The polis's innovation in making shared power the basis of government did not immediately change the course of history—monarchy later became once again the most common form of government in ancient Western civilization—but it was important as proof that power sharing was not just a workable system of political organization but also a desirable one.

Religion in the Greek City-State. The Greek polis was not only a political entity. Like all earlier ancient communities, Greek city-states were officially religious communities: as well as worshipping many deities, each city-state honored a particular god or goddess as its special protector, such as Athena at Athens. Different communities could choose the same deity: Sparta, Athens's chief rival in later times, also chose Athena as its de-

fender. Greeks envisioned the twelve most important gods banqueting atop Mount Olympus, the highest peak in mainland Greece. Zeus headed this pantheon; the others were Hera, his wife; Aphrodite, goddess of love; Apollo, sun god; Ares, war god; Artemis, moon goddess; Athena, goddess of wisdom and war; Demeter, earth goddess; Dionysus, god of pleasure, wine, and disorder; Hephaestus, fire god; Hermes, messenger god; and Poseidon, sea god. Like Homer's warriors, the Olympian gods were competitive, both with each other and with human beings, and they resented any slights to their honor. "I am well aware that the gods are competitively jealous and disruptive towards humans," remarked the sixth-century Athenian statesman Solon. The Greeks believed that their gods occasionally experienced temporary pain or sadness in their dealings with one another but were immune to permanent suffering because they were immortal.

Greek religion's core belief was that humans, both as individuals and as communities, must honor the gods to thank them for blessings received and to receive more blessings in return. Furthermore, the Greeks believed that the gods sent both good and bad into the world. The relationship between gods and humans

A Greek Woman at an Altar
This red-figure vase painting (contrast the black-figure vase on page 32) from the center of a large drinking cup shows a woman in rich clothing pouring a libation to the gods onto a flaming altar. In her other arm, she carries a religious object that we cannot securely identify. This scene illustrates the most important and frequent role of women in Greek public life: participating in religious ceremonies, both at home and in community festivals. Greek women (and men) commonly wore sandals; why do you think they are usually depicted without shoes in vase paintings? *(The Toledo Museum of Art, Toledo, Ohio; Purchased with funds from the Libbey Endowment, Gift of Edward Drummond Libbey [1972.55].)*

Cyrene Records Its Foundation as a Greek Colony

The Greeks living in Cyrene in North Africa (in modern Libya) set up this inscription recording the foundation of their polis by colonists dispatched about 630 B.C.E. from Thera (a polis on an island north of Crete). The text we have, which is damaged and therefore uncertain in places (marked by brackets), comes from the fourth century B.C.E., but it was based on earlier documents. Cyrene was one of the few colonies originally established by a polis instead of by entrepreneurs.

The Oath of the Colonists

The assembly of Thera decided:

Since the god Apollo of Delphi spontaneously instructed Battus and the Therans to settle Cyrene, the Therans decided to send Battus to North Africa as leader and king and for the Therans to sail as his companions. They are to sail on equal and fair terms according to their households and one adult son [from each household] is to be selected, and grown young men [are to be selected], and of the other Therans only those who are free can sail. And if the colonists establish a colony, a man from the households who subsequently sails to North Africa shall share in citizenship and public office and shall be given a portion from land that has no owner. But if they do not establish a colony and the Therans are unable to provide aid, but the colonists suffer hardship for five years, they are allowed to leave the land without fear and return to Thera and their property and to be citizens. If any man is not willing to sail when the polis sends him, he will be subject to the death penalty and his property shall be confiscated. Any man who harbors or hides such a man, whether a father his son, or a brother his brother, will be subject to the same penalty as the man who is not willing to sail. Those who stayed at home and those who sailed to found the colony swore oaths on these terms, and they invoked curses against those who break the oaths and fail to keep them, whether they were those who settled in North Africa or those who remained at home.

Source: R. Meiggs and D. Lewis, eds., *A Selection of Greek Historical Inscriptions to the End of the Fifth Century B.C.* (1969), no. 5. Translation by Thomas R. Martin.

---

generated sorrow as well as joy, punishment in the here and now, and only a limited hope for favored treatment in this life and in the underworld after death. Greeks did not expect to reach paradise at some future time when evil forces would be vanquished forever.

The idea of reciprocity between gods and humans underlay the Greek understanding of the nature of the gods. Deities did not love humans. Rather, they protected people who paid them honor and did not offend them. Gods could punish offenders by sending calamities such as famine, earthquake, epidemic disease, or defeat in war.

City-states honored gods by sacrificing animals such as cattle, sheep, goats, and pigs; decorating their sanctuaries with works of art; and celebrating festivals with songs, dances, prayers, and processions. A seventh-century B.C.E. bronze statuette, which a man named Mantiklos gave to a sanctuary of Apollo to honor the god, makes clear why individuals gave such gifts. On its legs the donor inscribed his understanding of the transaction: "Mantiklos gave this from his share to the Far Darter of the Silver Bow [Apollo]; now you, Apollo, do something for me in return."

People's greatest religious difficulty lay in anticipating what might offend a deity. Mythology hinted at the gods' expectations of proper human behavior. For example, the Greeks told stories of the gods demanding hospitality for strangers, proper burial for family members, and punishment for human arrogance and murderous violence. Oracles, dreams, divination, and the prophecies of seers provided clues about what humans might have done to anger the gods. The most important oracle was at Delphi, in central Greece, where a priestess in a trance provided Apollo's answers to questions. Offenses could be acts such as performing a sacrifice improperly, violating the sanctity of a temple area, or breaking an oath or sworn agreement. People believed that the deities were attentive to some wrongdoings, such as violating oaths, but generally uninterested in common crimes, which humans had to police themselves. Homicide was such a serious offense, however, that the gods were thought to punish it by casting a miasma (ritual contamination) on the murderer and on all those around him or her. Unless the members of the affected group purified themselves by punishing the murderer, they could all expect to suffer divine punishment, such as bad harvests or disease.

A community and individuals alike paid homage and respect to each deity through a **cult**, a set of official, publicly funded religious activities for a deity overseen by priests and priestesses. To carry out their duties, people prayed, sang hymns of praise, offered sacrifices, and presented gifts at the deity's sanctuary. In these holy places a person could honor and thank the deities for blessings and beg them for relief when misfortune struck the community or the petitioner. Individuals could also offer sacrifices at home with the household gathered around; sometimes the family's slaves were allowed to participate.

Priests and priestesses chosen from the citizen body conducted the sacrifices of public cults; they did not use their positions to influence political or social matters. Their special knowledge consisted in knowing how to perform traditional religious rites. They were not guardians of correct religious thinking because Greek polytheism had no scripture or uniform set of beliefs and practices. It required its adherents only to support the community's local rituals and to avoid religious pollution.

Citizenship for Rich and Poor.   Greeks devised the concept of citizenship to organize their city-states; it meant free people agreeing to form a political community that was supposed to be a partnership of privileges and duties in common affairs under the rule of law. Citizenship was a distinctive political concept because, even in Greek city-states organized as tyrannies or oligarchies (rule by a small group), it bestowed a basic level of political and legal equality. Most important, it carried the expectation (although not always the fulfillment) of equal treatment under the law for male citizens regardless of their social status or wealth. Women had the protection of the law, but they were barred from participation in politics on the grounds that female judgment was inferior to male. Regulations governing sexual behavior and control of property were stricter for women than for men.

In the most dramatic version of political equality, all free, adult male citizens in a Greek city-state shared in governance by attending and voting in a political assembly, where the laws and policies of the community were ratified. The degree of power sharing varied. In oligarchic city-states where the social elite had a stranglehold on

politics, small groups or even a single family could dominate the process of legislating. Other city-states eventually introduced direct democracy, which gave all free men the right to propose laws and policies in the assembly and to serve on juries. Even in democratic city-states, however, citizens did not enjoy perfect political equality. The right to hold office, for example, could be restricted to citizens possessing a certain amount of property. Equality prevailed most strongly in the justice system, in which all male citizens were treated the same, regardless of wealth or status.

Because monarchy and legal inequality had characterized the history of the ancient Near East and Greece in earlier times, making equality the principle for the reorganization of Greek society and politics in the Archaic Age was a radical innovation. The polis — with its emphasis on equal protection of the laws for rich and poor alike — remained the preeminent form of political and social organization in Greece until the beginning of Roman control six centuries later.

The Greek city-states' free poor enjoyed the privileges and duties of citizenship alongside the rich throughout this long period. How the poor gained those privileges remains a mystery. The population increase in the late Dark Age and the Archaic Age was greatest among the poor. These families raised more children to help farm more land, which had been vacant after the depopulation brought on by the worst of the Dark Age. (See "Taking Measure," page 55.) There was no precedent in Western civilization for extending even limited political and legal equality to this growing number of poorer people, but the Greek city-states did so.

Until recently, historians cited a hoplite revolution as the reason for expanded political rights, but recent research has undermined this interpretation. A **hoplite** was an infantryman who wore metal body armor and attacked with a thrusting spear; the hoplites constituted the main strike force of the militia that defended each city-state; there were no permanent Greek armies at this period. Hoplites marched into combat arrayed in a rectangular formation called a phalanx. Staying in line and working together were the secrets to successful phalanx tactics. Greeks had fought in phalanxes for a long time, but until the eighth century B.C.E. only the elite could afford hoplite equipment. In the eighth century B.C.E., however, a growing number of men had become prosperous

---

cult: In ancient Greece, a set of official, publicly funded religious activities for a deity overseen by priests and priestesses.

hoplite: A heavily armed Greek infantryman. Hoplites constituted the main strike force of a city-state's militia.

A Hoplite's Breastplate

This bronze armor protected the chest of a sixth-century B.C.E. hoplite. It had to be fitted to his individual body; the design is meant to match the musculature of his chest and symbolize his manliness. The Greek soldier would have worn a cloth or leather shirt underneath to prevent the worst chafing, but such a heavy and hot device could never be comfortable, and soldiers often removed them despite the danger. A slave would have carried the soldier's armor for him, and the soldier would have donned his protective gear just before facing the enemy.

(Olympia Museum © Archaeological Receipts Fund.)

tance of so-called light troops has been seriously underestimated in the study of Greek warfare and that poor men earned respect by fighting to defend the community, just as hoplites did. Fighting as lightly armed skirmishers, poor men could disrupt an enemy's heavy infantry by slinging barrages of rocks or shooting arrows. It is also possible that tyrants—sole rulers who seized power for their families in some city-states (see "Tyranny in Corinth," page 60)—boosted the status of poor men. Tyrants may have granted greater political rights to poor men as a means of gathering popular support. No matter how the poor became citizens who possessed a rough equality of political freedom and legal rights with the rich, this unprecedented decision and its effect on politics constituted Greek society's most daring innovation in the Archaic Age.

The Expansion of Greek Slavery. The growth of freedom and equality in Greece produced a corresponding expansion of slavery, as free citizens protected their status by drawing harsh lines between themselves and slaves. Many slaves were war captives; pirates or raiders seized others in the rough regions to the north and east of Greek territory. The fierce bands in these areas also captured and sold one another to slave dealers. Rich families prized Greek-speaking and educated slaves because they could use them to tutor their children, since no schools existed in this period.

City-states as well as individuals owned slaves. Public slaves enjoyed limited independence, living on their own and performing specialized tasks. In Athens, for example, special slaves were trained to detect counterfeit coinage. Temple slaves belonged to the deity of the sanctuary, for whom they worked as servants.

Slaves made up about one-third of the total population in some city-states by the fifth century B.C.E. They became cheap enough that even middle-class people could afford one or two. Still, small landowners and their families continued to do much work themselves, sometimes hiring free laborers. Not even wealthy Greek landowners acquired large numbers of agricultural slaves because maintaining gangs of hundreds of enslaved workers year-round would have been uneconomical. Most crops required short periods of intense labor punctuated by long stretches of inactivity, and owners did not want to feed slaves who had no work.

Slaves did all kinds of jobs. Household slaves, often women, cleaned, cooked, fetched water from public fountains, helped the wife with the weaving, watched the children, accompanied the hus-

enough to buy metal weapons, especially because the use of iron had made such weapons more readily available.

It seems probable that these new hoplites, because they bought their own equipment and trained hard to learn phalanx tactics to defend their community, felt they should also enjoy political rights. According to the hoplite revolution theory, these new hoplites forced the social elite to share political power by threatening to refuse to fight, which would cripple military defense. This interpretation correctly assumes that new hoplites had the power to demand and receive a voice in politics but ignores that hoplites were not poor. How then did poor men, too, win political rights? The hoplite revolution theory cannot account for the extension of rights to poor men. Furthermore, archaeology shows that not many men were wealthy enough to afford hoplite armor until the middle of the seventh century B.C.E., well after the earliest city-states had emerged.

The most likely explanation for the extension of political rights to the poor is that the impor-

TAKING MEASURE

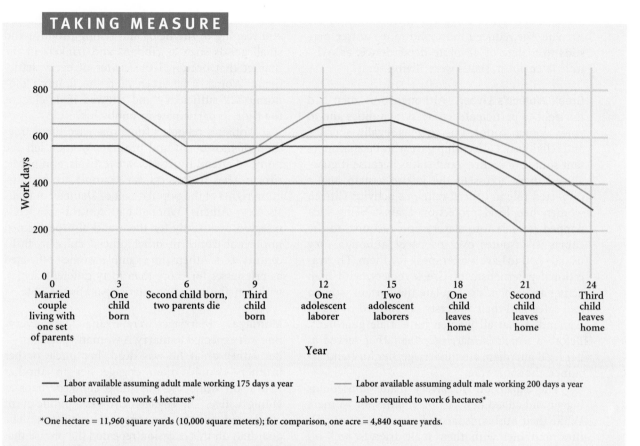

— Labor available assuming adult male working 175 days a year   — Labor available assuming adult male working 200 days a year
— Labor required to work 4 hectares*   — Labor required to work 6 hectares*

*One hectare = 11,960 square yards (10,000 square meters); for comparison, one acre = 4,840 square yards.

Greek Family Size and Agricultural Labor in the Archaic Age
Modern demographers have calculated the changing relationship in the Archaic Age between a farm family's productive capacity to work the land and the number of people in the family over time. The graph shows how valuable healthy teenage children were to the family's prosperity. When the family had two adolescent laborers available, it could farm over 50 percent more land, increasing its productivity significantly and thus making life more prosperous. *(Adapted from Thomas W. Gallant,* Risk and Survival in Ancient Greece: Reconstructing the Rural Domestic Economy *(1991), Fig. 4.10.)*

band as he did the marketing, and performed other domestic chores. Neither female nor male slaves could refuse if their masters demanded sexual favors. Owners often labored alongside their slaves in small manufacturing businesses and on farms, although rich landowners might appoint a slave supervisor to oversee work in the fields. Slaves toiling in the narrow, landslide-prone tunnels of Greece's silver and gold mines had the worst lot: many died doing this dangerous, dark, backbreaking work.

Since slaves existed as property, not people, owners could legally beat or even kill them. But probably few owners hurt or executed slaves because it made no economic sense—the master would be crippling or destroying his own property. Under the best conditions, household workers with humane masters lived lives free of violent punishment; they may have even been allowed to join their owners' families on excursions and attend religious rituals. However, without the right to a family of their own, without property, and without legal or political rights, slaves remained alienated from regular society. In the words of an ancient commentator, slaves lived lives of "work, punishment, and food." Sometimes owners liberated their slaves, and some promised freedom at a future date to encourage their slaves to work hard. Those slaves who gained their freedom did not become citizens in Greek city-states but instead mixed into the population of *metics*—noncitizens officially allowed to live in the community. Freed slaves were still expected to help out their former masters when called on.

Greek slaves rarely revolted on a large scale, except in Sparta, because they were usually of too many different origins and nationalities and too scattered to organize. No Greeks called for the abolition of slavery. The expansion of slavery in the Archaic Age reduced more and more unfree persons to a state of absolute dependence; as Aristotle later put it, slaves were "living tools."

Greek Women's Lives.   Although only men had the right to participate in city-state politics and to vote, women counted as citizens legally, socially, and religiously. Citizenship gave women an important source of security and status because it guaranteed them access to the justice system and a respected role in official religious activity. Citizen women had legal protection against being kidnapped for sale into slavery and recourse to the courts in disputes over property, although they usually had to have a man speak for them. The traditional paternalism of Greek society, with men acting as "fathers" to regulate the lives of women and safeguard their interests (as defined by men) demanded that all women have male guardians. Before a woman's marriage, her father served as her legal guardian; after marriage, her husband assumed the same role.

The expansion of slavery made households bigger and added new responsibilities for women. While their husbands farmed, participated in politics, and met with their male friends, well-off wives managed the household: raising the children, supervising the preservation and preparation of food, keeping the family's financial accounts, weaving fabric for clothing, directing the work of the slaves, and tending them when they were ill.

Poor women worked outside the home, hoeing and reaping in the fields and selling produce and small goods such as ribbons and trinkets in the market that occupied the center of every settlement. Women's labor ensured the family's economic self-sufficiency and allowed male citizens the time to participate in public life.

Women's religious functions gave them freedom of movement and prestige. Women left the home to attend funerals, state festivals, and public rituals. They had access, for example, to the initiation rights of the popular cult of Demeter at Eleusis, near Athens. Women had control over cults reserved exclusively for them and also performed important duties in other official cults; in fifth-century B.C.E. Athens, for example, women officiated as priestesses for more than forty different deities, with benefits including salaries paid by the state.

Marriage.   Marriages were arranged, and everyone was expected to marry. A woman's guardian — her father or, if he was dead, her uncle or her brother — would often engage her to another man's son while she was still a child, perhaps as young as five. The engagement was a public event conducted in the presence of witnesses. The guardian on this occasion repeated the phrase that expressed the primary aim of the marriage: "I give you this woman for the plowing [procreation] of legitimate children." The wedding took place when the girl was in her early teens and the groom ten to fifteen years older. Hesiod advised a man to

A Bride's Preparation
This special piece of pottery was designed to fit over a woman's thigh to protect it while she sat down to spin wool. As a woman's tool, it appropriately carried a picture from a woman's life: a bride being helped to prepare for her wedding by her family, friends, and servants. The inscriptions indicate that this fifth-century B.C.E. piece shows the mythological bride Alcestis, famous for sacrificing herself to save her husband and then being rescued from Death by the hero Heracles. (*Deutsches Archäologisches Institut-Athens. DAI Neg. No. INM5126. Photo: E.M. Czako.*)

marry a virgin in the fifth year after her first menstruation, when he himself was "not much younger than thirty and not much older." A legal wedding consisted of the bride moving to her husband's dwelling; the procession to his house served as the ceremony. The woman brought to the marriage a dowry of property (perhaps land yielding an income, if she was wealthy) and personal possessions that formed part of the new household's assets and could be inherited by her children. Her husband was legally obliged to preserve the dowry and to return it in case of a divorce. A husband could expel his wife from his home; a wife could legally leave her husband to return to the guardianship of her male relatives, but her husband could force her to stay.

Except in certain cases in Sparta, monogamy was the rule in ancient Greece, as was a nuclear family (husband, wife, and children living together without other relatives in the same house). Citizen men, married or not, were free to have sexual relations with slaves, foreign concubines, female prostitutes, or willing pre-adult citizen males. Citizen women, single or married, had no such freedom. Sex between a wife and anyone other than her husband carried harsh penalties for both parties, except in Sparta.

Greek citizen men placed Greek citizen women under their guardianship both to regulate marriage and procreation and to maintain family property. According to Greek mythology, women were a necessary evil: men needed them to have a family but could expect troubles as the price. Zeus supposedly created the first woman, Pandora, as a punishment for men in his vendetta against Prometheus for giving fire to humans. To see what was in a container that had come as a gift from the gods, Pandora lifted its lid and accidentally freed the evils that had been penned inside into the previously trouble-free world. When she finally slammed the lid back down, only hope still remained in the container. Hesiod described women as "big trouble" but thought any man who refused to marry to escape the "troublesome deeds of women" would come to "destructive old age" alone, with no heirs. In other words, a man needed a wife so that he could father children who would later care for him and preserve his property after his death. This paternalistic attitude allowed men to control human reproduction and consequently the distribution of property.

REVIEW: How did the physical, social, and intellectual conditions of life in the Archaic Age promote the emergence of the Greek city-state?

New Directions for the Polis, 750–500 B.C.E.

Greek city-states developed three forms of social and political organization based on citizenship: oligarchy, tyranny, and democracy. Sparta provided Greece's most famous example of an oligarchy, in which a small number of men dominated policymaking in an assembly of male citizens. For a time Corinth had the best-known tyranny, in which one man seized control of the city-state, ruling it for the advantage of his family and loyal supporters, while acknowledging the citizenship of all (thereby distinguishing a tyrant from a king, who ruled over subjects). Athens developed Greece's best-known democracy by allowing all male citizens to participate in governing. Although assemblies of men had influenced some ancient Near Eastern kings (see "Contrasting Views," page 58), Greek democracies gave their male citizens an unprecedented degree of equality and political power.

The Archaic Age polis is justly famous as the incubator for democratic politics; it also provided the environment in which Greeks created new forms of artistic expression and new ways of thought. In this period they formulated innovative ways of employing reason to understand the physical world, their relations to it, and their relationships with one another. This intellectual innovation laid the foundation for the gradual emergence of scientific thought and logic in Western civilization.

Oligarchy in Sparta, 700–500 B.C.E.

Unique among the Greek city-states, Sparta organized its society with laws directed at a single purpose: military readiness. This oligarchic city-state developed the mightiest infantry force in Greece during the Archaic Age. Its citizens were renowned for their militaristic self-discipline. Sparta's urban center nestled in an easily defended valley on the Peloponnesian peninsula twenty-five miles from the Mediterranean coast. This separation from the sea kept the Spartans from becoming adept sailors; their strength lay on land.

The Spartan oligarchy included three components of rule. First came the two hereditary,

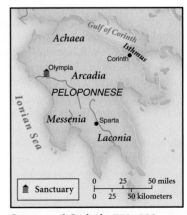

Sparta and Corinth, 750–500 B.C.E.

Persians Debate Democracy, Oligarchy, and Monarchy

According to the Greek historian Herodotus, after a group of seven eminent Persians overthrew a false king in 522 B.C.E., they debated what would be the best type of government to establish in Persia. Otanes argued for democracy (or, as he calls it, "putting things in the middle"), Megabyzus for oligarchy, and Darius for monarchy. Four of the seven voted in favor of monarchy, and Darius became the new, legitimate king. Herodotus also says that some Greeks refused to believe that the debate ever took place, perhaps because there was no evidence that any system other than monarchy had ever been possible in Persia. In any case, these speeches present the earliest recorded contrasting views on systems of government, with special attention to the characteristics of monarchy.

Otanes recommended to the Persians to put things in the middle by saying this: "It doesn't seem right to me that one of us should be the monarch. There is nothing sweet or good about it. You know to what lengths violent arrogance [hubris] carried our former king Camybses, and you experienced that violent arrogance under the recent false king. How could monarchy be a suitable thing, when it allows the ruler to do whatever he wishes without any official accountability? Even the best of men would change his usual ideas if he had such a position of rule. Violent arrogance comes to him from the good things that he possesses, and jealousy has been part of human nature from the start. In having these two characteristics he has total bad character. Sated with his violent arrogance and jealousy, he does many outrageous things. A ruler with tyrannical power ought to be free of envy, for he possesses every good thing. But the opposite is true of his relations with the citizens. He is jealous if the best ones stay alive, delighted if the worst ones do; he's the best at listening to accusations. He is most difficult of men to deal with: if you only praise him in moderation, he gets angry because he is not being energetically flattered, but if someone flatters him energetically, he gets angry because the person is a flatterer. And now I am going to say the worst things of all: he overturns traditional customs, he rapes women, and he kills people without a trial. When the people are the ruler, the government has the best name: equality before the law. It does nothing of the things that a monarch does. It fills offices by lottery, its rule is subject to official accountability, and it has the community make all decisions. My judgment is that we should get rid of the monarchy and increase the power of the masses. For in the many is everything."

Otanes offered this judgment, but Megabyzus said they should entrust the government to an oligarchy, saying this: "What Otanes said about not having tyranny, I agree with, but as for giving power to the masses, he has missed the best judgment.

There is nothing less intelligent or more violently arrogant than a useless crowd. It is certainly intolerable for men to flee the violent arrogance of the tyrant, only to fall victim to the violent arrogance of the people, who have no restraints upon them. If a tyrant does something, he does it from knowledge, but there is no knowledge in the people. How could someone have knowledge when he hasn't been taught anything fine and doesn't know it innately? He rushes into things without thought, like a river in its winter flood. Let those who intend evil to the Persians push for democracy, but let us choose a group of the best men and endow them with power. For we will be part of this group, and it is likely that the best plans will come from the best men."

Megabyzus offered this judgment, and Darius was the third to reveal his judgment, saying: "Megabyzus seems to me to speak correctly in what he says about the masses, but not correctly about oligarchy. For if we consider for argument's sake that all three systems are the best they can be—the best democracy, the best oligarchy, the best monarchy—then monarchy is far superior. For clearly nothing is better than the one best man. Relying on judgment that is the best he would direct the masses faultlessly, and he would be especially good at making plans against hostile men without them being divulged. In an oligarchy, where many men want to use their excellence for common interests, intense private hatreds tend to arise. For each one wants to be the head man and to win with his judgments, and they create great hatreds among themselves. From this come violent factions, and from factions comes murder, and from murder the system turns to monarchy. And in this one sees by how much monarchy is the best. Again, when the people rule, it is impossible that there not be evildoing. Moreover, when there is evildoing for the common interests, hatred doesn't arise among the evildoers; instead, strong friendships arise. For the evildoers act together to corrupt the common interests. This sort of thing happens until one man becomes the head of the people and stops these evildoers. With these actions he amazes the people, and being the object of amazement he clearly becomes a monarch. So, in this way, too, it is clear that monarchy is the strongest. To say it all together in one word: from where did our [i.e., Persian] freedom come, and who gave it to us? From the people, or an oligarchy, or a monarch? It is my judgment that, having obtained our freedom through one man, we should maintain our freedom in the same way, and we should also not do away with our sound traditional customs; for this is not better."

Source: Herodotus, *The Histories*, Book 3, chapters 80–82. Translation by Thomas R. Martin.

prestigious military leaders called kings, who served as the state's religious heads and the generals of its army. Despite their title, they were not monarchs but just one part of the ruling oligarchy. The second part was a council of twenty-eight men over sixty years old (the elders), and the third part consisted of five annually elected officials called *ephors* (overseers), who made policy and enforced the laws.

In principle, legislation had to be approved by an assembly of all Sparta's free adult males, who were called the Alike to stress their common status and purpose. The assembly had only limited power to amend the proposals put before it, however, and the council would withdraw a proposal when the assembly's reaction proved negative. "If the people speak crookedly," according to Spartan tradition, "the elders and the leaders of the people shall be withdrawers." The council would then resubmit the proposal after marshaling support for its passage.

Spartan society demanded strict compliance with all laws. When the ephors took office, for example, they issued an official proclamation to Sparta's males: "Shave your mustache and obey the laws." The laws' importance was emphasized by the official story that the god Apollo had given them to Sparta. Unlike other Greeks, the Spartans never wrote down their laws. Instead, they preserved their system with a unique, highly structured way of life. All Spartan citizens were expected to put service to their city-state before personal concerns because their state's survival was continually threatened by its own economic foundation: the great mass of Greek slaves, called helots, who did almost all the work for citizens.

The Helots.   A **helot** was a slave owned by the Spartan city-state; such slaves came from neighboring parts of Greece that the Spartans conquered. Most helots lived in Messenia, to the west, which Sparta had conquered by around 700 B.C.E. The helots outnumbered Sparta's free citizens. Harshly treated by their Spartan masters, helots constantly looked for chances to revolt.

Helots had a semblance of family life because they were expected to produce children to maintain their population, and they could own some personal possessions and practice their religion. They labored as farmers and household slaves so that Spartan citizens would not have to do such nonmilitary work. Spartan men wore their hair very long to show they were warriors rather than laborers, for whom long hair was inconvenient.

Helots lived under the constant threat of officially sanctioned violence. Every year the ephors formally declared war between Sparta and the helots, allowing any Spartan to kill a helot without legal penalty or fear of offending the gods by unsanctioned murder. By beating the helots frequently, forcing them to get drunk in public as an object lesson to young Spartans, and humiliating them by making them wear dog-skin caps, the Spartans emphasized their slaves' "otherness." In this way Spartans created a moral barrier to justify their harsh abuse of fellow Greeks. Contrasting the freedom of Spartan citizens from ordinary work with the lot of the helots, a later Athenian observed, "Sparta is the home of the freest of the Greeks, and of the most enslaved."

Spartan Communal Life.   With helots to work the fields, male citizens could devote themselves to full-time preparation for war, training to protect their state from hostile neighbors and its own slaves. Boys lived at home only until their seventh year, when they were sent to live in barracks with other males until they were thirty. They spent most of their time exercising, hunting, practicing with weapons, and learning Spartan values by listening to tales of bravery and heroism at communal meals, where adult males ate most of the time instead of at home. Discipline was strict, and the boys were purposely underfed so that they would learn stealth by stealing food. If they were caught, punishment and disgrace followed immediately. One famous Spartan tale shows how seriously boys were supposed to fear such failure: having successfully stolen a fox, which he was hiding under his clothing, a Spartan youth died because he let the panicked animal rip out his insides rather than be detected in the theft. A Spartan male who could not survive the tough training was publicly disgraced and denied the status of being an Alike.

Spending so much time in shared quarters schooled Sparta's young men in their society's values. This communal existence took the place of a Spartan boy's family and school when he was growing up and remained his main social environment even after he reached adulthood. There he learned to call all older men Father to emphasize that his primary loyalty was to the group instead of his biological family. The environment trained him for the one honorable occupation for Spartan men: obedient soldier. A seventh-century B.C.E. poet expressed the Spartan male ideal: "Know that it is good for the city-state and the whole people

---

helot: A slave owned by the Spartan city-state; such slaves came from parts of Greece conquered by the Spartans.

Hunt Painting in a Spartan Cup
This black-figure drinking cup with a picture of a hunt on its interior was made in Sparta about 560 B.C.E. Hunting large, dangerous wild game was an important way for Spartan men to show their courage and acquire meat for their communal meals. The painter has chosen a "porthole" style, as if we were looking through a circular window. The alignment of the figures' legs, torsos, and heads reflect the influence of Egyptian art. By the classical period, the Spartans' overwhelming military focus ended their creation of art. *(Reunion Des Musées Nationaux / Art Resource, NY.)*

when a man takes his place in the front row of warriors and stands his ground without flinching."

An adolescent boy's life often involved what in today's terminology would be called a homosexual relationship, although the ancient concepts of heterosexuality and homosexuality did not match modern notions. An older male would choose a teenager as a special favorite, in many cases engaging him in sexual relations. Their bond of affection was meant to make each ready to die for the other, at whose side he would march into battle. Numerous city-states included this form of homosexuality among their customs, although some forbade it. The physical relationship could be controversial; the Athenian author Xenophon (c. 430–355 B.C.E.) wrote a work on the Spartan way of life denying that sex with boys existed there because he thought it demeaning to the Spartans' reputation for virtue. However, the evidence shows such relationships did exist in Sparta and else-

where. (The first modern histories of Greece suppressed discussion of this topic because their writers saw it as a form of child abuse.)

In such relationships the elder partner (the "lover") was supposed to help educate the young man (the "beloved") in politics and community values, and not just exploit him for physical pleasure. The relationship would not be lasting or exclusive: beloveds would grow up to get married, as lovers were, and would eventually become the older member of a new pair. Sex between adult males was considered disgraceful, as was sex between females of all ages (at least according to men).

Spartan women were known throughout the Greek world for their personal freedom. Since their husbands were so rarely at home, women directed the households, which included servants, daughters, and sons until they left for their communal training. Consequently, Spartan women exercised more power in the household than did women elsewhere in Greece. They could own property, including land. Wives were expected to stay physically fit so that they could bear healthy children to keep up the population. They were also expected to drum Spartan values into their children. One mother became legendary for handing her son his shield on the eve of battle and admonishing him, "Come back with it or [lying dead] on it."

Demography determined Sparta's long-term fate. The population of Sparta was never large; adult males — who made up the army — numbered between eight and ten thousand in the Archaic period. Over time, the problem of producing enough children to keep the Spartan army from shrinking became desperate, probably because losses in war far outnumbered births. Men became legally required to marry, with bachelors punished by fines and public ridicule. If everyone agreed, a woman could legitimately have children by a man other than her husband.

Because the Spartans' survival depended on the exploitation of enslaved Greeks, they believed changes in their way of life must be avoided because any change might make them vulnerable to internal revolts. Some Greeks criticized the Spartan way of life as repressive and monotonous, but the Spartans' discipline and respect for their laws gained them widespread admiration.

Tyranny in Corinth, 657–585 B.C.E.

In some city-states, competition among the social elite for political leadership became so bitter that

The Archaic Temple of Apollo at Corinth
This temple was built in the sixth century B.C.E. near the base of Corinth's acropolis, the
massive rock formation soaring in the background. One of the earliest stone temples from
Greece, it was constructed in Doric style, with its fluted columns resting directly on the
foundation and topped by flattened disks. Earthquakes over the centuries have toppled
most of the temple's columns and all its walls. (The walls in the foreground are from
later buildings.) *(The Art Archive/Dagli Orti.)*

a single family would suppress all its rivals and establish itself in rule for a time. The family's leader
thus became a tyrant, a dictator who gained political dominance by force and was backed by his relatives and other supporters. Tyrants usually rallied
support by promising privileges to poor citizens in
city-states where they lacked full citizenship or felt
disfranchised in political life. Successful tyrants
kept their elite rivals at bay by cultivating the goodwill of the masses with economic policies favoring
their interests, such as public employment schemes.
Since few tyrants successfully passed their popularity on to their heirs, tyrannies tended to be
short-lived.

Tyrants usually preserved their city-states' existing laws and political institutions. If a city-state
had an assembly, for example, the tyrant would allow it to continue to meet, expecting it to follow
his direction. Although today the word *tyrant* indicates a brutal or unwanted leader, tyrants in Archaic Greece did not always fit that description.

Ordinary Greeks evaluated tyrants according to
their behavior, opposing the ruthless and violent
ones but welcoming the fair and helpful ones.

The most famous early tyranny arose at
Corinth in 657 B.C.E., when the family of Cypselus
rebelled against the city's harsh oligarchic leadership. This takeover attracted wide attention in the
Greek world because Corinth was such an important city-state. Its location on the isthmus controlling land access to the Peloponnese and a huge
amount of seaborne trade made it the most prosperous city-state of the Archaic Age (see Map 2.4).
Cypselus rallied popular support for his political
coup. "He became one of the most admired of
Corinth's citizens because he was courageous, prudent, and helpful to the people, unlike the oligarchs in power, who were insolent and violent,"
according to a later historian. Cypselus's son succeeded him at his death in 625 B.C.E. and aggressively continued Corinth's economic expansion
by founding colonies to increase trade. He also

pursued commercial contacts with Egypt. Unlike his father, the son lost popular support by ruling harshly. He held on to power until his death in 585 B.C.E., but the hostility he had provoked soon led to the overthrow of his heir. The social elite, to prevent tyranny, installed an oligarchic government based on a board of officials and a council.

Democracy in Athens, 632–500 B.C.E.

Only democracy, which the Greeks invented, instituted genuine political power sharing in the polis. Athens, located at the southeastern corner of central Greece, became the most famous of the democratic city-states because its government gave political rights to the greatest number of people, financed magnificent temples and public buildings, and, in the fifth century B.C.E., became militarily strong enough to force numerous other city-states to follow Athenian leadership in a maritime empire. Athenian democracy did not reach its full development until the mid-fifth century B.C.E., but its first steps in the Archaic Age allowed all male citizens to participate meaningfully in making laws and administering justice. Democracy has remained so important in Western civilization that understanding why and how Athenian democracy worked remains a vital historical quest.

Athens's early development of a populous middle class was a crucial factor in opening this new path for Western civilization. The Athenian population apparently expanded at a phenomenal rate when economic conditions improved rapidly from about 800 to 700 B.C.E. The ready availability of good farmland in Athenian territory and opportunities for seaborne trade along the long coastline allowed many families to achieve modest prosperity. These hardworking entrepreneurs evidently felt that their self-won economic success entitled them to a say in government. The democratic cohesiveness forged by the Athenian masses was evident as early as 632 B.C.E., when the people rallied "from the fields in a body," according to Herodotus, to foil the attempt by an elite Athenian to install a tyranny.

By the seventh century B.C.E., all freeborn adult male citizens of Athens had the right to vote

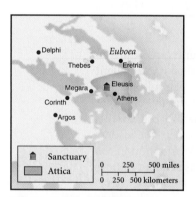

Athens and Central Greece, 750–500 B.C.E.

on public matters in the assembly, whose meetings regularly attracted several thousand participants. They also elected high officials called archons, who ran the judicial system by rendering verdicts in disputes and criminal accusations. Members of the elite dominated these offices; because archons received no pay, poor men could not afford to serve.

An extended economic crisis beginning in the late seventh century B.C.E. almost suffocated Athens's infant democracy. The first attempt to solve the problem was the emergency appointment around 621 B.C.E. of a man named Draco to revise the laws. Like the Mesopotamian kings before them, Athens's leaders believed that reforming and clarifying the laws would bring social harmony through justice. Unfortunately, Draco's changes, which made death the penalty for even minor crimes, proved too harsh to work; later Greeks said Draco (whose harshness inspired the word *draconian*) had written his laws in blood, not ink. By 600 B.C.E., economic conditions had become so dire that poor farmers had to borrow constantly from richer neighbors and deeply mortgage their land. As the crisis grew worse, impoverished citizens were sold into slavery to pay off debts. Civil war seemed next.

Solon's Democratic Reforms. Desperate, Athenians appointed another emergency official in 594 B.C.E., a war hero named **Solon**. To head off violence, Solon gave both rich and poor something of what they wanted, a compromise called the "shaking off of obligations." He canceled private debts, which helped the poor but displeased the rich; he decided not to redistribute land, which placated the wealthy while disappointing the poor. He banned selling citizens into slavery to settle debts and liberated citizens who had become slaves in this way. His elimination of debt slavery was a significant recognition of what today would be called citizen rights, and Solon celebrated his success in poetry: "To Athens, their home established by the gods, I brought back many who had been sold into slavery, some justly, some not."

Solon balanced political power between rich and poor by reordering Athens's traditional ranking of citizens into four groups. Most important, he made the top-ranking division depend solely on wealth, not birth. This change eliminated formal aristocracy at Athens. The groupings did not affect a man's treatment at law, only his eligibility for government office. The higher a man's ranking, the

---

Solon: Athenian political reformer whose changes promoted early democracy.

higher the post to which he could be elected; men at the poorest level, called laborers, were not eligible for any office. Solon did, however, confirm the laborers' right to vote in the legislative assembly. His classification scheme was another step toward democracy because it allowed for upward social mobility: a man who increased his wealth could move up the scale of eligibility for office.

Since the process of making decisions by persuasion can be glacially slow in large groups, the creation of a smaller council to prepare the agenda for the assembly was a crucial development in making Athenian democracy efficient. It may have been Solon (some evidence suggests the council came later) who created the council of four hundred men that decided what the assembly needed to discuss. The practice of choosing council members annually by lottery—the most democratic method possible—from the adult male citizen body prevented the social elite from capturing too many seats.

Even more than his changes to the government, Solon's two changes in the judicial system promoted democratic principles of equality. First, he mandated that any male citizen could bring charges on behalf of any crime victim. Second, he gave people the right to appeal an archon's judgment to the assembly. With these two measures, Solon empowered ordinary citizens in the administration of justice. Characteristically, he balanced these democratic reforms by granting broader powers to the "Council which meets on the Hill of the god of war Ares," the Areopagus Council. This select body, limited to ex-archons, wielded great power because its members judged the most important cases—accusations against archons themselves.

Solon's reforms broke the traditional pattern of government limited to the elite; they extended power broadly through the citizen body and created a system of law that applied more equally than before to all the community's free men. A critic once challenged Solon, "Do you actually believe your fellow citizens' injustice and greed can be kept in check this way? Written laws are more like spiders' webs than anything else: they tie up the weak and the small fry who get stuck in them, but the rich and the powerful tear them to shreds." Solon replied that communal values assure the rule of law: "People abide by their agreements when neither side has anything to gain by breaking them. I am writing laws for the Athenians in such a way that they will clearly see it is to everyone's advantage to obey the laws rather than to break them."

Some elite Athenians wanted oligarchy and therefore vehemently disagreed with Solon. Their jealousy of one another kept them from uniting, but the unrest they caused opened the door to tyranny at Athens. Peisistratus, helped by his upper-class friends and the poor whose interests he championed, made himself tyrant in 546 B.C.E. Like the Corinthian tyrants, he promoted the economic, cultural, and architectural development of Athens and curried the masses' favor. He helped poorer men, for example, by hiring them to build roads, a huge temple to Zeus, and fountains to increase the supply of drinking water. He boosted Athens's economy and its image by minting new coins stamped with Athena's owl and organizing a great annual festival honoring the god Dionysus that attracted people from near and far to see its musical and dramatic performances.

Peisistratus's family could not maintain public goodwill after his death. Hippias, his eldest son, ruled harshly and was denounced as unjust by a rival elite family. These rivals convinced the Spartans, the self-proclaimed champions of Greek freedom, to "liberate" Athens from tyranny by expelling Hippias and his family in 510 B.C.E.

Cleisthenes, "Father of Athenian Democracy."

Peisistratus's support for the interests of ordinary people evidently had the unintended consequence of making them think that they deserved political equality. In this way, tyranny at Athens opened the way to the most important step in developing Athenian democracy, the reforms of Cleisthenes. A member of the social elite, in 508 B.C.E. Cleisthenes found himself losing against rivals for election to office. He seized the opportunity to capitalize on popular feeling by offering greater democracy to the masses as his political program. Ordinary people so strongly favored his plan, especially his promise of equality before the law, that they spontaneously rallied to repel a Spartan army that Cleisthenes' bitterest rival had convinced Sparta's leaders to send to block the reforms.

By about 500 B.C.E. Cleisthenes had ensured direct participation in government by as many adult male citizens as possible. First he created constituent units for the city-state's new political organization by grouping country villages and urban neighborhoods into units called **demes**. The demes chose council members annually by lottery in proportion to the size of their populations. To

---

demes (DEEMZ): The villages and city neighborhoods that formed the constituent political units of Athenian democracy in the late Archaic Age.

allow for greater participation, Solon's council of four hundred was expanded to five hundred members. Finally, Cleisthenes required candidates for public office to be spread widely throughout the demes.

Cleisthenes helped his reforms succeed by grounding them in preexisting social conditions favorable to democracy. The creation of demes, for example, suggests that democratic notions stemmed from traditions of small-community life, in which each man was entitled to his say in running local affairs and had to persuade—not force—others to agree. For his reforms, Athenians remembered Cleisthenes as the father of their democracy. It took another fifty years of political struggle, however, before Athenian democracy reached its full development.

New Ways of Thought and Expression, 630–500 B.C.E.

The idea that persuasion, rather than force or status, should drive political decisions matched the spirit of intellectual change rippling through Greece in the late Archaic Age. In city-states all over the Greek world, artists, poets, and philosophers pursued new ways of thought and new forms of expression. Through their contacts with the Near East, the Greeks encountered traditions to learn from and, in some cases, to alter for their own purposes.

Archaic Age Art and Literature. Early in the Archaic period Greek artists took inspiration from the Near East, but by the sixth century B.C.E., they had introduced innovations of their own. In ceramics, painters experimented with different clays and colors to depict vivid scenes from mythology and daily life. They became expert at rendering three-dimensional figures in an increasingly realistic style. Sculptors gave their statues balanced poses and calm, smiling faces.

Greek poets built on the Near Eastern tradition of poetry expressing personal emotions by creating a new form called lyric poetry. This poetry sprang from popular song and was performed to the accompaniment of the lyre (a kind of harp that gives its name to the poetry). Greek lyric poems were short, rhythmic, and diverse in subject. Lyric poets wrote songs both for choruses and for individual performers. Choral poems honored deities on public occasions, celebrated famous events in a city-state's history, praised victors in athletic contests, and enlivened weddings.

Solo lyric poems generated controversy because they valued individual expression and opinion over conventional views. Solon wrote poems justifying his reforms. Other poets criticized traditional values, such as strength in war. **Sappho**, a lyric poet from Lesbos born about 630 B.C.E. and famous for her poems on love, wrote, "Some would say the most beautiful thing on our dark earth is an army of cavalry, others of infantry, others of ships, but I say it's whatever a person loves." In this poem Sappho was expressing her longing for a woman she loved, who was now far away. Archilochus of Paros, who probably lived in the early seventh century B.C.E., became famous for poems mocking militarism, lamenting friends lost at sea, and regretting love affairs gone wrong. He became infamous for his lines about throwing away his shield in battle so that he could run away to save his life: "Oh, the hell with it; I can get another one just as good." When he taunted a family in verse after the father had ended Archilochus's affair with one of his daughters, the power of his ridicule reportedly caused the father and his two daughters to commit suicide.

Vase Painting of a Music Lesson

This sixth-century B.C.E. red-figure vase shows a young man (seated on the left, without a beard) holding a lyre and watching an older, bearded man play the same instrument, while an adolescent boy and an older man listen. They all wear wreaths to show they are in a festive mood. The youth is evidently a pupil learning to play. Instruction in performing music and singing lyric poetry was considered an essential part of an upper-class Greek male's education. The teacher's lyre has a sounding board made from a turtle shell, as was customary for this instrument. *(Staatliche Antikensammlungen und Glypothek.)*

Sappho (SAF oh): The most famous woman lyric poet of ancient Greece, a native of Lesbos.

Greek Philosophy and Science. The study of philosophy ("love of wisdom") began in the seventh and sixth centuries B.C.E. when Greek thinkers created prose writing to express their innovative ideas, in particular their radically new explanations of the human world and its relation to the gods. Most of these philosophers lived in Ionia, on Anatolia's western coast, where they came in contact with Near Eastern knowledge in astronomy, mathematics, and myth. Because there were no formal schools in the Archaic Age, philosophers communicated their ideas by teaching privately and giving public lectures. Some also composed poetry to explain their theories. People who studied with these philosophers or heard their presentations helped spread the new ideas.

Working from Babylonian discoveries about the regular movements of the stars and planets, Ionian philosophers such as Thales (c. 625–545 B.C.E.) and Anaximander (c. 610–540 B.C.E.), both of Miletus, reached the revolutionary conclusion that unchanging laws of nature (rather than gods' whims) governed the universe. Pythagoras, who emigrated from the island of Samos to the Greek city-state Croton in southern Italy about 530 B.C.E., taught that numerical relationships explained the world; he initiated the Greek study of mathematics and the numerical aspects of musical harmony.

Ionian philosophers insisted that natural phenomena were neither random nor arbitrary. They applied the word *cosmos*—meaning "an orderly arrangement that is beautiful"—to the universe. The cosmos encompassed not only the motions of heavenly bodies but also the weather, the growth of plants and animals, and human health. Because the universe was ordered, it was knowable; because it was knowable, thought and research could explain it. Philosophers therefore looked for the first or universal cause of all things, a quest that scientists still pursue. These first philosophers believed they needed to give reasons for their conclusions and to persuade others by arguments based on evidence; that is, they believed in logic. This new way of thought, called **rationalism**, became the foundation for the study of science and philosophy. This rule-based view of the causes of events and

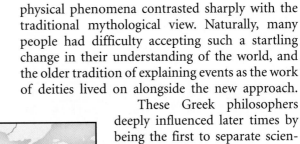

Ionia and the Aegean, 750–500 B.C.E.

physical phenomena contrasted sharply with the traditional mythological view. Naturally, many people had difficulty accepting such a startling change in their understanding of the world, and the older tradition of explaining events as the work of deities lived on alongside the new approach.

These Greek philosophers deeply influenced later times by being the first to separate scientific thinking from myth and religion. Their idea that people must give reasons to justify their beliefs, rather than simply make assertions that others must accept without evidence, was their most important achievement. This insistence on rationalism, coupled with the belief that the world could be understood as something other than the plaything of the gods, gave people hope that they could improve their lives through their own efforts. As Xenophanes of Colophon (c. 570–c. 478 B.C.E.) concluded, "The gods have not revealed all things from the beginning to mortals, but, by seeking, human beings find out, in time, what is better." This saying expressed the value Archaic Age philosophers gave to intellectual freedom, corresponding to the value that citizens gave to political freedom in the city-state.

> **REVIEW:** What were the main differences among the various forms of government in the Greek city-states?

Conclusion

Over different spans of time and with different results, both the Near East and Greece recovered from their Dark Ages, brought on by the calamities of the period 1200–1000 B.C.E. After its Dark Age, the Near East quickly revived its traditional pattern of social and political organization: empire with a strong central authority (monarchy). The Neo-Assyrians, the Neo-Babylonians, and the Persians succeeded one another as imperial powers. The moral dualism of Persian religion, Zoroastrianism, influenced later religions. The Hebrews' development of monotheism based on scripture changed the course of religious history in Western civilization.

Greece's recovery from its Dark Age produced a new form of political and social organization: the

---

rationalism: The philosophic idea that people must justify their claims by logic and reason, not myth.

MAPPING THE WEST

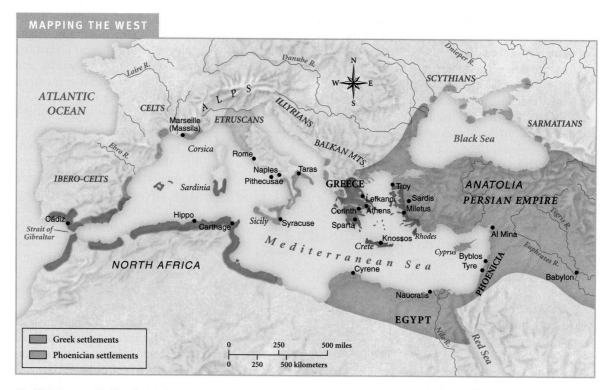

Greek settlements

Phoenician settlements

Mediterranean Civilizations, c. 500 B.C.E.
At the end of the sixth century B.C.E., the Persian Empire was far and away the most powerful civilization touching the Mediterranean. Its riches and its unity gave it resources that no Phoenician or Greek city could match. The Phoenicians dominated economically in the western Mediterranean, while the Greek city-states in Sicily and southern Italy rivaled the power of those in the heartland. In Italy, the Etruscans were the most powerful civilization; the Romans were still a small community struggling to replace monarchy with a republic.

polis, a city-state based on citizenship and shared governance. The rapidly growing population of the Archaic Age developed the sense of communal identity, personal freedom, and divine justice instituted by citizens that underlay the city-state. The degree of power sharing and the form of the political system varied in the Greek city-states. Some, like Sparta, were oligarchies; in others, like Corinth, rule was by tyranny. Over time, Athens developed the most thoroughgoing democracy, in which political power extended to the greatest number of male citizens.

Just as revolutionary as the invention of democracy were the new methods of artistic expression and new ways of thought that Greeks developed. Building on Near Eastern traditions, Greek poets created lyric poetry to express personal emotion. Greek philosophers argued that laws of nature controlled the universe and that humans could discover these laws through reason and research, thereby establishing rationalism as the conceptual basis for science and philosophy.

The political and intellectual innovations of the Greek Archaic Age, which so profoundly affected later Western civilization, were almost lost to history. By about 500 B.C.E., Persia's awesome empire threatened the Greek world and its new values.

FOR FURTHER EXPLORATION

■ **For suggested references, including Web sites, for topics in this chapter,** see page SR-1 at the end of the book.

■ **For additional primary-source material from this period,** see Chapter 2 in *Sources of THE MAKING OF THE WEST*, Third Edition.

■ **For Web sites and documents related to topics in this chapter,** see *Make History* at bedfordstmartins.com/hunt.

CHAPTER REVIEW

KEY TERMS AND PEOPLE

Cyrus (37)   cult (53)

moral dualism (39)   hoplite (53)

Torah (40)   helot (59)

Diaspora (42)   Solon (62)

aretê (44)   demes (63)

Homer (44)   Sappho (64)

polis (47)   rationalism (65)

REVIEW QUESTIONS

1. In what ways was religion important in the Near East from c. 1000 B.C.E. to c. 500 B.C.E.?

2. What factors proved most important in the Greek recovery from the troubles of the Dark Age?

3. How did the physical, social, and intellectual conditions of life in the Archaic Age promote the emergence of the Greek city-state?

4. What were the main differences among the various forms of government in the Greek city-states?

MAKING CONNECTIONS

1. What characteristics made the Greek city-state a different form of political and social organization from that in Near Eastern city-states?

2. How were the ideas of the Ionian philosophers different from mythic traditions?

> **For practice quizzes, a customized study plan, and other study tools,** see the Online Study Guide at bedfordstmartins.com/hunt.

IMPORTANT EVENTS

1000–750 B.C.E.	Greece experiences its Dark Age
900 B.C.E.	Neo-Assyrian Empire emerges
800 B.C.E.	Greeks learn to write with an alphabet
776 B.C.E.	Olympic Games founded in Greece
750 B.C.E.	Greeks begin to create the polis
700 B.C.E.	Spartans conquer Messenia and enslave its inhabitants as helots
700–500 B.C.E.	Ionian philosophers invent rationalism
657 B.C.E.	Cypselus becomes tyrant in Corinth
630 B.C.E.	The lyric poet Sappho is born
597 and 586 B.C.E.	Hebrews are exiled to Babylon
594 B.C.E.	Solon's reforms promote early democracy in Athens
546–510 B.C.E.	Peisistratus's family rules Athens as tyrants
539 B.C.E.	Persian king Cyrus captures Babylon and permits the Hebrews to return to Canaan
508–500 B.C.E.	Cleisthenes' reforms secure democracy in Athens

The Greek Golden Age

c. 500–c. 400 B.C.E.

A failure in international negotiations fueled the greatest foreign danger ever to threaten Greece. In 507 B.C.E., Athens feared an attack from Sparta, its more powerful rival. The Athenian assembly therefore sent ambassadors to the Persian king, Darius I (r. 522–486 B.C.E.), to plead for a defensive alliance. The Athenian diplomats arranged for a meeting with the king's governor in Ionia (the western coast of modern Turkey), who controlled the Greeks living in that region. After the Athenians made their plea, the governor asked, "But who in the world are these people and where do they live that they are begging for an alliance with the Persians?" The mutual misunderstandings that resulted from this confused exchange helped start a prolonged conflict between mainland Greece and Persia in the early fifth century B.C.E.

This incident reveals external and internal reasons why war dominated Greece's history throughout that century, first with Greeks fighting Persians and then with Greeks fighting Greeks. The Persian king was eager to make more Greek city-states his subjects (those in Ionia had been his subjects for forty years) because their trade and growing wealth made them desirable prizes and because the Persians' traditions encouraged their kings to expand their empire. Unity seemed the Greeks' best defense, but the mainland city-states were so intensely competitive and suspicious of each other that they had never yet been able to come together to combat the Persians, not even to try to liberate the Greek city-states in Ionia from Persian control. Athens and

---

Greek against Persian in Hand-to-Hand Combat (detail)
This red-figure painting appears on the interior of the kind of cup that the Greeks used to drink wine. Painted about 480 B.C.E. (during the Persian Wars), it shows a Greek hoplite (armored infantry man) striking a Persian warrior in hand-to-hand combat with swords. The Greek has lost his principal weapon, a spear, and the Persian can no longer shoot his, the bow and arrow. The Greek artist has designed the painting to express multiple messages: the Persian's colorful outfit with sleeves and pants stresses the "otherness" of the enemy in Greek eyes, and their serene expressions at such a desperate moment dignify the horror of killing in war. Greek warriors often had heroic symbols painted on their shields, such as the winged horse Pegasus, an allusion to the brave exploits of Bellerophon. (© *The Trustees of the National Museums of Scotland.*)

Sparta so mistrusted each other that the Athenians appealed to foreigners for help against fellow Greeks.

Conflicting interests and mutual misunderstandings between Persia and Greece ignited a great conflict at the start of the fifth century B.C.E.: the so-called Persian Wars (499–479 B.C.E.), in which Persia invaded Greece. The Persian invasions threatened the independence of the Greek mainland and Aegean islands. So dire was the threat that thirty-one Greek states (out of hundreds) temporarily laid aside their traditional competition to form an alliance to defeat the Persians; in victory, however, they lost their unity and fell to fighting one another. In the midst of nearly constant warfare spanning the century, Greeks (especially in Athens) created what later ages judged to be their most famous innovations in architecture, art, and theater. These cultural achievements have led historians to call this period from around 500 to around 400 B.C.E. the Golden Age. This Golden Age is the first part of the period called the Classical Age of Greece, which lasted from around 500 B.C.E. to the death of Alexander the Great in 323 B.C.E.

Athens provides almost all of the surviving evidence for the Golden Age because most of the cultural achievements took place there and because the surviving literary and archaeological sources preserve few details about this period in other important city-states, such as Corinth and Syracuse. Many famous plays, histories, inscriptions, buildings, and sculptures survive from fifth-century B.C.E. Athens. For these reasons, studying the Greek Golden Age primarily means studying the Athenian Golden Age.

The confidence the Greeks gained from repelling the Persian invasions, combined with their traditional competitiveness, produced brilliant innovations in art, architecture, literature, education, and philosophy in the Golden Age. The new ideas in education and philosophy became hotly controversial at the time but have had a lasting influence on Western civilization. Such ideas angered many people because the changes seemed to attack ancient traditions, especially religion; they feared the gods would punish them for abandoning ancestral ways.

Political change also characterized the Athenian Golden Age. First, Athenian citizens made their city-state government more democratic than ever. Second, Athens also grew internationally powerful by using its navy to establish rule over other Greeks in a system dubbed "empire" by modern scholars. This naval power also promoted seaborne trade, and revenues from rule and trade brought Athens enormous prosperity. This newfound wealth supported cultural and political innovation because Athens's citizens voted to use the funds to finance new public buildings, art, and competitive theater festivals, and to pay for poorer men to serve as officials and jurors in an expanded democratic government.

The Golden Age ended when Sparta defeated Athens in the Peloponnesian War (431–404 B.C.E.) and the Athenians then fought a brief but bloody civil war (404–403 B.C.E.). The fifth century B.C.E., so famous for its cultural innovation, therefore both began and ended with fierce wars, with Greeks standing together in the first one and tearing each other apart in the concluding one. Victory in the Persian Wars spurred the growth of Athens's naval power and seaborne trade; the added income from military victories and international commerce financed political and cultural development; losing the Peloponnesian War bankrupted and divided Athens, turning its Golden Age to lead.

> **FOCUS QUESTION:** Did war bring more benefit or more harm — politically, socially and intellectually — to Golden Age Athens?

■ 500–323 Classical Age

■ 499–479 Persian Wars

■ Early 450s Pericles introduces pay for public office

■ 454 Athenian fleet defeated in Egypt

500 B.C.E. | **475 B.C.E.** | **450 B.C.E.**

■ 490 Battle of Marathon

■ 480–479 Xerxes' invasion of Greece

■ 480 Battle of Salamis

■ 461 Ephialtes' court reform begins

■ 451 Athenian citizenship law

■ 450 Sophists begin teaching in Athens

Wars between Persia and Greece, 499–479 B.C.E.

The Persian Wars had their roots in Athens's request for help from Persia in 507 B.C.E. The Athenian ambassadors agreed to the standard Persian requirement for an alliance: presenting tokens of earth and water to acknowledge submission to the Persian king. The Athenian assembly erupted in outrage at their diplomats' capitulation but failed to inform King Darius that it rejected his terms; he continued to believe that Athens had intended to submit to him. This misunderstanding planted the seed for two Persian attacks on Greece, one small and one huge. Since the Persian Empire far outstripped the Greek city-states in soldiers and money, the conflict pitted the equivalent of a huge bear against a pack of undersized dogs.

From the Ionian Revolt to the Battle of Marathon, 499–490 B.C.E.

When the Ionian Revolt led to the Persian Wars, the lesser conflict sparked a greater one—a common occurrence in the history of war. In 499 B.C.E., the Greek city-states in Ionia revolted against their Persian-installed tyrants, who were ruling harshly and unjustly, and the king's demand that the Ionians send still more soldiers for his army. The Spartans refused to help the Ionian rebels, but the Athenians sent troops because they regarded the Ionians as close kin. A Persian counterattack sent the Athenians fleeing home and crushed the revolt by 494 B.C.E. (Map 3.1, page 72). Darius exploded in anger when he learned that the Athenians had attacked in Ionia; after all, he thought they were faithful allies. So bitter was this perceived betrayal that, according to the historian Herodotus, Darius ordered a slave to repeat three times at every meal, "Lord, remember the Athenians."

In 490 B.C.E., Darius sent a small fleet to punish Athens and install a puppet tyrant. He expected Athens to surrender without a fight. The Athenians refused to back down, however, confronting the invaders near the village of Marathon. The Athenian soldiers were stunned by the Persians' strange garb—they wore colorful pants instead of the short tunics and bare legs that Greeks regarded as proper dress (see the picture at the opening of this chapter)—but the Greek commanders in a tactical innovation spurred the hoplites (armored infantry) to charge the enemy at a dead run instead of their usual slow advance. Running cut the time that the Athenians were exposed to the enemy's archers. The Greek soldiers, each wearing seventy pounds of metal armor, clanked across the Marathon plain through a hail of Persian arrows. In the hand-to-hand combat, the Greek hoplites used their heavier weapons to overwhelm the Persian infantry.

The Athenian infantry then hurried the twenty-six miles from Marathon to Athens to guard the city against the Persian navy. (Today's marathon races commemorate the legend of a runner speeding ahead to announce the victory, and then dropping dead.) When the Persians sailed home, the Athenians rejoiced in disbelief; thereafter, a family's greatest honor was to count a "Marathon fighter" among its ancestors.

Their unexpected success at Marathon evidently strengthened the Athenians' sense of community. When a fabulously rich strike was made in Athens's publicly owned silver mines in 483 B.C.E., a far-sighted leader named **Themistocles** convinced the assembly to spend the money on doubling the size of the navy to defend against possible foreign attack instead of distributing the money to the citizens to spend on themselves.

Themistocles (thuh MIST uh kleez): Athens's leader during the great Persian invasion of Greece.

- 446–445 Athens/Sparta peace treaty
- 441 B.C.E. Sophocles, *Antigone*
- 411 Aristophanes, *Lysistrata*
- 420s Herodotus, *Histories*

425 B.C.E.   **400 B.C.E.**

- 431–404 Peloponnesian War
- 415–413 Athenian defeat in Sicily
- 404–403 Thirty Tyrants rule
- 403 Restoration of democracy

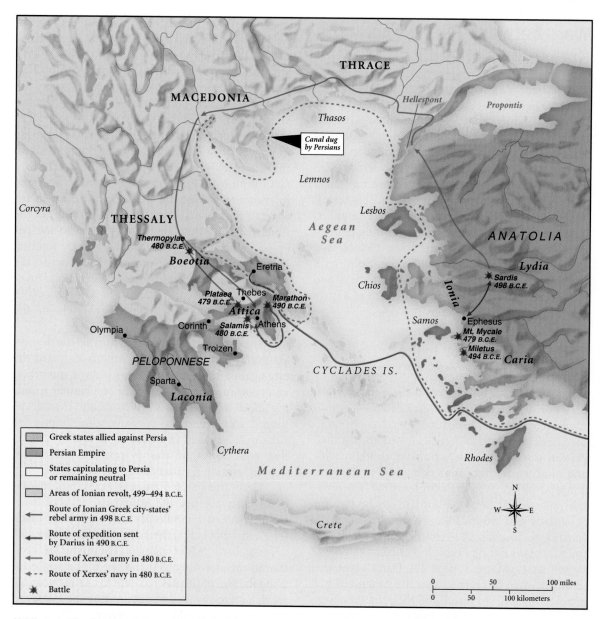

MAP 3.1 The Persian Wars, 499–479 B.C.E.
Following the example of the founder of the Persian kingdom, King Cyrus (d. 530 B.C.E.), King Cambyses (r. 530–522 B.C.E.) and King Darius I (r. 522–486 B.C.E.) expanded their empire eastward and westward. Darius invaded Thrace more than fifteen years before the conflict against the Greeks that we call the Persian Wars. The Persians' unexpected defeat in Greece put an end to their attempt to extend their power into Europe.

The Great Persian Invasion, 480–479 B.C.E.

Themistocles' foresight proved valuable when Darius's son Xerxes I (r. 486–465 B.C.E.) assembled an immense force to invade Greece to avenge his father's defeat and add the mainland city-states to the many lands paying him tribute. The Persians spared no expense, even digging a great canal through a peninsula in northern Greece to give their fleet safe passage. So huge was Xerxes' army, the Greeks claimed, that it took seven days and seven nights for the entire force to cross the Hellespont, the strip of sea between Anatolia and Greece, when the invasion began in 480 B.C.E. Xerxes thought the Greek city-states would immediately surrender; some did, but thirty-one made a decision new in Greek history: to unite as allies to defend their city-states' political freedom.

Their coalition became known as the Hellenic League, but it hardly represented the entire Greek world. The allies desperately wanted the major Greek city-states in Italy and Sicily to join the league because these western states were rich naval powers, but they refused. Syracuse, for example, the most powerful Greek state at the time, controlled a regional empire built on agriculture in Sicily's plains and seaborne commerce through its harbors astride the Mediterranean's western trading routes. The tyrant ruling Syracuse rejected the league's appeal for help because he was fighting his own war against Carthage, a Phoenician city in North Africa, over control of the trade routes.

The Hellenic League chose Sparta to lead because of its reputation for military valor; the Athenians swallowed their competitive pride and agreed to follow. The Spartans demonstrated their courage in 480 B.C.E. when three hundred of their infantry blocked Xerxes' army for several days at the narrow pass called Thermopylae ("Gate of Hot Springs") in central Greece. When told the Persian archers were so numerous that their arrows darkened the sun, one Spartan reportedly remarked, "That's good news; we'll get to fight in the shade." They did—to the death. Their tomb's memorial proclaimed, "Go tell the Spartans that we lie buried here obedient to their orders."

When the Persians marched south, the Athenians, knowing they could not defend the city, evacuated their residents to the Peloponnese rather than surrender; the Persians then burned Athens. The panicked allies decided to retreat to the Peloponnese, but in the summer of 480 B.C.E. Themistocles and his Athenian political rival Aristides cooperated to win a tough argument with the other city-states' generals, convincing them to stay and fight a naval battle. Themistocles then tricked the Persian king into sending his ships into battle against the Greek fleet in the channel between the island of Salamis and the west coast of Athens: the narrowness of the channel prevented Xerxes from sending all his fleet (twice or more the size of the Greeks') into battle at the same time. The heavier Greek warships then prevailed by ramming the flimsier Persian craft in the tight space. The battle of Salamis turned the tide of the war, and Xerxes retreated to Persia. The following summer (479 B.C.E.), the Spartans led the Greek infantry to dual victories over the remaining Persian land forces on the Greek mainland and, now on the offensive against the enemy, on the Anatolian coast. Superior generalship and the Greek competitive spirit of aretê

A Persian Royal Guard
This six-foot-high panel of polychrome glazed brick formed part of the decoration of a courtyard in the palace at Susa built by the Persian king Darius I (r. 522–486 B.C.E.). Susa was the most important administrative center of the Persian Empire, and the king and his court spent part of each year there. The warrior shown here perhaps represents one of the royal guards known as "immortals." An inscription reports that the craftsmen who made these panels came from Babylon, where there was a long tradition of this sort of architectural decoration. *(The Granger Collection, New York.)*

(excellence) underlay these successes. When the victorious allies met to award a prize to the war's best Greek commander, Themistocles won the competition—every general voted for himself first and Themistocles second!

The Greeks won their battles against the Persians because their generals, especially Themistocles, had better strategic foresight, their soldiers had stronger body armor, their warships were more effective in close combat, and their tactics minimized the Persian advantage in numbers of troops and ships. Above all, the Greeks won the war because enough of them took the innovative step of uniting to fight together for their independence. Because the Greek forces included not only the social elites but also thousands of poorer men who rowed the warships, the victory over the Persians showed that rich and poor Greeks alike treasured the ideal of political freedom for their city-states that had emerged during the Archaic Age.

The Delian and Peloponnesian Leagues

REVIEW: How did the Greeks overcome the challenges presented by the Persian invasions?

Athenian Confidence in the Golden Age, 478–431 B.C.E.

The struggle against the Persians was one of the rare occasions when at least some Greek city-states cooperated. Victory fractured this alliance, however, because the allies resented the harshness of Spartan command and the Athenians had gained the confidence to compete with the Spartans for leadership of Greece. No longer were Athenians satisfied to be followers of Sparta; now they dreamed of a much grander role for themselves. From this desire arose the so-called Athenian Empire. The growth of Athenian power over other Greeks inspired yet more confidence, which created a broader democracy willing to spend vast amounts on pay for officials and jurors, public buildings, art, and religious festivals in which citizens competed for public recognition in music and drama.

The Establishment of the Athenian Empire

After the Persian Wars, Sparta and Athens built up separate alliances to strengthen their own positions because each believed that their security depended on winning a competition for power. Sparta led strong infantry forces from the Peloponnese region, and its ally Corinth had a sizable navy. Called the Peloponnesian League, the Spartan alliance had an assembly to decide policy, but Sparta dominated.

Athens, with Aristides as lead negotiator, allied with city-states in northern Greece, on the islands of the Aegean Sea, and along the Ionian coast—the places most in need of protection from Persian retaliation. This alliance, whose treasury was originally located on the Aegean island of Delos, was built on naval power and today is called the **Delian League**.

The Delian League started out as a democratic alliance for collective security, but Athens came to control it through the allies' willingness to allow the Athenians to command and to set the financing arrangements for the league's fleet. At its height, the league included some three hundred city-states. Each paid dues (called tribute) according to its size. Larger city-states paid by sending **triremes**—warships propelled by 170 rowers on three levels and equipped with a battering ram at the bow (see Figure 3.1 on page 75)—complete with trained crews and their pay; smaller states could share the cost of one ship or contribute cash instead.

Over time, more and more Delian League members voluntarily paid cash because it was easier. Athens then used their tribute to construct triremes and pay men to row them; oarsmen who brought a slave to row alongside them earned double pay. Drawn primarily from the poorest citizens, rowers gained both income and political influence in Athenian democracy because the navy became the city-state's main force. These benefits made poor citizens eager to expand

Delian (DEE lee un) **League:** The naval alliance led by Athens in the Golden Age that became the basis for the Athenian Empire.

triremes (TRY reems): Greek wooden warships rowed by 170 oarsmen sitting on three levels and equipped with a battering ram at the bow.

Athens's power over other Greeks. The increase in Athenian naval power thus promoted the development of a wider democracy at home, but it undermined the democracy of the Delian League.

Since most Delian League allies had not kept up their own navies, the Athenian assembly could use the league fleet to compel disobedient allies to pay tribute. As the Athenian historian Thucydides commented, rebellious allies "lost their independence, and the Athenians became no longer as popular as they used to be." Athens's heavy-handed dominance of the Delian League, backed up by the threat of force, has led modern historians to label it the Athenian Empire.

Unpopularity among most allies was the price Athens paid for making itself the major naval power in the eastern Mediterranean: by about 460 B.C.E. the Delian League's fleet had expelled remaining Persian garrisons from northern Greece and driven the enemy fleet from the Aegean Sea. This sweep eliminated the Persian threat for the next fifty years and proved the effectiveness of Athenian leadership.

Military success made Athens prosperous by bringing in spoils and tribute, making seaborne trade safe, and benefiting rich and poor alike—the poor men who rowed the Delian League's navy earned good pay, while elite commanders enhanced their chances for election to high office by spending their spoils on public festivals and buildings. The Athenian assembly debated how Athens should treat its league allies, but the majority consistently rejected complaints on the grounds that the league was fulfilling its original duty by protecting everyone from Persian attack. In this way, democracy for its own citizens, pay, and imperialism were directly linked in Golden Age Athens.

Radical Democracy and Pericles' Leadership, 461–431 B.C.E.

As the Delian League grew, the Athenian fleet's oarsmen realized that they provided the cornerstone for Athens's new power and prosperity. In the late 460s B.C.E., they decided that the time had come to increase their political power by making the court system of Athens just as democratic as the legislative assembly, in which all free adult male citizens could already participate. They wanted laws and political institutions that would finally make Cleisthenes' promise of equality before the law a reality for everyone, so that they would no longer be liable to unfair verdicts at the hands of the elite in criminal cases and civil suits. Members

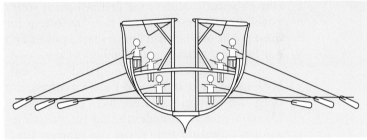

FIGURE 3.1 Triremes, the Foremost Classical Greek Warships
Innovations in military technology and training fueled a naval arms race in the fifth century B.C.E. when Greek shipbuilders devised larger and faster ramming ships powered by 170 rowers seated in three rows, one above each other. (See the illustration of the rowers, from behind, at the top of this page.) Called triremes, these ships were expensive to build and required extensive crew training. Only wealthy and populous city-states such as Athens could afford to build and man large fleets of triremes. This relief sculpture found on the Athenian acropolis and dating from about 400 B.C.E. gives a glimpse of what a trireme looked like from the side when being rowed into battle. (Sails were used to power the ship only when not in combat.) *(The Art Archive/Acropolis Museum Athens/Dagli Orti.)*

of the elite led this push for judicial reform, hoping to win popular support for election to high office by speaking out for the interests of the masses. A member of one of Athens's most distinguished families, **Pericles** (c. 495–429 B.C.E.), became Golden Age Athens's dominant politician by spearheading reforms to democratize its judicial system and provide pay for many public offices.

Pericles (PEHR uh kleez): Athens's political leader during the Golden Age.

Creating Radical Democracy. The changes to Athenian democracy in the 460s and 450s B.C.E. have led historians to label the system *radical* (literally, "from the roots") because it gave direct political power in the assembly and participation in the court system to all adult male citizens. The government consisted of the assembly open to all these men, the Council of Five Hundred chosen annually by lottery, the Council of the Areopagus of ex-archons serving for life, an executive board of ten annually elected "generals," nine archons (now chosen by lottery every year), hundreds of other annual minor officials (most chosen by lottery), and the court system.

Athens's **radical democracy** balanced two competing principles: participation by as many ordinary male citizens as possible in direct (not representative) democracy and selective leadership by elite citizens. To achieve the first, Athenian voters established (1) random selection by lottery for most public offices, term limits, shared power, and pay for most officials and members of the Council of Five Hundred (which prepared the assembly's agenda and supervised public matters); (2) open investigation and punishment of corruption; (3) equal protection under the law for citizens regardless of wealth; and (4) pay and random selection for jurors. To achieve the second principle, the highest-level officials were elected, rather than chosen by lottery. The top officials (the board of ten generals, who oversaw military and financial affairs) ran for election every year, could be reelected an unlimited number of times, and received no pay so that they would not seek election just for financial rewards. A successful general could stay in office indefinitely; Pericles, for example, won reelection fifteen years in a row in one stretch of his political career.

The changes in the judicial system did the most to create radical democracy. Previously, archons and the ex-archons of the Council of the Areopagus, who tended to be members of the elite, had decided most legal cases. As with Cleisthenes, reform took place when an elite man proposed it to support ordinary men's political rights and simultaneously win their votes against his rivals: in 461 B.C.E. Ephialtes won popular support by getting the assembly to establish a new system that took away jurisdiction from the archons and gave it to courts manned by citizen jurors. To make it more democratic and prevent bribery, jurors were selected by lottery from male citizens over thirty years old. They received a daily stipend to serve on juries numbering from several hundred to several thousand members. No judges or lawyers existed, and jurors voted by secret ballot after hearing speeches from the persons involved. As in the assembly, a majority vote decided matters; no appeals of verdicts were allowed.

Ostracism and Majority Rule. Athenian radical democracy included notions of privacy and legal protection for individuals, but majority rule could override those notions on matters of public policy. A striking example was **ostracism** (from *ostrakon*, a piece of broken pottery used as a ballot). Once a year, all male citizens could cast a ballot on which they scratched the name of one man they thought should be exiled for ten years. If at least six thousand ballots were cast, the man whose name appeared on the greatest number was expelled from Athens. He suffered no other penalty; his family and property remained undisturbed.

Usually a man was ostracized because he had become so popular that a majority feared he would overthrow the democracy to rule as a tyrant.

Potsherd Ballots for Ostracism
These two shards (*ostraka*) were broken from the same pot (as the breakage line shows) and inscribed for use as ballots in an ostracism at Athens. The lower fragment carries the name of Themistocles, the leader who engineered the Greek fleet's success against the Persian navy off the island of Salamis in 480 B.C.E.; the upper one bears the name of Cimon, the Delian League's most famous general. Political competition led to Themistocles' ostracism sometime in the late 470s B.C.E. and Cimon's in 461 B.C.E. Therefore, if these two ballots were intended for the same ostracism, it must have been that of Themistocles, or an earlier one when he was still in Athens.

radical democracy: The Athenian system of democracy established in the 460s and 450s B.C.E. that extended direct political power and participation in the court system to all adult male citizens.

ostracism (AHS truh sizm): An annual procedure in Athenian radical democracy by which a man could be voted out of the city-state for ten years; its purpose was to prevent tyranny.

Sometimes a leader was ostracized when his political competitors ganged up to vote against him; this was the fate of Themistocles, who in a great irony ended up living in Persia as a favorite of King Xerxes, who valued his former enemy's intelligence. There was no guarantee of voters' motives in an ostracism, as a story about Aristides illustrates. He was nicknamed "the Just" because he had proved himself so fair-minded in setting the original level of dues for Delian League members. On the day of an ostracism, an illiterate citizen handed him a pottery fragment and asked him to scratch a name on it:

> "Certainly," said Aristides. "Which name shall I write?" "Aristides," replied the man. "All right," said Aristides as he inscribed his own name, "but why do you want to ostracize Aristides? What has he done to you?" "Oh, nothing. I don't even know him," sputtered the man. "I just can't stand hearing everybody refer to him as 'the Just.'"

True or not, this tale demonstrates that most Athenians believed the right way to support democracy was to trust a majority vote regardless of its possible injustice to a particular individual.

Not all citizens approved of radical democracy. Some socially elite citizens bitterly criticized what they saw as its disregard for social merit in giving political power to the poor. Opponents of democracy blamed it for promoting the interests of those whom they called the "wicked" (i.e., the poor) over the interests of "useful" citizens (i.e., themselves, the rich). These critics became particularly vocal when Athens's democracy suffered periods of crisis, as at certain points in the great war with Sparta that was to erupt at the end of the Golden Age. They insisted that oligarchy—the rule of the few—was morally superior to radical democracy because they believed that the poor lacked the education and moral values needed for leadership and would use their majority rule to strip the rich of their wealth by passing laws to make them pay for expensive public programs.

Pericles' Leadership. Pericles became the most influential leader of his era by using his political vision and spellbinding skill in public speaking to convince the assembly to pass reforms strengthening the equality that poor citizens prized. He began his career by supporting Ephialtes' reform of the court system. Then, in the early 450s B.C.E., he boosted mass participation in democracy by introducing pay for service in the public offices filled by lottery. This reform used public funds to pay men for serving in numerous government posts, on the Council of Five Hundred, and on juries. Previously, because these offices had been unpaid,

only wealthy men could afford to fill them. Now, poor citizens could serve. In 451 B.C.E., Pericles sponsored a law restricting citizenship to those whose mother and father were both Athenian by birth. Previously, wealthy men had often married foreign women from elite families. This change both increased the status of Athenian women, rich or poor, as potential mothers of citizens and made Athenian citizenship more valuable by reducing the number of people eligible for its legal and financial benefits. In a complementary measure to enforce exclusiveness, officials reviewed everyone's citizenship and, some sources report, struck thousands from the rolls.

Pericles also promoted aggressive naval campaigns (and thus provided poor Athenians an income as rowers) when war with Sparta broke out in the 450s over Athenian actions against Peloponnesian League states. He also supported sending the fleet against Persian garrisons in Cyprus, Egypt, and the eastern Mediterranean to expand the Delian League's power and win war spoils. The voters in the assembly were so eager to compete for international power against both Greeks and Persians that they authorized up to three major expeditions at the same time. This exuberant militarism slowed in the late 450s B.C.E. after a horrendous defeat at the hands of Persian forces in Egypt in 454 B.C.E. killed tens of thousands of oarsmen; the Athenians had sent a large naval force to aid an Egyptian rebellion against Persian rule, hoping to weaken Persian power in the eastern Mediterranean. In the winter of 446–445 B.C.E., Pericles engineered a peace treaty with Sparta with the goal of stabilizing the balance of power in Greece for thirty years and thus preserving Athenian control of the Delian League.

The Urban Landscape

Golden Age Athens prospered from Delian League dues, war plunder, and taxes on booming international seaborne trade. Its harbor in Piraeus promoted cross-Mediterranean commerce, its navy made its empire's numerous ports safe for merchants and travelers from far-flung locations, and its courts resolved legal disputes. Its artisans produced goods traded far and wide; the Etruscans in central Italy, for example, imported countless painted vases for wine drinking at Greek-style dinner parties. The economic activity and international traffic of the mid-fifth century B.C.E. boosted Athens to its greatest prosperity ever.

Athenians spent their new riches not just on broadening participation in democratic government but also on their city's public buildings, art, and religious festivals. In private life, rich urban dwellers splurged on luxury goods influenced by Persian designs, but most houses retained their traditional modest size and plainness. Farmhouses could cluster in villages or stand isolated, while homes and apartments in the city wedged tightly against one another along narrow, winding streets. Recent archaeological study of the city of Olynthus in northeastern Greece shows that urban one-family homes were built on varying patterns, but one favorite plan grouped bedrooms, storerooms, and dining rooms around open-air courtyards. Poor city residents rented small apartments. Wall paintings or decorative artworks were rare, furnishings sparse. Toilets consisted of pots and a pit outside the front door; the city paid collectors to dump the dung outside its fortification walls.

Generals who wanted to display their excellence (aretê) and also win the people's favor spent their war spoils on running tracks, shade trees, and public buildings. A popular building project was a stoa, a narrow structure open along one side that offered shelter from the weather. The super-rich commander Cimon, for example, paid for the Painted Stoa to be built on the edge of Athens's **agora**, the central market square. There, crowds of shoppers could admire the stoa's bright paintings depicting his family's military exploits, especially his father's leadership in the battle of Marathon. This sort of contribution was voluntary, but the laws required wealthy citizens to pay for festivals and equipping warships. This financial obligation on the rich was essential because Athens, like most Greek city-states, had no regular property or income taxes.

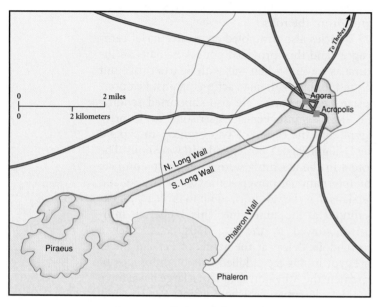

MAP 3.2 Fifth-Century B.C.E. Athens
The urban center of Athens, with the agora and acropolis at its heart, measured about one square mile, surrounded by a stone wall with a circuit of some four miles. Gates guarded by towers and various smaller entries allowed traffic in and out of the city; much of the Athenian population lived in the many demes (villages) of the surrounding countryside. Most of the city's water supply came from wells and springs inside the walls, but, unusually for a Greek city, Athens also had water piped in from outside. The Long Walls provided a protected corridor connecting the city to its harbor at Piraeus, where the Athenian navy was anchored and grain was imported to feed the people.

The Parthenon.   On Athens's acropolis (the rocky hill at the city's center, Map 3.2, left), Pericles had the two most famous buildings of Golden Age Athens erected during the 440s and 430s B.C.E.: a mammoth gateway and an enormous marble temple of Athena called the **Parthenon**. Comparing a day's wage then and now, we can estimate that these buildings together cost more than the equivalent of a billion dollars, a phenomenal sum for a Greek city-state; Pericles' political rivals

agora (AH gore uh): The central market square of a Greek city-state, a popular gathering place for conversation.

Parthenon (PAR thuh non): The massive temple to Athena as a warrior goddess built atop the Athenian acropolis in the Golden Age of Greece.

FIGURE 3.2 Styles of Greek Capitals
The Greeks decorated the capitals, or tops, of columns in these three styles to fit the different architectural "canons" (their word for precise mathematical systems of proportions) that they devised for designing buildings. These styles were much imitated in later times, as on many U.S. state capitols and the U.S. Supreme Court Building in Washington, D.C.

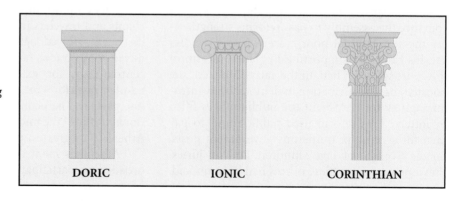

DORIC   IONIC   CORINTHIAN

slammed him for spending too much public money on the project and diverting Delian League funds to domestic uses.

The Parthenon (literally, "the virgin goddess's house") has become the foremost symbol of Athens's Golden Age. The Parthenon honored Athena, the city's patron deity, as the divine champion of Athenian military power and proclaimed that she had a real presence in the city. Inside the temple, a gold-and-ivory statue nearly forty feet high depicted the goddess in armor, holding in her outstretched hand a six-foot statue of Nike, the goddess of victory.

Like all Greek temples, the Parthenon was meant as a house for its divinity, not as a gathering place for worshippers. Its design followed standard temple architecture: a rectangular box on a raised platform studded with columns, a plan the Greeks probably derived from the stone temples of Egypt. The Parthenon's soaring columns fenced in a porch surrounding the interior chamber on all sides. They were carved in the simple style called Doric, in contrast to the more elaborate Ionic and Corinthian styles often imitated in columns on modern buildings (Figure 3.2, facing page).

The Parthenon's massive size and innovative style proclaimed the self-confidence of Golden Age Athens and its competitive drive to build a monument more spectacular than any other in Greece. Constructed from twenty thousand tons of Attic marble, the temple stretched some 230 feet long and 100 feet wide, with eight columns across the ends instead of the six normally found in Doric style and seventeen instead of thirteen along the sides. The temple's sophisticated architecture demonstrated the Athenian ambition to use human

---

The Acropolis of Athens
Most Greek city-states, including Athens, sprang up around a prominent rocky hill, called an acropolis ("height of the city"; compare the picture of Corinth on page 61). The summit of the acropolis usually housed sanctuaries for the city's protective deities and could serve as a fortress for the population during an enemy attack. Athens's acropolis boasted several elaborately decorated marble temples honoring the goddess Athena; the largest one was the Parthenon, seen here from its west (back) side. Recent research suggest that the ruins of a temple burned by the Persians when they captured Athens in 480 B.C.E. remained in place right next to the Parthenon; the Athenians left its charred remains to remind themselves of the sacrifices they had made in defending their freedom. (The walls in the lower foreground are from a theater built in Roman times.) *(akg-images.)*

Scene from the Parthenon Frieze

The Parthenon, the Athenian temple honoring Athena as a warrior goddess and patron of the Delian League, dominated the summit of the city's acropolis. A frieze (band of sculpture in relief), of which this is a small section, ran around the top of the temple's outside wall. Here, riders line up in the Pan-Athenaic festival's procession to the Parthenon; the artist layered the horses' legs to show depth. The original blazed with bright colors and details fashioned from metal, such as the horses' bridles. The elaborate folds of the riders' garments display the rich style characteristic of clothed figures in Classical Age sculpture. How would you compare the style of this relief to that of the Persian relief on page 73? *(The Art Archive/Acropolis Museum Athens/Dagli Orti.)*

skill to improve nature: because perfectly rectilinear architecture appears curved to the human eye, subtle curves and inclines were built into the Parthenon to produce an illusion of completely straight lines and emphasize its massiveness.

The Parthenon's many sculptures communicated confident messages: the gods ensure triumph over the forces of chaos, and Athenians enjoy the gods' goodwill more than any other city-state's citizens do. The sculptures in each pediment (a triangular space atop the columns at either end of the temple) portrayed Athena as the city-state's benefactor. The metopes (panels sculpted in relief above the outer columns around all four sides) portrayed victories over hostile centaurs and other enemies of civilization. Most strikingly of all, a frieze (a continuous band of figures carved in relief) ran around the top of the walls inside the

porch and was painted in bright colors to make it more visible. The Parthenon's frieze was special because usually only Ionic-style buildings had one. Although it had no inscription to state its subject, the frieze most likely portrayed Athenian men, women, and children on parade in the presence of the gods, the procession shown in motion like the pictures in a graphic novel or cartoon today.

The Parthenon frieze made a bold statement about how Athenians perceived their relationship to the gods—no other Greeks had ever adorned a temple with representations of themselves. Its sculpture staked a claim of unique intimacy between the city-state and the gods, reflecting the Athenians' confidence after helping turn back the Persians, achieving leadership of a powerful naval alliance, and amassing great wealth. Their success, the Athenians believed, proved that the gods were on their side, and their fabulous buildings signaled their gratitude.

Sculpture's New Message. Like the unique Parthenon frieze, the innovations that Golden Age artists made in representing the human body shattered tradition. By the time of the Persian Wars, Greek sculptors had begun replacing the stiffly balanced style of Archaic Age statues with statues in motion in new poses. This style of movement in stone expressed an energetic balancing of competing forces, echoing a theme evident in radical democracy's principles.

Sculptors also began carving anatomically realistic but perfect-looking bodies, suggesting that humans could be confident in their potential for beauty and perfection. Female statues, for example, now displayed the shape of the curves underneath their clothing, while male ones showed bodybuilders' muscles. The faces showed a self-confident reserve rather than the rigid smiles of archaic statues.

As with relief sculptures on temples, Golden Age freestanding statues were erected to be seen by the public, whether they were paid for with private or government funds. Privately commissioned statues of gods were placed in sanctuaries as symbols of devotion. Wealthy families commissioned statues of their deceased members, especially if they had died young in war, to be placed above their graves as memorials of their excellence and signs of the family's social status.

REVIEW: What factors produced political change in fifth-century B.C.E. Athens?

Tradition and Innovation in Athens's Golden Age

Golden Age Athens's prosperity and international contacts created unprecedented innovations in architecture, art, drama, education, and philosophy, but central aspects of its social and religious customs remained traditional, as did such customs throughout Greece. This contrast between cultural change and social continuity generated tension between the desire to innovate and the pressure to preserve traditional ways, especially with regard to the conduct of women and to the practice of religion. In keeping with tradition, Athenian women, along with other Greek women, were expected to limit their public role to participation in religious ceremonies; in private life they were to manage their households and, if they were poor, work to help support their families. The startling new ideas of competitive philosophers and teachers called Sophists and the Athenian philosopher Socrates' views on personal morality and responsibility caused many people to fear that the gods would be angered. The most famous response to the clash between innovation and tradition was the development of publicly funded drama festivals, whose contests for tragic and comic plays examined problems in city-state life, especially the social and personal hardships caused by war.

Religious Tradition in a Period of Change

Greeks maintained religious tradition publicly by participating in the city-state's sacrifices and festivals, and privately by seeking a personal relationship with the gods in the rituals of hero cults and mystery cults. Each cult had its own rituals, including sacrifices ranging from the slaughter of large animals to bloodless offering of fruits, vegetables, and small cakes. The speechwriter Lysias (c. 445–380 B.C.E.), a Syracusan residing in Athens, explained the reason for publicly funded sacrifices:

> Our ancestors handed down to us the most powerful and prosperous community in Greece by performing the prescribed sacrifices. It is therefore proper for us to offer the same sacrifices as they, if only for the sake of the success which has resulted from those rites.

The public sacrifice of a large animal provided an occasion for the community to reaffirm its ties to the divine world and for the worshippers to benefit by feasting on the roasted meat of the sacrificed beast. For poor people, the free food provided at religious festivals might be the only meat they ever tasted.

Golden Age Athens used its riches to pay for more religious festivals than any other city-state; nearly half the days of the year included one. The biggest festivals featured parades as well as contests with valuable prizes in music, dancing, poetry, and athletics. Laborers' contracts specified how many days off they received to attend such ceremonies. Some festivals were for women only, such as the three-day festival for married women in honor of Demeter, goddess of agriculture and fertility.

Privately, people took a keen interest in actions meant to improve their personal relations with the divine. Families marked significant events such as birth, marriage, and death with prayers, rituals, and sacrifices. They honored their ancestors with offerings made at their tombs, consulted seers about the meanings of dreams and omens, and paid magicians for spells to improve their love lives or curses to harm their enemies. Particularly important were hero cults and mystery cults. Hero cults included rituals performed at the tomb of an extraordinarily famous man or woman. Heroes' remains were thought to retain special power to reveal the future by inspiring oracles, healing sickness, and providing protection in battle. The strongman Herakles (or Hercules, as the Romans spelled his name) had cults all over the Greek world because his superhuman reputation gave him international appeal. **Mystery cults** involved a set of prayers, hymns, ritual purification, sacrifices, and other forms of worship that initiated members into secret knowledge about the divine and human worlds. Initiates believed that they gained divine protection from the cult's god or gods.

The Athenian mystery cult of Demeter and her daughter Persephone attracted worshippers from all parts of the world because it offered hope for protection on earth and in the afterlife. The cult's central rite was the Mysteries: a series of initiation ceremonies into secret knowledge. So important were these Mysteries that the Greek states observed an international truce—as with the Olympic Games—to allow travel even from distant corners of the world to attend them. The Mysteries were open to any free, Greek-speaking individuals—women and men, adults and children—if they were free of ritual pollution (for example, if they had not been convicted of murder, committed sacrilege, or had recent contact with a corpse or blood from a

---

mystery cults: Religious worship that provided initiation into secret knowledge and divine protection, including hope for a better afterlife.

birth). Some slaves who worked in the sanctuary were also eligible. The main stage of initiation took almost two weeks, culminating in the revelation of Demeter's central secret after a day of fasting. So seriously did Greeks take the initiation that no one ever revealed the secret during the cult's thousand-year history. Being initiated promised a better fate on earth and after death. As a sixth-century B.C.E. poem says, "Richly blessed is the mortal who has seen these rites; but whoever is not an initiate and has no share in them, that one never has an equal portion after death, down in the gloomy darkness."

Mystery cults reveal that ancient Greeks thought their gods required action from their worshippers to receive blessings. Preserving religious tradition mattered deeply to most people because they saw it as a safeguard against the precariousness of life.

Women, Slaves, and Metics

Women, slaves, and **metics** (foreigners granted permanent residence status in return for paying taxes and serving in the military) made up the majority of Athens's population, but they lacked political rights. Women who were citizens enjoyed legal privileges and social status denied slaves and foreigners, and they earned respect through their roles in the family and in religion. Upper-class women managed their households, visited female friends, and participated in religious cults at home and in public. Poor women worked as small-scale merchants, crafts producers, and agricultural laborers. Slaves and metics also contributed much to Athens's prosperity, but they always remained outsiders in the city-state.

Property, Inheritance, and Marriage. Bearing children in marriage earned women status because it was literally the source of family—the heart of Greek society. To defend this fundamental social institution, men were expected to respect and support their wives. Childbirth was dangerous under the medical conditions of the time. In *Medea*, a play of 431 B.C.E. by Euripides, the heroine shouts in anger at her husband, who has selfishly betrayed her: "People say that we women lead a safe life at home, while men have to go to war. What fools they are! I would much rather fight in battle three times than give birth to a child even once."

Athenian wives were expected to be partners with their husbands in owning and managing the

household's property to help the family thrive. (See "Contrasting Views," page 84.) Rich women acquired property, including land—the most valued possession in Greek society because it could be farmed or rented out for income—through inheritance and dowry (the family property a daughter received at marriage). The husband was legally required to preserve the dowry and use it to support his wife and their children. A man often had to put up valuable land of his own as collateral to guarantee the safety of his wife's dowry.

Like fathers, mothers were expected to hand down property to their children to keep it in the family. This expectation shows up most clearly in Athenian law about heiresses (daughters whose fathers died without any sons, which happened in about one in every five families): the closest male relative of the heiress's father—her official guardian after her father's death—was required to marry her. The goal was to produce a son to inherit the father's property. This rule applied regardless of whether the heiress was already married (unless she had sons) or whether the male relative already had a wife; the heiress and the male relative were both supposed to divorce their present spouses and marry each other. In real life, however, people often used legal technicalities to get around this requirement so that they could remain with their chosen partners.

Requiring property to be passed down in this way met two traditional goals of male-dominated Greek society: continuing the father's bloodline and preventing property from piling up in the hands of unmarried women (and therefore out of the control of men). At Sparta, the renowned scholar Aristotle (384–322 B.C.E.) reported, the inheritance laws were different (and, in his opinion, deficient); he claimed that women came to own 40 percent of Spartan territory.

Women's Daily Lives. Tradition restricted women's freedom of movement in public; men claimed that this restriction protected women by limiting opportunities for seducers and rapists. Men wanted to ensure that their children were truly theirs, that family property went only to genuine heirs, and that the city had only legitimate citizens. Well-off women in the city were expected to avoid contact with male strangers and mainly to spend their time at home or with women friends in their houses. Recent research has exploded the idea that Greek homes had a set "women's quarter" to which women were confined; rather, women were granted privacy in certain rooms. If the house in-

---

metic: A foreigner granted permanent residence status in Athens in return for paying taxes and serving in the military.

cluded an interior courtyard, women could walk there in the open air and talk with other members of the household, male and female. In the safety of her home, a well-to-do woman would spin wool for clothing, converse with visiting friends, direct her children, supervise the slaves, and present her opinions on various matters, including politics, to the men of the house as they came and went. Poor women had little time for such activities because they—like their husbands, sons, and brothers—had to leave the house, usually a crowded rental apartment, to set up small stalls to sell bread, vegetables, simple clothing, or trinkets they had made.

An elite woman careful of her reputation left home only for appropriate reasons, such as religious festivals, funerals, childbirths at the houses of relatives and friends, and trips to workshops to buy shoes or other domestic articles. Often her husband escorted her, but sometimes she took only a slave, setting her own itinerary.

Women who bore legitimate children merited increased respect and freedom, as an Athenian man explained in his speech (written by Lysias) defending himself for having killed his wife's adulterer:

> After my marriage, I initially refrained from bothering my wife very much, but neither did I allow her too much independence. I kept an eye on her. . . . But after she had a baby, I started to trust her more and put her in charge of all my things, believing we now had the closest of relationships.

Bearing male children brought a woman special honor because sons meant security. Sons could appear in court to support their parents in lawsuits and protect them in the streets of Athens, which for most of its history had no regular police force. By law, sons were required to support elderly parents. So intense was the pressure to produce sons that stories circulated of women who smuggled in male babies born to slaves and passed them off as their own.

Most upper-class women probably viewed their limited contact with men outside the household as a badge of superior social status. For example, a pale complexion, from staying inside so much, was much admired as a sign of an enviable life of leisure and wealth. Many women used powdered white lead as makeup, unaware of the health risk, to give themselves a fashionable lack of color in their skin.

Extraordinary Women.   A few women in Athens escaped traditional restrictions by working as what

Vase Painting of a Woman Buying Shoes (detail)
Greek vases frequently displayed scenes from daily life instead of mythological stories. Here, a woman is being fitted for a pair of custom-made shoes by a craftsman and his apprentice. Her husband has accompanied her, as was often the case for shopping, and he appears to be participating in the discussion of the purchase. This vase was painted in so-called black-figure technique, in which the figures are dark and have their details incised on a background of red clay. (Henry Lillie Pierce Fund. Photograph © 2007 Museum of Fine Arts, Boston.)

■ **For more help analyzing this image,** see the visual activity for this chapter in the Online Study Guide at **bedfordstmartins.com/hunt**.

Greeks called a **hetaira** (literally, "companion"). Companions, usually foreigners, were unmarried, physically attractive, witty in speech, and skilled in music and poetry. Men hired them to entertain at a symposium (a drinking party to which wives were not invited) with their playful conversation. Their much-admired skill at clever teasing and verbal insults allowed companions a freedom of speech denied to "proper" women; they nevertheless lacked the social respectability and status that wives and mothers possessed.

Sometimes companions also sold sex for a high price, and they could control their own sexuality by choosing their clients. Athenian men (but not women) could buy sex as they pleased without legal hindrance. "Certainly you don't think men father children out of sexual desire?" wrote the upper-class author Xenophon. "The streets and

---

hetaira (heh TYE ruh): A witty and attractive woman who charged fees to entertain at a symposium.

The Nature of Women and Marriage

Greeks believed that women had different natures from men and that both genders were capable of excellence, but in their own ways (Documents 1 and 2). Marriage was supposed to bring these natures together in a partnership of complementary strengths and obligations to each other (Document 3). Marriage contracts (Document 4), similar to modern prenuptial agreements, became common to define the partnership's terms.

1. Pericles Addresses the Athenians in the First Year of the Peloponnesian War (431–430 B.C.E.)

According to Thucydides, Pericles concluded his Funeral Oration, a solemn public occasion commemorating the valor of soldiers killed in battle and the virtues expected of citizens, with these terse remarks to the women in the audience. His comments reveal two ancient Greek assumptions: that women had a different nature from men and that women best served social harmony by not becoming subjects of gossip. He kept these comments to a bare minimum in his long speech.

If it is also appropriate now for me to say something about what constitutes excellence for women, I will signal all my thinking with this short piece of advice to those of you present who are now widows of the war dead: your reputation will be great if you don't fall short of your innate nature and men talk about you the least whether in praise of your excellence or blaming your faults.

Source: Thucydides, *History of the Peloponnesian War*, Book 2.45. Translation by Thomas R. Martin.

2. Melanippe Explains Why Men's Criticism of Women Is Baseless (late fifth century B.C.E.)

The Athenian playwright Euripides often portrays female characters denouncing men for misunderstanding and criticizing women. The heroine of his tragedy Melanippe the Captive *is a mother who overcomes hardship and treachery to save her family. Preserved only on damaged papyrus scraps, Melanippe's speech unfortunately breaks off before finishing.*

Men's blame and criticism of women are empty, like the twanging sound a bow string makes without an arrow. Women are superior to men, and I'll demonstrate it. They make contracts with no need of witnesses [to swear they are honest]. They manage their households and keep safe the valuable possessions, shipped from abroad, that they have inside their homes; without a woman, no household is elegant or happy. And then in the matter of people's relationship with the gods—this I judge to be most important of all—there we have the greatest role. For women prophesy the will of Apollo in his oracles [at Delphi], and at the hallowed oracle of Dodona by the sacred oak tree a woman reveals the will of Zeus to all Greeks who seek it. And then there are the sacred rites of initiation performed for the Fates and the Goddesses Without Names: these can't be done with holiness by men, but women make them flourish in every way. In this way women's role in religion is right and proper.

Therefore, should anyone put down women? Won't those men stop their empty fault-finding, the ones who strongly believe that all women should be blamed if a single one is found to be bad? I will make a distinction with the following argument: nothing is worse than a bad woman, but nothing is more surpassingly superior than a worthy one.

Source: Euripides, *Melanippe the Captive*, fragment 660 Mette. Translation by Thomas R. Martin.

3. Socrates Discusses Gender Roles in Marriage (late fifth century B.C.E.)

Socrates, who was dedicated to discovering the nature of human virtue, often discussed family life because it revealed the qualities of women as well as men. When his upper-class friend Ischomachus married a young wife, as was common, the philosopher quizzed him about their marriage; the new husband explained that it was a partnership based on the complementary natures of male and female.

Ischomachus: I said to her: . . . I for my sake and your parents for your sake [arranged our marriage] by considering who would be the best partner for forming a household and having children. I chose you, and your parents chose me as the best they could find.

the brothels are swarming with ways to take care of that." Men (but, again, not women) could also have sex freely with female or male slaves, who could not refuse their masters.

Less successful companions lived precarious lives of exploitation and even violence at the hands of their male customers, but the most skilled of them attracted admirers from the highest levels of society and earned enough to live in luxury on their own. The most famous companion in Athens was Aspasia from Miletus, who became Pericles' lover and bore him a son. She dazzled men with her brilliant talk and wide knowledge; Pericles fell so deeply in love with her that he wanted to make her an "honest woman" by marrying her, despite his own law of 451 B.C.E. restricting citizenship, which meant their children could not be citizens without a special law passed by the assembly.

If God should give us children, we will then plan how to raise them in the best possible way. For our partnership provides us this good: the best mutual support and the best maintenance in our old age. We have this sharing now in our household, because I've contributed all that I own to the common resources of the household, and so have you. We're not going to count up who brought more property, because the one who turns out to be the better partner in a marriage has made the greater contribution.

Ischomachus's wife (no name is given): But how will I be able to partner you? What ability do I have? Everything rests on you. My mother told me my job was to behave with thoughtful moderation.

Ischomachus: Well, my father told me the same thing. Thoughtful moderation for a man as for a woman means behaving in such a way that their possessions will be in the best possible condition and will increase as much as possible by good and just means. . . . So, you must do what the gods made you naturally capable of and what our law requires. . . . With great forethought the gods have yoked together male and female so that they can form the most beneficial partnership. This yoking together keeps living creatures from disappearing by producing children, and it provides offspring to look after parents in their old age, at least for people. [He then explains that human survival requires outdoor work — to raise crops and livestock — and indoor work — to preserve food, raise infants, and manufacture clothing.] . . . And since the work both outside and inside required effort and care, God, it seems to me, from the start fashioned women's nature for indoor work and men's for outdoor. Therefore he made men's bodies and spirits more able to endure cold and heat and travel and marches, giving them the outside jobs, while assigning indoor tasks to women, it seems, because their bodies are less hardy. . . .

But since both men and women have to manage things, [God] gave them equal shares in memory and attentiveness; you can't tell which gender has more of these qualities. And God gave both an equal ability to practice self-control, with the power to benefit the most from this quality going to whoever is better at it — whether man or woman. Precisely because they have different natures, they have greater need of each other and their yoking together is the most beneficial, with the one being capable where the other one is lacking. And as God has made them partners for their children, the law makes them partners for the household.

Source: Xenophon, *Oeconomicus* 7.10–30. Translation by Thomas R. Martin.

4. Greek Marriage Contract from Egypt (311–310 B.C.E.)

Greeks living abroad customarily drew up written contracts to define the duties of each partner in a marriage because they wanted their traditional expectations to remain legally binding regardless of the local laws. The earliest surviving such contract comes from Elephantine, the site of a Greek military garrison far up the Nile.

Marriage contract of Heraclides and Demetria. Heraclides [of Temnos] takes as his lawful wife Demetria of Cos from her father Leptines of Cos and her mother Philotis. He is a free person; she is a free person. She brings a dowry of clothing and jewelry worth 1,000 drachmas. Heraclides must provide Demetria with everything appropriate for a freeborn wife. We will live together in whatever location Leptines and Heraclides together decide is best.

If Demetria is apprehended doing anything bad that shames her husband, she will forfeit all her dowry; Heraclides will have to prove any allegations against her in the presence of three men, whom they both must approve. It will be illegal for Heraclides to bring home another wife to Demetria's harm or to father children by another woman or to do anything bad to Demetria for any reason. If he is apprehended doing any of these things and Demetria proves it in the presence of three men whom they both approve, Heraclides must return her dowry in full and pay her 1,000 drachmas additional. Demetria and those who help her in getting this payment will have legal standing to act against Heraclides and all his property on land and sea. . . . Each shall have the right to keep a personal copy of this contract. [A list of witnesses follows.]

Source: *Elephantine Papyri*, ed. O. Rubensohn (Berlin, 1907), no. 1. Translation by Thomas R. Martin.

QUESTIONS TO CONSIDER

1. What evidence and arguments for differing natures for men and women do these documents offer?
2. Do you think Athenian women would have found these arguments convincing? Why or why not?

Great riches could also free a woman from tradition, allowing her to speak to men openly and bluntly. The most outspoken Athenian woman of wealth was Elpinike, Cimon's sister. When controversy erupted over a speech by Pericles supporting Athens's attack on a rebellious Delian League ally, Elpinike publicly rebuked him by sarcastically remarking in front of a group of women who were praising him, "This really is wonderful, Pericles. . . . You have caused the loss of many good citizens, not in battle against Phoenicians or Persians . . . but in suppressing an allied city of fellow Greeks."

Other sources, especially comic drama and fourth-century B.C.E. oratory, imply that not-so-rich women, too, had strong opinions about politics. They customarily expressed their views to their husbands and male relatives at home in private.

Vase Painting of a Symposium
Upper-class Greek men often spent their evenings at a symposium, a drinking party that always included much conversation and usually featured music and entertainers; wives were not included. The discussions could range widely, from literature to politics to philosophy. The man on the right is about to fling the dregs of his wine, playing a messy game called *kottabos*. The nudity of the female musician indicates she is a hired prostitute. *(Reproduced by permission of the Syndics of the Fitzwilliam Museum, Cambridge. Master and Fellows of Corpus Christi College, Cambridge.)*

Slaves and Metics. Traditional social and legal restrictions in Golden Age Athens made outsiders of slaves and metics, despite all the work they did in and for the city-state. Individuals and the city-state alike owned slaves, who could be purchased from traders or bred in the household. Unwanted newborns abandoned by their parents (an accepted practice called infant exposure) were often picked up by others and raised as slaves. Athens's commercial growth in this period increased the demand for slaves, who in Pericles' time made up around 100,000 of the city-state's total of perhaps 250,000 inhabitants (the numbers are extremely uncertain extrapolations from ancient reports of the army's numbers and probable household sizes). Slaves worked in homes, on farms, and in crafts shops; rowed alongside their owners in the navy; and, if they were really unlucky, toiled in Athens's dangerous silver mines. Unlike those at Sparta, Athens's slaves almost never rebelled, probably because they originated from too many different places to be able to unite. Many mining slaves did run away to the Spartan base established in Athenian territory during the Peloponnesian War; the Spartans probably resold them.

Golden Age Athens's wealth and cultural vitality attracted many metics, who flocked to the city from all around the Mediterranean, hoping to make money as importers, crafts producers, entertainers, and laborers. By the start of the Pelopon-

nesian War in 431 B.C.E., metics constituted perhaps 50,000 to 75,000 of the estimated 150,000 free men, women, and children in the city-state. Metics paid for the privilege of living and working in Athens through a special foreigners' tax and military service. Athenians valued metics' contributions to the city's prosperity, but their insistence on exclusive citizenship meant they were unwilling to share its legal and financial benefits with immigrants.

Innovations in Education and Philosophy

Building on the intellectual foundation of rationalism laid in the Archaic Age, innovative ideas in education, philosophy, historical writing, and medicine developed in the Greek Golden Age. These innovations delighted some fifth-century Greeks, but they deeply upset others, who feared that these drastic changes from older ways of life and thought would undermine the traditions that held society together, especially religion, thereby provoking punishment from the angry gods. These controversial changes opened the way to the development of scientific study as an enduring characteristic of Western civilization.

Education and philosophy provided the hottest battles between tradition and innovation. Earlier, education had stressed the preservation of old ways; parents controlled what children learned at home and from hired tutors (there were no public schools). Controversy erupted when Sophists appeared in the mid-fifth century B.C.E. and offered, for pay, classes to teenage and young-adult males that taught nontraditional philosophic and religious doctrines and novel techniques for public speaking. Some philosophers' ideas about the nature of the cosmos challenged traditional religious views. The philosopher Socrates, who did not work as a Sophist, expounded such strict views on personal morality and responsibility that he provoked an equally fierce controversy. In historical writing and medicine, innovators created models of interpretation and scientific method that stimulated argument over how to understand human experience and the body.

Disagreement over whether these changes in intellectual life were dangerous for Athenian society contributed to the political tension that had arisen at Athens by the 430s B.C.E. concerning Athens's harsh treatment of its own allies and its economic sanctions against those allied with Sparta. This interaction occurred because the political, intellectual, and religious dimensions of life in ancient Athens were closely intertwined. Athenians would connect philosophic ideas about the nature of justice with their decisions about the city-state's domestic and foreign policy, while also being concerned about the attitude of the gods toward the community. (See Document, "Athenian Regulations for a Rebellious Ally," page 88.)

Education. The only formal education available came from private teachers, to whom well-to-do families sent their sons to learn to read, write, play a musical instrument or sing, and develop athletic skills suitable for war. Physical training was considered a vital part of men's education because it both made their bodies beautiful and prepared them for service in the militia (to which they could be summoned anytime between ages eighteen and sixty). Therefore, men exercised nude every day in gymnasia, which were public open-air facilities paid for by wealthy families. Men frequently discussed politics and exchanged news at these gymnasia. The daughters of wealthy families usually received instruction at home from educated slaves, who were expensive because they were rare. The young girls learned reading, writing, and arithmetic so that they would be ready to help their future husbands by managing the household.

Poor girls and boys received no formal education; they learned a trade and perhaps a little reading, writing, and calculating by assisting their parents in their daily work or by serving as appren-

The Masculine Ideal
This sculpture of a male warrior/athlete, found in a shipwreck off the coast of Riace in southern Italy, was cast in bronze in the mid-fifth century B.C.E. Greeks preferred bronze over marble for top-rank statues, but few have survived because they were usually melted down and their metal reused (e.g., to make guns in later ages). The figure's relaxed pose displays the asymmetry—the head looking to one side, the arms in different positions, the torso tilted—that made Greek statues from the Classical Age appear less stiff than Archaic Age ones. The cap on his head was what warriors wore to cushion their helmet. The body displays the ideal build that Greek men strove to achieve through daily workouts. For male statues, nudity indicated a heroic ideal. *(Eric Lessing/Art Resource, NY.)*

tices to skilled crafts workers. Scholars disagree about how many people could read well, but most likely they were a minority. Weak reading skills were less of a problem then than they are today because Greeks could always find someone to read aloud any written text; in fact, oral communication was at the center of Greek life, whether in political speeches or in songs, plays, and stories from literature and history.

Athenian Regulations for a Rebellious Ally

The city-state of Chalcis on the island of Euboea rebelled from the Athenian-dominated Delian League in 446 B.C.E. After defeating the rebels, the Athenians forced the Chalcidians to swear compliance with new regulations, which were inscribed on stone in both cities. The text reveals that the terms were not the same for the two sides.

The Athenian Council and the jurors shall swear an oath in this form: "I will not expel Chalcidians from Chalcis nor will I reduce the city to ruins nor deprive any individual of his citizen rights nor punish him with exile nor imprison him nor kill him nor take property from anyone who has not had a trial without approval from the People [i.e., the assembly] of the Athenians, nor will I have a vote taken against the community or any single individual without their being called to trial, and when an embassy arrives, I will introduce them to the Council and People within ten days when I am in charge of the procedure, so far as I am able. These things I will guarantee the Chalcidians if they obey the People of the Athenians."

The Chalcidians shall swear an oath in this form: "I will not rebel from the People of the Athenians either by cunning or by any way at all either by word or by deed, and I will not obey anyone who rebels, and if anyone does rebel, I will denounce him to the Athenians, and I will pay the tribute to the Athenians which I persuade the Athenians [to levy on me], and as an ally I will be the best and most just that I am able, and I will give support to and defend the People of the Athenians, if anyone wrongs the People of the Athenians, and I will obey the People of the Athenians."

Source: *Inscriptiones Graecae*, 3rd ed. (1981), no. 40. Translation by Thomas R. Martin.

After their early education, young men from prosperous families would learn how to participate in public life, and especially Athenian democracy, not by taking formal lessons but by observing their fathers, uncles, and other older men as they debated in the Council of Five Hundred and the assembly, served in public office, and spoke in court. Often an older man would choose an adolescent boy as his special favorite to educate. The teenager would learn about public life by spending time with the older man. During the day the boy would listen to his mentor talking politics in the agora, help him perform his duties in public office, and work out with him in a gymnasium. They would spend their evenings at a symposium, whose agenda could range from serious political and philosophical discussion to riotous partying.

This older mentor–younger favorite relationship could lead to sexual relations between the youth and the older male, who would usually be married. Sex between mentors and favorites was considered acceptable in elite circles in many city-states, including Athens, Sparta, and Thebes; other places banned this behavior because they believed, as the Athenian author Xenophon suggests, that it sprang from a man's shameful inability to control his lustful desires.

Sophists and Philosophers as a Threat to Tradition.

By the time of radical democracy in Athens, young men eager to develop the essential political skill of public speaking could obtain higher education in a new way: pay an expensive professional teacher to train them. These teachers, called **Sophists** ("men of wisdom"), sparked controversy because they strongly challenged traditional beliefs by teaching new skills of persuasion in speaking and new ways of thinking based on rational arguments. The term *sophist* later acquired a negative connotation (preserved in the English word *sophistry*) because clever Sophists could use complex reasoning to make deceptive arguments.

Starting about 450 B.C.E. Athens's booming economy and lively intellectual activity attracted Sophists from around the Greek world. They were individual entrepreneurs competing with one another to attract pupils who could pay the hefty prices they charged for their innovative courses. As in every part of Greek intellectual life, the competition for prominence was intense. Sophists competed by offering specialized training in rhetoric—the skill of speaking persuasively. Every ambitious man craved rhetorical training because it promised power in Athens's assembly, councils, and courts. The Sophists alarmed many tradition-minded Athenians, who feared their teachings would undermine established social and political traditions. Speakers trained by silver-tongued

Sophists (SAH fists): Competitive intellectuals and teachers in ancient Greece who offered expensive courses in persuasive public speaking and new ways of philosophic and religious thinking beginning around 450 B.C.E.

Sophists, they believed, might be able to mislead the assembly by persuading it to accept bad decisions promoting their private interests.

Prominent older leaders, Pericles among them, often joined the Sophists for discussions of their new ideas. The most notorious Sophist was Protagoras, a contemporary of Pericles from Abdera, in northern Greece. Protagoras moved to Athens around 450 B.C.E., when he was around forty, and spent most of his career there. His views on the nature of truth and morality outraged many Athenians: he argued that rationally there could be no absolute standard of truth because every issue had two irreconcilable sides. For example, if one person feeling a breeze thinks it warm whereas another person thinks it cool, neither judgment can be absolutely correct because the wind simply is warm to one and cool to the other. Protagoras summed up this subjectivism—the belief that there is no absolute reality behind and independent of appearances—in his work *Truth:* "The human being is the measure of all things, of the things that are that they are, and of the things that are not that they are not." According to Protagoras, the individual, male or female, is the sole judge of his or her own impressions.

The subjectivism of Protagoras and other Sophists contained two main ideas: (1) human institutions and values are only matters of convention, custom, or law (*nomos*) and not creations of nature (*physis*), and (2) since truth is subjective, speakers should be able to argue either side of a question with equal persuasiveness and rationality. The first view implied that traditional human institutions were arbitrary and transient rather than natural and permanent, whereas the second seemed to many people to make questions of right and wrong irrelevant. (See Document, "Sophists Arguing Both Sides of a Case," page 90.)

The Sophists' critics therefore charged them with teaching moral relativism and threatening the shared public values of the democratic city-state. Aristophanes, author of comic plays, satirized Sophists for harming Athens by instructing students in persuasive techniques "to make the weaker argument the stronger." Protagoras, for one, energetically responded that his doctrines were not hostile to democracy, arguing that every person had a natural capability for excellence and that human society depended on the rule of law based on a sense of justice. Members of a community, he explained, must be persuaded to obey the laws, not because they were based on absolute truth, which did not exist, but because rationally it was advantageous for everyone to be law-abiding. A thief, for example, who might claim that stealing was a part of nature, would have to be persuaded by reason that a man-made law forbidding theft was to his advantage because it protected his own property and the community in which he, like all humans, had to live in order to survive.

Even more disturbing than the Sophists' ideas about truth were their ideas about religion. Protagoras angered people with his agnosticism (the belief that supernatural phenomena are unknowable): "Whether the gods exist I cannot discover, nor what their form is like, for there are many impediments to knowledge, [such as] the obscurity of the subject and the brevity of human life." His implication that even religious belief must be based on knowledge acquired through evidence was in keeping with the development of Greek rationalism and scientific thought, but it upset those who thought he was saying that conventional religion had no meaning. They worried that his words would provoke divine anger against the community that gave him a home.

Other fifth-century B.C.E. philosophers and thinkers, though not working as Sophists, also proposed new scientific theories about the nature of the cosmos and the origin of religion that offended believers in traditional religion. A philosopher friend of Pericles, for example, argued that the sun was a lump of flaming rock, not a god. Another philosopher invented an atomic theory of matter to explain how change was constant in the universe. Everything, he argued, consisted of tiny, invisible particles in eternal motion. Their random collisions caused them to combine and recombine in an infinite variety of forms, with no divine purpose guiding their collisions and combinations. These ideas seemed to invalidate traditional religion, which explained events as governed by the gods' will. Even worse was the idea advanced by the wealthy aristocrat Critias, who wrote a play in which religion was denounced as a clever but false system invented by powerful men to fool ordinary people into obeying moral standards through fear of divine punishment.

The Sophists' techniques of persuasion and ways of thought based on rational arguments helped their students advance their political opinions forcefully and defend themselves in court. But because only wealthy men could afford their classes, the Sophists threatened Athenian democracy by giving yet another advantage to the rich in the assembly's debates or speeches in court. In addition, moral relativism and the physical explanation of the universe struck many Athenians as dangerous: they feared that such teachings, by offending the gods, would destroy the divine goodwill they believed Athens enjoyed. These ideas so

DOCUMENT

Sophists Argue Both Sides of a Case

The Sophist Protagoras taught his students to argue both sides of any case, but he insisted he did not teach this skill for immoral purposes. Some teachers following in his footsteps were less ethical. This excerpt comes from an anonymous handbook of the late fifth century B.C.E. *entitled* Double Arguments, *which provided examples of how Sophists could make arguments in the fashion of Protagoras.*

Greek philosophers put forward double arguments concerning the good and the bad. Some say that the good is one thing and the bad another, but others say that they are the same, and that a thing might be good for some persons but bad for others, or at one time good and at another time bad for the same person. I myself agree with those who hold the latter opinion, which I shall examine using as an example human life and its concern for food, drink, and sexual pleasures: these things are bad for a man if he is sick but good if he is healthy and needs them. And, further, overindulgence in these things is bad for the one who overindulges but good for those who make a profit by selling these things. And again, sickness is bad for the sick but good for the doctors. And death is bad for those who die but good for the undertakers and makers of grave monuments. . . . Shipwrecks are bad for the ship owners but good for the ship builders. When tools are blunted and worn away it is bad for others but good for the blacksmith. And if a pot gets smashed, this is bad for everyone else but good for the potter. When shoes wear out and fall apart it is bad for others but good for the shoemaker. . . . In the *stadion* race for runners, victory is good for the winner but bad for the losers.

Source: *Dissoi Logoi* 1.1–6. Translation adapted from Rosamund Kent Sprague, ed., *The Older Sophists* (Columbia: University of South Carolina Press, 1972), 279–80.

---

infuriated some Athenians that in the 430s B.C.E., they sponsored a law allowing citizens to bring charges of impiety against "those who fail to respect divine things or teach theories about the cosmos." Not even Pericles could prevent his philosopher friend from being convicted on this charge and expelled from Athens.

Socrates on Ethics. Socrates (469–399 B.C.E.), the most famous philosopher of the Golden Age, became well known in his home state of Athens during this troubled time of the 430s, when people were anxious not just about the Sophists but also about the growing threat of war with Sparta. Socrates devoted his life to questioning people about their beliefs, but he insisted he was not a Sophist because he offered no courses and took no pay. Above all, he fought against the view that justice should be equated with power over others. By insisting that true justice was better than injustice under any and all circumstances, he gave a new direction to Greek philosophy: an emphasis on ethics (the study of ideal human values and moral duties). Although other thinkers before him (especially poets and authors of plays) had dealt with similar issues, Socrates was the first philosopher to make ethics his central concern.

Socrates lived an eccentric life that attracted constant attention. Sporting a stomach, in his words, "a bit too big to be convenient," he wore the same cheap cloak summer and winter and scorned shoes no matter how cold the weather. His physical stamina — including both his tirelessness as a soldier in Athens's infantry and his ability to out-drink anyone at a symposium — was legendary. Unlike the high-priced Sophists, he lived in poverty and disdained material possessions, though somehow managing to support a wife and several children; he probably inherited some money and accepted gifts from wealthy admirers.

Socrates spent his time in conversations all over Athens: participating in a symposium, strolling in the agora, or watching young men exercise in a gymnasium. In this behavior he resembled his fellow Athenians, who placed great value on the importance and pleasure of speaking with one another at length. He wrote nothing; our knowledge of his ideas comes from others' writings, especially those of his famous follower Plato (c. 428–348 B.C.E.). Plato portrays Socrates as a relentless questioner of his fellow citizens, foreign friends, and leading Sophists. Socrates' questions had the goal of making his conversational partners examine the basic assumptions of their way of life. Giving few answers, Socrates never directly instructed anyone; instead, he led them to draw conclusions in response to his probing questions and refutations of their cherished assumptions. Today this procedure is called the **Socratic method**.

Socratic method: The Athenian philosopher Socrates' method of teaching through conversation, in which he asked probing questions to make his listeners examine their most cherished assumptions.

Socrates frequently upset and even outraged people because his method made them feel ignorant and baffled. Socrates' questions forced them to admit that they did not in fact know what they had assumed they knew very well. Even more painful to them was Socrates' fiercely argued view that the way they lived their lives — pursuing success in politics or business or art — was merely an excuse for avoiding the hard work of understanding and developing genuine aretê. Socrates insisted that he was ignorant of the best definition of excellence and the good but that his wisdom consisted of knowing that he did not know. He vowed he was trying to improve, not undermine, people's ethical beliefs, even though, as a friend put it, a conversation with Socrates made a man feel numb — as if a jellyfish had stung him.

Socrates especially wanted to use reasoning to discover universal, objective standards that justified individual ethics. He attacked the Sophists for their relativistic claim that conventional standards of right and wrong were merely "the fetters that bind nature." This view, he protested, equated human happiness with power and "getting more."

Socrates insisted that the only way to achieve true happiness was to behave in accordance with a universal, transcendent standard of just behavior that people could grasp rationally. Essentially, he argued that just behavior and excellence were identical to knowledge and that true knowledge of justice would inevitably lead people to choose good over evil. They would therefore have truly happy lives, regardless of how rich or poor they were. Since Socrates believed that ethical knowledge was all a person needed for the good life, he argued that no one knowingly behaved unjustly and that behaving justly was always in the individual's interest. It was simply ignorant to believe that the best life was the life of unlimited power to pursue whatever one desired. The most desirable human life was concerned with virtue and guided by reason, not by dreams of personal gain.

Though very different from the Sophists' doctrines, Socrates' ideas proved just as disturbing because they rejected the Athenians' traditional way of life. His ridicule of commonly accepted ideas about the importance of wealth and public success infuriated many people. Unhappiest of all were the fathers whose sons, after listening to Socrates' questions reduce someone to utter bewilderment, came home to try the same technique on their parents, employing rational arguments to criticize as old-fashioned and worthless the values their family held dear. Men who experienced this reversal of the traditional educational hierarchy — the father was supposed to educate the son — felt that Socrates

Statuette of the Philosopher Socrates
The controversial Socrates, the most famous philosopher of Athens in the fifth century B.C.E., joked that he had a homely face and a bulging stomach. This small statue is an artist's impression of what Socrates looked like; we cannot be sure of the truth. Socrates was renowned for his irony, and he may have purposely exaggerated his physical unattractiveness to show his disdain for ordinary standards of beauty and his own emphasis on the quality of one's soul as the true measure of one's worth. Compare his body to that of the athletes shown in the vase painting on page 45 or of the statue of the warrior/athlete on page 87. (© Copyright The Trustees of the British Museum.)

was undermining the stability of society by making young men question Athenian traditions. Socrates evidently did not teach women, but Plato portrays him as ready to learn from exceptional women, such as Pericles' companion Aspasia.

The worry that Socrates' ideas presented a danger to conventional society inspired Aristophanes to write his comedy *The Clouds* (423 B.C.E.). This play portrays Socrates as a cynical Sophist who, for a fee, offers instruction in Protagoras's technique of making the weaker argument the stronger. When the curriculum of Socrates' school

("The Thinkery") transforms a youth into a public speaker who argues that a son has the right to beat his parents, his father burns the place down. None of these plot details seems to have been real; what was genuine was the fear that Socrates' radical views on individual morality endangered the city-state's traditional practices. This anxiety only grew worse as the Peloponnesian War dragged on with ever more casualties, and many citizens began to feel that their best hope for victory lay in strengthening tradition, not weakening it.

Historical Writing. Just as the Sophists and Socrates antagonized many people with their new ideas, the inventors of historical writing drew attention because they took a critical attitude in their descriptions of the past. Herodotus of Halicarnassus (c. 485–425 B.C.E.) and Thucydides of Athens (c. 455–399 B.C.E.) became Greece's most famous historians and established Western civilization's tradition of history writing. The fifth-century B.C.E.'s unprecedented events—a coalition Greek victory over the world's greatest power and then the longest war ever between Greeks—apparently inspired them to create history as a subject based on strenuous research. They explained that they wrote histories because they wanted people to remember the past and to understand why wars had taken place. In the 420s B.C.E., Herodotus finished a long, groundbreaking work called *Histories* (meaning "inquiries" in Greek) to explain the Persian Wars as a clash between the cultures of the East and West; by Roman times he had been dubbed the Father of History. A typically competitive Greek intellectual, Herodotus made the justifiable claim that he surpassed all previous recording of the past by taking an in-depth and investigative approach to evidence, being interested in the culture of non-Greeks as well as Greeks, and expressing explicit and implicit judgments about people's actions. Because Herodotus recognized the necessity (and the delight) of studying other cultures for historical research, he pushed his inquiries deep into the past, looking for long-standing cultural differences that helped explain the Persian-Greek conflict. Unlike poets and playwrights, he did not make the gods the driving force in history, instead putting the focus on human psychology and interaction.

Thucydides redirected historical inquiry—and overtly competed with Herodotus—by writing contemporary history and inventing the kind of analysis of power that today informs political science. His *History of the Peloponnesian War*, published after the end of the war, made power politics, not divine intervention, history's primary force. Deeply affected by the war's brutality, he used his experiences as a politician and failed military commander (he was exiled for losing a key outpost) to make his narrative vivid and frank in describing human moral failings. His insistence that historians should spare no effort in seeking out the most reliable sources and evaluating their testimony with objectivity set a high standard for later writers. Like Herodotus, he challenged tradition by revealing that Greek history was not just a story of glorious achievements but also had its share of shameful actions (such as the Athenian punishment of Melos in the Peloponnesian War—see page 98).

Hippocrates and the Birth of Scientific Medicine. Hippocrates of Cos, a fifth-century B.C.E. contemporary of Thucydides, challenged tradition by grounding medical diagnosis and treatment in clinical observation; his fame continues today in the oath bearing his name that doctors swear at the beginning of their professional careers. Previously, medicine had depended on magic and ritual; illness was believed to be caused by evil spirits, and various cults in Greek religion offered healing to patients through divine intervention. Competing to refute these earlier doctors' theories, Hippocrates insisted that only physical factors caused disease. He may have been the author of the view, dominant in later medicine, that four humors (fluids) made up the human body: blood, phlegm, black bile, and yellow bile. Health depended on keeping the proper balance among them; being healthy was to be in "good humor." This system for understanding the body corresponded to the division of the inanimate world into four parts: the elements earth, air, fire, and water.

Hippocrates taught that the physician's most important duty was to base his knowledge on careful observation of patients and their response to different treatments. Clinical experience, not abstract theory or religious belief, was the proper principle for establishing effective cures. By putting his innovative ideas and practices to the test in competition with those of traditional medicine, Hippocrates established the truth of his principle, which later became a cornerstone of scientific medicine.

The Development of Greek Tragedy

Greek ideas about the problematic relationship between gods and humans inspired Golden Age Athens's most prominent cultural innovation:

Divine Healing
This relief sculpture shows the god Asclepius healing Archinus (his name is inscribed below). Patients sought Asclepius's help by going to sleep and dreaming in his sanctuary, as shown at right; the god in the form of a snake is licking the patient's shoulder to heal it. At left, the god's power is symbolized by showing him as a heroic-sized figure, who is directly treating the injured shoulder. The Athenians brought Asclepius's cult from abroad to their city in 420 B.C.E. during the Peloponnesian War to try to alleviate epidemic disease and war injuries. The famous doctor and medical theorist Hippocrates challenged tradition by rejecting this kind of divine healing. *(The Art Archive/National Archaeological Museum, Athens/Dagli Orti.)*

tragic drama. Plays called tragedies were presented over three days at the major annual festival of the god Dionysus in a contest for playwrights, in keeping with the competitive spirit characteristic of Greek cultural life. Tragedies presented shocking stories involving fierce conflict and characters representing powerful forces, usually from myth but occasionally from history, that could be related to controversial issues in contemporary Athens. Therefore, these plays stimulated their large audiences to ponder the danger that ignorance, arrogance, and violence presented to the city-state's democratic society. Following the tradition of Homer and Hesiod, Golden Age playwrights explored topics ranging from the roots of good and evil to the nature of individual freedom and responsibility in the family and the political community. As with other ancient texts, most tragedies have not survived: only thirty-three still exist from the hundreds that were produced at Athens.

The competition took place every year, with an archon choosing three authors from a pool of applicants. Each of these finalists presented four plays during the festival: three tragedies in a row (a trilogy), followed by a semicomic play featuring satyrs (mythical half-man, half-animal beings) to end the day on a lighter note. Tragedies were written in verses of solemn language; they were often based on stories about the violent possibilities when gods and humans interacted. The plots often ended with a resolution to the trouble—but only after prolonged suffering.

Athenian tragedies in performance bore little resemblance to modern plays. As in many other cities in Greece, they took place during the daytime in an outdoor theater. At Athens, the theater was sacred to the god Dionysus and built into the southern slope of Athens's acropolis. This theater held about fourteen thousand spectators overlooking an open, circular area in front of a slightly raised stage. A tragedy had eighteen cast members, all of whom were men: three actors to play the speaking roles (both male and female characters) and fifteen chorus members. Although the chorus leader sometimes engaged in dialogue with the actors, the chorus primarily performed songs and dances in the circular area in front of the stage, called the orchestra.

A successful tragedy offered a vivid spectacle. The chorus wore elaborate costumes and performed intricate dance routines. The actors, who wore masks, used broad gestures and booming voices to reach the upper tier of seats. A powerful voice was crucial to a tragic actor because words represented the heart of the plays, in which dialogue and long speeches predominated over physical action. Special effects were part of the spectacle. For example, a crane allowed actors playing the roles of gods to fly suddenly onto the stage. The actors playing lead roles, called the protagonists (literally, "first competitors"), competed against one another for the designation of best actor. So important was a first-rate protagonist to a play's success that actors were assigned by lottery to the

Theater of Dionysus at Athens
Tragedies, satyr plays, and comedies were produced at Athens during the daytime in this outdoor theater honoring the god Dionysus. Temporary wooden installations provided seating, the stage, and the scenery during the Classical Age; the seats and the stone stage building foundations that are visible here come from later eras. The theater seated about fourteen thousand or more people, and subsidies kept ticket prices reasonable. Since Athens's drama festivals featured multiple plays each day, spectators spent long hours in the theater to see them all. *(John Elk III/Bruce Coleman, Inc. www.bciusa.com.)*

competing playwrights to give all three an equal chance to have a winning cast. Great protagonists became enormously popular, although they were not usually members of the social elite.

Playwrights were from the elite because only men of some wealth could afford the amount of time and learning this work demanded: as author, director, producer, musical composer, choreographer, and sometimes even actor. As citizens, playwrights also fulfilled the normal military and political obligations of Athenian men. The best-known Athenian tragedians—Aeschylus (525–456 B.C.E.), Sophocles (c. 496–406 B.C.E.), and Euripides (c. 485–406 B.C.E.)—all served in the army, and Sophocles was elected to Athens's highest public office. Authors of plays competed from a love of honor, not money: the prizes, determined by a board of judges, awarded high prestige but little cash. The competition was regarded as so important that any judge who took a bribe to award a prize was put to death.

Athenian tragedy was a public art form subsidized by tax revenues and mandatory contribu-

tions by the rich. Tragedy's plots explored the difficulties of telling right from wrong when humans came into conflict with one another in the city-state and the gods became involved. Even though most tragedies were based on stories that referred to a legendary time before city-states existed, such as the period of the Trojan War, the moral issues the plays illuminated always pertained to the society and obligations of citizens in a city-state. For example, Aeschylus in his trilogy *Oresteia* (458 B.C.E.) uses the story of how the gods stop the murderous violence in the family of Orestes, son of Agamemnon, the Greek leader against Troy, to explain the divine origins of democratic Athens's court system. The plays suggest that human beings learn only by suffering but that the gods provide justice in the long run. Sophocles' *Antigone* (441 B.C.E.) presents the story of the cursed family of Oedipus of Thebes as a drama of harsh conflict between a courageous woman, Antigone, and the city-state's stern male leader, her uncle Creon. After her brother dies in a failed rebellion, Antigone insists on her family's moral obligation to bury its dead in obedience to divine command, while Creon takes harsh action to preserve order and protect community values by prohibiting the burial of his nephew the traitor. In a horrifying story of raging anger and suicide that features one of the most famous heroines of Western literature, Sophocles exposes the right and wrong on each side of the conflict. His play offers no easy resolution of the competing interests of divinely sanctioned moral tradition and the state's political rules.

Ancient sources tell us that the audiences reacted strongly to the messages of the tragedies presented in the drama competition of the Dionysian festival. For one thing, they could see that the central characters of the plays were figures who fell into disaster even though they held positions of power and prestige. The characters' reversals of fortune came about not because they were absolute villains but because, as humans, they were susceptible to a lethal mixture of error, ignorance, and **hubris** (violent arrogance that, according to the Greeks, drove the competitive spirit to excess). The Athenian Empire was at its height when audiences at Athens attended the tragedies of these and other popular playwrights. Thoughtful spectators could reflect on the possibility that Athens's current power and prestige, managed as they were by humans, might fall prey to the same kind of mistakes and conflicts that brought down the heroes and heroines of tragedy. Thus, tragedies not only entertained through their spectacle but also educated through their stories and words. In particular, they reminded male citizens, who governed the city-state in its assembly, council, and courts, that success created complex moral problems that self-righteous arrogance never solved.

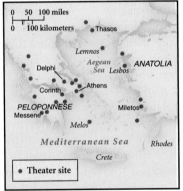

Theaters of Classical Greece

The Development of Greek Comedy

Golden Age Athens developed comedy as its second distinctive form of public theater. Like tragedies, comedies were written in verse, performed in Dionysus festivals, and subsidized with public funds and contributions from the rich. Unlike tragedies, comedies commented directly on public policy and criticized current politicians and intellectuals. They did this with plots and casts presenting outrageous fantasies of contemporary life. For example, comic choruses, which had twenty-four dancing singers, could be colorfully dressed as talking birds or dancing clouds, or an actor could fly on a giant dung beetle to visit the gods.

Comic playwrights vied to win the award for the festival's best comedy by creating beautiful poetry, raising laughs with constant jokes and puns, and skewering pretentious citizens and political leaders. Much of the humor concerned sex and bodily functions, delivered in a stream of imaginative profanity. Well-known men of the day were targets for insults as cowards or effeminate weaklings.

Statuettes of Comic Actors
Although these little statues are dressed in the kinds of masks and costumes that came into vogue later than the style of comedy that Aristophanes and his contemporaries wrote in the fifth century B.C.E. (for which no such pieces exist), they give a vivid sense of the exaggerated buffoonery that characterized the acting in Greek comedy. In Aristophanes' day, the grotesque unreality of comic costumes would have been even more striking because the male actors wore large leather phalluses (penises) attached below their waists that could be props for all sorts of ribald jokes. The use of masks in certain kinds of theater performances continued into Roman times. (*Bildarchiv Preussischer Kulturbesitz/Art Resource, NY.*)

---

hubris (HYOO bris): The Greek term for violent arrogance.

Women characters portrayed as figures of fun and ridicule seem to have been fictional, to protect the dignity of actual female citizens.

Athenian comedies often made fun of political leaders. As the leading politician of radical democracy, Pericles came in for fierce criticism in comedy. Comic playwrights mocked his policies, his love life, even the shape of his skull ("Old Turnip Head" was a favorite insult). Aristophanes (c. 455–385 B.C.E.), Athens's most famous comic playwright, so fiercely ridiculed Cleon, the city's most prominent leader early in the Peloponnesian War, that Cleon sued him. A citizen jury ruled in Aristophanes' favor, upholding the Athenian tradition of free speech.

In several of Aristophanes' comedies, the main characters are powerful women who compel the men of Athens to change their policy to preserve family life and the city-state. These plays even criticize the assembly's policy during wartime. Most famous is *Lysistrata* (411 B.C.E.), named after the female lead character of the play. In this fantasy, the women of Athens and Sparta unite to force their husbands to end the Peloponnesian War. To make the men agree to a peace treaty, they first seize the acropolis, where Athens's financial reserves are kept, to prevent the men from squandering them further on the war. They then use sarcasm and pitchers of cold water to beat back an attack on their position by the old men who have remained in Athens while the younger men are out on campaign. Above all, the women steel themselves to refuse to sleep with their husbands when they return from battle. The effects of their sex strike on the men, portrayed in a series of explicit episodes, finally compel the warriors to make peace.

Lysistrata presents women acting bravely and aggressively against men who seem bent on destroying traditional family life—they are staying away from home for long stretches while on military campaign and are ruining the city-state by prolonging a pointless war. Lysistrata insists that women have the intelligence and judgment to make political decisions: "I am a woman, and, yes, I have brains. And I'm not badly off for judgment. Nor has my education been bad, coming as it has from my listening often to the conversations of my father and the elders among the men." Her old-fashioned training and good sense allow her to see what needs to be done to protect the community. Like the heroines of tragedy, Lysistrata is a conservative, even a reactionary; she wants to put things back the way they were before the war ruined family life. To do that, however, she has to act like an impatient revolutionary. That irony sums up the

challenge that fifth-century B.C.E. Athens faced in trying to resolve the tension between the dynamic innovation of its Golden Age and the importance of tradition in Greek life.

The remarkable freedom of speech of Athenian comedy allowed frank, even brutal, commentary on current issues and personalities. It cannot be an accident that this energetic, critical drama emerged in Athens at the same time as radical democracy, in the mid-fifth century B.C.E. The feeling that all citizens should have a stake in determining their government's policies evidently fueled a passion for using biting humor to keep the community's leaders from becoming arrogant and aloof.

> **REVIEW:** How did new ways of thinking in the Golden Age change traditional ways of life?

The End of the Golden Age, 431–403 B.C.E.

A war between Athens and Sparta that lasted a generation (431–404 B.C.E.) ended the Golden Age; it is called the Peloponnesian War today because it pitted Sparta's Peloponnese-based alliance against Athens and the Delian League. The war started, according to Thucydides, because the growth of Athenian power alarmed the Spartans, who feared that their interests and allies would fall to the Athenians' restless drive. Pericles, the most powerful politician in Athens at the time, persuaded its assembly to take a hard line when the Spartans demanded that Athens ease restrictions on city-states allied with Sparta. Corinth and Megara, crucial Spartan allies, complained bitterly to Sparta about Athens; finally, Corinth told Sparta to attack Athens, or else Corinth and its navy would change sides to the Athenian alliance. Sparta's leaders therefore gave Athens an ultimatum—stop mistreating our allies. Pericles convinced the Athenian assembly to reject the ultimatum on the grounds that Sparta had refused to settle the dispute through the third-party arbitration process called for by the 446–445 B.C.E. treaty. Pericles' critics claimed he was insisting on war against Sparta to revive his fading popularity; his supporters replied that he was defending Athenian honor and protecting foreign trade, a linchpin of the economy. By 431 B.C.E. these disputes had shattered the peace treaty between Athens and Sparta negotiated by Pericles in 446–445 B.C.E.

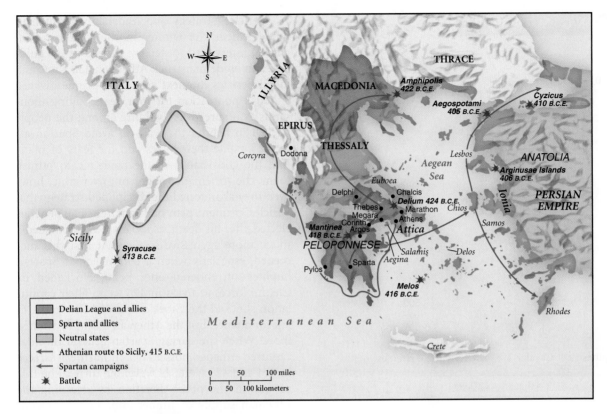

MAP 3.3 The Peloponnesian War, 431–404 B.C.E.
For the first ten years, the Peloponnesian War's battles took place largely in mainland Greece. Sparta, whose armies usually avoided distant campaigns, shocked Athens when its general Brasidas led successful attacks against Athenian forces in northeast Greece. Athens stunned the entire Greek world in the war's next phase by launching a huge naval expedition against Spartan allies in far-off Sicily. The last ten years of the war saw the action move to the east, on and along the western coast of Anatolia and its islands, on the boundary of the Persian Empire, which helped the Spartans build a navy there to defeat the famous Athenian fleet. ■ Look at the route of Athens's expedition to Sicily; why do you think the Athenians took this longer voyage, rather than a more direct route?

The Peloponnesian War, 431–404 B.C.E.

Lasting longer than any previous war in Greek history, the Peloponnesian War (Map 3.3) took place above all because Spartan leaders believed they had to fight now to keep the Athenians from using their superior long-distance offensive power—the Delian League's naval forces—to destroy Sparta's control of the Peloponnesian League. (See "Taking Measure.") Sparta made the first strike of the war, but the conflict dragged on so long because the Athenian assembly failed to negotiate peace with Sparta when it had the chance and because the Spartans were willing to deal with Persia for money to build a fleet and thereby win the war.

Dramatic evidence for the angry feelings that fueled the war comes from Thucydides' version of Pericles' stern oration to the Athenian assembly about not yielding to Spartan pressure:

If we do go to war, harbor no thought that you went to war over a trivial affair. For you this trifling matter is the assurance and the proof of your determination. If you yield to their demands, they will immediately confront you with some larger demand, since they will think that you only gave way on the first point out of fear. But if you stand firm, you will show them that they have to deal with you as equals. . . . When our equals, without agreeing to arbitration of the matter under dispute, make claims on us as neighbors and state those claims as commands, it would be no better than slavery to give in to them, no matter how large or how small the claim may be.

When Sparta invaded Athenian territory, Pericles advised a two-pronged strategy to win what he saw would be a long war: (1) use the navy to raid the lands of Sparta and its allies, and (2) avoid large infantry battles with the superior land forces of the Spartans, even when the enemy hoplites plundered the Athenian countryside outside the city. Athens's citizens could retreat to safety behind

TAKING MEASURE

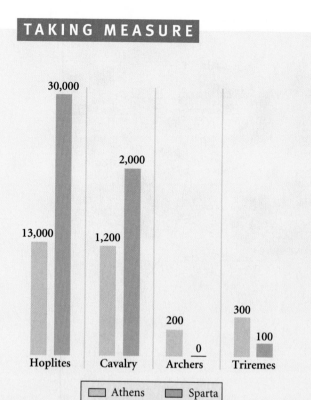

Military Forces of Athens and Sparta at the Beginning of the Peloponnesian War (431 B.C.E.)
This chart compares the military forces of the Athenian side and the Spartan side when the Peloponnesian War broke out in 431 B.C.E. The numbers come from ancient sources, above all the Athenian general and historian Thucydides, who fought in the war. The bar graph starkly reveals the different characteristics of the competing forces: Athens relied on its navy of triremes and its archers (the fifth-century B.C.E. equivalent of artillery and snipers), while Sparta was preeminent in the forces needed for pitched land battles—hoplites (heavily armed infantry) and cavalry (shock troops used to disrupt opposing phalanxes). These differences dictated the differing strategies and tactics of the two sides: Athens in guerrilla fashion launching surprise raids from the sea, and Sparta trying to force decisive confrontations on the battlefield.
(From Pamela Bradley, Ancient Greece: Using Evidence *(Melbourne: Edward Arnold, 1990), 229.)*

Pericles' strategy and leadership might have made Athens the winner in the long run, but chance intervened to deprive Athens of his guidance: an epidemic struck Athens in 430 B.C.E. and killed Pericles the next year. This plague ravaged Athens's population for four years, killing thousands as it spread like wildfire among the people packed in behind the walls to avoid Spartan attacks. Despite their losses and the fears of many that the gods had sent the epidemic to punish them, the Athenians fought on; over time, however, they abandoned the disciplined strategy that Pericles' prudent plan had required. The generals elected after his death, especially Cleon, pursued a much more aggressive strategy. At first this succeeded, especially when a contingent of Spartan hoplites surrendered after being blockaded by Cleon's forces at Pylos in 425 B.C.E. Their capitulation shocked the Greek world and led Sparta to ask for a truce, but the Athenian assembly wanted more. When the daring Spartan general Brasidas captured Athens's possessions in northern Greece in 424 and 423 B.C.E., however, he turned the tide of war in the other direction by crippling the Athenian supply of timber and precious metals from this crucial region. When Brasidas and Cleon were both killed in 422 B.C.E., Sparta and Athens made peace in 421 B.C.E. out of mutual exhaustion.

Athens's most innovative and confident new general, Alcibiades, soon persuaded the assembly to reject the peace and to attack Spartan allies in 418 B.C.E. In 416–415 B.C.E., the Athenians and their allies overpowered the tiny and strategically meaningless Aegean island of Melos because it refused to abandon its allegiance to Sparta. Thucydides dramatically represents Athenian messengers telling the Melians they had to be conquered to show that Athens permitted no defiance to its dominance. Following their victory the Athenians executed the Melian men, sold the women and children into slavery, and colonized the island.

The turning point in the war came soon thereafter when, in 415 B.C.E., Alcibiades persuaded the Athenian assembly to launch the greatest and most expensive campaign in Greek history. The expedition of 415 B.C.E. was directed against Sparta's allies in Sicily, far to the west; Alcibiades had dazzled his fellow citizens with the dream of conquering that rich island and especially its greatest city, Syracuse. Alcibiades' political rivals had him deposed from his command, however, and lesser generals blundered into catastrophic defeat in Sicily in 413 B.C.E. (see Map 3.3). The victorious Syracusans destroyed the allied invasion fleet and packed the survivors like human sardines into quarries under the

the city's impregnable fortification walls, massive barriers of stone that encircled the city and the harbor, with the Long Walls protecting the land corridor between the urban center and the port. He insisted that Athenians should sacrifice their vast and valuable country property to save their population. In the end, he predicted, Athens, with its superior resources, would win a war of attrition, especially because the Spartans, lacking a base in Athenian territory, could not support long invasions.

blazing sun, with no toilets and only half a pint of drinking water and a handful of grain a day.

On the advice of Alcibiades, who had deserted to their side in anger at having lost his command, the Spartans in 413 B.C.E. seized a permanent base of operations in the Athenian countryside for year-round raids, now that Athens was too weak to drive them out. Constant Spartan attacks devastated Athenian agriculture, and twenty thousand slave workers crippled production in Athens's silver mines by deserting to the enemy. The democratic assembly became so upset over these losses that in 411 B.C.E. it voted itself out of existence in favor of an emergency government run by the wealthier citizens. When an oligarchic group illegally took charge, however, the citizens restored the radical democracy and kept fighting for another seven years. They even recalled Alcibiades, seeking better generalship, but the end came when Persia gave the Spartans money to build a navy; the Persian king thought it was in his interest to see Athens defeated. Aggressive Spartan naval action forced Athens to surrender in 404 B.C.E. After twenty-seven years of near-continuous war, the Athenians were at their enemy's mercy.

Athens Humbled: Tyranny and Civil War, 404–403 B.C.E.

Following Athens's surrender, the Spartans installed a regime of antidemocratic Athenians known as the Thirty Tyrants who were willing to collaborate with the victors. The collaborators were members of the social elite, and some, including their notoriously violent leader Critias, infamous for his criticism of religion, had been well-known pupils of Sophists. Brutally suppressing democratic opposition, these oligarchs embarked on an eight-month period of murder and plunder in 404–403 B.C.E. The speechwriter Lysias, for example, reported that Spartan henchmen murdered his brother in order to steal the family's valuables, even ripping the gold rings from the ears of his brother's wife. Outraged at the violence and greed of the Thirty Tyrants, citizens who wanted to restore democracy banded together outside the city to fight to regain control of Athens. Fortunately for them, a feud between Sparta's two most important leaders paralyzed the Spartans, and they failed to send help to the Athenian collaborators. The democratic rebels defeated the forces of the Thirty Tyrants in a series of bloody street battles in Athens.

Democracy was thereby restored, but the city-state still seethed with anger and unrest. To settle the internal strife that threatened to tear Athens apart, the newly restored democratic assembly voted the first known amnesty in Western history, a truce agreement forbidding any official charges or recriminations stemming from the crimes of 404–403 B.C.E. Agreeing not to pursue grievances in court was the price of peace. As would soon become clear, however, some Athenians harbored grudges that no amnesty could dispel. In addition, Athens's financial and military strength had been shattered. At the end of the Golden Age, Athenians worried about how to remake their lives and restore the luster that their city-state's innovative accomplishments had produced.

> **REVIEW:** What factors determined the course of the Peloponnesian War?

Conclusion

When at the beginning of the fifth century B.C.E. some Greek city-states temporarily united to resist the Persian Empire, they surprised themselves by defeating the Persian invaders, who threatened their political independence. When the Persians retreated, however, so too did Greek unity. Following the Greek victory, Athens competed with Sparta for power; the Athenian Golden Age that followed the Persian Wars was based on empire and trade, and the city's riches funded the widening of democracy and brilliant cultural accomplishments.

As the money poured in, Athens built glorious and expensive temples, instituted pay for service in many government offices to strengthen democracy, and assembled the Mediterranean's most powerful navy. The poor men who rowed the ships demanded greater democracy; such demands led to political and legal reforms that guaranteed fair treatment for all. Pericles became the most famous politician of the Golden Age by leading the drive for radical democracy.

Religious practice and women's lives reflected the strong grip of tradition on everyday life, but dramatic innovations in education and philosophy created social tension. The Sophists' relativistic views disturbed tradition-minded people, as did Socrates' definition of virtue, which questioned ordinary people's love of wealth and success. Art and architecture broke out of old forms, promoting an impression of balanced motion rather than stability, while medicine gained a more scientific basis. Tragedy and comedy developed at Athens as pub-

MAPPING THE WEST

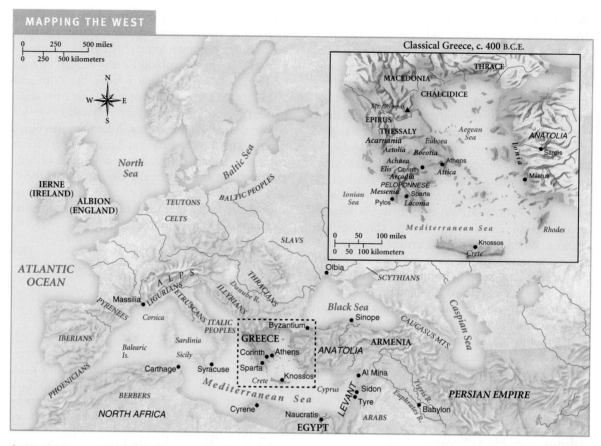

Greece, Europe, and the Mediterranean, 400 B.C.E.
No single power controlled the Mediterranean region at the end of the fifth century B.C.E. In the west, the Phoenician city of Carthage and the Greek cities on Sicily and in southern Italy were rivals for the riches to be won by trade. In the east, the Spartans, emboldened by their recent victory over Athens in the Peloponnesian War, tried to become an international power outside the mainland for the first time in their history by sending campaigns into Anatolia. This aggressive action aroused stiff opposition from the Persians because it was a threat to their westernmost imperial provinces. There was to be no peace and quiet in the Mediterranean even after the twenty-seven years of the Peloponnesian War.

lic art forms commenting on contemporary social and political issues.

Wars framed the Golden Age. The Persian Wars sent the Athenians soaring to imperial power and prosperity, but their high-handed treatment of allies and enemies combined with Spartan fears about Athenian power to bring on the disastrous Peloponnesian War. Nearly three decades of battle brought the stars of the Greek Golden Age crashing to earth: by 400 B.C.E. the Athenians found themselves in the same situation as in 500 B.C.E., fearful of Spartan power and worried whether the world's first democracy could survive. As it turned out, the next great threat to Greek stability and independence would once again come from a neighboring monarchy, this time not from Persia (to the east) but from Macedonia (to the north).

FOR FURTHER EXPLORATION

- **For suggested references, including Web sites, for topics in this chapter,** see page SR-1 at the end of the book.

- **For additional primary-source material from this period,** see Chapter 3 in *Sources of THE MAKING OF THE WEST*, Third Edition.

- **For Web sites and documents related to topics in this chapter,** see *Make History* at bedfordstmartins.com/hunt.

CHAPTER REVIEW

KEY TERMS AND PEOPLE

Themistocles (71)

Delian League (74)

triremes (74)

Pericles (75)

radical democracy (76)

ostracism (76)

agora (78)

Parthenon (78)

mystery cults (81)

metic (82)

hetaira (83)

Sophists (88)

Socratic method (90)

hubris (95)

REVIEW QUESTIONS

1. How did the Greeks overcome the challenges presented by the Persian invasions?

2. What factors produced political change in fifth-century B.C.E. Athens?

3. How did new ways of thinking in the Golden Age change traditional ways of life?

4. What factors determined the course of the Peloponnesian War?

MAKING CONNECTIONS

1. What were the most significant differences between Archaic Age Greece and Golden Age Greece?

2. For what sorts of things did Greeks of the Golden Age spend public funds? Why did they believe these things were worth the expense?

For practice quizzes, a customized study plan, and other study tools, see the Online Study Guide at bedfordstmartins.com/hunt.

IMPORTANT EVENTS

500–323 B.C.E.	Classical Age of Greece
499–479 B.C.E.	Wars between Persia and Greece
490 B.C.E.	Battle of Marathon
480–479 B.C.E.	Xerxes' invasion of Greece
480 B.C.E.	Battle of Salamis
461 B.C.E.	Ephialtes reforms the Athenian court system
Early 450s B.C.E.	Pericles introduces pay for officeholders in Athenian democracy
454 B.C.E.	Catastrophic defeat of Athenian fleet by Persians in Egypt
451 B.C.E.	Pericles restricts Athenian citizenship to children whose parents are both citizens
450 B.C.E.	Protagoras and other Sophists begin to teach in Athens
446–445 B.C.E. (winter)	Peace treaty between Athens and Sparta; intended to last thirty years
441 B.C.E.	Sophocles presents the tragedy *Antigone*
431–404 B.C.E.	Peloponnesian War
420s B.C.E.	Herodotus finishes *Histories*
415–413 B.C.E.	Enormous Athenian military expedition against Sicily
411 B.C.E.	Aristophanes presents the comedy *Lysistrata*
404–403 B.C.E.	Rule of the Thirty Tyrants at Athens
403 B.C.E.	Restoration of democracy in Athens

From the Classical to the Hellenistic World

400–30 B.C.E.

About 255 B.C.E., an Egyptian camel trader far from home paid a scribe to write his Greek employer, Zeno, back in Egypt, to protest how Zeno's assistant, Krotos, was cheating him:

> You know that when you left me in Syria with Krotos I followed all your instructions concerning the camels and behaved blamelessly towards you. But Krotos has ignored your orders to pay me my salary; I've received nothing despite asking him for my money over and over. He just tells me to go away. I waited a long time for you to come, but when I no longer had life's necessities and couldn't get help anywhere, I had to run away ... to keep from starving to death.... I am desperate summer and winter.... They have treated me like dirt because I am not a Greek. I therefore beg you, please, command them to pay me so that I won't go hungry just because I don't know how to speak Greek.

The trader's plea shows that not speaking Greek hurt him. His needing help from a foreigner holding power in his homeland reflects the changes in the eastern Mediterranean world during the Hellenistic Age (323–30 B.C.E.). The movement of Greeks into the Near East and their contacts with local peoples increased the cultural interaction of the Greek and the Near Eastern worlds to the highest level ever, forging a multicultural synthesis that set a new course for Western civilization in politics, art, philosophy, science, and religion. War fueled these changes. The first stage came after the Peloponnesian War, when thousands of Greeks became mercenary soldiers serving Near Eastern rulers. Alexander the Great (356–323 B.C.E.) then changed the course of history by conquering the Persian Empire, leading an army of Greeks and Macedonians to the border of India, taking Near Easterners into his army and imperial administration, and planting colonies of Greeks as far east as Afghanistan. His amazing expedition shocked the world because his exploits seemed superhuman, and it gave new creative energy

The Rosetta Stone
This inscription found near Rosetta, in the Nile River delta, unlocked the lost secrets of how to read Egyptian hieroglyphs. The bands of text repeat the same message (priests praising King Ptolemy V in 196 B.C.E.) in hieroglyphs, demotic (a cursive form of Egyptian invented around 600 B.C.E.), and Greek. Bilingual texts were necessary to reach the mixed population of Hellenistic Egypt. Scholars deciphered the hieroglyphs by comparing them to the Greek version. They started with the hieroglyphs surrounded by an oval, which they guessed were royal names. *(Art Resource, NY.)*

to Western civilization by acting like a cultural whirlwind that swirled together Greek and Near Eastern traditions as never before.

Politics changed in the Greek world after Alexander's death when his successors revived monarchy by carving out territories to rule as their personal kingdoms. These new kingdoms, which became the dominant powers of the Hellenistic Age, restricted the freedom of Greece's city-states; the city-states retained local rule but lost their independence to compete with each other in foreign policy. The Hellenistic kings now controlled international affairs. They imported Greeks to fill royal offices, man their armies, and run businesses. This demographic change created tension with the kings' non-Greek subjects. Immigrant Greeks, such as Zeno in Egypt, formed a social elite that lorded it over the kingdoms' local populations. Egyptians, Syrians, or Mesopotamians who wanted to rise in society had to win the support of these Greeks and learn their language. Otherwise, they were likely to find themselves as powerless as the hungry camel merchant.

Over time, the Near East's local cultures interacted with the Greek overlords' culture to spawn a multicultural synthesis. Locals married Greeks, shared their artistic and religious traditions with the newcomers, passed along their agricultural and scientific knowledge, and learned Greek to win administrative jobs. Although Hellenistic royal society always remained hierarchical, with Greeks at the top, and never eliminated tension between rulers and ruled, its kings and queens did finance innovations in art, philosophy, religion, and science that combined Near Eastern and Greek traditions. The Hellenistic kingdoms fell in the second and first centuries B.C.E. when the Romans overthrew them one by one.

All this happened during an era of constant warfare. Cultural interaction, a characteristic of Western civilization from the beginning, reached a new level of intensity as an unintended consequence of Alexander's military campaigns. The new contacts between diverse peoples and the emergence of new ideas strongly influenced Roman civilization and therefore later Western civilization. In particular, Hellenistic artistic, scientific, philosophical, and religious innovations persisted even after the glory of Greece's Golden Age had faded, especially since Hellenistic religion provided the background for Christianity.

FOCUS QUESTION: What were the major political and cultural changes in the Hellenistic Age?

Classical Greece after the Peloponnesian War, 400–350 B.C.E.

The Greek city-states gradually regained their economic and political stability after the Peloponnesian War (431–404 B.C.E.), but daily life remained hard, especially for working people. The war's aftermath dramatically affected Greek philosophy. At Athens, citizens who blamed Socrates for inspiring the worst of the Thirty Tyrants brought him to trial; the jury condemned him to death. His execution helped persuade the philosophers Plato and Aristotle to detest democracy and develop new ways of thinking about right versus wrong and how human beings should live.

Although the city-states recovered after the war, their continuing competition for power in the fourth century B.C.E. undermined their independence. After failing to control defeated Athens, the Spartans tried to expand their power into central Greece and Anatolia by collaborating with the Persians. This policy stirred up violent resistance from Thebes and from Athens, which had rebuilt its naval empire. By the 350s B.C.E., the strife among the Greek city-states so weakened all of them that

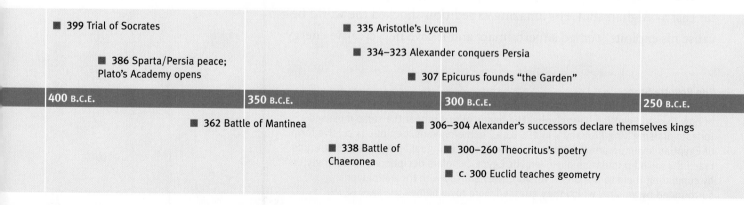

■ 399 Trial of Socrates

■ 386 Sparta/Persia peace; Plato's Academy opens

■ 335 Aristotle's Lyceum

■ 334–323 Alexander conquers Persia

■ 307 Epicurus founds "the Garden"

| 400 B.C.E. | 350 B.C.E. | 300 B.C.E. | 250 B.C.E. |

■ 362 Battle of Mantinea

■ 338 Battle of Chaeronea

■ 306–304 Alexander's successors declare themselves kings

■ 300–260 Theocritus's poetry

■ c. 300 Euclid teaches geometry

they were unable to prevent the Macedonian kingdom (Alexander the Great's homeland) from gaining control of Greece.

Restoring Daily Life in Athens

Athens provides the most evidence for Greek life after the Peloponnesian War. The devastation of Athens's rural economy by Spartan raids and the overcrowding in the wartime city produced friction between refugees from the countryside and city dwellers. Life became difficult for middle-class women whose husbands and brothers had died during the conflict. Traditionally, they had woven cloth at home for their families and supervised the household slaves, but the men had earned the family's income by farming or working at a trade. Now, with no man to provide for them and their children, many war widows had to work outside the home. The only jobs open to them—such as wet-nursing, weaving, or laboring in vineyards—were low-paying.

Resourceful Athenians found ways to profit from women's skills. The family of one of Socrates' friends, for example, became poverty-stricken when several widowed sisters, nieces, and female cousins moved in. The friend complained to Socrates that he was too poor to support his new family of fourteen plus their slaves. Socrates replied that the women knew how to make men's and women's cloaks, shirts, capes, and smocks, "the work considered the best and most fitting for women." He suggested they begin to sell the clothes outside the home. This plan succeeded financially, but the women complained that Socrates' friend was the household's only member who ate without working. Socrates advised the man to reply that the women should think of him as sheep did a guard dog—he earned his share of the food by keeping the wolves away.

Athens's postwar economy recovered because small-business owners and households engaged in

Vase Painting of Women Fetching Water (detail)
This vase painting depicts women filling water jugs at a public fountain to take back to their homes. Both freeborn and slave women fetched water for their households, as few Greek homes had running water. Cities built attractive fountain houses such as this one, which dispensed fresh water from springs or piped it in through small aqueducts (compare the large Roman aqueduct on page 146). Women often gathered at fountains for conversation with people from outside their household. *(William Francis Warden Fund. Photograph © 2007 Museum of Fine Arts, Boston (61.195).)*

trade and produced manufactured goods. Greek businesses, usually family-run, were small; the largest known was a shield-making company with 120 slave workers. Some changes occurred in occupations formerly defined by gender. For example, men began working alongside women in cloth production when the first commercial weaving shops outside the home sprang up. Some women made careers in the arts, especially painting and music, which men had traditionally dominated.

The rebuilding by 393 B.C.E. of Athens's destroyed Long Walls, which connected the city to the port, boosted the economy. Exports of grain, wine, pottery, and silver from Athens's mines resumed. The refortified harbor also allowed Athens

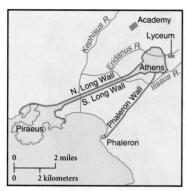

Athens's Long Walls as Rebuilt after the Peloponnesian War

to begin to rebuild its navy, which increased employment opportunities for poor men.

Even in an improving economy, daily life remained difficult for working people. Most workers earned barely enough to feed and clothe their families. They ate two meals a day, a light one at mid-morning and a heavier evening meal. Bread baked from barley provided their main food; only rich people could afford wheat bread. A family bought bread from small bakery stands, often run by women, or made it at home, with the wife directing the slaves in grinding the grain, shaping the dough, and baking it in a clay oven heated by charcoal. People topped their bread with greens, beans, onions, garlic, olives, fruit, and cheese. The few households rich enough to afford meat boiled or grilled it over a fire. Everyone of all ages drank wine, diluted with water, with every meal.

The Long Walls of Athens
In the fifth century B.C.E., Athens—which was several miles from Piraeus, its port—connected its city center to the port by extending its fortification walls in a corridor called the Long Walls. This section near the port shows the walls' close-fitting exterior. The Spartans forced the Athenians to demolish the Long Walls after the Peloponnesian War. When the Athenians regained their freedom in 403 B.C.E., they spent ten years repairing the Long Walls so that they could rebuild their naval empire. *(Photo: Craig and Marie Mauzy.)*

The Execution of Socrates, 399 B.C.E.

Socrates, Athens's most famous philosopher in the Golden Age, fell victim to the bitterness many Athenians felt about the rule of the Thirty Tyrants following the Peloponnesian War. Since the amnesty proclaimed by the restored democratic assembly prohibited prosecutions for crimes committed under the tyrants' reign of terror, angry citizens had to bring other charges against those they hated. Some prominent Athenians hated Socrates because his follower Critias had been one of the Thirty Tyrants' most violent leaders.

These prominent citizens charged Socrates with impiety, a serious crime, claiming that he had angered the gods with his ideas and therefore threatened the city with divine punishment. In 399 B.C.E., they argued their case to a jury of 501 male citizens. They presented religious and moral arguments: Socrates, they claimed, rejected the city-state's gods, introduced new divinities, and lured young men away from Athenian moral traditions. Speaking in his own defense, Socrates refused to beg for sympathy, as was customary in trials; instead, he repeated his dedication to goading his fellow citizens into examining their preconceptions about how to live justly. He vowed to remain their stinging gadfly no matter what.

When the jurors narrowly voted to convict the philosopher, Athenian law required them to decide between the penalty proposed by the prosecutors and that proposed by the defendant. The prosecutors proposed death. Everyone expected Socrates to offer exile as an alternative and the jury to accept it. The philosopher, however, said that he deserved a reward rather than punishment, until his friends made him propose a fine as his penalty. The jury chose death, requiring him to drink a poison concocted from powdered hemlock. Socrates accepted his sentence calmly because, as he put it, "no evil can befall a good man either in life or in death." Ancient sources report that many Athenians soon came to regret Socrates' punishment as a tragic mistake and a severe blow to their reputation.

The Philosophy of Plato

Socrates' death made his follower and Greece's most famous philosopher, **Plato** (429–348 B.C.E.), hate democracy. From a well-to-do family and related to the infamous Critias, whom he mentions favorably, Plato started out as a political consultant promoting the rule of philosopher-tyrants as the best form of government. He traveled to Sicily to advise Dionysius, tyrant of Syracuse, but when he failed to turn Dionysius into an ideal ruler, he gave up hope that political action could stop violence and greed. Instead, he turned to talking and writing about philosophy as the guide to life and established a philosophical school, the Academy, in Athens around 386 B.C.E. The Academy was an informal association of people who studied philosophy, mathematics, and theoretical astronomy under the leader's guidance. It attracted intellectuals to Athens for the next nine hundred years, and Plato's ideas about the nature of reality, ethics, and politics have remained central to philosophy and political science to this day.

Plato's Ethical Thought.   Plato's intellectual interests covered astronomy, mathematics, political philosophy, **metaphysics** (ideas about the ultimate nature of reality beyond the reach of the human senses), and ethics. His radical views on reality underlay his ethics. He presented his ideas in dialogues, which usually featured Socrates conversing with a variety of people. Plato wrote to provoke readers into thoughtful reflection, not to prescribe a set of beliefs. Nevertheless, he always maintained one essential idea based on his view of reality: ultimate moral qualities are universal, unchanging, and absolute, not relative. He thus rejected the relativism that the Sophists had taught.

Plato's dialogues explain his theory that justice, goodness, beauty, and equality exist on their own in a higher realm beyond the daily world. He used the word *Forms* (or *Ideas*) to describe the abstract, invariable, and ultimate realities of such ethical qualities. According to Plato, the Forms are the only genuine reality; all things that humans perceive with their senses on earth are only dim and imperfect copies of these metaphysical realities. Forms are not defined by human experience of them—any earthly examples can always display the opposite quality. For example, returning a bor-

Mosaic Depicting Plato's Academy
This Roman-era mosaic shows philosophers talking at Plato's school in Athens, the Academy. Founded about 386 B.C.E., the Academy became one of Greece's longest-lasting institutions, attracting scholars and students for more than nine hundred years. The columns and the tree in the mosaic express the harmonious blend of the natural and built environment of the Academy, which was meant to promote discussion. What message do the philosophers' bare chests convey? *(Erich Lessing/Art Resource, NY.)*

rowed item might seem like justice. But what if the borrowed item is a weapon and the lender wants it back to commit murder? Returning the borrowed item would then support injustice. Therefore, every ethical quality is relative in the world that humans experience, but not in reality. Human experiences are like shadows of ultimate realities cast on the wall of a cave. The difficult notion of Forms made metaphysics an important issue in philosophy.

Plato's ideas about the soul also profoundly influenced later thought. He believed that humans possess immortal souls distinct from their bodies; this idea established the concept of **dualism**, a separation between soul (or mind) and body. Plato further explained that the human soul possesses preexisting knowledge put there by a god. The

---

Plato: A follower of Socrates who became Greece's most famous philosopher.

metaphysics: Philosophical ideas about the ultimate nature of reality beyond the reach of human senses.

dualism: The philosophical idea that the human soul (or mind) and body are separate.

world has order because a rational deity created it. The god wanted to reproduce the Forms' perfect order in the material world, but the world turned out imperfect because matter is imperfect. Humans' present, impure existence is only a temporary stage in cosmic existence because, while the body does not last, the soul is immortal.

Building on earlier Greek rationalism, Plato argued that people must seek perfect order and purity in their souls by using rational thought to control irrational and therefore harmful desires. People who yield to irrational desires fail to consider the future of their body and soul. The desire to drink too much alcohol, for example, is irrational because the binge drinker fails to consider the hangover that will follow.

Plato's *Republic*. Plato presented his most famous ideas on politics in his dialogue *The Republic*. This work, whose Greek title means "System of Government," discusses the nature of justice and the reasons people should shun injustice. Democracy cannot create justice because people on their own cannot rise above narrow self-interest to knowledge of any universal truth. Justice can come only under the rule of an enlightened oligarchy or monarchy. Therefore, a just society requires a strict hierarchy.

Plato's *Republic* envisions an ideal society with a hierarchy of three classes distinguished by their ability to grasp the truth of Forms. The highest class is the rulers, or "guardians," who must be educated in mathematics, astronomy, and metaphysics. Next come the "auxiliaries," who defend the community. "Producers" make up the bottom class; they grow food and make objects for everyone.

Women can be guardians because they possess the same virtues and abilities as men, except for a disparity in physical strength between the average woman and the average man. To minimize distraction, guardians are to have neither private property nor nuclear families. Male and female guardians are to live in houses shared in common, eat in the same dining halls, and exercise in the same gymnasia. They are to have sex with various partners so that the best women can mate with the best men to produce the best children. The children are to be raised together by special caretakers. Guardians who achieve the highest level of knowledge can rule as philosopher-kings. Plato did

not think humans could actually create the ideal society described in *The Republic,* but he did believe that imagining it was an important way to help people learn to live justly. For Plato, philosophy was an essential guide to human life.

Aristotle, Scientist and Philosopher

Aristotle (384–322 B.C.E.) was another Greek thinker who believed in the importance of philosophy as a guide to life. At the age of seventeen, he joined Plato's Academy. From 342 to 335 B.C.E. he earned a living by tutoring the teenage Alexander the Great in Macedonia. Returning to Athens in 355 B.C.E., Aristotle founded his own school, the Lyceum, and taught his own life-guiding philosophy, based on logic, scientific knowledge, and practical experience. Like Plato, he thought Athenian democracy was a bad system because it did not restrict decision making to the most educated and moderate citizens. His vast writings made him one of the world's most influential thinkers.

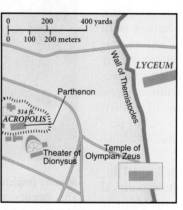

Aristotle's Lyceum, established 335 B.C.E.

Aristotle's reputation rests on his scientific investigation of the natural world, development of rigorous systems of logical argument, and practical ethics. He regarded science and philosophy as the disciplined search for knowledge in every aspect of everyday life. That search brought the good life and genuine happiness. Aristotle lectured with dazzling intelligence on biology, medicine, anatomy, psychology, meteorology, physics, chemistry, mathematics, music, metaphysics, rhetoric, literary criticism, political science, and ethics. He also invented a system of logic for precise argumentation. By creating ways to identify valid arguments, Aristotle established grounds for distinguishing a logically sound case from a merely persuasive one.

Aristotle required explanations to be based on strict rationality and common sense rather than metaphysics. He rejected Plato's theory of Forms because, he said, the separate existence Plato postulated for Forms was not subject to demonstrable proof. Aristotle believed that the best way to understand anything was to observe it in its natural setting. He coupled detailed investigation with

---

Aristotle: Greek philosopher famous for his scientific investigations, development of logical argument, and practical ethics.

Aristotle on the Nature of the Greek Polis

Aristotle's book Politics *discussed the origins of political states and the different ways to organize them. Here, Aristotle argues that the city-state (polis) was a creation of nature.*

Since we see that every city-state is a type of partnership and that every partnership is established for the sake of some good, for everything that everyone does is motivated by what seems to them to be a good, it is clear that, with all partnerships aiming at some good, the most authoritative partnership, which includes all other partnerships, does this the most of all and aims at the most authoritative of all goods. This is what is called the city-state, that is, the political partnership. . . .

If one looks at things as they grow from the beginning, one will make the best observations, on this topic and all others. Necessity first brings together those who cannot exist without each other, that is, on the one hand, the female and the male for the purpose of reproduction, and this is not a matter of choice, but just as with the other animals and with plants, it is a matter of nature to desire to leave behind another of the same kind; on the other hand, [necessity brings together] the ruler and the one who is naturally ruled for the sake of security, for the one who is able to foresee things with his mind is by nature a ruler and by nature a master, while the one who is able to do things with his body is the one who is ruled and is by nature a slave. For this reason the same thing benefits master and slave. . . .

From these two partnerships comes first the household, and Hesiod spoke correctly, saying, "First of all, [get yourself] a house and a wife and an ox for plowing,"[1] because the ox is a household slave for a poor man. Therefore, the partnership that is established first by nature for everyday purposes is the household. . . .

The partnership that first arises from multiple households for the sake of more than everyday needs is the village. The village seems by nature to be a colony from the household. . . .

The final partnership of multiple villages is the city-state, which possesses the limit of self-sufficiency, so to speak. It comes into being for the sake of living, but it exists for the sake of living well. Every city-state therefore exists by nature, if it is true that the first partnerships do. . . . It is clear that the city-state belongs to the things existing by nature, and that humans are beings who by nature live in a city-state, and that the one who has no city-state by nature and not by chance is either a fool or a superhuman. . . .

[1] A quotation from *Works and Days*, line 405.

Source: Aristotle, *Politics*, Book 1.1–2, 1252a1–1253a19. Translation by Thomas R. Martin.

---

perceptive reasoning in biology, botany, and zoology. He was the first investigator to try to collect and classify all available information on animal species, recording facts and advancing knowledge about more than five hundred different kinds of animals, including insects. His recognition that whales and dolphins are mammals, for example, was overlooked by later writers on animals and not rediscovered for another two thousand years.

Some of Aristotle's views justified inequalities characteristic of his time. He regarded slavery as natural, arguing that some people were slaves by nature because their souls lacked the rational part that should rule in a human. He also concluded, on the basis of faulty biological observations, that nature made women inferior to men. He wrongly believed, for example, that in procreation the male's semen actively gave the fetus its design, whereas the female passively provided its matter. Erroneous biological information led Aristotle to evaluate females as incomplete males, a conclusion with disastrous results for later thought. At the same time, he believed that human communities could be successful and happy only if women and men both contributed. (See Document, "Aristotle on the Nature of the Greek Polis," page 109.)

In ethics, Aristotle emphasized the need to develop practical habits of just behavior to achieve happiness. People should achieve self-control by training their minds to win out over instincts and passions. Self-control meant finding "the mean," or balance, between denying and indulging physical pleasures. Aristotle claimed that the mind must rule in finding the balance leading to true happiness because the intellect is the finest human quality and the mind is the true self—indeed, the godlike part of a person.

Aristotle influenced ethics by insisting that standards of right and wrong have merit only if they are grounded in character and aligned with the good in human nature; they cannot work if they consist of abstract reasons for just behavior. That is, an ethical system must be relevant to real human situations. He argued that the life of the mind and experience of the real world are inseparable in defining a worthwhile and happy existence.

Greek Political Disunity

In the same period that Plato and Aristotle were developing their philosophies as guides to life, the Greek city-states were in a constant state of war. Sparta, Thebes, and Athens competed to dominate Greece. None succeeded. Their endless fighting sapped their spirit and their finances, leaving Greek independence vulnerable to external threat.

The Spartans provoked the competition by trying to conquer other city-states in central Greece and in Anatolia in the 390s B.C.E. Thebes, Athens, Corinth, and Argos then formed an anti-Spartan coalition. The Spartans checkmated the alliance by negotiating with the Persian king. Betraying their traditional claim to defend Greek freedom, the Spartans acknowledged the Persian ruler's right to control the Greek city-states of Anatolia—in return for permission to wage war in Greece without Persian interference. This agreement of 386 B.C.E., called the King's Peace, sold out the Greeks of Anatolia, returning them to subordination to Persia, just as before the Persian Wars.

The Athenians rebuilt their military to compete with Sparta. The Long Walls restored Athens's invulnerability to invasion, and a new kind of light infantry—the *peltast*, armed with a small leather shield, javelins, and sword—fighting alongside hoplites gave Athenian ground forces greater tactical mobility and flexibility. Most important, Athens rebuilt its navy so that by 377 B.C.E. it had again become the leader of a naval alliance of Greek city-states. This time the league members insisted that their rights be specified in writing to prevent Athenian domination.

The Thebans became Greece's main power in the 370s B.C.E. through brilliant generalship. They crushed the Spartan invasion of Theban territory in 371 B.C.E. and then invaded the Spartan homeland in the Peloponnese. They greatly weakened Sparta by freeing many helots. The Thebans' success alarmed the Athenians, whose city was only forty miles from Thebes, so they allied with their hated enemies, the Spartans. Their armies confronted the Thebans in the battle of Mantinea in the Peloponnese in 362 B.C.E. Thebes won the battle but lost the war when its best general was killed and no capable replacement could be found.

The battle of Mantinea left the Greek city-states in disunity and weakness. As a commentator said, "Everyone had supposed that this battle's winners would become Greece's rulers and its losers their subjects; but there was only more confusion and disturbance in Greece after Mantinea than before." This judgment was confirmed when the Athenian naval alliance fell apart in a war between Athens and its allies over the negotiations some allies were conducting with Persia and Macedonia.

By the 350s B.C.E., no Greek city-state had the power to rule anything except its own territory. Their competition for supremacy over one another finally died out in a stalemate of exhaustion. By failing to cooperate, the Greeks opened the way for the rise of a new power—the kingdom of Macedonia—that would end their independence in international politics. The Macedonian kings did not literally enslave the Greeks, as the Spartans did the helots, or usually even change their local governments, but they took away the city-states' freedom to manage their international affairs.

> **REVIEW:** How did daily life, philosophy, and the political situation change in Greece during the period 400–350 B.C.E.?

The Rise of Macedonia, 359–323 B.C.E.

The kingdom of Macedonia's rise to superpower status counts as one of the greatest surprises in ancient military and political history. In little more than a generation, the Macedonian kingdom, located just north of central Greece, took advantage of the Greek city-states' disunity to rocket from being a minor state to ruling the Greek and Near Eastern worlds. Two aggressive and charismatic Macedonian kings produced this transformation: Philip II (r. 359–336 B.C.E.) and his son **Alexander the Great** (r. 336–323 B.C.E.). Their conquests ended the Greek Classical Age and set in motion the Hellenistic Age's cultural changes.

The Roots of Macedonian Power

The Macedonians' power sprang from the characteristics of their monarchy and their people's ethnic pride. Macedonian kings had to listen to their

---

Alexander the Great: The fourth-century B.C.E. Macedonian king whose conquest of the Persian Empire led to the greatly increased cultural interactions of Greece and the Near East in the Hellenistic Age.

The Rule of Philip II, 359–336 B.C.E.

King Philip II forged Macedonia into an international power against heavy odds. Before his reign, frequent strife between royals and the elite plus attacks from hostile neighbors had kept the kingdom weak. Princes married young, soon after the age of twenty, and possibly more than one wife, to try to produce male heirs to provide strong rule protecting the kingdom.

A military disaster in 359 B.C.E. brought Philip to the throne at a desperate moment. The Illyrians had slaughtered the previous king and four thousand troops. Philip restored the Macedonian army's confidence by teaching his troops an unstoppable new tactic with their thrusting spears, which reached a length of sixteen feet and took two hands to wield: arranging them in the traditional phalanx formation, he created deep blocks of soldiers whose front lines bristled with outstretched spears like a lethal porcupine. Then he trained them to move around in battle in different directions without losing their formation. By moving as a unit, a mobile phalanx armed with such long spears could splinter the enemy's infantry. Deploying cavalry as a strike force to soften up the enemy while also protecting the infantry's flanks, Philip used his reorganized army to rout the Illyrians in the field, while at home he eliminated his local rivals for kingship.

Philip next moved southward into Greece, employing diplomacy, bribery, and military action to bulldoze the city-states into following him. A Greek contemporary labeled Philip "insatiable and extravagant; he did everything in a hurry ... he never spared the time to reckon up his income and expenses." By the late 340s B.C.E., Philip had cajoled or coerced most of northern and central Greece into alliance with him. Seeking glory for

people, who had freedom of speech. The king governed by maintaining the elite's support because they ranked as his social equals and controlled many followers. Men spent their time training for war, hunting, and drinking heavily. The king had to excel in these activities to show that he deserved to lead the state. Queens and royal mothers received respect because they came from powerful families or the ruling houses of neighboring regions. In the king's absence these royal women wielded power at court.

Macedonian kings thought of themselves as ethnically Greek; they spoke Greek as well as they did their native Macedonian. Macedonians as a whole, however, looked down on the Greeks as too soft to survive life in their northern land. The Greeks reciprocated this contempt. The famed Athenian orator Demosthenes (384–322 B.C.E.) scorned Philip II as "not only not a Greek nor related to the Greeks, but not even a barbarian from a land worth mentioning; no, he's a pestilence from Macedonia, a region where you can't even buy a slave worth his salt."

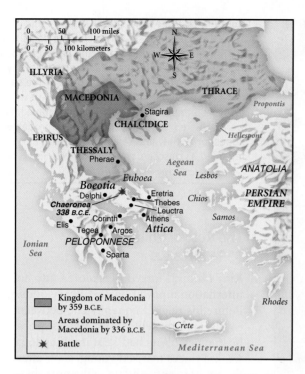

MAP 4.1 Expansion of Macedonia under Philip II, 359–336 B.C.E.

King Philip II expanded Macedonian power southward: mountainous terrain and warlike people blocked the way northward. The Macedonian royal house saw itself as ethnically Greek, and Philip made himself the leader of Greece by defeating a Greek coalition led by Athens at the battle of Chaeronea in 338 B.C.E. Sparta, far from Macedonia in the southern Peloponnese, did not join the coalition. Philip ignored it; Sparta's shrinking number of citizens made it too weak to matter.

Greece and fearing the instability his reinvigorated army would create in his kingdom if the soldiers had nothing to do, he decided to lead a united Macedonian and Greek army to conquer the Persian Empire.

Philip justified attacking Persia as revenge for its invasion of Greece 150 years earlier. Some Greeks remained unconvinced. At Athens, Demosthenes bitterly criticized Greeks for not resisting Philip. They stood by, he thundered, "as if Philip were a hailstorm, praying that he would not come their way, but not trying to do anything to head him off." Moved by his words, Athens and Thebes rallied a coalition of southern Greek city-states to combat Philip, but in 338 B.C.E. the Macedonian king and his Greek allies trounced the coalition's forces at the battle of Chaeronea in Boeotia (Map 4.1). The defeated city-states retained their internal freedom, but Philip compelled them to join his alliance. The battle of Chaeronea marked a turning point in Greek history: never again

would the city-states of Greece be independent actors in foreign policy. City-states remained Greece's central social and economic units, but they were always looking over their shoulders, worrying about the powerful kings who wanted to control them.

The Rule of Alexander the Great, 336–323 B.C.E.

If Philip had not been murdered by a Macedonian acquaintance in 336 B.C.E., we might be calling him Philip the Great. Instead, his assassination brought his son Alexander III to power. Rumors swirled that the son and his mother, Olympias, had instigated Philip's murder to procure the throne for the twenty-year-old Alexander, but the best guess is that the murderer acted out of personal anger at the king. Alexander secured his rule by killing his internal rivals and defeating Macedonia's enemies to the west and north in several lightning-fast strikes. Finally, Alexander compelled the southern Greeks, who had defected from the alliance at the news of Philip's death, to rejoin. To demonstrate the price of disloyalty, in 335 B.C.E. Alexander destroyed Thebes for having rebelled.

Conquering the Persian Empire. In 334 B.C.E., Alexander launched the most astonishing military campaign in ancient history by leading a Macedonian and Greek army against the Persian Empire to fulfill Philip's dream of avenging Greece. Alexander's conquest of all the lands from Turkey to Egypt to Uzbekistan while still in his twenties led later peoples to call him Alexander the Great. In his own time, he became a legend by leading cavalry charges to disrupt the enemy's infantry and by motivating his men to victory after victory in hostile, unknown regions far from Macedonia.

Alexander inspired his troops by exhibiting reckless disregard for his own safety in battle. He often led the charge against the enemy's front line, riding his warhorse Bucephalus ("Oxhead"). Everyone saw him speeding ahead in his plumed helmet, polished armor, and vividly colored cloak. He was so intent on conquest that he rejected advice to delay the war until he had fathered an heir. He gave away nearly all of his land to strengthen ties with his army officers. "What," one adviser asked, "do you have left for yourself?" "My hopes," Alexander replied. Alexander's hopes centered on making himself a warrior as famous as Achilles in Homer's *Iliad*; he always kept a copy of *The Iliad* under his pillow—and a dagger.

Alexander displayed his heroic ambitions as his army advanced. In Anatolia, he visited

Gordion, where an oracle had promised the lord-ship of Asia to whoever could untie a massive knot of rope tying the yoke of an ancient chariot. Alexander, so the story goes, cut the Gordian knot with his sword. When Alexander later captured the Persian king's wives and daughters, he treated the women with respect. His honorable behavior toward the Persian royal women enhanced his claim to be the legitimate king of all Asia.

Building on Near Eastern traditions of siege technology and Philip's innovations, Alexander developed better military technology. When Tyre, a heavily fortified city on an island off the eastern Mediterranean, refused to surrender to him in 332 B.C.E., he built a massive stone pier as a platform for artillery towers, armored battering rams, and catapults flinging boulders to breach Tyre's walls. The successful use of this siege technology against Tyre showed that walls alone could no longer protect city-states. The knowledge that Alexander's army could overcome their fortifications made enemies much readier to negotiate a deal.

In his conquest of Egypt and the Persian heartland, Alexander revealed his strategy for ruling a vast empire: keeping an area's traditional administrative system in place while sprinkling cities of Greeks and Macedonians in conquered territory. In Egypt, he established his first new city, naming it Alexandria after himself. In Persia, he proclaimed himself the king of Asia and left the existing governing units intact, retaining selected Persian administrators. For local populations, Alexander's becoming their king changed their lives not a bit. They continued to send the same taxes to a remote master.

To India and Back.   Alexander led his army past the Persian heartland farther east into territory hardly known to the Greeks (Map 4.2). He aimed to outdo the heroes of legend by marching to the end of the world. Shrinking his army to reduce the need for supplies, he marched northeast into what is today Afghanistan and Uzbekistan. On the Jaxartes River, he founded a city called Alexandria the Furthest to show that he had penetrated deeper into this region than even Cyrus, the founder of the Persian Empire. Unable to subdue the local guerrilla forces, Alexander settled for an alliance sealed by his marriage to the Bactrian princess Roxane.

Alexander then headed east into India. Seventy days of marching through monsoon rains extinguished his soldiers' fire for conquest. In the spring of 326 B.C.E., they mutinied on the banks of the Hyphasis River and forced Alexander to turn back. The return journey through southeastern

Alexander the Great
This marble portrait of Alexander (a copy of a bronze original) has him wearing a lion's head as a helmet to recall the hero Hercules (Hercules), whose myth said he killed the fiercest beast in Greece and wore its head as proof. Alexander gazes into the distance; he commanded that his portraits show him with this visionary expression. Why do you think he wanted the world to see him with these attributes? *(The Art Archive/National Archaeological Museum, Athens/Dagli Orti [A].)*

Iran's deserts cost many casualties from hunger and thirst; the survivors finally reached safety in the Persian heartland in 324 B.C.E. Alexander immediately began planning an invasion of the Arabian peninsula and, after that, of North Africa.

Alexander ruled more harshly after his return and began treating the Greeks as subjects instead of allies. He ordered the city-states to restore citizenship to the many exiles created by war, whose status as stateless persons was causing unrest. Even more striking was Alexander's announcement that he wished to receive the honors due a god. Most Greek city-states complied by sending religious delegations to him. A Spartan expressed the only prudent position on Alexander's deification: "If Alexander wishes to be a god, then we'll agree that he be called a god."

Personal motives best explain Alexander's announcement. He had come to believe he was truly the son of Zeus; after all, Greek myths said Zeus had mated with many human females who pro-

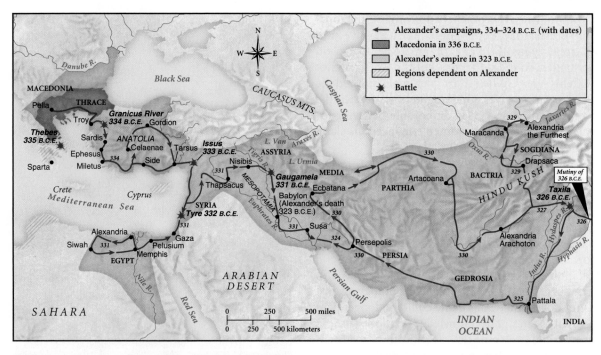

MAP 4.2 Conquests of Alexander the Great, 336–323 B.C.E.
From the time Alexander led his army against Persia in 334 B.C.E. until his death in 323 B.C.E., he was continually fighting military campaigns. His charismatic and fearless generalship, combined with effective intelligence gathering about his targets, generated an unbroken string of victories and made him a legend. His founding of garrison cities and preservation of local governments kept his conquests largely stable during his lifetime.

duced children. Since Alexander's superhuman accomplishments demonstrated that he had achieved godlike power, he must be a god himself. Alexander's divinity was, in ancient terms, a natural consequence of his power.

Alexander's premature death from a fever and heavy drinking in 323 B.C.E. aborted his plan to conquer Arabia and North Africa. His death followed months of depression provoked by the death of his best friend, Hephaistion. Some modern historians conclude that Alexander and Hephaistion were lovers, but no surviving ancient source reports this. Unfortunately for the stability of Alexander's immense conquests, by the time of his death he had not fathered an heir who could take over his rule. Roxane gave birth to their son only after Alexander's death. The story goes that, when at Alexander's deathbed his commanders asked him to whom he left his kingdom, he replied, "To the most powerful."

Alexander's Impact. Scholars disagree on almost everything about Alexander, from whether his claim to divinity was meant to justify his increasingly authoritarian attitude toward the Greek city-states, to what he meant to achieve through conquest, to the nature of his character. Was he a bloodthirsty monster obsessed with war, or a romantic visionary intent on creating a multiethnic world open to all cultures? The ancient sources suggest that Alexander had interlinked goals reflecting his restless and ruthless nature: both to conquer and administer the known world and to explore and colonize new territory beyond.

The ancient world agreed that Alexander was a marvel. An Athenian orator expressed the bewilderment many people felt over the events of Alexander's lifetime: "What strange and unexpected event has not occurred in our time? The life we have lived is no ordinary human one, but we were born to be an object of wonder to posterity." Alexander's fame increased after his death. Stories of reality-defying exploits attributed to him became popular folktales throughout the ancient world, even in distant regions such as southern Africa, where Alexander never set foot.

Alexander's conquests had consequences in many areas. His explorations benefited scientific fields from geography to botany because he took along knowledgeable writers to collect and catalog new knowledge. He had vast quantities of scientific observations dispatched to his old tutor Aristotle. Alexander's new cities promoted trade between Greece and the Near East. Most of all, his career brought these cultures into closer contact than ever before. This contact represented his career's most enduring impact.

> **REVIEW:** What were the accomplishments of Alexander the Great and what was their effect, both for the ancient world and for later Western civilization?

The Hellenistic Kingdoms, 323–30 B.C.E.

Alexander's empire fragmented after his death, and new kingdoms arose. The period that extends from Alexander's death in 323 B.C.E. to the death of Cleopatra VII, the last Macedonian queen of Egypt, in 30 B.C.E. is known as the Hellenistic Age, a name given it by modern scholars. The word **Hellenistic** ("Greek-like") conveys the most significant characteristic of this period: the emergence in the eastern Mediterranean world of a mixture of Greek and Near Eastern traditions that generated innovations in politics, literature, art, philosophy, and religion. War stirred up this cultural mixing, and tension persisted between conquerors and subjects. The process promoted regional diversity: Greek ideas and practices had their greatest impact on the urban populations of Egypt and southwestern Asia, while the many people who farmed in the countryside had much less contact with Greek ways of life.

New kingdoms formed the Hellenistic period's dominant political structures. They reintroduced monarchy into Greek culture, kings having been almost nonexistent in Greece since the fall of Mycenaean civilization nearly a thousand years earlier. Commanders from Alexander's army created the kingdoms after his death by seizing portions of his empire and proclaiming themselves kings in these new states. This process of state formation took more than fifty years of war. The self-proclaimed kings—called Alexander's successors—had to transform their families into dynasties and accumulate enough power to compel the Greek city-states to give control of foreign policy to these new overlords. This process of transfor-

---

Hellenistic: An adjective meaning "Greek-like" that is today used as a chronological term for the period 323–30 B.C.E.

Greek-style Buddha
The style of this statue of the founder of Buddhism, who expounded his doctrines in India, shows the mingling of eastern and western art. The Buddha's appearance, gaze, and posture stem from Indian artistic traditions, while the flowing folds of his garment recall Greek traditions. Compare the garment that Socrates is wearing on page 91. This combination of styles is called Gandhara, after the region in northwestern India where it began. *(Borromeo/Art Resource, NY.)*

mation reinforced the hierarchical nature of Hellenistic society. Eventually, wars with the Romans brought all the Hellenistic kingdoms to an end.

Creating New Kingdoms

Alexander's untimely death left his succession an open question. His only legitimate son, Alexander IV, was born a few months later. Alexander's mother, Olympias, tried to protect her grandson,

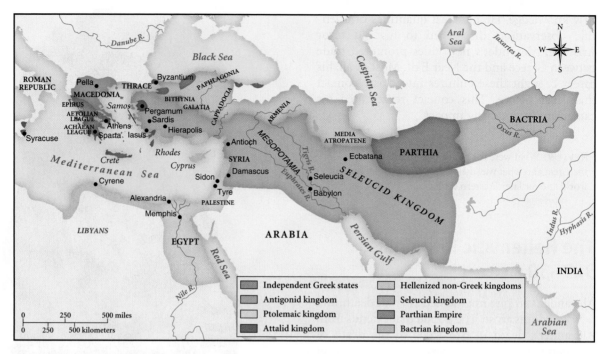

MAP 4.3 Hellenistic Kingdoms, 240 B.C.E.
Monarchy became the dominant political system in the areas of Alexander's conquests. By about eighty years after his death, the three major kingdoms established by his successors had settled their boundaries, after the Seleucids gave up their easternmost territories to an Indian king and the Attalids carved out their kingdom in western Anatolia.

but Alexander's former commanders executed Olympias in 316 B.C.E. and later murdered the boy and his mother, Roxane; having eradicated the royal family, the successors divided Alexander's conquests among themselves. Antigonus (c. 382–301 B.C.E.) took over Anatolia, the Near East, Macedonia, and Greece; Seleucus (c. 358–281 B.C.E.) seized Babylonia and the East as far as India; and Ptolemy (c. 367–282 B.C.E.) grabbed Egypt. These successors had to create their own form of monarchy based on military power and personal prestige because they did not inherit their positions legitimately: they were self-proclaimed rulers with no connection to Alexander's royal line. Several years after the elimination of Alexander's line, however, they announced that they were now kings.

In the beginning, the new kings' biggest enemies were one another. They fought constantly in the decades after Alexander's death, trying to annex more territory to their individual kingdoms. By the middle of the third century B.C.E., the three Hellenistic kingdoms had established their home territories (Map 4.3). The Antigonids had been reduced to a kingdom in Macedonia, but they also compelled the mainland Greek city-states to follow royal foreign policy. The Seleucids ruled in Syria and Mesopotamia, but they had to cede their

easternmost territory to the Indian king Chandragupta (r. 323–299 B.C.E.). They also lost most of Persia to the Parthians, a northern Iranian people. The Ptolemies ruled the rich land of Egypt.

These territorial arrangements were never completely stable because the Hellenistic monarchs never stopped competing. Conflicts repeatedly arose over border areas. The Ptolemies and the Seleucids, for example, fought to control the eastern Mediterranean coast, just as the Egyptians and Hittites had done centuries earlier. The wars between the major kingdoms left openings for smaller, regional kingdoms to establish themselves. The most famous of these was the kingdom of the Attalids in western Anatolia, with the wealthy city of Pergamum as its capital. In Bactria in Central Asia, the Greeks—originally colonists settled by Alexander—broke off from the Seleucid kingdom in the mid-third century B.C.E. to found their own regional kingdom, which flourished for a time from the trade in luxury goods between India and China and the Mediterranean world.

The Structure of Hellenistic Kingdoms

The Hellenistic kingdoms imposed foreign rule by Macedonian kings and queens on indigenous populations. The kings incorporated local traditions into their rule to build legitimacy. The Seleucids combined Macedonian with Near Eastern traditions, while the Ptolemies mixed Macedonian with Egyptian ones. The Ptolemaic royal family, for example, observed the Egyptian royal tradition of brother-sister marriage. Royal power was the ultimate source of control over the kingdoms' subjects, in keeping with the Near Eastern monarchical tradition that Hellenistic kings adopted. This tradition persisted above all in defining justice. Seleucus justified his rule on what he claimed as a universal truth of monarchy: "It is not the customs of the Persians and other people that I impose upon you, but the law which is common to everyone, that what is decreed by the king is always just." Hellenistic kings had to do more to survive than simply assert a right to rule, however. The survival of their dynasties depended on their ability to create strong armies, effective administrations, and close ties to urban elites. A letter from a Greek city summed up the situation while praising the Seleucid king Antiochus I (c. 324–261 B.C.E.): "His rule depends above all on his own excellence [aretê], and on the goodwill of his friends, and on his forces."

Royal Military Forces and Administration. Hellenistic royal armies and navies provided internal and external security. Professional soldiers manned these forces. To develop their military might, the Seleucid and Ptolemaic kings encouraged immigration by Greeks and Macedonians, who received land grants in return for military service. When this source of manpower gave out, the kings had to employ more local men as troops. Military competition put tremendous financial pressure on the kings to pay growing numbers of mercenaries and to purchase expensive new military technology. To compete effectively, a Hellenistic king had to provide giant artillery, such as catapults capable of flinging a 170-pound projectile up to two hundred yards. His navy cost a fortune because warships were now huge, requiring crews of several hundred men. War elephants, whose bellowing charges frightened opposing infantry, became popular after Alexander's encounters with them in India, and they were extremely costly to maintain.

Hellenistic kings needed effective administrations to collect revenues. Initially, they recruited mostly Greek and Macedonian immigrants to fill high-level posts. Following Alexander's example, however, the Seleucids and the Ptolemies also employed non-Greeks for middle- and lower-level positions, where officials had to be able to deal with the subject populations and speak their languages. Local men who wanted a government job bettered their chances if they could read and write Greek in addition to their native language. Bilingualism qualified them to fill positions communicating the orders of the highest-ranking officials, all Greeks and Macedonians, to local farmers, builders, and crafts producers. Non-Greeks who had successful government careers were rarely admitted to royal society because Greeks and Macedonians saw themselves as too superior to mix with locals. Greeks and non-Greeks therefore tended to live in separate communities.

Hellenistic royal administrations recalled those of the earlier Assyrian, Babylonian, and Persian empires. Administrators' principal responsibilities were to maintain order and to direct the kingdoms' tax systems. Officials mediated disputes whenever possible, but they could call on soldiers to serve as police. The Ptolemaic administration used methods of central planning and control inherited from earlier Egyptian history. Its officials continued to administer royal monopolies, such as that on vegetable oil, to maximize the king's revenue. They decided how much land farmers could sow in oil-bearing plants, supervised production and distribution of the oil, and set prices for every stage of the oil business. The king, through his officials, also often entered into partnerships with private investors to produce more revenue.

Cities and Urban Elites. Cities were the Hellenistic kingdoms' economic and social hubs. Many Greeks and Macedonians lived in new cities founded by Alexander and the Hellenistic kings in Egypt and the Near East, and they also immigrated to existing cities there. Hellenistic kings promoted this urban immigration by adorning their new cities with the features of classical Greek city-states, such as gymnasia and theaters. Although these cities often retained the city-state's political institutions, such as councils and assemblies for citizen men, the need to follow royal policy limited their freedom; they made no independent decisions on international affairs. In addition, the cities taxed their populations to send money demanded by the king.

Monarchy's reemergence in the Greek world also created a new relationship between rulers and the social elites, because the crucial element in the Hellenistic kingdom's political and social structure was the system of mutual rewards by which the kings and their leading urban subjects became partners in government and public finance. Wealthy people in the cities had the crucial responsibility of collecting taxes from the surrounding countryside as well as from their city and sending the money on to the royal treasury; the royal military and the administration were too small to perform these duties themselves. The kings honored and flattered the cities' Greek and Macedonians elites because they needed their co-operation to ensure a steady flow of tax revenues. When writing to a city's council, the king would express himself in the form of polite requests, but the recipients knew he was giving commands.

This system thus continued the Greek tradition of requiring the wealthy elite to contribute to the common good. Cooperative cities received gifts from the king to pay for expensive public works like theaters and temples or for reconstruction after natural disasters such as earthquakes. Wealthy men and women in turn helped keep the general population peaceful by subsidizing teachers and doctors, financing public works, and providing donations and loans to ensure a reliable supply of grain to feed the city's residents.

This system also required the kings to establish relationships with well-to-do non-Greeks living in the old cities of Anatolia and the Near East to keep their vast kingdoms peaceful and profitable. In addition, non-Greeks and non-Macedonians from eastern regions began moving westward to the new Hellenistic Greek cities in increasing numbers. Jews in particular moved from their ancestral homeland to Anatolia, Greece, and Egypt. The Jewish community eventually became an influential minority in Egyptian Alexandria, the most important Hellenistic city. In Egypt, as the Rosetta stone shows, the king also had to build good relationships with the priests who controlled the temples of the traditional Egyptian gods because the temples owned large tracts of rich land worked by tenant farmers.

The Layers of Hellenistic Society

Hellenistic monarchy reinforced social hierarchy. At the top were the royal family and the king's friends. The Greek and Macedonian elites of the major cities ranked next. Then came indigenous urban elites, leaders of large minority urban populations, and local lords in rural regions. Merchants, artisans, and laborers made up the free population's bottom layer. Slaves remained where they had always been, without any social status.

The kingdoms' growth increased the demand for slave labor throughout the eastern Mediterranean; the island of Delos established a market where up to ten thousand slaves a day were bought and sold. The fortunate ones were purchased as servants for the royal court or elite households and lived physically comfortable lives, so long as they

pleased their owners; the luckless ones toiled, and often died, in the mines. Enslaved children could be taken far from home to work: for example, a sales contract from 259 B.C.E. records that Zeno, to whom the camel trader wrote, bought a girl about seven years old named Gemstone to work in an Egyptian textile factory. Originally from an eastern Mediterranean town, she had previously labored as the slave of a Greek mercenary soldier employed by a Jewish cavalry commander in the Transjordan region.

The Poor. The majority of the population continued to live in country villages. Poor people performed almost all the agricultural labor required to support the Hellenistic kingdoms' economies.

Emotion in Hellenistic Sculpture
Hellenistic sculptors introduced a new style into Greek art by depicting people's emotions. This statue of an elderly woman, for example, shows an expression of pain, disheveled clothing, and a body stooped from age and from carrying a basket of chickens and vegetables. The statue probably portrays a poor woman trying to survive by hawking food in the street. This new style strove to produce an emotional response in its viewers. The statue is probably a later copy of a Hellenistic original.
(The Metropolitan Museum of Art, Rogers Fund, 1909 (09.39). Photograph © 1997 The Metropolitan Museum of Art.)

Many worked on the royal family's huge estates, but free peasants still worked their own small plots in addition to laboring for wealthy landowners. Rural people rose with the sun and began working before the heat became unbearable, raising the same kinds of crops and animals as their ancestors had with the same simple hand tools. Perhaps as many as 80 percent of all adult men and women had to work the land to produce enough food to sustain the population. Poverty often meant hunger, even in fertile lands such as Egypt. In cities, poor women and men could work as small merchants, peddlers, and artisans, producing and selling goods such as tools, pottery, clothing, and furniture. Men could sign on as deckhands on the merchant ships that sailed the Mediterranean Sea and Indian Ocean.

Many country people in the Seleucid and Ptolemaic kingdoms existed in a state of dependency between free and slave. The peoples, as they were called, were tenants who farmed the estates belonging to the king. Although they could not be sold like slaves, they were not allowed to move away or abandon their tenancies. They owed a large quota of produce to the king, and this compulsory rent gave these tenant farmers little chance to escape poverty.

Women's Lives. Hellenistic women's social and political status depended on their rank in the kingdom's hierarchy. Hellenistic queens commanded enormous riches and honors. The kingdoms buttressed their legitimacy from the female as well as the male side. Hellenistic queens exercised power as the representatives of distinguished families, the mothers of a line of royal descendants, and patrons of artists, thinkers, and even cities. Later Ptolemaic queens essentially co-ruled with their husbands. Queens ruled on their own when no male heir existed. For example, Arsinoe II (c. 316–270 B.C.E.), the daughter of Ptolemy I, first married the Macedonian successor Lysimachus, who gave her four towns as her personal domain. After his death she married her brother Ptolemy II of Egypt and exerted at least as much influence on policy as he did. The virtues publicly praised in a queen reflected traditional Greek values for women. A city decree from about 165 B.C.E. honored Queen Apollonis of Pergamum by praising her piety toward the gods, reverence toward her parents, distinguished conduct toward her husband, and harmonious relations with her "beautiful children born in wedlock."

Some queens paid special attention to the condition of women. About 195 B.C.E., for example, the Seleucid queen Laodice gave a ten-year endow-

Egyptian-Style Statue of Queen Arsinoe II
Arsinoe II (c. 316–270 B.C.E.), daughter of Alexander's general Ptolemy, was one of the most remarkable women of the Hellenistic period. After surviving twenty-five years of dynastic intrigue and family murders, she married her brother Ptolemy II. Hailed as Philadelphoi ("Brother-Loving"), the couple set a precedent for brother-sister marriages in the Ptolemaic dynasty that ruled Egypt until the death of Cleopatra VII in 30 B.C.E. Arsinoe was the first Ptolemaic ruler whose image was placed in Egyptian temples as a "temple-sharing goddess." This eight-foot-tall red granite statue portrays Arsinoe in the traditional sculptural style of the pharaohs. Why would a Hellenistic queen wish to be depicted in traditional Egyptian royal style? *(© Vatican Museums.)*

ment to a city to provide dowries for needy girls. That Laodice funded dowries shows that she recognized the importance to women of controlling property, the surest guarantee of respect in their households.

Most women remained under the control of men. "Who can judge better than a father what is to his daughter's interest?" remained the dominant creed of fathers; once a woman married, the words *husband* and *wife* replaced *father* and *daughter*. Most of the time, elite women continued to be separated from men outside of their families, while poor women still worked in public. Greeks continued to abandon infants they did not want to raise—girls more often than boys—but other populations, such as the Egyptians and the Jews, did not practice abandonment, or infant exposure. Exposure differed from infanticide in that the parents expected someone to find the child and rear it, usually as a slave. A third-century B.C.E. comic poet overstated the case by saying, "A son, one always raises even if one is poor; a daughter, one exposes, even if one is rich." Daughters of wealthy parents were not usually abandoned, but scholars have estimated that up to 10 percent of other infant girls were.

In some ways, women achieved greater control over their lives in the Hellenistic period than before. A woman of exceptional wealth could enter public life by making donations or loans to her city and in return be rewarded with an official post in local government. In Egypt, women acquired greater say in married life because marriage contracts (see Chapter 3, "Contrasting Views," page 85) evolved from an agreement between the bride's parents and the groom to one in which the bride made her own arrangements with the groom.

The Wealthy. Rich people showed increasing concern for the welfare of the less fortunate during the Hellenistic period. They were following the lead of the royal families, who emphasized philanthropy to build a reputation for generosity that would buttress their legitimacy. Sometimes wealthy citizens funded a foundation to distribute free grain to eliminate food shortages, and they also funded schools for children in various Hellenistic cities. In some places, girls as well as boys could attend school. Many cities also began sponsoring doctors to improve medical care: patients still had to pay, but at least they could count on finding a doctor.

The donors funding these services were repaid by the respect and honor they earned from their fellow citizens. Philanthropy even touched international relations. When an earthquake devastated Rhodes, many cities joined kings and queens in sending donations to help the residents recover. In return, they showered honors on their benefactors by appointing them to prestigious municipal offices and erecting inscriptions expressing the city's gratitude. In this system, the masses' welfare depended more and more on the voluntary generosity of the rich; without democracy, the poor had no political power to demand support.

The End of the Hellenistic Kingdoms

All the Hellenistic kingdoms eventually fell to the Romans. Rome repeatedly intervened in the squabbles of the Greek city-states to try to maintain peace on its eastern frontier, causing wars that established Roman dominance over the Antigonid kingdom by the middle of the second century B.C.E.

The Seleucid kingdom fell to the Romans in 64 B.C.E. The Ptolemaic kingdom in Egypt survived a bit longer. By the 50s B.C.E., its royal family had split into warring factions; the resulting disunity and weakness forced the rivals for the throne to seek Roman support. The end came when the famous queen Cleopatra, the last Macedonian to rule Egypt, chose the losing side in the civil war between Mark Antony and the future emperor Augustus in the late first century B.C.E. An invading Roman army ended Ptolemaic rule in 30 B.C.E. Rome thus became the heir to all the Hellenistic kingdoms (see Mapping the West, page 130).

REVIEW: What were the political and social structures of the new Hellenistic kingdoms?

Hellenistic Culture

Hellenistic culture reflected three principal influences: the overwhelming impact of royal wealth, increased emphasis on private life and emotion, and greater interaction of diverse peoples. The kings drove developments in literature, art, science, and philosophy by deciding which scholars and artists to put on the royal payroll. Their obligation to the kings meant that authors and artists did not have freedom to criticize public policy; their works therefore concentrated on everyday life and individual emotion.

Cultural interaction between Greek and Near Eastern traditions occurred most prominently in language and religion. These developments deeply influenced the Romans as they took over the Hellenistic world; the Roman poet Horace (65–8 B.C.E.) described the effect of Hellenistic culture on his own by saying that "captive Greece captured its fierce victor."

The Arts under Royal Patronage

Hellenistic kings became the patrons of scholarship and the arts on a vast scale, competing with one another to lure the best scholars and artists to their capitals with lavish salaries. They funded intellectuals and artists because they wanted to boost their reputations by having these famous people produce books, poems, sculptures, and other prestigious creations at their courts.

The Ptolemies turned Alexandria into the Mediterranean's leading arts and sciences center, establishing the world's first scholarly research institute and a massive library. The librarians were instructed to collect all the books in the world. The library grew to hold half a million scrolls, an enormous number for the time. Linked to it was the building in which the hired research scholars dined together and produced encyclopedias of knowledge such as *The Wonders of the World* and *On the Rivers of Europe*. We still use the name of the research institute's building, the Museum ("place of the Muses," the Greek goddesses of learning and the arts), to designate institutions preserving knowledge. The Alexandrian scholars produced prodigiously. Their champion was the scholar Didymus (c. 80–10 B.C.E.), nicknamed "Brass Bowels" for writing nearly four thousand books commenting on literature. Sadly, not a single one has survived because the library was later destroyed by fire in wartime.

Literature at Court. The writers and artists whom Hellenistic kings paid had to please their patrons with their works. The poet Theocritus (c. 300–260 B.C.E.) spelled out the deal underlying royal patronage in a poem flattering King Ptolemy II: "The spokesmen of the Muses [that is, poets] celebrate Ptolemy in return for his benefactions." Poets such as Theocritus avoided political topics and stressed the social gap between the intellectual elite—to which the kings belonged—and the uneducated masses. They filled their new poetry with erudite references to make it difficult to understand and therefore exclusive. Only people with a deep literary education could appreciate the mythological allusions that studded these authors' elaborate poems.

Theocritus was the first Greek poet to express the divide between town and countryside, a poetic stance corresponding to a growing Hellenistic reality. His *Idylls* emphasized the discontinuity between urban life and the country bumpkins' bucolic existence, reflecting the Ptolemaic social division between the food consumers in the town and the food producers in the countryside. Theocritus presented a city dweller's idealized dream that country life was peaceful and stress-free, a fiction that deeply influenced later literature.

No Hellenistic women poets seem to have enjoyed royal patronage; rather, they created their art independently. They excelled in writing **epigrams**, a style of short poem originally used for funeral epitaphs. Elegantly worded poems by women from diverse regions of the Hellenistic world still survive (see Document, "Epigrams by Women Poets," page 122). Many epigrams were about women, from courtesans to respectable matrons, and the writer's personal feelings. No other Hellenistic literature better conveys the depth of human emotion than the epigrams of women poets.

Hellenistic comedies also emphasized stories about emotions and stayed away from politics. Comic playwrights presented plays concerning the troubles of fictional lovers. These comedies of manners, as they are called, became enormously popular because, like modern situation comedies, they offered humorous views of daily life. Papyrus discoveries have restored comedies of Menander (c. 342–289 B.C.E.), the most famous Hellenistic

comic poet, noted for his skill in depicting human personality (see "New Sources, New Perspectives," page 124). Hellenistic tragedy could take a multicultural approach: Ezechiel, a Jew living in Alexandria, wrote *Exodus*, a tragedy in Greek about Moses leading the Hebrews out of captivity in Egypt.

Emotion in Sculpture and Painting. Hellenistic sculptors and painters also featured emotions in their works. Classical artists had given their subjects' faces an idealized serenity, but now sculptures depicted personal feelings. A sculpture from Pergamum (below), for example, commemorating the Attalid victory over invading Gauls (one of the

---

Dying Barbarians

Hellenistic artists excelled in portraying emotional scenes, such as this murder-suicide of a Celtic warrior who is slaying himself after killing his wife, to prevent their capture by the enemy. (Celtic women followed their men to the battlefield.) The original was in bronze, forming part of a large sculptural group that Attalus I (r. 241–197 B.C.E.) erected at Pergamum to commemorate his victory over these barbarian raiders. Why did Attalus celebrate his victory by erecting a monument portraying the defeated enemy as brave and noble? *(Erich Lessing/Art Resource, NY.)*

■ For more help analyzing this image, see the visual activity for this chapter in the Online Study Guide at **bedfordstmartins.com/hunt**.

---

epigrams: Short poems written by women in the Hellenistic Age; many were about other women and the writer's personal feelings.

Epigrams by Women Poets

Anyte, Nossis, and Erinna were three of the most famous women poets of the Hellenistic period. They composed short poems about death, love, and sex, often centered on women. They also invented the tradition of writing poems about speaking animals. None of them was hired by a Hellenistic king to be a resident poet at court, so they had to create their poetic masterpieces on their own.

Anyte on Mourning a Young Woman

The virgin Antibia I mourn for; many
young men came to her father's house
  seeking to marry her,
drawn by the fame of her beauty and
  wisdom. But everyone's
hopes deadly Fate tossed away.

Anyte on a Dolphin Speaking after Death

No longer taking joy in surging seas
will I stretch out my neck as I leap from
  the depths,
no longer around the lovely bows of the
  ship
will I jump, delighting in the figurehead,
  my likeness.
No, the purple surge of the sea cast me
  onto the land;
here I lie on this narrow strip of beach.

Nossis on the Joy of Sex

Nothing is sweeter than sexual passion;
  every other blessing is second;
I spit out from my mouth even honey.
This is what Nossis says: anyone that
  Aphrodite has not kissed
doesn't know what kind of flowers her
  roses are.

Nossis on a Woman's Present to Aphrodite

The picture of herself Callo dedicated in
  the temple of blond Aphrodite,
having her portrait made to look exactly
  like herself.
How gracefully it stands; see how great is
  the grace that blooms on it.

Best wishes to her! For she has no blame
  in her life.

Erinno on the Death of the Bride Baukis

I am the grave marker of the bride
  Baukis. As you pass by
this most wept-for pillar, say this to
  Hades in the underworld:
"You are jealous of Baukis, Hades!" The
  lovely letters that you see
announce the brutal fate Chance brought
  to Baukis,
how with the pine-torches from the wedding that they were using to worship
  Hymenaeus [the god of marriage]
the groom's father set afire her funeral
  pyre.
And you, Hymenaeus, the tuneful song
  of the wedding
converted to the sad cries of
  lamentation.

Source: *Palatine Anthology* 7.490, 7.215, 5.170, 9.605, 7.712. Translations by Thomas R. Martin.

Celtic peoples from what is now France), showed a defeated Celtic warrior stabbing himself after having killed his wife to prevent her enslavement by the victors.

The artists created their works mainly on commission from royalty and from the urban elites who wanted to show they had the same artistic taste as their royal superiors. The increasing diversity of subjects that emerged in Hellenistic art presumably represented a trend approved by kings, queens, and the elites. Sculpture best reveals this new preference for depicting people never before appearing in art: pitiable enemies, drunkards, battered athletes, wrinkled old people. The female nude became common. A statue of Aphrodite by Praxiteles, which portrayed the goddess completely nude for the first time, became renowned as a religious object and tourist attraction in the city of Cnidos, which had commissioned it. The king of Bithynia offered to pay off the citizens' en-

tire public debt if he could have the work of art. They refused.

Philosophy for a New Age

New philosophies arose in the Hellenistic period, all asking the same question: What is the best way to live? They recommended different paths to the same answer: individuals must attain personal tranquillity to achieve freedom from the turbulence of outside forces, especially chance. It is easy to see why these philosophies had appeal: outside forces—the Hellenistic kings—had robbed the Greek city-states of their independence in foreign policy, and their citizens' fates ultimately rested in the hands of unpredictable monarchs. More than ever, human life seemed out of individuals' control. It therefore was appealing to look to philosophy for personal, private solutions to the unsettling new conditions of Hellenistic life.

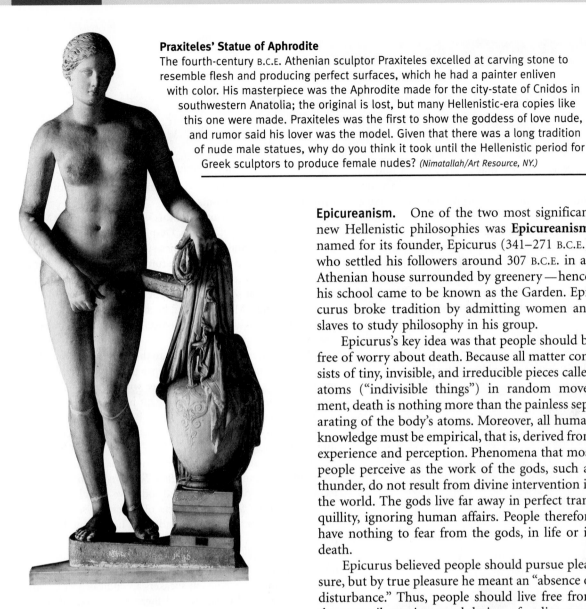

Praxiteles' Statue of Aphrodite
The fourth-century B.C.E. Athenian sculptor Praxiteles excelled at carving stone to resemble flesh and producing perfect surfaces, which he had a painter enliven with color. His masterpiece was the Aphrodite made for the city-state of Cnidos in southwestern Anatolia; the original is lost, but many Hellenistic-era copies like this one were made. Praxiteles was the first to show the goddess of love nude, and rumor said his lover was the model. Given that there was a long tradition of nude male statues, why do you think it took until the Hellenistic period for Greek sculptors to produce female nudes? *(Nimatallah/Art Resource, NY.)*

Hellenistic philosophers concentrated on **materialism**, the doctrine that only things made of matter truly exist. Materialism denied Plato's metaphysical concept of the soul and indeed of all nonmaterial phenomena, following up Aristotle's doctrine that only things identified through logic or observation exist. Hellenistic philosophy was divided into three areas: (1) logic, the process for discovering truth; (2) physics, the fundamental truth about the nature of existence; and (3) ethics, how humans should achieve happiness and well-being through logic and physics. Materialism greatly influenced Roman thinkers and the many important Western philosophers who later read those thinkers' works.

Epicureanism.   One of the two most significant new Hellenistic philosophies was **Epicureanism**, named for its founder, Epicurus (341–271 B.C.E.), who settled his followers around 307 B.C.E. in an Athenian house surrounded by greenery — hence, his school came to be known as the Garden. Epicurus broke tradition by admitting women and slaves to study philosophy in his group.

Epicurus's key idea was that people should be free of worry about death. Because all matter consists of tiny, invisible, and irreducible pieces called atoms ("indivisible things") in random movement, death is nothing more than the painless separating of the body's atoms. Moreover, all human knowledge must be empirical, that is, derived from experience and perception. Phenomena that most people perceive as the work of the gods, such as thunder, do not result from divine intervention in the world. The gods live far away in perfect tranquillity, ignoring human affairs. People therefore have nothing to fear from the gods, in life or in death.

Epicurus believed people should pursue pleasure, but by true pleasure he meant an "absence of disturbance." Thus, people should live free from the turmoil, passions, and desires of ordinary existence. A sober life spent with friends and separated from the cares of the common world provided Epicurean pleasure. Epicureanism therefore represented a serious challenge to the Greek tradition of political participation by citizens.

Stoicism.   The other important new Hellenistic philosophy, **Stoicism**, prohibited an isolationist life. Its name derives from the Painted Stoa in Athens, where Stoic philosophers discussed their doctrines. Stoics believed that fate controls people's lives but that individuals should still make the

---

materialism: A philosophical doctrine of the Hellenistic Age that denied metaphysics and claimed instead that only things consisting of matter truly exist.

Epicureanism (eh puh KYUR ee uh nizm): The philosophy founded by Epicurus of Athens to help people achieve a life of true pleasure, by which he meant "absence of disturbance."

Stoicism: The Hellenistic philosophy whose followers believed in fate but also in pursuing virtue by cultivating good sense, justice, courage, and temperance.

Papyrus Discoveries and Menander's Comedies

Fourth-century B.C.E. Greek playwrights invented a kind of comedy, called New Comedy, that is today's most popular entertainment—the sitcom. They wrote comedies that concentrated on the conflicts between personality types in everyday situations. The rocky course of love and marriage drove most plots. Avoiding political satire, comedians created type characters such as bubble-headed lovers, cranky fathers, rascally servants, and boastful soldiers, as revealed by their titles: *The Country Boob*, *Pot-Belly*, *The Stolen Girl*, *The Bad-Tempered Man*, and so on. Confusions of identity leading to hilarious misunderstandings were frequent, as were jokes about marriage, such as:

First Man: "He's married, you know."

Second Man: "What's that you say? Actually married? How can that be? I just left him alive and walking around!"

Pompeian Wall Painting of Menander
A wealthy Roman had this painting of Menander put on a wall in his house at Pompeii. The owner appears to have loved Greek plays—he had the room's other walls decorated with images of the tragedian Euripides and possibly the Muses of Tragedy and Comedy. The faded lettering on the scroll identified the playwright: "Menander: he was the first to write New Comedy." The ivy wreath on his head symbolizes the poet's victory in the contests of comedies presented at the festivals of the god Dionysus, the patron of drama. *(Scala/Art Resource, NY.)*

These comic plays inspired many imitations, especially Roman comedies, which inspired William Shakespeare (1564–1616) in England and Molière (1622–1673) in France; their comedies, in turn, led to today's sitcoms.

The most famous author of this kind of comedy was Menander (343–291 B.C.E.) of Athens. Despite antiquity's "two thumbs up," none of Menander's comedies survived into modern times. Works of Greek and Roman literature had to be copied over and over by hand for centuries if they were to survive. For unknown reasons, people at some point stopped recopying New Comedy. So scholars knew Menander had been a star but had never read any of his plays—until archaeologists began finding ancient paper in Egypt.

The Egyptians made paper from the papyrus plant, and their super-arid climate preserved the paper that people used to wrap mummies or simply threw away after writing on it. The French emperor Napoleon's conquest of Egypt in 1798–1801 inspired a European craze for collecting papyrus. By unwrapping mummies and excavating ancient trash dumps, scholars have discovered thousands of texts of all kinds.

Incredibly, some of Menander's comedies turned up in these discoveries, beginning with *The Bad-Tempered Man*. Further detective work has yielded more, and today we can also read most of *The Girl from Samos* and parts of other plays. In this way, Menander's characters, stories, and jokes have come back from the dead.

Recovering plays from papyrus is difficult. The handwriting is often difficult to decipher, there are no gaps between words, punctuation is minimal, changes in speakers are indicated by colons or dashes rather than by names, and there are no stage directions. Sometimes the papyrus has been chewed by mice and insects, burned, or torn. One part of a play can turn up in the wrapping of one mummy and another part in a different one. However, the collaboration of archaeologists, historians, and literary scholars has brought back to life the ancestors of what remains our most crowd-pleasing form of comedy.

QUESTIONS TO CONSIDER
1. What makes situation comedy so appealing?
2. Why would Greeks living in the fourth century B.C.E. prefer situation comedy to political satire or darker forms of humor?

FURTHER READING
Bagnall, Roger. *Reading Papyri, Writing Ancient History.* 1995.
Menander: Plays and Fragments. Translated with an introduction by Norma Miller. 1987.
Parkinson, Richard, and Stephen Quirke. *Papyrus.* 1995.

pursuit of virtue their goal. Stoic virtue meant putting oneself in harmony with the divine, rational force of universal nature by cultivating good sense, justice, courage, and temperance. These doctrines applied to women as well as men. In fact, some Stoics advocated equal citizenship for women, unisex clothing, and abolition of marriage and families.

The Stoic belief in fate raised the question of whether humans have free will. Stoic philosophers concluded that purposeful human actions do have significance even if fate rules. Nature, itself good, does not prevent evil from occurring, because virtue would otherwise have no meaning. What matters in life is striving for good. A person should therefore take action against evil by, for example, participating in politics. To be a Stoic also meant to shun desire and anger while calmly enduring pain and sorrow, an attitude that yields the modern meaning of the word *stoic*. Through endurance and self-control, adherents of Stoic philosophy attained tranquillity. They did not fear death because they believed that people live the same life over and over again. This repetition occurred because the world is periodically destroyed by fire and then re-formed.

Competing Philosophies.   Several other Hellenistic philosophies competed with Epicureanism and Stoicism. Some of these philosophies built on the work of earlier giants such as Pythagoras and Plato. Others struck out in new directions. Skeptics, for example, aimed at the same state of personal calm as did Epicureans, but from a completely different premise. They believed that secure knowledge about anything was impossible because the human senses yield contradictory information about the world. All people can do, they insisted, is depend on appearances while suspending judgment about their reality. These ideas had been influenced by the Indian ascetics (who practiced self-denial as part of their spiritual discipline) encountered on Alexander the Great's expedition.

For their part, Cynics rejected every convention of ordinary life, especially wealth and material comfort. The name *Cynic*, which meant "like a dog," came from the notion that dogs had no shame. Cynics believed that humans should aim for complete self-sufficiency and that whatever was natural was good and could be done without shame before anyone; therefore, even public defecation and fornication were fine. Women and men alike should be free to follow their sexual inclinations. Above all, Cynics disdained life's comforts. The most famous early Cynic, Diogenes (d. 323

Gemstone
Showing Diogenes in His Jar
This engraved gem from the Roman period shows the famous philosopher Diogenes (c. 412–c. 324 B.C.E.) living in a storage jar and talking with a man holding a scroll. Diogenes was born at Sinope on the Black Sea but was exiled in a dispute over monetary fraud; he then lived at Athens and Corinth, becoming infamous as the founder of Cynic ("doglike") philosophy. To defy social convention, he lived as shamelessly as a dog, hence the name given to his philosophical views and the dog usually shown beside him in art. What kind of person do you think would have wanted this gemstone as a piece of jewelry?
(Thorvaldsen Museum, Copenhagen.)

B.C.E.), wore borrowed clothing and slept in a storage jar. Almost as notorious was Hipparchia, a female Cynic of the late fourth century B.C.E. who once bested a philosophical opponent named Theodorus the Atheist with the following remarks: "That which would not be considered wrong if done by Theodorus would also not be considered wrong if done by Hipparchia. Now if Theodorus strikes himself, he does no wrong. Therefore, if Hipparchia strikes Theodorus, she does no wrong."

Philosophy in the Hellenistic Age reached a wider audience than ever before. Although the working poor were too busy to attend philosophers' lectures, well-off members of society studied philosophy in growing numbers. Kings competed to attract famous philosophers to their courts, and Greek settlers took their interest in philosophy with them to even the most remote Hellenistic cities. Archaeologists excavating a city located thousands of miles from Greece in Afghanistan uncovered a Greek philosophical text as well as inscriptions of moral advice imputed to Apollo's oracle at Delphi. Sadly, this site, called Ai-Khanoum, was devastated in the twentieth century during the Soviet war in Afghanistan.

Scientific Innovation

Scientific investigation was separated from philosophy in the Hellenistic period. Science so benefited from this divorce that historians have called this era ancient science's golden age. Scientific innovation flourished because Alexander's expedition had encouraged curiosity and increased knowledge about the world's extent and diversity, royal patronage supported scientists financially, and the concentration of scientists in Alexandria promoted the exchange of ideas.

Advances in Geometry and Mathematics. The greatest advances in scientific knowledge came in geometry and mathematics. Euclid, who taught at Alexandria around 300 B.C.E., made revolutionary discoveries in analyzing two- and three-dimensional space. The utility of Euclidean geometry still endures. Archimedes of Syracuse (287–212 B.C.E.) calculated the approximate value of pi and devised a way to manipulate very large numbers. He also invented hydrostatics (the science of the equilibrium of fluid systems) and mechanical devices such as a screw for lifting water to a higher elevation or cranes to disable enemy warships. Archimedes' shout of delight when he solved a problem while soaking in his bathtub has been immortalized in the modern expression "Eureka!" meaning "I have found it!"

Advances in Hellenistic mathematics energized other fields that required complex computation. Early in the third century B.C.E. Aristarchus was the first to propose the correct model of the solar system: the earth revolving around the sun. Later astronomers rejected Aristarchus's heliocentric model in favor of the traditional geocentric one (with the earth at the center) because conclusions drawn from his calculations of the earth's orbit failed to correspond to the observed positions of celestial objects. Aristarchus had assumed a circular orbit instead of an elliptical one, an assumption not corrected until much later. Eratosthenes (c. 275–194 B.C.E.) pioneered mathematical geography. He calculated the circumference of the earth with astonishing accuracy by simultaneously measuring the length of the shadows of widely separated but identically tall structures. Together, these researchers gave Western scientific thought an important start toward its fundamental procedure of reconciling theory with observed data through measurement and experimentation.

Tower of the Winds
This forty-foot octagonal tower, built in Athens about 150 B.C.E., used scientific knowledge developed in Hellenistic Alexandria to tell time and predict the weather. Eight sundials (now missing) carved on the walls displayed the time of day all year, a huge interior water clock showed hours, days, and phases of the moon, and a vane on the top showed wind direction. The carved figures represented the winds, which the Greeks saw as gods. Each figure's clothing predicted the typical weather from that direction, with the cold northern winds wearing boots and heavy cloaks, while the mild southern ones have bare feet and gauzy clothes. *(The Art Archive/Dagli Orti.)*

Discoveries in Science and Medicine. Hellenistic science and medicine made gains through royal support, especially in Alexandria, although rigorous experimentation was impossible because no technology existed to measure very small amounts of time or matter. The science of the age was as quantitative as it could be given these limitations.

Ctesibius invented pneumatics by creating machines operated by air pressure. He also built a working water pump, an organ powered by water, and the first accurate water clock. Hero continued this development of mechanical ingenuity by building a rotating sphere powered by steam. As in most of Hellenistic science, these inventions did not lead to viable applications in daily life. The scientists and their royal patrons were more interested in new theoretical discoveries than in practical results, and the technology did not exist to produce the pipes, fittings, and screws needed to build metal machines.

Hellenistic science produced noteworthy military technology, such as more powerful catapults and huge siege towers on wheels. The most famous large-scale application of technology for nonmilitary purposes was the construction of the Pharos, a lighthouse three hundred feet tall, for the harbor at Alexandria. Using polished metal mirrors to reflect the light from a large bonfire, the Pharos shone many miles out over the sea. Awestruck sailors called it one of the wonders of the world.

Medicine also benefited from the Hellenistic quest for new knowledge as medical researchers delved into the mysteries of anatomy. Increased contact between Greeks and people of the Near East made Mesopotamian and Egyptian medical knowledge better known in the West and promoted research on human health and illness. Hellenistic medical researchers discovered the value of measuring the pulse in diagnosing illness and studied anatomy by dissecting human corpses and, it was rumored, condemned criminals still alive; they had access to these subjects because the king authorized the research. Some of the terms then invented are still used, such as *diastolic* and *systolic* for blood pressure. Other Hellenistic advances in anatomy included the discovery of the nerves and nervous system.

Cultural and Religious Transformations

Wealthy non-Greeks increasingly adopted a Greek lifestyle to conform to the Hellenistic world's social hierarchy. Greek became the common language for international commerce and cultural exchange. The widespread use of the simplified form of the Greek language called **Koine**

("shared" or "common") reflected the emergence of an international culture based on Greek models; this was the reason that the Egyptian camel trader stranded in Syria (recall the story at the beginning of this chapter) had to communicate in Greek with a high-level official in Egypt. The most striking evidence of this cultural development comes from Afghanistan. There, King Ashoka (r. c. 268–232 B.C.E.), who ruled most of the Indian subcontinent, used Greek as one of the languages in his public inscriptions. These texts announced his plan to teach his subjects Buddhist self-control, such as abstinence from eating meat. Local languages did not disappear in the Hellenistic kingdoms, however. In one region of Anatolia, for example, people spoke twenty-two different languages. This sort of diversity was common in the Hellenistic world.

Changes in Greek and Egyptian Religion. Diversity in religion also grew. Traditional Greek cults remained popular, but new cults, especially those deifying kings, reflected changing political and social conditions. Preexisting cults that previously had only local significance gained adherents all over the Hellenistic world. In many cases, Greek cults and local cults from the eastern Mediterranean influenced each other. Their beliefs meshed well because these cults shared many assumptions about how to remedy the troubles of human life. In other instances, local cults and Greek cults existed side by side and even overlapped. Some Egyptian villagers, for example, continued worshipping their traditional crocodile god and mummifying their dead according to the old ways but also paid homage to Greek deities. Since they were polytheists (believers in multiple gods), people could worship in both old and new cults.

New cults incorporated a prominent theme of Hellenistic thought: concern for the relationship between the individual and what seemed the arbitrary power of divinities such as Tychê (whose name means "chance" or "luck"). Since advances in astronomy had revealed the mathematical precision of the universe's celestial sphere, religion now had to address the disconnection between that heavenly uniformity and the shapeless chaos of earthly life. One increasingly popular approach to bridging that gap was to rely on astrology for advice deduced from the movement of the stars and planets, thought of as divinities. Another very common choice was to worship Tychê in the hope of securing good luck in life.

The most revolutionary approach in seeking protection from Tychê's unpredictable tricks was

---

Koine (koy NAY): The "common" or "shared" form of the Greek language that became the international language in the Hellenistic period.

Underground Labyrinth for Healing
This underground stone labyrinth formed part of the enormous healing sanctuary of the god Asclepius at Epidaurus in Greece. Patients flocked to the site from all over the Mediterranean world. They descended into the labyrinth, which was covered and dark, as part of their treatment, which centered on reaching a trance state to receive dreams that would provide instructions on their healing and, sometimes, miraculous surgery. *(The Art Archive/Dagli Orti.)*

to pray for salvation from deified kings, who expressed their divine power in what are now called **ruler cults**. Various populations established these cults in recognition of great benefactions. The Athenians, for example, deified the Macedonian Antigonus and his son Demetrius as savior gods in 307 B.C.E., when they liberated the city and bestowed magnificent gifts on it. Like most ruler cults, this one expressed the populations' spontaneous gratitude and a desire to flatter the rulers in the hope of obtaining additional favors, and the rulers' wish to have their power made clear. Many cities in the Ptolemaic and Seleucid kingdoms instituted ruler cults for their kings and queens. An inscription put up by Egyptian priests in 238 B.C.E. concretely described the qualities appropriate for a divine king and queen:

> King Ptolemy III and Queen Berenice, his sister and wife, the Benefactor Gods, . . . have provided good govern-

ment . . . and [after a drought] sacrificed a large amount of their revenues for the salvation of the population, and by importing grain . . . they saved the inhabitants of Egypt.

As these words make clear, the Hellenistic monarchs' tremendous power and wealth gave them the status of gods to the ordinary people who depended on their generosity and protection. The idea that a human being could be a god, present on earth to be a savior who delivered people from evils, was now firmly established and would prove influential later in Roman imperial religion and Christianity.

Healing divinities offered another form of protection to anxious individuals. Scientific Greek medicine had rejected the notion of supernatural causes and cures for disease ever since Hippocrates in the fifth century B.C.E. Nevertheless, the cult of the god Asclepius, who offered cures for illness and injury at his many shrines, grew popular during the Hellenistic period. Suppliants seeking Asclepius's help would sleep in special locations at his shrines to await dreams in which he prescribed

---

ruler cults: Cults that involved worship of a Hellenistic ruler as a savior god.

healing treatments. These prescriptions emphasized diet and exercise, but numerous inscriptions commissioned by grateful patients also testified to miraculous cures and surgery performed while the sufferer slept. The following example is typical:

> Ambrosia of Athens was blind in one eye. . . . She . . . ridiculed some of the cures [described in inscriptions in the sanctuary] as being incredible and impossible. . . . But when she went to sleep, she saw a vision; she thought the god was standing next to her. . . . He split open the diseased eye and poured in a medicine. When day came she left cured.

People's faith in divine healing gave them hope that they could overcome the constant danger of illness, which appeared to strike at random; there was no knowledge of germs as causing infections.

Mystery cults proffered secret knowledge as a key to worldly and physical salvation. The cults of the Greek god Dionysus and, in particular, the Egyptian goddess Isis attracted many followers in this period. Isis was beloved because her powers protected her worshippers in all aspects of their lives. King Ptolemy I boosted her popularity by establishing a headquarters for her cult in Alexandria. The cult of Isis, who became the most popular female divinity in the Mediterranean, involved extensive ceremonies, rituals, and festivals incorporating features of Egyptian religion mixed with Greek elements. Disciples of Isis hoped to achieve personal purification, as well as the aid of the goddess in overcoming the demonic power of Tychê. That an Egyptian deity like Isis could achieve such popularity among Greeks (and, later, Romans) is the best evidence of the cultural cross-fertilization of the Hellenistic world.

Hellenistic Judaism.   Cultural interaction between Greeks and Jews produced important changes in Judaism during the Hellenistic period. King Ptolemy II made the Hebrew Bible accessible to a wide audience by having his Alexandrian scholars produce a Greek translation—the Septuagint. Many Jews, especially those in the large Jewish communities that had grown up in Hellenistic cities outside their homeland, began to speak Greek and adopt Greek culture. These Greek-style Jews mixed Jewish and Greek customs, while retaining Judaism's rituals and rules and not worshipping Greek gods.

Internal dissension among Jews erupted in second-century B.C.E. Palestine over how much Greek tradition was acceptable for traditional Jews. The Seleucid king Antiochus IV (r. 175–163 B.C.E.) intervened to support Greek-style Jews in Jerusalem, who had taken over the high priesthood

that ruled the Jewish community. In 167 B.C.E., Antiochus converted the great Jewish temple in Jerusalem into a Greek temple and outlawed the practice of Jewish religious rites, such as observing the Sabbath and circumcision. This action provoked a revolt led by Judah the Maccabee, which won Jewish independence from Seleucid control after twenty-five years of war. The most famous episode in this revolt was the retaking of the Jerusalem temple and its rededication to the worship of the Jewish god, Yahweh, commemorated by the Hanukkah holiday. That Greek culture attracted some Jews in the first place provides a striking example of the transformations that affected many—though far from all—people of the Hellenistic world. By the time of the Roman Empire, one of those transformations would be Christianity, whose theology had roots in the cultural interaction of Hellenistic Jews and Greeks and their ideas on apocalypticism (religious ideas revealing the future) and divine human beings.

> **REVIEW:** How did the political changes of the Hellenistic period affect art, science, and religion?

Conclusion

The aftermath of the Peloponnesian War led ordinary people as well as philosophers like Plato and Aristotle to question the basis of morality. The disunity of Greek international politics allowed Macedonia's aggressive leaders Philip II (r. 359–336 B.C.E.) and Alexander the Great (r. 336–323 B.C.E.) to make themselves the masters of the competing city-states. Inspired by Greek heroic ideals, Alexander the Great conquered the Persian Empire and set in motion the Hellenistic period's momentous political, social, and cultural changes.

When Alexander's commanders transformed themselves into Hellenistic kings after his death, they reintroduced monarchy into the Greek world, adding to the conquered lands' existing governments an administrative layer of Greeks and Macedonians. Local elites cooperated with the new Hellenistic monarchs in governing and financing their hierarchical society, which was divided along ethnic lines, with the Greek and Macedonian elite ranking above local elites. To enhance their own reputations, Hellenistic kings and queens funded writers, artists, scholars, philosophers, and scientists, thereby energizing intellectual life. The traditional city-states continued to exist in Hellenistic

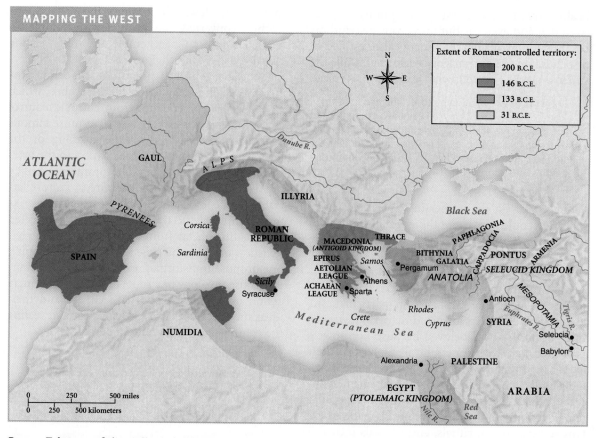

Roman Takeover of the Hellenistic World, to 30 B.C.E.
By the death of Cleopatra VII of Egypt in 30 B.C.E., the Romans had taken over the Hellenistic kingdoms of the eastern Mediterranean. This territory became the eastern half of the Roman Empire. Compare the political divisions on this map with those on the map at the end of Chapter 3 to see the differences from the Classical Age.

Greece, but their freedom extended only to local governance; the Hellenistic kings controlled foreign policy.

Increased interaction between diverse peoples promoted greater cultural interchange in the Hellenistic world. Artists and writers expressed emotion in their works in new ways, philosophers discussed how to achieve true happiness, and scientists explored the mysteries of nature and the human body. Political and cultural change increased people's anxiety about the role of chance and luck in life. In response, they looked for new religious experiences to satisfy their yearning for protection and health. In the midst of so much novelty, the ancient world's fundamental elements remained unchanged—the labor, the poverty, and the necessarily limited horizons of the mass of ordinary people working in its fields, vineyards, and pastures. What changed most of all was the Romans' culture once they took over the Hellenistic kingdoms' territory and came into close con-

tact with their diverse peoples' traditions. Rome's rise to power took centuries, however, because Rome originated as a tiny, insignificant place that no one except Romans ever expected to amount to anything on the world stage.

FOR FURTHER EXPLORATION

■ **For suggested references, including Web sites, for topics in this chapter,** see page SR-1 at the end of the book.

■ **For additional primary-source material from this period,** see Chapter 4 in *Sources of THE MAKING OF THE WEST,* Third Edition.

■ **For Web sites and documents related to topics in this chapter,** see *Make History* at bedfordstmartins.com/hunt.

CHAPTER REVIEW

KEY TERMS AND PEOPLE

Plato (107)

metaphysics (107)

dualism (107)

Aristotle (108)

Alexander the Great (110)

Hellenistic (115)

epigrams (121)

materialism (123)

Epicureanism (123)

Stoicism (123)

Koine (127)

ruler cults (128)

MAKING CONNECTIONS

1. What made ancient people see Alexander as "great"? Would he be regarded as "great" in today's world?

2. What are the advantages and disadvantages of governmental support of the arts and sciences? Compare such support in the Hellenistic kingdoms to that in the United States today (e.g., through the National Endowment for the Humanities, National Endowment for the Arts, and the National Science Foundation).

REVIEW QUESTIONS

1. How did daily life, philosophy, and the political situation change in Greece during the period 400–350 B.C.E.?

2. What were the accomplishments of Alexander the Great and what was their effect, both for the ancient world and for later Western civilization?

3. What were the political and social structures of the new Hellenistic kingdoms?

4. How did the political changes of the Hellenistic period affect art, science, and religion?

For practice quizzes, a customized study plan, and other study tools, see the Online Study Guide at bedfordstmartins.com/hunt.

IMPORTANT EVENTS

399 B.C.E.	Execution of Socrates
386 B.C.E.	In King's Peace, Sparta cedes control of Anatolian Greek city-states to Persia; Plato founds the Academy
362 B.C.E.	Battle of Mantinea leaves power vacuum in Greece
338 B.C.E.	Battle of Chaeronea allows Macedonian Philip II to become the leading power in Greece
335 B.C.E.	Aristotle founds the Lyceum
334–323 B.C.E.	Alexander the Great leads Greeks and Macedonians to conquer the Persian Empire
307 B.C.E.	Epicurus founds his philosophical group in Athens
306–304 B.C.E.	The successors of Alexander declare themselves kings
300–260 B.C.E.	Theocritus writes poetry at the Ptolemaic court
C. 300 B.C.E.	Euclid teaches geometry at Alexandria
195 B.C.E.	Seleucid queen Laodice endows dowries for girls
167 B.C.E.	Maccabee revolt after Antiochus IV turns temple in Jerusalem into a Greek sanctuary
30 B.C.E.	Death of Cleopatra VII and takeover of the Ptolemaic Empire by Rome

The Rise of Rome
753–44 B.C.E.

The Romans treasured legends about their state's transformation from a tiny village to a world power. They especially loved stories about their first king, Romulus, famous as a hot-tempered but shrewd leader. According to the tale later called "The Rape of the Sabine Women," Romulus's Rome needed more women to bear children to increase its population and build a strong army. The king therefore begged Rome's neighbors for permission for Romans to marry their women. Everyone turned him down, scorning Rome's poverty and weakness. Enraged, Romulus hatched a plan to use force where diplomacy had failed. Inviting the neighboring Sabines to a religious festival, he had his men kidnap the unmarried women. The Roman kidnappers promptly married the Sabine women, promising to cherish them as beloved wives and new citizens. When the Sabine men attacked Rome to rescue their kin, the women rushed into the midst of the bloody battle, begging their brothers, fathers, and new husbands either to stop slaughtering one another or to kill them to end the war. The men immediately made peace and agreed to merge their populations under Roman rule.

This legend emphasizes that Rome, unlike the city-states of Greece, expanded by absorbing outsiders into its citizen body, sometimes violently, sometimes peacefully. Rome's growth became the ancient world's greatest expansion of population and territory, as a people originally housed in a few huts gradually created a state that fought countless wars and relocated an unprecedented number of citizens to gain control of most of Europe, North Africa, Egypt, and the eastern Mediterranean lands. The social, cultural, political, legal, and economic traditions that Romans developed in ruling this vast area created closer

The Wolf Suckling Romulus and Remus
This bronze statue depicts the myth that a she-wolf suckled the twin brothers Romulus and Remus, the offspring of the war god Mars and the future founders of Rome. Romans treasured this story because it implied that Mars loved their city so dearly that he dispatched a wild animal to nurture its founders after a cruel tyrant had forced their mother to abandon the infants. The myth also taught Romans that their state had been born in violence: Romulus killed Remus in an argument over who would lead their new settlement. The wolf is an Etruscan sculpture from the fifth century B.C.E.; the babies were added in the Renaissance. *(Scala/Art Resource, NY.)*

interconnections between its diverse peoples than ever before or since. Unlike the Greeks and Macedonians, the Romans maintained the unity of their state for centuries. Its political longevity allowed many Roman values and traditions to become essential components of Western civilization.

Roman values and traditions originated with ancient Italy's many peoples, but Greek literature, art, and philosophy influenced Rome's culture most of all. This cross-cultural contact that so deeply influenced Rome was a kind of competition in innovation between equals, not "inferior" Romans imitating "superior" Greek culture. Like other ancient peoples, Romans often learned from their neighbors, but they adapted foreign traditions to their own purposes and forged their own cultural identity.

The kidnapping legend belongs to Rome's earliest history, when kings ruled (753–509 B.C.E.). Rome's most important history comes afterward, divided into two major periods of about five hundred years each — the republic and the empire. Under the republic (founded 509 B.C.E.), the people elected their officials and laws were passed by assemblies (although an oligarchy of the social elite controlled politics); under the empire, monarchs once again ruled. Rome's greatest expansion came during the republic. Romans' belief in a divine destiny fueled this tremendous growth; they believed that the gods wanted them to rule the world by military might and law and improve it through social and moral values. Their faith in a divine destiny is illustrated by the legend of the Sabine women, in which the earliest Romans used a religious festival as a ruse. Their conviction that values should drive politics showed in their determination to persuade the Sabine women that loyalty and love would wipe out the crime of kidnapping.

Roman values emphasized family loyalty, selfless political and military service to the community, individual honor and public status, the importance of the law, and shared decision making. Unfortunately, these values conflicted with one another in the long run. By the first century B.C.E., power-hungry leaders such as Sulla and Julius Caesar had plunged Rome into civil war. By putting their personal ambition before the good of the state, they destroyed the republic.

FOCUS QUESTION: How did traditional Roman values affect both the rise and the downfall of the Roman republic?

Roman Social and Religious Traditions

Roman social and religious traditions shaped the history of the Roman republic. Rome's citizens believed that eternal moral values connected them to one another and required them to honor the gods in return for divine support. Hierarchy affected all of life: people at all social levels were obligated to patrons or clients; in families, fathers dominated; in religion, sacrifices, rituals, and prayers were due the gods who protected the family and the state.

Roman Moral Values

Roman values defined relationships with other people and with the gods. Romans guided their lives by the **mos maiorum** ("the way of the elders"), or values handed down from their ancestors. The Romans preserved these values because, for them, *old* equaled "tested by time" whereas *new* implied "dangerous." Roman morality emphasized virtue, faithfulness, and respect; moral conduct earned public respect.

Virtus was a primarily masculine quality comprising courage (especially in war), strength, and

---

mos maiorum: Literally, "the way of the elders"; the set of Roman values handed down from the ancestors.

■ **753** Rome's founding as a monarchy

■ **396** Defeat of Veii

■ **509** Roman republic established

■ **387** Gauls sack Rome

| 700 B.C.E. | 600 B.C.E. | 500 B.C.E. | 400 B.C.E. |

■ **509–287** Struggle of the orders

■ **451–449** Twelve Tables created

loyalty. It also included wisdom and moral purity, qualities that the social elite were expected to display in their public and private lives. In this broader sense, virtus applied to women as well as to men. In the second century B.C.E., the Roman poet Lucilius defined it this way:

> *Virtus* is to know the human relevance of each thing,
> To know what is humanly right and useful and
>   honorable,
> And what things are good and what are bad, useless,
>   shameful, and dishonorable. . . .
> Virtus is to pay what in reality is owed to honorable
>   status,
> To be an enemy and a foe to bad people and bad values,
> But a defender of good people and good values. . . .
> And, in addition, *virtus* is putting the country's interests
>   first,
> Then our parents', with our own interests third and last.

Fides (FEE dehs, "faithfulness") meant keeping one's obligations no matter the cost. Failing to meet an obligation offended the community and the gods. Faithful women remained virgins before marriage and monogamous afterward. Men demonstrated faithfulness by keeping their word, paying their debts, and treating everyone with justice—which did not mean treating everyone equally, but rather treating each person appropriately, according to whether he or she was a social superior, an equal, or an inferior.

Religion was part of faithfulness. Showing devotion to the gods and to one's family was its supreme form. Romans respected the superior authority of the gods and of the elders and ancestors of their families. Performing religious rituals properly was crucial: Romans believed they had to worship the gods faithfully to maintain the divine favor that protected their community.

Roman values required that each person maintain self-control and limit displays of emotion. So strict was this value that not even wives and husbands could kiss in public without seeming emotionally out of control. It also meant that

An Aristocrat Holding Death Masks of His Ancestors
This marble statue shows an elderly aristocrat holding death masks of his ancestors. It illustrates the Romans' commitment to the *mos maiorum*, the way of the elders. A historian explained, "The masks are portraits, carefully made to resemble the dead person in shape and form. Romans display them at public sacrifices, and when a prominent family member dies, they carry them in the funeral procession, having them worn by those who most resemble the dead ancestor in stature and build." This statue may come from the first century C.E., but if so, it imitated one from the republic. Compare its realistic style with that of the relief of an ex-slave family on page 136. *(Scala/Art Resource, NY.)*

a person should never give up no matter how hard the situation. Persevering and doing one's duty were instilled from a young age.

The reward for living these values was respect from others. Women earned respect by bearing legitimate children and educating them morally; their reward was a good reputation among their families and friends. Respected men relied on their

300 B.C.E.	200 B.C.E.	100 B.C.E.	0
■ 264–241 First Punic War	■ 149–146 Third Punic War		■ 49–45 Civil War; Caesar wins
■ 218–201 Second Punic War		■ 91–87 Social War	
			■ 60 First Triumvirate
	■ 220 Rome controls Italy south of the Po River	■ 133 Tiberius Gracchus elected tribune, assassinated	■ 45–44 Cicero writes on *humanitas*
	■ 168–149 Cato, *The Origins*		■ 44 Caesar appointed dictator, assassinated
		■ 146 Carthage and Corinth destroyed	

reputations to help them win election to government posts. A man of the highest reputation commanded so much respect that others would obey him regardless of whether he held an office with formal power over them. A man with this much prestige was said to possess authority.

The concept of authority based on respect reflected the Roman belief that some people were inherently superior to others and that society had to be hierarchical to be just. Thus, they determined status both by family history and by wealth. Romans believed that aristocrats, or people born into the best families, automatically deserved high respect. In return, aristocrats were supposed to live strictly by the highest values and serve the community.

In Roman legends about the early days, a person could be poor and still remain a proud aristocrat. Over time, however, money became overwhelmingly important to the Roman elite, for spending on showy luxuries, large-scale entertaining, and lavish gifts to the community. In this way, wealth became necessary to maintain high social status. By the later centuries of the Roman republic, ambitious men often trampled on other values to acquire riches and high status.

Sculpted Tomb of a Family of Ex-Slaves
The inscription on this tomb monument from, probably, the first century B.C.E. reveals that the couple started life as slaves but became free and thus Roman citizens. Their son (his head has been knocked off) is shown in the background holding a pet pigeon. This family had done well enough financially to afford a sculpted tomb, and the tablets the man is holding and the woman's hairstyle are meant to show that their family was literate and stylish. Compare the man's realistically lined face with the woman's softer, more idealized one. *(German Archeological Institute/Madeline Grimoldi.)*

The Patron-Client System

The **patron-client system** underlay status in Roman society. It was an interlocking network of personal relationships that obligated people to one another. A patron was a man of superior status who could provide benefits, as they were called, to lower-status people who paid him special attention. These were his clients, who in return owed him duties. In this hierarchical system, a patron was often himself the client of a higher-status man.

Benefits and duties centered on financial and political help. A patron would help a client get started in a political career by supporting his candidacy and would provide gifts or loans. A patron's most important obligation was to support a client and his family if they got into legal trouble.

Clients had to aid their patrons' campaigns for public office by swinging votes their way. They also had to lend money when patrons incurred large expenses to provide public works and to fund their daughters' dowries. A patron expected his clients to gather at his house at dawn to accompany him to the forum, the city's public center, because it was a mark of great status to have numerous clients thronging around. A Roman leader needed a large house to hold this throng and to entertain his social equals; a crowded house signified social success.

Patrons' and clients' mutual obligations endured for generations. Ex-slaves, who became the clients for life of the masters who freed them, often passed this relationship on to their children. Romans with contacts abroad could acquire clients among foreigners; Roman generals sometimes had entire foreign communities obligated to them. The patron-client system enshrined the Roman view that social stability and well-being were achieved by faithfully maintaining established ties.

The Roman Family

The family was Roman society's bedrock because it taught values and determined the ownership of property. Men and women shared the duty of teaching their children values, though by law the father possessed the *patria potestas* ("father's power") over his children, no matter how old, and his slaves. This power made him the sole owner of all his dependents' property. As long as he was alive, no son

---

patron-client system: The interlocking network of mutual obligations between Roman patrons (social superiors) and clients (social inferiors).

patria potestas (PAH tree uh po TEHS tahs): Literally, "father's power"; the legal power a Roman father possessed over the children and slaves in his family, including owning all their property and having the right to punish them, even with death.

Sculpture of a Woman Running a Store
This sculpture portrays a woman selling food from a small shop while customers make purchases or chat. Since Roman women could own property, it is possible that the woman is the store owner. The man standing behind her could be her husband or a servant. Much like malls of today, markets in Roman towns were packed with small stores. (*Art Resource, NY.*)

or daughter could officially own anything, accumulate money, or possess any independent legal standing. Unofficially, however, adult children did acquire personal property and money, and favored slaves could build up savings. Fathers also held legal power of life and death over these members of their households, but they rarely exercised this power except, like the Greeks, through exposure of newborns, an accepted practice to limit family size and dispose of physically imperfect infants.

Patria potestas did not allow a husband to control his wife because "free" marriages—in which the wife formally remained under her father's power as long as the father lived—became common. But in the ancient world, few fathers lived long enough to oversee the lives of their married daughters or sons; four out of five parents died before their children reached age thirty. A woman without a living father was relatively independent. Legally she needed a male guardian to conduct her business, but guardianship was largely an empty formality by the first century B.C.E. Upper-class women could even demonstrate publicly to express their opinions. In 195 B.C.E., for example, a group of women blocked Rome's streets for days, until the men rescinded a wartime law meant to reduce tensions between rich and poor by limiting the amount of gold jewelry and fine clothing women could wear and where they could ride in carriages. A later legal expert commented on women's freedom of action: "The common belief,

that because of their instability of judgment women are often deceived and that it is only fair to have them controlled by the authority of guardians, seems more false than true. For women of full age manage their affairs themselves."

A Roman woman had to grow up fast to assume her duties as teacher of values to her children and manager of her household's resources. Tullia (c. 79–45 B.C.E.), daughter of Rome's most famous orator, Cicero (106–43 B.C.E.), was engaged at twelve, married at sixteen, and widowed by twenty-two. Like every other wealthy married Roman woman, she managed the household slaves, monitored the nurturing of the young children by wet nurses, kept account books to track the property she personally owned, and accompanied her husband to dinner parties—something a Greek wife never did.

A mother's responsibility for shaping her children's values constituted the foundation of female virtue. Women like Cornelia, a famous aristocrat of the second century B.C.E., won enormous respect for loyalty to family. When her husband died, Cornelia refused an offer of marriage from King Ptolemy of Egypt so that she could continue to oversee the family estate and educate her surviving daughter and two sons. (Her other nine children had died.) The boys, Tiberius and Gaius Gracchus, grew up to be among the most influential political leaders in the late republic. The number of children Cornelia bore exemplified the fertility and stamina required of a Roman wife to ensure the survival of her husband's family line. Cornelia also became renowned for her stylish letters, which were still being read a century later.

Roman women had no official political role, but wealthy women like Cornelia could influence politics indirectly through their male relatives. Marcus Porcius Cato (234–149 B.C.E.), a renowned politician and author, described this clout: "All mankind rule their wives, we [Roman men] rule all mankind, and our wives rule us."

Women could acquire property through inheritance and entrepreneurship; archaeological discoveries reveal that by the end of the republic some women owned large businesses. Because both women and men could control property, prenuptial agreements determining the property rights of husband and wife were common. Divorce was legally simple, with fathers usually keeping the children. Most poor women, like poor men, had to toil for a living as field laborers or hawkers selling trinkets in cities. Women and men both worked in manufacturing, which mostly happened in the home. The men worked the raw materials, cutting, fitting, and polishing wood, leather, and metal, while the women sold the finished goods. The poorest women earned money through prostitution, which was legal but considered disgraceful.

Education for Public Life

Roman education aimed to make men and women effective speakers and exponents of traditional values. Most children received their education at home; there were no public schools, and only the rich could afford private teachers. Wealthy parents bought literate slaves to educate their children; by the late republic, they often chose Greek slaves so that their children could learn to speak Greek and read Greek literature. Lessons emphasized memorization, and teachers used corporal punishment to keep pupils attentive. In upper-class families, both daughters and sons learned to read. The girls were also taught literature and perhaps some music, and how to make educated conversation at dinner parties. The principal aim of women's education was to prepare them to instill traditional social and moral values in their children.

Sons received physical training and learned to fight with weapons, but rhetorical training dominated an upper-class Roman boy's education because a successful political career depended on the ability to speak persuasively. A boy would learn winning techniques by listening to speeches in public meetings and arguments in court cases. As the orator Cicero said, young men must learn to "excel in public speaking. It is the tool for controlling men at Rome."

Public and Private Religion

Romans followed Greek models in religion. Their chief deity, Jupiter, corresponded to the Greek god Zeus and was seen as a powerful, stern father. Juno (Greek Hera), queen of the gods, and Minerva (Greek Athena), goddess of wisdom, joined Jupiter to form the state religion's central triad. These three deities shared Rome's most revered temple.

Protecting Rome's safety and prosperity was the gods' major function. They were supposed to help Rome defeat enemies in war, but divine support for agriculture was also indispensable. Official prayers requested the gods' aid in ensuring good crops, healing disease, and promoting reproduction for animals and people. In times of crisis, Romans sought foreign gods for help, such as when the government imported the cult of the healing god Asclepius from Greece in 293 B.C.E., hoping he would save Rome from a plague.

The republic supported many other cults, including that of Vesta, goddess of the hearth and therefore protector of the family. Her shrine housed Rome's official eternal flame, which guaranteed the state's permanent existence. The Vestal Virgins, six unmarried women sworn to chastity and Rome's only female priests, tended Vesta's shrine. Their chastity was considered crucial to preserving Rome. They earned high status and freedom from their fathers' control by performing their most important duty: keeping the flame from going out. If the flame went out, the Romans assumed that one of the Vestal Virgins had had sex and buried her alive.

Religion was important in Roman family life. Each household maintained small shrines housing statuettes of the spirits of the household and those of the ancestors, who were believed to protect the family's health and morality. Upper-class families kept death masks of ancestors hanging in the main room and wore them at funerals to commemorate the family's heritage and the current generation's responsibility to live up to the ancestors' values.

Because Romans believed that divine spirits participated in crucial events such as birth, marriage, and death, they performed many rituals seeking protection. Rituals also accompanied everyday activities, such as breast-feeding babies or fertilizing crops. Many public religious gatherings promoted the community's health and stability. For example, during the February 15 Lupercalia festi-

Household Shrine from Pompeii

This shrine stood inside the entrance to a house at Pompeii owned by successful businessmen, who spent heavily to decorate their home with 188 colorful wall paintings. This type of shrine housed statuettes of the deities protecting the household, shown here also in a painting, flanking a figure representing the spirit of the family's father. What do you think it signifies that the deities are dancing? The snake below, which is about to drink from a bowl probably holding milk, also symbolizes a protective force. The scene sums up the role Romans expected their gods to play: preventing harm and bad luck. *(Scala/Art Resource, NY.)*

val (whose name recalled the wolf, *luper* in Latin, who legend said had reared Romulus and his twin, Remus), naked young men streaked around the Palatine hill, lashing any woman they met with strips of goatskin. Women who had not yet borne children would run out to be struck, believing this would help them to become fertile.

Like the Greeks, Romans did not regard the gods as the guardians of human morality. Cicero's description of Jupiter's titles explained public religion's closer ties to security and prosperity than to personal behavior: "We call Jupiter the Best and Greatest not because he makes us just or sober or wise but, rather, healthy, unharmed, rich, and prosperous." Roman officials preceded important actions with the ritual called "taking the auspices," which sought Jupiter's approval by observing natural signs such as the direction of the flights of birds, their eating habits, or the appearance of thunder and lightning. Action proceeded only if the auspices were favorable.

Romans linked values and religion by regarding values as divine forces. *Pietas*, for example, which meant devotion and duty to family, friends, the state, and the gods, had a temple at Rome with a statue personifying pietas as a female divinity. This personification of abstract moral qualities provided a focus for cult rituals.

The duty of Roman religious officials was to ensure peace with the gods. Socially prominent men served as priests, conducting sacrifices, festivals, and prayers. They were not professionals devoting their lives to religious activity; they were citizens performing public service. The chief priest, the *pontifex maximus* ("greatest bridge-builder"), served as the head of state religion and the ultimate authority on religious matters affecting government. The political powers of this priesthood motivated Rome's most ambitious men to seek it.

Disrespect for religious tradition brought punishment. Admirals, for example, took the auspices by feeding sacred chickens on their warships: if the birds ate energetically, Jupiter favored the Romans and an attack could begin. In 249 B.C.E., the commander Publius Claudius Pulcher grew frustrated when his chickens, probably seasick, refused to eat. Determined to attack, he finally hurled the birds overboard in a rage, sputtering, "Well then, let them drink!" When he promptly suffered a huge defeat, he was fined heavily.

> **REVIEW:** What common themes underlay Roman values? How did Romans' behavior reflect those values?

From Monarchy to Republic

Romans' values and their belief in a divine destiny fueled their astounding growth from a tiny settlement into the Mediterranean's greatest power. This process took centuries, as the Romans developed their government and expanded their territory through war. From the eighth to the sixth century B.C.E., they were ruled by kings, but the later kings' violence provoked members of the social elite to overthrow the monarchy and create a new political system—the republic—which lasted from the fifth through the first century B.C.E. The republic—from the Latin *res publica* (meaning "the people's matter" or "the public business")—distributed power by electing officials and making laws in open meetings of male citizens. This model of republican government, rather than Athens's direct democracy, influenced the founders of the United States in organizing the new nation as a federal republic. Rome gained land and population by winning aggressive wars and by absorbing other peoples. Its economic and cultural growth depended on contact with many other peoples around the Mediterranean.

Roman Society under the Kings, 753–509 B.C.E.

Legend taught that Rome's original government had seven kings, ruling from 753 to 509 B.C.E. The kings created Rome's most famous and enduring government body: the Senate, a group of distinguished men chosen as the king's personal council. This council played the same role—advising government leaders—for a thousand years, as Rome changed from a monarchy to a republic and back to a monarchy (the empire). It was always a Roman tradition that one should never make decisions by oneself but only after consulting advisers and friends.

The kings began Rome's expansion by taking in outsiders whom they conquered, as reflected in the story of Romulus's assimilating the Sabines. This inclusionary policy of making others into citizens, which contrasted sharply with the exclusionary laws of the Greeks, proved crucial for Rome's growth and promoted ethnic diversity. Even more remarkably, Romans, unlike Greeks, granted citizenship to freed slaves. These freedmen and freedwomen owed special obligations to their former owners, and they could not hold elective office or serve in the army. In all other ways, however, exslaves enjoyed citizens' rights, such as legal marriage. Their children possessed citizenship without any limits. By the late republic, many Roman citizens descended from freed slaves.

Expansion and Cross-Cultural Contact.   By approximately 550 B.C.E., Rome had grown to between

thirty and forty thousand people and, through war and diplomacy, had won control of three hundred square miles of surrounding territory. Rome's geography propelled its further expansion. It possessed fertile farmland and controlled a river crossing on a major north–south route. Most important, Rome was ideally situated for international trade: the peninsula it was on stuck so far out into the Mediterranean that east–west seaborne traffic naturally encountered it (Map 5.1), and the city had a good port nearby.

War and trade promoted Romans' contact with other peoples and profoundly influenced their cultural development. Their closest neighbors were

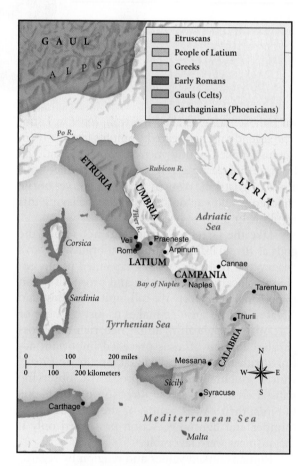

MAP 5.1 Ancient Italy, 500 B.C.E.
When the Romans ousted the monarchy to found a republic in 509 B.C.E., they inhabited a relatively small territory in central Italy. Many different peoples lived in Italy at this time, with the most prosperous occupying fertile agricultural land and sheltered harbors on the peninsula's west side. The early republic's most urbanized neighbors were the Etruscans to the north and the Greeks in the city-states to the south, including on the island of Sicily. Immediately adjacent to Rome were the people of Latium, called Latins.
■ How did geography aid Roman expansion?

---

res publica (REHS POOB lih kuh): Literally, "the people's matter" or "the public business"; the Romans' name for their republic and the source of our word *republic*.

Banquet Scene in an Etruscan Tomb
Painted around 480–470 B.C.E., this scene decorated a wall in an Etruscan tomb at Tarquinia. Wealthy Etruscans filled their tombs with paintings, which probably represented the funeral feasts held to celebrate the life of the dead person and simultaneously the social pleasures experienced in this life and expected in the next. Here the banqueters recline on their elbows, one of the many ways in which the Greeks influenced the Etruscans. The Greeks themselves had probably adopted their dining customs from Near Eastern precedents. Why do you think the men's robes are more colorful than those worn by the men in the mosaic depicting Plato's Academy on page 107? *(Scala/Art Resource, NY.)*

poor villagers like the earliest Romans and spoke the same Indo-European language, Latin. To the south in Italy and Sicily, however, lived Greeks, and contact with them had the greatest effect on Roman cultural development. Greek culture reached its most famous flowering in the fifth century B.C.E., at the time when the Roman republic was taking shape and centuries before Rome had its own literature, theater, or monumental architecture. Romans developed a love-hate relationship with Greece, admiring its literature and art but despising its lack of military unity. They adopted many elements from Greek culture—from deities for their national cults to models for their poetry, prose, and architectural styles.

The Etruscans. The Etruscans, a people to the north, also influenced Roman culture. Magnificently colored wall paintings in tombs, portraying funeral banquets and games, reveal the splendor of Etruscan society. In addition to producing their own art, jewelry, and sculpture, the Etruscans also imported luxurious objects from Greece and the Near East. Most of the intact Greek vases known today were found in Etruscan tombs.

The relationship between the Etruscan and Roman cultures remains a controversial topic. Scholars had concluded that the Etruscans completely reshaped Roman culture during a period of supposed political domination in the sixth century B.C.E. New research, however, shows the Romans' independence in developing their own cultural traditions: they borrowed from the Etruscans, as from the Greeks, whatever appealed to them and adapted these borrowings to their own circumstances.

Romans adopted ceremonial features of Etruscan culture, such as the design of magistrates' robes, musical instruments, and religious rituals. The Romans also learned from the Etruscans the practice of divining the will of the gods by examining organs of slaughtered animals. The custom of wives joining husbands at dinner parties may also have come from the Etruscans.

Other features of Roman culture formerly seen as deriving from Etruscan influence were probably part of the ancient Mediterranean's shared cultural environment. The organization of the Roman army, a citizen militia of heavily armed infantry troops fighting in formation, reflected the practice of many other peoples. The alphabet, which the Romans first learned from the Etruscans, was actually Greek; the Greeks had gotten it through their contact with the earlier alphabets of eastern Mediterranean peoples. Foreign trade and urban planning are other features of Etruscan life that Romans are said to have assimilated, but it is too simplistic to assume these cultural developments resulted from a superior culture instructing a less developed one. Rather, at this time in Mediterranean history, similar cultural developments were under way in many places.

The Early Roman Republic, 509–287 B.C.E.

The Roman social elite's hatred of monarchy motivated the creation of the republic. Aristocrats believed that power would inevitably corrupt a sole ruler. This belief was enshrined in the most famous legend about the fall of the monarchy, the rape of Lucretia by the king's son and her subsequent suicide (see Document, "The Rape and Suicide of Lucretia," page 144). Declaring themselves Rome's liberators from tyranny, in 509 B.C.E. Lucretia's relatives and friends from the social elite drove out the king and founded the republic. Thereafter, the Romans prided themselves on having created a political system freer than that of many of their neighbors.

The Struggle of the Orders. The Romans struggled for nearly 250 years to shape a stable government for the republic. Roman social hierarchy split the population into two **orders** — the patricians (a small group of the most aristocratic families) and the plebeians (the rest of the citizens). Bitter power struggles pitted the orders against one another; historians call this turmoil the struggle of the orders. The conflict finally ended in 287 B.C.E. when plebeians won the right to make laws in their own assembly.

Social and economic disputes created the struggle. Patricians constituted a tiny percentage of the population — numbering only about 130 families in all — but their inherited status entitled them to control public religion. Soon after the republic's founding, they used this power to monopolize political office. In this early period, many patricians were much wealthier than most plebeians. Some plebeians, however, were also rich, and they resented the patricians' dominance, especially their ban on intermarriage with plebeians. Patricians enflamed tensions by wearing special red shoes to set themselves apart; later they changed to black shoes adorned with a small metal crescent.

The struggle began when rich plebeians clamored for the right to marry patricians as social equals, while poor plebeians demanded farmland and relief from crushing debts. To pressure the patricians, the plebeians periodically refused military service. This tactic worked because Rome's army depended on plebeian manpower; the patricians were too few to defend Rome by themselves. The patricians therefore agreed to written laws guaranteeing greater equality and social mobility. The earliest Roman law code, the **Twelve Tables**, was enacted between 451 and 449 B.C.E. in response to this tactic. The Tables formalized early Rome's legal customs in simply worded laws such as "If plaintiff calls defendant to court, he shall go," or "If a wind causes a neighbor's tree to be bent and lean over your farm, action may be taken to have that tree removed." These laws prevented the patrician public officials who judged most legal cases from rendering arbitrary decisions. The Twelve Tables became so important a symbol of the commitment to justice for all citizens that children were required to memorize them. The Roman belief in fair laws as the best protection against social unrest helped keep the republic united until the late second century B.C.E.

The Consuls, the Ladder of Offices, and the Senate. Elected officials ran Roman republican government, whose elections took place in and near the forum in the center of the city (Map 5.2). All officials operated as committees, numbering from two to more than a dozen members, in accordance with the Roman value that rule should be shared. The highest officials, two elected each year, were called consuls. Their most important duty was commanding the army. Winning a consulship was the greatest political honor a Roman man could achieve and bestowed high status on his descendants forever.

To be elected consul, a man had to win elections all the way up a **ladder of offices**. First, however, came ten years of military service from about age twenty to thirty. The ladder's first step was getting elected quaestor, a financial administrator. Continuing to climb the ladder, a man sought election as an aedile (supervisors of Rome's streets, sewers, aqueducts, temples, and markets). Few men reached the next step, election as praetor. Praetors performed judicial and military duties. The most successful praetors competed for the consulship. Ex-consuls competed to become one of the censors, elected every five years to conduct censuses of the citizen body and to appoint new

---

orders: The two groups of people in the Roman republic — patricians (aristocratic families) and plebeians (plih BEE uhns) (all other citizens).

Twelve Tables: The first written Roman law code, enacted between 451 and 449 B.C.E.

ladder of offices: The series of Roman elective government offices from quaestor to aedile to praetor to consul.

senators. To be eligible for selection to the Senate, a man had to have been at least a quaestor.

The patricians tried to monopolize the highest offices, but after violent struggle from about 500 to 450 B.C.E., the plebeians forced the patricians to create ten annually elected plebeian officials, called tribunes, who could stop actions that would harm plebeians and their property. The tribunate did not count as a regular ladder office. Tribunes derived their special power from the plebeians' sworn oath to protect them and their power to block officials' actions, prevent laws from being passed, suspend elections, and—most controversially—contradict the Senate's advice. The tribunes' extraordinary power to veto government action often made them catalysts for political strife. By 367 B.C.E., the plebeians had forced passage of a law requiring that at least one consul every year be a plebeian.

In keeping with Roman values, men were supposed to compete for public office to win respect and glory, not money. Only well-off men could run for election because officials earned no salaries. In fact, they were expected to spend their own money lavishly to win popular support by paying for expensive public shows featuring gladiators and wild animals, such as lions imported from Africa. Financing such exhibitions could put a candidate deeply in debt. Once elected, a magistrate had to spend his money building and maintaining roads, aqueducts, and temples.

Early republican officials' only reward was the respect they earned for public service. As Romans conquered more and more overseas territory, however, their desire for money to finance electoral campaigns overcame their adherence to traditional Roman values of faithfulness and honesty. By the second century B.C.E., military officers enriched themselves not only legally by seizing booty from foreign enemies but also illegally by extorting bribes as administrators of newly conquered territories. Over time, acquiring money became more important than public service.

The Senate retained the role it had played under the monarchy: shaping government policy by giving advice to its highest officials. Strictly speaking, the Senate did not make law, but the senators' high social standing gave their opinions the moral force of law. If a consul rejected or ignored the Senate's advice, a political crisis resulted. The Senate thus guided the republic in every area: decisions on war, domestic and foreign policy, state finance, official religion, and all types of legislation. To make their status visible, the senators wore black high-top shoes and robes with a broad purple stripe.

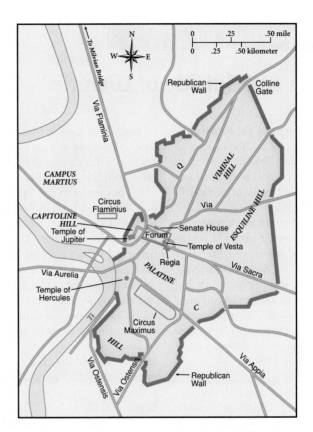

MAP 5.2 The City of Rome during the Republic
Roman tradition said that a king built Rome's first defensive wall in the sixth century B.C.E., but archaeology shows that the first wall encircling the city's center and seven hills on the east bank of the Tiber River belongs to the fourth century B.C.E.; this wall covered a circuit of about seven miles. By the second century B.C.E., the wall had been extended to soar fifty-two feet high and had been fitted with catapults to protect the large gates. Like the open agora surrounded by buildings at the heart of a Greek city, the forum remained Rome's political and social heart. ■ Would modern cities be better off with a large public space at their center?

The Assemblies. Male citizens meeting in three different assemblies decided legislation, government policy, election outcomes, and judgment in certain trials. The Centuriate Assembly, which elected praetors and consuls, was dominated by patricians and richer plebeians. The Plebeian Assembly, which excluded patricians, elected the tribunes. In 287 B.C.E., its resolutions, called **plebiscites**, became legally binding on all Romans. The Tribal Assembly mixed patricians with plebeians and became the republic's most important

plebiscites (PLEH buh sites): Resolutions passed by the Plebeian Assembly; such resolutions gained the force of law in 287 B.C.E.

The Rape and Suicide of Lucretia

This story explaining why the Roman elite expelled the monarchy in 509 B.C.E., thus opening the way to the republic, centered on female virtue and courage, as did other stories about significant political changes in early Roman history. The values ascribed to Lucretia obviously reflect men's wishes for women's behavior, but it would be a mistake to assume that women could not hold the same views. The historian Livy, the source of this document, wrote in the late first century B.C.E., at another crucial point in Roman history—the violent transition from republic to empire—when Romans were deeply concerned with the values of the past as a guide to the present.

The king of Rome's son, Sextus Tarquinius, came to Lucretia's home. She greeted him warmly and asked him to stay. Crazy with desire, he waited until he was sure the household was sleeping. Drawing his sword, he snuck into Lucretia's bedroom and placed the blade against her left breast, whispering, "Quiet, Lucretia; I am Sextus Tarquinius, and I am holding a sword. If you cry out, I'll kill you!" Rudely awakened, the desperate woman realized that no one could help her and that she was close to death. Sextus Tarquinius said he loved her, begging and threatening her in turn, trying everything to wear her down. When she wouldn't give in, even in the face of threats of murder, he added another intimidation. "After I've murdered you, I am going to put the naked corpse of a slave next to your body, and everybody will say that you were killed during a disgraceful adultery." This final threat defeated her, and after raping her he left, having stolen her honor.

Lucretia, overwhelmed by sadness and shame, sent messengers to her husband, Tarquinius Conlatinus, who was away, and her father at Rome, telling them, "Come immediately, with a good friend, because something horrible has happened." Her father arrived with a friend, and her husband came with Lucius Junius Brutus. . . . They found Lucretia in her room, overcome with grief. When she saw them, she started weeping. "How are you?" her husband asked. "Very bad," she replied. "How can anything be fine for a woman who has lost her honor? Traces of another man are in our bed, my husband. My body is defiled, though my heart is still pure; my death will be the proof. But give me your right hand and promise that you will not let the guilty escape. It was Sextus Tarquinius who returned our hospitality with hostility last night. With his sword in his hand, he came to have his fun, to my despair, but it will also be his sorrow—if you are real men." They pledged that they would catch him, and they tried to ease her sadness, saying that the soul did wrong, not the body, and where there were no bad intentions there could be no blame. "It is your responsibility to ensure that he gets what he deserves," she said; "I am blameless, but I will not free myself from punishment. No dishonorable woman shall hold up Lucretia as an example." Then she grabbed a dagger hidden underneath her robe and stabbed herself in the heart. She fell dead, as her husband and father cried out.

Brutus, leaving them to their tears, pulled the blade from Lucretia's wound and held it up drenched in blood, shouting, "By this blood, which was completely pure before the crime of the king's son, I swear before you, O gods, to drive out the king himself, his criminal wife, and all their children, by sword, fire, and everything in my power, and never to allow a king to rule Rome ever again, whether from that family or any other."

Source: Livy, *From the Foundation of the City* 1.57–59. Translation by Thomas R. Martin.

---

assembly for making policy, passing laws, and, until separate courts were created, holding trials.

Assemblies met outdoors and were only for voting, not debates; discussions of a sort took place before assembly meetings when orators gave speeches about the issues. Everyone, including women and noncitizens, could listen to these pre-vote speeches. The crowd expressed its agreement or disagreement with the speeches by applauding or hissing. This process mixed a small measure of democracy with the republic's oligarchic government. A significant restriction on democracy in the assemblies, however, was that voting took place by group, not by individuals. Each assembly was divided into groups of different sizes determined by status and wealth; each group had one vote.

The Judicial System. The republic's judicial system developed overlapping institutions. Early on, the praetors decided many legal cases; especially serious trials could be transferred to the assemblies. A separate jury system arose in the second century B.C.E., and senators repeatedly clashed with other upper-class Romans over whether these juries should consist exclusively of senators.

As in Greece, Rome had no state-paid prosecutors or defenders. Accusers and accused had to speak for themselves in court or have friends speak for them. Priests dominated in legal knowledge until the third century B.C.E., when senators with legal expertise began to offer legal advice. Called jurists, they operated as private citizens, not as officials. Developed over centuries and gradually incorporating laws from other peoples, Roman law, especially on civil matters, became the basis for European legal codes still in use today.

The republic's complex system of political and judicial institutions evolved in response to conflicts over power. Laws could emerge from different assemblies, and legal cases could be decided by various institutions. Rome had no single highest court, such as the U.S. Supreme Court, to give final verdicts. The republic's stability therefore depended on maintaining the mos maiorum. Because they defined this tradition, the most socially prominent and richest Romans dominated politics and the courts.

> **REVIEW:** How and why did the Roman republic develop its complicated political and judicial systems?

Roman Imperialism and Its Consequences

Expansion through war made conquest and military service central to Romans' lives; it also caused a huge number of citizens to migrate and settle in new communities that the government established as anchors in newly conquered areas. From the fifth to the third century B.C.E., the Romans fought war after war in Italy until Rome became the most powerful state on the peninsula. In the third and second centuries B.C.E., Romans warred far from home in every direction, above all against Carthage to the south. Their success in these campaigns made Rome the premier power in the Mediterranean by the first century B.C.E.

Fear of attacks and the desire for wealth propelled Roman imperialism. The senators' worries about national security made them advise preemptive attacks against potential enemies, while everyone longed to capture plunder and new farmland. Poorer soldiers hoped to pull their families out of poverty; the elite, who commanded the armies, wanted to strengthen their campaigns for office by acquiring glory and greater wealth.

The wars in Italy and abroad transformed Roman life. The contact with others that conquest brought stimulated the first Roman written works of history and poetry; astonishingly, Rome had no literature until around 240 B.C.E. War's harshness also influenced Roman art, especially portraiture. On the social side, endless military service away from home created stresses on small farmers and undermined the stability of Roman society; so, too,

did the relocation of so many citizens and the importation of countless war captives to work as slaves on rich people's estates. Rome's great conquests thus turned out to be a two-edged sword: they brought expansion and wealth, but their unexpected social and political consequences disrupted traditional values and the community's stability.

Expansion in Italy, 500–220 B.C.E.

After defeating their Latin neighbors in the 490s B.C.E., the Romans spent the next hundred years warring with the nearby Etruscan town of Veii. Their 396 B.C.E. victory doubled Roman territory. By the fourth century B.C.E., the Roman infantry legion of five thousand men had surpassed the Greek and Macedonian phalanx as an effective fighting force because its soldiers were trained to throw javelins from behind their long shields and then rush in to finish off the enemy with swords. A devastating sack of Rome in 387 B.C.E. by marauding Gauls (Celts) from beyond the Alps proved only a temporary setback, though it made Romans forever fearful of foreign invasion. By around 220 B.C.E., Rome controlled all of Italy south of the Po River.

Rome and Central Italy, Fifth Century B.C.E.

The Romans combined brutality with diplomacy to control conquered people and territory. Sometimes they enslaved the defeated or forced them to surrender large parcels of land. Other times they struck generous peace terms with former enemies but required them to render military aid against other foes, for which they received a share of the booty, chiefly slaves and land. In this way, the Romans co-opted opponents by making them partners in the spoils of conquest.

To buttress homeland security, the Romans planted numerous colonies of relocated citizens and constructed roads up and down the peninsula to allow troops to march faster. By connecting Italy's diverse peoples, these roads promoted a unified culture dominated by Rome. Latin became the com-

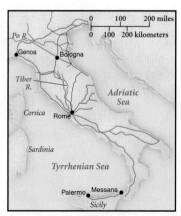

Roman Roads, 110 B.C.E.

mon language, although local tongues lived on, especially Greek in the south.

The wealth captured in the first two centuries of expansion attracted hordes of people to the capital because it financed new aqueducts to provide fresh, running water—a treasure in the ancient world—and a massive building program that employed the poor. By 300 B.C.E., about 150,000 people lived within Rome's walls (see Map 5.2). Outside the city, around 750,000 free Roman citizens inhabited various parts of Italy on land taken from local peoples. Much conquered territory was declared public land, open to any Roman for grazing cattle.

Rich plebeians and patricians cooperated to exploit the expanding Roman territories; the old distinction between the orders had become largely a technicality. This merged elite derived its wealth mainly from agricultural land and plunder acquired during military service. Since Rome levied no regular income or inheritance taxes, families could pass down their wealth from generation to generation.

Wars with Carthage and in the East, 264–121 B.C.E.

Rome's leaders, remembering the Gauls' attack on the city in 387 B.C.E., feared foreign invasions and also saw imperialism as the route to riches. The republic therefore fought its three most famous wars against the wealthy city of Carthage in North Africa. In the third century B.C.E., Carthage, also governed as a republic, controlled a powerful empire emphasizing seaborne trade. Geography meant that an expansionist Rome would sooner or later come into conflict with Carthage. To Romans, Carthage seemed both a dangerous rival and a fine prize because it had grown so prosperous from agriculture and international commerce. Horror at the Carthaginians' tradition of incinerating infants to placate their gods in times of trouble also fed Roman hostility.

First Wars Abroad. Rome's three wars with Carthage are called the Punic Wars, and the first one (264–241 B.C.E.) erupted over Sicily, where

Aqueduct at Nîmes in France

The Romans excelled at building complex delivery systems of tunnels, channels, bridges, and fountains to transport fresh water from far away. Compare the Greek city fountain shown in the vase painting on page 105. One of the best-preserved sections of a major aqueduct is the so-called Pont-du-Gard near Nîmes (ancient Nemausus) in France, erected in the late first century B.C.E. to serve the flourishing town there. Built of stones fitted together without clamps or mortar, the span soars 160 feet high and 875 feet long, carrying water along its topmost level from thirty-five miles away in a channel constructed to fall only one foot in height for every three thousand feet in length so that the flow would remain steady but gentle. What sort of social and political organization would be necessary to construct such a system? *(Hubertus Kanus/Photo Researchers, Inc.)*

■ **For more help analyzing this image,** see the visual activity for this chapter in the Online Study Guide at **bedfordstmartins.com/hunt**.

Carthage wanted to preserve its trading settlements and Rome wanted to prevent Carthaginian troops from being close to their territory. This long conflict revealed why the Romans won wars: the large Italian population provided deep manpower reserves, and the Roman government was prepared to sacrifice as many troops, spend as much money, and fight as long as it took to prevail. Previously unskilled at naval warfare, the Romans expended vast sums to build warships to combat Carthage's experienced navy; they lost more than five hundred ships and 250,000 men while learning how to win at sea. (See "Taking Measure," page 148.)

The Romans' victory in the First Punic War made them masters of Sicily, where they set up their first province (a foreign territory ruled and taxed by Roman officials). This innovation proved so profitable that they soon seized the islands of Sardinia and Corsica from the Carthaginians to create another province. These first successful foreign conquests whetted the Romans' appetite for more (Map 5.3). Fearing a renewal of Carthage's power, the Romans cemented alliances with local peoples in Spain, where the Carthaginians were expanding from their southern trading posts.

A Roman ultimatum forbidding further expansion convinced the Carthaginians that another war was inevitable, so they decided to strike back. In the Second Punic War (218–201 B.C.E.), the daring Carthaginian general Hannibal astonished the Romans by marching troops and war elephants over the Alps into Italy. Slaughtering more than thirty thousand at Cannae in 216 B.C.E. in the bloodiest Roman loss ever, Hannibal tried to convince Rome's Italian allies to desert, but most refused to rebel. Hannibal's alliance in 215 B.C.E. with the king of Macedonia forced the Romans to fight on a second front in Greece. Still, they refused to crack despite Hannibal's ravaging of Italy from 218

MAP 5.3 Roman Expansion, 500–44 B.C.E.
During its first two centuries, the Roman republic used war and diplomacy to extend its power north and south in the Italian peninsula. In the third and second centuries B.C.E., conflict with Carthage in the south and west and the Hellenistic kingdoms in the east extended Roman power outside Italy and led to the creation of provinces from Spain to Greece. The first century B.C.E. saw the conquest of Syria by Pompey and of Gaul by Julius Caesar (d. 44 B.C.E.).

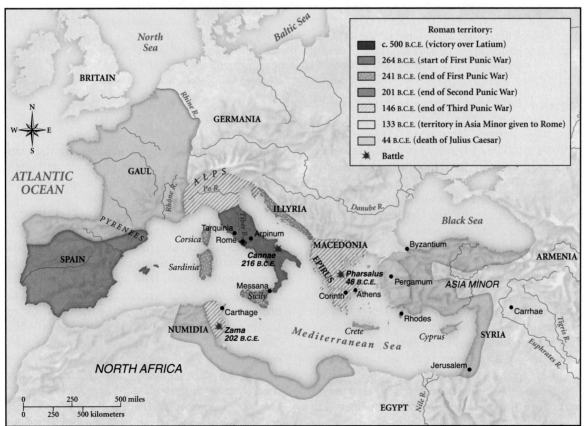

TAKING MEASURE

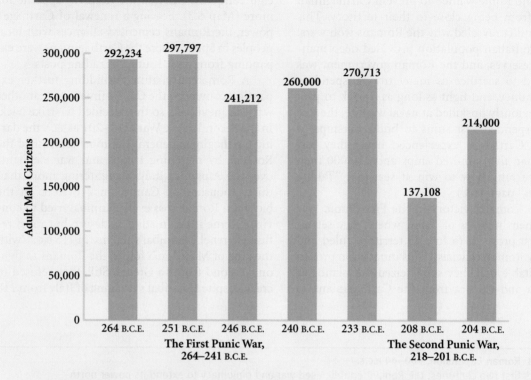

Census Records during the First and Second Punic Wars
Livy (59 B.C.E.–17 C.E.) and Jerome (c. 347–420 C.E.) provide these numbers from Rome's censuses, which counted only adult male citizens (the men eligible for Rome's regular army), conducted during and between the first two wars against Carthage. The drop in the total for 246 B.C.E., compared with the total for 264 B.C.E., reflects losses in the First Punic War. The low total for 208 B.C.E. reflects both losses in battle and defections of citizenship-holding communities. Since the census did not include the Italian allies fighting on Rome's side, the census numbers understate the wars' total casualties; scholars estimate that they took the lives of nearly a third of Italy's adult male population, which would have meant perhaps a quarter of a million soldiers killed. *(Tenney Frank, An Economic Survey of Ancient Rome, vol. I (New York: Farrar, Straus and Giroux, 1959), p. 56.)*

to 203 B.C.E. Then the Romans turned the tables: invading the Carthaginians' homeland, the Roman army prevailed at the battle of Zama in 202 B.C.E. The Senate imposed a punishing settlement on the enemy in 201 B.C.E., forcing Carthage to scuttle its navy, pay huge war indemnities, and hand over its lucrative holdings in Spain, which Rome made into provinces prosperous from their mines.

Dominance in the Mediterranean. The Third Punic War (149–146 B.C.E.) began when the Carthaginians, who had revived financially, retaliated against the aggression of the king of Numidia, a Roman ally. After winning the war, the Romans heeded the crusty senator Cato's repeated opinion, "Carthage must be destroyed!" They razed the city and converted its territory into a province. This disaster did not obliterate Carthaginian culture,

however, and under the Roman Empire this part of North Africa flourished economically and intellectually, creating a synthesis of Roman and Carthaginian traditions.

The Punic War victories extended Roman power beyond Spain and North Africa to Macedonia, Greece, and western Asia Minor. Hannibal's alliance with the king of Macedonia had brought Roman troops east of Italy for the first time. After thrashing the Macedonian king for revenge and to prevent any threat of his invading Italy, the Roman commander proclaimed the "freedom of the Greeks" in 196 B.C.E. to show respect for Greece's glorious past. The Greek cities and federal leagues understood the proclamation to mean that they could behave as they liked. They misunderstood. The Romans expected them to behave as clients and follow their new patrons' advice, while the

Greeks thought, as "friends" of Rome, that they were truly free.

The Romans repeatedly intervened to make the kingdom of Macedonia and the Greeks observe their obligations as clients; the Senate in 146 B.C.E. ordered Corinth destroyed for asserting its independence and converted Macedonia and Greece into a province. In 133 B.C.E., the Attalid king increased Roman power with a stupendous gift: in his will he bequeathed his Asia Minor kingdom to Rome. In 121 B.C.E., the Romans made the lower part of Gaul across the Alps (modern France) into a province. By the late first century B.C.E., then, Rome governed and profited from two-thirds of the Mediterranean region; only the easternmost Mediterranean lay outside its control (see Map 5.3).

Greek Influence on Roman Literature and the Arts

Roman imperialism generated extensive cross-cultural contact with Greece. Although Romans looked down on Greeks for their military weakness, Roman authors and artists looked to Greek models. About 200 B.C.E., the first Roman historian used Greek to write his narrative of Rome's foundation and the wars with Carthage. The earliest Latin poetry was a translation of Homer's *Odyssey* by a Greek ex-slave, composed sometime after the First Punic War.

Roman literature combined the foreign and the familiar. Many famous early Latin authors were not native Romans, but came from different regions of Italy, Sicily, and even North Africa. All found inspiration in Greek literature. Roman comedies, for example, took their plots and stock characters from Hellenistic comedy, which featured jokes about family life and stereotyped personalities, such as the braggart warrior and the obsessed lover. (See Actors in a Comedy, page 150.)

Some Romans distrusted the effect of Greek culture on their own. In the mid-second century B.C.E., Cato, although he studied Greek himself, thundered against the influence of the "effete" Greeks on the "sturdy" Romans. His history of Rome, *The Origins*, and his instructions on running a large farm, *On Agriculture*, established Latin prose. Cato predicted that if the Romans ever adopted Greek values, they would lose their power. In truth, despite its debt to Greek literature, early Latin literature reflected traditional Roman values. For example, the path-breaking Latin epic *Annals*, a poetic version of Roman history by the poet Ennius, shows the influence of Greek epic, but it praises ancestral Roman traditions, as in this famous line: "On the ways and the men of old rests the Roman commonwealth."

Later Roman writers also took inspiration from Greek literature in both content and style. The first-century B.C.E. poet Lucretius wrote *On the Nature of Things* to persuade people not to fear death, a terror that only inflamed "the running sores of life." His ideas reflected Greek philosophy's "atomic theory," which said that matter was composed of tiny, invisible particles. Dying, the poem taught, simply meant the dissolution of the union of atoms, which had come together temporarily to make up a person's body. There could be no eternal punishment or pain after death, indeed no existence at all, because a person's soul, itself made up of atoms, perished along with the body.

COMPARISON OF ANCIENT GREEK AND ROMAN DEVELOPMENTS, c. 750 B.C.E.–146 B.C.E.		
	GREECE	**ROME**
750 B.C.E.	Polis begins to develop	
750–700 B.C.E.	First Greek poetry (Homer and Hesiod)	
753 B.C.E.		Traditional date for the founding of Rome
509 B.C.E.		Overthrow of monarchy and establishment of the republic
508–500 B.C.E.	Cleisthenes' reforms to strengthen Athenian democracy	
500–450 B.C.E.		Struggle to establish office of tribune to protect the people
461 B.C.E.	Ephialtes' reforms to democratize Athens's courts	
451–449 B.C.E.		Rome's first law code established (Twelve Tables)
420s B.C.E.	The first Greek history (Herodotus)	
200 B.C.E.		First Roman history in Greek
240–210 B.C.E.		First poetry in Latin (translation of Homer's *Odyssey*)
168–149 B.C.E.		First Roman history in Latin (Cato)
146 B.C.E.	Rome makes Greece a province	

Actors in a Comedy
This sculpture from the first century C.E. shows actors portraying characters in one of the several kinds of comedy popular during the Roman republic. In this variety, which derived from Hellenistic comedy, the actors wore exaggerated masks designating stock personality types and acted broad, slapstick comedy. The plots ranged from burlesques of famous myths to stereotypes of family problems. Here, on the right, a son returns home after a night of binge drinking, leaning on his slave and accompanied by a hired female musician. On the left, his enraged father is being restrained by a friend from beating his drunken son with a cane. *(Scala/Art Resource, NY.)*

Hellenistic Greek authors inspired Catullus in the first century B.C.E. to write witty poems ridiculing prominent politicians for their sexual behavior (see Document 2 in "Contrasting Views," page 156) and lamenting his own disastrous love life. His most famous love poems revealed his obsession with a married woman named Lesbia, whom he begged to think only of immediate pleasures:

> Let us live, my Lesbia, and love; the gossip of stern old men is not worth a cent. Suns can set and rise again; we, when once our brief light has set, must sleep one neverending night. Give me a thousand kisses, then a hundred, then a thousand more.

The orator **Cicero** wrote speeches, letters, and treatises on political science, philosophy, ethics, and theology; he adapted Greek philosophy to Roman life and infused his writings with an appreciation of each person's uniqueness. His doctrine of *humanitas* ("humaneness, the quality of human-

---

Cicero (SIH suh roh): Rome's most famous orator and author of the doctrine of *humanitas*.

humanitas: The Roman orator Cicero's ideal of "humaneness," meaning generous and honest treatment of others based on natural law.

ity") expressed an ideal for human life based on generous and honest treatment of others and a commitment to morality based on natural law (the inherent rights of all people, independent of the differing laws and customs of different societies). The spirit of humanitas that Cicero passed on to later Western civilization was one of the ancient world's most attractive ideals.

Greece also influenced Rome's art and architecture, from the style of sculpture and painting to the design of public buildings. Romans adapted Greek models to their own purposes, as portrait sculpture reveals. Hellenistic sculptors had pioneered a realistic style showing the ravages of age and infirmity on the human body. They portrayed only stereotypes, however, such as the "old man" or the "drunken woman," not specific people. Individual portrait sculpture presented actual individuals in the best possible light, much like an airbrushed photograph today.

Roman artists applied Greek realism to male portraiture, as contemporary Etruscan sculptors also did. They sculpted men without hiding their unflattering features: long noses, receding chins, deep wrinkles, bald heads, careworn looks. Portraits of women, by contrast, were more idealized, probably representing the traditional vision of the bliss of family life (see the image of the sculpted family tomb on page 136). Because the men depicted in the portraits (or their families) paid for the busts, they must have wanted their faces sculpted realistically—showing the toll of age and effort—to emphasize how hard they had worked to serve the republic.

Stresses on Republican Society

The wars of the third and second centuries B.C.E. proved disastrous for small farmers, confronting the republic with grave social and economic difficulties. The long deployments of troops abroad disrupted Rome's agricultural system, the economy's foundation. Before this time, Roman warfare had followed a pattern of short campaigns timed not to interfere with farmers' work. Now, however, a farmer absent during a protracted war had two unhappy choices: rely on a hired hand or slave to manage his crops and animals, or have his wife work in the fields in addition to her usual domestic tasks.

The story of the consul Regulus, who won a great victory in Africa in 256 B.C.E., revealed the problems prolonged absence caused. When the man who managed Regulus's farm died while the consul was away fighting, a worker stole all the farm's tools and livestock. Regulus begged the Senate to send a replacement so that he could return to save his wife and children from starving. The senators sent help to preserve Regulus's family and property because they wanted to keep him in the field.

The Poor. Ordinary soldiers could expect no such special aid, and economic troubles hit their families particularly hard when, in the second century B.C.E., for reasons that remain unclear, there was not enough farmland to support the population. Scholars have usually concluded that the rich had deprived the poor of land, but recent research suggests that the problem stemmed from an astonishing increase in the number of young people. Not all regions of Italy suffered as severely as others, and some impoverished farmers and their families managed to survive by working as agricultural laborers for others. Still, the number of poor people with no way to make a living created a social crisis by the late second century B.C.E. Many homeless people relocated to Rome, where the men begged for work as day laborers and women sought piecework making cloth but often had to become prostitutes to survive.

This flood of desperate people increased the poverty-level population of Rome, and the landless poor became an explosive swing element in Roman politics. They backed any politician who promised to address their need for food, and the government had to feed them to avert riots. Like Athens in the fifth century B.C.E., Rome by the late second century B.C.E. needed to import grain to feed its swollen urban population. The poor's demand for low-priced (and eventually free) food distributed at state expense became one of the most divisive issues in late republican politics.

The Rich. While the landless poor struggled, imperialism brought Rome's elite rich political and financial rewards. The need for commanders to lead military campaigns abroad created opportunities for successful generals to enrich their families. The elite enhanced their reputa-

tions by using their gains to finance public works that benefited the general population. Building new temples, for example, was thought to increase everyone's security because the Romans believed it pleased their gods to have many shrines. In 146 B.C.E., a victorious general paid for Rome's first marble temple, finally bringing this Greek style to the capital city.

The economic distress of small farmers benefited rich landowners because they could buy bankrupt farms to create large estates. They further increased their holdings by illegally occupying public land carved out of the territory seized from defeated enemies. The rich worked their huge farms, called *latifundia*, with free laborers as well as slaves, a ready supply of which were available from the huge numbers taken captive in the same wars that displaced so many farmers. Thus, the victories won by free but poor Roman citizens cre-

Bedroom in a Rich Roman House
The bedroom from about 40 B.C.E. was in the house of a rich Roman family near Naples; it was buried—and preserved—by the eruption of the volcano Vesuvius in 79 C.E. The bright paintings showed a dazzling variety of outdoor scenes and architecture. The mosaic stone floor helped create a sensation of coolness in the summer. *(Image copyright © The Metropolitan Museum of Art/Art Resource, NY.)*

ated a slave workforce with which they could not compete. The growing size of the slave crews working on latifundia was a mixed blessing for their wealthy owners. Although they did not have to pay these laborers, the presence of so many slave workers in one place led to periodic revolts that required military intervention.

The elite profited from Rome's expansion in that they filled the governing offices in the new provinces and could get enormously rich by ruling corruptly. Since provincial officials ruled by martial law, no one in the provinces could curb a greedy governor's appetite for graft, extortion, and plunder. Some governors ruled honestly, but others used their power to squeeze the provincials. Often such offenders faced no punishment because their colleagues in the Senate excused one another's crimes.

The new opportunities for rich living strained the traditional values of moderation and frugality. Previously, a man like Manius Curius (d. 270 B.C.E.) became legendary for his life's simplicity: despite glorious military victories, he boiled turnips for his meals in a humble hut. Now, in the second century B.C.E., the elite acquired showy luxuries, such as large country villas for entertaining friends and clients. Money had become more valuable to them than the ancestral values of the republic.

> **REVIEW:** What advantages and disadvantages did Rome's victories over foreign peoples create for both rich and poor Romans?

Upheaval in the Late Republic

In the late second and first centuries B.C.E., members of the Roman elite set the republic on the road to civil war. Senators introduced violence to politics by murdering the tribunes Tiberius and Gaius Gracchus when the brothers pushed for reforms to help the poor by giving them land. When a would-be member of the elite, Gaius Marius, opened military service to the poor to boost his personal status, his creation of "client armies" undermined faithfulness to the general good of the community. When the people's unwillingness to share citizenship with Italian allies sparked a war in Roman territory and then the clashing ambitions of the "great men" Sulla, Pompey, and Julius Caesar burst into civil war, the republic fractured, never to recover.

The Gracchus Brothers and Factional Politics, 133–121 B.C.E.

Tiberius and Gaius Gracchus based their political careers on pressing the rich to make concessions to strengthen the state. They came from the cream of Roman society: their grandfather had defeated Hannibal, and their mother was the Cornelia whom the king of Egypt had courted. Their policies supporting the poor angered many of their fellow elite. Tiberius explained the tragic circumstances that motivated them politically:

> The wild beasts that roam over Italy have their dens. . . . But the men who fight and die for Italy enjoy nothing but the air and light; without house or home they wander about with their wives and children. . . . They fight and die to protect the wealth and luxury of others; they are styled masters of the world, and have not a clod of earth they call their own.

When Tiberius won election as a tribune in 133 B.C.E., his opponents blocked his attempts at reform. He therefore took the radical step of disregarding the Senate's advice by having the Plebeian Assembly pass reform laws to redistribute public land to landless Romans. He further broke with tradition by circumventing the Senate to finance his agrarian reform, having the people pass a law to use the Attalid king's bequest of his kingdom to equip new farms on the redistributed land.

Tiberius then announced he would run for re-election as tribune for the following year, violating the prohibition against consecutive terms. His opponents had had enough: Tiberius's cousin, an ex-consul, led a band of senators and their clients in a sudden attack on him, shouting, "Save the republic." Pulling up their togas over their left arms so they would not trip in a fight, they clubbed the tribune to death, along with many of his followers.

Gaius, whom the people elected tribune for 123 B.C.E. and, contrary to tradition, again for the next year, also pushed measures that outraged the elite: more agrarian reform, subsidized prices for grain, public works projects to employ the poor, and colonies abroad with farms for the landless. His most revolutionary measures proposed Roman citizenship for many Italians and new courts to try senators accused of corruption as provincial governors. The new juries would be manned not by senators but by **equites** ("equestrians" or "knights"). These were elite landowners who, in the earliest republic, had been men rich enough to

---

equites (EHK wih tehs): Wealthy Roman businessmen who chose not to pursue a government career.

provide horses for cavalry service but were now wealthy businessmen, whose careers in commerce instead of government made their interests different from the senators'. Because they did not serve in the Senate, the equites could convict criminal senators free of peer pressure. Gaius's proposal marked the equites' emergence as a political force in Roman politics, to the senators' dismay.

When in 121 B.C.E. the senators blocked Gaius's plans, he assembled an armed group to threaten them. They responded by telling the consuls "to take all measures necessary to defend the republic," meaning the use of force. To escape being murdered, Gaius had one of his slaves cut his throat; the senators then killed hundreds of his supporters and their servants.

The violence provoked by the Gracchus brothers introduced factions (strongly aggressive interest groups) into Roman politics. From that point on, members of the elite identified themselves as either supporters of the people, the ***populares*** faction, or supporters of "the best," the ***optimates*** faction. Some chose a faction from genuine allegiance to its policies; others supported whichever side better promoted their own political advancement. The elite's splintering into bitterly hostile factions remained a source of violent conflict until the end of the republic.

Marius and the Origin of Client Armies, 107–100 B.C.E.

The republic needed imaginative commanders to combat slave revolts and foreign invasions in the late second and early first centuries B.C.E. A new kind of leader arose to meet this need: the "new man," an upper-class man without a consul among his ancestors, who relied on sheer ability and often political violence to force his way to fame, fortune, and—his ultimate goal—the consulship.

Gaius Marius (c. 157–86 B.C.E.), who came from the equites class, set the pattern for this new kind of leader. Ordinarily, a man of Marius's status had no chance to crack the ranks of Rome's ruling oligarchy. Capitalizing on his brilliant military record as a junior officer and on the people's anger at the current war leadership, Marius won election as a consul for 107 B.C.E. In Roman terms

this election made him a "new man"—that is, the first man in his family's history to become consul. Marius's continuing success as a commander, first in North Africa and next against German tribes who attacked southern France and then Italy, led the people to elect him consul six times, breaking all tradition.

For his victories, the Senate voted Marius a triumph, Rome's ultimate military honor. In the ceremony, as he rode in a chariot through the streets of Rome, huge crowds cheered him, while his army pricked him with off-color jokes, to ward off the evil eye at this moment of supreme glory. For a former small-town member of the equites class like Marius, this honor was a supreme social coup. Yet, despite his triumph, the optimates never accepted Marius because they viewed him as an upstart. His support came from the common people, whom he had won over with his reform of entrance requirements for the army. Previously, only men with property could enroll as soldiers. Marius opened the ranks to **proletarians**, men who had no property and could not afford weapons on their own. For them, serving in the army meant an opportunity to better their lot by acquiring booty and a grant of land. (See Document, "Polybius on Roman Military Discipline," page 154.)

Marius's reform changed Roman history by creating armies more loyal to their commander than to the republic. Proletarian troops felt immense goodwill toward a commander who led them to victory and then divided the spoils with them generously. The crowds of poor Roman soldiers thus began to behave like an army of clients following their commander as patron. In keeping with the patron-client system, they supported his personal ambitions. Marius was the first to promote his own career in this way. He lost his political importance after 100 B.C.E. when, no longer consul, he foolishly tried to win favor with the optimates. Commanders after Marius used client armies to advance their political careers more ruthlessly than he had, thereby accelerating the republic's disintegration.

Sulla and Civil War, 91–78 B.C.E.

One such commander, Lucius Cornelius Sulla (c. 138–78 B.C.E.), took advantage of uprisings in Italy and Asia Minor in the early first century B.C.E. to use his client army to seize Rome's highest offices and compel the Senate to support his poli-

---

populares (poh poo LAH rehs): The Roman political faction supporting the common people; established during the late republic.

optimates (op tee MAH tehs): The Roman political faction supporting the "best," or highest, social class; established during the late republic.

---

proletarians: In the Roman republic, the mass of people so poor they owned no property.

DOCUMENT

Polybius on Roman Military Discipline

Polybius, a Greek commander who spent years on campaign with Roman armies in the second century B.C.E., describes the ideal centurion (an experienced soldier appointed to discipline the troop) and the importance of harsh punishments and the fear of disgrace for maintaining military discipline.

The Romans want centurions not so much to be bold and eager to take risks but rather to be capable of leadership and steady and solid in character. Nor do they want them to initiate attacks and precipitate battle. They want men who will hold their position and stay in place even when they are losing the battle and will die to hold their ground. . . . Soldiers [convicted of neglecting sentry duty] who manage to live [after being beaten or stoned as punishment] don't thereby secure their safety. How could they? For they are not permitted to return to their homeland, and none of their relatives would dare to accept such a man into their households. For this reason men who have once fallen into this misfortune are completely ruined. . . . Even when clearly at risk of being wiped out by enor-mously superior enemy forces, troops in tactical reserve units are not willing to desert their places in the battle line, for fear of the punishment that would be inflicted by their own side. Some men who have lost a shield or sword or another part of their arms in battle heedlessly throw themselves against the enemy, hoping either to recover what they lost, or to escape the inevitable disgrace and the insults of their relatives by suffering [injury or death].

Source: Polybius, *Histories*, Book 6.24, 37. Translation by Thomas R. Martin.

cies. His career revealed the dirty secret of politics in the late republic: traditional values no longer restrained commanders who prized their own advancement and the enrichment of their troops above peace and the good of the community.

The Social War.   The uprisings in Italy occurred because many of Rome's Italian allies lacked Roman citizenship and therefore had no vote in decisions concerning their own interests. They became increasingly unhappy as wealth from conquests piled up in the late republic; their upper classes wanted a greater share of the prosperity that war had brought to the citizen elite. Romans rejected the allies' demand for citizenship, from fear that sharing such status would lessen their own privileges.

The Italians' discontent erupted in 91–87 B.C.E. in the Social War (so named because the Latin word for "ally" is *socius*). Forming a confederacy to fight Rome, the allies demonstrated their commitment by the number of their casualties — 300,000 dead. Although Rome's army prevailed, the rebels won the political war: the Romans granted citizenship and the vote to all freeborn peoples in Italy south of the Po River. The Social War's bloodshed therefore reestablished Rome's tradition of strengthening the state by granting cit-izenship to outsiders. The war's other significant outcome was that Sulla's successful generalship won him election as consul for 88 B.C.E.

Plunder Abroad and Violence at Home.   Sulla gained supreme power by taking advantage of events in Asia Minor in 88 B.C.E., when Mithridates VI (120–63 B.C.E.), king of Pontus on the Black Sea's southern coast, instigated a rebellion against Roman control. The peoples of Asia Minor hated Rome's tax collectors, who tried to make provincials pay much more than was required. Denouncing the Romans as "the common enemies of all mankind," Mithridates persuaded the locals to kill all the Italians there — tens of thousands of them — in a single day.

In retaliation for this treachery, the Senate advised a military expedition; victory would mean unimaginable booty from Asia Minor's wealthy cities. Born to a patrician family that had lost much of its status and all of its money, Sulla craved the command. When the Senate gave it to him, his jealous rival Marius, now an old man, immediately plotted to have it transferred to himself by plebiscite. Outraged, Sulla marched his client army against Rome itself. All his officers except one deserted him in horror at this unthinkable outrage, but his common soldiers followed him to a man. Neither they

The Kingdom of Mithridates VI, 88 B.C.E.

nor their commander shrank from starting a civil war. After capturing Rome, Sulla killed or exiled his opponents and let his men rampage through the city. He then led them off to Asia Minor, ignoring a summons to stand trial and sacking Athens on the way. In Sulla's absence, Marius embarked on his own reign of terror in Rome to try to regain his former preeminence. In 83 B.C.E., Sulla returned victorious, having allowed his soldiers to plunder Asia Minor. Civil war recommenced for two years until Sulla crushed his enemies at home.

Sulla then exterminated everyone who had opposed him. To speed the process, he devised a horrific procedure called proscription—posting a list of people supposedly traitors so that anyone could hunt them down and execute them. Because proscribed men's property was confiscated, the victors fraudulently added to the list anyone's name whose wealth they coveted. The terrorized Senate appointed Sulla dictator—an emergency office supposed to be held only temporarily—without any limitation of term. As dictator, he reorganized the government to favor the optimates—his social class—by making senators the only ones allowed to judge cases against their colleagues and forbidding tribunes to sponsor legislation or hold any other office after their term.

The Effects of Sulla's Career.

Sulla died before he could permanently remake republican government, but his murderous career revealed the strengths and weaknesses of Roman values. First, success in war had changed from defending the community to accumulating plunder for common soldiers as well as commanders. Second, the patron-client system led proletarian soldiers to feel stronger ties of obligation to their generals than to the republic.

Finally, the traditional desire for status worked both for and against political stability. When that value motivated men to seek office to promote the community's welfare—the traditional ideal of a public career—it exerted a powerful force for social unity and prosperity. But pushed to its extreme, as in the case of Sulla, the drive for prestige and wealth could overshadow all considerations of public service and weaken the republic.

The Republic's Downfall, 83–44 B.C.E.

Powerful generals after Sulla took him as their model: while professing allegiance to the state, they ruthlessly pursued their own advancement. Two Roman aristocrats' competition for power and money flared into a civil war that ruined the re-

public and opened the way for the return of monarchy. Those competitors were Gnaeus Pompey and Julius Caesar. (See "Contrasting Views," page 156.)

Pompey's Irregular Career.

Pompey (106–48 B.C.E.) was a better general than a politician. In his early twenties he won victories supporting Sulla. In 71 B.C.E. Pompey won the mop-up battles defeating a massive slave rebellion led by a fugitive gladiator named Spartacus, stealing the glory from the real victor, Marcus Licinius Crassus. (Spartacus had terrorized southern Italy for two years and defeated consuls with his army of 100,000 escaped slaves.) Pompey demanded the consulship for 70 B.C.E., long before he had reached the legal age of forty-two or been elected to any other office. Three years later, he received a command with unlimited powers to exterminate the pirates then infesting the Mediterranean, a task he accomplished in a matter of months. This success made him wildly popular with many groups: the urban poor, who depended on a steady flow of imported grain; merchants, who depended on safe sea lanes; and coastal communities, which were vulnerable to pirates' raids. In 66 B.C.E., he defeated Mithridates, who was still stirring up trouble in Asia Minor. By annexing Syria as a province in 64 B.C.E., Pompey ended the Seleucid kingdom and extended Rome's power to the Mediterranean's eastern coast.

People compared Pompey to Alexander the Great and nicknamed him Magnus ("the Great"). His actions show the degree to which Roman foreign policy had become the personal business of "great men." He ignored the tradition of commanders consulting the Senate about conquering and administering

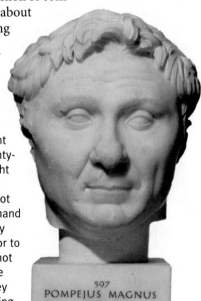

Bust of Pompey
Pompey (106–48 B.C.E.) became Julius Caesar's main political opponent, until Caesar defeated him in the civil war that fractured the republic. Pompey was a brilliant general, even when young. At twenty-three he raised a client army to fight on Sulla's side. So frightening was Pompey's power that Sulla could not refuse the youth's astonishing demand for a triumph—the ultimate military honor. Awarding the supreme honor to such a young man, who had held not a single public office, shattered the republic's traditions. But as Pompey told Sulla, "People worship the rising, not the setting, sun."
(© Ny Carslberg Glyptotek, Copenhagen, Denmark/The Bridgeman Art Library.)

What Was Julius Caesar Like?

Julius Caesar provoked strong reactions among people: some loved him, some hated him, some ridiculed him (Document 2), and some changed their minds (Document 3)—but only fools failed to recognize his extraordinary energy and will (Document 1). These excerpts, including one in his own words (Document 4), offer sample assessments of what this most famous Roman was like. The biographer Suetonius presented a balanced view of Caesar's strengths and faults (Document 5).

1. Caesar and the Pirates

Plutarch also wrote a biography of Caesar, which illustrated Caesar's personality with this story of the eighteen-year-old being captured by pirates, after he refused Sulla's politically motivated order to divorce his wife and fled Rome to escape being murdered by the dictator.

[To escape Sulla], Caesar sailed to King Nicomedes in Bithynia (in Asia Minor). On his voyage home, pirates from Cilicia captured him and held him on an island. When they demanded twenty talents [a huge sum] for his ransom, he laughed at them for not knowing who he was, and spontaneously promised to give them fifty talents instead. Next, after he had dispatched friends to various cities to gather the money, he had only one friend and two attendants left while a captive of the most murderous men in the world. Nevertheless, he felt so superior to them that whenever he wanted to sleep, he would order them to be quiet.

For thirty-eight days, as if the pirates were not his kidnappers but rather his bodyguards, he participated in their games and exercises with a carefree spirit. He also composed poems and speeches that he read aloud to them, and anyone who failed to admire his work he would call an illiterate barbarian to his face, and often with a laugh threatened to string them all up. The pirates loved this, and attributed his free speech to simplemindedness and youthful spirit.

After Caesar had paid the ransom and was released, he immediately manned ships and put to sea against the pirates. He caught them still anchored, and captured most of them. He took their loot as his booty and threw the men into prison, telling the Roman provincial governor that it was his job to punish them. But since the governor had his eyes on the pirates' rich loot and kept saying that he would consider their case when he had time, Caesar took the pirates out of prison and crucified them all, just as he had often warned them on the island that he was going to do, when they thought he was joking.

Source: Plutarch, *Life of Julius Caesar*, 1–2 (excerpted). Translation by Thomas R. Martin.

2. A Poet Mocks Caesar about Sex

In about 58 B.C.E., the twenty-something Catullus ridiculed Caesar (in his early forties) and his follower Mamurra in several acid-tongued poems. The biographer Suetonius (Life of Julius Caesar 73) reports that Caesar said the ridicule inflicted a permanent blot on his name, but that when Catullus apologized, Caesar invited the poet to dinner that very same day.

They're a pretty good match, those fags,
Mamurra and that queer, Caesar.
And no wonder. They've both got the same stains,
One of them a City guy and the other from Formiae,
And they won't wash out.
One's just as sick as the other, those twins,
Two little brainiacs on the same little couch,
This one's just as greedy an adulterer as the other,
They're allies competing even for little girlies;
So, they're a pretty good match, those fags.

Source: Catullus, Poem 57. Translation by Thomas R. Martin.

3. Cicero Writes to a Friend about Caesar

Cicero, Rome's most famous orator, wrote many private letters that have survived. In this one, written to his friend Atticus a few days after Caesar began the civil war by crossing the Rubicon River in January 49 B.C.E., Cicero worriedly expresses his opinion of Caesar at the time.

What's going on? I'm in the dark. . . . That awful fool Caesar, who has never had even the slightest thought of "the good and the fair!" He claims he's doing all this for the sake of honor? But how can you have honor if you have no ethics? Is it ethical to lead an army without official confirmation of your command, to capture cities of Roman citizens to force your way more easily to our mother city, to plot abolition of debts and the recall of exiles, a thousand outrages, "all to obtain the greatest of divinities, sole rule"?

In this letter, written on March 1 of the same year, Cicero offers a different opinion.

Just look at the kind of man who has taken over the republic: clear thinking, sharp, on the ball. By god, if he doesn't murder anyone and doesn't take away people's property, the very people who lived in fear of him will worship him the most.

Source: Cicero, *Letters to Atticus*, 7.11, 8.13. Translation by Thomas R. Martin.

4. Caesar Explains Why He Fought the Civil War

In his memoirs, Caesar provided his own account of the civil war that made him Rome's most powerful man. Here he reports what he said to the Senate on April 1, 49 B.C.E., after Pompey left the capital and Caesar took it without a struggle. Curiously, in his writing Caesar refers to himself in the third person, so the "he" in this excerpt is Caesar.

A meeting of the Senate convened, and he spoke about the wrongs his enemies had done him. He explained that he had only wanted a usual office [i.e., consul] . . . and was content with what any citizen could obtain. . . . He emphasized his moderation in asking on his own initiative that both his army and Pompey's be disbanded [to prevent war], a concession that would have cost him both status and office. He talked about how bitter his enemies had been . . . and how they had not laid down their command and armies, even at the cost of anarchy. He stressed how unfair they had been to try to deprive him of his legions, and how savage and arrogant in putting restrictions on the tribunes [who favored him]. He spoke about the offers he had made, the meeting that he had suggested but they had rejected. Given all this, he encouraged, he asked the Senators to take responsibility for the state and govern it together with him. But, he added, if they ran away out of fear, he would not run away from the job and would govern the state by himself. His opinion was that the Senate should send delegates to Pompey to arrange a settlement; he was not cowed by Pompey's recent remark in the Senate that to receive a delegation implied authority but sending it implied fear. That sort of thought revealed a weak and superficial spirit. He, by contrast, wished to win the competition to be just and fair in the same way in which he had striven to excel in his achievements.

Source: Julius Caesar, *The Civil War*, 1.32. Translation by Thomas R. Martin.

5. A Biographer Describes Caesar's Character

These excerpts come from Suetonius's biography, written about 150 years after Caesar's assassination.

Caesar was somewhat overly concerned with how he looked, and he always had a careful haircut and shave, and even had excess hair removed. . . . His baldness embarrassed him because his enemies made fun of it. He therefore used to comb his little remaining hair forward, and more than any other honor bestowed by the Senate and people he treasured and used the right to wear a wreath of laurel leaves on his head all the time. . . .

The only sexual impropriety in his reputation was his relationship with the king of Bythinia, but that accusation was serious and lasted; everybody insulted him about it. . . . He seduced lots of women. . . . and had love affairs with queens. . . . He drank only very little.

Both as a military commander and as a public official at Rome he used every trick to accumulate money. . . . As a public speaker and a general he either equaled or outstripped the fame of the most outstanding men of the past. . . . He wrote memoirs . . . which Cicero says "deserve the highest praise— they're simple and elegant at the same time."

On military campaigns he showed incredible endurance. . . . It's hard to say whether as a commander he relied more on caution or boldness because he never led his army into a spot where it could be ambushed without first making a careful scouting of the territory. . . . He never let concern for religious scruples deter him from action or slow him down. . . . Whenever his troops started to retreat, he often rallied them himself, using his body to block their way . . . even grabbing them by the throat and making them turn around to face the enemy. . . . He judged his soldiers not by their character or luck but only by how skilled they were, and he treated them all with the same strictness and the same indulgence. . . . He would sometimes overlook their mistakes and didn't punish them strictly according to the rules, but he always kept careful watch for soldiers deserting or mutinying, and these he punished with great harshness. . . . So, he made his men very devoted to him and also very brave.

Even as a young man he treated his clients faithfully. . . . He was always kind to his friends. . . . He never became so much of an enemy to anyone that he couldn't make them a friend when the chance came. . . . Even in seeking revenge he was naturally very merciful . . . and he certainly showed wonderful self-restraint and mercy while fighting the civil war and after he won. . . .

In the end, however, his other words and deeds outbalance all this, and there is the opinion that he abused his rule and that it was justice that he was murdered.

Source: Suetonius, *Life of Julius Caesar*, 45–76. Translation by Thomas R. Martin.

QUESTIONS TO CONSIDER

1. What characteristics made Julius Caesar such a remarkable individual?
2. How and why do an individual's personal characteristics matter for political success?

foreign territories, behaving like an independent king rather than a Roman official. He summed up his attitude by replying to some foreigners who criticized his actions as unjust: "Stop quoting the laws to us," he told them. "We carry swords."

Pompey's enemies at Rome sought popular support by proclaiming their concern for the common people's plight. By the 60s B.C.E., Rome's urban population had soared to more than half a million. Hundreds of thousands of the poor lived crowded together in slum apartments, surviving on subsidized food distributions. Jobs were scarce. Danger haunted the streets because the city had no police force. Even property owners were in trouble: Sulla's confiscations had caused land values to plummet and produced a credit crunch by flooding the real estate market with properties for sale. Overextended investors were trying to borrow their way back to financial security, without success.

The First Triumvirate. The Senate, eager to curb Pompey's power, blocked his reorganization of the former Seleucid kingdom and his distribution of land to his army veterans. Pompey therefore negotiated with his fiercest political rivals, Crassus and Caesar (100–44 B.C.E.). In 60 B.C.E., these three formed an unofficial arrangement called the **First Triumvirate**. Pompey then forced through laws confirming his earlier plans, thus reinforcing his status as a great patron. Caesar got the consulship for 59 B.C.E. and a special command in Gaul, where he could seize booty to build his own client army, and Crassus received financial breaks for the Roman tax collectors in Asia Minor, who supported him politically and financially.

This coalition of political rivals revealed how private relationships had largely replaced communal values in republican politics. To cement their political bond, Caesar arranged to have his daughter, Julia, married to Pompey in 59 B.C.E., even though she had been engaged to another man. Pompey soothed Julia's jilted fiancé by having him marry his own daughter, who had been engaged to yet somebody else. Through these marital machinations, the two powerful antagonists now had a common interest: the fate of Julia, Caesar's only daughter and Pompey's new wife. (Pompey had earlier divorced his second wife after Caesar allegedly seduced her.) Pompey and Julia apparently fell deeply in love in their arranged marriage. As long as Julia lived, Pompey's affection for her kept him from breaking with her father.

First Triumvirate: The coalition formed in 60 B.C.E. by Pompey, Crassus, and Caesar. (The word *triumvirate* means "group of three.")

Civil War. During the 50s B.C.E., Caesar won his soldiers' loyalty with victories and plunder in Gaul, which he added to the Roman provinces, and where he awed his troops with his daring by crossing the channel to campaign in Britain. His political enemies in Rome dreaded him even more as his military successes mounted, and the bond linking him to Pompey shattered in 54 B.C.E. when Julia died in childbirth. The two leaders' rivalry then exploded into violence: gangs of their supporters battled each other in the streets of Rome. The violence reached such a pitch in 53 B.C.E. that it was impossible to hold elections. The First Triumvirate soon dissolved, and in 52 B.C.E. Caesar's enemies convinced the Senate to make Pompey consul by himself, an outrageous repudiation of the republican tradition of shared rule.

Civil war erupted when the Senate ordered Caesar to surrender his command. Like Sulla, Caesar led his army against Rome. As he crossed the Rubicon River, the official northern boundary of Italy, in early 49 B.C.E., he uttered the famous words signaling that he had made an irrevocable choice: "The die is cast." His troops followed him without hesitation, and the people in the countryside cheered him on. He had many backers in Rome, too: the masses counting on his legendary generosity for handouts, and impoverished members of the elite hoping to recoup their fortunes through proscriptions of the rich.

The support for Caesar induced Pompey and most senators to flee to Greece. Caesar entered Rome peacefully, left to defeat Roman enemies in Spain, and then sailed to Greece. There he nearly lost the war when his supplies ran out, but his soldiers stayed loyal even when they were reduced to eating bread made from roots. When Pompey saw what Caesar's men were willing to subsist on, he cried, "I am fighting wild beasts." Caesar's nail-hard troops defeated the army of Pompey and the Senate at the battle of Pharsalus in central Greece in 48 B.C.E. Pompey fled to Egypt, where the ministers of the teenaged pharaoh Ptolemy XIII (63–47 B.C.E.) treacherously murdered him.

Caesar next invaded Egypt, winning a difficult campaign that ended when he restored Cleopatra VII (69–30 B.C.E.) to the throne of Egypt. As ruthless as she was intelligent, Cleopatra charmed Caesar into sharing her bed and supporting her rule. Their love affair shocked the general's friends and enemies alike: they thought Rome should seize power from foreigners, not share it with them.

Caesar's Dictatorship and Murder. By 45 B.C.E., Caesar had won the civil war. He now had to decide how to rule a shattered republic. He appar-

Coin Portrait of Julius Caesar
Julius Caesar (100–44 B.C.E.) was the first living Roman to have his portrait on a coin, defying the tradition of showing only dead persons (the same rule applies to U.S. currency). After he won the civil war in 45 B.C.E., Caesar broke that tradition, as he did many others, to show that he was Rome's supreme leader. Here he wears the laurel wreath of a conquering general. The portrait conforms to late republican style, in which the subject is shown realistically. Caesar's wrinkled neck and careworn expression emphasize the suffering he had endured—and imposed on others—to reach the pinnacle of success. *(Bibliothèque nationale de France.)*

ently believed that only a sole ruler could end the chaotic violence of factional politics, but the republic's oldest tradition prohibited monarchy. Still, Caesar decided to rule as a king, but without the title, taking instead the traditional Roman title of *dictator*, used for a temporary emergency ruler. In 44 B.C.E., he announced he would continue as dictator without a term limit. "I am not a king," he insisted. The distinction, however, was meaningless. As dictator, he controlled the government. Elections for offices continued, but Caesar manipulated the results by recommending candidates to the assemblies, which his supporters dominated.

Caesar's policies as dictator were meant to improve the financial situation and reward his supporters: a moderate cancellation of debts; a cap on the number of people eligible for subsidized grain; a large program of public works, including public libraries; colonies for his veterans in Italy and abroad; rebuilding Corinth and Carthage as commercial centers; and citizenship for more non-Romans.

Unlike Sulla, Caesar did not proscribe his enemies. Instead, he exercised clemency; its beneficiaries were obligated to be his grateful clients. His foregoing revenge earned him unprecedented honors, such as a special golden seat in the Senate house and the renaming of the seventh month of the year after him (July). He also regularized the Roman calendar by having each year include 365 days, a calculation based on an ancient Egyptian calendar that forms the basis for our modern one.

Caesar's dictatorship suited the people but outraged the optimates. (See "Contrasting Views," page 156.) They resented being dominated by one of their own, a "traitor" who had deserted to the people's faction. Some senators, led by Caesar's former close friend Brutus and inspired by the memory of Brutus's ancestor, who headed the overthrow of Rome's first monarchy five hundred years before, conspired to murder him. They stabbed Caesar repeatedly in a shower of blood in the Senate house on March 15 (the Ides of March in the Roman calendar), 44 B.C.E. When his friend Brutus struck him, Caesar gasped his last words—in Greek: "You, too, child?" He collapsed dead at the foot of a statue of Pompey.

The liberators, as they called themselves, had no new plans for government. They naively thought the traditional republic would revive automatically after Caesar's murder, ignoring the political violence of the past forty years and the deadly imbalance in Roman values, with "great men" placing their private interests above the community's. The liberators were stunned when the people rioted at Caesar's funeral to vent their anger against the upper class that had robbed them of their generous patron. Instead of then forming a united front, the elite resumed their personal vendettas. Old republican values had failed to save the republic.

REVIEW: What factors generated the conflicts that caused the republic's downfall?

Conclusion

The most remarkable features of the Roman republic's history were its phenomenal expansion and its violent disintegration. Rome expanded because it incorporated outsiders, its small farmers produced agricultural surpluses to support a growing population and army, and its leaders

Ides of March Coin Celebrating Caesar's Murder
Roman coins were the most widely distributed form of art and communication in the Roman world. Their messages became topical and contemporary during the crisis of the late republic. Caesar's assassins, led by Marcus Junius Brutus (85–42 B.C.E.), issued this coin celebrating the murder and their claim to be liberators. The daggers refer to their method, while the conical cap stands for liberation—it was the kind of headgear worn by slaves who had won their freedom. The inscription gives the date of the assassination, the Ides of March (March 15). What political message was intended by putting pictures of murder weapons on a coin? *(© Copyright The Trustees of the British Museum.)*

MAPPING THE WEST

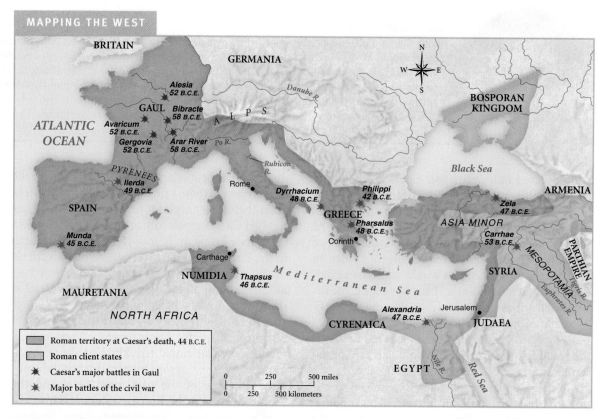

The Roman World at the End of the Republic, 44 B.C.E.
Upon Julius Caesar's assassination in 44 B.C.E., the territory that would be the Roman Empire was almost complete. Caesar's young relative Octavian (the future Augustus) would conquer and add Egypt in 30 B.C.E. Geography, distance, and formidable enemies were the primary factors inhibiting further expansion, which Romans never stopped wanting, even when lack of money and political discord rendered it purely theoretical. The deserts of Africa and the resurgent Persian kingdom in the Near East worked against expansion southward or eastward, while trackless forests and fierce resistance from local inhabitants made expansion into central Europe and the British Isles impossible to maintain.

respected the traditional values stressing the common good. The Romans' willingness to endure great loss of life and property—the proof of their faithfulness—made their army unstoppable in prolonged conflicts: Rome might lose battles, but never wars. Because wars of conquest brought profits to leaders and the common people alike, peace seemed a wasted opportunity.

But the republic's victories against Carthage and in Macedonia and Greece had unexpected consequences. Long military service ruined many farming families, and security needs forced many others to relocate. Many poor people flocked to Rome to live on subsidized food, becoming an unstable political force. Members of the upper class escalated their competition with each other for the increased career opportunities presented by constant war. These rivalries became unmanageable when successful generals began acting as patrons to client armies of poor troops. In this dog-eat-dog atmosphere, violence and murder became the preferred means for settling political disputes. Com-

munal values were drowned in the blood of civil war. No reasonable Roman could have been optimistic about the chances for an enduring peace following Caesar's assassination in 44 B.C.E.; that Caesar's adopted son Octavian—a teenage student at the time of the murder—would eventually forge peace by devising a new political system as Augustus would have seemed an impossible dream.

FOR FURTHER EXPLORATION

■ **For suggested references, including Web sites, for topics in this chapter,** see page SR-1 at the end of the book.

■ **For additional primary-source material from this period,** see Chapter 5 in *Sources of THE MAKING OF THE WEST,* Third Edition.

■ **For Web sites and documents related to topics in this chapter,** see *Make History* at bedfordstmartins.com/hunt.

CHAPTER REVIEW

KEY TERMS AND PEOPLE

mos maiorum (134)

patron-client system (136)

patria potestas (136)

res publica (140)

orders (142)

Twelve Tables (142)

ladder of offices (142)

plebiscites (143)

Cicero (150)

humanitas (150)

equites (152)

populares (153)

optimates (153)

proletarians (153)

First Triumvirate (158)

MAKING CONNECTIONS

1. How do the political and social values of the Roman republic compare to those of the Greek city-state in the Classical Age?

2. What were the positive and the negative consequences of war for the Roman republic?

For practice quizzes, a customized study plan, and other study tools, see the Online Study Guide at bedfordstmartins.com/hunt.

REVIEW QUESTIONS

1. What common themes underlay Roman values? How did Romans' behavior reflect those values?

2. How and why did the Roman republic develop its complicated political and judicial systems?

3. What advantages and disadvantages did Rome's victories over foreign peoples create for both rich and poor Romans?

4. What factors generated the conflicts that caused the republic's downfall?

IMPORTANT EVENTS

753 B.C.E.	Traditional date of Rome's founding as a monarchy	168–149 B.C.E.	Cato writes *The Origins*, the first history of Rome in Latin
509 B.C.E.	Roman republic established	149–146 B.C.E.	Rome and Carthage fight Third Punic War
509–287 B.C.E.	Struggle of the orders	146 B.C.E.	Carthage and Corinth destroyed
451–449 B.C.E.	Creation of the Twelve Tables, Rome's first written law code	133 B.C.E.	Tiberius Gracchus elected tribune; assassinated in same year
396 B.C.E.	Defeat of the Etruscan city of Veii; first great expansion of Roman territory	91–87 B.C.E.	Social War between Rome and its Italian allies
387 B.C.E.	Gauls sack Rome	60 B.C.E.	First Triumvirate of Caesar, Pompey, and Crassus
264–241 B.C.E.	Rome and Carthage fight First Punic War	49–45 B.C.E.	Civil war, with Caesar the victor
220 B.C.E.	Rome controls Italy south of the Po River	45–44 B.C.E.	Cicero writes his philosophical works on *humanitas*
218–201 B.C.E.	Rome and Carthage fight Second Punic War	44 B.C.E.	Caesar appointed dictator for life; assassinated in same year

The Roman Empire
44 B.C.E.–284 C.E.

I n 203 C.E., Vibia Perpetua, wealthy and twenty-two years old, sat in a Carthage jail, nursing her infant while awaiting execution; she had received the death sentence for refusing to sacrifice to the gods for the Roman emperor's health and safety. One morning the jailer dragged her off to the city's main square, where a crowd had gathered. Perpetua described in a journal what happened when the local governor tried to persuade her to save her life:

> My father came carrying my son, crying "Perform the sacrifice; take pity on your baby!" Then the governor said, "Think of your old father; show pity for your little child! Offer the sacrifice for the imperial family's welfare." "I refuse," I answered. "Are you a Christian?" asked the governor. "Yes." When my father would not stop trying to change my mind, the governor ordered him flung to the earth and whipped with a rod. I felt sorry for my father; it seemed they were beating me. I pitied his pathetic old age.

The brutality of Perpetua's punishment failed to break her: gored by a wild cow and stabbed by a gladiator, she died professing her faith.

Perpetua went to her death because she believed that her Christian faith required her not only to disregard the traditional Roman value of faithfulness to her family obligations but also to refuse the state's demand to show loyalty. Her decision to put her personal religious commitment ahead of her civic duty was a different version of the republic's commanders' fighting civil wars because they valued their individual success above service to the common good.

Following Julius Caesar's assassination in 44 B.C.E., Augustus (63 B.C.E.–14 C.E.) eventually forged peace by reforming Roman

Executing a Criminal in the Amphitheater
This mosaic shows a condemned man being mauled by a leopard in the arena of an amphitheater. Being condemned to the beasts, as the execution was called, was the most spectacularly gruesome of punishments. Martyrs charged with treason, such as Vibia Perpetua, were often executed in this way. Here the prisoner is tied to a stake on a chariot so that the handlers can propel him into the face of the leopard to provoke an angry leap; wild animals often refused to attack without this provocation. This scene formed part of a larger mosaic showing gladiators and other performers before a large crowd in the arena. Laid about 200 C.E., the mosaic covered a floor in a North African villa; it belonged to the same time and region of the Roman Empire as did Perpetua. The villa's owner probably ordered these subjects for the mosaic to show that he paid for the expensive spectacle that included the execution. *(Roger Wood/Corbis.)*

government. Ever after, Rome's rulers feared disloyalty above all because it threatened to rekindle the civil wars that had consumed the republic. The refusal of Christians such as Perpetua to perform traditional sacrifice was considered treason—the ultimate disloyalty—because Romans believed the gods would punish the entire community for harboring such impious people.

The Roman Empire, the modern name applied to the period from Augustus onward, opened with a bloodbath: seventeen years of civil war followed Caesar's funeral. Finally, in 27 B.C.E., Augustus created a disguised monarchy—the *principate*—to end the violence, ingeniously masking his creation as a restoration of the republic. He retained the republic's name and its institutions for sharing power—the Senate, the consuls, the courts—while in reality making himself sole ruler. He concealed his monarchy by referring to himself not as a *rex* ("king") but only with the informal title *princeps* ("first man among social equals"), an honorary designation from the republic indicating general agreement about who was the leading individual of the time, or who was the most distinguished Roman senator. *Princeps* is therefore the position we call "emperor." Each new *princeps* was supposed to be designated only with the Senate's approval, but in practice each ruler chose his own successor, as in a monarchy. More than a thousand years would pass before republican government reappeared in Western civilization.

The challenge for Romans during the empire was to maintain political stability and prosperity. Augustus's political system brought peace for two hundred years, except for a struggle between generals for rule in 69 C.E. This **Pax Romana** (from

the Latin for "Roman peace") allowed agriculture and trade to flourish in the provinces, but war still determined Rome's long-term future because of its financial effects. Under the republic, foreign wars had won huge amounts of land and money for Romans, but now the distances were too great, the adjoining lands too rough, and the foreign enemies too strong for continued conquest. The army became no longer a offensive weapon for expansion but instead a defense force protecting the frontier regions. This change during the Pax Romana slowly created a financial crisis that weakened the principate and destabilized the empire. The emergence of Christianity created a new religion that would over centuries transform the Roman world, but this change also created tension because the growing presence of Christians made other Romans worry about punishment from the gods. In the third century C.E., a crisis developed when generals competing to rule reignited prolonged civil war. By the 280s C.E., Roman government teetered once more on the brink of disintegration.

> **FOCUS QUESTION:** How did Augustus's "restored republic" successfully keep the Pax Romana for more than two centuries, and why did it fail in the third century?

Creating the Pax Romana

Inventing tradition takes time. Augustus created his new political system gradually; as his biographer expressed it, Augustus "made haste slowly." Augustus succeeded because he won the struggle for power, reinvented government, and built legitimacy and loyalty by communicating an image of himself as a dedicated leader. His professed respect for tradition and his reign's length established

---

principate: Roman political system invented by Augustus as a disguised monarchy with the *princeps* ("first man") as emperor.

Pax Romana: The two centuries of relative peace and prosperity in the Roman Empire under the early principate begun by Augustus.

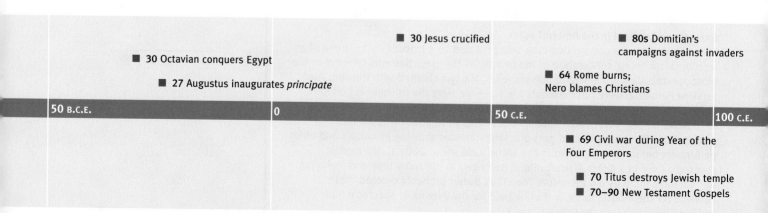

■ 30 Octavian conquers Egypt

■ 27 Augustus inaugurates *principate*

■ 30 Jesus crucified

■ 80s Domitian's campaigns against invaders

■ 64 Rome burns; Nero blames Christians

| 50 B.C.E. | 0 | 50 C.E. | 100 C.E. |

■ 69 Civil war during Year of the Four Emperors

■ 70 Titus destroys Jewish temple
■ 70–90 New Testament Gospels

monarchy as Rome's political system and saved the state from anarchy. Succeeding where Caesar had failed, he did it by making the new look old.

From Republic to Principate, 44–27 B.C.E.

Aristocrats competing for power after Caesar's assassination in 44 B.C.E. started a civil war that lasted until 30 B.C.E. The main competitors were Caesar's friend Mark Antony and Caesar's eighteen-year-old grandnephew and adopted son, Octavian (the future Augustus). Octavian won over Caesar's soldiers by promising them rewards from their murdered general's wealth, which he had inherited. Marching these troops to Rome, the teenager forced the Senate to make him consul in 43 B.C.E., disregarding the rule that a man had to climb the ladder of offices before becoming consul.

Octavian and Antony put aside their differences—for a time—and with a general named Lepidus joined forces against Caesar's assassins and anyone else they thought dangerous. In late 43 B.C.E., the trio formed the so-called Second Triumvirate and compelled the Senate to recognize them as an official panel for reconstituting the state. They then proscribed their enemies, including their own relatives, and confiscated their property.

Octavian and Antony next forced Lepidus into retirement and began fighting each other. Antony controlled the eastern provinces by allying with the Ptolemaic queen Cleopatra VII (69–30 B.C.E.), who had earlier allied with Caesar. Dazzled by her intelligence and personal magnetism, Antony, who was married to Octavian's sister, fell in love with Cleopatra. Octavian rallied support by claiming that Antony planned to make this foreign queen Rome's ruler. He made the residents of Italy and the western provinces swear an oath of allegiance to him. His victory in the naval battle of Actium in northwest Greece in 31 B.C.E. won the war.

Cleopatra and Antony fled to Egypt, where they both committed suicide in 30 B.C.E. The general first stabbed himself, bleeding to death in his lover's embrace. The queen then ended her life by allowing a poisonous snake to bite her. Octavian's profits from capturing Egypt made him Rome's richest citizen.

Augustus's "Restoration of the Republic," 27 B.C.E.–14 C.E.

After distributing land to army veterans and creating colonies in the provinces, in 27 B.C.E. Octavian, in his own words, "returned the state from my own power to the control of the Roman Senate and the people" and said they should decide how to preserve it. His action triggered a turning point in Roman history: recognizing Octavian's overwhelming power, the senators asked him to safeguard the restored republic, granted him special civil and military powers, and bestowed on him the honorary name **Augustus**, meaning "divinely favored."

Inventing the Principate.   In reality, the arrangements of 27 B.C.E. changed Rome's political system, but Augustus, as everyone now called him, kept up the appearance and the name of republican government. Consuls were elected, the Senate gave advice, and the assemblies met. Augustus periodically served as consul, but mostly he let others be consuls. To preserve the tradition that no official should hold more than one post at a time, he had the Senate grant him a tribune's powers without holding the office; that is, he possessed the authority to act and to veto as if he were a tribune protecting the rights of the people, but he left all the

---

Augustus: The honorary name meaning "divinely favored" that the Roman Senate bestowed on Octavian; it became shorthand for "Roman imperial ruler."

■ **161–180** Multiethnic bands attack northern frontiers

■ **230s–280s** Third-century crisis

| 150 C.E. | 200 C.E. | 250 C.E. |

■ **212** Caracalla extends Roman citizenship

■ **249–251** Decius persecutes Christians

Cameo Celebrating Augustus
This cameo, about eight by nine inches, was carved early in the Roman Empire from a stone with layers of blue and white. Interpretations of the scenes vary, but the upper scene probably shows Augustus being crowned for saving Roman citizens by a standing female figure representing the Inhabited World. The seated female figure represents Rome and resembles Augustus's wife, Livia, his partner in rule. The man stepping out of a chariot is Tiberius, Augustus's choice to succeed him as princeps. Why do you think Tiberius carries a scepter like that held by Augustus? The lower scene shows defeated enemies subjected to Roman power. How do you think the lower scene relates to the upper scene? *(Kunsthistorisches Museum, Wien.)*

Livia, his wife, played a prominent role under his regime as his political adviser and partner in upholding old-fashioned values.

Augustus's choice of *princeps* as his public, though unofficial, title was a brilliant symbolic move because it used tradition to give legitimacy to revolution. He claimed that he commanded public affairs only through the respect and *auctoritas* ("moral authority") he merited; he had no more *potestas* ("formal power"), he insisted, than any other leader. He invented the principate to disguise a monarchy as a corrected and restored republic, headed by an emperor cloaked as a princeps ruling only by auctoritas. Roman emperors after Augustus used the same propaganda: they always called the Roman state "the republic." In truth, Augustus revolutionized the underlying power structure of Rome's government: no one previously could have exercised the powers of both tribune and "superior" consul simultaneously while also controlling the state's money and troops.

Augustus made the military the foundation of his power by turning the republic's citizen militia into a professional, full-time army and navy. He established regular lengths of service and a substantial retirement benefit, changes that made the princeps the troops' patron and solidified their loyalty to him. To pay the added costs, Augustus imposed Rome's first inheritance tax on citizens, angering the rich. His other major military innovation was to station several thousand soldiers in Rome for the first time ever. These soldiers—the **praetorian guard**—would later play a crucial role in imperial politics by selecting the princeps. Augustus meant them to provide security for him and prevent rebellion in the capital by serving as a visible reminder that the princeps's superiority was grounded in the threat of force.

Communicating the Emperor's Image. In keeping with his policy of using both force and symbols, Augustus constantly communicated his image as patron and public benefactor (see Doc-

tribunates open for plebeians to occupy, just as under the republic. In 23 B.C.E., the Senate agreed that he should also have a consul's power to command—with the crucial addition that his power would be superior to the power of the actual consuls.

Holding the power of a tribune and the "superior power" of a consul meant that Augustus exercised supreme power, and future emperors claimed these same powers as the basis of their rule. The naked truth was that Augustus and the emperors after him ruled because they controlled the army and the treasury. Augustus knew, however, that symbols affect people's perception of reality, so he dressed and acted modestly, like a regular republican citizen, not an arrogant king.

---

praetorian (pree TOR ee uhn) **guard:** The group of soldiers stationed in Rome under the emperor's control; first formed by Augustus.

ument, "Augustus, *Res Gestae*," page 168). He used media as small as coins and as large as buildings. The only mass-produced medium for official messages, Roman coins functioned like modern political advertising. They proclaimed slogans such as "Father of His Country" to remind Romans of the princeps's moral authority, or "Roads have been built" to emphasize his generosity in paying for highway construction.

Augustus used his personal fortune to erect spectacular public buildings in Rome. The huge Forum of Augustus, dedicated in 2 B.C.E., best illustrates his skill at sending messages through architecture (Figure 6.1). This public gathering space centered on a temple to Mars, the Roman god of war, where Julius Caesar's sword was preserved as a national treasure. Two-story colonnades extended from the temple like wings, sheltering statues of famous Roman heroes to serve as inspirations to future leaders. Augustus's forum provided space for religious rituals and the coming-of-age ceremonies of upper-class boys, but it also stressed his justifications for his rule: peace and security restored through military power, the foundation of a new age, devotion to the gods who protected Rome, respect for tradition, and his generosity in spending money for public purposes.

Augustus's Motives.

Augustus never revealed his motives for establishing the principate, but his challenge was the one every Roman leader faced— balancing the need for peace and Rome's traditional commitment to its citizens' freedom of action with his own ambitions. Augustus's solution was to employ traditional values to justify changes, as with his reinvention of the meaning of the word *princeps*. Above all, he transferred the traditional paternalism of social relations—the patron-client system—to politics by making the princeps everyone's most important patron, with the moral authority to guide their lives. This process culminated in 2 B.C.E. when the Senate joined the Roman people in formally proclaiming Augustus "Father of His Country" (a title that Julius Caesar had also received). The title emphasized that the principate gave Romans a sole ruler who governed them like a father: stern but caring, expecting obedience and loyalty from his children, and obligated to nurture them in return. The goal of such an arrangement was a combination of stability and order, not political freedom.

Augustus ruled until his death at age seventy-five in 14 C.E. The length of his reign—forty-one years—solidified his transformation of Roman government. As the historian Tacitus (c. 56–120

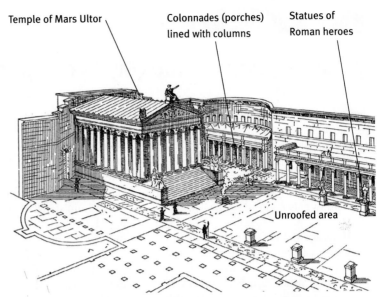

FIGURE 6.1 Cutaway Reconstruction of the Forum of Augustus Augustus built this large forum (120 × 90 yards) to commemorate his victory over the assassins of Julius Caesar. The centerpiece was a marble temple to Mars Ultor ("The Avenger"), and inside the temple were statues of Mars, Venus (the divine ancestor of Julius Caesar), and Julius Caesar (as a god), as well as works of art and Caesar's sword. The two apses flanking the temple featured statues of Aeneas and Romulus, Rome's founders. The high stone wall behind the temple protected it from fire, a constant threat in the crowded neighborhood just behind.

C.E.) remarked, by the time Augustus died, "almost no one was still alive who had seen the republic." Through his longevity, command over the army, rapport with the capital's urban masses, and manipulation of political symbols and language to mask his power, Augustus restored political stability and transformed republican Rome into imperial Rome.

Augustan Rome

Archaeological and literary sources reveal a composite picture of life in Augustan Rome. Although some of the sources refer to times after Augustus and to cities other than Rome, they help us understand the Augustan period because economic and social conditions were essentially the same in Roman cities throughout the Pax Romana.

Augustan Rome's population of nearly one million was vast for the ancient world. No European city would have this many people again until London in the 1700s. Many people had no regular jobs and too little to eat. The streets were packed: "One man jabs me with his elbow, another whacks me with a pole; my legs are smeared with mud, and big feet step on me from all sides" was

Augustus, *Res Gestae* (My Accomplishments)

Augustus, the first Roman emperor, had an autobiographical report of his accomplishments displayed around the empire. These excerpts reveal his justifications for his rule. Many of the sections not included here list his numerous and expensive personal contributions to public works.

1. At the age of nineteen, on my own initiative and at my own expense, I raised an army, which I used to liberate the republic, which had been oppressed by the tyranny of a faction. For this reason the Senate passed honorary votes for me and made me a member [in 43 B.C.E.], at the same time granting me the rank of a consul in its voting, and it gave me the power of military command [*imperium*]. It ordered me as propraetor to see to it, along with the consuls, that no harm came to the state. Moreover, in the same year, when both consuls had died in the war, the people elected me consul and a triumvir with the duty of establishing the republic. . . .

3. I waged many wars, civil and foreign, throughout the whole world by land and by sea, and as victor I spared all citizens who asked for pardons. Foreign peoples who could safely be pardoned I preferred to spare rather than destroy. Approximately 500,000 Roman citizens swore military oaths to me. A little more than 300,000 of these, when their terms of service were ended, I settled in colonies or sent back to their own municipalities; I allotted lands or granted money to all of them as rewards for military service. . . .

5. I refused to accept the dictatorship offered to me [in 22 B.C.E.] by the people and by the senate, both in my absence and my presence. During a severe scarcity of grain I accepted the supervision of the grain supply, which I so administered that within a few days I freed the whole people from imminent panic and danger by my expenditures and effort. The consulship, too, which was offered to me at that time as an annual office for life, I refused to accept.

6. [In 19, 18, and 11 B.C.E.], although the Roman Senate and people in unison agreed that I should be elected sole guardian of the laws and morals with supreme power, I refused to accept any office offered to me that was contrary to our ancestors' traditions [*mos maiorum*]. The measures that the Senate desired me to take at that time I carried out under the tribunician power. While holding this power I five times voluntarily requested and was given a colleague by the senate.

7. . . . I have been ranking senator [*princeps senatus*] for forty years, up to the day on which I wrote this document. [There follows a list of priesthoods he held, including that of "the greatest priest," *pontifex maximus*.]

8. . . . By new legislation that I sponsored I restored many precedents from our ancestors that were becoming dead letters in our generation, and I myself handed down precedents in many spheres for posterity to imitate. . . .

34. In my sixth and seventh consulships [28 and 27 B.C.E.], after I had put an end to the civil wars, having gained possession of everything through the consent of everyone, I returned the state from my own power [*potestas*] to the control of the Roman Senate and the people. As reward for this meritorious service, I received the title of Augustus by vote of the Senate, and the doorposts of my house were publicly decked with laurels, the civic crown was affixed over my doorway, and a golden shield was set up in the Julian Senate house, which, as the inscription on this shield testifies, the Roman Senate and people gave me in recognition of my valor, clemency, justice, and devotion. After that time I excelled all in authority [*auctoritas*], but I possessed no more power [*potestas*] than the others who were my colleagues in each magistracy.

35. When I held my thirteenth consulship [2 B.C.E.], the Senate, the equestrian order, and the entire Roman people gave me the title of "father of the country" [*pater patriae*] and voted that this title should be inscribed in the vestibule of my house, in the Julian Senate house, and in the Augustan Forum on the pedestal of the chariot which was set up in my honor by vote of the Senate. At the time I wrote this document I was in my seventy-sixth year.

Source: Herbert W. Benario, ed., *Caesaris Augusti Res Gestae et Fragmenta*, 2nd ed. (1990). Translation by Thomas R. Martin.

how the poet Juvenal described walking in Rome in the early second century. To ease congestion in the narrow streets, the city banned carts and wagons in the daytime. This regulation made nights noisy with the creaking of axles and the shouting of drivers caught in traffic jams.

The Precariousness of City Life. Most urban residents lived in small apartments in multistoried buildings called islands. Outnumbering private houses by more than twenty to one, the islands' first floors housed shops, bars, and restaurants. Graffiti of all kinds—political endorsements, the posting of rewards, personal insults, and advertising—covered the exterior walls. The higher the floor, the cheaper the rent. Well-off tenants occupied the lower stories, while the poorest people lived in single rooms rented by the day on the top floors. Aqueducts delivered a plentiful supply of fresh water to public fountains, but apartment dwellers had to lug heavy jugs up the stairs. The wealthy few had piped-in water at ground level. Most tenants lacked bathrooms and had to use the public latrines or pots for toilets at home. Some buildings had cesspits, but most people had to carry buckets of excrement down to the streets to be emptied by sewage collectors. Lazy tenants flung these containers' foul-smelling contents out the window. Sanitation was an enormous problem in a city that generated sixty tons of human waste every day.

To keep clean, residents used public baths. Because admission fees were low, almost everyone could afford to bathe daily. Baths existed all over the city; like modern health clubs, they served as centers for exercising and socializing (see Document, "The Scene at a Roman Bath," page 170). Bath patrons progressed through a series of increasingly warm, humid areas until they reached a sauna-like room. Bathers swam naked in their choice of hot or cold pools. Women had access to the public baths, but men and women bathed apart. Since bathing was thought to be helpful for sick people, communal baths unintentionally contributed to the spread of communicable diseases.

Augustus's care for citizens' everyday lives helped them accept his political changes. He did all he could to improve Rome's public safety and health. Since fire presented a constant danger, Augustus gave Rome the first public fire department in Western history. He also established the first permanent police force, despite his fondness for watching the frequent brawls in Rome's crowded streets. There were challenges in urban life, however, that not even his power and money could overcome. He greatly enlarged the city's main sewer, but its contents still emptied untreated into the Tiber River. The technology for sanitary disposal of waste did not exist. People often left human and animal corpses in the streets, to be gnawed by vultures and dogs. The poor were not the only people affected by such conditions: a stray mutt once brought a human hand to the table where Vespasian, who would be emperor from 69 to 79 C.E., was eating lunch. Flies everywhere and a lack of refrigeration contributed to frequent gastrointestinal ailments: the most popular jewelry of the time was supposed to ward off stomach trouble.

A Roman Street
Like Pompeii, the town of Herculaneum on the Bay of Naples was frozen in time by the volcanic eruption of Mount Vesuvius in 79 C.E. Mud from the eruption buried the town and preserved its buildings. Herculaneum's straight roads paved with flat stones and sidewalks were typical for a Roman town. Balconies jutted from the houses, offering a shady viewing point for life in the streets. Roman houses often enclosed a garden courtyard instead of having yards in front or back. Why do you think urban homes had this arrangement? *(Scala/Art Resource, NY.)*

Although the wealthy could not avoid such problems, they made their lives more pleasant with luxuries such as snow rushed from the mountains to ice their drinks and slaves to clean their houses, which were built around courtyards and gardens.

City residents faced hazards beyond infectious disease. Apartment dwellers often hurled broken pots and debris out their windows, where it rained down on pedestrians. "If you are walking to a dinner party in Rome," Juvenal warned, "you would be foolish not to make out your will first. For every open window is a source of potential disaster." Apartment buildings could be dangerous because they sometimes collapsed. Roman architects built public structures from concrete, brick, and stone that lasted centuries, but crooked contractors cut costs by cheating on materials for private build-

DOCUMENT

The Scene at a Roman Bath

The Roman philosopher Seneca (4 B.C.E.–65 C.E.) wrote to a friend describing the commotion that he had to endure to keep up his studies while living in a rented apartment over a public bath of the kind that existed in every sizable community in the Roman Empire.

I am staying in an apartment directly above a public bath. Imagine all the kinds of voices that I hear, enough to make me hate having ears! When the really strong guys are working out with heavy lead weights, when they are working hard or at least pretending to work hard, I hear their grunts; and whenever they exhale the breath they've been holding in, I hear them hissing and panting harshly. When I happen to notice some sluggish type getting a cheap rubdown, I hear the slap of the hand pounding his shoulders, changing its sound according to whether it's a blow with an open or a closed fist. If a serious ball-player comes along and starts keeping score out loud, then I'm done for. Add to this the bruiser who likes to pick fights, the pickpocket who's been caught, and the man who loves to hear the sound of his own voice in the bath. And there are those people who jump into the swimming pool with a tremendous splash and lots of noise. Besides all the ones who have awful voices, imagine the "armpit hair plucker-outer" with his high, shrill voice — so he'll be noticed — always chattering and never shutting up, except when he is plucking armpits and making his customer yell instead of yelling himself. And there are also all the different cries from the sausage seller, and the fellow selling pastries, and all the food vendors screaming out what they have to sell, all of them with their own special tones.

Source: Seneca, *Moral Epistles*, 56.1–2. Translation by Thomas R. Martin.

---

ings. Augustus imposed a height limit of seventy feet on new apartment buildings to limit the danger.

As Rome's patron, Augustus used his own money to import grain to feed the urban poor. State distribution of some grain had long been a tradition, but Augustus's welfare plan reached 250,000 recipients. Counting the recipients' families, more than 700,000 people depended on the princeps to survive. Poor Romans cooked this grain into soup or bread, washed down with cheap wine. If they were lucky, they might add beans, leeks, or cheese. The rich ate more delectable dishes, such as roast pork or crayfish, flavored with sweet-and-sour sauce concocted from honey and vinegar.

Wealthy Romans increasingly spent money on luxuries and political careers instead of raising families. Fearing that the falling birthrate would destroy the elite on whom Rome relied for public service, Augustus granted legal privileges to the parents of three or more children. To strengthen marriages, he made adultery a crime and supported this reform so strongly that he exiled his own daughter — his only child — and a granddaughter for sex scandals. His legislation had little effect, however, and the prestigious old families dwindled over the coming centuries. Recent research suggests that up to three-quarters of senatorial families either lost their official status by spending all their money or died out every generation by failing to have children. Equestrians and provincials who won imperial favor took their places in the social hierarchy and the Senate.

Roman Slavery. Unlike other ancient states, Rome gave citizenship to freed slaves. All slaves could hope to acquire the rights of a free citizen, and their descendants, if they became wealthy, could become members of the social elite. This policy gave slaves reason to persevere and cooperate with their masters. It also meant that most Romans had slave ancestors.

The harshness of slaves' lives varied widely. Slaves in agriculture and manufacturing lived a grueling existence. Most such workers were men, although women might assist the foremen who managed gangs of rural laborers. The second-century novelist Apuleius described the grim situation of slaves in a flour mill: "Through the holes in their ragged clothes you could see all over their bodies the scars from whippings. Some wore only loincloths. Letters had been branded on their foreheads and irons manacled their ankles." Worse than the mills were the mines, where the foremen whipped the miners to keep them working in such a dangerous environment.

Household slaves lived better. Most Romans owned slaves as home servants; modestly well-off families had one or two, while rich houses and the

Gladiator after a Kill
This first-century C.E. mosaic covered a villa floor in North Africa. It shows a gladiator staring at the opponent he has just killed. What feelings do you think his expression conveys? Gladiatorial combats originated as part of wealthy people's funeral ceremonies, symbolizing the human struggle to avoid death. Training an expert gladiator took many years and great expense. Like boxers today, gladiators fought only a couple of times a year. Because it cost so much to replace a dead gladiator, most fights were not to the death intentionally; however, kills often happened in the fury of combat. *(Photo: Helmut Ziegert/University of Hamburg.)*

imperial palace owned hordes. Domestic slaves were often women, working as nurses, maids, kitchen helpers, and clothes makers. Some male slaves ran businesses for their masters, and they were often allowed to keep part of the profits as an incentive; they saved to purchase their freedom someday. Women had less opportunity to earn money, though masters sometimes granted tips for sexual favors to female and male slaves. Many female prostitutes were slaves working for a master. Slaves with savings would sometimes buy other slaves, especially to have a mate. They could then live as a shadow family, barred from legal marriage because they and their children remained their master's property. Fortunate slaves could buy themselves from their masters or be freed in their masters' wills. Some tomb inscriptions record a master's affection for a slave, but even household slaves endured inhumane treatment if their masters were cruel. Slaves had no legal recourse, and if they attacked their owners, the punishment was death.

Violence in Public Entertainment.   Potential violence defined slaves' lives; actual violence defined much Roman public entertainment. The emperors regularly provided spectacles featuring hunters killing fierce beasts, wild African animals mangling condemned criminals, mock naval battles in flooded arenas, blood-drenched gladiatorial com-

bats, and wreck-filled chariot races. Spectators packed arenas for these shows, seated according to their social rank and gender following an Augustan law. The emperor and senators sat close to the action, while women and the poor were relegated to the upper tiers, to display the hierarchy that Romans believed necessary to social stability.

War captives, criminals, slaves, and free volunteers fought as gladiators; most were men, though women sometimes competed. Daughters trained by their gladiator fathers had first competed during the republic, and women continued to compete occasionally until the emperor Septimius Severus (r. 193–211 C.E.) banned their appearance. Gladiatorial shows had originated as part of rich funerals, but Augustus made them popular entertainment. Gladiators were often wounded or killed because the fights were so dangerous, but their contests rarely required a fight to the death, unless they were captives or criminals; professional fighters could have extended careers and win riches and celebrity. To make the fights unpredictable, pairs of gladiators often competed with different weapons. One favorite bout pitted a lightly armored "net man," who used a net and a trident, against a more heavily armored "fish man," so named from the design of his helmet crest. Betting was popular, the crowds rowdy. As a Christian commentator complained: "Look at the mob coming to the show—already they're out of their minds! Aggressive, thoughtless, already in an uproar about their bets! They all share the same suspense, the same madness, the same voice."

Public entertainment served as two-way communication between ruler and ruled. Emperors provided gladiatorial shows, chariot races, and theater productions for the masses, and ordinary citizens staged protests at these festivals to express their wishes to the emperors, who were expected to attend. Poor Romans, for example, rioted to protest shortfalls in the free grain supply.

Imperial Education, Literature, and Art

Elite culture changed in the Augustan period to serve the same goal as public entertainment: legitimizing the transformed political system. Oratory — the highest attainment of Roman education — lost its freedom. Under the republic, the ability to make frank speeches criticizing political opponents had been such a powerful weapon that it could catapult a "new man" like Cicero to a leadership role. Under the principate, the emperor's supremacy ruled out honest political debate. Now ambitious men required rhetorical skills to praise the emperor. Criticism of the established political system in both oratory and the arts was too risky.

Imperial Education. Education in oratory remained a privilege of the wealthy. Rome had no free public schools, so the poor received no formal education. Most people had time for learning only practical skills. A character in a Roman satirical novel expresses this utilitarian attitude: "I didn't study geometry and literary criticism and worthless junk like that. I just learned how to read the letters on signs and how to work out percentages, and I learned weights, measures, and the values of the different kinds of coins."

Servants attended rich boys and girls, who attended private elementary schools from ages seven to eleven to learn reading, writing, and basic arithmetic. Some children went on to the next three years of school, in which they studied literature, history, and grammar. Only a few boys then proceeded to the study of rhetoric. Advanced studies concerned literature, history, ethical philosophy, law, and dialectic (reasoned argument). Mathematics and science were rarely studied as separate subjects, but engineers and architects became proficient at calculation despite the difficulty of using Roman numerals for complex math.

Ideals in Literature and Sculpture. So much literature blossomed during the Augustan period that scholars call it the Golden Age of Latin literature. The emperor, himself an author, served as a patron for writers and artists. His favorites were Horace (65–8 B.C.E.) and Virgil (70–19 B.C.E.). Horace entranced audiences with the rhythms and irony of his poems on public and private subjects. His poem celebrating Augustus's victory at Actium became famous for its opening line: "Now we have to drink!"

Virgil became the most famous Roman poet for his long poem *The Aeneid*, which both praised and — very indirectly — criticized the principate. Inspired by Homer's epics, *The Aeneid* told the story of the Trojan Aeneas, the legendary founder of Rome. Virgil balanced his praise for Roman civilization with recognition of the price in freedom to be paid for peace. *The Aeneid* thus revealed the complex mix of gain and loss created by Augustus's transformation of Roman politics.

Literacy and Social Status
This twenty-six-inch-high wall painting of a woman and her husband was found in a comfortable house in Pompeii, buried by twelve feet of ash from Mount Vesuvius's volcanic eruption in 79 C.E. The couple may have owned the bakery that adjoined the house. Both are depicted with items showing that they were literate and therefore deserving of social status. She holds the notepad of the time, a hinged wooden tablet filled with wax for writing on with the stylus (thin stick) that she touches to her lips; he holds a scroll of papyrus or animal skin, the standard form for books at the time. Her hairstyle was one popular in the mid-first century C.E. *(Erich Lessing/Art Resource, NY.)*

Authors with a more independent streak had to be careful. The historian Livy (54 B.C.E.–17 C.E.) composed a history of Rome in which he recorded Augustus's ruthlessness in the civil war after Caesar's murder. The emperor scolded but did not punish Livy because his work proclaimed that stability and prosperity depended on traditional values of loyalty and self-sacrifice. The poet Ovid (43 B.C.E.–17 C.E.), however, wrote *Art of Love* and *Love Affairs* to mock the emperor's moral legislation with witty advice for conducting sexual affairs and picking up other men's wives. His work *Metamorphoses* undermined the idea of hierarchy as natural by telling bizarre stories of supernatural shape-changes, with people becoming animals and confusion between the human and the divine. In 8 B.C.E., after Ovid became embroiled in the scandal involving Augustus's granddaughter, the emperor exiled him.

Public sculpture also reflected the emperor's influence. When Augustus was growing up, portraits were starkly realistic. The sculpture that Augustus ordered displayed an idealized style based on classical Greek models. In works such as the Prima Porta statue, Augustus had himself portrayed as serene and dignified, not careworn and sick, as he often was. As with architecture, Augustus used sculpture to project a calm and competent image of himself as the "restorer of the republic" and founder of a new age for Rome.

REVIEW: How did the peace gained through Augustus's "restoration of the republic" affect Romans' lives?

Maintaining the Pax Romana

Augustus made political changes to promote stability and prosperity (and his personal glory)—above all by preventing civil war—but his new system lacked a way to block struggles for power when

Marble Statue of Augustus from Prima Porta
At six feet eight inches high, this statue of Augustus stood a foot taller than he did. Found at his wife Livia's country villa at Prima Porta ("First Gate"), the portrait was probably done about 20 B.C.E., when Augustus was in his forties; however, it shows him as younger, using the idealizing techniques of classical Greek art. Compare his smooth face to the realistic portraiture in Chapter 5. The statue's symbols communicate Augustus's image: his bare feet hint he is a near-divine hero, the Cupid refers to the Julian family's descent from the goddess Venus, and the breastplate's design shows a Parthian surrendering to a Roman soldier under the gaze of personified cosmic forces admiring the peace Augustus's regime has created.
(Scala/Art Resource, NY.)

■ **For more help analyzing this image,** see the visual activity for this chapter in the Online Study Guide at **bedfordstmartins.com/hunt**.

the princeps died. Since he claimed not to have created a monarchy, no successor could automatically inherit his power without the Senate's approval. Augustus therefore decided to identify an heir whom he wished the senators to recognize as princeps after his death. This strategy succeeded and kept rule in his family, called the **Julio-Claudians**, until the death in 68 C.E. of Augustus's last descendent, the infamous Nero. It established the tradition that family dynasties ruled the "restored republic" of imperial Rome.

Under the principate, the emperor's main goals were preventing unrest, building loyalty, and financing the administration while governing the diverse provinces. Augustus set the pattern for effective imperial rule: take special care of the army, communicate the emperor's image as a just and generous ruler, and promote Roman law and

Julio-Claudians: The ruling family of the early principate from Augustus through Nero, descended from the aristocratic families of the Julians and the Claudians.

culture as universal standards. The citizens, in return for their loyalty, expected the emperors to be generous patrons—but the difficulties of long-range communication imposed practical limits on imperial intervention in the lives of the residents of the provinces.

Making Monarchy Permanent, 14–180 C.E.

Augustus's claim that the republic continued meant that he needed the Senate's cooperation to give legitimacy to his successor. He had no son, so he adopted Livia's son by a previous marriage, Tiberius (42 B.C.E.–37 C.E.). Since Tiberius had a distinguished record as a general, the army supported Augustus's choice. Augustus had Tiberius granted the power of a tribune and the power of a consul equal to his own so that he would be recognized as princeps after Augustus's death. The senators did just that when Augustus died in 14 C.E., allowing the Julio-Claudian dynasty to begin.

The First Dynasty: The Julio-Claudians, 14–68 C.E.

Tiberius (r. 14–37 C.E.) stayed in power for twenty-three years because he had the most important qualification for succeeding as emperor: the army's respect. He built the praetorian guard a fortified camp in Rome so that its soldiers could better protect the emperor. This change had the unintended consequence of guaranteeing the guards a role in determining all future successions—no emperor could come to power without their support. Tiberius described his position by saying, "I am the master of the slaves, the commander of the soldiers, and the princeps of the rest."

Tiberius's long reign provided the protracted transition period that the principate needed to endure, establishing the compromise on power between the elite and the emperor essential for political stability. The traditional offices of consul, senator, and provincial governor continued, with elite Romans filling them and basking in their prestige, but the emperors decided who received the offices and controlled law and government policy. In this way, the social elite performed valuable service, especially by keeping the peace and overseeing the collection of taxes while governing provinces that the emperor allotted them (though the provinces with strong military forces he governed through his assistants). Everyone saved face by pretending that the republic's political offices retained their original power.

Tiberius paid a bitter price to rule. To strengthen their family tie, Augustus forced Tiberius to divorce his beloved wife, Vipsania, to marry Augustus's daughter, Julia—and the marriage proved disastrously unhappy. When Tiberius's sadness led him to spend his reign's last decade in seclusion far from Rome, his neglect of the government permitted abuses in the capital and kept him from training a decent successor for the Senate's approval.

Tiberius designated Gaius (r. 37–41 C.E.), better known as Caligula, to be the next emperor because Gaius was Augustus's great-grandson and Tiberius's fawning supporter, not because he had leadership qualities. The third Julio-Claudian emperor might have been successful because he knew about soldiering: *Caligula* means "baby boots," the nickname the soldiers gave him as a child because he wore little leather shoes like theirs when he was growing up in the military garrisons his father (Tiberius's nephew and adopted son Germanicus) commanded. Unfortunately, Gaius's enormous appetites dominated his feeble virtues. Cruel and violent, he bankrupted the treasury to humor his desires. His biographer labeled him a monster for his murders and sexual crimes; the latter, gossip said, included incest with his sisters. He outraged the elite by fighting in mock gladiatorial combats and appearing in public in women's clothing or costumes imitating gods. As he said, "I'm allowed to do anything." The praetorian commanders murdered him in 41 C.E. to avenge personal insults.

The senators then debated the idea of truly restoring the republic by refusing to approve a new emperor. They capitulated, however, when Claudius (r. 41–54 C.E.), Augustus's grandnephew and Caligula's uncle, bribed the praetorian guard to back him. Claudius's succession revealed that the soldiers would insist on there always being an emperor so that they would have a patron to pay them and that senatorial yearnings for the republic's return would never be fulfilled.

Claudius was an active emperor, commanding a successful invasion of Britain in 43 C.E. that made much of the island into a Roman province. He opened the way for provincial elites to expand their participation in government by enrolling men from Gaul in the Senate. In return for keeping their regions peaceful and ensuring tax payments, they would receive offices at Rome and imperial patronage. Claudius also transformed imperial bureaucracy by employing freed slaves as powerful administrators; since they owed their positions to the emperor, they could be expected to be loyal.

Power corrupted Claudius's teenage successor, Nero (r. 54–68 C.E.). Emperor at sixteen, he loved music and acting, not governing. The spectacles he sponsored and the cash he distributed kept him popular with Rome's poor. His generals put down the revolt in Britain led by the woman commander Boudica in 60 C.E. and fought the Jewish rebels who tried to throw off Roman rule in Judaea in 66 C.E., but he himself had no military career. A giant fire in 64 C.E. (the event behind the legend that Nero fiddled while Rome burned) aroused suspicions that he ordered the conflagration to make space for a new palace. Nero scandalized the senatorial class by appearing onstage to sing, and he emptied the treasury by building a palace called the Golden House. To raise money he faked treason charges against senators and equites to seize their property. When his generals toppled his regime, Nero had a servant help him cut his own throat as he dug his grave, wailing, "I'm dying reduced to a laborer's status!"

The Flavian Dynasty and the Imperial Cult, 69–96 C.E.

Nero's fall sparked a year of civil war in which four generals vied for power (69 C.E., the Year of the Four Emperors). Vespasian (r. 69–79 C.E.) won. His victory proved that the principate would continue because the elite and the army demanded it. To give his new dynasty—the Flavian, from his family name—legitimacy, Vespasian had the Senate grant him the same powers as previous emperors, pointedly leaving Caligula and Nero off the list. He encouraged the spread of the imperial cult (worship of the emperor as a living god and sacrifices for his household's welfare) in the provinces but not in Italy, where this innovation would have disturbed traditional Romans. The imperial cult communicated the same image of the emperor to the provinces as Rome's architecture and sculpture did: he was superhuman, provided benefactions, and deserved loyalty. Vespasian reportedly did not believe in his own divinity, to judge from his witty remark on his deathbed: "Oh me! I think I'm becoming a god."

Vespasian's sons, Titus (r. 79–81 C.E.) and Domitian (r. 81–96 C.E.), conducted hardheaded fiscal policy and high-profile military campaigns. Titus finally suppressed the Jewish revolt by capturing Jerusalem in 70 C.E. He sent relief to Pompeii and Herculaneum when, in 79 C.E., Mount Vesuvius's volcanic eruption buried these towns. He built a state-of-the-art site for public entertainment by finishing Rome's **Colosseum**, outfitting the amphitheater seating fifty thousand spectators with awnings to shade the crowd. The Colosseum was deliberately constructed on the site of the former fishpond in Nero's Golden House to demonstrate the new dynasty's public-spiritedness.

During his reign, Domitian balanced the budget and campaigned against Germanic tribes threatening the empire's northern frontiers, but his arrogance turned the senators against him; once he sent them a letter announcing, "Our lord god, myself, orders you to do this." Alarmed by an elite general's rebellion, Domitian executed numerous upper-class citizens as conspirators. Fearful that they, too, would become victims, his wife and members of his court murdered him in 96 C.E.

The Five "Good Emperors," 96–180 C.E.

As Domitian's fate showed, the principate had not solved monarchy's inevitable weakness: rivalry among the elite for rule. The danger of civil war persisted, whether generated by ambitious generals or the emperor's jealous heirs. No one could predict whether a good ruler or a bad one would emerge. As Tacitus commented, emperors were like the weather: "We just have to wait for bad ones to pass and hope for good ones to appear." Fortunately for Rome, fair weather dawned with the next five emperors—Nerva (r. 96–98 C.E.), Trajan (r. 98–117 C.E.), Hadrian (r. 117–138 C.E.), Antoninus Pius (r. 138–161 C.E.), and Marcus Aurelius (r. 161–180 C.E.). Historians call this period the Roman political Golden Age because it had peaceful successions for nearly a century. Nevertheless, it saw ample war and strife: Trajan fought to expand Roman control across the Danube River into Dacia (today Romania) and eastward into Mesopotamia (Map 6.1); Hadrian executed several senators as alleged conspirators, punished a Jewish revolt by turning Jerusalem into a military colony, and withdrew Roman forces from Mesopotamia. Marcus Aurelius faithfully did his duty by spending difficult years fighting off invasions in the Danube region.

Still, the five "good emperors" did preside over a political and economic Golden Age. They succeeded one another without murder or conspiracy—the first four, having no surviving sons, used adoption to find the best possible successor. The economy provided enough money to finance building projects such as the fortification wall Hadrian built across Britain. Most important, they kept the army obedient. Their reigns marked Rome's longest stretch without a civil war since the second century B.C.E.

Colosseum: Rome's fifty-thousand-seat amphitheater built by the Flavian dynasty for gladiatorial combats and other spectacles.

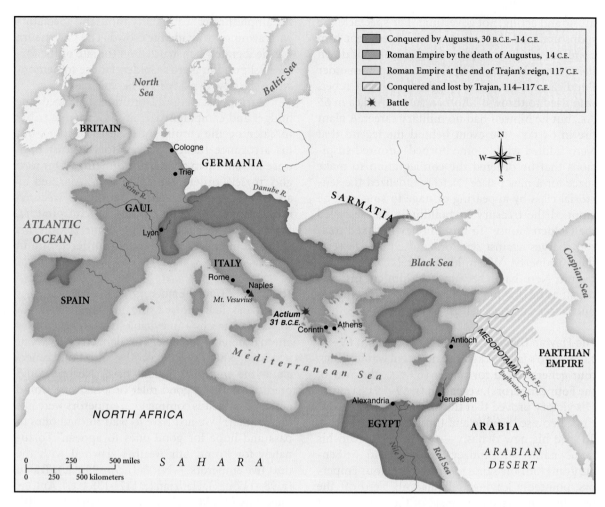

MAP 6.1 The Expansion of the Roman Empire, 30 B.C.E.–117 C.E.
When Octavian (the future Augustus) captured Egypt in 30 B.C.E. after the suicides of Mark Antony and Cleopatra, he greatly boosted Rome's economic strength. The land produced enormous amounts of grain and gold, and Roman power now almost encircled the Mediterranean Sea. When the emperor Trajan took over the southern part of Mesopotamia in 114–117 C.E., imperial conquest reached its height; Rome's control had never extended so far east. Egypt remained part of the empire until the Arab conquest in 642 C.E., but Mesopotamia was immediately abandoned by Hadrian, Trajan's successor, probably because it seemed too distant to defend. ■ How did territorial expansion both strengthen and weaken the Roman Empire?

Life in the Roman Golden Age, 96–180 C.E.

Peace and prosperity in Rome's Golden Age depended on defense by a loyal military, public-spiritedness by provincial elites in local administration and tax collection, common laws enforced throughout the empire, and a healthy population reproducing itself. The empire's vast size and the relatively small numbers of soldiers and imperial officials in the provinces meant that emperors had only limited control over these factors.

Imperial Military Aims and the Army. In theory, Rome's military goal remained perpetual expan-sion, because conquest brought land, money, and glory. Virgil expressed this notion in *The Aeneid* by portraying Jupiter, the king of the gods, as promising Rome "imperial rule without limit." In reality, the emperors lacked the resources to ex-pand the empire permanently much beyond what Augustus had controlled and had to concentrate on defending imperial territory.

Most provinces were peaceful and had no need for garrisons. Even Gaul, which had fiercely resisted Roman control, was, according to one contemporary witness, "kept in order by 1,200 troops—hardly more soldiers than it has towns." Most legions (units of five thousand troops) were stationed on frontiers to prevent invasions from barbarians to the north and Persians to the east. The Pax Romana supported the Golden Age's prosperity and promoted long-distance trade for luxury goods, such as spices and silk, from as far away as India and China.

The army, which included both Romans and noncitizens from the provinces, reflected the population's diversity. Serving under Roman officers, the non-Romans could learn to speak Latin and to practice Roman customs. Upon discharge, they received Roman citizenship. Thus, the army helped spread a common way of life.

Financing Government and Defense.

Paying for imperial government became an insoluble problem. In the past, foreign wars had brought in huge amounts of capital through booty and through prisoners of war sold into slavery. Conquered territory also provided additional tax revenues. Now the army was no longer making big conquests, but the soldiers had to be paid well to maintain discipline. As the army's patrons, emperors at their accession and other special occasions supplemented soldiers' regular pay with substantial bonuses. These rewards made a soldier's career desirable but cost the emperors dearly.

A tax on agriculture in the provinces (Italy was exempt) now provided the principal source of revenue for the imperial government and the army. The administration itself required relatively little money because it was small compared with the size of the territory being governed: no more than several hundred top officials governed a population of about fifty million. Most locally collected taxes stayed in the provinces for expenditures there, especially legionnaires' pay. Senatorial and equestrian governors with small staffs ran the provinces, which eventually numbered about forty. In Rome, the emperor employed a large staff of freedmen and slaves, while equestrian officials called prefects managed the city.

The government's finances depended on tax collection carried out by provincial elites. Serving as **decurions** (municipal senate members), these wealthy men were required personally to guarantee that their area's financial responsibilities were met. If there was a shortfall in tax collection or local finances, the decurions had to make up the difference from their own pockets. Wise emperors kept taxes moderate. As Tiberius put it when refusing a request for tax increases from provincial governors, "I want you to shear my sheep, not skin them alive." The financial liability could make holding civic office expensive, but the accompanying prestige made the elite willing to take the risk. Some decurions received priesthoods in the imperial cult as a reward, an honor open to both men and women.

The system worked because it observed tradition: the local elites were their communities' patrons and the emperor's clients. As long as there were enough rich, public-spirited provincials participating, the principate functioned by fostering the republican ideal of communal values.

The Impact of Roman Culture on the Provinces.

The provinces contained diverse peoples who spoke different languages, observed different customs, dressed differently, and worshipped different divinities (Map 6.2). In the countryside, Roman conquest only lightly affected local customs. Where new towns sprang up around Roman forts or settlements of army veterans, Roman influence prevailed. Modern cities such as Trier and Cologne, in Germany, started as such towns. Roman culture had the greatest effect on western Europe, permanently rooting Latin (and the languages that would emerge from it) as well as Roman law and customs there. Over time, social and cultural distinctions lessened between the provinces and Italy. Eventually, emperors came from citizen-families in the provinces; Trajan, from Spain, was the first.

Romanization, as historians call the spread of Roman law and culture in the provinces, raised the standard of living for many by providing roads and bridges, increasing trade, and establishing peaceful conditions for agriculture. The army's need for supplies created business for farmers and merchants. The prosperity that provincials enjoyed under Roman rule made Romanization acceptable. In addition, Romanization was not a one-way street. In western regions as diverse as Gaul, Britain, and North Africa, interaction between the local people and Romans produced new, mixed cultural traditions, especially in religion and art. Therefore, the process led to a gradual merging of Roman and local culture, not the unilateral imposition of the conquerors' way of life. (See Roman Architecture in North Africa on page 179.)

Romanization affected the eastern provinces less, and they largely retained their Greek and Near Eastern character. Huge Hellenistic cities such as Alexandria (in Egypt) and Antioch (in Syria)

---

decurions (dih KYUR ee uhns): Municipal senate members in the Roman Empire responsible for collecting local taxes.

Romanization: The spread of Roman law and culture in the provinces of the Roman Empire.

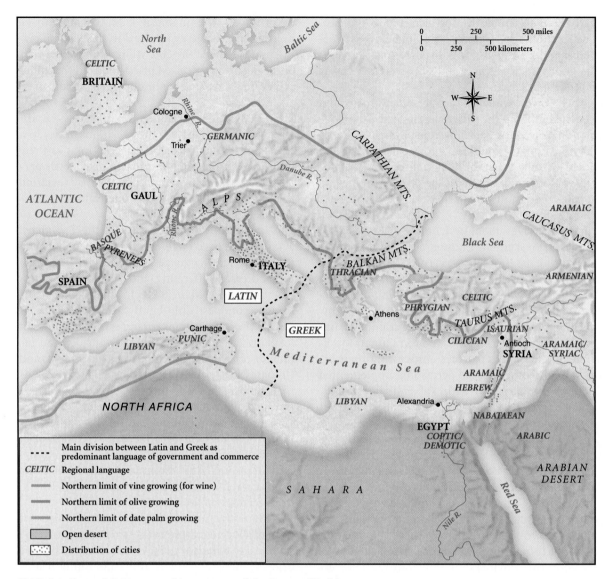

MAP 6.2 Natural Features and Languages of the Roman World
The environment of the Roman world included a large variety of topography, climate, and languages.
The inhabitants of the Roman Empire, estimated to have numbered as many as fifty million, spoke
dozens of different tongues, many of which survived well into the late empire. The two predominant
languages were Latin in the western part of the empire and Greek in the eastern. Latin remained the
language of law even in the eastern empire. Vineyards and olive groves were important agricultural
resources because wine was regarded as an essential beverage, and olive oil was the principal source
of fat for most people as well as being used to make soap, perfume, and other products for daily life.
Dates and figs were popular sweets in the Roman world, which had no sugar.

rivaled Rome in size and splendor. The eastern
provincial elites readily accepted Roman governance because Hellenistic royal traditions had prepared them to see the emperor as their patron and
themselves as his clients.

New Trends in Literature.   The continuing vitality of Greek language and culture contributed to
a flourishing of Roman literature. New trends,
often harking back to classical literature, blos-

somed. Lucian (c. 117–180 C.E.) composed satirical
dialogues fiercely mocking stuffy and superstitious
people. The essayist and philosopher Plutarch
(c. 50–120 C.E.) wrote *Parallel Lives*, biographies of
matching Greek and Roman men. His exciting stories made him favorite reading for centuries;
William Shakespeare (1564–1616) based several
plays on Plutarch's work.

So vigorous was the growth of Latin literature
that scholars rank the late first and early to mid-

Roman Architecture in North Africa

The Roman town of Thysdrus (today El Djem in Tunisia) built this amphitheater for public entertainment in the early third century C.E. Seating thirty-two thousand spectators (more than the town's total population), it imitated the larger Colosseum in Rome and was the seventh biggest such building in the empire. Its arched walls soared more than a hundred feet high, and storerooms under the arena floor had three elevators to lift wild animals to the surface. Thysdrus also had a track for chariot racing and a smaller amphitheater. *(Erich Lessing/Art Resource, NY.)*

second centuries C.E. as the Silver Age of Latin literature, second only to the Augustan Golden Age. Tacitus (c. 56–120 C.E.) composed historical works that exposed the Julio-Claudian emperors' ruthlessness. Juvenal (c. 65–130 C.E.) wrote poems mocking pretentious Romans while bemoaning the indignities of living broke in the capital. Apuleius (c. 125–170 C.E.) excited readers with his *Golden Ass*, a sexually explicit novel about a man turned into a donkey who regains his body and his soul through the kindness of the Egyptian goddess Isis.

Law and Order through Equity. Romans prided themselves on their ability to order their society through law. As Virgil said, their divine mission was "to establish law and order within a framework of peace." Roman law influenced most modern European legal systems. It featured the principle of equity, which meant doing what was "good and fair" even if that meant ignoring the letter of the law. This principle taught that the intent in a contract outweighed its words, and that accusers should prove the accused guilty because it

was unfair to make defendants prove their innocence. The emperor Trajan ruled that no one should be convicted on the grounds of suspicion alone because it was better for a guilty person to go unpunished than for an innocent person to be condemned. (See "Contrasting Views," page 186.)

The Roman notion of hierarchy required formal distinctions in society. The elites constituted a tiny portion of the population. Only about one in every fifty thousand had enough money to qualify for the senatorial order, the highest-ranking class, while about one in a thousand belonged to the equestrian order, the second-ranking class. Different purple stripes on clothing identified these orders. The third highest order consisted of decurions, the local senate members in provincial towns.

Republican law had made a legal distinction between "better people" and "humbler people" that became even stricter under the principate. "Better people" included senators, equites, decurions, and retired army veterans. Everybody else — except slaves, who counted as property, not people — made up the vastly larger group of

Midwife's Sign

Childbirth was dangerous for women because of possible death from infection or internal hemorrhage. This terra-cotta sign from Ostia, the ancient port city of Rome, probably hung outside a midwife's room to announce her expertise in helping women give birth. It shows a pregnant woman clutching the sides of her chair, with an assistant supporting her from behind and the midwife crouched in front to help deliver the baby. Why do you think the woman is seated for delivery instead of lying down? Such signs were especially effective for people who were illiterate; a person did not have to read to understand the services that the specialist inside could provide. *(Scala/Art Resource, NY.)*

"humbler people." The law imposed harsher penalties on them than on "better people" for the same crime. "Humbler people" convicted of capital crimes were regularly executed by being crucified or torn apart by wild animals before a crowd of spectators. "Better people" rarely suffered the death penalty; if they did, they received a quicker and more dignified execution by the sword. "Humbler people" could also be tortured in criminal investigations, even if they were citizens. Romans regarded these differences as fair on the grounds that an elite person's higher status required of him or her a higher level of responsibility for the common good. As one provincial governor expressed it, "Nothing is less equitable than mere equality itself."

Reproduction and Marriage.   Nothing mattered more to the empire's strength than steady population levels. Concern about reproduction filled Roman society. The upper-class government official Pliny, for example, sent the following report to the grandfather of his third wife, Calpurnia: "You will be very sad to learn that your granddaughter has suffered a miscarriage. She is a young girl and did not realize she was pregnant. As a result she was more active than she should have been and paid a high price."

Complications in childbirth could easily lead to the mother's death because doctors could not stop internal bleeding or cure infections. They possessed sturdy instruments for surgery and physical examinations, but they misunderstood the biology of reproduction. Gynecologists erroneously recommended the days just after menstruation as the best time to become pregnant, when the woman's body was "not congested." Many doctors were freedmen from the provinces, usually with only informal training. People considered their occupation of low status, unless they served the upper class.

As in earlier times, girls often wed in their early teens, to have as many years as possible to bear children. Wealthy women hired wet nurses to breastfeed their babies. Because so many babies died young, families had to produce numerous offspring to keep from disappearing. The tombstone of Veturia, a soldier's wife married at eleven, tells a typical story: "Here I lie, having lived for twenty-seven years. I was married to the same man for sixteen years and bore six children, five of whom died before I did." The propertied classes usually arranged marriages between spouses who hardly knew each other, although husband and wife could grow to love each other in a partnership devoted to family.

The emphasis on childbearing brought many health hazards to women, but to remain single and childless represented social failure for women and men. When Romans wanted to control family size, they practiced contraception by obstructing the female organs or by administering drugs to the female partner, or they abandoned unwanted infants.

The emperors tried to support reproduction. They aided needy children to encourage larger families. Following the emperors' lead, wealthy people often adopted children in their communities. One North African man supported three hundred boys and three hundred girls each year until they grew up.

REVIEW: In the early Roman Empire, what was life like in the cities and in the country for the elite and for ordinary people?

The Emergence of Christianity

Christianity began as what scholars call "the Jesus Movement," a Jewish splinter group in Judaea, where, as elsewhere under Roman rule, Jews were allowed to practice their ancestral religion. The new faith was slow to attract believers; three centuries after the death of Jesus, Christians were still a minority. Moreover, from time to time they aroused official suspicion and hostility. The new religion grew, if slowly, because it had an appeal based on Jesus's charismatic career, its message of salvation, its early believers' sense of mission, and the strong bonds of community it inspired. Ultimately, Christianity's emergence proved the most significant development in Roman history.

Jesus and His Teachings

Jesus (c. 4 B.C.E.–30 C.E.) grew up in a troubled region. Harsh Roman rule in Judaea had angered the Jews, and the provincial authorities worried about rebellion. Jesus's execution reflected the Roman policy of eliminating any threat to social order. In the two decades after his crucifixion, his followers, particularly Paul of Tarsus, spread his teachings beyond his region's Jewish community to the wider Roman world.

Jewish Apocalypticism and Christianity. Christianity offered an answer to a difficult question about divine justice raised by the Jews' long history of oppression under the kingdoms of the ancient and Hellenistic Near East: If God was just, as Hebrew monotheism taught, how could he allow the wicked to prosper and the righteous to suffer? Nearly two hundred years before Jesus's birth, persecution by the Seleucid king Antiochus IV (r. 175–164 B.C.E.) had provoked the Jews into revolt, a struggle that generated the concept of apocalypticism (see Chapter 2, page 41). According to this doctrine, evil powers controlled the world, but God would end their rule by sending the Messiah ("anointed one," *Mashiach* in Hebrew, **Christ** in Greek) to conquer them. A final judgment would soon follow, punishing the wicked and rewarding the righteous for eternity. Apocalypticism especially influenced the Jews living in Judaea under Roman rule and later inspired Christians and Muslims.

Christ: Greek for "anointed one," in Hebrew *Mashiach* or in English *Messiah*; in apocalyptic thought, God's agent sent to conquer the forces of evil.

During Jesus's life, Jews disagreed among themselves about what form Judaism should take in such troubled times. Some favored accommodation with the Romans, while others preached rejection of the non-Jewish world and its spiritual corruption. Their local ruler, installed by the Romans, was Herod the Great (r. 37–4 B.C.E.). His Greek style of life, flouting Jewish law, made him unpopular with many locals, despite his magnificent rebuilding of the great Jewish temple in Jerusalem. When a decade of unrest followed Herod's death, Augustus installed a Roman administration to stop the trouble. Judaea had thus turned into a powder keg by Jesus's lifetime.

The Life and Ministry of Jesus. Jesus began his career as a teacher and healer during the reign of Tiberius. The books that would later become the New Testament Gospels, composed around 70 to 90 C.E., offer the earliest accounts of his life. Jesus wrote nothing down, and others' accounts of his words and deeds are varied. He taught not through direct instruction but by telling stories and parables that challenged his followers to reflect on what he meant.

Jesus's public ministry began with his baptism by John the Baptist, who preached a message of repentance before the approaching final judgment. The Jewish ruler Herod Antipas, a son of Herod the Great, executed John because he feared that John's apocalyptic preaching might instigate riots. After John's death, Jesus continued his mission by traveling around Judaea's countryside teaching that God's kingdom was coming and that those who heard him needed to prepare spiritually for it. Some saw Jesus as the Messiah, but his apocalypticism did not call for immediate revolt against the Romans. Instead, he taught that God's true kingdom was to be found not on earth but in heaven. He stressed that this kingdom was open to believers regardless of their social status or apparent sinfulness. His emphasis on God's love for humanity and people's responsibility to love one another reflected Jewish religious teachings, such as the scriptural interpretations and moral teachings of the scholar Hillel, who lived in the time of Jesus.

Realizing that he had to reach more than country people to make an impact, Jesus took his message to the Jewish population of Jerusalem, the region's main city. His miraculous healings and ex-

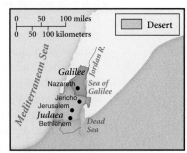

Palestine in the Time of Jesus, 30 C.E.

orcisms, combined with his powerful preaching, created a sensation. So popular was he that his followers created the Jesus movement; it was not yet Christianity but rather a Jewish sect, of which there were several, such as the Saducces and Pharisees, competing for authority at the time. Jesus attracted the attention of Jewish leaders, who assumed that he aspired to replace them. Fearing Jesus might ignite a Jewish revolt, the Roman governor Pontius Pilate ordered his crucifixion in Jerusalem in 30 C.E.

The Mission of Paul of Tarsus. Jesus's followers reported that they had seen him in person after his death, proclaiming that God had raised him from the dead. They convinced a few other Jews that he would soon return to judge the world and begin God's kingdom. At this time, his closest disciples, the twelve Apostles (Greek for "messengers"), still considered themselves faithful Jews and continued to follow the commandments of Jewish law. Their leader was Peter, who won acclaim as the greatest miracle worker of the Apostles, an ambassador to Jews interested in the Jesus movement, and the most important messenger proclaiming Jesus's teachings in the imperial capital; the later Christian church called him the first bishop of Rome.

A radical change took place with the conversion of Paul of Tarsus (c. 10–65 C.E.), a pious Jew and a Roman citizen who had violently opposed Jews who accepted Jesus as the Messiah. A spiritual vision on the road to Damascus in Syria, which Paul interpreted as a divine revelation, inspired him to become a follower of Jesus as the Messiah, or Christ—a Christian, as members of the movement came to be known. Paul taught that accepting Jesus as divine and his crucifixion as the ultimate sacrifice for the sins of humanity was the only way of becoming righteous in the eyes of God. In this way alone could one expect to attain salvation in the world to come.

Seeking converts outside Judaea, Paul traveled to preach to Jews and Gentiles (non-Jews) who had adopted some Jewish practices in Asia Minor (today Turkey), Syria, and Greece. Although he stressed the necessity of ethical behavior as defined by Jewish tradition, especially the rejection of sexual immorality and polytheism, Paul also taught that converts need not keep all the provisions of Jewish law. To make conversion easier, he did not require male converts to undergo the Jewish initiation rite of circumcision. This tenet and his teachings that his congregations did not have to observe Jewish dietary restrictions or festivals led to tensions with Jewish authorities in Jerusalem as well as with the followers of Jesus living there, who still believed that Christians had to follow Jewish law. Roman authorities arrested Paul as a troublemaker, and he was executed in about 65 C.E.

Hatred of Roman rule provoked Jews to revolt in 66 C.E. After crushing the rebels in 70 C.E., the Roman emperor Titus destroyed the Jerusalem temple and sold most of the city's population into slavery. In the aftermath of this catastrophe, Christianity began to be separated from Judaism, giving birth to a different religion now that the Jewish community had lost its religious center.

Paul's importance in early Christianity shows in the number of letters—thirteen—attributed to him among the twenty-seven Christian writings that were put together as the New Testament by around 200 C.E. Followers of Jesus regarded the New Testament as having equal authority with the Jewish Bible, which they then called the Old Testament. Since teachers like Paul preached mainly in the cities to reach large crowds, congregations of Christians sprang up in urban areas. In early Christianity, women in some locations could be leaders, such as Lydia, a businesswoman who founded the congregation in Philippi in Greece, but many men, such as Paul, opposed women's leadership.

Growth of a New Religion

Christianity faced serious obstacles as a new religion. Imperial officials, suspecting Christians such as Vibia Perpetua of being traitors, could prosecute them for refusing to perform traditional sacrifices. Christian leaders had to build an organization from scratch to administer their growing congregations. Finally, Christians had to settle the dispute over a leadership role for women.

The Rise of Persecution and Martyrdom. The Roman emperors found Christians baffling and troublesome. Unlike Jews, Christians professed a new faith rather than their ancestors' traditional religion; Roman law therefore granted them no special treatment. Most Romans feared that Christians' denial of the old gods and the imperial cult would provoke divine retribution. Christians' secret rituals led to accusations of cannibalism and sexual promiscuity because they symbolically ate the body and drank the blood of Jesus during communal dinners, called Love Feasts, which men and women attended together.

Not surprisingly, Romans were quick to blame Christians for disasters. Following Rome's great fire in 64 C.E., Nero punished Christians as arsonists by draping them in wild animal skins to be

Catacomb Painting of Christ as the Good Shepherd
Catacombs (underground tombs), cut into soft rock outside various cities of the Roman Empire, served as meeting rooms and vast underground burial chambers for Jews and Christians. Rome alone had 340 miles of catacombs. Painted in the third century C.E. on the wall of a Christian catacomb just outside Rome, this fresco depicts Jesus as the Good Shepherd (John 10:10–11). In addition to the tired or injured sheep, Jesus carries a pot of milk and perhaps honey, which new Christians received after their baptism as a symbol of their entry into the Promised Land of the Hebrew Bible. Such catacomb paintings were the earliest Christian art. *(Scala/Art Resource, NY.)*

torn to bits by dogs, or fastened to crosses and set on fire to light the streets at night. The cruelty of Nero's punishments earned Christians sympathy from Rome's population.

Persecutions like Nero's were infrequent and sporadic. No law forbade Christianity, but officials could punish Christians, as they could other citizens, to maintain public order. Pliny's actions as a provincial governor in Asia Minor illustrated the situation. (See "Contrasting Views," page 186.) In about 112 C.E., Pliny asked some people accused of practicing this new religion if they were really Christians and urged those who confessed to reconsider. He freed those who denied Christianity, so long as they sacrificed to the gods, vowed loyalty through the imperial cult, and cursed Christ. He executed those who persisted in their faith. Advocates of Christianity argued that Romans had nothing to fear from their faith. Far from spreading immorality and subversion, they insisted, Christianity taught an elevated moral code and respect for authority. It was not a foreign superstition but the true philosophy, combining the best features of Judaism and Greek rational thought.

The sporadic persecutions of the early empire did not stop Christianity. Christians like Perpetua regarded public executions as an opportunity to become a **martyr** (Greek for "witness"), someone

who dies for his or her religious faith. Martyrs' belief that their deaths would send them directly to paradise allowed them to face torture; some Christians actively sought martyrdom. Tertullian (c. 160–240 C.E.) proclaimed that "martyrs' blood is the seed of the Church." Ignatius (c. 35–107 C.E.), bishop of Antioch, begged Rome's congregation, which was becoming the most prominent Christian group, not to ask the emperor to show him mercy after his arrest: "Let me be food for the wild animals [in the arena] through whom I can reach God," he pleaded. "I am God's wheat, to be ground up by the teeth of beasts so that I may be found pure bread of Christ." Stories reporting the martyrs' courage inspired the faithful to accept hostility from non-Christians and helped shape the new religion as a creed that gave its believers the spiritual power to endure suffering.

Bishops and Christian Hierarchy. First-century C.E. Christians expected Jesus to return to pass judgment on the world during their lifetimes. When he did not, they began transforming their religion from an apocalyptic Jewish sect expecting the immediate end of the world into one that could survive indefinitely. This transformation was painful because early Christians fiercely disagreed about what they should believe, how they should live, and who had the authority to decide these questions. Some insisted Christians should withdraw from the everyday world to escape its evil,

---

martyr: Greek for "witness," the term for someone who dies for his or her religious beliefs.

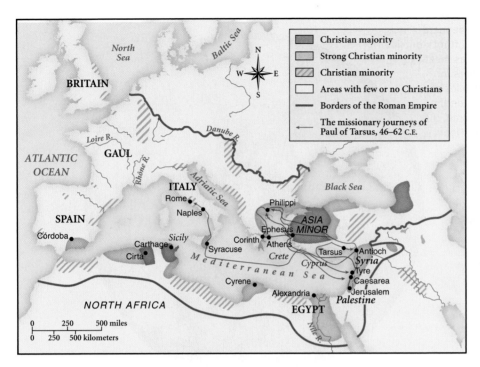

MAP 6.3 Christian Populations in the Late Third Century C.E.
Christians were still a minority in the Roman world three hundred years after Jesus's crucifixion. Certain areas of the empire, however, especially Asia Minor, where Paul had preached, had a concentration of Christians. Most Christians lived in cities and towns, where the missionaries had gone to find crowds to hear their message. *Paganus*, a Latin word for "country person" or "rural villager," came to mean a believer in traditional polytheistic cults—hence the word *pagan* often found in modern works on this period. Paganism lived on in rural areas for centuries.

abandoning their families and shunning sex and reproduction. Others believed they could live by Christ's teachings while living ordinary lives. Many Christians worried they could not serve as soldiers without betraying their faith because the army participated in the imperial cult. This dilemma raised the further issue of whether Christians could remain loyal subjects of the emperor. Disagreement over these doctrinal questions raged in the many congregations that arose in the early empire around the Mediterranean, from Gaul to Africa to the Near East (Map 6.3).

The need to deal with such tensions and to administer the congregations led Christians to create a hierarchical organization, headed by bishops with authority to define Christian doctrine and regulate congregations. The emergence of bishops became the most important institutional development in early Christianity. Bishops received their positions based on the principle later called **apostolic succession**, which states that the Apostles appointed the first bishops as their successors, granting these new officials the authority Jesus had originally given to the Apostles. Those designated by the Apostles in turn appointed their own successors. Bishops had authority to ordain priests with the holy power to administer the sacraments, above all baptism and communion, which believ-

ers regarded as necessary for achieving eternal life. Bishops also controlled their congregations' memberships and finances; the money financing the early church flowed from members' gifts.

The bishops tried to suppress the disagreements splintering the new religion. They claimed the authority to define **orthodoxy** (true doctrine) and **heresy** (false doctrine). The meetings of the bishops of different cities constituted the church's organization in this period. Today it is common to refer to this loose organization as the early Catholic (Greek for "universal") church. Since the bishops themselves often disagreed about doctrine, unity remained an unachieved goal.

Women in the Church. When bishops came to power, they demoted women from positions of leadership. This change reflected their view that in Christianity women should be subordinate to men, just as in Roman imperial society in general.

Some congregations took a long time to accept this shift, however, and women still claimed authority in some groups in the second and third centuries C.E. In late second-century C.E. Asia Minor, for example, Prisca and Maximilla declared themselves prophetesses with the power to baptize believers in anticipation of the coming end of the

---

apostolic (ah puh STAH lihk) succession: The principle by which Christian bishops traced their authority back to the apostles of Jesus.

orthodoxy: True doctrine; specifically, the beliefs defined for Christians by councils of bishops.

heresy: False doctrine; specifically, the beliefs banned for Christians by councils of bishops.

Mithras Slaying the Bull
Hundreds of shrines to the mysterious god Mithras have been found in the Roman Empire. Scholars debate the symbolic meaning of the bull slaying so prominent in art connected to Mithras's cult, as in this wall painting of about 200 C.E. from the shrine at Marino, south of Rome. Here, a snake and a dog lick the sacrificial animal's blood, while a scorpion pinches its testicles as it dies in agony. The ancient sources do not clarify the scene's meaning. What do you think could be the explanation for this type of sacrifice? *(Scala/Art Resource, NY.)*

world. They spread the apocalyptic message that the heavenly Jerusalem would soon descend in their region.

Excluded from leadership posts, many women chose a life without sex to demonstrate their devotion to Christ. Their commitment to celibacy gave these women the power to control their own bodies. Other Christians regarded women achieving this special closeness to God as holy and socially superior. By rejecting the traditional roles of wife and mother in favor of spiritual excellence, celibate Christian women achieved independence and status otherwise denied them.

Competing Beliefs

Three centuries after Jesus's death, the overwhelming majority of the Roman Empire's population still practiced traditional polytheism. Its beliefs, centered on deities worshiped in varying ways in different places, never became a unified religion. The principate's success and prosperity gave traditional believers confidence that the old gods and the imperial cult protected them. Even those who preferred religious philosophy, such as Stoicism's idea of divine providence, respected the old cults because they embodied Roman tradition. By the third century C.E., the growth of Christianity, along with the persistence of Judaism and polytheistic cults, meant that people could choose from a number of competing beliefs. Especially appealing were beliefs that offered people hope that they could change their present lives for the better and also look forward to an afterlife.

Polytheistic, or pagan, religion had as its goal gaining the favor of all the divinities who could affect human life. Its deities ranged from the state cults' major gods, such as Jupiter and Minerva, to spirits thought to inhabit groves and springs. International cults such as the Mysteries of Demeter and Persephone outside Athens remained popular; the emperor Hadrian traveled there to be initiated.

Isis and Mithras.   The cults of Isis and Mithras demonstrate how polytheism could provide a religious experience arousing strong emotions and

Christians in the Empire: Conspirators or Faithful Subjects?

Romans worried that new religions would disrupt the "peace with the gods" that guaranteed their national safety and prosperity. Groups whose religious beliefs seemed likely to offend the traditional deities could therefore be accused of treason, but Christians insisted that they were loyal subjects who prayed for the safety of the emperors (Document 1). The early emperors tried to forge a policy that was fair both to Christian subjects and to those citizens who feared them (Document 2).

1. Tertullian's Defense of His Fellow Christians, 197 C.E.

A sharp-tongued theologian from North Africa, Tertullian insisted that Christians supported the empire. He explained that, even though Christians refused to pray to the emperor, they prayed for him and thus for the community's health and safety.

So that is why Christians are public enemies — because they will not give the emperors vain, false, and reckless honors; because, being men of a true religion, they celebrate the emperors' festivals more in heart than in frolic. . . .

On the contrary, the name faction may properly be given to those who join to hate the good and honest, who shout for the blood of the innocent, who use as a pretext to defend their hatred the absurdity that they take the Christians to be the cause of every disaster to the state, of every misfortune of the people. If the Tiber reaches the walls, if the Nile does not rise to water the fields, if the sky does not move [i.e., if there is no rain] or the earth does, if there is famine, if there is plague, the cry at once arises: "The Christians to the lions!"

For we invoke the eternal God, the true God, the living God for the safety of the emperors. . . . Looking up to heaven, the Christians — with hands outspread, because innocent, with head bare because we do not blush, yes! and without a prompter because we pray from the heart — are ever praying for all the emperors. We pray for a fortunate life for them, a secure rule, a safe house, brave armies, a faithful senate, a virtuous people, a peaceful world. . . .

Should not our sect [i.e., Christianity] have been classed among the legal associations, when it commits no such actions as are commonly feared from unlawful associations? For unless I am mistaken, the reason for prohibiting associations clearly lay in forethought for public order — to save the state from being torn into factions, a thing very likely to disturb election assemblies, public gatherings, local senates, meetings, even the public games, with the clashing and rivalry of partisans. . . . We, however, whom all the passion for glory and rank leave cold, have no need to combine; nothing is more foreign to us than the state. One state we recognize for all — the universe.

Source: Tertullian, *Apology*, 10.1, 23.2–3, 35.1, 40.1–2. Translation by T. R. Glover, 1931.

2. Pliny on Early Imperial Policy toward Christians, 112 C.E.

As governor of the province of Bithynia, Pliny had to decide the fate of Christians accused of crimes by their neighbors. Knowing of no precedent to guide him, he tried to be fair and wrote to the emperor Trajan to ask if he had acted correctly. The emperor's reply set out official policy concerning Christians in the early empire.

[Pliny to the emperor Trajan]

It is my practice, my lord, to refer to you all matters concerning which I am in doubt. For who can better give guidance

demanding a moral way of life. The Egyptian goddess Isis had already attracted Romans by the time of Augustus, who tried to suppress her cult because it was Cleopatra's religion. But the fame of Isis as a kind, compassionate goddess who cared for her followers made her cult too popular to crush: the Egyptians said it was her tears for starving humans that caused the Nile to flood every year and bring them good harvests. Her image was that of a loving mother, and in art she was often depicted nursing her son. Her cult's central doctrine concerned the death and resurrection of her husband, Osiris; Isis promised her believers a similar life after death.

Isis required her followers to behave righteously. Many inscriptions expressed her high moral standards by listing her own civilizing accomplishments: "I broke down the rule of tyrants; I put an end to murders; I caused what is right to be mightier than gold and silver." The hero of Apuleius's novel *The Golden Ass* shouts out his into my hesitation or inform my ignorance? I have never participated in trials of Christians. I therefore do not know what offenses it is the practice to punish or investigate, and to what extent. . . .

In the case of those who were denounced to me as Christians, I have observed the following procedure: I interrogated these as to whether they were Christians; those who confessed I interrogated a second and a third time, threatening them with punishment; those who persisted I ordered executed. For I had no doubt that, whatever the nature of their creed, stubbornness and inflexible obstinacy surely deserve to be punished. There were others possessed of the same madness; but because they were Roman citizens, I signed an order for them to be transferred to Rome.

Soon accusations spread, as usually happens, because of the proceedings going on, and several incidents occurred. An anonymous document was published containing the names of many persons. Those who denied that they were or had been Christians, when they invoked the gods in words dictated by me, offered prayer with incense and wine to your image, which I had ordered to be brought for this purpose together with statues of the gods, and moreover cursed Christ—none of which those who are really Christians, it is said, can be forced to do—these I thought should be set free. Others named by the informer declared that they were Christians, but then denied it, asserting that they had been but had ceased to be, some three years before, others many years, some as much as twenty-five years. They all worshiped your image and the statues of the gods, and cursed Christ.

They asserted, however, that the sum and substance of their fault or error had been that they were accustomed to meet on a fixed day before dawn and sing responsively a hymn to Christ as to a god, and to bind themselves by oath, not to some crime, but not to commit fraud, theft, or adultery, not to break their word, nor to refuse to return a trust when called upon to do so. When this was over, it was their custom to depart and to assemble again to eat together—but ordinary and innocent food. Even this, they affirmed, they had stopped doing after my edict by which, in accordance with your instructions, I had forbidden political asso-

ciations. Accordingly, I judged it all the more necessary to find out what the truth was by torturing two female slaves who were called attendants. But I discovered nothing else but depraved, excessive superstition.

I therefore postponed the investigation and hastened to consult you. For the matter seemed to me to require consulting you, especially because of the numbers involved. For the infection of this superstition has spread not only to the cities but also to the villages and farms. But it seems possible to check and cure it. It is certainly quite clear that the temples, which had been almost deserted, have begun to be frequented, that the established religious rites, long neglected, are being resumed, and that from everywhere sacrificial animals are coming, for which until now very few purchasers could be found. Hence it is easy to imagine what a multitude of people can be reformed if an opportunity for repentance is afforded.

[The emperor Trajan to Pliny]

You followed proper procedure, my dear Pliny, in handling the cases of those who had been denounced to you as Christians. For it is not possible to lay down any general rule to serve as a kind of fixed standard. They are not to be searched for; if they are denounced and proved guilty, they are to be punished, with this reservation, that whoever denies that he is a Christian and really proves it—that is, by worshiping our gods—even though he was under suspicion in the past, shall obtain pardon through repentance. But anonymously posted accusations ought to have no place in any prosecution. For this is both a dangerous kind of precedent and out of keeping with [the spirit of] our age.

Source: Pliny, *Letters*, Book 10, nos. 96 and 97. Translation (modified) by Betty Radice, 1969.

QUESTIONS TO CONSIDER

1. Do you think that Pliny's procedure in dealing with the accused Christians respected the Roman legal principle of equity? Explain.
2. How should a society treat a minority of its members whose presence severely disturbs the majority?

tense joy after his rescue and spiritual rebirth through Isis: "O holy and eternal guardian of the human race, who always cherishes mortals and blesses them, you care for the troubles of miserable humans with a sweet mother's love. Neither day nor night, nor any moment of time, ever passes by without your blessings." Other cults also required worshippers to lead upright lives. Inscriptions from Asia Minor, for example, record people's confessions to sins such as sexual trans-

gressions for which their local god had imposed severe penance.

Archaeology reveals that the cult of Mithras had many shrines under the Roman Empire, but no texts survive to explain its mysterious rituals and symbols, which Romans believed had originated in Persia. Mithras's legend said that he killed a bull in a cave, apparently as a sacrifice for the benefit of his worshippers. As pictures show (see Mithras Slaying the Bull, page 185), this was no ordinary sacrifice because the animal did not die without struggling. Initiates in Mithras's cult proceeded through rankings named, from bottom to top, Raven, Male Bride, Soldier, Lion, Persian, Sunrunner, and Father, this last a title of great honor.

Philosophy as Guide.   Many upper-class Romans guided their lives by Greek philosophy. The most popular choice was Stoicism, which required self-discipline and duty (see Chapters 4 and 5). Philosophic individuals put together their own set of beliefs, such as those on duty expressed by the emperor Marcus Aurelius in his memoirs, entitled *To Myself* (or *Meditations*).

Christian and polytheist intellectuals debated Christianity's relationship to Greek philosophy. Origen (c. 185–255 C.E.) argued that Christianity was superior to Greek philosophical doctrines as a guide to correct living. At about the same time, Plotinus (c. 205–270 C.E.) developed the most religiously influential formulation of philosophic belief. His spiritual philosophy was influenced by Persian religious ideas and, above all, Plato's philosophy, for which reason it is called **Neoplatonism**. Plotinus's ideas deeply influenced many Christian thinkers as well as polytheists. He wrote that ultimate reality is a trinity of The One, Mind, and Soul. By turning away from the life of the body and relying on reason, individual souls could achieve a mystic union with The One, who, in Christian thought, would be God. To succeed in this spiritual quest required strenuous self-discipline in personal morality and spiritual purity as well as in philosophical contemplation.

> **REVIEW:** Which factors supported the growth of Christianity, and which opposed it?

The Third-Century Crisis

In the third century C.E., military expenses provoked a financial crisis that fed a political crisis lasting from the 230s to the 280s C.E. Invasions on the northern and eastern frontiers had forced the emperors to expand the army for defense, but no new revenues came in to meet the additional costs. The emperors' desperate schemes to finance defense costs damaged the economy and infuriated the population. This anger at the regime encouraged generals to imitate the behavior that had de-

Neoplatonism: Plotinus's spiritual philosophy, based mainly on Plato's ideas, which was very influential for Christian intellectuals.

War Scene on Trajan's Column
The emperor Trajan erected a hundred-foot-tall column carved with some twenty-five hundred figures to show his conquest of Dacia (territory north of the Danube River). Our knowledge of Roman military equipment largely comes from the pictures on the column. The scenes spiral up the column in a continuing story, showing Trajan leading his troops and making sacrifices to the gods, with his soldiers preparing to march, crossing the river, building camps, and (as here) fighting hand-to-hand battles with the Dacians, who fought with no armor except shields. (© *Vittoriano Rastelli/Corbis.*)

stroyed the republic: commanding client armies to seize power. They created civil war that lasted fifty years. Earthquakes and scattered epidemics added to people's misery. By 284 C.E., this combination of troubles had shredded the Pax Romana.

Defending the Frontiers

Emperors since Domitian in the first century had combated invaders. The most aggressive attackers were the multiethnic bands that crossed the Danube and Rhine rivers to raid Roman territory. Constant fighting against the Roman army helped these poorly organized northerners develop military discipline, and they mounted dangerous invasions during the reign of Marcus Aurelius (r. 161–180 C.E.). A major threat also appeared at the eastern edge of the empire, when a new dynasty, the Sasanids, defeated the Parthian Empire and reenergized the ancient Persian kingdom. By the early third century C.E., Persia's military resurgence compelled the emperors to concentrate forces in the rich eastern provinces, at the expense of the defense of the northern frontiers.

Recognizing the northern warriors' bravery, the emperors had begun hiring them as auxiliary soldiers for the Roman army in the late first century C.E. and settling them on the frontiers as buffers against other invaders. By around 200 C.E., the army had expanded to enroll perhaps as many as 450,000 troops (the size of the navy remains unknown). Training constantly, soldiers had to be able to carry forty-pound packs twenty miles in five hours, swimming rivers on the way. Since the early second century C.E., the emperors had built many stone camps for permanent garrisons, but on the march an army constructed a fortified camp every night; soldiers transported all the makings of a wooden walled city everywhere they went. As one ancient commentator noted, "Infantrymen were little different from loaded pack mules." At one temporary fort in a frontier area, archaeologists found a supply of a million iron nails—ten tons' worth. The same encampment required seventeen miles of timber for its barracks' walls. To outfit a single legion with tents required fifty-four thousand calves' hides.

The increased demand for pay and supplies strained imperial finances because successful conquests had become rare. The army had become a source of negative instead of positive cash flow to the treasury, and the economy had not expanded to make up the difference. To make matters worse, inflation had driven up prices. A principal cause of inflation may have been, ironically, the principate's long period of peace, during which demand for the economy's relatively static production of goods and services had increased.

In desperation, some emperors attempted to curb inflation by debasing imperial coinage to cut government costs. **Debasement of coinage** meant putting less silver in each coin without changing its

debasement of coinage: Putting less silver in a coin without changing its face value; practiced during the third-century C.E. crisis in Rome.

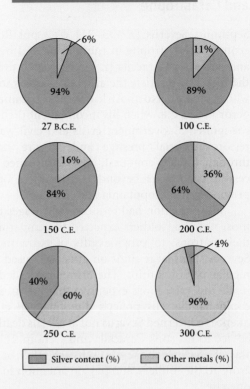

TAKING MEASURE

The Value of Roman Imperial Coinage, 27 B.C.E.–300 C.E. Ancient silver coinage derived its value from its metallic content; the less silver in a coin, the less the coin was worth. When government and military expenses rose but revenues fell because no conquests were being made, emperors debased the coinage by reducing the amount of silver and increasing the amount of other, cheaper metals in each coin. These pie charts reveal that devaluation of the coinage was gradual until the third century C.E., when military expenses skyrocketed. By 300 C.E., coins contained only a trace amount of silver. Debasement fueled inflation because merchants and producers had to raise their prices for goods and services when they were paid with currency that was increasingly less valuable. (Adapted from Kevin Greene, The Archeology of the Roman Empire (London: B. T. Batsford, Ltd., 1986), 60.)

face value; the emperors hoped in this way to create more cash from the same amount of precious metal. (See "Taking Measure" on this page.) But merchants soon raised prices to make up for the debased coinage's reduced value; this in turn produced more inflation. By 200 C.E., the furious spiral of rising prices had spun into a financial tornado. Still, the soldiers demanded that their patrons, the emperors, pay them well. This pressure drove imperial finances into collapse by the 250s C.E.

The Severan Emperors and Catastrophe

Septimius Severus (r. 193–211 C.E.) put Rome's economic catastrophe in motion: he and his son and successor Caracalla (r. 211–217 C.E.) drained the treasury to satisfy the army. A soldier's soldier who came from North Africa, Severus became emperor in 193 C.E. when his incompetent predecessor ignited a government crisis and civil war. To restore imperial prestige and acquire money through foreign conquest, Severus pursued successful campaigns beyond the frontiers of the provinces in Mesopotamia and Scotland.

Since inflation had reduced their wages to almost nothing, soldiers expected the emperors, as their patrons, to provide gifts of extra money. Severus spent large sums on gifts and raised their regular pay by a third. The army's expanded size made this raise more expensive than the treasury could handle. His policy's dire financial consequences concerned Severus not at all. His deathbed advice to his sons Caracalla and Geta in 211 C.E. was to "stay on good terms with each other, be generous to the soldiers, and pay no attention to anyone else."

Caracalla and Civil War. Severus's sons followed his advice only on the last two points. Caracalla, after murdering his brother, ended the Roman Golden Age of peace and prosperity with his reckless spending and cruelty. He increased the soldiers' pay by another 40 to 50 percent and spent gigantic sums on building projects, including the largest public baths Rome had ever seen, covering blocks and blocks of the city. His extravagant spending put unbearable pressure on the local provincial officials responsible for collecting taxes and on the citizens, whom the officials in turn squeezed for ever larger payments.

In 212 C.E., Caracalla took his most famous step to try to fix the budget crisis: he granted Roman citizenship to almost every man and woman in imperial territory except slaves. Since only citizens paid inheritance taxes and fees for freeing slaves, an increase in citizens meant an increase in revenues, most of which was earmarked for the army. But too much was never enough for Caracalla, whose brutal treatment of anyone who displeased him made contemporaries whisper that he was insane. His attempted conquests of new territory failed to bring in enough funds, and he wrecked the imperial budget. Once when his mother upbraided him for his excesses he replied, as he drew his sword, "Never mind, we won't run out of money as long as I have this."

Financial troubles fueled a period of political instability that flared into a half century of civil war. Compounded by natural disasters, this stretch of violent struggle broke the principate's back. For fifty years, a parade of emperors and pretenders fought to rule; more than two dozen men, often

Emperor Severus and His Family
This portrait of the emperor Septimius Severus; his wife, Julia Domna; and their sons, Caracalla (on the right) and Geta (with his face obliterated) was painted in Egypt about 200 C.E. The males hold scepters, symbolic of rule, but all four family members wear bejeweled golden crowns fit for royalty. Severus arranged to marry Julia without ever meeting her because her horoscope predicted she would become a queen, and she served as her husband's valued adviser. They hoped their sons would share rule, but when Severus died in 211 C.E., Caracalla murdered Geta so that he could rule alone. Why do you think the portrait's owner rubbed out Geta's face? *(Bildarchiv Preussischer Kulturbesitz/Art Resource, NY.)*

several at a time, held or claimed power in that time. Their only qualification was their ability to command a frontier army and to reward the troops for loyalty to their general instead of to the state.

This civil war devastated the population and the economy; violence and hyperinflation made life miserable in many regions. Agriculture withered as farmers could not keep up normal production when armies searching for food ravaged their crops. City council members faced constantly escalating demands for tax revenues from the swiftly changing emperors; the endless financial pressure destroyed members' will to serve their communities.

Foreign enemies to the north and east took advantage of the Roman civil wars to attack. Roman fortunes hit bottom when Shapur I, king of the Sasanid Empire of Persia, invaded the province of Syria and captured the emperor Valerian (r. 253–260 C.E.). Imperial territory was in constant danger of fragmenting by the later third century C.E. Zenobia, the warrior queen of Palmyra in Syria, for example, seized Egypt and Asia Minor; the emperor Aurelian (r. 270–275 C.E.) recovered these provinces only with great difficulty. He also had to encircle Rome with a larger wall to ward off attacks from northern raiders, who were smashing their way into Italy from the north.

Historians dispute how severely natural disaster worsened the crisis, but earthquakes and epidemics did strike some of the provinces in the mid-third century. The population declined significantly as food supplies became less dependable, civil war killed soldiers and civilians alike, and infection flared over large regions. The loss of population meant fewer soldiers for the army, whose strength as a defense and police force had been gutted by political and financial chaos. This weakness made frontier areas more vulnerable to raids and allowed roving bands of robbers to range unchecked inside the borders.

Persecution of Christians.   Polytheists explained the third-century crisis in the traditional way: the state gods were angry about something. But what? The obvious answer was the presence of Christians, who denied the existence of the Roman gods and refused to participate in their worship. The emperor Decius (r. 249–251 C.E.) therefore launched a systematic persecution to eliminate Christians and restore the goodwill of the gods. He proclaimed himself Restorer of the Cults while declaring, "I would rather see a rival to my throne than another bishop of Rome." He ordered all the empire's inhabitants to prove their loyalty to the state's well-being by sacrificing to its gods. Christians who refused were killed. This persecution did not stop the civil war, economic failure, and natural disasters that threatened Rome's empire. By the 280s C.E., the principate was near to fragmenting.

> **REVIEW:** What were the causes and the effects of the Roman crisis in the third century C.E.?

Conclusion

Augustus created the principate and the Pax Romana by installing a disguised monarchy while insisting that he was restoring the republic. He succeeded because he ensured the army's loyalty and exploited the traditional patron-client system. The principate made the emperor the army's and the people's patron. Provincials found this arrangement acceptable because it replicated the kind of top-down government that they had grown used to before Roman conquest. The imperial cult provided a focus for building and displaying loyalty to the emperor.

So long as the emperors had enough money to keep their millions of clients satisfied, stability prevailed. They provided food to the poor, built baths and arenas for public entertainment, and paid their troops well. The emperors of the first and second centuries expanded the military to protect their distant territories stretching from Britain to North Africa to Syria. By the second century, peace and prosperity had created an imperial Golden Age. Long-term financial difficulties set in, however, because the army, now concentrating on defense, no longer brought money in through frequent conquests. Severe inflation made the situation desperate. Since the elites could no longer meet the demand for increased taxes without draining their fortunes, they lost their public-spiritedness and avoided their communal responsibilities. Loyalty to the state became too expensive.

The emergence of Christianity added to the instability because Roman officials doubted Christians' loyalty. The new religion evolved from Jewish apocalypticism to a hierarchical organization. Its believers disputed with each other and with the authorities; martyrs such as Vibia Perpetua worried the government with the depth of their beliefs. Citizens placing loyalty to a divinity ahead of loyalty to the state was a new and inexplicable phenomenon for Roman officialdom.

When financial ruin, civil war, and natural disasters combined to weaken the principate in the

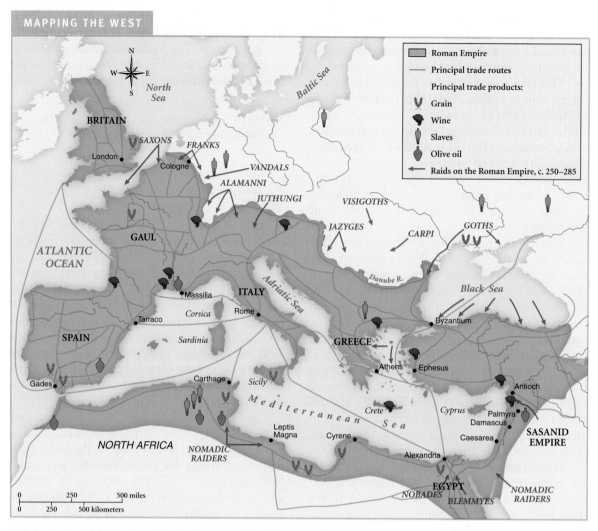

The Roman Empire in Crisis, 284 C.E.

By the 280s C.E., fifty years of civil war had torn the principate apart. Imperial territory retained the outlines inherited from the time of Augustus (compare Map 6.1 on page 176), except for the loss of Dacia to the Goths a few years before. Attacks from the north and east had repeatedly penetrated the frontiers, however. Long-distance trade had always been important to the empire's prosperity, but the decades of violence had made transport riskier and therefore more expensive, contributing to the crisis. ■ What do you think would have been the greatest challenges in ruling such a vast empire in an age without swift communications or fast travel?

mid-third century C.E., the emperors lacked the money and the popular support to end the crisis. Not even persecutions of Christians could convince the gods to restore Rome's good fortunes, and the Pax Romana fell apart. The empire, threatened with fragmentation, had to be transformed politically and religiously. That transformation took place under the emperors Diocletian (r. 284–305 C.E.) and Constantine (r. 306–337 C.E.).

FOR FURTHER EXPLORATION

■ **For suggested references, including Web sites, for topics in this chapter,** see page SR-1 at the end of the book.

■ **For additional primary-source material from this period,** see Chapter 6 in *Sources of THE MAKING OF THE WEST*, Third Edition.

■ **For Web sites and documents related to topics in this chapter,** see *Make History* at bedfordstmartins.com/hunt.

CHAPTER REVIEW

KEY TERMS AND PEOPLE

principate (164)
Pax Romana (164)
Augustus (165)
praetorian guard (166)
Julio-Claudians (173)
Colosseum (175)
decurions (177)
Romanization (177)

Christ (181)
martyr (183)
apostolic succession (184)
orthodoxy (184)
heresy (184)
Neoplatonism (188)
debasement of coinage (189)

REVIEW QUESTIONS

1. How did the peace gained through Augustus's "restoration of the republic" affect Romans' lives?

2. In the early Roman Empire, what was life like in the cities and in the country for the elite and for ordinary people?

3. Which factors supported the growth of Christianity, and which opposed it?

4. What were the causes and the effects of the Roman crisis in the third century C.E.?

MAKING CONNECTIONS

1. What were the similarities and differences between the crisis in the first century B.C.E. that undermined the republic and the crisis in the third century C.E. that undermined the principate?

2. If you had been a first-century Roman emperor under the principate, what would you have done about the Christians and why? What if you had been a third-century emperor?

> **For practice quizzes, a customized study plan, and other study tools,** see the Online Study Guide at **bedfordstmartins.com/hunt**.

IMPORTANT EVENTS

30 B.C.E.	Octavian (the future Augustus) conquers Ptolemaic Egypt	**70–90 C.E.**	New Testament Gospels are written
27 B.C.E.	Augustus inaugurates the *principate*	**80s C.E.**	Domitian leads campaigns against multiethnic invaders on northern frontiers
30 C.E.	Jesus crucified in Jerusalem	**161–180 C.E.**	Multiethnic bands attack the northern frontiers
64 C.E.	Much of Rome burns in mammoth fire; Nero blames Christians	**212 C.E.**	Caracalla extends Roman citizenship to almost all free inhabitants of the provinces
69 C.E.	Civil war during the Year of the Four Emperors	**249–251 C.E.**	Decius persecutes Christians
70 C.E.	Titus captures Jerusalem and destroys the Jewish temple	**230s–280s C.E.**	Third-century crisis

The Transformation of the Roman Empire
284–600 C.E.

In 376 C.E., bands of Visigoths, desperate to escape the deadly attacks of the Huns, begged the Roman emperor Valens (r. 364–378) to let them cross the Danube River from their homelands into Roman territory. As emperors before him had done, Valens admitted them into the empire because he wanted to use their warriors in place of Romans, who could buy their way out of military service by paying for barbarian—that is, northern foreign—mercenaries to substitute for them. Roman officers charged with helping the barbarians instead greedily extorted bribes; they even forced the starving refugees to sell some of their own people into slavery to buy dogs to eat.

Furious, the barbarians massacred Valens's army at the battle of Adrianople (or Hadrianopolis) in Thrace in 378. Valens trampled on the bleeding corpses of his men as he tried to escape. He failed, and his body was never found. Some said he was incinerated while cowering in a farmhouse, eerily fulfilling the wishes of citizens who often expressed their unhappiness with his reign by rioting in the streets and yelling, "We want Valens to burn alive!" Theodosius I (r. 379–395), Valens's successor, then had to allow the barbarians to settle permanently inside the borders in a kingdom under their own laws and give them annual "gifts" of money, in return for their fighting alongside Romans as federates (allies) protecting the empire.

The battle of Adrianople, Rome's bloodiest defeat since Hannibal had invaded Italy six hundred years earlier, illustrates the love-hate

Vandal General Stilicho and His Family
This ivory diptych ("folding tablet") from around 400 C.E. shows Stilicho, the top general in the Roman army in Europe and close adviser to the western Roman emperor, with Stilicho's wife, Serena, and their son Eucherius. Born to a barbarian (non-Roman) father from the Vandal tribe in Germany and a Roman mother, Stilicho rose to prominence in Roman imperial government and society; he married the adoptive daughter of the emperor, and his daughter Maria married the emperor's son. Stilicho's parentage reveals the mixing of cultures in the later Roman Empire, while the depiction of the dual rulers points to the political and geographical fragmentation that also took place. Stilicho is shown dressed in the richly decorated clothing appropriate for a member of the Roman elite, and he wears a metal clasp to fasten his robe, a symbol of his father's ethnicity. The images on his shield of the two emperors then ruling the divided Roman Empire proclaimed his loyalty. *(Basilica di San Giovanni Battista, Monza, Italy/The Bridgeman Art Library.)*

relationship that the emperors had with the barbarian peoples north and east of the Danube and Rhine rivers in Europe: for centuries, Rome's rulers, recognizing the barbarians' bravery, had hired them as soldiers and let them bring their families into the empire, while at the same time looking down on them for their non-Roman ways and often allowing imperial officials to exploit them so cruelly that they rebelled. This relationship had unintentional consequences that helped change the course of history by pushing the Roman Empire toward fragmentation into two halves with different destinies.

Competition between ambitious generals and would-be emperors had fueled the empire's third-century crisis. The emperor Diocletian (r. 284–305) finally stopped Romans from fighting one another. Tough enough to impose peace, he was also flexible enough to reorganize the administration by appointing a co-emperor and two assistant emperors. Regaining social stability proved more difficult because of religious tensions between Christians and followers of traditional polytheistic cults concerning who was responsible for the divine anger that, they all believed, had sent the crisis. Diocletian pushed his co-rulers to persecute the Christians, whom he blamed. His successor Constantine (r. 306–337) ended this brutality by converting to Christianity and supporting it with imperial funds and a policy of religious toleration. Even with official support, however, it took nearly a hundred years more for the new faith to become the state religion, and the church from early on was rocked by fierce disagreements over doctrine. The social and cultural transformations produced by the Christianization of the Roman Empire settled in even more slowly because many Romans clung to their traditional beliefs; Christian emperors had to employ non-Christians if they wanted to get the best possible administrators and generals.

Diocletian's rescue of the empire only postponed the splintering of imperial territory: less than twenty years after the battle of Adrianople, Theodosius I split the empire in two, with one of his sons ruling the west and the other the east. The two emperors were supposed to cooperate, but in the long run this system of divided rule could not cope with the different pressures affecting the two regions.

In the western empire, military and political events provoked social and cultural change when barbarian newcomers began living side by side with Romans. Both sides changed, with the barbarians creating kingdoms and laws based on Roman traditions and adopting Christianity, while wealthy Romans increasingly fled from cities to seek safety in country estates when the western central government became ineffective. These changes in turn transformed the political landscape of western Europe

Coin Portrait of Emperor Constantine
Constantine had these special, extra-large coins minted to depict him for the first time as an overtly Christian emperor. The jewels on his helmet and crown, the fancy bridle on the horse, and the scepter indicate his status as emperor, while his armor and shield signify his military accomplishments. He proclaims his Christian rule with his scepter's new design—a cross with a globe—and the round badge sticking up from his helmet that carries the monogram signifying "Christ" (see page 202) that he had his soldiers paint on their shields to win God's favor in battle. *(Staatliche Munzsammlung, Münich.)*

■ 293 Tetrarchy created

■ 301 Diocletian's Edict on Maximum Prices and Wages

■ 303 Diocletian launches Great Persecution of Christians

■ 312 Battle of the Milvian Bridge; Constantine converts to Christianity

■ 361–363 Julian the Apostate tries to reinstate traditional religion

■ 391 Theodosius I makes Christianity the official religion

300 C.E.   **350 C.E.**   **400 C.E.**

■ 313 Edict of Milan

■ 323 Pachomius establishes first monasteries in Upper Egypt

■ 324 Constantine wins civil war; Constantinople becomes "new Rome"

■ 325 Council of Nicaea

■ 378 Battle of Adrianople

■ 395 Empire divided into western and eastern halves

■ 410 Visigoths sack Rome

in ways that foreshadowed Europe's later political states. In the east, the empire, economically vibrant and politically united, lived on for a thousand years beyond its disintegration and transformation in the west and helped pass on the memory of classical traditions to later Western civilization by preserving much ancient Greek and Roman literature. Despite financial pressures and the gradual loss of territory, the eastern half endured as the continuation of the Roman Empire until Turkish invaders conquered it in 1453.

> **FOCUS QUESTION:** What were the most important sources of unity and of division in the Roman Empire from the reign of Diocletian to the reign of Justinian, and why?

Reorganizing the Empire, 284–395

Diocletian and Constantine pulled Roman government out of its extended crisis by increasing the emperors' authority, reorganizing the empire's defense, restricting workers' freedom, and changing the tax system to try to raise the money to pay for all these changes. The two emperors also believed that they had to win back divine favor to ensure their people's safety. This duty, however, was now complicated by concern about the gods' goodwill that the growing number of Christians provoked among followers of Rome's traditional religion.

Diocletian and Constantine believed that they could best resolve the empire's problems by becoming more autocratic. Since for Romans strength had to be visible to be effective, they transformed their appearance as rulers to make their power seem awesome beyond compare, hoping that this display of supremacy would help keep the empire united. In the long run, however, their desire to preserve the empire on the scale created by Augustus became only an empty longing.

From Reform to Fragmentation

No one could have predicted Diocletian's success: he began life as an uneducated peasant in the Balkans, far from the center of power in Rome. In the third-century crisis, however, military talent counted for more than connections. Diocletian's leadership, courage, and intelligence propelled him through the ranks until the army made him emperor in 284. He slammed the gate on half a century of anarchy by imposing the most autocratic system of rule in Roman history.

Inventing the Dominate. The foremost symbol of Diocletian's new system was the title that he used after becoming emperor: *dominus*, meaning "lord" or "master" — what slaves called their owners. Historians refer to Roman rule from Diocletian onward as the **dominate**. Like the emperors before them, the emperors of the dominate continued to refer to their government as the Roman republic (see, for example, the first line in the document "Diocletian's Edict on Maximum Prices and Wages," page 201), but they ruled autocratically as "lords and masters." This new system eliminated any sharing of authority with the Senate, for the emperors of the dominate recognized no social equals. Senators, consuls, and other positions from the ancient republic continued to exist but only as posts of honor; these officials had the responsibil-

---

dominate: The blatantly authoritarian style of Roman rule from Diocletian (r. 284–305) onward; the word was derived from *dominus* ("master" or "lord") and contrasted with *principate*.

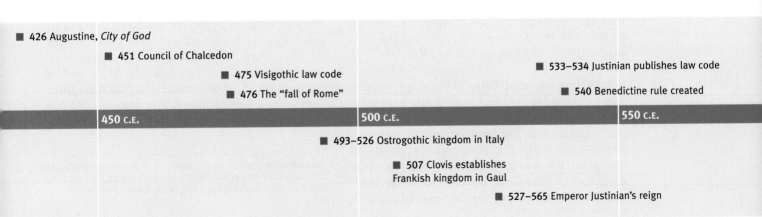

■ 426 Augustine, *City of God*

    ■ 451 Council of Chalcedon

        ■ 475 Visigothic law code

        ■ 476 The "fall of Rome"

            ■ 533–534 Justinian publishes law code

            ■ 540 Benedictine rule created

450 C.E.	500 C.E.	550 C.E.

    ■ 493–526 Ostrogothic kingdom in Italy

    ■ 507 Clovis establishes Frankish kingdom in Gaul

    ■ 527–565 Emperor Justinian's reign

ity to pay for public services, especially chariot races and festivals, but no power to govern. Imperial administrators were increasingly chosen from lower ranks of society according to their competence and their loyalty to the emperor.

The grandiose style of the dominate recalled the monarchies of the ancient Near East rather than the modest manner of Augustus's principate. The dominate's emperors flaunted their majesty by surrounding themselves with courtiers and ceremony, presiding from a raised platform, and sparkling in jeweled crowns, robes, and shoes. Constantine initiated the tradition that emperors set themselves apart by wearing a diadem, a purple gem-studded headband, as a visible boast of supremacy that recalled the decorated ribbon Alexander the Great put on his head after conquering the Persian king. In an echo of Persian monarchy, a series of veils separated the palace's waiting rooms from the interior room where the emperor listened to people's pleas for help or justice, further emphasizing the difference between the emperor and ordinary people. Officials marked their rank in the rigidly hierarchical administration by wearing special shoes and belts and claiming grandiose titles such as "most perfect."

The dominate's emperors also asserted their supreme power through laws and punishments. Their word alone made law; indeed, they came to be above the law because they were not bound even by the decisions of their predecessors. To impose order, they raised punishments to often brutal levels. Violent criminals were executed in traditional fashion: tied in a leather sack with poisonous snakes and drowned in a river. New punishments included Constantine's order that the "greedy hands" of officials who took bribes "shall be cut off by the sword." The guardians of a young girl who allowed a lover to seduce her were executed by having molten lead poured into their mouths. Penalties grew ever harsher for the majority of the population, legally designated as "humbler people" to indicate they could be punished more severely than the "better people" for comparable offenses. In this way, the dominate strengthened the divisions between ordinary people and the rich.

Subdividing Imperial Rule. Diocletian realized that he needed to reform imperial rule to prevent civil war and defend against invaders from the north and the east. The principle underlying his reforms—subdivide the government's power to strengthen it—was daring because it increased the chance of more civil war between ambitious leaders. By 293, he had put the first part of his plan

into practice. He divided imperial territory into four loosely defined administrative districts, two in the west and two in the east. He then appointed three "partners" (a co-emperor and two assistant emperors, who were the designated successors) to join him in this new subdivision of power, called a **tetrarchy** ("rule by four"). Each ruler controlled one of the four districts. Diocletian served as supreme ruler and was supposed to receive the loyalty of the others. This system was Diocletian's attempt to put imperial government into closer contact with the empire's frontier regions, where the danger of invasion or rebellious troops loomed.

Diocletian also subdivided the territory of the provinces themselves, thereby doubling their number to almost a hundred. He then grouped these smaller administrative units into twelve regions (dioceses) under separate governors, who reported to the four emperors' assistants, the praetorian prefects (Map 7.1). Finally, he tried to prevent provincial administrators from rebelling by separating their civil and military authority, granting them control only of legal and financial affairs while entrusting defense to separate commanders, a process that Constantine completed.

Although Diocletian's successors dropped the tetrarchy, his principle of subdividing rule endured. It also ended Rome's thousand years as the capital city. Diocletian—who lived in Nicomedia, in Asia Minor—did not even visit Rome until 303, nearly twenty years after becoming emperor. He chose his four new capitals for their utility as military command posts close to the frontiers: Milan, in northern Italy; Sirmium, near the Danube River border; Trier, near the Rhine River border; and Nicomedia. Italy became just another section of the empire, on an equal footing with the other provinces and subject to the same taxation system, except for the district of Rome itself—the last vestige of the city's traditional primacy.

Creating Eastern and Western Empires. Diocletian's reforms failed to guarantee political stability. After he resigned in 305 for unknown reasons, rivals for power fought off and on in civil wars until 324, when Constantine finally defeated all contenders outside his own family. At the end of his reign in 337, Constantine designated his three sons as joint heirs, admonishing them to continue the new imperial system of co-emperorship.

---

tetrarchy: The "rule by four," consisting of two co-emperors and two assistant emperors/designated successors, initiated by Diocletian to subdivide the ruling of the Roman Empire into four regions.

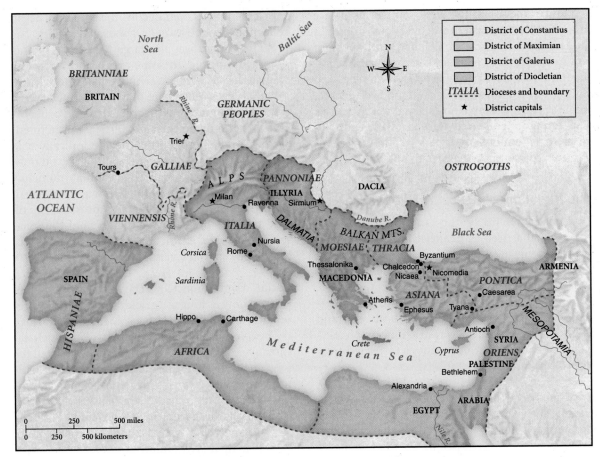

MAP 7.1 Diocletian's Reorganization of 293
Anxious to avoid further civil war, Emperor Diocletian reorganized imperial territory for tighter control by placing the Roman Empire under the rule of the tetrarchy's four partners, each the head of a large district. He subdivided the preexisting provinces into smaller units and grouped them into twelve dioceses, each overseen by a regional administrator. The four districts as shown here reflect the arrangement recorded by the imperial official Sextus Aurelius Victor in about 360. ■ What were the advantages and disadvantages of subdividing the empire?

Plunging into war with one another, they failed to govern together as violently as had the sons of Septimius Severus a century earlier.

When their rivalry ruined any chance of genuinely shared rule, they put their forces in positions that roughly split the Roman Empire on a north–south line along the Balkan peninsula. Theodosius made this territorial division official in 395. He intended for the eastern empire and the western empire to cooperate, but the permanent division launched the empire's halves on different futures.

Each half had its own capital city. Constantinople ("Constantine's City") — formerly the ancient city of Byzantium (today Istanbul, Turkey) — was the eastern capital. Constantine had renamed it after himself in 324, boasting that it was a "new Rome." He had made it his capital because of its strategic military and commercial location: it lay at the mouth of the Black Sea on an easily fortified peninsula astride principal routes for trade and troop movements. To recall the glory of Rome and thus claim for himself the political legitimacy of the old capital, Constantine constructed a forum, an imperial palace, a hippodrome for chariot races, and monumental statues of the traditional gods in his refounded city. Constantinople grew to be the greatest city in the Roman Empire.

Geography determined the site of the western capital as well. Honorius, Theodosius's

The Empire's East/West Division, 395

son and successor in the west, wanted his palace in a city that was easier to defend than Rome. In 404, he chose the port of Ravenna, an important commercial center on Italy's northeastern coast that housed a main naval base. Great marshes and walls protected it from attack by land, while access to the sea kept it from being starved out in a siege. The emperors enhanced Ravenna with churches covered in multicolored mosaics, but it never rivaled Constantinople in size or splendor.

The High Cost of Rescuing the Empire

Diocletian's rescue of the empire carried high costs, social as well as financial ones. To support the huge army needed to keep peace inside the empire and defend its frontiers, Diocletian imposed a new taxation system and price and wage controls, hoping to raise more revenue and control inflation. These measures squeezed both rich and poor financially, while new restrictions on people's rights to choose their occupations restricted freedoms for many in the empire.

Price and Wage Controls and Tax Increases.

Diocletian struggled to reduce the hyperinflation brought on by the third-century civil wars. As prices rose ever higher, people hoarded whatever they could buy. "Hurry and spend all my money you have; buy me any kinds of goods at whatever prices they are available," wrote one official to his servant, trying to salvage something of the value of his savings by converting his money into things. Hoarding, however, only worsened the problem.

In 301, the inflation was so severe that Diocletian took the radical step of imposing harsh price and wage controls in the worst-hit areas (see Document, "Diocletian's Edict on Maximum Prices and Wages," page 201). This mandate, which blamed high prices on profiteers' "unlimited and frenzied avarice," forbade hoarding of goods and set ceilings on what could legally be charged or paid for about one thousand goods and services. However, merchants refused to cooperate and government officials were unable to enforce the mandate, despite the threat of death or exile as the penalty for violations.

The civil wars that followed Diocletian's resignation stoked the government's insatiable appetite for revenue. The emperors increased taxes mostly to support the army, which required enormous amounts of grain, meat, salt, wine, vegetable oil, horses, camels, and mules. The major sources of payments were a tax on land, assessed according to its productivity, and a head tax on individuals. To supplement taxes paid in coin, the emperors began collecting some revenue in goods and services.

The empire was too large to enforce the tax system uniformly. In some areas, both men and women ages twelve to sixty-five paid the full tax, but in others women paid only one-half the tax assessment or none at all. Workers in cities probably owed taxes only on their property, perhaps to encourage crafts production. They periodically paid "in kind," that is, by laboring without pay on public works projects such as cleaning municipal drains or repairing buildings. Owners of urban businesses, from shopkeepers to prostitutes, still paid taxes in money, while members of the senatorial class were exempt from ordinary taxes but had to pay special levies.

Social Consequences.

The new tax system worked only as long as agricultural production remained stable and the government kept track of the people liable for the head tax (see "Taking Measure," page 202). Diocletian therefore restricted the movement of tenant farmers, called *coloni* ("cultivators"), whose work provided the empire's economic base. Coloni had traditionally been free to move to another farm to work for a new landlord as long as their debts were paid. Now, male coloni, as well as their wives in areas where women were assessed for taxes, were increasingly tied to a particular plot of land. Their children were also bound to the family plot, making farming a hereditary obligation.

The government also regulated other occupations deemed essential. Bakers, who were required to produce free bread for Rome's many poor, a tradition begun under the republic to prevent food riots, could not leave their jobs, and anyone who acquired a baker's property had to assume that occupation. From Constantine's reign on, the military was another hereditary lifetime career: the sons of military veterans were obliged to serve in the army.

The emperors decreed equally oppressive regulations for the **curials**, the social elite in the cities and towns. During this period, almost all men in the curial class were obliged to serve as unsalaried members of their city senate (*curia*) and to spend

---

coloni (kuh LOH ny): Literally, "cultivators"; tenant farmers in the Roman Empire who became bound by law to the land they worked and whose children were legally required to continue to farm the same land.

curials (KYUR ee uhls): The social elite in Roman empires' cities and towns, most of whom were obliged to serve on municipal senates and collect taxes for the imperial government, paying any shortfalls themselves.

DOCUMENT

Diocletian's Edict on Maximum Prices and Wages

To try to control rampant inflation caused by soaring government expenditures, Diocletian and his co-emperors issued an edict in 301 C.E. setting maximum prices and wages for the first time in Roman history. Their orders proved impossible to enforce across the vast empire. The high-sounding language was typical of imperial bureaucracy under the dominate.

Recalling the wars that we have successfully waged, it is to the fortune of our republic, next to the immortal gods, that we owe the peaceful state of our world, located in the lap of the deepest tranquillity, and the benefits of peace, which we worked for with great effort. Our honorable public and Rome's respectability and majesty long for this fortune to be faithfully established and suitably adorned. Therefore, we, who with the kind support of the gods in the past overcame the blazing raids of the barbarian peoples by slaughtering those nations, must fortify the tranquillity that we established for eternity with the necessary defenses of justice. . . .

It is agreed that we [the co-emperors], who are the parents of the human race, are to bring decisive justice to the situation, so that what humanity has long hoped for but not been able to provide will be conferred by the solutions of our foresight for the common improvement of everyone. . . .

Who then could be unaware that audacity lies in wait to attack the public interest wherever the common well-being of everyone demands that our armies be directed, not only in villages or towns but on every march, jacking up prices for goods for sale not four or eight times, but to such a height that the system of human speech cannot find names for this pricing and this deed. And so the result is that the sale of a single item deprives the soldier of his bonus and his pay, and that all the taxes paid by the entire world to support the armies fall victim to this detestable profit seeking. . . .

It is our decision that, if anyone makes an effort through daring to go against this edict, he shall be subject to capital punishment. . . .

Listed below are the prices for the sale of individual items; no one may exceed them. *[These examples are selections from the edict's long list of maximum allowed prices and wages. A sextarius was about half a liter; the Roman pound was about three-quarters of a U.S. pound. The silver coin was the denarius. A soldier at this date earned eighteen hundred silver coins per year.]*

Prices for food

Sextarius of first-quality old wine
  24 silver coins
Sextarius of country wine   8 silver coins

Sextarius of beer from Gaul   4 silver coins
Sextarius of beer from Egypt   2 silver coins
Pound of pork   12 silver coins
Pound of goat or sheep   8 silver coins
Fattened pheasant   250 silver coins
Pair of chickens   60 silver coins
Pound of second-quality fish   16 silver coins

Wages for workers

Daily pay for a farm laborer, with food
  25 silver coins
Daily pay for a finish carpenter, with food   50 silver coins
Baker, with food   50 silver coins
Mule doctor, for trimming and preparing hoofs   6 silver coins per animal
Scribe, for first-quality writing   25 silver coins per 100 lines
Scribe, for second-quality writing   20 silver coins per 100 lines
Elementary teacher   50 silver coins per student per month
Greek, Latin, or geometry teacher   200 silver coins per student per month
Public speaking teacher   250 silver coins per student per month
Legal expert or speaker in court   1,000 silver coins per case

Source: *Diocletiani edictum de pretiis rerum venalium.* Translation by Thomas R. Martin.

their own funds to support the community. Their financial responsibilities ranged from maintaining the water supply to feeding troops, but their most expensive duty was paying for shortfalls in tax collection. The emperors' demands for more and more revenue made this duty a crushing obligation, compounding the damage that the third-century crisis had inflicted on local elites.

For centuries, the empire's welfare had depended on a steady supply of property owners filling crucial local posts in return for honor and the

emperor's favor. Now this tradition broke down as wealthy people avoided public service to escape financial ruin. So distorted had the situation become that service on a municipal council could be imposed as punishment for a crime. Eventually, to prevent curials from escaping their obligations, imperial policy forbade them to move away from the town where they had been born. Members of the elite tried frantically to win exemptions from public service by petitioning the emperor, bribing imperial officials, or taking up

TAKING MEASURE

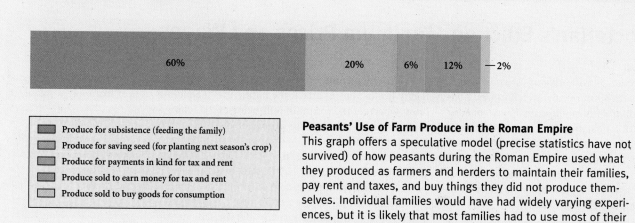

60%	20%	6%	12%	—2%

- ▮ Produce for subsistence (feeding the family)
- ▮ Produce for saving seed (for planting next season's crop)
- ▮ Produce for payments in kind for tax and rent
- ▮ Produce sold to earn money for tax and rent
- ▮ Produce sold to buy goods for consumption

Peasants' Use of Farm Produce in the Roman Empire
This graph offers a speculative model (precise statistics have not survived) of how peasants during the Roman Empire used what they produced as farmers and herders to maintain their families, pay rent and taxes, and buy things they did not produce themselves. Individual families would have had widely varying experiences, but it is likely that most families had to use most of their production just to maintain a subsistence level—a description of poverty by modern standards. *(Adapted from Keith Hopkins,* Conquerors and Slaves: Sociological Studies in Roman History *(New York: Cambridge University Press, 1978), 17.)*

an occupation that freed them from curial obligations (the military, imperial administration, or church governance). The most desperate simply fled, abandoning home and property to avoid fulfilling their traditional duties.

The restrictions on personal freedom caused by the viselike pressure for higher taxes thus eroded the communal values that had long motivated wealthy Romans. The squeeze to increase revenues also produced social discontent among poorer citizens: the tax rate on land eventually reached one-third of the land's gross yield, impoverishing small farmers. Financial troubles, especially severe in the west, kept the empire from ever regaining the prosperity of its Golden Age and contributed to increasing friction between government and citizens.

The Emperors and Official Religion

Diocletian concluded that the gods' anger had caused the empire's third-century crisis. To restore divine goodwill, he called on citizens to follow the ancient gods who had guided Rome to power and virtue in the past: "Through the providence of the immortal gods, eminent, wise, and upright men have in their wisdom established good and true principles. It is wrong to oppose these principles or to abandon the ancient religion for some new one." Christianity was the novel faith he meant.

From Persecution to Conversion. To eliminate what he saw as a threat to national security, Dio-

cletian in 303 launched the so-called **Great Persecution** to suppress Christianity. He expelled Christians from official posts, seized their property, tore down churches, and executed anyone who refused to participate in official religious rituals. His three partners in the tetrarchy applied the policy unevenly. In the western empire, official violence against Christians stopped after about a year; in the east, it continued for a decade. The public executions of Christians were so gruesome that they aroused the sympathy of some polytheists. The persecution, like the edict on price and wages, ultimately failed: it undermined social stability without destroying Christianity.

Constantine changed the world's religious history forever by converting to the new faith. He had learned to have a favorable view of Christians from his father, one of the empire's co-rulers, and believed that the Christian God brought him victory in a crucial battle that secured his political power. During the civil war that Constantine fought after Diocletian stepped down, on the eve of the battle of the Milvian Bridge in Rome in 312, Constantine reportedly experienced a dream promising him God's support and saw Jesus's cross in the sky surrounded by the words "In this sign you shall be the victor." Constantine ordered his soldiers to paint a monogram signifying "Christ" on their shields and won a great victory that ended the civil

---

Great Persecution: The violent program initiated by Diocletian in 303 to make Christians convert to traditional religion or risk confiscation of their property and even death.

DOCUMENT

The Edict of Milan on Religious Liberty

In 313 C.E., Constantine, recently converted to Christianity, and his co-emperor, Licinius, a follower of traditional Roman religion, met to discuss official policy on religion. They agreed to abolish restrictions on Christianity and proclaim religious liberty in the eastern parts of the empire; Constantine had done this as early as 306 in the west. The document contains the letter of instructions later sent to governors in the eastern provinces; it is the best surviving evidence for the new policies. The long sentences (which are shortened here) and lofty language reflect the official imperial style.

When I, Constantine Augustus, and I, Licinius Augustus, had a successful meeting at Milan and discussed everything pertaining to the public benefit and security, among other things that we regarded as going to be of use to many people, we believed that first place should go to those matters having to do with reverence for divinity, so that we might give the Christians and everyone the free power of worshipping in the religion that they wish. In this way, whatever divinity exists in the heavenly seat may be appeased and be kind to us and to all those who are established under our power. And thus, believing that we should initiate this policy on a wholesome and most upright basis, we thought that to no one whatsoever should the opportunity be denied, whether he dedicates his mind to the worship of the Christians or to that religion, which he felt best suited him. Our purpose is so that the highest divinity, whose religion we follow with free minds, may provide his customary favor and kindness in all things. Wherefore it has pleased us for your Devotedness [the provincial governor] to know that all the restrictions on the Christian name set forth in letters given to your office previously are completely removed and that whatever seemed utterly sinister and foreign to our clemency should be repealed, and that now any person of those also wishing to observe the religion of the Christians may strive to do so freely and plainly without any worry or interference. We believed that these things should be made completely clear to your Solicitude so that you would know that we have given a free and absolute permission to these Christians to practice their religion. When you see that we have granted this to them, your Devotedness will know that we have likewise conceded an open and free power to others to practice their religion for the sake of the tranquillity of our age, so that each person may have free permission to worship in the manner he has chosen. We did this so that we shall not seem to have detracted from any observance or religion.

[The emperors next order people who bought or received Christians' property confiscated in the Great Persecution to return it at no cost and then to apply to an imperial representative for reimbursement through the emperors' "clemency."]

On all these matters you will be obligated to provide your most effectual aid to the body of Christians mentioned above, so that our orders may be carried out more quickly, whereby public tranquillity may be served also by our clemency. In this way it will happen, as was explained above, that divine favor toward us, which we have experienced in so many things, will endure for all time to give prosperity to our successes in company with the public happiness. Moreover, so that the content of this ordinance and of our kindness may come to everyone's attention, it should be put up everywhere above an announcement of your own and brought to the knowledge of everyone, so that this ordinance of our kindness shall not be concealed.

Source: Lactantius, *On the Deaths of the Persecutors*, 48, and Eusebius, *Ecclesiastical History*, 10.5.2–14. Translation by Thomas R. Martin.

---

war. Thus, he attributed his success to the Christian God's miraculous power and goodwill and declared himself a Christian emperor.

Edict of Milan of 313. Following his conversion to the new faith, Constantine neither outlawed polytheism nor made Christianity the official religion. Instead, he compelled the empire's co-rulers to allow religious liberty, a policy that, following his father's lead, he had put into practice in the west as early as 306. The best evidence for this change survives in the so-called **Edict of Milan** of 313 (see Document, "The Edict of Milan on Religious Liberty," above). It proclaimed that Constantine and his polytheist co-emperor Licinius decreed free choice of religion for everyone and referred to the empire's protection by "the highest divinity" — an imprecise term meant to satisfy both polytheists and Christians.

Constantine tried to avoid angering traditional believers, who still greatly outnumbered Christians, but he also promoted his newly chosen religion. These conflicting goals called for a careful balancing act that continued the principle of subdividing power to achieve stability. In this case, he subdivided official support and respect for religion. For example, he returned all property confiscated from Christians during the Great Per-

Edict of Milan: The proclamation of Roman co-emperors Constantine and Licinius decreeing free choice of religion in the empire.

The Empire's Four Rulers
The sculpture shows the four rulers of the tetrarchy, the system of shared rule that the emperor Diocletian created in the 290s C.E. to try to administer and defend the Roman Empire more effectively. The sculptor divided the rulers into two pairs, each showing an emperor and a co-emperor (the junior member of the pair). Their gestures symbolize the closeness that the pairs were supposed to display in the tetrarchy, while their nearly identical faces imply that individuality was secondary to cooperation in the new system of governing. Their hands on swords emphasize that they were ready to use force to defend Roman territory and tradition. Originally erected in Constantinople, the capital of the eastern empire, the sculpture was probably looted when crusaders sacked that city in 1204. It was then carried back to Venice, where it was built into the wall of St. Mark's cathedral. *(Basilica di San Marco, Venice, Italy/The Bridgeman Art Library.)*

secution, but he had the treasury compensate those who had bought it. When in 321 he made the Lord's Day of each week a holy occasion on which no official business or manufacturing work could be performed, he called it Sunday to blend Christian and traditional notions in honoring two divinities, God and the sun. He adorned his new capital of Constantinople with statues of traditional gods. Most conspicuously, he respected tradition by continuing to hold the office of *pontifex maximus* ("chief priest"), which emperors had filled ever since Augustus.

> **REVIEW:** How did Diocletian's policies end the third-century crisis, and why did they fail to work in the long run?

Christianizing the Empire, 312–c. 540

Constantine's conversion in 312 set the empire on the path to official Christianization. The process was gradual: not until the end of the fourth century was Christianity proclaimed the state religion, and even thereafter many people worshipped the traditional gods in private. Eventually, however, Christianity became the religion of the overwhelming majority by attracting converts among women and men of all classes, assuring believers of personal salvation, offering the social advantages and security of belonging to the emperors' religion, nourishing a strong sense of shared identity, developing a hierarchy to govern the church, and creating communities of devoted monks (male and female). The transformation from polytheist empire into Christian state was the Roman Empire's most important influence on Western civilization.

Changing Religious Beliefs

The empire's Christianization provoked passionate responses because ordinary people cared fervently about religion. (See "Seeing History," page 206.) Polytheists and Christians shared some similar beliefs. Both regarded spirits and demons as powerful and ever-present forces in life. For some, it seemed safest to ignore neither faith. A silver spoon used in the worship of the polytheist forest spirit Faunus, for example, has been found engraved with a fish, the common symbol whose Greek spelling (*ichthys*) was taken as an acronym for the Greek words "Jesus Christ the Son of God, the Savior."

The Persistence of Polytheism.
The differences between polytheists' and Christians' beliefs far outweighed their similarities, however. People debated heatedly whether there was one God or many and what kind of interest the divinity (or divinities) took in the world of humans. Polytheists participated in frequent festivals and sacrifices to many different gods. Why, they wondered, did these joyous occasions not satisfy everyone's yearnings for contact with divinity?

Equally incomprehensible to them was belief in a savior who promised eternal salvation for believers yet had not only failed to overthrow Roman rule but had even been executed as a common criminal. The traditional gods, by contrast, had bestowed a world empire on their worshippers. Moreover, polytheists pointed out, cults such as that of the goddess Isis and philosophies such as Stoicism insisted that only the pure of heart and mind could be admitted to their fellowship. Christians, by contrast, embraced sinners. Why, wondered perplexed polytheists, would anyone want to associate with such people? In short, as the Greek philosopher Porphyry argued, Christians had no right to claim they possessed the sole version of religious truth, for no one had ever discovered a doctrine that provided "the sole path to the liberation of the soul." The slow pace of religious change revealed how strong polytheism remained in this period, especially at the highest social levels. In fact, the emperor known as **Julian the Apostate** (r. 361–363) rebelled against his family's Christianity—the word *apostate* means "renegade from the faith"—by trying to reverse official support of the new religion in favor of his own philosophical interpretation of polytheism. He, too, believed in a supreme deity, but he based his religion on Greek philosophy when he said, "This divine and completely beautiful universe, from heaven's highest arch to earth's lowest limit, is tied together by the continuous providence of god, has existed ungenerated eternally, and is imperishable forever."

Making Christianity Official.
Julian was killed in a military expedition against Persia, and the suc-

Relief Sculpture of Saturn from North Africa
This pillar depicts the solar divinity known to Romans as Saturn and to Carthaginians as Ba'al Hammon, from the cult of the Phoenician founders of Carthage. This syncretism (identifying deities as the same even though they carried different names in different places) was typical of ancient polytheism and allowed Roman and non-Roman cults to merge. The inscription dates the pillar to 323. Other objects testify to the prevalence of polytheistic cults in the Roman Empire until the end of the fourth century. What in this sculpture indicates that it depicts a god? *(© Martha Cooper/Peter Arnold, Inc.)*

ceeding emperors were Christians, who provided government support for their religion while denying it to traditional cults. They dropped the title *pontifex maximus* and ceased government-funded sacrifices. Symmachus (c. 340–402), a polytheist senator who held the prestigious post of prefect (mayor) of Rome, objected to this suppression of religious diversity. In a last public protest against the new religious order, he echoed Porphyry: "We all have our own way of life and our own way of worship. . . . So vast a mystery cannot be approached by only one path."

Christianity officially replaced traditional polytheism as the state religion in 391 when **Theodosius I** successfully enforced a ban on polytheist sacrifices, even if private individuals paid for the animals, and announced that all polytheist temples had to close. Nevertheless, some famous shrines, such as the Parthenon in Athens, remained open for a long time; temples were gradually converted to churches during the fifth and sixth centuries. Non-Christian schools were not forced to close—the Academy, founded by Plato in Athens in the early fourth century B.C.E., endured for 140

Julian the Apostate: The Roman emperor (r. 361–363), who rejected Christianity and tried to restore traditional religion as the state religion. *Apostate* means "renegade from the faith."

Theodosius I: The Roman emperor (r. 379–395) who made Christianity the state religion by ending public sacrifices in the traditional cults and closing their temples; in 395 he also divided the empire into western and eastern halves to be ruled by his sons.

Changing Religious Beliefs: Pagan and Christian Sarcophagi

Christianity became Rome's state religion in 391 when the emperor Theodosius I banned polytheist sacrifices, but the Christianization of the empire had begun long before. Over time, Christians found ways to testify publicly to their beliefs, often making creative use of methods previously employed to honor Rome's traditional gods. We can see this process in action by comparing scenes from two sarcophagi (stone coffins), one from the first century and one from the mid-fourth century. These decorated coffins were meant to be seen, not hidden in the ground, to make a statement about their owner's beliefs.

The left-hand image, from a pagan Roman sarcophagus, shows a religious

Scene of a Procession in Honor of the God Dionysus. Marble Sarcophagus, Roman, First Century C.E.
(Erich Lessing/Art Resource, NY.)

years after Theodosius's reign — but Christians received advantages in official careers.

Jews posed a special problem for the Christian emperors. They seemed entitled to special treatment because Jesus had been a Jew. Previous emperors had allowed Jews to practice their religion, but the Christian emperors now burdened them with legal restrictions. Imperial decrees banned Jews from holding government posts but still required them to assume the financial burdens of cu-

rials without the status. By the late sixth century, the law barred Jews from marrying Christians, making wills, receiving inheritances, or testifying in court.

These restrictions began the long process that made Jews into second-class citizens in later European history, but they did not destroy Judaism. Magnificent synagogues continued to exist in Palestine, where some Jews still lived, though most had been dispersed throughout the cities of the

procession by members of the cult of the god Dionysus. The worship of Dionysus as god of wine and theater was so complex as even to seem contradictory, ranging from violent passion to peaceful rest; it showed both the good that could come from pleasure and the evil that resulted from going too far. Lively processions in his honor, some led by women, were popular. Dionysus is shown here in one of his many different forms: a chubby, lusty, old drunkard, whom the Romans called Bacchus. He reclines on a cart with a jar of wine, pulled by a horse and some kind of half man, half beast, perhaps a centaur. His entourage also includes female musicians, who dance along playing horns and beating tambourines. What other details can you make out? Do they offer hints about the values of the cult of Dionysus?

Compare this scene with the one shown on the right, a detail from the most spectacular surviving example of an early Christian sarcophagus. This coffin, from 359, held the remains of a prominent Roman official. Carved from marble in a classical style, the scenes are all taken from the Bible and center on the story of Christ. The absence of references to polytheistic mythology, which had been standard on earlier Christian sarcophagi, illustrates Christians' growing confidence in their own religious traditions, which they display in the same way that pagans had previously done. What other shifts in attitude and competing values are revealed by comparing this detail from the Garden of Eden (when Eve is seduced by the snake into eating the

Adam and Eve on the Sarcophagus of Junius Bassus, 359 C.E. *(Erich Lessing/Art Resource, NY.)*

forbidden fruit and she and Adam are cast out of paradise by God) with the procession in honor of Dionysus? What accounts for the position of Adam and Eve's hands? What do the scenes suggest about the roles of women in pagan and Christian religion?

empire and the lands to the east. Jewish scholarship flourished in this period, culminating in the fifth-century C.E. texts known as the Palestinian and the Babylonian Talmuds (collections of learned opinions on Jewish law) and the scriptural commentaries of the Midrash (explanation of the meaning of the Hebrew Bible), compiled from around 200 to 800. These works of religious scholarship laid the foundation for later Jewish life and practice.

Christianity's Growing Appeal. Christianity's official status attracted new believers, especially in the military. Now soldiers could convert and still serve in the army; previously, Christians had sometimes created disciplinary problems by renouncing their military oath. As one senior infantryman had said at his court-martial in 298 for refusing to continue his duties, "A Christian serving the Lord Christ should not serve the affairs of this world." Once the emperors had become Christians, how-

Jesus as Sun God
This heavily damaged mosaic, perhaps from the mid-third century, depicts Jesus like the Greek god of the sun, Apollo, riding in a chariot pulled by horses with rays of light shining forth around his head. This symbolism—God is light—reached back to ancient Egypt; Christian artists used it to portray Jesus because he had said, "I am the light of the world" (John 8:12). The mosaic artist has arranged the sunbeams to suggest the shape of the Christian cross. The cloak flaring from Jesus's shoulder suggests the spread of his motion across the heavens.
(Scala/Art Resource, NY.)

■ **For more help analyzing this image,** see the visual activity for this chapter in the Online Study Guide at **bedfordstmartins.com/hunt**.

ever, soldiers saw military duty as serving Christ's regime.

Christianity's social values contributed to its appeal by offering believers a strong sense of shared identity in this world. Wherever Christians traveled, they could find a warm welcome in the local congregation (Map 7.2). The faith also won adherents by promoting the tradition of charitable works characteristic of Judaism and some polytheist cults, which emphasized caring for the poor, widows, and orphans. By the mid-third century, for example, Rome's congregation was supporting fifteen hundred widows and poor people. Fellowship and philanthropy to support believers who were poor contributed to the faith's growth.

Women were deeply involved in the new faith. **Augustine** (354–430), bishop of Hippo, in North Africa, and perhaps the most influential theologian in Western civilization, recognized women's contribution to the strengthening of Christianity in a letter he wrote to the unbaptized husband of a baptized woman: "O you men, who fear all the burdens imposed by baptism! Your women easily best you. Chaste and devoted to the faith, it is their presence in large numbers that causes the church to grow." Women could win renown by giving their property to their congregation or by renouncing marriage to dedicate themselves to Christ. Consecrated virgins and widows who chose not to remarry thus joined large donors as especially respected women. These women's choices challenged the traditional social order, in which women were supposed to devote themselves to raising families. Even these sanctified women, however, were excluded from leadership positions as the church's hierarchy came more and more to resemble the male-dominated world of imperial rule.

Hierarchy in the Church. The Christianization of the Roman Empire depended on creating a hierarchy based on the authority of male bishops, who had replaced early Christianity's relatively loose, communal organization in which women could also lead. Bishops selected priests to conduct the church's sacraments, such as baptism and communion, the rituals that guaranteed eternal life. They also oversaw their congregations' memberships and finances. Over time, the bishops replaced the curials as the emperors' partners in local rule, in return earning the right to control the distribution of imperial subsidies to the people. Regional councils of bishops appointed new bishops and addressed doctrinal disputes. The bishops in the largest cities became the most powerful leaders in the church. The main bishop of Carthage, for example, oversaw at least one hundred local bishops in the surrounding area. The bishop of Rome eventually emerged as the church's supreme leader in the western empire, reserving for himself a title previously applied to many bishops: pope (from *pappas*, Greek for "father"), the designation still used for the head of the Roman Catholic church.

The bishops of Rome justified their leadership over other bishops by citing the New Testament, where Jesus addresses Peter, his head apostle: "You

Augustine: Bishop in North Africa whose writings defining religious orthodoxy made him the most influential theologian in Western civilization.

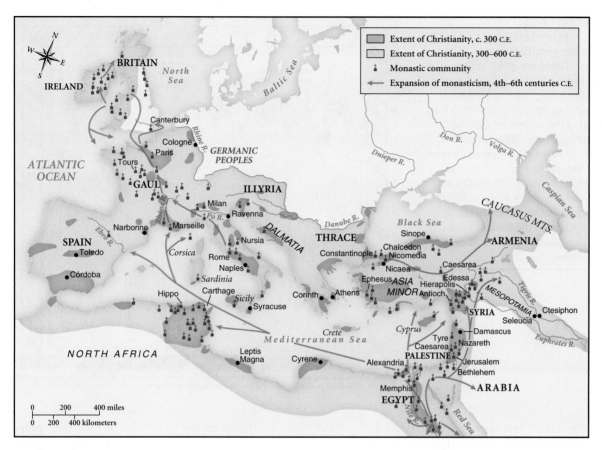

MAP 7. 2 The Spread of Christianity, 300–600
Christians were distinctly a minority in the Roman Empire in 300, although congregations existed in many cities and towns, especially in the eastern provinces. The emperor Constantine's conversion to Christianity in the early fourth century gave a boost to the new religion; it gained further strength during that century as the Christian emperors supported it financially and eliminated subsidies for the polytheist cults that had previously made up the religion of the state. By 600, Christianity reached from end to end of the empire. *(From Henry Chadwick and G. R. Evans,* Atlas of the Christian Church *(Oxford: Andromeda Oxford Ltd., 1987), 28. Reproduced by permission of Andromeda Oxford Limited.)*

are Peter, and upon this rock I will build my church. . . . I will entrust to you the keys of the kingdom of heaven. Whatever you bind on earth shall be bound in heaven. Whatever you loose on earth shall be loosed in heaven" (Matt. 16:18–19). Because Peter's name in Greek means "rock" and because Peter was believed to have been the first bishop of Rome, later bishops in Rome claimed that this passage recognized their direct succession from Peter and thus their supremacy in the church.

Establishing Christian Orthodoxy

Jesus himself left no written teachings, and early Christians frequently argued over what their savior had meant them to believe. The church's expanding hierarchy pushed hard for uniformity in belief and worship to ensure its members' spiritual purity and to maintain its authority over them. Bishops as well as rank-and-file believers often disagreed about theology, however, and doctrinal disputes repeatedly threatened the unity of the church.

Controversy centered on what was orthodoxy and what was heresy. (See Chapter 6, page 184.) After Christianity became official, the emperor was ultimately responsible for enforcing orthodox creed (a summary of correct beliefs) and could use force to compel agreement when disputes led to violence.

Arguing about God: Arianism. Subtle theological questions about the nature of the Christian Trinity — Father, Son, and Holy Spirit — seen by the orthodox as a unified, co-eternal, and identical divinity, caused the deepest divisions. The doc-

Mosaic of a Family from Edessa

This mosaic, found in a cave tomb from c. 218–238 C.E., depicts an elite family of Edessa in the late Roman Empire. Their names are given in Syriac, the dialect of Aramaic spoken in their region, and their colorful clothing reflects local Iranian traditions. The mosaic's border uses decorative patterns from Roman art, illustrating the mixture of cultural traditions in the Roman Empire. Edessa was the capital of the small kingdom of Osrhoëne, annexed by Rome in 216. It became famous in Christian history because its king Agbar (r. 179–216) was remembered as the first monarch to convert to Christianity, well before Constantine. The eastern Roman emperors proclaimed themselves the heirs of King Agbar. *(From* Vanished Civilizations *ed. Edward Bacon, Thames & Hudson Ltd., London.)*

trine called **Arianism** generated fierce controversy for centuries. Named after its founder, Arius (c. 260–336), a priest from Alexandria, it maintained that Jesus as God's son had not existed eternally; rather, God the Father "begot" (created) his son from nothing and bestowed on him his special status. Thus, Jesus was not co-eternal with God and not identical with God the Father. This view implied that the Trinity was divisible and that Christianity's monotheism was not absolute. Arianism found widespread support—the emperor Valens and his barbarian opponents were Arian Christians. Its appeal perhaps came from its eliminating the difficulty of understanding how a son could be as old as his father and because its subordination of son to father corresponded to the norms of family life. Arius used popular songs to make his views known, and people everywhere became engrossed in the controversy. "When you ask for your change from a shopkeeper," one observer remarked in describing Constantinople, "he harangues you about the Begotten and the Unbegotten. If you inquire how much bread costs, the reply is that 'the Father is superior and the Son inferior.'"

Many Christians became so incensed over this apparent demotion of Jesus that Constantine had to intervene to try to restore ecclesiastical peace and lead the bishops in determining religious truth. In 325, he convened 220 bishops at the Council of Nicaea to discuss Arianism. The majority of bishops voted to come down hard on the heresy: they banished Arius to Illyria, a rough Balkan region, and declared in the **Nicene Creed** that the Father and the Son were "of one substance" (*homoousion*) and co-eternal. So difficult were the issues, however, that Constantine later changed his mind twice, first recalling Arius from exile and then reproaching him again not long after. The doctrine lived on: Constantine's third son, Constantius II (r. 337–361), favored Arianism, and his missionaries converted many of the non-Roman peoples who later poured into the empire.

Monophysitism, Nestorianism, and Donatism. Numerous other disputes about the nature of Christ divided believers. The orthodox position held that Jesus's divine and human natures commingled within his person but remained distinct. Monophysites (a Greek term for "single-nature believers") argued that the divine took precedence

---

Arianism: The Christian doctrine named after Arius, who argued that Jesus was "begotten" by God and did not have an identical nature with God the Father.

Nicene Creed: The doctrine agreed on by the council of bishops convened by Constantine at Nicaea in 325 to defend orthodoxy against Arianism; it declared that God the Father and Jesus were "of one substance" (*homoousion*).

over the human in Jesus and that he therefore had essentially only a single nature. They split from the orthodox hierarchy in the sixth century to found independent churches in Egypt (the Coptic church), Ethiopia, Syria, and Armenia.

Nestorius, who became the bishop of Constantinople in 428, disagreed with the orthodox version of how Jesus's human and divine natures were related to his birth, insisting that Mary gave birth to the human that became the temple for the indwelling divine. Nestorianism enraged orthodox Christians by rejecting the designation *theotokos* (Greek for "bearer of God") for Mary. The bishops of Alexandria and Rome had Nestorius deposed and his doctrines officially rejected at councils held in 430 and 431; they condemned his writings in 435. Refusing to accept these decisions, Nestorian bishops in the eastern empire formed a separate church centered in Persia, where for centuries Nestorian Christians flourished under the tolerance of non-Christian rulers. They later became important agents of cultural diffusion by establishing communities that still endure in Arabia, India, and China.

Donatism best illustrates the level of ferocity that Christian disputes could generate. A conflict erupted in North Africa over whether to readmit to their old congregations Christians who had cooperated with imperial authorities during the Great Persecution. The Donatists (followers of the North African priest Donatus) insisted that the church should not be polluted with such "traitors." So bitter was the clash that it even sundered Christian families. One son threatened his mother, "I will join Donatus's followers, and I will drink your blood."

With emotions at a fever pitch, the church promoted orthodoxy as religious truth. The Council of Chalcedon (a suburb of Constantinople) in 451 was the most important attempt to forge agreement on orthodoxy. Its conclusions form the basis of what most Christians in the West still accept as doctrine. At the time, however, it failed to create unanimity, especially in the eastern empire, where Monophysites flourished.

Augustine on Order.

The ideas of Augustine became the foundation of Christian orthodoxy in the western empire. By around 500, Augustine and other influential theologians such as Ambrose (c. 339–397) and Jerome (c. 345–420) earned the

Original Areas of Christian Splinter Groups

informal title "church fathers" because their views were cited as authoritative in disputes over orthodoxy. Augustine became the most famous of this group of patristic (from the Greek for "father," *pater*) authors, and for the next thousand years his works would be the most influential texts in western Christianity except the Bible. He wrote so prolifically about religion and philosophy that a later scholar was moved to declare: "The man lies who says he has read all your works."

Augustine deeply affected later thinkers with his views on order in human life, expressed in the *City of God*, a "large and arduous work," as he called it, published in 426 after thirteen years of writing. In it, Augustine asserted that the basic dilemma for humans lay between the desire for earthly pleasures and spiritual purity. Emotion, especially love, was natural and desirable, but only when directed toward God. Humans were misguided to look for value in life on earth. Only life in God's eternal city had meaning.

Nevertheless, Augustine wrote, law and government were required on earth because humans are imperfect. God's original creation was perfect, but after Adam and Eve disobeyed God, humans lost their initial perfection and inherited a permanently flawed nature. According to this doctrine of original sin—a subject of theological debate since at least the second century—Adam and Eve's disobedience bequeathed to people a hereditary moral disease that made the human will a divisive force. This corruption necessitated governments that could suppress evil. The state therefore had a duty to compel people to remain loyal to the church, by force if necessary.

For Augustine, the purpose of secular authority was to maintain a social order based on a moral order. To help maintain order, Christians had a duty to obey the emperor and participate in political life. Soldiers, too, had to follow their orders. Order was so essential, Augustine argued, that it even justified what he admitted was the unjust institution of slavery. Although detesting slavery, he believed it was a lesser evil than the social disorder that he thought its abolition would create.

In *City of God*, Augustine argued that history has a divine purpose, even if people could not see it. All that Christians could know with certainty was that history progressed toward an ultimate goal, but only God could know the meaning of each day's events:

> To be truthful, I myself fail to understand why God created mice and frogs, flies and worms. Nevertheless, I recognize that each of these creatures is beautiful in its own way. For when I contemplate the body and limbs of any living creature, where do I not find proportion, number, and order exhibiting the unity of concord? Where one discovers proportion, number, and order, one should look for the craftsman.

The repeated *I* in this passage indicates the intense personal engagement Augustine brought to matters of faith and doctrine. Many other Christians shared this intensity, a trait that energized their disagreements over orthodoxy and heresy.

Augustine and Sexual Desire. Next to the nature of Christ, the question of how to understand and regulate sexual desire presented Christians with the thorniest problem in the search for religious truth. Augustine became the most influential source of the idea that sex enmeshed human beings in evil and that they should therefore strive for **asceticism**, the practice of self-denial, especially through spiritual discipline. Augustine knew from personal experience how difficult it was to accept this doctrine. In his autobiographical work *Confessions*, written about 397, he described the deep conflict he felt between his sexual desires and his religious beliefs. Only after a long period of reflection and doubt, he wrote, did he find the inner strength to commit to chastity as part of his conversion to Christianity.

He advocated sexual abstinence as the highest course for Christians because he believed that Adam and Eve's disobedience had forever ruined the perfect harmony God created between the human will and human passions. According to Augustine, God punished his disobedient children by making sexual desire a disruptive force that human will would always struggle to control. He reaffirmed the value of marriage in God's plan, but he insisted that sexual intercourse even between loving spouses carried the melancholy reminder of humanity's fall from grace. A married couple should "descend with a certain sadness" to the task of procreation, the only acceptable reason for sex; sexual pleasure could never be a human good.

This doctrine ennobled virginity and sexual renunciation as the highest virtues; in the words of the ascetic biblical scholar Jerome, they counted

as "daily martyrdom." By the end of the fourth century, Christians valued virginity as an ascetic virtue so highly that congregations began to call for virgin priests and bishops.

The Emergence of Christian Monks

Christian asceticism reached its peak with the emergence of monks: men and women who withdrew from everyday society to live a life of extreme self-denial imitating Jesus's suffering, while praying for divine mercy on the world. In this movement, called monasticism, at first monks lived alone, but soon they formed communities for mutual support in the pursuit of holiness.

The Appeal of Monasticism. Polytheists and Jews had strong ascetic traditions, but Christian monasticism was distinctive for the huge numbers of people drawn to it and the high status that they earned in the Christian population. Monks' renown came from their rejection of ordinary pleasures and comforts. They left their families and congregations, renounced sex, worshipped almost constantly, wore rough clothes, and ate only enough to survive. To achieve inner peace detached from daily concerns, monks fought a constant spiritual battle against fantasies of earthly delights—plentiful, tasty food and the joys of sex.

The earliest monks emerged in Egypt in the second half of the third century. Antony (c. 251–356), the son of a well-to-do family, was among the first to renounce regular existence. After hearing a sermon stressing Jesus's command to a rich young man to sell his possessions and give the proceeds to the poor (Matt. 19:21), in about 285 he left his property and withdrew into the desert to devote the rest of his life to worshipping God through extreme self-denial.

Antony achieved fame for his ascetic life, illustrating a principal appeal of monasticism: the chance to achieve excellence and recognition, a traditional ideal in the ancient Western world. This opportunity seemed especially valuable after the end of the Great Persecution. Becoming a monk—a living martyrdom—served as the substitute for dying a martyr's death and emulated the sacrifice of Christ. Hermit monks went to great lengths to attract attention to their dedication. In Syria, "holy women" and "holy men" sought fame through feats of pious endurance; Symeon (390–459), for example, lived atop a tall pillar for thirty years, preaching to the people gathered at the foot of his perch. Egyptian Christians came to believe that their monks' supreme piety made them living he-

---

asceticism (uh SEH tuh sih zuhm): The practice of self-denial, especially through spiritual discipline; a doctrine for Christians emphasized by Augustine.

roes who ensured the annual flooding of the Nile, an event once associated with the pharaohs' religious power.

The influence of ascetics with reputations for exceptional holiness continued after their deaths. Their relics—body parts or clothing—became treasured sources of protection and healing. Projecting the enduring power of saints (people venerated after their deaths for their holiness), relics gave believers faith in divine favor. Christian reverence for relics continued a long-standing tradition: the fifth-century B.C.E. Athenians, for example, had believed that good fortune followed from the recovery of bones identified as the remains of Theseus, their legendary founder.

The Rise of Monastic Communities.   In about 323, an Egyptian Christian named Pachomius or-

ganized the first monastic community, establishing the tradition of single-sex settlements of male or female monks helping one another along the harsh path to holiness. This communal monasticism dominated Christian asceticism ever after. Communities of men and women were often built close together to share labor, with women making clothing, for example, while men farmed.

All monastic groups imposed military-style discipline, but they differed in their degree of internal austerity and contact with the outside world (see Monastery of St. Catherine at Mount Sinai). Some strove for complete self-sufficiency to avoid transactions with outsiders. The most isolationist groups lived in the eastern empire, but the followers of Martin of Tours (c. 316–397), an ex-soldier famed for his pious deeds, founded communities in the west as austere as any. Basil of Caesarea

Monastery of St. Catherine at Mount Sinai
The sixth-century eastern Roman emperor Justinian enclosed this monastery in the desert at the foot of Mount Sinai (on the peninsula between Egypt and Arabia) with a wall. Justinian fortified the monastery to promote orthodoxy in a region dominated by Monophysite Christians. The monastery gained its name in the ninth century when the story was circulated that angels had recently brought the body of Catherine of Alexandria there. Catherine was said to have been martyred in the fourth century for refusing to marry the emperor because, in her words, she was the bride of Christ.
(Erich Lessing/Art Resource, NY.)

(c. 330–379), in Asia Minor, started an alternative tradition of monasteries in service to society. Basil (later dubbed "the Great") required monks to perform charitable deeds, especially ministering to the sick, a development that led to the foundation of the first hospitals, attached to monasteries.

A milder code of monastic conduct became the standard in the west beginning about 540. Called the Benedictine rule after its creator, Benedict of Nursia (c. 480–553), in central Italy, it mandated the monastery's daily routine of prayer, scriptural readings, and manual labor. This was the first time in Greek and Roman history that physical work was seen as noble, even godly. The rule divided the day into seven parts, each with a compulsory service of prayers and lessons, called the office. Unlike the harsh regulations of other monastic communities, Benedict's code did not isolate the monks from the outside world or deprive them of sleep, adequate food, or warm clothing. Although it gave the abbot (the head monk) full authority, it instructed him to listen to other members of the community before deciding important matters. He was not allowed to beat disobedient monks, as sometimes happened under other systems. Communities of women, such as those founded by Basil's sister Macrina and Benedict's sister Scholastica, generally followed the rules of the male monasteries, with an emphasis on the decorum thought necessary for women.

The thousands upon thousands of Christians who joined monasteries from the fourth century onward abandoned the outside world for social as well as theological reasons. Monastic piety held special appeal for women and the rich. Jerome wrote, "[As monks] we evaluate people's virtue not by their gender but by their character, and deem those to be worthy of the greatest glory who have renounced both status and riches." Some monks did not choose their life; they were given as babies to monasteries by parents who could not raise them or were fulfilling pious vows, a practice called oblation. Jerome once gave this advice to a mother who decided to send her young daughter to a monastery:

> Let her be brought up in a monastery, let her live among virgins, let her learn to avoid swearing, let her regard lying as an offense against God, let her be ignorant of the world, let her live the angelic life, while in the flesh let her be without the flesh, and let her suppose that all human beings are like herself.

When the girl reached adulthood as a virgin, he added, she should avoid the baths so that she would not be seen naked or give her body pleasure by dipping in the warm pools. Jerome emphasized traditional values favoring males when he promised that God would reward the mother with the birth of sons in compensation for the dedication of her daughter.

Since monasteries were self-governing, they could find themselves in conflict with the church hierarchy. Bishops resented members of their congregations who withdrew into monasteries, especially because they then gave money and property to their new community instead of to their local churches. Moreover, monks represented a threat to bishops' authority because holy men and women earned their special status not by having it bestowed from the church hierarchy but through their own actions; strengthening the bishops' right to discipline monks who resisted their authority was one of the goals of the Council of Chalcedon. At bottom, however, bishops and monks shared a spiritual goal — salvation and service to God.

> **REVIEW:** How did Christianity both unite and divide the Roman Empire?

Non-Roman Kingdoms in the West, c. 370–550s

The residents of the western empire had special reason to pray for God's help because their territory came under great pressure from the many incursions of non-Roman peoples — barbarians, the Romans called them, meaning "brave but uncivilized" — that took place in the fourth and fifth centuries. These multiethnic groups from east of the Rhine River and north of the Danube River were sometimes admitted to the empire but more often fought their way in from the northeast. The barbarians had two strong motivations to move westward: to flee attacks by the Huns (nomads from central Asia) and to share in Roman prosperity. By the 370s, this human tide had swollen to a flood, provoking violence and a loss of order in the western empire. Over the coming decades, the immigrants transformed themselves from loosely organized, multiethnic tribes into kingdoms with newly defined identities. By the 470s, one of their commanders ruled Italy — the political change that has been said to mark the so-called fall of the Roman Empire. In fact, the interactions of these non-Roman peoples with the empire's residents in western Europe and North Africa are better understood as causing a political, social, and cultural transformation—admittedly based on force more than cooperation—that made the immigrants the heirs of the western Roman Empire and led to the formation of medieval Europe.

Non-Roman Migrations

The non-Roman peoples who flooded into the empire had diverse origins; scholars in the past referred to them generically as Germanic peoples, but this label misrepresents the variety of languages and customs among these multiethnic groups. What we must remember is that the diverse barbarian peoples had no strongly established sense of ethnic identity; many of them had had previous contact with Romans through trade and service in the Roman army. Like earlier emperors, fourth-century emperors at first encouraged the movement of non-Romans into imperial territory, recruiting the men to serve in the Roman army. By late in the century, these warriors' families had followed them into the empire. Hordes of men, women, and children crossed the Roman border as refugees. They came with no political or military unity and no clear plan. Loosely organized into tribes that often warred with one another, they shared only their terror of the Huns and their custom of conducting raids for a living.

The inability to prevent immigrants from crossing the border or to control them once they arrived fatally weakened the western central government. Persistent economic weakness rooted in the third-century crisis underlay this failure. Tenant farmers and landlords fleeing crushing taxes had left as much as 20 percent of arable territory unfarmed in the most seriously affected areas. The loss of revenue made the government unable to afford enough soldiers to control the situation. Over time, the immigrating non-Roman peoples forced the Roman government to grant them territory in the empire. Remarkably, they then began to develop separate ethnic identities and formed new societies for themselves and the Romans living under their control.

Immigrant Traditions. The traditions the newcomers brought with them from their eastern homelands poorly prepared them for ruling others. There they had lived in small settlements whose economies depended on farming, herding, and ironworking; they had no experience with running kingdoms built on strong central authority.

In their homelands the barbarians had lived in chiefdom societies, whose members could only be persuaded, not ordered, to follow the chief. Chiefs maintained their status by giving gifts to their followers and leading raids to capture cattle and slaves. They led clans—groups of households organized on kinship lines, following maternal as well as paternal descent. Members of a clan were supposed to keep peace among themselves, and violence against a fellow clan member was the worst possible offense. Clans in turn grouped themselves into tribes—loose and fluctuating multiethnic coalitions that anyone could join. Tribes differentiated themselves by their clothing, hairstyles, jewelry, weapons, religious cults, and oral stories.

Family life was patriarchal: men headed households and held authority over women, children, and slaves. Warfare preoccupied men, as their ritual sacrifices of weapons preserved in northern European bogs have shown. Women were valued for their ability to bear children, and rich men could have more than one wife and perhaps concubines as well. A division of labor made women responsible for growing crops, making pottery, and producing textiles, while men worked iron and herded cattle. Women enjoyed certain rights of inheritance and could control property, and married women received a dowry of one-third of their husband's property.

Assemblies of free male warriors made major decisions in the tribes. Their leaders' authority was restricted mostly to religious and military matters. Tribes could be unstable and prone to internal conflict—clans frequently feuded, with bloody consequences. Tribal law tried to determine what forms of violence were and were not acceptable in seeking revenge, but laws were oral, not written, and thus open to wide dispute.

Fleeing the Huns. The migrations avalanched when the Huns invaded eastern Europe in the fourth century. Perhaps distantly related to the Hiung-nu, a central Asian people who had earlier attacked China and Persia, the Huns arrived on the Russian steppes shortly before 370 as the vanguard of Turkish-speaking nomads. Their warriors' appearance terrified their victims, who reported skulls elongated from having been bound between boards in infancy, faces grooved with decorative scars, and arms fearsome with elaborate tattoos. Huns excelled as raiders, launching cavalry attacks far and wide. Skilled as horsemen, they could shoot their powerful bows accurately while riding full tilt and stay mounted for days, sleeping atop their horses and carrying snacks of raw meat between their thighs and the animal's back.

Later in the fourth century the Huns moved westward toward the Hungarian plain north of the

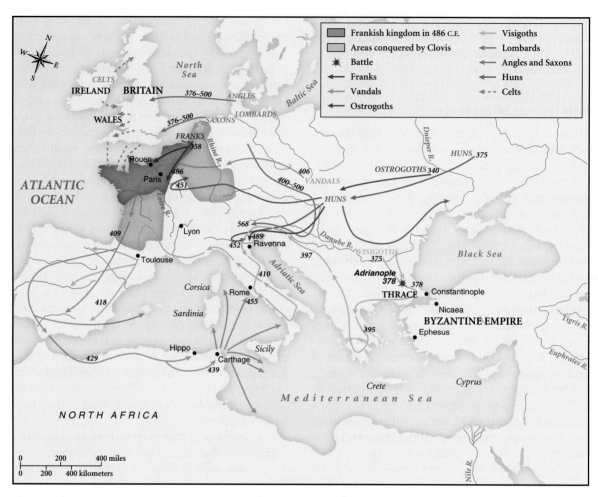

MAP 7.3 Migrations and Invasions of the Fourth and Fifth Centuries
The movements of non-Roman peoples into imperial territory transformed the Roman Empire. These migrations had begun as early as the reign of Domitian (r. 81–96), but in the fourth century they increased greatly when the Huns' attacks pushed numerous barbarian bands into the empire's northern provinces. Print maps offer only a static representation of dynamic processes such as movements of populations, but this map helps illustrate the variety of peoples involved, the wide extent of imperial territory that they affected, and their prominence in the western empire.

Danube, terrifying the peoples there and launching raids southward into the Balkans. The emperors in Constantinople began paying the Huns to spare their territory, so the most ambitious Hunnic leader, Attila (r. c. 440–453), pushed his domain westward toward the Alps. In 451, he led his forces as far west as central France, and in 452 into northern Italy. At Attila's death in 454, the Huns lost their fragile cohesiveness and faded from history. By this time, however, the terror that they had inspired in the peoples living in eastern Europe had provoked the migrations that eventually transformed the western empire.

Visigoths: The First New Society.   The first non-Roman group that coalesced inside the empire to create a new society were the barbarians who

defeated Valens at Adrianople (Map 7.3). Their history illustrates the pattern of the migrations: desperate barbarians in barely organized groups with no uniform ethnic identity, seeking asylum from Roman government in return for service but being mistreated, and then rebelling to form their own, new kingdom.

When the emperor Theodosius died in 395, the barbarians whom he had allowed to settle in the empire as semi-autonomous allies rebelled. United by Alaric into a tribe known as the **Visigoths**, they fought their way into the western empire. In 410, they stunned the world by sacking Rome itself. For

Visigoths: The name given to the barbarians whom Alaric united and led on a military campaign into the western Roman Empire to establish a new kingdom; they sacked Rome in 410.

the first time since the Gauls eight hundred years before, a foreign force occupied the ancient capital. They terrorized the population: when Alaric demanded all the citizens' goods, the Romans asked, "What will be left to us?" "Your lives," he replied.

Too weak to fend off the invaders, the western emperor Honorius in 418 reluctantly agreed to settle the newcomers in southwestern Gaul (present-day France), where they completed their unprecedented transition from tribe to kingdom, organizing a political state and creating their identity as Visigoths. In this process they followed the only model available: Roman tradition. They established mutually beneficial relations with local Roman elites, who used time-tested ways of flattering their new superiors to gain advantages. Sidonius Apollinaris (c. 430–479), for example, a well-connected noble from Lyon, once purposely lost a backgammon game to the Visigothic king as a way of winning a favor.

How the new non-Roman kingdoms raised revenues has become a much-debated question. Did the newcomers become landed proprietors by forcing Roman landowners to redistribute a portion of their lands, slaves, and movable property to them? Or did Romans directly pay the expenses of the kingdom's soldiers, who lived mostly in urban garrisons? Whatever the new arrangements were, the Visigoths found them profitable enough to expand into Spain within a century of establishing themselves in southwestern Gaul.

The Vandals and the Spiral of Violence.   The western government's concessions to the Visigoths emboldened other groups to seize territory and create new kingdoms and identities. In 406, the Vandals, fleeing the Huns, crossed the Rhine into Roman territory. This huge group cut a swath through Gaul all the way to the Spanish coast. (The modern word *vandal*, meaning "destroyer of property," perpetuates their reputation for warlike ruthlessness.)

In 429, eighty thousand Vandals ferried to North Africa, where they soon broke their agreement to become federates and captured the region. They crippled the western empire by seizing North Africa's tax payments of grain and vegetable oil and disrupting the importation of food to Rome, and they frightened the eastern empire with their strong navy. In 455, they set the western government tottering by plundering Rome. The Vandals caused tremendous hardship for local Africans by confiscating property rather than (like the Visigoths) allowing owners to make regular payments to "ransom" their land, and as Arian Christians they persecuted North African Christians whose doctrines they considered heresy.

The Anglo-Saxons at the Empire's Western Edge. Small non-Roman groups took advantage of the disruption caused by bigger bands to break off distant pieces of the weakened western empire. The most significant group for later history was the Anglo-Saxons. Composed of Angles from what is now Denmark and Saxons from northwestern Germany, this mixed group invaded Britain in the 440s after the Roman army had been recalled from the province to defend Italy against the Visigoths. The Anglo-Saxons captured territory from the local Celtic peoples and the remaining Roman inhabitants. Gradually, their culture replaced the local traditions of the island's eastern regions; the Celts there lost most of their language, and Christianity gave way to Anglo-Saxon beliefs, surviving only in Wales and Ireland.

The Fall of Rome and the Ostrogoths.   Another barbarian group, the Ostrogoths, carved out a kingdom in Italy in the fifth century. By the time the Ostrogothic king Theodoric (r. 493–526) came to power, there had not been a western Roman emperor for nearly twenty years, and there never would be again—the change that has traditionally, but simplistically, been called the fall of the Roman Empire. (See "New Sources, New Perspectives," page 218.) The story's details reveal the complexity of the political transformation of the western empire under the new kingdoms. The weakness of the western emperors' army had obliged them to hire foreign officers to lead the defense of Italy. By the middle of the fifth century, one non-Roman general after another decided who would serve as puppet emperor under his control. The employees were running the company.

The last such unfortunate puppet was only a child; his father, a former aide to Attila, tried to establish a royal house by proclaiming his young son as western emperor in 475. He gave the boy ruler the name Romulus Augustulus ("Romulus the Little Augustus") to match his tender age and recall both Rome's founder and its first emperor. In 476, following a dispute over pay, the emperor's non-Roman soldiers murdered his father and deposed him; pitied as an innocent child, Little Augustus was given safe refuge and a generous pension. The rebels' leader, Odoacer, did not appoint another emperor. Instead, he had the Roman Senate petition Zeno, the eastern emperor, to recognize his leadership in return for his acknowledging Zeno as sole emperor over west and east. Odoacer thereafter oversaw Italy nominally as the eastern emperor's viceroy, but in fact he ruled as he liked.

In 488, Zeno plotted to rid himself of an ambitious non-Roman general then resident in

NEW SOURCES, NEW PERSPECTIVES

Was There a Decline and Fall of the Roman Empire?

In 1776, the Englishman Edward Gibbon (1737–1794) became a celebrity by publishing the first installment of his best-selling, multivolume work *The Decline and Fall of the Roman Empire.* The reading public loved his writing for its stinging style. Gibbon's title grew so famous that, if there is anything commonly "known" about the Roman Empire, it is that it declined and fell. Many historians, however, find this idea misleading. Gibbon later regretted his choice of a title because his work continued the story far beyond 476 C.E., the year when a non-Roman general took over the western empire. In fact, Gibbon's final volume (published in 1788) reached 1453, when the Turks toppled the eastern empire by taking Constantinople.

Various sources of new information and analysis have challenged the idea that the Roman Empire fell once and for all in 476. This is not to say that no disasters occurred in the fourth and fifth centuries: clearly, important conditions of life—economic security and prosperity, opportunities for leisure and entertainment, and even nutrition—became awful for many people as non-Romans entered the western empire with great violence, and the center of power shifted to its eastern half. Still, these changes for the worse are not the whole story. It seems more accurate to describe the empire's fate as a complex transformation—completed with much death and destruction—rather than as a simple decline and fall.

Art and archaeology have provided some of the most intriguing sources for this new perspective, either looking at long-known objects in new ways or discovering new objects. Past scholars, for example, considered Gothic culture inferior because its art, unlike classical art, did not

Eagle Brooches (Fibulae) from Gothic Spain *(The Walters Art Gallery, Baltimore, Maryland.)*

emphasize the human figure or symmetry. Instead, it focused on animal motifs and abstract patterns. This tendency did not mean that it could not communicate as powerfully as classical art; it just meant that observers had to be able to understand the art's conventions and goals. Recent archaeological research has shown that Goths used everyday art objects to convey crucial meanings—in particular, assertions of the growing sense of ethnic identity that emerged during their migrations into the Roman Empire. When in the fifth century C.E. Visigoths took up permanent residence in Spain, the women expressed their identity by emphasizing an old custom from their traditional Danube region: fastening their clothes at the shoulders with two artfully crafted brooches instead of just one. Previously, this style had not served to identify separate groups; now it said, "I am a Visigothic woman."

Above all, Gothic art expressed the transformation of the empire. A clear example comes in the spectacular eagle pins that elite Goths favored. Dazzlingly fashioned in gold and semiprecious stones, these small works of art took their inspiration from the traditions of the Huns and the Romans, both of whom highlighted the eagle as a symbol of power. Goths had never previously used eagles this way, but now they adapted the traditions of others to express their own transformation into powerful members of imperial politics and society. From their perspective, the empire's fate was hardly a decline and fall.

QUESTIONS TO CONSIDER

1. What is the difference between seeing works of art as evidence for history and as sources of beauty? What are the advantages and disadvantages of each approach?
2. How do people determine whether art is "superior" or "inferior"? Are such judgments important to make?

FURTHER READING

Greene, K. "Gothic Material Culture." In Ian Hodder, ed. *Archaeology as Long-Term History.* 1987. 117–42.

Heather, Peter. *The Goths.* 1996. Chapter 10.

Hoxie, Albert. "Mutations in Art." In Lynn White Jr., ed. *The Transformation of the Roman World: Gibbon's Problem after Two Centuries.* 1966. 266–90.

Constantinople — Theodoric — by sending him to fight Odoacer, whom the emperor had found too independent. Successfully eliminating Odoacer by 493, Theodoric then established his own Ostrogothic kingdom, ruling Italy from the capital at Ravenna.

Theodoric and his Ostrogothic nobles wanted to enjoy the luxurious life of the empire's elite, not destroy it, and to preserve the empire's prestige and status. They therefore left the Senate and consulships intact. An Arian Christian, Theodoric followed Constantine's example by announcing a policy of religious toleration. Like the other non-Romans, the Ostrogoths appropriated Roman traditions that supported the stability of their own rule. For these reasons, some scholars consider it more accurate to speak of the western empire's "transformation" than of its "fall."

The Enduring Kingdom of the Franks. The Franks were the people who transformed Roman Gaul into Francia (from which the name *France* comes). Roman emperors had allowed some of the Franks to settle in a rough northern border region (now in the Netherlands) in the early fourth century; by the late fifth century they were a major presence in Gaul. In 507, their king Clovis (r. 485–511), with support from the eastern Roman emperor, overthrew the Visigothic king in Gaul. When the emperor named him an honorary consul, Clovis celebrated this ancient honor by having himself crowned with a diadem in the style of the emperors since Constantine. He carved out western Europe's largest new kingdom in what is today mostly France, overshadowing the neighboring and rival kingdoms of the Burgundians and Alemanni in eastern Gaul. Probably persuaded by his wife, Clotilda, a Christian, to believe that God had helped him defeat the Alemanni, Clovis proclaimed himself an orthodox Christian and renounced Arianism, which he had reportedly embraced previously. To build stability, he carefully fostered good relations with the bishops as the regime's intermediaries with the population.

Clovis's dynasty, called Merovingian after the legendary Frankish ancestor Merovech, endured for another two hundred years, foreshadowing the kingdom that would emerge much later as the forerunner of modern France. The Merovingians survived so long because, better than any other kingdom, they successfully combined their own traditions of military valor with Roman social and legal traditions. In addition, their location in far western Europe kept them out of the reach of the destructive invasions sent against Italy by the eastern emperor Justinian in the sixth century to reunite the Roman world.

Mixing Traditions

Western Europe's political transformation — the gradual replacement of imperial government by the new kingdoms — set in motion a social and cultural transformation (Map 7.4). The newcomers and their Roman subjects created novel ways of life by combining old traditions, as the Visigoth king Athaulf (r. 410–415) explained after marrying a Roman noblewoman:

> At the start I wanted to erase the Romans' name and turn their land into a Gothic empire, doing myself what Augustus had done. But I have learned that the Goths' freewheeling wildness will never accept the rule of law, and that state with no law is no state. Thus, I have more wisely chosen another path to glory: reviving the Roman name with Gothic vigor. I pray that future generations will remember me as the founder of a Roman restoration.

This process of social and cultural transformation promoted stability by producing new law codes but undermined long-term security by weakening the economic situation.

Visigothic and Frankish Law. Roman law was the most influential precedent for the new kings in their efforts to construct stable states. Their original tribal societies never had written laws, but their new states required legal codes to create a sense of justice and keep order. The Visigothic kings were the first to issue a written law code. Published in Latin in about 475, it made fines and compensation the primary method for resolving disputes. Clovis also emphasized written law for the Merovingian kingdom. His code, also published in Latin between about 507 and 511, promoted social order through clear penalties for specific crimes. In particular, he formalized a system of fines intended to defuse feuds and vendettas between individuals and clans. The most prominent component of this system was **wergild**, the payment a murderer had to make as compensation for his crime, to prevent feuds of revenge. The king received about one-third of the fine, with the rest paid to the victim's family.

Since laws indicate social values, the differing amounts of wergild in Clovis's code suggest the rel-

---

wergild: Under Frankish law, the payment that a murderer had to make as compensation for the crime, to prevent feuds of revenge.

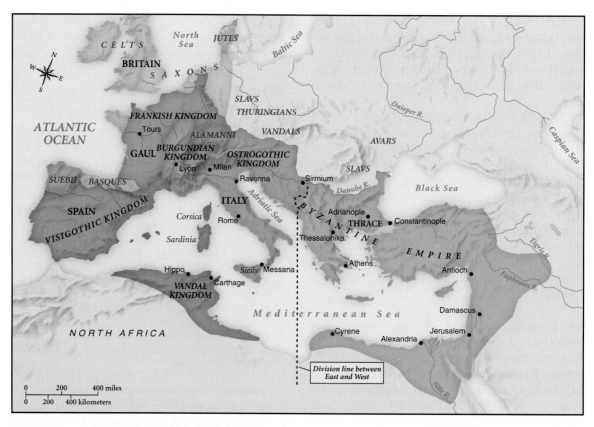

MAP 7.4 Peoples and Kingdoms of the Roman World, 526
The provinces of the Roman Empire had always been home to a population diverse in language and ethnicity. By the early sixth century, the territory of the western empire had become a mixture of diverse political units as well. Italy and most of the former western provinces were ruled by kingdoms organized by different non-Roman peoples, who had moved into former imperial territory over several centuries. The eastern empire remained under the political control of the emperor in Constantinople.

ative values of different categories of people in his kingdom. Murdering a woman of childbearing age, a boy under twelve, or a man in the king's retinue incurred a massive fine of six hundred gold coins, enough to buy six hundred cattle. A woman past childbearing age (specified as sixty years), a young girl, or a freeborn man was valued at two hundred. Ordinary slaves rated thirty-five.

A Transformed Economic Landscape. The migrations that transformed the western empire harmed its already weakened economy. The Vandals' violent sweep severely damaged many towns in Gaul, hastening a decline in urban population. In the countryside, now outside the control of any central government, wealthy Romans built sprawling villas on extensive estates, staffed by tenants bound to the land like slaves. These establishments strove to operate as self-sufficient units by producing all they needed, defending themselves against barbar-

ian raids, and keeping their distance from any authorities. Craving isolation, the owners shunned municipal offices and tax collection, the public services that had supplied the lifeblood of Roman administration. Provincial government disappeared, and the new kingdoms never matured sufficiently to replace their services fully.

The situation only grew grimmer as the effects of these changes multiplied. The infrastructure of trade — roads and bridges — fell into disrepair with no public-spirited elite to maintain them. The elite holed up in their fortress-like households. They could afford to protect themselves: the annual income of the richest of them rivaled the revenue of an entire province in the old western empire.

In some cases, these fortunate few helped transmit Roman learning to later ages. Cassiodorus (c. 490–585), for one, founded a monastery on his ancestral estate in Italy in the 550s after a career in imperial administration. He gave the monks the

Mosaic of Women Exercising
This picture covered a floor in a fourth-century country villa in Sicily that had more than forty rooms decorated with thirty-five hundred square meters of mosaics. The women shown in this mosaic were perhaps dancers getting in shape for public appearances, or athletes performing as part of a show. Members of the Roman elite built such enormous and expensive houses as the centerpieces of estates meant to insulate them from increasingly dismal conditions in cities and protect them from barbarian attack. In this case, the strategy apparently failed: the villa was likely seriously damaged by Vandal invaders. *(Erich Lessing/Art Resource, NY.)*

task of copying manuscripts to keep their contents from disappearing as old ones disintegrated. His own book *Institutions* encapsulated what he saw as the foundation of ancient Greek and Roman culture by listing the books an educated person should read; it included ancient literature as well as Christian texts. The most lasting effort to keep classical traditions alive, however, came in the eastern empire.

REVIEW: How did the barbarian migrations and invasions change the Roman Empire and Roman society?

The Roman Empire in the East, c. 500–565

The eastern Roman Empire (later called the Byzantine Empire — see Chapter 8) avoided the massive transformations that reshaped western

Europe. Trade and agriculture kept the eastern empire from poverty, while its emperors used force, diplomacy, and bribery to prevent invasions from the north and repel attacks by the Sasanid kingdom in Persia, which was still making periodic strikes against the eastern empire.

The eastern emperors believed it their duty to continue the Roman Empire and prevent barbarians from debasing its culture. The most famous eastern Roman emperor, **Justinian** (r. 527–565), and his wife and partner in rule, **Theodora** (500–548), took this mission so seriously that for decades the eastern empire waged war against the barbarian kingdoms in the west, aiming to reunite the empire and restore the imperial glory of the Augustan period. Like Diocletian, Justinian increased imperial authority and tried to purify religion to provide what he saw as the strong lead-

Justinian and Theodora: Sixth-century emperor and empress of the eastern Roman Empire, famous for waging costly wars to reunite the empire.

ership and divine favor necessary in unsettled times. He and his successors in the eastern empire also contributed to the preservation of the memory of classical Greek and Roman culture by preserving a great deal of earlier literature, non-Christian and Christian.

Imperial Society in the East

The sixth-century eastern empire enjoyed a vitality that had vanished in the west. Its elite spent freely on luxuries such as silk, precious stones, and pepper and other spices imported from China and India. Markets in its large cities teemed with merchants from far and wide. Its churches' soaring domes testified to its confidence in the Christian God as its divine protector.

In keeping with Roman tradition, the eastern emperors sponsored religious festivals and entertainments on a massive scale to rally public support. Rich and poor alike crowded city squares, theaters, and hippodromes on these lively occasions. Chariot racing aroused the hottest passions. Constantinople's residents divided themselves into competitive factions called Blues and Greens after the racing colors of their favorite charioteers. Emperors sometimes backed one gang or the other to intimidate potential rivals.

Preserving "Romanness." The eastern emperors worked to maintain Roman tradition and identity, believing that "Romanness" was the best defense against what they saw as the barbarization of the western empire. They hired many foreign mercenaries, but they also tried to keep their subjects from adopting foreign ways. Styles of dress figured largely in this struggle. Eastern emperors ordered Constantinople's residents not to wear barbarian-style clothing (especially heavy boots and fur clothing) instead of traditional Roman garb (sandals or light shoes and cloth robes), overlooking the favored clothing of the chariot factions.

The quest for cultural unity was hopeless because society in the eastern empire was thoroughly multilingual and multiethnic. The eastern empire's inhabitants regarded themselves as the heirs of ancient Roman culture: they referred to themselves as Romans, even though most of them spoke Greek as their native language and used Latin only for government and military communication. Many people retained their traditional languages, such as Phrygian and Cappadocian in western Asia Minor, Armenian farther east, and Syriac and other Aramaic dialects along the eastern Mediterranean

coast. The streets of Constantinople reportedly rang with seventy-two languages.

Romanness definitely included Christianity, but the eastern empire's theological diversity rivaled its ethnic complexity. Bitter controversies over doctrine divided eastern Christians; neither the emperors nor the bishops succeeded in imposing orthodoxy. Emperors used violence against heretics when persuasion failed. They had to resort to extreme measures, they believed, to save lost souls and preserve the empire's religious purity and divine goodwill. The persecution of Christian subjects by Christian emperors illustrates the disturbing consequences that the quest for a unitary identity required.

Women in Society and at Court. Most women in eastern Roman society lived according to ancient Mediterranean tradition: they concentrated on their households and minimized contact with men outside that circle. Law barred them from performing many public functions, such as witnessing wills. Subject to the authority of their fathers and husbands, women veiled their heads (though not their faces) to show modesty. Since Christian theologians exceeded Roman tradition in restricting sexuality and reproduction, divorce became more difficult and remarriage was discouraged even for widows. Sexual offenses carried stiffer legal penalties. Female prostitution remained legal and common, but emperors raised the penalties for those who forced women under their control (children or slaves) into prostitution.

Women in the imperial family could achieve prominence unattainable for ordinary women. Empress Theodora demonstrated the influence women could achieve in the eastern empire. Uninhibited by her humble origins (she was the daughter of a bear trainer and had been an actress with a scandalous reputation), she came to rival anyone in influence and wealth (see the mosaic of Theodora on page 223). She had a hand in every aspect of Justinian's rule, advising him on personnel for his administration, pushing for her religious views in disputes over Christian doctrine, and rallying his courage at times of crisis. John Lydus, a contemporary government official and high-ranking administrator, judged her "superior in intelligence to any man."

Social Class and Government Services. Government in the eastern empire aggravated social divisions because it provided services according to people's wealth. Officials demanded fees for countless activities, from commercial permits to legal

Theodora and Her Court in Ravenna
This resplendent mosaic shows the empress Theodora and members of her court presenting a gift to the church at San Vitale in Ravenna. It faced the matching scene of her husband Justinian and his attendants (page 224). Theodora wears the jewels, pearls, and rich robes characteristic of eastern Roman monarchs. (Compare the style of the clothes in these two mosaics to those shown in the cameo from Augustus's time on page 166. What were the different styles of dress meant to convey about the leaders in each period?) Theodora extends in her hands a gem-encrusted wine cup as her present; her gesture imitates the gift-giving of the Magi to the baby Jesus, the scene illustrated on the hem of her garment. The circle around her head, called a nimbus (Latin for "cloud"), indicates special holiness. (Scala/Art Resource, NY.)

grievances. Nothing got done without payment. People with money and status found this process easy: they relied on their social connections to get a hearing from the right official and on their wealth to pay bribes to move matters along quickly. Whether seeking preferential treatment or just spurring administrators to do what they were supposed to do, the rich could make the system work. The poor, by contrast, could not afford the hefty amounts that government officials extorted.

This fee-based system allowed the emperors to pay their civil servants tiny salaries and spend imperial funds for other purposes. John Lydus, for example, reported that he earned thirty times his annual salary in payments from petitioners during his first year in office. To keep the system from destroying itself through limitless extortion, the emperors published an official list of the maximum bribes that their employees could demand.

The Reign of Justinian, 527–565

Justinian won his reputation by waging war to reunite the empire as it had been in the days of Augustus, making imperial rule more autocratic, constructing costly buildings in Constantinople, and instituting legal and religious reforms. The most intellectual emperor since Julian the Apostate two centuries earlier, Justinian had the same aims as all his predecessors: to preserve social order based on hierarchy and maintain divine goodwill (see the mosaic of Justinian on page 224). Unfortunately, the cost of his plans forced him to raise taxes, generating civil strife.

Taxes and Social Unrest.   Justinian faced bitter resistance to his plans and their enormous cost. His unpopular taxes provoked a major riot in 532. Known as the Nika Riot, it arose when the Blue and Green factions, gathering to watch chariot races, unexpectedly united against the emperor, shouting "Nika! Nika!" ("Win! Win!") as their battle cry. After nine days of violence that left much of Constantinople in ashes, Justinian was ready to abandon his throne and flee in panic. But Theodora sternly rebuked him: "Once born, no one can escape dying, but for one who has held imperial power it would be unbearable to be a fugitive. May I never take off my imperial robes of purple, nor live to see the day when those who meet me will not greet me as their ruler." Her husband then sent in troops, who quelled the disturbance by slaughtering thirty thousand rioters trapped in the racetrack.

Justinian and His Court in Ravenna
This mosaic scene dominated by the eastern Roman emperor Justinian stands opposite
Theodora's mosaic (page 223) in San Vitale's Church in Ravenna. The emperor is shown presenting
a gift to the church. Justinian and Theodora finished building the church, which the Ostrogothic
king Theodoric had started, to commemorate their successful campaign to restore Italy to the
Roman Empire and reassert control of the western capital, Ravenna. The inclusion of the portrait
of Maximianus, bishop of Ravenna, standing on Justinian's left and identified by name, stresses
the theme of cooperation between bishops and emperors in ruling the world. What do you think
the inclusion of the soldiers at the left is meant to indicate? *(Scala/Art Resource, NY.)*

Justinian's most ambitious goal was to restore
the empire to a unified territory, religion, and culture. Invading the former western provinces, his
generals defeated the Vandals and Ostrogoths after campaigns that in some cases took decades to
complete. At an enormous price in lives and
money, Justinian's armies restored the old empire's
geography, with its territory stretching from the
Atlantic to the western edge of Mesopotamia.

Justinian's success in reuniting the western and
eastern empires had unintended consequences: destruction of the west's infrastructure and depletion
of the east's finances. Italy endured the most physical damage; the war there against the Goths spread
death and destruction on a massive scale. The east
suffered because Justinian squeezed even more
taxes out of his already overburdened population
to finance the western wars and bribe the Persian
kingdom not to attack while his home defenses
were depleted. The tax burden crippled the economy, leading to constant banditry in the country-

side. Crowds poured into the capital from rural areas, seeking relief from poverty and robbers.

Natural disaster compounded Justinian's
problems. In the 540s, a horrific epidemic killed a
third of his empire's inhabitants; a quarter of a million, half the capital's population, succumbed in
Constantinople alone. This was only the first of
many pandemics that erased millions of people in
the eastern empire over the next two centuries. Serious earthquakes, always a danger in this region,
increased the death toll. The loss of so many people created a shortage of army recruits, requiring
the hire of expensive mercenaries, and left countless farms vacant, reducing tax revenues.

Strengthening Central Authority.   The threats to
his regime made Justinian crave stability, which he
sought by strengthening his authority in two ways:
emphasizing his closeness to God and increasing
the autocratic power of his rule. These traits became characteristic of eastern Roman emperors.

Moreover, Justinian proclaimed the emperor the "living law," recalling the Hellenistic royal doctrine that the ruler's decisions defined law.

His building program in Constantinople communicated his overpowering supremacy and religiosity. Most spectacular of all was his reconstruction of Constantine's Hagia Sophia (Church of the Holy Wisdom). Creating a new design for churches, Justinian's architects erected a huge building on a square plan capped by a dome 107 feet across and 160 feet high. Its interior walls glowed like the sun from the light reflecting off their four acres of gold mosaics. Imported marble of every color added to the sparkling effect. When he first entered his masterpiece, dedicated in 538, Justinian exclaimed, "Solomon, I have outdone you," claiming to have bested the glorious temple that the ancient king built for the Hebrews.

Justinian's autocratic rule reduced the autonomy of the empire's cities. Their councils ceased to govern; imperial officials took over instead. Provincial elites still had to ensure full payment of their area's taxes, but no longer could they decide local matters. Now the central government determined all aspects of decision making and social status. Men of property from the provinces who aspired to power and prestige could satisfy their ambitions only by joining the imperial administration in the capital.

Legal and Religious Reform. To solidify his authority, Justinian codified the laws of the empire to bring uniformity to the confusing mass of decisions that earlier emperors had announced. The final version of his *Codex* appeared in 534. A team of scholars also condensed millions of words of regulations to produce the *Digest* in 533, intended to expedite legal cases and provide a syllabus for law schools. This collection, like the *Codex* written in Latin and therefore readable in the western empire, influenced legal scholars for centuries. Justinian's legal experts also compiled a textbook for students, the *Institutes*, which appeared in 533 and remained on law school reading lists until modern times.

To fulfill the emperor's sacred duty to secure the welfare of his people, Justinian acted to enforce their religious purity. Like the polytheist and Christian emperors before him, he believed his world could not flourish if its divine protector became angered by the presence of religious offend-

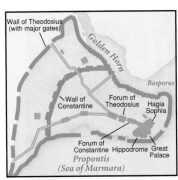

Constantinople during the Rule of Justinian

ers. As emperor, Justinian decided who the offenders were. Zealously enforcing laws against polytheists, he compelled them to be baptized or forfeit their lands and official positions. He also relentlessly purged heretical Christians who rejected his version of orthodoxy. In pursuit of sexual purity, his laws made male homosexual relations illegal for the first time in Roman history. Homosexual marriage, apparently allowed earlier, had been officially prohibited in 342, but civil sanctions had never before been imposed on men engaging in homosexual activity. All the previous emperors, for example, had simply taxed male prostitutes. The legal status of homosexual activity between women is less clear; it probably counted as adultery when married women were involved and thus constituted criminal behavior.

A brilliant theologian in his own right, Justinian labored mightily to reconcile orthodox and Monophysite Christians by having the creed of the Council of Chalcedon revised. But the church leaders in Rome and Constantinople had become too bitterly divided and too jealous of the others' prominence to agree on a unified church; the eastern and western churches were by now firmly launched on the diverging courses that would result in formal schism five hundred years later. Justinian's own ecumenical council in Constantinople ended in conflict in 553 when he jailed Rome's defiant Pope Vigilius while also managing to alienate Monophysite bishops. Probably no one could have done better, but his efforts to compel religious unity only drove Christians further apart and undermined his vision of a restored Roman world.

Preserving Classical Traditions

Since knowledge of a culture can disappear if its texts are not preserved, Christianization of the empire endangered the memory of classical traditions. The greatest danger to the survival of the plays, histories, philosophical works, poems, speeches, and novels of classical Greece and Rome — which were polytheist and therefore potentially subversive of Christian belief — stemmed not so much from active censorship as simple neglect. As Christians became authors, which they did in great numbers, their works displaced ancient Greek and Roman texts as the most important literature of the age. Fortunately for later

The Soaring Architecture of Hagia Sophia
Golden mosaics originally reflected a dazzling light from the interior of Hagia Sophia ("Holy Wisdom"), the huge church that the eastern emperor Justinian built in the 530s near his palace in Constantinople. A central dome, 184 feet high and supported by four arches resting on massive piers, capped the church's vast interior; the ring of windows at the base of the dome is just visible at the top of the picture. Hagia Sophia became a mosque after the Turks captured the city in 1453; the large medallions contain religious quotations in Arabic. Now a museum, Hagia Sophia continues to host people offering prayers. (© Adam Woolfit/Corbis.)

times, however, the eastern empire played a crucial role in passing on the intellectual legacy of the past to later Western civilization.

Classical texts survived because Christian education and literature depended on non-Christian models, Latin and Greek. In the eastern empire, the region's original Greek culture remained the dominant influence, but Latin literature continued to be read because the administration was bilingual, with official documents and laws published in Latin along with Greek translations. Latin scholarship in the east received a boost when Justinian's Italian wars impelled Latin-speaking scholars to flee for safety to Constantinople. Their labors in the capital helped to conserve many works that might otherwise have disappeared. Scholars preserved classical literature because they regarded it as a crucial part of a high-level education. In other words, much of the classical literature available today survived because it served as schoolwork for Christians. At least a rudimentary knowledge of some pre-Christian classics was required for a good career in government service, the goal of every ambitious student. An imperial decree from 360 stated, "No person shall obtain a post of the first rank unless it shall be shown that he excels in long practice of liberal studies, and that he is so polished in literary matters that words flow from his pen faultlessly."

Another factor promoting the preservation of classical literature was that the principles of classical rhetoric provided the guidelines for the most effective presentation of Christian theology. When Ambrose, bishop of Milan from 374 to 397, composed the first systematic description of Christian ethics for young priests, he consciously imitated the great classical orator Cicero. Theologians refuted heretical Christian doctrines by employing the dialogue form pioneered by Plato, and polytheist traditions of biography praising heroes inspired the hugely popular genre of saints' lives. Similarly, Christian artists incorporated polytheist traditions in communicating their beliefs and emotions in paintings, mosaics, and carved reliefs. A favorite artistic motif of Christ with a sunburst surrounding his head, for example, took its inspiration from polytheist depictions of the radiant Sun as a god. (See Jesus as Sun God, page 208.)

The proliferation of Christian literature generated a technological innovation used also to preserve classical literature. Polytheist scribes had written books on sheets of parchment (made from thin animal skin) or paper (made from papyrus). They then glued the sheets together and attached rods at both ends to form a scroll. Readers faced a cumbersome task in unrolling scrolls to read. For ease of use, Christians produced their literature in the form of the codex—a book with bound pages that not only was less susceptible to damage from rolling and unrolling but also contained text more efficiently than scrolls. Eventually the codex became the standard form of book production.

Despite the continuing importance of classical Greek and Latin literature in education and rhetoric, its survival remained precarious in a war-torn world dominated by Christians. Knowledge of Greek in the turbulent west faded so drastically that by the sixth century almost no one there could read the original versions of Homer's *Iliad* and *Odyssey*, the traditional foundations of a classical literary education. Latin fared better, and scholars such as Augustine and Jerome knew Rome's ancient literature extremely well. But they also saw its classics as potentially too seductive for a pious Christian because the pleasure that came from reading them could be a distraction from the worship of God. Jerome in fact once had a nightmare of being condemned on Judgment Day for having been more dedicated to Cicero than to Christ.

The closing around 530 of the Academy, founded in Athens by Plato more than nine hundred years earlier, vividly demonstrated the dangers for classical learning lurking in the later Roman Empire. This most famous of classical schools finally went out of business when many of its scholars emigrated to Persia to escape harsher restrictions on polytheists and its revenues dwindled because the Athenian elite, its traditional supporters, were increasingly Christianized. The Neoplatonist school at Alexandria, by contrast, continued; its leader John Philoponus (c. 490–570) was a Christian. In addition to Christian theology, Philoponus wrote commentaries on the works of Aristotle; some of his ideas anticipated those of Galileo a thousand years later. With his work, he achieved the kind of synthesis of old and new that was one of the fruitful possibilities in the ferment of the late Roman world—he was a Christian subject of the eastern Roman Empire in sixth-century Egypt, heading a school founded long before by polytheists, studying the works of an ancient Greek philosopher as the inspiration for his forward-looking scholarship. The strong possibility that present generations could learn from the past would continue as Western civilization once again remade itself in medieval times.

REVIEW: What policies did Justinian undertake to try to restore and strengthen the Roman Empire?

Conclusion

The third-century civil wars brought the Roman Empire to a crisis that Diocletian's creation of the dominate and reorganization of government relieved, but his reforms could only delay the empire's fragmentation. In the late fourth century, migrations of non-Roman peoples fleeing the Huns brought intense pressures on the central government. Emperor Theodosius I divided the empire into western and eastern halves in 395 to try to improve its administration and defense. When Roman authorities bungled the task of integrating immigrant barbarian tribes into Roman society, the newcomers created kingdoms that eventually replaced imperial government in the west. Roman history increasingly divided into two regional streams, even though emperors as late as Justinian in the sixth century retained the dream of reuniting the empire and restoring its glory.

The large-scale immigration of barbarian tribes into the Roman Empire transformed not only the west's politics, society, and economy but also the tribes themselves, as they developed their own ethnic identities while organizing themselves into kingdoms inside Roman territory. The economic deterioration and political weakness that accompanied these often violent changes destroyed the public-spiritedness of the elite, which had been one of the foundations of imperial stability, as wealthy nobles retreated to self-sufficient country estates and shunned municipal office.

The eastern empire fared better economically than the western and avoided the worst violence of the migrations. Eastern emperors attempted to preserve "Romanness" by maintaining Roman culture and political traditions. The financial drain of trying to reunite the empire by wars against the new kingdoms increased social discontent by driving tax rates to punitive levels, while the concentration of greater central authority in the capital weakened local communities.

The great change that unified—but also divided—the empire was its Christianization. Constantine's conversion in 312 marked an epochal turning point in Western history. Conversion to Christianity throughout the empire occurred gradually, and it was not until 391 that it became the official state religion and public polytheist worship was completely banned. Christians disagreed among themselves over fundamental doctrines of faith, even to the point of deadly violence. The church developed a hierarchy to combat disunity, but believers proved remarkably defiant in

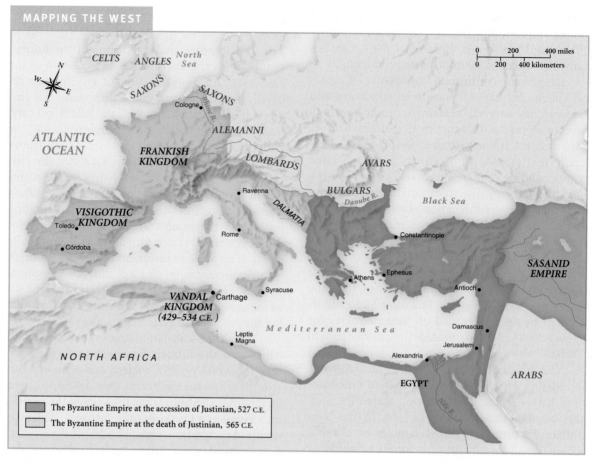

Western Europe and the Eastern Roman Empire, 600

The eastern Roman emperor Justinian employed brilliant generals and expended huge sums of money to reconquer Italy, North Africa, and part of Spain to reunite the western and eastern halves of the former Roman Empire. His wars to regain Italy and North Africa eliminated the Ostrogothic and Vandal kingdoms, respectively, but at a huge cost in effort, time—the war in Italy took twenty years—and expense. The resources of the eastern empire were so depleted that his successors could not maintain the reunification. By the early seventh century, the Visigoths had taken back all of Spain. Africa, despite serious revolts by indigenous Berber tribes, remained under imperial control until the Arab conquest of the seventh century; however, within five years of Justinian's death, the Lombards had set up a new kingdom controlling a large section of Italy. Never again would anyone attempt to reestablish a universal Roman Empire.

the face of authority. Many Christians attempted to come closer to God by abandoning everyday society to live as monks. Monastic life redefined the meaning of holiness by creating communities of God's heroes who withdrew from this world to devote their service to glorifying the next. In the end, then, the imperial vision of unity faded before the divisive forces of religious strife combined with the powerful dynamics of political and social transformation. Nevertheless, the memory of Roman power and culture remained potent and present, providing an influential inheritance to the peoples and states that would become Rome's heirs in the next stage of Western civilization.

FOR FURTHER EXPLORATION

■ **For suggested references, including Web sites, for topics in this chapter,** see page SR-1 at the end of the book.

■ **For additional primary-source material from this period,** see Chapter 7 in *Sources of THE MAKING OF THE WEST*, Third Edition.

■ **For Web sites and documents related to topics in this chapter,** see *Make History* at bedfordstmartins.com/hunt.

CHAPTER REVIEW

KEY TERMS AND PEOPLE

dominate (197)

tetrarchy (198)

coloni (200)

curials (200)

Great Persecution (202)

Edict of Milan (203)

Julian the Apostate (205)

Theodosius I (205)

Augustine (208)

Arianism (210)

Nicene Creed (210)

asceticism (212)

Visigoths (216)

wergild (219)

Justinian and
   Theodora (221)

REVIEW QUESTIONS

1. How did Diocletian's policies end the third-century crisis, and why did they fail to work in the long run?

2. How did Christianity both unite and divide the Roman Empire?

3. How did the barbarian migrations and invasions change the Roman Empire and Roman society?

4. What policies did Justinian undertake to try to restore and strengthen the Roman Empire?

MAKING CONNECTIONS

1. What were the main similarities and differences between the political reality and the political appearance of the principate and the dominate?

2. What were the main similarities and differences between traditional Roman religion and Christianity as official state religions?

> **For practice quizzes, a customized study plan, and other study tools,** see the Online Study Guide at bedfordstmartins.com/hunt.

IMPORTANT EVENTS

293	Diocletian creates the tetrarchy
301	Diocletian issues the Edict on Maximum Prices and Wages
303	Diocletian launches Great Persecution of Christians
312	Constantine wins the battle of the Milvian Bridge and converts to Christianity
313	Religious toleration proclaimed in the Edict of Milan
323	Pachomius in Upper Egypt establishes the first monasteries
324	Constantine wins the civil war and refounds Byzantium as Constantinople, the "new Rome"
325	Council of Nicaea defends Christian orthodoxy against Arianism
361–363	Julian the Apostate tries to reinstate traditional religion as official state religion
378	Barbarian massacre of Roman army in battle of Adrianople
391	Theodosius I makes Christianity the official state religion
395	Theodosius I divides the empire into western and eastern halves
410	Visigoths sack Rome
426	Augustine publishes *City of God*
451	Council of Chalcedon attempts to forge agreement on Christian orthodoxy
475	Visigoths publish law code
476	The "fall of Rome" (German commander Odoacer deposes the final western emperor, the boy Romulus Augustulus)
493–526	Ostrogothic kingdom in Italy
507	Clovis establishes Frankish kingdom in Gaul
527–565	Reign of eastern Roman emperor Justinian
533–534	Justinian publishes law code and handbooks
540	Benedict devises his rule for monasteries

Islam, Byzantium, and the West

600–750

I n the eighth century, a Syrian monk named Joshua wrote about the first appearance of Islam in Roman territory: "The Arabs conquered the land of Palestine and the land as far as the great river Euphrates. The Romans fled," he marveled, and then continued:

> The first king was a man among them named Muhammad, whom they also called Prophet because he turned them away from cults of all kinds and taught them that there was only one God, creator of the universe. He also instituted laws for them because they were much entangled in the worship of demons.

Joshua was wrong about Muhammad leading the conquest of Palestine—Muhammad died in 632, six years before the fall of Palestine. But he was right to see the Arab movement as a momentous development, for in the course of a few decades the Arabs conquered much of the Persian and Roman empires. Joshua was also right to emphasize Muhammad's teachings, for it was the fervor of Islam that brought the Arabs out of the Arabian peninsula and into the regions that hugged the Mediterranean in one direction and led to the Indus River in the other.

In the sixth century, as the western and eastern parts of the Roman Empire were going their separate ways, a third power—Arab and Muslim—was taking shape. These three powers have continued in various forms to the present day: the western Roman Empire became western Europe; the eastern Roman Empire, occupying what is now Turkey, Greece, and some of the Balkans, became part of eastern Europe and helped to create Russia; and the Arab world endures in North Africa and the Middle East (the ancient Near East).

The Dome of the Rock at Jerusalem (691)
Rivaling the great churches of Christendom, the mosque in Jerusalem called Dome of the Rock borrowed from late Roman and Byzantine forms even while asserting its Islamic identity. The columns and capitals atop them, the round arches, the dome, and the mosaics that decorate them are all from Byzantine models. In fact, the columns were taken from older buildings at Jerusalem. But the strips of Arabic writing on the dome itself—and in many other parts of the building—assert Islamic doctrine. *(Erich Lessing/Art Resource, NY.)*

As diverse as these cultures are today, they share many of the same roots. All were heirs of Hellenistic and Roman traditions. All adhered to monotheism. The western and eastern halves of the Roman Empire had Christianity in common, although they differed at times in interpreting it. Adherents of Islam, the Arab world's religion, believed in the same God as the Jews and Christians. They understood Jesus, however, as God's prophet rather than his son.

The history of the seventh and eighth centuries is a story of adaptation and transformation. Historians consider the changes so important that they use a new term—Byzantium or Byzantine Empire—to describe the eastern Roman Empire. They also speak of the end of one era—antiquity—and the beginning of another—the Middle Ages. (See "Terms of History," page 233.) Use of the term *Byzantium* or *Byzantine Empire*, which comes from the old Greek name of the city of Constantinople, rightly implies that the center of power and culture in the old eastern half of the Roman Empire was now concentrated in this one city. During the course of many centuries, the Byzantine Empire shrank, expanded, and even nearly disappeared—but it hung on, in one form or another, until 1453.

During the period 600 to 750, all three heirs of the Roman Empire combined elements of their heritage with new values, interests, and conditions. The divergences among them resulted from disparities in geography and climate, material and human resources, skills, beliefs, and local traditions. But these differences should not obscure the fact that the Byzantine, Muslim, and western European worlds were related cultures.

> **FOCUS QUESTION:** What three cultures took the place of the Roman Empire, and to what extent did each of them both draw on and reject Roman traditions?

Islam: A New Religion and a New Empire

In the sixth century, a religion that called on all to submit to the will of one God began in Arabia (today Saudi Arabia). Islam, which means "submission to God," emerged under Muhammad (c. 570–632), a merchant-turned-holy-man from the city of Mecca. While the great majority of people living in Arabia were polytheists, Muhammad recognized one God, the same one worshipped by Jews and Christians. He understood himself to be God's last prophet—and thus he is called the Prophet—the person to receive and in turn repeat God's final words to humans. Invited by the disunited and pagan people of the city of Medina to come and act as a mediator for them, Muhammad exercised the powers of both a religious and a secular leader. This dual role became the model for his successors, known as caliphs. Through a combination of persuasion and force, Muhammad and his co-religionists, the Muslims ("those who submit to Islam"), converted most of the Arabian peninsula. By the time Muhammad died in 632, conquest and conversion had begun to move northward, into Byzantine and Persian territories. In the next generation, the Arabs conquered most of Persia and all of Egypt and were on their way across North Africa to Spain. Yet within the territories they conquered, daily life went on much as before.

Nomads and City Dwellers

In the seventh century, the vast deserts of the Arabian peninsula were populated by both sedentary and nomadic peoples. The sedentary peoples—who lived in one place—far outnumbered the nomads. Some of the sedentary groups made their living by farming, while others lived in oases, where they raised dates, a highly prized food. Some

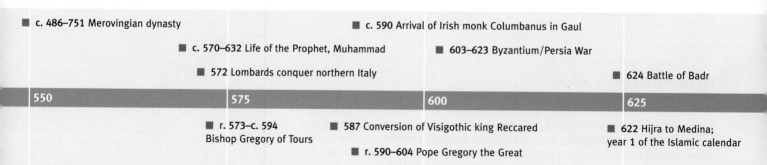

■ c. 486–751 Merovingian dynasty

■ c. 590 Arrival of Irish monk Columbanus in Gaul

■ c. 570–632 Life of the Prophet, Muhammad

■ 603–623 Byzantium/Persia War

■ 572 Lombards conquer northern Italy

■ 624 Battle of Badr

550   575   600   625

■ r. 573–c. 594
Bishop Gregory of Tours

■ 587 Conversion of Visigothic king Reccared

■ 622 Hijra to Medina;
year 1 of the Islamic calendar

■ r. 590–604 Pope Gregory the Great

oases were prosperous enough to support merchants and artisans. The nomads, which also included semi-nomads, were called Bedouins; they lived in the desert, where they herded goats, sheep, or camels, surviving largely on the products of their animals: leather, milk, and meat. (The rich camel nomads called themselves Arabs.) The Bedouins were warriors who raided one another to capture slaves or wives and to take belongings. They valued honor, bravery, and generosity. Although they lacked written literature, their oral culture of poetry expressed many things, including the bravado of a boast, the trials of a journey, and longing for a lost love.

> To remember Salma! to recall
> times spent with her
> is folly, conjecture about the other side,
> a casting of stones.

The "follies of love" were part of a culture in which men practiced polygyny (having more than one wife at a time).

Islam began as a religion of the sedentary city dwellers, but it soon found support and military strength among the nomads. It had its start in Mecca, a major oasis and commercial center located near the coast of the Red Sea. Mecca was also a religious center, the home of the Ka'ba, a shrine that contained the images of many gods. The Ka'ba was a sacred place within which war and violence among all tribes were prohibited. The tribe that dominated Mecca, the Quraysh, controlled access to the shrine, taxing the pilgrims who flocked there and selling them food and drink. Visitors, assured of their safety, bartered on the sacred grounds, transforming the plunder from raids into trade.

The Prophet Muhammad and the Faith of Islam

Muhammad was born in Mecca. Orphaned at the age of six, he lived two years with his grandfather

TERMS OF HISTORY

Medieval

How did the word *medieval* come into being, and why is it a derogatory term today? No one who lived in the Middle Ages thought of himself or herself as "medieval." People did not say they lived in the "Middle Ages." The whole idea of the Middle Ages began in the sixteenth century. At that time, writers decided that their own age, known as the Renaissance (French for "rebirth"), and the ancient Greek and Roman civilizations were much alike. They dubbed the period in between—from about 600 to about 1400—with a Latin term: the *medium aevum*, or the "middle age." It was not a flattering term. Renaissance writers considered the *medium aevum* a single unfortunate, barbaric, and ignorant period.

Only with the Romantic movement of the nineteenth century and the advent of history as an academic discipline did writers begin to divide that middle age into several ages. Often, they divided it into three periods: Early (c. 600–1100), High (c. 1100–1300), and Late (c. 1300–1400). Today there is no hard-and-fast rule about this terminology: Chapter 11 of this book, for example, covers the period 1150–1215 as the High Middle Ages.

The period before the High Middle Ages was sometimes called the Dark Ages, a term that immediately brings to mind doom and gloom. However, recent research disputes this view of the period, stressing instead its creativity, multiethnicity, and localism.

Newspaper reporters and others still sometimes use *medieval* as a negative term: for example, by calling a primitive prison system "medieval." Little do they know that when they do that, they are stuck in the sixteenth century.

and then came under the care of his uncle, a leader of the Quraysh tribe. Eventually, Muhammad became a trader. At the age of twenty-five, he married Khadija, a rich widow who had once employed him. They had at least four daughters and lived (to all appearances) happily and comfortably. Yet Muhammad sometimes left home and

661–750 Umayyad caliphate

726–787 Byzantine iconoclasm

| 650 | 675 | 700 | 725 |

664 Synod of Whitby

DOCUMENT

The Fatihah of the Qur'an

The Fatihah is the prayer that begins the Qur'an. It emphasizes God's compassion for the believer, who needs to be guided "along the road straight"—God's highway. The translation here uses no punctuation in order to convey the fluid nature of the phrases, which relate to one another in many ways and have no one meaning.

The Opening

In the name of God
    the Compassionate the Caring
Praise be to God
    lord sustainer of the worlds
the Compassionate the Caring
master of the day of reckoning
To you we turn to worship
    and to you we turn in time of need
Guide us along the road straight
the road of those to whom you are giving
    not those with anger upon them
    not those who have lost the way

Source: Approaching the Qur'an: The Early Revelations, intro. and trans. Michael Sells (Ashland, OR: White Cloud Press, 1999), 42.

the "one of great power." In an early Sura, Muhammad has a vision of this power:

> This is a revelation
> taught him by one of great power
> and strength that stretched out over
> while on the highest horizon—
> then drew near and came down
> two bows' lengths or nearer

Here the object of Muhammad's vision never quite reveals itself; nevertheless, it teaches him about its great power and strength, its astonishing ability to stretch to the horizon, and its willingness at the same time almost to touch him.

Beginning with the Fatihah (or opening), frequently also said as an independent prayer, the Qur'an continues with Suras of gradually decreasing length, which cover the gamut of human experience and the life to come (see Document, "The Fatihah of the Qur'an," on this page). For Muslims, the Qur'an contains the foundations of history, prophecy, and the legal and moral code by which men and women should live: "Do not set up another god with God.... Do not worship anyone but Him, and be good to your parents.... Give to your relatives what is their due, and to those who are needy, and the wayfarers." The Qur'an emphasizes the nuclear family—a man, his wife (or wives), and children—as the basic unit of Muslim society. For its adherents, Islam replaced the identity and protection of the tribe with a new identity as part of the *ummah*, the community of believers, who share both a belief in one God and a set of religious practices.

Stressing individual belief in God and adherence to the Qur'an, Islam has no priests or sacraments, though in time it came to have authoritative religious leaders who interpreted the Qur'an and related texts. The Ka'ba, with its many gods, had gathered together tribes from the surrounding vicinity. Muhammad, with his one God, forged an even more universal religion.

Growth of Islam, c. 610–632

The first convert to Muhammad's faith was his wife, Khadija. A few friends and members of their immediate family joined them. Eventually, as Muhammad preached the new faith, others became adherents. Soon the new faith polarized Meccan society. Muhammad's insistence that the cults of all other gods be abandoned in favor of one brought him into conflict with leading members of the Quraysh tribe, whose control over the Ka'ba had given them prestige and wealth. As a result, they insulted Muhammad and harassed his adherents.

spent a few days in a nearby cave in prayer and contemplation, practicing a type of piety similar to that of the early Christians.

In about 610, on one of these retreats, Muhammad heard a voice and had a vision that summoned him to worship Allah, the God of the Jews and Christians. (*Allah* means "the God" in Arabic.) He accepted the call as coming from God. Over the next years, he received messages that he understood to be divine revelation. Later, when these messages had been written down and compiled—a process that was completed in the seventh century, but after Muhammad's death—they became the **Qur'an**, the holy book of Islam. (See a page from the Qur'an above.) Qur'an means "recitation"; each of the book's parts, or Suras, is understood to be God's revelation as told to Muhammad by the archangel Gabriel, then recited by Muhammad to others. Written entirely in verse, the Qur'an changed the focus of traditional Bedouin poetry, which had emphasized the here and now. In the Qur'an the focus is on the divine,

Qur'an (Kur AN/Koo RAHN): The holy book of Islam, considered the word of God (Allah) as revealed to the Prophet Muhammad.

Hijra: Muhammad's Journey from Mecca to Medina.

Disillusioned with the people of Mecca, Muhammad looked elsewhere for a place and a population receptive to his message. In particular, he expected support from Jews, whose monotheism, in Muhammad's view, prepared them for his own faith. When a few of Muhammad's converts from Medina promised to protect him if he would join them there, he eagerly accepted the invitation, in part because Medina had a significant Jewish population. In 622, Muhammad emigrated to Medina, an oasis about two hundred miles north of Mecca. This journey—called the **Hijra**—proved to be a crucial event for the new faith. At Medina, Muhammad found people ready to listen to his religious message and to accept him as the leader of their community. They expected him to act as a neutral and impartial judge in their interclan disputes. Muhammad's political position in the community set the pattern by which Islamic society would be governed afterward; rather than simply adding a church to political and cultural life, Muslims made their political and religious institutions inseparable. After Muhammad's death, the year of the Hijra was named the first year of the Islamic calendar; it marked the beginning of the new Islamic era.[1]

Although successful at Medina, the Muslims felt threatened by the Quraysh at Mecca, who actively opposed the public practice of Islam. For this reason, Muhammad led raids against them. At the battle of Badr in 624, Muhammad and his followers killed forty-nine of the Meccan enemy, took numerous prisoners, and confiscated rich booty. Thus, from the time of this conflict, the Bedouin tradition of plundering was grafted onto the Muslim duty of jihad (literally, "striving").[2]

The battle of Badr was a great triumph for Muhammad, who was now able to secure his position at Medina, gaining new adherents and silencing all doubters, including Jews. The Jews of Medina had not converted to Islam as Muhhamad had expected. Suspecting them of supporting his enemies, he expelled two Jewish tribes from Medina and executed the male members of another. Although Muslims had originally prayed in the direction of Jerusalem, the center of Jewish worship, Muhammad now had them turn in the direction of Mecca.

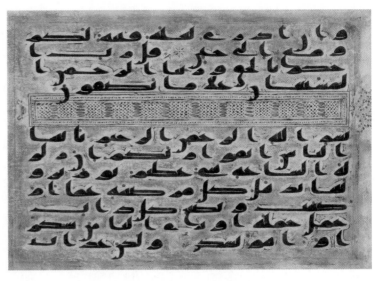

Qur'an
More than a holy book, the Qur'an represents for Muslims the very words of God that were dictated to Muhammad by the archangel Gabriel. In the Umayyad period, the Qur'an was written, as here, on pages wider than long. The first four lines on the top give the last verses of Sura 21. *(Freer Gallery of Art, Smithsonian Institution, Washington, D.C., F1945.16.)*

Defining the Faith.

As Muhammad broke with the Jews, he instituted new practices to define Islam as a unique religion. Among these were the *zakat*, a tax on possessions to be used for alms; the fast of Ramadan, which took place during the ninth month of the Islamic year, the month in which the battle of Badr had been fought; the *hajj*, the pilgrimage to Mecca during the last month of the year, which each Muslim was to make at least once in his or her lifetime; and the *salat*, formal worship at least three times a day (later increased to five). The salat could include the *shahadah*, or profession of faith—"There is no divinity but God, and Muhammad is the messenger of God." Detailed regulations for these practices, sometimes called the **Five Pillars of Islam**, were worked out in the eighth and early ninth centuries.

Meanwhile, Muhammad sent troops to subdue Arabs north and south. In 630, he entered Mecca with ten thousand men and took over the city, assuring the Quraysh of leniency and offering alliances with its leaders. As the prestige of Islam grew, clans elsewhere converted. Through a combination of force, conversion, and negotiation,

---

[1] Thus, 1 A.H. (1 *anno Hegirae*) on the Muslim calendar is equivalent to 622 C.E.

[2] *Jihad* means "striving" and is used in particular in the context of striving against unbelievers. In that sense, it is often translated as "holy war." But it can also mean striving against one's worst impulses.

Hijra (HIJ ruh): The emigration of Muhammad from Mecca to Medina. Its date, 622, marks the year 1 of the Islamic calendar.

Five Pillars of Islam: The five essential practices of Islam, namely, the *zakat* (alms); the fast of Ramadan; the *hajj* (pilgrimage to Mecca); the *salat* (formal worship); and the *shahadah* (profession of faith).

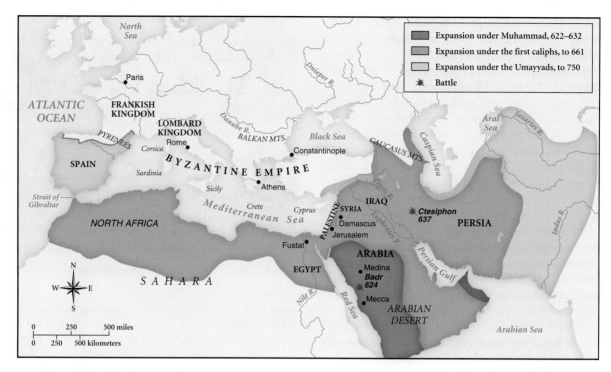

MAP 8.1 Expansion of Islam to 750
In little more than a century, Islamic armies conquered a vast region that included numerous different people, cultures, climates, and living conditions. Yet under the Umayyads, these disparate territories were administered by one ruler from the capital city at Damascus. The uniting force was the religion of Islam, which gathered all believers into one community, the *ummah*.

Muhammad was able to unite many, though by no means all, Arabic-speaking tribes under his leadership by the time of his death in 632.

Muhammad was responsible for social as well as religious change. The ummah included both men and women; as a result, women's status was enhanced. At first, Muslim women joined men during the prayer periods that punctuated the day, but beginning in the eighth century, women began to pray apart from men. Men were allowed to have up to four wives at one time, but were obliged to treat them equally; their wives received dowries and had certain inheritance rights. Islam prohibited all infanticide, a practice that Arabs had long used largely against female infants. Like Judaism and Christianity, Islam retained the practices of a patriarchal society in which women's participation in community life was limited.

Even though the Islamic ummah was a new sort of community, in many ways it functioned as a tribe, or rather a "supertribe," obligated to fight common enemies, share plunder, and resolve peacefully any internal disputes. Muslims participated in group rituals, such as the salat and public recitation. The Qur'an was soon publicly sung by professional reciters, much as the old tribal poetry had been. Most significant for the eventual

spread of Islam was that, as the Bedouin tribesmen converted to Islam, they turned their traditional warrior culture to its cause. Along the routes once taken by caravans to Syria, Muslim armies reaped profits at the point of a sword. But this differed from intertribal fighting; it was the jihad of people who were carrying out God's command against unbelievers as recorded in the Qur'an: "Strive, O Prophet, against the unbelievers and the hypocrites, and deal with them firmly. Their final abode is Hell: And what a wretched destination!"

The Caliphs, Muhammad's Successors, 632–750

In the new political community he founded in Arabia, Muhammad reorganized traditional Arab society by cutting across clan allegiances and welcoming converts from every tribe. He forged the Muslims into a formidable military force, and his successors, the caliphs, used this force to take the Byzantine and Persian worlds by storm.

War and Conquest.   To the north and west, the Muslims easily took Byzantine territory in Syria and moved into Egypt in the 640s (Map 8.1). To the east, they invaded the Sasanid Empire, defeating the Persians at the very gates of their capital, Ctesiphon, in 637. The whole of Persia was in Muslim hands by 651. During the last half of the seventh century and the beginning of the eighth, Islamic warriors extended their sway westward to Spain and eastward to India.

How were such widespread conquests possible, especially in so short a time? First, the Islamic forces came up against weakened empires. The Byzantine and Sasanid states were exhausted from fighting each other, and the cities that they fought over were depopulated and demoralized. Second, discontented Christians and Jews welcomed Muslims into both Byzantine and Persian territories. The Monophysite Christians in Syria and Egypt, for example, who had suffered persecution under the Byzantines, were glad to have new, Islamic overlords.

These were the external reasons for Islamic success. There were also internal reasons. Arabs had long been used to intertribal warfare. Now united as a supertribe, inspired by religious fervor, and under the banner of jihad, they exercised their skills as warriors not against one another but rather against unbelievers. Fully armed and mounted on horseback, using camels as convoys to carry supplies and provide protection, they conquered with amazing ease. To secure their victories, they built garrison cities from which their soldiers requisitioned taxes and goods. Sometimes whole Arab tribes, including women and children, were resettled in conquered territory, as happened in parts of Syria. In other regions, such as Egypt, one small Muslim settlement sufficed to gather the spoils of conquest.

The Politics of Succession. Falling ill in the midst of preparations for an invasion of Syria, Muhammad died quietly at Medina in 632. The question of who should succeed him as leader of the new Islamic state was the origin of the tension between Shi'ite and Sunni Muslims that continues today. The caliphs who followed Muhammad came not from the traditional tribal elite but rather from the inner circle of men who had participated in the Hijra and remained close to the Prophet. The first two caliphs ruled without serious opposition, but the third caliph, Uthman (r. 644–656), a member of the Umayyad clan and son-in-law (by marriage to two daughters) of Muhammad, aroused discontent among other members of the inner circle and soldiers unhappy with his distribution of high offices and revenues. Accusing Uthman of favoritism, they supported his rival, Ali, a member of the Hashim clan (to which Muhammad had belonged) and the husband of Muhammad's only surviving child, Fatimah. After a group of discontented soldiers murdered Uthman, civil war broke out between the Umayyads and Ali's faction. It ended when Ali was killed by one of his own former supporters, and the caliphate remained in Umayyad hands from 661 to 750.

Despite defeat, the *Shi'at Ali*, or Ali's faction, did not fade away. Ali's memory lived on among groups of Muslims (the Shi'ites) who saw in him a symbol of justice and righteousness. For them, Ali's death was the martyrdom of the only true successor to Muhammad. They remained faithful to his dynasty, shunning the mainstream caliphs of the other Muslims (Sunni Muslims, as they were later called, from *Sunna*, the practices of Muhammad). The Shi'ites awaited the arrival of the true leader — the imam — who in their view could come only from the house of Ali.

Peace and Prosperity in Islamic Lands

Ironically, the definitive victories of the Muslim warriors ushered in times of peace. While the conquerors stayed within their fortified cities or built magnificent hunting lodges in the deserts of Syria, the conquered went back to work, to study, to play, and — in the case of Christians and Jews, who were considered protected subjects — to worship as they pleased in return for the payment of a special tax. Under the **Umayyad caliphate**, which lasted from 661 to 750, the Muslim world became a state with its capital at Damascus, the historic capital of Syria — and today's as well. Borrowing from institutions well known to the civilizations they had just conquered, the Muslims issued coins and hired Byzantine and Persian officials as civil servants. (See "Seeing History," page 239.) They made Arabic a tool of centralization, imposing it as the language of government on regions not previously united linguistically. At the same time, the Islamic world was startlingly multiethnic, including Arabs, Syrians, Egyptians, Iraqis, and many other peoples. It was also multireligious, for although the Muslims fought against unbelievers, they tolerated other "people of the book" — Jews and Christians of every sort. Taking advantage of the vigorous economy in both the rural and urban sectors, the Umayyads presided over a new literary and artistic flowering. At Damascus, local artists and craftspeople worked on the lavish decorations for a

---

Umayyad caliphate (oo MAH yuhd KAY luhf ayt): The caliphs (successors of Muhammad) who traced their ancestry to Umayyah, a member of Muhammad's tribe. The dynasty lasted from 661 to 750.

Great Mosque at Damascus
Like the Dome of the Rock, the Umayyad mosque at Damascus in Syria, built at the beginning of the eighth century, drew on Byzantine forms. In this mosaic, which is one of many that decorates the interior of the mosque, the style is Byzantine. But the harmonious intertwining of trees, buildings, rocks, and water picks up on an Islamic theme: the new faith's conquest over both civilization and nature. (© Umayyad Mosque, Damascus, Syria/Bildarchiv Steffens/The Bridgeman Art Library.)

created new forms of prose writing in Arabic— official documents as well as essays on topics ranging from hunting to ruling. Umayyad poetry explored new worlds of thought and feeling. Supported by the caliphs, for whom written poetry served as an important source of propaganda and reinforcement for their power, the poets also reached a wider audience that delighted in their clever use of words, their satire, and their verses celebrating courage, piety, and sometimes erotic love:

> I spent the night as her bed-companion, each enamored of the other,
> And I made her laugh and cry, and stripped her of her clothes.
> I played with her and she vanquished me; I made her happy and I angered her.
> That was a night we spent, in my sleep, playing and joyful,
> But the caller to prayer woke me up.

Such poetry scandalized conservative Muslims, brought up on the ascetic tenets of the Qur'an. But this love poetry was a by-product of the new urban civilization of the Umayyad period, during which wealth, cultural mix, and the confidence born of conquest inspired diverse and experimental literary forms. By the time the Umayyad caliphate ended in 750, Islamic civilization was multiethnic, urban, and sophisticated, a true heir of Roman and Persian traditions.

REVIEW: How and why did the Muslims conquer so many lands in the period 632–750?

Byzantium: A Christian Empire under Siege

Even more than the Muslims, the Byzantines made use of Roman traditions. Emperor Justinian (r. 527–565) had tried to re-create the old Roman Empire. On the surface, he succeeded. His empire once again included Italy, North Africa, and the Balkans. Vestiges of the old Roman society persisted: an educated elite maintained its prestige, town governments continued to function, and old myths and legends were retold in poetry and depicted on silver plates and chests. Around 600, however, the eastern half of the Roman Empire began to undergo a transformation as striking as the one that had earlier remade the western half. Almost constant war, beginning in the last third of the sixth century and continuing through the seventh century, shrank its territory drastically. Cul-

mosque that used Roman motifs. At Jerusalem, the mosque called the Dome of the Rock used Christian building models for its octagonal form and its interior arches, which rested on columns and piers (see the chapter-opening photo).

During the seventh and eighth centuries, Muslim scholars wrote down the formerly mostly oral Arabic literature. They determined the definitive form for the Qur'an and compiled pious narratives about Muhammad, called hadith literature. Scribes composed these works in exquisite handwriting; Arab calligraphy became an art form. A literate class, consisting mainly of the old Persian and Syrian elite who had now converted to Islam,

Who Conquered Whom?
A Persian and an Arabic Coin Compared

D o you see any differences between these coins? One is Persian; the other is Arabic and comes from a later period. Both were minted for use in Iran and Iraq, but at different times, when these lands were under different rule. The coin on the top is Persian and shows the image of a Sasanid King of Kings. In the margin are three crescents, each with little stars. It was minted under Chosroes II (r. 591–628), the ambitious conqueror of Jerusalem. The coin on the bottom was minted by an Umayyad provincial governor in 696/697, after Islamic armies had conquered Persia. True, one branch of Islam barred depicting the human form, but the Ummayads were less condemning and saw nothing wrong with imitating traditional numismatic models. Although the image on the Arabic coin is still of a Sasanid ruler, the governor had his own name added in Arabic — it's in the right half of the central roundel, perpendicular to the nose. He also added in the margin of the coin an Arabic inscription that mentions Allah several times. What do these images suggest about how much the Islamic world borrowed from the Persian Empire that it conquered?

Persian Silver Coin (minted 606). *(© The Trustees of the British Museum.)*

Consider these coins in conjunction with supplemental evidence. The Arabic word for this type of coin, *dirham*, comes from the Greek *drachma*, a monetary unit used under the Byzantines. In areas that had been under Byzantine rule, the early Umayyad rulers adopted Byzantine coin forms, reusing *their* images — just as here they used the face of a Sasanid ruler. In general, the Umayyad fiscal system, which preserved the Byzantine land taxes, was administered by Syrians, who had often served Byzantine rulers in the same capacity. What advantages did the Arabs derive from adopting these institutions? From this evidence, how might you argue that both Greek and Persian institutions captured the conquering Arabs?

Umayyad Silver Dirham (minted 696/697). *(© The Trustees of the British Museum.)*

tural and political change came as well. Cities decayed, and the countryside became the focus of governmental and military administration. In the wake of these shifts, the old elite largely disappeared and classical learning gave way to new forms of education, mainly religious in content. The traditional styles of urban life, dependent on public gathering places and community spirit, faded away. Historians have good reason to stop speaking of the eastern Roman Empire and call this something new — the Byzantine Empire.

At the same time, the transformations should not be exaggerated. An emperor continued to rule at Constantinople with all the claims of a Constantine. Roman laws and taxes remained in place. The

cities, while shrunken, nevertheless survived, and Constantinople itself had a flourishing economic and cultural life even in Byzantium's darkest hours. The Byzantines continued to call themselves Romans. For them, the empire never ended: it just moved to Constantinople.

Wars on the Frontiers, c. 570–750

From about 570 to 750, the Byzantines waged war against invaders. One key challenge came from an old enemy, Persia. Another involved many new groups — Lombards, Slavs, Avars, Bulgars, and Muslims. In the wake of these onslaughts, Byzantium became smaller but tougher.

Invasions from Persia. In the sixth century, before the Muslims came on the scene, the Sasanid Empire of Persia was the great challenger to Byzantine power. Since the third century, the Sasanid kings and Roman emperors had fought off and on but never with decisive effect on either side. But in the middle of the sixth century, the Sasanids, using the revenues from new taxes to strengthen the army, decided to invade major areas of the Roman Empire.

Modeling their capital city at Ctesiphon after the great Byzantine city of Antioch in Syria (in fact, they gave it the title "Better-than-Antioch"), the Sasanid kings promoted an exalted view of themselves. They took the title "King of Kings" and gave the men at their court titles such as "priest of priests" and "scribe of scribes." Dreams of military and imperial glory accompanied the display of splendor. The Sasanid king Chosroes II (r. 591–628) decided to re-create the Persian Empire of Darius and Xerxes, which had extended down through Syria all the way to Egypt. (See Chapter 2, Mapping the West, page 66.) Between 611 and 614, Chosroes took Syria and Jerusalem; he conquered Egypt in 620. The fall of Jerusalem particularly shocked the pious Byzantines, since Chosroes took as plunder the relic of the Holy Cross (on which Christ was said to have died).

Responding to this affront, the Byzantine emperor **Heraclius** reorganized his army and inspired his troops to avenge the sack of Jerusalem. By 627, the Byzantines had regained all their lost territory. But the wars had changed much: Syrian, Egyptian, and Palestinian cities had grown used to being under Persian rule, and Christians who did not adhere to the orthodoxy at Byzantium preferred their Persian overlords. The constant wars and plundering sapped the wealth of the region and the energy of its people.

Attack on All Fronts. Preoccupied by war with the Sasanids, Byzantium was ill equipped to deal with other groups pushing into parts of the empire at about the same time (Map 8.2). The **Lombards**, a Germanic people, entered northern Italy in 568 and by 572 were masters of the Po valley and some inland regions in Italy's south. In addition to Rome, the Byzantines retained only Bari, Calabria,

and Sicily and a narrow swath of land through the middle called the Exarchate of Ravenna.

The Byzantine army could not contend any more successfully with the Slavs and other peoples just beyond the Danube River. The Slavs conducted lightning raids on the Balkan countryside (part of Byzantium at the time); and, joined by the Avars, they attacked Byzantine cities as well. Meanwhile, the Bulgars entered what is now Bulgaria in the 670s, defeating the Byzantine army and in 681 forcing the emperor to recognize their new state.

Even as the Byzantine Empire was facing military attacks on all fronts, its power was being whittled away by more peaceful means. For example, as Slavs and Avars, who were not subject to Byzantine rulers, settled in the Balkans, they often intermingled with the native peoples there, absorbing local agricultural techniques and burial practices while imposing their language and establishing religious cults.

Consequences of Constant Warfare. Byzantium's loss of control over the Balkans through both peaceful and military means meant the shrinking of its empire. More important over the long term was that the Balkans could no longer serve, as it had previously, as a major link between Byzantium and Europe. The loss of the Balkans exacerbated the growing separation between the eastern and western parts of the former Roman Empire. The political division between the Greek-speaking and Latin-speaking halves had begun in the fourth century. The events of the seventh century, however, made the split both physical and cultural. Avar and Slavic control of the Balkans effectively cut off trade and travel between Constantinople and the cities of the Dalmatian coast, while the Bulgar state threw a political barrier across the Danube. Perhaps as a result of this physical separation, historians in the East ceased to be interested in the western part of Europe, and Byzantine scholars no longer bothered to learn Latin. The two halves of the former Roman Empire communicated very little in the seventh century.

Byzantium's wars with the Sasanid Empire exhausted both Persian and Byzantine military strength. Both empires were now vulnerable to attack by the Muslim Arabs, whose military conquests, as we have seen, created a new empire and introduced a new religion.

From an Urban to a Rural Way of Life

As Byzantium shrank (see Map 8.2 inset), Byzantines in the conquered regions had to contend with new rulers and learn to accommodate to them.

Heraclius (her uh KLY uhs): The Byzantine emperor who reversed the fortunes of war with the Persians in the first quarter of the seventh century.

Lombards: The people who settled in Italy during the sixth century, following Justinian's reconquest. A king ruled the north of Italy, while dukes ruled the south. In between was the papacy, which felt threatened both by Lombard Arianism and by the Lombards' geographical proximity to Rome.

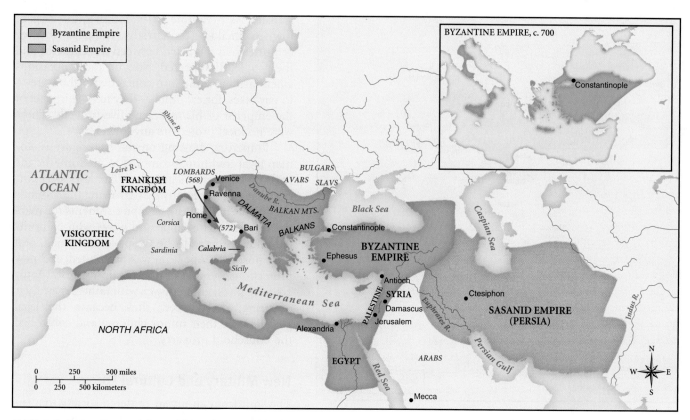

MAP 8.2 Byzantine and Sasanid Empires, c. 600
Justinian hoped to re-create the old Roman Empire, but just a century after his death Italy was largely conquered by the Lombards. Meanwhile, the Byzantine Empire had to contend with the Sasanid Empire to its east. In 600, these two major powers faced each other uneasily. Three years later, the Sasanid king attacked Byzantine territory. The resulting wars, which lasted until 627, exhausted both empires and left them open to invasion by the Arabs. By 700, the Byzantine Empire was quite small. ■ Compare the inset map here with Map 8.1, on page 236. Where had the Muslims made significant conquests of Byzantine territory?

Byzantine subjects in Syria and Egypt who came under Arab rule adapted to the new conditions, paying a special tax to their conquerors and practicing their Christian and Jewish religions in peace. Cities remained centers of government, scholarship, and business, and rural dwellers were permitted to keep and farm their lands. In the Balkans, some cities disappeared as people fled to hilltop settlements and Slavs and Bulgars came to dominate the peninsula. Nevertheless, the newcomers recognized the Byzantine emperor's authority, and they soon began to flirt with Christianity.

Some of the most radical transformations for seventh- and eighth-century Byzantines occurred not in the territories lost but in the shrunken empire itself. Under the ceaseless barrage of invaders, many towns, formerly bustling centers of trade and the imperial bureaucracy, vanished or became unrecognizable. The public activity of large, open marketplaces, theaters, and town squares largely ended. City baths, once places where people gos-

siped, made deals, and talked politics and philosophy, disappeared in most Byzantine towns—with the significant exception of Constantinople. Warfare reduced some cities to rubble, and the limited resources available for rebuilding went to construct thick city walls and solid churches instead of spacious marketplaces and baths. Traders and craftspeople sold their goods on overcrowded streets that looked much like the bazaars of the modern Middle East. People under siege sought protection at home or in a church and avoided public activities. In the Byzantine city of Ephesus, the citizens who built the new walls in the seventh century enclosed not the old public edifices but rather homes and churches (Map 8.3). Despite the new emphasis on church buildings, many cities were too impoverished even to repair their churches. (See "Taking Measure," page 243.)

Despite the general urban decay, the capital of Constantinople and a few other urban centers retained some of their old vitality. The manufacture

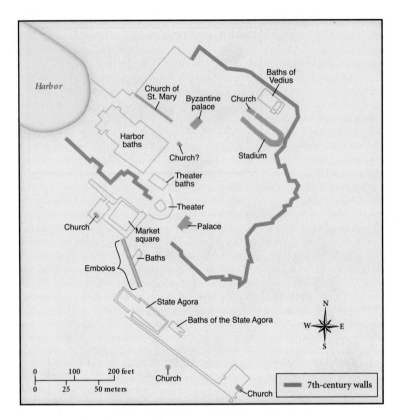

MAP 8.3 Diagram of the City of Ephesus

Before the seventh century, Ephesus sprawled around its harbor. Nearest the harbor were baths and churches including, by 500, the bishop's Church of St. Mary. To the south was the Embolos—a long, marble-paved avenue adorned with fountains, statues, and arcades and bordered by well-appointed homes. The earthquakes, plague, and invasions of the seventh century changed much. A new wall was built to embrace the area around the harbor. The Embolos was neglected, and even within the narrow precinct protected by the new wall, baths were allowed to go to ruin, while people made their homes within the debris. After the Arabs invaded, the bishop moved out of the city altogether.

and trade of fine silk textiles continued. Even though Byzantium's economic life became increasingly rural and barter-based in the seventh and eighth centuries, the skills, knowledge, and institutions of urban workers remained. Centuries of devastating wars, however, prevented full use of these resources until after 750.

As urban life declined, agriculture, always the basis of the Byzantine economy, became the center of its social life as well. This social world was small and local. Unlike Europe, where an extremely rich and powerful elite dominated the agricultural economy, the Byzantine Empire of the seventh century was principally a realm of free and semi-free peasant farmers, who grew food, herded cattle, and tended vineyards on small plots of land. Farmers interacted mostly with members of their families or with monks at local monasteries; two or three neighbors were enough to ratify a land

transfer. As Byzantine cities declined, the class of town councilors (the curials), the elite who for centuries had mediated between the emperor and the people, disappeared. Now on those occasions when farmers came into contact with the state—to pay taxes, for example—they felt the impact of the emperor or his representatives directly. There were no local protectors any longer.

Emperors, drawing on the still-vigorous Roman legal tradition, promoted local, domestic life with new imperial legislation. The laws strengthened the nuclear family by narrowing the grounds for divorce and setting new punishments for marital infidelity. Husbands and wives who committed adultery were to be whipped and fined, and their noses slit. Abortion was prohibited, and new protections were set in place against incest. Mothers were given equal power with fathers over their offspring; if widowed, they became the legal guardians of their minor children and controlled the household property.

New Military and Cultural Forms

The shift from an urban-centered society to a rural way of life not only changed Byzantine social life and the economy but also affected the empire's military and cultural institutions. The Byzantine navy fought successfully at sea with its powerful weapon of "Greek fire," a combustible oil that floated on water and burst into flames upon hitting its target. Determined to win wars on land as well, the imperial government tightened its control over the military by wresting power from other elite families and encouraging the formation of a middle class of farmer-soldiers. In the seventh century, an emperor, possibly Heraclius, divided the empire into military districts called *themes* and put all civil as well as military matters in each district into the hands of one general, a *strategos*. Landless men were lured to join the army with the promise of land and low taxes; they fought side by side with local farmers, who provided their own weapons and horses. The new organization effectively countered frontier attacks.

The disappearance of the old cultural elite meant a shift in the focus of education. Whereas the curial class had cultivated the study of the pagan classics, hiring tutors or sending their children (primarily their sons) to school to learn to read the works of Greek poets and philosophers, eighth-century parents showed far more interest in giving their children, both sons and daughters, a religious education. Even with the decay of urban centers, cities and villages often retained an elementary school. There teachers used the Book of

TAKING MEASURE

a) Major church repairs at Constantinople.

b) Major church repairs at Rome.

Church Repair, 600–900

The impoverishment of the period 600–750 is clear from graph (a), which shows a major slump in church repair at Constantinople. Had there been any money to spend on building repairs, it would undoubtedly have gone to the churches first. By contrast, graph (b) shows that Rome was not so hard hit as Constantinople, even though it was part of the Byzantine Empire. There was, to be sure, a dramatic reduction in the number of church repairs in Rome in the period 500–600. But from 700 to 800, there was a clear, if small, increase. Taken together, the two graphs help show the toll taken by the invasions and financial hardships of the period 600–750.

(Data adapted from Klavs Randsborg, "The Migration Period: Model History and Treasure," in The Sixth Century: Production, Distribution and Demand, *eds. Richard Hodges and William Bowden [Leiden: Brill, 1998].)*

Psalms (the Psalter) as their primer. Secular, classical learning remained decidedly out of favor throughout the seventh and eighth centuries; dogmatic writings, biographies of saints, and devotional works took center stage.

Silver Censer from Cyprus

This small dish, used for burning incense (and thus called a censer), was used during the Christian church service; it was carried and swung on three chains attached to the round rings on the lip of the censer. Each of the six sides shows a holy figure; in this case the Virgin Mary is flanked by Saints John and James. By the seventh century, such precious objects were common in churches throughout the Byzantine Empire.

(© The Trustees of the British Museum.)

Religion, Politics, and Iconoclasm

The importance placed on religious learning and piety complemented both the autocratic imperial ideal and the powers of the bishops in the seventh century. Although the curial elite had disappeared, bishops and their clergy continued to form a rich and powerful upper class, even in declining cities. Since the spiritual and secular realms were considered inseparable, the bishops wielded political power in their cities, while Byzantine emperors ruled as both religious and political figures. In theory, imperial and church power were separate but interdependent. In fact, the emperor exercised considerable power over the church; he influenced the appointment of the chief religious official, the patriarch of Constantinople; he called church councils to determine dogma; and he regularly used bishops as local governors. Beginning with Heraclius, the emperors considered it one of their duties to baptize Jews forcibly, persecuting those who would not convert. In the view of the imperial court, this was part of the ruler's role in upholding orthodoxy.

Powerful Bishops and Monks. Bishops functioned as state administrators in their cities. They served as judges and tax collectors. They distributed food in times of famine or siege, provisioned troops, and set up military fortifications. As part of their charitable work, they cared for the sick and the needy. Byzantine bishops were part of a three-tiered system: they were appointed by metropolitans, bishops who headed an entire province; and the metropolitans, in turn, were appointed by the patriarchs, bishops with authority over whole regions.

Theoretically, monasteries were under the limited control of the local bishop, but in fact they were enormously powerful institutions that often defied the authority of bishops and even emperors. Because monks commanded immense prestige as the holiest of God's faithful, they could influence the many issues of church doctrine that racked the Byzantine church.

Conflict over Icons.   The most important issue of the Byzantine church in this period revolved around icons. Icons are images of holy people—

Icon of the Virgin and Child
Surrounded by two angels in the back and two soldier-saints at either side, the Virgin Mary and the Christ Child are depicted with still, otherworldly dignity. The sixth-century artist gave the angels transparent halos to emphasize their spiritual natures, while depicting the saints as earthly men, with hair and beards, and feet planted firmly on the ground. Icons like this were used for worship both in private homes and in Byzantine monasteries. *(Erich Lessing/Art Resource, NY.)*

Christ, his mother (Mary), and the saints (see Icon of the Virgin and Child, on this page). To Byzantine Christians, icons were far more than mere representations: they were believed to possess holy power that directly affected people's daily lives as well as their chances for salvation.

Many seventh-century Byzantines made icons the focus of their religious devotion. To them, the images were like the incarnation of Christ: they turned spirit into material substance. That is, an icon manifested in physical form the holy person it depicted. Some Byzantines actually worshipped icons; others, particularly monks, considered icons a necessary part of Christian piety. Protected by his Muslim overlords, the Christian Syrian St. John of Damascus wrote a thundering defense of icons (see Document, "On Holy Images," page 245).

Other Byzantines abhorred icons. Most numerous of these were the soldiers on the frontiers. Unnerved by Arab triumphs, they attributed their misfortunes to disregard of the biblical command against graven (carved) images: "You shall not make for yourself a graven image, or any likeness of anything that is in heaven above, or that is in the earth beneath, or that is in the water under the earth" (Exod. 20:4). When they compared their defeats to Muslim successes, Byzantine soldiers could not help but notice that Islam prohibited all visual images of the divine. To these soldiers and others who shared their view, icons revived pagan idolatry and desecrated Christian divinity. As iconoclastic (anti-icon or, literally, icon-breaking) feeling grew, some churchmen became outspoken in their opposition to icons.

Byzantine emperors shared these religious objections, and they also had important political reasons for opposing icons. In fact, the issue of icons became a test of their authority. Icons diffused loyalties, creating intermediaries between worshippers and God that undermined the emperor's exclusive place in the divine and temporal order. In addition, the emphasis on icons in monastic communities made the monks potential threats to imperial power; the emperors hoped to use this issue to break the power of the monasteries. Above all, though, the emperors opposed icons because the army did, and they needed to retain the loyalty of their troops.

After Emperor Leo III the Isaurian (r. 717–741) defeated the Arabs besieging Constantinople at the beginning of his reign, he turned his attention to consolidating his political position. Officers of the imperial court tore down the great golden icon of Christ at the gateway of the palace and replaced it with a cross. A crowd of women protested this action by going on a furious ram-

DOCUMENT

On Holy Images

At Constantinople, no one could publicly oppose iconoclasm. But Christians in the Arab world had more freedom. John of Damascus (c. 675–749) was born in Syria after it came under Islamic rule. His father, though Christian, worked for the Arab governor there, and John soon did so as well. John wrote this ringing defense of icons shortly before he joined a monastery near Jerusalem.

I believe in one God, the source of all things, without beginning, uncreated, immortal, everlasting, incomprehensible, bodiless, invisible, uncircumscribed [i.e., in no one place], without form. I believe in one supersubstantial being [i.e., beyond all substance], one divine Godhead in three entities, the Father, the Son, and the Holy Ghost, and I adore Him alone with the worship [due God alone]. I adore one God, one Godhead but three Persons, God the Father, God the Son made flesh, and God the Holy Ghost, one God. I do not adore creation more than the Creator, but I adore the creature created as I am, adopting creation freely and spontaneously that He might elevate our nature and make us partakers of His divine nature. Together with my Lord and King I worship Him clothed in the flesh, not as if it were a garment or He constituted a fourth person of the Trinity — God forbid. That flesh is divine, and endures after its assumption. Human nature was not lost in the Godhead, but just as the Word made flesh remained the Word, so flesh became the Word remaining flesh, becoming, rather, one with the Word through union. Therefore I venture to draw an image of the invisible God, not as invisible, but as having become visible for our sakes through flesh and blood. I do not draw an image of the immortal Godhead. I paint the visible flesh of God, for if it is impossible to represent a spirit, how much more God who gives breath to the spirit.

Source: *St. John Damascene on Holy Images*, trans. Mary H. Allies (London: Thomas Baker, 1898), 1 (slightly modified).

---

page in support of icons. But Leo would not budge. In 726, he ordered all icons destroyed, a ban that remained in effect, despite much opposition, until 787. This is known as the period of **iconoclasm** in Byzantine history. A modified ban would be revived in 815 and last until 843.

Iconoclasm had an enormous impact on daily life. At home, where people had their own portable icons, it forced changes in private worship: the devout had to destroy their icons or worship them in secret. The ban on icons meant ferocious attacks on the monasteries: splendid collections of holy images were destroyed; vast properties were confiscated; and monks, who were staunch defenders of icons, were ordered to leave the monastery, give up their vocation, and marry. In this way iconoclasm destroyed communities that might otherwise have served as centers of resistance to imperial power. Reorganized and reoriented, Byzantium was ready to confront the Arabs with vigor.

> **REVIEW:** What stresses did the Byzantine Empire endure in the seventh and eighth centuries, and how was iconoclasm a response to those stresses?

---

iconoclasm: Literally, "icon breaking"; referring to the destruction of icons, or images of holy people. Byzantine emperors banned icons from 726 to 787; a modified ban was revived in 815 and lasted until 843.

Western Europe: A Medley of Kingdoms

In contrast to Byzantium, where an emperor still ruled as the successor to Augustus and Constantine, drawing on an unbroken chain of Roman legal and administrative traditions, political power in western Europe was more diffuse. With the end of Roman imperial government in the western half of the empire, the region was divided into a number of kingdoms: various monarchs ruled in Spain, Italy, England, and Gaul. The primary foundations of power and stability in all of these kingdoms were kinship networks, church patronage, royal courts, and wealth derived from land and plunder. There were kings, to be sure; but in some places churchmen and rich magnates were even more powerful than royalty. Icons were not very important in the West, but in their place was the power of the saints as exercised through their relics — the bodies and body parts, even clothes and dust from the tombs of holy people. These represented and wielded the divine forces of God. Although the patterns of daily life and the procedures of government in western Europe remained recognizably Roman, they were also in the process of change, borrowing from and adapting to local traditions and to the very powerful role of the Christian religion in every aspect of society.

TABLE 8.1   The Three Monotheistic Religions, c. 750*

RELIGION	FOUNDER/ PROPHET	CHIEF RELIGIOUS HEAD(S)	PLACE OF WORSHIP	IMPORTANT ELEMENTS OF WORSHIP	KEY RELIGIOUS TEXTS	MATERIAL AIDS TO WORSHIP
Christianity						
Roman Catholic	Jesus	Bishops, increasingly pope at Rome	Church	Mass, prayer, fasting	Bible, especially the Psalms	Relics
Byzantine	Jesus	Patriarch of Constantinople	Church	Mass, prayer, fasting	Bible, especially the Psalms	Icons
Judaism	Abraham	Rabbis	Synagogue	Prayer, fasting	Hebrew Scriptures and rabbinic legal literature (Talmud)	Torah (first five books of the Bible)
Islam	Muhammad	Caliphs or, increasingly, religious scholars	Mosque	Prayer, fasting	Qur'an and commentaries on it	Qur'an

*None of these religions remained fixed in the form they had in 750. See Chapter 14, in particular, for changes in Christianity.

Amphitheater at Arles
In what is today the south of France, the ruins of a Roman amphi-theater still dwarf the surrounding buildings of the modern city of Arles. This huge edifice was even more striking in the seventh century, when the city was impoverished and depopulated. Plague, war, and the dislocation of Roman trade networks forced most people to abandon the cities to live on the land. Only the bishop and his clergy—and individuals who could make a living servicing them—stayed in the cities. There were monasteries at Arles as well, and some of them were thriving. In the mid-sixth century there were perhaps two hundred nuns at one of the female convents there. *(Bridgeman-Giraudon/Art Resource, NY.)*

Frankish Kingdoms with Roman Roots

The most important kingdoms in post-Roman Europe were Frankish. During the sixth century, the Franks had established themselves as dominant in Gaul, and by the seventh century the limits of their kingdoms roughly approximated the eastern borders of present-day France, Belgium, the Netherlands, and Luxembourg (Map 8.4). More-over, the Frankish rulers known as the Merovingian kings (the name of the dynasty derived from Merovech, a reputed ancestor), had subjugated many of the peoples beyond the Rhine, foreshad-owing the contours of the western half of modern Germany. These northern and eastern regions were little Romanized, but the inhabitants of the rest of the Frankish kingdoms lived with the vestiges of Rome all around them.

Roman Ruins.   Travelers making a trip to Paris in the seventh century, perhaps on a pilgrimage to visit the relics of St. Denis, would probably have relied on river travel, even though some Roman roads were still in fair repair. (They would have preferred water routes because land travel was very slow and because even large groups of travelers on the roads were vulnerable to attacks by robbers.) Like the roads, other structures in the landscape would have seemed familiarly Roman. Coming up the Rhône River from the south, voyagers would have passed Roman amphitheaters and farmlands neatly and squarely laid out by Roman land surveyors. The great stone palaces of villas would still have dotted the countryside. (See Amphitheater at Arles, page 246.)

What would have been missing, to observant travelers, were thriving cities. Only the hulks of cities remained, still serving as the centers of church administration; but during the late Roman period, many urban centers lost their commercial and cultural vitality. Depopulated, they survived as mere skeletons. Moreover, if the travelers had approached Paris from the northeast, they would have passed through dense, nearly untouched forests and land more often used as pasture for animals than for cultivation of cereal crops. These areas were not much influenced by Romans; they represented far more the farming and village settlement patterns of the Franks. Yet even on the northern and eastern fringes of the Merovingian kingdoms, some structures of the Roman Empire remained. Fortresses were still standing at Trier (near Bonn, Germany, today), and great stone villas, such as the one excavated by archaeologists near Douai (today in France, near the Belgian border), loomed over the more humble wooden dwellings of the countryside.

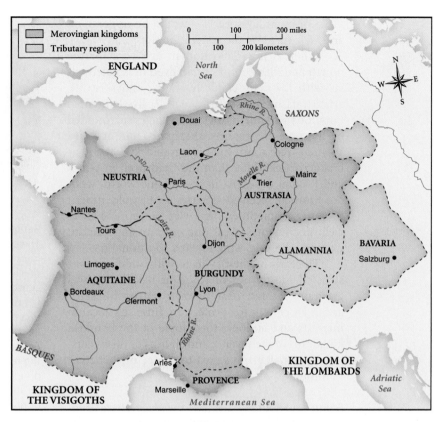

MAP 8.4 The Merovingian Kingdoms in the Seventh Century
By the seventh century, there were three powerful Merovingian kingdoms: Neustria, Austrasia, and Burgundy. The important cities of Aquitaine were assigned to these major kingdoms, while Aquitaine as a whole was assigned to a duke or other governor. Kings did not establish capital cities; they did not even stay in one place. Rather, they continually traveled throughout their kingdoms, making their power felt in person.

Frankish Settlement and Society. In the south, gangs of slaves still might occasionally be found cultivating the extensive lands of wealthy estate owners, as they had done since the days of the late Roman republic. Scattered here and there, independent peasants worked their own small plots as they had for centuries. But for the most part, seventh-century travelers would have found semi-free peasant families settled on small holdings, their manses—including a house, a garden, and cultivable land—for which they paid dues and owed labor services to a landowner. Some of these peasants were descendants of the *coloni* (tenant farmers) of the late Roman Empire; others were the sons and daughters of slaves, now provided with a small plot of land; and a few were people of free Frankish origin who for various reasons had come down in the world. At the lower end of the social scale, the status of Franks and Romans had become identical.

Romans (or, more precisely, Gallo-Romans) and Franks had also merged at the upper end of

the social scale. Although people south of the Loire River continued to be called Romans and people to the north Franks, their cultures were strikingly similar: they shared language, settlement patterns, and religion. (See "New Sources, New Perspectives," page 249.) There were many dialects in the Frankish kingdoms in the seventh century, but most were derived from Latin, though no longer the Latin of Cicero. "Though my speech is rude," Bishop **Gregory of Tours** (r. 573–c. 594), wrote at the end of the sixth century, "[. . .] to my surprise, it has often been said by men of our day, that few understand the learned words of the rhetorician but many the rude language of the common people." This beginning to Gregory's *Histories*, a valuable source for the Merovingian period (c. 486–751), testifies to Latin's transformation; Gregory expected that his "rude" Latin—the plain

---

Gregory of Tours: Bishop of Tours (in Gaul) from 573 to 594, the chief source for the history and culture of the Merovingian kingdoms.

Latin of everyday speech—would be understood and welcomed by the general public.

Whereas the Gallo-Roman aristocrat of the fourth and fifth centuries had lived in isolated villas with his wife, children, slaves, and servants, aristocrats of the seventh century lived in more populous settlements: in small villages surrounded by the huts of peasants, shepherds, and artisans. Women were more fully integrated into the general activities of life than they had been in Greek and Roman times. As in the Islamic world, western women received dowries and could inherit property. Sometimes they were entrepreneurs as well; documents reveal one enterprising peasant woman who sold wine to earn additional money.

The early medieval village, with buildings constructed mostly out of wood or baked clay, was generally located near a waterway or forest or around a church for protection. Intensely local in interests and outlook, the people in the Frankish kingdoms of the seventh and eighth centuries clustered in small groups next to protectors, whether rich men or saints.

Saints and Relics.   Tours—the place where Gregory was bishop—exemplified this new-style settlement. Once a Roman city, Tours's main focus was now outside the city walls, where a church had been built. The population of the surrounding countryside was pulled to this church as if to a magnet, for it housed the remains of the most important and venerated person in the locale: St. Martin. This saint, a fourth-century soldier-turned-monk, was long dead, but his relics remained at Tours, where he had served as bishop. There, in the succeeding centuries, he acted as the representative of God's power: a protector, healer, and avenger. In Gregory's view, Martin's relics (or rather God *through* Martin's relics) had prevented armies from plundering local peasants. Martin was not the only human thought to have such great power; all of God's saints were miracle workers.

This veneration of saints and their relics was a major departure from the classical world in which the dead had been banished from the presence of the living. In the medieval world, the holy dead held the place of highest esteem. The church had no formal procedures for proclaiming saints in the

Reliquary
The cult of relics necessitated housing the precious parts of the saints in equally precious containers. This reliquary—made of cloisonné enamel (bits of enamel framed by metal), garnets, glass gems, and a cameo—is in the shape of a miniature sarcophagus. On the back is the inscription "Theuderic the priest had this made in honor of Saint Maurice." Theuderic must have given the reliquary to the monastery of Saint-Maurice d'Agaune (today in Switzerland), which was renowned for its long and elaborate liturgy—its daily schedule of prayer—in the late seventh century. *(From* The Dark Ages, *ed. David Talbot Rice, Thames and Hudson Ltd., London.)*

Tours, c. 600
(Nancy Gauthier and Henri Galinié, eds., Gregoire de Tours et l'espace gaulois (Tours: Actes du congrès internationale, 1997), 70.)

Map labels:
0 750 1,500 feet
0 400 meters
Loire R.
Church of St. Martin
Bishop's church
Bishop's palace
Baptistery
Fortifications built c. 400
■ House
∴ Cemetery
‡ Church/monastery
Area inhabited in 4th century
Zone of pilgrimage and semi-permanent habitation, c. 600

early Middle Ages, but holiness was "recognized" by influential local people and the local bishop. When, for example, miracles were observed at the supposed tomb of the martyr Benignus in Dijon, the common people went there regularly to ask for help. But only after the martyr himself appeared to the local bishop in a vision, thus dispelling doubts about the tomb, was Benignus accorded saintly status. No one at Tours doubted that Martin had been a saint, however, and to tap into the power of his relics, the local bishop built a church directly over his tomb. For a man like Gregory of Tours and his flock, the church building was above all a home for the relics of the saints.

Economic Activity in a Peasant Society

As a bishop, Gregory was aware of some of the sophisticated forms of economic activity that existed in early medieval Europe, such as long-distance trade. Yet most people lived on the very edge of survival. Studies of Alpine peat bogs show that from the fifth to the mid-eighth century glaciers advanced and the mean temperature in Europe dropped. This climatic change spelled shortages in crops. Chronicles, histories, and biographies of saints also describe crop shortages, famines, and diseases as a normal part of life. For the year 591

Anthropology, Archaeology, and Changing Notions of Ethnicity

At the end of the nineteenth century, scholars argued that ethnicity was the same as race and that both were biological. They measured skeletal features and argued that different human groups—blacks, whites, Jews, and Slavs, for example—were biologically distinct and that some were better than others according to "scientific" criteria. This same view was shared by historians, who spoke of the various groups who entered the Roman Empire—Franks, Visigoths, Saxons, Lombards—as if these people were biologically different from Romans and from one another. They thought, for example, that there was a real biological group called the Lombards that had migrated into the Roman Empire and set up the "Lombard kingdom" in Italy by conquering another real biological group called the Romans.

Some anthropologists challenged this view. In the early 1900s, for example, the anthropologist Franz Boas showed that American Indians were not biologically different from any other human group; their "ethnicity" was cultural. Boas meant that the characteristics that made Indians "Indian" were not physical but rather a combination of practices, beliefs, language, dress, and sense of identity. Soon archaeologists came to realize that no physical difference distinguished a Frankish skeleton from a Lombard or a Roman or a Slav skeleton. It was only the artifacts associated with skeletons in grave excavations—jewelry, weapons—that revealed to what ethnicity a person belonged.

If ethnicity were biological, it would be fixed. No one could be a Lombard unless he or she had been born into the group. But since ethnicity is cultural, "outsiders" can join, while "insiders" can be shed. Historians—especially those associated with the University of Vienna—have shown in detail how this was the case with the peoples that the Romans called barbarians. Walter Pohl, for example, has demonstrated how ethnic groups like the Lombards and Franks were made up of men and women from all sorts of backgrounds. Their sense of being Lombard or Frankish was a product of common myths that they accepted about themselves. The Lombards, for example, thought that their name came from a trick played by their women, who tied their long hair around their chins, humoring the war god Woden into calling them "Longbeards" and giving their men victory in battle. The Avars, for their part, were held together by their loyalty to their leader, the *khagan*. Avars who broke away from the khagan's political dominance were no longer considered part of the group—they were considered Bulgarians instead. In contrast, the less centrally organized Slavs recognized all sorts of people living in their territory as Slavs; their ethnicity was based on language and other cultural traditions, which could be learned even by newcomers.

Seeing ethnicity as cultural allows us to understand the origins of European states not as the result of the conquest of one well-defined group by another but rather as a historical process. France, Germany, and England were not created by fixed entities known for all time as, respectively, the Franks, the Germans, and the Angles. Rather, they were created and shaped by the will and imagination of men and women who intermingled, interacted, and adapted to one another over time.

QUESTIONS TO CONSIDER

1. The society of the United States has been called a melting pot. In what ways might the same be said about European societies?
2. How do common myths nourish contemporary notions of ethnicity?

FURTHER READING

Geary, Patrick J. *The Myth of Nations: The Medieval Origins of Europe.* 2002.

Pohl, Walter, with Helmut Reimitz. *Strategies of Distinction: The Construction of Ethnic Communities, 300–800.* 1998.

Wolfram, Herwig. "The Shaping of the Early Medieval Kingdom." *Viator* 1 (1970): 1–20.

---

alone, Gregory reported that

> a terrible epidemic killed off the people in Tours and in Nantes.... In the town of Limoges a number of people were consumed by fire from heaven for having profaned the Lord's day by transacting business.... There was a terrible drought which destroyed all the green pasture. As a result there were great losses of flocks and herds.

Subsistence and Gift Economies. An underlying reason for the calamities of the Merovingian period was the weakness of the agricultural economy.

Even the meager population of the Merovingian world was too large for its productive capacities. The dry, light soil of the Mediterranean region could be easily tilled with wooden implements. But the northern soils of most of the Merovingian world were heavy, wet, and difficult to turn and aerate. Technological limitations meant a limited food supply, and agricultural work was not equitably or efficiently allocated and managed. A leisure class of landowning warriors and churchmen lived off the work of peasant men, who tilled

Early Medieval Accounting
In the seventh century, peasants in western Europe were lucky to produce more grain than they sowed. To make sure that it got its share of this meager production, at least one enterprising landlord, the monastery of St.-Martin at Tours, kept a kind of ledger. This extremely unusual parchment sheet, dating from the second half of the seventh century, lists the amount of grain and wood owed to the monastery by its tenants. *(Bibliothèque nationale de France.)*

the fields, and peasant women, who wove cloth, gardened, brewed, and baked.

Occasionally surpluses developed, either from good harvests in peacetime or plunder in warfare, and these were traded, although not in an impersonal, commercial manner. Most economic transactions of the seventh and eighth centuries were part of a gift economy, a system of give and take: booty was taken, tribute demanded, harvests hoarded, and coins minted, all to be redistributed to friends, followers, and dependents. Kings and other rich and powerful men and women amassed gold, silver, ornaments, and jewelry in their treasuries and grain in their storehouses to mark their power, add to their prestige, and demonstrate their generosity. Those benefiting from the gifts of the rich included religious people and institutions: monks, nuns, bishops, monasteries, and churches. We still have a partial gift economy today. At holidays, for example, goods change hands for social purposes: to consecrate a holy event, to express love and friendship, to show off wealth and status. In the Merovingian world, the gift economy was the dynamic behind most of the exchanges of goods and money.

Trade and Traders. Some economic activity in this period was purely commercial and impersonal, especially long-distance trade, for which Europe supplied slaves and raw materials such as furs and honey, and in return received luxuries and manufactured goods such as silks and papyrus. Trading voyages, diplomatic ventures, and pilgrimages were the ways in which the Byzantine, Islamic, and western European descendants of the Roman Empire kept in tenuous contact with one another. Seventh- and eighth-century sources speak of Byzantines, Syrians, and Jews as the chief intermediaries of any long-distance trade that existed. Many of these intermediaries lived in the still-thriving port cities of the Mediterranean. Gregory of Tours associated Jews with commerce, complaining that they sold things "at a higher price than they were worth."

Although the population of the Merovingian world was overwhelmingly Christian, Jews were integrated into every aspect of secular life. They used Hebrew in worship, but otherwise they spoke the same languages as Christians and used Latin in their legal documents. Their children were often given the same names as Christians (and, in turn, Christians often took Old Testament biblical names); they dressed as everyone else dressed; and they engaged in the same occupations. Many Jews planted and tended vineyards, in part because of the importance of wine in synagogue services and in part because the surplus could easily be sold. Some Jews were rich landowners, with slaves and dependent peasants working for them; others were independent peasants of modest means. Some Jews lived in towns with a small Jewish quarter where their homes and synagogues were located, but most Jews, like their Christian neighbors, lived on the land. Only much later, in the eleventh century, would the status of Jews change, setting them markedly apart from Christians.

The Powerful in Merovingian Society

Monarchs and aristocrats held political power in Merovingian society. The Merovingian elite—who included monks and bishops as well as laypeople—obtained their power through hereditary wealth, status, and personal influence.

The Aristocrats. Many aristocrats were extremely wealthy. The will drawn up by a bishop and aristocrat named Bertram of Le Mans, for example, shows that he had estates—some from his family, others given him as gifts—scattered over much of Gaul.

Along with administering their estates, many male aristocrats of the period spent their time honing their proficiency as warriors. To be a great warrior in Merovingian society, just as in the otherwise very different world of the Bedouin, meant more than just fighting: it meant perfecting the virtues necessary for leading armed men. Merovingian warriors affirmed their skills and comradeship in the hunt, they proved their worth in the regular taking of booty, and they rewarded their followers afterward at generous banquets. At these feasts, in keeping with the gift economy, the lords combined fellowship with the redistribution of wealth as they gave abundantly to their dependents.

Merovingian aristocrats also valued bedtime. The bed—including procreation—was the focus of their marriage. Important both to the survival of aristocratic families and to the transmission of their property and power, marriage was an expensive institution. There was more than one form of marriage: in the most formal, the man gave a generous dowry of clothes, livestock, and land to his bride; after the marriage was consummated, he gave her a "morning gift" of furniture. Very wealthy men also might support one or more concubines, who enjoyed a less formal type of marriage, receiving a morning gift but no dowry. In this period, churchmen had many ideas about the value of marriages, but in practice they had little to do with the matter. Marriage was a family decision and a family matter; no one was married in a church.

Some sixth-century aristocrats still patterned their lives on those of the Romans, teaching their children classical Latin poetry and writing to one another in phrases borrowed from Virgil. But already in the seventh century their spoken language had become very different from literary Latin. Some still learned Latin, but they cultivated it mainly to read the Psalms. Just as in Byzantium, a religious culture that emphasized Christian piety over the classics was developing in Europe.

The arrival (c. 590) on the continent of the Irish monk St. Columbanus (d. 615) energized this heightened emphasis on religion. Columbanus's brand of monasticism, which stressed exile, devotion, and discipline, found much favor among the Merovingian elite. The monasteries St. Columbanus established in both Gaul and Italy attracted local recruits from the aristocracy, some of them grown men and women. Others were young children, given to the monastery by their parents. This practice, called oblation, was not only accepted but also often considered essential for the spiritual

Praying Man
This incised brick, formed in the shape of a church, was a decorative element in an edifice (perhaps itself a church) built in the eighth century. The figure is a bearded man in prayer. Prior to the tenth or eleventh century, people did not pray with hands pressed together but rather with hands raised up on either side of the head. Here the artist gave the gesture special importance by exaggerating the man's arms and hands; his feet hardly matter. *(Touraine Archaeological and Historical Museum, Hotel Gouin, Tours, France.)*

well-being of both the children and their families. Irish monasticism introduced aristocrats on the continent to a deepened religious devotion. Those aristocrats who did not join or patronize a monastery still often read (or listened to others read) books about penitence, and they chanted the Psalms.

Bishops ranked among the most powerful men in Merovingian society. Gregory of Tours, for example, considered himself the protector of "his citizens" at Tours. When representatives of the king came to collect taxes, Gregory stopped them in their tracks, warning them that St. Martin would punish anyone who tried to tax his people. "That very day," Gregory reported, "the man who had produced the tax rolls caught a fever and died."

Like other aristocrats, many bishops were married, even though church councils demanded celibacy. As the overseers of priests and guardians of morality, however, bishops were expected to refrain from sexual relations with their wives. Since bishops were ordinarily appointed late in life, long after they had raised a family, this restriction did not threaten the ideal of a procreative marriage.

Women of Power. Noble parents decided whom their daughters would marry, for such unions bound together not only husbands and wives but entire extended families as well. Like brides of the lower classes, aristocratic wives received a dowry—usually land, over which they had some control; if they were widowed without children, they were allowed to sell, give away, exchange, or rent out their dowry estates as they wished. Moreover, men could give their women kinfolk property outright in written testaments. Because fathers often wanted to share their property with their daughters, an enterprising author created a formula for scribes to follow when drawing up wills in such cases. It began:

> For a long time an ungodly custom has been observed among us that forbids sisters to share with their brothers the paternal land. I reject this impious law: I make you, my beloved daughter, an equal and legitimate heir in all my patrimony [inheritance].

Such bequests, dowries, and other gifts made many aristocratic women very rich. Childless widows frequently gave generous gifts to the church from their vast possessions. But a woman need not have been a widow to control enormous wealth. In 632, for example, the nun Burgundofara, who had never married, drew up a will giving her monastery the land, slaves, vineyards, pastures, and forests she had received from her two brothers and her father. She bequeathed other property that she owned to her brothers and sister.

Though legally under the authority of her husband, a Merovingian woman often found ways to exercise some power and control over her life. Tetradia, wife of Count Eulalius, left her husband, taking all his gold and silver, because, as Gregory of Tours tells us,

> he was in the habit of sleeping with the women-servants in his household. As a result he neglected his wife. . . . As a result of his excesses, he ran into serious debt, and to meet this he stole his wife's jewelry and money.

A court of law ordered Tetradia to repay Eulalius four times the amount she had taken from him, but she was allowed to keep and live on her own property.

Other women were able to exercise behind-the-scenes control through their sons. Artemia, for example, used the prophecy that her son Nicetius would become a bishop to prevent her husband from taking the bishopric himself. After Nicetius became a bishop (here fulfilling the prophecy), he remained at home with his mother well into his thirties, working alongside the servants and teaching the younger children to read the Psalms.

Some women exercised direct power. Rich widows with fortunes to bestow wielded enormous influence. Some Merovingian women were abbesses, rulers in their own right over female monasteries and sometimes over "double monasteries," with separate facilities for men and women. Monasteries under the control of abbesses could be substantial centers of population: the convent at Laon, for example, had three hundred nuns in the seventh century. Because women lived in populous convents or were monopolized by rich men able to support several wives or mistresses at one time, unattached aristocratic women were scarce in society and therefore valuable.

The Power of Kings.   Atop the aristocracy were the Merovingian kings, rulers of the Frankish kingdoms. The **Merovingian dynasty** (c. 486–751) owed its longevity to good political sense: it had allied itself with local lay aristocrats and ecclesiastical (church) authorities. The kings relied on these men to bolster the power they derived from other sources: their leadership in war; their access to the lion's share of plunder; and their takeover of the taxation system, public lands, and legal framework of Roman administration. The kings' courts functioned as schools for the sons of the elite, tightening the bonds and loyalties between royal and aristocratic families. When kings sent officials— counts and dukes—to rule in their name in various regions of their kingdoms, these regional governors worked with and married into the aristocratic families who had long controlled local affairs.

Both kings and aristocrats had good reason to want a powerful royal authority. The king acted as arbitrator and intermediary for the competing interests of the aristocrats while taking advantage of local opportunities to appoint favorites and garner prestige by giving out land and privileges to supporters and religious institutions. Gregory of Tours's history of the sixth century is filled with stories of bitter battles between Merovingian kings, as royal brothers fought continuously over territories, wives, and revenues. Yet what seemed to the bishop like royal weakness and violent chaos was in fact one way the kings contained local aristocratic tensions, organizing them on one side or another, and preventing them from spinning out of royal control. By the beginning of the seventh century, three relatively stable Frankish kingdoms had emerged: Austrasia to the northeast; Neustria to the west, with its capital city at Paris; and Burgundy, incorporating the southeast (see Map 8.4). In an age that depended on local face-to-face contact, these divisions were so useful to aristocrats and Merovingian kings alike that even when royal power was united in the hands of one king, Clothar II (r. 613–623), he made his son the independent king of Austrasia.

As the power of the kings in the seventh century increased, however, so did the might of their chief court official, the mayor of the palace. In the

Merovingian (mehr oh VIN jian) **dynasty:** The royal dynasty that ruled Gaul from about 486 to 751.

following century, allied with the Austrasian aristocracy, one mayoral family would displace the Merovingian dynasty and establish a new royal line, the Carolingians.

Christianity and Classical Culture in the British Isles

The Merovingian kingdoms exemplify some of the ways in which Roman and non-Roman traditions combined; the British Isles show others. Ireland had never been part of the Roman Empire, but it was early converted to Christianity, as were Roman Britain and parts of Scotland. Invasions by various Celtic and Germanic groups—particularly the Anglo-Saxons, who gave their name to England, "the land of the Angles"—redrew the religious boundaries. Ireland, largely free of invaders, remained Christian; Scotland, also relatively untouched by invaders, had been slowly Christianized by the Irish from the west and in early years by the British from the south; England, which emerged from the invasions as a mosaic of about a dozen kingdoms ruled by separate Anglo-Saxon kings, became largely pagan.

Competing Church Hierarchies in Anglo-Saxon England.
Christianity was introduced to Anglo-Saxon England from two directions. In the north of England, Irish monks brought their own brand of Christianity. Converted in the fifth century by St. Patrick and other missionaries, the Irish had evolved a church organization that corresponded to its rural clan organization. Abbots and abbesses, generally from powerful dynasties, headed monastic *familiae*, communities composed of blood relatives, servants, slaves, and of course monks or nuns. Bishops were often under the authority of abbots, since the monasteries rather than cities were the centers of population in Ireland. The Irish missionaries to England were monks, and they set up monasteries modeled on those at home.

In the south of England, Christianity came via missionaries sent by Pope Gregory the Great (r. 590–604) in 597. The missionaries, under the leadership of Augustine (not the same Augustine as the bishop of Hippo), intended to convert the king and people of Kent, the southernmost kingdom, and then work their way northward. But Augustine and his party brought with them Roman practices at odds with those of Irish Christianity, stressing ties to the pope and the organization of the church un-

York Helmet
This fine helmet, once belonging to a very wealthy warrior named Oshere living near York, England, in the second half of the eighth century, was intended for both display and real battle. The helmet, made of iron, and the back flap, made of flexible chain mail, gave excellent protection against sword blades. The cheek pieces were probably originally pulled close to the warrior's face by a leather tie. The nose piece, decorated with interlaced animals, protected his nose. Over the top, two bands of copper meet at the middle. They were inscribed "In the name of our Lord Jesus, the Holy Spirit, God, and with all, we pray. Amen. Oshere. Christ." *(York Castle Museum, York Museums Trust.)*

der bishops rather than abbots. Using the Roman model, they divided England into territorial units called dioceses headed by an archbishop and bishops. Augustine, for example, became archbishop of Canterbury. As he was a monk, he set up a monastery right next to his cathedral, and it became a characteristic of the English church to have a community of monks attached to the bishop's church. Later a second archbishopric was added at York.

A major bone of contention between the Roman and Irish churches involved the calculation of the date of Easter, celebrated by Christians as the day on which Christ rose from the dead. The Roman church insisted that Easter fall on the first Sunday following the first full moon after the spring equinox. The Irish had a different method of determining when Easter should fall, and therefore they celebrated Easter on a different day. Because everyone agreed that believers could not be saved unless they observed Christ's resurrection properly and on the right date, the conflict was bitter. It was resolved by Oswy, king of Northumbria, who organized a meeting of churchmen, the **Synod of Whitby,** in 664. Convinced by the synod that Rome spoke with the voice of St. Peter, who was said in the New Testament to hold the keys of the kingdom of heaven, Oswy chose the Roman date. His decision

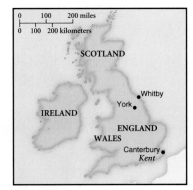

The British Isles

Synod of Whitby: The meeting of churchmen and King Oswy of Northumbria in 664 that led to the adoption of the Roman brand of Christianity in England.

paved the way for the triumph of the Roman brand of Christianity in England.

Literary Culture. St. Peter was not the only reason for favoring Roman Christianity. For many English churchmen, Rome had great prestige because it was a treasure trove of knowledge, piety, and holy objects. Benedict Biscop (c. 630–690), the founder of two important English monasteries, made many difficult trips to Rome, bringing back relics, liturgical vestments, and even a cantor to teach his monks the proper melodies in a time before written musical notation. Above all, he went to Rome to get books. At his monasteries in the north of England, he built up a grand library. In Anglo-Saxon England, as in Scotland and Ireland, all of which lacked a strong classical tradition from Roman times, a book was considered a precious object, to be decorated as finely as a garnet-studded brooch. (See Lindisfarne Gospels, below.)

The Anglo-Saxons and Irish Celts had a thriving oral culture but extremely limited uses for writing. Books became valuable only when these societies converted to Christianity. Just as Islamic reliance on the Qur'an made possible a literary culture under the Umayyads, so Christian dependence on the Bible, liturgy, and the writings of the church fathers helped make England and Ireland centers of literature and learning in the seventh and eighth centuries. Archbishop Theodore (r. 669–690), who had studied at Athens and was one of the most learned men of his day, founded a school at Canterbury where students studied Latin and even some Greek in order to comment on biblical texts. Men like Benedict Biscop soon sponsored other centers of learning, using the texts from the classical past. Although women did not establish famous schools, many abbesses ruled over monasteries that stressed Christian learning. Here as elsewhere, Latin writings, even pagan texts, were studied diligently, in part because Latin was so foreign a language that mastering it required systematic and formal study. One of Benedict Biscop's pupils was Bede (673–735), an Anglo-Saxon monk and a historian of extraordinary breadth. Bede in turn taught a new generation of monks who became advisers to eighth-century rulers.

Much of the vigorous pagan Anglo-Saxon oral tradition was adapted to Christian culture. Bede encouraged and supported the use of the Anglo-Saxon language, urging priests, for example, to use it when they instructed their flocks. In contrast to other European regions, where Latin was the primary written language in the seventh and eighth centuries, England made use of the vernacular—the language normally spoken by the people. Writ-

Lindisfarne Gospels
The lavishly illuminated manuscript known as the Lindisfarne Gospels, of which this is one page, was probably produced in the first third of the eighth century. For the monks at Lindisfarne and elsewhere in the British Isles, books were precious objects, to be decorated much like pieces of jewelry. (Compare the treatment of the letters here with the decoration of the eagle brooches on page 218.) The page depicted here is the beginning of the Gospel according to St. Matthew, which begins with the words "Liber generationis." Note how elaborately the first letter, L, is treated and how the decoration gradually recedes, so that the last line, while still very embellished, is quite plain in comparison with the others. *(By permission of the British Library.)*

ten Anglo-Saxon (or Old English) was used in every aspect of English life, from government to entertainment.

The decision at the Synod of Whitby favoring Roman Christianity tied the English church to the church of Rome by doctrine, friendship, and conviction. The Anglo-Saxon monk and bishop Wynfrith even changed his name to the Latin Boniface to symbolize his loyalty to the Roman church. Preaching on the continent, Boniface (680–754) set up churches in Germany and Gaul that, like those in England, looked to Rome for leadership and guidance. Boniface's efforts would give the papacy new importance in Europe.

Unity in Spain, Division in Italy

In contrast to the British Isles, southern Gaul, Spain, and Italy had long been part of the Roman Empire and preserved many of its traditions. Nevertheless, as they were settled and fought over by new peoples, their histories diverged dramatically. When the Merovingian king Clovis defeated the Visigoths in 507, their vast kingdom, which had sprawled across southern Gaul into Spain, was dismembered. By midcentury, the Franks came into possession of most of the Visigothic kingdom in southern Gaul.

In Spain, the Visigothic king Leovigild (r. 569–586) established territorial control by military might. But no ruler could hope to maintain his position in Visigothic Spain without the support of the Hispano-Roman population, which included both the great landowners and leading bishops; and their backing was unattainable while the Visigoths remained Arian Christians (see page 210). Leovigild's son Reccared (r. 586–601) took the necessary step in 587, converting to Roman Catholic Christianity. Two years later, at the Third Council of Toledo, most of the Arian bishops followed their king by announcing their conversion to Catholicism.

Thereafter, the bishops and kings of Spain cooperated to a degree unprecedented in other regions. While the king gave the churchmen free rein to set up their own hierarchy (with the bishop of Toledo at the top) and to meet regularly at synods to regulate and reform the church, the bishops in turn supported their Visigothic king, who ruled as a minister of the Christian people. Rebellion against him was tantamount to rebellion against Christ. The Spanish bishops reinforced this idea by anointing the king, daubing him with holy oil in a ritual that paralleled the ordination of priests and demonstrated divine favor. Toledo, the city where the highest bishop presided, was also where

the kings were "made" through anointment. While the bishops in this way made the king's cause their own, their lay counterparts, the great landowners, helped supply the king with troops, allowing him to maintain internal order and repel his external enemies.

Ironically, it was precisely the centralization and unification of the Visigothic kingdom that proved its undoing. When the Arabs arrived in 711, they needed only to kill the king, defeat his army, and capture Toledo to take the kingdom.

By contrast, in Italy the Lombard king constantly faced a hostile papacy in the center of the peninsula and virtually independent dukes in the south. Theoretically royal officers, the dukes of Benevento and Spoleto in fact ruled on their own behalf. Although many Lombards were Catholics, others, including important kings and dukes, were Arian. The "official" religion of Lombards in Italy varied with the ruler in power. Rather than signal a major political event, the conversion of the Lombards to Catholic Christianity occurred gradually, ending only around the mid-seventh century. Partly as a result of this slow development, the Lombard kings, unlike the Visigoths, Franks, or even the Anglo-Saxons, never enlisted the full support of any particular group of churchmen.

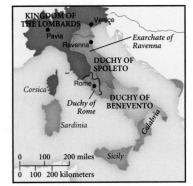

Lombard Italy, Early Eighth Century

Although lacking united religious support, Lombard royal power still had strengths. Chief among these were the traditions of leadership associated with the royal dynasty, the kings' military ability and their control over large estates in northern Italy, and the Roman institutions that survived in Italy. The Italian peninsula had been devastated by the wars between the Ostrogoths and the Byzantine Empire, but the Lombard kings took advantage of the still-urban organization of Italian society and the economy, assigning dukes to city bases and setting up a royal capital at Pavia. Recalling emperors like Constantine and Justinian, the kings built churches, monasteries, and other places of worship in the royal capital; they maintained the city walls, issued laws, and minted coins. Revenues from tolls, sales taxes, port duties, and court fines filled their treasuries, although their inability to revive the Roman land tax was a major weakness. The greatest challenge for the Lombard kings came from sharing the peninsula with Rome. As soon as the kings began to make serious headway into southern Italy against the duchies of Spoleto and Benevento, the pope began to fear for his own position and called on the Franks for help.

Political Tensions and the Power of the Pope

In the year 600, the pope's position was ambiguous: he was both a ruler and a subordinate. On the one hand, believing he was the successor of St. Peter and head of the church, he wielded real secular power. The pope known as **Gregory the Great** (r. 590–604) in many ways laid the foundations for the papacy's spiritual and temporal ascendancy. During his reign, Gregory the Great became the greatest landowner in Italy; he organized the defenses of Rome and paid for its army; he heard court cases, made treaties, and provided welfare services. The missionary expedition Gregory sent to England was only a small part of his involvement in the rest of Europe. He also maintained close ties with the churchmen in Spain who were working to convert the Visigoths from Arianism to Catholicism. He wrote letters to the Byzantine emperor and to European kings and queens. He admonished Brunhild, a Frankish queen well known to Gregory of Tours, to reform the church in Gaul:

> Evil priests cause ruin for the people . . . [so] see that you send us a letter of yours, and we shall send over a person with the assent of your authority, if you give the order, who together with other priests should inquire into these acts with great care, and correct them according to God's will.

A prolific author of spiritual works and biblical commentaries, Gregory digested and simplified the ideas of church fathers like St. Augustine of Hippo, making them accessible to a wider audience. His book *Pastoral Rule* was used as a guide for bishops throughout Europe.

Yet the pope was not independent. He was only one of many bishops in the Roman Empire, which was now ruled from Constantinople, and he was therefore subordinate to the emperor at Byzantium. For a long time the emperor's views on dogma, discipline, and church administration prevailed at Rome. This authority began to unravel in the seventh century. In 691, Emperor Justinian II convened a council that determined 102 rules for the church, and he sent them to Rome for papal endorsement. Most of the rules were unobjectionable, but Pope Sergius I (r. 687 or 689–701)

was unwilling to agree to the whole because it permitted priests to marry (which the Roman church did not want to allow) and prohibited fasting on Saturdays in Lent (which the Roman church required). Outraged by Sergius's refusal, Justinian tried to arrest him, but Italian armies (theoretically under the emperor) came to the pope's aid, while Justinian's arresting officer cowered under the pope's bed. As this incident reveals, some local forces were already willing to rally to the side of the pope against the emperor. Constantinople's influence and authority over Rome was dwindling. Sheer distance, as well as diminishing imperial power in Italy, meant that the popes were, in effect, the leaders of the parts of Italy not controlled by the Lombards.

The gap between Byzantium and Rome widened in the early eighth century as Emperor Leo III tried to increase the taxes on papal property to pay for his war against the Arab invaders. The pope responded by leading a general tax revolt. Meanwhile, Leo's fierce policy of iconoclasm collided with the pope's tolerance of images. In Italy, as in other European regions, Christian piety focused more on relics than on icons. Nevertheless, the papacy would not allow sacred images and icons to be destroyed. The pope argued that holy images should be respected but not worshipped as if God. His support of images reflected popular opinion as well. A later commentator wrote that iconoclasm so infuriated the inhabitants of Ravenna and Venice that "if the pope had not prohibited the people, they would have attempted to set up a [different] emperor over themselves."

These difficulties with the emperor were matched by increasing friction between the pope and the Lombards. The Lombard kings had gradually managed to bring under their control the duchies of Spoleto and Benevento as well as part of the Exarchate of Ravenna. By the mid-eighth century, the popes feared that Rome would fall to the Lombards, and Pope Zachary (r. 741–752) looked northward for friends. He created an ally by giving his approval to the removal of the last Merovingian king and his replacement by the first Carolingian king, Pippin III (r. 751–768). In 753, Pope Stephen II (r. 752–757) called on Pippin to march to Italy with an army to fight the Lombards. Thus, events at Rome had a major impact on the history not only of Italy but of the Frankish kingdom as well.

Gregory the Great: The pope (r. 590–604) who sent missionaries to Anglo-Saxon England, wrote influential books, tried to reform the church, and had contact with the major ruling families of Europe and Byzantium.

REVIEW: What were the similarities and differences among the kingdoms that emerged in western Europe, and how did their histories combine and diverge?

Mosaic at Santo Stefano Rotondo
The church of Santo Stefano, built by Pope Simplicius (r. 468–483), was round, like a classical temple. It made up part of the papal Lateran palace complex, in the southeastern zone of Rome. Later popes continued to beautify and adorn Santo Stefano, drawing on the artistic styles of their own time. Pope Theodore (r. 642–649) moved the relics of two Roman martyrs, Primus and Felician, from a small church outside of Rome to Santo Stefano. To celebrate the event, he commissioned the mosaic shown here, in which the figures of Primus and Felician flank a giant cross. The heavy outlines and gold surroundings echo mosaics done at Byzantium around the same time, attesting to political, cultural, and theological links between Rome and Constantinople. *(Madeline Grimoldi.)*

■ **For more help analyzing this image,** see the visual activity for this chapter in the Online Study Guide at **bedfordstmartins.com/hunt.**

Conclusion

The Islamic world, Byzantium, and western Europe were heirs of the Roman Empire, but they built on its legacies in different ways. Muslims were the newcomers to the Roman world, but their religion, Islam, was influenced by both Jewish and Christian monotheism, each with roots in Roman culture. Under the guidance of Muhammad the Prophet, Islam became both a coherent theology and a tightly structured way of life. Once the Muslim Arabs embarked on military conquests, they became the heirs of Rome in other ways: preserving Byzantine cities, hiring Syrian civil servants, and adopting Mediterranean artistic styles. Drawing on Roman and Persian traditions, the Umayyad dynasty created a powerful Islamic state, with a capital city in Syria and a culture that generally tolerated a wide variety of economic, religious, and social institutions so long as the conquered paid taxes to their Muslim overlords.

Byzantium directly inherited the central political institutions of Rome: its people called themselves Romans; its emperor was the Roman emperor; and its capital, Constantinople, was considered to be the new Rome. Byzantium also inherited the cities, laws, and religion—Christianity—of Rome. The changes of the seventh and eighth centuries—contraction of territory, urban decline, disappearance of the old elite, and a ban on icons—whittled away at this Roman character. By 750, Byzantium was less Roman than it was a new, resilient political and cultural entity, a Christian state on the borders of the new Muslim empire.

Western Europe also inherited—and transformed—Roman institutions. The Frankish kings built on Roman traditions that had earlier been modified by provincial and Germanic custom. In Anglo-Saxon England, once the far-flung northern outpost of the Roman Empire, parts of the Roman legacy—Latin learning and the Christian religion—had to be reimported in the seventh century. In Spain, the Visigothic kings converted

MAPPING THE WEST

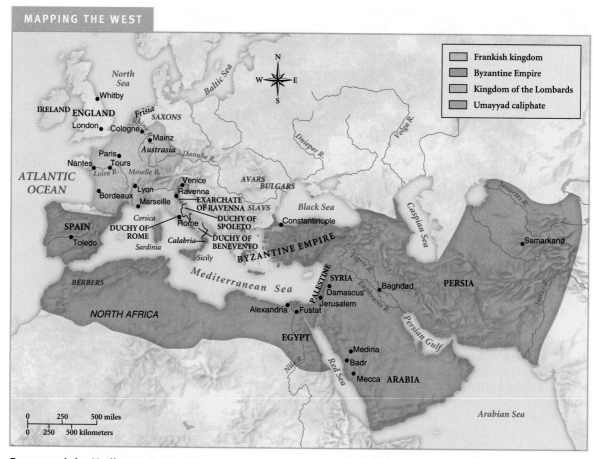

	Frankish kingdom
	Byzantine Empire
	Kingdom of the Lombards
	Umayyad caliphate

Europe and the Mediterranean, c. 750
The major political fact of the period 600–750 was the emergence of Islam and the creation of an Islamic state that reached from Spain to the Indus River. The Byzantine Empire, once a great power, was dwarfed—and half swallowed up—by its Islamic neighbor. To the west were fledgling barbarian kingdoms, mere trifles on the world stage. The next centuries, however, would prove their resourcefulness and durability.

from Arian to Roman Christianity and allied themselves with a Hispano-Roman elite that maintained elements of the organization and intellectual traditions of the late empire. In Italy and at Rome itself, the traditions of the classical past endured. The roads remained, the cities of Italy survived (although depopulated), and both the popes and the Lombard kings ruled according to the traditions of Roman government.

Muslim, Byzantine, and western European societies all suffered the ravages of war. In each one, the social hierarchy became simpler, with the loss of "middle" groups like the curials at Byzantium and the near-suppression of tribal affiliations among Muslims. All tied politics to religion more tightly than ever before. In Byzantium, the emperor was a religious force, presiding over the destruction of icons. In the Islamic world, the caliph was the successor to Muhammad, a religious and political leader. In western Europe the kings allied with churchmen in order to rule. Despite their

many differences, all these leaders had a common understanding of their place in a divine scheme: they were God's agents on earth, ruling over God's people. In the next century they would consolidate their power. Little did they know that, soon thereafter, local elites would be able to assert greater authority than ever before.

FOR FURTHER EXPLORATION

- ■ **For suggested references, including Web sites, for topics in this chapter,** see page SR-1 at the end of the book.

- ■ **For additional primary-source material from this period,** see Chapter 8 in *Sources of THE MAKING OF THE WEST,* Third Edition.

- ■ **For Web sites and documents related to topics in this chapter,** see *Make History* at bedfordstmartins.com/hunt.

CHAPTER REVIEW

KEY TERMS AND PEOPLE

Qur'an (234)

Hijra (235)

Five Pillars of Islam (235)

Umayyad caliphate (237)

Heraclius (240)

Lombards (240)

iconoclasm (245)

Gregory of Tours (247)

Merovingian dynasty (252)

Synod of Whitby (253)

Gregory the Great (256)

REVIEW QUESTIONS

1. How and why did the Muslims conquer so many lands in the period 632–750?

2. What stresses did the Byzantine Empire endure in the seventh and eighth centuries, and how was iconoclasm a response to those stresses?

3. What were the similarities and differences among the kingdoms that emerged in western Europe, and how did their histories combine and diverge?

MAKING CONNECTIONS

1. What were the similarities and the differences in political organization in the Islamic, Byzantine, and western European worlds in the seventh century?

2. Compare and contrast the role of religion in the Islamic, Byzantine, and western European societies in the seventh century.

> For practice quizzes, a customized study plan, and other study tools, see the Online Study Guide at bedfordstmartins.com/hunt.

IMPORTANT EVENTS

c. 486–751	Merovingian dynasty	603–623	War between Byzantium and Persia
c. 570–632	Life of Muhammad, prophet of Islam	622	Hijra to Medina; year 1 of the Islamic calendar
572	Lombards conquer northern Italy	624	Muhammad and Meccans fight battle of Badr
r. 573–c. 594	Bishop Gregory of Tours	661–750	Umayyad caliphate
587	Conversion of Visigothic king Reccared	664	Synod of Whitby; English king opts for Roman form of Christianity
c. 590	Arrival of Irish monk Columbanus in Gaul	726–787	Period of iconoclasm at Byzantium
r. 590–604	Papacy of Pope Gregory the Great		

Emperors, Caliphs, and Local Lords

750–1050

I n 841, a fifteen-year-old boy named William went to serve at the court of Charles the Bald, king of the Franks. William's father was Bernard, an extremely powerful noble. His mother was Dhuoda, a well-educated, pious, and able woman; she administered the family's estates in the south of France while her husband occupied himself in court politics and royal administration. In 841, however, politics had become a dangerous business. King Charles was fighting with his brothers over his portion of the Frankish Empire, and Bernard (who had been a supporter of Charles's father, Louis the Pious) held a precarious position at the young king's court. In fact, William was sent to Charles's court as a kind of hostage, to ensure Bernard's loyalty. Anxious about her son, Dhuoda wrote a handbook of advice for William, outlining what he ought to believe about God; about politics and society; about obligations to his family; and, above all, about his duties to his father, which she emphasized even over loyalty to the king:

> In the human understanding of things, royal and imperial appearance and power seem preeminent in the world, and the custom of men is to account those men's actions and their names ahead of all others. . . . But despite all this . . . I caution you to render first to him whose son you are special, faithful, steadfast loyalty as long as you shall live. . . . So I urge you again, most beloved son William, that first of all you love God. . . . Then love, fear, and cherish your father.

William heeded his mother's words, with tragic results: when Bernard ran afoul of Charles and was executed, William died in a failed attempt to avenge his father.

Dhuoda's handbook reveals the volatile political atmosphere of the mid-ninth century, and her advice to her son points to one of its causes: a crisis of loyalty. Loyalty to emperors, caliphs, and kings—all of whom were symbols of unity cutting across regional and family

Carolingian Mother
This depiction of a nursing mother is a detail from a full-page illustration of the biblical story of the Creation and Fall in a Carolingian Bible manuscript made in the ninth century. The mother is Eve, cast out of the Garden of Eden and suckling her firstborn, Cain. Christian mothers had an important model in Mary, the mother of Jesus, and Eve's dignified placement within a bower of garlands may reflect this association. *(By permission of the British Library.)*

ties — competed with allegiances to local authorities; and those, in turn, vied with family loyalties. The period 600–750 had seen the startling rise of Islam, the whittling away of Byzantium, and the beginnings of stable political and economic development in an impoverished Europe. The period 750–1050 would see all three societies contend with internal issues of diversity even as they became increasingly conscious of their unity and uniqueness. At the beginning of this period, rulers built up and dominated strong, united political communities. By the end, these realms had fragmented into smaller, more local units. While men and women continued to feel some loyalty toward faraway emperors and caliphs, their most powerful allegiances often focused on local lords closer to home.

In Byzantium, the military triumphs of the emperors brought them enormous prestige. A renaissance (that is, an important revival; French for "rebirth") of culture and art took place at Constantinople. Yet at the same time new elites began to dominate the Byzantine countryside. In the Islamic world, a dynastic revolution in 750 ousted the Umayyads from the caliphate and replaced them with a new family, the Abbasids. The new caliphs moved their capital from Damascus to the former Persia, setting up a new capital at Baghdad. Even though their power began to ebb as regional Islamic rulers came to the fore, the Islamic world, too, saw a renaissance. In western Europe, Charlemagne — a Frankish king from a new dynasty, the Carolingians — forged a huge empire and presided over yet another cultural renaissance. Yet this newly unified kingdom was fragile, disintegrating within a generation of Charlemagne's death. In western Europe, even more than in the Byzantine and Islamic worlds, power fell into the hands of local lords.

Along the borders of these realms, new political entities began to develop, shaped by the religion and culture of their more dominant neighbors. Russia grew up in the shadow of Byzan-

tium, as did Bulgaria and Serbia. Western Europe cast its influence over central European states. In the west, the borders of the Islamic world remained stable or were pushed back. (By contrast, Muslim expansion to the east changed the shape of central Asia.) By the year 1050, the contours of what were to become modern Europe and the Middle East were dimly visible.

> **Focus Question:** What forces led to the dissolution — or weakening — of centralized governments in the period 750–1050, and what institutions took their place?

The Emperor and Local Elites in the Byzantine Empire

Between 750 and 850, Byzantium staved off Muslim attacks in Asia Minor and began to rebuild. After 850, it went on the attack. Military victories brought new wealth and power to the imperial court, and the emperors supported a vast program of literary and artistic revival — the Macedonian renaissance — at Constantinople. But while the emperor dominated at the capital, a new landowning elite began to control the countryside. On its northern frontier, Byzantium helped create new Slavic realms.

Imperial Power

While the *themes*, with their territorial military organization, took care of attacks on Byzantine territory, new mobile armies made up of the best troops (*tagmata*) moved aggressively outward, beginning around 850. By 1025, the empire extended from the Danube in the north to the Euphrates in the south (Map 9.1). The Byzantines had not controlled so much territory since their wars with the Sasanid Persians four hundred years earlier.

■ 750–c. 950 Abbasid caliphate

■ 786–809 Caliphate of Harun al-Rashid

750	800	850	900

■ 751 Pippin III becomes king of the Franks

■ 843 Treaty of Verdun

■ 768–814 Charlemagne's rule (Frankish kingdom)

■ 871–899 King Alfred's rule (England)

■ 800 Charlemagne crowned emperor

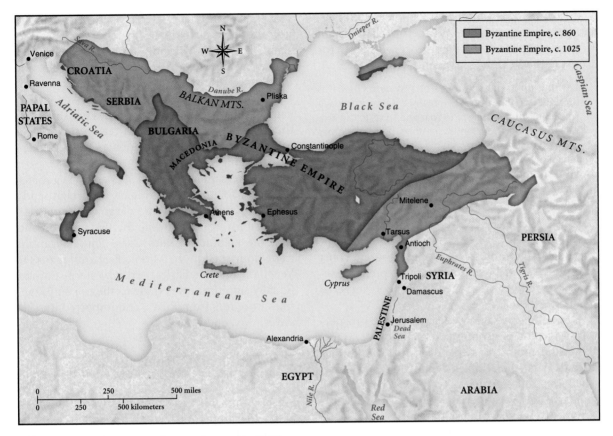

MAP 9.1 The Expansion of Byzantium, 860–1025

In 860, the Byzantine Empire was only a fraction of its former size. To the west, it had lost most of Italy, to the east, it held only part of Asia Minor. On its northern flank, the Bulgarians had set up an independent state. By 1025, however, the empire had ballooned, its western half embracing the entire area of the Balkans, its eastern arm extending around the Black Sea, and its southern fringe reaching nearly to Tripoli. The year 1025 marked the Byzantine Empire's greatest size after the rise of Islam.

Military victories gave new prestige and wealth to the army and to the imperial court. The emperors drew revenues from vast and growing imperial estates. They could demand services and money from the general population at will—requiring citizens to build bridges and roads, to offer lodging to the emperor and his attendants, and to pay taxes in cash. Emperors used their wealth to create a lavish court culture, surrounding themselves with servants, slaves, family members, and civil servants. Eunuchs (castrated men who could not pose a threat to the imperial line) were entrusted with some of the highest posts in government. From their powerful position, the emperors negotiated with other rulers, exchanging ambassadors and receiving and entertaining diplomats

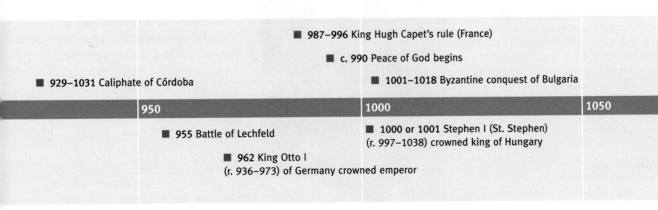

■ 987–996 King Hugh Capet's rule (France)

■ c. 990 Peace of God begins

■ 929–1031 Caliphate of Córdoba

■ 1001–1018 Byzantine conquest of Bulgaria

950   **1000**   **1050**

■ 955 Battle of Lechfeld

■ 1000 or 1001 Stephen I (St. Stephen) (r. 997–1038) crowned king of Hungary

■ 962 King Otto I (r. 936–973) of Germany crowned emperor

with elaborate ceremonies. One such diplomat, Liutprand, bishop of the northern Italian city of Cremona, reported on his audience with Emperor Constantine VII Porphyrogenitos (r. 913–959):

> Leaning upon the shoulders of two eunuchs I was brought into the emperor's presence. At my approach [mechanical] lions began to roar and birds to cry out, each according to its kind. . . . After I had three times [bowed] to the emperor with my face upon the ground, I lifted my head, and behold! the man whom just before I had seen sitting on a moderately elevated seat had now changed his [clothing] and was sitting on the level of the ceiling. How it was done I could not imagine, unless perhaps he was lifted up by some such sort of device as we use for raising the timbers of a wine press.

Although Liutprand mocked this elaborate court ceremony, it had a real function: to express the serious, sacred, concentrated power of imperial majesty.

The emperor's wealth derived from a prosperous agricultural economy organized for trade. Byzantine commerce depended on a careful balance of state regulation and individual enterprise. The emperor controlled craft and commercial guilds to ensure imperial revenues and a stable supply of valuable and useful commodities, while entrepreneurs organized most of the markets held throughout the empire (see Document, "The Book of the Prefect," page 265). Foreign merchants traded within the empire, either at Constantinople (where they were lodged at state expense) or in border cities. Because this international trade intertwined with foreign policy, the Byzantine government considered trade a political as

The Crowning of Constantine Porphyrogenitos
This ivory relief was carved at Constantinople in the mid-tenth century. The artist wanted to emphasize hierarchy and symbolism, not nature. Christ is shown crowning Emperor Constantine Porphyrogenitos (r. 913–959). What message do you suppose the artist wanted to telegraph by making Christ higher than the emperor and by having the emperor slightly incline his head and upper torso to receive the crown? (*Hirmer Fotoarchiv.*)

■ **For more help analyzing this image,** see the visual activity for this chapter in the Online Study Guide at bedfordstmartins.com/hunt.

well as an economic matter. Emperors issued privileges to certain "nations" (as the Venetians, Russians, and Jews, among others, were called), regulating the fees they were obliged to pay and the services they had to render. At the end of the tenth century, for example, the Venetians bargained to reduce their customs dues per ship from thirty *solidi* (coins) to two; in return they promised to transport Byzantine soldiers to Italy whenever the emperor wished.

At the same time, the emperors negotiated privileges for their own traders in foreign lands. Byzantine merchants were guaranteed protection in Syria, for example, while the two governments split the income on sales taxes. Thus, Byzantine trade flourished in the Middle East and, thanks to Venetian intermediaries, with western Europe. Equally significant was trade to the north. Byzantines wore furs from Russia and imported Russian slaves, wax, and honey.

The Macedonian Renaissance, c. 870–c. 1025

Flush with victory and recalling Byzantium's past glory, the emperors revived classical intellectual pursuits. Basil I (r. 867–886) from Macedonia founded the imperial dynasty that presided over the so-called Macedonian renaissance. This renaissance was made possible by an intellectual elite, who came from families that—even in the anxious years of the eighth century—had persisted in studying the classics in spite of the trend toward a simple religious education.

Now, with the empire slowly regaining its military eminence and with icons permanently restored in 843, this scholarly elite thrived again. Byzantine artists produced new works, and emperors and other members of the new court society, liberated from the sober taboos of the iconoclastic period, sponsored lavish artistic productions. Emperor Constantine Porphyrogenitos wrote books of geography and history and financed the work of other scholars and artists. He even supervised the details of his craftspeople's prod-

The Book of the Prefect

Claiming to control all aspects of Byzantine life, emperors issued rules and regulations for every sort of profession. The Book of the Prefect was a decree issued in 911 or 912 by the emperor. It regulated numerous traders and craftspeople, including silk merchants, perfume dealers, candle makers, butchers, bakers, and—as illustrated here—notaries and jewelers. The prefect was the chief city official at Constantinople.

Preface

God, after having created all things that are and given order and harmony to the universe, with his own finger engraved the Law on the tables and published it openly so that men, being well directed thereby, should not shamelessly trample upon one another and the stronger should not do violence to the weaker but that all things should be apportioned with just measure. Therefore it has seemed good for Our Serenity [i.e., the emperor] also to lay down the following ordinances based on the statutes in order that the human race may be governed fittingly and no person may injure his fellow.

I. The Notaries [writers of legal or official documents]

1. Whoever wishes to be appointed a notary must be elected by a vote and decision both of the *primicerius* [the chief of the guild of notaries] and the notaries acting with him to ensure that he has a knowledge and understanding of the laws, that he excels in handwriting, that he is not garrulous [overly talkative] or insolent, and that he does not lead a corrupt life, but on the contrary is serious in his habits, guileless in his thoughts, eloquent, intelligent, a polished reader, and accurate in his diction, to guard against his being easily led to give a false meaning in places to what he writes or to insert deceptive clauses. And if at any time a notary is found to be doing something contrary to the law and the authorized written regulations, those who have acted as his witnesses shall be responsible.

2. The candidate must know by heart the forty titles of the *Manual of Law* [a short compilation of imperial laws] and must also know the sixty books of the Basilika [a much longer compilation]. He shall also have received a general education so that he may not make mistakes in formulating his documents and be guilty of errors in his reading. He shall also have abundant time to give proof of his ability both mental and physical. Let him prepare a handwritten document in a meeting of the guild, so that he may not later commit unforeseen errors; but if he should then be detected in any, let him be expelled, from the order. . . .

II. The Jewelers

1. We ordain that the jewelers may, if any one invites them, buy the things that pertain to them, such as gold, silver, pearls, or precious stones; but not bronze and woven linens or any other materials which others should purchase rather than they. However, they are not hereby prevented from buying anything they wish for private use.

2. They must not depreciate or increase the price of things for sale to the detriment of the vendors, but shall appraise them at their just value. If anyone acts deceitfully in this, he shall forfeit the appraised value of the things to the vendor. . . .

4. If a jeweler discovers a woman offering for sale objects of gold or silver, or pearls, or precious stones, he shall inform the Prefect of these things to prevent their being exported to foreign peoples.

5. If anyone adulterates uncoined metal and manufactures things for sale from it, he shall have his hand cut off.

Source: A. E. R. Boak, "Notes and Documents: The Book of the Prefect," *Journal of Economic and Business History* 1 (1929); 600–602, 604 (slightly modified).

ucts, insisting on exacting standards: "Who could enumerate how many artisans the Porphyrogenitos corrected? He corrected the stonemasons, the carpenters, the goldsmiths, the silversmiths, and the blacksmiths," wrote a historian supported by the same emperor's patronage.

The emperors were not alone in their support of the arts. Other members of the imperial court also sponsored writers, philosophers, and historians. Scholars wrote summaries of classical literature, encyclopedias of ancient knowledge, and commentaries on classical authors. Some copied manuscripts of religious and theological commentaries, such as homilies, liturgical texts, Bibles, and Psalters. The merging of classical and Christian traditions is clearest in manuscript illuminations (painted illustrations or embellishments in hand-copied manuscripts). For example, to depict King David, the supposed poet of the Psalms, an artist illuminating a Psalter turned to a model of Orpheus, the enchanting musician of ancient Greek mythology. (See The Macedonian Renaissance, page 266.) Both in Byzantium and in the West, artists chose their subjects by considering the texts they were to illustrate and the ways in which previous artists had handled particular themes. As with the illustration of King David, they drew on traditional models to make their subjects identifiable. Like

The Macedonian Renaissance
This manuscript illumination, made at Constantinople in the mid-ninth century, combines Christian and classical elements in a harmonious composition. David, author of the Psalms, sits in the center. Like the classical Orpheus, he plays music that attracts and tames the beasts. In the right-hand corner, a figure labeled "Bethlehem" is modeled on a lounging river or mountain god. *(Bibliothèque nationale de France.)*

modern illustrators of Santa Claus who rely on a tradition dictating a plump man with a bushy white beard — Santa's "iconography" — medieval artists used particular visual cues to alert viewers to the identity of their subjects.

The *Dynatoi*: A New Landowning Elite

At Constantinople the emperor reigned supreme. But outside the capital, especially in the border regions of Anatolia, where army leaders of the tagmata became famous as military heroes, extremely powerful military families began to compete with imperial power. The *dynatoi*, as this new hereditary elite was called, got rich on booty and new lands taken in the aggressive wars of the tenth cen-

---

dynatoi (DY nuh toy): The "powerful men" who dominated the countryside of the Byzantine Empire in the tenth and eleventh centuries and to some degree challenged the authority of the emperor.

tury. They took over or bought up whole villages, turning the peasants' labor to their benefit. For the most part they exercised their power locally, but they also sometimes occupied the imperial throne.

The Phocas family exemplifies the strengths as well as the weaknesses of the dynatoi. Probably originally from Armenia, they possessed military skills and exhibited loyalty to the emperor that together brought them high positions in both the army and at court in the last decades of the ninth century. In the tenth century, with new successes in the east, the Phocas family gained independent power. After some particularly brilliant victories, Nicephorus Phocas was declared emperor by his armies and ruled at Constantinople from 963 to 969. But opposing factions of the dynatoi brought him down. The mainstay of Phocas family power, as of that of all the dynatoi, was outside the capital, on the family's great estates.

As the dynatoi gained power, the social hierarchy of Byzantium began to resemble that of western Europe, where land owned by aristocratic lords was farmed by peasants bound by tax and service obligations to the fields they cultivated.

In Byzantium's Shadow: Bulgaria, Serbia, Russia

The shape of what was to become modern eastern Europe was created during the period 850–950. By 800, Slavic settlements dotted the area from the Danube River down to Greece and from the Black Sea to Croatia. The ruler of the Bulgarians, called a *khagan*, presided over the largest realm, northwest of Constantinople. Under Khagan Krum (r. c. 803–814) and his son, Bulgarian rule stretched west to the Tisza River in modern Hungary. At about the same time as Krum's triumphant expansion, however, the Byzantine Empire began its own campaigns to conquer, convert, and control these Slavic regions, today known as the Balkans.

Bulgaria and Serbia. The Byzantine offensive to the north and west began under Emperor Nicephorus I (r. 802–811), who waged war against the Slavs of Greece in the Peloponnesus, set up a new Christian diocese there, organized it as a new military theme, and forcibly resettled Christians in the area to counteract Slavic paganism. The Byzantines followed this pattern of conquest as they pushed northward. By 900, Byzantium ruled all of Greece.

Still under Nicephorus, the Byzantines launched a massive attack against the Bulgarians, took the chief city of Pliska, plundered it, burned it to the ground, and then marched against Krum's encampment in the Balkan mountains. Krum, however, attacked the imperial troops, killed Nicephorus, and brought home the emperor's skull in triumph. Cleaned out and lined with silver, the skull served as the victorious Krum's drinking goblet. In 816, the two sides agreed to a peace that lasted for thirty years. But hostility remained, and intermittent skirmishes between the Bulgarians and Byzantines gave way to longer wars throughout the tenth century. Emperor **Basil II** (r. 976–1025) led the Byzantines in a slow, methodical conquest (1001–1018). Aptly called the Bulgar-Slayer, Basil brought the entire region under Byzantine control and forced its ruler to accept the Byzantine form of Christianity. Around the same time, the Serbs, encouraged by Byzantium to oppose the Bulgarians, began to form the political community that would become Serbia.

Religion played an important role in the Byzantine conquest of the Balkans. In 863, the brothers Cyril and Methodius were sent as Christian missionaries from the Byzantines to the Slavs. Well educated in both classical and religious texts, they spoke one Slavic dialect fluently and devised an alphabet for Slavic (until then an oral language) based on Greek forms. It was the ancestor of the modern Cyrillic alphabet used in Bulgaria, Serbia, and Russia today.

Kievan Russia.   The region that would eventually become Russia lay outside the sphere of direct Byzantine rule in the ninth and tenth centuries. Like Serbia and Bulgaria, however, it came under increasingly strong Byzantine cultural and religious influence. In the ninth century, the Vikings—Scandinavian adventurers who ranged over vast stretches of ninth-century Europe seeking trade, booty, and land—had penetrated Russia from the north and imposed their rule over the Slavs inhabiting the broad river valleys. Like the Bulgars in Bulgaria, the Scandinavian Vikings gradually blended into the larger Slavic population. At the end of the ninth century, a chief named Oleg had established control over most of the tribes in southwestern Russia and forced peoples farther away to pay him tribute. The tribal association he created formed the nucleus of Kievan

The Balkans, c. 850–950

Russia, named for Kiev, the city that had become the commercial center of the region and today is the capital of Ukraine.

The relationship between Kievan Russia and Byzantium began with war, developed through trade agreements, and was finally sustained by religion. Around 905, Oleg launched a military expedition to Constantinople, forcing the Byzantines to pay him a large fee and open their doors to Russian traders in exchange for peace. At the time, only a few Christians lived in Russia—together with Jews and probably some Muslims—alongside a largely pagan population. The Russians' conversion to Christianity was spearheaded by a Russian ruler later in the century. Vladimir (r. c. 980–1015), the grand prince of Kiev and all Russia, and the Byzantine emperor Basil II agreed that Vladimir should adopt the Byzantine form of Christianity. Vladimir took a variant of the name Basil in honor of the emperor and married the emperor's sister Anna; then he reportedly had all the people of his realm baptized in the Dnieper River.

Vladimir's conversion represented a wider pattern of the Christianization of Europe, in which an emerging split between orthodox Byzantine Christianity in the eastern half of the former Roman Empire and Roman Catholicism in the west was reinforced. Slavic realms such as Moravia, Serbia, and Bulgaria adopted the Byzantine form of Christianity, while the rulers and peoples of Poland, Hungary, Denmark, and Norway were converted under the auspices of the Roman church. Russia's conversion to Christianity was especially significant, because Russia was geographically as close to the Islamic world as to the Christian and could conceivably have become an Islamic land. By converting to Byzantine Christianity, Russians made themselves heir to Byzantium and its church, customs, art, and political ideology. Adopting Christianity linked Russia to the Christian world, but choosing the Byzantine form of Christianity, rather than the Roman Catholic, served later on to isolate Russia from western Europe, as in the course of the centuries the Byzantine (Greek-speaking) and Roman (Latin-speaking) churches became estranged.

Wishing to counteract such isolation, Russian rulers at times sought to cement relations with central and western Europe, which were tied to Catholic Rome. Prince Iaroslav the Wise (r. 1019–1054) forged such links through his own marriage and

---

Basil II: The Byzantine emperor (r. 976–1025) who presided over the end of the Bulgar threat (earning the name Bulgar-Slayer) and the conversion of Kievan Russia to Christianity.

Mosaic of Mary in the Cathedral of St. Sophia
Imitating Justinian's church of St. Sophia at Constantinople, the cathedral of St. Sophia in Kiev was built by Yaroslav the Wise around 1050. Here the Virgin Mary, who looms at the very center of the cathedral, is portrayed in a praying position. Compare her to the Icon of the Virgin and Child on page 244 to see how much the Russian artists borrowed from Byzantine styles. (© Cathedral of St. Sophia, Kiev, Russia/Vadim Gippenreiter/The Bridgeman Art Library.)

those of his sons and daughters to rulers and princely families in France, Hungary, and Scandinavia. Iaroslav encouraged intellectual and artistic developments that would connect Russian culture to the classical past. At his own church of St. Sophia, in Kiev, which copied the one at Constantinople, Iaroslav created a major library.

When Iaroslav died, his kingdom was divided among his sons. Civil wars broke out between the brothers and eventually between cousins, shredding what unity Russia had known. Massive invasions by outsiders, particularly from the east, further weakened Kievan rulers, who were eventually displaced by princes from northern Russia. At the crossroads of East and West, Russia could meet and absorb a great variety of traditions; but its geographical position also opened it to unremitting

military pressures, including some from the Islamic world.

> **REVIEW:** What were the effects of expansion on the power of the Byzantine emperor?

The Caliphate and Its Fragmentation

A new dynasty of caliphs — the Abbasids — first brought unity and then, in their decline, fragmentation to the Islamic world. Caliphs ruled in name only, as regional rulers took over the actual government in Islamic lands. Local traditions based on religious and political differences played an increasingly important role in people's lives. Yet, even in the eleventh century, the Islamic world had a clear sense of its own unity, based on language, commerce, and artistic and intellectual achievements that transcended regional boundaries.

The Abbasid Caliphate, 750–c. 950

In 750, a civil war ousted the Umayyads and raised the **Abbasids** to the caliphate. The Abbasids found support in an uneasy coalition of Shi'ites (the faction of Islam loyal to Ali's memory) and non-Arabs who had been excluded from Umayyad government and now demanded a place in political life. With the new regime, the center of Islamic rule shifted from Damascus, with its roots in the Roman tradition, to Baghdad, a new capital city, built by the Abbasids right next to Ctesiphon, which had been the Sasanid capital. Here the Abbasid caliphs adhered even more firmly than the Umayyads to Persian courtly models. Their administration grew more and more centralized: the caliph's staff grew, and he controlled the appointment of regional governors.

From Baghdad, the Abbasid caliph Harun al-Rashid (r. 786–809) presided over a flourishing empire. His contemporary Frankish ruler, Charlemagne, was impressed with the elephant Harun sent him as a gift, along with monkeys, spices, and medicines. These items were mainstays of everyday commerce in Harun's Iraq. A mid-ninth-century catalog of imports listed "tigers, panthers, elephants, panther skins, rubies, white sandal, ebony, and coconuts" from India as well as "silk,

---

Abbasids (A buh sihds): The dynasty of caliphs that, in 750, took over from the Umayyads in all of the Islamic realm except for Spain (al-Andalus). From their new capital at Baghdad, they presided over a wealthy realm until the late ninth century.

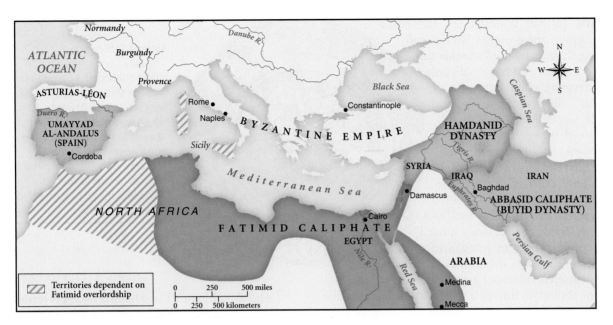

MAP 9.2 Islamic States, c. 1000
A glance back at Map 8.1 on page 236 will quickly demonstrate the fragmentation of the once united Islamic caliphate. In 750, one caliph ruled territory stretching from Spain to India. In 1000, there was more than one caliphate as well as several other ruling dynasties. The most important were the Fatimids, who began as organizers of a movement to overthrow the Abbasids. By 1000, they had conquered Egypt and claimed hegemony over all of North Africa.

chinaware, paper, ink, peacocks, racing horses, saddles, felts [and] cinnamon" from China.

The Abbasid dynasty began to decline after Harun's death. Obliged to support a huge army and increasingly complex civil service, the Abbasids found their tax base inadequate. They needed to collect revenues from their provinces, such as Syria and Egypt, but the governors of those regions often refused to send the revenues. After Harun's death, ex-soldiers seeking better salaries recognized different caliphs and fought for power in savage civil wars. The caliphs tried to bypass the regular army, made up largely of free Muslim foot soldiers, by turning to Turkish slaves—Mamluks—bought and armed to serve as mounted cavalry. But the caliphate's dwindling revenues could not sustain a loyal or powerful military force, and in the tenth century the caliphs became figureheads only, as independent rulers established themselves in the various Islamic regions. For military support, many of these new rulers turned to independent military commanders who led Mamluk troops. Well paid to maintain their mounts and arms, many Mamluks gained renown and, after being freed by their masters, high positions at the courts of regional rulers. In the thirteenth century, some of them became rulers themselves.

Thus, in the Islamic world, as in the Byzantine, new regional lords challenged the power of the central ruler. But the process was soon much more advanced in Islamic than in Byzantine territories. Map 9.1 (page 263) correctly omits any indication of regional dynatoi because the key center of power in the Byzantine Empire continued to be Constantinople. Map 9.2, on the other hand, shows the fragmentation of the Abbasid caliphate, as local dynasties established themselves.

Regional Diversity in Islamic Lands

A faraway caliph could not command sufficient allegiance from local leaders once he demanded more in taxes than he gave back in favors. The forces of fragmentation were strong in the Islamic world: it was, after all, based on the conquest of many diverse regions, each with its own deeply rooted traditions and culture. The Islamic religion, with its Sunni/Shi'ite split, also became a source of polarization. Western Europeans knew almost nothing about Muslims, calling all of them Saracens (from the Latin word for "Arabs") without distinction. But, in fact, like today, Muslims were of different ethnicities, practiced different customs, and identified with different regions. With the fragmentation of political and religious unity, each of the tenth- and early-eleventh-century Islamic states built on local traditions under local rulers.

The Fatimid Dynasty. In the tenth century, one group of Shi'ites, calling themselves the **Fatimids** (after Fatimah, Muhammad's only surviving child and wife of Ali), allied with the Berbers in North Africa and established themselves in 909 as rulers in the region now called Tunisia. The Fatimid Ubayd Allah claimed to be not only the true imam—the descendant of Ali—but also the *mahdi*, the "divinely guided" messiah, come to bring justice on earth. In 969, the Fatimids declared themselves rulers of Egypt. Their dynasty lasted for about two hundred years. Fatimid leaders also controlled North Africa, Arabia, and even Syria for a time. They established a court that rivaled the one at Baghdad, and they supported industries, such as lusterware (see Fatimid Tableware on this page), that had once been a monopoly of the Abbasids.

The Spanish Emirate. Whereas the Shi'ites dominated Egypt, Sunni Muslims ruled al-Andalus, the Islamic central and southern heart of Spain. Unlike the other independent Islamic states, which were forged during the ninth and tenth centuries, the Spanish emirate of Córdoba (so called because its ruler took the secular title *emir*, "commander," and fixed his capital at Córdoba) was created near the start of the Abbasid caliphate, in 756. During the Abbasid revolution, Abd al-Rahman—a member of the Umayyad family—fled to Morocco, gathered an army, invaded Spain, and was declared emir after only one battle. He and his successors ruled a broad range of peoples, including many Jews and Christians. After the initial Islamic conquest of Spain, the Christians adopted so much of the new Arabic language and so many of the customs that they were called Mozarabs, that is, "like Arabs." The Arabs allowed them freedom of worship and let them live according to their own laws. Some Mozarabs were content with their status, others converted to Islam, and still others intermarried—most commonly, Christian women married Muslim men and raised their children as Muslims, since the religion of the father determined that of the children.

Fatimid Tableware
The elites under the Fatimid rulers cultivated a luxurious lifestyle that including dining on porcelain tableware, which was glazed and fired several times to produce the effect seen here. Trade contacts with China inspired the Islamic world to mimic Chinese pottery. (© 2008 by Benaki Museum, Athens.)

Abd al-Rahman III (r. 912–961) was powerful enough to take the title of caliph, and the caliphate of Córdoba that he created lasted from 929 to 1031. Under Abd al-Rahman's rule, members of all religious groups in al-Andalus were given not only freedom of worship but also equal opportunity to rise in the civil service. The caliph also initiated diplomatic contacts with Byzantine and European rulers, ignoring the weak and tiny Christian kingdoms squeezed into northern Spain. Yet under later caliphs, al-Andalus experienced the same political fragmentation that was occurring everywhere else. The caliphate of Córdoba broke up in 1031, and rulers of small, independent regions, called *taifas*, took power.

Unity of Commerce and Language

Although the regions of the Islamic world were culturally and politically diverse, they maintained a measure of unity through trade networks and language. Their principal bond was Arabic, the language of the Qur'an. At once poetic and sacred, Arabic was also the language of commerce and government from Baghdad to Córdoba. Moreover, despite political differences, borders were open: an artisan could move from Córdoba to Cairo; a landowner in Morocco might very well own property in al-Andalus; a young man from North Africa would think nothing of going to Baghdad to find a wife; a young girl purchased as a slave in Mecca might become part of a prince's household in Baghdad. With few barriers to commerce (though every city and town had its own customs dues), traders regularly dealt in various, often exotic, goods.

Although the primary reason for these open borders was Islam itself, the openness extended to non-Muslims as well. The commercial activities of the Tustari brothers, Jewish merchants from

---

Fatimids (FAT ih mihds): Members of the tenth-century Shi'ite dynasty who derived their name from Fatimah, the daughter of Muhammad and wife of Ali; they dominated in parts of North Africa, Egypt, and even Syria.

southern Iran, were typical in the Arabic-speaking world. By 1026, the Tustaris had established a flourishing business in Egypt. Although they did not have "branch offices," informal contacts with friends and family allowed them to import fine textiles from Iran to sell in Egypt and to export Egyptian fabrics to sell in Iran. Dealing in fabrics could yield fabulous wealth, for cloth was essential not only for clothing but also for home decoration: textiles covered walls; curtains separated rooms. The Tustari brothers held the highest rank in Jewish society and had contacts with Muslim rulers. The son of one of the brothers converted to Islam and became vizier (chief minister) to the Fatimids in Egypt.

The sophisticated Islamic society of the tenth and eleventh centuries supported commercial networks even more vast than those of the Tustari family. Muslim merchants brought tin from England; salt and gold from Timbuktu in west-central Africa; amber, gold, and copper from Russia; and slaves from every region. Equally widespread was the reach of the Islamic renaissance.

The Islamic Renaissance, c. 790–c. 1050

The dissolution of the caliphate into separate political entities multiplied the centers of learning and intellectual productivity. Unlike the Macedonian renaissance, which was concentrated in Constantinople, the Islamic renaissance occurred throughout the Islamic world. It was particularly dazzling in capital cities such as Córdoba, where tenth-century rulers presided over a brilliant court culture, patronizing scholars, poets, and artists. The library at Córdoba contained the largest collection of books in Europe at that time. (See Document, "When She Approached," page 272.)

Elsewhere, already in the eighth century, the Abbasid caliphs endowed research libraries and set up centers for translation where scholars culled the writings of the ancients, including the classics of Persia, India, and Greece. Many scholars read, translated, and commented on the works of ancient philosophers. Others worked on astronomy (see A Dancing Constellation, above), and still others wrote on mathematical matters. Al-Kwarazmi (d. 850) wrote a book on algebra (the word itself is from the Arab *al-jabr*) and another on the Indian method of calculation, using the numbers 1, 2, and 3. He introduced the zero, essential for differentiating 1 from 10, for example. When these numerals were introduced into western Europe in the twelfth century, they were known as Arabic, as they are still called today.

A Dancing Constellation
The study of sciences such as medicine, physics, and astronomy flourished in the tenth and eleventh centuries in the cosmopolitan Islamic world. This whimsical depiction of Andromeda C, a constellation in the Northern Hemisphere, illustrates the *Book of Images of the Fixed Stars*, an astronomical treatise written around 965 by al-Sufi at the request of his pupil, the ruler of Iran. Al-Sufi drew from classical treatises, particularly the *Almagest* by Ptolemy. This copy of his book, probably made by his son in 1009, also draws on classical models for the illustrations; but instead of Greek clothing, Andromeda wears the pantaloons and skirt of an Islamic dancer.
(Bodleian Library, University of Oxford. Shelfmark MS. Marsh 14, 2523c. 24.)

The newly independent Islamic rulers supported science as well as mathematics. Ibn Sina (980–1037), known in Christian Europe as Avicenna, wrote books on logic, the natural sciences, and physics. His *Canon of Medicine* systematized earlier treatises and reconciled them with his own experience as a physician. Active in the centers of power, he served as vizier to various rulers. In his autobiography, he spoke with pleasure and pride about his intellectual development:

One day I asked permission [of the ruler] to go into [his doctors'] library, look at their books, and read the medical ones. He gave me permission, and I went into a

DOCUMENT

When She Approached

The tenth and eleventh centuries marked the golden age of Arabic poetry in al-Andalus. In the first of these centuries, the poets' patron was the caliph at Córdoba. In the eleventh century, as al-Andalus broke up into taifas (see page 270), each taifa ruler supported his own artists. Ibn Darraj al-Quastali (958–1030), the author of When She Approached *revealed his most intimate feelings when he wrote about leaving wife and child behind to find employment at the court of a taifa ruler.*

> When she approached to bid me farewell,
> her sighs and moans breaking down my endurance,
> reminding me of the times of love and joy,
> while in the crib a little one gurgles,
> unable to talk, but the sounds he makes
> firmly lodge in the heart's whims. . . .
> I disobeyed the promptings of my heart to stay with him,
> led on by a habit of constant travel day and night,
> and the wing of parting took off with me, while the fear
> of parting flew high with many wings.

Source: Salma Khadra Jayyusi, "Andalusi Poetry: The Golden Period," in *The Legacy of Muslim Spain*, ed. Salma Khadra Jayyusi, 2 vols. (Leiden: Brill, 1994), 1:335.

palace of many rooms, each with trunks full of books, back-to-back. In one room there were books on Arabic and poetry, in another books on jurisprudence, and similarly in each room books on a single subject. . . . When I reached the age of eighteen, I had completed the study of all these sciences.

Long before there were universities in Europe, there were institutions of higher learning in the Islamic world. Rich Muslims, often members of the ruling elite, demonstrated their piety and charity by establishing schools. Each school, or madrasa, was located within or attached to a mosque. Sometimes visiting scholars held passionate public debates at these schools. More regularly, professors held classes throughout the day on the interpretation of the Qur'an and other literary or legal texts. Students, all male, attended the classes that suited their achievement level and interest. Most students paid a fee for learning, but there were also scholarship students. One tenth-century vizier was so solicitous of the welfare of the scholars he supported that each day he set out iced refreshments, candles, and paper for them in his own kitchen.

The use of paper, made from flax and hemp or rags and vegetable fiber, points to a major difference among the Islamic, Byzantine, and (as we shall see) Carolingian renaissances. Byzantine scholars worked to enhance the prestige of the ruling classes. Their work, written on expensive parchment (made from animal skins), kept manuscripts out of the hands of all but the very rich. This was true of scholarship in Europe as well. By contrast, Islamic scholars had goals that cut across all social classes: to be physicians to the rich, teachers to the young, and contributors to passionate religious debates. Their writings, on paper (less expensive than parchment), were widely available.

> **REVIEW:** What forces fragmented the Islamic world in the tenth and eleventh centuries, and what forces held it together?

The Creation and Division of a New European Empire

Just as in the Byzantine and Islamic worlds, so too in Europe the period 750–1050 saw first the formation of a strong empire, ruled by one man, and then its fragmentation as local rulers took power into their own hands. A new dynasty, the Carolingians, came to rule in the Frankish kingdom at almost the very moment (c. 750) that the Abbasids gained the caliphate. Charlemagne, the most powerful Carolingian monarch, conquered new territory, took the title of emperor, and presided over a revival of Christian classical culture known as the Carolingian renaissance. He ruled at the local level through counts and other military men. Nevertheless, the unity of the Carolingian Empire — based largely on conquest, a measure of prosperity, and personal allegiance to Charlemagne — was shaky. Its weaknesses were exacerbated by attacks from Viking, Muslim, and Magyar invaders. Charlemagne's successors divided his empire among themselves and saw it divided further as local leaders took defense — and rule — into their own hands.

The Rise of the Carolingians

The Carolingians were among many aristocratic families on the rise during the Merovingian period, but they gained exceptional power by monopolizing the position of "palace mayor" — a sort of prime minister — under the Merovingian kings. Charles Martel, mayor 714–741, gave the name

Carolingian (from *Carolus*, the Latin for "Charles") to the dynasty. Renowned for defeating an invading army of Muslims from al-Andalus near Poitiers in 732, he also contended vigorously against other aristocrats who were carving out independent lordships for themselves. Charles and his family turned aristocratic factions against one another, rewarded supporters, crushed enemies, and dominated whole regions by supporting monasteries that served as focal points for both religious piety and land donations.

The Carolingians also allied themselves with the Roman papacy and its adherents. They supported Anglo-Saxon missionaries like Boniface (see page 255), who went to areas on the fringes of the Carolingian realm as the pope's ambassador. Reforming the Christianity that these regions had adopted, Boniface set up a hierarchical church organization and founded monasteries dedicated to the Benedictine rule. His newly appointed bishops were loyal to Rome and the Carolingians. Pippin III (d. 768), Charles Martel's son, turned to the pope even more directly. When he deposed the Merovingian king in 751, taking over the kingship himself, Pippin petitioned Pope Zachary to legitimize the act. The pope agreed. The Carolingians returned the favor a few years later when the pope asked for their help against hostile Lombards. That papal request signaled a major shift. Before 754, the papacy had been part of the Byzantine Empire; after that, it turned to Europe for protection. Pippin launched a successful campaign against the Lombard king that ended in 756 with the so-called Donation of Pippin, a peace accord between the Lombards and the pope. The treaty gave back to the pope cities that had been taken by the Lombard king. The new arrangement recognized what the papacy had long ago created: a territorial "republic of St. Peter" ruled by the pope, not by the Byzantine emperor. Henceforth, the fate of Italy would be tied largely to the policies of the pope and the Frankish kings to the north, not to the emperors of the East.

Partnership with the Roman church gave the Carolingian dynasty a Christian aura, expressed in symbolic form by anointment. Bishops rubbed holy oil on the foreheads and shoulders of Carolingian kings during the coronation ceremony, imitating the Old Testament kings who had been anointed by God.

Charlemagne and His Kingdom, 768–814

The most famous Carolingian king was Charles (r. 768–814), called the Great (*le Magne* in Old French) by his contemporaries — thus, **Charlemagne**. For various — though always admiring — views of Charlemagne by people who lived during or just after his lifetime, see "Contrasting Views" on pages 276–277. Modern historians are less dazzled than his contemporaries were, noting that Charlemagne was complex, contradictory, and sometimes brutal. He loved listening to St. Augustine's *City of God* as it was read aloud, and he supported major scholarly enterprises; yet he never learned to write. He was devout, building a beautiful chapel at his major residence at Aachen (see Charlemagne's Chapel, page 274), yet he flouted the advice of churchmen when they told him to convert pagans rather than force baptism on them. He admired the pope, yet he was furious when a pope placed the imperial crown on his head. He waged many successful wars, yet he thereby destroyed the buffer states surrounding the Frankish kingdoms, unleashing a new round of invasions even before his death.

Behind these contradictions, however, lay a unifying vision. Charlemagne dreamed of an empire that would unite the martial and learned traditions of the Roman and Germanic worlds with the legacy of Christianity. This vision lay at the core of his political activity, his building programs, and his support of scholarship and education.

Territorial Expansion.   During the early years of his reign, Charlemagne conquered lands in all directions (Map 9.3). He invaded Italy, seizing the crown of the Lombard kings and annexing northern Italy in 774. He then moved northward and began a long and difficult war against the Saxons, concluded only after more than thirty years of fighting, during which he forcibly annexed Saxon territory and converted the Saxon people to Christianity through mass baptisms at the point of the sword. To the southeast, Charlemagne fought the Avars. Charlemagne's courtier and biographer Einhard described this campaign as follows: "All the money and treasure that had been amassed over many years was seized, and no war in which the Franks have ever engaged within the memory of man brought them such riches and such booty."

Carolingian: The Frankish dynasty that ruled a western European empire from 751 to the late 800s; its greatest vigor was in the time of Charlemagne (r. 768–814) and Louis the Pious (r. 814–840).

Charlemagne (SHAR luh mayn): The Carolingian king (r. 768–814) whose conquests greatly expanded the Frankish kingdom. He was crowned emperor on December 25, 800.

Charlemagne's Chapel
Charlemagne was the first Frankish king to build a permanent capital city. The decision to do so was made in 789, and the king chose Aachen because of its natural warm springs. There he built a palace complex that, besides a grand living area for himself and his retinue, included a chapel (a small semiprivate church), still standing today, modeled on the Byzantine church of San Vitale in Ravenna. (© Aachen Cathedral, Aachen, Germany/Bildarchiv Steffens/The Bridgeman Art Library.)

To the southwest, Charlemagne led an expedition to al-Andalus. Although suffering a defeat at Roncesvalles in 778 (immortalized later in the medieval epic *The Song of Roland*), he did set up a march, or military buffer region, between al-Andalus and his own realm.

By the 790s, Charlemagne's kingdom stretched eastward beyond the Elbe River (today in Germany), southeast to what is today Austria, and south to Spain and Italy. Such power in the West was unheard of since the time of the Roman Empire. Charlemagne began to imitate aspects of the imperial model: he sponsored building programs to symbolize his authority, standardized weights and measures, and acted as a patron of intellectual and artistic efforts. He built a capital city

at Aachen, complete with a church patterned on one built by Justinian at Ravenna.

To discourage corruption, Charlemagne appointed special officials, called *missi dominici* (meaning "those sent out by the lord king"), to oversee his regional governors—the counts—on the king's behalf. The missi—lay aristocrats or bishops—traveled in pairs throughout the kingdom. As one of Charlemagne's capitularies (summaries of royal decisions) put it, the missi "are to make diligent inquiry wherever people claim that someone has done them an injustice, so that the missi fully carry out the law and do justice for everyone everywhere, whether in the holy churches of God or among the poor, orphans, or widows."

Imperial Coronation. While Charlemagne was busy imitating Roman emperors through his conquests, his building programs, his legislation, and his efforts at church reform, the papacy was beginning to claim imperial power for itself. At some point, perhaps in the 760s, members of the papal chancery (writing office) created a document called the Donation of Constantine, which declared the pope the recipient of the fourth-century emperor Constantine's crown, cloak, and military rank along with "all provinces, palaces, and districts of the city of Rome and Italy and of the regions of the West." (The document was much later proved a forgery.) The tension between the imperial claims of the Carolingians and those of the pope was heightened by the existence of an emperor at Constantinople who also had rights in the West.

Pope Leo III (r. 795–816) upset the delicate balance among these three powers. In 799, accused of adultery and perjury by a faction of the Roman aristocracy, Leo narrowly escaped being blinded and having his tongue cut out. He fled northward to seek Charlemagne's protection. (See an anonymous poet's account of this event in Document 2 in "Contrasting Views," page 276.) Charlemagne had the pope escorted back to Rome under royal protection, and he soon arrived there himself to an imperial welcome orchestrated by Leo. On Christmas Day, 800, Leo put an imperial crown on Charlemagne's head and the clergy and nobles who were present acclaimed the king Augustus, the title of the first Roman emperor. The pope hoped in this way to exalt the king of the Franks, to downgrade the Byzantine ruler, and to claim for himself the role of "emperor maker."

About twenty years later, when Einhard wrote about this coronation, he said that the imperial title at first displeased Charlemagne "so much that he stated that, if he had known in advance of the

MAP 9.3 Expansion of the Carolingian Empire under Charlemagne
The conquests of Charlemagne temporarily united almost all of western Europe under one ruler. Although this great empire broke apart (see the inset showing the divisions of the Treaty of Verdun), the legacy of that unity remained, even serving as one of the inspirations behind today's European Union.

pope's plan, he would not have entered the church that day." In fact, for more than a year afterward, Charlemagne used no title but *king*. However, it is unlikely that he was completely surprised by the imperial title; his advisers certainly had been thinking about it for him. He might have hesitated to adopt the title because he feared the reaction of the Byzantines, as Einhard went on to suggest, or he might have objected to the papal role in his crowning rather than to the crown itself. When Charlemagne finally did call himself emperor, after establishing a peace with the Byzantines, he used a long and revealing title: "Charles, the most serene Augustus, crowned by God, great and peaceful Emperor who governs the Roman Empire and who is, by the mercy of God, king of the Franks and the Lombards." According to this title, Charlemagne was not the Roman emperor

crowned by the pope but rather God's emperor, who governed the Roman Empire along with his many other duties.

The Carolingian Renaissance, c. 790–c. 900

Charlemagne inaugurated—and his successors continued to support—a revival of learning designed to enhance the glory of the kings, educate their officials, reform the liturgy, and purify the faith. Like the renaissances of the Byzantine and Islamic worlds, the Carolingian renaissance resuscitated the learning of the past. Scholars studied Roman imperial writers such as Suetonius and Virgil, read and commented on the works of the church fathers, and worked to establish complete and accurate texts of everything they read and prized.

Charlemagne: Roman Emperor, Father of Europe, or the Chief Bishop?

Charlemagne was crowned emperor, but was he really one of the successors of Augustus? Einhard (Document 1) thought so. An anonymous poet at Charlemagne's court claimed still more (Document 2): the king was the "father of Europe." Even while these secular views of Charlemagne were being expressed, other people—both in and outside the court—were stressing the king's religious functions and duties. Later on, these views became even more grandiose, as Notker the Stammerer's statement (Document 3) reveals.

1. Charles as Emperor

Probably at some point in the mid 820s, Einhard, who had spent time at the Carolingian court and knew Charlemagne well, wrote a biography of the emperor that took as its model the Lives of the Caesars *by Suetonius (c. 70–130). Although he did not emphasize Charlemagne's imperial title per se, Einhard stressed the classical moral values of his hero, including his "greatness of spirit" and steadfast determination (see pages 134–136 for the traditional Roman virtues).*

It is widely recognized that, in these ways [i.e., through conquests, diplomacy, and patronage of the arts], [Charles] protected, increased the size of, and beautified his kingdom. Now I should begin at this point to speak of the character of his mind, his supreme steadfastness in good times and bad, and those other things that belong to his spiritual and domestic life.

After the death of his father [in 768], when he was sharing the kingdom with his brother [Carloman], he endured the pettiness and jealousy of his brother with such great patience, that it seemed remarkable to all that he could not be provoked to anger by him. Then [in 770], at the urging of his mother [Bertrada], he married a daughter of Desiderius, the king of the Lombards, but for some unknown reason he sent her away after a year and took Hildegard [758–783], a Swabian woman of distinct nobility. . . .

[Charles] believed that his children, both his daughters and his sons, should be educated, first in the liberal arts, which he himself had studied. Then, he saw to it that when the boys had reached the right age they were trained to ride in the Frankish fashion, to fight, and to hunt. But he ordered his daughters to learn how to work with wool, how to spin and weave it, so that they might not grow dull from inactivity and [instead might] learn to value work and virtuous activity. . . .

Source: *Charlemagne's Courtier: The Complete Einhard*, ed. and trans. Paul Edward Dutton (Peterborough, Ont.: Broadview Press, 1998), 27–28.

2. The "Father of Europe"

Shortly after Pope Leo III fled northward to seek Charlemagne's help (799), an anonymous poet at the royal court composed an extremely flattering poem about the king. Here Charlemagne's virtues became larger than life.

The priests and the joyful people await the pope's advent.

Now father Charles [i.e., Charlemagne] sees his troops arrayed on the wide field;

He knows that Pepin [his son] and the highest pastor [the pope] are fast approaching;

The English scholar Alcuin (c. 732–804), a member of the circle of scholars whom Charlemagne recruited to form a center of study, brought with him the traditions of Anglo-Saxon scholarship that had been developed by men such as Benedict Biscop and Bede. Invited to Aachen, Alcuin became Charlemagne's chief adviser, writing letters on the king's behalf, counseling him on royal policy, and tutoring the king's household, including the women and girls. He also prepared an improved edition of the Vulgate, the Latin Bible used by the clergy in all church services.

The Carolingian renaissance depended on an elite staff of scholars such as Alcuin, yet its educational program had broader appeal. In one of his capitularies, Charlemagne ordered that the cathedrals and monasteries of his kingdom teach reading and writing to all who were able to learn. Some churchmen expressed the hope that schools for children would be established even in small villages and hamlets. Although this dream was never realized, it shows that, at just about the same time as the Islamic world was organizing its madrasas, the Carolingians were thinking about the importance of religious education for more than a small elite.

Art, like scholarship, served Carolingian political and religious goals. Carolingian artists turned to models from Byzantium (perhaps some refugees from Byzantine iconoclasm joined them)

He orders his people to wait for them.

He divides his troops into a ring-like shape,

In the center of which, he himself, that blessed one, stands,

Awaiting the advent of the pope, but higher up than his comrades

On the summit of the ring; he rises above the assembled [Franks].

Now Pope Leo approaches and crosses the front line of the ring.

He marvels at the many peoples from many lands whom he sees,

At their differences, their strange tongues, dress, and weapons.

At once Charles hastens to pay his reverent respects,

Embraces the great pontiff, and kisses him.

The two men join hands and walk together, speaking as they go.

The entire army prostrates itself three times before the pope,

And the suppliant throng three times pays its respects.

The pope prays from his heart for the people three times.

The king, the father of Europe, and Leo, the world's highest pastor,

Walk together and exchange views,

Charles inquiring as to the pope's case and his troubles.

He is shocked to learn of the wicked deeds of the [Roman] people.

He is amazed by the pope's eyes which had been blinded,

But to which sight had now returned,

And he marveled that a tongue mutilated with tongs now spoke. . . .

Source: *Carolingian Civilization: A Reader*, 2d ed., ed. Paul Edward Dutton, (Peterborough, Ont.: Broadview Press, 2004), 64–65.

3. The Chief Bishop

A monk at the Swiss monastery of St. Gall, Notker the Stammerer, wrote a Life of Charlemagne *in 884 at the request of Charlemagne's great-grandson Charles the Fat. Here the emphasis is on Charlemagne's religious authority.*

The Devil, who is skilful in laying ambushes and is in the habit of setting snares for us in the road which we are to follow, is not slow to trip us up one after another by means of some vice or other. The crime of fornication was imputed to a certain princely bishop—in such a case the name must be omitted. This matter came to the notice of his congregation, and then through tale-tellers it eventually reached the ears of the most pious Charles, the chief bishop of them all. . . . Charlemagne, that most rigorous searcher after justice, sent two of his court officials who were to turn aside that evening to a place near to the city in question and then come unexpectedly to the bishop at first light and ask him to celebrate Mass for them. If he should refuse, then they were to compel him in the name of the Emperor to celebrate the Holy Mysteries in person. The bishop did not know what to do, for that very night he had sinned before the eyes of the Heavenly Observer [God], and yet he did not dare to offend his visitors. Fearing men more than he feared God, he bathed his sweaty limbs in ice-cold spring-water and then went forward to offer the awe-inspiring sacraments. Behold, either his conscience gripped his heart tight, or the water penetrated his veins, for he was seized with such frosty chill that no attention from his doctors was of use to him. He was brought to his death by a frightful attack of fever and compelled to submit his soul to the decree of the strict and eternal Judge.

Source: *Einhard and Notker the Stammerer: Two Lives of Charlemagne*, trans. Lewis Thorpe (Harmondsworth, England: Penguin Books, 1969), 121–22.

and Italy to illustrate Gospels, Psalters, scientific treatises, and literary manuscripts.

The ambitious Carolingian program endured, even after the Carolingian dynasty had faded to a memory. The work of locating, understanding, and transmitting models of the past continued in a number of monastic schools. In the twelfth century, scholars would build on the foundations laid by the Carolingian renaissance. The very print of this textbook depends on one achievement of the period: modern letter fonts are based on the clear and beautiful letter forms, called Caroline minuscule, invented in the ninth century to standardize manuscript handwriting—and make it more readable—across the whole empire.

Charlemagne's Successors, 814–911

Charlemagne's son Louis the Pious (r. 814–840) took his role as leader of the Christian empire even more seriously than his father did. He brought the monastic reformer Benedict of Aniane to court and issued a capitulary in 817 imposing a uniform way of life, based on the Benedictine rule, on all the monasteries of the empire. Although some monasteries opposed this legislation, and in the years to come the king was unable to impose his will directly, this moment marked the effective adoption of the Benedictine rule as the monastic standard in Europe.

Vivian Bible
In this sumptuously illustrated bible made for King Charles the Bald, Charlemagne's grandson, David, as the composer of the Psalms, plays the harp and dances on a cloud. Above and below him are his musicians with their instruments. The influence of earlier models is clear in the two figures flanking David, who are dressed like soldiers in the late Roman Empire. *(Bibliothèque nationale de France.)*

In a new development of the coronation ritual, Louis's first wife, Ermengard, was crowned empress by the pope in 816. In 817, their firstborn son, Lothar, was given the title emperor and made co-ruler with Louis. Their other sons, Pippin and Louis (later called Louis the German), were made subkings under imperial rule. Louis the Pious hoped in this way to ensure the unity of the empire while satisfying the claims of all his sons. Should any son die, only his firstborn could succeed him, a measure intended to prevent further splintering. But Louis's hopes were thwarted by events. Ermengard died, and Louis married Judith, reputed to be the most beautiful woman in the kingdom. In 823, she and Louis had a son, Charles (later known as Charles the Bald, to whose court Dhuoda's son William was sent). The sons of Ermengard, bitter over the birth of another royal heir, rebelled against their father and fought one another for more than a decade. Finally, after Louis's death

in 840, the **Treaty of Verdun** (843) divided the empire among the three remaining brothers (Pippin had died in 838) in an arrangement that would roughly define the future political contours of western Europe (see the inset in Map 9.3). The western third, bequeathed to Charles the Bald (r. 843–877), would eventually become France; the eastern third, handed to Louis the German (r. 843–876), would become Germany. The "Middle Kingdom," which was given to Lothar (r. 840–855) along with the imperial title, had a different fate: parts of it were absorbed by France and Germany, and the rest eventually formed what were to become the modern states of the Netherlands, Belgium, Luxembourg, Switzerland, and Italy.

By 843, the European-wide empire of Charlemagne had dissolved. Forged by conquest, it had been supported by a small group of privileged aristocrats with lands and offices stretching across its entire expanse. Their loyalty—based on shared values, friendship, expectations of gain, and sometimes formal ties of vassalage and fealty (see page 282)—was crucial to the success of the Carolingians. The empire had also been supported by an ideal, shared by educated laymen and churchmen alike, of conquest and Christian belief working together to bring good order to the earthly state. But powerful forces operated against the Carolingian Empire. Once the empire's borders were fixed and conquests ceased, the aristocrats could not hope for new lands and offices. They put down roots in particular regions and began to gather their own followings. Powerful local traditions such as different languages also undermined imperial unity. Finally, as Dhuoda revealed, some people disagreed with the imperial ideal. By asking her son to put his father before the emperor, she demonstrated her belief in the primacy of the family and the personal ties that bound it together. Her ideal represented a new sensibility that saw real value in the breaking apart of Charlemagne's empire into smaller, more intimate local units.

Land and Power

The Carolingian economy, based on trade and agriculture, contributed to both the rise and the dissolution of the Carolingian Empire. At the onset, the empire's wealth came from land and plunder. After the booty from war ceased to pour in, the Carolingians still had access to money and goods. To the north, in Viking trading stations

---

Treaty of Verdun: The treaty that, in 843, split the Carolingian Empire into three parts; its borders roughly outline modern western European states.

such as Haithabu (today Hedeby, in northern Germany), archaeologists have found Carolingian glass and pots alongside Islamic coins and cloth, evidence that the Carolingian economy intermingled with that of the Abbasid caliphate. Silver from the Islamic world probably came north up the Volga River through Russia to the Baltic Sea. There the coins were melted down, the silver traded to the Carolingians in return for wine, jugs, glasses, and other manufactured goods. The Carolingians turned the silver into coins of their own, to be used throughout the empire for small-scale local trade. The weakening of the Abbasid caliphate in the mid-ninth century, however, disrupted this far-flung trade network and contributed to the weakening of the Carolingians at about the same time.

Land provided the most important source of Carolingian wealth and power. Like the landholders of the late Roman Empire and the Merovingian period, Carolingian aristocrats held many estates, scattered throughout the Frankish kingdoms. But in the Carolingian period, these estates were reorganized and their productivity carefully calculated. Modern historians often call these estates manors.

A typical manor was Villeneuve Saint-Georges, which belonged to the monastery of Saint-Germain-des-Prés (today in Paris) in the ninth century. Villeneuve consisted of arable fields, vineyards, meadows where animals could roam, and woodland, all scattered about the countryside rather than connected in a compact unit. The land was not tilled by slave gangs, as had been the custom on great estates of the Roman Empire, but by peasant families, each one settled on its own manse, which consisted of a house, a garden, and small sections of the arable land. The families farmed the land that belonged to them and also worked the demesne, the very large manse of the lord, in this case the abbey of Saint-Germain.

These peasant farms, cultivated by households, marked a major social and economic development. Slaves had not been allowed to live in family units. By contrast, the peasants of Villeneuve and on other Carolingian manors could not be separated involuntarily from their families or displaced from their manses. In this sense, the peasant household of the Carolingian period was the precursor of the modern nuclear family.

Peasants at Villeneuve practiced the most progressive sort of plowing, known as the three-field system, in which they farmed two-thirds of the arable land at one time. They planted one-third with winter wheat and one-third with summer crops, leaving the remaining third fallow to restore its fertility. The crops sown and the fallow field then rotated so that land use was repeated only every three years. This method of organizing the land produced larger yields (because two-thirds of the land was cultivated each year) than the still-prevalent two-field system, in which only half of the arable land was cultivated one year, while the other half lay fallow.

All the peasants at Villeneuve were dependents of the monastery and owed dues and services to Saint-Germain. Their obligations varied enormously. One family, for example, owed four silver coins, wine, wood, three hens, and fifteen eggs every year, and the men had to plow the fields of the demesne land. Another family owed the intensive labor of working the vineyards. One woman was required to weave cloth and feed the chickens. Peasant women spent much time at the lord's house in the *gynaeceum* — the women's workshop, where they made and dyed cloth and sewed garments — or in the kitchens, as cooks. Peasant men spent most of their time in the fields.

Manors organized on the model of Villeneuve were profitable. Like other lords, the Carolingians benefited from their extensive manors. Nevertheless, farming was still too primitive to return great surpluses, and as the lands belonging to the king were divided up in the wake of the partitioning of the empire and new invasions, Carolingian dependence on manors scattered throughout their kingdom proved to be a source of weakness.

Viking, Muslim, and Magyar Invasions, c. 790–955

Carolingian kings and counts confronted new groups — Vikings, Muslims, and Magyars — along their borders (Map 9.4). As royal sons fought one another and as counts and other powerful men sought to carve out their own principalities, some allied with the newcomers, helping to integrate them swiftly into European politics.

Vikings. About the same time as they made their forays into Russia, the Vikings moved westward as well. The Franks called them Northmen; the English called them Danes. They were, in fact, much less united than their victims thought. When they began their voyages at the end of the eighth century, they did so in independent bands. Merchants and pirates at the same time, Vikings followed a chief, seeking profit, prestige, and land. Many traveled as families: husbands, wives, children, and slaves.

The Vikings perfected the art of navigation. They crossed the Atlantic in their longships, not only settling Iceland and Greenland but also (in about the year 1000) landing on the coast of North

America. Other Viking bands navigated the rivers of Europe. The Vikings were pagans, and to them monasteries and churches—with their reliquaries, chalices, and crosses—were simply storehouses of booty.

Parts of the British Isles were especially hard hit. In England, for example, the Vikings raided regularly in the 830s and 840s; by midcentury, they were spending winters there. The Vikings did not just destroy. In 876, they settled in the northeast of England, plowing the land and preparing to live on it. The region where they settled and imposed their own laws was later called the Danelaw. (See England in the Age of King Alfred, page 288.)

In Wessex, the southernmost kingdom of England, King Alfred the Great (r. 871–899) bought time and peace by paying tribute and giving hostages. Such tribute, later called *Danegeld*, eventually became the basis of a relatively lucrative taxation system in England. In 878, Alfred led an army that, as his biographer put it, "gained the victory through God's will. He destroyed the Vikings with great slaughter and pursued those who fled . . . hacking them down." Thereafter, the pressures of invasion eased as Alfred reorganized his army, set up strongholds, and deployed new warships.

On the continent, too, Viking invaders set up trading stations and settled where originally they had raided. Beginning about 850, their attacks became well-organized expeditions for regional control. At the end of the ninth century, one contingent settled in the region of France that soon took the name Normandy, the land of the Northmen. The new inhabitants converted to Christianity during the tenth century. Rollo, the Viking leader in Normandy, accepted Christianity in 911; at the same time, Normandy was formally ceded to him by the Frankish king Charles the Simple.

Normandy was not the only new Christian polity created in the north during the tenth and eleventh centuries. Scandinavia itself was transformed with the creation of the powerful kingdom of Denmark. There had been kings in Scandinavia before the tenth century, but they had been weak, their power challenged by nearby chieftains. The Vikings had been led by these chieftains, each competing for booty to win prestige, land, and power back home. During the course of their raids, they and their followers came into contact with new cultures and learned from them. Meanwhile the Carolingians and the English supported missionaries in Scandinavia. By the middle of the tenth century, the Danish kings and their people had become Christian. Following the model of the Christian kings to their south, they built up an effective monarchy, with a royal mint and local agents who depended on them. By about 1000, the Danes had extended their control to parts of Sweden, Norway, and even England under King Cnut (also spelled Canute) (r. 1017–1035).

Muslims. The dynasty that preceded the Fatimids in Egypt developed a navy that, over the ninth and tenth centuries, gradually conquered Sicily, which had been under Byzantine rule. By the middle of the tenth century, independent Islamic princes ruled all of Sicily. Around the same time, other raiders from North Africa set up bases on other Mediterranean islands, while pirates from al-Andalus built a stronghold in Provence (in southern France). Liutprand of Cremona was outraged:

> [Muslim pirates from al-Andalus], disembarking under cover of night, entered the manor house unobserved and murdered—O grievous tale!—the Christian inhabitants. They then took the place as their own. . . [fortified it and] started stealthy raids on all the neighboring country. . . . Meanwhile the people of Provence close by, swayed by envy and mutual jealousy, began to cut one another's throats, plunder each other's substance, and do every sort of conceivable mischief. . . . [Furthermore, they called upon the Muslims] and in company with them proceeded to crush their neighbors.

In this way the Muslims, although outsiders, were drawn into local Provençal disputes.

Magyars. The Magyars, a nomadic people from the Urals (today northeastern Russia) who spoke a language unrelated to any other in Europe

Viking Picture Stone
Picture stones—some elaborate, others with simple incisions—were made on the island of Gotland, today part of Sweden, from the fifth to the twelfth century. This one, dating from the eighth or ninth century, has four interrelated scenes. The bottom scene is a battle between people defending a farm and archers outside. The woman in the enclosure above is either Gudrun mourning her brother Gunnar, who was thrown into a snake pit, or Sigyn, the faithful wife of the god Loke, catching in a bowl the venom that a snake pours down on her chained husband. The ship in the next scene is the ship of death that takes heroes to heaven. At the very top is heaven—Valhalla, where the heroes hunt and feast for all eternity. (*Photo: Raymond Hejdstrom.*)

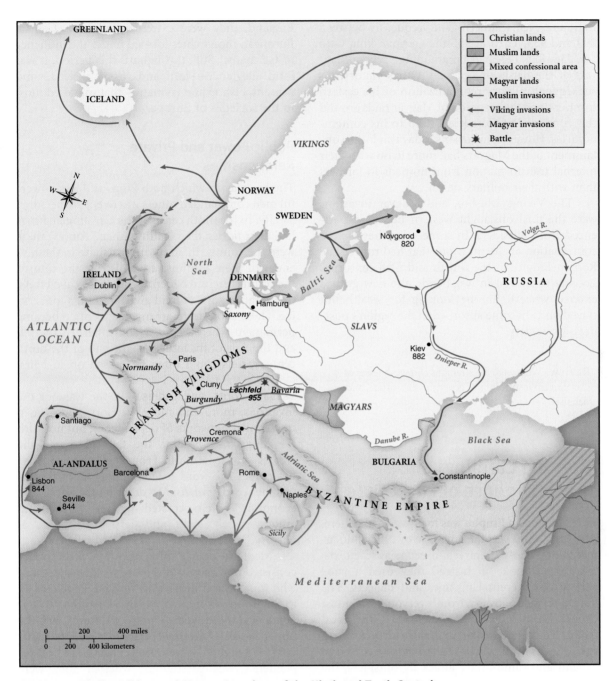

MAP 9.4 Muslim, Viking, and Magyar Invasions of the Ninth and Tenth Centuries
Bristling with multicolored arrows, this map suggests that western Europe was continually and
thoroughly pillaged by outside invaders for almost two centuries. That impression is only partially
true; it must be offset by several factors. First, not all the invaders came at once. The Viking raids
were nearly over when the Magyar attacks began. Second, the invaders were not entirely unwelcome.
The Magyars were for a time enlisted as mercenaries by an Italian ruler, and some Muslims were
allied to local lords in Provence. Third, the invasions, though widespread, were local in effect.
Note, for example, that the Viking raids were largely limited to rivers or coastal areas.
■ Why might the Vikings have raided primarily along these areas?

(except Finnish), arrived around 899 in the
Danube basin, a region that until then had been
predominantly Slavic. The Magyars drove a wedge
between the Slavs near the Frankish kingdom and
those bordering on Byzantium; the Bulgarians,

Serbs, and Russians were driven into the Byzantine orbit, while the Slavs nearer the Frankish kingdom came under the influence of Germany.

From their bases in present-day Hungary, the
Magyars raided far to the west, attacking Germany,

Italy, and even southern Gaul frequently between 899 and 955. Then in 955 the German king Otto I (r. 936–973) defeated a marauding party of Magyars at the battle of Lechfeld. Otto's victory, his subsequent military reorganization of his eastern frontiers, and the cessation of Magyar raids around this time made Otto a great hero to his contemporaries. However, historians today think the containment of the Magyars had more to do with their internal transformation from nomads to farmers than with their military defeat.

The Viking, Muslim, and Magyar invasions were the final onslaught western Europe experienced from outsiders. In some ways they were a continuation of the invasions that had rocked the Roman Empire in the fourth and fifth centuries. Loosely organized in war bands, the new groups entered western Europe looking for wealth but stayed on to become absorbed in the region's post-invasion society.

> **REVIEW:** What were the strengths and weaknesses of Carolingian institutions of government, warfare, and defense?

After the Carolingians: The Emergence of Local Rule

The Carolingian Empire was too diverse to cohere. Although Latin was the language of official documents and most literary and ecclesiastical texts, few people spoke it; instead they used a wide variety of different languages and dialects. The king demanded loyalty from everyone, but most people knew only his representative, the local count. The king's power ultimately depended on the count's allegiance, but as the empire ceased to expand and came under attack by outsiders, the counts and other powerful men stopped looking to the king for new lands and offices and began to develop and exploit what they already had. Commanding allegiance from vassals, controlling the local peasantry, building castles, setting up markets, collecting revenues, and keeping the peace, they regarded themselves as independent regional rulers. In this way, a new warrior class of lords and vassals came to dominate post-Carolingian society.

Not all of Europe, however, came under the control of rural leaders. In northern and central Italy, where cities had never lost their importance, urban elites ruled over the surrounding countryside. Everywhere kings retained a certain amount of power; in some places, such as Germany and

England, they were extremely effective. Central European monarchies formed under the influence of Germany.[1] Still, throughout this period, it was local allegiance—lord and vassal, castellan and peasant, bishop and layman—that mattered most to the societies of Europe.

Public Power and Private Relationships

The key way in which both kings and less powerful men commanded others was to ensure personal loyalty. In the ninth century, the Carolingian kings had their *fideles*, their "faithful men." Among these were the counts. In addition to a share in the revenues of their administrative district, the county, the counts received benefices, later also called **fiefs**, temporary grants of land given in return for service. These short-term arrangements often became permanent when a count's son inherited the job and the fiefs of his father. By the end of the ninth century, fiefs could often be passed on to heirs.

Vassals, Lords, and Ladies. In the wake of the invasions, more and more warriors were drawn into similar networks of dependency, but not with the king: they became the faithful men—the vassals—of local lords. From the Latin word for fief comes the word *feudal*, and some historians use the word *feudalism* to describe the social and economic system created by the relationship among vassals, lords, and fiefs. (See "Terms of History," page 283.)

Medieval people often said that their society consisted of three groups: those who prayed, those who fought, and those who worked. People of all these groups were involved in a hierarchy of dependency and linked by personal bonds, but the upper classes—the prayers (monks) and the fighters (the knights)—were free. Their brand of dependency was prestigious, whether they were vassals, lords, or both. In fact, a typical warrior was lord of several vassals even while serving as the vassal of another lord. Monasteries normally had vassals to fight for them, and their abbots in turn were often vassals of a king or other powerful lord.

Vassalage served both as an alternative to public power and as a way to strengthen what little

---

[1]Terms such as *Germany*, *France*, and *Italy* are used here for the sake of convenience. They refer to regions, not to the nation-states that would eventually become associated with those names.

---

fiefs: Grants of land, theoretically temporary, from lords to their noble dependents (*fideles* or, later, vassals) given in recognition of services, usually military, done or expected in the future; also called *benefices*.

public power there was. Given the impoverished economic conditions of western Europe, its primitive methods of communication, and its lack of unifying traditions, kings relied on vassals personally loyal to them to muster troops, collect taxes, and administer justice. When in the ninth century the Carolingian Empire broke up politically and power fell into the hands of local lords, those lords, too, needed "faithful men" to protect them and carry out their orders. And vassals needed lords. At the low end of the social scale, poor vassals depended on their lords to feed, clothe, house, and arm them. They hoped that they would be rewarded for their service with a fief of their own, with which they could support themselves and a family. At the upper end of the social scale, vassals looked to lords to give them still more land.

Many upper-class laywomen participated in the society of fighters and prayers as wives and mothers of vassals and lords. A few women were themselves vassals, and some were lords (or, rather, ladies, the female counterpart). Other women entered convents and became members of the social group that prayed. Through its abbess or a man standing in for her, a convent often had vassals as well. Many elite women engaged in property transactions, whether alone, with other family members, or as part of a group, such as a convent. (See "Taking Measure," page 284).

Becoming a vassal often involved both ritual gestures and verbal promises. In a ceremony witnessed by others, the vassal-to-be knelt and, placing his hands between the hands of his lord, said, "I promise to be your man." This act, known as homage, was followed by the promise of fealty—fidelity, trust, and service—which the vassal swore with his hand on relics or a Bible. Then the vassal and the lord kissed. In an age when many people could not read, a public ceremony such as this represented a visual and verbal contract. Vassalage bound the lord and vassal to one another with reciprocal obligations, usually military. Knights, as the premier fighters of the day, were the most desirable vassals.

Lords and Peasants. At the bottom of the social scale were those who worked—the peasants. In the Carolingian period, many peasants were free; they did not live on a manor or, if they did, they owed very little to its lord. But as power fell into the hands of local rulers, fewer and fewer peasants remained free. Rather, they were made dependent on lords, not as vassals but as serfs. A serf's dependency was completely unlike that of a vassal. Serfdom was not voluntary but rather inherited. No serf did homage or fealty to his lord; no serf

TERMS OF HISTORY

Feudalism

Feudalism is a modern word, like *capitalism* and *communism*. No one in the Middle Ages used it, or any of its related terms, such as *feudal system* or *feudal society*. Many historians today think that it is a misleading word and should be discarded. The term poses two serious problems. First, historians have used it to mean different things. Second, it implies that one way of life dominated the Middle Ages, when in fact social, political, and economic arrangements varied widely.

Consider the many different meanings that *feudalism* has had. Historians influenced by Karl Marx's powerful communist theory used (and still use) the word *feudalism* to refer to an economic system in which nobles dominated subservient peasant cultivators. When they speak of feudalism, they are speaking of manors, lords, and serfs. Other historians, however, call that system *manorialism*. They reserve the word *feudalism* for a system consisting of vassals (who never did agricultural labor but only military service), lords, and fiefs. For example, in an influential book written in the mid-1940s, *Feudalism*, F. L. Ganshof considered the tenth to the thirteenth centuries to be the "classical age of feudalism" because during this period lords regularly granted fiefs to their vassals, who fought on their lord's behalf in return.

But, writing around the same time as Ganshof, Marc Bloch included in his definition of feudalism every aspect of the political and social life of the Middle Ages, including peasants, fiefs, knights, vassals, the fragmentation of royal authority, and even the survival of the state.

Today many historians argue that talking about feudalism distorts the realities of medieval life. The fief—whose Latin form, *feodum*, gave rise to the word *feudalism*—was by no means important everywhere. And even where it was important, it did not necessarily have anything to do with lords, vassals, or military obligations. For such historians, feudalism is a myth.

kissed his lord as an equal. Vassals served their lords as warriors. Serfs worked as laborers on their lord's land and paid taxes and dues to their lord. Peasants constituted the majority of the population, but unlike knights, who were celebrated in song, they were barely noticed by the upper classes—except as a source of revenue. While there were still free peasants who could lease land or till their own soil without paying dues to a lord, serfs—who could not be kicked off their land but who were also not free to leave it—became the norm.

New methods of cultivation and a slightly warmer climate helped transform the rural landscape, making it more productive and thus able to

TAKING MEASURE

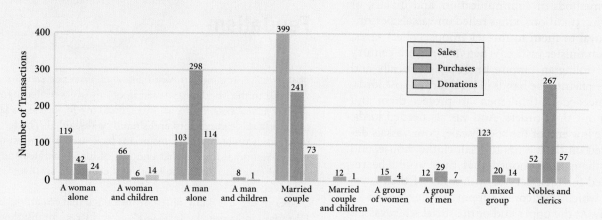

Sellers, Buyers, and Donors, 800–1000

How did ladies get their wealth, and what did they do with it? Two counties in northeastern Spain, Osona and Manresa, are particularly rich in documentation for the period 880–1000. We have 2,121 charters (legal documents) attesting to sales, purchases, and donations of land from this period. As the graph shows, few women purchased property, which suggests that they gained their lands mainly through inheritance. As for what they did with it: by themselves they were more likely to sell property than men alone, and as part of a married couple, they were often involved in sales. They were less likely than men to make donations, many of which went to churches or monasteries. *(From Lluís to Figueras, "Dot et douaire dans la société rurale de Catalogne," in* Dots et douaires dans le haut moyen âge, *ed. F. Bougard, L. Feller, and R. Le Jan (École française de Rome, 2002), 193, Table 1.)*

support a larger population. Along with a growing number of men and women to work the land, however, population increase meant more mouths to feed and the threat of food shortages. Landlords began reorganizing their estates to run more efficiently. In the tenth century, the three-field system became more prevalent; heavy plows that could turn the heavy northern soils came into wider use; and horses (more effective than oxen) were harnessed to pull the plows. The result was surplus food and a better standard of living for nearly everyone.

In search of greater profits, some lords lightened the dues and services of peasants to allow them to open up new lands by draining marshes and cutting down forests. Some landlords converted dues and labor services into money payments, a boon for both lords and peasants. Rather than receiving hens and eggs they might not need, lords now received money to spend on what they wanted. Peasants benefited because their dues were fixed despite inflation. Thus, as the prices of their hens and eggs went up, they could sell them, reaping a profit in spite of the payments they owed their lords.

By the tenth century, many peasants lived in populous rural settlements, true villages. Surrounded by arable land, meadow, wood, and wasteland, villages developed a sense of community. Boundaries—sometimes real fortifications, sometimes simple markers—told nonresidents to keep out and to find shelter in huts located outside the village limits.

The church often formed the focal point of village activity. There people met, received the sacraments, drew up contracts, and buried their dead. Religious feasts and festivals joined the rituals of farming to mark the seasons. The church dominated the village in another way: men and women owed it a tax called a tithe (equivalent to one-tenth of their crops or income, paid in money or in kind), which was first instituted on a regular basis by the Carolingians.

Village peasants developed a sense of common purpose based on their interdependence, as they shared oxen or horses for the teams that pulled the plow or turned to village craftsmen to fix their wheels or shoe their horses. A sense of solidarity sometimes encouraged people to band together to ask for privileges as a group. Near Verona, in northern Italy, for example, twenty-five men living around the castle of Nogara joined together in 920 to ask their lord, the abbot of Nonantola, to allow them to lease plots of land, houses, and pasturage there in return for a small yearly rent and the promise to defend the castle. The abbot granted their request.

Village solidarity could be compromised, however, by conflicting loyalties and obligations. A peasant in one village might very well have one piece of land connected with a certain manor and another bit of arable field on a different estate; and he or she might owe several lords different kinds of dues. Even peasants of one village working for one lord might owe him varied services and taxes.

Obligations differed even more strikingly across the regions of Europe than within particular villages. The principal distinction was between free peasants—such as small landowners in Saxony and other parts of Germany, who had no lords—and serfs, who were especially common in France and England. In Italy, peasants ranged from small independent landowners to leaseholders (like the tenants at Nogara); most were both, owning a parcel in one place and leasing another nearby.

As the power of kings weakened, the system of peasant obligations became part of a larger system of local rule. When landlords consolidated their power over their manors, they collected not only dues and services but also fees for the use of their flour mills, bake houses, and breweries. Some built castles, fortified strongholds, and imposed the even wider powers of the ban: the rights to collect taxes, hear court cases, levy fines, and muster men for defense.

In France, for example, as the king's power waned, political control fell into the hands of counts and other princes. By 1000, castles had become the key to their power. In the south of France, power was so fragmented that each man who controlled a castle—a **castellan**—was a virtual ruler, although often with a very limited reach. In northwestern France, territorial princes, basing their rule on the control of *many* castles, dominated much broader regions. For example, Fulk Nera, count of Anjou (987–1040), built more than thirteen castles and captured others from rival counts. By the end of his life, he controlled a region extending from Blois to Nantes along the Loire valley.

Castellans extended their authority by subjecting everyone near their castle to their ban. Peasants, whether or not they worked on his estates, had to pay the castellan a variety of dues for his "protection" and judicial rights over them. Castellans also established links with wealthy landholders in the region, tempting or coercing them to become vassals. Lay castellans often supported local monasteries and controlled the appointment of local priests. But churchmen themselves sometimes held the position of territorial lord, as did, for example, the archbishop of Milan in the eleventh century.

The development of virtually independent local political units, dominated by a castle and controlled by a military elite, marks an important turning point in western Europe. Although this development did not occur everywhere simultaneously (and in some places it hardly occurred at all), the social, political, and cultural life of Europe was now dominated by landowners who saw themselves as military men and regional leaders.

Warriors and Warfare

Not all warriors were alike. At the top of this elite group were the kings, counts, and dukes. Below them, but on the rise, were the castellans; and still further down the social scale were ordinary knights. Yet all shared in a common lifestyle.

Knights and their lords fought on horseback. High astride his steed, wearing a shirt of chain mail and a helmet of flat metal plates riveted together, the knight marked a military revolution. The war season started in May, when the grasses were high enough for horses to forage. Horseshoes allowed armies to move faster than ever before and to negotiate rough terrain previously unsuitable for battle. Stirrups, probably invented by nomadic Asiatic tribes, allowed the mounted warrior to hold his seat and thrust at the enemy with heavy lances. The light javelin of ancient Roman warfare was abandoned.

Lords and their vassals often lived together. In the lord's great hall they ate, listened to entertainment, and bedded down for the night. They went out hunting together, competed with one another in military games, and went off to the battlefield as a group. Some powerful vassals—counts, for example—lived on their own fiefs. They hardly ever saw their lord (probably the king), except when doing homage and fealty—once in their lifetime—or serving him in battles, for perhaps forty days a year (as was the custom in eleventh-century France). But they themselves were lords of knightly vassals who were not married and who lived and ate and hunted with them.

---

castellan (KAS tuh luhn): The holder of a castle. In the tenth and eleventh centuries, castellans became important local lords, taking over the rights of the ban (to call up men to military service, to collect taxes, or to administer justice).

Two Cities Besieged
In about 900, the monks of the monastery of St. Gall produced a Psalter with numerous illuminations. The illustration for Psalm 59, which tells of King David's victories, used four pages. This page was the fourth. On the top level, David's army besieges a fortified city from two directions. On the right are foot soldiers, one of whom holds a burning torch to set the city afire; on the left are horsemen—led by their standard-bearer—with lances and bows and arrows. Within the city, four soldiers protect themselves with shields, while four other men seem to be cowering behind the city. In the bottom register, a different city burns fiercely (note the towers on fire). This city lacks defenders; the people within it are unarmed. Although this illumination purports to show David's victories, in fact it nicely represents the equipment and strategies of ninth-century warfare. *(Stiftsbibliothek St. Gallen, Switzerland.)*

mid-ninth century, Count Everard and his wife, for example, willed their large estates, scattered from Belgium to Italy, to their four sons and three daughters (although they gave the boys far more than the girls, and the oldest boy far more than the others).

By 1000, however, adapting to diminished opportunities for land and office and wary of fragmenting the estates they had, French nobles changed both their conception of their family and the way property passed to the next generation. Recognizing the overriding claims of one son, often the eldest, they handed down their entire inheritance to him. (The system of inheritance in which the heir is the eldest son is called primogeniture.) The heir, in turn, traced his lineage only through the male line, backward through his father and forward through his own eldest son. Such patrilineal families left many younger sons without an inheritance and therefore without the prospect of marrying and founding a family; instead, the younger sons lived at the courts of the great as youths, or they joined the church as clerics or monks. The development of territorial rule and patrilineal families went hand in hand, as fathers passed down to one son not only manors but also titles, castles, and the authority of the ban.

Patrilineal inheritance tended to bypass daughters and so worked against aristocratic women, who lost the power that came with inherited wealth. In families without sons, however, widows and daughters did inherit property. And wives often acted as lords of estates when their husbands were at war. Moreover, all aristocratic women played an important role in this warrior society, whether in the monastery (where they prayed for the souls of their families) or through their marriages (where they produced children and helped forge alliances between their own natal families and the families of their husbands).

Efforts to Contain Violence

Warfare benefited territorial rulers in the short term, but in the long run their revenues suffered as armies plundered the countryside and sacked walled cities. (See Two Cities Besieged on this page.) Bishops, members of the class of lords and warriors, worried about the dangers to church property. Peasants cried out against wars that destroyed their crops or forced them to join regional infantries. Monks and religious thinkers were appalled at violence that was not in the service of an anointed king. By the end of the tenth century, all classes clamored for peace.

No matter how old they might be, unmarried knights who lived with their lords were called youths by their contemporaries. Such perpetual bachelors were something new, the result of a profound transformation in the organization of families and inheritance. Before about 1000, noble families had recognized all their children as heirs and had divided their estates accordingly. In the

Sentiment against local violence was united in a movement called the **Peace of God**, which began in the south of France around 990 and by 1050 had spread over a wide region. Meetings of bishops, counts, and lords and often crowds of lower-class men and women set forth the provisions of this peace, which prohibited certain acts of violence: "No man in the counties or bishoprics shall seize a horse, colt, ox, cow, ass, or the burdens which it carries. . . . No one shall seize a peasant, man or woman," ran the decree of one early council. Anyone who violated this peace was to be excommunicated: cut off from the community of the faithful, denied the services of the church and the hope of salvation.

The peace proclaimed at local councils like this limited some violence but did not address the problem of conflict between armed men. A second set of agreements, the Truce of God, soon supplemented the Peace of God. The truce prohibited fighting between warriors at certain times: on Sunday because it was the Lord's day, on Saturday because it was a reminder of Holy Saturday, on Friday because it symbolized Good Friday, and on Thursday because it stood for Holy Thursday. Enforcement of the truce fell to the local knights and nobles, who swore over saints' relics to uphold it and to fight anyone who broke it.

The Peace of God and Truce of God were only two of the mechanisms that attempted to contain or defuse violent confrontations in the tenth and eleventh centuries. At times, lords and their vassals mediated wars and feuds at grand judicial assemblies. In other instances, monks or laymen tried to find solutions to disputes that would leave the honor of both parties intact. Rather than establishing guilt or innocence, winners or losers, these methods of adjudication often resulted in compromises on both sides.

Political Communities in Italy, England, and France

The political systems that emerged following the breakup of the Carolingian Empire were as varied as the regions of Europe. In northern and central Italy, cities were the centers of power, still reflecting, if feebly, the political organization of ancient Rome. In England, strong kings came to the fore. In France, where the king was relatively weak, great lords dominated the countryside.

Urban Power in Northern and Central Italy. Unlike their counterparts in France, where great landlords built their castles in the countryside, Italian elites tended to construct their family castles within the walls of cities such as Milan and Lucca. Also built within the city walls were churches, as many as fifty or sixty, the proud work of rich laymen and laywomen or of bishops. From their perch within the cities, the great landholders, both lay and religious, dominated the countryside.

Italian cities also served as marketplaces where peasants sold their surplus goods, artisans and merchants lived within the walls, and foreign traders offered their wares. These members of the lower classes were supported by the wealthy elite, who depended, here more than elsewhere, on cash to satisfy their desires. In the course of the ninth and tenth centuries, the peasants in the countryside became renters who paid in currency, helping to satisfy their landlords' need for cash.

Family organization in Italy was quite different from that of the patrilineal families of France. To stave off the partitioning of their properties among heirs, Italian families became a kind of economic corporation in which all male members shared the profits of the family's inheritance and all women were excluded. In the coming centuries, this successful model would also serve as the foundation of most early Italian businesses and banks.

Alfred and His Successors: Kings of All the English. Whereas much of Italy was urban, most of England was rural. Having successfully repelled the Viking invaders, **Alfred the Great**, king of Wessex (r. 871–899), developed new mechanisms of royal government, instituting reforms that his successors continued. He fortified settlements throughout Wessex and divided the army into two parts, one with the duty of defending these fortifications, the other operating as a mobile unit. Alfred also started a navy. The money to pay for these military innovations came from assessments on peasants' holdings.

Alfred sought to strengthen his kingdom's religious integrity as well as its regional fortifications. In the ninth century, people interpreted invasions as God's punishment for sin. Hence, Alfred began a program of religious reform by bringing scholars to his court to write and to educate others. Above all, Alfred wanted to translate

---

Peace of God: A movement begun by bishops in the south of France around 990, first to limit the violence done to property and to the unarmed, and later, with the Truce of God, to limit fighting between warriors.

Alfred the Great: King of Wessex (r. 871–899) and the first king to rule over most of England. He organized a successful defense against Viking invaders, had key Latin works translated into the vernacular, and wrote a law code for the whole of England.

key religious works from Latin into Anglo-Saxon (or Old English). He was determined to "turn into the language that we can all understand certain books which are the most necessary for all men to know." Alfred and scholars under his guidance translated works by church fathers such as Gregory the Great and St. Augustine. Even the Psalms, until now sung only in Hebrew, Greek, and Latin, were rendered into Anglo-Saxon. In most of ninth- and tenth-century Europe, Latin remained the language of scholarship, government, and writing, separate from the language people spoke. In England, however, the vernacular—the common spoken language—was also a literary language. With Alfred's reign giving it greater legitimacy, Anglo-Saxon came to be used alongside Latin for both literature and royal administration.

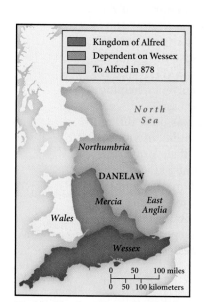

England in the Age of King Alfred, 871–899

Alfred's reforms strengthened not only defense, education, and religion but also royal power. He consolidated his control over Wessex and fought the Danish kings, who by the mid-870s had taken Northumbria, northeastern Mercia, and East Anglia. Eventually, as he successfully fought the Danes who were pushing south and westward, he was recognized as king of all the English not under Danish rule. He issued a law code, the first by an English king since 695. Unlike earlier codes, which had been drawn up for each separate kingdom of England, Alfred drew his laws from and for all of the English kingdoms. In this way, Alfred became the first king of all the English.

Alfred's successors rolled back the Danish rule in England. "Then the Norsemen departed in their nailed ships, bloodstained survivors of spears," wrote one poet about a battle the Vikings lost in 937. But many Vikings remained. Converted to Christianity, their great men joined Anglo-Saxons in attending the English king at court. As peace returned, new administrative subdivisions for judicial and tax purposes were established throughout England: shires (a bit like counties) and hundreds (smaller units). The powerful men of the kingdom swore fealty to the king, promising to be enemies of his enemies, friends of his friends. England was united and organized to support a strong ruler.

Alfred's grandson Edgar (r. 957–975) commanded all the possibilities early medieval king-

ship offered. He was the sworn lord of all the great men of the kingdom. He controlled appointments to the English church and sponsored monastic reform. In 973, following the continental fashion, he was anointed king. The fortifications of the kingdom were in his hands, as was the army, and he took responsibility for keeping the peace by proclaiming certain crimes—arson and theft—to be under his special jurisdiction and by mobilizing the machinery of the shire and the hundred to find and punish thieves.

Despite its apparent centralization, England was not a unified state in the modern sense, and the king's control was often tenuous. Many royal officials were great landowners who (as on the continent) worked for the king because it was in their best interest. When it was not, they allied with different claimants to the throne. This political fragility may have helped the Danish king Cnut to conquer England. King there from 1017 to 1035, Cnut reinforced the already strong connections between England and Scandinavia while keeping intact much of the administrative, ecclesiastical, and military apparatus already established in England by the Anglo-Saxons. By Cnut's time, Scandinavian traditions had largely merged with those of the rest of Europe and the Vikings were no longer an alien culture.

Capetian Kings of Franks: Weak but Prestigious.

French kings had a harder time than the English coping with invasions because their realm was much larger. They had no chance to build up their defenses slowly from one powerful base. During most of the tenth century, Carolingian kings alternated on the throne with kings from a family that would later be called the Capetian. As the Carolingian dynasty waned, the most powerful men of the kingdom—dukes, counts, and important bishops—came together to elect as king Hugh Capet (r. 987–996), a lord of great prestige yet relatively little power. His choice marked the end of Carolingian rule and the beginning of the new **Capetian dynasty** that would hand down the royal title from father to son until the fourteenth century.

In the eleventh century, territorial lordships limited the reach of the Capetian kings. The king's scattered but substantial estates lay in the north of France, in the region around Paris—the Île-de-France (literally, "island of France"). His castles and his vassals were there. Independent castellans, however, controlled areas nearby. In the sense that

---

Capetian (kuh PAY shuhn) **dynasty:** A long-lasting dynasty of French kings, taking their name from Hugh Capet (r. 987–996).

he was a neighbor of castellans and not much more powerful militarily than they, the king of the Franks—who would only later take the territorial title of king of France—was just another local leader. Yet the Capetian kings had considerable prestige. They were anointed with holy oil, and they represented the idea of unity inherited from Charlemagne. Most of the counts, at least in the north of France, became their vassals. They did not promise to obey the king, but they did vow not to try to kill or depose him.

The Kingdom of the Franks under Hugh Capet, 987–996

Emperors and Kings in Central and Eastern Europe

In contrast with the development of territorial lordships in France, Germany's fragmentation had hardly begun before it was reversed. The **Ottonian kings** of Germany consolidated their rule there; took the title emperor; and then, hand in hand with the papacy, fostered the emergence of new Christian monarchies. Aligned with the Roman church, these new kingdoms were the ancestors of today's Czech and Slovak Republics, Poland, and Hungary.

Ottonian Power in Germany. Five duchies (regions dominated by dukes) emerged in Germany in the late Carolingian period, each much larger than the counties and castellanies of France. When Louis the Child, the last Carolingian king in Germany, died in 911, the dukes elected one of themselves as king. Then, as the Magyar invasions increased, the dukes gave the royal title to the duke of Saxony, Henry I (r. 919–936), who proceeded to set up fortifications and reorganize his army, crowning his efforts with a major defeat of a Magyar army in 933.

Otto I (r. 936–973), the son of Henry I, was an even greater military hero. In 951, he marched into Italy and took the Lombard crown. His defeat of the Magyar forces in 955 at Lechfeld gave him prestige and helped solidify his dynasty. Against the Slavs, with whom the Germans shared a border, Otto created marches (border regions

specifically set up for defense) from which he could make expeditions and stave off counterattacks. After the pope crowned him emperor in 962, Otto claimed the Middle Kingdom carved out by the Treaty of Verdun and cast himself as the agent of Roman imperial renewal. His Kingdom became the Empire, as if it were the old Roman Empire revived.

Otto's victories brought tribute and plunder, ensuring him a following but also raising the German nobles' expectations for enrichment. He and his successors, Otto II (r. 973–983), Otto III (r. 983–1002)—for which reason the dynasty is called the Ottonian—and Henry II (r. 1002–1024), were not always able or willing to provide the gifts and inheritances their family members and followers expected. To maintain centralized rule, for example, the Ottonians did not divide their kingdom among their sons: like castellans in France, they created a patrilineal pattern of inheritance. But the consequence was that younger sons and other potential heirs felt cheated, and disgruntled royal kin led revolt after revolt against the Ottonian kings. The rebels found followers among the aristocracy, where the trend toward the patrilineal family prompted similar feuds and thwarted expectations.

Relations between the Ottonians and the German clergy were more harmonious.

The Ottonian Empire, 936–1002

With a ribbon of new bishoprics along his eastern border, Otto I appointed bishops, gave them extensive lands, and subjected the local peasantry to their overlordship. Like Charlemagne, Otto believed that the well-being of the church in his kingdom depended on him. The Ottonians placed the churches and many monasteries of Germany under their control. They gave bishops the powers of the ban, allowing them to collect revenues and call men to arms. Answering to the king and furnishing him with troops, the bishops became royal officials, while also carrying out their religious duties.

Ottonian (ah TOH nee uhn) **kings:** The tenth- and early-eleventh-century kings of Germany; beginning with Otto I (r. 936–973), they claimed the imperial crown and worked closely with their bishops to rule a vast territory.

Otto III Receiving Gifts
This triumphal image is in a book of Gospels made for Otto III (r. 983–1002). The crowned women on the left are personifications of the four parts of Otto's empire: Sclavinia (the Slavic lands), Germania (Germany), Gallia (Gaul), and Roma (Rome). Each offers a gift in tribute and homage to the emperor, who sits on a throne holding the symbols of his power (orb and scepter) and flanked by representatives of the church (on his right) and of the army (on his left). Why do you suppose the artist separated the image of the emperor from that of the women? What does the body language of the women indicate about the relations Otto wanted to portray between himself and the parts of his empire? Can you relate this manuscript, which was made in 997–1000, to Otto's conquest over the Slavs in 997? (Bayerische Staatsbibliothek, Munich.)

German kings claimed the right to select bishops, even the pope at Rome, and to "invest" them by participating in the ceremony that installed them in office. The higher clergy joined royal court society. Most came to the court to be schooled; in turn, they taught the kings, princes, and noblewomen there.

Like all the strong rulers of the day, whether in Europe or in the Byzantine and Islamic worlds, the Ottonians presided over a renaissance of learning. For example, the tutor of Otto III was Gerbert, the best-educated man of his time. Placed on the papal throne as Pope Sylvester II (r. 999–1003), Gerbert knew how to use the abacus and to calculate with Arabic numerals. He spent "large sums of money to pay copyists and to acquire copies of authors," as he put it. He studied the Latin classics as models of rhetoric and argument, and he reveled in logic and debate. Not only did churchmen and kings support Ottonian scholarship, but to an

unprecedented extent noblewomen in Germany also acquired an education and participated in the intellectual revival. Aristocratic women spent much of their wealth on learning. Living at home with their kinfolk and servants or in convents that provided them with comfortable private apartments, noblewomen wrote books and occasionally even Roman-style plays. They also supported other artists and scholars.

Despite their military and political strength, the kings of Germany faced resistance from dukes and other powerful princes, who hoped to become regional rulers themselves. The Salians, the dynasty that succeeded the Ottonians, tried to balance the power among the German dukes but could not meld them into a corps of vassals the way the Capetian kings tamed their counts. In Germany, vassalage was considered beneath the dignity of free men. Instead of relying on vassals, the Salian kings and their bishops used ministerials (specially designated men who were legally serfs) to collect taxes, administer justice, and fight on horseback. Ministerials retained their servile status even though they often rose to wealth and high position. Under the Salian kings, ministerials became the mainstay of the royal army and administration.

Supported by their prestige, their churchmen, and their ministerials, the German kings expanded their influence eastward, into the region from the Elbe River to Russia. Otto I was so serious about expansion that he created an extraordinary "elastic" archbishopric: it had no eastern boundary, so it could extend as far as future conquests and conversions to Christianity would allow.

The Emergence of Catholic Bohemia, Poland, and Hungary.

Hand in hand with the popes, German kings insisted on the creation of new, Catholic polities along their eastern frontier. The Czechs, who lived in the region of Bohemia, converted under the rule of Václav (r. 920–929), who thereby gained recognition in Germany as the duke of Bohemia. He and his successors did not become kings, remaining politically within the German sphere. Václav's murder by his younger brother made him a martyr and the patron saint of Bohemia, a symbol around which later movements for independence rallied.

The Poles gained a greater measure of independence than the Czechs. In 966, Mieszko I (r. 963–992), the leader of the Slavic tribe known as the Polanians, accepted baptism to forestall the attack that the Germans were already mounting against pagan Slavic peoples along the Baltic coast and east of the Elbe River. Busily engaged in bringing the other Slavic tribes of Poland under his control, he adroitly shifted his alliances with various German princes to suit his needs. In 991, Mieszko placed his realm under the protection of the pope, establishing a tradition of Polish loyalty to the Roman church. Mieszko's son Boleslaw the Brave (r. 992–1025) greatly extended Poland's boundaries, at one time or another holding sway from the Bohemian border to Kiev. In 1000, he gained a royal crown with papal blessing.

Hungary's case was similar to that of Poland. The Magyars settled in the region known today as Hungary. They became landowners, using the native Slavs to till the soil and imposing their language. At the end of the tenth century, the Magyar ruler Stephen I (r. 997–1038) accepted Roman Christianity. In return, German knights and monks helped him consolidate his power and convert his people. According to legend, the crown placed on Stephen's head at his coronation (in late 1000 or early 1001) was sent to him by the pope. To this day, the crown of St. Stephen (Stephen was canonized in 1083) remains the most hallowed symbol of Hungarian nationhood.

Symbols of rulership such as crowns, consecrated by Christian priests and accorded a prestige almost akin to saints' relics, were among the most vital sources of royal power in central Europe. The economic basis for the power of central European rulers gradually shifted from slave raids to agriculture. This change encouraged a proliferation of regional centers of power that challenged monarchical rule. From the eleventh century onward, all the medieval Slavic realms faced the constant problem of internal division.

> **REVIEW:** After the dissolution of the Carolingian Empire, what political systems developed in western, northern, eastern, and central Europe, and how did these systems differ from one another?

Conclusion

In 800, the three heirs of the Roman Empire all appeared to be organized like their parent: centralized, monarchical, imperial. Byzantine emperors writing their learned books, Abbasid caliphs holding court in their new resplendent palace at Baghdad, and Carolingian emperors issuing their directives for reform all mimicked the Roman emperors. Yet leaders in all three realms confronted tensions and regional pressures that tended to put political power into the hands of local lords. Byzantium felt this fragmentation least, yet even there the emergence of a new elite, the *dynatoi*, led to the emperor's loss of control over the countryside. In the Islamic world, economic crisis, religious tension, and the ambitions of powerful local rulers decisively weakened the caliphate and opened the way to separate successor states. In Europe, powerful independent landowners strove with greater or lesser success (depending on the region) to establish themselves as effective rulers. By 1050, most of the states that are now in Europe — western, central, and eastern — had begun to form.

In western Europe, local conditions determined political and economic organizations. Between 900 and 1000, for example, French society was transformed by the development of territorial lordships, patrilineal families, and ties of vassalage. These factors figured less prominently in Germany, where a central monarchy remained,

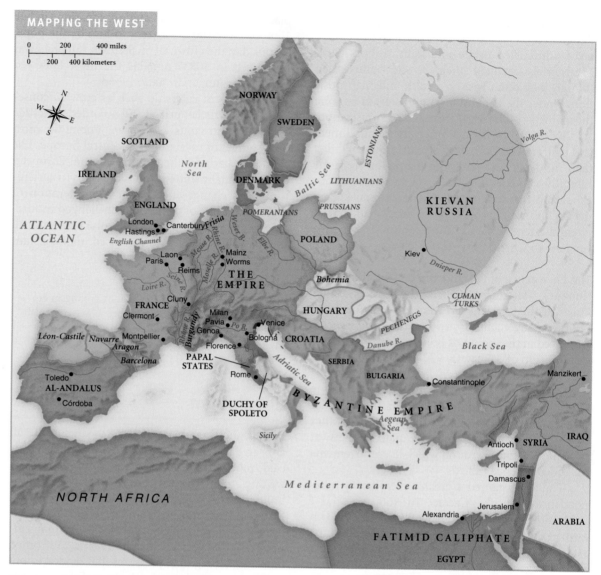

Europe and the Mediterranean, c. 1050
The Empire here refers to the area ruled by the Ottonian emperors. But the clear borders and distinct colors of the "states" on this map distort an essential truth: none of the areas shown had centralized governments that controlled whole territories, as in modern states. Instead, there were numerous regional rulers within each, and there were numerous overlapping claims of jurisdiction. The eleventh and twelfth centuries would show both the weaknesses and surprising strengths of this fragmentation.

buttressed by churchmen, ministerials, and conquests to the east.

After 1050, however, the German king would lose his supreme position as a storm of church reform whirled around him. The economy changed, becoming more commercial and urban, and the papacy would assert itself with new force in the life of Europe.

FOR FURTHER EXPLORATION

■ **For suggested references, including Web sites, for topics in this chapter,** see page SR-1 at the end of the book.

■ **For additional primary-source material from this period,** see Chapter 9 in *Sources of THE MAKING OF THE WEST,* Third Edition.

■ **For Web sites and documents related to topics in this chapter,** see *Make History* at bedfordstmartins.com/hunt.

CHAPTER REVIEW

KEY TERMS AND PEOPLE

dynatoi (266)

Basil II (267)

Abbasids (268)

Fatimids (270)

Carolingian (273)

Charlemagne (273)

Treaty of Verdun (278)

fiefs (282)

castellan (285)

Peace of God (287)

Alfred the Great (287)

Capetian dynasty (288)

Ottonian kings (289)

REVIEW QUESTIONS

1. What were the effects of expansion on the power of the Byzantine emperor?

2. What forces fragmented the Islamic world in the tenth and eleventh centuries?

3. What were the strengths and weaknesses of Carolingian institutions of government, warfare, and defense?

4. After the dissolution of the Carolingian Empire, what political systems developed in western, northern, eastern, and central Europe, and how did these systems differ from one another?

MAKING CONNECTIONS

1. How were the Byzantine, Islamic, and European economies similar? How did they differ? How did these economies interact?

2. How were the powers and ambitions of castellans similar to, and how were they different from, those of the dynatoi of Byzantium and of Muslim provincial rulers?

3. Compare the effects of the barbarian invasions into the Roman Empire with the effects of the Viking, Muslim, and Magyar invasions into Carolingian Europe.

> **For practice quizzes, a customized study plan, and other study tools,** see the Online Study Guide at bedfordstmartins.com/hunt.

IMPORTANT EVENTS

750–c. 950	The Abbasid caliphate		955	Battle of Lechfeld
751	Pippin III becomes king of the Franks, establishing Carolingian rule		962	King Otto I (r. 936–973) of Germany crowned emperor
768–814	Charlemagne rules as king of the Franks		987–996	Reign of King Hugh Capet of France
786–809	Caliphate of Harun al-Rashid		c. 990	Peace of God movement begins
800	Charlemagne crowned emperor at Rome		1000 or 1001	Stephen I (St. Stephen) (r. 997–1038) crowned king of Hungary
843	Treaty of Verdun		1001–1018	Byzantine conquest of Bulgaria
871–899	King Alfred of England			
929–1031	Caliphate of Córdoba			

Merchants and Kings, Popes and Crusaders
1050–1150

In the middle of the twelfth century, a sculptor was hired to add some friezes depicting scenes from the Old and New Testaments to the facade of the grand new hilltop cathedral at Lincoln, England. He portrayed in striking fashion the deaths of the poor man Lazarus and the rich man Dives. Their fates could not have been more different. While Lazarus was carried to heaven by two angels, a contented-looking devil poked Dives and two other rich men straight into the mouth of hell—headfirst.

The sculptor's work reflected a widespread change in attitudes toward money. In the Carolingian and post-Carolingian period, wealth was considered, in general, a very good thing. Rich kings were praised for their generosity, sumptuous manuscripts were highly prized, and splendid churches like Charlemagne's chapel at Aachen were widely admired. This view changed over the course of the eleventh century. A new money economy, burgeoning cities, and the growth of a well-heeled merchant and trading class led many observers to condemn wealth and to emphasize its corrupting influence. Even the participants in the new economy shared this perspective: Lincoln's new cathedral was built right next to a marketplace, and its twelfth-century bishops—who were themselves rich men—wanted to warn moneymaking parishioners about the perils of wealth.

The most striking feature of the period 1050–1150 was the rise of a money economy in western Europe. Cities, trade, and agricultural production swelled. The resulting worldliness met with a wide variety of responses. Some people fled it altogether, seeking isolation and poverty. Others, like the bishops of Lincoln, condemned it or tried to reform it. Almost everyone else embraced it in some way, some eagerly, others cautiously.

Dives and Lazarus
At the time this sculpted depiction of Dives and Lazarus was made, the town of Lincoln was expanding both within and without its Roman walls. Within the walls were the precincts of the fishmongers, the grain sellers, and the poultry merchants. Outside the walls were the bakers, the soapmakers, and the salt sellers. The town was highly attuned to moneymaking—both its pleasures and its dangers. *(Conway Library, Courtauld Institute of Art, London.)*

The development of a profit-based economy quickly transformed western Europe. Many villages and fortifications became cities where traders, merchants, and artisans conducted business. In some places, town dwellers began to determine their own laws and administer their own justice. Although most people still lived in sparsely populated rural areas, their lives were touched in many ways by the new cash economy. Economic concerns helped drive changes within the church, where a movement for reform gathered steam and exploded in three directions: the Investiture Conflict, new monastic orders emphasizing poverty, and the Crusades. Money even helped popes, kings, and princes to redefine the nature of their power.

> **FOCUS QUESTION:** How did the commercial revolution affect religion and politics?

The Commercial Revolution

As the population of Europe continued to expand in the eleventh century, cities, long-distance trade networks, local markets, and new business arrangements meshed to create a profit-based economy. With improvements in agriculture and more land in cultivation, the great estates of the eleventh century produced surpluses that helped feed — and therefore make possible — a new urban population.

Commerce was not new to the history of western Europe, but the commercial revolution of the Middle Ages spawned the institutions that would be the direct ancestors of modern businesses: corporations, banks, accounting systems, and, above all, urban centers that thrived on economic vitality. Whereas ancient cities had primarily religious, social, and political functions, medieval cities were centers of production and economic activity. Wealth meant power: it allowed city dwellers to become self-governing.

Fairs, Towns, and Cities

In many places, markets met weekly to sell local surplus goods. Fairs — which lasted anywhere from several days to a few months — took place once a year and drew traders from longer distances (Map 10.1). Some fairs specialized in particular goods: at Skania, in southern Sweden, the chief product was herring. At Saint-Denis, a monastery near Paris that had had a fair since at least the seventh century, the star attraction was wine. But most fairs offered a wide variety of products: at six different fairs in Champagne, merchants arrived from Flanders with woolen fabrics, from Lucca with silks, from Spain with leather goods, from Germany with furs. Bankers attended as well, exchanging coins from one currency into another — and charging for their services. Local inhabitants did not have to pay taxes or tolls, but traders from the outside — protected by guarantees of safe conduct — were charged stall fees as well as entry and exit fees. Local landlords reaped great profits, and as the fairs came under royal control, kings did so as well.

Permanent commercial centers — cities and towns — developed around castles and monasteries and within the walls of ancient Roman towns. Great lords in the countryside — and this included monasteries — were eager to take advantage of the profits that their estates generated. In the late tenth century, they reorganized their lands for greater productivity, encouraged their peasants to cultivate new land, and converted services and dues to money payments. With ready cash, they not only fostered the development of local markets and yearly fairs, where they could sell their surpluses and buy luxury goods, but also encouraged traders and craftspeople to settle down near them.

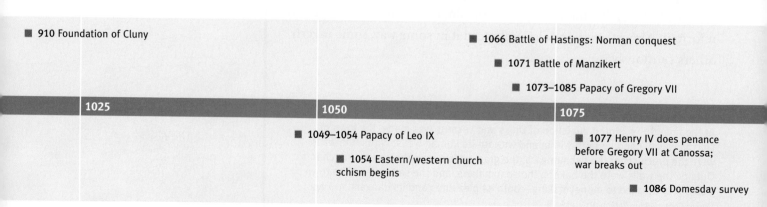

■ 910 Foundation of Cluny

■ 1066 Battle of Hastings: Norman conquest

■ 1071 Battle of Manzikert

■ 1073–1085 Papacy of Gregory VII

1025	1050	1075

■ 1049–1054 Papacy of Leo IX

■ 1054 Eastern/western church schism begins

■ 1077 Henry IV does penance before Gregory VII at Canossa; war breaks out

■ 1086 Domesday survey

For example, at Bruges (today in Belgium), the local lord's castle became the magnet around which a city formed. As a medieval chronicler observed:

> To satisfy the needs of the people in the castle at Bruges, first merchants with luxury articles began to surge around the gate: then the winesellers came; finally the innkeepers arrived to feed and lodge the people who had business with the prince. . . . So many houses were built that soon a great city was created.

Other commercial centers clustered around monasteries and churches. Still other markets formed just outside the walls of older cities; these gradually merged into new and enlarged urban communities as town walls were built around them to protect their inhabitants. Sometimes informal country markets were housed in permanent structures. Along the Rhine and in other river valleys, cities sprang up to service the merchants who traversed the route between Italy and the north.

The Jews in the Cities.   Many of the long-distance traders were Italians and Jews. They supplied the fine wines, spices, and fabrics beloved by lords and ladies, their families, and their vassals. Italians took up long-distance trade because of Italy's proximity to Byzantine and Islamic ports, their opportunities for plunder and trade on the high seas, and their never entirely extinguished urban traditions. The Jews of Mediterranean regions—especially Italy and Spain—had been involved in commerce since Roman times. That trade had centered on the Mediterranean; now it extended to the north as well. For Jews living in the port cities of the old Roman Empire, little had changed. But for many Jews in northern Europe, the story was different. They had settled on the land alongside other peasants, and during the Carolingian period, their properties bordered those of their Christian neighbors. As political power fragmented in the course

Synagogue Inscription from the City of Worms
This inscription is the oldest artifact we have from a synagogue in Europe. It says that Jacob ben David and his wife Rahel used their fortune to construct and furnish the synagogue, which was completed in 1034. They express the belief that this act of piety is as pleasing to God as having children. *(Jüdisches Museum im Raschihaus, Worms, Germany.)*

of the tenth century—and the countryside was reorganized under the ban (controlling powers) of local lords—Jews were driven off the land. They found refuge in the new towns and cities. Some became scholars, doctors, and judges within their communities; many became small-time pawnbrokers; and still others became moneylenders and financiers.

By the eleventh century, most Jews lived in cities, but they were not citizens. They were, in general, serfs of the king or, in the Rhineland, under the safeguard of the local bishop. This status was ambiguous: they were "protected" but also exploited, since their protectors constantly demanded steep taxes. Jews could not join the regular town trade and craft organizations or the governments that towns often set up. Nevertheless, they had their own institutions, centered on the synagogue, their place of worship (see Synagogue Inscription from the City of Worms, this page). Although they were often assigned a "Jewish quarter," they were not forcibly segregated from other

■ **1095** Council of Clermont; Pope Urban II calls the First Crusade

■ **1096–1099** First Crusade   ■ **1122** Concordat of Worms   ■ **1147–1149** Second Crusade

1100   **1125**   **1150**

■ **1097** Establishment of commune at Milan   ■ **c. 1140** Gratian, *Decretum*

■ **1108–1137** Reign of Louis VI

■ **1109** Establishment of the crusader states

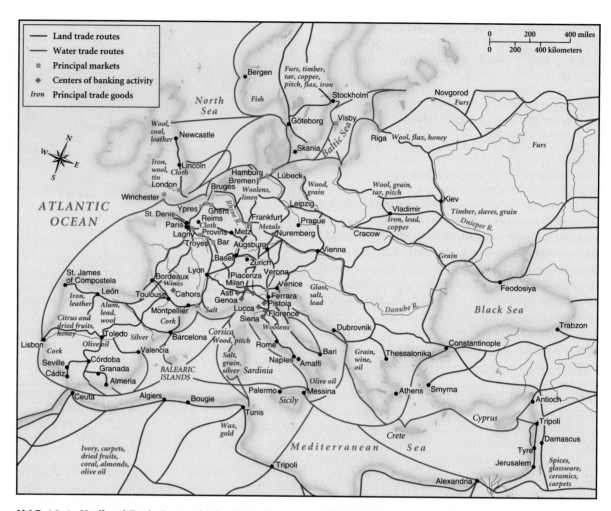

MAP 10.1 Medieval Trade Routes in the Eleventh and Twelfth Centuries
In the medieval world, bulk goods from the north (furs, fish, and wood) were traded for luxury goods from the south (ivory and spices, including medicines, perfumes, and dyes). Already regions were beginning to specialize. England, for example, supplied raw wool, but Flanders (Ypres, Ghent) specialized in turning that wool into cloth and shipping it farther south, to the fairs of Champagne (whose capital was Troyes) or Germany. Italian cities channeled goods from the Muslim and Byzantine worlds northward and exported European goods southward and eastward.

townspeople. In many cities, they lived near Christians, purchased products from Christian craftspeople, and hired Christians as servants. In turn, Christians purchased luxury goods from Jewish long-distance traders and often borrowed money from Jewish lenders.

The "Unplanned" Town. The fact that Jews and Christians could live side by side had less to do with tolerance than with lack of planning. Most towns grew haphazardly. Typically, towns had a center, where the church and town governments had their headquarters, and around this were the shops of tradespeople and craftspeople, generally grouped by specialty. Around the marketplace at Reims, for example, was a network of streets whose

names (many of which still exist) revealed their commercial functions: Street of the Butchers, Street of the Wool Market, Street of the Wheat Market.

The look and feel of such developing cities varied enormously, but nearly all included a marketplace, a castle, and several churches. Most had to adapt to increasingly crowded conditions. Archaeologists have discovered that at the end of the eleventh century in Winchester, England, city plots were still large enough to accommodate houses parallel to the street; but the swelling population soon necessitated destroying these houses and building instead long, narrow, hall-like tenement houses, constructed at right angles to the thoroughfare. These were built on a frame made

Baptismal Font at Liège, 1107–1118
This detail from a large bronze baptismal font cast at Liège (a city today in Belgium) illustrated the words of Luke 3:12–14: "Tax collectors also came to be baptized, and said to [Jesus], 'Teacher, what shall we do?' And he said to them, 'Collect no more than is appointed you.' Soldiers also asked him, 'And we, what shall we do?' And he said to them, 'Rob no one . . . and be content with your wages.'" In this representation, the tax collectors are dressed like twelfth-century city dwellers, while a soldier is dressed like a knight of the period. *(akg-images.)*

from strips of wood filled with wattle and daub—twigs woven together and covered with clay. If they were like the stone houses built in the late twelfth century (a period about which we know a good deal), they had two stories: a shop or warehouse on the lower floor and living quarters above. Behind this main building was the kitchen and perhaps also enclosures for livestock, as archaeologists have found at Southampton, England. Even city dwellers clung to rural pursuits, living largely off the food they raised themselves.

The construction of houses and markets was part of a building boom that began in the tenth century and continued at an accelerated pace through the thirteenth. Specialized buildings for trade and city government were put up—charitable houses for the sick and indigent, city halls, and warehouses. Walls surrounded medieval cities. By 1100, three rings of walls encircled Speyer (today in Germany): the first had been put up around its cathedral, the second went just beyond the parish church of St. Moritz, and the last was built still farther out to protect the marketplace. Within the walls lay a network of streets—often narrow, dirty, dark, and winding—made of packed clay or gravel. New bridges were built to span the rivers. Before the eleventh century, Europeans had depended on boats and waterways for bulky long-distance transport; in the twelfth century, carts could haul items overland because new roads through the countryside linked the urban markets.

Although commercial centers developed throughout western Europe, they grew fastest and most densely in regions along key waterways: the Mediterranean coasts of Italy, France, and Spain; northern Italy along the Po River; the Rhône-Saône-Meuse river system; the Rhineland; the English Channel; the shores of the Baltic Sea. During the eleventh century, these waterways became part of a single interdependent economy.

What did townspeople look like? We can get an idea from a baptismal font cast in Liège in the twelfth century that shows St. John speaking to the soldiers and publicans: the soldier is dressed as a medieval knight, while the publicans wear the caps and clothes of well-to-do city dwellers (see Baptismal Font at Liège).

Organizing Crafts and Commerce

In modern capitalism, there are few craftspeople: machines weave textiles, for example, and people sew pieces (a collar, perhaps) rather than whole garments. Piecework was just beginning in the Middle Ages, when most manufactured goods were produced by hand or with primitive machines and tools (see Comb for Wool, page 300). Nevertheless, most medieval industries, though not mechanized, were highly organized. The fundamental unit of organization was the guild, a sort of "club" for craftspeople and tradespeople. Similarly, the ancestors of modern business corporations—which rely on capital pooled from various sources—had their origins in the Middle Ages.

Guilds. It was not by chance that city streets were named for various occupations: in a medieval city, crafts and trades were collective endeavors. Each was organized as a **guild**. Originally these were religious and charitable associations of people in the same line of trade. In Ferrara, Italy, for example, the shoemakers' guild started as a prayer confraternity, an association whose members gathered and prayed for one another. But soon guilds became professional corporations defined by statutes and rules. They charged dues, negotiated with lords and town governments, set the standards of their trade, and controlled their membership.

The manufacture of finished products often required the cooperation of several guilds. The production of wool cloth, for example, involved numerous guilds — shearers, weavers, fullers (who thickened the cloth), dyers — generally working under the supervision of the merchant guild that imported the raw wool. Some guilds were more prestigious than others: in Florence, for example, professional guilds of notaries and judges ranked above craft guilds. Within each guild of artisans, merchants, or professionals existed another kind of hierarchy. Apprentices were at the bottom, journeymen and journeywomen (that is, day laborers) in the middle, and masters at the top. Apprentices were boys and occasionally girls placed under the tutelage of a master for a number of years to learn a trade. At Paris, it took four years of apprenticeship to become a baker; at Genoa, it took ten to become a silversmith.

Learning a trade was not the same as becoming a master. A young person would spend many years as a day laborer hired by a master who needed extra help. Unlike apprentices, these journeymen and journeywomen did not live with their masters;

they worked for them for a wage. This marked an important stage in the economic history of the West. For the first time, many workers were neither slaves nor dependents but free and independent wage earners. At least a few day workers were female; invariably, they received wages far lower than those of their male counterparts. Sometimes a married couple hired themselves out as a team. Often journeymen and journeywomen were required to be guild members — so that they would pay dues and so their masters could keep tabs on them.

Masters occupied the top of the guild hierarchy, dominating the offices and policies of the guild. They drew up the guild regulations and served as its chief overseers, inspectors, and treasurers. Because the number of masters was few and the turnover of official posts frequent, most masters eventually had a chance to serve as guild officers. Occasionally they were elected, but more often they were appointed by town governments or local rulers.

Partnerships, Contracts, and the Rise of Industry.

In the course of the eleventh and twelfth centuries, people created new kinds of business arrangements through partnerships, contracts, and large-scale productive enterprises — the ancestors of modern capitalism. Although they took many forms, all of these business agreements had the common purpose of bringing people together to pool their resources and finance larger initiatives. Short-lived partnerships were set up for the term of one sea voyage; longer-term partnerships were created for land trade. In northern and central Italy, for example, long-term ventures took the form of a *compagnia* formed by extended families. Everyone who contributed to the compagnia bore joint and unlimited liability for all losses and debts. This provision enhanced family solidarity, because each member was responsible for the debts of all the others, but it also risked bankrupting everyone in the family.

The commercial revolution also fostered the development of contracts for sales, exchanges, and loans. Loans were the most problematic. In the Middle Ages, as now, interest payments were the chief inducement for an investor to supply money. To circumvent the church's ban on usury (profiting from loans), a contract often disguised interest as a "penalty for late payment." The new willingness to finance business enterprises with loans signaled a changed attitude toward credit: risk was acceptable if it brought profit.

Contracts and partnerships made large-scale productive enterprises possible. In fact, light in-

---

guild: A trade organization within a city or town that controlled product quality and cost and outlined members' responsibilities. Guilds were also social and religious associations.

Comb for Wool

This stout wooden comb, which was used in the first half of the eleventh century to remove the tangles in raw wool, had two sets of teeth. (*Collection Musée dauphinois (inv.90.14.81), Grenoble — France.*)

dustry began in the eleventh century. One of the earliest products to benefit from new industrial technologies was cloth. Water mills powered machines such as flails to clean and thicken cloth and presses to extract oil from fibers. Machines also exploited raw materials more efficiently: new deep-mining technology provided Europeans with hitherto untapped sources of metals. At the same time, forging techniques improved, and iron was for the first time regularly used for agricultural tools and plows. Iron tools, in turn, made farming more productive, which in turn fed the commercial revolution. People also fashioned metals into objects ranging from weapons and armor to ornaments and coins.

Communes: Self-Government for the Towns

Both to themselves and to outsiders, townspeople seemed different. Tradespeople, artisans, ship captains, innkeepers, and money changers did not fit into the old categories of medieval types — those who pray, those who fight, and those who labor. Just knowing they were different gave townspeople a sense of solidarity. But practical reasons also contributed to their feeling of common purpose: they lived in close quarters, and they shared a mutual interest in reliable coinage, laws to facilitate commerce, freedom from servile dues and services, and independence to buy and sell as the market dictated. Already in the early twelfth century, the king of England granted to the citizens of Newcastle-upon-Tyne the privilege that any unfree peasant who lived there unclaimed by his lord for a year and a day would thereafter be a free person. To townspeople, freedom meant having their own officials and law courts. They petitioned the political powers that ruled them — bishops, kings, counts, castellans — for the right to govern themselves. Often they had to fight for this freedom and, if successful, paid a hefty sum for the privilege. Town institutions of self-government were called **communes**; citizens swore allegiance to the commune, forming a legal corporate body.

Communes were especially common in northern and central Italy, France, and Flanders. Italian cities were centers of regional political power even before the commercial revolution. Castellans constructed their fortifications and bishops ruled the countryside from such cities.

The commercial revolution swelled the Italian cities with tradespeople, whose interest in self-government was often fueled by religious as well as economic concerns. At Milan in the second half of the eleventh century, popular discontent with the archbishop, who effectively ruled the city, led to numerous armed clashes. In 1097, the Milanese succeeded in transferring political power from the archbishop and his clergy to a government of leading men of the city, who called themselves consuls. The title recalled the government of the ancient Roman republic, affirming the consuls' status as representatives of the people. As the archbishop's power had done, the consuls' rule extended beyond the town walls into the *contado*, the outlying countryside.

Outside Italy, movements for city independence took place within the framework of larger kingdoms or principalities. Such movements were sometimes violent, as at Milan, but at other times they were peaceful. For example, William Clito, who claimed the county of Flanders (today in Belgium), willingly granted the citizens of St. Omer the rights they asked for in 1127 in return for their support of his claims: he recognized them as legally free, gave them the right to mint coins, allowed them their own laws and courts, and lifted certain tolls and taxes. Whether violently or peacefully, the men and women of many towns and cities gained a measure of self-rule.

The Commercial Revolution in the Countryside

The countryside itself was caught in the new networks of trade. Country people brought local products to markets and fairs. By 1150, rural life in many regions was organized for the marketplace. The commercialization of the countryside opened up opportunities for both peasants and lords, but it also burdened some with unwelcome obligations.

Great lords hired trained, literate agents to administer their estates, calculate profits and losses, and make marketing decisions. Aristocrats needed money not only because they relished luxuries but also because their honor and authority continued to depend on their personal generosity, patronage, and displays of wealth. In the twelfth century, when some townsmen could boast fortunes that rivaled the riches of the landed aristocracy, the economic pressures on the nobles increased as their extravagance exceeded their income. Many went into debt.

The lord's need for money integrated peasants, too, into the developing commercial econ-

---

commune: In a medieval town, a sworn association of citizens who formed a legal corporate body. The commune appointed or elected officials, made laws, kept the peace, and administered justice.

omy. The increase in population and the resultant greater demand for food required bringing more land under cultivation. By the middle of the twelfth century, isolated and sporadic attempts to cultivate new land had become a regular and co-ordinated activity. Great lords offered special privileges to peasants who would do the backbreaking work of plowing marginal land or draining marshes. In 1106, for example, the archbishop of Hamburg-Bremen gave colonists from Holland swampland in his diocese and the right to hear their own court cases. In return, he expected them to drain the swamps, bring the region under cultivation, and give him regular payments. Similarly enterprising landlords were to be found throughout Europe, especially in northern Italy, England, Flanders, and Germany. In Flanders, where land was regularly inundated by seawater, the great monasteries sponsored drainage projects. Canals linking the cities to the agricultural districts let boats ply the waters to virtually every nook and cranny of the region. With its dense population, Flanders provided not only a natural meeting ground for long-distance traders from England and France but also numerous markets for local traders.

Sometimes free peasants acted on their own to clear land and relieve the pressure of overpopulation, as when the small freeholders in England's Fenland region cooperated to build banks and dikes to reclaim the land that led out to the North Sea. Villages were founded on the drained land, and villagers shared responsibility for repairing and maintaining the dikes even as each peasant family farmed its new holding individually.

On old estates, the rise in population strained to the breaking point the manse organization that had developed in Carolingian Europe, where each household was settled on the land that supported it. Now, in the twelfth century, twenty peasant families might live on what had been, in the tenth century, the manse of one family. With the manse supporting so many more people, labor services and dues had to be recalculated, and peasants and their lords often turned services and dues into money rents, payable once a year. Peasants sometimes joined together in collectives like communes to buy their liberty for a high price, paid out over many years to their lord. Like town citizens, they gained a new sense of identity and solidarity as they bargained with a lord keen to increase his income at their expense.

The commercial revolution and the resulting money economy brought both benefits and burdens to peasants. They gained from rising prices, which made their fixed rents less onerous. They had access to markets where they could sell their surplus and buy what they lacked. Increases in land under cultivation and the use of iron tools meant greater productivity. Peasants also gained increased personal freedom, as they shook off direct control by lords. Nevertheless, these advantages were partially canceled out by their cash obligations. Peasants touched by the commercial revolution ate better than their forebears had eaten, but they also had to spend more.

REVIEW: What new institutions resulted from the commercial revolution?

Church Reform

The commercial revolution affected the church no less than it affected other institutions of the time. Bishops ruled over many cities, and many were appointed by kings or powerful local lords. This transaction involved gifts: churchmen gave gifts and money to secular leaders in return for their offices. Soon these transactions were being condemned by the same sorts of people who appreciated the fates of Dives and Lazarus. The impulse to free the church from "the world" — from rulers, wealth, sex, money, and power — was as old as the origins of monasticism; but, beginning in the tenth century and increasing to fever pitch in the eleventh, reformers demanded that the church as a whole remodel itself and become free of secular entanglements.

This freedom was, from the start, as much a matter of power as of religion. Most people had long believed that their ruler — whether king, duke, count, or castellan — reigned by the grace of God and had the right to control the churches in his territory. But by the second half of the eleventh century, more and more people saw a great deal wrong with secular power over the church. They looked to the papacy to lead the movement of church reform. The matter came to a head during the so-called Investiture Conflict, when Pope Gregory VII clashed with Emperor Henry IV (whose empire embraced both Germany and Italy). The Investiture Conflict ushered in a major civil war in Germany and a great upheaval in the distribution of power across western Europe. By the early 1100s, a reformed church — with the pope at its head — was penetrating into areas of life never before touched by churchmen. Church reform began as a way to free the church from the world, but in the end the church was thoroughly involved in the new world it had helped to create.

Beginnings of Reform

The project of freeing the church from the world began in the tenth century with no particular plan and only a vague idea of what it might mean. Local reformers—both clerical and lay—took some early steps to make the clergy not only celibate but also independent of laymen. But church reform did not take final shape until the papacy embraced it and turned it into a blueprint for reorganizing the church under papal leadership. The movement to "liberate the church" in fact began in unlikely circles: with the very rulers who were controlling churches and monasteries, appointing churchmen, and using bishops as their administrators.

Cluniac Reform. The Benedictine monastery of Cluny may serve to represent the early phases of the reform. Cluny was founded in 910 by the duke and duchess of Aquitaine, who endowed it with property. Then they did something new. Instead of retaining control over the monastery, as other monastic founders did, they gave it and its worldly possessions to Saints Peter and Paul. In this way, they put control of the monastery into the hands of heaven's two most powerful saints. They designated the pope, as the successor of St. Peter, to be the monastery's worldly protector if anyone should bother or threaten it. The whole notion of "freedom" at this point was vague. But Cluny's prestige was great because of its status as St. Peter's property and the elaborate round of prayers that the monks carried out there with scrupulous devotion. The Cluniac monks fulfilled the role of "those who pray" in a way that dazzled their contemporaries. Through their prayers, they seemed to guarantee the salvation of all Christians. Rulers, bishops, rich landowners, and even serfs (if they could) donated land to Cluny, joining their contributions to the land of St. Peter and the fate of their souls to Cluny's powerful prayers. Powerful men and women called on the Cluniac monks to reform other monasteries along the Cluniac model.

The abbots of Cluny came to see themselves as reformers of the world as well. They advocated clerical celibacy, arguing against the prevailing norm in which parish priests and even some bishops were married. They also thought that the laity could be reformed, become more virtuous, and cease its oppression of the poor. In the eleventh century, the Cluniacs began to link their program of internal monastic and external worldly reform to the papacy. When bishops and laypeople encroached on their lands, they appealed to the popes for help. At the same time, the papacy itself was becoming interested in reform.

Church Reform in the Empire. Around the time the Cluniacs were joining their fate to that of the popes, a small group of clerics and monks in the Empire, the political entity created by the Ottonians, began calling for systematic reform within the church. They buttressed their arguments with new interpretations of canon law—the laws decreed over the centuries at church councils and by bishops and popes. They concentrated on two breaches of those laws: clerical marriage and **simony** (buying church offices).[1] Later they added the condemnation of **lay investiture**—the installation of clerics into their offices by lay rulers. Most of the men who promoted the reform lived in the most commercialized regions of the empire—Italy and the regions along the northern half of the Rhine River. Familiar with the impersonal practices of a profit economy, they regarded the gifts that churchmen were used to giving in return for their offices as no more than crass purchases.

Emperor Henry III (r. 1039–1056) supported the reformers. Taking seriously his position as the anointed of God, Henry felt responsible for the well-being of the church in his empire. He denounced simony and refused to accept money or gifts when he appointed bishops to their posts. When in 1046 three men, each representing a different faction of the Roman aristocracy, claimed to be pope, Henry, as ruler of Rome, traveled to Italy to settle the matter. The Synod of Sutri (1046), over which he presided, deposed all three popes and elected another. In 1049, Henry appointed a bishop from the Rhineland to the papacy as Leo IX (r. 1049–1054). But this appointment did not work out as Henry had expected, for Leo set out to reform the church under his own, not the emperor's, control.

Leo IX and the Expansion of Papal Power. During Leo's tenure, the pope's role expanded. (For one artist's image of Leo, see the picture on the

---

[1] The word *simony* comes from the name Simon Magus, the magician in the New Testament who wanted to buy the gifts of the Holy Spirit from St. Peter.

simony (SY muh nee): The sin of giving gifts or paying money to get a church office.

lay investiture: The installation of clerics into their offices by lay people, normally rulers or lords.

right.) He traveled to France and Germany, holding councils to condemn bishops guilty of simony. He sponsored the creation of a canon law textbook—the *Collection in 74 Titles*—that emphasized the pope's power. To the papal court, Leo brought the most zealous reformers of his day, including Humbert of Silva Candida and Hildebrand (later Gregory VII).

At first, clergy and secular rulers alike ignored Leo's claims to new power over the church hierarchy. Only a few bishops attended the Council of Reims, which Leo called in 1049; the king of France boycotted it entirely. Nevertheless, the pope made the council into a forum for exercising his authority. Placing the relics of St. Remigius (the patron saint of Reims) on the altar of the church, he demanded that the attending bishops and abbots say whether or not they had purchased their offices. A few confessed, some did not respond, and others gave excuses. New and extraordinary was the fact that all present felt accountable to the pope and accepted his verdicts.

In 1054, his last year as pope, Leo sent Humbert of Silva Candida to Constantinople on a diplomatic mission to argue against the patriarch of Constantinople on behalf of the new, lofty claims of the pope. Furious at the contemptuous way he was treated by the patriarch, Humbert excommunicated him. In retaliation, the patriarch excommunicated Humbert and his party, threatening them with eternal damnation. Clashes between the two churches had occurred before and had been patched up, but this one, the schism between the eastern and western churches, proved insurmountable.[2] Thereafter, the Roman Catholic and the Greek Orthodox churches were largely separate (see Document, "A Byzantine View of Papal Primacy," page 305).

Leo also had to confront a new power to his south. Under Count Roger I (c. 1040–1101), the Normans created a county that would eventually stretch from Capua to Sicily (see map on page 306). Leo, threatened by this great power, tried to curtail it: in 1053 he sent a military force to Apulia, but it was soundly defeated. Leo's successors were obliged to change their policy. In 1058, the reigning pope "invested"—in effect, gave—Apulia, nearby Calabria, "and in the future, with the help of God and St. Peter," even Sicily to Roger's brother, even though none of this was the pope's to give. The papacy was particularly keen to see the Nor-

Leo IX

This eleventh-century manuscript shows not so much a portrait of Pope Leo IX as an idealized image of his power and position. What does the halo signify? Why do you suppose he stands at least three heads taller than the other figure in the picture, Warinus, the abbot of St. Arnulf of Metz? What is Leo doing with his right hand? With his left hand he holds a little church (symbol of a real one) that is being presented to him by Warinus. What did the artist intend to convey about the relationship of this church to papal power? *(Burgerbibliothek Bern cod. 292f.73r.)*

mans conquer Sicily. Once part of the Byzantine Empire, it had been taken by Muslims in the tenth century. Now the pope hoped to bring it under Catholic control. Thus, the pope's desires to convert Sicily nicely meshed with the territorial ambitions of Roger and his brother. The agreement of 1058 included a promise that all of the churches of southern Italy and Sicily would be placed under papal jurisdiction. No wonder that when the Investiture Conflict broke out, Roger and his army played an important role as a military arm of the papacy.

The popes were in fact becoming more and more involved in military enterprises. They participated in wars of expansion in Spain, for example. There the political fragmentation of al-

---

[2] Despite occasional thaws and liftings of the sentences, the mutual excommunications of pope and patriarch largely remained in effect until 1965, when Pope Paul VI and the Greek Orthodox patriarch, Athenagoras I, publicly deplored them.

DOCUMENT

A Byzantine View of Papal Primacy

A continual source of friction between the Roman and Greek churches was the question of papal primacy (the pope's place at the head of the church). Even after the schism between eastern and western churches of 1054, the two sides continued to argue over the matter. In 1136, a debate at Constantinople pitted a German bishop, Anselm of Havelburg — who argued that the pope had jurisdiction over the Greek church — against Nicetas, the Greek bishop of Nicomedia. In the following passage, Nicetas presents a moderate view.

I neither deny nor do I reject the Primacy of the Roman Church whose dignity you have extolled. As a matter of fact, we read in our ancient histories that there were three patriarchal sees closely linked in brotherhood, Rome, Alexandria, and Antioch, among which Rome, the highest see in the empire, received the primacy. . . .

But the Bishop of Rome himself ought not to be called the Prince of the Priesthood, nor the Supreme Priest nor anything of that kind, but only the Bishop of the first see. Thus it was that Boniface III [pope during the year 607], who was Roman by nationality, and the son of John, the Bishop of Rome, obtained from the Emperor Phocas [at Byzantium] confirmation of the fact that the apostolic see of Blessed Peter was the head of all the other Churches, since at that time, the Church of Constantinople was saying that it was the first see because of the transfer of the Empire. . . .

But the Roman Church to which we do not deny the Primacy among her sisters, and whom we recognize as holding the highest place in any general council, the first place of honor, that Church has separated herself from the rest by her pretensions. She has appropriated to herself the monarchy which is not contained in her office and which has divided the bishops and the churches of the East and the West since the partition of the [Roman] Empire. When, as a result of these circumstances, she gathers a council of the Western bishops without making us (in the East) a part of it, it is fitting that her bishops should accept its decrees and observe them with the veneration that is due to them . . . but although we are not in disagreement with the Roman Church in the matter of the Catholic faith, how can we be expected to accept these decisions which were taken without our advice and of which we know nothing, since we were not at that same time gathered in council? If the Roman Pontiff, seated upon his sublime throne of glory, wishes to fulminate against us and to launch his orders from the height of his sublime dignity, if he wishes to sit in judgment on our Churches with a total disregard of our advice and solely according to his own will, as he seems to wish, what brotherhood and what fatherhood can we see in such a course of action? Who could ever accept such a situation? In such circumstances we could not be called nor would we really be any longer sons of the Church but truly its slaves.

Source: Deno John Geanakoplos, *Byzantium: Church, Society, and Civilization Seen through Contemporary Eyes* (Chicago: University of Chicago Press, 1984), 214–15, quoting in turn from F. Dvornik, *Byzantium and the Roman Primacy,* trans. Edwin A. Quain, S.J. (New York: Fordham University Press, 1966/1979), 145–46. Footnote omitted.

Andalus into small and weak *taifas* (see page 270) made it fair game for the Christians to the north. Slowly the idea of the ***reconquista***, the Christian "reconquest" of Spain from the Muslims, took shape, fed by religious fervor as well as by greed for land and power. In 1063, just before a major battle, the pope issued an indulgence to all who would fight — a grant that, if it did not go so far as to forgive all sins, nevertheless fulfilled the knights' current obligation to do penance.

The Gregorian Reform and the Investiture Conflict, 1073–1122

The papal reform movement is above all associated with Gregory VII (r. 1073–1085) and is therefore often called the **Gregorian reform**. Beginning as a lowly Roman cleric named Hildebrand, with the job of administering the papal estates, he rose slowly through the hierarchy. A passionate advocate of papal primacy (the theory that the pope was the head of the church), Gregory was not afraid to clash head-on with the emperor, **Henry IV** (r. 1056–1106), theoretical ruler of Germany and much of Italy, over leadership of the church. In Gregory's view — an astonishing one at the time, given the religious and spiritual roles associated with rulers — the emperor was just a layman who had no right to meddle in church affairs.

---

reconquista (ray con KEE stuh): The collective name for the wars waged by the Christian princes of Spain against the Muslim-ruled regions to their south. These wars were considered holy, akin to the crusades.

Gregorian reform: The papal movement for church reform associated with Gregory VII (r. 1073–1085); its ideals included ending the purchase of church offices, clerical marriage, and lay investiture.

Henry IV: King of Germany (r. 1056–1106), crowned emperor in 1084. From 1073 until his death, he was embroiled in the Investiture Conflict with Pope Gregory VII.

Gregory was and remains an extraordinarily controversial figure. He certainly thought that as pope he was acting as the vicar, or representative, of St. Peter on earth. Describing himself, he declared, "I have labored with all my power that Holy Church, the bride of God, our Lady Mother, might come again to her own splendor and might remain free, pure, and Catholic." He thought that the reforms he advocated and the upheavals he precipitated were necessary to free the church from the evil rulers of the world. But his great nemesis, Henry IV, had a very different view of Gregory. He considered him an ambitious and evil man who "seduced the world far and wide and stained the Church with the blood of her sons." Not surprisingly, modern historians are only a bit less divided in their assessment of Gregory. Few deny his sincerity and deep religious devotion, but many speak of his pride, ambition, and single-mindedness. He was not an easy man.

Henry IV was less complex. He was raised in the traditions of his father, Henry III, a pious church reformer who considered it part of his duty to appoint bishops and even popes to ensure the well-being of both church and state. The emperor believed that he and his bishops—who were, at the same time, his most valuable supporters and administrators—were the rightful leaders of the church. He had no intention of allowing the pope to become head of the church.

The Investiture Conflict. The great confrontation between Gregory and Henry that historians call the **Investiture Conflict**[3] began over the appointment of the archbishop of Milan. Gregory disputed Henry's right to "invest" churchmen. In the investiture ritual, the emperor or his representative symbolically gave the church and the land that went with it to the priest or bishop or archbishop chosen for the job. When, in 1075, Henry insisted

The World of the Investiture Conflict, c. 1070–1122

on investing a new archbishop of Milan, the emperor and the pope began hurling denunciations at each other. The next year Henry called a council of German bishops who demanded that Gregory, that "false monk," resign. In reply, Gregory called a synod that both excommunicated and suspended Henry from office:

> I deprive King Henry, son of the emperor Henry, who has rebelled against [God's] Church with unheard-of audacity, of the government over the whole kingdom of Germany and Italy, and I release all Christian men from the allegiance which they have sworn or may swear to him, and I forbid anyone to serve him as king.

It was this part of the decree that made it politically explosive, because it authorized anyone in Henry's kingdom to rebel against him. Henry's enemies, mostly German princes (as German aristocrats were called), now threatened to elect another king. They were motivated partly by religious sentiments, as many had established links with the papacy through their support of reformed monasteries, and partly by political opportunism, as they had chafed under the strong German king, who had tried to keep their power in check. Some bishops joined forces with Gregory's supporters. This was a great blow to royal power because Henry desperately needed the troops supplied by his churchmen.

Attacked from all sides, Henry traveled to intercept Gregory, who was journeying northward to visit the rebellious princes. In early 1077, king and pope met at a castle belonging to Matilda, countess of Tuscany, at Canossa, high in central Italy's snowy Apennine Mountains. Gregory was inside a fortress there; Henry stood outside as a penitent, begging forgiveness. Henry's move was astute, for no priest could refuse absolution to a penitent; Gregory had to lift the excommunication and receive Henry back into the church. But Gregory now had the advantage of enjoying the king's humiliation before the majesty of the pope.

Although Henry was technically back in the church's fold, nothing of substance had been resolved. The princes elected an antiking (a king chosen illegally), and Henry and his supporters elected an antipope. From 1077 until 1122, papal and imperial armies and supporters waged intermittent war in both Germany and Italy.

---

[3] This movement is also called the Investiture Controversy, Investiture Contest, or Investiture Struggle. The epithets all refer to the same thing: the disagreement and eventually war between the pope and the emperor over the right to invest churchmen in particular and power over the church hierarchy in general.

Investiture Conflict: The confrontation between Gregory VII and Henry IV that began in 1073 over lay investiture and the nature of church leadership. It was resolved in 1122 by the Concordat of Worms.

Matilda of Tuscany
Matilda, countess of Tuscany and key supporter of Pope Gregory VII, here sits on a throne. She is the dominant figure in this picture, which was made around 1115 to illustrate a book about her life. To her right is Hugh, the abbot of Cluny. Beneath them both, in a gesture of supplication, is Emperor Henry IV, who asks them to intervene with the pope on his behalf.
(© Biblioteca Apostolica Vaticana (Vatican) Vat. Lat. 4922, f. 49.)

Outcome of the Investiture Conflict. The Investiture Conflict was finally resolved long after Henry IV and Gregory VII had died. The **Concordat of Worms** of 1122 ended the fighting with a compromise. The emperor gave up the right in the investiture ceremony to confer the ring and the pastoral staff— symbols of spiritual power. But he retained, in Germany, the right to be present when bishops were elected. In effect, he would continue to have influence over those elections. In both Germany and Italy he also had the right to give the scepter to the churchman in a gesture meant to indicate the transfer of the temporal, or worldly, powers and possessions of the church—the lands by which it was supported.

Superficially, nothing much had changed; secular rulers would continue to have a part in choosing and investing churchmen. In fact, however, few people would now claim that a king could act as head of the church. Just as the concordat broke the investiture ritual into two parts—one spiritual, with ring and staff, the other secular, with the

scepter—so too it implied a new notion of kingship that separated it from priesthood. The Investiture Conflict did not produce the modern distinction between church and state—that would develop slowly—but it set the wheels in motion.

The most important changes brought about by the Investiture Conflict, however, were on the ground: the political landscape in both Italy and Germany was irrevocably transformed. In Germany, the princes consolidated their lands and their positions at the expense of royal power. In Italy, the emperor lost power to the cities. The northern and central Italian communes were formed in the crucible of the war between the pope and the emperor. In fierce communal struggles, city factions, often created by local grievances but claiming to fight on behalf of the papal or the imperial cause, created their own governing bodies. In the course of the twelfth century, these Italian cities became accustomed to self-government.

The Sweep of Reform

Church reform involved much more than the clash of popes, emperors, and their supporters. It penetrated into the daily lives of ordinary Christians, inspired new ways to think about church institutions such as the sacraments, brought about a new systemization of church law, changed the way the papacy operated, inspired new monastic orders dedicated to poverty, and led to the crusades.

New Emphasis on the Sacraments. According to the Catholic church, the sacraments were the regular means by which God's heavenly grace infused mundane existence. But this did not mean that Christians were clear about how many sacraments there were, how they worked, or even what their significance was. (The sacraments included rites such as baptism, taking communion, and marriage.) Eleventh-century church reformers began the process—which would continue into the thirteenth century—of emphasizing the importance of the sacraments and the special nature of the priest, whose chief role was to administer them.

In the sacrament of marriage, for example, the effective involvement of the church in the wedding of husband and wife came only after the Gregorian reform. Before the twelfth century, priests had little to do with weddings, which were family affairs. After the twelfth century, however, priests were expected to consecrate marriages. When the knight Arnulf of Ardres got married in 1194, for example, priests blessed and sprinkled him and his wife with holy water as the couple lay in their nuptial bed. Churchmen also began to assume juris-

---

Concordat of Worms: The agreement between pope and emperor in 1122 that ended the Investiture Conflict.

diction over marital disputes, not simply in cases involving royalty (as they had always done) but also in those involving lesser aristocrats. Because the nobility kept its inheritance intact by transferring it to a single male heir, the heir's marriage was crucial to the family strategy. The clergy's prohibition of marriage partners as distant as seventh cousins (marriage between such cousins was considered incest) had the potential to control dynastic alliances.

At the same time, churchmen began to stress the sanctity of marriage. Hugh of St. Victor, a twelfth-century scholar, dwelled on the sacramental meaning of marriage:

> Can you find anything else in marriage except conjugal society which makes it sacred and by which you can assert that it is holy? . . . Each shall be to the other as a same self in all sincere love, all careful solicitude, every kindness of affection, in constant compassion, unflagging consolation, and faithful devotedness.

Hugh saw marriage as a matter of Christian love.

The reformers also proclaimed the special importance of the sacrament of the Eucharist or holy communion, received by eating the wafer (the body of Christ) and drinking wine (the blood of Christ) during the Mass. Gregory VII called the Mass "the greatest thing in the Christian religion." No layman, regardless of how powerful, and no woman of any class or status at all could perform anything equal to it, for the Mass was the key to salvation.

Clerical Celibacy. The new emphasis on the sacraments, which were now more thoroughly and carefully defined, along with the desire to set priests clearly apart from the laity, led to vigorous enforcement of an old element of church discipline: the celibacy of priests. The demand for a celibate clergy had far-reaching significance for the history of the church. It distanced western clerics even further from their eastern Orthodox counterparts (who did not practice celibacy), exacerbating the east-west church schism of 1054. It also broke with traditional local practices, as clerical marriage was customary in some places. Gregorian reformers exhorted every cleric from the humble parish priest to the exalted bishop to refrain from marriage or to abandon his wife. Naturally, many churchmen resisted. The historian Orderic Vitalis (1075–c. 1142) reported that one zealous archbishop in Normandy

> fulfilled his duties as metropolitan [bishop] with courage and thoroughness, continually striving to separate immoral priests from their mistresses [and wives]: on one occasion when he forbade them to keep concubines he was stoned out of the synod.

Undaunted, the reformers persisted, and in 1123 the pope proclaimed all clerical marriages invalid. With its new power, the papacy was largely able to enforce the rule.

The Papal Monarchy. Some of the new powers of the papacy rested on the consolidation and imposition of canon, or church, law. These laws had begun simply as rules determined at church councils. Later they were supplemented with papal declarations. Several attempts to gather together and organize these laws had been made before the eleventh century. But the proliferation of rules during that century, along with the desire of Gregory's followers to clarify church law as they saw it, made a systematic collection of rules even more necessary. Around 1140, a teacher of canon law named Gratian achieved this goal with a landmark synthesis, the *Decretum*. Collecting nearly two thousand passages from the decrees of popes and councils as well as the writings of the church fathers, Gratian intended to demonstrate their essential agreement. In fact, his book's original title was *Harmony of Discordant Canons*. If he found any discord in his sources, Gratian usually imposed the harmony himself by arguing that the passages dealt with different situations. A bit later, another legal scholar revised and expanded the *Decretum*, adding ancient Roman law to the mix.

Even while Gratian was writing, the papal curia, or government, centered in Rome, resembled a court of law with its own collection agency. In the course of the eleventh and twelfth centuries, the papacy developed a bureaucracy to hear cases and rule on petitions, such as disputed elections of bishops. Churchmen not involved in litigation went to the papal curia for other purposes as well: to petition for privileges for their monasteries or to be consecrated by the pope. All these services were also expensive, requiring lawyers, judges, hearing officers, notaries, and collectors. The lands owned by the papacy were not sufficient to support the growing cost of its administrative apparatus, and the petitioners and litigants themselves had to pay, a practice they resented. A satire written about 1100, in the style of the Gospels, made bitter fun of papal greed:

> There came to the court a certain wealthy clerk, fat and thick, and gross. . . . He first gave to the dispenser, second to the treasurer, third to the cardinals. But they thought among themselves that they should receive more. The Lord Pope, hearing that his cardinals had received many gifts, was sick, nigh unto death. But the rich man sent to him a couch of gold and silver and immediately he was made whole. Then the Lord Pope called his cardinals and ministers to him and said to them: "Brethren, look, lest anyone deceive you with vain

words. For I have given you an example: as I have grasped, so you grasp also."

The pope, with his law courts, bureaucracy, and financial apparatus, had become a monarch.

New Monastic Orders of Poverty

Like the popes, the monks of Cluny and other Benedictine monasteries were reformers. Unlike the popes, they spent nearly their entire day in large and magnificently outfitted churches singing a long and complex liturgy consisting of Masses, prayers, and psalms. These "black monks"—so called because they dyed their robes black—reached the height of their popularity in the eleventh century. Their monasteries often housed hundreds of monks—though convents for Benedictine nuns were usually less populated. Cluny was one of the largest monasteries, with some four hundred brothers in the mid-eleventh century.

In the twelfth century, this lifestyle came under attack by groups seeking a religious life of poverty. They considered the opulence of a huge and gorgeous monastery like Cluny to be a sign of greed rather than honor. (See the photograph of Cluny on this page.) The Carthusian order founded by Bruno of Cologne in the 1080s was one such group. Each monk took a vow of silence and lived as a hermit in his own small hut. Monks occasionally joined others for prayer in a common prayer room, or oratory. When not engaged in prayer or meditation, the Carthusians copied manuscripts. They considered this task part of their religious vocation, a way to preach God's word with their hands rather than their mouths. The Carthusian order grew slowly. Each monastery was limited to only twelve monks, the number of the Apostles.

The Cistercians, by contrast, expanded rapidly. Their guiding spirit was **St. Bernard** (c. 1090–1153), who arrived at the Burgundian monastery of Cîteaux (in Latin, Cistercium, hence the name of the monks) in 1112 along with about thirty friends and relatives. Soon he became abbot of Clairvaux, one of a cluster of Cistercian monasteries in Burgundy. By the mid-twelfth century, more than three hundred monasteries spread throughout Europe were following what they took to be the customs of Cîteaux. Nuns too—as eager as monks to live the life of simplicity and poverty that they believed the Apostles had enjoyed and endured—adopted Cistercian customs. By the end of the twelfth century, the Cistercians were an order: all

Cluny (twelfth century)
The church of the monastery of Cluny was the largest and grandest in all of Christendom in the twelfth century. In its cavernous stone building, the sounds of the liturgy echoed throughout the day. *(akg-images.)*

of their houses followed rules determined at a General Chapter, a meeting at which the abbots met to hammer out legislation.

Although they held up the rule of St. Benedict as the foundation of their monastic life, the Cistercians created a style of life all their own, largely governed by the goal of simplicity. Rejecting even the conceit of blackening their robes, they left them undyed (hence their nickname, the "white monks"). Cistercian monasteries were remarkably standardized. As shown in Figure 10.1, there were two halves to each monastery: the eastern half was for the monks, and the western half was for the lay brothers. The lay brothers did the hard manual labor necessary to keep the other monks—the "choir" monks—free to worship.

Cistercian churches reflected the order's emphasis on poverty. The churches were small, made of smoothly hewn, undecorated stone. Wall paintings and sculpture were prohibited. St. Bernard wrote a scathing attack on the sort of decorative sculpture shown in this chapter's opening

---

St. Bernard: The most important Cistercian abbot (early twelfth century) and the chief preacher of the Second Crusade.

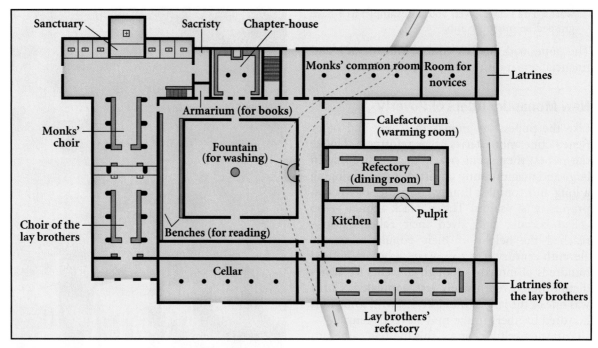

FIGURE 10.1 Floor Plan of a Cistercian Monastery
Cistercian monasteries seldom deviated much from this standard plan, which perfectly suited their double lifestyle — one half for the lay brothers, who worked in the fields, the other half for the monks, who performed the devotions. This plan shows the first floor. Above were the dormitories. The lay brothers slept above their cellar and refectory, the monks above their chapter house, common room, and room for novices. No one had a private bedroom, just as the rule of St. Benedict prescribed. *(Adapted from Wolfgang Braunfels,* Monasteries of Western Europe *(Princeton, NJ: Princeton University Press, 1972), 75.)*

illustration, Dives and Lazarus:

> What is the point of ridiculous monstrosities in the cloister where there are brethren reading—I mean those extraordinary deformed beauties and beautiful deformities? What are those lascivious apes doing, those fierce lions, monstrous centaurs, half-men and spotted leopards? . . . It is more diverting to decipher marble than the text before you.

The Cistercians had no such visual diversions, but the simplicity of their buildings and of their clothing also had its beauty. Illuminated by the pure white light that came through clear glass windows, Cistercian churches like the one at Eberbech (see page 311) were luminous, cool, and serene.

True to this emphasis on purity, the communal liturgy of the Cistercians was simplified and shorn of the many additions found in the houses of the black monks. Instead, the white monks dedicated themselves to monastic administration as well as to private prayer and contemplation. Each house had large and highly organized farms and grazing lands called granges. Cistercian monks spent much of their time managing their estates and flocks, both of which yielded handsome profits by the end of the twelfth century. Although they reacted against the wealth of the commercial rev-

olution, the Cistercians became part of it, and managerial expertise was an integral part of their monastic life.

At the same time, the Cistercians emphasized a spirituality of intense personal emotion. As St. Bernard said:

> Often enough when we approach the altar to pray our hearts are dry and lukewarm. But if we persevere, there comes an unexpected infusion of grace, our breast expands as it were, and our interior is filled with an overflowing love.

The Cistercians emphasized not only human emotion but also Christ's and Mary's humanity. While pilgrims continued to stream to the tombs and reliquaries of saints, the Cistercians dedicated all their churches to the Virgin Mary (for whom they had no relics) because for them she signified the model of a loving mother. Indeed, the Cistercians regularly used maternal imagery (as St. Bernard's description invoking the metaphor of a flowing breast illustrates) to describe the nurturing care that Jesus provided to humans. The Cistercian Jesus was approachable, human, protective, even mothering.

Many who were not members of the Cistercian order held similar views of God; their spiri-

Eberbech
Eberbech, a Cistercian church, was built between 1170 and 1186. It is relatively small and compact and has no wall paintings or sculpture—nothing to distract from the interior life of the worshipper. *(akg-images.)*

tuality signaled wider changes. For example, around 1099, St. Anselm wrote a theological treatise entitled *Why God Became Man*, arguing that since man had sinned, only a sinless man could redeem him. St. Anselm's work represented a new theological emphasis on the redemptive power of human charity, including that of Jesus as a human being. As Anselm was writing, the crusaders were heading for the very place of Christ's crucifixion, making his humanity more real and powerful to people who walked in the holy "place of God's humiliation and our redemption," as one chronicler put it. This new stress on the loving bonds that tied Christians together also led to the persecution of non-Christians, especially Jews and Muslims.

REVIEW: What were the causes and consequences of the Gregorian reform?

The Crusades

The crusades were the culmination of two separate historical movements: pilgrimages and holy wars. As pilgrimages to the Holy Land, the place where Christ had lived and died, they drew on a long tradition of making pious voyages to sacred shrines to petition for help or cure. The relics of Christ's crucifixion in Jerusalem, and even the region around it, attracted pilgrims long before the First Crusade was called in 1095.

As holy wars blessed by church leaders, the crusades also had a prehistory. The Truce of God depended on knights ready to go to battle to uphold it. The Normans' war against Sicily had the pope's approval. Already one early battle in the reconquista of Spain was fought with a papal indulgence.

The crusades established Europeans in the Middle East for two hundred years. A tiny strip of crusader states along the eastern Mediterranean survived—perilously—until 1291. Although the crusades ultimately failed, in the sense that the crusaders did not succeed in permanently retaining the Holy Land for Christendom, they were a pivotal episode in Western civilization. They marked the first stage of European overseas expansion, which would later become imperialism.

Calling the Crusade

The events leading to the First Crusade began with the entry of the Seljuk Turks into Asia Minor (Map 10.2). As noted in Chapter 9, the Muslim world had splintered into numerous small states during the 900s. Weakened by disunity, they were easy prey for the fierce Seljuk Turks—Sunni Muslims inspired by religious zeal to take over Islamic and infidel (unbeliever) regions. By the 1050s, they had captured Baghdad, subjugated the Abbasid caliphate, and begun to threaten Byzantium. The difficulties the Byzantine emperor Romanus IV had in pulling together an army to attack the Turks reveal how weak his position had become. Unable to muster Byzantine troops—which were either busy defending their own districts or were under the control of *dynatoi* (see page 266) wary of sending support to the emperor—Romanus had to rely on a mercenary army made up of Normans, Franks, Slavs, and even Turks. This motley force met the Seljuks at Manzikert in what is today eastern Turkey. The battle was a disaster for Romanus: the Seljuks routed the Byzantine army and captured the emperor. The battle of Manzikert (1071) marked the end of Byzantine domination in the region.

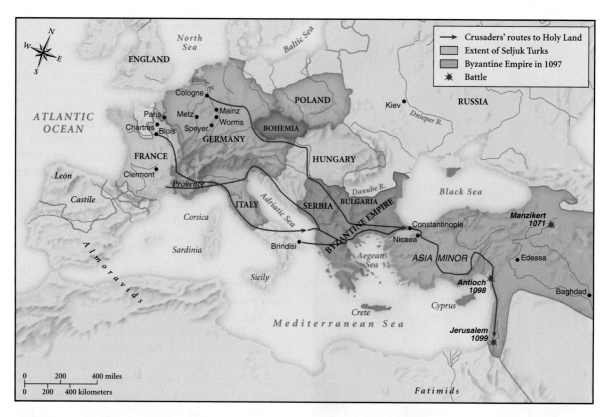

MAP 10.2 The First Crusade, 1096–1099

The First Crusade was a major military undertaking that required organization, movement over both land and sea, and enormous resources. Four main groups were responsible for the conquest of Jerusalem. One began at Cologne, in northern Germany; a second group started out from Blois, in France; the third originated just to the west of Provence; and the fourth launched ships from Brindisi, at the heel of Italy. All joined up at Constantinople, where their leaders negotiated with Alexius for help and supplies in return for a pledge of vassalage to the emperor.

Gradually settling in Asia Minor, the Turks extended their control across the empire and beyond, all the way to Jerusalem, which had been under Muslim control since the seventh century, but more recently had been under the rule of the Shi'ite Fatimids. In 1095, the Byzantine emperor **Alexius I (Alexius Comnenus)** (r. 1081–1118) appealed for help to Pope Urban II, hoping to get new mercenary troops for a fresh offensive.

Urban II (r. 1088–1099) chose to interpret the request in his own way. He made a long voyage through France, consecrating churches and cemeteries and other holy places. Arriving in Clermont in 1095, he attended a church council there and, after it had finished the usual business of proclaiming the Truce of God and condemning simony

among the clergy, Urban moved outside the church and addressed an already excited throng:

> Oh, race of Franks, race from across the mountains, race beloved and chosen by God. . . . Let hatred depart from among you, let your quarrels end, let wars cease, and let all dissensions and controversies slumber. Enter upon the road to the Holy Sepulcher; wrest that land from the wicked race, and subject it to yourselves.

The crowd reportedly responded with one voice: "God wills it." Urban offered all who made the difficult trek to the Holy Land an indulgence — the forgiveness of sins. The pains of the trip would substitute for ordinary penance.

Historians remain divided over Urban's motives for his massive call to arms. Certainly he hoped to win Christian control of the Holy Land. He was also anxious to fulfill the goals of the Truce of God by turning the entire "race of Franks" into a peace militia dedicated to holy purposes, an army of God. Just as the Truce of God mobilized whole communities to fight against anyone who broke the truce, so the First Crusade mobilized armed

Alexius I (Alexius Comnenus): The Byzantine emperor (r. 1081–1118) whose leadership marked a new triumph of the *dynatoi*. His request to Pope Urban II for troops to fight the Turks turned into the First Crusade.

Urban II: The pope (r. 1088–1099) responsible for calling the First Crusade in 1095.

groups sworn to free the Holy Land of its enemies. Finally, Urban's call placed the papacy in a new position of leadership, one that complemented in a military arena the position the popes had gained in the church hierarchy.

Inspired by local preachers, men and women, rich and poor, young and old, laypeople and clerics heeded Urban's call to go on the **First Crusade** (1096–1099). Between 60,000 and 100,000 people abandoned their homes and braved the rough journey to the Holy Land to fight for God. They also went — especially younger sons of aristocrats, who because of the tradition of primogeniture could not expect an inheritance — because they wanted land. Some knights went because they were obligated to follow their lord. Others hoped for plunder. Although women were discouraged from going on the crusades (one, who begged permission from her bishop, was persuaded to stay home and spend her wealth on charity instead), some crusaders were accompanied by their wives. (See A Crusader and His Wife, at right.) Other women went as servants; a few may have been fighters. Children and old men and women, not able to fight, made the cords for siege engines — giant machines used to hurl stones at enemy fortifications. As more crusades were undertaken during the twelfth century, the transport and supply of these armies became a lucrative business for the commercial classes of maritime Italian cities such as Venice, strategically located on the route eastward.

The First Crusade

The armies of the First Crusade were organized not as one military force but rather as separate militias, each commanded by a different individual. Fulcher of Chartres (c. 1059–c. 1127), an eyewitness, reported: "There grew armies of innumerable people coming together from everywhere. Thus a countless multitude speaking many languages and coming from many regions was to be seen." Fulcher was speaking of the armies led by nobles and authorized by the pope. There were also irregular armies with their own agendas; most were soon decimated. The main forces, despite numerous difficulties, managed to achieve their goal to take Jerusalem.

First Crusade: The massive armed pilgrimage to Jerusalem that lasted from 1096 to 1099. It resulted in the massacre of Jews in the Rhineland (1095), the sack of Jerusalem (1099), and the setting up of the crusader states.

A Crusader and His Wife
How do we know that the man on the left is a crusader? On his shirt is a cross, the sign worn by all men going on the crusades. In his right hand is a pilgrim's staff, a useful reminder that the crusades were sometimes considered less a matter of war than of penance and piety. What does the crusader's wife's embrace imply about marital love in the twelfth century? (© Musée Lorrain, Nancy/photo: P. Mignot.)

Attacking the Jews. A number of armed groups, not heeding the pope's official departure date in August, took off in late spring. Historians have called these loosely affiliated groups the People's (or Peasants') Crusade. Some of the participants were peasants, others knights. Inspired by the fiery and charismatic orator Peter the Hermit and others like him, they took off for the Holy land via the Rhineland.

This unlikely route was no mistake. The crusaders took it to kill Jews. By 1095, three cities of the Rhineland — Speyer, Worms, and Mainz — had especially large and flourishing Jewish populations. (See the illustrations Synagogue Inscription from the City of Worms, page 297, and Window from a Mikvah, page 316.) They had long-established relationships with the local bishops, and in 1090 Emperor Henry IV had granted the Jews of Speyer and Worms a privilege of special protection.

Jewish Communities Attacked during the First Crusade
(Adapted from Angus Mackay with David Ditchburn, eds., Atlas of Medieval Europe [New York: Routledge, 1997].)

CONTRASTING VIEWS

The First Crusade

When Urban II preached the First Crusade at Clermont in 1095, he unleashed a movement that was seen and interpreted in many different ways. Document 1 is an early and almost official account begun around 1100 by Fulcher of Chartres, who considered the crusade a wonderful historical movement and participated in it himself. Jews in the Rhineland who experienced the virulent attacks of some of the crusading forces had a very different view (Document 2). Document 3 presents an Arab view of the crusaders' capture of Jerusalem.

1. The Chronicle of Fulcher of Chartres (early twelfth century)

Fulcher of Chartres, a chaplain for one of the crusade leaders, wrote his account of the First Crusade for posterity. His chronicle is ordinarily very accurate, and he is careful to note the different experiences of different participants. It is all the more significant, therefore, that he expresses the public view of the First Crusade by making liberal use of biblical quotations and imagery to describe the event. He saw it as the fulfillment of God's plan for humanity.

In March of the year 1096 from the Lord's Incarnation, after Pope Urban had held the Council, which has been described, at Auvergne in November, some people, earlier prepared than others, hastened to begin the holy journey. Others followed in April or May, June or July, and also in August, September, or October, whenever the opportunity of securing expenses presented itself.

In that year, with God disposing, peace and a vast abundance of grain and wine overflowed through all the regions of the earth, so that they who chose to follow Him with their crosses according to His commands did not fail on the way for lack of bread. [Fulcher then names the "leaders of the pilgrims."] . . .

So, with such a great band proceeding from western parts, gradually from day to day on the way there grew armies of innumerable people coming together from everywhere. Thus a countless multitude speaking many languages and coming from many regions was to be seen. However, all were not assembled into one army until we arrived at the city of Nicaea.

What more shall I tell? The islands of the seas and all the kingdoms of the earth were so agitated that one believed that the prophecy of David was fulfilled, who said in his Psalm: "All nations whom Thou hast made shall come and worship before Thee O Lord" [Ps. 86:9]; and what those going all the way there later said with good reason: "We shall worship in the place where His feet have stood" [Ps. 132:7]. We have read much about this in the Prophets which it is tedious to repeat.

Source: Edward Peters, ed., *The First Crusade: The Chronicle of Fulcher of Chartres and Other Source Materials* (Philadelphia: University of Pennsylvania Press, 1971), 35–37.

2. The Jewish Experience as Told by Solomon Bar Simson (mid-twelfth century)

Around 1140, Solomon Bar Simson, a Jew from Mainz, published a chronicle of the First Crusade. This excerpt shows that the Jewish community interpreted the coming of the crusaders as a punishment from God, hence their prayers and fasting and their conviction that those killed by the crusaders were martyrs for God.

At this time arrogant people, a people of strange speech, a nation bitter and impetuous, Frenchmen and Germans, set out for the Holy City, which had been desecrated by barbaric nations, there to seek their house of idolatry and banish the Ishmaelites [Muslims] and other denizens of the land and conquer the land for themselves. . . . Now it came to pass that as they passed through the towns where Jews dwelled, they said to one another: "Look now, we are going a long way to seek out the profane shrine and to avenge ourselves on the Ishmaelites, when here, in our very midst, are the Jews—they whose forefathers murdered and

It was against such Jewish communities that the People's Crusade—joined by local nobles, knights, and townspeople—vented its fury. As one commentator put it, the crusaders considered it ridiculous to attack Muslims when other infidels lived in their own backyards: "That's doing our work backward." The Rhineland Jews faced either forced conversion or death. Some of their persecutors relented when the Jews paid them money; others, however, attacked. Many of the Jews of Speyer found refuge in the bishop's castle, but at Worms and Mainz hundreds were massacred. Similar pogroms—systematic persecutions of the Jews—took place a half century later, when the preaching of the Second Crusade led to new attacks on the Jews (see "Contrasting Views," above.)

Miserable as it was to die, it was glorious to be a martyr. The Rhineland Jews met their persecutors with uncustomary fervor, preferring to kill themselves and their children rather than be polluted by the enemy's sword. A new kind of Hebrew literature was created, celebrating the "beautiful death" of those who died in this way:

crucified [Christ] for no reason. Let us first avenge ourselves on them and exterminate them from among the nations so that the name of Israel will no longer be remembered, or let them adopt our faith and acknowledge the offspring of promiscuity."

When the Jewish communities became aware of their intentions, they resorted to the custom of our ancestors, repentance, prayer, and charity. The hands of the Holy Nation turned faint at this time, their hearts melted, and their strength flagged. They hid in their innermost rooms to escape the swirling sword. They subjected themselves to great endurance, abstaining from food and drink for three consecutive days and nights, and then fasting many days from sunrise to sunset, until their skin was shriveled and dry as wood upon their bones. And they cried out loudly and bitterly to God. . . .

On the eighth day of Iyar, on the Sabbath, the foe attacked the community of Speyer and murdered eleven holy souls who sanctified their Creator on the holy Sabbath and refused to defile themselves by adopting the faith of their foe. There was a distinguished, pious woman there who slaughtered herself in sanctification of God's name. She was the first among all the communities of those who were slaughtered. The remainder were saved by the local bishop without defilement [baptism], as described above.

On the twenty-third day of Iyar they attacked the community of Worms. The community was then divided into two groups; some remained in their homes and others fled to the local bishop seeking refuge. Those who remained in their homes were set upon by the steppe-wolves who pillaged men, women, and infants, children and old people. They pulled down the stairways and destroyed the houses, looting and plundering; and they took the Torah Scroll, trampled it in the mud, and tore and burned it.

Source: Patrick J. Geary, ed., *Readings in Medieval History* (Peterborough, Ontario, Canada: Broadview Press, 1989), 433–34.

3. The Seizure of Jerusalem as Told by Ibn Al-Athir (early thirteenth century)

Ibn Al-Athir (1160–1233) was an Arab historian who drew on earlier accounts for this recounting of the crusaders' conquest of Jerusalem. He stresses the greed and impiety of the crusaders, who pillaged Muslim holy places, and their pitiless slaughter.

After their vain attempt to take Acre by siege, the Franks moved on to Jerusalem and besieged it for more than six weeks. They built two towers, one of which, near Sion, the Muslims burnt down, killing everyone inside it. It had scarcely ceased to burn before a messenger arrived to ask for help and to bring the news that the other side of the city had fallen. In fact Jerusalem was taken from the north on the morning of Friday 22 sha'ban 492 [July 15, 1099]. The population was put to the sword by the Franks who pillaged the area for a week. A band of Muslims barricaded themselves into the Oratory of David and fought on for several days. They were granted their lives in return for surrendering.

The Franks honored their word, and the group left by night for Ascalon. In the Masjid al-Aqsa [a mosque] the Franks slaughtered more than 70,000 people, among them a large number of Imams and Muslim scholars, devout and ascetic men who had left their homelands to live lives of pious seclusion in the Holy Place. The Franks stripped the Dome of the Rock [a place holy to the Muslims, upon which was built the mosque that the Crusaders plundered] of more than forty silver candelabra, each of them weighing 3,600 drams, and a great silver lamp weighing forty-four Syrian pounds, as well as a hundred and fifty smaller silver candelabra and more than twenty gold ones, and a great deal more booty. Refugees from Syria reached Baghdad in ramadan [the month of fasting].

Source: Patrick J. Geary, ed., *Readings in Medieval History* (Peterborough, Ontario, Canada: Broadview Press, 1989), 443.

QUESTIONS TO CONSIDER
1. What commonalities, if any, do you detect between the religious ideas of the crusaders and those whom they attacked?
2. What were the similarities and what were the differences in the experiences of the Jews in Rhineland cities and the Arabs in Jerusalem?
3. What were the motives of the crusaders?

Youths like saplings pleaded with their fathers:
"Hurry! Hasten to do our Maker's Will!
The One God is our portion and destiny
Our days are over, our end has come."

Taking the Holy Land. Some members of the People's Crusade died or dropped out; the rest continued through Hungary to Constantinople, where Alexius Comnenus promptly shipped them across the Bosporus — most to meet their death in Asia Minor. In the autumn, the main armies of the crusaders began to arrive, their leaders squabbling with Alexius as their expectations and his clashed. Eventually, they promised that whatever they conquered they would return to the Byzantine empire. They didn't keep the promise.

Spared by the Turks on their arrival across the Bosporus (the Turks thought they were too weak to bother with), the crusaders made their way south to the Seljuk capital at Nicaea. At first, their armies were uncoordinated and their food supplies uncertain, but soon the crusaders organized themselves, setting up a "council of princes" that included their best leaders, while the Byzantines

Window from a Mikvah
A mikvah is a ritual bathhouse. Within each one is a pool of water deep enough for a person to be totally immersed. The mikvah is used in purification rituals, most typically when Jewish women purify themselves in the pool after their menstrual period. This mikvah window at Speyer was carved by the same people who made the Speyer Cathedral windows, attesting to the close relations between Christians and Jews in that city before the attacks of the First Crusade.
(Historisches Museum der Pfalz, Speyer.)

supplied food at a nearby port. The crusaders managed to defeat a Turkish army that attacked from nearby, and, surrounding Nicaea and besieging it with catapults and other war machines, they took the city on June 18, 1097, dutifully handing it over to Alexius.

Gradually, the crusaders left the Byzantine orbit. Most of them went toward Antioch, which stood in the way of their conquest of Jerusalem, but one led his followers to Edessa, where they took over the city and its outlying area, creating the first of the crusader states: the county of Edessa. Meanwhile, the main body of crusaders remained stymied before the thick and heavily fortified walls of Antioch for eight months. Then, in a surprise turnaround, they entered the town and found themselves besieged by Turks from the outside. Their mood grim, they rallied when a peasant named Peter Bartholomew reported that he had seen buried in the main church in Antioch the Holy Lance that had pierced Christ's body. (Antioch had a flourishing Christian population even under Muslim rule.) Believing, after a night of feverish digging, that they had found the Holy Lance, the crusaders prepared for a decisive confrontation with the Turks: "Then with God's right hand fighting with us," wrote Fulcher of Chartres, "we forced them to drive together to flee, and to leave their camps with everything in them."

From Antioch, it was only a short march to Jerusalem. But disputes among the leaders delayed that next step for over a year. One of them claimed Antioch. Another eventually took charge—provisionally—of the expedition to Jerusalem. Quarrels among Muslim rulers eased his way, and an alliance with one of them allowed free passage through what would have been enemy territory. In early June 1099, a large force of crusaders amassed before the walls of Jerusalem and set to work to build siege engines—some an astonishing three stories high. In mid-July they attacked and soon breached the walls and entered the city. "Now that our men had possession of the walls and towers, wonderful sights were to be seen," wrote Raymond d'Aguiliers, a priest serving one of the crusade leaders. He continued:

> Some of our men (and this was the more merciful) cut off the heads of their enemies; others shot them with arrows, so that they fell from the towers; others tortured them longer by casting them into the flames. Piles of heads, hands, and feet were to be seen in the streets of the city. . . . In the Temple and porch of Solomon, men rode in blood up to their knees and bridle reins. Indeed, it was a just and splendid judgment of God that this place should be filled with the blood of the unbelievers, since it had suffered so long from their blasphemies.

The Crusader States

The main objective of the First Crusade—to wrest the Holy Land from the Muslims and subject it to Christian rule—had now been accomplished. The territories conquered were not given to Alexius; they were retained by the leaders of the expedition. By 1109 they had carved out several tiny states in the Holy Land.

Because the crusader states were created by conquest, they were treated as lordships. The rulers granted fiefs to their own vassals, and some of these men in turn gave portions of their holdings as fiefs to their own vassals. Many other vassals simply lived in the households of their lords. Since most Europeans went home after the First Crusade, the

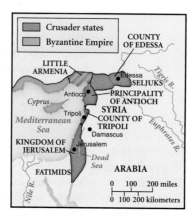

The Crusader States in 1109

rulers who remained learned to coexist with the indigenous population, which included Muslims, Jews, and Greek Orthodox Christians (see "New Sources, New Perspectives," page 318). They encouraged a lively trade at their ports, visited by merchants from Italy, Byzantium, and Islamic cities.

The main concerns of these rulers, however, were military. They set up castles and recruited knights from Europe. So organized for war was this society that it produced a new and militant kind of monasticism: the Knights Templar. The Templars vowed themselves to poverty and chastity. But unlike monks, the Templars, whose name came from their living quarters in the area of the former Jewish Temple at Jerusalem, devoted themselves to warfare. Their first mission—to protect the pilgrimage routes from Palestine to Jerusalem—soon diversified. They manned the town garrisons of the crusader states, and they transported money from Europe to the Holy Land. In this way, the Templars became enormously wealthy, with branch "banks" in major cities across Europe.

The Disastrous Second Crusade

The presence of the Knights Templar did not prevent a new Seljuk chieftain, Zengi, from taking the county of Edessa in 1144. This was the beginning of the slow but steady shrinking of the crusader states, and it sparked the Second Crusade (1147–1149). Called by Pope Eugenius III (r. 1145–1153), it attracted, for the first time, ruling monarchs to the cause: Louis VII of France and Emperor Conrad III in Germany. (The First Crusade had been led by counts and dukes.) St. Bernard, the charismatic and influential Cistercian abbot, was its tireless preacher. But Bernard and the pope were equally interested in other ventures. Eugenius supported Alfonso VI of Castile in his bid to continue the reconquista of Spain. He also encouraged German nobles to turn their interest in crusade eastward—to conquer the pagans on the Baltic coast—rather than to the Holy Land. St. Bernard inspired Flemings and Germans to attack the Portuguese city of Lisbon, aiding the king of Portugal in his own bid to expand into Muslim territory.

Little organization or planning went into the Second Crusade. The emperor at Byzantium was hardly involved. Louis VII and Conrad had no coordinated strategy, and it was too late, after they had crossed the Bosporus to Asia Minor, for Louis to beg Conrad to wait for him. As a chronicler of the crusade remarked, "Those whose common will had undertaken a common task should also use a common plan of action."

In fact, the Germans themselves had no clear plan, breaking into two groups that went their separate ways. All the armies—both French and German—were badly hurt by Turkish attacks. Furthermore, they largely acted at cross-purposes with the Christian rulers still in the Holy Land.

At last the leaders met at Acre and agreed to storm Damascus, which was under Muslim control and a thorn in the side of the Christian king of Jerusalem. On July 24, 1148, they were on the city's outskirts, but, encountering a stiff defense, they abandoned the attack after five days, suffering many losses as they retreated. The crusade was over.

The Second Crusade had one decisive outcome: it led Louis VII to divorce his wife, Eleanor, the heiress of Aquitaine. He was already primed to do this, since she had provided him with a daughter but no son. During the crusade, on which she accompanied her husband, he came to suspect her of infidelity, and after she gave birth to yet another daughter, their marriage was "dissolved" by the pope—that is, found to have been uncanonical in the first place. Eleanor promptly married Henry, count of Anjou and duke of Normandy. This marriage had far-reaching consequences, as we shall see, when Henry became King Henry II of England in 1154.

The Long-Term Impact of the Crusades

The success of the First Crusade was a mirage. The European toehold in the Middle East could not last. Numerous new crusades were called, and eight major ones were fought between the first in 1096 and the last at the end of the thirteenth century. But most Europeans were not willing to commit the vast resources and personnel that would have been necessary to maintain the crusader states, which fell to the Muslims permanently in 1291. In Europe, the crusades to the Holy Land became a sort of myth—an elusive goal that receded before more pressing ventures nearer to home. Yet they inspired new far-flung expeditions like Columbus's in 1492. Although they stimulated trade a bit, especially enhancing the prosperity of Italian cities like Venice, the commercial revolution would have happened without them. In the end, the main impact of the crusades on the West was on its imagination.

In the Middle East, the crusades worsened—but did not cause—Islamic disunity. Initially, the Muslims were perplexed by Europeans meddling in a region that had had only peripheral importance to them as a place of pilgrimage. Before the

The Cairo Geniza

What do historians know about the daily life of ordinary people in the Middle Ages? Generally speaking, very little. We have writings from the intellectual elite and administrative documents from monasteries, churches, and courts. But these rarely mention ordinary folk, and if they do, it is always from the standpoint of those who are not ordinary themselves. Glimpsing the concerns, occupations, and family relations of medieval people as they went about their daily lives is very difficult—except at old Cairo (now called Fustat), in Egypt.

Cairo is exceptional because of a cache of unusual sources that were discovered in the *geniza*, or "depository" of the Jewish synagogue near the city. Because their writings might include the name of God, members of the Jewish community left everything that they wrote, including their notes, letters, and even shopping lists, in the geniza to await ceremonial burial. Cairo was not the only place where this was the practice. But by chance at Cairo, the papers were left untouched in the depository and not buried. In 1890, when the synagogue was remodeled, workers tore down the walls of the geniza and discovered literally heaps of documents.

Many of these documents were purchased by American and English collectors and ended up in libraries in New York, Philadelphia, and Cambridge, England, where they remain. As is often the case in historical research, the questions that scholars ask are just as important as the sources themselves. At first, historians did not ask what the documents could tell them about everyday life. They wanted to know how to transcribe and read them;

they wanted to study the evolution of their handwriting (a discipline called paleography). They also needed to organize the material. Dispersed among various libraries, the documents were a hodgepodge of lists, books, pages, and fragments. For example, the first page of a personal letter might be in one library, the second page in a completely different location. For decades, scholars were busy simply transcribing the documents with a view to printing and publishing their contents. Not until 1964 was a bibliography of these published materials made available.

Only then, when they knew where to find the sources and how to piece them together, did historians, most notably S. D. Goitein, begin to work through the papers for their historical interest. What Goitein learned through the remains of the geniza amplified historians' understanding of the everyday life of much of the Mediterranean world. He discovered a cosmopolitan community occupied with trade, schooling, marriages, divorces, poetry, litigation—all the common issues and activities of a middle-class society. For example, some documents showed that middle-class Jewish women disposed of their own property and that widows often reared and educated their children on their own.

More recently, Mark R. Cohen has looked at the underclass—the poor and needy—represented in the geniza documents. He has discovered workers down on their luck, starving children, and refugees in need of aid. At moments of crisis, these people wrote letters appealing for help. These were private messages, usually addressed to wealthier individuals or

a small group: "I have been earning a livelihood, just managing to get by," wrote a man named Yahya sometime around 1100 to a hoped-for benefactor. He continued:

> I have responsibility for children and a family and an old mother advanced in years and blind. I incurred losses because of debts owed to Muslims in Alexandria. I remained in hiding. . . . Unable to go out, I began watching my children and old mother starve. . . . I heard that your excellency has a heart for his fellow Jews and is a generous person, who acts to receive reward from God and seeks to do good works, so I throw myself before God and you to help me.

So think twice the next time you throw away a piece of paper. If a historian of the year 3000 were to read your notes, lists, or letters, what would he or she learn about your culture?

QUESTIONS TO CONSIDER
1. What do the documents in the geniza tell us about Muslim as well as Jewish life in medieval Cairo?
2. What new questions might historians explore with the geniza documents?

FURTHER READING
Cohen, Mark R. *The Voice of the Poor in the Middle Ages: An Anthology of Documents from the Cairo Geniza.* 2005.

Goitein, S. D. *A Mediterranean Society: The Jewish Communities of the Arab World as Portrayed in the Documents of the Cairo Geniza.* 6 vols. 1967–1983.

Source: Quote is from Mark R. Cohen, *The Voice of the Poor in the Middle Ages: An Anthology of Documents from the Cairo Geniza* (Princeton: Princeton University Press, 2005), pp. 22–23.

---

crusades, Muslims had a complex relationship with the Christians in their midst—taxing but not persecuting them, allowing their churches to stand and be used, permitting pilgrims into Jerusalem to visit the holy sites of Christ's life and death. In many ways, the split between Shi'ite and Sunni Muslims was more serious than the rift between Muslims and Christians. The crusades, and especially the conquest of Jerusalem, which was extraordinarily brutal, shocked and dismayed

Muslims: "We have mingled blood with flowing tears," wrote one of their poets, "and there is no room left in us for pity."

> **REVIEW:** How and why was the First Crusade a success, and how and why was it a failure?

The Revival of Monarchies

Even as the papacy was exercising its new authority by annulling marriages and calling crusades, kings and other rulers were, for the most part, enhancing and consolidating their own power. They created new ideologies and dusted off old theories to justify their hegemony, they hired officials to work for them, and they found vassals and churchmen to support them. Money gave them greater effectiveness, and the new commercial economy supplied them with increased revenues. The exception was the emperor in Germany, weakened by the Investiture Conflict.

Reconstructing the Empire at Byzantium

Ten years after the disastrous battle at Manzikert, Alexius Comnenus became the Byzantine emperor. He was an upstart—from a family of dynatoi—who saw the opportunity to seize the throne in a time of crisis. The people of Constantinople were suffering under a combination of high taxes and rising living costs. In addition, the empire was under attack on every side—from Normans in southern Italy, Seljuk Turks in Asia Minor, and new groups in the Balkans. It is no wonder that an artist of his times hopefully pictured Alexius receiving Christ's blessing (see the illustration on this page). In fact, the emperor managed to avert the worst dangers. We have already seen how astutely he handled the crusaders who arrived on his doorstep.

To wage all the wars he had to fight, Alexius relied on mercenaries and allied dynatoi, armed and mounted like European knights and accompanied by their own troops. In return for their services, he gave these nobles lifetime possession of large imperial estates and their dependent peasants. Meanwhile, Alexius satisfied the urban elite by granting them new offices. He normally got on well with the patriarch and Byzantine clergy, for emperor and church depended on each other to suppress heresy and foster orthodoxy. The emperors of the Comnenian dynasty (1081–1185) thus

Alexius Comnenus Stands before Christ
In this twelfth-century manuscript illumination, the Byzantine emperor Alexius is shown in the presence of Christ. Note that both are almost exactly the same height, and the halos around their heads are the same size. What do you suppose is the significance of Christ sitting on a throne while the emperor is standing? Compare this image of the emperor with that on page 264. What statement is the twelfth-century artist making about the relationship between Christ and Alexius?
(© Biblioteca Apostolica Vaticana (Vatican) Vat. Lat.)

gained in prestige and military might, but at the price of significant concessions to the nobility.

England under Norman Rule

In the twelfth century, the kings of England were the most powerful monarchs of Europe in large part because they ruled their whole kingdom by right of conquest. When the Anglo-Saxon king Edward the Confessor (r. 1042–1066) died childless in 1066, three main contenders vied for the English throne: Harold, earl of Wessex, an Englishman close to the king but not of royal blood; Harald Hardrada, the king of Norway, who had unsuccessfully attempted to conquer the Danes and now turned hopefully to England; and William, duke of Normandy, who claimed that Edward had promised him the throne fifteen years earlier. On his deathbed, Edward had named Harold of Wessex to succeed him, and a royal advisory committee that had the right to choose the king had confirmed the nomination.

The Norman Invasion, 1066.

When he learned that Harold had been anointed and crowned, William (1027–1087) prepared for battle. Appealing to the pope, he received the banner of St. Peter and with this symbol of God's approval launched the invasion of England, filling his ships with warriors recruited from many parts of France. Just before William's invasion force landed, Harold defeated Harald Hardrada at Stamford Bridge, near York, in the north of England. When he heard of William's arrival, Harold turned his forces south, marching them 250 miles and picking up new soldiers along the way to meet the Normans.

The two armies clashed at the **battle of Hastings** on October 14, 1066, in one of history's rare decisive battles. Both armies had about seven or eight thousand men, Harold's in defensive position on a slope, William's attacking from below. All the men were crammed into a very small space as they began the fight. Most of Harold's men were on foot, armed with battle-axes and stones tied to sticks, which could be thrown with great force. William's army consisted of perhaps three thousand mounted knights, a thousand archers, and the rest infantry. At first William's knights broke rank, frightened by the deadly battle-axes thrown by the English; but then some of the English also broke rank as they pursued the knights. William removed his helmet so his men would know him, rallying them to surround and cut down the English who had broken away. Gradually Harold's troops were worn down, particularly by William's archers, whose arrows flew a hundred yards, much farther than an Englishman could throw his battle-axe. (Some of the archers are depicted on the lower margin of the Bayeux "Tapestry," page 321.) By dusk, King Harold was

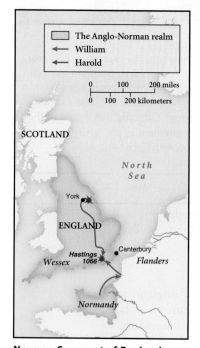

Norman Conquest of England, 1066

dead and his army utterly defeated. No other army gathered to oppose the successful claimant. (See Document, "Penances for the Invaders," page 322.)

Some people in England gladly supported William, considering his victory a verdict from God and hoping to gain a place in the new order themselves. But William — known to posterity as William the Conqueror — wanted to replace, not assimilate, the Anglo-Saxons. During William's reign, families from the continent almost totally supplanted the English aristocracy. Although the English peasantry remained — now with new lords — they were severely shaken. A twelfth-century historian claimed to record William's deathbed confession:

> I have persecuted [England's] native inhabitants beyond all reason. Whether gentle or simple, I have cruelly oppressed them; many I unjustly disinherited; innumerable multitudes, especially in the county of York, perished through me by famine or the sword.

Modern historians estimate that one out of five people in England died as a result of the Norman conquest and its immediate aftermath.

Institutions of Norman Kingship.

Although the Normans destroyed a generation of English men and women, they preserved and extended many Anglo-Saxon institutions. For example, the new kings used writs — terse written instructions — to communicate orders, and they retained the old administrative divisions and legal system of the shires (counties). The Norman kings also drew from continental institutions. They set up a graded political hierarchy, culminating in the king, whose strength was reinforced by his castles and made visible to all. Because all of England was the king's by conquest, he could treat it as his booty; William kept about 20 percent of the land for himself and divided the rest, distributing it in large but scattered fiefs to a relatively small number of his barons and family members, lay and ecclesiastical, as well as to some lesser men, such as personal servants and soldiers. In turn, these men maintained their own vassals; they owed the king military service (and the service of a fixed number of their vassals) along with certain dues, such as reliefs (money paid upon inheriting a fief) and aids (payments made on important occasions).

Domesday.

Apart from the revenues and rights expected from the nobles, the king of England commanded the peasantry as well. Twenty years after his conquest, in 1086, William ordered a survey and census of England, popularly called Domesday because, like the records of people judged at doomsday, it provided facts that could

---

battle of Hastings: The battle of 1066 that replaced the Anglo-Saxon king with a Norman one and thus tied England to the rest of Europe as never before.

Bayeux "Tapestry" (detail)
This famous "tapestry" is misnamed; it is really an embroidery, 231 feet long and 20 inches wide, that was made to tell the story of the Norman conquest of England from William's point of view. In this detail, the Norman archers are lined up along the lower margin, in a band below the armies. In the central band, the English warriors are on foot (the one at the farthest right holds a long battle-axe), while the Norman knights are on horseback. Who seems to be winning? Compare the armor and fighting gear shown here with that shown on page 286. *(Tapisserie de Bayeux. By special permission of the City of Bayeux, France.)*

■ **For more help analyzing this image,** see the visual activity for this chapter in the Online Study Guide at **bedfordstmartins.com/hunt**.

not be appealed. It was the most extensive inventory of land, livestock, taxes, and population that had ever been compiled in Europe. (See "Taking Measure," page 323.) The king

> sent his men over all England into every shire and had them find out how many hundred hides [a measure of land] there were in the shire, or what land and cattle the king himself had in the country, or what dues he ought to receive every year from the shire. . . . So very narrowly did he have the survey to be made that there was not a single hide or yard of land, nor indeed . . . an ox or a cow or a pig left out.

The king's men conducted local surveys by consulting Anglo-Saxon tax lists and by taking testimony from local jurors, men sworn to answer a series of formal questions truthfully. From these inquests, scribes wrote voluminous reports filled with facts and statements from villagers, sheriffs, priests, and barons. These reports were then summarized in Domesday itself, a concise record of England's resources that supplied the king and his officials with information such as how much and what sort of land England had, who held it, and what revenues — including the lucrative Danegeld, which was now in effect a royal tax — could be expected from it.

England and the Continent. The Norman conquest tied England to the languages, politics, institutions, and culture of the continent. Modern English is an amalgam of Anglo-Saxon and Norman French, the language the Normans spoke. English commerce was linked to the wool industry in Flanders. St. Anselm, the archbishop of Canterbury and author of *Why God Became Man*, was born in Italy and served as the abbot of a monastery in Normandy before crossing the Channel to England.

The barons of England retained their estates in Normandy and elsewhere, and the kings of England often spent more time on the continent than they did on the island. When William's son Henry I (r. 1100–1135) died without male heirs, civil war soon erupted: the throne of England was fought over by two French counts, one married to Henry's daughter, the other to his sister. The story of England after 1066 was, in miniature, the story of Europe.

Praising the King of France

The twelfth-century kings of France were much less obviously powerful than their English and Byzantine counterparts. Yet they, too, took part in the monarchical revival. Louis VI, called Louis the

DOCUMENT

Penances for the Invaders (1070)

Although William's conquest of England took place with papal blessing, nevertheless the church still insisted that the shedding of blood was a sin requiring penance. This explains why the indulgence (forgiveness of sins) offered by the pope to those who went on the First Crusade was so important. Such an indulgence was not available at the time of the invasion of England. In this document the Norman bishops impose penances on those who participated in the invasion and conquest.

This is an institution of penance according to the decrees of the bishops of the Normans, confirmed by the authority of the pope through his legate Ermenfrid, bishop of [Sion, Switizerland]. It is to apply to those men whom William, duke of the Normans [commanded], and who gave him military service as their duty.

Anyone who knows that he killed a man in the great battle [of Hastings] must do penance for one year for each man that he killed.

Anyone who wounded a man, and does not know whether he killed him or not, must do penance for forty days for each man he thus struck (if he can remember the number), either continuously or at intervals.

Anyone who does not know the number of those he wounded or killed must, at the discretion of his bishop, do penance for one day in each week for the remainder of his life; or, if he can, let him redeem his sin by a perpetual alms [charity], either by building or by endowing a church.

The [churchmen] who fought, or who were armed for fighting, must do penance as if they had committed these sins in their own country, for they are forbidden by the canons [church law] to do battle.

Source: *English Historical Documents*, vol. 2: *1041–1189*, ed. David C. Douglas and George W. Greenaway, 2d ed. (London: Routledge, 1981), 649.

Fat (r. 1108–1137), so heavy that he had to be hoisted onto his horse by a crane, was a tireless defender of royal power. We know a good deal about him and his reputation because a contemporary and close associate, Suger (1081–1152), abbot of Saint-Denis, wrote Louis's biography.

Although a churchman, Suger was a propagandist for his king. When Louis set about consolidating his rule in the Île-de-France, Suger portrayed him as a righteous hero. He thought that the king had rights over the French nobles because they were his vassals. He believed that the king had a religious role as the protector of the church and the poor. He saw Louis as another Charlemagne, a ruler for all society, not merely an overlord of the nobility. In Suger's view, Louis waged war to keep God's peace. To be sure, the Gregorian reform had made its mark: Suger did not claim Louis was the head of the church. But he nevertheless emphasized the royal dignity and its importance to the papacy. When a pope arrived in France, Louis, not yet king, and his father, Philip I (r. 1052–1108), bowed low, but (Suger wrote), "the pope lifted them up and made them sit before him like devout sons of the apostles. In the manner of a wise man acting wisely, he conferred with them privately on the present condition of the church." In this passage Suger shows the pope in need of royal advice. Meanwhile, Suger stressed Louis's piety and active defense of the faith:

Helped by his powerful band of armed men, or rather by the hand of God, he abruptly seized the castle [of Crécy] and captured its very strong tower as if it were simply the hut of a peasant. Having startled those criminals, he piously slaughtered the impious.

When Louis VI died in 1137, Suger's notion of the might and right of the king of France reflected reality in an extremely small area. Nevertheless, Louis laid the groundwork for the gradual extension of royal power in France. As the lord of vassals, the king could call on his men to aid him in times of war, though the most powerful among them sometimes disregarded the call and chose not to help. As a king and landlord, he could obtain many dues and taxes. He also drew revenues from Paris, a thriving city not only of commerce but also of scholarship. Officials called provosts enforced his royal laws and collected taxes. With money and land, Louis dispensed the favors and gave the gifts that added to his prestige and his power. Louis VI and Suger together created the territorial core and royal ideal of the future French monarchy.

Surviving as Emperor

Henry IV, emperor and king of both Germany and Italy, was a powerful ruler who began his reign by commanding important resources of both the church and the state. He had the right to appoint and invest important churchmen, many of whom worked for him as governmental ministers. He also profited from the wealth of silver mines and imperial estates in Germany as well as from flourishing trade in northern Italy. At the same time, Germany was not united behind him; from the very beginning of his reign, Henry had to fight a bitter war with rebellious Saxons.

The challenge of the Investiture Conflict was to find a new basis for power once the old underpinnings were gone. The emperor could no longer control the church hierarchy in Germany and northern Italy, nor could he depend on bishops to work as government officials. The rebellion of the princes of Germany during the conflict was a symptom of his lack of support there, and the growing independence of the Italian cities ended his control over them and their revenues.

When Henry IV died and his son, Henry V (r. 1105–1125), came to the throne, the Investiture Conflict was still raging. As we have seen, years of fruitless negotiations and numerous wars ended only in 1122 with the Concordat of Worms. This conceded considerable power within the church to the king, since he was understood to invest the bishops with their temporal goods—including the church buildings, estates, and taxes that belonged to them. But the concordat said nothing about the ruler's relations with the German princes or the Italian cities. When Henry V died childless in 1025, the position of the emperor was extremely uncertain.

When a German king died childless, the great bishops and princes would meet together to elect the next emperor. Numerous candidates were put forward; the winner, Lothar III (r. 1125–1137), was chosen largely because he was *not* the person designated by Henry V. He had little time to reestablish royal control before he, too, died childless, leaving the princes to elect Conrad III. It was Conrad's nephew, Frederick Barbarossa, who would have a chance to find new sources of imperial power in a post-Gregorian age.

> **REVIEW:** Which ruler—Alexius, William the Conqueror, or Louis VI—was the strongest, which the feeblest, and why?

Conclusion

The commercial revolution and the building boom it spurred profoundly changed Europe. New trade, wealth, and business institutions became common in its thriving cities. Merchants and artisans became important people. Mutual and fraternal organizations like the guilds and communes expressed and reinforced the solidarity and economic interest of

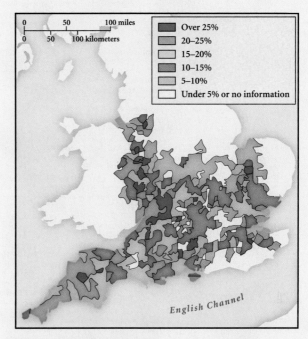

Slaves in England in 1086
Domesday provided important data for the English king in 1086, and those data remain important for historians today. We can see from this distribution map based on the data in Domesday, for example, that slavery was an important institution in eleventh-century England. The slaves, who were bought and sold, had no land of their own; they cultivated the land of their lord. Slavery was most important in the west of England, while free peasants dominated in the east. *(Adapted from H. C. Darby,* Domesday England *[Cambridge: Cambridge University Press, 1977]).*

city dwellers. The countryside became reorganized for the market.

Sensitized by the commercial revolution to the corrupting effects of money and inspired by the model of Cluny, which seemed to "free the church from the world," reformers at the papal court began to demand a new and purified church. They were joined by ordinary laypeople, who feared that their immortal souls were jeopardized by married and simoniacal priests. Under Pope Gregory VII, the reform asserted a new vision of the church with the pope at the top. But too many people— especially rulers—depended on the old system, in which kings and bishops together kept the temporal and spiritual peace. Emperor Henry IV was particularly affected, and for him the Gregorian reform meant war: the Investiture Conflict. Although officially ended by a compromise, the conflict in fact greatly enhanced the power of the papacy and weakened that of the emperor.

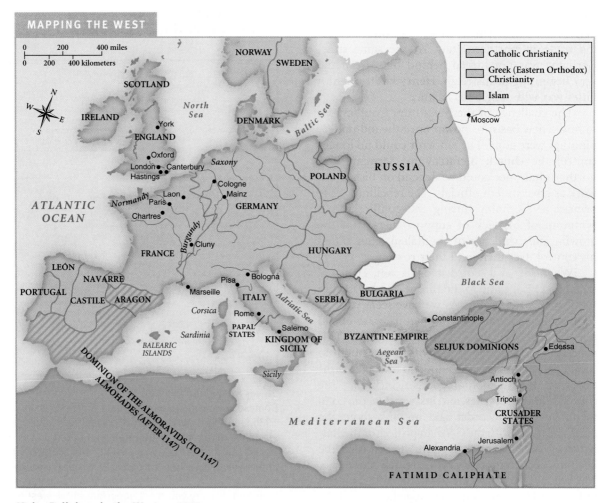

MAPPING THE WEST

Major Religions in the West, c. 1150
The broad washes of color on this map tell a striking story: by 1150, there were three major religions, each corresponding to a broad region. To the west, north of the Mediterranean Sea, Catholic Christianity held sway; to the east, the Greek Orthodox Church was ascendant; all along the southern Mediterranean, Islam triumphed. Only a few places defied this logic: one was a tiny outpost of Catholic crusaders who ruled over a largely Muslim population. What this map does not show, however, are the details: Jewish communities in many cities, lively varieties of Islamic beliefs within the Muslim world, communities of Coptic Christians in Egypt, and scattered groups of heretics in Catholic lands.

The First Crusade was both cause and effect of the new power of the papacy. But the crusades were not just papal projects. They were fueled by enormous popular piety as well as the ambitions of European rulers. They resulted in a ribbon of crusader states along the Eastern Mediterranean that lasted until 1291.

Apart from the emperor, rulers in the period after the Investiture Conflict gained new prestige and, with the wealth of the commercial revolution, the ability to hire civil servants and impose their will as never before. The Norman conquest of England is a good example of the new-style king; William was interested not only in waging war but also in setting up the most efficient possible taxation system in times of peace. The successes of

these rulers signaled a new era: the flowering of the Middle Ages.

FOR FURTHER EXPLORATION

- **For suggested references, including Web sites, for topics in this chapter,** see page SR-1 at the end of the book.

- **For additional primary-source material from this period,** see Chapter 10 in *Sources of THE MAKING OF THE WEST*, Third Edition.

- **For Web sites and documents related to topics in this chapter,** see *Make History* at **bedfordstmartins.com/hunt**.

CHAPTER REVIEW

KEY TERMS AND PEOPLE

guild (300)
commune (301)
simony (303)
lay investiture (303)
reconquista (305)
Gregorian Reform (305)
Henry IV (305)
Investiture Conflict (306)

Concordat of Worms (307)
St. Bernard (309)
Alexius I (Alexius Comnenus) (312)
Urban II (312)
First Crusade (313)
battle of Hastings (320)

REVIEW QUESTIONS

1. What new institutions resulted from the commercial revolution?

2. What were the causes and consequences of the Gregorian reform?

3. How and why was the First Crusade a success, and how and why was it a failure?

4. Which ruler — Alexius, William the Conqueror, or Louis VI — was the strongest, which the feeblest, and why?

MAKING CONNECTIONS

1. What were the similarities — and what were the differences — between the powers wielded by the Carolingian kings and those wielded by twelfth-century rulers?

2. How may the First Crusade be understood as a consequence of the Gregorian reform?

> **For practice quizzes, a customized study plan, and other study tools,** see the Online Study Guide at bedfordstmartins.com/hunt.

IMPORTANT EVENTS

910	Founding of Cluny
1049–1054	Papacy of Leo IX
1054	Schism between eastern and western churches begins
1066	Battle of Hastings: Norman conquest of England under William I
1071	Battle between Byzantines and Seljuk Turks at Manzikert
1073–1085	Papacy of Gregory VII
1077	Henry IV does penance before Gregory VII at Canossa; war breaks out
1086	Domesday survey
1095	Council of Clermont; Pope Urban II calls the First Crusade
1096–1099	First Crusade
1097	Establishment of commune at Milan
1108–1137	Reign of Louis VI
1109	Establishment of the crusader states
1122	Concordat of Worms ends the Investiture Conflict
c. 1140	Gratian's *Decretum*, a systematic collection of canon law, published
1147–1149	Second Crusade

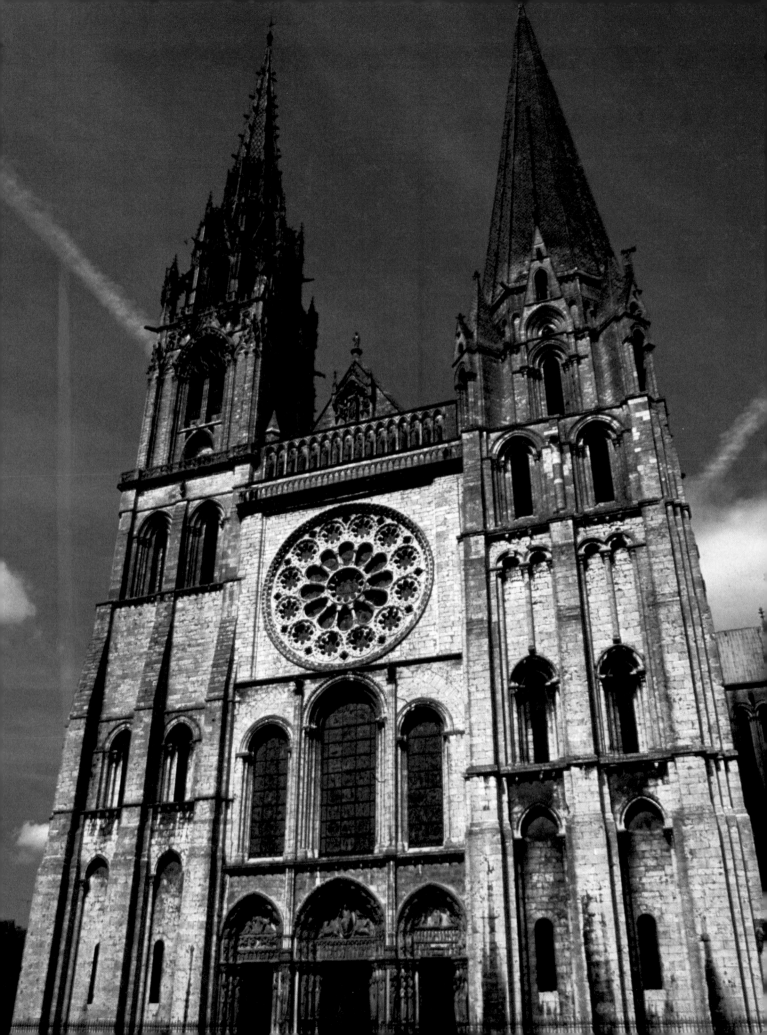

The Flowering of the Middle Ages

1150–1215

I n 1194 a raging fire burned most of the town of Chartres, in France — including its cathedral. Worried citizens feared that their most prized relic, the sacred tunic worn by the Virgin Mary when Christ was born, had gone up in flames as well. Had the Virgin abandoned the town? Suddenly the bishop and his clerics emerged from the cathedral crypt, carrying the sacred tunic, which had remained unharmed. Not only had the Virgin *not* abandoned her city, but she had made clear that she wanted a new and more magnificent cathedral to house her relic. The town dedicated itself to the task; the bishop, his clerics, the town guilds — all gave generously to pay for stonecutters, carvers, glaziers, countless other workmen, and a master builder. Donations poured in from the counts and dukes of France and from the royal house. The new cathedral was finished in an incredible twenty-six years — in an age when such churches usually took a century or more to build. Its vault soared 116 feet high; its length stretched more than one hundred yards, longer than a modern football field. On its western portals, which had been spared the flames, it retained the sculptural decoration — carved around 1150 — of the old church: three doorways surrounded and surmounted by figures that demonstrated the close relationship between the truths of divine wisdom, the seven liberal arts, and the French royal house.

The new cathedral at Chartres sums up in stone the key features that characterized the period 1150–1215 and would mark the rest of the Middle Ages. Its Gothic style — with its high vault, flying buttresses, and enormous stained-glass windows — became the quintessential style of medieval architecture. The celebration of the liberal arts at Chartres mirrors the new schools that flourished in the twelfth century and culminated in the universities of the thirteenth. Its twenty-four statues of Old Testament figures meant to prefigure the kings of France demonstrate the extraordinary importance of powerful princes in this period,

Chartres Cathedral
Rebuilt after a fire in 1194, the cathedral of Chartres reconciled old and new. The three doorways of its west end (shown here) were remnants of the former church. But they were crowned by a rose window, a form newly in vogue. *(The Art Archive/Neil Setchfield.)*

when monarchies and principalities ceased to be the personal creation of each ruler and became — with varying success in different places — permanent institutions, with professional bureaucratic staffs. The outpouring of popular support that culminated in the building of the cathedral is evidence of a vibrant vernacular (non-Latin-speaking) culture, which expressed itself not only in stone but in literature as well. Finally, the emphasis at Chartres on the divine wisdom echoes the age's fervor about Christian truths, a zeal that led to the creation of new religious movements even as it stoked the fires of the crusade movement.

> **FOCUS QUESTION:** What tied together the cultural and political achievements of the late twelfth century?

New Schools and Churches

Key to the flowering of Middle Ages were a new emphasis on learning and a new form of church architecture — the Gothic style. In many ways, these developments were the foundations for other trends of the period. The princely bureaucrats who kept governments running efficiently even when the ruler himself was absent were literate men trained in the schools; the new religious fervor — and dissent — of the period was fed by theological speculation and debate, a product of the schools as well. The new architectural style gave special luster to its rich patrons. At the same time, without the support of rich rulers, neither the new institutions of learning nor the new style of architecture would have had a chance to flourish.

The New Learning and the Rise of the University

Schools had been connected to monasteries and cathedrals since the Carolingian period. They served to train new recruits to become either monks or priests. Some were better endowed with books and masters (or teachers) than others; a few developed a reputation for a certain kind of theological approach or specialized in a branch of learning, such as literature, medicine, or law. By the end of the eleventh century, the best schools were generally in the larger cities: Reims, Paris, and Montpellier in France and Bologna in Italy.

Eager students sampled nearly all of them. The young monk Gilbert of Liège was typical: "Instilled with an insatiable thirst for learning, whenever he heard of somebody excelling in the arts, he rushed immediately to that place and drank whatever delightful potion he could draw from the master there." For Gilbert and other students, a good lecture had the excitement of theater. Teachers at cathedral schools found themselves forced to find larger halls to accommodate the crush of students. Other teachers simply declared themselves "masters" and set up shop by renting a room. If they could prove their mettle in the classroom, they had no trouble finding paying students (see A Teacher and His Students, page 329).

Wandering scholars like Gilbert were probably all male, and because schools had hitherto been the training ground for clergymen, all students were considered clerics, whether or not they had been ordained. Wandering became a way of life as the consolidation of castellanies, counties, and kingdoms made violence against travelers less frequent. Markets, taverns, and lodgings sprang up in urban centers to serve the needs of transients.

Using Latin, Europe's common language, students could drift from, say, Italy to Spain, Germany, England, and France, wherever a noted master had settled. Along with crusaders, pilgrims, and merchants, students made the roads of Europe very crowded indeed. What the students sought, above all, was knowledge of the seven liberal arts. Grammar, rhetoric, and logic (or dialectic) belonged to the beginning arts, the so-called trivium.

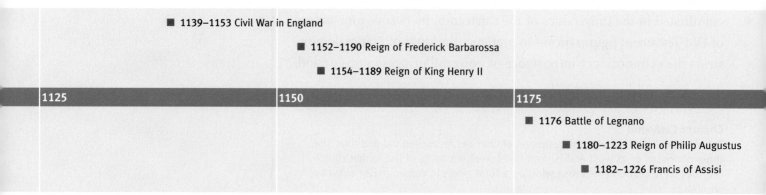

■ 1139–1153 Civil War in England

■ 1152–1190 Reign of Frederick Barbarossa

■ 1154–1189 Reign of King Henry II

| 1125 | 1150 | 1175 |

■ 1176 Battle of Legnano

■ 1180–1223 Reign of Philip Augustus

■ 1182–1226 Francis of Assisi

Logic, involving the technical analysis of texts as well as the application and manipulation of mental constructs, was a transitional subject leading to the second part of the liberal arts, the quadrivium. This comprised four areas of study that we might call theoretical math and science: arithmetic, geometry, music (theory), and astronomy.

Of all these arts, twelfth-century students were most interested in logic. Medieval students and masters were convinced that logic could bring together, order, and clarify every issue, even questions about the nature of God. St. Anselm, a major theologian as well as an abbot and archbishop, saw logic as a way for faith to "seek understanding." Emptying his mind of all ideas except that of God, he attempted to use the tools of logic to prove God's existence.

After studying the trivium, students went on to schools of medicine, theology, or law. Paris was renowned for theology, Montpellier for medicine, and Bologna for law. All of these schools trained men for jobs. The law schools, for example, taught men who went on to serve popes, bishops, kings, princes, and communes. Scholars interested in the quadrivium, by contrast, tended to pursue those studies outside of the normal school curriculum, and few gained their living through such pursuits.

The remarkable renewal of scholarship in the twelfth century had an unexpected benefit: we know a great deal about the men involved in it—and a few of the women—because they wrote so much, often about themselves. Three important figures may serve to typify the scholars of the period: Abelard and Heloise, who were early examples of the new learning; and Peter the Chanter, a product of a slightly later period.

Abelard and Heloise. Born into a family of the petty (lesser) French Breton nobility and destined for a career as a warrior and lord, Peter Abelard (1079–1142) instead became one of the twelfth

A Teacher and His Students
This miniature, which illustrates the hierarchical relationship between students and teachers in the twelfth century, appears in a late-twelfth-century manuscript of a commentary written by Gilbert (d. 1154), bishop of Poitiers. Some considered Gilbert's ideas in this commentary to be heretical. Nevertheless, Gilbert escaped condemnation. The artist asserts Gilbert's orthodoxy by depicting Gilbert with a halo, in the full dress of a bishop, speaking from his throne. Below Gilbert are three of his disciples, also with halos. The artist's positive view of Gilbert is echoed by modern historians, who recognize Gilbert as a pioneer in his approach to scriptural commentary. *(Bibliothèque Municipale de Valenciennes.)*

■ 1189–1192 Third Crusade   ■ 1214 Battle of Bouvines

   ■ 1202–1204 Fourth Crusade ■ 1215 Magna Carta

   ■ 1204 Fall of Constantinople to crusaders

| 1200 | 1225 | 1250 |

   ■ 1204 Philip takes Normandy, Anjou, Maine, Touraine, and Poitou from John

   ■ 1209–1229 Albigensian Crusade

   ■ 1212 Battle of Las Navas de Tolosa; triumph of the reconquista

Hildegard of Bingen
Unlike Heloise, Hildegard of Bingen (1098–1179) did not actively seek to become a scholar. Placed in a German convent as a young girl, she received her schooling there and took vows as a nun. Later she became an abbess and began to write and to preach, an activity normally reserved for bishops. This miniature represents Hildegard at the beginning of her book *Scivias,* illustrating her inspiration: "Heaven was opened and a fiery light . . . came and permeated my whole brain. . . . And immediately I knew the meaning of the . . . Scriptures." *(Erich Lessing/Art Resource, NY.)*

century's greatest thinkers. In his autobiographical account, *The Story of My Misfortunes,* Abelard describes his shift from the life of the warrior to the life of the scholar:

> I was so carried away by my love of learning, that I renounced the glory of a soldier's life, made over my inheritance and rights of the eldest son to my brothers, and withdrew from the court of Mars [war] in order to kneel at the feet of Minerva [learning].

Arriving eventually at Paris, Abelard studied with one of the best-known teachers of his day, William of Champeaux, but soon challenged his teacher's scholarship. He had nothing but scorn for William's position on "universals," one of the most controversial topics of the day. The question in dispute was whether a universal—something that can be said

of more than one thing, such as *cat* may be said of Puffy and Fluffy—is real or just a mental category or manner of speaking. William taught that the species, such as *cat,* was indeed real. (We call such thinkers realists.) Others (people who were later called nominalists) claimed that the species was just a word. Abelard took a middle position, maintaining that the species did have a sort of reality—*cat* would be the common "status" of Puffy and Fluffy.

Later in the twelfth century, scholars discovered that Aristotle had elaborated tools of logic to solve this and other problems. But until midcentury, very little of Aristotle's work was available in Europe because it had not been translated from Greek into Latin. By the end of the century, however, that situation had been rectified by translators who traveled to cities such as Córdoba in Spain and Syracuse in Sicily, where they found Islamic scholars who had already translated Aristotle's Greek into Arabic and could help them translate from Arabic to Latin.

After his confrontation with William of Champeaux, Abelard began to lecture and to gather students of his own. Around 1122–1123, he composed a textbook for his students, his *Sic et Non,* which consisted of opposing positions on 156 subjects, among them "That God is one and the contrary," "That all are permitted to marry and the contrary," "That it is permitted to kill men and the contrary." Arrayed on both sides of each question were passages from the Bible, the church fathers, the letters of popes, and other sources. The juxtaposition of authoritative sentences was nothing new; what was new was calling attention to their contradictions. Abelard's students loved the challenge: they were eager to find the origins of the quotes, consider the context of each one carefully, and seek to reconcile the opposing sides. Abelard wrote that his methods "excite young readers to the maximum of effort in inquiring into the truth." In fact, in Abelard's view the inquiring student followed the model of Christ himself, who as a boy sat among the rabbis, asking them questions.

Abelard's fame as a teacher was such that a Parisian cleric named Fulbert gave Abelard room and board and engaged him as tutor for Heloise (c. 1100–c. 1163/1164), Fulbert's niece. Heloise is one of the few learned women of the period who left written traces. Brought up under Fulbert's guardianship, Heloise had been sent as a young girl to a convent school, where she received a thorough grounding in a literary education. Her uncle had hoped to continue her education at home by hiring Abelard. Abelard, however, became Heloise's lover as well as her tutor. "Our desires left no stage of love-making untried," wrote Abelard in his *Mis-*

fortunes. At first their love affair was secret. But Heloise became pregnant, and Abelard insisted they marry. They did so clandestinely to prevent damaging Abelard's career, for the new emphasis on clerical celibacy meant that Abelard's professional success and prestige would have been compromised if news of his marriage were made public. After they were married, Heloise and Abelard rarely saw one another; their child, Astrolabe, was raised by Abelard's sister. Fulbert, suspecting foul play, plotted a cruel punishment: he paid a servant to castrate Abelard. Soon after, Abelard and Heloise entered separate monasteries.

For Heloise, separation from Abelard was a lasting blow. Although she became a successful abbess, carefully tending to the physical and spiritual needs of her nuns, she continued to call on Abelard for "renewal of strength." In a series of letters addressed to him, she poured out her feelings as "his handmaid, or rather his daughter, wife, or rather sister":

> You know, beloved, as the whole world knows, how much I have lost in you, how at one wretched stroke of fortune that supreme act of flagrant treachery robbed me of my very self in robbing me of you. . . . You alone have the power to make me sad, to bring me happiness or comfort.

For Abelard, however, the loss of Heloise and even his castration were not the worst disasters of his life. The cruelest blow came later, and it was directed at his intellect. He wrote a book that applied "human and logical reasons" (as he put it) to the Trinity; the book was condemned at the Council of Soissons in 1121, and he was forced to throw it, page by page, into the flames. Bitterly weeping at the injustice, Abelard lamented, "This open violence had come upon me only because of the purity of my intentions and love of our Faith, which had compelled me to write."

Peter the Chanter. In the second half of the twelfth century numerous masters were at work. Many of them were at Paris, though others taught at Montpellier, Bologna, and Oxford in England. Peter the Chanter (d. 1197) was one of the most influential and prolific of these masters. Like Abelard, he came from a family of the petty nobility. He studied at the cathedral school at Reims and was given the honorary title of chanter of Notre Dame in Paris in 1183. The chant, as we shall see, consisted of the music and words of the church liturgy. But Peter had his underlings work with the choir singers: he was far more interested in lecturing, disputing, and preaching.

Like all masters, Peter lectured. The lecture began with the recitation of a passage from an important text. The master then explained the text, giving his comments. He then "disputed" — mentioning other explanations and refuting them, often drawing on the logic of Aristotle, which by Peter's time was fully available. Sometimes masters held public debates on their interpretations.

Peter chose to comment on biblical texts. There were many ways to interpret the Bible. Some commentators chose to talk about it as an allegory. Others preferred to stress its literal meaning. Peter was interested in the morals it taught. While most theology masters commented on just the Psalms and the New Testament, Peter taught all the books of the Bible. He wrote two important treatises and was particularly interested in exploring social issues and the sacrament of penance.

Peter also took the fruits of his classroom experience to the people. His sermons have not survived, but he inspired a whole group of men around him to preach in and around Paris. One of his protégés, for example, was renowned for turning prostitutes, usurers, and immoral clerics from their sinful ways.

Universities. Shortly after Peter's death, the pope wrote to the masters of theology, church law, and the liberal arts at Paris, calling them a *universitas* — a corporation. They may well have been organized as a guild even before this. The schools of Bologna and Oxford were also turning into guilds at this time.

Like guilds, universities were regulatory institutions, controlling student discipline, scholastic proficiency, and housing while overseeing the masters' behavior in equal detail. For example, masters at the University of Paris were required to wear long black gowns, follow a particular order in their lectures, and set the standards by which students could become masters themselves. The University of Bologna was unique in having two guilds, one of students and one of masters. At Bologna, the students participated in the appointment of masters and paid their salaries.

The University of Bologna was unusual because it was principally a school of law, where the students were often older men, well along in their careers and used to wielding power. The University of Paris, however, attracted younger students, drawn particularly by its renown in the liberal arts and theology. The universities of Salerno and Montpellier specialized in medicine. Oxford, once a sleepy town where students clustered around one or two masters, became a center of royal administration, and its university soon developed a reputation for teaching the liberal arts, theology and — extraordinarily — science.

University curricula differed in content and duration. At the University of Paris in the early thirteenth century, for example, a student had to spend at least six years studying the liberal arts before he could begin to teach. If he wanted to continue his studies with theology, he had to attend lectures on the subject for at least another five years. As we have already seen in the case of Peter the Chanter, lectures were the most important way in which material was conveyed to students. Books were expensive and not readily available, so students committed their teachers' lectures to memory.

Within the larger association of the university, students found more intimate groups with which to live. These groups, called nations, were linked to the students' place of origin. At Bologna, for example, students incorporated themselves into two nations, the Italians and the non-Italians. Each nation protected its members, wrote statutes, and elected officers.

With few exceptions, masters and students were considered clerics. This had two important consequences. First, it meant that there were no university women. And second, it ensured that university men would be subject to church courts rather than to the secular jurisdiction of towns or lords. Many universities received generous privileges from popes and kings, who valued the ser-vices of scholars. Thus, for example, in 1200 the king of France promised that "neither our provost nor our judges shall lay hands on a student [at the University of Paris] for any offense whatever." The combination of clerical status and special privileges made universities virtually self-governing corporations within the towns. This sometimes led to friction. For example, when a student at Oxford was suspected of killing his mistress and the townspeople tried to punish him, the masters protested by refusing to teach and leaving town. Incidents such as this explain why historians speak of the hostility between "town" and "gown." Yet, as in our own time, university towns depended on scholars to patronize local restaurants, shops, and hostels. Town and gown normally learned to negotiate with each other to their mutual advantage.

Architectural Style: From Romanesque to Gothic

While Peter the Chanter lectured at Notre Dame, the cathedral itself was going up around him — in Gothic style. At the time, this was a new architectural fashion, attempted only in the Île-de-France and nearby cities. It was associated with the luster of the Capetian kings of France. Elsewhere — in France, Germany, Italy — the reigning style was Romanesque. But in the course of the thirteenth century Gothic style took Europe by storm, and by the fourteenth it was the quintessential cathedral style.

Romanesque Solidity. *Romanesque* is the term art historians use to describe the massive church buildings of eleventh-century monasteries like Cluny. Heavy, serious, and solid, Romanesque churches were decorated with brightly colored wall paintings and sculpture. (See Painted Vault, this page.) The various parts of the church — the chapels in the *chevet*, or apse (the east end), for example — were handled as discrete units, with the forms of cubes, cones, and cylinders (Figure 11.1). Inventive sculptural reliefs, both inside and outside the church, enlivened these pristine geometrical forms. Emotional and sometimes frenzied,

Painted Vault

This fresco of Christ as ruler of the universe, his hand raised in a gesture of blessing, is one of many paintings in the Romanesque church of San Isidore de León, built in northwest Spain in the eleventh century. Surrounding Christ are the symbols of the four evangelists: the ox for Luke, the lion for Mark, the eagle for John, and the man for Matthew. *(The Art Archive.)*

Romanesque sculpture depicted themes ranging from the beauty of Eve to the horrors of the Last Judgment. (See Dives and Lazarus on page 294 for an example.)

Romanesque churches were above all houses for prayer, which was neither silent nor private. Prayer was sung in a musical style called plainchant, or Gregorian chant. Plainchant melodies are sung in unison and without instrumental accompaniment. Although rhythmically free, lacking a regular beat, chant's melodies range from extremely simple to highly ornate and embellished. By the twelfth century, a large repertoire of melodies had grown up, at first through oral composition and transmission and then, starting in the Carolingian period, in written notation. Echoing within the stone walls and the cavernous choirs, plainchant worked well in a Romanesque church.

Gilded reliquaries (where sacred relics were housed) and altars made of silver, precious gems, and pearls were considered the fitting accoutrements of worship in Romanesque churches. The prayer, decoration, and music complemented the gift economy of the period before the commercial revolution: wearing vestments of the finest materials, intoning the liturgy in the most splendid of churches, monks and priests offered up the gift of prayer to God, begging in return the gift of salvation of their souls and the souls of all the faithful.

Gothic style. **Gothic architecture**, to the contrary, was a style of the cities, reflecting the self-confidence and wealth of merchants, guildspeople, bishops, and kings.[1] Usually a cathedral—the bishop's principal church—rather than a monastic church, the Gothic church was the religious, social, and commercial focal point of a city. The style, popular from the twelfth to fifteenth centuries, was characterized by pointed arches. These began as architectural motifs but were soon adopted in every art form. Gothic churches appealed to the senses the way that Peter the Chanter's lectures and disputations appealed to human logic and reason: both were designed to lead people to knowledge that touched the divine. Being in a Gothic church was a foretaste of heaven.

The style had its beginnings around 1135, with the project of Abbot Suger, the close associate of

---

[1]*Gothic* is a modern term. It was originally meant to denigrate the style's "barbarity," but most contemporary observers now use the word admiringly.

Gothic architecture: The style of architecture that started in the Île-de-France in the twelfth century and eventually became the quintessential cathedral style of the Middle Ages, characterized by pointed arches, ribbed vaults, and stained-glass windows.

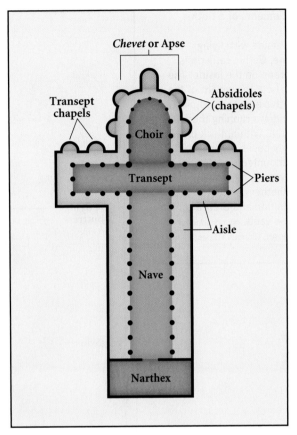

FIGURE 11.1 Floor Plan of a Romanesque Church
As churchgoers entered a Romanesque church, they passed through the narthex, an anteroom decorated with sculptures depicting scenes from the Bible. Walking through the portal of the narthex, they entered the church's nave, at the east end of which — just after the crossing of the transept and in front of the choir — was the altar. Walking down the nave, they passed tall, massive piers leading up to the vaulting (the ceiling) of the nave. Each of these piers was decorated with sculpture, and the walls were brightly painted. Romanesque churches were both lively and colorful (because of their decoration) and solemn and somber (because of their heavy stones and massive scale.)

King Louis the Fat of France (see page 322), to remodel portions of the church of Saint-Denis. Suger's rebuilding was part of the fruitful melding of royal and ecclesiastical interests and ideals in the north of France. At the west end of his church, the place where the faithful entered, Suger decorated the portals with figures of Old Testament kings, queens, and patriarchs, signaling the links between the present king and his illustrious predecessors. Within the church, Suger rebuilt the *chevet*, using pointed arches and stained glass to let in light, which Suger believed would transport the worshipper from the "slime of earth" to the "purity of Heaven." Suger

FIGURE 11.2 Elements of a Gothic Cathedral

Bristling on the outside with flying buttresses of stone, Gothic cathedrals were lofty and serene on the inside. The buttresses, which held the weight of the vault, allowed Gothic architects to pierce the walls with windows running the full length of the church. Within, thick piers anchored on sturdy bases became thin columns as they mounted over the triforium and clerestory, blossoming into ribs at the top. Whether plain or ornate, the ribs gave definition and drew attention to the high pointed vault. *(Figure adapted from Michael Camille,* Gothic Art: Glorious Visions *[New York: Abrams, 1996].)*

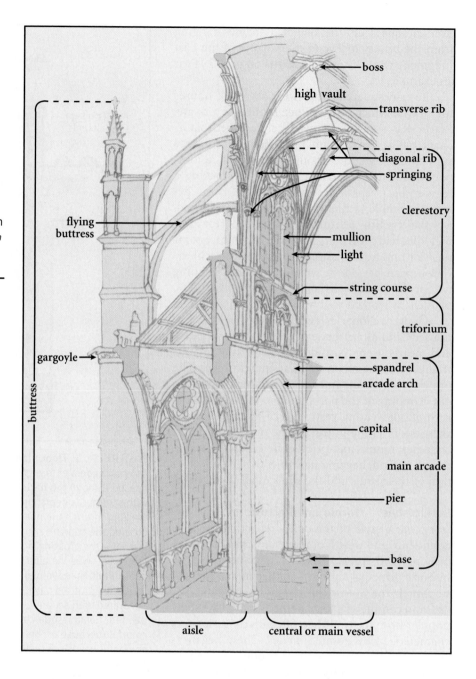

said that the father of lights, God himself, "illuminated" the minds of the beholders through the light that filtered through the stained-glass windows.

The technologies that made Gothic churches possible were all known before the twelfth century. But Suger's church showed how they could be used together to achieve a particularly dazzling effect. Gothic techniques included ribbed vaulting, which gave a sense of precision and order; the pointed arch, which produced a feeling of soaring height; and flying buttresses, which took the weight of the vault off the walls. The buttresses permitted much of the wall to be cut away and the open spaces to be filled with glass. Soaring above the west, north, south, and often east ends of many Gothic churches is a rose window: a large round window shaped like a flower.

Unlike Romanesque churches, whose exteriors prepare visitors for what they will see within them, Gothic cathedrals surprise. The exterior of a Gothic church has an opaque, bristling, and forbidding look owing to the dark surface of its stained glass and its flying buttresses. The interior, however, is just the opposite. All is soaring lightness, harmony, and order. (See "Seeing History," page 335.)

By the mid-thirteenth century, Gothic architecture had spread from France to other European countries. The style varied by region, most dramatically in Italy. At Sant'Andrea in Vercelli, shown

Romanesque versus Gothic: The View Down the Nave

When you enter a church, which, in the Middle Ages, you always did from the west end, you find yourself looking down its nave, toward the choir and the altar (the focal points of the church). That view changed over time, and the change tells us a lot about new architectural tastes in the Middle Ages. The church on the left, Saint-Savin, built near Poitiers, in France, in the early twelfth century, is a representative Romanesque church. The one on the right is Bourges,

a Gothic church built (about a hundred miles to the east of Saint-Savin) around a century later. Comparing the views down the nave systematically will allow us to discover what makes the Romanesque and Gothic styles distinctive. You might first consider the vaults. Which one is more like a tunnel, and what contributes to that effect? Does one interior create more of a soaring effect? How? What elements of the architecture contribute to this impression? Which one has paintings? Which one lets

in the most light, as reflected on the vault and also coming from the eastern end? What architectural features make this possible? In which church are the capitals of the columns (the very tops) elaborately carved? In which one are the columns themselves highly articulated, with multiple pillars? From these considerations, name the features that make a Gothic church "Gothic." What twelfth-century social and cultural trends are reflected in the shift from Romanesque to Gothic?

Saint-Savin-sur-Gartempe (begun 1095).
(Bridgeman–Giraudon/Art Resource, NY.)

Bourges (begun 1195). *(Scala/Art Resource, NY.)*

Sant'Andrea
The church of Sant'Andrea at Vercelli suggests that Italian church architects and patrons adopted what they liked of French Gothic, particularly its pointed arches, while remaining uninterested in soaring heights and grand stained-glass windows. The real interest of the interior of Sant'Andrea is its inventive and lively use of contrasting light and dark stone. *(Scala/Art Resource, NY.)*

above, for example, there are only two stories, and light filters in from small windows. Yet with its pointed arches and ribbed vaulting, it is considered a Gothic church. At its east end is a rose window.

REVIEW: What was new about the learning in the schools and the architecture of church buildings in the twelfth and early thirteenth centuries?

Governments as Institutions

By the end of the twelfth century, western Europeans for the first time spoke of their rulers not as kings of a people (for example, the king of the Franks) but as kings of a territory (for example, the king of France). This new designation reflected an important change in medieval rulership. However strong earlier rulers had been, their political power had been personal (depending on ties of kinship, friendship, and vassalage) rather than territorial (touching all who lived within the borders of their state). Renewed interest in Roman law, a product of the schools, served as a foundation for strong, central rule. Money allowed kings to hire salaried professionals—talented, literate officials, many of whom had been schooled in the new institutions of learning cropping up across Europe—to carry out the new ideology. The process of state building had begun.

In England, the governmental system was institutionalized early, with royal officials administering both law and revenues. In other regions, such as France and Germany, bureaucratic administration did not develop so far. In eastern Europe, it hardly existed at all. At Byzantium, the bureaucracy that had long been in place frayed badly, leaving the state open to conquest by western crusaders.

England: Unity through Common Law

In the mid-twelfth century, the government of England was by far the most institutionalized in Europe. The king hardly needed to be present: royal government functioned smoothly without him, with officials handling all the administrative matters and record keeping. The very circumstances of the English king favored the growth of an administrative staff: his frequent travels to and from the continent meant that officials needed to work in his absence, and his enormous wealth meant that he could afford them. **Henry II** (r. 1154–1189) was the driving force in extending and strengthening the institutions of English government.

Accession of Henry II, 1154. Henry II became king in the wake of a terrible civil war. Henry I (r. 1100–1135), son of William the Conqueror, had no male heir. Before he died, he called on the

***

Henry II: King of England (r. 1154–1189) who ended the period of civil war there and affirmed and expanded royal powers. He is associated with the creation of common law in England.

great barons to swear that his daughter Matilda would rule after him. The effort failed; the Norman barons could not imagine a woman ruling over them. Many were glad to see Stephen of Blois (r. 1135–1154), Henry's nephew, take the throne. With Matilda's son, the future Henry II, only two years old when Stephen took the crown, the struggle for control of England during Stephen's reign became part of a larger territorial contest between the house of Anjou (Henry's family) and the house of Blois (Stephen's family) (Figure 11.3). Continual civil war (1139–1153) in England benefited the English barons and high churchmen, who gained new privileges and powers as the monarch's authority waned. Newly built private castles, already familiar on the continent, now appeared in England as symbols of the rising power of the English barons. Stephen's coalition of barons, high clergymen, and townsmen eventually fell apart, and he agreed to the accession of Matilda's son, Henry of Anjou. Thus began what would be known as the Angevin (from Anjou) dynasty.[2]

Henry's marriage to Eleanor of Aquitaine in 1152, after her marriage to Louis VII of France was annulled, brought the enormous inheritance of the duchy of Aquitaine to the English crown. Although he remained the vassal of the king of France for his continental lands, Henry in effect ruled a territory that stretched from England to southern France (Map 11.1).

Eleanor brought Henry not only an enormous inheritance but also the sons that he needed to maintain his dynasty. He gave her much less. As queen of France, Eleanor had enjoyed an important position: she disputed with St. Bernard, the Cistercian abbot who was the most renowned churchman of the day, and when she accompanied Louis on the Second Crusade, she brought more troops than he did. Of independent mind, she determined to separate from Louis even before he considered leaving her. But with Henry, she lost much of her power, for he dominated her just as he came to dominate his barons. Turning to her

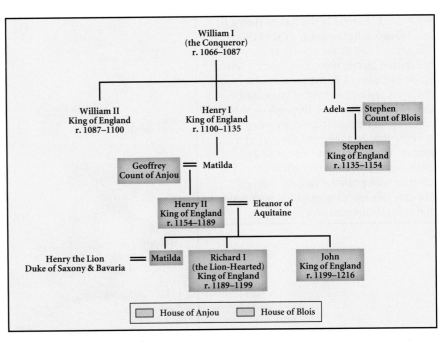

FIGURE 11.3 Genealogy of Henry II
King William I of England was succeeded by his sons, William II and Henry I. When Henry died, the succession was disputed by two women and their husbands. One was William I's daughter, Adela, married to Stephen, count of Blois; the other was Henry's daughter, Matilda, wife of the count of Anjou. Although the English crown first went to the house of Blois, it reverted in midcentury to the house of Anjou, headed by Matilda's son, Henry. Henry II thus began the Angevin dynasty in England.

offspring in 1173, Eleanor, disguised as a man, tried to join her eldest son, Henry the Younger, in a plot against his father. But the rebellion was put down, and she spent most of her years thereafter, until her husband's death in 1189, confined under guard at Winchester Castle.

Royal Authority and Common Law. When Henry II became king of England, he immediately set about to undo the damage to the monarchy caused by the civil war. He destroyed or confiscated the new castles and regained crown land. Then he proceeded to extend monarchical power, above all by imposing royal justice.

Henry's judicial reforms built on an already well-developed English system. The Anglo-Saxon kings had royal district courts: the king appointed sheriffs to police the shires, muster military levies, and haul criminals into court. The Norman kings retained these courts, which all the free men of the shire were summoned to attend. To these established institutions, Henry II added a system of judicial visitations called eyres (from the Latin *iter*, "journey"). Under this system, royal justices made regular trips to every locality in England. Henry declared that some crimes, such as murder, arson, and

---

[2]Henry's father, Geoffrey of Anjou, was nicknamed "Plantagenet" from the *genet*, a shrub he liked. Historians sometimes use the name to refer to the entire dynasty, so Henry II was the first Plantagenet as well as the first Angevin king of England.

MAP 11.1 Europe in the Age of Henry II and Frederick Barbarossa, 1150–1190

The second half of the twelfth century was dominated by two men, King Henry II and Emperor Frederick Barbarossa. Of the two, Frederick seemed to control more land, but this was deceptive. Although he was emperor, he had great difficulty ruling the territory that was theoretically part of his empire. Frederick's base was in central Germany, and even there he had to contend with powerful vassals. Henry II's territory was more compact but also more surely under his control.

rape, were so heinous that they violated the "king's peace" no matter where they were committed. The king required local representatives of the knightly class to meet during each eyre and either give the sheriff the names of those suspected of committing crimes in the vicinity or arrest the suspects themselves and hand them over to the royal justices.

During the eyres, the justices also heard cases between individuals, today called civil cases. Free men and women (that is, people of the knightly class or above) could bring their disputes over such matters as inheritance, dowries, and property claims to the king's justices. Earlier courts had generally relied on duels between litigants to determine verdicts. Henry's new system offered a different option, an inquest under royal supervision.

The new system of **common law**—law that applied to all of England—was praised for its ef-

common law: Begun by Henry II (r. 1154–1189), the English royal law carried out by the king's justices in eyre (traveling justices). It applied to the entire kingdom and thus was "common" to all.

ficiency, speed, and conclusiveness in a twelfth-century legal treatise known as *Glanvill* (after its presumed author): "This legal institution emanates from perfect equity. For justice, which after many and long delays is scarcely ever demonstrated by the duel, is advantageously and speedily attained through this institution." *Glanvill* might have added that the king also speedily gained a large treasury. The exchequer, as the financial bureau of England was called, recorded all the fines paid for judgments and the sums collected for writs. The amounts, entered on parchment sewn together and stored as rolls, became the Receipt Rolls and Pipe Rolls, the first of many such records of the English monarchy and an indication that writing had become a mechanism for institutionalizing royal power in England.

The stiffest opposition to Henry's extension of royal courts came from the church, where a separate system of trial and punishment had long been available to the clergy and to others who enjoyed church protection. The punishments for crimes

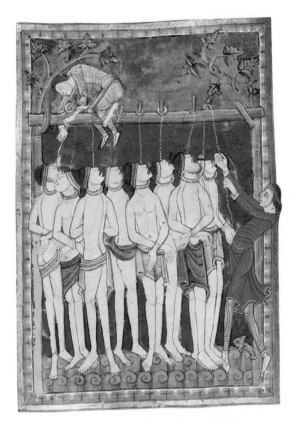

Hanging Thieves

The development of common law in England meant mobilizing royal agents to bring charges and arrest people throughout the land. In 1124, the royal justice Ralph Basset hanged forty-four thieves. It could not have been very shocking in that context to see, in this miniature from around 1130, eight thieves hanged for breaking into the shrine of St. Edmund. Under Henry II, all cases of murder, arson, and rape were considered crimes against the king himself. The result was not just the enhancement of the king's power but also new definitions of crime, more thorough policing, and more systematic punishments. Even so, hanging was probably no more frequent than it had been before. *(The Pierpont Morgan Library/Art Resource, NY.)*

meted out by these courts were generally quite mild. Protective of their special status, churchmen refused to submit to the jurisdiction of Henry's courts. Henry insisted, and the ensuing contest between Henry II and his archbishop, Thomas Becket (1118–1170), became the greatest battle between the church and the state in the twelfth century. The conflict simmered for six years, with Becket refusing to allow "criminous clerics" — clergy suspected of committing a crime — to come before royal courts. Then Henry's henchmen murdered Thomas, right in his own cathedral. The desecration unintentionally turned Becket into a martyr. Although Henry's role in the murder remained ambiguous, he was forced by the general outcry to do public penance for the deed. In the end, both church and royal courts expanded to address the concerns of an increasingly litigious society. (See The Murder of Thomas Becket, this page.)

Henry II was an English king with an imperial reach. He was lord over almost half of France, though much of this territory was in the hands of his vassals, and he was, at least theoretically, vassal to the French king. (See Map 11.1.) In England, he made the king's presence felt everywhere through his system of royal courts that traveled the length and breadth of the country. On the continent, he maintained his position through a combination of war and negotiation, but rebellions

The Murder of Thomas Becket

Almost immediately after King Henry II's knights murdered Archbishop Thomas Becket in his church at Canterbury, Becket was viewed as a martyr. In this early depiction of the event, one of the murderers knocks off Becket's cap, while another hits the arm of Becket's supporter, who holds the bishop's cross-staff. *(British Library, London, UK/The Bridgeman Art Library.)*

■ **For more help analyzing this image,** see the visual activity for this chapter in the Online Study Guide at bedfordstmartins.com/hunt.

begun by his own sons with help from the king of France dogged him throughout his life.

Henry's Successors.   Under Henry and his sons Richard I (r. 1189–1199) and John (r. 1199–1216), the English monarchy was omnipresent and rich. Its omnipresence derived largely from its eyre system of justice and its administrative apparatus. Its wealth came from court fees, income from numerous royal estates both in England and on the continent, taxes from cities, and customary feudal dues (reliefs and aids) collected from barons and knights. These dues were paid on such occasions as the knighting of the king's eldest son and the marriage of the king's eldest daughter. Enriched by the commercial economy of the late twelfth century, the English kings encouraged their knights and barons not to serve them personally in battle but instead to pay the king a tax called scutage in lieu of service. The monarchs preferred to hire mercenaries both as troops to fight external enemies and as police to enforce the king's will at home.

Richard I was known as the Lion-Hearted for his boldness. Historians have often criticized him for being an "absentee" king, yet it is hard to see what he might have done differently. He went on the Third Crusade the very year he was crowned; on his way home, he was captured and held for a long time for ransom by political enemies; and he died defending his possessions on the continent. Richard's real tragedy was that he died young.

Richard's successor, John, has also been widely faulted. Even in his own day, he was accused of asserting his will in a highhanded way. To understand John, it is necessary to appreciate how desperate he was to keep his continental possessions. In 1204, the king of France, **Philip II (Philip Augustus)** (r. 1180–1223), confiscated the northern French territories held by John. Between 1204 and 1214, John did everything he could to add to the crown revenues so that he could pay for an army to win back the territories. He forced his vassals to pay ever-increasing scutages and extorted money in the form of new feu-

dal dues. He compelled the widows of his vassals to marry men of his choosing or pay him a hefty fee if they refused. Despite John's heavy investment in this war effort, his army was defeated in 1214 at the battle of Bouvines. The defeat caused discontented English barons to rebel openly against the king. At Runnymede in June 1215, John was forced to agree to the charter of baronial liberties that has come to be called **Magna Carta**, or "Great Charter."

Magna Carta, 1215.   The English barons intended Magna Carta to be a conservative document defining the "customary" obligations and rights of the nobility and forbidding the king to break from these customs without consulting his barons. It also maintained that all free men in the land had certain rights that the king was obligated to uphold. (See "Contrasting Views," pages 342–343.) In this way, Magna Carta implied that the king was not above the law. The growing royal power was matched by the self-confidence of the English barons, certain of their rights and eager to articulate them. In time, as the definition of *free men* expanded to include all the king's subjects, Magna Carta came to be seen as a guarantee of the rights of Englishmen in general.

France: Consolidation and Conquest

Whereas the power of the English king led to a baronial movement to curb it, the weakness of the French monarchy ironically led to its expansion. In 1180, the French crown passed from the Capetian king Louis VII (first husband of Eleanor of Aquitaine) to his young son, Philip Augustus. When the new king came to the throne, the royal domain, the Île-de-France, was sandwiched between territory controlled by the counts of Flanders, Champagne, and Anjou. By far the most powerful ruler on the continent was King Henry II of England. He was the count of Anjou and the duke of Normandy, and he held the duchy of Aquitaine through his wife. He also controlled Poitou and Brittany (see Map 11.1).

Henry and the counts of Flanders and Champagne vied to con-

The Consolidation of France under Philip Augustus, 1180–1223

Map legend:
- French royal domain (Île-de-France), c. 1180
- Acquired by Philip Augustus, 1180–1223
- French royal fiefs
- ✳ Battle

Philip II (Philip Augustus): King of France (r. 1180–1223) who bested the English king John and won most of John's continental territories, thus immeasurably strengthening the power of the Capetian dynasty.

Magna Carta: The charter of baronial liberties that King John was forced to agree to in 1215. It implied that royal power was subject to custom and law.

trol the newly crowned fourteen-year-old king of France. Philip, however, quickly learned to play them off against one another, in particular by setting the sons of Henry II against their father. Contemporaries were astounded when Philip successfully gained territory: he wrested land from Flanders in the 1190s and Normandy, Anjou, Maine, the Touraine, and Poitou from King John of England in 1204. No wonder he was given the epithet *Augustus*, after the first Roman emperor.

After Philip's army confirmed its triumph over most of John's continental territories in 1214, the French monarch could boast that he was the richest and most powerful ruler in France. Most important, Philip had sufficient support and resources to keep a tight hold on Normandy.[3] He received homage and fealty from most of the Norman aristocracy, and his officers carried out their work there in accordance with Norman customs. For ordinary Normans, the shift from English duke to French king brought few changes.

Wherever he ruled, Philip instituted new administrative practices, run by officials who kept accounts and files. Before Philip's day, most French royal arrangements were committed to memory rather than to writing. If decrees were recorded at all, they were saved by the recipient, not by the government. The king did keep some documents, which he generally carried with him in his travels like personal possessions. But in 1194, in a battle with the king of England, Philip lost his meager cache of documents along with much treasure when he had to abandon his baggage train. After 1194, the king had all his decrees written down, and he established permanent repositories in which to keep them.

Like the English king, Philip relied largely on members of the lesser nobility — knights and clerics, many of whom were masters educated in the city schools of France. They served as officers of his court, tax collectors, and overseers of the royal estates, making the king's power felt locally as never before.

Germany: The Revived Monarchy of Frederick Barbarossa

Theoretically, Henry V and his successors were kings of Germany and Italy, and at Rome they received the crown and title of emperor from the popes as well. But the Investiture Conflict had reduced their power and authority. Meanwhile, the

German princes strengthened their position, enjoying near independence as they built castles on their properties and established control over whole territories. When they elected a new king, they made sure that he would give them new lands and powers. These kings were in a difficult position. They had to balance the many conflicting interests of their royal and imperial offices, their families, and the German princes. They had to contend with the increasing influence of the papacy and the Italian communes, which made alliances with one another and with the German princes. All this prevented the consolidation of power under a strong German monarch during the first half of the twelfth century.

During the Investiture Conflict, the two sides (imperial and papal) were represented by two noble families. Leading the imperial party were the Staufer, or Hohenstaufen, clan; opposing them were the Welfs. (Two later Italian factions, the Ghibellines and the Guelphs, corresponded, respectively, to the

Frederick Barbarossa
In this image of Frederick, made during his lifetime, the emperor is dressed as a crusader, and the inscription tells him to fight the Muslims. The small figure on the right is the abbot of the Monastery of Schäftlarn, who gives Frederick a book that contains an account of the First Crusade. (© *Biblioteca Apostolica Vaticana [Vatican]. Vat. Lat. 2001 fol. 1 recto.*)

---

[3]Philip was particularly successful in imposing royal control in Normandy; later French kings gave most of the other territories to collateral members of the royal family.

CONTRASTING VIEWS

Magna Carta

Magna Carta, today considered a landmark of constitutional government, began as a demand by English barons and churchmen for specific rights and privileges. Reacting to King John's "abuses," they forced him in 1215 to affix his seal to a "charter of liberties," the "Great Charter" (Magna Carta, Document 1). It set forth the customs that the king was expected to observe and, in its sixty-first clause, in effect allowed the king's subjects to declare war against him if he failed to carry out the charter's provisions.

In 1225, Henry III, John's son, issued a definitive version of the charter. By then, it had become more important as a symbol of liberty than for its specific provisions. It was, for example, invoked by the barons in 1242 when they were summoned to one of the first Parliaments (Document 2).

1. Magna Carta, 1215

In these excerpts, the provisions that were dropped in the definitive version of 1225 are starred. Explanatory notes are in brackets. The original charter had sixty-three clauses. In every clause John refers to himself by the royal "we."

1. First of all [we, i.e., John] have granted to God, and by this our present charter confirmed for us and our heirs for ever that the English church shall be free, and shall have its rights undiminished and its liberties unimpaired. . . .

8. No widow shall be forced to marry so long as she wishes to live without a husband, provided that she gives security [a pledge or deposit] not to marry without our consent if she holds [her land] from us, or without the consent of her lord of whom she holds, if she holds of another.

9. Neither we nor our bailiffs will seize for any debt any land or rent, so long as the chattels [property] of the debtor are sufficient to repay the debt. . . .

*10. If anyone who has borrowed from the Jews any sum, great or small, dies before it is repaid, the debt shall not bear interest as long as the heir is under age, of whomsoever [lord] he holds [his land]; and if the debt falls into our hands [which might happen, as Jews were serfs of the crown], we will not take anything except the principal mentioned in the bond.

*12. No scutage or aid [money payments owed by a vassal to his lord] shall be imposed in our kingdom unless by common counsel of our kingdom, except for ransoming our person, for making our eldest son a knight, and for once marrying our eldest daughter; and for these only a reasonable aid shall be levied. . . .

30. No sheriff, or bailiff of ours, or anyone else shall take the horses or carts of any free man [for the most part, a member of the elite] for transport work save with the agreement of that freeman.

31. Neither we nor our bailiffs will take, for castles or other works of ours, timber which is not ours, except with the agreement of him whose timber it is. . . .

39. No free man shall be arrested or imprisoned or disseised [deprived of his land] or outlawed or exiled or in any way victimized, neither will we attack him or send anyone to attack him, except by the lawful judgment of his peers or by the law of the land. . . .

*61. Since . . . we have granted all these things aforesaid . . . we give and grant [the barons] the under-written security, namely, that the barons shall choose any twenty-five barons of the kingdom they wish, who must with all their might observe, hold, and cause to be observed, the peace and liberties which we have granted and confirmed to them by this present charter of ours, so that if we, or our justiciar [the king's chief minister], or our bailiffs or any one of our servants offend in any way against anyone or transgress any of

---

Hohenstaufens and the Welfs.) The enmity between these families was legendary, and warfare between the groups raged even after the Concordat of Worms in 1122. Exhausted from constant battles, by 1152 all parties longed for peace. In an act of rare unanimity, they elected **Frederick I** (r. 1152–1190), who was called **Barbarossa**, as king. In Frederick they seemed to have a candidate

who could end the strife: his mother was a Welf, his father a Staufer. Contemporary accounts of the king's career represented Frederick in the image of Christ as the cornerstone that joined two houses and reconciled enemies.

New Foundations of Power. Frederick's appearance impressed his contemporaries — the name *Barbarossa* referred to his red-blond hair and beard. But beyond appearances, Frederick impressed those around him by what they called his firmness. He affirmed royal rights, even when he handed out duchies and allowed others to name

---

Frederick I (Barbarossa): King of Germany (r. 1152–1190) and emperor (crowned 1155) who tried to cement the power of the German king through conquest (for example, of northern Italy) and the bonds of vassalage.

the articles of the peace or the security . . . , [the barons] shall come to us . . . and laying the transgression before us, shall petition us to have that transgression corrected without delay. And if we do not correct the transgression . . . within forty days . . . those twenty-five barons together with the community of the whole land shall distrain and distress us in every way they can, namely, by seizing castles, lands, possessions, and in such other ways as they can, saving [not harming] our person.

Source: *English Historical Documents*, vol. 3, ed. Harry Rothwell (London: Eyre & Spottiswoode, 1975), 317–23.

2. The Barons at Parliament Refuse to Give the King an Aid, 1242

Henry III convoked the barons to a meeting (parliament), expecting them to ratify his request for money to wage war for his French possessions. As this document makes clear, the barons considered his request an excessive imposition. Magna Carta thus became a justification for their flat rejection of the king's request.

Since he had been their ruler they had many times, at his request, given him aid, namely, a thirteenth of their movable property, and afterwards a fifteenth and a sixteenth and a fortieth. . . . Scarcely, however, had four years or so elapsed from that time, when he again asked them for aid, and, at length, by dint of great entreaties, he obtained a thirtieth, which they granted him on the condition that neither that exaction nor the others before it should in the future be made a precedent of. And regarding that he gave them his charter. Furthermore, he then [at that earlier time] granted them that all the liberties contained in Magna Carta should thenceforward be fully observed throughout the whole of his kingdom. . . .

Furthermore, from the time of their giving the said thirtieth, itinerant justices have been continually going on eyre [moving from place to place] through all parts of England, alike for

John's Seal on Magna Carta

King John did not sign Magna Carta; he sealed it. From the thirteenth through the fifteenth century, kings, queens, and many other individuals and groups at all levels of society used seals to authenticate their charters — what we would call "legal documents." The seal itself was made of wax or lead that was melted and pressed with a matrix of hard metal, such as gold or brass, that was carved in the negative, to produce a raised image. These seals reminded the public of the status as well as the name of the sealer. What image did John wish to project? (*© Copyright The Trustees of the British Museum.*)

pleas of the forest [to enforce the king's monopoly on forests] and all other pleas, so that all the counties, hundreds, cities, boroughs, and nearly all the vills of England are heavily amerced [fined]; wherefore, from that eyre alone the king has, or ought to have, a very large sum of money, if it were paid, and properly collected. They therefore say with truth that all in the kingdom are so oppressed and impoverished by these amercements and by the other aids given before that they have little or no goods left. And because the king had never, after the granting of the thirtieth, abided by his charter of liberties [namely, Magna Carta], nay had since then oppressed them more than usual . . . they told the king flatly that for the present they would not give him an aid.

Source: *English Historical Documents*, 3:355–56.

QUESTIONS TO CONSIDER

1. From the clauses of Magna Carta that say what will henceforth *not* be done, speculate about what the king *had been* doing.
2. How did the barons of 1242 use Magna Carta as a symbol of liberty?

---

bishops, because in return for these political powers Frederick required the princes to concede formally and publicly that they held their rights and territories from him as their lord. By making them his vassals, although with nearly royal rights within their principalities, Frederick defined the princes' relationship to the German king: they were powerful yet personally subordinate to him. In this way, Frederick hoped to save the monarchy and to coordinate royal and princely rule, thus ending Germany's chronic civil wars. Frederick used the lord–vassal relationship to give him a free hand to rule while placating the princes.

As the king of Germany, Frederick had the traditional right to claim the imperial crown. When, in 1155, he marched to Rome to be crowned emperor, the fledgling commune there protested that it alone had the right to give him the crown. Frederick interrupted them, asserting that the glory of Rome, together with its crown, came to him by right of conquest (see Document, "Frederick I's Reply to the Romans," page 344). He was equally insistent to the pope, who wrote to tell him that Rome belonged to St. Peter. Frederick replied that his imperial title gave him rights over the city. In part, Frederick was influenced by the revival

DOCUMENT

Frederick I's Reply to the Romans

Frederick I's conception of his rights and powers is well illustrated by the speech that he reportedly gave upon his entry into Rome in 1155 for his imperial coronation. The pope considered it his right to confer the crown on the king. But when Frederick came to Rome, envoys from the new city government that had been established there greeted him with an offer to give him the crown instead. Frederick reacted forcefully: the crown was not theirs to give; it was his by right. The gist of his reply to the Romans was recorded by his counselor and chronicler, Bishop Otto of Freising.

We have heard much heretofore concerning the wisdom and the valor of the Romans, yet more concerning their wisdom. Wherefore we cannot wonder enough at finding your words insipid with swollen pride rather than seasoned with the salt of wisdom. You set forth the ancient renown of your city. You extol to the very stars the ancient status of your sacred republic. Granted, granted! To use the words of your own writer, "There was, *there was once*, virtue in this republic." "Once," I say. And oh that we might truthfully and freely say "now"! Your Rome — nay, ours also — has experienced the vicissitudes of time. She could not be the only one to escape a fate ordained by the Author of all things for all that dwell beneath the orb of the moon. What shall I say? It is clear how first the strength of your nobility was transferred from this city of ours to the royal city of the East [Constantinople], and how for the course of many years the thirsty Greekling sucked the breasts of your delight. Then came the Frank, truly noble, in deed as in name, and forcibly possessed himself of whatever freedom was still left to you. Do you wish to know the ancient glory of your Rome? The worth of the senatorial dignity? The impregnable disposition of the camp? The virtue and the discipline of the equestrian order, its unmarred and unconquerable boldness when advancing to a conflict? Behold our state. All these things are to be found with us. All these have descended to us, together with the empire.

Source: Brian Tierney, *The Crisis of Church and State, 1050–1300: With Selected Documents* (Englewood Cliffs, NJ: Prentice Hall, 1964), 103–4.

of Roman law — the laws of Theodosius and Justinian — that was taking place in the schools of Italy. In part, too, he was convinced of the sacred — not just secular — origins of the imperial office. Frederick called his empire *sacer*, "sacred," asserting that it was in its own way as precious, worthwhile, and God-given as the church.

Frederick buttressed this high view of his imperial right with worldly power. He married Beatrice of Burgundy, whose vast estates in Burgundy and Provence enabled him to establish a powerful political and territorial base centered in Swabia (today southwestern Germany).

Frederick and Italy. Frederick then looked south to Italy. Its flourishing commercial cities could make him rich. Taxes on agricultural production there alone yielded thirty thousand silver talents annually, an incredible sum equal to the annual income of the richest ruler of the day, the king of England. Swabia and northern Italy together would give Frederick a compact and centrally located territory.

No emperor could leave Italy alone. The very title came from the Roman emperor, who had controlled the city of Rome and all of Italy. It would have seemed laughable to be "emperor" without holding at least some of this territory. Some historians have faulted Frederick for "entangling" himself in Italy. But Frederick's title pushed him to intervene there.

Nevertheless, Frederick's ambitions in Italy were problematic. Since the Investiture Conflict, the emperor had ruled Italy in name only. The communes of the northern cities guarded their liberties jealously, while the pope considered Italy his own sphere of influence. Frederick's territorial base just north of Italy threatened those interests (see Map 11.1). In 1157, soon after Frederick's imperial coronation, the pope's envoys arrived at a meeting called by the emperor with a letter detailing the dignities, honors, and other *beneficia* the papacy had showered on Frederick. The word *beneficia* angered Frederick and his supporters because it meant not only "benefits" but also "fiefs," casting Frederick as the pope's vassal. The incident opened old wounds from the Investiture Conflict and revealed the gulf between papal and imperial conceptions of worldly authority.

Despite the opposition of the cities and the pope, Frederick was determined to conquer northern Italy. Alternately negotiating and fighting, especially with Milan, the major city there, Frederick achieved military control over the cities in 1158. Adopting an Italian solution for governing the communes — appointing outsiders as magistrates — Frederick appointed his own men to these powerful positions. Here is where Frederick made his mistake. He chose German officials who lacked a sense of Italian communal traditions. The heavy hand of Frederick's magistrates created enormous resentment. For example, the magistrates at Milan immediately ordered an inventory of all taxes due the emperor and levied new and demeaning labor duties, even demanding that citizens carry the wood and stones of their plundered city to Pavia, twenty-five miles away, for use in constructing new houses there. By 1167, most of the cities of northern Italy had joined with the pope to form the Lombard League against Frederick. Defeated by the league at the battle of Legnano in 1176, Frederick made peace and withdrew most of his forces from Italy. The battle marked the triumph of the city over the crown in Italy, which would not have a centralized government until the nineteenth century; its political history would instead be that of its various regions and their dominant cities.

Frederick Barbarossa was the victim of traditions that were rapidly being outmoded. He based much of his rule in Germany on the bond of lord and vassal at the very moment when rulers elsewhere were relying less on such personal ties and more on salaried officials. He lived up to the meaning of *emperor*, with all its obligations to rule Rome and northern Italy, when other leaders were consolidating their territorial rule bit by bit. In addition, as "universal" emperor, he did not recognize the importance of local pride, language, customs, and traditions; he tried to rule Italian communes with his own men from the outside, and he failed.

Henry the Lion: Lord and Vassal.

Frederick also had problems in Germany, where he had to contend with princes of near-royal status who acted as independent rulers of their principalities, though acknowledging Frederick as their feudal lord. One of the most powerful was Henry the Lion (c. 1130–1195). Married to Matilda, daughter of the English king Henry II and Eleanor of Aquitaine, Henry was duke of Saxony and Bavaria, which gave him important bases in both the north and the south of Germany. (See Henry the Lion and Matilda, this page.) A self-confident and aggressive ruler, Henry dominated his territory by investing bishops (usurping the role of the emperor as outlined in the Concordat of Worms), collecting dues from his estates, and exercising judicial rights over his duchies. He also actively extended his rule, especially in Slavic regions, pushing northeast past the Elbe River to reestablish dioceses and to build the commercial city of Lübeck.

Henry was lord of many vassals and ministerials (people of unfree status but high prestige). With his army reinforced by Slavs, Henry expanded into new territories. He also organized a staff of clerics and ministerials to collect taxes and tolls and to write up his legal acts. Here, as elsewhere, administration no longer depended entirely on the personal involvement of the ruler.

Yet like kings, princes could fall. Henry's growing power so threatened other princes and even Frederick that in 1179 Frederick called Henry to the king's court for violating the peace. When Henry chose not to appear, Frederick exercised his

Henry the Lion and Matilda
In this deluxe manuscript of a liturgical book made for Henry the Lion, the duke and his wife are shown being crowned from heaven. Behind them are their royal and ducal forefathers.
(Herzog August Bibliothek Wolfenbüttel: Cod. Guelf. 105 Noviss. 2, 171 v.)

authority as Henry's lord and charged him with violating his duty as a vassal. Because Henry refused the summons to court and avoided serving his lord in Italy, Frederick condemned him, confiscated his holdings, and drove him out of Germany in 1180.

Late-twelfth-century kings and emperors often found themselves engaged in a balancing act of ruling yet placating their powerful vassals. The process was almost always risky. Successfully challenging one recalcitrant prince/vassal meant negotiating costly deals with the others, since their support was vital. Frederick wanted to retain Henry's duchy for himself, as Philip Augustus had managed to do with Normandy. But Frederick was not powerful enough to do so and was forced to divide and distribute it to the supporters he had relied on to enforce his decrees against Henry.

Eastern Europe and Byzantium: Fragmenting Realms

The importance of governmental and bureaucratic institutions such as those developed in England and France is made especially clear by comparing the experience of regions where they

Eastern Europe and Byzantium, c. 1200

were not established. In eastern Europe, the characteristic pattern was for states to form under the leadership of one great ruler and then to fragment under his successor. For example, King Béla III of Hungary (r. 1172–1196) built up a state that looked superficially like a western European kingdom. He married a French princess, sent his officials to Paris to be educated, and built his palace in the French Romanesque style. The annual income from his estates, tolls, dues, and taxes equaled that of the richest western monarchs. But he did not set up enduring governmental institutions, and in the decades that followed his death, wars between Béla's sons splintered his monarchical holdings, and aristocratic supporters divided the wealth.

Russia underwent a similar process. Although twelfth-century Kiev was politically fragmented, autocratic princes to the north constructed Suzdal, the nucleus of the later Muscovite state. The borders of Suzdal were clearly defined, well-to-do towns prospered, monasteries and churches dotted the countryside, and the other princes of Russia recognized its ruler as the "grand prince." Yet in 1212, this nascent state began to crumble as the sons of Grand Prince Vsevolod III (r. 1176–1212) fought one another for territory, much as Béla's sons had done in Hungary.

Although the Byzantine Empire was already a consolidated, bureaucratic state, after the mid-twelfth century it gradually began to show weaknesses. Traders from the west—the Venetians especially—dominated its commerce. The Byzantine emperors who ruled during the last half of the twelfth century downgraded the old civil servants, elevated imperial relatives to high offices, and favored the military elite, who nevertheless rarely came to the aid of the emperor. As Byzantine rule grew more personal and European rule became more bureaucratic, the two gradually became more like one another.

The Byzantine Empire might well have continued like this for a long time. Instead, its heart was knocked out by the warriors of the Fourth Crusade (1202–1204). At the instigation of Venice, the crusaders made a detour to Constantinople on their way to the Holy Land, capturing the city in 1204. Although one of the crusade leaders was named "emperor" and ruled in Constantinople and its surrounding territory, the Byzantine Empire itself continued to exist, though disunited and weak (see Mapping the West, page 356). In 1261 it retook Constantinople, but it never regained the power that it had had in the eleventh century.

REVIEW: What new sources and institutions of power became available to rulers in the second half of the twelfth century?

The Growth of a Vernacular High Culture

With their consolidation of territory, wealth, and power in the last half of the twelfth century, kings, barons, princes, and their wives and daughters supported new kinds of literature and music. For the first time on the continent, though long true in England, poems and songs were written in the vernacular, the spoken language, rather than in Latin. They celebrated the lives of the nobility and were meant to be read or sung aloud, sometimes with accompanying musical instruments. They provided a common experience for aristocrats at court. Whether in the cities of Italy or the more isolated courts of northern Europe, patrons and patronesses, enriched by their estates and commerce, now spent their profits on the arts. Their support helped develop and enrich the spoken language while it heightened their prestige as aristocrats.

The Troubadours: Poets of Love and Play

Already at the beginning of the twelfth century, Duke William IX of Aquitaine (1071–1126), the grandfather of Eleanor, had written lyric poems in Occitan, the vernacular of southern France. Perhaps influenced by Arabic and Hebrew love poetry from al-Andalus, his own poetry in turn provided a model for poetic forms that gained popularity through repeated performances. The final four-line stanza of one such poem demonstrates the composer's skill with words:

Per aquesta fri e tremble,	For this one I shiver and tremble,
quar de tan bon' amor l'am;	I love her with such a good love;
qu'anc no cug qu'en nasques semble	I do not think the like of her was ever born
en semblan de gran linh n'Adam.	in the long line of Lord Adam.

The rhyme scheme of this poem appears to be simple—*tremble* goes with *semble*, *l'am* with *n'Adam*—but the entire poem has five earlier verses, all six lines long and all containing the -*am*, -*am* rhyme in the fourth and sixth lines, while every other line within each verse rhymes as well.

Troubadours, lyric poets who wrote in Occitan, varied their rhymes and meters endlessly to dazzle their audiences with brilliant originality. Most of their rhymes and meters resemble Latin religious poetry of the same time, indicating that the vernacular and Latin religious cultures overlapped. Such similarity is also evident in the troubadours' choice of subjects. The most common topic, love, echoed the twelfth-century church's emphasis on the emotional relationship between God and humans.

The troubadours invented new meanings for old images. When William IX sang of his "good love" for a woman unlike any other born in the line of Adam, the words could be interpreted in two ways. They reminded listeners of the Virgin Mary, a woman unlike any other, but they also referred to William's lover, recalled in another part of the poem, where he had complained

> If I do not get help soon
> and my lady does not give me love,
> by Saint Gregory's holy head I'll die
> if she doesn't kiss me in a chamber or under a tree.

His lady's character is ambiguous: she is like the Virgin Mary, but she is also his mistress.

Troubadours, both male and female, expressed prevalent views of love much as popular singers do today. The Contessa de Dia (flourished c. 1160) wrote about her unrequited love for a man:

> So bitter do I feel toward him
> whom I love more than anything.
> With him my mercy and fine manners [cortesia]
>   are in vain.

The key to troubadour verse is the idea of *cortesia*. It refers to courtesy, the refinement of people living at court, and to their struggle to achieve an ideal of virtue.

Historians and literary critics used to use the term *courtly love* to emphasize one of the themes of courtly literature: overwhelming love for a beautiful married noblewoman who is far above the poet in status and utterly unattainable. But this theme was only one of many aspects of love that the troubadours sang about: some of the songs boasted of sexual conquests, others played with the notion of equality between lovers, and still others preached that love was the source of virtue. The real overall theme of this literature is not courtly love; it is the power of women. No wonder Eleanor of Aquitaine and other aristocratic women patronized the troubadours: they enjoyed the image that it gave them of themselves. Until recently, historians thought that the image was a delusion and that twelfth-century aristocratic women were valuable mainly as heiresses to marry and as mothers of sons. But new research reveals that there were many powerful female lords in southern France. They owned property, had vassals, led battles, decided disputes, and entered into and broke political alliances as their advantage dictated. Both men and women appreciated troubadour poetry, which recognized and praised women's power even as it eroticized it.

Music was part of troubadour poetry, which was always sung, typically by a *jongleur*, a medieval musician. No written troubadour music exists from before the thirteenth century, and even then we have music for only a fraction of the poems. This music was written on four- and five-line staves, so scholars can at least determine relative pitches, and modern musicians can sing some troubadour songs with the hope of sounding rea-

---

troubadours: Vernacular poets in southern France in the twelfth and early thirteenth centuries who sang of love, longing, and courtesy.

FIGURE 11.4 Troubadour Song: "I Never Died for Love"
This music is the first part of a song that the troubadour poet Peire Vidal wrote sometime between 1175 and 1205. It has been adapted here for the treble clef. There is no time signature, but the music may easily be played by calculating one beat for each note, except for the two-note slurs, which fit into one beat together. *(From Samuel N. Rosenberg, Margaret Switten, and Gerard Le Vot, eds.,* Songs of the Troubadours and Trouvères. *Copyright © 1997 by Samuel N. Rosenberg, Margaret Switten, and Gerard Le Vot. Reprinted by permission of Taylor & Francis/Garland Publishing, http://www.taylorandfrancis.com.)*

sonably like the original. This is the earliest popular music that can be re-created authentically (Figure 11.4).

From southern France, the troubadours' songs spread to Italy, northern France, England, and Germany. Similar poetry appeared in other vernacular languages: the *minnesingers* (literally, "love singers") sang in German; the *trouvères* sang in the Old French of northern France. One trouvère was the English king Richard the Lion-Hearted. Taken prisoner on his return from the Third Crusade, Richard wrote a poem expressing his longing not for a lady but for the good companions of war, the knightly "youths" he had joined in battle:

> They know well, the men of Anjou and Touraine,
> those bachelors, now so magnificent and safe,
> that I am arrested, far from them, in another's hands.
> They used to love me much, now they love me not at all.
> There's no lordly fighting now on the barren plains,
> because I am a prisoner.

The Literature of Epic and Romance

The yearning for the battlefield was not as common a topic in lyric poetry as love, but long nar-

rative poems about heroic deeds, called **chansons de geste**, appeared frequently in vernacular writing. Such poems followed a long oral tradition and appeared at about the same time as love poems. Like the songs of the troubadours, these epic poems implied a code of behavior for aristocrats, in this case on the battlefield.

By the end of the twelfth century, warriors wanted a guide for conduct and a common identity. Nobles and knights had begun to merge into one class as they felt threatened from below by newly rich merchants and from above by newly powerful kings. Their ascendancy on the battlefield, where they unhorsed one another with lances and long swords and took prisoners rather than kill their opponents, was also beginning to wane in the face of mercenary infantrymen who wielded long hooks and knives that ripped easily through chain mail. A knightly ethos and sense of group solidarity emerged in the face of these social, political, and military changes. Thus, the protagonists of heroic poems yearned not for love but for battle:

> The armies are in sight of one another. . . . The cowards tremble as they march, but the brave hearts rejoice for the battle.

Examining the moral issues that made war both tragic and inevitable, poets played on the contradictory values of their society, such as the conflicting loyalties of friendship and vassalage or a vassal's right to a fief versus a son's right to his father's land.

These vernacular narrative poems, later called epics, focused on war. Other long poems, later called romances, explored the relationships between men and women. Romances reached their zenith of popularity during the late twelfth and early thirteenth centuries. The legend of King Arthur inspired many of them. For example, in a romance by the poet Chrétien de Troyes (c. 1150–1190) the heroic knight, Lancelot, who is in love with King Arthur's wife, Queen Guinevere, comes across a comb bearing some strands of her radiant hair:

> Never will the eye of man see anything receive such honor as when [Lancelot] begins to adore these tresses. . . . Even for St. Martin and St. James he has no need.

Chrétien is evoking the familiar imagery of relics, such as bits of hair or the bones of saints, as items of devotion. Making Guinevere's hair an object of adoration not only conveys the depth of Lancelot's feeling but also pokes a bit of fun at him. Like the

---

chansons de geste (shahn SOHN duh ZHEST): Epic poems of the twelfth century about knightly and heroic deeds.

troubadours, the romantic poets enjoyed the interplay between religious and amorous feelings. Just as the ideal monk merged his will in God's will, Lancelot loses his will to Guinevere. When she sees him — the greatest knight in Christendom — fighting in a tournament, she tests him by asking him to do his "worst." The poor knight is obliged to lose all his battles until she changes her mind.

Lancelot was the perfect chivalric knight. The word *chivalry* derives from the French word *cheval* ("horse"); the fact that the knight was a horseman marked him as a warrior of the most prestigious sort. Perched high on his horse, his heavy lance couched in his right arm, the knight was an imposing and menacing figure. Chivalry made him gentle — except to his enemies on the battlefield. The chivalric hero was a knight constrained by a code of refinement, fair play, piety, and devotion to an ideal. Historians debate whether real knights lived up to the codes implicit in epics and romances, but there is no doubt that knights saw themselves mirrored there. They were the poets' audience; sometimes they were the poets' subject as well. For example, when the knight William the Marshal died, his son commissioned a poet to write his biography. In it, William was depicted as a model knight, courteous with the ladies and brave on the battlefield.

> **REVIEW:** What do the works of the troubadours and vernacular poets reveal about the nature of entertainment — its themes, its audience, its performers — in the twelfth century?

Religious Fervor and Crusade

The new vernacular culture was merely one reflection of the growing wealth, sophistication, and self-confidence of the late twelfth century. New forms of religious life were another. Unlike the reformed orders of the early half of the century, which had fled the cities, the new religious groups embraced (and were embraced by) urban populations. Rich and poor, male and female joined these movements. They criticized the existing church as too wealthy, impersonal, and spiritually superficial. Intensely focused on the life of Christ, men and women in the late twelfth century made his childhood, agony, death, and presence in the Eucharist — the bread and wine that became the body and blood of Christ in the Mass — the most important experiences of their own lives.

Religious fervor mixed with greed in new crusades that had little success in the Holy Land but were victorious on the borders of Europe and, as we have already seen, at Constantinople. These were the poisonous flowers of the Middle Ages.

New Religious Orders in the Cities

The quick rebuilding of the cathedral at Chartres reveals the religious fervor of late-twelfth-century city dwellers. New religious orders in the cities do so as well. Appealing to people who did not want to leave urban society but who, nevertheless, wished to deepen their religious lives, the new orders — including the Franciscans and the Beguines — had enormous success. Some of these urban movements, however, so threatened established doctrine and church hierarchy that they were condemned as heresies.

Francis and the Franciscans. St. Francis (c. 1182–1226) founded the most famous orthodox religious movement — the **Franciscans**. Francis was a child of city life and commerce. Expected to follow his well-to-do father in the cloth trade at Assisi in Italy, Francis began to experience doubts, dreams, and illnesses, which spurred him to religious self-examination. Eventually, he renounced his family's wealth, dramatically marking the decision by casting off all his clothes and standing naked before his father, a crowd of spectators, and the bishop of Assisi. Francis then put on a simple robe and went about preaching penance to anyone who would listen.

Clinging to poverty as if, in his words, "she" were his "lady" (and thus borrowing the vocabulary of chivalry), he accepted no money, walked without shoes, and wore only one coarse tunic. Francis brought religious devotion out of the monastery and into the streets. Intending to follow the model of Christ, he received, as his biographers put it, a miraculous gift of grace: the stigmata, bleeding sores corresponding to the wounds Christ suffered on the cross.

By all accounts Francis was a spellbinding speaker, and he attracted many followers. Because they went about begging, those followers were called mendicants, from the Latin verb *mendicare*, meaning "to beg." Recognized as a religious order by the pope, the Brothers of St. Francis (or friars, from the Latin term for "brothers") spent their time preaching, ministering to lepers, and doing manual labor. Eventually they dispersed, setting up

---

Franciscans: A religious order, founded by St. Francis (c. 1182–1226), dedicated to poverty and preaching, particularly in towns and cities.

fraternal groups throughout Italy and then in France, Spain, the Holy Land, Germany, and England. The friars sought town society, preaching to crowds and begging for their daily bread. St. Francis converted both men and women. In 1212, an eighteen-year-old noblewoman, Clare, formed the nucleus of a community of pious women, which became the Order of the Sisters of St. Francis. At first, the women worked alongside the friars; but both Francis and the church hierarchy disapproved of their activities in the world, and soon Franciscan sisters were confined to cloisters under the rule of St. Benedict.

The Beguines.   Clare was one of many women who sought a new kind of religious expression. Some women joined convents; others became recluses, living alone, like hermits; still others sought membership in new lay sisterhoods. In northern Europe at the end of the twelfth century, laywomen who lived together in informal pious communities were called Beguines. Without permanent vows or an established rule, the Beguines chose to be celibate (though they were free to leave and marry) and often made their living by weaving cloth or tending to the sick and old. Some of them may have prepared and illustrated their own reading materials. (See the Beguine Psalter, this page.) Although their daily occupations were ordinary, the Beguines' spiritual lives were often emotional and ecstatic, infused with the combined imagery of love and religion so pervasive in both monasteries and courts. One renowned Beguine, Mary of Oignies (1177–1213), who, like St. Francis, was said to have received stigmata, felt herself to be a pious mother entrusted with the Christ child. As her biographer, Jacques de Vitry, wrote, "Sometimes it seemed to her that for three or more days she held [Christ] close to her so that He nestled between her breasts like a baby, and she hid Him there lest He be seen by others."

Heresies.   In addition to the orthodox religious movements that took off at the end of the twelfth century, there was a veritable explosion of ideas and doctrines that contradicted those officially accepted by church authorities and were therefore labeled heresies. Heresies were not new in the twelfth century. But the eleventh-century Gregorian reform had created for the first time in the West a clear church hierarchy headed by a pope who could enforce a single doctrine and discipline. Clearly defined orthodoxy meant that people in western Europe now perceived heresy as a serious problem. When intense religious feeling led to the fervent espousal of new religious ideas, established

Beguine Psalter
Although emphasizing labor and caring for others, most Beguines were also literate. The Psalter (book of Psalms) illustrated here was probably made by Beguines. The painting focuses on Mary: in the bottom tier is the Annunciation, when she learns that she will give birth to the Savior. At the top she reigns as Queen of Heaven, with a crown on her head and the baby Jesus on her lap. *(By permission of the British Library.)*

authorities often felt threatened and took steps to preserve their power.

Among the most visible heretics were dualists who saw the world as being torn between two great forces, one good, the other evil. Already important in Bulgaria and Asia Minor, dualism became a prominent ingredient in religious life in Italy and the Rhineland by the end of the twelfth century. Another center of dualism was Languedoc, an area of southern France; there the dualists were called Albigensians, a name derived from the town of Albi.

Calling themselves "Christ's poor" — though modern historians have given them the collective name Cathars — these men and women believed that the devil had created the material world. Therefore, they renounced the world, abjuring wealth, meat, and sex. Their repudiation of sex reflected some of the attitudes of eleventh-century church reformers (whose orthodoxy, however, was never in doubt), while their rejection of wealth echoed the same concerns that moved St. Francis to embrace poverty. In many ways, the dualists simply took these attitudes to an extreme; but unlike orthodox reformers, they also challenged the efficacy and legitimacy of the church hierarchy. Attracting both men and women, young and old, literate and unlettered, and giving women access to all but the highest positions in their church, the dualists saw themselves as followers of Christ's original message. But the church called them heretics.

The church also condemned other, nondualist groups as heretical, not on doctrinal grounds but because these groups allowed their lay members to preach, challenging the authority of the church hierarchy. In Lyon (in southeastern France) in the 1170s, for example, a rich merchant named Waldo decided to take literally the Gospel message "If you wish to be perfect, then go and sell everything you have, and give to the poor" (Matt. 19:21). The same message had inspired countless monks and would worry the church far less several decades later, when St. Francis established his new order. But when Waldo went into the street and gave away his belongings, announcing, "I am not really insane, as you think," he scandalized not only the bystanders but the church as well. Refusing to retire to a monastery, Waldo and his followers — men and women who called themselves the Poor of Lyon but were called Waldensians by their enemies — lived in poverty. They spent their time preaching, quoting the Gospel in the vernacular so that everyone would understand. But the papacy rebuffed Waldo's bid to preach freely; and his community — denounced, excommunicated, and expelled from Lyon — wandered to Languedoc, Italy, northern Spain, and the Moselle valley in Germany. Most were persecuted and eventually exterminated, but a few remnants survived and their descendents were absorbed into the sixteenth-century Protestant Reformation.

Disastrous Crusades to the Holy Land

Did religious fervor also inspire the new crusades of the later twelfth century? At least some Europeans thought so. The pope called the Third Crusade "an opportunity for repentance and doing good." A poet in Bavaria wrote, "If any man now will not have pity upon [Christ's] cross and his Sepulcher [in Jerusalem], then he will not be given heavenly bliss."

Following the crushing defeat of the crusaders in the Second Crusade, the Muslim hero Nur al-Din united Syria and presided over a renewal of Sunni Islam. His successor, Saladin (1138–1193), fought the Christian king of Jerusalem over Egypt, which Saladin ruled, together with Syria, by 1186. Caught in a pincer, Jerusalem fell to Saladin's armies in 1187. The Third Crusade, an unsuccessful bid to retake Jerusalem, marked a military and political turning point for the crusader states. The European outpost survived, but it was reduced to a narrow strip of land. Christians could continue to enter Jerusalem as pilgrims, but Islamic hegemony over the Holy Land would remain a fact of life for centuries.

The Third Crusade, 1189–1192. Led by the greatest rulers of Europe — Emperor Frederick I Barbarossa, Philip II of France, Leopold of Austria, and Richard I of England — the Third Crusade reflected political tensions among the European ruling class. Richard, in particular, seemed to cultivate enemies. The most serious of these was Leopold, whom he offended at the siege of Acre. But the apparent personal tensions indicated a broader hostility between the kings of England and France. In this, Leopold was Philip's ally. On his return home, Richard was captured by Leopold and held for a huge ransom. He had good reason to write his plaintive poem bemoaning his captivity and the lost "love" of former friends.

The Third Crusade accomplished little and exacerbated tensions with Byzantium. Frederick I went overland on the crusade, passing through Hungary and Bulgaria and descending into the Byzantine Empire (Map 11.2). Before his untimely death by drowning in Turkey, he spent most of his time harassing the Byzantines.

The Fourth Crusade, 1202–1204. The hostilities that surfaced during the Third Crusade made it a dress rehearsal for the Fourth. Resentment had built up against the Byzantine Greeks ever since the First Crusade, when they had abandoned the crusaders after the battle of Nicaea (see page 316). During the **Fourth Crusade** prejudice and religious zeal combined to persuade many of the crusaders to change their plans and capture Constantinople rather than Jerusalem (see Map 11.2). (Some, disgusted by the new goal, went home.)

The Venetians instigated the change of plans. After the pope called the crusade, the Venetians

---

Fourth Crusade: The crusade that lasted from 1202 to 1204; its original goal was to recapture Jerusalem, but the crusaders ended up conquering Constantinople instead.

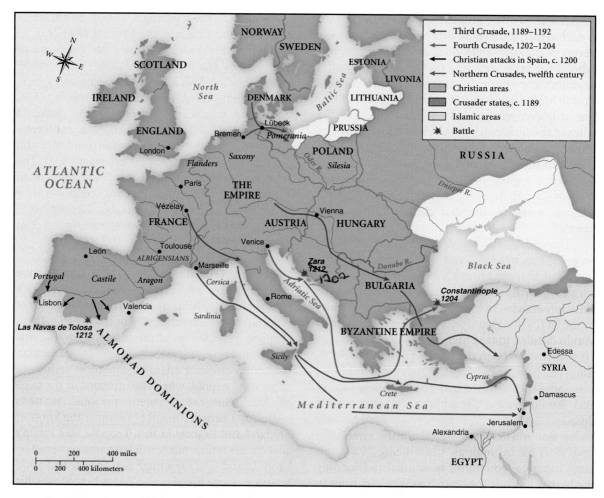

MAP 11.2 Crusades and Anti-Heretic Campaigns, 1150–1204
Europeans aggressively expanded their territory during the second half of the twelfth century. To the north, German knights pushed into Pomerania; to the south, Spanish warriors moved into the remaining strip of al-Andalus; to the east, new crusades were undertaken to shore up the tiny European outpost in the Holy Land. Although most of these aggressive activities had the establishment of Christianity as at least one motive, the conquest of Constantinople in 1204 had no such justification. It grew in part out of general European hostility toward Byzantium but mainly out of Venice's commercial ambitions.

fitted out a fine fleet of ships and galleys for the expedition. But when the crusaders arrived in Venice, there were far fewer fighters to pay for the transport than had been anticipated. To defray the costs of the ships and other expenses, the Venetians convinced the crusaders to do them some favors before taking off against the Muslims. First, they had the crusaders attack Zara, a Christian city in Dalmatia (today's Croatia) but Venice's competitor in the Adriatic. Then they urged the army to attack Constantinople itself, where they hoped to gain commercial advantage over their rivals. Convinced of the superiority of their brand of Christianity over that of the Byzantines, the crusaders plundered, killed, and ransacked the city for treasure and relics. "Never," wrote a contemporary, "was so great an enterprise undertaken by any

people since the creation of the world." When one crusader discovered a cache of relics, a chronicler recalled, "he plunged both hands in and, girding up his loins, he filled the folds of his gown with the holy booty of the Church."

The pope decried the sack of Constantinople, but he also took advantage of it, ordering the crusaders to stay there for a year to consolidate their gains. Plans to go on to the Holy Land were never carried out. The crusade leaders chose one of themselves—Baldwin of Flanders—to be emperor, and he, the other princes, and the Venetians divided the conquered lands among themselves.

Popes continued to call crusades to the Holy Land until the mid-fifteenth century, but the Fourth Crusade marked the last major mobilization of men and leaders for such an enterprise.

Working against these expeditions were the new values of the late twelfth century, which placed a premium on the interior pilgrimage of the soul and wanted rulers to stay home and care for their people. (See Document, "The Children's Crusade," page 355.)

Victorious Crusades in Europe and on Its Frontiers

Armed expeditions against those perceived as infidels were launched not only to the Holy Land but also much nearer to home. In the second half of the twelfth century, the Spanish reconquista continued with increasing success and virulence, new wars of conquest were waged at the northern edge of Europe, and a crusade was launched against the Albigensians living in Europe itself.

The War in Spain. In the second half of the twelfth century, Christian Spain achieved the political configuration that would last for centuries, dominated to the east by the kingdom of Aragon; in the middle by Castile, whose ruler styled himself emperor; and in the west by Portugal, whose ruler similarly transformed his title from prince to king. The three leaders competed for territory and power, but above all they sought an advantage against the Muslims to the south (Map 11.3).

Muslim disunity aided the Christian conquest of Spain. The Muslims of al-Andalus were themselves beset from the south by waves of new groups of Berber Muslims from North Africa. Claiming religious purity, these North African zealots declared their own holy war against the Andalusians. Beset from north and south, the Muslim leaders of Spain tried to negotiate with their Christian neighbors, sometimes even swearing vassalage to them.

But the crusading ideal held no room for such subtleties. The reconquista was set back by Berber victories, and competition between the Christian Spanish states prevented a coordinated effort. Nevertheless, piecemeal conquests—followed by the granting of law codes to regulate relations among new Christian settlers as well as the Muslims, Mozarabs (Christians who had lived under the Muslims), and Jews who remained—gradually brought more territory under the control of the north. In 1212, a crusading army of Spaniards led by the kings of Aragon and Castile defeated the Muslims decisively at the battle of Las Navas de Tolosa. "On their side 100,000 armed men or more fell in the battle," the king of Castile wrote afterward, "but of the army of the Lord . . . incredible

Reconquista
In the north of Spain, the Christians adopted the figure of St. James, considered the Apostle to Spain, as the supernatural leader of their armies against the Muslims to the south. On this tympanum—the space within the archway over a door—from the cathedral of St. James (Santiago) at Compostela, James is shown as a knight on horseback, holding a flag and a sword. He was known as "the Moor-Slayer"—slayer of Muslims. Was the reconquista a holy war? How was it like the crusades, and how was it different? *(Institut Amatller de Arte Hispanico. Arxiu Mas.)*

though it may be, unless it be a miracle, hardly 25 or 30 Christians of our whole army fell. O what happiness! O what thanksgiving!" The decisive turning point in the reconquista had been reached, though all of Spain came under Christian control only in 1492.

The Northern Crusades. Christians flexed their military muscle along Europe's northern frontiers as well. By the twelfth century, the peoples living along the Baltic coast—partly pagan, mostly Slavic- or Baltic-speaking—had learned to glean a living and a profit from the inhospitable soil and climate. Through fishing and trading, they supplied the rest of Europe and Russia with slaves, furs, amber, wax, and dried fish. Like the earlier Vikings, they combined commercial competition with outright raiding, so that the Danes and the Germans of Saxony both benefited and suffered from their presence. As noted in Chapter 10 (page 317), during the Second Crusade a number of campaigns had been launched against the people on the Baltic coast. Thus began the Northern Crusades, which continued intermittently until the early fifteenth century.

The Danish king Valdemar I (r. 1157–1182) and the Saxon duke Henry the Lion led the first

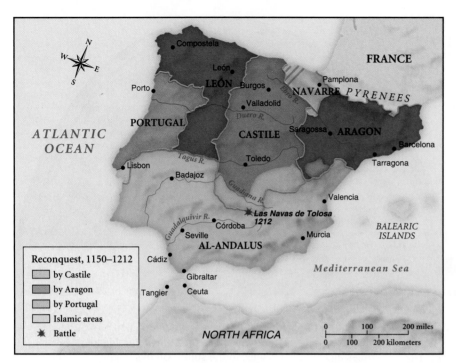

MAP 11.3 The Reconquista, 1150–1212
Slowly but surely the Christian kingdoms of Spain encroached on al-Andalus, taking Las Navas de Tolosa, deep in Islamic territory, in 1212. At the center of this activity was Castile. It had originally been a tributary of León, but in the twelfth century it became a power in its own right. (In 1230, León and Castile merged into one kingdom.) Meanwhile, the ruler of Portugal, who had also been dependent on León, began to claim the title of king, which was recognized officially in 1179, when he put Portugal under the protection of the papacy. Navarre was joined to Aragon until 1134, when it became, briefly, an independent kingdom. (In 1234, the count of Champagne came to the throne of Navarre, and thereafter its history was as much tied to France as to Spain.)

phase of the Northern Crusades. Their initial attacks on the Slavs were uncoordinated—in some instances, the Danes and Saxons even fought each other. But in key raids in the 1160s and 1170s, the two leaders worked together briefly to bring much of the region west of the Oder River under their control. They took some land outright—Henry the Lion apportioned conquered territory to his followers, for example—but more often the Slavic princes surrendered and had their territories reinstated once they became vassals of the Christian rulers. Meanwhile, churchmen arrived: the Cistercians came long before the first phase of fighting had ended, confidently building their monasteries to the very banks of the Oder River. Slavic peasants surely suffered from the conquerors' fire and pillage, but the Slavic ruling classes ultimately benefited from the crusades. Once converted to Christianity, they found it advantageous for both their eternal salvation and their worldly profit to join new crusades to areas still farther east.

Meanwhile German traders, craftspeople, and colonists poured in, populating new towns and cities along the Baltic coast and dominating the shipping that had once been controlled by non-Christians. The leaders of the crusades gave these townsmen some political independence but demanded a large share of the cities' wealth in return.

Although less well known than the crusades to the Holy Land, the Northern Crusades had far more lasting effects: they settled the Baltic region with German-speaking lords and peasants and forged a permanent relationship between northeastern Europe and its neighbors to the south and west. With the Baltic dotted with churches and monasteries and its peoples dipped into baptismal waters, the region would gradually adopt the institutions of western medieval society—cities, guilds, universities, castles, and manors. The Livs (whose region was eventually known as Livonia) were conquered by 1208, and their bishop sent knights northward to conquer the Estonians. A cooperative venture between the Polish and German aristocracy conquered the Prussians, and German peasants eventually settled Prussia. Only the Lithuanians managed to resist western conquest, settlement, and conversion.

The Albigensian Crusade. The first crusade to be launched within Europe itself was against the Cathars in southern France. It began with papal missions to preach to the people there, convert the heretics, and, if necessary use force. The Dominican Order had its start in this way. Its founder, St. Dominic (1170–1221), recognized that preachers of Christ's word who came to the region on horseback, followed by a crowd of servants and wearing fine clothes, had no moral leverage with their audience. Dominic and his followers, like their heretical adversaries, rejected material riches and instead went about on foot, preaching and begging. They resembled the Franciscans, both organizationally and spiritually, and were also called friars.

The missions did not have the success anticipated, however, and in 1208, the murder of a

DOCUMENT

The Children's Crusade (1212)

In some regions, intense lay piety led groups of unarmed young people, accompanied by priests and other adults, to attempt to free the Holy Sepulcher at Jerusalem. Chroniclers recorded their activities, some with dismay, others with amusement or admiration. The account below comes from the Ebersheim Chronicle, *written in Germany.*

Unheard-of events appeal to us from their outset, challenging us to preserve their memory. A certain little boy named Nicholas, who came from the region of Cologne, spurred on a great gathering of children through some unknown coun-

sel, claiming that he could walk across the waves of the sea without wetting his feet and could provide sufficient provisions for those following him. The rumor of such a marvelous deed resounded through the cities and towns, and however many heard him, boys or girls, they abandoned their parents, marked themselves as crusaders, and prepared to cross the sea. And so throughout all Germany and France an infinite number of serving-boys, handmaids, and maidens followed their leader and came to Vienne, which is a city by the sea.[1] There they were taken on board some ships, carried

off by pirates, and sold to the Saracens. Some who tried to return home wasted away with hunger; and many girls who were virgins when they left were pregnant when they returned. Thus, one can clearly see that this journey issued from the deception of the devil because it caused so much loss.

Source: *Medieval Popular Religion 1000–1500: A Reader,* ed. John Shinners, 2nd ed. (Peterborough, Ontario: Broadview Press, 2007), 418–19.

---

[1] Vienne isn't by the sea, but the crusaders did get to various Mediterranean port cities.

---

papal legate in southern France prompted the pope to demand that northern princes take up the sword, invade Languedoc, wrest the land from the heretics, and populate it with orthodox Christians. The Albigensian Crusade (1209–1229) marked the first time the pope offered warriors fighting an enemy within Christian Europe all the spiritual and temporal benefits of a crusade to the Holy Land. The crusaders' monetary debts were suspended, and they were promised that their sins would be forgiven after forty days' service. Like all other crusades, the Albigensian Crusade had political as well as religious dimensions. It pitted southern French princes, who often had heretical sympathies, against northern leaders eager to demonstrate their piety and win new possessions. After twenty years of fighting, the dynasty of the Capetian kings of France took over leadership of the crusade in 1229. Southern resistance was broken, and Languedoc was brought under the French crown.

The Albigensian Crusade, 1209–1229

REVIEW: How did the idea of crusade change from the time of the original expedition to the Holy Land?

Conclusion

In the second half of the twelfth century, Christian Europe expanded from the Baltic Sea to the southern Iberian peninsula. European settlements in the Holy Land, by contrast, were nearly obliterated. When western Europeans sacked Constantinople in 1204, Europe and the Islamic world became the dominant political forces in the West.

Powerful territorial kings and princes established institutions of bureaucratic authority. They hired staffs to handle their accounts, record acts, collect taxes, issue writs, and preside over courts. A money economy provided the finances necessary to support the personnel now hired by medieval governments. Cathedral schools and universities became the training grounds for the new administrators. A new lay vernacular culture celebrated the achievements and power of the ruling class, while Gothic architecture reflected above all the pride and power of the cities.

New religious groups blossomed. Beguines, Franciscans, Dominicans, and heretics — however dissimilar the particulars of their beliefs and lifestyles — all reflected the fact that people,

MAPPING THE WEST

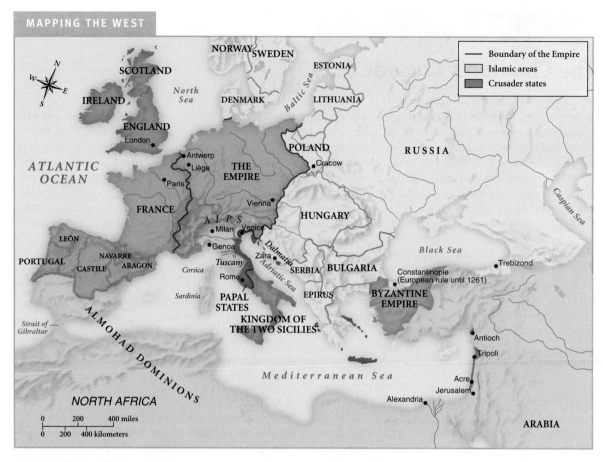

Europe and Byzantium, c. 1215
The major transformation in the map of the West between 1150 and 1215 was the conquest of Constantinople and the setting up of European rule there until 1261. The Byzantine Empire was now a mere shell. A new state, Epirus, emerged in the power vacuum to dominate Thrace. Bulgaria once again gained its independence. If Venice had hoped to control the Adriatic by conquering Constantinople, it must have been disappointed, for Hungary became its rival over the ports of the Dalmatian coast.

especially city dwellers, yearned for a deeper spirituality.

Intense religiosity helped fuel the flames of crusades, which were now fought more often and against an increasing variety of foes, not only in the Holy Land but also in Spain, in southern France, and on Europe's northern frontiers. With heretics voicing criticisms and maintaining their beliefs, the church, led by the papacy, now defined orthodoxy and declared dissenters its enemies. The peoples on the Baltic coast became targets for new evangelical zeal; the Byzantines became the butt of envy, hostility, and finally enmity. European Christians still considered Muslims arrogant heathens, and the deflection of the Fourth Crusade did not stem the zeal of popes to call for new crusades to the Holy Land.

Confident and aggressive, the leaders of Christian Europe in the thirteenth century would attempt to impose their rule, legislate morality,

and create a unified worldview impregnable to attack. But this drive for order would be countered by unexpected varieties of thought and action, by political and social tensions, and by intensely personal religious quests.

FOR FURTHER EXPLORATION

■ **For suggested references, including Web sites, for topics in this chapter,** see page SR-1 at the end of the book.

■ **For additional primary-source material from this period,** see Chapter 11 in *Sources of THE MAKING OF THE WEST,* Third Edition.

■ **For Web sites and documents related to topics in this chapter,** see *Make History* at bedfordstmartins.com/hunt.

CHAPTER REVIEW

KEY TERMS AND PEOPLE

Gothic architecture (333)
Henry II (336)
common law (338)
Philip II (Philip Augustus) (340)
Magna Carta (340)
Frederick I (Barbarossa) (342)
troubadours (347)
chansons de geste (348)
Franciscans (349)
Fourth Crusade (351)

REVIEW QUESTIONS

1. What was new about the learning in the schools and the architecture of church buildings in the twelfth and early thirteenth centuries?

2. What new sources and institutions of power became available to rulers in the second half of the twelfth century?

3. What do the works of the troubadours and vernacular poets reveal about the nature of entertainment — its themes, its audience, its performers — in the twelfth century?

4. How did the idea of crusade change from the time of the original expedition to the Holy Land?

MAKING CONNECTIONS

1. What were the chief differences that separated the ideals of the religious life in the period 1150–1215 from those of the period 1050–1150?

2. How was the gift economy associated with Romanesque architecture and the money economy with the Gothic style?

> **For practice quizzes, a customized study plan, and other study tools,** see the Online Study Guide at bedfordstmartins.com/hunt.

IMPORTANT EVENTS

1139–1153	Civil War in England
1152–1190	Reign of Frederick Barbarossa
1154–1189	Reign of King Henry II
1176	Battle of Legnano
1180–1223	Reign of Philip II Augustus
1182–1226	Francis of Assisi
1189–1192	The Third Crusade
1202–1204	The Fourth Crusade
1204	Fall of Constantinople to crusaders
1204	Philip takes Normandy, Anjou, Maine, Touraine, and Poitou from John
1209–1229	Albigensian Crusade
1212	Battle of Las Navas de Tolosa; triumph of the reconquista
1214	Battle of Bouvines
1215	Magna Carta

The Medieval Search for Order
1215–1340

In the second half of the thirteenth century, a wealthy patron asked a Parisian workshop specializing in manuscript illuminations to decorate Aristotle's *On the Length and Shortness of Life.* Most Parisian illuminators knew very well how to illustrate the Bible, liturgical books, and the writings of the church fathers. But Aristotle was a Greek who had lived before the time of Christ, and he was skeptical about the possibility of an afterlife. His treatise on the length of life ended with death. The workshop's artists did not care about this fact. They illustrated Aristotle's work as if he had been a Christian and had believed in the immortal soul. As shown in the illustration opposite this page, for the first initial of the book (the large, highly decorated letter that opened the text), the artists depicted the Christian Mass for the dead, a rite that is performed for the eternal salvation of Christians. In this way, the artists subtly but surely made Aristotle part of the orderly system of Christian belief and practice.

In the period 1215–1340, people at all levels, from workshop artisans to kings and popes, expected to find order and unity in a world they believed was created by God. Sometimes, as in the case of the illumination made for Aristotle's work, or in the writings of scholars seeking to harmonize faith and reason, such order was made manifest. Because of this general search for unity, historians sometimes speak of the "medieval synthesis." But often disorder was the result of the search: kings and popes debated without resolution the limits of their power, while theologians fought over the place of reason in matters of faith. Discord continually threatened expectations of unity, harmony, and synthesis.

New institutions of power and control were created to ensure order. In 1215, a comprehensive set of church laws for both clergy and laity was set forth. Designed to create an orderly Christian society, these

Christianizing Aristotle
This illumination was created for a thirteenth-century Latin translation of Aristotle's *On the Length and Shortness of Life.* Although Aristotle did not believe in the eternity of the soul, the artists nevertheless placed a depiction of the Christian Mass for the dead in one of the book's initials, in this way revealing their conviction that the ancient teachings of Aristotle and Christian practice worked together. *(© Biblioteca Apostolica Vaticana (Vatican) Vat. Lat. 2071, f. 297.)*

laws sought to regulate lay life and suppress heresy. They led to the establishment of courts of inquisition designed to find and punish those who dissented from church teachings and authority.

At the same time, many Christian laypeople spontaneously sought new ways to express their religious fervor. This resulted in new devotional practices but also in the persecution of others — such as Jews and lepers — who were seen as contaminating the purity of Christian life.

But the most important characteristic of the period was not to stamp out opposition but to reconcile opposites and differences. Medieval thinkers, writers, musicians, and artists attempted to reconcile faith and reason and to find the commonalities in the sacred and secular realms. At the level of philosophy, this quest led to a new method of inquiry and study known as scholasticism.

To impose greater order, kings and other rulers found new ways to extend their influence over their subjects. They used the tools of taxes, courts, and even representative institutions to control their realms. Yet the laws did not prevent dissent, and rulers often did not gain all the power that they wanted. During this period the Empire weakened, the papacy was forced to move out of Rome, and the Mongols challenged Christian rulers. Soon natural disasters — crop failures and famine — added to the tension and further challenged the search for order.

> **FOCUS QUESTION:** In what areas of life did thirteenth-century Europeans try to impose order, and how successful were these attempts?

The Church's Mission

The church had long sought to reform the secular world. In the eleventh century, during the Gregorian reform, such efforts focused on the king. In the thirteenth century, however, the church hoped to purify all of society. It tried to strengthen its institutions of law and justice to combat heresy and heretics, and it supported preachers who would bring the official views of the church to the streets. In this way, the church attempted to reorder the world in the image of heaven, with everyone following one rule of God in order and harmony. To some degree, the church succeeded in this endeavor; but it also came up against the limits of control, as dissident voices and forces clashed with its vision.

Innocent III and the Fourth Lateran Council

Innocent III (r. 1198–1216), whose portrait appears on page 361, was the most powerful, respected, and prestigious of medieval popes. As pope, he allowed St. Francis's group of impoverished followers to become a new church order, and he called the Fourth Crusade, which mobilized a large force drawn from every level of European society. The first pope to be trained at universities, Innocent studied theology at Paris and law at Bologna. From theology, he learned to tease new meaning out of canonical writings to magnify papal authority: he thought of himself as ruling in the place of Christ the King, with kings and emperors existing to help the pope. From law, Innocent gained his conception of the pope as lawmaker and of law as an instrument of moral reformation.

Innocent used the traditional method of declaring church law: a council. Presided over by Innocent, the **Fourth Lateran Council** (1215)

Innocent III: The pope (r. 1198–1216) who called the Fourth Lateran Council; he was arguably the most powerful, respected, and prestigious of medieval popes.

Fourth Lateran Council: The council that met in 1215 and covered the important topics of Christianity, among them the nature of the sacraments, the obligations of the laity, and policies toward heretics and Jews.

■ **1188** King Alfonso IX summons townsmen to the *cortes*

■ **1212–1250** Reign of Frederick II

■ **1215** Fourth Lateran Council

■ **1240** Mongols capture Kiev

| 1175 | 1200 | 1225 | 1250 |

■ **1226–1270** Reign of Louis IX (St. Louis)

■ **1232** Frederick II, Statute in Favor of the Princes

attempted to regulate all aspects of Christian life. The comprehensive legislation it produced aimed at reforming both the clergy and the laity. Innocent and the bishops who met at the council hoped in this way to create a society united under God's law. They expected that Christians, lay and clerical alike, would work together harmoniously to achieve the common goal of salvation. They did not anticipate either the sheer variety of responses to their message or the persistence of those who defied it altogether.

The Laity and the Sacraments. For laymen and laywomen, perhaps the most important canons (church laws) of the Fourth Lateran Council concerned the sacraments, the rites the church believed Jesus had instituted to confer sanctifying grace. Building on the reforms of the eleventh century, the council made the obligations that the sacraments imposed on the laity more precise and detailed. One canon required Christians to attend Mass and to confess their sins to a priest at least once a year. The increasing importance of the Eucharist as God's powerful instrument of salvation was reinforced by the council's definition:

Innocent III

Pope Innocent III appears young, aristocratic, and impassive in this thirteenth-century fresco in the lower church of Sacro Speco, Subiaco, about thirty miles east of Rome and not far from Innocent's birthplace. Innocent claimed full power over the whole church, in all regions. Moreover, he thought the pope had the right to intervene in any issue where sin might be involved—and that meant most matters. While these were only theoretical claims, difficult to put into practice given his meager resources and inefficient staff, Innocent was a major force in his day. *(Scala/Art Resource, NY.)*

> [Christ's] body and blood are truly contained in the sacrament of the altar under the forms of bread and wine, the bread and wine having been changed in substance [transubstantiated], by God's power, into his body and blood, so that in order to achieve this mystery of unity we receive from God what he received from us. Nobody can effect this sacrament except a priest who has been properly ordained according to the church's keys, which Jesus Christ himself gave to the apostles and their successors.

The Council's emphasis on this moment of transformation gave the host—the bread taken at communion—new importance.

Other canons of the Fourth Lateran Council codified the traditions of marriage. The church de-

clared that it had the duty to discover any impediments to a union (such as a close relationship by blood), and it claimed jurisdiction over marital disputes. The canons further insisted that children conceived within clandestine or forbidden marriages be declared illegitimate; they were not to inherit from their parents or become priests.

The impact of these provisions was perhaps less dramatic than church leaders hoped. Well-to-do London fathers included their bastard children in their wills. On English manors, sons conceived out of wedlock regularly took over their parents' land. Men and women continued to marry in secret, and even churchmen had to admit that the

■ 1265 English commons
summoned to Parliament

■ 1265–1321 Dante Alighieri

■ 1302 First Meeting of the
French Estates General

1275   **1300**   **1325**

■ 1273 Thomas Aquinas, *Summa Theologiae*   ■ 1309–1378 Avignon papacy

■ 1315–1322 Great Famine

consent of both parties made any marriage valid. Nevertheless, many men and women took to heart the obligation to take communion (the Eucharist consecrated by a priest) and confess once a year, and priests proceeded to call out the banns (announcements of marriages) to discover any impediments to them.

Labeling the Jews. Innocent III had wanted the council to condemn Christian men who had sexual intercourse with Jewish women and then claimed ignorance as their excuse. But, building on the anti-Jewish feelings that had been mounting throughout the twelfth century, the Fourth Lateran Council went even further, requiring all Jews to advertise their religion by some outward sign: "We decree that [Jews] of either sex in every Christian province at all times shall be distinguished from other people by the character of their dress in public."

As with all church rules, these took effect only when local rulers enforced them. In many instances, they did so with zeal, not so much because they were eager to humiliate Jews but rather because they could make money selling exemptions to Jews who were willing to pay to avoid the requirements. Nonetheless, sooner or later Jews almost everywhere had to wear a badge as a sign of their second-class status.

In southern France and in a few places in Spain, Jews were supposed to wear round badges. In England, Oxford required a rectangular badge, while Salisbury demanded that Jews wear special clothing. In Vienna and Germany, they were told to put on pointed hats. (See Jewish Couple, page 366.)

The Suppression of Heretics. The Fourth Lateran Council's longest decree blasted heretics: "Those condemned as heretics shall be handed over to the secular authorities for punishment." If the secular authority did not carry out the punishment, the heretic was to be excommunicated. If he or she had vassals, they were to be released from their oaths of fealty. The lands of heretics were to be taken over by orthodox Christians.

Rulers heeded these declarations. Already some had taken up arms against heretics in the Albigensian Crusade (1209–1229). As a result of this crusade, southern France, which had been the home of most Albigensians, came under French royal control. The continuing presence of heretics there and elsewhere led church authorities inspired by the Fourth Lateran Council to set up a court of papal inquisitors. The Inquisition became permanent in 1233.

The Inquisition

The word *inquisition* simply means "inquiry"; secular rulers had long used the method to summon people together, either to discover facts or to uncover and punish crimes. In its zeal to end heresy and save souls, the thirteenth-century church used the Inquisition to ferret out "heretical depravity." Calling suspects to testify, inquisitors, aided by secular authorities, rounded up virtually entire villages and interrogated everyone. (See "New Sources, New Perspectives," page 364.)

Typically, the inquisitors first called the people of a district to a "preaching," where they gave a sermon and promised clemency to those who promptly confessed their heresy. Then, at a general inquest, they questioned each man and woman who seemed to know something about heresy: "Have you ever seen any heretics? Have you heard them preach? Attended any of their ceremonies? Adored heretics?" The judges assigned relatively lenient penalties to those who were not aware that they held heretical beliefs and to heretics who quickly recanted. But unrepentant heretics were punished severely because the church believed that such people threatened the salvation of all. (See "Taking Measure," page 363.)

In the thirteenth century, for the first time, long-term imprisonment became a tool to repress heresy, even if the heretic confessed. "It is our will," wrote one tribunal, "that [Raymond Maurin and Arnalda, his wife,] because they have rashly transgressed against God and holy church . . . be thrust into perpetual prison to do [appropriate] penance, and we command them to remain there in perpetuity." The inquisitors also used imprisonment to force people to recant, to give the names of other heretics, or to admit a plot. As the quest for religious control spawned wild fantasies of conspiracy, the inquisitors pinned their fears on real people.

Lay Piety

The church's zeal to reform the laity was matched by the desire of many laypeople to become more involved in their religion. They flocked to hear the preaching of friars and took what they heard to heart. Some women found new outlets for their piety by focusing on the Eucharist.

Preaching Friars and Receptive Townspeople. The friars made themselves a permanent feature of the towns. At night they slept in their friaries, but they spent their days preaching. So, too, did other men, often trained in the universities and willing to take to the road to address throngs of townsfolk. When Berthold, a Franciscan who trav-

TAKING MEASURE

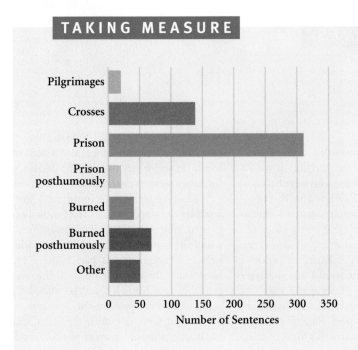

Sentences Imposed by an Inquisitor, 1308–1323
How harsh was the Inquisition? Did its agents regularly burn people alive? The register of offenses and punishments kept by Bernard Gui, an inquisitor in Languedoc from 1308 to 1323, shows that only a relatively small number of people were burned alive. Nearly half of the guilty were sentenced to prison, usually for life. *(From J. Given, "A Medieval Inquisitor at Work," in* Portraits of Medieval and Renaissance Living, *ed. S. K. Cohn and S. A. Epstein (Ann Arbor: University of Michigan Press, 1996), 215.)*

eled the length and breadth of Germany giving sermons, came to a town, a high tower was set up for him outside the city walls. A pennant advertised his presence and let people know which way the wind would blow his voice. St. Anthony of Padua preached in Italian to huge audiences that had lined up hours in advance to be sure they would have a place to hear him.

Townspeople flocked to hear such preachers because they wanted to know how the Christian message applied to their daily lives. They were concerned, for example, about the ethics of money-making, sex in marriage, and family life. In turn, the preachers represented the front line of the church. They met the laity on their own turf, spoke in the vernacular that all could understand, and taught them to shape their behaviors to church teachings.

Laypeople further tied their lives to the mendicants, particularly the Franciscans, by becoming tertiaries. They adopted the practices of the friars — prayer and works of charity, for example — while continuing to live in the world, raising families and tending to the normal tasks of daily life, whatever their occupation. Even kings and queens became tertiaries.

The Piety of Women.   All across Europe, women in the thirteenth century sought outlets for their intense piety. As in previous centuries, powerful families founded new nunneries, especially within towns and cities. On the whole, these were set up for the daughters of the very wealthy. Ordinary

Friars and Usurers

Although clerics sometimes borrowed money, the friars had a different attitude. St. Francis, son of a merchant, refused to touch money altogether. In this illumination from about 1250, a Franciscan (in light-colored robes) and a Dominican (in black) reject offers from two usurers, whose profession they are thus shown to condemn. Other friars, including Thomas Aquinas, worked out justifications for some kinds of moneymaking professions, though not usury. *(Bibliothèque nationale de France.)*

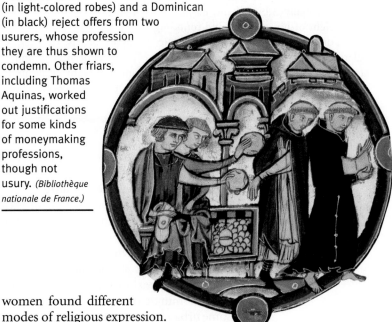

women found different modes of religious expression.
Some sought the lives of quiet activity and rapturous mysticism of the Beguines, others chose the lives of charity and service of women's mendicant orders, and still others decided on domestic lives of marriage and family punctuated by religious devotions. Elisabeth of Hungary, who married a German prince at the age of fourteen, raised three children. At the same time, she devoted her life to fasting, prayer, and service to the poor.

The Peasants of Montaillou

While historians can learn from material evidence how medieval peasants lived and worked, it is nearly impossible to find out what peasants thought. Almost all of our written sources come from the elite classes who, if they noticed peasants at all, certainly did not care about their ideas. How, then, can historians hear and record the voices of peasants themselves? Until the 1960s, historians cared little about hearing those voices. They wanted to know about economic structures rather than peasant mentalities.

For that reason, historians did not notice an extremely important source of peasant voices, the Inquisition register made at the command of Bishop Fournier of Pamiers in the years 1318–1325. Fournier was a zealous anti-heretic, and when he became bishop of a diocese that harbored many Albigensians, he put the full weight of his office behind rounding them up. He concentrated on one particularly "heretic-infested" village, Montaillou, in the south of France near the Spanish border. Interrogating a total of 114 people, including 48 women, over seven years, he committed their confessions and testimony to parchment with a view to punishing those who were heretics. Fournier was not interested in the peasants' "voices": he simply wanted to know their religious beliefs and every other detail of their lives and thoughts. However, the long-term result of Fournier's zealous inquest—though he would not be happy to hear it—was to preserve the words of a whole village of peasants, shepherds, artisans, and shopkeepers. Fournier's register sat in the Vatican archives for centuries, gathering dust, until it was transcribed and published in 1965. Only in 1975 was its great potential for peasant history made clear; in that year, Emmanuel Le Roy Ladurie published *Montaillou: The Promised Land of Error*, which for the first time brought a medieval peasant village to life.

Le Roy Ladurie's book reveals the myths, beliefs, rivalries, tensions, love affairs, tendernesses, and duplicities of a small peasant community where all the people, even those who were better off, worked with their hands; where wealth was calculated by the size of a family's herd of livestock; and where the church's demands for tithes seemed outrageously unfair.

The register shows a community torn apart by the opportunities the Inquisition gave to informers. The village priest, from a well-off family, was very clear about why he was denouncing his parishioners. He liked the Albigensians, he said (he was probably one himself), but he added: "I want to be revenged on the peasants of Montaillou, who have done me harm, and I will avenge myself in every possible way." However, the register also shows a community united by love: parents cared about their children, husbands and wives loved one another, and illicit lovers were caught up in passion. One affair took place between the village priest and Béatrice, a woman of somewhat higher rank. The priest courted her for half a year, and after she gave in, they met two or three nights a week. In the end, though, Béatrice decided to marry someone else and left the village.

Béatrice was not the only person of independent mind in Montaillou. Many

Many women were not as devout as Elisabeth. In the countryside, they cooked their porridge, brewed their ale, and raised their children. They attended church regularly, but only on major feast days or for churching—the ritual of purification after a pregnancy. In the cities, working women scratched out a meager living. They sometimes made pilgrimages to relic shrines to seek help or cures. Religion was a part of these women's lives, but it did not dominate them.

For some urban women, however, religion was the focus of life, and the church's attempt to define and control the Eucharist had some unintended results. The new emphasis on the holiness of the transformed wine and bread induced some of these pious women to eat nothing but the Eucharist. One such woman, Angela of Foligno, reported that the consecrated bread swelled in her mouth, tasting sweeter than any other food. For these women, eating the Eucharist was truly eating God. This is how they understood the church's teaching that the consecrated bread was actually Christ's body. In the minds of these holy women, Christ's crucifixion was the literal sacrifice of his body, to be eaten by sinful men and women as the way to redeem themselves and others. Renouncing all other foods became part of a life of service, because many of these devout women gave the poor the food they refused to eat.

These women both accepted and challenged the pronouncements of the Fourth Lateran Council about the meaning of the Eucharist. They agreed that only priests could say Mass, but some of them bypassed their own priests, receiving the Eucharist (as they explained) directly from Christ in the form of a vision. Although men dominated the institutions that governed political, religious, and economic affairs, these women found ways to control their own lives and to some extent the lives of those around them, both those whom they

people there were indeed heretics in the sense that their beliefs defied the teachings of the church. But they called themselves "good Christians." Other villagers remained in the Catholic fold. And still others in the region had their own ideas, as may be seen from Raimond de l'Aire's testimony, below.

Fournier's register became a "new" source because Le Roy Ladurie had new questions and sought a way to answer them, treating his evidence the way ethnographers treat reports by native peoples they have interviewed. Today, some historians question Le Roy Ladurie's approach, arguing that an Inquisition record cannot be handled in the same way that ethnographers consider information from their informants. For example, they point out that the words of the peasants were translated from Occitan, the language they spoke, to Latin for the official record. What readers hear are not the voices of the peasants but rather their ideas filtered through the vocabulary and summaries of the elite. Moreover, the peasants called before the tribunal were held in prison, feared for their lives, and were forced to talk about events that had taken place ten or more years earlier. In light of these circumstances, to what extent is their testimony a direct window onto their lives? Nevertheless, the register remains a precious source for learning at least something about what ordinary people thought and felt in a small village about seven hundred years ago.

Raimond de l'Aire's Testimony

One of the witnesses recorded by Fournier was Raimond de l'Aire. He was not from Montaillou but rather from Tignac, a small town in Fournier's diocese. In this testimony, he reports on the beliefs of one of his acquaintances:

> An older man told [Raimond de l'Aire] that a mule has a soul as good as a man's; "and from this belief he had by himself deduced that his own soul and those of other men are nothing but blood, because when a person's blood is taken away, he dies. He also believed that a dead person's soul and body both die, and that after death nothing human remains. . . . From this he believed that the human soul after death [is] neither good nor evil, and that there is no hell or paradise in another world where human souls are rewarded or punished."

QUESTIONS TO CONSIDER
1. In what ways are modern court cases like Fournier's Inquisition register? In what ways are they unlike such a source? Could you use modern court cases to reconstruct the life of a community?
2. What are the advantages and the pitfalls of using a source such as the register for historical research?
3. Do you think that Raimond might have made up his testimony? Why or why not?
4. What does this testimony suggest about the impact of church doctrines in the French countryside?

FURTHER READING
Boyle, Leonard. "Montaillou Revisited: Mentalité and Methodology." In J. A. Raftis, ed., *Pathways to Medieval Peasants.* 1981.
Le Roy Ladurie, Emmanuel. *Montaillou: The Promised Land of Error.* 1978. The original French version was published in 1975.
Resaldo, Renato. "From the Door of His Tent: The Fieldworker and the Inquisitor." In James Clifford and George E. Marcus, eds., *Writing Culture: The Poetics and Politics of Ethnography.* 1986.

Source: *Heresy and Authority in Medieval Europe: Documents in Translation,* ed. Edward Peters (Philadelphia: University of Pennsylvania Press, 1980), 253.

served and those they lived with. Typically involved with meal preparation and feeding, like other women of the time, these holy women found a way to use their control over ordinary food to gain new kinds of social and religious power.

Jews and Lepers as Outcasts

The First and Second Crusades gave outlet to anti-Jewish feeling. Nevertheless, they were abnormal episodes in the generally stable if tense relationship between Christians and Jews in Europe up to the middle of the twelfth century. Then things changed dramatically, as kings became more powerful, popular piety deepened, and church law singled Jews out for particular discrimination.

Jews were not alone in this new segregation. Lepers, too, had to wear a special costume, were forbidden to touch children, could not eat with those not afflicted, and were kept in leper houses.

Jews Exploited and Expelled. As noted earlier (see Chapter 10), when Christian lords came to dominate the countryside, Jews were forced off the manors and into the cities. Their opportunities narrowed with the growing monopoly of guilds, which prohibited Jewish members. Thus in many places Jews were barred from the crafts and trades. In effect, they were compelled to become usurers (moneylenders) because other fields were closed to them. Even with Christian moneylenders available (for some existed despite the Gospel prohibition against charging interest for loans), lords, especially kings, borrowed from Jews and encouraged others to do so because, along with their newly asserted powers, European rulers claimed the Jews as their serfs and Jewish property as their own. In England, where Jews had arrived with the Norman conquest in 1066, a special royal exchequer of the Jews was created in 1194 to collect unpaid debts due after the death of a Jewish creditor.

Jewish Couple
In this illustration from a Hebrew manuscript, a couple is shown on their wedding night. They sit holding hands in a garden under a leafy bower. Even though the manuscript was made for Jews, it shows them with demeaning symbols. The man wears a pointed hat, as Jews were forced to do, while the woman is blindfolded, echoing artistic depictions of the Synagogue, the Jewish house of worship. *(Staats-und Universitats-bibliothek Hamburg Carl von Ossietzky, Cod. Levy 37, fol. 169.)*

and encouraging a wellspring of elite and popular anti-Jewish feeling.

Attacks against Jews were inspired by more than resentment against Jewish money and the desire for power and control. They also, ironically, grew out of the codification of Christian religious doctrine and the anxiety of Christians about their own institutions. For example, in the twelfth century, the newly rigorous definition of the Eucharist represented by the word *transubstantiation* meant to many pious Christians that the body of Christ literally lay upon the altar. Reflecting this unsettling view, sensational stories, originating in clerical circles but soon widely circulated, told of Jews who secretly sacrificed Christian children in a morbid revisiting of the crucifixion of Jesus.

In 1144, in one of the earliest instances of this charge, the body of a young boy named William was found in the woods near Norwich (England). His uncle, a priest, accused local Jews of killing the child. A monk connected to the cathedral at Norwich, Thomas of Monmouth, took up the cause. He had visions that told him to exhume the body from the cemetery and bring it into the monastery. Miracles followed, and soon Thomas wrote *The Life and Martyrdom of St. William of Norwich.* According to his account, the Jews carefully prepared at Passover for the horrible ritual slaughter of the boy, whom they had chosen "to be mocked and sacrificed in scorn of the Lord's passion."

This charge, called blood libel by historians, was made frequently about other "martyrs" and led to massacres of Jews in cities in England, France, Spain, and Germany. (In fact, however, Jews had no rituals involving blood sacrifice at all.)

Even before 1194, the king of England had imposed new and arbitrary taxes on the Jewish community. Similarly in France, persecuting Jews and confiscating their property benefited both the treasury and the authoritative image of the king. In 1198, the French king declared that Jews must be moneylenders or money changers exclusively. Their activities were to be taxed and monitored by royal officials.

Limiting Jews to moneylending in an increasingly commercial economy clearly served the interests of kings. But lesser lords who needed cash also benefited: they borrowed money from Jews and then, as happened in York (England) in 1190, they orchestrated an attack to rid themselves of their debts and of the Jews to whom they owed money. Churchmen, too, used credit in a money economy but resented the fiscal obligations it imposed. With their drive to create centralized territorial states and their desire to make their authority known and felt, powerful rulers of Europe — churchmen and laymen alike — exploited and coerced the Jews while drawing on

Blood Libel Charges in Europe, c. 1100–1300 *(Adapted from Angus Mackay with David Ditchburn, eds.,* Atlas of Medieval Europe *[New York: Routledge, 1997].)*

Disgusted by the Jews, some communities simply expelled them: at Bury-Saint-Edmunds, which was under the jurisdiction of the abbot of the monastery, a chronicler of the time described the event:

> And when they had been sent forth and conducted under armed escort to other towns [in England], the abbot ordered that all those who from that time forth should receive Jews or harbor them in the town of St. Edmund should be solemnly excommunicated in every church and at every altar.

Eventually, in 1291, the Jews were cast out from the entire kingdom of England. Most dispersed to France and Germany, but to a sad welcome. In 1306, for example, King Philip the Fair (r. 1285–1314) had them driven from France, though they were allowed to reenter, tentatively, in 1315.

Fearing the Contamination of Lepers. Lepers played a small role in medieval society until the eleventh century. Then, beginning around 1075 and extending to the fourteenth century, lepers became the objects of both charity and disgust. Houses for lepers, isolated from other habitations, were set up both for charitable reasons and to segregate lepers from everyone else.

Lepers were not allowed to live in ordinary society because their disease disfigured them horribly, was associated with sin in the Bible, and was contagious. In 1179, the Third Lateran Council took note of the fact that "lepers cannot dwell with the healthy or come to church with others" and asked that, where possible, special churches and cemeteries be set aside for them. No doubt this inspired a boom in the foundation of leper houses, which peaked between 1175 and 1250.

Before the leper went to such a house, he or she was formally expelled from the community of Christians via a ceremony of terrible solemnity. In northern France, for example, the leper had to stand in a cemetery, his or her face veiled. Mass was intoned, and the priest threw dirt on the leper as if he or she were being buried. "Be dead to the world, be reborn in God," the priest said, continuing:

> I forbid you to ever enter the church or monastery, fair, mill, marketplace, or company of persons. I forbid you to ever leave your house without your leper's costume [usually gloves and a long robe], in order that one recognize you and that you never go barefoot. I forbid you to wash your hands or any thing about you in the stream or in the fountain and to ever drink.

In 1321, the prohibition against drinking in the stream or fountain gained more sinister meaning as rumors spread that Muslims had recruited both Jews and lepers to poison all the wells of Christendom.

REVIEW: How did people respond to the teachings and laws of the church in the early thirteenth century?

The Medieval Synthesis

Just as the church wanted to regulate worldly life in accordance with God's plan for salvation, so contemporary thinkers, writers, musicians, and artists sought to harmonize the secular with the sacred realms. Scholars wrote treatises that reconciled faith with reason, poets and musicians sang of the links between heaven and human life on earth, and artists expressed the same ideas in stone and sculpture and on parchment. In the face of many contradictions, all of these groups were largely successful in communicating an orderly image of the world.

Scholasticism: Harmonizing Faith and Reason

Scholasticism was the culmination of the method of logical inquiry and exposition pioneered by masters like Peter Abelard and Peter the Chanter (see Chapter 11). In the thirteenth century, the method was used to summarize and reconcile all knowledge. Many of the thirteenth-century scholastics (those who practiced scholasticism) were members of the Dominican and Franciscan orders and taught in the universities. On the whole, they were confident that knowledge obtained through the senses and reason was compatible with the knowledge derived from faith and revelation. One of their goals was to demonstrate this harmony. The scholastic summa, or summary of knowledge, was a systematic exposition of the answer to every possible question about human morality, the physical world, society, belief, action, and theology. Another goal of the scholastics was to preach the conclusions of these treatises. As one scholastic put it, "First the bow is bent in study, then the arrow is released in preaching": first you study the summa and then you hit your mark — convert people — by preaching. Many of the preachers who came to the towns were students and disciples of scholastic university teachers.

The method of the summa borrowed much of the vocabulary and many of the rules of logic long ago outlined by Aristotle. Even though Aristotle

---

scholasticism: The method of logical inquiry used by the scholastics, the scholars of the medieval universities; it applied Aristotelian logic to biblical and other authoritative texts in an attempt to summarize and reconcile all knowledge.

was a pagan, scholastics considered his coherent and rational body of thought the most perfect that human reason alone could devise. Because they had the benefit of Christ's revelations, the scholastics believed they could take Aristotle's philosophy one necessary step further and reconcile human reason with Christian faith. Confident in their method and conclusions, scholastics embraced the world and its issues.

Some scholastics considered questions about the natural world. Albertus Magnus (c. 1200–1280) was a major theologian who also contributed to the fields of biology, botany, astronomy, and physics. His reconsideration of Aristotle's views on motion led the way to distinctions that helped scientists in the sixteenth and seventeenth centuries arrive at the modern notion of inertia.

St. Thomas Aquinas (c. 1225–1274) was perhaps the most famous scholastic. Huge of build and renowned for his composure in scholastic disputation, Thomas came from a noble Neapolitan family that had hoped to see him become a powerful bishop rather than a poor university professor. When he was about eighteen years old, he thwarted his family's wishes and joined the Dominicans. Soon he was studying at Cologne with Albertus Magnus. At thirty-two, he became a master at the University of Paris.

Like many other scholastics, Thomas considered Aristotle to be "the Philosopher," the authoritative voice of human reason, which he sought to reconcile with divine revelation in a universal and harmonious scheme. In 1273, he published his monumental *Summa Theologiae* (sometimes called the *Summa Theologica*), intended to cover all important topics, human and divine. He divided these topics into questions, exploring each one thoroughly and systematically and concluding with a decisive position and a refutation of opposing views. Yet even Thomas departed from Aristotle, who had explained the universe through human reason alone. In Thomas's view, God, nature, and reason were in harmony, so even though Aristotle's arguments could be used to explore both the human and the divine order, there were some exceptions. "Certain things that are true about God wholly surpass the capability of human reason, for instance that God is three and one," Thomas wrote. But he thought these exceptions were rare.

Many of Thomas's questions spoke to the keenest concerns of his day. He asked, for example, whether it was lawful to sell something for more than its worth. (See Friars and Usurers, page 363.) Thomas arranged his argument systematically, first quoting authorities that seemed to declare every sort of selling practice, even deceptive

ones, to be lawful. This was the *sic* (or "yes") position. Then he quoted an authority that opposed selling something for more than its worth. This was the *non*. Following that, he gave his own argument, prefaced by the words "I answer that." Like Peter Abelard, but now systematically, Thomas came to clear conclusions that harmonized both the yes and the no responses. In the case of selling something for more than it was worth, he pointed out that price and worth depended on the circumstances of the buyer and seller. He concluded that charging more than a seller had originally paid could be legitimate at times, as, for example, "when a man has great need of a certain thing, while another man will suffer if he is without it."

For townspeople engaged in commerce and worried about biblical prohibitions on money-making, Thomas's ideas about selling practices addressed burning questions. Hoping to go to heaven as well as reap the profits of their business ventures, laypeople listened eagerly to preachers who delivered their sermons in the vernacular but who based their ideas on the Latin summae (the plural of summa) of Thomas and other scholastics. Thomas's conclusions aided townspeople in justifying their worldly activities.

Scholastics like Thomas were enormous optimists. They believed that everything had a place in God's scheme of things, that the world was orderly, and that human beings could make rational sense of it. This optimism filled the classrooms, spilled into the friars' convents, and found its way to the streets where artisans and shopkeepers lived and worked. Scholastic philosophy helped give ordinary people a sense of purpose and a guide to behavior.

Yet even among scholastics, unity was elusive. In his own day, Thomas was accused of placing too much emphasis on reason and relying too fully on Aristotle. Later scholastics argued that reason could not find truth through its own faculties and energies. In the summae of John Duns Scotus (c. 1266–1308), for example, the world and God were less compatible. John, whose name Duns Scotus reveals his Scottish origin, was a Franciscan who taught at both Oxford and Paris. For John, human reason could know truth only through the "special illumination of the uncreated light," that is, by divine illumination. But unlike his predecessors, John believed that this illumination came not as a matter of course but only when God chose to intervene. John—and others—experienced God as sometimes willful rather than reasonable. Human reason could not soar to God; God's will alone determined whether or not a person could know him. In this way, John separated the divine and secular realms. The search for order was thwarted by discord.

New Syntheses in Writing and Music

Thirteenth-century writers and musicians, like scholastics, presented complicated ideas and feelings as harmonious and unified syntheses. Writers explored the relations between this world and the next, whereas musicians found ways to bridge sacred and secular forms of music.

Vernacular Literature Comes of Age.   Vernacular literature may be said to have reached its full development with the work of Dante Alighieri (1265–1321), who harmonized the scholastic universe with the mysteries of faith and the poetry of love. Born in Florence in a time of political turmoil, Dante incorporated the major figures of history and his own day into his most famous poem, the *Commedia*, written between 1313 and 1321. Later known as the *Divine Comedy*, Dante's poem describes the poet taking an imaginary journey from Hell to Purgatory and finally to Paradise.

The poem is an allegory in which every person and object must be read at more than one level. At the most literal level, the poem is about Dante's travels. At a deeper level, it is about the soul's search for meaning and enlightenment and its ultimate discovery of God in the light of divine love. Just as Thomas Aquinas employed Aristotle's logic to reach important truths, so Dante used the pagan poet Virgil as his guide through Hell and Purgatory. And just as Thomas believed that faith went beyond reason to even higher truths, so Dante found a new guide representing earthly love to lead him through most of Paradise. That guide was Beatrice, a Florentine girl with whom Dante had fallen in love as a boy and whom he never forgot. But only faith, in the form of the divine love of the Virgin Mary, could bring Dante to the culmination of his journey—a blinding and inexpressibly awesome vision of God:

> What I then saw is more than tongue can say. Our human speech is dark before the vision. The ravished memory swoons and falls away.

Dante's poem electrified a wide audience. By elevating one dialect of Italian—the language that ordinary Florentines used in their everyday life—to a language of exquisite poetry, Dante was able to communicate the scholastics' orderly and optimistic vision of the universe in an even more exciting and accessible way. So influential was his work that it is no exaggeration to say that modern Italian is based on Dante's Florentine dialect.

DOCUMENT

The Debate between Reason and the Lover

Jean de Meun's portion of the Romance of the Rose *is organized as a dialogue between the Lover and various figures he meets on his quest for the rose. The figure of Reason gives the following jaundiced definition of love.*

If I know anything of love, it is
Imaginary illness freely spread
Between two persons of opposing sex,
Originating from disordered sight,
Producing great desire to hug and kiss
And see enjoyment in a mutual lust.

To which the lover responds:

Madam, you would betray me; should I scorn
All folk because the God of Love now frowns?
Shall I no more experience true love,
But live in hate? Truly, so help me God,
Then were I moral sinner worse than thief!

Source: Guillaume de Lorris and Jean de Meun, *The Romance of the Rose*, trans. Harry W. Robbins (New York: Dutton, 1962), 97, 102.

Other writers of the period used different methods to express the harmony between heaven and earth. The anonymous author of the *Quest of the Holy Grail* (c. 1225), for example, wrote about the adventures of some of the knights of King Arthur's Round Table to convey the doctrine of transubstantiation and the wonder of the vision of God. In *The Romance of the Rose*, begun by one poet and finished by another, a lover seeks the rose, his true love. In the long dream that the poem describes, the narrator's search for the rose is thwarted by personifications of Love, Shame, Reason, Abstinence, and so on. They present him with arguments for and against love. In the end, sexual love is made part of the divine scheme—and the lover plucks the rose. (See Document, "The Debate between Reason and the Lover," above.)

Polyphony and the Motet.   Plainchant (see Chapter 11) is orderly, consisting of a particular sequence of notes for a given text. The earliest plainchant was sometimes embellished by having two voices sing exactly the same melody an interval apart. This was the first form of polyphony, the simultaneous sounding of two or more melodies. In the twelfth century, musicians experimented with freer melodies. One voice might go up the scale, for example, while the other went down, achieving even so a pleasing harmony. Or one voice might hold a pitch while the other danced around it.

In the thirteenth century, some musicians tried even bolder combinations, seeking order in complex melodies played together harmoniously. This was true of the most distinctive musical form of the thirteenth century, the motet (from the French *mot*, meaning "word"). The motet was a unique merging of the sacred and the secular. It probably originated in Paris, the center of scholastic culture as well. Before about 1215, most polyphony was sacred; purely secular polyphony was not common before the fourteenth century.

The typical thirteenth-century motet has two or three melody lines (or "voices"). The lowest,

usually from a liturgical chant melody, has only one or two words; it may have been played on an instrument rather than sung. The remaining melodies have different texts, either Latin or French (or one of each), which are sung simultaneously. Latin texts are usually sacred, whereas French ones are secular, dealing with themes such as love and springtime. The motet thus weaves the sacred (the chant melody in the lowest voice) and the secular (the French texts in the upper voices) into a sophisticated tapestry of words and music. Like the scholastic summae, motets were written by and for a clerical elite. (See Singing a Motet, at left.) Yet they incorporated the music of ordinary people, such as the calls of street vendors and the boisterous songs of students. In turn, they touched the lives of everyone, for polyphony influenced every form of music, from the Mass to popular songs that entertained laypeople and churchmen alike.

Complementing the motet's complexity was the development of a new notation for rhythm. A primitive form of musical notation had been created in the ninth century; by the eleventh century, composers could indicate pitch but had no way to show the duration of the notes. Music theorists of the thirteenth century, however, developed increasingly precise methods to indicate rhythm. Franco of Cologne, for example, in his *Art of Measurable Song* (c. 1280), used different shapes to mark the number of beats each note should be held. His system became the basis of modern musical notation. Because each note could now be allotted a specific duration, written music could express new and complicated rhythms. The music of the thirteenth century reflected both the melding of the secular and the sacred and the possibilities of greater order and control.

Singing a Motet

In this fourteenth-century English Psalter, the artist has illustrated the first letter of Psalm 96, which begins, "O sing to the Lord a new song," with a depiction of three clerics singing a motet. Its words and musical notation are written on a scroll draped over a lectern. *(By permission of the British Library.)*

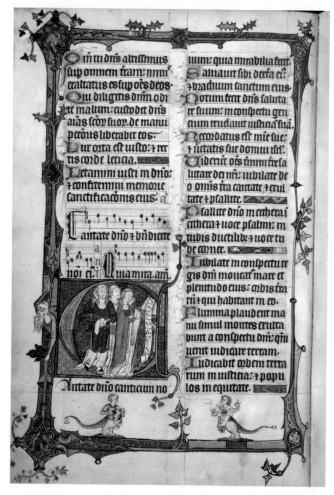

Gothic Art

By the end of the thirteenth century, the Gothic style in architecture, which had its beginnings at Saint-Denis and Chartres, had spread over most of Europe. Elements of Gothic style began to appear as well in other forms of art: stained glass, sculpture, painting, and the decorative motifs in manuscript illuminations.

Stained Glass. Because pointed arches and flying buttresses allowed the walls of a Gothic church to be pierced with large windows, stained glass became a newly important art form. (See Sainte-Chapelle, page 371.) The adjective *stained* is a misnomer. To make this glass, workers added chemicals to sand, which was then heated until liquid, blown, and flattened. For example, adding cobalt produced blue glass; copper oxide made red. Yellow, a rare color, was produced by painting clear glass with silver nitrate, then firing it in a kiln. Artists cut shapes from these colored glass sheets and held them in place with lead strips. They painted details right on the glass. As the sun shown through the finished windows, they glowed like jewels.

The size of the windows allowed glaziers to depict complicated themes. The windows at Sainte-Chapelle, for example, tell the story of salvation in 1,134 scenes, starting with events of the Old Testament and ending with the Apocalypse. All such windows are read from bottom to top. At Reims cathedral, which was begun in 1211 after a great fire, one of the archbishops had himself portrayed in stained glass (see "The Archbishop of Reims" on this page). Above him in the same window is the crucifixion. Reading from bottom to top associates the archbishop directly with Christ.

Sculpture. Gothic cathedrals were decorated with sculpture. This was not new: Romanesque ar-

chitecture had also featured sculpture (see the opening illustration for Chapter 10, page 294). But Gothic figures were separated from their background and sculpted in the round. They turned, moved, and interacted; at times, they even smiled. (See The Annunciation, page 372.) Taken together, they were often meant to be "read" like a scholastic summa. The south portal of Chartres cathedral is a good example of the way in which Gothic sculpture could be used to sum up a body of truths. The sculptures in each massive doorway have related themes: the left doorway depicts the martyrs, the right the confessors, and the center the Last Judgment. Like Dante's *Divine Comedy*, these portals tell the story of the soul's pilgrimage from the suffering of this world to eternal life.

Gothic sculpture began in France and was adopted, with many varia-

---

Sainte-Chapelle
Gothic architecture opened up the walls of the church to windows, as may be seen at Sainte-Chapelle, the private chapel of the French king Louis IX (St. Louis). Consecrated in 1248, it was built to house Christ's crown of thorns and other relics of the Passion. This photo shows the interior of the upper chapel looking east. *(Bridgeman-Giraudon/Art Resource, NY.)*

The Archbishop of Reims
This stained glass window not only associates the archbishop with Christ but, by featuring a chalice that catches Christ's blood at the foot of the cross, shows the archbishop's crucial role in the sacrament of the Mass.
(Alain Lonchampt © Centre des monuments nationaux, Paris.)

tions, elsewhere in Europe during the thirteenth century. The Italian sculptor Nicola Pisano (c. 1220–1278?), for example, crafted dignified figures inspired by classical forms. German sculptors created excited, emotional figures that sometimes gestured dramatically to one another.

Painting. By the early fourteenth century, the naturalistic sculptures so prominent in architecture were reflected in painting as well. This new style is evident in the work of Giotto (1266–1337), a Florentine artist who changed the emphasis of painting, which had been predominantly symbolic, decorative, and intellectual. When Giotto filled the walls of a private chapel at Padua with paintings depicting scenes of Christ's life, he experimented with the illusion of depth. Giotto's figures, appearing weighty and voluminous, express a range of emotions as they move across interior and exterior spaces. (See Giotto's *Birth of the Virgin*, below.) In bringing sculptural naturalism to a flat surface, Giotto stressed three-dimensionality, illusional space, and human emotion. By fusing earthly forms with religious meaning, Giotto found yet another way to bring together the natural and divine realms.

Gothic style also appeared in paintings as a decorative motif. Manuscript illuminations feature the shape of stained-glass windows and pointed vaults as common background themes. (See the portrait of Louis IX and Blanche of Castile, page 375, for one example.) The colors of Gothic manuscripts echo the rich hues of stained glass.

> **REVIEW:** How did artists, musicians, and scholastics try to link this world with the divine?

Giotto's *Birth of the Virgin*
This depiction of the Virgin Mary's birth pays attention to the homey details of a thirteenth-century Florentine aristocratic household. The baby is bathed and swaddled by maidservants in the bottom tier, while above she is handed to her mother, St. Anne, who reaches out eagerly for the child. *(The Art Archive/Scrovegni Chapel, Padua/Dagli Orti [A].)*

The Annunciation
At Gothic churches, such as this one at Reims (in northern France), the figures were carved in the round. Here the angel Gabriel (on the left) turns and smiles joyfully at Mary, who looks down modestly as he announces that she will give birth to Jesus.
(Scala/Art Resource, NY.)

The Politics of Control

The quest for order, control, and harmony also became part of the political agendas of princes, popes, and cities. These rulers and institutions imposed—or tried to impose—their authority ever more fully and systematically through taxes, courts, and sometimes representative institutions. The ancestors of modern European parliaments and of the U.S. Congress can be traced to this era.

Louis IX of France is a good example of a ruler whose power increased during this period. However, while some rulers, like Louis, were strengthened, others were not: the emperor—who once claimed both Germany and Italy—gave up most of his power in Germany and lost it in Italy as well, while the papacy moved from Rome to Avignon, a real blow to its prestige. In Italy the rise of *signori* (lords) meant that the communes, which had long governed many cities, gave way to rule by one strong man.

A new political entity, the Mongols, directly confronted the rulers of Russia, Poland, and Hungary. Installing themselves in Russia, the Mongols became a new fixture in the west. In the end, they vitalized European trade, opening up routes to the east. But just as this was taking place, a new challenge to the political and economic order came in the form of the calamities known collectively as the Great Famine.

The Weakening of the Empire

During the thirteenth century, both popes and emperors sought to dominate Italy. In the end, the emperor lost control not only of Italy but of Germany as well.

The clash of the German emperor and the papacy had its origins in Frederick Barbarossa's failure to control northern Italy, which was crucial to imperial policy. The model of Charlemagne required his imperial successors to exercise hegemony there. Moreover, Italy's prosperous cities beckoned as rich sources of income. When Barbarossa failed in the north, his son tried a new approach to gain Italy: he married Constance, the heiress of Sicily. From this base near the southern tip of Italy, he hoped to make good his imperial title. But he died suddenly, leaving his three-year-old son, Frederick II, to take up his plan. It was a perilous moment.

While Frederick was a child, the imperial office became the plaything of the German princes and the papacy. Both wanted an emperor, but a virtually powerless one. Thus, when Frederick's uncle attempted to become interim king until

Frederick reached his majority, many princes and the papacy blocked the move. They supported Otto of Brunswick, the son of Henry the Lion and an implacable foe of Frederick's family. Otto promised the pope that he would not intervene in Italy, and Pope Innocent III crowned him emperor in return.

But Innocent had miscalculated. No emperor worthy of the name could leave Italy alone. Almost immediately after his coronation, Otto invaded Sicily, and Innocent excommunicated him in 1211. In 1212, Innocent gave the imperial crown to **Frederick II** (r. 1212–1250), now a young man ready to take up the reins of power.

Frederick was an amazing ruler: *stupor mundi* ("wonder of the world") his contemporaries called him. Heir to two cultures, Sicilian on his mother's side and German on his father's, he cut a worldly and sophisticated figure. In Sicily, he moved easily within a diverse culture of Jews, Muslims, and Christians. Here he could play the role of all-powerful ruler. In Germany, he was less at home. There Christian princes, often churchmen with ministerial retinues, were acutely aware of their crucial role in royal elections and jealously guarded their rights and privileges.

Both emperor and pope needed to dominate Italy to maintain their power and position (Map 12.1). The papacy under Innocent III was expansionist, gathering money and troops to make good its claim to the Papal States, the band of territory stretching from Rome to Ferrara in the North and Fermo in the east. The pope expected dues and taxes, military service, and the profits of justice from this region. To ensure its survival, the pope refused to tolerate any imperial claims to Italy.

Frederick, in turn, could not imagine ruling as an emperor unless he controlled Italy. He attempted to do this throughout his life, as did his heirs. Frederick had a three-pronged strategy. First, he revamped the government of Sicily to give him more control and yield greater profits. His *Constitutions of Melfi* (1231), an eclectic body of laws, set up a system of salaried governors who worked according to uni-

Italy at the End of the Thirteenth Century

Frederick II: The king of Sicily and Germany, as well as emperor (r. 1212–1250), who allowed the German princes a free hand as he battled the pope for control of Italy.

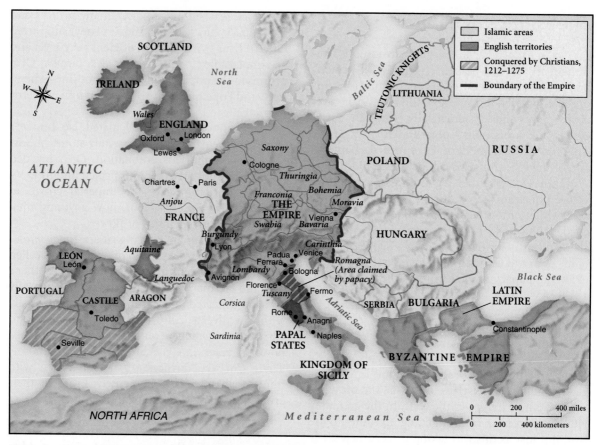

MAP 12.1 Europe in the Time of Frederick II, r. 1212–1250
King of Sicily and Germany and emperor as well, Frederick ruled over territory that encircled—and threatened—the papacy. Excommunicated several times, Frederick spent much of his career fighting the pope's forces. In the process he made so many concessions to the German princes that the emperor thenceforth had little power in Germany. Meanwhile, rulers of smaller states, such as England, France, and Castile-León, were increasing their power and authority.

form procedures. The *Constitutions* called for nearly all court cases to be heard by royal courts, regularized commercial privileges, and set up a system of taxation. Second, to ensure that he would not be hounded by opponents in Germany, Frederick granted them important concessions in his **Statute in Favor of the Princes**, finalized in 1232. These privileges allowed the German princes to turn their principalities into virtually independent states. Third, Frederick sought to enter Italy through Lombardy, as his grandfather had done.

The four popes who came between the deaths of Innocent (1216) and Frederick (1250) followed Frederick's every move and excommunicated the emperor a number of times. The most serious of these condemnations came in 1245, when the pope and other churchmen assembled at the Council of

Lyon, excommunicated and deposed Frederick, absolving his vassals and subjects of their fealty to him and, indeed, forbidding anyone to support him. By 1248, papal legates were preaching a crusade against Frederick and all his followers. Frederick's death soon after ensured their triumph.

The fact that Frederick's vision of the empire failed is of less long-term importance than the way it failed. His concessions to the German princes meant that Germany would not be united until the nineteenth century. The political entity now called Germany was simply a geographical expression, divided under many independent princes. Between 1254 and 1273, the princes kept the German throne empty. Splintered into factions, they elected two different foreigners, who spent their time fighting each other. In one of history's great ironies, it was during this low point of the German monarchy that the term *Holy Roman Empire* was coined. In 1273, the princes at last united and elected a German, Rudolf (r. 1273–1291), whose

---

Statute in Favor of the Princes: A statute finalized by Frederick II in 1232 that gave the German princes sovereign power within their own principalities.

Louis IX and Blanche of Castile
This miniature shows St. Louis, portrayed as a young boy, sitting opposite his mother, Blanche of Castile. Blanche served as regent twice in Louis's lifetime, once when he was too young to rule and a second time when he was away on crusade. The emphasis on the equality of queen and king may be evidence of Blanche's influence on and patronage of the artist. *(The Pierpont Morgan Library/Art Resource, NY.)*

■ **For more help analyzing this image,** see the visual activity for this chapter in the Online Study Guide at **bedfordstmartins.com/hunt**.

family, the Habsburgs, was new to imperial power. Rudolf used the imperial title to help him consolidate control over his own principality, Swabia, but he did not try to fulfill the meaning of the imperial title elsewhere. For the first time, the word *emperor* was freed from its association with Italy and Rome. For the Habsburgs, the title *Holy Roman Emperor* was a prestigious but otherwise meaningless honorific.

The failure of Frederick II in Italy meant that the Italian cities would continue their independent course. In Sicily, the papacy ensured that the heirs of Frederick would not continue their rule by calling successively on other rulers to take over the island—first Henry III of England and then Charles of Anjou. Forces loyal to Frederick's family turned to the king of Aragon (Spain). The move left two enduring claimants to Sicily's crown—the kings of Aragon and the house of Anjou—and it spawned a long war impoverishing the region.

The popes won the war against Frederick, but at a cost. Even the king of France criticized the popes for doing "new and unheard-of things." By making its war against Frederick part of its crusade against heresy, the papacy came under attack for using religion as a political tool.

Louis IX and a New Ideal of Kingship

In hindsight, we can see that Frederick's fight for an empire that would stretch from Germany to Sicily was doomed. The successful rulers of me-

dieval Europe were those content with smaller, more compact, more united polities. The future was reserved for "national" states, like France and England. (However, that, too, may just be one phase of Western civilization.) In France, the new ideal of a "stay-at-home" monarch started in the thirteenth century with the reign of **Louis IX** (r. 1226–1270). His two crusades to the Holy Land made clear to his subjects just how much they needed him in France, even though his place was ably filled the first time by his mother, Blanche of Castile. The two are pictured on this page.

Louis was revered not because he was a military leader but because he was an administrator, judge, and "just father" of his people. On warm summer days, he would sit under a tree in the woods near his castle at Vincennes on the outskirts of Paris, hearing disputes and dispensing justice personally. Through his administrators, he vigorously imposed his laws and justice over much of France. At Paris he appointed a salaried chief magistrate, who could be supervised and fired if necessary. During his reign, the influence of the parlement of Paris (the royal court of justice) increased significantly. Originally a changeable and movable body, part of the king's personal entourage when he dealt with litigation, the parlement was now permanently housed in Paris and staffed by professional judges who heard cases and recorded their decisions.

Louis IX: A French king (r. 1226–1270) revered as a military leader and a judge; he was declared a saint after his death.

Unlike his grandfather Philip Augustus, Louis did not try to expand his territory. He inherited a large kingdom that included Poitou and Languedoc (Map 12.2), and he was content. Although Henry III, the king of England, attacked him continually to try to regain territory lost under Philip Augustus, Louis remained unprovoked. Rather than prolong the fighting, he conceded a bit and made peace in 1259. At the same time, Louis was a zealous crusader. He took seriously the need to defend the Holy Land when most of his contemporaries were weary of the idea.

Louis was respectful of the church and the pope; he accepted limits on his authority in relation to the church and never claimed power over spiritual matters. Nevertheless, he vigorously maintained the dignity of the king and his rights. He expected royal and ecclesiastical power to work in harmony, and he refused to let the church dictate how he should use his temporal authority. For example, French bishops wanted royal officers to support the church's sentences of excommunica-

tion. But Louis declared that he would authorize his officials to do so only if he was able to judge each case himself, to see if the excommunication had been justly pronounced or not. The bishops refused, and Louis held his ground. Royal and ecclesiastical power would work side by side, neither subservient to the other.

Many modern historians fault Louis for his policies toward Jews. His hatred of them was well known. He did not exactly advocate violence against them, but he sometimes subjected them to arrest, canceling the debts owed to them (but collecting part into the royal treasury), and confiscating their belongings. In 1253, he ordered them to live "by the labor of their hands" or leave France. He meant that they should no longer lend money, in effect taking away their one means of livelihood. Louis's contemporaries did not criticize him for his Jewish policies. If anything, his hatred of Jews enhanced his reputation.

In fact, many of Louis's contemporaries considered him a saint, praising his care for the poor and sick, the pains and penances he inflicted on himself, and his regular participation in church services. In 1297, Pope Boniface VIII canonized him as St. Louis. The result was enormous prestige for the French monarchy. This prestige, joined with the renown of Paris as the center of scholarship and the repute of French courts as the hubs of chivalry, made France the cultural model of Europe.

The Birth of Representative Institutions

As thirteenth-century monarchs and princes expanded their powers, they devised a new political tool to enlist more broadly based support: all across Europe, from Spain to Poland, from England to Hungary, rulers summoned parliaments. These grew out of the ad hoc advisory sessions kings had held in the past with men from the two most powerful classes, or "orders," of medieval society—the nobility and the clergy. In the thirteenth century, the advisory sessions turned into solemn, formal meetings of representatives of the orders to the kings' chief councils—the precursor of parliamentary sessions. Eventually these bodies became organs through which people not ordinarily present at court could articulate their wishes.

In practice, thirteenth-century kings did not so much command representatives of the orders to come to court as they simply summoned the most powerful members of their realm—whether clerics, nobles, or important townsmen—to support their policies. In thirteenth-century León (part of present-day Spain), for example, the king

MAP 12.2 France under Louis IX, r. 1226–1270
Louis IX did not expand his kingdom as dramatically as his grandfather Philip Augustus had done. He was greatly admired nevertheless, for he was seen by contemporaries as a model of Christian piety and justice. After his death, he was recognized as a saint and thus posthumously enhanced the prestige of the French monarchy.

sometimes called only the clergy and nobles; sometimes he sent for representatives of the towns, especially when he wanted the help of town militias. As townsmen gradually began to participate regularly in advisory sessions, kings came to depend on them and their support. In turn, commoners became more fully integrated into the work of royal government.

Spanish *Cortes*.   The *cortes* of Castile-León were among the earliest representative assemblies called to the king's court and the first to include townsmen. Enriched by plunder, fledgling villages soon burgeoned into major commercial centers. Like the cities of Italy, Spanish towns dominated the countryside. Hence, it was no wonder that King Alfonso IX (r. 1188–1230) summoned townsmen to the cortes in the first year of his reign, getting their representatives to agree to his plea for military and financial support and for help in consolidating his rule. Once convened at court, the townsmen joined bishops and noblemen in formally counseling the king and assenting to royal decisions. Beginning with Alfonso X (r. 1252–1284), Castilian monarchs regularly called on the cortes to participate in major political and military decisions and to assent to new taxes to finance them.

English Parliament.   The English Parliament also developed as a new tool of royal government.[1] In this case, however, the king's control was complicated by the power of the barons, manifested, for example, in Magna Carta. In the twelfth century, King Henry II had consulted prelates and barons at Great Councils, using these parliaments as his tool to ratify and gain support for his policies. Although Magna Carta had nothing to do with such councils, the barons thought the document gave them an important and permanent role in royal government as the king's advisers and a solid guarantee of their customary rights and privileges. Henry III (r. 1216–1272) was crowned at the age of nine and therefore was king in name only for the first sixteen years of his reign. Instead, England was governed by a council consisting of a few barons, university-trained administrators, and a papal legate. Although not quite "government by Parliament," this council set a precedent for baronial participation in government.

A parliament that included commoners came only in the midst of war and as a result of political weakness. Henry III so alienated nobles and commoners alike by his wars, debts, choice of advisers, and demands for money that the barons threatened to rebel. At a meeting at Oxford in 1258, they forced Henry to dismiss his foreign advisers, rule with the advice of a Council of Fifteen chosen jointly by the barons and the king, and limit the terms of his chief officers. However, this new government was itself riven by strife among the barons, and civil war erupted in 1264. At the battle of Lewes in the same year, the leader of the baronial opposition, Simon de Montfort (c. 1208–1265), routed the king's forces, captured the king, and became England's de facto ruler. Because only a minority of the barons followed Simon, he sought new support by convening a parliament in 1265, to which he summoned not only the earls, barons, and churchmen who backed him but also representatives from the towns, the "commons" — and he appealed for their help. Thus, for the first time the commons were given a voice in government. Even though Simon's brief rule ended that very year and Henry's son Edward I (r. 1272–1307) became a rallying point for royalists, the idea of representative government in England had emerged, born out of the interplay between royal initiatives and baronial revolts.

The Weakening of the Papacy

In France, the development of representative institutions originated in the conflict between Pope **Boniface VIII** (r. 1294–1303) and King Philip IV (r. 1285–1314), known as Philip the Fair. At the time, this confrontation seemed to be just one more episode in the ongoing struggle between medieval popes and secular rulers for power and authority. But at the end of the thirteenth century, kings had more power, and the standoff between Boniface and Philip became a turning point that weakened the papacy and strengthened the monarchy.

Taxing the Clergy.   For centuries, the clergy had maintained a special status within the medieval state. Since the twelfth century, popes had declared

---

[1]Although *parlement* and *Parliament* are similar words, both deriving from the French word *parler* ("to speak"), the institutions they named were very different. The parlement of France was a law court, whereas the English Parliament, although beginning as a court to redress grievances, had by 1327 become above all a representative institution. The major French representative assembly, the Estates General, first convened at the beginning of the fourteenth century.

---

cortes (kawr TEHZ): The earliest European representative institution, called initially to consent to royal wishes; first convoked in 1188 by the king of Castile-León.

Boniface VIII: The pope (r. 1294–1303) who unsuccessfully asserted the special place of the pope in the church and the spiritual subordination of the king.

the clergy under their jurisdiction. Clerics were not taxed except in the case of religious wars; they were not tried except in clerical courts. At the end of the thirteenth century, royal challenges to these principles provoked angry papal responses. The clashes began over taxing the clergy. Philip the Fair and the English king Edward I both financed their wars (mainly against one another) by taxing the clergy along with everyone else. The new principle of national sovereignty that they were claiming led them to assert jurisdiction over all people, even churchmen, who lived within their borders. For the pope, however, the principle at stake was his role as head of the clergy. Thus, Pope Boniface VIII, whose heavy, dignified image is illustrated on this page, declared that only the pope could authorize taxes on clerics. Threatening to excommunicate kings who taxed prelates without papal permission, he called on clerics to disobey any such royal orders.

Edward and Philip reacted swiftly. Taking advantage of the role English courts played in protecting the peace, Edward declared that all clerics who refused to pay his taxes would be considered outlaws—literally "outside the law." Clergymen who were robbed, for example, would have no recourse against their attackers; if accused of crimes, they would have no defense in court. Relying on a different strategy, Philip forbade the exportation of precious metals, money, or jewels—effectively sealing the French borders. Immediately, the English clergy cried out for legal protection, while the papacy itself cried out for the revenues it had long enjoyed from French pilgrims, litigants, and travelers. Boniface was forced to back down, conceding in 1297 that kings had the right to tax their clergy in emergencies. But this concession did not end the confrontation.

Boniface VIII

For the sculptor who depicted Pope Boniface VIII, Arnolfo di Cambio (d. 1302), not much had changed since the time of Innocent III. Compare this sculpture with the picture of Innocent on page 361. In both representations, the popes are depicted as young, majestic, authoritative, sober, and calm. Yet Boniface could not have been very calm, for his authority was challenged at every turn. *(Scala/Art Resource, NY.)*

The King's New Tools: Propaganda and Popular Opinion. In 1301, Philip the Fair tested his jurisdiction in southern France by arresting Bernard Saisset, the bishop of Pamiers, on a charge of treason for slandering the king by comparing him to an owl, "the handsomest of birds which is worth absolutely nothing." Saisset's imprisonment violated the principle, maintained both by the pope and by French law, that a clergyman was not subject to lay justice. Boniface reacted angrily, and Philip seized the opportunity to deride and humiliate him, orchestrating a public relations campaign against Boniface. (See Document, "*Ausculta Fili,*" page 379.) Philip convened representatives of the clergy, nobles, and townspeople to explain, justify, and propagandize his position. This new assembly, which met in 1302, was the ancestor of the French representative institution, the Estates General. The pope's reply, the bull[2] *Unam Sanctam* (1302), intensified the situation to fever pitch by declaring bluntly "that it is altogether necessary to salvation for every human creature to be subject to the Roman Pontiff." At meetings of the king's inner circle, Philip's agents declared Boniface a false pope, accusing him of sexual perversion, various crimes, and heresy.

Papal Defeat. In 1303, royal agents, acting under Philip's orders, invaded Boniface's palace at Anagni (southeast of Rome) to capture the pope, bring him to France, and try him. Fearing for the pope's life, however, the people of Anagni joined forces and drove the French agents out of town. Yet even after such public support for the pope, the king made his power felt. Boniface died very shortly thereafter, and the next two popes quickly pardoned Philip and his agents for their actions.

Just as Frederick II's failure revealed the weakness of the empire, so Boniface's humiliation demonstrated the limits of papal control. The two powers that claimed "universal" authority had very little weight in the face of new, limited, but tightly controlled national states such as France and England. After 1303, popes continued to denounce kings and emperors, but their words had less and less impact. In the face of newly powerful medieval states—undergirded by vast revenues, judicial apparatuses, representative institutions, and even the loyalty of churchmen—the papacy could make little headway. The delicate balance between church and state, a hallmark of the years of St. Louis, one that reflected a sense of universal order, broke down at the end of the thirteenth century.

---

[2]An official papal document is called a bull, from the *bulla,* or seal, that was used to authenticate it.

DOCUMENT

Ausculta Fili (Listen, Beloved Son)

In 1301, Philip the Fair of France asserted his power over the bishops of France through the arrest, trial, and punishment of Bishop Saisset. He asked Pope Boniface VIII to ratify his actions, and predictably the pope responded with a flurry of papal bulls, calling for a council of French bishops to meet at Rome the next year. Boniface also wrote a "personal" letter to Philip in the tone of a superior admonishing an inferior — Ausculta Fili (Listen, Beloved Son). Philip burned the letter and released a parody of it to inflame popular opinion. Taking advantage of the antipapal mood, he convened the first meeting of the Estates General in France.

Listen, beloved son, to the precepts of a father and pay heed to the teaching of a master who holds the place on earth of Him who alone is lord and master; take into your heart the warning of holy mother church and be sure to act on it with good effect so that with a contrite heart you may reverently return to God from whom, as is known, you have turned away through negligence or evil counsel and conform yourself to His will and ours.... You have entered the ark of the true Noah outside of which no one is saved, that is to say the Catholic church, the "one dove," the immaculate bride of the one Christ, in which the primacy is known to belong to Christ's vicar, the successor of Peter, who, having received the keys of the kingdom of heaven, is acknowledged to have been established by God as judge of the living and the dead; and it belongs to him, sitting in the seat of judgment, to abolish all evil by his sentence....

Moved by our conscience and urgent necessity we will explain to you more clearly, O son, why we are writing these things to you. For, although our merits are insufficient, God has set us over kings and kingdoms and has imposed on us the yoke of apostolic service to root up and to pull down, to waste and to destroy, to build and to plant in his name and according to his teaching (see Jeremias 1:10)... wherefore, dearest son, let no one persuade you that you have no superior or that you are not subject to the head of the ecclesiastical hierarchy, for he is a fool who so thinks, and whoever affirms it pertinaciously is convicted as an unbeliever and is outside the fold of the good shepherd.

Source: *The Crisis of Church and State, 1050–1300*, ed. Brian Tierney (Medieval Academy Reprints for Teaching, No. 21 [publ. by University of Toronto Press; orig. publ. 1964]), 185–86.

The quest for control led not to order but to confrontation and extremism.

The Avignon Papacy.   In 1309, forced from Rome by civil strife, the papacy settled at Avignon, a city technically in the Holy Roman Empire but very close to, and influenced by, France. Here the popes remained until 1378, and thus the period 1309–1378 is called the **Avignon papacy**. Europeans sensitive to the calamity of having popes living far from Rome called it the Babylonian captivity. They were thinking of the Old Testament story of the Jews captured and brought into slavery in ancient Babylon.[3] The Avignon popes, many of them French, established a sober and efficient organization that took in regular revenues and gave the papacy more say than ever before in the appointment of churchmen. Slowly, they abandoned the idea of leading all of Christendom, tacitly recognizing the growing power of the secular states to regulate their internal affairs.

---

[3]See 2 Kings 24–25.

Avignon (AH vee NYAW) **papacy:** The period (1309–1378) during which the popes ruled from Avignon rather than from Rome.

The Rise of the *Signori*

During the thirteenth century, new groups, generally made up of the non-noble classes — the *popolo*, the "people," who fought on foot — attempted to take over the reins of power in many Italian communes. The popolo incorporated members of city associations such as craft and merchant guilds, parishes, and the commune itself. In fact, the popolo was a kind of alternative commune. Armed and militant, the popolo demanded a share in city government, particularly to gain a voice in matters of taxation. In 1223 at Piacenza, for example, the popolo's members and the nobles worked out a plan to share the election of their city's government. Such power sharing was a typical result of the popolo's struggle. In some cities, however, nobles dissolved the popolo, while in others the popolo virtually excluded the nobles from government. Such factions turned northern Italian cities into centers of civil discord.

Weakened by this constant friction, the communes were tempting prey for great regional nobles who, allying with one or another faction, often succeeded in establishing themselves as *signori* (singular *signore*, "lord") of the cities, keeping the peace at the price of repression. Thirteenth-century

Piacenza was typical: first dominated by nobles, the popolo gained a voice by 1225; but then by midcentury both the nobles and the popolo were eclipsed by the power of a signore.

The Mongol Takeover

Europeans were not the only warring society in the thirteenth century: to the east, the Mongols (sometimes called Tatars or Tartars) created an aggressive army under the leadership of Chingiz (or Genghis) Khan (c. 1162–1227) and his sons. In part, economic necessity drove them out of Mongolia: changes in climate had reduced the grasslands that sustained their animals and their nomadic way of life. But they were also inspired by Chingiz's hope of conquering the world. By 1215, the Mongols held Beijing and most of northern China. Some years later, they moved through central Asia and skirted the Caspian Sea (Map 12.3).

The Golden Horde in Russia.
In the 1230s, the Mongols began concerted attacks in Russia, Poland, and Hungary, where native princes were weak. Only the death of the Great Khan, Chingiz's son Ogodei (1186–1241), and disputes over his succession prevented a concentrated assault on Germany. In the 1250s, the Mongols took Iran, Iraq, and Syria. From the point of view of the Muslim world, the Mongol challenge was much more serious than any western crusade.

The Mongols' sophisticated military tactics contributed to their overwhelming success. They devised two- and three-flank operations. The invasion of Hungary, for example, was two-pronged with divisions arriving from Russia, Poland, and Germany. The Mongols—fighting mainly on horseback with heavy lances and powerful bows and arrows whose shots traveled far and penetrated deeply—crushed the Hungarian army of mixed infantry and cavalry.

In the west, the Mongol rule in Russia lasted the longest. Their most important victory there was the capture of Kiev in 1240. Making the mouth of the Volga River the center of their power in Russia, the Mongols dominated all of Russia's principalities for about two hundred years. The Mongol Empire in Russia, later called the **Golden Horde** (*golden* probably from the color of their leader's tent; *horde* from a Turkish word meaning "camp"), adopted much of the local government apparatus and left many of the old institutions in

---

Golden Horde: The political institution set up by the Mongol Empire in Russia, lasting from the thirteenth to the fifteenth century.

---

place. They allowed Russian princes to continue ruling as long as they paid homage and tribute to the khan, and they tolerated the Russian church, exempting it from taxes. The Mongols' chief undertaking was a series of population censuses on the basis of which they recalculated taxes and recruited troops.

The Opening of China to Europeans.
The Mongol invasion changed the political configuration of Europe and Asia. Because the Mongols were willing to deal with westerners, one effect of their conquests was to open China to European travelers for the first time. Missionaries, diplomats, and merchants went to China over land routes and via the Persian Gulf. Some of these voyagers hoped to enlist the aid of the Mongols against the Muslims; others expected to make new converts to Christianity; still others dreamed of lucrative trade routes.

The most famous of these travelers was Marco Polo (1254–1324), son of a merchant family from Venice. Marco's father and uncle had already been to China once and returned when Marco joined them on a second expedition. He stayed in China for nearly two years. Others stayed even longer. In fact, evidence suggests that an entire community of Venetian traders lived in the city of Yangzhou in the mid-fourteenth century.

Merchants paved the way for missionaries. Friars (preachers to the cities of Europe) became missionaries to new continents as well. In 1289, the pope made the Franciscan John of Monte Corvino his envoy to China. Preaching in India along the way, John arrived in China four or five years after setting out, converting one local ruler, and building a church. A few years later, now at Beijing, he boasted that he had converted six thousand people, constructed two churches, and translated the New Testament and Psalms into the native language.

The long-term effect of the Mongols on the West was to open up new land routes to the East that helped bind together the two halves of the known world. Travel stories such as Marco Polo's account of his journeys stimulated others to seek out the fabulous riches—textiles, ginger, ceramics, copper—of China and other regions of the East. In a sense, the Mongols initiated the search for exotic goods and missionary opportunities that culminated in the European "discovery" of a new world, the Americas.

The Great Famine

While the Mongols stimulated the European economy, natural disasters coupled with political ineptitude brought on a terrible period of famine in

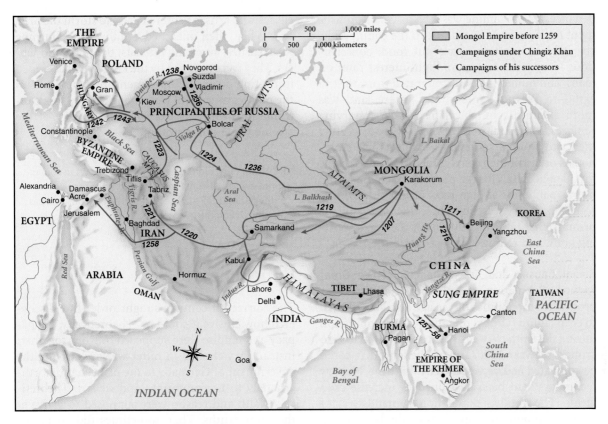

MAP 12.3 The Mongol Invasions to 1259

The Mongols were the first people to tie the eastern world to the west. Their conquest of China, which took place at about the same time as their invasions of Russia and Iran, created a Eurasian economy.
■ Compare this map with the Mapping the West map on page 356. Why were the Mongol invasions a threat to the Muslim world?

northern Europe. The **Great Famine** (1315–1322) left many hungry, sick, and weak while it fueled social antagonisms.

Hunger and Its Effects. An anonymous chronicler looking back on the events of 1315 wrote,

> The floods of rain have rotted almost all the seed, so that the prophecy of Isaiah might seem now to be fulfilled, . . . and in many places the hay lay so long under water that it could neither be mown nor gathered. Sheep generally died and other animals were killed in a sudden plague. . . . [In the next year, 1316,] the dearth of grain was much increased. Such a scarcity has not been seen in our time in England, nor heard of for a hundred years. For the measure of wheat sold in London and the neighboring places for forty pence [a very high price], and in other less thickly populated parts of the country thirty pence was a common price.

Thus did the chronicler name the three main hardships of the famine: uncommonly heavy rains,

which washed up or drowned the crops; the death of farm animals that were key to agricultural life not only for their meat and fleeces but also for their labor; and finally, the economic effects in the cities as scarcity drove up the prices of ordinary foods. All of these led to hunger, disease, and death.

Had the rains gone back to normal, the European economy would no doubt have recovered. But the rains continued, and the crops kept failing. In many regions, the crisis lasted for a full seven years. Hardest hit were the peasants and the poor. In rural areas, wealthy lords and churches and monasteries profited from the newly high prices they could charge. In the cities, some merchants and ecclesiastical institutions benefited as well. But on the whole, even the well-to-do suffered, as both rural and urban areas lost fully 5 to 10 percent of their population. The impact was enormous, for loss of population meant erosion of manpower and falling productivity.

The search for order included attempts to cope with and contain these disasters. The clergy offered up prayers and urged their congregations to do

---

Great Famine: The shortage of food and accompanying social ills that besieged northern Europe between 1315 and 1322.

penance, for the famine was seen as God's punishment for the sins of humanity. In the countryside, charitable monasteries gave out food; conscientious kings tried to control high interest rates on loans; and hungry peasants migrated from west to east — to Poland, for example, where land was more plentiful. In the cities, where starving refugees from rural areas flocked for food, wealthy men and women sometimes opened their storehouses or distributed coins. Other rich townspeople founded hospitals for the poor. Town councils sold municipal bonds at high rates of interest, gaining some temporary solvency. These towns became the primary charitable institutions of the era, importing grain and selling it at cost or a bit less.

Social Causes and Consequences of the Great Famine. Population growth that challenged the productive capabilities of the age also contributed to crop failure. The exponential leap in population during the tenth to twelfth centuries slowed to zero around the year 1300, and all the land that could be cultivated had been settled by this time. No new technology had been developed to increase crop yields. The swollen population demanded a lot from the productive capacities of the land. Just a small shortfall could dislocate the whole system of distribution.

The policies of rulers added to the problems of too many people and too little food. The anonymous chronicler who considered "plentiful rain" the cause of the famine also observed "that in Northumbria [the north of England] dogs and horses and other unclean things were eaten. For there, on account of the frequent raids of the Scots, work is more irksome, as the accursed Scots despoil the people daily of their food." Scottish troops were not the only ones who destroyed the crops. The king of England sent his soldiers to ravage Scotland in turn. The kings of Norway, Denmark, and Sweden regularly fought one another. The king of France was at war with rebellious Flemings to control Flanders. These wars not only ruined the crops but also diverted manpower and resources to arms and castles, at the same time disrupting normal markets and trade routes.

In order to wage wars, rulers imposed heavy taxes and, as the famine became worse, requisitioned grain to support their troops. Consequently, the effects of the famine grew worse, and in many regions people rose up in protest. In France, the merchants were enraged to see their grain taken off the open market, where they could hope to profit. The king tried to mollify them. In England, peasants resisted tax collectors. In a more violent reaction, poor French shepherds, outcasts,

clerics, and artisans entered Paris to storm the prisons. They then marched southward — burning royal castles, attacking officials, the Jews, and lepers. They were pursued by the king, who succeeded in putting down the movement. But the limits of the politics of control were made clear in this confrontation, which exacerbated the misery of the famine while doing nothing to contain it.

> **REVIEW:** How did the search for order result in cooperation — and confrontation — between the secular rulers of the period 1215–1340 and other institutions, such as the church and the towns?

Conclusion

The thirteenth century sought order but discovered how elusive it could be. Theoretically, the papacy and empire were supposed to work together; instead they clashed in bitter warfare, leaving the government of Germany to the princes and northern Italy to its communes and *signori*. Theoretically, faith and reason were supposed to arrive at the same truths. They sometimes did so in the hands of scholastics, but not always. Theoretically, all Christians were expected to practice the same rites and follow the teachings of the church. In fact, local enforcement determined which church laws took effect — and to what extent. Moreover, the search for order was never able to bring together all the diverse peoples, ideas, and interests of thirteenth-century society. Heretics and Jews were set apart.

Order was more achievable in the arts. Depictions in stained glass and sculpture explored the orderly progression from the Old to the New Testaments. Musicians wove together disparate melodic and poetic lines into motets. Writers melded heroic and romantic themes with theological truths and mystical visions.

Political leaders also aimed at order and control to increase their revenues, expand their territories, and enhance their prestige. The kings of England and France and the governments of northern and central Italian cities partially succeeded in these goals, while the king of Germany failed miserably. Germany and Italy remained fragmented until the nineteenth century. Within the new, compact governments, however, the quest for orderly procedures and hierarchies succeeded to a degree. Kings and representative institutions worked well together on the whole, and clergy and laypeople came to feel that they were part of the same political entity, whether that entity was

MAPPING THE WEST

Europe, c. 1340

The Empire, now called the Holy Roman Empire, still dominated the map of Europe in 1340, but the emperor himself had little power. Each principality—often each city—was ruled separately and independently. To the east, the Ottoman Turks were just beginning to make themselves felt. In the course of the next century, they would disrupt the Mongol hegemony and become a great power.

France or a German principality. Ironically, the Mongols, who began as invaders in the west, helped unify areas that were far apart by opening trade routes.

Events at the end of the thirteenth century thwarted the search for order. The balance between church and state achieved under St. Louis in France disintegrated into irreconcilable claims to power under Pope Boniface VIII and Philip the Fair. The carefully constructed tapestry of St. Thomas's summae began to unravel in the teachings of John Duns Scotus. An economy stretched to the breaking point resulted in a terrible period of famine. Disorder and anxiety—but also extraordinary creativity—would mark the next era.

FOR FURTHER EXPLORATION

- **For suggested references, including Web sites, for topics in this chapter,** see page SR-1 at the end of the book.

- **For additional primary-source material from this period,** see Chapter 12 in *Sources of THE MAKING OF THE WEST,* Third Edition.

- **For Web sites and documents related to topics in this chapter,** see *Make History* at bedfordstmartins.com/hunt.

CHAPTER REVIEW

KEY TERMS AND PEOPLE

Innocent III (360)

Fourth Lateran
Council (360)

scholasticism (367)

Frederick II (373)

Statute in Favor of the
Princes (374)

Louis IX (375)

cortes (377)

Boniface VIII (377)

Avignon papacy (379)

Golden Horde (380)

Great Famine (381)

REVIEW QUESTIONS

1. How did people respond to the teachings and laws of the church in the early thirteenth century?

2. How did artists, musicians, and scholastics try to link this world with the divine?

3. How did the search for order result in cooperation—and confrontation—between the secular rulers of the period 1215–1340 and other institutions, such as the church and the towns?

MAKING CONNECTIONS

1. Why was Innocent III more successful than Boniface VIII in carrying out his objectives?

2. What impact did the Mongol invasions have on the medieval economy?

> **For practice quizzes, a customized study plan, and other study tools,** see the Online Study Guide at bedfordstmartins.com/hunt.

IMPORTANT EVENTS

1188	King Alfonso IX summons townsmen to the *cortes*	1265	English commons summoned to Parliament
1212–1250	Reign of Frederick II	1265–1321	Dante Alighieri
1215	Fourth Lateran Council	1273	Thomas Aquinas publishes the *Summa Theologiae*
1226–1270	Reign of Louis IX (St. Louis)	1302	First Meeting of the French Estates General
1232	Frederick II finalizes Statute in Favor of the Princes	1309–1378	Avignon papacy
1240	Mongols capture Kiev	1315–1322	Great Famine

Crisis and Renaissance
1340–1492

I n 1453, the Ottoman Turks turned their cannons on Constantinople and blasted the city's walls. The fall of Constantinople, which spelled the end of the Byzantine Empire, was an enormous shock to Europeans. Some, like the pope, called for a crusade against the Ottomans; others, like the writer Lauro Quirini, sneered, calling them "a barbaric, uncultivated race, without established customs, or laws, [who lived] a careless, vagrant, arbitrary life."

But the Turks didn't consider themselves uncultivated or arbitrary. In fact, they shared many of the values and tastes of the Europeans who were so hostile to them. Sultan Mehmed II employed European architects to construct his new palace — the Topkapi Saray — in what was once Constantinople and was now popularly called Istanbul. He commissioned the Venetian Gentile Bellini to paint his portrait, the latest trend in European art.

Mehmed's actions and interests sum up the dual features of the period of crisis and Renaissance that took place from the middle of the fourteenth century to the late fifteenth century. What was a crisis from one point of view was at the same time stimulus for what historians call the Renaissance. This word, French for "rebirth," describes a period when people discovered new value in ancient, classical culture. The classical revival provided the stimulus for new styles of living, ruling, and thinking. A new vocabulary drawn from classical literature as well as astonishing new forms of art and music based on ancient precedents were used both to confront and to mask the crises of the day.

The extraordinary calamities of the period from 1340 to 1492 were matched by equally significant gains. The plague, or Black Death, tore at the fabric of communities and families — but the survivors and their children reaped the benefits of higher wages and better living standards.

Portrait of Mehmed II
The Ottoman ruler Mehmed II saw himself as a Renaissance patron of the arts, and he called upon the most famous artists and architects of the day to work for him. The painter of this portrait, Gentile Bellini, was from a well-known family of artists in Venice and served at Mehmed's court in 1479–1480. The revival of portraiture, so characteristic of Renaissance tastes, was as important to the Turkish sultans as to European rulers. *(Erich Lessing/Art Resource, NY.)*

The Hundred Years' War, fought between France and England from 1337 until 1453 (and involving many smaller states in its slaughter), brought untold misery to the French countryside — but it also helped create the glittering court of Burgundy, patron of new art and music. By the war's end, both the French and the English kings were more powerful than ever. Following their conquest of Constantinople, the Ottoman Turks penetrated far into the Balkans; but this was a calamity only from the European point of view. Well into the sixteenth century, the Ottomans were part of the culture that nourished the artistic achievements of the Renaissance. A crisis in the church overlapped with the crises of disease and war as a schism within the papacy — pitting pope against pope — divided Europe into separate camps. The Renaissance played a role in this crisis as well, since Renaissance writers attended the church council that eventually resolved the papal schism.

> **FOCUS QUESTION:** How were the crises of the fourteenth and fifteenth centuries and the Renaissance related?

Crisis: Disease, War, and Schism

In the mid-fourteenth century, a series of crises shook the West. The Black Death swept through Europe and decimated the population, especially in the cities. Two major wars redrew the map of Europe during the period from 1340 to 1492. The first was the Hundred Years' War, which began in 1337 and lasted for *more* than one hundred years, until 1453. This war turned a dynastic struggle over the kingdom of France into a military confrontation that transformed the nature of warfare

itself. The second war began with the Ottoman domination of Byzantium in the 1360s and culminated in the Ottoman conquest of Constantinople in 1453 — the same year that the Hundred Years' War ended. The capture of Constantinople marked a major shift in global power as the last buffer between Europe and the Islamic world fell. The Ottomans now had a secure base from which to move into Europe. As the wars raged and attacks of the plague came and went, a crisis in the church also weighed on Europeans. Attempts to bring the pope at Avignon (see page 379) back to Rome resulted in the Great Schism (1378–1417), when first two and then three rival popes asserted universal authority. In the wake of these crises, many ordinary folk sought solace in new forms of piety, some of them heretical.

The Black Death, 1346–1353

The **Black Death**, so named by later historians, was a calamitous disease. It decimated the population wherever it struck and wrought havoc on social and economic structures. Yet in the wake of this plague, those fortunate enough to survive benefited from an improved standard of living. Unprofitable farms were abandoned, and a more diversified agriculture developed. Birthrates climbed, and new universities were established to educate the post-plague generations.

A "pestilential disease."   The Black Death began in 1346, perhaps in the region between the Black and Caspian seas. A year later, the Byzantine scholar Nicephorus Gregoras was already familiar with it. Calling it a "pestilential disease," he described its symptoms: "The prominent signs of this disease, signs indicating early death, were tumor-

---

Black Death: The term historians give to the plague that swept through Europe in 1346–1353.

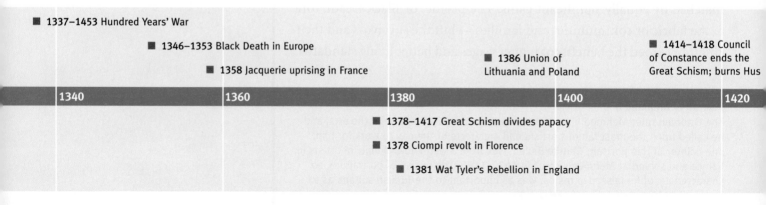

■ 1337–1453 Hundred Years' War

■ 1346–1353 Black Death in Europe

■ 1358 Jacquerie uprising in France

■ 1386 Union of Lithuania and Poland

■ 1414–1418 Council of Constance ends the Great Schism; burns Hus

| 1340 | 1360 | 1380 | 1400 | 1420 |

■ 1378–1417 Great Schism divides papacy

■ 1378 Ciompi revolt in Florence

■ 1381 Wat Tyler's Rebellion in England

TAKING MEASURE

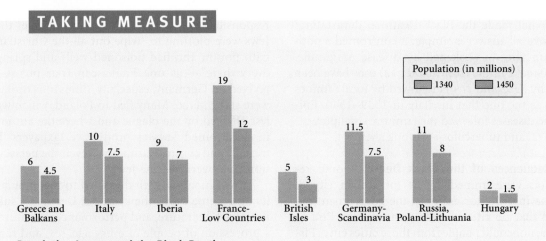

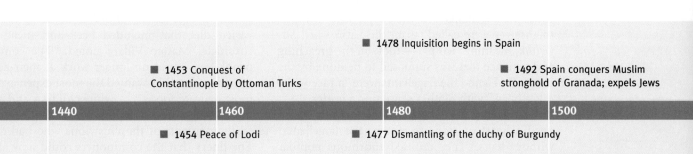

Population Losses and the Black Death

The bar chart represents dramatically the impact of the Black Death and the recurrent plagues between 1340 and 1450. More than a century after the Black Death, none of the regions of Europe had made up for the losses of population. The population of 1450 stood at about 75–80 percent of the pre-plague population. The areas hardest hit were France and the Low Countries, which also suffered from the devastations of the Hundred Years' War. *(From Carlo M. Cipolla, ed.,*
Fontana Economic History of Europe: The Middle Ages *(Great Britain: Collins/Fontana Books, 1974), 36.)*

ous outgrowths at the roots of thighs and arms and simultaneously bleeding ulcerations." Most historians think that the Black Death was caused by the bacterium *Yersinia pestis*, the same organism responsible for outbreaks of plague today. From its breeding ground it traveled westward, to the Middle East, the North African coast, and Europe. Carried by fleas traveling on the backs of rats, it hitched boat rides with spices, silks, and porcelain. In 1347, people in the Genoese colony in Caffa, on the north edge of the Black Sea, contracted the disease. By January 1348, it arrived in Europe—in Sicily, Sardinia, Corsica, and Marseille. Six months later, it had spread to Aragon, all of Italy, the Balkans, and most of France. Soon it crept northward to Germany, England, and Scandinavia, reaching the Russian city of Novgorod in 1351. It

spread to the Islamic world as well—to Baghdad, north Africa, and al-Andalus.

This was just the beginning. The plague recurred every ten to twelve years throughout the fourteenth century (though only the attack of 1346–1353 is called the Black Death), and it continued, though at longer intervals, until the eighteenth century.

The effects of the Black Death were spread across Europe yet oddly localized. At Florence, in Italy, nearly half of the population died, yet two hundred miles to the north, Milan suffered very little. Conservative estimates put the death toll in Europe at between one-third and one-half of the entire population, but some historians put the mortality rate as high as 60 percent. (See "Taking Measure," above.)

1478 Inquisition begins in Spain

1453 Conquest of
Constantinople by Ottoman Turks

1492 Spain conquers Muslim
stronghold of Granada; expels Jews

| 1440 | 1460 | 1480 | 1500 |

1454 Peace of Lodi   **1477** Dismantling of the duchy of Burgundy

What made the Black Death so devastating? The overall answer is simple: it confronted a population already weakened by disease or famine. The Great Famine (see Chapter 12) may have been over by 1322, but it was followed by local famines such as the one that hit Italy in 1339–1340. Epidemic diseases followed the famines: smallpox, influenza, and tuberculosis all took their toll.

Consequences of the Black Death. Some responses were immediate. At the Italian city of Pistoia in 1348, for example, the government decreed that no citizen could go to nearby Pisa or Lucca, nor could people from those cities enter Pistoia; in effect, Pistoia set up a quarantine. In the same set of ordinances, the Pistoians, thinking that "bad air" brought the plague, provided for better sanitation, declaring that "butchers and retailers of meat shall not stable horses or allow any mud or dung in the shop or other place where they sell meat." Elsewhere reactions were religious. The archbishop of York in England, for example, tried to prevent the plague from entering his diocese by ordering "that devout processions [be] held every Wednesday and Friday in our cathedral church . . . and in every parish church in our city and diocese."

Some people took more extreme measures. Lamenting their sins—which they believed had brought on the plague—and attempting to placate God, men and women wandered from city to city with whips in their hands. Entering a church, they took off their shirts or blouses, lay down one by one on the church floor, and, according to the chronicler Henry of Hervordia (d. 1370),

> one of them would strike the first with a whip, saying, "May God grant you remission [forgiveness] of all your sins. Arise." And he would get up, and do the same to the second, and all the others in turn did the same. When they were all on their feet, and arranged two by two in procession, two of them in the middle of the column would begin singing a hymn in a high voice, with a sweet melody.

The church did not approve of this practice because the flagellants—as the people who whipped themselves were called (from the Latin word *flagellum*, meaning "whip")—took on the preaching and penance that was supposed to be done by the clergy. To Henry, the flagellants were "a race without a head," with neither sense nor a leader.

Yet Henry also thought that "a man would need a heart of stone to watch [the flagellants] without tears." They aroused enormous popular feeling wherever they went. This religious enthusiasm often culminated in violence against the Jews, as rumors circulated that the Jews were

responsible for the Black Death. Old charges that Jews were plotting to "wipe out all the Christians with poison and had poisoned wells and springs everywhere"—as one Franciscan friar put it—revived. In Germany, especially, thousands of Jews were slaughtered. Many fled to Poland, which was less affected by the plague and where the authorities welcomed Jews as productive taxpayers. In western and central Europe, however, the persecutions impoverished the Jews.

Preoccupation with death led to the popularity of a theme called the Dance of Death as a subject of art, literature, and performance. It featured a procession of people of every age, sex, and rank making their way to the grave. In works of art, skeletal figures of Death, whirling about, laughed as they abducted their prey. These were often life-size paintings that ran horizontally for many feet. They were meant to be "mirrors" in which viewers could see themselves. The Dance of Death was also sometimes performed—in a church or at a princely court. Preachers talked about the theme; poets wrote dialogues between Death and his victims. "Thus Death takes us all; that is certain," one poet concluded.

At the same time that it helped inspire this bleak view of the world, the Black Death brought new opportunities for those who survived its murderous path. With a smaller population to feed, less land was needed for farming. Marginal land that had been cultivated was returned to pasture, meadow, or forest. Landlords diversified their products. Wheat had been the favored crop before the plague, but barley—the key ingredient of beer—turned out to be more profitable afterward. Animal products continued to fetch a high price, and some landlords switched from farming to animal husbandry.

These changes in agriculture meant a better standard of living. The peasants and urban workers who survived the plague were able to negotiate better conditions or higher wages from their landlords or employers. With more money to spend, people could afford a better and more varied diet that included beer and meat. The chronicler Matteo Villani noted, "The common people . . . would no longer work at their accustomed trades; they wanted the most expensive and most delicate foods, . . . while children and common women dressed themselves in all the fair and costly garments of the illustrious who had died." The finery that the commoners could now afford threatened to erase the lines between the nobles and everyone else, and many Italian cities passed laws to prohibit ostentatious dress among every

Dance of Death
A stiff Holy Roman Emperor and a slightly more animated empress — both flanked by gleeful, dancing skeletons — dominate the center of a large canvas of the Dance of Death, which was painted at Reval (today Tallinn, Estonia) in the fifteenth century. At the left end of the canvas (not pictured here) is a preacher who warns all that their fate is death. After him comes the pope, then the emperor and empress, then the cardinal and the king. The rest of the painting is lost, but its message is clear: even the exalted end up in the grave. *(© St. Nicholas' Church, Art Museum of Estonia, Tallinn, Estonia/The Bridgeman Art Library.)*

class of citizens. These laws were generally ineffective, however; families continued to announce their rank and prestige by wearing lavish clothes.

Each attack of the plague brought with it, a few years later, a slight jump in the birthrate. It is unlikely that women became more fertile after the plague. Rather, the cause of the increased birthrate was more subtle: with good employment opportunities, couples married at younger ages and with greater frequency than they had previously. For example, before the Black Death, about seventeen couples per year married at Givry, a small town in Burgundy. But once the plague hit, an average of forty-seven couples there wed each year. "After the end of the epidemic," one chronicler wrote, "the men and women who stayed alive did everything to get married."

The Black Death also had an effect on patterns of education. The post-plague generations needed schooling. The pestilential disease spared neither the students nor the professors of the old universities. As the disease ebbed, new local colleges and universities were built, partly to train a new generation for the priesthood and partly to satisfy

local donors — many of them princes — who, riding on a sea of wealth left behind by the dead, wanted to be known as patrons of education. Thus, in 1348, in the midst of the plague, Holy Roman Emperor Charles IV chartered a university at Prague. The king of Poland founded Cracow University, and a Habsburg duke created a university at Vienna. Rather than travel to Paris or Bologna, young men living east of the Rhine River now tended to study nearer home.

The Hundred Years' War, 1337–1453

Adding to the miseries of the Black Death were the ravages of war. One of the most brutal was the Hundred Years' War, which pitted England against France. Since the Norman invasion of England in the eleventh century (see page 320), the king of England had held land on the continent. The French kings continually chipped away at it, however, and by the beginning of the fourteenth century England retained only the area around Bordeaux, called Guyenne. In 1337, after a series of challenges and skirmishes, King Philip VI of

France declared Guyenne to be his; King Edward III of England, in turn, declared himself king of France. The **Hundred Years' War** had begun.

The war had four phases. The first three saw the progressive weakening of French power, the strengthening of England, and the creation of a new kingdom, Burgundy, which for a crucial time allied itself with England. The fourth phase, which began when King Henry V of England invaded France and achieved a great victory at the battle of Agincourt in 1415, ended in a complete reversal and the ousting of the English from the continent for good (Map 13.1).

Joan of Arc. How did the French achieve this turnaround? The answer largely lies in the inspiration of a sixteen-year-old peasant girl who presented herself at the court of the dauphin (the man who had been designated as king but had not yet been anointed and crowned) as the heaven-sent savior of France. Inspired by visions in which God told her to lead the war against the English, and calling herself "the Maid" (a virgin), **Joan of Arc** (1412–1431) arrived at court in 1429 wearing armor, riding a horse, and leading a small army. Full of charisma and confidence at a desperate hour, Joan was carefully questioned and examined (to be sure of her virginity) before her message was accepted. She convinced the French that she had been sent by God when she fought courageously (and was wounded) in the successful battle of Orléans. At her urging, the dauphin traveled deep into enemy territory to be anointed and crowned as King Charles VII at the cathedral in Reims, following the tradition of French monarchs.

The victory at Orléans and the anointing of Charles began the French about-face, but Joan herself suffered greatly. A promise to take Paris proved empty, and she was captured and turned over to the English. Tried as a witch, she was burned at the stake in 1431. (See "Contrasting Views," page 394.)

The Hundred Years' War as a World War. The Hundred Years' War drew other countries of Europe into its vortex. Both the English and the French hired mercenaries from Germany, Switzerland, and the Netherlands; the best crossbow-

Joan of Arc
This manuscript illumination of Joan of Arc, painted circa 1420, shows Joan in plate armor, holding a sword in one hand and a banner decorated with angels in the other—clear symbols of her role as a soldier and a messenger of God. *(akg-images.)*

men came from Genoa. Since the economies of England and Flanders were interdependent, with England exporting the wool that Flemish workers turned into cloth, it was inevitable that Flanders would be drawn into the conflict. In fact, once the war broke out, Flemish townsmen allied with England against their count, who supported the French king.

The duchy of Burgundy became involved in the war as well when the marriage of the heiress to Flanders and the duke of Burgundy in 1369 created a powerful new state. Calculating shrewdly which side—England or France—to support and cannily entering the fray when it suited them, the dukes of Burgundy created a glittering court, a center of art and culture. Had Burgundy maintained its alliance with England, the map of Europe would be entirely different today. But the alliance fell apart when Burgundy's attempt to expand clashed with the interests of the Swiss Confederation. In 1474, Swiss soldiers defeated the Burgundians on the battlefield. This was the beginning of the end of the Burgundian state.

Hundred Years' War: The long war between England and France, 1337–1453; it produced numerous social upheavals yet left both states more powerful than before.

Joan of Arc: A peasant girl (1412–1431) whose conviction that God had sent her to save France in fact helped France win the Hundred Years' War.

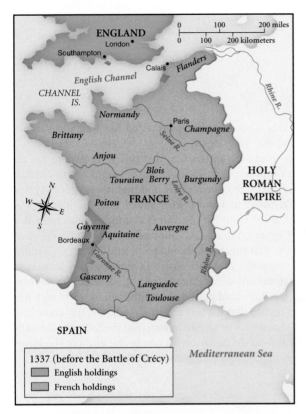

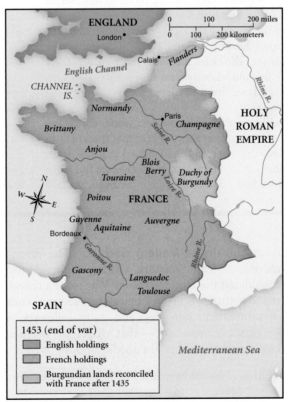

MAP 13.1 The Hundred Years' War, 1337–1453

During the Hundred Years' War, English kings—aided by the new state of Burgundy—contested the French monarchy for the domination of France. For many decades, the English seemed to be winning, but the French monarchy prevailed in the end.

CONTRASTING VIEWS

Joan of Arc: Who Was "the Maid"?

The figure of Joan of Arc gives shape to the confused events and personalities of the Hundred Years' War. But who was this young woman? Joan herself emphasized her visions and divine calling (Document 1). The royal court was unsure whether to consider her a fraud (or, worse, the devil's tool) or a gift from heaven (Document 2). A neighbor of the young Joan recalled her as an ordinary young country girl (Document 3).

1. Joan the Visionary

Joan first referred to her visions at length after her capture by her enemies, who were eager to prove that she was inspired by the devil. The light and voices that she testified to echoed the experiences of many medieval visionaries. But we do not have Joan's exact words; her account was written up by her examiners, who composed it in Latin even though Joan spoke in French.

She confessed that when she was aged thirteen, she had a voice from God to help her to guide herself. And the first time she was greatly afraid. And this voice came around noon, in summer, in the garden of her father, and Joan had not fasted on the preceding day. She heard the voice on the right-hand side, towards the church, and she rarely heard it without a light. This light came from the same side that she heard the voice, but generally there was a great light there. And when Joan came to France [Lorraine, where Joan was raised, was not considered part of France], she often heard this voice. . . .

She said, in addition, that if she was in a wood, she clearly heard the voices coming to her. She also said that it seemed to her that it was a worthy voice and she believed that this voice had been sent from God, and that, after she had heard this voice three times, she knew that this was the voice of an angel. She said

also that this voice had always protected her well and that she understood this voice clearly.

Asked about the instruction that this voice gave to her for the salvation of her soul, she said that it taught her to conduct herself well, to go to church often, and that it was necessary that she should travel to France. Joan added that her interrogator would not learn from her, on this occasion, in what form that voice had appeared to her. . . . She said moreover that the voice had told her that she, Joan, should go to find Robert de Baudricourt in the town of Vaucouleurs [a tiny holdout in eastern France that was not under English control], of which he was captain, and that he would provide her with men to travel with her. Joan then replied that she was a poor girl who did not know how to ride on horseback or to lead in war. [But she followed through, met with Robert de Baudricourt, and in the end got the escort that she needed to go to the court of the dauphin, the future Charles VII.]

Source: *Joan of Arc: La Pucelle*, trans. and annotated by Craig Taylor (Manchester: Manchester University Press, 2006), 141–42.

2. Messenger of God?

When Joan appeared at the court of the dauphin, her reputation as the messenger of God had preceded her. The French court received her with a mixture of wonder, curiosity, and skepticism. There was debate among the dauphin's counselors about whether Joan should be taken seriously, and the dauphin referred the case to a panel of theologians to determine whether Joan's mission was of divine origin. The following account of Joan's first visit to the dauphin was given by Simon Charles, president of the royal Chamber of Accounts at an investigation begun in 1455 to nullify Joan's sentence of 1429.

From Chivalry to Modern Warfare. The French chronicler Jean Froissart, writing around 1400, considered the Hundred Years' War to be a chivalric adventure—chivalry being the medieval code of refinement, fair play, and piety followed by knights on horseback—that displayed the gallantry and bravery of the medieval nobility:

> In order that the honorable enterprises, noble adventure, and deeds of arms which took place during the wars waged by France and England should be fittingly related and preserved for posterity, so that brave men should be inspired thereby to follow such examples, I wish to place on record these matters of great renown.

In his account of the war, Froissart described knights like the Englishman Walter de Manny, who was so

eager to show off his prowess that he privately gathered a group of followers and attacked the French town of Mortagne to fulfill a vow made "in the hearing of ladies and lords that, 'If war breaks out, . . . I'll be the first to arm myself and capture a castle or town in the kingdom of France.'"

But even Froissart could not help but notice that most of the men who went to battle were not wealthy knights on a lark like Walter de Manny. Nor were they ordinary foot soldiers, who had always made up a large portion of all medieval armies. The soldiers of the Hundred Years' War were primarily mercenaries: men who fought for pay and plunder, heedless of the king for whom they were supposed to be fighting. During lulls in the war, these so-called Free Companies lived

Questioned first on what he could depose and testify . . . [Simon Charles] said and declared upon oath that he only knew what follows: . . . that when Joan arrived at the town of Chinon, the council discussed whether the King should hear her or not. She was first asked why she had come and what she wanted. Although she did not wish to say anything except to the King, she was nevertheless forced on behalf of the King to reveal the purpose of her mission. She said that she had two commands from the King of Heaven, that is to say one to raise the siege of Orléans, and the other to conduct the King to Reims for his coronation and consecration. Having heard this, some among the King's councilors said that the King should not have any faith in this Joan, and the others said that, since she declared that she had been sent by God and that she had certain things to say to the King, the King should at least hear her. But the King decided that she should first be examined by the clerks and churchmen, which was done.

Source: Ibid., pp. 317–18.

3. Normal Girl?

At the same trial, various inhabitants in and near Domremy, Joan's village, recalled her as a normal young girl. The following account was given by Jean Morel, a laborer from a town near Joan's. He knew her as Jeannette.

He declared upon oath that the Jeannette in question was born at Domremy and was baptized at the parish church of Saint-Rémy in that place. Her father was named Jacques d'Arc, her mother Isabelle, both laborers living together at Domremy as long as they lived. They were good and faithful Catholics, good laborers, of good reputation, and of honest behavior. . . .

He declared upon oath that from her earliest childhood, Jeannette was well brought up in the faith as was appropriate, and instructed in good morals, as far as he knew, so that almost everyone in the village of Domremy loved her. Just like the other young girls she knew the *Credo*, the *Pater Noster*, and the *Ave Maria* [all three basic texts of Christian belief].

He declared that Jeannette was honest in her behavior, just as any similar girl is, because her parents were not very rich. In her childhood, and right up to her departure from her family home, she followed the plough and sometimes minded the animals in the fields; she did the work of a woman, spinning and making other things.

He declared upon oath that, as he saw, this Jeannette often went to church willingly to the extent that sometimes she was mocked by the other young people. . . .

He declared upon oath that on the subject of the tree called "of the Ladies," he once heard it said that women or supernatural persons—they were called fairies—came long ago to dance under that tree. But, so it is said, since a reading of the gospel of St. John, they did not come there any more. He also declared that in the present day . . . the young girls and lads of Domremy went under this tree to dance [on a particular Sunday in Lent], and sometimes also in the spring and summer on feast days; sometimes they ate at that place. On their return, they went to the spring of Thorns, strolling and singing, and they drank from the water of this spring, and all around they had fun gathering flowers. He also declared that Joan the Pucelle [the Maid] went there sometimes with the other girls and did as they did; he never heard it said that she went alone to the tree or to the spring, which is nearer to the village than the tree, for any other reason than to walk about and to play just like the other young girls.

Source: Ibid., pp. 267–68.

QUESTIONS TO CONSIDER

1. Given the norms of the time, in what ways was Joan ordinary?
2. How fixed were male and female roles in fifteenth-century France?

---

off the French countryside, terrorizing the peasants and exacting "protection" money. Froissart wrote of "men-at-arms and irregulars from various countries, who subdued and plundered the whole region between the Seine and the Loire. . . . They ranged the country in troops of twenty, thirty, or forty, and they met no one capable of putting up a resistance to them."

The ideal chivalric knight fought on horseback with other armed horsemen. But in the Hundred Years' War, foot soldiers and archers were far more important than swordsmen. The French tended to use crossbows, whose heavy, deadly arrows were released by a mechanism that even a townsman could master. The English employed longbows, which could shoot five arrows for every one launched on the crossbow. The volley of arrows fired by large groups of English archers could wreak havoc. Meanwhile, gunpowder was slowly being introduced and cannons forged. Handguns were beginning to be used, their effect about equal to that of crossbows.

By the end of the war, chivalry was only a dream—though one that continued to inspire soldiers even up to the First World War. Heavy artillery and foot soldiers, tightly massed together in formations of many thousands of men, were the face of the new military. Moreover, the army was becoming more professional and centralized. In the 1440s the French king created a permanent army of mounted soldiers. He paid them a wage and subjected them to regular inspection. Private armies—such as the one Walter de Manny recruited for his own ambitions—were prohibited.

The War's Progeny: Uprisings in Flanders, the Jacquerie, and Wat Tyler's Rebellion.

The outbreak of the Hundred Years' War led to revolts in Ghent and other great Flemish textile centers. Dependent on England for the raw wool they processed, Flemish cities could not afford to have their count side with the French. In 1338, the cities revolted and succeeded for a time in ousting the count, who fled to France. But discord among the cities and within each town allowed the count's successor, Louis de Male, to return in 1348. Revolts continued to flare up thereafter, but Louis allowed a measure of self-government to the towns, maintained some distance from French influence, and managed on the whole to keep the peace.

In France, the Parisians chafed against the high taxes they were forced to pay to finance the war. When the English captured the French king John at the battle of Poitiers in 1358, Étienne Marcel, provost of the Paris merchants, and other disillusioned members of the estates of France (the representatives of the clergy, nobility, and commons) met in Paris to discuss political reform, the incompetence of the French army, and taxes. Under Marcel's leadership, a crowd of Parisians killed some nobles and for a short while took control of the city. But troops soon blockaded Paris and cut off its food supply. Later that year, Marcel was assassinated and the Parisian revolt came to an end.

Also in that year, peasants, weary of the Free Companies—who were ravaging the countryside—and disgusted by the military incompetence of the nobility, rose up in protest. Opponents of this movement—the French nobility—called it the **Jacquerie**, probably taken from a derisive name for male peasants: Jacques Bonhomme (Jack Goodfellow). Froissart was scandalized by the peasants' behavior:

> They banded together and went off . . . unarmed except for pikes and knives, to the house of a knight who lived near by. They broke in and killed the knight with his lady and his children, big and small, and set fire to the house. Next they went to another castle and did much worse.

If the peasants were in fact guilty of these atrocities, the nobles soon gave as good as they got. The revolts were put down with exceptional brutality. Froissart described the moment with relish: "They [the nobles] began to kill those evil men [the peasants] and to cut them to pieces without mercy."

Similar revolts took place in England. The movement known as Wat Tyler's Rebellion, for example, started as an uprising in much of southern and central England when royal agents tried to collect poll taxes (a tax on each household) to finance the Hundred Years' War. Refusing to pay and refusing to be arrested, the commons—peasants and small householders—rose up in rebellion in 1381. They massed in various groups, vowing "to slay all lawyers, and all jurors, and all the servants of the King whom they could find," as one chronicler put it. Marching to London to see the king, whom they professed to support, they began to make a more radical demand: an end to serfdom. Although the rebellion was put down and its leaders executed, the death knell of serfdom in England had been sounded, as peasants returned home to bargain with their lords for better terms. (See Document, "Wat Tyler's Rebellion," page 398.)

The Ottoman Conquest of Constantinople, 1453

The end of the Hundred Years' War coincided with an event that was even more decisive for all of Europe: the conquest of Constantinople by the Ottoman Turks. The Ottomans, who were converts to Islam, were one of several tribal confederations in central Asia. Starting as a small enclave between the Mongol Empire and Byzantium, and taking their name from Osman I (r. 1280–1324), a potent early leader, the Ottomans began to expand in the fourteenth century in a quest to wage holy war against infidels, or unbelievers.

During the next two centuries, the Ottomans took over the Balkans and Anatolia by both negotiations and arms (Map 13.2). Under Murad I (r. 1360–1389), they reduced the Byzantine Empire to the city of Constantinople and treated it as a vassal state. At the Maritsa River in 1364, Murad defeated a joint Hungarian-Serbian army, setting off a wave of crusading fervor in Europe that led (in the end) to only a few unsuccessful expeditions. In 1389, Murad's forces won the battle of Kosovo—still invoked in Serbia today as a great struggle between Christians and Muslims, even though a number of Serbian princes fought on the Ottoman side.

After a lull, when the Ottoman thrust was stopped, Sultan Mehmed I (r. 1410–1421) resumed the conquests and his grandson **Mehmed II**

Jacquerie (zhah kuh REE): The 1358 uprising of French peasants against the nobles amid the Hundred Years' War; it was brutally put down.

Mehmed II: The sultan under whom the Ottoman Turks conquered Constantinople in 1453.

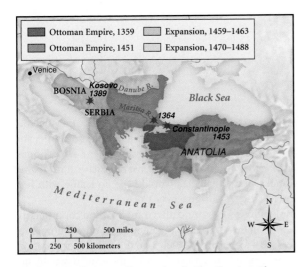

MAP 13.2 Ottoman Expansion in the Fourteenth and Fifteenth Centuries
The Balkans were the major theater of expansion for the Ottoman Empire. The Byzantine Empire was reduced to the city of Constantinople and surrounded by the Ottomans before its final fall in 1453.

(r. 1451–1481) determined to take the city of Constantinople itself. Preparations began about a year in advance, when Mehmed II built an enormous fortress near the capital and fitted it out with a large number of soldiers and several brass cannons. In March 1453, he launched the attack. Perhaps eighty thousand men confronted some three thousand defenders (the entire population of the city of Constantinople was no more than fifty thousand) and a fleet from Genoa. The city held out until the end of May, when Mehmed's forces attacked by both land and sea. The decisive moment came when his cannons breached the city's land walls. Mehmed's troops entered the city and plundered it thoroughly, killing the emperor and displaying his head in triumph.

The conquest of Constantinople marked the end of the Byzantine Empire. But that was not the way Mehmed saw the matter. He conquered Constantinople in part to be a successor to the Roman emperors—a Muslim successor, to be sure. He turned Hagia Sophia, the great church built by Justinian (see page 225), into a mosque, as he did with most of the other Byzantine churches. He retained the city's name, the City of Constantine—Qustantiniyya in Turkish—though it was popularly referred to as Istanbul, meaning "the city."

Like the French and English kings after the Hundred Years' War, the Ottoman sultans were central monarchs who guaranteed law and order. The core of their army consisted of European Christian boys, who were requisitioned as tribute

every five years. Trained in arms and converted to Islam, they made up the Janissaries—a highly disciplined military force also used to supervise local administrators throughout formerly Byzantine regions. Building a system of roads that crisscrossed their empire, the sultans made long-distance trade easy and profitable.

Once Constantinople was his, Mehmed embarked on an ambitious program of expansion and conquest. He brought all of Serbia under Ottoman control in 1458; he crossed the Aegean Sea and took over Athens and the Peloponnese by 1460; six years later, he gained Bosnia. By 1500, the Ottoman Empire was a new and powerful state bridging Europe and the Middle East.

The Great Schism, 1378–1417

Even as war and disease threatened their material and physical well-being, a crisis in the church, precipitated by a scandal in the papacy, tore at Europeans' spiritual life. The move of the papacy from Rome to Avignon in 1309 (see Chapter 12) had caused an outcry, especially among Italians, distraught by the election of French popes and anxious to see the papacy return to Rome. Some critics, such as Marsilius of Padua, were disillusioned with the institution of the papacy itself. Marsilius, a physician and lawyer by training, argued in *The Defender of the Peace* (1324) that the source of all power lay with the people: "the law-making power or the first and real effective source of law is the people or the body of citizens or the prevailing part of the people according to its election or its will expressed in general convention by vote." Applied to the papacy, Marsilius's argument meant that Christians themselves formed the church and that the pope should be elected by a general council representing all Christians.

William of Ockham (c. 1285–1349), an English Franciscan who was one of the most eminent theologians of his age, was an even more thoroughgoing critic of the papacy. He believed that church power derived from the congregation of the faithful, both laity and clergy, not from the pope or a church council. Rejecting the confident synthesis of Christian doctrine and Aristotelian philosophy by Thomas Aquinas, Ockham believed that universal concepts had no reality in nature but instead existed only as mere representations, names in the mind—a philosophy that came to be called nominalism. Perceiving and analyzing such concepts as "man" or "papal infallibility" offered no assurance that the concepts expressed truth. Observation and human reason were limited tools with which to understand the universe

Wat Tyler's Rebellion (1381)

An anonymous chronicler wrote about Wat Tyler's Rebellion shortly after it took place in 1381. The author was hostile to the rebels yet understood their motives quite well. After converging on London from various parts of southern England, the rebels, led by men like Wat Tyler, demanded that the king end the unjust taxes collected by local officials. The fourteen-year-old Richard II (r. 1377–1399) eventually met with them and seemed to give in to their demands, but another meeting the next day led to Tyler's death and the dispersal of the demonstrators. The excerpt here chronicles the very beginning of the movement, before the march on London.

Because in the year 1380 the subsidies [taxes] were over lightly granted at the Parliament of Northampton and because it seemed to various Lords and to the commons that the said subsidies were not honestly levied, but commonly exacted from the poor and not from the rich, to the great profit and advantage of the tax-collectors and to the deception of the King and the commons, the Council of the King ordained certain commissions to make inquiry in every township how the tax had been levied. Among these commissions, one for Essex was sent to one Thomas Bampton [one of the tax collectors]. . . . He summoned before him the townships of a neighboring hundred and wished to have from them new contributions. . . .

Among these townships was Fobbing, whose people made answer that they would not pay a penny more because they already had a receipt from himself for the said subsidy. On which the said Thomas threatened them angrily. . . . And for fear of his malice the folks of Fobbing took counsel with the folks of Corringham, and the folks of these two places . . . sent messages to the men of Stanford. . . . Then the people of these three townships came together to the number of a hundred or more, and with one assent went to the said Thomas Bampton, and roundly gave him answer that they would have no traffic with him nor give him a penny. . . .

And afterwards the said commons assembled together . . . to the number of some 50,000, and they went to the manors and townships of those who would not rise with them, and cast their houses to the ground or set fire to them. At this time they caught three clerks of Thomas Bampton, and cut off their heads, and carried the heads about with them for several days stuck on poles as an example to others. For it was their purpose to slay all lawyers, and all jurors, and all the servants of the King whom they could find.

Source: Charles Oman, *The Great Revolt of 1381* (New York: Greenwood Press, 1969), 186–90.

---

and to know God. The insistence that simple explanations were superior to complex ones became known as Ockham's razor. Imprisoned by Pope John XXII for heresy in 1328, Ockham escaped that very year and found refuge with Emperor Louis of Bavaria.

Stung by his critics, Pope Gregory XI (r. 1370–78) left Avignon to return to Rome in 1377. The scandal of the Avignon papacy seemed to be over. But Rome itself presented a problem. Glad to have the papacy back, the Romans were determined never to lose it again. When the cardinals—many of whom came from Spain, Italy, and France—met to elect Gregory's successor, the *popolo*, who controlled the city, demanded that they choose a Roman: "A Roman! A Roman! A Roman or at least an Italian! Or else we'll kill them all." Expecting to gain an important place in papal government, the cardinals chose an Italian, who took the name Urban VI. But Urban had no intention of kowtowing to the cardinals: he exalted the power of the pope and began to reduce the cardinals' wealth and privileges. The cardinals from France decided that they had made a big mistake.

Many left Rome for a meeting at Anagni, where they claimed that Urban's election had been irregular and called on him to resign. When he refused, they elected a Frenchman as pope; he took the name Clement VII and soon moved his papal court to Avignon, but not before he and Urban had excommunicated each other. The **Great Schism** (1378–1417) had begun.

All of Europe was drawn into the dispute. The king of France supported Clement; the king of England favored Urban. Some European states—Burgundy, Scotland, and Castile, for example—lined up on the side of France. Others—the Holy Roman Empire, Poland, and Hungary—supported Urban. Portugal switched sides four times, depending on which alliance offered it the most advantages. Each pope declared that those who followed the other were to be deprived of the rights of church membership; in effect, everyone in Europe was in effect excommunicated by one or another pope.

Great Schism: The papal dispute of 1378–1417 when the church had two or even three popes. The Great Schism was ended by the Council of Constance.

The Conciliar Movement.　Contrary to the ideas of Marsilius, church law said that only a pope could summon a general council of the church—a sort of parliament of high churchmen. But given the state of confusion in Christendom, many intellectuals argued that the crisis justified calling a general council to represent the body of the faithful, even against the wishes of an unwilling pope—or popes. They spearheaded the conciliar movement—a movement to have the cardinals or the emperor call a council.

In 1408, long after Urban and Clement had passed away and new popes had followed, the conciliar movement succeeded when cardinals from both sides met and declared their resolve "to pursue the union of the Church . . . by way of abdication of both papal contenders." With support from both England and France, the cardinals called for a council to be held at Pisa in 1409. Both popes refused to attend, and the council deposed them, electing a new pope.

But the "deposed" popes refused to budge, even though most of the European powers abandoned them. There were now three popes. The successor of the newest one, John XXIII, turned to the emperor to arrange for another council.

The Council of Constance (1414–1418) met to resolve the papal crisis as well as to institute church reforms. The delegates deposed John XXIII and accepted the resignation of the pope at Rome. After long negotiations with rulers still supporting the Avignon pope, all allegiance to him was withdrawn and he was deposed. The council then elected Martin V, who was recognized as pope by every important ruler of Europe. Finally, the Great Schism had come to an end.

New Forms of Piety.　The Great Schism, no doubt abetted by the miseries of the plague and the distresses of war, caused enormous anxiety among ordinary Christians. Worried about the salvation of their souls, pious men and women eagerly sought new forms of religious solace. The plenary indulgence—full forgiveness of sins, which had been originally offered to crusaders who died while fighting for the cause—was now offered to those who made a pilgrimage to Rome and other designated holy places during declared Holy Years. Sins could be wiped away through confession and contrition, but some guilt remained that could be removed only through good deeds or in purgatory. As the idea of purgatory—the place where sins were fully purged—took full form, new indulgences were offered for good works to reduce the time in purgatory. Thus, for example, the duchess

of Brittany was granted a hundred days off of her purgatorial punishments when she allowed the Feast of Corpus Christi to be preached in her chapel. Lesser folk might obtain indulgences in more modest ways.

Both clergy and laity became more interested than ever in the education of young people as a way to deepen their faith and spiritual life. The Brethren of the Common Life—laypeople, mainly in the Low Countries, who devoted themselves to pious works—set up a model school at Deventer, and humanists in Italy emphasized primary school education. Priests were expected to teach the faithful the basics of the Christian religion.

Home was equally a place for devotion. Portable images of Mary, the mother of God, and of the life and passion of Christ proliferated. They were meant to be contemplated by ordinary Christians at convenient moments throughout the day. People purchased or commissioned copies of Books of Hours, which contained prayers to be said on the appropriate day at the hours of the monastic office (see Chapter 7 for the "office" of the Benedictine Rule). Books of Hours included calendars, sometimes splendidly illustrated with depictions of the seasons and labors of the year. Other illustrations reminded their users of the life and suffering of Christ.

On the streets of towns, priests marched in dignified processions, carrying the sanctified bread of the Mass—the very body of Christ—in tall and splendid monstrances that trumpeted the importance and dignity of the Eucharistic wafer. Like images of the Lord's life and crucifixion, the monstrance emphasized Christ's body. Christ's blood was perhaps even more important. It was considered "wonderful blood," the blood that brought man's redemption. Thus, the image of a bleeding, crucified Christ was repeated over and over in depictions of the day. Viewers were meant to think about Christ's pain and feel it themselves, mentally participating in his death on the cross. Flagellants, as we have seen, literally drew their own blood.

New Heresies: The Lollards and the Hussites.
Religious anxieties, intellectual dissent, and social unrest combined to create new heretical movements in England and Bohemia. In England were the Lollards—a name given them by their opponents from the Middle Dutch *lollaerd*, or "mumbler." The Lollards were inspired by the Oxford scholar John Wycliffe (c. 1330–1384), who, like Marsilius of Padua and William of Ockham in an earlier generation, came to believe that the true church was the community of believers rather than

Book of Hours

This illustration for June in a Book of Hours made for the duke of Berry was meant for the contemplation of a nobleman. In the background is a fairy-tale depiction of the duke's palace and the tower of a Gothic church, while in the foreground graceful women rake the hay and well-muscled men swing their scythes. *(Bridgeman-Giraudon/Art Resource, NY.)*

■ **For more help analyzing this image,** see the visual activity for this chapter in the Online Study Guide at **bedfordstmartins.com/hunt.**

the clerical hierarchy. Wycliffe criticized monasticism, excommunication, and the Mass. He emphasized Bible reading in the vernacular, arguing that true believers, not corrupt priests, formed the church.

Wycliffe's followers included scholars and members of the gentry (lesser noble) class as well as artisans and other humbler folk. His supporters translated the Bible into English and produced many sermons to publicize his views. They influenced the priest John Ball, who was one of the leaders of Wat Tyler's Rebellion. Ball rallied the crowds with the chant "When Adam dug and Eve spun / Who then was the gentleman?" From questioning the church hierarchy, some Lollards came to challenge social inequality of every sort.

After Wycliffe's death, the Lollards were persecuted in England. But groups of them

remained underground, to reemerge with the coming of the Reformation there (see Chapter 14).

The Bohemian Hussites— named after one of their leaders, Jan Hus (1372?–1415)—had greater success. Their central demand—that the faithful receive not just the bread (the body) but also the wine (the blood) at Mass—brought together several passionately held desires and beliefs. The blood of Christ was particularly important to the devout, and the Hussite call to allow the laity to drink the wine from the chalice reflected this focus on the blood's redemptive power. Furthermore, the call for communion with *both* bread and wine signified a desire for equality. Bohemia was an exceptionally divided country, with an urban German-speaking elite, including merchants, artisans, bishops, and scholars, and a Czech-speaking nobility and peasantry that was beginning to seek better opportunities. (Hus himself was a Czech of peasant stock who became a professor at the University of Prague.) When priests celebrated Mass, they had the privilege of drinking the wine. The Hussites, who were largely Czech laity, wanted the same privilege and, with it, recognition of their dignity and worth.

Condemned by the church as a heretic, Hus was protected by the Bohemian nobility until he was lured to the Council of Constance by the Holy Roman Emperor Sigismund "to justify himself before all men." Though promised safe conduct, Hus was arrested when he arrived at the council. After refusing to recant his views, he was declared a heretic and burned at the stake.

Hus's death caused a national uproar, and his movement became a full-scale national revolt of Czechs against Germans. Sigismund called crusades against the Hussites, but all of his expeditions were soundly defeated. Radical groups of Hus-

The Hussite Revolution, 1415–1436

Areas under Hussite control

0   200   400 miles
0   200   400 kilometers

TEUTONIC KNIGHTS

HOLY
ROMAN
EMPIRE
Nuremberg
Prague
Tabor   Kutná Hora
Bohemia
Constance

POLAND

HUNGARY

Monstrance

Elaborate church vessels like this gilded copper monstrance from Salzburg became popular in the fifteenth century. The monstrance, a term that comes from a Latin word meaning "to show," displayed the consecrated Eucharist (bread) in fitting splendor to churchgoers. *(Erich Lessing/Art Resource, NY.)*

sites organized several new communities in southern Bohemia at Mount Tabor, named after the New Testament spot where the Transfiguration of Christ was thought to have taken place (Matt. 7:1–8). Here the radicals attempted to live according to the example of the first apostles. They recognized no lord, gave women some political rights, and created a simple liturgy that was carried out in the Czech language. Negotiations with Sigismund and his successor led by 1450 to the Hussites' incorporation into the Bohemian political system, although they were largely marginalized. They had, however, won the right to receive communion in "both kinds" (wine and bread), and they had made Bohemia intensely aware of its Czech, rather than German, identity.

REVIEW: What crises did Europeans confront in the fourteenth and fifteenth centuries, and how did they handle them?

The Renaissance: New Forms of Thought and Expression

Some Europeans confronted the crises they faced with the culture of the Renaissance, a word that means "rebirth." The period associated with the Renaissance, about 1350 to 1600, revived elements of the classical past — the Greek philosophers before Aristotle, Hellenistic artists, and Roman rhetoricians. (See "Terms of History", page 402.) Humanists modeled their writing on the Latin of Cicero, architects looked back to ancient notions of public space, artists adopted classical forms, and musicians used classical texts. Much of the work of Renaissance writers and artists built on medieval precedents but gave them a new feel.

Renaissance Humanism

Three of the delegates at the Council of Constance — Cincius Romanus, Poggius Bracciolinus, and Bartholomaeus Politianus — decided to take time off for a rescue mission. Cincius described the escapade to one of his Latin teachers back in Italy:

> In Germany there are many monasteries with libraries full of Latin books. This aroused the hope in me that some of the works of Cicero, Varro, Livy, and other great men of learning, which seem to have completely vanished might come to light, if a careful search were instituted. A few days ago, [we] went by agreement to the town of St. Gall. As soon as we went into the library [of the monastery there], we found *Jason's Argonauticon,* written by C. Valerius Flaccus in verse that is both splendid and dignified and not far removed from poetic majesty. Then we found some discussion in prose of a number of Cicero's orations.

Cicero, Varro, Livy, and Valerius Flaccus were pagan Latin writers. Even though Cincius and his friends were working for Pope John XXIII, they loved the writings of the ancients, whose Latin was, in their view, "splendid and dignified," unlike the Latin that was used in their own time, which they found debased and faulty. They saw themselves as the resuscitators of ancient language, literature, and culture. Cincius continued:

> When we carefully inspected the nearby tower of the church of St. Gall in which countless books were kept like captives and the library neglected and infested with dust, worms, soot, and all the things associated with the destruction of books, we all burst into tears. . . . Truly if this library could speak for itself, it would cry loudly: ". . . Snatch me from this prison. . . ." There were in that monastery an abbot and monks totally devoid of any knowledge of literature. What barbarous hostility to the Latin tongue! What damned dregs of humanity!

Renaissance

The word *renaissance* has been employed numerous times in this book. Recall the Macedonian renaissance, the Islamic renaissance, and the renaissance of the twelfth century. All those renaissances involved a rebirth of classical culture—or aspects of classical culture—in the medieval period.

Renaissance was first used in the sixteenth century to refer to a historical moment. At that time it meant the rebirth of classical poetry, prose, and art of that period alone. Only later did historians borrow the word to refer to earlier rebirths. One of the first persons to herald the fifteenth-century Renaissance was the Italian painter and architect Giorgio Vasari (1511–1574) in his *Lives of the Most Excellent Italian Architects, Painters, and Sculptors* (1550). Vasari argued that Greco-Roman art declined after the dissolution of the Roman Empire, to be followed by a long period of barbarity. Only in the past generations had Italian artists begun to restore the perfection of the arts, according to Vasari, a development he called *rinascita*, the Italian for "rebirth." It was the French equivalent—*renaissance*—that stuck.

Referring initially to a rebirth in the arts and literature, the word *Renaissance* came to mean a new consciousness of modernity and individuality. Prizing the ancient world, the humanists were convinced that they lived in a new age that recalled that lost glory. They called the period between their age and the ancient one "the Middle Age." They reveled in their human potential and their individuality.

The Renaissance was an important movement in Italy, France, Spain, the Low Countries, and central Europe. The word itself acquired widespread recognition with the publication of Jakob Burckhardt's *The Civilization of the Renaissance in Italy* in 1860. A historian at the University of Basel, Burckhardt considered the Renaissance a watershed in Western civilization. For him, the Renaissance ushered in a spirit of modernity, freeing the individual from the domination of society and creative impulses from the repression of the church; the Renaissance represented the beginning of secular society and the preeminence of individual creative geniuses.

Although very influential, Burckhardt's ideas have also been strongly challenged by many recent scholars. Some point out the various continuities between the Middle Ages and the Renaissance, others argue that the Renaissance was not a secular but a profoundly religious age, and still others see the Renaissance as only the beginning of a long period of transition from the Middle Ages to modernity. The consensus among scholars today is that the Renaissance represents a distinct cultural period lasting from the fourteenth to the sixteenth century, centered on the revival of classical learning. Historians disagree about its significance, but they generally understand it to represent some of the complex changes that characterized the passing from medieval society to modernity.

The monks were barbarians, and Cincius and his companions were heroic raiders swooping in to liberate the captive books. **Humanism** was a literary and linguistic movement—an attempt to revive classical Latin (and later Greek) as well as the values and sensibilities that came with the language. It began among men and women living in the Italian city-states, where many saw parallels between their urban, independent lives and the experiences of the city-states of the ancient world. Humanism was a way to confront the crises—and praise the advances—of the fourteenth through sixteenth centuries. Humanists wrote poetry, history, moral philosophy, and grammar books, all patterned on classical models, especially the writings of Cicero.

That Cincius was employed by the pope yet considered the monks of St. Gall barbarians was no oddity. Most humanists combined sincere Christian piety with a new appreciation of the pagan past. Besides, they needed to work in order to live, and they took employment where they found it. Some humanists worked for the church, others were civil servants, and still others were notaries. A few were rich men who had a taste for literary subjects.

The first humanist, most historians agree, was **Francis Petrarch** (1304–1374). He was born in Arezzo, a town about fifty miles southeast of Florence. As a boy, he moved around a lot (his father was exiled from Florence), ending up in the region of Avignon, where he received his earliest schooling and fell in love with classical literature. After a brief flirtation with legal studies at the behest of his father, Petrarch gave up law and devoted himself to writing poetry, both in Italian and in Latin. When writing in Italian, he drew on the traditions of the troubadours, dedicating poems of longing to an unattainable and idealized woman named Laura; who she really was, we do not know. When writing in Latin, he was much influenced by classical poetry.

On the one hand, a boyhood in Avignon made Petrarch sensitive to the failings of the church: he was the writer who coined the phrase "Babylonian captivity" to liken the Avignon papacy to the biblical Jewish captivity in Babylonia. On the other hand, he took minor religious orders there, which

---

humanism: A literary and linguistic movement cultivated in particular in the fourteenth through the sixteenth centuries and founded on reviving classical Latin and Greek texts, styles, and values.

Francis Petrarch: An Italian poet (1304–1374) who revived the styles of classical authors; he is considered the first Renaissance humanist.

gave him a modest living. Struggling between what he considered a life of dissipation (he fathered two children out of wedlock) and a religious vocation, he resolved the conflict at last in his book *On the Solitary Life*, in which he claimed that the solitude needed for reading the classics was akin to the solitude practiced by those who devoted themselves to God. For Petrarch, humanism was a vocation, a calling.

Less famous, but for that reason perhaps more representative of humanists in general, was Lauro Quirini (1420–1475?), the man who (as we saw at the start of this chapter) wrote disparagingly about the Turks as barbarians. Educated at the University of Padua, Quirini eventually got a law degree there. He wrote numerous letters and essays, corresponding with other humanists on topics such as the nature of the state and the character of true nobility. He spent the last half of his life in Crete, where he traded various commodities—alum, cloth, wine, Greek books. Believing that the Ottomans had destroyed the libraries of Constantinople, he wrote to Pope Nicholas V, "The language and literature of the Greeks, invented, augmented, and perfected over so long a period with such labor and industry, will certainly perish." But the fact that he himself participated in the lively trade of Greek books proves his prediction wrong.

If Quirini represents the ordinary humanist, Giovanni Pico della Mirandola (1463–1494) was perhaps the most flamboyant. Born near Ferrara of a noble family, Pico received a humanist education at home before going on to Bologna to study law and to Padua to study philosophy. Soon he was picking up Hebrew, Aramaic, and Arabic. A convinced eclectic, he thought that Jewish mystical writings supported Christian scriptures, and in 1486 he proposed that he publicly defend at Rome nine hundred theses drawn from diverse sources. The church found some of the theses heretical, however, and banned the whole affair. But Pico's *Oration on the Dignity of Man*, which he intended to deliver before his defense, summed up the humanist view of humanity: the creative individual, armed only with his (or her) "desires and judgment," could choose to become a boor or an angel. Humanity's potential was unlimited. (See Document, "Giovanni Pico della Mirandola, *Oration on the Dignity of Man*," page 404.)

Christine de Pisan (c.1365–c.1430) exemplifies a humanist who chose to fashion herself into a writer and courtier. Born in Venice and educated in France, Christine de Pisan was married and then widowed young. Forced to support herself, her mother, and her three young children, she began

to write poems inspired by classical models, depending on patrons to admire her work and pay her to write more. Many members of the upper nobility supported her, including Duke Philip the Bold of Burgundy, Queen Isabelle of Bavaria, and the English earl of Salisbury. But this cast of characters did not mean she sided with the English during the Hundred Years' War. On the contrary, she lamented the violence on all sides, and Joan of Arc's early victories inspired her to write a hymn to the Maid:

> We've never heard
> About a marvel quite so great,
> For all the heroes who have lived
> In history can't measure up
> In bravery against the Maid.

The Arts

The lure of the classical past was as strong in the arts as in literature—and for many of the same reasons. Architects and artists admired ancient Athens and Rome, but they also modified these classical models, melding them with medieval artistic traditions. In music, Renaissance composers incorporated classical texts and allusions into songs that were based on the motet and other forms of polyphony. Working for patrons—whether churchmen, secular rulers, or republican governments—Renaissance artists and musicians used both past and present to express the patriotism, religious piety, and prestige of their benefactors.

The Ducal Palace at Urbino
Duke Federico, a friend of the Renaissance architect Alberti, commissioned this courtyard, a spacious and airy counterpoint to the monumental and grand exterior of the building. *(Scala/Art Resource, NY.)*

Giovanni Pico della Mirandola, *Oration on the Dignity of Man*

A prelude to the nine hundred theses that Pico della Mirandola (1463–1494) hoped to argue at Rome, the Oration on the Dignity of Man *retold the story of creation. God made the universe and its creatures, but when he came to fashion humans, he had nothing more to give. So he endowed men (and women) with the ability to take on any of the characteristics they chose of God's other creatures. In this way, people in effect created themselves. Similar ideas about human self-fashioning were expressed in other humanist writings.*

I have come to understand why man is the most fortunate of creatures and consequently worthy of all admiration and what precisely is that rank which is his lot in the universal chain of Being — a rank to be envied not only by brutes but even by the stars and by minds beyond this world. It is a matter past faith and a wondrous one. Why should it not be? For it is on this very account that man is rightly called and judged a great miracle and a wonderful creature indeed.

But hear, Fathers [the audience that was to listen to Pico's arguments], exactly what this rank is. . . . God the Father, the supreme Architect, had already built this cosmic home we behold, the most sacred temple of His godhead, by the laws of His mysterious wisdom. . . . But, when the work was finished, the Craftsman kept wishing that there were someone to ponder the plan of so great a work, to love its beauty, and to wonder at its vastness. Therefore, when everything was done (as Moses and Timaeus [a character in a Platonic dialogue on the origins of the universe] bear witness), He finally took thought concerning the creation of man. . . . [But] all things had been assigned to the highest, the middle, and the lowest orders [of the universe]. . . .

At last the best of artisans ordained that that creature to whom He had been able to give nothing proper to himself should have joint possession of whatever had been peculiar to each of the different kinds of being. He therefore took man as a creature of indeterminate nature and, assigning him a place in the middle of the world, addressed him thus: "Neither a fixed home nor a form that is yours alone nor any function peculiar to yourself have we given you, Adam, to the end that according to your longing and according to your judgment, you may have and possess what home, what form, and what functions you yourself shall desire. The nature of all other beings is limited and constrained within the bounds of laws prescribed by us. You, constrained by no limits, in accordance with your own free will, in whose hand we have placed you, shall ordain for yourself the limits of your nature."

Source: *Oration on the Dignity of Man*, trans. Elizabeth Livermore Forbes in *The Renaissance Philosophy of Man*, ed. Ernst Cassirer, Paul Oskar Kristeller, and John Herman Randall Jr. (Chicago: University of Chicago Press, 1948), 223–25.

From Agora to Piazza. Medieval cities had grown without planning. Streets turned back on themselves. Churches sat cheek-by-jowl with private houses. In the Renaissance, however, the whole city was reimagined as a place of order and harmony. The Florentine architect Leon Battista Alberti (1404–1472) proposed that each building in a city be proportioned to fit harmoniously with all the others and that city spaces allow for all necessary public activities — there should be market squares, play areas, grounds for military exercises. In Renaissance cities, the agora and forum (the open, public spaces of the classical world) appeared once again, but in a new guise, as the piazza — a plaza or open square. Architects carved out spaces around their new buildings, and they built graceful covered walkways (porticos) of columns and arches through which passersby could walk. The artist Pietro Perugino (1445–1523) depicted Christ giving the keys of the kingdom of heaven to the apostle Peter in an idealized city piazza, at the center of which was a perfectly proportioned church.

The same principles applied to the architecture of the Renaissance court. At Urbino, Duke Federico, a great patron of humanists and artists, commissioned a new palace. The architect, probably Luciano Laurana, designed its courtyard as a public space, a sort of piazza within a palace (see illustration, page 403). Later the courtier Baldassare Castiglione reminisced about this building: "[Duke Federico] built on the rugged site of Urbino a palace thought by many the most beautiful to be found anywhere in all Italy, and he furnished it so well with every suitable thing that it seemed not a palace but a city in the form of a palace." A city had both public and private spaces; similarly, public rooms at the ducal palace gave way to a modest space for the duke's private quarters, a bedroom, a bathroom, a chapel, and, most important of all, his study, filled with books.

Pietro Perugino, *Christ Giving the Keys to St. Peter*
In this fresco on one of the side walls of the Sistine Chapel in the papal palace at Rome (now the Vatican), the artist Perugino depicted the transfer of power in Christ's church. Inspired by the architecture of the ancient world, Perugino set the action in a large piazza flanked by Roman triumphal arches.
(© Vatican Museums and Galleries, Vatican City, Italy/The Bridgeman Art Library.)

The Gothic cathedral of the Middle Ages was a cluster of graceful spikes and soaring arches. Renaissance architects appreciated its vigor and energy, but they tamed it with regular geometrical forms inspired by classical buildings. Classical forms were applied to previously built structures as well as new ones. Florence's Santa Maria Novella, for example, had been a typical Gothic church when it was first built. But when Alberti, the man who believed in public spaces and harmonious buildings, was commissioned to replace its facade, he drew on Roman temple forms.

Sculpture and Painting. In 1400, the Florentines sponsored a competition for new bronze doors for their baptistery. The entry of Lorenzo Ghiberti (1378?–1455) depicted the sacrifice of Isaac, the Old Testament story in which God tested Abraham's faith by ordering him to sacrifice his son (see page 406). Cast in one piece, a major technological feat at the time, it shows a young, nude Isaac modeled on a classical sculpture such as the masculine ideal on page 87. At the same time, Ghiberti drew on medieval models for his depiction of Abraham and for his quatrefoil frame. In this way, he gracefully melded old and new elements—and won the contest.

In addition to using the forms of classical art, Renaissance artists also mined the ancient world for new subjects. Venus, the Roman goddess of love and beauty, had numerous stories attached to her name. At first glance, *The Birth of Venus* by Sandro Botticelli (c. 1445–1510) seems simply an illustra-

tion of the tale of Venus's rise from the sea (see page 407). In fact, however, Botticelli's work is much more complicated, drawing on the ideas of Marsilio Ficino (1433–1499) and the poetry of Angelo Poliziano (1454–1494). According to Ficino, Venus was "humanitas"—the essence of the

The Renaissance Facade at Santa Maria Novella
When Italians wished to transform their churches into the Renaissance style, they did not tear them down; they gave them a new facade. At Santa Maria Novella in Florence, the architect Leon Battista Alberti designed a facade that was inspired by classical models—hence the round-arched entranceway and columns. At the same time, he paid tribute to the original Gothic church by including a round window.
(Scala/Art Resource, NY.)

Lorenzo Ghiberti, *Sacrifice of Isaac*
This bronze relief, which decorates one of the doors of the San Giovanni Baptistry in Florence, captures the dramatic moment when the angel intervenes as Abraham prepares to kill Isaac, a story told in the Hebrew Scriptures. *(Scala/Art Resource, NY.)*

humanities. For Poliziano, she was

> fair Venus, mother of the cupids.
> Zephyr bathes the meadow with dew
> spreading a thousand lovely fragrances:
> wherever he flies he clothes the countryside
> in roses, lilies, violets, and other flowers.

In Botticelli's painting, Zephyr, one of the winds, blows while Venus herself is clothed in a fine robe embroidered with leaves and flowers.

The Sacrifice of Isaac and *The Birth of Venus* show some of the ways in which Renaissance artists used ancient models. Other artists perfected perspective—the illusion of three-dimensional space—to a degree that even classical antiquity had not anticipated. The development of the laws of perspective accompanied the introduction of long-range weaponry, such as cannons. In fact, some of perspective's practitioners—Leonardo da Vinci (1452–1519), for example—were military engineers as well as artists. In Leonardo's painting *The Annunciation*, sight lines meeting at a point on the horizon open wide precisely where the angel kneels and Mary responds in surprise.

Ghiberti, Botticelli, and Leonardo were all Italian artists. While they were creating their works, a northern Renaissance was taking place as well. At the court of France during the Hundred Years' War, kings commissioned portraits of themselves—sometimes unflattering ones—just as Roman leaders had once commissioned their own busts. Soon it was the fashion for everyone who could afford it to have his portrait made, as naturalistically as possible. Compare the image of Louis IX and his mother on page 375 with the painting of the Virgin Mary and Chancellor Nicolas Rolin completed by the Dutch artist Jan van Eyck around 1433 (page 408). The artist who depicted Louis

and his mother wanted to show a young king—any young king. The image was meant to be symbolic. By contrast, van Eyck and his patron wanted to show a particular person—Nicolas Rolin. The very wrinkles of Rolin's neck proclaim his individuality. Moreover, Rolin, though in a pious pose, is the key figure in the picture; the Virgin and baby Jesus sit a bit to the back and in shadow. Meanwhile, the grand view of a city spreads behind them, underscoring Rolin's prominence in the community: van Eyck was a master of perspective, and he used it to emphasize Rolin's gravity and importance.

In fact Rolin *was* an important man: he worked for the duke of Burgundy and was also the founder of a hospital at Beaune and a religious order of nurses to serve it. Renaissance portraiture emphasized the individuality and dignity of the subject.

New Harmonies in Music.   Using music to add glamour and glory to their courts and reputations, Renaissance rulers spent as much as 6 percent of their annual revenue to support musicians and composers. The Avignon papacy, in its own way one such court, was a major sponsor of sacred music. Whether secular or religious, music was appreciated for its ability to express the innermost feelings of the individual.

Every proper court had its own musicians. Some served as chaplains, writing music for the ruler's private chapel—the place where his court and household heard Mass. When Josquin Desprez (1440–1521) served as the duke of Ferrara's chaplain, he wrote a Mass that used the musical equivalents of the letters of the duke's name (the Italian version of *do re mi*) as its theme. Isabella d'Este (1474–1539), the daughter of the duke, employed her own musicians—singers, woodwind and string players, percussionists, and keyboard players—while her husband, the duke of Mantua, had his own band. Tromboncino was Isabella's favorite musician. When her brother sent her poems to recopy, she had Tromboncino set them to music. This was one of the ways in which humanists and musicians worked together: the poems that interested Tromboncino were of the newest sort, patterned on classical forms. He and Isabella particularly favored Petrarch's poems.

The church, too, was a major sponsor of music. Every feast required music, and the papal schism inadvertently encouraged more musical production than usual, as rival popes tried to best

Sandro Botticelli, *The Birth of Venus*
Venus had been depicted in art before Botticelli's painting, but he was the first artist since
antiquity to portray her in the nude. (*© Galleria degli Uffizi, Florence, Italy/Giraudon/The Bridgeman Art Library.*)

Leonardo da Vinci, *The Annunciation*
Working with a traditional Christian theme (the moment when the angel Gabriel announced to the Virgin
Mary that she would give birth to Christ), Leonardo produced a work of great originality, drawing the
viewer's eye from a vanishing point in the distance to the subject of the painting. The ability to subordinate
the background to the foreground was a great contribution of Renaissance perspective. (*Scala/Art Resource, NY.*)

Jan van Eyck, *The Virgin of Chancellor Rolin*
Van Eyck portrays the Virgin and Chancellor Rolin as if they were contemporaries sharing a nice chat. Only the angel, who is placing a crown on the Virgin's head, suggests that something out of the ordinary is happening. *(Erich Lessing/Art Resource, NY.)*

Music for a Banquet
This manuscript illustration depicts a royal couple at a large table. As servants begin to place delicacies before them — under the supervision of the maître d'hôtel — their dinner is heralded by the sound of trumpets. *(Bibliothèque publique et universitaire, Genève.)*

one another in the realm of pageantry and sound. Churches needed choirs of singers, and many composers got their start as choirboys. But the job could last well into adulthood: in the fourteenth century, the men who sang in the choir at Reims received a yearly stipend and an extra fee every time they sang the Mass and the liturgical offices of the day.

When the composer Johannes Ockeghem — chaplain for three French kings — died in 1497, his fellow musicians vied in expressing their grief in song. Josquin Desprez was among them, and his composition illustrates how the addition of classical elements to very traditional musical forms enhanced music's emotive power. Josquin's work combines personal grief with religious liturgy and the feelings expressed in classical elegies. The piece uses five voices. Inspired by classical mythology, four of the voices sing in the vernacular French about the "nymphs of the wood" coming together to mourn. But the fifth voice intones the words of the liturgy: "Requiescat in pace" — May he rest in peace. At the very moment in the song that the four vernacular voices lament Ockeghem's burial in the dark ground, the liturgical voice sings of the heavenly light. The contrast makes the song more moving. By drawing on the classical past, Renaissance musicians found new ways in which to express emotion.

> **REVIEW:** How and why did Renaissance humanists, artists, and musicians revive classical traditions?

Consolidating Power

The shape of Europe changed during the period 1340–1492. Eastern Europe consolidated when the capital of the Holy Roman Empire moved to Prague and the duke of Lithuania married the queen of Poland, uniting those two states. In western Europe, a few places organized and maintained themselves as republics; the Swiss, for example, consolidated their informal alliances in the Swiss Confederation. Italy, which at the beginning of the period was dotted with numerous small city-states, was by the end dominated by five major powers: Milan, the papacy, Naples, and the republics of Venice and Florence. Most western European states, however, became centralized monarchies. The union of Aragon and Castile via the marriage of their respective rulers created Spain. In England and France, consolidation meant the strengthening of the central government. Whether monarchies, principalities, or republics, states throughout

Europe used their new powers to finance humanists, artists, and musicians—and to persecute heretics, Muslims, and Jews with new vigor.

New Political Formations in Eastern Europe

In the eastern half of the Holy Roman Empire, Bohemia had gained new status as the seat of the Luxembourg imperial dynasty (Emperor Sigismund was its last representative). This development bred a religious and political crisis when the Hussites clashed with Sigismund (see page 400). The chief beneficiary of the violence was the nobility, both Catholic and Hussite, but they quarreled among themselves, especially about who should be king. No Joan of Arc appeared to declare the national will, and most of Europe considered Bohemia a heretic state. Countering this isolation from the rest of Europe, the Bohemian king Vladislav Jagiello (r. 1471–1516) borrowed some Renaissance architectural motifs for his palace.

Farther north, it was the cities rather than the landed nobility that held power. Allied cities, known as *Hanse*, were common. The most successful alliance was the **Hanseatic League**, a loose federation of mainly north German cities formed to protect their mutual interests in defense and trade—and art. The Dance of Death, for example, painted at the Hanse town of Reval (see page 391), was made by the artist Bernt Notke, who hailed from Lübeck, another Hanse town. The Hanseatic League linked the Baltic coast with Russia, Norway, the British Isles, France, and even (via imperial cities like Augsburg and Nuremberg) the cities of Italy. When threatened by rival powers in Denmark and Norway in 1367–1370, the league waged war and won the peace. But in the fifteenth century it confronted new rivals and began a long and slow decline.

To the east of the Hanseatic cities, two new monarchies took shape in northeastern Europe: Poland and Lithuania. Poland had begun to form in the tenth century. Powerful nobles soon dominated it, and Mongol invasions devastated the land. But recovery was under way by 1300. Unlike almost every other part of Europe, Poland expanded demo-

Vladislav Hall

The interior of this hall, built by Bohemian king Vladislav to house grand tournaments, is largely based on Gothic forms. Note, for example, the elaborate ribs of the vault. But the rectangular windows are based on Renaissance architecture, the first such borrowing north of the Alps. *(© Franz-Marc Frei/Corbis.)*

graphically and economically during the fourteenth century. Jews migrated there to escape persecutions in western Europe, and both Jewish and German settlers helped build thriving towns like Cracow. Monarchical consolidation began thereafter.

On Poland's eastern flank was Lithuania, the only major holdout from Christianity in eastern Europe. But as it expanded into southern Russia, its grand dukes flirted with both the Roman Catholic and Orthodox varieties. In 1386, Grand Duke Jogailo (c. 1351–1434), taking advantage of a hiatus in the Polish ruling dynasty, united both states when he married Queen Jadwiga of Poland, received a Catholic baptism, and was elected by the Polish nobility as King Wladyslaw II Jagiello. As

Hanseatic League: A league of northern European cities formed in the fourteenth century to protect their mutual interests in trade and defense.

- • Important Hanseatic towns
- ▲ Hanseatic trading partners

0   250   500 miles
0   250   500 kilometers

Bergen

NORWAY   SWEDEN

Reval

SCOTLAND

North Sea

Riga

DENMARK

Baltic Sea

TEUTONIC KNIGHTS

ENGLAND   Hamburg

Lübeck

LITH.

London   Bruges

POLAND

HOLY ROMAN EMPIRE

Nuremburg

FRANCE

Augsburg

HUNGARY

PAPAL STATES

Hanseatic League

part of the negotiations prior to these events, he promised to convert Lithuania, and after his coronation he sent churchmen there to begin the long, slow process. The union of Poland and Lithuania lasted, with some interruptions, until 1772. (See Mapping the West, page 415.)

Powerful States in Western Europe

Four powerful states dominated western Europe during the fifteenth century. The kingdom of Spain and the duchy of Burgundy were created by marriage; the newly powerful kingdoms of France and England were forged in the crucible of war. By the end of the century, however, Burgundy had disappeared, leaving three exceptionally powerful monarchies.

Spain. Decades of violence on the Iberian peninsula ended when Isabella of Castile and Ferdinand of Aragon married in 1469 and restored law and order in the decades that followed. Castile was the powerhouse, with Aragon its lesser neighbor and Navarre a pawn between the two. When the king and queen joined forces, they ruled together over their separate dominions, allowing each to retain its traditional laws and privileges. The union of Castile and Aragon was the first step toward a united Spain and a centralized monarchy there.

Relying on a lucrative taxation system, pliant meetings of the *cortes* (the representative institution that voted taxes), and an ideology that glorified the monarchy, Ferdinand and Isabella consolidated their power. They had an extensive bureaucracy for financial matters and a well-staffed writing office. They sent their own officials to rule over towns that had previously been self-governing, and they established regional courts of law.

Burgundy. The duchy of Burgundy—created when the duke of Burgundy and heiress of Flanders married in 1369—was dis-

Spain before Unification, Late Fifteenth Century

[Map: Spain before Unification, Late Fifteenth Century — showing PORTUGAL, NAVARRE 1512, FRANCE, CASTILE 1469, ARAGON 1469, GRANADA 1492, BALEARIC IS., with scale 0 100 200 miles / 0 100 200 kilometers]

united linguistically and geographically. Its success and expansion in the fifteenth century was the result of military might and careful statecraft.

Part of the French royal house, the Burgundian dynasty expanded its power rapidly by acquiring land, primarily in the Netherlands. Between 1384 and 1476, the Burgundian state filled the territorial gap between France and Germany, extending from the Swiss border in the south to Friesland (Germany) in the north. Through purchases, inheritance, and conquests, the dukes ruled over French-, Dutch-, and German-speaking subjects, creating a state that resembled a patchwork of provinces and regions, each jealously guarding its laws and traditions. The Low Countries, with their flourishing cities, constituted the state's economic heartland, while the region of Burgundy itself, which gave the state its name, offered rich farmlands and vineyards. Unlike England, whose island geography made it a natural political unit; or France, whose borders were forged in the national experience of repelling English invaders; or Spain, whose national identity came from centuries of warfare against Islam, Burgundy was an artificial creation whose coherence depended entirely on the skillful exercise of statecraft.

At the heart of Burgundian politics was the personal cult of its dukes. Philip the Good (r. 1418–1467) and his son Charles the Bold (r. 1467–1477) were very different kinds of rulers, but both were devoted to enhancing the prestige of their dynasty and the security of their dominion. Philip was a lavish patron of the arts who commissioned numerous illuminated manuscripts, chronicles, tapestries, paintings, and music in his efforts to glorify Burgundy. Charles, by contrast, spent more time on war than at court. Renowned for his courage (hence his nickname), he died in 1477 when his army was routed by the Swiss at Nancy, a loss that marked the end of Burgundian power.

The Burgundians' success depended in large part on their personal relationship with their subjects. Not only did the dukes travel constantly from one part of their dominion to another, they also staged elaborate ceremonies to enhance their power and promote their legitimacy. Their en-

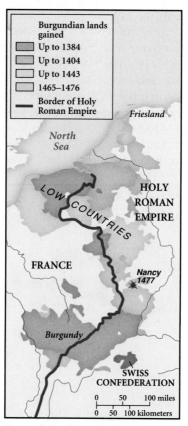

Expansion of Burgundy, 1384–1476

[Map legend: Burgundian lands gained — Up to 1384, Up to 1404, Up to 1443, 1465–1476, Border of Holy Roman Empire. Labels: North Sea, Friesland, LOW COUNTRIES, HOLY ROMAN EMPIRE, FRANCE, Nancy 1477, Burgundy, SWISS CONFEDERATION. Scale 0 50 100 miles / 0 50 100 kilometers]

tries into cities and their presence at weddings, births, and funerals became the centerpieces of a "theater state" in which the dynasty provided the only link among diverse territories. New rituals became propaganda tools. Philip's revival of chivalry at court transformed the semi-independent nobility into courtiers closely tied to the prince. But when Charles the Bold died without heirs in 1477, France and the Holy Roman Empire divided up his duchy for themselves: the Low Countries went to the Holy Roman Empire, while the rest went to France.

France.   France was powerful enough to take a large bite out of Burgundy because of its quick recovery from the Hundred Years' War. Under Louis XI (r. 1461–1483), the French monarchy both expanded its territory and consolidated its power. Soon after Burgundy fell to him, Louis inherited most of southern France after the Anjou dynasty died out. When the French king inherited claims to the duchy of Milan and the kingdom of Naples, he was ready to exploit other opportunities in Italy. By the end of the century, France had doubled its territory, assuming boundaries close to its modern ones, and was looking to expand even further.

To strengthen royal power at home, Louis promoted industry and commerce, imposed permanent salt and land taxes, maintained western Europe's first standing army (created by his predecessor), and dispensed with the meetings of the Estates General, which included the clergy, the nobility, and representatives from the major towns of France. The French kings had already increased their power with important concessions from the papacy. The 1438 Pragmatic Sanction of Bourges asserted the superiority of a general church council over the pope. Harking back to a long tradition of the high Middle Ages, the Sanction of Bourges established what would come to be known as Gallicanism (after Gaul, the ancient Roman name for France), in which the French king would effectively control ecclesiastical revenues and the appointment of French bishops.

England.   In England the Hundred Years' War led to intermittent civil wars that came to be called the Wars of the Roses. They ended with the victory of Henry Tudor, who took the title of Henry VII (r. 1485–1509). Though long, the Wars of the Roses caused relatively little damage; the battles were generally short and, in the words of one chronicler, "neither the country, nor the people nor the houses, were wasted, destroyed or demolished, but the calamities and misfortunes of the war fell only upon the soldiers, and especially on the nobility."

As a result, the English economy continued to grow during the fifteenth century. The cloth industry expanded considerably, and the English used much of the raw wool that they had been exporting to the Low Countries to manufacture goods at home. London merchants, taking a vigorous role in trade, also assumed greater political prominence, not only in governing London but also as bankers to kings and members of Parliament. In the countryside the landed classes — the nobility, the gentry (the lesser nobility), and the yeomanry (free farmers) — benefited from rising farm and land-rent income as the population increased slowly but steadily. The Tudor monarchs took advantage of the general prosperity to bolster both their treasury and their power.

Republics

Within the fifteenth-century world of largely monarchical power were three important exceptions: Switzerland, Venice, and Florence. Republics, they prided themselves on traditions of self-rule. At the same time, however, they were in every case dominated by elites — or even by one family.

The Swiss Confederation.   The cities of the Alpine region of the Holy Roman Empire, like those of the Hanseatic League in the Baltic, had long had alliances with one another. In the fourteenth century, their union became more binding, and they joined with equally well-organized communities in rural and forested areas in the region. Their original purpose was to keep the peace, but soon they also pledged to aid one another against the Holy Roman Emperor. By the end of the fourteenth century, they had become an entity: the Swiss Confederation. While not united by a comprehensive constitution, they were nevertheless an effective political force.

Wealthy merchants and tradesmen dominated the cities of the Swiss Confederation, and in the fifteenth century they managed to supplant the landed nobility. At the same time, the power of the rural communes gave some ordinary folk political importance. No king, duke, or count ever became head of the confederation. In its fiercely independent stance against the empire, it became a symbol of republican freedom. On the other hand, poor Swiss foot soldiers made their

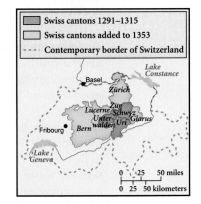

Growth of the Swiss Confederation, 1291–1386

living by hiring themselves out as mercenaries, fueling the wars of kings in the rest of Europe.

The Republic of Venice.

By the fifteenth century, Venice, a city built on a lagoon, ruled an extensive empire. Its merchant ships plied the waters stretching from the Black Sea to the Mediterranean and out to the Atlantic Ocean. It had an excellent navy. Now, for the first time in its career, it turned to conquer land in northern Italy. In the early fifteenth century, Venice took over Brescia, Verona, Padua, Belluno, and many other cities, eventually coming up against the equally powerful city-state of Milan to its west. Between 1450 and 1454, two coalitions, one led by Milan, the other by Venice, fought for territorial control of the eastern half of northern Italy. Financial exhaustion and fear of an invasion by France or the Ottoman Turks led to the Peace of Lodi in 1454. Italy was no longer a collection of small cities and their contados (surrounding countryside) but of large territorial city-states.

Italy at the Peace of Lodi, 1454

It is no accident that the Peace of Lodi was signed one year after the Ottoman conquest of Constantinople: Venice wanted to direct its might against the Turks. But the Venetians also knew that peace was good for business; they traded with the Ottomans, and the two powers influenced each other's art and culture: Gentile Bellini's portrait of Mehmed is a good example of the importance of the Renaissance at the Ottoman court.

Ruled by the Great Council, which was dominated by the most important families, Venice was never ruled by a *signore* ("lord"). Far from being a hereditary monarch, the doge—the leading magistrate at Venice—was elected by the Great Council. The great question is why the lower classes at Venice did not rebel and demand their own political power as happened in so many other Italian cities. The answer may be that its foundation on water demanded so much central planning, citywide efforts to maintain buildings and services, and the dedication of public funds to provide the population with necessities that it fostered a greater sense of common community than could be found elsewhere.

While Venice was not itself a center of humanism, its conquest of Padua in 1405 transformed its culture. After studying rhetoric at the University of Padua, young Venetian nobles returned home convinced of the values of a humanistic education for administering their empire. Lauro Quirini was one such man; his time at Padua was followed by a long period on Crete, which was under Venetian control.

Like humanism, Renaissance art also became part of the fabric of the city. Because of its trading links with Byzantium, Venice had long been influenced by Byzantine artistic styles. As it acquired a land-based empire in northern Italy, however, its artists adopted the Gothic styles prevalent elsewhere. In the fifteenth century, Renaissance art forms began to make inroads as well. Venice achieved its own unique style, characterized by strong colors, intense lighting, and sensuous use of paint—adapting the work of classical antiquity for its own purposes. Most Venetian artists worked on commission from churches, but lay confraternities—lay religious organizations devoted to charity—also sponsored paintings.

Florence.

Florence, like Venice, was also a republic. But unlike Venice, its society and political life were turbulent, as social classes and political factions competed for power. The most important of these civil uprisings was the so-called Ciompi Revolt of 1378. Named after the wool workers (*ciompi*), laborers so lowly that they had not been allowed to form a guild, the revolt led to the creation of a guild for them, along with a new distribution of power in the city. But by 1382, the upper classes were once again monopolizing the government, and now with even less sympathy for the commoners.

By 1434, the **Medici** family had become the dominant power in this unruly city. The patriarch of this family, Cosimo de'Medici (1389–1464), founded his political power on the wealth of the Medici bank, which handled papal finances and had numerous branch offices in Italian and northern European cities. Backed by his money, Cosimo took over Florentine politics. He determined which men could take public office, and he established new committees made up of men loyal to him to govern the city. He kept the old forms of the Florentine constitution intact, governing behind the scenes, not by force but through a broad consensus among the ruling elite.

Cosimo's grandson Lorenzo "the Magnificent" (1449–1492), who assumed power in 1467, bolstered the regime's legitimacy with his patronage of the humanities and the arts. He himself was a

---

Medici (MEH dih chee): The ruling family of Florence during much of the fifteenth to the seventeenth centuries.

Gentile Bellini, *Procession in Piazza San Marco*
After he returned to Venice from Istanbul, Bellini was commissioned by a prestigious confraternity—the Grand School of St. John—to paint a large canvas of the procession of the Holy Cross for the school's new Renaissance-style Great Hall. Bellini set the scene in the Piazza San Marco, Venice's central square.
(Erich Lessing/Art Resource, NY.)

poet and avid collector of antiquities. He intended to build a grand library made of marble at his palace but died before it was complete. More successful was his sculpture garden, which he filled with ancient works and entrusted to the sculptor Bertoldo di Giovanni to tend. Serving on various Florentine committees in charge of building, renovating, and adorning the churches of the city, Lorenzo employed important artists and architects to work on his own palaces. He probably encouraged the young Michelangelo; he certainly patronized the poet Angelo Poliziano, whose verses inspired Botticelli's *Venus*. No wonder humanists and poets sang his praises.

But the Medici family also had enemies. In 1478, Lorenzo narrowly escaped an assassination attempt, and his successor was driven out of Florence in 1494. The Medici returned to power in 1512, only to be driven out again in 1527. In 1530, the republic fell for good as the Medici once again took power, this time declaring themselves dukes of Florence.

The Tools of Power

Whether monarchies, duchies, or republics, the newly consolidated states of the fifteenth century exercised their powers more thoroughly than ever before. Sometimes they reached into the intimate lives of their subjects or citizens; at other times they persecuted undesirables with new efficiency.

New Taxes, New Knowledge. A good example of the ways in which governments peeked into the lives of their citizens—and picked their pockets—is the Florentine *catasto*. This was an inventory of households within the city and its outlying territory made for the purposes of taxation in 1427. The Domesday survey conducted in England in 1086 had been the most complete census of its day. But the catasto bested Domesday in thoroughness and inquisitiveness. It inquired about names, types of houses, and animals. It asked people to name their trade, and their answers reveal the levels of Florentine society, ranging from agricultural laborers with no land of their own to soldiers, cooks, grave diggers, scribes, great merchants, doctors, wine dealers, innkeepers, and tanners. The list seems endless. The catasto inquired about private and public investments, real estate holdings, and taxable assets. Finally, it turned to the sex of the head of the family, his or her age and marital status, and the number of mouths to feed in the household. An identification number was assigned to each household.

The catasto shows that in 1427 Florence and its outlying regions had a population of more than 260,000. Although the city itself had only thirty-eight thousand inhabitants (about 15 percent of the total population), it held 67 percent of the wealth. Some 60 percent of the Florentine households in the city belonged to the "little people"—artisans and small merchants. The "fat people" (what we would call the upper middle class) made up 30 percent of the urban population and included wealthy merchants, leading artisans, notaries, doctors, and other professionals. At the very bottom of the hierarchy were slaves and servants, largely women from the surrounding countryside employed in domestic service. At the top, a tiny elite of wealthy patricians, bankers, and wool merchants controlled the state and owned more than one-quarter of its wealth. This was the group that produced the Medici family.

Most Florentine households consisted of at least six people, not all of whom were members of the family. Wealthier families had more children, while childless couples existed almost exclusively among the poor. The rich gave their infants to wet nurses to breastfeed, while the poor often left their children to public charity. Florence was rightly proud of its orphanage: it both provided for the city's poorer children and was built in the newest and finest Renaissance style.

Driving Out Muslims, Heretics, and Jews. European kings had long fought Muslims and expelled Jews from their kingdoms. But in the fifteenth century, their powers became concentrated and centralized. Newly rich from national taxes, buttressed by political theories that glorified their power, masters of the new, expensive technologies of war (like cannons and mercenary armies), fifteenth-century kings in western Europe—England, France, Spain—commanded what we may call modern states. They used the full force of their new powers against their internal and external enemies.

Spain is a good example of this new trend. Once Ferdinand and Isabella established their rule over Castile and Aragon, they sought to impose religious uniformity and purity. They began systematically to persecute the *conversos* (converts). The conversos were Jews who converted to Christianity in the aftermath of vicious attacks on Jews at Seville, Cordova, Toledo, and other Spanish towns in 1391. During the first half of the fifteenth century they and their descendants (still called conversos, even though their children were born and baptized in the Christian faith) took advantage of the opportunities open to educated Christians, in many instances rising to high positions in both the church and the state and marrying into so-called Old Christian families. The conversos' success bred resentment, and their commitment to Christianity was questioned as well. Local massacres of conversos began. In Toledo in 1467, two conversos were caught and hanged "as traitors and captains of the heretical conversos." The terms *traitors* and *heretics* are telling. Conversos were no longer Jews, so their persecution was justified by branding them as heretics who undermined the monarchy. In 1478, Ferdinand and Isabella set up the Inquisition in Spain to do on behalf of the crown what the towns had started. Treating the conversos as heretics, the inquisitors imposed harsh sentences, expelling or burning most of them. That was not enough (in the view of the monarchs) to purify the land. In 1492, Ferdinand and Isabella decreed that all Jews in Spain must convert or leave the country. Some did indeed convert, but the experiences of the former conversos soured most on the prospect, and most Jews—perhaps 150,000—left Spain, scattering around the Mediterranean.

Meanwhile, Ferdinand and Isabella determined to rid Spain of its last Muslim stronghold, Granada. Disunity within the ruling family at Granada allowed the conquest to proceed, and in January 1492—just a few months before they expelled the Jews—Ferdinand and Isabella made their triumphal entry into the Alhambra, the former residence of the Muslim king of Granada. While they initially promised freedom of religion to the Muslims who chose to remain, the royal couple also provided a fleet of boats to take away those who chose exile. In 1502, they demanded that all Muslims adopt Christianity or leave the kingdom.

> **REVIEW:** How did the monarchs and republics of the fifteenth century use (and abuse) their newly consolidated powers?

Conclusion

The years from 1340 to 1492 marked a period of crisis in Europe. The Hundred Years' War broke out in 1337, and nine years later, in 1346, the Black Death hit, taking a heavy toll. In 1378, crisis shook the church when first two and then three popes claimed universal authority. Revolts and riots plagued the cities and countryside. The Ottoman Turks took Constantinople in 1453, changing the very shape of Europe and the Middle East.

The revival of classical literature, art, architecture, and music helped men and women cope with these crises and gave them new tools for dealing

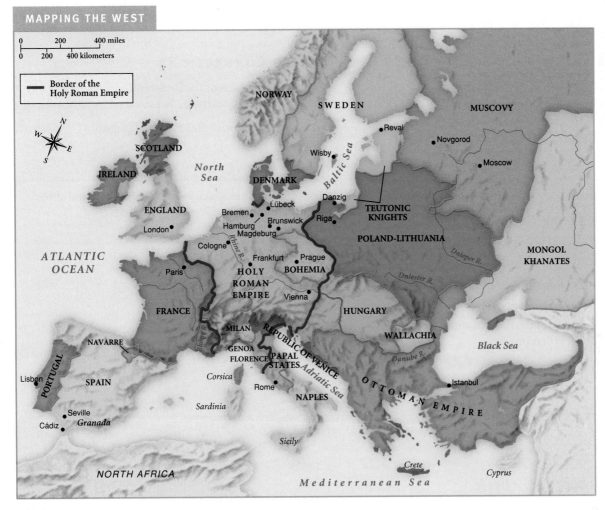

Europe, c. 1492
By the end of the fifteenth century, the shape of early modern Europe was largely fixed as it would remain until the eighteenth century. The chief exception was the disappearance of an independent Hungarian kingdom after 1529.

with them. The Renaissance began mainly in the city-states of Italy, but it spread — via the education and training of humanists, artists, sculptors, architects, and musicians — throughout much of Europe. At the courts of great kings and dukes — even of the sultan — Renaissance music, art, and literature served as a way to celebrate the grandeur of rulers who controlled more of the apparatuses of government — armies, artillery, courts, and taxes — than ever before.

Consolidation was the principle underlying the new states of the Renaissance. Venice absorbed nearby northern Italian cities, and the Peace of Lodi confirmed its new status as a power on land as well as the sea. In eastern Europe, marriage joined together the states of Lithuania and Poland. A similar union took place in Spain when Isabella of Castile and Ferdinand of Aragon married. The Swiss Confederation became a permanent entity.

The king of France came to rule over all of the area that we today call France. The consolidated modern states of the fifteenth century would soon look to the Atlantic Ocean and beyond for new lands to explore and conquer.

FOR FURTHER EXPLORATION

■ **For suggested references, including Web sites, for topics in this chapter,** see page SR-1 at the end of the book.

■ **For additional primary-source material from this period,** see Chapter 13 in *Sources of THE MAKING OF THE WEST*, Third Edition.

■ **For Web sites and documents related to topics in this chapter,** see *Make History* at bedfordstmartins.com/hunt.

CHAPTER REVIEW

KEY TERMS AND PEOPLE

Black Death (388)

Hundred Years' War (392)

Joan of Arc (392)

Jacquerie (396)

Mehmed II (396)

Great Schism (398)

humanism (402)

Francis Petrarch (402)

Hanseatic League (409)

Medici (412)

REVIEW QUESTIONS

1. What crises did Europeans confront in the fourteenth and fifteenth centuries, and how did they handle them?

2. How and why did Renaissance humanists, artists, and musicians revive classical traditions?

3. How did the monarchs and republics of the fifteenth century use (and abuse) their powers?

MAKING CONNECTIONS

1. How did the rulers of the fourteenth century make use of the forms and styles of the Renaissance?

2. On what values did Renaissance humanists and artists agree?

> **For practice quizzes, a customized study plan, and other study tools,** see the Online Study Guide at bedfordstmartins.com/hunt.

IMPORTANT EVENTS

1337–1453	Hundred Years' War
1346–1353	Black Death in Europe
1358	Jacquerie uprising in France
1378–1417	Great Schism divides papacy
1378	Ciompi revolt in Florence
1381	Wat Tyler's Rebellion in England
1386	Union of Lithuania and Poland
1414–1418	Council of Constance ends the Great Schism; burns Hus
1453	Conquest of Constantinople by Ottoman Turks; end of Hundred Years' War
1454	Peace of Lodi
1477	Dismantling of the duchy of Burgundy
1478	Inquisition begins in Spain
1492	Spain conquers Muslim stronghold of Granada; expels the Jews.

Global Encounters and Religious Reforms

1492–1560

I n Tlaxcala, New Spain (present-day Mexico), Indians newly converted to Christianity performed a pageant organized in 1539 by Catholic missionaries. The festivities celebrated a truce recently concluded between the Habsburg emperor Charles V and the French king Francis I. *The Conquest of Jerusalem*, as the drama was called, featured a combined army from Spain and New Spain fighting to protect the pope, defeat the Muslims, and win control of the holy city of Jerusalem. In the play, a miracle saves the Christian soldiers, and the Muslims give up and convert to Christianity. Although it is hard to imagine what the Indians made of this celebration of places and people far away, the event reveals a great deal about the Europeans: still preoccupied with battling the Muslims and still fighting among themselves, Europeans now pursued their interests worldwide. Yet even as their explorations and conquests transformed the New World, disputes over the "true" religion divided Europeans into hostile camps. Catholic missionaries saw their success in converting Indians as a sign of God's favor in the struggle against the Protestant reformers, who had begun to spread their message in Europe not long before the pageant in Tlaxcala took place.

Led first by the Portuguese and then Spanish explorers, Europeans sailed into contact with peoples and cultures hitherto unknown to Latin Christendom. Motivated by the desire to find gold, win personal glory, extend the reach of Christianity, and chart the unknown, European

---

Cortés

In this Spanish depiction of the landing of Hernán Cortés in Mexico in 1519, the ships and arms of the Spanish are a commanding presence, especially in comparison to the nakedness and lack of firearms among the Indians and the kneeling stance of their leader. A Spanish artist painted this miniature, which measures only 6⅛ inches by 4¼ inches. It probably accompanied an account of the Spanish conquest of Mexico. On the back of the picture is a small map of the west coast of Europe and Africa and the east coast of Central America. Europeans relied on such images, and especially on maps, to help them make sense of all the new information flooding into Europe from faraway places. Many Spaniards viewed Cortés's conquests as a sign of divine favor in a time of religious division. Some even believed that Cortés was born the same day, or at least the same year, as Martin Luther, the German monk who had initiated the Protestant Reformation just two years before Cortés's landing (in fact, Luther was born two years before Cortés). *(Erich Lessing/Art Resource, NY.)*

voyagers subjugated native peoples, declared their control over vast new lands, and established a new system of slavery linking Africa and the New World. Millions of Indians died of diseases unknowingly imported by the Europeans. The discovery of new crops—corn, potatoes, tobacco, coffee, and cocoa—and of gold and silver mines brought new patterns of consumption, and new objects of conflict, to Europe. This spiral of changes in ecology, agriculture, and social patterns is so momentous that historians now call it the Columbian exchange after Christopher Columbus, who started the process.

The invention of the printing press in the 1440s helped spread news of the European explorations, but it had an even more significant impact when it hastened the breakup of Christian unity under the impact of the Protestant Reformation. After the German Catholic monk Martin Luther criticized corrupt church practices in 1517, printed broadsheets, pamphlets, and books quickly spread his message and helped make the Protestant break with Roman Catholicism permanent. Religious division soon engulfed the German states and reached into Switzerland, France, and England. Responding to the desire for reform that fed the Protestant movement, Catholics undertook their own renewal. When radical Protestants threatened to overthrow the social and political order, more mainstream Protestants, like Catholics, insisted that the state oversee religious, moral, and social matters.

Confrontations between Protestants and Catholics complicated the long-standing rivalries between princes. Traditional sources of enmity between the Christian powers did not disappear, and the Ottomans continued their thrust into Hungary. Now, however, the Catholic Habsburg emperor had to wage war against Protestant German princes and religious divisions threatened the stability of the monarchy in England and Scotland. Divisions between Catholics and Protestants

would shape the course of European history for several generations.

> **FOCUS QUESTION:** Why did Christian unity break up in Europe just when Europeans began to expand their influence overseas in dramatic fashion?

Widening Horizons

The maritime explorations of Portugal and Spain brought Europe to the attention of the rest of the world. Fourteenth-century Mongols had been more interested in conquering China and Persia—lands with sophisticated cultures—than in invading Europe; Persian historians of the early fifteenth century dismissed Europeans as "barbaric Franks"; and China's Ming dynasty rulers, who sent maritime expeditions to Southeast Asia and East Africa around 1400, seemed unaware of the Europeans, even though Marco Polo and other Italian merchants had appeared at the court of the preceding Mongol Yuan dynasty. By the end of the fifteenth century, in contrast, Europeans could no longer be ignored. The Portuguese and Spanish, inspired by a crusading spirit against Islam and by riches to be won through trade in spices and gold, sailed across the Atlantic, Indian, and Pacific oceans. The English, French, and Dutch followed a century later, creating a new global exchange of people, crops, and diseases that would shape the modern world. As a result of these European expeditions, the people of the Americas for the first time confronted forces that threatened to destroy not only their culture but even their existence.

Portuguese Explorations

The first phase of European overseas expansion began in 1433 with Portuguese exploration of the West African coast and culminated in 1519–1522

■ **1492** Columbus reaches the Americas

■ **1516** Erasmus publishes Greek New Testament; More, *Utopia*

1490	1500	1510	1520

■ **1494** Italian Wars begin; Treaty of Tordesillas

■ **1517** Luther composes ninety-five theses

■ **1520** Luther publishes three treatises; Zwingli breaks from Rome

with Spanish circumnavigation of the globe. Looking back, the sixteenth-century Spanish historian Francisco López de Gómora described the Iberian maritime voyages to the East and West Indies as "the greatest event since the creation of the world, apart from the incarnation and death of him who created it."

The Portuguese hoped to find a sea route to the spice-producing lands of South and Southeast Asia in order to bypass the Ottoman Turks, who controlled the traditional land routes between Europe and Asia. Rumors of vast gold mines in West Africa and the legend of a mysterious Christian kingdom established by Prester John and surrounded by Muslims drew sailors to voyages despite the possibilities of shipwreck and death. Success in the voyages of exploration depended on several technological breakthroughs, including the caravel, a small, easily maneuvered three-masted ship that used triangular lateen sails adapted from the Arabs. (The sails permitted a ship to tack against headwinds.) Prince Henry the Navigator of Portugal (1394–1460) personally financed many voyages with revenues from a noble crusading order. The first triumphs of the Portuguese attracted a host of Christian, Jewish, and even Arab sailors, astronomers, and cartographers to the service of Prince Henry and King John II (r. 1481–1495). They compiled better tide calendars and books of sailing directions for pilots that enabled sailors to venture farther into the oceans and reduced — though did not eliminate — the dangers of sea travel.

Searching for gold and then slaves, the Portuguese gradually established forts down the West African coast. In 1487–1488, they reached the Cape of Good Hope at the tip of Africa; ten years later, Vasco da Gama led a Portuguese fleet around the cape and reached as far as Calicut, India, the center of the spice trade. His return to Lisbon with twelve pieces of Chinese porcelain for the Portuguese king set off two centuries of porcelain

mania. Until the early eighteenth century, only the Chinese knew how to produce porcelain (in vases or dinnerware), so over the next two hundred years Western merchants would import no fewer than seventy million pieces of porcelain, still known today as "china." In 1512, Ferdinand Magellan, a Portuguese sailor in Spanish service, led the first expedition to circumnavigate the globe. By 1517, a chain of Portuguese forts dotted the Indian Ocean — at Mozambique, Hormuz (at the mouth of the Persian Gulf), Goa (in India), Colombo (in modern Sri Lanka), and Malacca (modern Malaysia) (Map 14.1).

The Voyages of Columbus

One of many sailors inspired by the Portuguese explorations, **Christopher Columbus** (1451–1506) opened an entirely new direction for discovery. Most likely born in Genoa of Italian parents, Columbus sailed the West African coast in Portuguese service between 1476 and 1485. Fifteenth-century Europeans already knew that the world was round (see "Seeing History," page 424). Columbus had studied *The Travels of Marco Polo*, written more than a century earlier, and wanted to sail west to reach "the lands of the Great Khan," unaware that the Mongol Empire had already collapsed in eastern Asia. Hugely underestimating the distance of such a voyage, Columbus dreamed of finding a new route to the East's gold and spices. After the Portuguese refused to fund his plan, Columbus turned to the Spanish monarchs Isabella of Castille and Ferdinand of Aragon, who agreed to finance his venture.

On August 3, 1492, with ninety men on board two caravels and one larger merchant ship for carrying supplies, Columbus set sail westward. His

---

Christopher Columbus: An Italian sailor (1451–1506) who opened up the New World by sailing west across the Atlantic in search of a route to Asia.

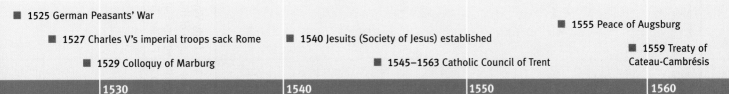

■ 1525 German Peasants' War

■ 1527 Charles V's imperial troops sack Rome

■ 1529 Colloquy of Marburg

■ 1540 Jesuits (Society of Jesus) established

■ 1545–1563 Catholic Council of Trent

■ 1555 Peace of Augsburg

■ 1559 Treaty of Cateau-Cambrésis

1530   **1540**   **1550**   **1560**

■ 1534 Henry VIII breaks with Rome; Affair of the Placards in France

■ 1547 Charles V defeats Protestants at Mühlberg

■ 1536 Calvin, *Institutes of the Christian Religion*

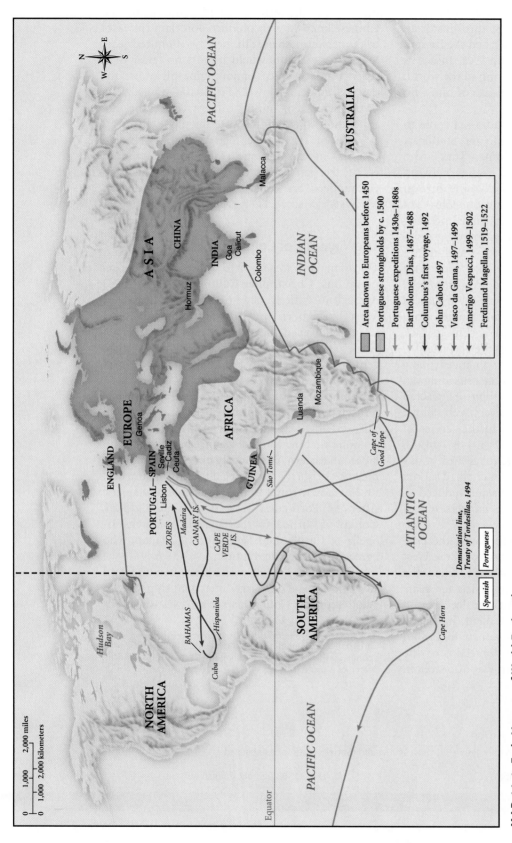

MAP 14.1 Early Voyages of World Exploration

Over the course of the fifteenth and early sixteenth centuries, European shipping dominated the Atlantic Ocean after the pioneering voyages of the Portuguese, who also first sailed around the Cape of Good Hope to the Indian Ocean and the Cape Horn to the Pacific. The search for spices and the need to circumnavigate the Ottoman Empire inspired these voyages.

Columbus Describes His First Voyage (1493)

In this famous letter to Raphael Sanchez, treasurer to his patrons, Ferdinand and Isabella, Columbus recounts his initial journey to the Bahamas, Cuba, and Hispaniola (today Haiti and the Dominican Republic), and tells of his achievements. This passage reflects the first contact between native Americans and Europeans; already the themes of trade, subjugation, gold, and conversion emerge in Columbus's own words.

Indians would give whatever the seller required; . . . Thus they bartered, like idiots, cotton and gold for fragments of bows, glasses, bottles, and jars; which I forbad as being unjust, and myself gave them many beautiful and acceptable articles which I had brought with me, taking nothing from them in return; I did this in order that I might the more easily conciliate them, that they might be led to become Christians, and be inclined to entertain a regard for the King and Queen, our Princes and all Spaniards, and that I might induce them to take an interest in seeking out, and collecting, and delivering to us such things as they possessed in abundance, but which we greatly needed. They practise no kind of idolatry, but have a firm belief that all strength and power, and indeed all good things, are in heaven, and that I had descended from thence with these ships and sailors, and under this impression was I received after they had thrown aside their fears. Nor are they slow or stupid, but of very clear understanding; and those men who have crossed to the neighbouring islands give an admirable description of everything they observed; but they never saw any people clothed, nor any ships like ours. On my arrival at that sea, I had taken some Indians by force from the first island that I came to, in order that they might learn our language, and communicate to us what they know respecting the country; which plan succeeded excellently, and was a great advantage to us, for in a short time, either by gestures and signs, or by words, we were enabled to understand each other. These men are still travelling with me, and although they have been with us now a long time, they continue to entertain the idea that I have descended from heaven.

Source: Christopher Columbus, *Four Voyages to the New World.* Translated by R. H. Major (New York: Corinth Books, 1961), 8–9.

contract stipulated that he would claim Castilian sovereignty over any new land and inhabitants and share any profits with the crown. Reaching what is today the Bahamas on October 12, Columbus mistook the islands to be part of the East Indies, not far from Japan. As the Spaniards explored the Caribbean islands, they encountered communities of peaceful Indians, the Arawaks, who were awed by the Europeans' military technology, not to mention their appearance. Although many positive entries in the ship's log testified to Columbus's personal goodwill toward the Indians, the Europeans' objectives were clear: find gold, subjugate the Indians, and propagate Christianity. (See Document, "Columbus Describes His First Voyage," above.)

Excited by the prospect of easy riches, many flocked to join Columbus's second voyage. When Columbus departed Cádiz in September 1493, he commanded a fleet of seventeen ships carrying some fifteen hundred men, many of whom believed that all they had to do was "to load the gold into the ships." Failing to find the imagined gold mines and spices, Columbus and his crew began capturing Caribs, enemies of the Arawaks, with the intention of bringing them back as slaves. In 1494, Columbus proposed setting up a regular slave trade based in Hispaniola. The Spaniards exported enslaved Indians to Spain, and slave traders sold them in Seville. When the Spanish monarchs realized the vast potential for material gain of their new dominions, they asserted direct royal authority by sending officials and priests to the Americas, which were named after the Italian Amerigo Vespucci, who led a voyage across the Atlantic in 1499–1502.

To head off looming conflicts between the Spanish and the Portuguese, Pope Alexander VI helped negotiate the Treaty of Tordesillas of 1494. It divided the Atlantic world between the two maritime powers, reserving for Portugal the West African coast and the route to India and giving Spain the oceans and lands to the west (see Map 14.1). The agreement allowed Portugal to claim Brazil in 1500, when it was accidentally "discovered" by Pedro Alvares Cabral (1467–1520) on a voyage to India.

A New Era in Slavery

The European voyages of discovery initiated a new era in slavery, both by expanding the economic scale of slave labor and by attaching race and color to servitude. Slavery had existed since antiquity and flourished in many parts of the world. Some slaves were captured in war or by piracy; others —

Expanding Geographic Knowledge: World Maps in an Age of Exploration

On the eve of Christopher Columbus's voyages, most Europeans knew that the world was round and many shared Columbus's view that new routes to Asia and its riches could be found by sailing west. Beyond that, however, geographic knowledge of what precisely lay on the other side of the Atlantic was sketchy at best. Even those regions familiar to Europe through trade and exploration—Africa and parts of Asia—were often shown inaccurately on maps of the day.

The hand-colored map at the top produced by a German geographer, Henricus Martellus, depicts the world as Europeans knew it just before Columbus's first voyage. How accurate is its rendition of Europe, the Mediterranean, and Africa? Note that the Americas are not shown as a separate continent, but rather are joined to the Asian landmass on the far right. (Scholars have identified several major Latin American rivers, including the Orinooko and the Amazon in part of lower right-hand quadrant of the map.) How does this map help explain Columbus's mistake about where he had landed in 1492? What else does it tell you about Europeans' perceptions of the world in this period?

By 1570, when Abraham Ortelius's map was printed, European knowledge of world geography had grown by leaps and bounds thanks to the voyages of exploration. Ortelius, a well-traveled and prominent geographer and cartographer, included this map in his *Theatrum Orbis Terrarum* (Theater of the World), considered to be the first modern atlas. Judging from this map, what areas of the world have come into greater focus? What areas are still inaccurately portrayed and rudimentary in some respects? How might you account for that? What advantages do accurate maps offer you, beyond knowing where you are headed? What else does the later map reveal about Europeans' knowledge of the world after less than a century of exploration?

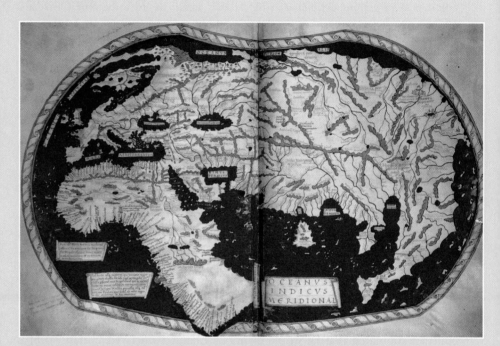

World Map by Henricus Martellus, 1489. *(The Art Archive/British Library.)*

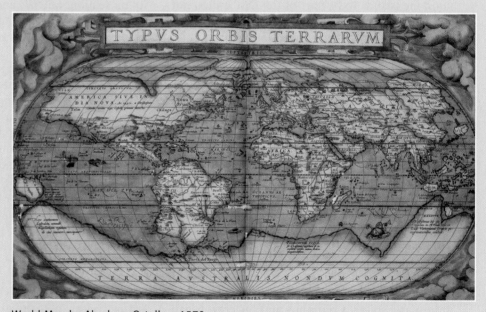

World Map by Abraham Ortelius, 1570. *(By permission of the British Library © British Library Board. All Rights Reserved. MAPS C2.c.3.)*

Africans—were sold by other Africans and Bedouin traders to Christian buyers; in western Asia, parents sold their children out of poverty into servitude; and many in the Balkans became slaves when their land was devastated by Ottoman invasions. Slaves could be Greek, Slav, European, African, or Turkish. Many served as domestics in European cities of the Mediterranean such as Barcelona or Venice. Others sweated as galley slaves in Ottoman and Christian fleets. Still others worked as agricultural laborers on Mediterranean islands. In the Ottoman army, slaves even formed an important elite contingent.

From the fifteenth century onward, Africans increasingly filled the ranks of slaves. Exploiting warfare between groups within West Africa, the Portuguese traded in gold and "pieces," as African slaves were called, a practice condemned at home by some conscientious clergy. Manoel Severim de Faria, for example, observed that "one cannot yet see any good effect resulting from so much butchery; for this is not the way in which commerce can flourish and the preaching of the gospel progress." Critical voices, however, could not deny the potential for profits that the slave trade brought to Portugal. Most slaves toiled in the sugar plantations of the Portuguese Atlantic islands and in Brazil. A fortunate few had somewhat easier lives as domestic servants in Portugal, where African freedmen and slaves, some thirty-five thousand in the early sixteenth century, constituted almost 3 percent of the population, a percentage that was much higher than in other European countries.

In the Americas, slavery would expand enormously in the following centuries. Even outspoken critics of colonial brutality toward indigenous peoples defended the development of African slavery. The Spanish Dominican Bartolomé de Las Casas (1474–1566), for example, argued that Africans were constitutionally more suitable for labor than native Americans and should therefore be imported to the plantations in the Americas to relieve the indigenous peoples, who were being worked to death.

Conquering the New World

In 1500, on the eve of European invasion, the native peoples of the Americas lived in a great diver-

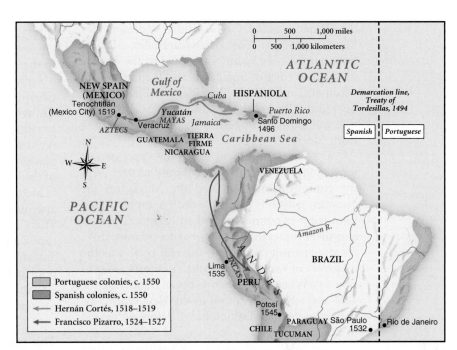

MAP 14.2 Spanish and Portuguese Colonies in the Americas, 1492–1560
The discovery of precious metals fueled the Spanish and Portuguese explorations and settlements of Central and South America, establishing the foundations of European colonial empires in the New World.

sity of social and political arrangements. Some were nomads roaming large, sparsely inhabited territories; others practiced agriculture in complexly organized states. Among the settled peoples, the largest groupings could be found in the Mexican and Peruvian highlands. Combining an elaborate religious culture with a rigid social and political hierarchy, the Aztecs in Mexico and the Incas in Peru ruled over subjugated Indian populations in their respective empires. From their large urban capitals, the Aztecs and Incas controlled large swaths of land and could be ruthless as conquerors.

The Spanish explorers organized their expeditions to the mainland of the Americas from a base in the Caribbean (Map 14.2). Two prominent commanders, **Hernán Cortés** (1485–1547) and Francisco Pizarro (c. 1475–1541), gathered men and arms and set off in search of gold. With them came Catholic priests intending to bring Christianity to supposedly uncivilized peoples. Some natives who resented their subjugation by the Aztecs joined Cortés and his soldiers. With a band of fewer than two hundred men, Cortés captured

Hernán Cortés: A Spanish explorer (1485–1547) who captured the Aztec capital, Tenochtitlán (present-day Mexico City), in 1519.

the Aztec capital, Tenochtitlán (present-day Mexico City), in 1519. Two years later, Mexico, then named New Spain, was added to the empire of the new ruler of Spain, Charles V, grandson of Ferdinand and Isabella. To the south, Pizarro conquered the Peruvian highlands. The Spanish Empire was now the largest in the world, stretching from Mexico to Chile.

The Aztecs and Incas fell to the superior war technology of the Spanish conquistadores. Next the conquistadores subdued the Mayas on the Yucatán peninsula, a people with a sophisticated knowledge of cosmology and arithmetic. The gold and silver mines in Mexico proved a treasure trove for the Spanish crown, but the real prize was the discovery of vast silver deposits in Potosí (today in Bolivia). When the Spaniards began importing the gold and silver they found in the New World, inflation soared in a fashion never before witnessed in Europe.

Not to be outdone by the Spaniards, other European powers joined the scramble for gold in the New World. In North America, the French went in search of a "northwest passage" to China. The French wanted to establish settlements in what became Canada, but the climate and the hostility of the indigenous peoples defeated them. Permanent European settlements in Canada and the present-day United States would succeed only in the seventeenth century, and by then the English had entered the contest for world mastery. Even before the French and the English, the Dutch entered the colonial competition. After they broke away from Spain late in the sixteenth century, the Dutch set about systematically and aggressively taking over Spanish and Portuguese trade routes. By the mid-seventeenth century, they had become the wealthiest people (per capita) in the world.

The discovery of the Americas resulted in a significant global movement of peoples, animals, plants, manufactured goods, and precious metals. Tobacco and cocoa were among the exotic items brought from the Americas to Europe. Voyages to the New World also brought diseases from Europe to the unsuspecting peoples of America. Without natural immunity, the Amerindians died in catastrophic numbers. Within fifty years of Columbus's first voyage, the indigenous populations of the Caribbean Islands had been wiped out.

> REVIEW: Which European countries led the way in maritime exploration, and what were their motives?

The Protestant Reformation

In the sixteenth century, religious reformers led by Martin Luther shattered the unity of Western Christendom, supplied by the Roman Catholic Church since the fourth century. The invention of printing with movable type proved crucial to the rapid spread of the Protestant message. The popular piety that swept Europe in the closing decades of the 1400s, along with Christian humanism, also helped pave the way for the reformers by focusing attention on corrupt practices and clerical abuses. The Catholic church might nonetheless have escaped a schism had it not been for the drive, talent, and theological brilliance of Luther and other reformers such as Huldrych Zwingli and John Calvin. They turned reform into protest—hence the name of their movement, Protestantism.

The Invention of Printing

Printing with movable type, developed in the 1440s by Johannes Gutenberg, a German goldsmith, marked a revolutionary departure from the old practice of copying works by hand or stamping pages with individually carved wood blocks. Printing itself predated movable type: the Chinese had been printing by woodblock since the tenth century, and woodcut pictures made their appearance in Europe in the early fifteenth century. Movable type, however, allowed entire manuscripts to be printed more quickly. Single letters, made in metal molds, could be emptied out of a frame and new ones inserted to print each new page. Also, the large-scale production of paper had paved the way for the invention of printing. Papermaking came to Europe from China via Arab intermediaries. By the fourteenth century, paper mills in Italy were producing paper that was more fragile but also much cheaper than parchment or vellum, the animal skins that Europeans had previously used for writing.

The invention of movable type in the West no doubt owed something to the twenty-six-character alphabets found in most European languages; setting twenty-six characters in metal type was much easier than trying to set the hundreds or even thousands of different picture-like characters that made up written Chinese. (See Printing Press, page 427.) In 1467, two German printers established the first press in Rome; within five years, they had produced twelve thousand volumes, a feat that in the past would have required a thousand scribes working full-time.

In the 1490s, the German city of Frankfurt became an international meeting place for printers and booksellers, establishing a book fair that remains an unbroken tradition to this day. Early printed books attracted an elite audience; their expense made them inaccessible to most literate people, who comprised a minority of the population in any case. Gutenberg's famous two-volume Latin Bible was a luxury item, and only 185 copies were printed. Gutenberg Bibles remain today a treasure that only the greatest libraries possess.

The invention of mechanical printing dramatically increased the speed at which knowledge could be transmitted and freed individuals from having to memorize everything that they learned. Printed books and pamphlets, even one-page flyers, might create a wider community of scholars no longer dependent on personal patronage or church sponsorship for texts. Printing thus encouraged the free expression and exchange of ideas, and its disruptive potential did not go unnoticed by political and religious authorities. Rulers and bishops in the German states, the birthplace of the printing industry, moved quickly to issue censorship regulations, but their efforts could not prevent the outbreak of the Protestant Reformation.

Popular Piety and Christian Humanism

The Christianizing of Europe had taken many centuries to complete, and by 1500 most people in Europe believed devoutly. However, the vast majority of them had little knowledge of Catholic doctrine. More popular forms of piety such as processions, festivals, and marvelous tales of saints' miracles captivated ordinary believers.

Urban merchants and artisans, more likely than the general population to be literate and critical of their local priests, yearned for a faith more meaningful to their daily lives and for a clergy more responsive to their needs. They wanted priests to preach edifying sermons, to administer the sacraments conscientiously, and to lead moral lives, so they generously donated money to establish new preaching positions for university-trained clerics. The merchants resented the funneling of the Catholic church's rich endowments to the younger children of the nobility who took up religious callings to protect the wealth of their families. The young, educated clerics funded by the merchants often came from cities themselves. They formed the backbone of **Christian humanism** and sometimes became reformers, too.

Christian humanism: A general intellectual trend in the sixteenth century that coupled love of classical learning, as in Renaissance humanism, with an emphasis on Christian piety.

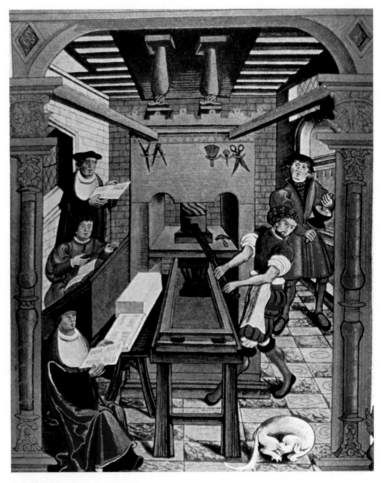

Printing Press
This illustration from a French manuscript of 1537 depicts typical printing equipment of the sixteenth century. An artisan is using the screw press to apply the inked type to the paper. Also shown are the composed type secured in a chase, the printed sheet (four pages of text printed on one sheet) held by the seated proofreader, and the bound volume. When two pages of text were printed on one standard-sized sheet, the bound book was called a folio. A bound book with four pages of text on one sheet was called a quarto ("in four"), and a book with eight pages of text on one sheet was called an octavo ("in eight"). The last is a pocket-size book, smaller than today's paperback. *(The Granger Collection, New York.)*

Humanism originated during the Renaissance in Italy among highly educated individuals attached to the personal households of prominent rulers. North of the Alps, however, humanists focused more on religious revival and the inculcation of Christian piety, through such means as the model school of the Brethren of the Common Life. The Brethren preached self-discipline and often criticized the local clergy for their inadequate training and lax morals. Two men, the Dutch scholar Desiderius Erasmus (c. 1466–1536) and the English lawyer Thomas More (1478–1535), stood out as representatives of these Christian humanists, who coupled their love of classical learning with the emphasis on Christian piety. They both longed for ideal societies based on peace and morality but faced a world that seemed bent on violent division instead.

Erasmus. Just as Cicero had dominated ancient Roman letters, Erasmus towered over the humanist world of early-sixteenth-century Europe. An intimate friend of kings and popes, he became known across Europe. Disseminated by the printing press, Erasmus's books made him famous. He devoted years to preparing a critical edition of the New Testament in Greek with a translation into Latin, which was finally published in 1516.

Only through education, Erasmus believed, could individuals reform themselves and society. He strove for a unified, peaceful Christendom in which charity and good works, not empty ceremonies, would mark true religion and in which learning and piety would dispel the darkness of ignorance. He elaborated many of these ideas in his *Handbook of the Militant Christian* (1503), an eloquent plea for a simple religion devoid of greed and the lust for power. In *The Praise of Folly* (1509), he satirized values held dear by his contemporaries. Modesty, humility, and poverty represented the true Christian virtues in a world that worshipped pomposity, power, and wealth. The wise appeared foolish, he concluded, for their wisdom and values were not of this world.

He instructed the young future emperor Charles V to rule as a just Christian prince and expressed deep sorrow about the brutal fighting that had ravaged Europe for decades. A man of peace and moderation, Erasmus soon found himself challenged by angry younger men and radical ideas once the Reformation took hold; he eventually chose Christian unity over reform and schism. His dream of Christian pacifism crushed, he lived to see dissenters executed—by Catholics and Protestants alike—for speaking their conscience. Erasmus spent his last years in Freiburg and Basel, isolated from the Protestant community, his writings condemned by many in the Catholic church. After the Protestant Reformation had been secured, the saying arose that "Erasmus laid the egg that Luther hatched." Some blamed the humanists for the emergence of Luther and Protestantism, despite the humanists' decision to remain in the Catholic church.

Thomas More. If Erasmus found himself abandoned by his times, his good friend across the English Channel, Thomas More, to whom *The Praise of Folly* was dedicated, met with even greater suffering. Like the humanists of Italy, More chose to

Albrecht Dürer, *The Knight, Death, and the Devil*
Dürer's 1513 engraving of the knight depicts a grim and determined warrior advancing in the face of devils, one of whom holds out an hourglass with a grimace while another wields a menacing pike. An illustration for Erasmus's *The Handbook of the Militant Christian*, this scene is often interpreted as portraying a Christian clad in the armor of righteousness on a path through life beset by death and demonic temptations. Yet the knight in early-sixteenth-century Germany had become a mercenary, selling his martial skills to princes. Some waylaid merchants, robbed rich clerics, and held citizens for ransom. The most notorious of these robber-knights, Franz von Sickingen, was declared an outlaw by the emperor and murdered in 1522. *(Bridgeman-Giraudon/Art Resource, NY.)*

■ **For more help analyzing this image,** see the visual activity for this chapter in the Online Study Guide at **bedfordstmartins.com/hunt.**

serve his prince. In 1529, he became lord chancellor, the chief officer of the English government. King Henry VIII had his own issues with the papacy and, in 1532, broke with the Roman Catholic church. He pulled England out from under papal control and began appointing his own bishops. In protest against Henry's newly asserted control of the clergy, More resigned his position and was executed in 1535 for refusing to subscribe to Henry VIII's version of the Protestant Reformation. By executing More, Henry created a martyr revered for centuries by Catholics and by those who believed in liberty of conscience.

From any perspective, More was an audacious, even eccentric thinker. In his best-known work, *Utopia* (1516), he describes an ideal imaginary land that stands in stark contrast to his own society. A just, equitable, and hardworking community, Utopia (meaning both "no place" and "best place" in Greek) was the opposite of England. In Utopia, everyone worked the land for two years; and since Utopians enjoyed public schools, communal kitchens, hospitals, and nurseries, they had no need for money or private property. Dedicated to the pursuit of knowledge and natural religion, with equal distribution of goods and few laws, Utopians knew neither crime nor internal discord.

Yet even in More's Utopia some oddities existed — voluntary slavery, for example, and strictly controlled travel. Although premarital sex brought severe punishment, prospective marriage partners could examine each other naked before making their final decisions. Men headed Utopia's households and exercised authority over women and children. And Utopians did not shy away from declaring war on their neighbors to protect their way of life. More nonetheless created an imaginary society that was paradise when compared with a Christian Europe battered by division and violence. The Christian humanists offered stirring visions of a better future, but peace, moderation, unity, and any idea of Utopia would all be submerged in the coming flood of radical religious change.

Martin Luther and the Holy Roman Empire

The Protestant Reformation began when the crisis of faith of one man, **Martin Luther** (1483–1546), started an international movement. Luther was an improbable spiritual revolutionary. Son of a miner and a deeply pious mother, he began his studies in the law. Caught in a storm on a lonely road one midsummer's night, the young student grew terrified by the thunder and lightning. He implored the help of St. Anne, the mother of the Virgin Mary, and promised to enter a monastery if she protected him. Luther abandoned his law studies and entered the Augustinian order. There he experienced his religious crisis and its resolution: the doctrine of faith alone as the means to salvation.

Even though as a monk Luther took up all the practices offered by the church to achieve personal salvation, he did not feel saved. He prayed, he took the sacraments, and as a priest he even said Mass. He did all the good works that the church prescribed yet still felt bereft of God's love. He came to believe that the church gave external behavior more weight than spiritual intentions. The sacrament of penance was a case in point. Instead of emphasizing the remorse that led the sinner to confess his sins to a priest and then receive forgiveness from the priest in God's name, the church emphasized the penance imposed by the priest. Some priests abused their authority by demanding sexual or monetary favors before granting forgiveness. Luther found peace inside himself when he became convinced that sinners were saved only through faith and that faith was a gift freely given by God. No amount of good works, he believed, could produce the faith on which salvation depended. Shortly before his death, Luther recalled his crisis:

> Though I lived as a monk without reproach, I felt that I was a sinner before God with an extremely disturbed conscience. I could not believe that he was placated by my satisfaction [in penance]. I did not love, yes, I hated the righteous God who punishes sinners, and secretly . . . I was angry with God. . . . At last, by the mercy of God, meditating day and night, I gave heed to the context of the words, namely, "In [the gospel] the righteousness of God is revealed, as it is written, 'He who through faith is righteous shall live.'" There I began to understand that the righteousness of God is that by which the righteous live by a gift of God, namely by faith.

Just as Luther was working out his own personal search for salvation, a priest named Johann Tetzel arrived in Wittenberg, where Luther was a university professor, to sell indulgences. Penance normally consisted of spiritual duties (prayers, pilgrimages), but the church also asked for monetary substitutions, called indulgences. Indulgences could even be bought for a deceased relative, which would forgive that person's time in purgatory and release the soul for heaven. Luther denounced what he, like so many of the Church's other crit-

---

Martin Luther: A German monk (1483–1546) who started the Protestant Reformation in 1517 by challenging the practices and doctrines of the Catholic church and advocating salvation through faith alone.

ics, saw as a corrupt practice, allowing sinners to buy rather than to earn forgiveness of their sins. But Luther's objections went far deeper. He believed that indulgences, like the sacrament of penance, were ultimately useless unless one had faith. No one, he felt, could be allowed to think that such a purchase had anything to do with salvation.

Armed with his sense of God's justice and grace, Luther composed ninety-five theses for academic debate in 1517. Among them were attacks on the sale of indulgences and the purchase of church offices. Printed, the theses became public and unleashed a torrent of pent-up resentment and frustration among the laypeople. What began as a theological debate in a provincial university soon engulfed the Holy Roman Empire. (See "Contrasting Views," page 431.) Luther's earliest supporters included younger Christian humanists and clerics who shared his critical attitude toward the church establishment. None of these Evangelicals, as they called themselves, came from the upper echelons of the church; many were from urban middle-class backgrounds, and most were university trained. The Evangelicals represented social groups most ready to challenge clerical authority — merchants, artisans, and literate urban laypeople. But illiterate artisans and peasants also rallied to Luther, sometimes with an almost fanatical zeal. They and he believed they were living in the last days of the world. Luther and his cause might be a sign of the approaching Last Judgment.

Initially, Luther presented himself as the pope's "loyal opposition," but in 1520, he burned his bridges with the publication of three fiery treatises. In *Freedom of a Christian*, written in Latin for the learned and addressed to Pope Leo X, Luther argued that faith, not good works, saved sinners from damnation, and he sharply distinguished between true Gospel teachings and invented church doctrines. Luther advocated "the priesthood of all believers," insisting that the Bible provided all the teachings necessary for Christian living and that a professional caste of clerics should not hold sway over laypeople. *Freedom of a Christian* circulated widely in an immediate German translation. Its principles "by faith alone," "by Scripture alone," and "the priesthood of all believers" became central features of the reform movement.

In his second treatise, *To the Nobility of the German Nation*, written in German, Luther ap-

Luther's World in the Early Sixteenth Century

pealed to German identity and to the nobles as the natural leaders of any reform movement. He denounced the corrupt Italians in Rome who were cheating and exploiting his compatriots and called on the German princes to defend their nation and reform the church. Luther's third treatise, *On the Babylonian Captivity of the Church*, condemned the papacy as the embodiment of the Antichrist.

From Rome's perspective, the "Luther Affair," as church officials called it, concerned only one unruly monk. When the pope ordered him to obey his superiors and keep quiet, Luther tore up the decree. Spread by the printing press, Luther's ideas circulated throughout the Holy Roman Empire, letting loose forces that neither the church nor Luther could control. Social, nationalist, and religious protests fused with lower-class resentments, much as in the Czech movement that Jan Hus had inspired a century earlier. Like Hus, Luther appeared before an emperor: in 1521, he defended his faith at the Imperial Diet of Worms before **Charles V** (r. 1519–1556), the newly elected Holy Roman Emperor who, at the age of nineteen, ruled over the Low Countries, Spain, Spain's Italian and New World dominions, and the Austrian Habsburg lands. Luther shocked Germans by declaring his admiration for the Czech heretic. But unlike Hus, Luther did not suffer martyrdom because he enjoyed the protection of Frederick the Wise, the elector of Saxony and Luther's lord. Frederick was one of the seven electors whom Charles V had bribed to become Holy Roman Emperor, and Charles had to treat him with respect. The emperor soon had cause to regret his reluctance to punish Luther.

Lutheran propaganda flooded German towns and villages. Hundreds of pamphlets lambasted the papacy and the Catholic clergy; others simplified the message of Luther for the common folk. Sometimes only a few pages in length, these broadsheets were often illustrated with crude satirical cartoons. City dwellers proved particularly receptive to Luther's teachings; they were literate and were eager to read the Bible for themselves. Magistrates began to curtail clerical privileges and

---

Charles V: Holy Roman Emperor (r. 1519–1556) and the most powerful ruler in sixteenth-century Europe; he reigned over the Low Countries, Spain, Spain's Italian and New World dominions, and the Austrian Habsburg lands.

Martin Luther: Holy Man or Heretic?

When Martin Luther criticized the papacy and the Catholic church, he was hailed as a godly prophet by some and condemned as a heretic by others. Both Protestants and Catholics used popular propaganda to argue their cause. They spread their message to a largely illiterate or semiliterate society through pamphlets, woodcuts, and broadsheets in which visual images took on increasing importance, to appeal to a wide public. These polemical works were distributed in the thousands to cities and market towns throughout the Holy Roman Empire. A few were even translated into Latin to reach an audience outside of Germany.

The 1521 woodcut by Matthias Gnidias represents Luther standing above his Catholic opponent, the Franciscan friar Thomas Murner, who is depicted here as a crawling dragon, Leviathan, the biblical monster (Document 1). Another positive image of Luther, also published in 1521, depicts him as inspired by the Holy Spirit (Document 2). An anti-Luther image from a few years later represents him as a seven-headed monster (Document 3), signifying that the reformer is the source of discord within Christianity. This image appeared in a book published in 1529 by the Dominican friar Johannes Cochlaeus, one of Luther's vociferous opponents.

Visual examples of religious propaganda worked effectively to demonize enemies and to contrast sharply good and evil. The 1520s saw the most intense production of these cheap polemical visual prints, but the use of visual propaganda would continue for more than a century in the religious conflict.

Luther as Monk. *(The Granger Collection, New York.)*

2. Luther as Monk, Doctor, Man of the Bible, and Saint (1521)

This woodcut by an anonymous artist appeared in a volume that the Strasbourg printer Johann Schott published in 1521. In addition to being one of the major centers of printing, Strasbourg was also a stronghold of the reform movement. Note the use of traditional symbols to signify Luther's holiness: the Bible in his hands, the halo, the Holy Spirit in the form of a dove, and his friar's robes. Although the cult of saints and monasticism came under severe criticism during the Reformation, the representation of Luther in traditional symbols of sanctity stressed his conservative values instead of his radical challenge to church authorities.

3. The Seven-Headed Martin Luther by Johannes Cochlaeus (1529)

The seven heads are labeled (from left to right) doctor, Martin, Luther, ecclesiast, enthusiast, visitirer, and Barrabas. The term en-thusiast represented a name of abuse, applied usually by the Catholic church to Anabaptists and religious radicals of all sorts. Visitirer is a pun in German on the word Tier, meaning "animal." Cochlaeus also mocks the new practice of Protestant clergy visiting parishes to check up on pastors' and parishioners' adherence to reformed doctrines and rituals in order to enforce Christian discipline. From left to right, Luther's many heads gradually reveal him to be a rebel, as Barrabas was condemned to die as a rabble-rouser by the Romans but instead was freed and his place taken by Jesus at the crucifixion. The number seven also alludes to the seven deadly sins.

Seven-Headed Luther. *(The Granger Collection, New York.)*

1. Matthias Gnidias's Representation of Luther and Leviathan (1521)

Luther and Leviathan

Dressed in a friar's robes, the Murner-Leviathan monster breathes "ignis, sumus, & sulphur"—fire, smoke, and sulphur. The good friar, Luther, holds the Bible in his hands, and is represented here as a prophet (foretelling the end of the world). The vertical Latin caption declares that the Lord will visit the earth with his sword and kill the Leviathan monster; he will trample underfoot lions and dragons; and the dragon, with a halter around its nostrils, will be dragged away on a hook.

QUESTIONS TO CONSIDER

1. Why did Johannes Cochlaeus condemn Martin Luther? How did he construct a negative image of Luther?
2. Evaluate the visual representations of Luther as a godly man. Which one is more effective?

subordinate the clergy to municipal authority. Luther's message—that each Christian could appeal directly to God for salvation—spoke to townspeople's spiritual needs and social vision. From Wittenberg, the many streams of the reform movement quickly merged and threatened to swamp all before it.

Huldrych Zwingli and John Calvin

Separate reform movements sprang up in Swiss cities. In 1520, just three years after Luther's initial break with Rome, the chief preacher of Zurich, Huldrych Zwingli (1484–1531), openly declared himself a reformer. Like Luther, Zwingli attacked corruption in the Catholic church hierarchy, and he also questioned fasting and clerical celibacy. Under Zwingli's leadership, Zurich served as the center for the Swiss and southern German reform movement. Luther and Zwingli did not agree on all points of doctrine. Luther insisted that Christ was both truly and symbolically present in the Eucharist, the central Christian sacrament that Christians partook of in communion; Zwingli, however, viewed the Eucharistic bread and wine as symbols of Christ's union with believers.

In 1529, troubled by these differences and other disagreements, Evangelical princes and magistrates assembled the major reformers in the Colloquy of Marburg, in central Germany. After several days of intense discussions, the reformers managed to resolve some differences over doctrine, but Luther and Zwingli failed to agree on the meaning of the Eucharist. The issue of the Eucharist would soon divide Lutherans and Calvinists as well.

Under the leadership of **John Calvin** (1509–1564), another wave of reform pounded at the gates of Rome. Born in Picardy, in northern France, Calvin studied in Paris and Orléans, where he took a law degree. A gifted intellectual attracted to humanism, Calvin could have enjoyed a brilliant career in government or the church. Instead, experiencing a crisis of faith, like Luther, he sought salvation through intense theological study. Calvin

read the works of the leading French humanists who sought to reform the church from within, and he also examined Luther's writings. Gradually, he came to question fundamental Catholic teachings.

On Sunday, October 18, 1534, Parisians found church doors posted with ribald broadsheets denouncing the Catholic Mass. Smuggled into France from the Protestant and French-speaking parts of Switzerland, the broadsheets provoked a wave of royal repression in the capital. In response to this so-called Affair of the Placards, the government arrested hundreds of French Protestants, executed some of them, and forced many more, including Calvin, to flee abroad.

On his way to Strasbourg, a haven for religious dissidents, Calvin detoured to Geneva—the French-speaking Swiss city-state where he would find his life's work. Genevans had renounced their allegiance to the Catholic bishop, and local supporters of reform begged Calvin to stay and labor there. Although it took some time for Calvin to solidify his position in the city, his supporters eventually triumphed and he remained in Geneva until his death in 1564.

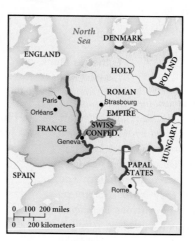

Calvin's World in the Mid-Sixteenth Century

Under Calvin's leadership, Geneva became a Christian republic on the model set out in his *Institutes of the Christian Religion*, first published in 1536. No reformer prior to Calvin had expounded on the doctrines, organization, history, and practices of Christianity in such a systematic, logical, and coherent manner. Calvin followed Luther's doctrine of salvation to its ultimate logical conclusion: if God is almighty and humans cannot earn their salvation by good works, then no Christian can be certain of salvation. Developing the doctrine of **predestination**, Calvin argued that God had ordained every man, woman, and child to salvation or damnation—even before the creation of the world. Thus, in Calvin's theology, God saved only the "elect"; he knew their identity eternally.

Predestination could terrify, but it could also embolden. A righteous life might be a sign of a person's having been chosen for salvation. Thus, Calvinist doctrine demanded rigorous discipline. The knowledge that only the elect, a small group,

---

John Calvin: French-born Christian humanist (1509–1564) and founder of Calvinism, one of the major branches of the Protestant Reformation; he led the reform movement in Geneva, Switzerland, from 1541 to 1564.

---

predestination: John Calvin's doctrine that God preordained salvation or damnation for each person before creation; those chosen for salvation were considered the "elect."

Ordinances for Calvinist Churches (1547)

The Calvinist churches, like others during the Protestant Reformation, emphasized the need for stricter moral regulation of individual behavior. These ordinances placed on churches in Geneva and surrounding areas show how all aspects of behavior, including popular entertainments, were subject to scrutiny.

Concerning the Times of Assembling at Church

That the temples be closed for the rest of the time [outside the time of services], in order that no one shall enter therein out of hours, impelled thereto by superstition; and if anyone be found engaged in any special act of devotion therein or nearby he shall be admonished for it: if it be found to be of a superstitious nature for which simple correction is inadequate then he shall be chastised.

Blasphemy.

Whoever shall have blasphemed, swearing by the body or by the blood of our Lord, or in similar manner, he shall be made to kiss the earth for the first offence; for the second to pay 5 sous, and for the third 6 sous, and for the last offence be put in the pillory for one hour.

Drunkenness.

1. That no one shall invite another to drink under penalty of 3 sous.
2. That taverns shall be closed during the sermon, under penalty that the tavern-keeper shall pay 3 sous, and whoever may be found therein shall pay the same amount.
3. If anyone be found intoxicated he shall pay for the first offence 3 sous and shall be remanded to the consistory [church council or governing body]; for the second offence he shall be held to pay the sum of 6 sous, and for the third 10 sous and be put in prison.
4. That no one shall make roiaumes [popular festivals] under penalty of 10 sous.

Songs and Dances.

If anyone sings immoral, dissolute or outrageous songs, or dance the virollet or other dance, he shall be put in prison for three days and then sent to the consistory.

Usury.

That no one shall take upon interest or profit more than five per cent., upon penalty of confiscation of the principal and of being condemned to make restitution as the case may demand.

Games.

That no one shall play at any dissolute game or at any game whatsoever it may be, neither for gold nor silver nor for any excessive stake [i.e., gambling], upon penalty of 5 sous and forfeiture of stake played for.

Source: George L. Burns, ed., in *Translations and Reprints from the Original Sources of European History*, 6 vols. (Philadelphia: University of Pennsylvania History Department, 1898–1912), vol. 1, 2–5.

would be saved should guide the actions of the godly in an uncertain world. Fusing church and society into what followers named the Reformed church, Geneva became a theocratic city-state dominated by Calvin and the elders of the Reformed church. Its people were rigorously monitored; detractors said that they were bullied. (See Document, "Ordinances for Calvinist Churches," above.)

Calvin tolerated no dissent. While passing through Geneva in 1553, the Spanish physician Michael Servetus was arrested because he had published books attacking Calvin and questioning the doctrine of the Trinity, the belief that there are three persons in one God — the Father, the Son (Christ), and the Holy Spirit. Upon Calvin's advice, the authorities executed Servetus. Despite the outcry over this action, Geneva became the new center of the Reformation, the place where pastors trained for missionary work and where books about Calvinist doctrines were produced and exported all over Europe. The Calvinist movement spread to France, the Low Countries, England, Scotland, the German states, Poland, Hungary, and eventually New England, becoming the established form of the Reformation in many of these countries.

The Anglican Church in England

England followed its own path, with reform led by the king rather than by men trained as Catholic clergy. Despite a tradition of religious dissent that went back to John Wycliffe, Protestantism gained few English adherents in the 1520s. King **Henry VIII** (r. 1509–1547) changed that when he broke

---

Henry VIII: The English king (r. 1509–1547) who first opposed the Protestant Reformation and then broke with the Catholic church, naming himself head of the Anglican church in the Act of Supremacy of 1534.

THE PROGRESS OF THE REFORMATION

1517	Martin Luther disseminates ninety-five theses attacking the sale of indulgences and other church practices
1520	Reformer Huldrych Zwingli breaks with Rome
1525	Peasants' War in German states divides reform movement
1529	Lutheran German princes protest the condemnation of religious reform by Charles V
1534	The Act of Supremacy establishes King Henry VIII as head of the Anglican church, severing ties to Rome
1534–1535	Anabaptists take over the German city of Münster in a failed experiment to create a holy community
1541	John Calvin establishes himself permanently in Geneva, making that city a model of Christian reform and discipline

with the Roman Catholic church for reasons that were both personal and political. The resulting Anglican church retained many aspects of Catholic worship but nonetheless aligned itself in the Protestant camp.

At first, Henry opposed the Reformation, even receiving the title Defender of the Faith from Pope Leo X for a treatise Henry wrote against Luther. A robust, ambitious, and well-educated man, Henry wanted to make his mark on history and, with the aid of his chancellors Cardinal Thomas Wolsey and Thomas More, he vigorously suppressed Protestantism and executed its leaders. But by 1527, the king wanted to divorce his wife, Catherine of Aragon (d. 1536), the daughter of Ferdinand and Isabella of Spain and the aunt of Charles V. The eighteen-year marriage had produced a daughter, Mary (known as Mary Tudor), but Henry desperately needed a male heir to consolidate the rule of the still-new Tudor dynasty. Moreover, he had fallen in love with Anne Boleyn, a lady at court and a strong supporter of the Reformation. Henry claimed that his marriage to Catherine had never been valid because she was the widow of his older brother, Arthur. Arthur and Catherine's marriage, which apparently was never consummated, had been annulled by Pope Julius II to allow the marriage between Henry and Catherine to take place. Now Henry asked the reigning pope, Clement VII, to declare his marriage to Catherine invalid.

Around "the king's great matter" unfolded a struggle for political and religious control. When Henry failed to secure papal approval of his divorce, he chose two Protestants as his new loyal servants: Thomas Cromwell (1485–1540) as chan-

cellor and Thomas Cranmer (1489–1556) as archbishop of Canterbury. Under their leadership, the English Parliament passed a number of acts that severed ties between the English church and Rome. The most important of these, the Act of Supremacy of 1534, made Henry the head of the Anglican church (the Church of England). Other legislation invalidated the claims of Mary, his daughter with Catherine, to the throne, recognized his marriage to Anne Boleyn, and allowed the English crown to embark on the dissolution of the monasteries. In an effort to consolidate support behind his version of the Reformation, Henry sold off monastic lands to the local gentry and aristocracy. Henry thus missed a golden opportunity to make the English crown as rich as its French counterpart by adding those lands to its own holdings.

By 1536, Henry had grown tired of Anne Boleyn, who had given birth to a daughter, the future Queen Elizabeth I, but had produced no sons. He ordered Anne beheaded on the charge of adultery, an act that he defined as treason. The king would go on to marry four other wives but father only one son, Edward. Thomas More had also been executed for treason, in 1535, and Cromwell suffered the same fate in 1540 after he lost the king's favor. When Henry died in 1547, the principle of royal supremacy in religious matters was firmly established, but much would now depend on who held the crown.

REVIEW: How did Luther, Zwingli, Calvin, and Henry VIII challenge the Roman Catholic church?

Reshaping Society through Religion

The religious upheavals of the sixteenth century affected European society in two contradictory ways: first, the reformers and their followers challenged political authority and the social order, and second, in reaction to the more extreme manifestations of the first, they underlined the need for discipline in worship and social behavior. Peasant rebels and radical Protestants known as Anabaptists wanted to push the Reformation in a more populist direction. They took the phrase "priesthood of all believers" quite literally and sided with the poor and the downtrodden. Like Catholics, Protestant authorities then became alarmed by the subversive potential of religious reforms. They viewed the Reformation not as a political and social movement, but as a way of instilling greater discipline in individual worship and church organization. Bible reading became a potent tool in the creation of this new, internally motivated person. At the same time, the Roman Catholic church undertook reforms of its own and launched an offensive against the Protestant Reformation, sometimes called the Counter-Reformation.

Protestant Challenges to the Social Order

When Luther described the freedom of the Christian, he meant an entirely spiritual freedom. But others interpreted his call for freedom in social and political terms. During the 1520s and 1530s, two movements emerged in the Holy Roman Empire to demand more far-reaching changes. In 1525, peasants and urban artisans rose up against the Catholic church and landed nobility and armed themselves to pursue their goals. Anabaptists experimented with new social and political doctrines. Some rejected violence, but one Anabaptist group tried to create a perfect Christian community in the German town of Münster. The results were disastrous.

The Peasants' War of 1525. The Catholic church was the largest landowner in the Holy Roman Empire: about one-seventh of the empire's territory consisted of ecclesiastical principalities in which bishops and abbots exercised both secular and churchly power. Luther's anticlerical message struck home with peasants who paid taxes to both their lord and the Catholic church. In the spring of 1525, many peasants in southern and central Germany, joined by urban workers, rose in rebellion (Map 14.3). In Thuringia (central/eastern Germany), the rebels followed an ex-priest, Thomas Müntzer (1468?–1525), who promised to chastise the wicked and thus clear the way for the Last Judgment.

The Peasants' War split the reform movement. Princes and city officials, ultimately supported by Luther, turned against the rebels. Catholic and Protestant princes joined hands to crush Müntzer and his supporters. All over the empire, princes

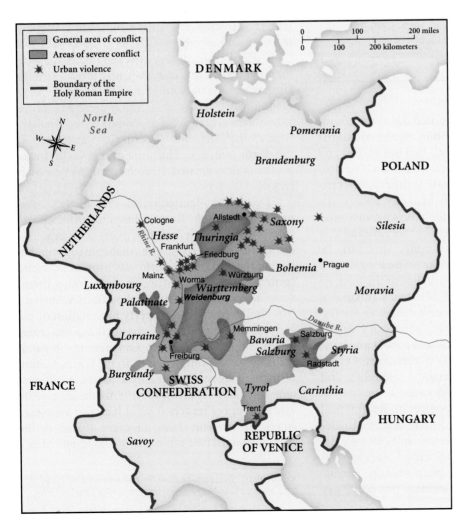

MAP 14.3 The Peasants' War of 1525
The centers of uprisings clustered in southern and central Germany, where the density of cities encouraged the spread of discontent and allowed for alliances between urban masses and rural rebels. The proximity to the Swiss Confederation, a stronghold of the Reformation movement, also inspired antiestablishment uprisings.

German Peasants' War of 1525
This colored woodcut depicts peasants attacking the
pope, a monk, and a nobleman during the massive
rural uprisings against the church that took place in
southern and central Germany in 1525. Even the
heavens show signs of trouble: a comet and clouds
in the shape of a goat signify bloodshed and sin.
(The Granger Collection, New York.)

trounced peasant armies, hunted down their leaders, and uprooted all opposition. By the end of the
year, more than 100,000 rebels had been killed and
many others maimed, imprisoned, or exiled. Initially, Luther had tried to mediate the conflict, criticizing the princes for their brutality toward the
peasants but also warning the rebels against mixing religion and social protest. Luther believed that
God ordained rulers, who must therefore be
obeyed even if they were tyrants. The kingdom of
God belonged not to this world but to the next, he
insisted. Luther considered Müntzer's mixing of
religion and politics the greatest danger to the Reformation, nothing less than "the devil's work."
When the rebels ignored Luther's appeal and continued to follow more radical preachers, Luther
called on the princes to slaughter the rebels and
restore the divinely ordained social order.

Fundamentally conservative in its political
philosophy, the Lutheran church henceforth depended on established political authority for its
protection. It lost supporters in rural areas and became an increasingly urban phenomenon. The ultimate victors were the German princes. They

defeated the peasants, sided with Luther, and confronted the Holy Roman Emperor, Charles V, who
declared Roman Catholicism the empire's only legitimate religion. The fragmentation of the Holy
Roman Empire only increased as people came to
support their Protestant princes against Charles's
Catholic orthodoxy.

Anabaptists.   While Zwingli challenged the Roman Catholic church in public, some laypeople in
Zurich secretly pursued their own path to reform.
Taking their cue from the New Testament's descriptions of the first Christian community, these
men and women believed that true faith came only
to those with reason and free will. How could a
baby knowingly choose Christ? Only adults could
believe and accept baptism; hence, the **Anabaptists**
(literally, "rebaptizers") rejected the validity of infant baptism and called for adult rebaptism. Many
were pacifists who also refused to acknowledge the
authority of law courts and considered themselves
a community of true Christians unblemished by
sin. The Anabaptist movement drew its leadership
primarily from the artisan class and its members
from the middle and lower classes—men and
women attracted by a simple but radical message
of peace and salvation.

Zwingli immediately attacked the Anabaptists
for their refusal to bear arms and swear oaths of
allegiance, sensing accurately that they were repu-
diating his theocratic (church-directed) order.
When persuasion failed to convince the Anabaptists, Zwingli urged Zurich magistrates to impose
the death sentence. Thus, the evangelical reformers themselves created the Reformation's first martyrs of conscience.

Despite condemnation in 1529 of the movement by the Holy Roman Emperor, Anabaptism
spread rapidly from Zurich to many cities in southern Germany. In 1534, one Anabaptist group, believing the end of the world was imminent, seized
control of the city of Münster. Proclaiming themselves a community of saints, the Münster Anabaptists abolished private property in imitation of the
early Christians and dissolved traditional marriages, allowing men, like Old Testament patriarchs, to have multiple wives, to the consternation
of many women. Besieged by a combined Protestant and Catholic army, the city fell in June 1535.
The Anabaptist leaders died in battle or were executed, their bodies hung in cages affixed to the
church tower. Their punishment was intended as a

Anabaptists: Sixteenth-century Protestants who believed that
only adults could truly have faith and accept baptism.

warning to all who might want to take the Reformation away from the Protestant authorities and hand it to the people. The Anabaptist movement in northwestern Europe nonetheless survived under the determined pacifist leadership of the Dutch reformer Menno Simons (1469–1561), whose followers were eventually named Mennonites.

New Forms of Discipline

Faced with the social firestorms ignited by religious reform, the middle-class urbanites who supported the Protestant Reformation urged greater religious conformity and stricter moral behavior. To gain more control over religious ferment, Protestant rulers and clergy encouraged Bible reading and a new work ethic. Ordinary men and women who learned how to behave as virtuous Christians at home and in Sunday worship applied what they learned in their households and their businesses. Protestants did not have monasteries or convents or saints' lives to set examples; they sought moral examples in their own homes, in the sermons of their preachers, and in their own reading of the Bible. The new emphasis on self-discipline led to growing impatience with the poor, now viewed as lacking personal virtue, and greater emphasis on regulation of marriage, now seen as critical to social discipline in general. Although some of these attitudes had medieval roots, the Protestant Reformation fostered their spread and Catholics soon began to embrace them.

Reading the Bible.   The only Bible authorized by the Catholic church was the Latin Bible, or Vulgate, even though it contained errors of translation from the Greek and Hebrew. In 1522, Martin Luther translated Erasmus's Greek New Testament into German, the first full vernacular translation in that language. A new Bible-centered culture began to take root, as more than 200,000 copies of Luther's New Testament were printed over twelve years, an immense number for the time. In 1534, Luther completed a translation of the Old Testament. Peppered with witty phrases and colloquial expressions, Luther's Bible was a treasure chest of the German language.

Found for the most part in urban and literate households, the German Bible occupied a central place in a family's history. Generations handed down valuable editions, and pious citizens often bound Bibles with family papers or other reading material. Bible reading became a common pastime undertaken in solitude or in family and church gatherings. To counter Protestant success, Catholic German Bibles soon appeared, thus sanctioning Bible reading by the Catholic laity, a sharp departure from medieval church practice. In the same year that Luther's German New Testament appeared in print, the French humanist Jacques Lefèvre d'Étaples (c. 1455–1536) translated the Vulgate (Latin) New Testament into French.

Catholic authorities did not always welcome translations, however. Sensing a potentially dangerous association between the vernacular Bible and heresy, England's Catholic church hierarchy had reacted swiftly against English-language Bibles. When William Tyndale (1495–1536) translated the Bible into English, he was burned at the stake as a heretic. After Henry VIII's break with Rome and adoption of the Reformation, in contrast, his government promoted an English Bible based on Tyndale's translation.

Public Relief for the Poor.   In the early sixteenth century, secular governments began to take over institutions of public charity from the church. This development, which took place in both Catholic and Protestant Europe, grew out of two trends: a new upsurge in poverty brought about by population growth and spiraling inflation, and the rise of a work ethic that included growing hostility toward the poor.

By 1500, the cycle of demographic collapse and economic depression triggered by the Black Death of 1346–1353 had passed. Between 1500 and 1560, rapid economic and population growth created prosperity for some and stress—caused or heightened by increased inflation—for many. Wanderers and urban beggars were by no means novel, but the reaction to poverty was. Sixteenth-century moralists decried the crime and sloth of vagabonds. Rejecting the notion that the poor played a central role in the Christian idea of salvation and that charity and prayers united rich and poor, these moralists distinguished between the genuine poor, or "God's poor," and vagabonds; they insisted that the latter, who were able-bodied, should be forced to work.

The Reformation provided an opportunity to restructure relief for the poor. Instead of decentralized, private initiatives often overseen by religious orders, Protestant magistrates appointed officials to head urban agencies that would certify the genuine poor and distribute welfare funds to them. This development progressed rapidly in urban areas, where poverty was most visible, and transcended religious divisions. During the 1520s, cities in the Low Countries, Italy, and Spain passed ordinances that prohibited begging and instituted public charity. In 1526, the Spanish humanist Juan Luis Vives, a Catholic, wrote *On the Support of the Poor*, a Latin treatise urging authorities to establish public poor relief; the work was soon translated into French, Italian, German, and English. National laws followed. In 1531, Henry VIII asked justices of the peace (unpaid local magistrates) to license the poor in England and to differentiate between those who could work and those who could not. In 1540, Charles V imposed a welfare tax in Spain to augment that country's inadequate system of private charity. In Spain, however, the religious orders continued to dominate the system of almsgiving.

Reforming Marriage. In their effort to establish order and discipline, Protestant reformers denounced sexual immorality and glorified the family. The early Protestant reformers like Luther championed the end of clerical celibacy and embraced marriage. Luther, once a celibate priest himself, married a former nun. The idealized patriarchal family provided protection against the forces of disorder and a place where reform values could be inculcated. Protestant magistrates established marital courts, passed new marriage laws, closed brothels, and inflicted harsher punishments for sexual deviance.

Prior to the Reformation, despite the legislation of church councils, marriages had largely been private affairs between families; some couples never even registered with the church. The Catholic church recognized any promise made between two consenting adults (with the legal age of twelve for females, fourteen for males) in the presence of two witnesses as a valid marriage. Many couples simply lived together as common-law husband and wife. Young men sometimes promised marriage in a passionate moment, only to renege later. The overwhelming number of cases in Catholic church courts involved young women seeking to enforce promises after they had exchanged their personal honor — that is, their virginity — for the greater honor of marriage.

The Reformation proved more effective than the late medieval church in suppressing common-law marriages. Protestant governments asserted greater official control over marriage, and Catholic governments followed suit. A marriage was legitimate only if registered by both a government official and a member of the clergy. In many Protestant countries, the new marriage ordinances also required parental consent, thus giving householders immense power in regulating not only marriage but also the transmission of family property.

In the fervor of the early Reformation years, the first generation of Protestant women attained greater marital equality than those of subsequent generations. Katharina Zell, wife of the reformer Matthew Zell, defended her equality by citing a Bible verse when a critic used St. Paul to support his argument that women should remain silent in church. Katharina retorted, "I would remind you of the word of this same apostle that in Christ there is no male nor female." Katharina helped feed and clothe the thousands of refugees who flooded Strasbourg after their defeat in the Peasants' War. In 1534, she published a collection of hymns. Outraged by the intolerance of a new breed of Protestant clergy, she reprimanded a prominent Lutheran pastor for his persecution of dissenters: "You young fellows tread on the graves of the first fathers of this church in Strasbourg and punish all who disagree with you, but faith cannot be forced."

Catholic Renewal

Like a slumbering giant finally awakened, the Catholic church decided in the 1540s to undertake drastic action to fend off the Protestant threat. Pope Paul III convened a general council of the

The Disciplined Home
Proper table manners reflected discipline and morality in the godly household, an ideal of the religious reformers of the sixteenth century. The householder, the father patriarch, leads his wife and children in prayer before a meal. The orderly behavior parallels the comfort (oven, smoked glass windows, chandeliers, timber ceiling, and cabinets) of a well-off patrician family. *(Staatsbibliothek Bamberg, Germany.)*

church in 1545 at Trent, a town on the border between the Holy Roman Empire and Italy. Meeting sporadically over nearly twenty years (1545–1563), the **Council of Trent** effectively set the course of Catholicism until the 1960s. Catholic leaders sought a renewal of religious devotion and spirituality as well as a clarification of church doctrine. New religious orders set out to win converts overseas or to reconvert Catholics who had turned to Protestantism. Catholic clergy emphasized the pageantry of ritual and the decoration of churches in order to counter the austerity of Protestant worship. At the same time, the church did not hesitate to root out dissent by giving greater powers to the Inquisition, including the power to censor books. The papal Index, or list of prohibited books, was established in 1557 and not abolished until 1966.

The Council of Trent. Italian and Spanish clergy predominated among the 255 bishops, archbishops, and cardinals attending the Council of Trent. Though its deliberations were interrupted first by an outbreak of the plague and then by warfare, the council came up with a remarkably wide-ranging series of decisions. It condemned the central doctrines of Protestantism. Salvation depended on faith and good works, not faith alone. On the sacrament of the Eucharist, the council reaffirmed that the bread of communion "really, truly" becomes Christ's body—a rejection of all Protestant positions on this issue so emphatic as to preclude compromise. It reasserted the supremacy of clerical authority over the laity; the church's interpretation of the Bible could not be challenged, and the Vulgate was the only authoritative version. The council rejected divorce, permitted by Protestants, and reaffirmed the legitimacy of indulgences. It also called for reform from within, however, insisting that bishops henceforth reside in their dioceses and decreeing that seminaries for the training of priests be established in every diocese.

The Council of Trent marked a watershed; henceforth, the schism between Protestant and Catholic remained permanent, and all hopes of reconciliation faded. The focus of the Catholic church turned now to rolling back the tide of dissent.

New Religious Orders. The energy of the Catholic renewal expressed itself most vigorously in the founding of new religious orders. Several were founded in early-sixteenth-century Italy and reflected an intense religious revival in the Italian cities from the 1490s to the 1520s. The most important of these, the Society of Jesus, or **Jesuits**, was established by a Spanish nobleman, Ignatius of Loyola (1491–1556). Inspired by tales of chivalric romances and the national glory of the *reconquista*, Ignatius eagerly sought to prove himself as a soldier. In 1521, while defending a Spanish border fortress against French attack, he sustained a severe injury. During his convalescence, Ignatius read lives of the saints; once he recovered, he abandoned his quest for military glory in favor of serving the church.

Attracted by his activist piety, young men gravitated to this charismatic figure. Thanks to a cardinal's intercession, Ignatius gained a hearing before the pope, and in 1540 the church recognized his small band. With Ignatius as its first general, the Jesuits became the most vigorous defenders of papal authority. The society quickly expanded; by the time of Ignatius's death in 1556, Europe had one thousand Jesuits. They established hundreds of colleges throughout the Catholic world, educating future generations of Catholic leaders. Jesuit missionaries played a key role in the global Portuguese maritime empire and brought Roman Catholicism to Africans, Asians, and native Americans. Together with other new religious orders, the Jesuits restored the confidence of the faithful in the dedication and power of the Catholic church. They also acquired a reputation for bringing controversy in their wake and for being drawn to power as counselors to powerful nobles and kings.

Missionary Zeal. To win new souls, Catholic missionaries set sail throughout the globe. They saw their effort as proof of the truth of Roman Catholicism and the success of their missions as a sign of divine favor, both particularly important in the face of Protestant challenge. But the missionary zeal of Catholics brought conflicting messages to indigenous peoples: for some, the message of a repressive and coercive alien religion; for others, a sweet sign of reason and faith. Frustrated in his efforts to convert Brazilian Indians, a Jesuit missionary wrote to his superior in Rome in 1563 that "for this kind of people it is better to be preaching with the sword and rod of iron."

To ensure rapid Christianization, European missionaries focused initially on winning over local elites. The recommendation of a Spanish royal

---

Council of Trent: A general council of the Catholic church that met at Trent between 1545 and 1563 to set Catholic doctrine, reform church practices, and defend the church against the Protestant challenge.

Jesuits: Members of the Society of Jesus, a Catholic religious order founded by Ignatius of Loyola (1491–1556) and approved by the pope in 1540. Jesuits served as missionaries and educators all over the world.

official in Mexico City was typical. He wrote to the crown in 1525:

> In order that the sons of caciques [chiefs] and native lords may be instructed in the faith, Your Majesty must command that a college be founded wherein they may be taught . . . to the end that they may be ordained priests. For he who shall become such among them, will be of greater profit in attracting others to the faith than will fifty [European] Christians.

Nevertheless, this recommendation was not adopted and the Catholic clergy in Spanish America remained overwhelmingly European.

After an initial period of relatively little racial discrimination, the Catholic church in the Americas and Africa adopted strict rules based on color. For example, the first Mexican Ecclesiastical Provincial Council in 1555 declared that holy orders were not to be conferred on Indians, mestizos (people of mixed European-Indian parentage), or mulattoes (people of mixed European-African heritage); along with descendants of Muslims, Jews, and persons who had been sentenced by the Spanish Inquisition, these groups were deemed "inherently unworthy of the sacerdotal [priestly] office." Europeans' sense of racial superiority led them to perceive native Americans' and Africans' resistance to domination as "treachery."

In East Asia, as in the Americas, Christian missionaries under Portuguese protection concentrated their efforts on the elites, preaching the Gospel to Confucian scholar-officials in China and to the samurai (the warrior aristocracy) in Japan. However, European missionaries in Asia greatly admired Chinese and Japanese civilization and thus used the sermon rather than the sword to win converts (see the illustration on this page). The Jesuit Francis Xavier preached in India and Japan, his work greatly assisted by a network of Portuguese trading stations. He died in 1552, awaiting permission to travel to China. A pioneer missionary in Asia, Xavier had prepared the ground for future missionary successes in Japan and China. The efforts of the Catholic missionaries seemed highly successful: vast multitudes of native Americans had become nominal Christians by the second half of the sixteenth century, and thirty years after Francis Xavier's 1549 landing in Japan, the Jesuits could claim more than 100,000 Japanese converts.

REVIEW: How did the forces for radical change unleashed by the Protestant Reformation interact with the urge for social order and stability?

The Portuguese in Japan
In this sixteenth-century Japanese black-lacquer screen painting of Portuguese missionaries, the Jesuits are dressed in black and the Franciscans in brown. At the lower right corner is a Portuguese nobleman depicted with exaggerated "Western" features. The Japanese considered themselves lighter in skin color than the Portuguese, whom they classified as "barbarians." In turn, the Portuguese classified Japanese (and Chinese) as "whites." The perception of ethnic differences in the sixteenth century, however, depended less on skin color than on clothing, eating habits, and other cultural signals. Color classifications were unstable and changed over time: by the late seventeenth century, Europeans no longer regarded Asians as "whites."
(Laurie Platt Winfrey, Inc.)

A Struggle for Mastery

In the sixteenth century, conflicts generated by the Reformation posed new challenges to the ambitions of rulers. Even as courts continued to sponsor the arts and literature of the Renaissance, princes and kings seized opportunities to build stronger states by fighting wars. Wars justified increased taxes, and growing revenues fostered the creation of a central bureaucracy housed at court. Victory on the battlefield translated into territory and just as important into reputation and awe. But victory required skills in making war; monarchs eagerly sought new military technology and battlefield ploys. One major obstacle complicated these efforts at state building: religious division. Could states maintain their authority if individuals were allowed to choose their religion? Almost everywhere, violence failed to settle religious differences. By 1560, an exhausted Europe had achieved a provisional peace, but one fraught with the seeds of future conflict.

The High Renaissance Court

At the center of art patronage, dynastic competition, and religious division lay the court, the focus of princely power and intrigue and the agent of state building. Kings, princes, and popes alike used their courts to keep an eye on their leading courtiers (cardinals in the case of popes) and impress their other subjects. Briefly defined, the court was the ruler's household. Around the prince gathered a community of household servants, noble attendants, councilors, officials, artists, and soldiers. Renaissance culture had been promoted by this political elite, and that culture now entered its "high" or most sophisticated phase. Its acclaimed representative was Michelangelo Buonarroti (1475–1564), an immensely talented Italian artist who sculpted a gigantic nude statue (see right) for officials in Florence and then painted the ceiling of the Sistine Chapel for the recently elected Pope Julius II.

Italian artists also flocked to the French court of Francis I (r. 1515–1547), which swelled to the largest in Europe. In addition to the king's own household, the queen and the queen mother each had her own staff of maids and chefs, as did each of the royal chil-

dren. The royal household employed officials to handle finances and provide guard duty, clothing, and food; in addition, physicians, librarians, musicians, dwarfs, animal trainers, and a multitude of hangers-on bloated its size. By 1535, the French court numbered 1,622 members. Although Francis built a magnificent Renaissance palace at Fontainebleau, where he hired Italian artists to produce paintings and sculpture, the French court often moved from palace to palace. It took no fewer than eighteen thousand horses to transport the people, furniture, and documents—not to mention the dogs and falcons for the royal hunt. Hunting was no mere diversion; it represented a form of mock combat, essential in the training of a military elite. Francis himself loved war games and almost lost his own life when, storming a house during one mock battle, he was hit on the head by a burning log.

Two Italian writers helped define the new culture of courtesy, or proper court behavior, that developed in such a setting: Ludovico Ariosto (1474–1533), in service at the Este court in Ferrara, and Baldassare Castiglione (1478–1529), a servant of the duke of Urbino and the pope. Considered one of the greatest Renaissance poets,

Michelangelo's *David*
Michelangelo combined the classical nude statue with the biblical figure of David in this larger-than-life sculpture showing the young man preparing for action against the giant Goliath. Originally commissioned by church officials in Florence, the statue ended up standing in front of city hall as a commemoration of the recapture of the city-state's freedom. Michelangelo's intentions are not easy to decipher. David's slingshot is barely visible on his left shoulder, and his easy slouch seems incongruous for a coming battle. An earlier drawing by Michelangelo showed David standing on the head of the defeated Goliath, a much more common depiction. What do you deduce from this portrayal?
(Nimatallah/Art Resource, NY.)

Ariosto composed a long epic poem, *Orlando Furioso*, which represented court culture as the highest synthesis of Christian and classical values. The poem's tales of combat, valor, love, and magic captivated the court's noble readers. In *The Courtier*, Castiglione represented court culture as a synthesis of military virtues and literary and artistic cultivation. His characters debate the qualities of an ideal courtier in a series of eloquent dialogues. The true courtier, Castiglione asserts, is a gentleman who speaks in a refined language and carries himself with nobility and dignity in the service of his prince and his lady.

Princes faced greater challenges than did their courtiers, and courtesy was not always their most cherished virtue. The greatest writer on politics of the age, Niccolò Machiavelli (1469–1527), underlined the need for pragmatic, even cold calculation in his controversial essay *The Prince*. Was it better, he asked, for a prince to be feared by his people or loved?

> It may be answered that one should wish to be both, but, because it is difficult to unite them in one person, is much safer to be feared than loved. . . . Because this is to be asserted in general of men, that they are ungrateful, fickle, false, cowardly, covetous, and as long as you succeed they are yours entirely; they will offer you their blood, property, life and children . . . when the need is far distant; but when it approaches they turn against you.

Machiavelli insisted that princes could benefit their subjects only by maintaining a firm grip on power, if necessary through deceit and manipulation. *Machiavellian* has remained ever since a term for using cunning and duplicity to achieve one's ends.

Dynastic Wars

Even as the Renaissance developed in the princely courts and the Reformation took hold in the German states, the Habsburgs (the ruling family in Spain and then the Holy Roman Empire) and the Valois (the ruling family in France) fought each other for domination of Europe (Map 14.4). French claims provoked the Italian Wars in 1494, which soon escalated into a general conflict that involved most Christian monarchs and the Muslim Ottoman sultan as well. From 1494 to 1559, the Valois and Habsburg dynasties, both Catholic, remained implacable enemies. The fighting raged in Italy and the Low Countries. During the 1520s,

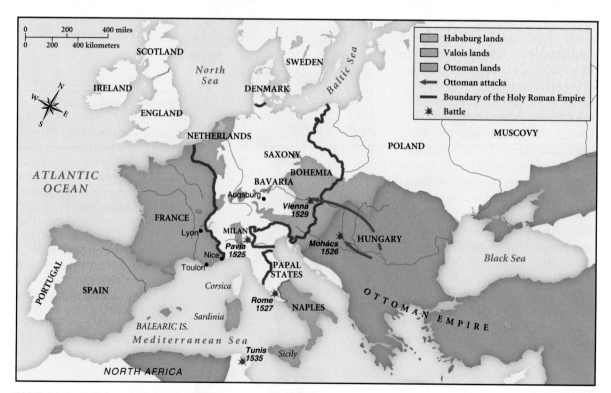

MAP 14.4 Habsburg-Valois-Ottoman Wars, 1494–1559
As the dominant European power, the Habsburg dynasty fought on two fronts: a religious war against the Islamic Ottoman Empire and a political war against the French Valois, who challenged Habsburg hegemony. The Mediterranean, the Balkans, and the Low Countries all became theaters of war.

Charles V and Francis I Make Peace
This fresco from the Palazzo Farnese in the town of Caprarola north of Rome shows French king Francis I and Holy Roman Emperor Charles V agreeing to the Truce of Nice in 1538, one of many peace agreements made and then broken during the wars between the Habsburgs and the Valois. Pope Paul III, who negotiated the truce, stands behind and between them. Charles is on the right pointing to Francis. The truce is the one celebrated in the Tlaxcala pageant described at the start of this chapter. *(The Art Archive/Palazzo Farnese Caprarola/Dagli Orti.)*

the Habsburgs enjoyed the upper hand. In 1525, the troops of Charles V crushed the French army at Pavia, Italy, counting among their captives the French king himself, Francis I. Forced to renounce all claims to Italian territory to gain his freedom, Francis furiously repudiated the treaty the moment he reached France, reigniting the conflict.

In 1527, Charles's troops captured and sacked Rome because the pope had allied with the French. Many of the imperial troops were German Protestant mercenaries, who pillaged Catholic churches and brutalized the Catholic clergy. Protestants and Catholics alike interpreted the sack of Rome by imperial forces as a punishment of God; even the Catholic church read it as a sign that reform was necessary. Finally, in 1559, the French gave up their claims in Italy and signed the Treaty of Cateau-Cambrésis, ending the conflict. As was common in such situations, marriage sealed the peace between rival dynasties; the French king Henry II married his sister to the duke of Savoy, an ally of the Habsburgs, and his daughter to the Habsburg king of Spain, Philip II.

The dynastic struggle (Valois versus Habsburg ruling family) had drawn in many other belligerents, who fought on one side or the other for their own benefit. Some acted purely out of power considerations, such as England, first siding with the Valois and then with the Habsburgs. Others fought for their independence, such as the papacy and the Italian states, which did not want any one power to dominate Italy. Still others chose sides for religious reasons, such as the Protestant princes in Germany, who exploited the Valois-Habsburg conflict to extract religious concessions from the emperor in 1555. The Ottoman Turks saw in this fight an opportunity to expand their territory.

The Ottoman Empire reached its height of power under Sultan Suleiman I, known as **Suleiman the Magnificent** (r. 1520–1566). In 1526, a Turkish expedition destroyed the Hungarian army at Mohács (see the illustration on page 443). Three years later, the Ottomans laid siege to Vienna; though unsuccessful, the attack sent shock waves throughout Christian Europe. In 1535, Charles V led a campaign to capture Tunis, the lair of North African pirates loyal to the Ottomans. Desperate to overcome Charles's superior Habsburg forces, the French king Francis I forged an alliance with the Turkish sultan. Coming to the aid of the French, the Turkish fleet besieged the Habsburg troops holding Nice, on the southern coast of France. Francis even ordered all inhabitants of nearby Toulon to vacate the town so that he could turn it into a Muslim colony for eight months, complete with a mosque and slave market. The French alliance with the Turks scandalized many Christians, but it reflected the spirit of the times:

Suleiman the Magnificent: Sultan of the Ottoman Empire (r. 1520–1566) at the time of its greatest power.

The Siege of Vienna, 1529
This illustration from an Ottoman manuscript of 1588 depicts the Turkish siege of Vienna (the siege guns can be seen in the center of the picture). Sultan Suleiman I (Suleiman the Magnificent) led an army of more than 100,000 men against Vienna, capital of the Austrian Habsburg lands. Several attacks on the city failed, and the Ottomans withdrew in October 1529. They maintained control over Hungary, but the logistics of moving so many men and horses kept them from advancing any farther westward into Europe. *(The Art Archive/Topkapi Museum Istanbul/Dagli Orti.)*

the age-old idea of the Christian crusade against Islam now had to compete with a new political strategy that considered religion only one factor among many in power politics. Religion could be sacrificed, if need be, on the altar of state building.

Constantly distracted by the challenges of the Ottomans to the east and the German Protestants at home, Charles V could not crush the French with one swift blow. Years of conflict drained the treasuries of all rulers, because warfare was becoming more expensive. The formula that war raises revenues that in turn build governments could devolve into an absurdity if wars could not be won. The race for battlefield superiority was on.

Financing War

The sixteenth century marked the beginning of superior Western military technology. All armies grew in size and their firepower became ever more deadly, increasing the cost of war. Heavier artillery pieces meant that the rectangular walls of medieval cities had to be transformed into fortresses with jutting ramparts and gun emplacements. Royal revenues could not keep up with war expenditures. To pay their bills, governments routinely devalued their coinage (the sixteenth-century equivalent of printing more paper money), causing prices to rise rapidly.

Charles V boasted the largest army in Europe, but like everyone else he sank into debt. Between 1520 and 1532, Charles borrowed 5.4 million ducats, primarily to pay his troops; from 1552 to 1556, his war loans soared to 9.6 million ducats. On his death in 1547, Francis I owed the bankers of Lyon almost 7 million French pounds — approximately the entire royal income for that year. The European powers literally fought themselves into bankruptcy. Taxation, the sale of offices, and outright confiscation failed to bring in enough money to satisfy the war machine. Both the Habsburg and the Valois kings looked to the leading bankers to finance their costly wars.

Foremost among these financiers was the Fugger bank, the largest such enterprise in sixteenth-century Europe. Based in the southern German imperial city of Augsburg, the Fugger family and their associates built an international financial empire that helped to make kings. The enterprise began with Jakob Fugger (1459–1525), who became personal banker to Charles V's grandfather Maximilian I. Constantly short of cash, Maximilian granted the Fugger family numerous mining and minting concessions. To pay for the service of providing and accepting bills of exchange, the Fuggers charged substantial fees and made handsome profits. By the end of his life, Maximilian was so deeply in debt to Jakob Fugger that he had to pawn the royal jewels.

In 1519, Fugger assembled a consortium of German and Italian bankers to secure the election of Charles V as Holy Roman Emperor. For the next three decades, the alliance between Europe's biggest international bank and its largest empire remained very close. Between 1527 and 1547, the Fugger bank's assets more than doubled; more than half came from loans to the Habsburgs. Charles stayed barely one step ahead of his creditors, and his successor in Spain gradually lost control of the Spanish state finances. Debt forced the Valois and the Habsburgs to sign the Treaty of Cateau-Cambrésis in 1559, ending more than sixty years of warfare, but the cycle of financial crises and warfare continued until the late eighteenth century.

Divided Realms

All European rulers viewed religious division as a dangerous challenge to the unity and stability of their rule. Subjects who considered their rulers heretics or blasphemers could only cause trouble, as the Peasants' War of 1525 had amply demonstrated. Moreover, religious differences encouraged the formation of competing noble factions, which easily led to violence when weak monarchs or children ruled.

France.   King Francis I tolerated Protestants until the Affair of the Placards in 1534. Even then, the government did not try to root out Protestantism, and the Reformed (Calvinist) church grew steadily. During the 1540s and 1550s, many French noble families—including some of the most powerful—converted to Calvinism and afforded the Protestants a measure of protection, es-

pecially in southern and western France. Francis and his successor, Henry II (r. 1547–1559), succeeded in maintaining a balance of power between Catholics and Calvinists, but after Henry's death the weakened monarchy could no longer hold together the fragile realm. The real drama of the Reformation in France took place after 1560, when the country plunged into four decades of religious wars, whose savagery was unparalleled elsewhere in Europe.

England and Scotland.   Religious divisions at the very top threatened the control of the English and Scottish rulers. Before his death in 1547, Henry VIII had succeeded in making England officially Protestant, but would they remain Protestants and if so, what kind of Protestants would his subjects become? Each of his children offered answers to that question, and the answers could not have been more contradictory. The advisers of the boy king Edward VI (r. 1547–1553) furthered the Reformation by welcoming prominent religious refugees from the continent. The refugees had been deeply influenced by Calvinism and wanted to see England move in that austere direction. But Edward died at age fifteen, opening the way to his Catholic half-sister, Mary Tudor, who had been restored to the line of succession by an act of Parliament under Henry VIII in 1544.

When Mary (r. 1553–1558) came to the throne, she restored Catholicism and persecuted Protestants. Nearly three hundred Protestants perished at the stake, and more than eight hundred fled to the Protestant German states and Switzerland. Finally, when Anne Boleyn's daughter, Elizabeth, succeeded her half-sister Mary, becoming Queen Elizabeth I (r. 1558–1603), the English Protestant cause again gained momentum. Under Elizabeth's leadership, Anglicanism eventually defined the character of the English nation. Catholics were tolerated only if they kept their opinions on religion and politics to themselves. A tentative but nonetheless real peace returned to England.

Still another pattern of religious politics unfolded in Scotland, where powerful noble clans directly challenged royal power. Protestants formed a small minority in Scotland until the 1550s. The most prominent Scottish reformer, John Knox (1514–1572), spent many of his early years in exile in England and on the continent because of his devout Calvinism. At the center of Scotland's conflict over religion stood Mary of Guise, a native French woman and Catholic married to the king of Scotland, James V. After he died in 1542, she surrounded herself and her daughter Mary Stuart, also a Catholic and heir to the throne, with French advisers. When Mary Stuart married Francis, the son of Henry II and the heir to the French throne, in 1558 many Scottish noblemen, alienated by this pro-French atmosphere, joined the pro-English, anti-French Protestant cause.

John Knox helped bring matters to a head when he published in 1558 a diatribe against both Mary Tudor of England and Mary of Guise. The era's suspicion of female rulers and regents also played a part in the work, *The First Blast of the Trumpet against the Monstrous Regiment [Rule] of Women*. In 1560, Protestant nobles gained control of the Scottish Parliament and dethroned the regent Mary of Guise. Eventually they forced her daughter, Mary, by then known as queen of Scots, to flee to England, and installed Mary's infant son James as king. Scotland would turn toward the Calvinist version of the Reformation and thus establish the potential for conflict with England and its Anglican church.

The German States. In the German states, the Protestant princes and cities formed the Schmalkaldic League in 1531. Headed by the elector of Saxony and Philip of Hesse (the two leading Protestant princes), the league included most of the imperial cities, the chief source of the empire's wealth. Opposing the league were Emperor Charles V, the bishops, and the few remaining Catholic princes. Although Charles had to concentrate on fighting the French and the Turks during the 1530s, he eventually secured the western Mediterranean and then turned his attention back home to central Europe to try to resolve the growing religious differences in his lands.

In 1541, Charles convened an Imperial Diet at Regensburg in an effort to mediate between Protestants and Catholics, only to see negotiations between the two sides rapidly break down. Rather than accept a permanent religious schism, Charles prepared to fight the Protestant Schmalkaldic League. To this end, he secured French neutrality in 1544 and papal support in 1545. War broke out in 1547, the year after Martin Luther's death. Using seasoned Spanish veterans and German allies, Charles occupied the German imperial cities in the south, restoring Catholic elites and suppressing the Reformation. In 1547, he defeated the Schmalkaldic League's armies at Mühlberg and captured the leading Lutheran princes. Jubilant, Charles restored Catholics' right to worship in Protestant lands while permitting Lutherans to keep their own rites. Protestant resistance to the declaration was deep and widespread: many pas-

tors went into exile, and riots broke out in many cities.

For Charles V, the reaction of his former allies proved far more alarming than Protestant resistance. His success frightened some Catholic powers. With Spanish troops controlling Milan and Naples, Pope Julius III (r. 1550–1555) feared that papal authority would be subjugated by imperial might. In the Holy Roman Empire, Protestant princes spoke out against "imperial tyranny." Jealously defending their traditional liberties against an overmighty emperor, the Protestant princes, led by Duke Maurice of Saxony, a former ally, raised another army to fight Charles. The princes declared war in 1552 and chased a surprised, unprepared, and practically bankrupt emperor back to Italy.

Forced to compromise, Charles V agreed to the **Peace of Augsburg** in 1555. The settlement recognized the Lutheran church in the empire; accepted the secularization of church lands but "reserved" the remaining ecclesiastical territories (mainly the bishoprics) for Catholics; and, most important, established the principle that all princes, whether Catholic or Lutheran, enjoyed the sole right to determine the religion of their lands and subjects. Significantly, Calvinist, Anabaptist, and other dissenting groups were excluded from the settlement. Ironically, the religious revolt of the common people had culminated in a princes' reformation. As the constitutional framework for the Holy Roman Empire, the Augsburg settlement preserved a fragile peace in central Europe until 1618, but the exclusion of Calvinists would prompt future conflict.

Exhausted by decades of war and disappointed by the disunity in Christian Europe, Emperor Charles V resigned his many thrones in 1555 and 1556, leaving his Netherlandish-Burgundian and Spanish dominions to his son, Philip II, and his Austrian lands to his brother, Ferdinand (who was also elected Holy Roman Emperor to succeed Charles). Retiring to a monastery in southern Spain, the most powerful of the Christian monarchs spent his last years quietly seeking salvation.

REVIEW: How did religious divisions complicate the efforts of rulers to maintain political stability and build stronger states?

Peace of Augsburg: The treaty of 1555 that settled disputes between Holy Roman Emperor Charles V and his Protestant princes. It recognized the Lutheran church and established the principle that all Catholic or Lutheran princes enjoyed the sole right to determine the religion of their lands and subjects.

Conclusion

Europe became a global power while at the same time undergoing a searing internal religious upheaval that permanently divided Christians. Even as Portuguese and Spanish explorers claimed new lands and Catholic missionaries gathered new souls for the church from Mexico to Japan, Luther, Calvin, and a host of others formed competing branches of Protestants in Europe. Lutherans, Calvinists, and Anglicans disagreed on many points of doctrine and church organization, but they all broke definitively from the Roman Catholic church. Protestant laypeople and priests established new Christian communities with new forms of ritual, new doctrines, new social prac-

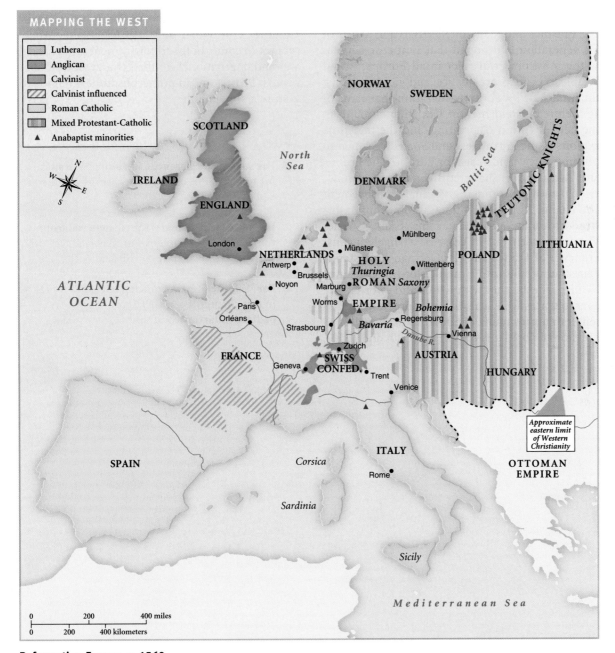

MAPPING THE WEST

Legend:
- Lutheran
- Anglican
- Calvinist
- Calvinist influenced
- Roman Catholic
- Mixed Protestant-Catholic
- ▲ Anabaptist minorities

Reformation Europe, c. 1560
The fortunes of Roman Catholicism were at their lowest point around 1560. Northern Germany and Scandinavia owed allegiance to the Lutheran church; England broke away under a national church headed by its monarchs; and the Calvinist Reformation would extend across large areas of western, central, and eastern Europe. Southern Europe remained solidly Catholic.

tices, and clergy with vastly different powers and personal lives from those of the Roman Catholic clergy. Catholic priests could not marry; Protestant clergymen could. Catholic clergymen said Mass and heard confessions; Protestant clergy preached the word of God and left confession and penance to the individual sinner, a matter between God and the human heart. Central to the Protestant cause was the belief that people are saved by faith alone; no amount of good works will bring salvation.

Erasmus and many intellectuals and artists of his generation had hoped that Emperor Charles V, the most powerful ruler in all Europe, would be able to bring peace, justice, and victory against the infidel Turks. For the generation that came of age before the Reformation, Christian humanism, the new invention of printing, and the maritime exploits of the Portuguese and Spanish seemed to promise a new golden age for Europe. The Protestant Reformation shattered their dream of powerful princes encouraging gradual improvement and change from within the Catholic church. Instead of leading a crusade against Islam, Charles V wore himself out in ceaseless struggle against Francis I of France and the German Protestants. Christianity split into a number of hostile camps battling one another with words and swords. The consequences were censorship, repression of dissenters, and, for many, death. After the brutal suppression of popular revolts in the 1520s and 1530s, religious persecution became a Christian institution: Luther called on the princes to kill rebellious peasants in 1525, Zwingli advocated the drowning of Anabaptists, and Calvin supported the death sentence for Michael Servetus. Executions in Catholic lands provided Protestants with a steady stream of martyrs. The two peace settlements in the 1550s failed to provide long-term solutions: the Peace of Augsburg gradually disintegrated as the religious struggles in the empire intensified, and the Treaty of Cateau-Cambrésis provided only a brief respite. Worse was yet to come. In the following generations, civil war and international conflicts would set Catholics against Protestants in numerous futile attempts to restore a single faith.

For Further Exploration

■ **For suggested references, including Web sites, for topics in this chapter,** see page SR-1 at the end of the book.

■ **For additional primary-source material from this period,** see Chapter 14 in *Sources of THE MAKING OF THE WEST*, Third Edition.

■ **For Web sites and documents related to topics in this chapter,** see *Make History* at bedfordstmartins.com/hunt.

CHAPTER REVIEW

KEY TERMS AND PEOPLE

Christopher Columbus (421)

Hernán Cortés (425)

Christian humanism (427)

Martin Luther (429)

Charles V (430)

John Calvin (432)

predestination (432)

Henry VIII (433)

Anabaptists (436)

Council of Trent (439)

Jesuits (439)

Suleiman the Magnificent (443)

Peace of Augsburg (446)

MAKING CONNECTIONS

1. Why was Charles V ultimately unable to prevent religious division in his lands?

2. How did the different religious groups respond to the opportunity presented by the printing press?

> **For practice quizzes, a customized study plan, and other study tools,** see the Online Study Guide at bedfordstmartins.com/hunt.

REVIEW QUESTIONS

1. Which European countries led the way in maritime exploration and what were their motives?

2. How did Luther, Zwingli, Calvin, and Henry VIII challenge the Roman Catholic church?

3. How did the forces for radical change unleashed by the Protestant Reformation interact with the urge for social order and stability?

4. How did religious divisions complicate the efforts of rulers to maintain political stability and build stronger states?

IMPORTANT EVENTS

1492	Columbus reaches the Americas
1494	Italian Wars begin; Treaty of Tordesillas divides Atlantic world between Portugal and Spain
1516	Erasmus publishes Greek edition of the New Testament; More writes *Utopia*
1517	Luther composes ninety-five theses to challenge Catholic church
1520	Luther publishes three treatises; Zwingli breaks from Rome
1525	German Peasants' War
1527	Charles V's imperial troops sack Rome
1529	Colloquy of Marburg assembles to address disagreements between German and Swiss church reformers
1534	Henry VIII breaks with Rome; Affair of the Placards in France
1536	Calvin publishes *Institutes of the Christian Religion*
1540	Jesuits (Society of Jesus) established as new Catholic order
1545–1563	Catholic Council of Trent condemns Protestant beliefs and confirms church doctrine and sacraments
1547	Charles V defeats Protestants at Mühlberg
1555	Peace of Augsburg ends religious wars and recognizes Lutheran church in German states
1559	Treaty of Cateau-Cambrésis ends wars between Habsburg and Valois rulers

Wars of Religion and the Clash of Worldviews
1560–1648

I n May 1618, Protestants in the kingdom of Bohemia furiously protested the Holy Roman Emperor's attempts to curtail their hard-won religious freedoms. Protestants wanted to build new churches; the Catholic emperor wanted to stop them. Tensions boiled over when two Catholic officials tried to dissolve the meetings of Protestants. On May 23, a crowd of angry Protestants surged up the stairs of the royal castle in Prague, trapped the two Catholic deputies, dragged them screaming for mercy to the windows, and hurled them to the pavement below. One of the rebels jeered: "We will see if your [Virgin] Mary can help you!" But because they landed in a dung heap, the Catholic deputies survived. One of the two limped off on his own; the other was carried by his servants to safety. Although no one died, the defenestration (from the French for "window," *la fenêtre*) of Prague touched off the Thirty Years' War (1618–1648), which eventually involved almost every major power in Europe. Before it ended, the fighting had devastated the lands of central Europe and produced permanent changes in European politics and culture.

The Thirty Years' War grew out of the religious conflicts initiated by the Reformation. When Martin Luther began the Protestant Reformation in 1517, few could have predicted that he would be unleashing such dangerous forces, but religious turmoil and warfare followed almost immediately upon Luther's break with the Catholic church. From its establishment in 1555 until the early 1600s, the Peace of Augsburg maintained relative calm in the lands of the Holy Roman Empire by granting each ruler the right to determine the religion of his territory. But in western Europe, religious strife increased dramatically after 1560 as Protestants made inroads in France, the Spanish-ruled Netherlands, and England. All in all, nearly constant warfare marked the century

The Defenestration of Prague, 1618
In this copper-plate engraving by Swiss artist Matthäus Merian (1593–1650), Czech Protestants attack the Catholic deputies sent to disband their meeting. The attackers are about to throw the two Catholics out of the windows of the royal castle (that is, the Catholics are about to suffer "defenestration"). The defenestration touched off the Thirty Years' War. *(Bildarchiv Preussischer Kulturbesitz/Art Resource, NY.)*

between 1560 and 1648. These struggles often began as religious conflicts, but religion was rarely the sole motive; political ambitions, commercial competition, and long-standing rivalries between the leading powers inevitably raised the stakes of conflict.

Although particularly dramatic and deadly, the church-state crisis was only one of a series of upheavals that shaped this era. In the early seventeenth century, a major economic downturn led to food shortages, famine, and disease in much of Europe. These catastrophes hit especially hard in the central European lands devastated by the fighting of the Thirty Years' War and helped shift the balance of economic power to northwestern Europe, away from the Mediterranean and central Europe. The deepening sense of crisis prompted some to seek new, nonreligious grounds for all forms of authority, whether artistic, political, or philosophical. The emergence of a secular worldview that relied on new scientific methods of research would ultimately reshape Western attitudes over the long term.

> **Focus Question:** What were the long-term political, economic, and intellectual consequences of the conflicts over religious belief?

Religious Conflicts Threaten State Power, 1560–1618

The Peace of Augsburg made Lutheranism a legal religion in the predominantly Catholic Holy Roman Empire, but it did not extend recognition to Calvinists. Although the followers of Martin Luther (Lutherans) and those of John Calvin (Calvinists) similarly refused the authority of the Catholic church, they disagreed with each other about religious doctrine and church organization. The rapid expansion of Calvinism after 1560 threatened to alter the religious balance of power in much of Europe. Calvinists challenged Catholic dominance in France, the Spanish-ruled Netherlands, Scotland, and Poland-Lithuania. In England, they sought to influence the new Protestant monarch, Elizabeth I. Calvinists were not the only source of religious contention, however. Philip II of Spain fought the Muslim Ottoman Turks in the Mediterranean and expelled the remnants of the Muslim population in Spain. To the east, the Russian tsar Ivan IV fought to make Muscovy the center of an empire based on Russian Orthodox Christianity.

French Wars of Religion, 1562–1598

Calvinism spread in France after 1555, when the Genevan Company of Pastors sent missionaries supplied with false passports and often disguised as merchants. The Calvinist pastors moved rapidly among their growing flock, which gathered in secret in towns near Paris or in the south. Calvinist nobles provided military protection to local congregations and helped set up a national organization for the French Calvinist — or Huguenot — church. In 1562, rival Huguenot and Catholic armies began fighting a series of wars that threatened to tear the French nation into shreds (Map 15.1).

Religious Division in the Nobility. Armed struggle erupted because the French kings could not keep a lid on religious conflict. By the end of the 1560s, nearly one-third of the nobles had joined the Huguenots, and they could raise their own armies. Conversion to Calvinism in French noble families often began with the noblewomen, some of whom sought intellectual independence as well as spiritual renewal in the new faith. Charlotte de

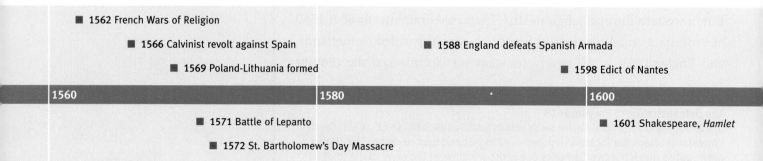

■ 1562 French Wars of Religion

■ 1566 Calvinist revolt against Spain

■ 1569 Poland-Lithuania formed

■ 1588 England defeats Spanish Armada

■ 1598 Edict of Nantes

1560	1580		1600

■ 1571 Battle of Lepanto

■ 1601 Shakespeare, *Hamlet*

■ 1572 St. Bartholomew's Day Massacre

Bourbon, for example, fled from a Catholic convent and eventually married William of Orange, the leader of the anti-Spanish resistance in the Netherlands. Calvinist noblewomen protected pastors, provided money and advice, and helped found schools and establish relief for the poor.

A series of family tragedies prevented the French kings from acting decisively to prevent the spread of Calvinism. King Henry II was accidentally killed during a jousting tournament in 1559 and his fifteen-year-old son, Francis, died soon after. Ten-year-old Charles IX (r. 1560–1574) became king, with his mother, **Catherine de Médicis**, as regent, or acting ruler. An ambassador commented on the weakness of Catherine's hold: "It is sufficient to say that she is a woman, a foreigner, and a Florentine to boot, born of a simple house, altogether beneath the dignity of the Kingdom of France." The Huguenots followed the lead of the Bourbon family, who were close relatives of the French king and stood first in line to inherit the throne if the Valois kings failed to produce a male heir. The most militantly Catholic nobles took their cues from the Guise family, who aimed to block Bourbon ambitions. Catherine tried to play the Bourbon and Guise factions against each other, but civil war erupted in 1562. Both sides committed terrible atrocities. Priests and pastors were murdered, and massacres of whole congregations became frighteningly commonplace.

Catherine de Médicis: Italian-born mother of French king Charles X; she served as regent and tried but failed to prevent religious warfare between Calvinists and Catholics.

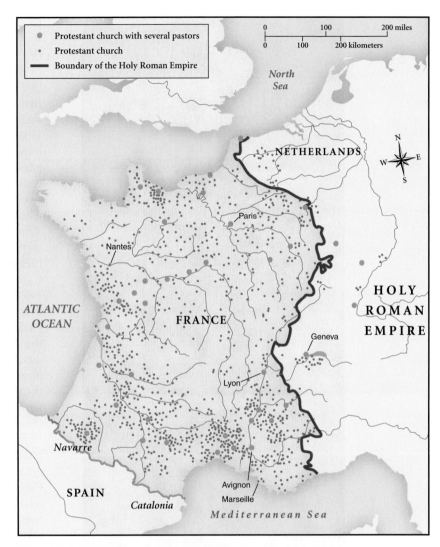

MAP 15.1 Protestant Churches in France, 1562
Calvinist missionaries took their message from their headquarters in Geneva across the border into France. The strongest concentration of Protestants was in southern France. The Bourbons, leaders of the Protestants in France, had their family lands in Navarre, a region in southwestern France that had been divided between France and Spain.

■ 1618 Thirty Years' War　　　■ 1635 French declare war on Spain

　　　　　　　　　　　　　　　　　　　　　　■ 1648 Peace of Westphalia

1620　　　　　　　　　**1640**　　　　　　　　　**1660**

　　■ 1625 Grotius, *The Laws of War and Peace*

　　　■ 1633 Galileo forced to recant

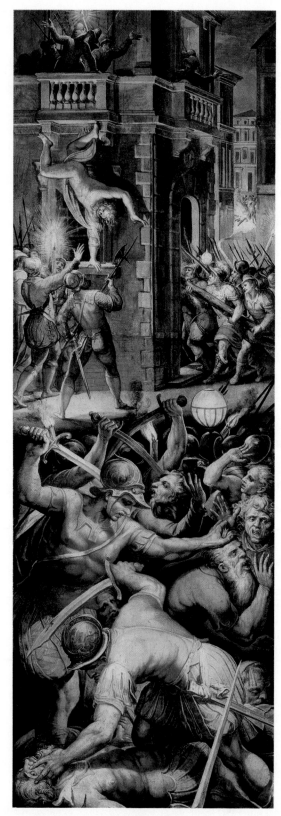

Massacre Motivated by Religion
The Italian artist Giorgio Vasari painted *St. Bartholomew's Night: The Massacre of the Huguenots* for a public room in Pope Gregory XIII's residence. How did the artist celebrate what he saw as a Catholic victory over Protestant heresy? *(Scala/Art Resource, NY.)*

St. Bartholomew's Day Massacre, 1572. Although a Catholic herself, Catherine feared the rise of Guise influence, so she arranged the marriage of the king's Catholic sister, Marguerite de Valois, to Henry of Navarre, a Huguenot and Bourbon. Just four days after the wedding in August 1572, assassins tried but failed to kill one of the Huguenot nobles allied with the Bourbons. Perhaps herself implicated in the botched plot and panicked at the thought of Huguenot revenge, Catherine convinced her son to go on the offensive by ordering the death of Huguenot leaders who had come to Paris for the wedding. Violence almost immediately spiraled out of control. On St. Bartholomew's Day, August 24, a bloodbath began, fueled by years of growing animosity between Catholics and Protestants. (See Massacre Motivated by Religion, at left.) In three days, Catholic mobs murdered three thousand Huguenots in Paris. Wherever Calvinists lacked military protection, they were at risk. Ten thousand Huguenots died in the provinces over the next six weeks. The pope joyfully ordered the church bells rung throughout Catholic Europe; Spain's Philip II wrote Catherine that it was "the best and most cheerful news which at present could come to me."

The massacre settled nothing. Huguenot pamphleteers now proclaimed their right to resist a tyrant who worshiped idols (a practice that Calvinists equated with Catholicism). This right of resistance was linked to a political notion of contract; upholding the true religion was part of the contract imagined as binding the ruler to his subjects. Both the right of resistance and the idea of a contract fed into the larger doctrine of constitutionalism—that a government's legitimacy rested on its upholding a constitution or contract between ruler and ruled. Constitutionalism was used to justify resistance movements from the sixteenth century onward. Protestants and Catholics alike now saw the religious conflict as an international struggle for survival that required aid to their fellow Catholics or Protestants in other countries. In this way, the French Wars of Religion paved the way for wider international conflicts over religion in the decades to come.

Henry IV and the Edict of Nantes. The religious division in France grew even more dangerous when Charles IX died and his brother Henry III (r. 1574–1589) became king. Like his brothers before him, Henry III failed to produce an heir. Next in line to the throne was none other than the Protestant Bourbon leader Henry of Navarre, a distant cousin of the Valois ruling family and brother-in-law of Charles and Henry. Convinced that Henry III lacked the will to root out Protestantism, the Guises formed the Catholic League, which requested help from Spanish king Philip II. Henry III responded with a fatal trick: in 1588, he summoned the two Guise leaders to a meeting and had his men kill them. A few months later, a fanatical monk stabbed Henry III to death, and Henry of Navarre became Henry IV (r. 1589–1610), despite Philip II's attempt to block his ascension with military intervention.

Henry IV soon concluded that to establish control over war-weary France he had to place the interests of the French state ahead of his Protestant faith. In 1593, he publicly embraced Catholicism, reputedly explaining his conversion with the statement "Paris is worth a Mass." Within a few years he defeated the ultra-Catholic opposition and drove out the Spanish. In 1598, he made peace with Spain and issued the **Edict of Nantes**, in which he granted the Huguenots a large measure of religious toleration. The approximately 1.25 million Huguenots became a legally protected minority within an officially Catholic kingdom of some 20 million people. Protestants were free to worship in specified towns and were allowed their own troops, fortresses, and even courts. Few believed in religious toleration, but Henry IV followed the advice of those moderate Catholics and Calvinists called *politiques* who urged him to give priority to the development of a durable state. Although their opponents hated them for their compromising spirit, the politiques believed that religious disputes could be resolved only in the peace provided by strong government.

The Edict of Nantes ended the French Wars of Religion, but Henry still needed to reestablish monarchical authority and hold the fractious nobles in check. He used court festivities and royal processions to rally subjects around him, and he allowed rich merchants and lawyers to buy offices and, in exchange for an annual payment, pass their positions on to their heirs to sell them to someone else. This new social elite was known as the "nobility of the robe" (named after the robes that magistrates wore, much like those judges wear today). Income raised by the increased sale of offices reduced the state debt and also helped Henry strengthen the monarchy. His efforts did not, however, prevent his enemies from assassinating him in 1610 after nineteen unsuccessful attempts.

Challenges to Spain's Authority

Although he failed to prevent Henry IV from taking the French throne in 1589, Philip II of Spain (r. 1556–1598) was the most powerful ruler in Europe (Map 15.2). In addition to the western Habsburg lands in Spain and the Netherlands, Philip had inherited from his father, Charles V, all the Spanish colonies recently settled in the New World of the Americas. Gold and silver funneled from the colonies supported his campaigns against the Ottoman Turks and the French and the English Protestants. But all of the money of the New World could not prevent Philip's eventual defeat in the Netherlands, where Calvinist rebels established an independent Dutch Republic that soon vied with Spain, France, and England for commercial supremacy.

Philip II, the Catholic King. A deeply devout Catholic, **Philip II** came to the Spanish throne at age twenty-eight determined to restore Catholic unity in Europe and lead the Christian defense against the Muslims. In his quest, Philip benefited from a series of misfortunes. His four wives all died, but through them he became part of four royal families: Portuguese, English, French, and Austrian. His brief marriage to Mary Tudor (Mary I of England) did not produce an heir, but it and his subsequent marriage to Elisabeth de Valois, the sister of Charles IX and Henry III of France, gave him reason enough for involvement in English and French affairs. In 1580, when the king of Portugal died without a direct heir, Philip took over this neighboring realm with its rich empire in Africa, India, and the Americas.

Philip insisted on Catholic unity in his own possessions and worked to forge an international Catholic alliance against the Ottoman Turks. In 1571, he achieved the single greatest military victory of his reign when he joined with Venice and the papacy to defeat the Turks in a great sea battle off the Greek coast at **Lepanto**. Fifty thousand sailors and soldiers fought on the allied side, and eight thousand died. Spain now controlled the western Mediterranean. But Philip could not rest on his laurels. Between 1568 and 1570, the Moriscos—Muslim converts to Christianity who

---

Edict of Nantes: The decree issued by French king Henry IV in 1598 that granted the Huguenots a large measure of religious toleration.

politiques (poh lih TEEK): Political advisers during the sixteenth-century French Wars of Religion who argued that compromise in matters of religion would strengthen the monarchy.

Philip II: King of Spain (r. 1556–1598) and the most powerful ruler in Europe; he reigned over the western Habsburg lands and all the Spanish colonies recently settled in the New World.

Lepanto: A site off the Greek coast where, in 1571, the allied Catholic forces of Spain's king Philip II, Venice, and the papacy defeated the Ottoman Turks in a great sea battle; the victory gave the Christian powers control of the Mediterranean.

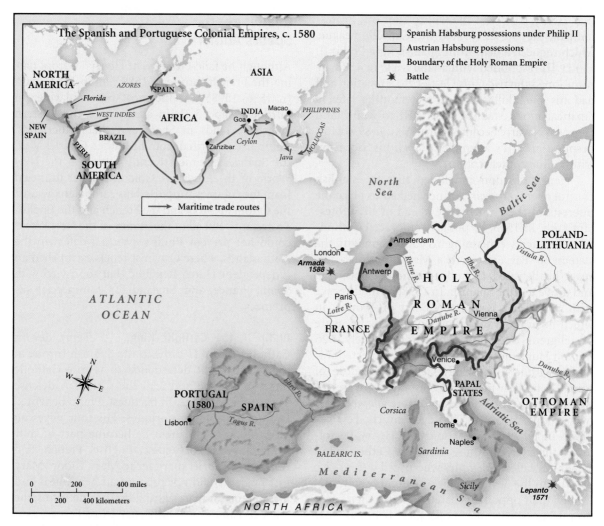

MAP 15.2 The Empire of Philip II, r. 1556–1598
Spanish king Philip II drew revenues from a truly worldwide empire. In 1580, he was
the richest European ruler, but the demands of governing and defending his control of
such far-flung territories eventually drained many of his resources.

remained secretly faithful to Islam — had revolted
in the south of Spain, killing ninety priests and fifteen hundred Christians. Philip retaliated by forcing fifty thousand to leave their villages and resettle
in other regions. In 1609, his suc-
cessor, Philip III, ordered their ex-
pulsion from Spanish territory,
and by 1614 some 300,000
Moriscos had been forced to relocate to North Africa.

The Revolt of the Netherlands.
The Calvinists of the Netherlands
were less easily intimidated than
the Moriscos: they were far from
Spain and accustomed to being
left alone. When Calvinists in the
Netherlands attacked Catholic

**The Netherlands during the
Revolt, c. 1580**

churches in 1566, smashing stained-glass windows
and statues of the Virgin Mary, Philip sent an army
to punish the rebels. Calvinist resistance continued despite this occupation, and in November

1576 Philip's long-unpaid armies
sacked Antwerp, then Europe's
wealthiest commercial city. In
eleven days of horror known as
the Spanish Fury, the Spanish
soldiers slaughtered seven thousand people. Led by Prince
William of Orange (whose name
came from the lands he owned in
southern France), the Netherlands' seven Protestant northern
provinces formally allied with the
ten Catholic southern provinces
and drove out the Spaniards. The

Philip II of Spain
The king of Spain is shown here (kneeling in black) with his allies at the battle of Lepanto, the doge of Venice on his left and Pope Pius V on his right. El Greco painted this canvas, sometimes called *The Dream of Philip II*, in 1578 or 1579. The painting is typically mannerist in the way it crowds figures into every available space, uses larger-than-life or elongated bodies, and creates new and often bizarre visual effects. What can we conclude about Philip II's character from the way he is depicted here? *(© The National Gallery, London.)*

southern provinces nonetheless remained Catholic, French-speaking in parts, and suspicious of the increasingly strict Calvinism in the north. In 1579, they returned to the Spanish fold. Despite the assassination in 1584 of William of Orange, Spanish troops never regained control in the north. Spain would not formally recognize Dutch independence until 1648, but by the end of the sixteenth century the Dutch Republic (sometimes called Holland after the most populous of its seven provinces) was a self-governing state sheltering a variety of religious groups.

Religious toleration thrived because the central government did not have the power to enforce religious orthodoxy. Urban merchant and professional families known as regents controlled the towns and provinces. In the absence of a national bureaucracy, a single legal system, or a central court, each province governed itself and sent delegates to the one common institution, the States General, which carried out the wishes of the strongest individual provinces and their ruling families. Although the princes of Orange resembled a ruling family, their powers paled next to those of local elites. One-third of the Dutch population remained Catholic, and local authorities allowed them to worship as they chose in private. The Dutch Republic also had a relatively large Jewish population because many Jews had settled there after being driven out of Spain and Portugal. From 1597, Jews could worship openly in their synagogues. This openness to various religions would help to make the Dutch Republic one of Europe's chief intellectual and scientific centers in the seventeenth and eighteenth centuries.

Well situated for maritime commerce, the Dutch Republic developed a thriving economy based on shipping and shipbuilding. Dutch merchants favored free trade in Europe because they could compete at an advantage. Whereas elites in other countries focused on their landholdings, the Dutch looked for investments in trade. After the Dutch gained independence, Amsterdam became the main European money market for two centuries. The city was also a primary commodities market and a chief supplier of arms—to allies, neutrals, and even enemies. Dutch entrepreneurs produced goods at lower prices than competitors and marketed them more efficiently. The Dutch controlled many overseas markets thanks to their preeminence in seaborne commerce: by 1670, the Dutch commercial fleet was larger than the English, French, Spanish, Portuguese, and Austrian fleets combined.

Elizabeth I's Defense of English Protestantism

As the Dutch revolt unfolded, Philip II became increasingly infuriated with **Elizabeth I** (r. 1558–1603), who had succeeded her half-sister Mary Tudor as queen of England. Philip had been married to Mary and had enthusiastically seconded Mary's efforts to return England to Catholicism. When Mary died in 1558, Elizabeth rejected Philip's proposal of marriage and promptly brought Protestantism back to England. Eventually, she provided funds and troops to the Dutch Protestant cause. As Elizabeth moved to solidify her personal power and the authority of the Anglican church (Church of England), she had to squash uprisings by Catholics in the north and at least two serious plots against her life. In the long run, however, her greater challenges came from the Calvinist Puritans and Philip II.

Puritanism and the Church of England. The **Puritans** were strict Calvinists who opposed all vestiges of Catholic ritual in the Church of England. After Elizabeth became queen, many Puritans returned from exile abroad, but Elizabeth resisted their demands for drastic changes in church ritual and governance. The Church of England's Thirty-Nine Articles of Religion, issued under her authority in 1563, incorporated elements of Catholic ritual along with Calvinist doctrines. Puritan ministers angrily denounced the Church of England's "popish attire and foolish disguising, . . . tithings, holy days, and a thousand more abominations." To accomplish their reforms, Puritans tried to undercut the crown-appointed bishops' authority by placing control of church administration in the hands of a local presbytery, that is, a group made up of the minister and the elders of the congregation. Elizabeth rejected this Calvinist presbyterianism.

Queen Elizabeth I of England

The Anglican (Church of England) Prayerbook of 1569 included a hand-colored print of Queen Elizabeth saying her prayers. As queen, Elizabeth was also official head of the Church of England—the scepter or sword at her feet symbolizes her power. She named bishops and made final decisions about every aspect of church governance. *(HIP/Art Resource, NY.)*

■ **For more help analyzing this image,** see the visual activity for this chapter in the Online Study Guide at bedfordstmartins.com/hunt.

Elizabeth I: English queen (r. 1558–1603) who oversaw the return of the Protestant Anglican church and, in 1588, the successful defense of the realm against the Spanish Armada.

Puritans: Strict Calvinists who opposed all vestiges of Catholic ritual in the Church of England.

The Puritans nonetheless steadily gained influence. Known for their emphasis on strict moral lives, the Puritans tried to close England's theaters and Sunday fairs. Every Puritan father—with the help of his wife—was to "make his house a little church" by teaching the children to read the Bible. At Puritan urging, a new translation of the Bible, known as the King James Bible after Elizabeth's successor, James I, was authorized in 1604. Believing themselves God's elect—those whom God has chosen for mercy and salvation—and England an "elect nation," the Puritans also pushed Elizabeth to help Protestants on the continent. Elizabeth initially resisted, but after Philip II annexed Portugal and began to interfere in French affairs, she sent funds to the Dutch rebels and in 1585 dispatched seven thousand soldiers to help them.

Triumph over Spain. Although enraged by Elizabeth's aid to the Dutch rebels against his rule, Philip II bided his time as long as Elizabeth remained unmarried and her Catholic cousin Mary Stuart, better known as Mary, Queen of Scots, stood next in line to inherit the English throne. In 1568, Scottish Calvinists forced Mary to abdicate the throne of Scotland in favor of her one-year-old son James (eventually James I of England), who was then raised as a Protestant. After her abdication, Mary spent nearly twenty years under house arrest in England, fomenting plots against Elizabeth. In 1587, when a letter from Mary offering her succession rights to Philip was discovered, Elizabeth overcame her reluctance to execute a fellow monarch and ordered Mary's beheading.

Now determined to act, Philip II sent his armada (Spanish for "fleet") of 130 ships from Lisbon toward the English Channel in May 1588. The English scattered the Spanish Armada by sending blazing fire ships into its midst. A great gale then forced the Spanish to flee around Scotland. When the armada limped home in September, half the ships had been lost and thousands of sailors were dead or starving. Protestants throughout Europe rejoiced. Philip and Catholic Spain suffered a crushing psychological blow. A Spanish monk lamented, "Almost the whole of Spain went into mourning."

Retreat of the Spanish Armada, 1588

By the time Philip II died in 1598, his great empire had begun to lose its luster. The costs of fighting the Dutch, the English, and the French had mounted, and an overburdened peasantry could no longer pay the taxes required to meet rising expenses. In his novel *Don Quixote* (1605), the Spanish writer Miguel de Cervantes captured the disappointment of thwarted imperial ambition. Cervantes himself had been wounded at Lepanto. His novel's hero, a minor nobleman, wants to understand "this thing they call reason of state," but he reads so many romances and books of chivalry that he loses his wits and wanders the countryside hoping to re-create the heroic deeds of times past.

England could never have defeated Spain in a head-to-head battle on land, but Elizabeth made the most of her limited means and consolidated the country's position as a Protestant power. In her early years, she held out the prospect of marriage to many political suitors; but in order to maintain her—and England's—independence, she never married. Her chosen successor, James I (r. 1603–1625), came to the throne as king of both Scotland and England. Shakespeare's tragedies *Hamlet* (1601), *King Lear* (1605), and *Macbeth* (1606), written around the time of James's succession, might all be read as commentaries on the uncertainties faced by Elizabeth and James. But Elizabeth's story, unlike Shakespeare's tragedies, had a happy ending; she left James secure in a kingdom of growing weight in world politics.

The Clash of Faiths and Empires in Eastern Europe

In the east, the most contentious border divided Christian Europe from the Islamic realm of the Ottoman Turks. Even after their defeat at Lepanto in 1571, the Ottomans continued their attacks, seizing Venetian-held Cyprus in 1573. In the Balkans, the Turks allowed their Christian subjects to cling to the Orthodox faith rather than forcibly converting them to Islam. They also tolerated many prosperous Jewish communities, which grew with the influx of Jews expelled from Spain.

The Muscovite tsars officially protected the Russian Orthodox church, which faced no competition within Russian lands. Building on the base laid by his grandfather Ivan III, Tsar Ivan IV (r. 1533–1584) stopped at nothing in his endeavor to make Muscovy the center of a mighty Russian empire. Given to unpredictable fits of rage, Ivan tortured priests, killed numerous *boyars* (nobles), and murdered his own son with an iron rod during a quarrel. His epithet "the Terrible" reflects not only the terror he unleashed but also the awesome impression he evoked. Cunning and cruel, Ivan came to embody barbarism in the eyes of Westerners. One English visitor commented disapprovingly that the Russian government "is very similar to the Turkish, which they apparently try to imitate."

Ivan initiated Russian expansion eastward into Siberia and also tried to gain new territory to the west, when he tried, unsuccessfully, to seize parts of present-day Estonia and Latvia to provide Russia direct access to the Baltic Sea. Two formidable foes blocked Ivan's plans for expansion: Sweden (which then included much of present-day Finland) and Poland-Lithuania. Their rulers hoped to annex the eastern Baltic provinces themselves. Poland and the grand duchy of Lithuania united into a single commonwealth in 1569 and controlled an extensive territory stretching from the Baltic Sea to deep within present-day Ukraine and Belarus. Poland-Lithuania, like the Dutch Republic, was one of the great exceptions to the general trend toward greater monarchical authority; the country's nobles elected their king and placed severe limits on his authority. Noble converts to Lutheranism or Calvinism feared religious persecution by the Catholic majority, so the Polish-Lithuanian nobles insisted that their kings accept the principle of religious toleration as a prerequisite for election.

Russia, Poland-Lithuania, and Sweden in the Late 1500s

Poland-Lithuania threatened the rule of Ivan's successors in Russia. After Ivan IV died in 1584, a terrible period of chaos known as the Time of Troubles ensued, during which the king of Poland-Lithuania tried to put his son on the Russian throne. In 1613, an army of nobles, townspeople, and peasants finally expelled the intruders and put on the throne a nobleman, Michael Romanov (r. 1613–1645), who established an enduring new dynasty. With the return of peace, Muscovite Russia resumed the process of state building.

REVIEW: How did state power depend on religious unity at the end of the sixteenth century and start of the seventeenth?

The Thirty Years' War, 1618–1648

Although the eastern states managed to avoid civil wars over religion in the early seventeenth century, the rest of Europe was drawn into the final and most deadly of the wars of religion, the Thirty Years' War. It began in 1618 with conflicts between Catholics and Protestants within the Holy Roman Empire and eventually involved most European states. By its end in 1648, many central European lands lay in ruins and the balance of power had shifted away from the Habsburg powers—Spain and Austria—toward France, England, and the Dutch Republic. Prolonged warfare created turmoil and suffering, but it also fostered the growth of armies and bureaucracies; out of the carnage would emerge centralized and powerful states that made increasing demands on ordinary people.

Origins and Course of the War

The fighting that devastated central Europe had its origins in a combination of religious dispute, ethnic competition, and political weakness. The Austrian Habsburgs officially ruled over the huge Holy Roman Empire, which comprised eight major ethnic groups. The emperor and four of the seven electors who chose him were Catholic; the other three electors were Protestants. The Peace of Augsburg of 1555 (see Chapter 14) was supposed to maintain the balance between Catholics and Lutherans, but it had no mechanism for resolving conflicts; tensions rose as the new Catholic religious order, the Jesuits, won many Lutheran cities back to Catholicism and as Calvinism, unrecognized under the peace, made inroads into Lutheran areas. By 1613, two of the three Protestant electors had become Calvinists.

These conflicts came to a head when the Catholic Habsburg heir Archduke Ferdinand was crowned king of Bohemia in 1617. The Austrian Habsburgs held not only the imperial crown of the Holy Roman Empire but also a collection of separately administered royal crowns, of which Bohemia was one. Once crowned, Ferdinand began to curtail the religious freedom previously granted to Protestants. The Czechs, the largest ethnic group in Bohemia, responded with the so-called defenestration of Prague and promptly established a Protestant assembly to spearhead resistance. A year later, when Ferdinand was elected emperor (as Ferdinand II, r. 1619–1637), the rebellious Bohemians deposed him and chose in his place the young Calvinist Frederick V of the Palatinate

(r. 1616–1623). A quick series of clashes ended in 1620 when the imperial armies defeated the outmanned Czechs at the battle of White Mountain, near Prague. Like the martyrdom of the religious reformer Jan Hus in 1415, White Mountain became an enduring symbol of the Czechs' desire for self-determination. They would not gain their independence until 1918.

White Mountain did not end the war, which soon spread to the German lands of the empire. Private mercenary armies (armies for hire) began to form during the fighting, and the emperor had little control over them. The meteoric rise of one commander, Albrecht von Wallenstein (1583–1634), showed how political ambition could trump religious conviction. A Czech Protestant by birth, Wallenstein offered in 1625 to raise an army for Ferdinand II and soon had in his employ 125,000 soldiers, who occupied and plundered much of Protestant Germany with the emperor's approval.

The Lutheran king of Denmark, Christian IV (r. 1596–1648), responded by invading northern Germany to protect the Protestants and to extend his own influence. Despite Dutch and English encouragement, Christian lacked adequate military support, and Wallenstein's forces defeated him. Emboldened by his general's victories, Ferdinand issued the Edict of Restitution in 1629, which outlawed Calvinism in the empire and reclaimed Catholic church properties confiscated by the Lutherans.

With Protestant interests in serious jeopardy, Gustavus Adolphus (r. 1611–1632) of Sweden marched into Germany in 1630. Declaring his support for the Protestant cause, he also intended to gain control over trade in northern Europe. His highly trained army of some 100,000 soldiers made Sweden, with a population of only one million, the supreme power of northern Europe. Hoping to block Spanish intervention in the war and win influence and perhaps territory in the Holy Roman Empire, the French monarchy's chief minister, Cardinal Richelieu (1585–1642), offered to subsidize the Lutheran Gustavus. This agreement between the Swedish Lutheran and French Catholic powers to fight the Catholic Habsburgs showed that state interests could outweigh all other considerations.

Gustavus defeated the imperial army and occupied the Catholic parts of southern Germany before he was killed at the battle of Lützen in 1632. Once again the tide turned, but this time it swept Wallenstein with it. Because Wallenstein was rumored to be negotiating with Protestant powers, Ferdinand dismissed his general and had him assassinated.

France openly joined the fray in 1635 by declaring war on Spain and soon after forged an alliance with the Calvinist Dutch to aid them in their ongoing struggle for official independence from Spain. Religion took a backseat to dynastic rivalry as the two Catholic powers France and Spain

---

The Violence of the Thirty Years' War
The French artist Jacques Callot produced this engraving of the Thirty Years' War as part of a series called *The Miseries and Misfortunes of War* (1633). It shows the rape, torture, and pillaging inflicted by soldiers on noncombatants they found in their path. *(The Granger Collection, New York.)*

DOCUMENT

The Horrors of the Thirty Years' War

Hans Grimmelshausen experienced the Thirty Years' War firsthand and then wrote about it in his novel The Adventures of a Simpleton *(published in 1669). He had been a Lutheran schoolboy when soldiers from an unidentified army looted his town. Later he served as a musketeer in the Catholic imperial armies and converted to Catholicism. In the novel, he writes from the point of view of a "simpleton," a naive peasant who does not understand what is happening around him as a group of cavalrymen ransack the village.*

What they did not intend to take along they broke and spoiled. Some ran their swords into the hay and straw, as if there hadn't been hogs enough to stick. Some shook the feathers out of beds and put bacon slabs, hams, and other stuff in the tick-ing, as if they might sleep better on these. Others knocked down the hearth and broke the windows, as if announcing an everlasting summer. They flattened out copper and pewter dishes and baled the ruined goods. They burned up bedsteads, tables, chairs, and benches, though there were yards of dry firewood outside the kitchen. Jars and crocks, pots and casseroles all were broken, either because they preferred their meat broiled or because they thought they'd eat only one meal with us. In the barn, the hired girl was handled so roughly that she was unable to walk away, I am ashamed to report. They stretched the hired man out flat on the ground, stuck a wooden wedge in his mouth to keep it open, and emptied a milk bucket full of stinking manure drippings down his throat; they called it a Swedish cocktail. He didn't relish it and made a very wry face. . . . Then they used thumb-screws, which they cleverly made out of their pistols, to torture the peasants, as if they wanted to burn witches. Though he had confessed to nothing as yet, they put one of the captured hayseeds in the bake-oven and lighted a fire in it. They put a rope around someone else's head and tightened it like a tourniquet until blood came out of his mouth, nose, and ears. In short, every soldier had his favorite method of making life miserable for peasants, and every peasant had his own misery.

Source: *The Adventures of Simplicius Simpliccissimus,* 2nd ed. Trans. George Schulz-Behrend (Columbia, S.C.: Camden House, 1993), 6–7.

---

pummeled each other. Advised by his minister Richelieu, who held the high rank of cardinal in the Catholic church, the French king Louis XIII (r. 1610–1643) hoped to profit from the troubles of Spain in the Netherlands and from the conflicts between the Austrian emperor and his Protestant subjects. The Swedes kept up their pressure in Germany, the Dutch attacked the Spanish fleet, and a series of internal revolts shook the cash-strapped Spanish crown. In 1640, peasants in the rich northeastern province of Catalonia rebelled, overrunning Barcelona and killing the viceroy; the Catalans resented government confiscation of their crops and demands that they house and feed soldiers on their way to the French frontier. The Portuguese revolted in 1640 and proclaimed independence like the Dutch. In 1643, the Spanish suffered their first major defeat at French hands. Although the Spanish were forced to concede independence to Portugal (part of Spain only since 1580), they eventually suppressed the Catalan revolt.

France, too, finally faced exhaustion after years of rising taxes and recurrent revolts. Richelieu died in 1642. Louis XIII followed him a few months later and was succeeded by his five-year-old son, Louis XIV. With yet another foreign queen mother—she was the daughter of the Spanish king—serving as regent and an Italian cardinal, Mazarin, providing advice, French politics once again moved into a period of instability, rumor, and crisis. All sides were ready for peace.

The Effects of Constant Fighting

When peace negotiations began in the 1640s, they did not come a moment too soon for the ordinary people of Europe. Some towns had faced up to ten or eleven prolonged sieges during the decades of fighting. Even worse suffering took place in the countryside. Peasants fled their villages, which were often burned down (see Document, "The Horrors of the Thirty Years' War," above). At times, desperate peasants revolted and attacked nearby castles and monasteries. War and intermittent outbreaks of plague cost some German towns one-third or more of their population. One-third of the inhabitants of Bohemia also perished.

Soldiers did not fare all that much better. An Englishman who fought for the Dutch army in 1633 described how he slept on the wet ground, got his boots full of water, and "at peep of day looked like a drowned ratt." Governments increasingly short of funds often failed to pay the troops, and frequent mutinies, looting, and pillaging resulted. Armies attracted all sorts of displaced people

MAP 15.3　The Thirty Years' War and the Peace of Westphalia, 1648
The Thirty Years' War involved many of the major continental European powers. The arrows marking invasion routes show that most of the fighting took place in central Europe in the lands of the Holy Roman Empire. The German states and Bohemia sustained the greatest damage during the fighting. None of the combatants emerged unscathed because even ultimate winners such as Sweden and France depleted their resources of men and money.

desperately in need of provisions. In the last year of the Thirty Years' War, the Imperial-Bavarian Army had 40,000 men entitled to draw rations — and more than 100,000 wives, prostitutes, servants, children, and other camp followers forced to scrounge for their own food.

The Peace of Westphalia, 1648

The comprehensive settlement provided by the **Peace of Westphalia** — named after the German province where negotiations took place — would serve as a model for resolving future conflicts among warring European states. For the first

time, a diplomatic congress convened to address international disputes, and those signing the treaties guaranteed the resulting settlement. A method still in use, the congress was the first to bring *all* parties together, rather than two or three at a time.

The Winners and Losers. France and Sweden gained most from the Peace of Westphalia. Although France and Spain continued fighting until 1659, France acquired parts of Alsace and replaced Spain as the prevailing power on the continent. Baltic conflicts would not be resolved until 1661, but Sweden took several northern territories from the Holy Roman Empire (Map 15.3).

The Habsburgs lost the most. The Spanish Habsburgs recognized Dutch independence after eighty years of war. The Swiss Confederation and the German princes demanded autonomy from the Austrian Habsburg rulers of the Holy Roman

Peace of Westphalia: The settlement (1648) of the Thirty Years' War; it established enduring religious divisions in the Holy Roman Empire by which Lutheranism would dominate in the north, Calvinism in the area of the Rhine River, and Catholicism in the south.

Empire. Each German prince gained the right to establish Lutheranism, Catholicism, or Calvinism in his state, a right denied to Calvinist rulers by the Peace of Augsburg in 1555. The independence ceded to German princes sustained political divisions that would remain until the nineteenth century and prepared the way for the emergence of a new power, the Hohenzollern Elector of Brandenburg, who increased his territories and developed a small but effective standing army. After losing considerable territory in the west, the Austrian Habsburgs turned eastward to concentrate on restoring Catholicism to Bohemia and wresting Hungary from the Turks.

The Peace of Westphalia permanently settled the distributions of the main religions in the Holy Roman Empire: Lutheranism would dominate in the north, Calvinism in the area of the Rhine River, and Catholicism in the south. Most of the territorial changes in Europe remained intact until the nineteenth century. In the future, international warfare would be undertaken for reasons of national security, commercial ambition, or dynastic pride rather than to enforce religious uniformity. As the politiques of the late sixteenth century had hoped, state interests now outweighed motivations of faith in political affairs.

Growth of State Authority. Warfare increased the reach of states: as armies grew to bolster the war effort, governments needed more money and more supervisory officials. The rate of land tax paid by French peasants doubled in the eight years after France joined the war. In addition to raising taxes, governments deliberately depreciated the value of the currency, which often resulted in inflation and soaring prices. Rulers also sold new offices and manipulated the embryonic stock and bond markets. When all else failed, they declared bankruptcy. The Spanish government, for example, did so three times in the first half of the seventeenth century. From Portugal to Muscovy, ordinary people resisted new taxes by forming makeshift armies and battling royal forces. With their colorful banners, unlikely leaders, strange names (the Nu-Pieds, or "Barefooted," in France, for instance), and crude weapons, the rebels usually proved no match for state armies, but they did keep officials worried and troops occupied.

To meet these new demands, monarchs relied on advisers who took on the role of modern prime ministers. Continuity in Swedish affairs, especially after the death of Gustavus Adolphus, largely depended on Axel Oxenstierna, who held office for more than forty years. Louis XIII's chief minister, Cardinal Richelieu, proclaimed the priority of *raison d'état* (reason of state), that is, the state's interest above all else. He silenced Protestants within France because they had become too independent, and he crushed noble and popular resistance to Louis's policies. He set up intendants—delegates from the king's council dispatched to the provinces—to oversee police, army, and financial affairs.

To justify the growth of state authority and the expansion of government bureaucracies, rulers carefully cultivated their royal images. (See The Arts and State Power, at left.) James I of England

The Arts and State Power
King Philip IV of Spain commissioned Diego Velázquez to paint this portrait in 1634–1635. He hung the painting in the new palace, called Buen Retiro, that he built near Madrid in the 1630s. Philip's court at Buen Retiro included formal gardens, artificial ponds, a huge iron bird cage (which led some critics to call the whole thing a chicken coop), a zoo, and a courtyard for bullfights as well as rooms filled with sculptures and paintings. Note that Philip looks completely in control, almost impassive, even though the horse is rearing. In this way the artist emphasizes the king's mastery. *(All rights reserved. © Museo Nacional del Prado—Madrid.)*

raison d'état (ray ZOHN day TAH): French for "reason of state," the political doctrine, first proposed by Cardinal Richelieu of France, which held that the state's interests should prevail over those of religion.

argued that he ruled by divine right and was accountable only to God: "The state of monarchy is the supremest thing on earth; for kings are not only God's lieutenant on earth, but even by God himself they are called gods." He advised his son to maintain a manly appearance (his own well-known homosexual liaisons did not make him seem less manly to his subjects): "Eschew to be effeminate in your clothes, in perfuming, preening, or such like." Appearance counted for so much that most rulers regulated who could wear which kinds of cloth and decoration, reserving the richest and rarest, such as ermine and gold, for themselves.

REVIEW: Why did a war fought over religious differences result in stronger states?

Economic Crisis and Realignment

The devastation caused by the Thirty Years' War deepened an economic crisis that was already under way. After a century of rising prices, caused partly by massive transfers of gold and silver from the New World and partly by population growth, in the early 1600s prices began to level off and even to drop, and in most places population growth slowed. With fewer goods being produced, international trade fell into recession. Agricultural yields also declined, and peasants and townspeople alike were less able to pay the escalating taxes needed to finance the wars. Famine and disease trailed grimly behind economic crisis and war, in some areas causing large-scale uprisings and revolts. Behind the scenes, the economic balance of power gradually shifted as northwestern Europe began to dominate international trade and broke the stranglehold of Spain and Portugal in the New World.

From Growth to Recession

Population grew and prices rose in the second half of the sixteenth century. Even though religious and political turbulence led to population decline in some cities, such as war-torn Antwerp, overall rates of growth remained impressive: in the sixteenth century, parts of Spain doubled in population and England's population grew by 70 percent. The supply of precious metals swelled, too. In the 1540s, new silver mines were discovered in Mexico and Peru. Spanish gold imports peaked in the 1550s,

silver in the 1590s. (See "Taking Measure," below.) This flood of precious metals combined with population growth to fuel an astounding inflation in food prices in western Europe — 400 percent in the sixteenth century — and a more moderate rise in the cost of manufactured goods. Wages rose much more slowly, at about half the rate of the increase in food prices. Governments always overspent revenues, and by 1600 most of Europe's rulers faced deep deficits.

Recession did not strike everywhere at the same time, but the warning signs were unmistakable. Foreign trade slumped as war and an uncertain money supply made business riskier. After 1625, silver imports to Spain declined, in part because so many of the native Americans who worked in Spanish colonial mines died from disease and in part because the mines themselves were progressively depleted. Textile production fell in many countries and in some places nearly

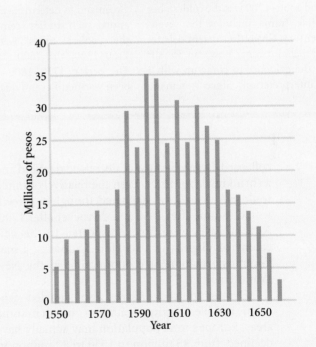

TAKING MEASURE

The Rise and Fall of Silver Imports to Spain, 1550–1660
Gold and silver from the New World enabled the king of Spain to pursue aggressive policies in Europe and around the world. At what point did silver imports reach their highest level? Was the fall in silver imports precipitous or gradual? What can we conclude about the resources available to the Spanish king? *(From Earl J. Hamilton,* American Revolution and the Price Revolution in Spain, 1501–1650 *[Cambridge, MA: Harvard University Press, 1934].)*

Tree Rings and the Little Ice Age

Global cooling helped bring about the economic crisis of the seventeenth century. Glaciers advanced, average temperatures fell, and winters were often exceptionally severe. Canals and rivers essential to markets froze over. Great storms disrupted ocean traffic — in fact, one storm changed the escape route of the Spanish Armada. Even in the valleys far from the mountain glaciers, cooler weather meant lower crop yields, which quickly translated into hunger and greater susceptibility to disease, leading in turn to population decline. Some historians of climate refer to the entire period 1600–1850 as the little ice age because glaciers advanced during this time and retreated only after 1850; others argue that the period 1550–1700 was the coldest, but either time frame includes the seventeenth century. Given the current debates about global warming, how can we sift through the evidence to come up with a reliable interpretation? Since systematic records of European temperatures were kept only from the 1700s onward, how do historians know that the weather was cooler?

Information about climate comes from various sources. The advance of glaciers can be seen in letters complaining to the authorities. In 1601, for example, panic-stricken villagers in Savoy (in the French Alps) wrote, "We are terrified of the glaciers . . . which are moving forward all the time and have just buried two of our villages." Yearly temperature fluctuations can be determined from the dates of wine harvests; growers harvested their grapes earliest when the weather was warmest and latest when it was coolest. Scientists study ice cores taken from Greenland to determine temperature variations; such studies seem to indicate that the coolest times were the periods 1160–1300; the 1600s; and 1820–1850. The period 1730–1800 appears to have been warmer. Recently, scientists have developed techniques for sampling corals in the tropics and sediments on oceanic shelves to provide evidence of climate change.

But the most striking are data gathered from tree rings (the science is called dendrochronology or dendroclimatology). Timber samples have been taken from very old oak trees and also from ancient beams in buildings and archaeological digs and from logs left long undisturbed in northern bogs and riverbeds. In cold summers, trees lay down thinner growth rings; in warm ones, thicker rings. Information about tree rings confirms the conclusions drawn from wine harvest and ice core samples: the seventeenth century was relatively cold. Recent tree ring studies have shown that some of the coldest summers were caused by volcanic eruptions; according to a study of more than one hundred sites in North America and Europe, the five coldest summers in the past four

collapsed, largely because of decreased demand and a shrinking labor force. Even the relatively limited trade in African slaves stagnated, though its growth would resume after 1650 and skyrocket after 1700. African slaves were first transported to the new colony of Virginia in 1619, foreshadowing a major transformation of economic life in the New World colonies.

Demographic slowdown also signaled economic trouble. Despite population growth in some areas, Europe's total population may actually have declined, from 85 million in 1550 to 80 million in 1650. In the Mediterranean, growth had already stopped in the 1570s. The most sudden reversal occurred in central Europe as a result of the Thirty Years' War: one-fourth of the inhabitants of the Holy Roman Empire perished in the 1630s and 1640s. Population growth continued only in England, the Dutch Republic and the Spanish Netherlands, and Scandinavia.

Where the population stagnated or declined, agricultural prices dropped because of less demand, and farmers who produced for the market suffered. The price of grain fell most precipitously, causing many farmers to convert grain-growing land to pasture or vineyards. In some places, peasants abandoned their villages and left land to waste, as had happened during the plague epidemic of the late fourteenth century. The only country that emerged unscathed from this downturn was the Dutch Republic, thanks to a growing population and tradition of agricultural innovation. Inhabiting Europe's most densely populated area, the Dutch developed systems of field drainage, crop rotation, and animal husbandry that provided high yields of grain for both people and animals. Their foreign trade, textile industry, crop production, and population all grew. After the Dutch, the English fared best; unlike the Spanish, the English never depended on infusions of New World gold and silver to shore up their economy, and unlike most continental European countries, England escaped the direct impact of the Thirty Years' War.

The Frozen Thames
This painting by Abraham Hondius of the frozen Thames River in London dates to 1677. In the 1670s and 1680s the Thames froze several times. Diarists recorded that shopkeepers even set up their stalls on the ice. The expected routines of daily life changed during the cooling down of the seventeenth century, and contemporaries were shocked enough by the changes to record them for posterity. *(© Museum of London.)*

hundred years were in 1601, 1641, 1669, 1699, and 1912 (four out of five in the seventeenth century), and all but the summer of 1699 came in years following recorded eruptions.

QUESTIONS TO CONSIDER
1. What were the historical consequences of global cooling in the seventeenth century?
2. Why would trees be especially valuable sources of information about climate?

FURTHER READING
Climate of the Past: **http://www.clim-past .net/recentpapers.html**
Jones, P. D., ed. *History and Climate: Memories of the Future?* 2001.

Historians have long disagreed about the causes of the early-seventeenth-century recession. Some cite the inability of agriculture to support a growing population by the end of the sixteenth century; others blame the Thirty Years' War, the states' demands for more taxes, the irregularities in money supply resulting from rudimentary banking practices, or the waste caused by middle-class expenditures in the desire to emulate the nobility. To this list of causes, recent researchers have added climatic changes. (See "New Sources, New Perspectives," page 466.) Cold winters and wet summers meant bad harvests, and these natural disasters ushered in a host of social catastrophes. When the harvest was bad, prices shot back up and many could not afford to feed themselves.

Consequences for Daily Life

The recession of the early 1600s had both short-term and long-term effects. In the short term, it aggravated the threat of food shortages, increased the outbreaks of famine and disease, and caused people to leave their families and homes. In the long term, it deepened the division between prosperous and poor peasants and fostered the development of a new pattern of late marriages and smaller families.

Famine and Disease. When grain harvests fell short, peasants immediately suffered because, outside of England and the Dutch Republic, grain had replaced more expensive meat as the essential staple of most Europeans' diets. By the end of the sixteenth century, the average adult European ate more than four hundred pounds of grain per year. Peasants lived on bread, soup with a little fat or oil, peas or lentils, garden vegetables in season, and only occasionally a piece of meat or fish. Usually the adverse years differed from place to place, but from 1594 to 1597 most of Europe suffered from shortages; the resulting famine triggered revolts from Ireland to Muscovy.

The Life of the Poor

This mid-seventeenth-century painting by the Dutch artist Adriaen Pietersz van de Venne depicts the poor peasant weighed down by his wife and child. An empty food bowl signifies their hunger. In retrospect, this painting seems unfair to the wife of the family; she is shown in clothes that are not nearly as tattered as her husband's and is portrayed entirely as a burden, rather than as a help in getting by in hard times. In reality, many poor men abandoned their homes in search of work, leaving their wives behind to cope with hungry children and what remained of the family farm. *(Allen Memorial Art Museum, Oberlin College, Mrs. F. F. Prentiss Fund, 1960. Inv # 1960.94.)*

to fear when hungry vagabonds, who sometimes banded together to beg for bread, became more aggressive, occasionally threatening to burn a barn if they were not given food.

Successive bad harvests led to malnutrition, which weakened people and made them more susceptible to such epidemic diseases as the plague, typhoid fever, typhus, dysentery, smallpox, and influenza. Disease did not spare the rich, although many epidemics hit the poor hardest. The plague was feared most: in one year it could cause the death of up to half of a town's or village's population, and it struck with no discernible pattern. Nearly 5 percent of France's entire population died just in the plague of 1628–1632.

The Changing Status of the Peasantry. Economic crisis widened the gap between rich and poor. Peasants shouldered many burdens, including rent and various fees for inheriting or selling land and tolls for using mills, wine presses, or ovens. States collected direct taxes on land and sales taxes on such consumer goods as salt, an essential preservative. Protestant and Catholic churches alike exacted a tithe (a tax equivalent to one-tenth of the parishioner's annual income); often the clergy took their tithe in the form of crops and collected it directly during the harvest. Any reversal of fortune could force peasants into the homeless world of vagrants and beggars, who numbered as much as 2 percent of the total population.

In England, the Dutch Republic, northern France, and northwestern Germany, the peasantry was disappearing. Improvements gave some peasants the means to become farmers who rented substantial holdings, produced for the market, and in good times enjoyed relative comfort and higher status. Those who could not afford to plant new crops such as maize (American corn) or to use techniques that ensured higher yields became simple laborers with little or no land of their own. One-half to four-fifths of the peasants did not have enough land to support a family. They descended deeper into debt during difficult times and often lost their land to wealthier farmers or to city officials intent on developing rural estates.

As the recession deepened, women lost some of their economic opportunities. Widows who had been able to take over their late husbands' trade now found themselves excluded by the urban guilds or limited to short tenures. Many women went into domestic service until they married, some for their entire lives. When town governments began to fear the effects of increased mo-

Most people, however, did not respond to their dismal circumstances by rebelling. They simply left their huts and hovels and took to the road in search of food and charity. Men left their families to search for better conditions in other parishes or even other countries. Those left behind might be reduced to eating chestnuts, roots, bark, and grass. Overwhelmed officials recorded pitiful tales of suffering. Women and children died while waiting in line for food at convents or churches. In eastern France in 1637, a witness reported, "The roads were paved with people. . . . Finally it came to cannibalism." Compassion sometimes gave way

bility from country to town and town to town, they carefully regulated the work of female servants, requiring women to stay in their positions unless they could prove mistreatment by a master.

Effects on Marriage and Childbearing.

European families reacted to economic downturn by postponing marriage and having fewer children. When hard times passed, more people married and had more children. But even in the best of times, one-fifth to one-quarter of all children died in their first year, and half died before age twenty. Childbirth still carried great risks for women, about 10 percent of whom died in the process. Even in the richest and most enlightened homes, childbirth often occasioned an atmosphere of panic. To allay their fears, women sometimes depended on magic stones, special pilgrimages, or prayers. Midwives delivered most babies; physicians were scarce, and even those who did attend births were generally less helpful than midwives. The Englishwoman Alice Thornton described in her diary how a doctor bled her to prevent a miscarriage after a fall (bloodletting, often by the application of leeches, was a common medical treatment); her son died anyway in a breech birth that almost killed her, too.

It might be assumed that families would have more children to compensate for high death rates, but beginning in the early seventeenth century and continuing until the end of the eighteenth, families in all ranks of society started to limit the number of children. Because methods of contraception were not widely known, they did this for the most part by marrying later; the average age at marriage during the seventeenth century rose from the early twenties to the late twenties. The average family had about four children. Poorer families seem to have had fewer children, wealthier ones more. Peasant couples, especially in eastern and southeastern Europe, had more children than urban couples because cultivation still required intensive manual labor — and having children was the most economical means of securing enough laborers.

The consequences of late marriage were profound. Young men and women were expected to put off marriage (and sexual intercourse) until their mid to late twenties — if they were among the lucky 50 percent who lived that long and not among the 10 percent who never married. Because both Protestant and Catholic clergy alike stressed sexual fidelity and abstinence before marriage, the number of births out of wedlock was relatively small (2–5 percent of births); premarital intercourse was generally tolerated only after a couple had announced their engagement.

The Economic Balance of Power

Just as the recession produced winners and losers among ordinary people, so too it created winners and losers among the competing states of Europe. The economies of southern Europe declined during this period, whereas those of the northwest emerged stronger. Competition in the New World reflected and reinforced this shift as the English, Dutch, and French rushed to establish trading outposts and permanent settlements to compete with the Spanish and Portuguese.

Regional Differences.

The new powers of northwestern Europe with their growing Atlantic trade gradually displaced the Mediterranean economies, which had dominated European commerce since the time of the Greeks and Romans. With expanding populations and geographical positions that promoted Atlantic trade, England and the Dutch Republic vied with France to become the leading mercantile powers. Northern Italian industries were eclipsed; Spanish commerce with the New World dropped. Amsterdam replaced Seville, Venice, Genoa, and Antwerp as the center of European trade and commerce. Even the plague contributed to this difference. Whereas central Europe and the Mediterranean countries took generations to recover from its ravages, northwestern Europe quickly replaced its lost population, no doubt because this area's people had suffered less from the effects of the Thirty Years' War and from the malnutrition related to the economic crisis.

All but the remnants of serfdom had disappeared in western Europe, yet in eastern Europe nobles reinforced their dominance over peasants, and the burden of serfdom increased. The price rise of the sixteenth century prompted Polish and eastern German nobles to increase their holdings and step up their production of grain for western markets. They demanded more rent and dues from their peasants, whom the government decreed must stay in their villages. In the economic downturn of the first half of the seventeenth century, peasants who were already dependent became serfs — completely tied to the land. A local official might complain of "this barbaric and as it were Egyptian servitude," but he had no power to fight the nobles. In Muscovy, the complete enserfment of the peasantry would eventually be recognized in the Code of Laws in 1649. Although enserfment produced short-term profits for landlords, in the long run it retarded economic development in eastern Europe and kept most of the population in a stranglehold of illiteracy and hardship.

Competition in the New World. Economic realignment also took place across the Atlantic ocean. Because Spain and Portugal had divided between themselves the rich spoils of South America, other prospective colonizers had to carve niches in seemingly less hospitable places, especially North America and the Caribbean (Map 15.4). Eventually, the English, French, and Dutch would dominate commerce with these colonies. Many European states, including Sweden and Denmark, rushed to join the colonial competition as a way of increasing national wealth. To this end, they chartered private joint-stock companies to enrich investors by importing fish, furs, tobacco, and precious metals, if they could be found, and to develop new markets for European products.

In establishing permanent colonies, the Europeans created whole new communities across the Atlantic. Careful plans could not always surmount the hazards of transatlantic shipping, however. Originally, the warm climate of Virginia made it an attractive destination for the Pilgrims, a small English sect that attempted to separate from the Church of England. But the *Mayflower*, which had sailed for Virginia with Pilgrim emigrants, landed far to the north in Massachusetts, where in 1620 the settlers founded New Plymouth Colony. By the 1640s, the British North American colonies had more than fifty thousand people — not including the Indians, whose numbers had been decimated in epidemics and wars — and the foundations of representative government in locally chosen colonial assemblies.

In contrast, French Canada had only about three thousand European inhabitants by 1640. Though thin in numbers, the French rapidly moved into the Great Lakes region. Fur traders sought beaver pelts to make the hats that had taken Paris fashion by storm. Jesuit missionaries lived with native American groups, learning their languages and describing their ways of life. Both England and France turned their attention to the Caribbean in the 1620s and 1630s when they occupied the islands of the West Indies after driving off the native Caribs. These islands would prove ideal for a plantation economy of tobacco and sugarcane.

Even as the British and French moved into North America and the Caribbean, Spanish explorers traveled the Pacific coast up to what is now northern California and pushed into New Mexico. On the other side of the world, in the Philippines, the Spanish competed with local Muslim rulers and indigenous tribal leaders to extend their control. Catholic missionaries printed tracts in Spanish and the islands' native Tagalog and established a university in 1611. Spanish officials

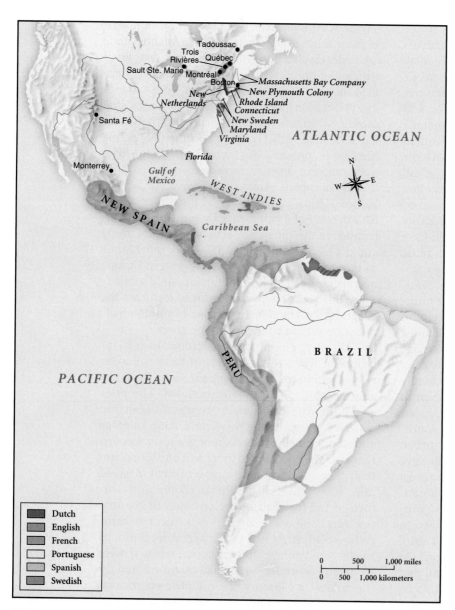

MAP 15.4 European Colonization of the Americas, c. 1640
Europeans coming to the Americas established themselves first in coastal areas. The English, French, and Dutch set up most of their colonies in the Caribbean and North America because the Spanish and Portuguese had already colonized the easily accessible regions in South America. Vast inland areas still remained unexplored and uncolonized in 1640.

"Savages" of the New World
The half-dressed savage appears much like a noble Italian in Paolo Farinati's 1595 painting *America*; he holds a crucifix in his right hand, signifying his conversion to Christianity. But to his left, a figure is roasting human flesh. Europeans were convinced that many native peoples were cannibals. What can we conclude from this painting about European attitudes toward peoples of the New World? *(Villa della Torre, Mezzane de Sotto, Verona.)*

worked closely with the missionaries to rule over a colony composed of indigenous peoples, Spaniards, and some Chinese merchants.

> **REVIEW:** What were the consequences of economic recession in the early 1600s?

The Rise of Secular and Scientific Worldviews

The countries that moved ahead economically in the first half of the seventeenth century — England, the Dutch Republic, and to some extent France — turned out to be the most receptive to new secular worldviews. In the long-term process known as **secularization**, religion became a matter of private conscience rather than public policy. Secularization did not entail a loss of religious faith, but it did prompt a search for nonreligious explanations for political authority and natural phenomena. During the late sixteenth and early seventeenth centuries, art, political theory, and science all began to break their bonds with religion. The visual arts, for example, more frequently depicted secular subjects. Scientists and scholars sought laws in nature to explain politics as well as

movements in the heavens and on earth. A scientific revolution was in the making. Yet traditional attitudes did not disappear. Belief in magic and witchcraft pervaded every level of society. People of all classes believed that the laws of nature reflected a divine plan for the universe. They accepted supernatural explanations for natural phenomena, a view only gradually and partially undermined by new ideas.

The Arts in an Age of Crisis

Two new forms of artistic expression — professional theater and opera — provided an outlet for secular values in an age of conflict over religious beliefs. The greatest playwright of the English language, William Shakespeare, never referred to religious disputes in his plays, and he always set his most personal reflections on political turmoil and uncertainty in faraway times or places. Religion played an important role in the new mannerist and baroque styles of painting, however, even though many rulers commissioned paintings on secular subjects for their own uses.

Theater in the Age of Shakespeare. The first professional acting companies performed before paying audiences in London, Seville, and Madrid in the 1570s. In previous centuries, traveling companies made their living by playing at major religious festivals and by repeating their performances in small towns and villages along the way. A huge outpouring of playwriting followed upon the formation of permanent professional theater

---

secularization: The trend toward making religious faith a private domain rather than one directly connected to state power and science; it prompted a search for nonreligious explanations for political authority and natural phenomena.

companies. The Spanish playwright Lope de Vega (1562–1635) alone wrote more than fifteen hundred plays. Theaters were extremely popular despite Puritan opposition in England and Catholic objections in Spain. Shopkeepers, apprentices, lawyers, and court nobles crowded into open-air theaters to see everything from bawdy farces to profound tragedies.

The most enduring and influential playwright of the time was the Englishman William Shakespeare (1564–1616), who wrote three dozen plays, comedies as well as tragedies, and acted in one of the chief troupes. Although Shakespeare's plays were not set in contemporary England, they reflected the concerns of his age: the nature of power and the crisis of authority. His tragedies in particular show the uncertainty and even chaos that result when power is misappropriated or misused. In *Hamlet* (1601), for example, Hamlet's mother marries the man who murdered his royal father and usurped the crown. In the end, Hamlet, his mother, and the usurper all die. One character in the final act describes the tragic story of Prince Hamlet as one "Of carnal, bloody, and unnatural acts;/Of accidental judgments, casual slaughters;/Of deaths put on by cunning and forced cause." Like many real-life people, Shakespeare's tragic characters found little peace in the turmoil of their times.

Mannerism and the Baroque in Art. Although painting did not always touch broad popular audiences in the ways that theater could, new styles in art and especially church architecture helped shape ordinary people's experience of religion. In the late sixteenth century, the artistic style known as mannerism emerged in the Italian states and soon spread across Europe. Mannerism was an almost theatrical style that allowed painters to distort perspective to convey a message or emphasize a theme. The most famous mannerist painter, called El Greco because he was of Greek origin, trained in Venice and Rome before he moved to Spain in the 1570s. The religious intensity of El Greco's pictures found a ready audience in Catholic Spain, which had proved immune to the Protestant suspicion of ritual and religious imagery (see Philip II of Spain, page 457).

The most important new style was the **baroque**, which, like mannerism, originated in the Italian states. In place of the Renaissance emphasis on harmonious design, unity, and clarity, the

baroque featured curves, exaggerated lighting, intense emotions, release from restraint, and even a kind of artistic sensationalism. Like many other historical designations, the word *baroque* was not used as a label by people living at the time; in the eighteenth century, art critics coined the word to mean shockingly bizarre, confused, and extravagant, and until the late nineteenth century, art historians and collectors largely disdained the baroque.

Closely tied to Catholic resurgence after the Reformation, the baroque melodramatically reaffirmed the emotional depths of the Catholic faith and glorified both church and monarchy (see "Seeing History," page 473). The style spread from Rome to other Italian states and then into central Europe. The Catholic Habsburg territories, including Spain and the Spanish Netherlands, embraced the style. The Spanish built baroque churches in their American colonies as part of their massive conversion campaign.

Opera. A new secular musical form, the opera, grew up parallel to the baroque style in the visual arts. First influential in the Italian states, opera combined music, drama, dance, and scenery in a grand sensual display, often with themes chosen to please the ruler and the aristocracy. Operas could be based on typically baroque sacred subjects or on traditional stories. Like many playwrights, including Shakespeare, opera composers often turned to familiar stories their audiences would recognize and readily follow. One of the most innovative composers of opera was Claudio Monteverdi (1567–1643), whose work contributed to the development of both opera and the orchestra. His earliest operatic production, *Orfeo* (1607), was based on Greek mythology. It required an orchestra of about forty instruments, and unlike previous composers, Monteverdi wrote parts for specific instruments as well as voices.

The Natural Laws of Politics

In reaction to the religious wars, writers not only began to defend the primacy of state interests over those of religious conformity but also insisted on secular explanations for politics. Machiavelli had pointed in this direction with his advice to Renaissance princes in the early sixteenth century, but this secular intellectual movement gathered steam in the aftermath of the religious violence unleashed by the Reformation. Adherents believed that religious toleration could not take hold until government could be organized on some principle other than one king, one faith. The French

---

baroque (buh ROHK): An artistic style of the seventeenth century that featured curves, exaggerated lighting, intense emotions, release from restraint, and even a kind of artistic sensationalism.

Religious Differences in Painting of the Baroque Period: Rubens and Rembrandt

Although the arts rarely reflect rigid religious or political divisions, artists do respond to the times in which they live. Protestant artists could not ignore the growing influence of the baroque style, but they also sought to distinguish themselves from it because of its association with the Catholic Counter-Reformation. The baroque style emphasized intense emotions, monumental decors, and even a kind of artistic sensationalism. Protestant artists, like Protestant preachers, wanted to produce strong reactions, too, but they placed more emphasis on the inner experience than on public display.

Here you see two paintings on the same biblical theme, one by Peter Paul Rubens (1577–1640), the great Catholic pioneer of the baroque style, and one by Rembrandt van Rijn (1606–1669), a Dutch Protestant. The subject of the paintings, taken from the Old Testament, is a scandalous one: when King David saw Bathsheba bathing, he fell in love with her, seduced her, and arranged for her husband to be killed in battle so that he might marry her.

Even though the central figure is the same in each painting, the artists' treatments are not. Look at the differences in settings, the number of people in the pictures, the colors, the lighting, and especially the facial expressions. In the Rubens, Bathsheba is about to receive a letter of summons from King David (shown on the balcony above), whereas in the Rembrandt she has just read the letter. What are the differences in feeling conveyed in the two depictions of Bathsheba? Why would Rembrandt draw attention to the sadness felt by Bathsheba, and how might this relate to the Protestant emphasis on each person's individual relationship to God? How do the setting and the lighting reinforce this emphasis on inwardness in the Rembrandt painting? Do not assume, however, that every difference in approach can be attributed to religious differences. Rembrandt created his own sensation by depicting Bathsheba almost entirely nude (and using his own mistress as the model).

Peter Paul Rubens, *Bathsheba at the Fountain*, c. 1635.

(© Gemaeldegalerie Alte Meister, Dresden, Germany/The Bridgeman Art Library.)

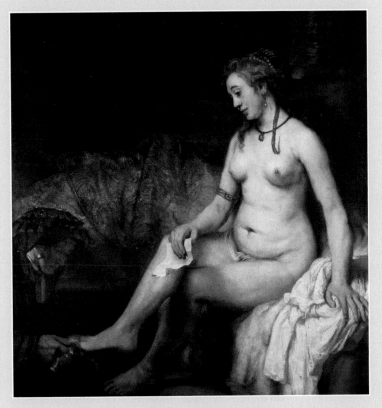

Rembrandt van Rijn, *Bathsheba at Her Bath*, 1654.

(© Louvre, Paris, France/Giraudon/The Bridgeman Art Library.)

politiques Michel de Montaigne and Jean Bodin started the search for those principles, and the Dutch legal scholar Hugo Grotius developed ideas on government that would influence John Locke and the American revolutionaries of the eighteenth century.

Montaigne and Bodin. Michel de Montaigne (1533–1592) was a French magistrate who resigned his office in the midst of the wars of religion to write about the need for tolerance and open-mindedness. Although himself a Catholic, Montaigne painted on the beams of his study the statement "All that is certain is that nothing is certain." To capture this need for personal reflection in a tumultuous age of religious discord, he invented the essay as a short and pithy form of expression. He revived the ancient doctrine of skepticism, which held that total certainty is never attainable — a doctrine, like toleration of religious differences, that was repugnant to Protestants and Catholics alike, both of whom were certain that their religion was the right one. He also questioned the common European habit of calling the native peoples of the New World barbarous and savage: "Everyone gives the title of barbarism to everything that is not in use in his own country."

The French Catholic lawyer Jean Bodin (1530–1596) sought systematic secular answers to the problem of disorder in *The Six Books of the Republic* (1576). Comparing the different forms of government throughout history, he concluded that there were three basic types of sovereignty: monarchy, aristocracy, and democracy. Only strong monarchical power offered hope for maintaining order, he insisted. Bodin rejected any doctrine of the right to resist tyrannical authority: "I denied that it was the function of a good man or of a good citizen to offer violence to his prince for any reason, however great a tyrant he might be" (and, it might be added, whatever his ideas on religion). While Bodin's ideas helped lay the foundation for absolutism, the idea that the monarch should be the sole and uncontested source of power, his systematic discussion of types of governments implied that they might be subject to choice and undercut the notion that monarchies were ordained by God, as most rulers maintained.

Grotius and Natural Law. During the Dutch revolt against Spain, Hugo Grotius (1583–1645) furthered secular thinking by attempting to systematize the notion of "natural law" — laws of nature that give legitimacy to government and stand above the actions of any particular ruler or religious group. Grotius argued that natural law stood beyond the reach of either secular or divine authority; it would be valid even if God did not exist (though Grotius himself believed in God). By this account, natural law — not scripture, religious authority, or tradition — should govern politics. Such ideas got Grotius into trouble with both Catholics and Protestants. His work *The Laws of War and Peace* (1625) was condemned by the Catholic church, while the Dutch Protestant government arrested him for taking part in religious controversies. Grotius's wife helped him escape prison by hiding him in a chest of books. He fled to Paris, where he got a small pension from Louis XIII and served as his ambassador to Sweden. The Swedish king Gustavus Adolphus claimed that he kept Grotius's book under his pillow even while at battle. Grotius was one of the first to argue that international conventions should govern the treatment of prisoners of war and the making of peace treaties.

Grotius's conception of natural law also challenged the widespread use of torture. Most states and the courts of the Catholic church used torture when a serious crime had been committed and the evidence seemed to point to a particular defendant but no definitive proof had been established. The judges ordered torture — hanging the accused by the hands with a rope thrown over a beam, pressing the legs in a leg screw, or just tying the hands very tightly — to extract a confession, which had to be given with a medical expert and notary present and had to be repeated without torture. Children, pregnant women, the elderly, aristocrats, kings, and even professors were exempt.

To be in accord with natural law, Grotius argued, governments had to defend natural rights, which he defined as life, body, freedom, and honor. Grotius did not encourage rebellion in the name of natural law or rights, but he did hope that someday all governments would adhere to these principles and stop killing their own and one another's subjects in the name of religion. Natural law and natural rights would play an important role in the founding of constitutional governments from the 1640s forward and in the establishment of various charters of human rights in our own time.

The Scientific Revolution

Although the Catholic and Protestant churches encouraged the study of science and many prominent scientists were themselves clerics, the search for a secular, scientific method of determining the laws of nature undermined traditional accounts of natural phenomena. Christian doctrine had incorporated the scientific teachings of ancient philosophers, especially Ptolemy and Aristotle; now these came into question. A revolution in astronomy contested the Ptolemaic view, endorsed by the Catholic church, which held that the sun revolved around the earth. Startling breakthroughs took place in medicine, too, which laid the foundations for modern anatomy and pharmacology. Supporters of these new developments argued for a **scientific method** that would combine experimental observation and mathematical deduction. The use of scientific method culminated in the astounding breakthroughs of Isaac Newton at the end of the seventeenth century. Newton's ability to explain the motion of the planets, as well as everyday objects on earth, gave science enormous new prestige.

The Revolution in Astronomy. The traditional account of the movement of the heavens derived from the second-century Greek astronomer Ptolemy, who put the earth at the center of the cosmos. Above the earth were fixed the moon, the stars, and the planets in concentric crystalline spheres; beyond these fixed spheres dwelt God and the angels. The planets revolved around the earth at the command of God. In this view, the sun revolved around the earth; the heavens were perfect and unchanging, and the earth was "corrupted." Ptolemy insisted that the planets revolved in perfectly circular orbits (because circles were more "perfect" than other figures). To account for the actual elliptical paths that could be observed and calculated, he posited orbits within orbits, or epicycles.

In 1543, the Polish clergyman Nicolaus Copernicus (1473–1543) began the revolution in astronomy by publishing his treatise *On the Revolution of the Celestial Spheres*. Copernicus attacked the Ptolemaic account, arguing that the earth and planets revolved around the sun, a view known as **heliocentrism** (a sun-centered universe). He discovered that by placing the sun instead of the earth at the center of the system of spheres, he could eliminate many epicycles from the calculations. In other words, he claimed that the heliocentric view simplified the mathematics. Copernicus died soon after publishing his theories, but when the Italian monk Giordano Bruno (1548–1600) taught helio-

centrism, the Catholic Inquisition (set up to seek out heretics) arrested him and burned him at the stake.

Copernicus's views began to attract widespread attention in the early 1600s, when astronomers systematically collected evidence that undermined the Ptolemaic view. A leader among them was the Danish astronomer Tycho Brahe (1546–1601), who designed his own instruments and observed a new star in 1572 and a comet in 1577. These discoveries called into question the traditional view that the universe was unchanging. Brahe still rejected heliocentrism, but the assistant he employed when he moved to Prague in 1599, Johannes Kepler (1571–1630), was converted to the Copernican view. Kepler continued Brahe's collection of planetary observations and used the evidence to develop his three laws of planetary motion, published between 1609 and 1619. Kepler's laws provided mathematical backing for heliocentrism and directly challenged the claim long held, even by Copernicus, that planetary motion was circular. Kepler's first law stated that the orbits of the planets are ellipses, with the sun always at one focus of the ellipse.

The Italian Galileo Galilei (1564–1642) provided more evidence to support the heliocentric view and also challenged the doctrine that the heavens were perfect and unchanging. After learning in 1609 that two Dutch astronomers had built a telescope, he built a better one and observed the earth's moon, four satellites of Jupiter, the phases of Venus (a cycle of changing physical appearances), and sunspots. The moon, the planets, and the sun were no more perfect than the earth, he insisted, and the shadows he could see on the moon could only be the product of hills and valleys like those on earth. Galileo portrayed the earth as a moving part of a larger system, only one of many planets revolving around the sun, not as the fixed center of a single, closed universe.

Because he recognized the utility of the new science for everyday projects, Galileo published his work in Italian, rather than Latin. But he meant only to instruct an educated elite of merchants and aristocrats. The new science, he claimed, suited "the minds of the wise," not "the shallow minds of the common people." After all, his discoveries challenged the commonsensical view that it is the sun that rises and sets while the earth stands still. If the Bible was wrong about motion in the universe, as Galileo's position implied, the error came from the Bible's use of common language to appeal to the lower orders. The Catholic church was not mollified by this explanation. In 1616, the church for-

---

scientific method: The combination of experimental observation and mathematical deduction that was used to determine the laws of nature and became the secular standard of truth.

heliocentrism: The view articulated by Polish clergyman Nicolaus Copernicus that the earth and planets revolve around the sun.

The Trial of Galileo

In this anonymous painting of the trial held in 1633, Galileo appears seated on a chair in the center facing the church officials who accused him of heresy for insisting that the sun, not the earth, was the center of the universe (heliocentrism). Catholic officials forced him to recant or suffer the death penalty. *(Erich Lessing/Art Resource, NY.)*

bade Galileo to teach that the earth moves; then, in 1633, it accused him of not obeying the earlier order. Forced to appear before the Inquisition, he agreed to publicly recant his assertion about the movement of the earth to save himself from torture and death. (See Document, "Sentence Pronounced against Galileo," page 477, and painting, The Trial of Galileo, above.) Afterward, he lived under house arrest and could publish his work only in the Dutch Republic, which had become a haven for iconoclastic scientists and thinkers.

Breakthroughs in Medicine. Just as astronomical knowledge was based on Ptolemy's work, medical knowledge in Europe was, until the mid-sixteenth century, based on the writings of the second-century Greek physician Galen, Ptolemy's contemporary. Galen derived his knowledge of the anatomy of the human body from partial dissections. In the same year that Copernicus challenged the traditional account in astronomy (1543), the Flemish scientist Andreas Vesalius (1514–1564) did the same for anatomy. Drawing on public dissections (which had been condemned by the Catholic church since 1300) he performed himself, Vesalius refuted Galen's work in his illustrated anatomical text, *On the Construction of the Human Body*. The German physician Paracelsus (1493–1541) went even further than Vesalius. In 1527, he burned Galen's text at the University of Basel, where he was a professor of medicine. Paracelsus performed operations (at the time, most academic physicians

taught medical theory, not practice) and pursued his interests in magic, alchemy, and astrology. He also experimented with new drugs and thus helped establish the modern science of pharmacology.

Like Vesalius, the Englishman William Harvey (1578–1657) used dissection to examine the circulation of blood within the body, demonstrating how the heart worked as a pump. The heart and its valves were "a piece of machinery," Harvey insisted. They obeyed mechanical laws just as the planets and earth revolved around the sun in a mechanical universe. Nature could be understood by experiment and rational deduction, not by following traditional authorities.

Scientific Method: Bacon and Descartes. In the 1630s, the European intellectual elite began to accept the new scientific views. Ancient learning, the churches and their theologians, and long-standing popular beliefs all seemed to be undercut by the scientific method. Two men were chiefly responsible for spreading the reputation of the scientific method in the first half of the seventeenth century: the English Protestant politician Sir Francis Bacon (1561–1626) and the French Catholic mathematician and philosopher René Descartes (1596–1650). They represented the two essential halves of the scientific method: inductive reasoning through observation and experimental research, and deductive reasoning from self-evident principles.

In *The Advancement of Learning* (1605), Bacon attacked reliance on ancient writers and optimisti-

Sentence Pronounced against Galileo (1633)

In 1633, the Roman Inquisition, a commit-tee of cardinals of the Catholic church, considered the case against Galileo and pronounced its final judgment. It found Galileo guilty of heresy against Catholic doctrine for defending heliocentrism but allowed him to recant and thus avoid the death penalty usual in cases of heresy. In 1980, Pope John Paul II appointed a commission to review the evidence and verdict. Four years later, the commission published its findings and concluded that the judges who condemned Galileo were wrong.

We say, pronounce, sentence, and declare that you, the above-mentioned Galileo, because of the things deduced in the trial and confessed by you as above, have rendered yourself according to this Holy Office [Inquisition] vehemently suspected of heresy, namely of having held and believed a doctrine which is false and contrary to the divine and Holy Scripture: that the sun is the center of the world and does not move from east to west, and the earth moves and is not the center of the world, and that one may hold and defend as probable an opinion after it has been declared and defined contrary to Holy Scripture. Consequently you have incurred all the censures and penalties imposed and promulgated by the sacred canons and all particular and general laws against such delinquents. We are willing to absolve you from them provided that first, with a sincere heart and unfeigned faith, in front of us you abjure, curse, and detest the above-mentioned errors and heresies, and every other error and heresy contrary to the Catholic and Apostolic Church, in the manner and form we will prescribe to you.

Furthermore, so that this serious and pernicious error and transgression of yours does not remain completely unpunished, and so that you will be more cautious in the future and an example for others to abstain from similar crimes, we order that the book *Dialogue* [*Dialogue Concerning the Two Chief World Systems*, published in 1632] by Galileo Galilei be prohibited by public edict.

Source: Maurice A. Finocchiaro, ed., *The Galileo Affairs: A Documentary History* (Berkeley: University of California Press, 1989), 291.

cally predicted that the scientific method would lead to social progress. The minds of the medieval scholars, he said, had been "shut up in the cells of a few authors (chiefly Aristotle, their dictator) as their persons were shut up in the cells of monasteries and colleges," and they could therefore produce only "cobwebs of learning" that were "of no substance or profit." Advancement would take place only through the collection, comparison, and analysis of information. Knowledge, in Bacon's view, must be empirically based (that is, gained by observation and experiment). Claiming that God had called the Catholic church "to account for their degenerate manners and ceremonies," Bacon looked to the Protestant English state, which he served as lord chancellor, for leadership on the road to scientific advancement.

Although Descartes agreed with Bacon's denunciation of traditional learning, he saw that the attack on tradition might only replace the dogmatism of the churches with the skepticism of Montaigne—that nothing at all was certain. Descartes aimed to establish the new science on more secure philosophical foundations, those of mathematics and logic. In his *Discourse on Method* (1637), he argued that mathematical and mechanical principles provided the key to understanding all of nature, including the actions of people and states. All prior assumptions must be repudiated in favor of one elementary principle: "I think, therefore I am." Everything else could—and should—be doubted, but even doubt showed the certain existence of someone thinking. Begin with the simple and go on to the complex, Descartes asserted, and believe only those ideas that present themselves "clearly and distinctly." He insisted that human reason could not only unravel the secrets of nature but also prove the existence of God. Although he hoped to secure the authority of both church and state, his reliance on human reason rather than faith irritated authorities, and his books were banned in many places. He moved to the Dutch Republic to work in peace. Scientific research, like economic growth, became centered in the northern, Protestant countries, where it was less constrained by church control than in the Catholic south.

Newton and the Consolidation of the Scientific Revolution. The power of the new scientific method was dramatically confirmed in the grand synthesis of the laws of movement developed by the English natural philosopher Isaac Newton (1642–1727). Born five years after the publication of Descartes's *Discourse on Method* and educated at Cambridge University, where he later became a professor, Newton attacked an astounding variety of problems in mathematics, mechanics, and optics. For example, he established the basis for the new mathematics of moving bodies, the infinitesimal calculus. After years of labor, he finally brought his most significant mathematical and mechanical discoveries together in his masterwork, *Principia Mathematica* (1687). In it, he developed his law of universal gravitation, which explained both movement on earth and the motion of the planets. His law held that every body in the universe exerts over every other body an attractive force directly proportional to the product of their masses and inversely proportional to the square of the distance between them. This law of universal gravitation explained Kepler's elliptical planetary orbits just as it accounted for the way an apple fell to the ground.

To establish his law of universal gravitation, Newton first applied mathematical principles to formulate three fundamental physical laws: (1) in the absence of force, motion continues in a straight line; (2) the rate of change in the motion of an object is a result of the forces acting on it; and (3) the action of one object on another has an equal and opposite reaction. Newtonian physics thus combined mass, inertia, force, velocity, and acceleration—all key concepts in modern science—and made them quantifiable. Newton knew that the stakes were high: "From the same principles [of motion] I now demonstrate the frame of the System of the World."

Once set in motion, in Newton's view, the universe operated like a masterpiece made possible by the ingenuity of God. Newton saw no conflict between faith and science. He believed that by demonstrating that the physical universe followed rational principles, natural philosophers could prove the existence of God and so liberate humans from doubt and the fear of chaos. Even while laying the foundation for modern physics, optics, and mechanics, Newton spent long hours trying to calculate the date of the beginning of the world and its end with the second coming of Jesus. Others, less devout than Newton, envisioned a clockwork universe that had no need for God's continuing intervention.

Some scientists, especially those on the continent, were reluctant to accept Newton's planetary theories. The Dutch scientist Christian Huygens, for example, declared the concept of attraction (action at a distance) "absurd." But within a couple of generations, Newton's work had gained widespread assent, partly because of experimental verification.

Magic and Witchcraft

Despite the new emphasis on clear reasoning, observation, and independence from past authorities, magic and science were still closely linked even in the greatest minds. Many scholars, like Paracelsus and Newton, studied alchemy alongside other scientific pursuits. Elizabeth I maintained a court astrologer who was also a serious mathematician, and many writers distinguished between "natural magic," which was close to experimental science, and demonic "black magic." The astronomer Tycho Brahe defended his studies of alchemy and astrology as part of natural magic.

In a world in which most people believed in astrology, magical healing, prophecy, and ghosts, it is hardly surprising that many of Europe's learned people also firmly believed in witchcraft, that is, the exercise of magical powers gained by a pact with the devil. The same Jean Bodin who argued against religious fanaticism insisted on death for witches—and for those magistrates who would not prosecute them. In France alone, 345 books and pamphlets on witchcraft appeared between 1550 and 1650. Trials of witches peaked in Europe between 1560 and 1640, the very time of the celebrated breakthroughs of the new science. Montaigne was one of the few to speak out against executing accused witches: "It is taking one's conjectures rather seriously to roast someone alive for them," he wrote in 1580.

Belief in witches was not new in the sixteenth century. Witches had long been blamed for de-

Giving a Child to Satan
This woodcut from Francesco Maria Guazzo's *Compendium Maleficarum* of 1608 shows witches giving a child to the devil. Many believed that witches made a pact with the devil to carry out his evil deeds. *(The Art Archive/Dagli Orti [A].)*

stroying crops and causing personal catastrophes ranging from miscarriage to madness. What was new was official persecution by state and religious authorities. In a time of economic crisis, plague, warfare, and the clash of religious differences, witchcraft trials provided an outlet for social stress and anxiety, legitimated by state power. Denunciation and persecution of witches coincided with the spread of reform, both Protestant and Catholic. Witch trials concentrated especially in the German lands of the Holy Roman Empire, the boiling cauldron of the Thirty Years' War.

The victims of the persecution were overwhelmingly female: women accounted for 80 percent of the accused witches in about 100,000 trials in Europe and North America during the sixteenth and seventeenth centuries. About one-third were sentenced to death. Before 1400, when witchcraft trials were rare, nearly half of those accused had been men. Why did attention now shift to women? Official descriptions of witchcraft oozed lurid details of sexual orgies, incest, homosexuality, and cannibalism, in which women acted as the devil's sexual slaves. Social factors help explain the prominence of women among the accused. Accusers were almost always better off than those they accused. The poorest and most socially marginal people in most communities were elderly spinsters and widows. Because they were thought likely to hanker after revenge on those more fortunate, they were singled out as witches.

Witchcraft trials declined when scientific thinking about causes and effects raised questions about the evidence used in court: how could judges or jurors be certain that someone was a witch? The tide turned everywhere at about the same time, as physicians, lawyers, judges, and even clergy came to suspect that accusations were based on popular superstition and peasant untrustworthiness. As early as the 1640s, French courts ordered the arrest of witch-hunters and released suspected witches. In 1682, a French royal decree treated witchcraft as fraud and imposture, meaning that the law did not recognize anyone as a witch. In 1693, the jurors who had convicted twenty witches in Salem, Massachusetts, recanted, claiming: "We confess that we ourselves were not capable to understand. . . . We justly fear that we were sadly deluded and mistaken." The Salem jurors had not stopped believing in witches; they had simply lost confidence in their ability to identify them. This was a general pattern. Popular attitudes had not changed; what had changed was the attitudes of the elites. When physicians and judges had believed in witches and carried out official persecutions, with torture, those accused of witchcraft had

gone to their deaths in record numbers. But when the same groups distanced themselves from popular beliefs, the trials and the executions stopped.

REVIEW: How could belief in witchcraft and the rising prestige of scientific method coexist?

Conclusion

The witchcraft persecutions reflected the traumas of these times of religious war, economic decline, and crises of political and intellectual authority. Faced with new threats, some people blamed poor widows or struggling neighbors for their problems; others joined desperate revolts, and still others emigrated to the New World to seek a better life. Even rulers confronted frightening choices: forced abdication, death in battle, or assassination often accompanied their religious decisions, and economic shocks could threaten the stability of their governments.

Deep differences over religion shaped the destinies of every European power in this period. These quarrels came to a head in the Thirty Years' War (1618–1648), which cut a path of destruction through central Europe and involved most of the European powers. Repulsed by the effects of religious violence on international relations, European rulers agreed to a peace that effectively removed disputes between Catholics and Protestants from the international arena. The growing separation of political motives from religious ones did not mean that violence or conflict had ended, however. Struggles for religious uniformity within states would continue, though on a smaller scale. Larger armies required more state involvement, and almost everywhere rulers emerged from these decades of war with expanded powers that they would seek to extend further in the second half of the seventeenth century. The growth of state power directly changed the lives of ordinary people: more men went into the armies, and most families paid higher taxes. The constant extension of state power is one of the defining themes of modern history; religious warfare gave it a jump-start.

For all their power and despite repeated efforts, rulers could not control economic, social, or intellectual trends. The economic downturn of the seventeenth century produced unexpected consequences for European states even while it made life miserable for many ordinary people; economic power and vibrancy shifted from the Mediterranean world to northwestern Europe because England, France, and the Dutch Republic,

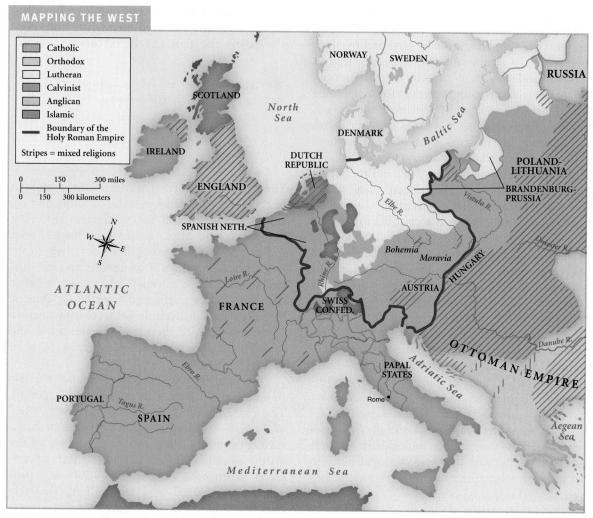

MAPPING THE WEST

Legend:
- Catholic
- Orthodox
- Lutheran
- Calvinist
- Anglican
- Islamic
- Boundary of the Holy Roman Empire
- Stripes = mixed religions

The Religious Divisions of Europe, c. 1648

The Peace of Westphalia recognized major religious divisions within Europe that have endured for the most part to the present day. Catholicism dominated in southern Europe, Lutheranism had its stronghold in northern Europe, and Calvinism flourished along the Rhine River. In southeastern Europe, the Islamic Ottoman Turks accommodated the Greek Orthodox Christians under their rule but bitterly fought the Catholic Austrian Habsburgs for control of Hungary.

especially, suffered less from the fighting of the Thirty Years' War and recovered more quickly from the loss of population and production during bad times.

In the face of violence and uncertainty, some began to look for secular alternatives in art, politics, and science. Although it would be foolish to claim that everyone's mental universe changed because of the clash between religious and secular worldviews, a truly monumental shift in attitudes had begun. Secularization encompassed the growing popularity of nonreligious forms of art, such as theater and opera; the search for nonreligious foundations of political authority; and the establishment of scientific method as the standard of truth. Proponents of these changes did not renounce their religious beliefs or even hold them less

fervently, but they did insist that attention to state interests and scientific knowledge could diminish religious violence and popular superstitions.

FOR FURTHER EXPLORATION

■ **For suggested references, including Web sites, for topics in this chapter,** see page SR-1 at the end of the book.

■ **For additional primary-source material from this period,** see Chapter 15 in *Sources of THE MAKING OF THE WEST*, Third Edition.

■ **For Web sites and documents related to topics in this chapter,** see *Make History* at bedfordstmartins.com/hunt.

CHAPTER REVIEW

KEY TERMS AND PEOPLE

Catherine de Médicis (453)

Edict of Nantes (455)

politiques (455)

Philip II (455)

Lepanto (455)

Elizabeth I (458)

Puritans (458)

Peace of Westphalia (463)

raison d'état (464)

secularization (471)

baroque (472)

scientific method (475)

heliocentrism (475)

REVIEW QUESTIONS

1. How did state power depend on religious unity at the end of the sixteenth century and start of the seventeenth?

2. Why did a war fought over religious differences result in stronger states?

3. What were the consequences of economic recession in the early 1600s?

4. How could belief in witchcraft and the rising prestige of scientific method coexist?

MAKING CONNECTIONS

1. How did the balance of power shift in Europe between 1560 and 1648? What were the main reasons for the shift?

2. Relate the new developments in the arts and sciences to the political and economic changes of this period of crisis.

> **For practice quizzes, a customized study plan, and other study tools,** see the Online Study Guide at bedfordstmartins.com/hunt.

IMPORTANT EVENTS

1562	French Wars of Religion begin	**1598**	French Wars of Religion end with Edict of Nantes
1566	Revolt of Calvinists in the Netherlands against Spain begins	**1601**	William Shakespeare, *Hamlet*
1569	Formation of commonwealth of Poland-Lithuania	**1618**	Thirty Years' War begins
1571	Battle of Lepanto marks victory of West over Ottomans at sea	**1625**	Hugo Grotius publishes *The Laws of War and Peace*
1572	St. Bartholomew's Day Massacre of French Protestants	**1633**	Galileo Galilei is forced to recant his support of heliocentrism
1588	English defeat of the Spanish Armada	**1635**	French join the Thirty Years' War by declaring war on Spain
		1648	Peace of Westphalia ends the Thirty Years' War

State Building and the Search for Order
1648–1690

I n May 1664, King Louis XIV of France organized a weeklong series of entertainments for his court at Versailles, where he had recently begun construction of a magnificent new palace. More than six hundred members of his court attended the series of spectacles called "The Delights of the Enchanted Island." The carefully orchestrated activities opened with an elaborate parade of the king and his courtiers, accompanied by an eighteen-foot-high float in the form of a chariot dedicated to Apollo, Greek god of the sun and Louis's personally chosen emblem. The king's favorite artists presented works specially prepared for the occasion, including ballets, plays, and musical concerts. Equestrian tournaments, visits to the king's personal collection of wild animals and birds, and a huge fireworks display captivated the audience. Every detail of the festivities appeared in an official program published the same year.

Louis XIV spared no expense in promoting his image, especially to those most dangerous to him, the leading nobles of his kingdom. Other mid-seventeenth-century rulers followed his example or explicitly rejected it, but they could not afford to ignore it. All governments faced the daunting task of rebuilding authority after the wars over religion and the economic recession of the early seventeenth century. As part of his campaign to underline his majesty, Louis encouraged leading nobles to dispense huge sums to entertain him and his court. He always spent even more in order to show that he was richer and more powerful than any noble or than any other monarch.

Louis XIV's model of state building was known as absolutism, a system of government in which the ruler claims sole and uncontestable power. Although absolutism exerted great influence beginning in the mid-1600s, especially in central and eastern Europe, it faced competition

---

Louis XIV and His Bodyguards
One of Louis XIV's court painters, the Flemish artist Adam Frans van der Meulen, depicted the king arriving at the palace of Versailles, still under construction (the painting dates from 1669). None of the gardens, pools, or statues had been installed. Louis is the only figure facing the viewer, and his dress is much more colorful than that of anyone else in the painting. (*Réunion des Musées Nationaux/Art Resource, NY.*)

from **constitutionalism**, a system in which the ruler shares power with an assembly of elected representatives. Constitutionalism led to weakness in Poland-Lithuania, but it provided a strong foundation for state power in England, the Dutch Republic, and the British North American colonies. Constitutionalism triumphed in England, however, only after one king had been executed as a traitor and another had been deposed. The English conflicts over the nature of authority found their most enduring expression in the writings of Thomas Hobbes and John Locke, which laid the foundations of modern political science.

Whether absolutist or constitutionalist, nations faced similar challenges in the mid-seventeenth century. Competition in the international arena required resources, and all states raised taxes in this period, provoking popular protests and rebellions. Monarchs still relied on religion to justify their divine right to rule, but they increasingly sought secular defenses of their powers, too. **Absolutism** and constitutionalism were the two main responses to the threat of disorder and breakdown left as a legacy of the wars over religion.

The search for order took place not only in government and politics but also in intellectual, cultural, and social life. Artists sought means of glorifying power and expressing order and symmetry in new fashion. As states consolidated their power, elites endeavored to distinguish themselves more clearly from the lower orders. The upper classes emulated the manners developed at court and tried in every way to distance themselves from anything viewed as vulgar or lower class. Officials, clergy, and laypeople all worked to reform the poor, now seen as a major source of disorder. Whether absolutist or constitutionalist, seventeenth-century states all aimed to extend control over their subjects' lives.

> **FOCUS QUESTION:** What were the most important differences between absolutism and constitutionalism, and how did they establish order?

Louis XIV: Absolutism and Its Limits

French king **Louis XIV** (r. 1643–1715) personified the absolutist ruler, who in theory shared his power with no one. Louis personally made all important state decisions and left no room for dissent. In 1655, he reputedly told the Paris high court of justice, *"L'état, c'est moi"* ("I am the state"), emphasizing that state authority rested in him personally. Louis cleverly manipulated the affections and ambitions of his courtiers, chose as his ministers middle-class men who owed everything to him, built up Europe's largest army, and snuffed out every hint of religious or political opposition. Yet the absoluteness of his power should not be exaggerated. Like all other rulers of his time, Louis depended on the cooperation of many people: local officials who enforced his decrees, peasants and artisans who joined his armies and paid his taxes, creditors who loaned crucial funds, clergy who preached his notion of Catholicism, and nobles who joined court festivities rather than staying home and causing trouble.

---

constitutionalism: A system of government in which rulers share power with parliaments made up of elected representatives.

absolutism: A system of government in which the ruler claims sole and uncontestable power.

Louis XIV: French king (r. 1643–1715) who personified the absolutist ruler; in theory he shared his power with no one, but in practice he had to gain the cooperation of nobles, local officials, and even the ordinary subjects who manned his armies and paid his taxes.

■ **1642–1646** English civil war

■ **1649** Charles I beheaded; new Russian legal code

■ **1651** Hobbes, *Leviathan*

■ **1660** Monarchy restored in England

1640   **1650**   **1660**

■ **1648** Peace of Westphalia; Fronde revolt in France; Ukranian Cossacks rebel; Dutch Republic recognized as independent

■ **1661** Barbados institutes slave code

The Fronde, 1648–1653

Louis XIV's absolutism built on a long French tradition of increasing centralization of state authority, but before he could establish his preeminence he had to weather a series of revolts known as the Fronde. Derived from the French word for a child's slingshot, the term was used by critics to signify that the revolts were mere child's play. In fact, however, they posed an unprecedented threat to the French crown. Louis was only five when he came to the throne in 1643 upon the death of his father, Louis XIII, who with his chief minister, Cardinal Richelieu, had steered France through increasing involvement in the Thirty Years' War, rapidly climbing taxes, and innumerable tax revolts. Louis XIV's mother, Anne of Austria, and her Italian-born adviser and rumored lover, Cardinal Mazarin (1602–1661), ruled in the young monarch's name.

To meet the financial pressure of fighting the Thirty Years' War, Mazarin sold new offices, raised taxes, and forced creditors to extend loans to the government. In 1648, a coalition of his opponents presented him with a charter of demands that, if granted, would have given the parlements (high courts) a form of constitutional power with the right to approve new taxes. Mazarin responded by arresting the leaders of the parlements. He soon faced the series of revolts that at one time or another involved nearly every social group in France.

The Fronde posed an immediate menace to the young king. Fearing for his safety, his mother and members of his court took Louis and fled Paris. With civil war threatening, Mazarin and Anne agreed to compromise with the parlements. The nobles saw an opportunity to reassert their claims to power against the weakened monarchy and renewed their demands for greater local control, which they had lost when the French Wars of Religion ended in 1598. Leading noblewomen often played key roles in the opposition to

Louis XIV, Conqueror of the Fronde
In this painting of 1654, Louis XIV is depicted as the Roman god Jupiter, who crushes the discord of the Fronde (represented on the shield by the Medusa's head made up of snakes). When the Fronde began, Louis was only ten years old; at the time of this painting, he was sixteen. The propaganda about his divine qualities had already begun. (*Réunion des Musées Nationaux/Art Resource, NY.*)

Mazarin, carrying messages and forging alliances, especially when male family members were in prison. While the nobles sought to regain power and local influence, the middle and lower classes chafed at the repeated tax increases. Conflicts erupted throughout the kingdom as nobles, parlements, and city councils all raised their own

■ 1667 First of Louis XIV's many wars

■ 1683 Austrian Habsburgs break Turkish siege of Vienna

■ 1685 Louis XIV revokes Edict of Nantes

1670   **1680**   **1690**

■ **1678** Madame de Lafayette, *The Princess of Clèves*

■ 1688 William and Mary crowned

■ 1690 Locke, *Two Treatises of Government*; *Essay Concerning Human Understanding*

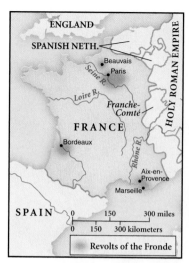

The Fronde, 1648–1653

armies to fight either the crown or each other, and rampaging soldiers devastated rural areas and disrupted commerce. The urban poor, such as those in the southwestern city of Bordeaux, sometimes revolted as well.

Neither the nobles nor the judges of the parlements really wanted to overthrow the king; they simply wanted a greater share in power. Mazarin and Anne eventually got the upper hand because their opponents failed to maintain unity in fighting the king's forces. But Louis XIV never forgot the humiliation and uncertainty that marred his childhood. His own policies as ruler would be designed to prevent the recurrence of any such revolts. Yet, for all his success, peasants would revolt against the introduction of new taxes on at least five more occasions in the 1660s and 1670s, requiring tens of thousands of soldiers to reestablish order. Absolutism was in part a fervent hope and not always a reality.

Court Culture as an Element of Absolutism

When Cardinal Mazarin died in 1661, Louis XIV, then twenty-two years old, decided to rule without a first minister. He described the dangers of his situation in memoirs he wrote later for his son's instruction: "Everywhere was disorder. My Court as a whole was still very far removed from the sentiments in which I trust you will find it." Louis listed many other problems in the kingdom, but none occupied him more than his attempts to control France's leading nobles, some of whom came from families that had opposed him militarily during the Fronde.

Typically quarrelsome, the French nobles had long exercised local authority by maintaining their own fighting forces, meting out justice on their estates, arranging jobs for underlings, and resolving their own conflicts through dueling. Louis set out to domesticate the warrior nobles by replacing violence with court ritual, such as the festivities at Versailles described at the beginning of this chapter. Using a systematic policy of bestowing pensions, offices, honors, gifts, and the threat of disfavor or punishment, Louis induced the nobles to cooperate with him and made himself the center of French power and culture. The aristocracy increasingly vied for his favor, attended the ballets and theatricals he put on, and learned the rules of etiquette he supervised—in short, became his clients, dependent on him for advancement. Great nobles competed for the honor of holding his shirt when he dressed, foreign ambassadors squabbled for places near him, and royal mistresses basked in the glow of his personal favor. Far from the court, however, nobles could still make considerable trouble for the king, and royal officials learned to compromise with them.

Those who did come to the king's court were kept on their toes. The preferred styles changed without notice, and the tiniest lapse in attention to etiquette could lead to ruin. Madame de

Louis XIV Visits the Royal Tapestry Workshop

This tapestry was woven at the Gobelins tapestry workshop between 1673 and 1680. It shows Louis XIV (wearing a red hat) and his minister Colbert (dressed in black, holding his hat) visiting the workshop on the outskirts of Paris. The workshop artisans scurry to show Louis all the luxury objects they manufacture. Louis bought the workshop in 1662 and made it a national enterprise for making tapestries and furniture. *(Bridgeman-Giraudon/Art Resource, NY.)*

DOCUMENT

Marie de Sévigné, Letter Describing the French Court (1675)

Marie de Rabutin-Chantal, marquise de Sévigné (1626–1696), was the most famous letter writer of her time. A noblewoman born in Paris, she frequented court circles and wrote about her experiences to her friends and relatives, especially her daughter. Although not published in her lifetime, her letters soon gained fame and were copied and read by those in her circle. She wrote her later letters with this audience in mind and so downplayed her own personal feelings, except those of missing her daughter to whom she was deeply attached. This letter from 1675 to her daughter recounts court intrigue surrounding Louis XIV's mistress and the shock when one of France's leading generals was killed in battle. Though Sévigné enjoyed spending time at Louis XIV's court, she could also write about it with biting wit.

They [the king and his court] were to set off today for Fontainebleau [one of the king's castles near Paris], where the entertainments were to become boring by their very multiplicity. Everything was ready when a bolt fell from the blue that shattered the joy. The populace says it is on account of *Quantova* [Sévigné's nickname for the king's mistress, Madame de Montespan, who gave birth to seven children fathered by Louis XIV], the attachment is still intense. Enough fuss is being made to upset the curé [priest] and everybody else, but perhaps not enough for her, for in her visible triumph there is an underlying sadness. You talk of the pleasures of Versailles, and at the time when they were off to Fontainebleau to plunge into joys, lo and behold M. De Turenne [commander of the French armies during the Dutch War] killed, general consternation, Monsieur le Prince [de Condé, another leading general], rushing off to Germany, France in desolation. Instead of seeing the end of the campaigns and having your brother back [Sévigné's son served in the army], we don't know where we are. There you have the world in its triumph and, since you like them, surprising events.

Source: *Madame de Sévigné: Selected Letters*, translated Leonard Tancock (New York: Penguin Books, 1982), 165.

Lafayette described the court in her novel *The Princess of Clèves* (1678): "The Court gravitated around ambition. Nobody was tranquil or indifferent — everybody was busily trying to better his or her position by pleasing, by helping, or by hindering somebody else." Elisabeth Charlotte, duchess of Orléans, the German-born sister-in-law of Louis, complained that "everything here is pure self-interest and deviousness." (See Document, "Marie de Sévigné, Letter Describing the French Court," above.)

Politics and the Arts. Louis XIV appreciated the political uses of every form of art. Mock battles, extravaganzas, theatrical performances, even the king's dinner — Louis's daily life was a public performance designed to enhance his prestige. Calling himself the Sun King, after Apollo, Greek god of the sun, Louis stopped at nothing to burnish this radiant image. He played Apollo in ballets performed at court; posed for portraits with the emblems of Apollo (laurel, lyre, and tripod); and adorned his palaces with statues of the god. He also emulated the style and methods of ancient Roman emperors. At a celebration for the birth of his first son in 1662, Louis dressed in Roman attire, and many engravings and paintings showed him as a Roman emperor. Commissioned histo-

ries vaunted his achievements, and coins and medals spread his likeness throughout the realm.

The king's officials treated the arts as a branch of government. The king gave pensions to artists who worked for him and sometimes protected writers from clerical critics. The most famous of these was the playwright Molière, whose comedy *Tartuffe* (1664) made fun of religious hypocrites and was loudly condemned by church leaders. Louis forced Molière to delay public performances of the play after its premiere at the festivities of May 1664 but resisted calls for his dismissal. Louis's ministers set up royal academies of dance, painting, architecture, music, and science and took control of the Académie française (French Academy), which to this day decides on correct usage of the French language. Louis's government also regulated the number and locations of theaters and closely censored all forms of publication.

Music and theater enjoyed special prominence. Louis commissioned operas to celebrate royal marriages, baptisms, and military victories. His favorite composer, Jean-Baptiste Lully, wrote sixteen operas for court performances as well as many ballets. Louis himself danced in the ballets if a role seemed especially important. Playwrights often presented their new plays first to the court. Pierre Corneille and Jean-Baptiste Racine wrote tragedies set in Greece or Rome that cele-brated the new aristocratic virtues that Louis aimed to inculcate: a reverence for order and self-control. All the characters were regal or noble, all the language lofty, all the behavior aristocratic.

The Palace of Versailles.   Louis glorified his im-age as well through massive public works projects. Veterans' hospitals and new fortified towns on the frontiers represented his military might. Urban improvements, such as the reconstruction of the Louvre palace in Paris, proved his wealth. But his most ambitious project was the construction of a new palace at Versailles, twelve miles from the tur-bulent capital (see illustration below).

Building began in the 1660s. By 1685, the fren-zied effort engaged thirty-six thousand workers, not including the thousands of troops who diverted a local river to supply water for pools and foun-tains. The gardens designed by landscape architect André Le Nôtre reflected the spirit of Louis XIV's rule: their geometrical arrangements and clear

lines showed that art and design could tame nature and that order and control defined the exercise of power. Le Nôtre's geometrical landscapes were later imitated in places as far away as St. Petersburg in Russia and Washington, D.C. Versailles symbol-ized Louis's success in reining in the nobility and dominating Europe, and other monarchs eagerly mimicked French fashion and often conducted their business in French.

Yet for all its apparent luxury and frivolity, life at Versailles was often cramped and cold. Fifteen thousand people crowded into the palace's apart-ments, including all the highest military officers, the ministers of state, and the separate households of each member of the royal family. Refuse col-lected in the corridors during the incessant build-ing, and thieves and prostitutes overran the grounds. By the time Louis actually moved from the Louvre to Versailles in 1682, he had reigned as monarch for thirty-nine years. After his wife's death in 1683, he secretly married his mistress, Françoise d'Aubigné, marquise de Maintenon, and

The Palace of Versailles
This painting by Jean-Baptiste Martin from the late seventeenth century gives a good view of one section of the palace and especially the geometrically arranged gardens. What would observers conclude about Louis XIV when they viewed this scene?
(Réunion des Musées Nationaux/Art Resource, NY.)

conducted most state affairs from her apartments at the palace. Her opponents at court complained that she controlled all the appointments, but her efforts focused on her own projects, including her favorite: the founding in 1686 of a royal school for girls from impoverished noble families. She also inspired Louis XIV to increase his devotion to Catholicism.

Enforcing Religious Orthodoxy

Louis believed that he reigned by divine right. He served as God's lieutenant on earth and even claimed certain godlike qualities. As Bishop Jacques-Benigne Bossuet (1627–1704) explained, "We have seen that kings take the place of God, who is the true father of the human species. We have also seen that the first idea of power which exists among men is that of the paternal power; and that kings are modeled on fathers." The king, like a father, should instruct his subjects in the true religion, or at least make sure that others did so. In religious questions, too, the king's endeavors to gain more complete control showed both his wide-ranging ambition and the nature of the obstacles he faced.

Louis's campaign for religious conformity first focused on the Jansenists, Catholics whose doctrines and practices resembled some aspects of Protestantism. Following the posthumous publication of the book *Augustinus* (1640) by the Flemish theologian Cornelius Jansen (1585–1638), the Jansenists stressed the need for God's grace in achieving salvation. They emphasized the importance of original sin and resembled the English Puritans in their austere religious practice. Prominent among the Jansenists was Blaise Pascal (1623–1662), a mathematician of genius, who wrote his *Provincial Letters* (1656–1657) to defend Jansenism against charges of heresy. Many judges in the parlements likewise endorsed Jansenist doctrine.

Some questioned Louis's understanding of the finer points of doctrine: according to his sister-in-law, Louis himself "has never read anything about religion, nor the Bible either, and just goes along believing whatever he is told." But Louis rejected any doctrine that gave priority to considerations of individual conscience over the demands of the official church hierarchy, especially when that doctrine had been embraced by some noble supporters of the Fronde. Louis preferred teachings that stressed obedience to authority. Therefore, in 1660 he began enforcing various papal bulls (decrees) against Jansenism and closed down Jansenist theological centers. Jansenists were forced underground for the rest of his reign.

After many years of escalating pressure on the Calvinist Huguenots, Louis decided in 1685 to eliminate all of the Calvinists' rights. Louis considered the Edict of Nantes (1598), by which his grandfather Henry IV granted the Protestants religious freedom and a degree of political independence, a temporary measure, and he fervently hoped to reconvert the Huguenots to Catholicism. His **revocation of the Edict of Nantes** closed their churches and schools, banned all their public activities, and exiled those who refused to embrace the state religion. Tens of thousands of Huguenots responded by emigrating to England, Brandenburg-Prussia, the Dutch Republic, or North America. Many now wrote for publications attacking Louis XIV's absolutism. Protestant European countries were shocked by this crackdown on religious dissent and would cite it in justification of their wars against Louis.

Extending State Authority at Home and Abroad

Louis XIV could not have enforced his religious policies without the services of a nationwide bureaucracy. **Bureaucracy**—a network of state officials carrying out orders according to a regular and routine line of authority—comes from the French word *bureau*, for "desk," which came to mean "office," both in the sense of a physical space and a position of authority. Louis personally supervised the activities of his bureaucrats and worked to ensure his supremacy in all matters. But he always had to negotiate with nobles and local officials who sometimes thwarted his will.

Bureaucracy and Mercantilism. Louis extended the bureaucratic forms his predecessors had developed, especially the use of intendants, officials who held their positions directly from the king rather than owning their offices, as crown officials had traditionally done. Louis handpicked an intendant for each region to represent his rule against entrenched local interests such as the parlements, provincial estates, and noble governors; they supervised the collection of taxes, the financing of public works, and the provisioning of the army. In 1673, Louis decreed that the parlements could no longer vote against his proposed laws or even speak against them. His

---

revocation of the Edict of Nantes: French king Louis XIV's decision to eliminate the rights of Calvinists granted in the edict of 1598; Louis banned all Calvinist public activities and forced those who refused to embrace the state religion to flee.

bureaucracy: A network of state officials carrying out orders according to a regular and routine line of authority.

intendants reduced local powers over finances and insisted on more efficient tax collection.

Louis's success in consolidating his authority depended on hard work, an eye for detail, and an ear to the ground. In his memoirs he described the tasks he set for himself:

> to learn each hour the news concerning every province and every nation, the secrets of every court, the mood and weaknesses of each Prince and of every foreign minister; to be well-informed on an infinite number of matters about which we are supposed to know nothing; to elicit from our subjects what they hide from us with the greatest care; to discover the most remote opinions of our courtiers and the most hidden interests of those who come to us with quite contrary professions [claims].

To gather all this information, Louis relied on a series of talented ministers, usually of modest origins, who gained fame, fortune, and even noble status from serving the king. Most important among them was Jean-Baptiste Colbert (1619–1683), the son of a wool merchant turned royal official. Colbert had managed Mazarin's personal finances and worked his way up under Louis XIV to become head of royal finances, public works, and the navy. He founded a family dynasty that eventually produced five ministers of state, an archbishop, two bishops, and three generals.

Colbert used the bureaucracy to establish a new economic doctrine, **mercantilism**. According to mercantilist policy, governments must intervene to increase national wealth by whatever means possible. Such government intervention inevitably increased the role and eventually the number of bureaucrats needed. Under Colbert, the French government established overseas trading companies, granted manufacturing monopolies, and standardized production methods for textiles, paper, and soap. A government inspection system regulated the quality of finished goods and compelled all craftsmen to organize into guilds, in which masters could supervise the work of the journeymen and apprentices. To protect French production, Colbert rescinded many internal customs fees but enacted high foreign tariffs, which cut imports of competing goods. To compete more effectively with England and the Dutch Republic, Colbert also subsidized shipbuilding, a policy that dramatically expanded the number of seaworthy vessels. Such mercantilist measures aimed to ensure France's prominence in world markets and to provide the resources needed to fight wars against the increasingly long list of en-

emies. Although later economists questioned the value of this state intervention in the economy, virtually every government in Europe embraced mercantilism.

Colbert's mercantilist projects extended to Canada, where in 1663 he took control of the trading company that had founded New France. He aimed to regulate all economic activity in the colonies. For example, he forbade colonial businesses from manufacturing anything already produced in mainland France. With the goal of establishing permanent settlements like those in the British North American colonies, he transplanted several thousand peasants from western France to the present-day province of Quebec, which France had claimed since 1608. He also tried to limit expansion westward, without success. Despite initial interruption of French fur-trading convoys by the Iroquois, in 1672 fur trader Louis Jolliet and Jesuit missionary Jacques Marquette reached the upper Mississippi River and traveled downstream as far as Arkansas. In 1684, French explorer Sieur de La Salle went all the way down to the Gulf of Mexico, claiming a vast territory for Louis XIV and calling it Louisiana after him. Colbert's successors embraced the expansion he had resisted, thinking it crucial to competing successfully with the English and the Dutch in the New World.

The Army and War. Colonial settlement occupied only a small portion of Louis XIV's attention, however, for his main foreign policy goal was to extend French power in Europe. In pursuing this purpose, he inevitably came up against the Spanish and Austrian Habsburgs, whose lands encircled his. To expand French power, Louis needed the biggest possible army. His powerful ministry of war centralized the organization of French troops. Barracks built in major towns received supplies from a central distribution system. The state began to provide uniforms for the soldiers and to offer veterans some hospital care. A militia draft instituted in 1688 supplemented the army in times of war and enrolled a hundred thousand men. Louis's wartime army could field a force as large as that of all his enemies combined.

Absolutist governments always tried to increase their territorial holdings, and as Louis extended his reach, he gained new enemies. In 1667–1668, in the War of Devolution (so called because Louis claimed that lands in the Spanish Netherlands should devolve to him since the Spanish king had failed to pay the dowry of Louis's Spanish bride), Louis defeated the Spanish armies

---

mercantilism: The doctrine that governments must intervene to increase national wealth by whatever means possible.

but had to make peace when England, Sweden, and the Dutch Republic joined the war. In the Treaty of Aix-la-Chapelle in 1668, he gained control of a few towns on the border of the Spanish Netherlands. Pamphlets sponsored by the Habsburgs accused Louis of aiming for "universal monarchy," or domination of Europe.

In 1672, Louis XIV opened hostilities against the Dutch because they stood in the way of his acquisition of more territory in the Spanish Netherlands. He declared war again on Spain in 1673. By now the Dutch had allied themselves with their former Spanish masters to hold off the French. Louis also marched his troops into territories of the Holy Roman Empire, provoking many of the German princes to join with the emperor, the Spanish, and the Dutch in an alliance against Louis, now denounced as a "Christian Turk" for his imperialist ambitions. But the French armies more than held their own. Faced with bloody but inconclusive results on the battlefield, the parties agreed to the Treaty of Nijmegen of 1678–1679, which ceded several Flemish towns and the Franche-Comté region to Louis, linking Alsace to the rest of France. French government deficits soared, and in 1675 increases in taxes touched off the most serious antitax revolt of Louis's reign.

Louis had no intention of standing still. Heartened by the Habsburgs' seeming weakness, he pushed eastward, seizing the city of Strasbourg in 1681 and invading the province of Lorraine in 1684. In 1688, he attacked some of the small German cities of the Holy Roman Empire. As Louis's own mental powers diminished with age, he apparently lost all sense of measure. His armies laid waste to German cities such as Mannheim; his government ordered the local military commander to "kill all those who would still wish to build houses there." Between 1689 and 1697, a coalition known as the League of Augsburg—made up of England, Spain, Sweden, the Dutch Republic, the Austrian emperor, and various German princes—fought Louis XIV to a stalemate. When hostilities ended in the Peace of Rijswijk in 1697, Louis returned many of his conquests made since 1678 with the exception of Strasbourg (Map 16.1). Louis never lost his taste for war, but his allies learned how to set limits on his ambitions. (See Chapter 17 for the end of Louis's reign.)

Louis was the last French ruler before Napoleon to accompany his troops to the battlefield. In later generations, as the military became more professional, French rulers left the fighting to their generals. Although Louis had eliminated

WARS OF LOUIS XIV

1667–1668	**WAR OF DEVOLUTION**
	Enemies: Spain, Dutch Republic, England, Sweden
	Ended by Treaty of Aix-la-Chapelle in 1668, with France gaining towns in Spanish Netherlands (Flanders)
1672–1678	**DUTCH WAR**
	Enemies: Dutch Republic, Spain, Holy Roman Empire
	Ended by Treaty of Nijmegen, 1678–1679, which gave several towns in Spanish Netherlands and Franche-Comté to France
1688–1697	**WAR OF THE LEAGUE OF AUGSBURG**
	Enemies: Holy Roman Empire, Sweden, Spain, England
	Ended by Peace of Rijswijk, 1697, with Louis returning all his conquests made since 1678 except Strasbourg

the private armies of his noble courtiers, he constantly promoted his own military prowess in order to keep his noble officers under his sway. He had miniature battle scenes painted on his high heels and commissioned tapestries showing his military processions into cities, even those he did not take by force. He seized every occasion to assert his supremacy, insisting that other fleets salute his ships first.

War required money and men, which Louis obtained by expanding state control over finances, conscription, and military supply. Thus, absolutism and warfare fed each other as the bureaucracy created new ways to raise and maintain an army and the army's success in war justified further expansion of state power. But constant warfare also eroded the state's resources. Further administrative and legal reform, the elimination of the buying and selling of offices, and the lowering of taxes—all were made impossible by the need for more money.

Ordinary people suffered the most for Louis's ambitions. By the end of the Sun King's reign, one in six Frenchmen had served in the military. Louis XIV's armies swelled to twice the size of the armies France fielded during the Thirty Years' War. In addition to the higher taxes paid by everyone, those who lived on the routes leading to the battlefields had to house and feed soldiers; only nobles were exempt from this requirement. Fulfilling these

MAP 16.1 Louis XIV's Acquisitions, 1668–1697
Every ruler in Europe hoped to extend his or her territorial control, and war was often the result. Louis XIV steadily encroached on the Spanish Netherlands to the north and the lands of the Holy Roman Empire to the east. Although coalitions of European powers reined in Louis's grander ambitions, he nonetheless incorporated many neighboring territories into the French crown.

demands could be difficult, if not impossible, especially during the months from November to March when weather made military campaigns difficult. Soldiers had to be fed, even when locals found themselves living off the food stored from the previous fall harvest. When food fell short, soldiers sometimes gave in to the temptation to pillage, extort, or steal from local residents.

REVIEW: How "absolute" was the power of Louis XIV?

Absolutism in Central and Eastern Europe

Central and eastern European rulers saw in Louis XIV a powerful model of absolutist state building, yet they did not blindly emulate the Sun King, in part because they confronted conditions peculiar to their regions. The ruler of Brandenburg-Prussia had to rebuild lands ravaged by the Thirty Years' War and unite far-flung territories. The Austrian Habsburgs needed to govern a mosaic of ethnic

TAKING MEASURE

State	Soldiers	Population	Ratio of soldiers/ total population
France	300,000	20 million	1:66
Russia	220,000	14 million	1:64
Austria	100,000	8 million	1:80
Sweden	40,000	1 million	1:25
Brandenburg-Prussia	30,000	2 million	1:66
England	24,000	10 million	1:410

*Figures for the end of the seventeenth century, ranging from 1688 for Prussia to 1710 for France

The Seventeenth-Century Army
The figures in this chart are only approximate, but they tell an important story. What conclusions can you draw about the relative weight of the military in the different European states? Why would England have such a smaller army than the others? Is the absolute or the relative size of the military the most important indicator?
(From André Corvisier, Armées et sociétés en Europe de 1494 à 1789 (Paris: Presses Universitaires de France, 1976), 126.)

and religious groups while fighting off the Ottoman Turks. The Russian tsars wanted to extend their power over an extensive but relatively impoverished empire. The great exception to absolutism in eastern Europe was Poland-Lithuania, where a long crisis virtually destroyed central authority and pulled much of eastern Europe into its turbulent wake.

Brandenburg-Prussia: Militaristic Absolutism

Brandenburg-Prussia began as a puny state on the Elbe River, but it had a remarkable future. In the nineteenth century, it would unify the disparate German states into modern-day Germany. The ruler of Brandenburg was an elector, one of the seven German princes entitled to select the Holy Roman Emperor. Since the sixteenth century the ruler of Brandenburg had also controlled the duchy of East Prussia; after 1618, the state was called Brandenburg-Prussia. Despite meager resources, **Frederick William of Hohenzollern**, who was the Great Elector of Brandenburg-Prussia (r. 1640–1688), succeeded in welding his scattered lands into an absolutist state.

Pressured first by the necessities of fighting the Thirty Years' War and then by the demands of re-

construction, Frederick William was determined to force his territories' estates (representative assemblies) to grant him a dependable income. The Great Elector struck a deal with the Junkers (nobles) of each province: in exchange for allowing him to collect taxes, he gave them complete control over their enserfed peasants and exempted them from taxation. The tactic worked. By the end of his reign, the estates met only on ceremonial occasions.

Supplied with a steady income, Frederick William could devote his attention to military and bureaucratic consolidation. Over forty years he expanded his army from eight thousand to thirty thousand men. (See "Taking Measure," above.) The army mirrored the rigid domination of nobles over peasants that characterized Brandenburg-Prussian society: peasants filled the ranks, and Junkers became officers. Nobles also took positions as bureaucratic officials, but military needs always had priority. The elector named special war commissars to take charge not only of military affairs but also of tax collection. To hasten military dispatches, he also established one of Europe's first state postal systems.

As a Calvinist ruler, Frederick William avoided the ostentation of the French court, even while following the absolutist model of centralizing state power. He boldly rebuffed Louis XIV by welcoming twenty thousand French Huguenot refugees after Louis's revocation of the Edict of Nantes. In pursuing foreign and domestic policies that promoted state power and prestige, Frederick William adroitly switched sides in Louis's wars and would

Frederick William of Hohenzollern: The Great Elector of Brandenburg-Prussia (r. 1640–1688) who brought his nation through the end of the Thirty Years' War and then succeeded in welding his scattered lands into an absolutist state.

stop at almost nothing to crush resistance at home. In 1701, his son Frederick I (r. 1688–1713) persuaded Holy Roman Emperor Leopold I to grant him the title "king in Prussia." Prussia had arrived as an important power.

An Uneasy Balance: Austrian Habsburgs and Ottoman Turks

Holy Roman Emperor Leopold I (r. 1658–1705) ruled over a variety of territories of different ethnicities, languages, and religions, yet in ways similar to his French and Prussian counterparts, he gradually consolidated his power. In addition to holding Louis XIV in check on his western frontiers, Leopold confronted the ever-present challenge of the Ottoman Turks to the east.

The Austrian Version of Absolutism. Like all the Holy Roman Emperors since 1438, Leopold was an Austrian Habsburg. He was simultaneously duke

of Upper and Lower Silesia, count of Tyrol, archduke of Upper and Lower Austria, king of Bohemia, king of Hungary and Croatia, and ruler of Styria and Moravia (Map 16.2). Some of these territories were provinces in the Holy Roman Empire; others were simply ruled from Vienna as Habsburg family holdings.

In response to the weakening of the Holy Roman Empire by the ravages of the Thirty Years' War, the emperor and his closest officials took control over recruiting, provisioning, and strategic planning and worked to replace the mercenaries hired during the war with a permanent standing army that promoted professional discipline. To pay for the army and staff his growing bureaucracy, Leopold gained the support of local aristocrats and chipped away at provincial institutions' powers.

Intent on replacing Bohemian nobles who had supported the 1618 revolt against Austrian authority, the Habsburgs promoted a new nobility made up of Czechs, Germans, Italians, Spaniards, and

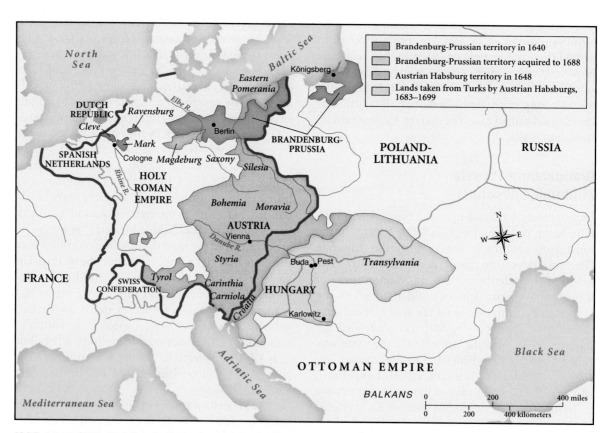

MAP 16.2 State Building in Central and Eastern Europe, 1648–1699
The Austrian Habsburgs had long contested the Ottoman Turks for dominance of eastern Europe, and by 1699 they had pushed the Turks out of Hungary. In central Europe, the Austrian Habsburgs confronted the growing power of Brandenburg-Prussia, which had emerged from relative obscurity after the Thirty Years' War to begin an aggressive program of expanding its military and its territorial base. As emperor of the Holy Roman Empire, the Austrian Habsburg ruler governed a huge expanse of territory, but the emperor's control was in fact only partial because of guarantees of local autonomy.

even Irish who used German as their common tongue, professed Catholicism, and loyally served the Austrian dynasty. Bohemia became a virtual Austrian colony. "Woe to you," lamented a Czech Jesuit in 1670, addressing Leopold, "the nobles you have oppressed, great cities made small. Of smiling towns you have made straggling villages." Austrian censors prohibited publication of this protest for over a century.

Battle for Hungary.   Austria had fought the Turks for control of Hungary for more than 150 years. In 1682, when war broke out again, Leopold I's Austria controlled the northwest section of Hungary; the Turks occupied the center; and in the east, the Turks demanded tribute from the Hungarian princes who ruled Transylvania. In 1683, the Turks pushed all the way to the gates of Vienna and laid siege to the Austrian capital. With the help of Polish cavalry, the Austrians finally broke the siege and turned the tide in a major counteroffensive (see illustration at right). By the Treaty of Karlowitz of 1699, the Ottoman Turks surrendered almost all of Hungary to the Austrians, marking the beginning of the decline of Ottoman power.

Hungary's "liberation" from the Turks came at a high price. The fighting laid waste vast stretches of Hungary's central plain, and the population may have declined by as much as 65 percent in the seventeenth century. Once the Turks had been beaten back, Austrian rule over Hungary tightened. In 1687, the Habsburg dynasty's hereditary right to the Hungarian crown was acknowledged by the Hungarian diet, a parliament revived by Leopold in 1681 to gain the cooperation of Hungarian nobles. The diet was dominated by a core of pro-Habsburg Hungarian aristocrats who would support the dynasty until it fell in 1918; Austrians and Hungarians looked down on the other ethnic groups, such as Croats and Romanians, who had enjoyed considerable autonomy under the Ottoman Turks. To root out remaining Turkish influence and assert Austrian superiority, Leopold systematically destroyed Turkish buildings and rebuilt Catholic churches, monasteries, roadside shrines, and monuments in the flamboyant Austrian baroque style.

Ottoman State Authority.   The Ottoman Turks also pursued state consolidation, but in a very different fashion from Leopold I and other European rulers. The Ottoman state extended its authority through a combination of settlement and military control. Hundreds of thousands of Turkish families moved with Turkish soldiers into the Balkan peninsula in the 1400s and 1500s. As locals con-

The Siege of Vienna, 1683
This detail from a painting by Franz Geffels shows the camp of the Ottoman Turks. The Turkish armies had surrounded Vienna since July 14, 1683. Jan Sobieski led an army of Poles who joined with Austrians and Germans to beat back the Turks on September 12, 1683.
(© The Art Archive/Corbis.)

verted to Islam, administration passed gradually into their hands. The Ottoman state would last longer than the French absolutist monarchy. Nevertheless, the seventeenth century marked a period of cultural decline in the eyes of the Turks themselves.

The Ottoman rulers, the sultans, were often challenged by mutinous army officers, but they rarely faced peasant revolts. Rather than resisting state authorities, Ottoman peasants periodically worked for the state as mercenaries. The sultans played elites off each other, absorbing some into the state bureaucracy and pitting one level of authority against another. Despite frequent palace coups and assassinations of sultans, the Ottoman state survived. This constantly shifting social and political system explains how the Ottoman state could appear weak in Western eyes and still pose a massive military threat on Europe's southeastern borders.

Russia: Setting the Foundations of Bureaucratic Absolutism

Seventeenth-century Russia seemed a world apart from the Europe of Leopold I and Louis XIV. Straddling Europe and Asia, the Russian lands stretched across Siberia to the Pacific Ocean. Western visitors either sneered or shuddered at the "barbarism" of Russian life, and Russians reciprocated by nursing deep suspicions of everything foreign. But under the surface, Russia was evolving as an absolutist state; the tsars wanted to claim unlimited autocratic power, but like their European counterparts they had to surmount internal disorder and come to an accommodation with noble landlords.

Serfdom and the Code of 1649.

When Tsar Alexei (r. 1645–1676) tried to extend state authority by imposing new administrative structures and taxes in 1648, Moscow and other cities erupted in bloody rioting. The government immediately doused the fire. In 1649, Alexei convened the Assembly of the Land (consisting of noble delegates from the provinces) to consult on a sweeping law code to organize Russian society in a strict social hierarchy that would last for nearly two centuries. The code of 1649 assigned all subjects to a hereditary class according to their current occupation or state needs. Slaves and free peasants were merged into a serf class. As serfs, they could not change occupations or move; they were tightly tied to the soil and to their noble masters. To prevent tax evasion, the code also forbade townspeople to move from the community where they resided. Nobles owed absolute obedience to the tsar and were required to serve in the army, but in return no other group could own estates worked by serfs. Serfs became the chattel of their lord, who could sell them like horses or land. Their lives differed little from those of the slaves on the plantations in the Americas.

Some peasants resisted enserfment. In 1667, **Stenka Razin**, the head of a powerful band of pirates and outlaws in southern Russia, led a rebellion that promised liberation from "the traitors and bloodsuckers of the peasant communes"— the great noble landowners, local governors, and Moscow courtiers. Captured four years later by the tsar's army, Razin was taken to Moscow, where he was dismembered in front of the public and his body thrown to the dogs (see illustration at left). Thousands of his followers also suffered grisly deaths, but his memory lived on in folk songs and legends. Landlords successfully petitioned for the abolition of the statute of limitations on runaway serfs, the use of state agents in searching for runaways, and harsh penalties against those who harbored runaways. The increase in Russian state authority went hand in hand with the enforcement of serfdom.

The Tsar's Absolute Powers.

To extend his power and emulate his western rivals, Tsar Alexei wanted a bigger army, exclusive control over state policy, and a greater say in religious matters. The size of the army increased dramatically from 35,000 in the 1630s to 220,000 by the end of the century. The Assembly of the Land, once an important source of noble consultation, never met again after 1653. Alexei also imposed firm control over the Russian Orthodox church. In 1666, a church council reaffirmed the tsar's role as God's direct representative on earth. The state-dominated church took action against a religious group called the Old Believers, who rejected church efforts to bring Russian worship in line with Byzantine tradition. Whole communities of Old Believers starved or burned themselves to death rather than submit. Religious schism opened a gulf between the Russian people and the crown.

Stenka Razin in Captivity

After leading a revolt of thousands of serfs, peasants, and members of non-Russian tribes of the middle and lower Volga region, Stenka Razin was captured by Russian forces and led off to Moscow, as shown here, where he was executed in 1671. He has been the subject of songs, legends, and poems ever since. *(RIA Novosti.)*

Stenka Razin: The head of a powerful band of pirates and outlaws in southern Russia, who in 1667 led a rebellion that promised peasants liberation from noble landowners and officials; Razin was captured by the tsar's army in 1671 and publicly executed in Moscow.

Nevertheless, modernizing trends prevailed. As the state bureaucracy expanded, adding more officials and establishing regulations and routines, the government intervened more and more in daily life. Decrees regulated tobacco smoking, card playing, and alcohol consumption and even dictated how people should leash and fence their pet dogs. Tsar Alexei set up the first Western-style theater in the Kremlin, and his daughter Sophia translated French plays. The most adventurous nobles began to wear German-style clothing. Some even argued that service and not just birth should determine rank. Russia's long struggle over Western influences had begun.

Poland-Lithuania Overwhelmed

Unlike Russia and the other eastern European powers, Poland-Lithuania did not follow the absolutist model. Decades of war weakened the monarchy and made the great nobles into virtually autonomous warlords. The great nobles dominated the Sejm (parliament), and to maintain an equilibrium among themselves, they each wielded an absolute veto power. This "free veto" constitutional system deadlocked parliamentary government. The monarchy lost its room to maneuver, and with it much of its remaining power.

In 1648, Ukrainian Cossack warriors revolted against the king of Poland-Lithuania, inaugurating two decades of tumult known as the Deluge. *Cossack* was the name given to runaway serfs and poor nobles who formed outlaw bands in the no-man's-land of southern Russia and Ukraine (Stenka Razin was a Cossack). The Polish nobles who claimed this potentially rich land scorned the Cossacks as troublemakers, but to the Ukrainian peasant population they were liberators. In 1654, the Cossacks offered Ukraine to Russian rule, provoking a Russo-Polish war that ended in 1667 when the tsar annexed eastern Ukraine and Kiev. Neighboring powers tried to profit from the chaos in Poland-Lithuania; Sweden, Brandenburg-Prussia, and Transylvania sent armies to seize territory.

Many towns were destroyed in the fighting, and as much as a third of the Polish population perished. The once prosperous Jewish and Protestant minorities suffered greatly: some fifty-six thousand Jews were killed by either the Cossacks, the Polish peasants, or the Russian troops, and thousands more had to flee or convert to Christianity. One rabbi wrote, "We were slaughtered each day, in a more agonizing way than cattle: they are butchered quickly, while we were being executed slowly." Surviving Jews moved from towns to shtetls (Jewish villages), where they took up petty trading, moneylending, tax gathering, and tavern leasing—activities that fanned peasant anti-Semitism. Desperate for protection amid the war, most Polish Protestants backed the violently anti-Catholic Swedes, and the victorious Catholic majority branded them as traitors. Some Protestant refugees fled to the Dutch Republic and England. In Poland-Lithuania it came to be assumed that a good Pole was a Catholic. The commonwealth had ceased to be an outpost of toleration.

The commonwealth revived briefly when a man of ability and ambition, Jan Sobieski (r. 1674–1696), was elected king. He gained a reputation throughout Europe when he led twenty-five thousand Polish cavalrymen into battle in the siege of Vienna in 1683. His cavalry helped rout the Turks and turned the tide against the Ottomans. Married to a politically shrewd French princess, Sobieski openly admired Louis XIV's France. Despite his efforts to rebuild the monarchy, he could not halt Poland-Lithuania's decline into powerlessness. The Polish version of constitutionalism fatally weakened the state and made it prey to neighboring powers.

Poland-Lithuania in the Seventeenth Century

> **REVIEW:** Why did absolutism flourish everywhere in eastern Europe except Poland-Lithuania?

Constitutionalism in England

In the second half of the seventeenth century, western and eastern European states began to move in different directions. In eastern Europe, nobles lorded over their serfs but owed almost slavish obedience in turn to their rulers. In western Europe, even in absolutist France, serfdom had almost entirely disappeared and nobles and rulers alike faced greater challenges to their control. The greatest challenges of all would come in England.

This outcome might seem surprising, for the English monarchs enjoyed many advantages compared with their continental rivals: they needed less money for their armies because they had stayed out of the Thirty Years' War, and their island kingdom's population was only one-fourth the size of France's and of relatively homogeneous ethnicity, making it, in theory at least, easier to rule. Yet the English rulers failed in their efforts to install absolutist policies. The English revolutions of 1642–1660 and 1688–1689 overturned two kings, confirmed the constitutional powers of an elected parliament, and laid the foundation for the idea that government must guarantee certain rights to the people under the law.

England Turned Upside Down, 1642–1660

Disputes about the right to levy taxes and the nature of authority in the Church of England had long troubled the relationship between the English crown and Parliament. For more than a hundred years, wealthy English landowners had been accustomed to participating in government through Parliament and expected to be consulted on royal policy. Although England had no single constitutional document, a variety of laws, judicial decisions, charters and petitions granted by the king, and customary procedures all regulated relations between king and Parliament. When Charles I tried to assert his authority over Parliament, a civil war broke out. It set in motion an unpredictable chain of events, which included an extraordinary ferment of religious and political ideas. Some historians view the English civil war of 1642–1646 as the last great war of religion because it pitted Puritans against those trying to push the Anglican church toward Catholicism; others see in it the first modern revolution because it gave birth to democratic political and religious movements.

Charles I versus Parliament. When Charles I (r. 1625–1649) succeeded his father, James I, he faced an increasingly aggressive Parliament that resisted new taxes and resented the king's efforts to extend his personal control. In 1628, Parliament forced Charles to agree to the Petition of Right, by which he promised not to levy taxes without its consent. Charles hoped to avoid further interference with his plans by simply refusing to call Parliament into session between 1629 and 1640. Without it, the king's ministers had to find every loophole possible to raise revenues. They tried to turn "ship money," a levy on seaports in times of emergency, into an annual tax collected everywhere in the country. The crown won the ensuing court case, but many subjects still refused to pay what they considered to be an illegal tax.

Religious tensions brought conflicts over the king's authority to a head. The Puritans had long

agitated for the removal of any vestiges of Catholicism, but Charles, married to a French Catholic, moved Anglicanism in the opposite direction in the 1630s. With Charles's encouragement, the archbishop of Canterbury, William Laud (1573–1645), imposed increasingly elaborate ceremonies on the Anglican church. Angered by these moves toward "popery," the Puritans poured forth reproving pamphlets and sermons. In response, Laud hauled them before the feared Court of Star Chamber, which the king personally controlled. The court ordered harsh sentences for Laud's Puritan critics; they were whipped, pilloried, branded, and even had their ears cut off and their noses split. When Laud tried to apply his policies to Scotland, however, they backfired completely: the stubborn Presbyterian Scots rioted against the imposition of the Anglican prayer book—the Book of Common Prayer—and in 1640 they invaded the north of England. To raise money to fight the war, Charles called Parliament into session and unwittingly opened the door to a constitutional and religious crisis.

The Parliament of 1640 did not intend revolution, but reformers in the House of Commons (the lower house of Parliament) wanted to undo what they saw as the royal tyranny of the 1630s. Parliament removed Laud from office, ordered the execution of an unpopular royal commander, abolished the Court of Star Chamber, repealed recently levied taxes, and provided for a parliamentary assembly at least once every three years, thus establishing a constitutional check on royal authority. Moderate reformers expected to stop there and resisted Puritan pressure to abolish bishops and eliminate the Anglican prayer book. But their hand was forced in January 1642, when Charles and his soldiers invaded Parliament and tried unsuccessfully to arrest those leaders who had moved to curb his power. Faced with mounting opposition within London, Charles quickly withdrew from the city and organized an army.

Civil War and the Challenge to All Authorities. The ensuing civil war between king and Parliament lasted four years (1642–1646) and divided the country. The king's army of royalists, known as Cavaliers, enjoyed the most support in northern and western England. The parliamentary forces, called Roundheads because they cut their hair short, had their stronghold in the southeast, including London. Although Puritans dominated on the parliamentary side, they were divided among themselves about the proper form of church government: the Presbyterians wanted a Calvinist church with some central authority, whereas the

Independents favored entirely autonomous congregations free from other church government (hence the term *congregationalism*, often associated with the Independents). The Puritans put aside their differences for the sake of military unity and united under an obscure member of the House of Commons, the country gentleman Oliver Cromwell (1599–1658), who sympathized with the Independents. After Cromwell skillfully reorganized the parliamentary troops, his New Model Army defeated the Cavaliers at the battle of Naseby in 1645. Charles surrendered in 1646.

England during the Civil War

Although the civil war between king and Parliament had ended in victory for Parliament, divisions within the Puritan ranks now came to the fore: the Presbyterians dominated Parliament, but the Independents controlled the army. The disputes between the leaders drew lower-class groups into the debate. (See "Contrasting Views," page 500.) When Parliament tried to disband the New Model Army in 1647, disgruntled soldiers protested. Called **Levellers** because of their insistence on leveling social differences, the soldiers took on their officers in a series of debates about the nature of political authority. The Levellers demanded that Parliament meet annually, that members be paid so as to allow common people to participate, and that all male heads of households be allowed to vote. Their ideal of political participation excluded servants, the propertyless, and women but offered access to artisans, shopkeepers, and modest farmers. Cromwell and other army leaders rejected the Levellers' demands as threatening to property owners. Cromwell insisted, "You have no other way to deal with these men but to break them in pieces. . . . If you do not break them they will break you."

Just as political differences between Presbyterians and Independents helped spark new political movements, so too their conflicts over church organization fostered the emergence of new religious doctrines. The new sects had in common only their emphasis on the "inner light" of individual religious inspiration and a disdain for hierarchical authority. Their emphasis on equality

before God and greater participation in church governance appealed to the middle and lower classes. The Baptists, for example, insisted on adult baptism because they believed that Christians should choose their own church and that every child should not automatically become a member of the Church of England. The Quakers demonstrated their beliefs in equality and the inner light by refusing to doff their hats to men in authority. Manifesting their religious experience by trembling, or "quaking," the Quakers believed that anyone — man or woman — inspired by a direct experience of God could preach.

Parliamentary leaders feared that the new sects would overturn the whole social hierarchy. Rumors abounded, for example, of naked Quakers

---

The World Turned Upside Down

The print from 1647 conveys the anxieties many people felt in the midst of religious and political upheaval. Nothing is as it should be: the feet are where the hands should be, the cart comes before the horse, a fish flies, and the wheelbarrow pushes the person. *(By permission of the British Library.)*

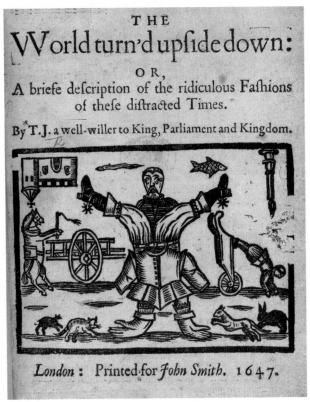

Levellers: Disgruntled soldiers in Cromwell's New Model Army who wanted to "level" social differences and extend political participation to all male property owners.

The English Civil War

The civil war between Charles I and Parliament (1642–1646) excited furious debates about the proper forms of political authority, debates that influenced political thought for two centuries or more. The Levellers, who served in the parliamentary army, wanted Parliament to be more accountable to ordinary men like themselves (Document 1). After the restoration of the monarchy in 1660, Lucy Hutchinson wrote a memoir in which she complained that Puritan *had become a term of political slander. Her memoir shows how religious terms had been politicized by the upheaval (Document 2). Thomas Hobbes, in his famous political treatise* Leviathan *(1651), develops the consequences of the civil war for political theory (Document 3).*

1. The Levellers, "The Agreement of the People, as Presented to the Council of the Army" (October 28, 1647)

Note especially two things about this document: (1) it focuses on Parliament as the chief instrument of reform, and (2) it claims that government depends on the consent of the people.

Since, therefore, our former oppressions and scarce-yet-ended troubles have been occasioned, either by want of frequent national meetings in Council [Parliament], or by rendering those meetings ineffectual, we are fully agreed and resolved to provide that hereafter our representatives be neither left to an uncertainty for the time nor made useless to the ends for which they are intended. In order whereunto we declare: — That the people of England, being at this day very unequally distributed by Counties, Cities, and Borough for the election of their deputies in Parliament, ought to be more indifferently [equally] proportioned according to the number of the inhabitants. . . . That the power of this, and all future Representatives of this Nation, is inferior only to theirs who choose them, and doth extend, without the consent or concurrence of any other person or persons [the king], to the enacting, altering, and repealing of laws, to the erecting and abolishing of offices and courts, to the appointing, removing, and calling to account magistrates and officers of all degrees, to the making of war and peace, to the treating with foreign States [in other words, Parliament is the supreme power, not the king]. . . . These things we declare to be our native rights, and therefore are agreed and resolved to maintain them with our utmost possibilities against all opposition whatsoever.

Source: Samuel Rawson Gardiner, ed., *The Constitutional Documents of the Puritan Revolution, 1625–1660* (Oxford: Clarendon Press, 1906), 333–35.

2. Lucy Hutchinson, Memoirs of the Life of Colonel Hutchinson (1664–1671)

Lucy Hutchinson wrote her memoir to defend her Puritan husband, who had been imprisoned upon the restoration of the monarchy.

If any were grieved at the dishonour of the kingdom, or the griping of the poor, or the unjust oppressions of the subject by a

---

running through the streets waiting for "a sign." Some sects did advocate sweeping change. The Diggers promoted rural communism — collective ownership of all property. Seekers and Ranters questioned just about everything. One notorious Ranter, John Robins, even claimed to be God. A few men advocated free love. These developments convinced the political elite that tolerating the new sects would lead to skepticism, anarchism, and debauchery.

In keeping with their notions of equality and individual inspiration, many of the new sects provided opportunities for women to become preachers and prophets. The Quakers thought women especially capable of prophecy. One such prophet, Anna Trapnel, explained her vocation: "For in all that was said by me, I was nothing, the Lord put all in my mouth, and told me what I should say." Women presented petitions, participated prominently in street demonstrations, distributed tracts, and occasionally even dressed as men, wearing swords and joining armies. The duchess of Newcastle complained in 1650 that women were "affecting a Masculinacy . . . practicing the behaviour . . . of men." The outspoken women in new sects like the Quakers underscored the threat of a social order turning upside down.

Oliver Cromwell. At the heart of the continuing political struggle was the question of what to do with the king, who tried to negotiate with the Presbyterians in Parliament. In late 1648, Independents in the army purged the Presbyterians from Parliament, leaving a "rump" of about seventy members. This Rump Parliament then created a high court to try Charles I. The court found him guilty of attempting to establish "an unlimited and tyrannical power" and pronounced a death sentence. On

thousand ways invented to maintain the riots of the courtiers and the swarms of needy Scots the king had brought in to devour like locusts the plenty of this land, he was a puritan; if any showed favour to any godly, honest person, kept them company, relieved them in want, or protected them against violent and unjust oppression, he was a puritan. . . . In short, all that crossed the views of the needy courtiers, the proud encroaching priests, the thievish projectors [speculators], the lewd nobility and gentry . . . all these were puritans; and if puritans, then enemies to the king and his government, seditious, factious hypocrites, ambitious disturbers of the public peace, and finally the pest of the kingdom.

Source: Christopher Hill and Edmund Dell, eds., *The Good Old Cause: The English Revolution of 1640–1660, Its Causes, Course and Consequences* (London: Lawrence and Wishart, 1949), 179–80.

3. Thomas Hobbes, *Leviathan* (1651)

In this excerpt, Hobbes depicts the anarchy of a society without a strong central authority, but he leaves open the question of whether that authority should be vested in "one Man" or "one Assembly of men," that is, a king or a parliament.

During the time men live without a common Power to keep them all in awe, they are in that condition which is called Warre; and such a warre, as is of every man, against every man. . . . In such condition, there is no place for Industry; because the fruit thereof is uncertain: and consequently no Culture of the Earth; no Navigation, nor use of the commodities that may be imported by Sea; no commodious Building; no Instrument of moving, and removing such things as require much force; no Knowledge of the face of the Earth; no account of Time; no Arts; no Letters; no Society; and which is worst of all, continuall feare, and danger of violent death; and the life of man, solitary, poore, nasty, brutish, and short. The only way to erect such a Common Power, as may be able to defend them from the invasion of Forraigners, and the injuries of one another, and thereby to secure them in such sort, as that by their owne industrie, and by the Fruites of the Earth, they may nourish themselves and live contentedly; is, to conferre all their power and strength upon one Man, or upon one Assembly of men, that may reduce all their wills, by plurality of voices, unto one Will. . . . This is more than Consent, or Concord; it is a reall Unitie of them all, in one and the same Person, made by Covenant of every man with every man. . . . This done, the Multitude so united in one Person, is called a COMMON-WEALTH, in latine CIVITAS. This is the Generation of that great LEVIATHAN, or rather (to speake more reverently) of that *Mortall God*, to which wee owe under the *Immortall God*, our peace and defence.

Source: Thomas Hobbes, *Leviathan*, ed. Richard E. Flathman and David Johnston (New York: Norton, 1997), 70, 95.

QUESTIONS TO CONSIDER
1. Why would both the king and the parliamentary leaders find the Levellers' views disturbing?
2. Why did Hobbes's arguments about political authority upset supporters of both monarchy and Parliament?

January 30, 1649, Charles was beheaded before an enormous crowd, which reportedly groaned as one when the axe fell. Although many had objected to Charles's autocratic rule, few had wanted him killed. For royalists, Charles immediately became a martyr, and reports of miracles, such as the curing of blindness by the touch of a handkerchief soaked in his blood, soon circulated.

The Rump Parliament abolished the monarchy and the House of Lords (the upper house of

Execution of Charles I
This print of the execution of English king Charles I appeared on the first page of the fictitious confessions of his executioner, Richard Brandon, who supposedly claimed to feel pains in his own neck from the moment he cut off Charles's head. (© *British Library, London, UK/The Bridgeman Art Library.*)

Printed in the year Year, of the Hang-mans down-fall, 1649.

Oliver Cromwell
In this painting of 1649, Robert Walker deliberately evokes previous portraits of English kings. Cromwell is shown preparing for battle in Ireland (note the shore and sea on Cromwell's right); he holds the baton of military command, and a young page is tying on a sash, symbol of his rank. Cromwell lived an austere life; he is depicted here without any sign of luxury. When he died, he was buried in Westminster Abbey, but in 1661 his body was exhumed and hanged in its shroud. His head was cut off and displayed outside Westminster Hall for nearly twenty years. *(National Portrait Gallery, London.)*

Parliament) and set up a Puritan republic with Oliver Cromwell (see illustration above) as chairman of the Council of State. Cromwell did not tolerate dissent from his policies. He saw the hand of God in events and himself as God's agent. Pamphleteers and songwriters ridiculed his red nose and accused him of wanting to be king, but few challenged his leadership. When his agents discovered plans for mutiny within the army, they executed the perpetrators; new decrees silenced the Levellers. Although Cromwell allowed the various Puritan sects to worship rather freely and permitted Jews with needed skills to return to England for the first time since the thirteenth century, Catholics could not worship publicly, nor could Anglicans use the Book of Common Prayer. The elites—many of them were still Anglican—were troubled by Cromwell's religious policies but pleased to see some social order reestablished.

The new regime aimed to extend state power just as Charles I had before. Cromwell laid the foundation for a Great Britain made up of England, Ireland, and Scotland by reconquering Scotland and subduing Ireland. Anti-English rebels in Ireland had seized the occasion of troubles between king and Parliament to revolt in 1641. When his position was secured in 1649, Cromwell went to Ireland with a large force and easily defeated the rebels, massacring whole garrisons and their priests. He encouraged expropriating the lands of the Irish "barbarous wretches," and Scottish immigrants resettled the northern county of Ulster. This seventeenth-century English conquest left a legacy of bitterness that the Irish even today call "the curse of Cromwell." In 1651, Parliament turned its attention overseas, putting mercantilist ideas into practice in the first Navigation Act, which allowed imports only if they were carried on English ships or came directly from the producers of goods. The Navigation Act was aimed at the Dutch, who dominated world trade; Cromwell tried to carry the policy further by waging naval war on the Dutch from 1652 to 1654.

At home, however, Cromwell faced growing resistance. His wars required a budget twice the size of Charles I's, and his increases in property taxes and customs duties alienated landowners and merchants. The conflict reached a crisis in 1653: Parliament considered disbanding the army, whereupon Cromwell abolished the Rump Parliament in a military coup and made himself Lord Protector. He now silenced his critics by banning newspapers and using networks of spies to read mail and keep tabs on his enemies. When Cromwell died in 1658, the diarist John Evelyn claimed, "There were none that cried but dogs." Cromwell intended that his son should succeed him, but his death only revived the prospect of civil war and political chaos. In 1660, a newly elected, staunchly Anglican Parliament invited Charles II, the son of the executed king, to return from exile.

The Glorious Revolution of 1688

The traditional monarchical form of government was reinstated in 1660, restoring Charles II (r. 1660–1685) to full partnership with Parliament. He promised "a liberty to tender consciences" in an attempt to extend religious toleration, especially to Catholics, with whom he sympathized. His successor James II (r. 1685–1688) pursued even more aggressive pro-Catholic policies, bringing dissent once more to a boil. In response, Parliament deposed James and installed his Protestant daughter, Mary, and her Dutch husband, William, as joint monarchs. This Glorious Revolution marked the final triumph of constitutionalism over absolutism in England.

The Restored Monarchy. Charles II moved quickly to reestablish royal authority. More than a thousand Puritan ministers lost their positions, and attending a service other than one conforming with the Anglican prayer book was illegal after 1664. Natural disasters also marred the early years of his reign. The plague stalked London's rat-infested streets in May 1665 and claimed more than thirty thousand victims by September. Then in 1666, the Great Fire (see illustration on this page) swept the city. Some in Parliament feared, not without cause, that the English government would come to resemble French absolutism. In 1670, Charles II made a secret agreement, soon leaked, with Louis XIV in which he promised to announce his conversion to Catholicism in exchange for money for a war against the Dutch. Charles never proclaimed himself a Catholic, but in his Declara-

tion of Indulgence (1673) he did suspend all laws against Catholics and Protestant dissenters. Parliament refused to continue funding the Dutch war unless Charles rescinded his Declaration of Indulgence. Asserting its authority further, Parliament passed the Test Act in 1673, requiring all government officials to profess allegiance to the Church of England and in effect disavow Catholic doctrine. Then in 1678, Parliament precipitated the so-called Exclusion Crisis by explicitly denying the throne to a Roman Catholic. This action was aimed at the king's brother and heir, James, an open convert to Catholicism. Charles refused to allow it to become law.

The dynastic crisis over the succession of a Catholic gave rise to two distinct factions in Parliament: the Tories, who supported a strong, hereditary monarchy and the restored ceremony of the Anglican church, and the Whigs, who advocated parliamentary supremacy and toleration of Protestant dissenters such as Presbyterians. Both labels were originally derogatory: *Tory* meant an Irish Catholic bandit; *Whig* was the Irish Catholic

Great Fire of London, 1666
This view of London shows the three-day fire at its height. The writer John Evelyn described the scene in his diary: "All the sky was of a fiery aspect, like the top of a burning oven, and the light seen above 40 miles round about for many nights. God grant mine eyes may never behold the like, who now saw above 10,000 houses all in one flame; the noise and cracking and thunder of people, the fall of towers, houses, and churches, was like an hideous storm." Everyone in London at the time felt overwhelmed by the catastrophe, and many attributed it to God's punishment for the upheavals of the 1640s and 1650s. (©*Museum of London.*)

designation for a Presbyterian Scot. The Tories favored James's succession despite his Catholicism, whereas the Whigs opposed a Catholic monarch. The loose moral atmosphere of Charles's court also offended some Whigs, who complained tongue in cheek that Charles was father of his country in much too literal a fashion (he had fathered more than one child by his mistresses but produced no legitimate heir).

Parliament's Revolt against James II. When he succeeded his brother, James seemed determined to force Catholicism on his subjects. Tories and Whigs joined together when a male heir—who would take precedence over James's two adult Protestant daughters—was born to James's second wife, an Italian Catholic, in 1688. They invited the Dutch ruler **William, prince of Orange**, and his wife, James's older daughter, Mary, to invade England. Mary was brought up as a Protestant and was willing to act with her husband against her father's pro-Catholic policies. James fled to France, and hardly any blood was shed. Parliament offered the throne jointly to William (r. 1689–1702) and Mary (r. 1689–1694) on the condition that they accept a bill of rights guaranteeing Parliament's full partnership in a constitutional government.

In the Bill of Rights (1689), William and Mary agreed not to raise a standing army or to levy taxes without Parliament's consent. They also agreed to call meetings of Parliament at least every three years, to guarantee free elections to parliamentary seats, and to abide by Parliament's decisions and not suspend duly passed laws. The agreement gave England's constitutional government a written, legal basis by formally recognizing Parliament as a self-contained, independent body that shared power with the rulers. Victorious supporters of the coup declared it the **Glorious Revolution** because it was achieved with so little bloodshed (at least in England).

The propertied classes who controlled Parliament prevented any resurgence of the popular turmoil of the 1640s. The Toleration Act of 1689 granted all Protestants freedom of worship, though non-Anglicans were still excluded from the universities; Catholics got no rights but were more often

left alone to worship privately. When the Catholics in Ireland rose to defend James II, William and Mary's troops brutally suppressed them. With the Whigs in power and the Tories in opposition, wealthy landowners now controlled political life throughout the realm. The factions' differences, however, were minor; essentially, the Tories had less access to the king's patronage. A contemporary reported that King William had said "that if he had good places [honors and land] enough to bestow, he should soon unite the two parties."

Social Contract Theory: Hobbes and Locke

Out of the turmoil of the English revolutions came a major rethinking of the foundations of all political authority. Although Thomas Hobbes and John Locke wrote in response to the upheavals of their times, they offered opposing arguments that were applicable to any place and any time, not just England of the seventeenth century. Hobbes justified absolute authority; Locke provided the rationale for constitutionalism. Yet both argued that all authority came not from divine right but from a **social contract** among citizens.

Hobbes. Thomas Hobbes (1588–1679) was a royalist who sat out the English civil war of the 1640s in France, where he tutored the future king Charles II. Returning to England in 1651, he published his masterpiece, *Leviathan* (1651), in which he argued for unlimited authority in a ruler. Absolute authority could be vested in either a king or a parliament; it had to be absolute, Hobbes insisted, in order to overcome the defects of human nature. Believing that people are essentially self-centered and driven by the "right to self-preservation," Hobbes made his case by referring to science, not religion. To Hobbes, human life in a state of nature—that is, any situation without firm authority—was "solitary, poor, nasty, brutish, and short." He believed that the desire for power and natural greed would inevitably lead to unfettered competition. Only the assurance of social order could make people secure enough to act according to law; consequently, giving up personal liberty, he maintained, was the price of collective security. Rulers derived their power, he concluded, from a contract in which absolute authority protects people's rights.

William, prince of Orange: Dutch ruler who, with his Protestant wife, Mary (daughter of James II), ruled England after the Glorious Revolution of 1688.

Glorious Revolution: The events of 1688 when Tories and Whigs replaced England's monarch James II with his Protestant daughter, Mary, and her husband, Dutch ruler William of Orange; William and Mary agreed to a Bill of Rights that guaranteed rights to Parliament.

social contract: The doctrine that all political authority derives not from divine right but from an implicit contract between citizens and their rulers.

Hobbes's notion of rule by an absolute authority left no room for political dissent or nonconformity, and it infuriated both royalists and supporters of Parliament. He enraged royalists by arguing that authority came not from divine right but from the social contract. Parliamentary supporters resisted Hobbes's claim that rulers must possess absolute authority to prevent the greater evil of anarchy; they believed that a constitution should guarantee shared power between king and Parliament, and protect individual rights under the law. Like Machiavelli before him, Hobbes became associated with a cynical, pessimistic view of human nature, and future political theorists often began their arguments by refuting Hobbes.

Locke.   Rejecting both Hobbes and the more traditional royalist defenses of absolute authority, John Locke (1632–1704) used the notion of a social contract to provide a foundation for constitutionalism. Locke experienced political life firsthand as physician, secretary, and intellectual companion to the earl of Shaftesbury, a leading English Whig. In 1683, during the Exclusion Crisis, Locke fled with Shaftesbury to the Dutch Republic. There he continued work on his *Two Treatises of Government,* which, when published in 1690, served to justify the Glorious Revolution of 1688. Locke's position was thoroughly antiabsolutist. He denied the divine right of kings and ridiculed the common royalist idea that political power in the state mirrored the father's authority in the family. Like Hobbes, he posited a state of nature that applied to all people. Unlike Hobbes, however, he thought people were reasonable and the state of nature peaceful.

Locke insisted that government's only purpose was to protect life, liberty, and property, a notion that linked economic and political freedom. Ultimate authority rested in the will of a majority of men who owned property, and government should be limited to its basic purpose of protection. A ruler who failed to uphold his part of the social contract between the ruler and the populace could be justifiably resisted, an idea that would become crucial for the leaders of the American Revolution a century later. For England's seventeenth-century landowners, however, Locke helped validate a revolution that consolidated their interests and ensured their privileges in the social hierarchy.

Locke defended his optimistic view of human nature in the immensely influential *Essay Concerning Human Understanding* (1690). He denied the existence of any innate ideas and asserted instead that each human is born with a mind that is a tabula rasa (blank slate). Not surprisingly, Locke devoted considerable energy to rethinking educational practices; he believed that education crucially shaped the human personality by channeling all sensory experience. Everything humans know, he claimed, comes from sensory experience, not from anything inherent in human nature. Locke's views promoted the belief that "all men are created equal," a belief that challenged absolutist forms of rule and ultimately raised questions about women's roles as well. Although Locke himself owned shares in the Royal African Company and justified slavery, his writings were later used by abolitionists in their campaign against slavery.

> **REVIEW:** What differences over religion and politics caused the conflict between king and Parliament in England?

Outposts of Constitutionalism

When William and Mary came to the throne in England in 1689, the Dutch and the English put aside the rivalries that had brought them to war against each other in 1652–1654, 1665–1667, and 1672–1674. Under William, the Dutch and the English together led the coalition that blocked Louis XIV's efforts to dominate continental Europe. The English and Dutch had much in common: oriented toward commerce, especially overseas, they were the successful exceptions to absolutism in Europe. Also among the few outposts of constitutionalism in the seventeenth century were the British North American colonies, which developed representative government while the English were preoccupied with their revolutions at home. Constitutionalism was not the only factor shaping this Atlantic world; as constitutionalism developed in the colonies, so too did the enslavement of black Africans as a new labor force.

The Dutch Republic

When the Dutch Republic gained formal independence from Spain in 1648, it had already established a decentralized, constitutional state. Rich merchants called regents effectively controlled the internal affairs of each province and through the Estates General named the *stadholder,* the executive officer responsible for defense and for representing the state at all ceremonial occasions. They

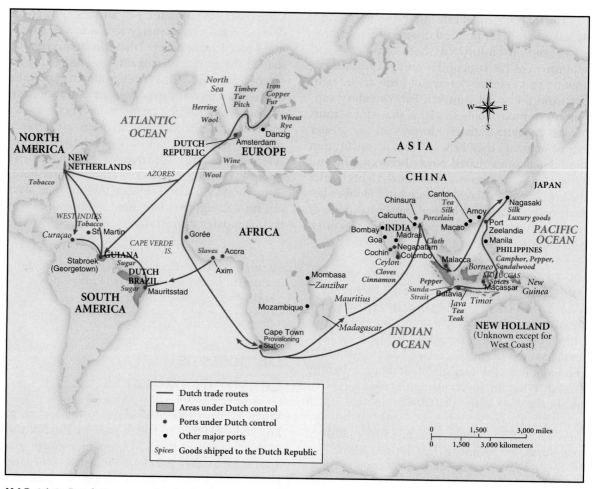

MAP 16.3 Dutch Commerce in the Seventeenth Century
Even before gaining formal independence from the Spanish in 1648, the Dutch had begun to compete with the Spanish and Portuguese all over the world. In 1602, a group of merchants established the Dutch East India Company, which soon offered investors an annual rate of return of 35 percent on the trade in spices with countries located on the Indian Ocean. Global commerce gave the Dutch the highest standard of living in Europe and soon attracted the envy of the French and the English.

almost always chose one of the princes of the house of Orange, but the stadholder resembled a president more than a king.

The decentralized state encouraged and protected trade, and the Dutch Republic soon became Europe's financial capital. The Bank of Amsterdam offered borrowers lower interest rates than those available in England and France. Praised for their industriousness, thrift, and cleanliness—and maligned as greedy, dull "butter-boxes"—the Dutch dominated overseas commerce with their shipping (Map 16.3). They imported products from all over the world: spices, tea, and silk from Asia; sugar and tobacco from the Americas; wool from England and Spain; timber and furs from Scandinavia;

grain from eastern Europe. A widely reprinted history of Amsterdam that appeared in 1662 described the city as "risen through the hand of God to the peak of prosperity and greatness. . . . The whole world stands amazed at its riches and from east and west, north and south they come to behold it."

The Dutch rapidly became the most prosperous and best-educated people in Europe. Middle-class people supported the visual arts, especially painting, to an unprecedented degree. Artists and engravers produced thousands of works, and Dutch artists were among the first to sell to a mass market. Whereas in other countries kings, nobles, and churches bought art, Dutch buyers were mer-

A Typical Dutch Scene from Daily Life
Jan Steen painted *The Baker Arent Oostward and His Wife* in 1658. Steen ran a brewery and tavern in addition to painting, and he was known for his interest in the details of daily life. Dutch artists popularized this kind of "genre" painting, which showed ordinary people at work and play.
(Rijksmuseum, Amsterdam.)

■ **For more help analyzing this image,** see the visual activity for this chapter in the Online Study Guide at **bedfordstmartins.com/hunt**.

chants, artisans, and shopkeepers. Engravings, illustrated histories, and oil paintings were all relatively inexpensive. One foreigner commented that "pictures are very common here, there being scarce an ordinary tradesman whose house is not decorated with them." Dutch artists focused on familiar daily details because for them ordinary people had religious as well as political significance; even children at play could be infused with radiant beauty. The family household, not the royal court, determined the moral character of this intensely commercial society. Relative prosperity decreased the need for married women to work, so Dutch society developed the clear contrast between middle-class male and female roles that would become prevalent elsewhere in Europe and in America more than a century later. As one contemporary Dutch writer explained, "The husband must be on the street to practice his trade; the wife must stay at home to be in the kitchen."

Extraordinarily high levels of urbanization and literacy created a large reading public. Dutch presses printed books censored elsewhere (printers or authors censored in one province simply shifted operations to another), and the University of Leiden attracted students and professors from all over Europe. Dutch tolerance extended to the works of Benedict Spinoza (1633–1677), a Jewish philosopher and biblical scholar who was expelled by his synagogue for alleged atheism but left alone by the Dutch authorities. Spinoza strove to reconcile religion with science and mathematics, but his work scandalized many Christians and Jews because he seemed to equate God and nature. Like nature, Spinoza's God followed unchangeable laws and could not be influenced by human actions, prayers, or faith.

Dutch learning, painting, and commerce all enjoyed wide renown in the seventeenth century, but this luster proved hard to maintain. The Dutch lived in a world of international rivalries in which strong central authority gave their enemies an advantage. Though inconclusive, the naval wars with England between 1652 and 1674 drained the state's revenues. Even more dangerous were the land wars with France, which continued into the eighteenth century. The Dutch survived these challenges but increasingly depended on alliances with other powers, especially England after the Glorious Revolution. At the end of the seventeenth century, the Dutch elites became more exclusive, more preoccupied with ostentation, and less tolerant of deviations from strict Calvinism. Rather than encouraging native Dutch styles, they became more concerned with imitating French ones. The Dutch "golden age" was over.

Freedom and Slavery in the New World

The Dutch also lost ground to the French and English in the New World colonies. While the Dutch concentrated on shipping, including the slave trade, the seventeenth-century French and English established settler colonies that would eventually provide fabulous revenues to the home countries. Many European governments encouraged private companies to vie for their share of the slave trade, and slavery began to take clear institutional form in the New World in this period. While whites found in the colonies greater political and religious freedom than in Europe, they subjected black Africans to the most degrading forms of bondage.

The Rise of the Slave Trade.

After the Spanish and Portuguese had shown that African slaves could be transported and forced to labor in South and Central America, the English and French endeavored to set up similar labor systems in their new Caribbean island colonies. White planters with large tracts of land bought African slaves to work fields of sugarcane; and as they gradually built up their holdings, the planters displaced most of the original white settlers, who moved to mainland North American colonies. After 1661, when Barbados instituted a slave code that stripped all Africans of rights under English law, slavery became codified as an inherited status that applied only to blacks. The result was a society of extremes: the very wealthy whites (about 7 percent of the population in Barbados) and the enslaved, powerless black majority. The English brought few of their religious or constitutional practices to the Caribbean.

Other Caribbean colonies followed a similar pattern of development. Louis XIV promulgated a "black code" in 1685 to regulate the legal status of slaves in the French colonies and to prevent non-Catholics from owning slaves. The code supposedly set limits on the violence planters could exercise and required them to house, feed, and clothe their slaves. But white planters simply ignored provisions of the code that did not suit them, and in any case, because the code defined slaves as property, slaves could not themselves bring suit in court to demand better treatment.

The governments of England, France, Spain, Portugal, the Dutch Republic, and Denmark all encouraged private companies to traffic in black Africans, while the highest church and government authorities in Catholic and Protestant countries alike condoned the gradually expanding slave trade. In 1600, about 9,500 Africans were exported from Africa to the New World every year; by 1700, this number had increased nearly fourfold to 36,000 annually. Historians advance several different ideas about which factors increased the slave trade: some claim that improvements in muskets made European slavers more effective; others cite the rising price for slaves, which made their sale more attractive for Africans; still others focus on factors internal to Africa such as the increasing size of African armies and their use of muskets in fighting and capturing other Africans for sale as slaves. The way had been prepared for the development of an Atlantic economy based on slavery.

Constitutional Freedoms in the English Colonies.

Virtually left to themselves during the upheavals in England, the fledgling English colonies in North America developed representative government on their own. Almost every colony had a governor and a two-house legislature. The colonial legislatures constantly sought to increase their power and resisted the efforts of Charles II and James II to reaffirm royal control. William and Mary reluctantly allowed emerging colonial elites more control over local affairs. The social and political elite among the settlers hoped to impose an English social hierarchy dominated by rich landowners. Ordinary immigrants to the colonies, however, took advantage of plentiful land to carve out their own farms using white servants and, later, in some colonies, African slaves.

For native Americans, the expanding European presence meant something else altogether. They faced death through disease and warfare and the accelerating loss of their homelands. Unlike white settlers, many native Americans believed that land was a divine gift provided for their collective use and not subject to individual ownership. Europeans' claims that they owned exclusive land rights consequently resulted in frequent skirmishes. In 1675–1676, for instance, three tribes allied under Metacomet (called King Philip by the English) threatened the survival of New England settlers, who savagely repulsed the attacks and sold their captives as slaves. Whites could portray native Americans as "noble savages," but when threatened they often depicted them as conspiring villains and sneaky heathens who were akin to Africans in their savagery. The benefits of constitutionalism were reserved for Europeans.

REVIEW: Why did constitutionalism thrive in the Dutch Republic and the British North American colonies, even as their participation in the slave trade grew?

The Search for Order in Elite and Popular Culture

Constitutionalism's emphasis on a social contract fostered the guarantee of individual freedoms, yet the constitutional governments pursued profits in the burgeoning slave trade just as avidly as the absolutist ones. Freedom did not mean liberty for everyone. One of the great debates of the time—and thereafter—concerned the meaning of freedom: for whom, under what conditions, with what justifiable limitations could freedom be claimed? Freedom of the press found its first champion in the English poet John Milton, and freedom to choose one's own religion began to attract adherents too. These freedoms posed their own dilemmas: should publishers be allowed to print anything they wished and would religious toleration undermine the state's authority or even promote skepticism about religion in general?

Poetry, painting, architecture, and even science at this time all reflected in some measure the attempts to ground authority—to define the relation between freedom and order—in new ways. Authority concerned not just rulers and subjects but also the hierarchy of groups in society. As European states consolidated their powers, elites worked to distinguish themselves from the lower classes. They developed new codes of correct behavior for themselves and tried to teach order and discipline to their social inferiors. Their repeated efforts show, however, that popular culture had its own dynamics which resisted control from above.

Freedom and Constraint in the Arts and Sciences

Most Europeans feared disorder above all else. The French mathematician Blaise Pascal vividly captured their worries in his *Pensées* (Thoughts) of 1660: "I look on all sides, and I see only darkness everywhere." Though Pascal made important contributions to the mathematical theory of probabilities, he was skeptical about the human ability to forge order out of chaos: "Nature presents to me nothing which is not a matter of doubt and concern. . . . It is incomprehensible that God should exist, and incomprehensible that He should not exist." Pascal urged his readers to accept the wager that God existed. Reason could not determine whether God existed or not, Pascal concluded. Poets, painters, and architects all grappled with similar issues of faith, reason,

and authority, but most of them came to more positive conclusions than Pascal about human capacities.

Milton.   The English Puritan poet John Milton (1608–1674) wrestled with the inevitable limitations on individual liberty. In 1643, in the midst of the civil war between king and Parliament, he published writings in favor of divorce. When Parliament enacted a censorship law aimed at such literature, Milton responded in 1644 with one of the first defenses of freedom of the press, *Areopagitica*. (See Document, "John Milton, Defense of Freedom of the Press," page 511.) In it, he argued that even controversial books about religion should be allowed because the state could not command religious belief. Milton favored limited

Gian Lorenzo Bernini, *Ecstasy of St. Teresa of Ávila* (c. 1650)
This ultimate statement of baroque sculpture captures all the drama and even sensationalism of a mystical religious faith. Bernini based his figures on a vision reported by St. Teresa in which she saw an angel: "In his hands I saw a great golden spear, and at the iron tip there appeared to be a point of fire. This he plunged into my heart several times so that it penetrated my entrails. When he pulled it out I felt that he took them with it, and left me utterly consumed by the great love of God." *(Scala/Art Resource, NY.)*

French Classicism

This painting by Nicolas Poussin, *Discovery of Achilles on Skyros* (1649–1650), shows the French interest in classical themes and ideals. In the Greek story, Thetis dresses her son Achilles as a young woman and hides him on the island of Skyros so he would not have to fight in the Trojan War. When a chest of treasures is offered to the women, Achilles reveals himself (he is the figure on the far right) because he cannot resist the sword. In telling the story, Poussin emphasizes harmony and almost a sedateness of composition, avoiding the exuberance and emotionalism of the baroque style. *(Photograph © 2007 Museum of Fine Arts, Boston.)*

religious toleration; that is, he wanted religious freedom for the many varieties of Protestants, but not for Catholics or non-Christians. Milton served as secretary to the Council of State during Cromwell's rule and earned the enmity of Charles II by writing a justification for the execution of his father, Charles I.

Forced into retirement after the restoration of the monarchy, Milton published his epic poem *Paradise Lost* in 1667. He used the biblical Adam and Eve's fall from grace to meditate on human freedom and the tragedies of rebellion. Although Milton wanted to "justify the ways of God to man," his Satan, the proud angel who challenges God and is cast out of heaven, is so compelling as to be heroic. In the end, Adam and Eve embrace moral responsibility for their actions. Individuals learn the limits to their freedom, yet personal liberty remains essential to their humanity.

The Varieties of Artistic Style. The dominant artistic styles of the time—the baroque and the classical—both submerged the ordinary individual in a grander design. The baroque style proved to be especially suitable for public displays of faith and power that overawed individual beholders. The combination of religious and political purposes in baroque art is best exemplified in the architecture and sculpture of Gian Lorenzo Bernini (1598–1680), the papacy's official artist. His architectural masterpiece was the gigantic square facing St. Peter's Basilica in Rome. Bernini's use of freestanding colonnades and a huge open space was meant to impress the individual observer with

the power of the popes and the Catholic religion. He also sculpted tombs for the popes and a large statue of Constantine, the first Christian emperor of Rome—perfect examples of the marriage of power and religion.

Although France was a Catholic country, French painters, sculptors, and architects, like their patron Louis XIV, preferred the standards of **classicism** to those of the baroque. French artists developed classicism to be a French national style, distinct from the baroque style that was closely associated with France's enemies, the Austrian and Spanish Habsburgs. As its name suggests, classicism reflected the ideals of the art of antiquity: geometric shapes, order, and harmony of lines took precedence over the sensuous, exuberant, and emotional forms of the baroque. Rather than being overshadowed by the sheer power of emotional display, in classicism the individual could be found at the intersection of converging, symmetrical, straight lines (see illustration above). These influences were apparent in the work of the leading French painters of the period, Nicolas Poussin (1594–1665) and Claude Lorrain (1600–1682), both of whom worked in Rome and tried to recreate classical Roman values in their mythological scenes and Roman landscapes.

Art could also serve the interests of science. One of the most skilled illustrators of insects and

classicism: A style of painting and architecture that reflected the ideals of the art of antiquity; in classicism, geometric shapes, order, and harmony of lines take precedence over the sensuous, exuberant, and emotional forms of the baroque.

DOCUMENT

John Milton, Defense of Freedom of the Press (1644)

In Areopagitica *(1644), the English poet John Milton rebuked Parliament for passing a bill to restrict freedom of the press by requiring licensing of every publication. The title came from Areopagus, the name of a court in ancient Athens. Milton argued that freedom of thought was essential to human dignity.*

I deny not but that it is of greatest concernment in the church and commonwealth to have a vigilant eye how books demean themselves as well as men; and thereafter to confine, imprison, and do sharpest justice on them as malefactors. For books are not absolutely dead things, but do contain a potency of life in them to be as active as that soul was whose progeny they are; nay, they do preserve as in a vial the purest efficacy and extraction of that living intellect that bred them. I know they are as lively and as vigorously productive as those fabulous dragon's teeth; and being sown up and down, may chance to spring up armed men. And yet, on the other hand, unless wariness be used, as good almost kill a man as kill a good book:

who kills a man kills a reasonable creature, God's image; but he who destroys a good book, kills reason itself, kills the image of God, as it were, in the eye. Many a man lives a burden to the earth; but a good book is the precious lifeblood of a master spirit, embalmed and treasured up on purpose to a life beyond life. 'Tis true, no age can restore a life, whereof perhaps there is no great loss; and revolutions of ages do not oft recover the loss of a rejected truth, for the want of which whole nations fare the worse. We should be wary, therefore, what persecution we raise against the living labors of public men, how we spill that seasoned life of man preserved and stored up in books; since we see a kind of homicide may be thus committed, sometimes a martyrdom; and if it extend to the whole impression, a kind of massacre, whereof the execution ends not in the slaying of an elemental life, but strikes at that ethereal and fifth essence, the breath of reason itself, slays an immortality rather than a life. But lest I should be condemned of introducing license, while I oppose licensing, I refuse not the pains to be so much histor-

ical as will serve to show what hath been done by ancient and famous commonwealths against this disorder, till the very time that this project of licensing crept out of the Inquisition, was caught up by our prelates, and hath caught some of our presbyters. [. . .] As therefore the state of man now is, what wisdom can there be to choose, what continence to forbear without the knowledge of evil? He that can apprehend and consider vice with all her baits and seeming pleasures, and yet abstain, and yet distinguish, and yet prefer that which is truly better, he is the true warfaring Christian. I cannot praise a fugitive and cloistered virtue, unexercised and unbreathed, that never sallies out and sees her adversary, but slinks out of the race where that immortal garland is to be run for, not without dust and heat. Assuredly we bring not innocence into the world, we bring impurity much rather: that which purifies us is trial, and trial is by what is contrary.

Source: John Milton, *Milton's Prose Writing* (London: J. M. Dant, 1961), 149–50, 158.

---

flowers was Maria Sibylla Merian (1646–1717), a German-born painter-scholar whose engravings were widely celebrated for their brilliant realism and microscopic clarity. Merian eventually separated from her husband and joined a sect called the Labadists (after its French founder, Jean de Labadie), whose members did not believe in formal marriage ties. After moving with her daughters to the Labadists' community in the northern Dutch province of Friesland, Merian went with missionaries from the sect to the Dutch colony of Surinam, in South America, and painted watercolors (see illustration, page 512) of the exotic flowers, birds, and insects she found in the jungle around the cocoa and sugarcane plantations. Many women became known for their still lifes, and especially their paintings of flowers, during this time.

Public Interest in Science. Despite the initial religious controversies associated with the scientific

revolution, absolutist rulers quickly saw the potential of the new science for enhancing their prestige and glory. Frederick William, the Great Elector of Brandenburg-Prussia, for example, set up agricultural experiments in front of his Berlin palace, and various German princes supported the work of Gottfried Wilhelm Leibniz (1646–1716), who claimed that he, and not Isaac Newton, had invented the calculus. A lawyer, diplomat, mathematician, and scholar who wrote about metaphysics, cosmology, and history, Leibniz also helped establish scientific societies in the German states.

Government involvement in science was greatest in France, where science became an arm of mercantilist policy; in 1666, Colbert founded the Royal Academy of Sciences, which supplied fifteen scientists with government stipends. It met in the King's Library in Paris, where for the first years the members devoted themselves to alchemical experiments and the study of mechanical devices.

European Fascination with Products of the New World
In this painting of a banana plant, Maria Sibylla Merian offers a scientific study of one of the many exotic plants and animals found by Europeans who traveled to the colonies overseas. Merian was fifty-one when she traveled to the Dutch South American colony of Surinam with her daughter. *(Courtesy of Hunt Institute for Botanical Documentation, Carnegie Mellon University, Pittsburgh, PA.)*

watch the exhibition of experiments. Labeled "mad" by her critics, she attacked the use of telescopes and microscopes because she detected in the new experimentalism a mechanistic view of the world that exalted masculine prowess and challenged the Christian belief in freedom of the will. Yet she urged the formal education of women, complaining that "we are kept like birds in cages to hop up and down in our houses." "Many of our Sex may have as much wit, and be capable of Learning as well as men," she insisted, "but since they want Instructions [lack education], it is not possible they should attain to it."

Women and Manners

Although excluded from the universities and the professions, women played important roles not only in the home but also in more formal spheres of social interaction, such as the courts of rulers. Women often took the lead in teaching manners or social etiquette. Poetry and painting might imaginatively explore the place of the individual within a larger whole, but real-life individuals had to learn to navigate their own social worlds. Women's importance in refining social relationships quickly became a subject of controversy.

The Cultivation of Manners.   The court had long been a central arena for the development of manners. Under the tutelage of their mothers and wives, nobles learned to hide all that was crass and to maintain a fine sense of social distinction. In some ways, aristocratic men were expected to act more like women; just as women had long been expected to please men, now aristocratic men had to please their monarch or patron by displaying proper manners and conversing with elegance and wit. The art of pleasing included foreign languages (especially French), dance, a taste for fine music, and attention to dress.

As part of the evolution of new aristocratic ideals, nobles learned to disdain all that was lowly. The upper classes began to reject popular festivals and fairs in favor of private theaters, where seats were relatively expensive and behavior was formal. Clowns and buffoons now seemed vulgar; the last king of England to keep a court fool was Charles I. Chivalric romances that had entranced the nobility since the time of Cervantes's *Don Quixote* (1605) now passed into popular literature.

Constitutional states supported science informally but provided an environment that encouraged its spread. The Royal Society of London, the counterpart to the one in Paris, grew out of informal meetings of scientists at London and Oxford rather than direct government involvement. It received a royal charter in 1662 but maintained complete independence. The society's secretary described its business to be "in the first place, to scrutinize the whole of Nature and to investigate its activity and powers by means of observations and experiments; and then in course of time to hammer out a more solid philosophy and more ample amenities of civilization." Whether the state paid for the work or not, thinkers of the day now tied science explicitly to social progress.

Because of their exclusion from most universities, women only rarely participated in the new scientific discoveries. In 1667, nonetheless, the Royal Society of London invited Margaret Cavendish, a writer of poems, essays, letters, and philosophical treatises, to attend a meeting to

The greatest French playwright of the seventeenth century, Molière (the pen name of Jean-Baptiste Poquelin, 1622–1673), wrote sparkling comedies of manners that revealed much about the new aristocratic behavior. His play *The Middle-Class Gentleman*, first performed for Louis XIV in 1670, revolves around the yearning of a rich, middle-class Frenchman, Monsieur Jourdain, to learn to act like a *gentilhomme* (meaning both "gentleman" and "nobleman"). Monsieur Jourdain buys fancy clothes; hires private instructors in dancing, music, fencing, and philosophy; and lends money to a debt-ridden noble in hopes that the noble will marry his daughter. Only his sensible wife and his daughter's love for a worthier commoner stand in his way. The message for the king's courtiers seemed to be a reassuring one: only true nobles by blood can hope to act like nobles. But the play also showed how the middle classes were learning to emulate the nobility; if one could learn to act nobly through self-discipline, could not anyone with some education and money pass himself off as noble?

As Molière's play demonstrated, new attention to manners trickled down from the court to the middle class. A French treatise on manners written in 1672 explained proper behavior:

> If everyone is eating from the same dish, you should take care not to put your hand into it before those of higher rank have done so. . . . Formerly one was permitted . . . to dip one's bread into the sauce, provided only that one had not already bitten it. Nowadays that would be a kind of rusticity. Formerly one was allowed to take from one's mouth what one could not eat and drop it on the floor, provided it was done skillfully. Now that would be very disgusting.

The key words *rusticity* and *disgusting* reveal the association of unacceptable social behavior with the peasantry, dirt, and repulsion. Similar rules governed spitting and blowing one's nose in public. Once the elite had successfully distinguished itself from the lower classes through manners, scholars became more interested in studying popular expressions. They avidly collected proverbs, folktales, and songs—all of these now curiosities.

Debates about Women's Roles. Courtly manners often permeated the upper reaches of society by means of the **salon**, an informal gathering held regularly in private homes and presided over by a socially eminent woman. In 1661, one French author claimed to have identified 251 Parisian women as hostesses of salons. The French government occasionally worried that these gatherings might challenge its authority, but the three main

topics of conversation were love, literature, and philosophy. Hostesses often worked hard to encourage the careers of budding authors. Before publishing a manuscript, many authors, including court favorites like Corneille and Racine, would read their compositions to a salon gathering.

Some women went beyond encouraging male authors and began to write on their own, but they faced many obstacles. Marie-Madeleine Pioche de La Vergne, known as Madame de Lafayette, wrote several short novels that were published anonymously because it was considered inappropriate for aristocratic women to appear in print. Following the publication of *The Princess of Clèves* in 1678, she denied having written it. Hannah Woolley, the English author of many books on domestic conduct, published under the name of her first husband. Women were known for writing wonderful letters, but the correspondence circulated only in handwritten form. In the 1650s, despite these limitations, French women began to turn out best sellers of a new type of literary form, the novel. Their success prompted the philosopher Pierre Bayle to remark in 1697 that "our best French novels for a long time have been written by women."

The new importance of women in the world of manners and letters did not sit well with everyone. Although the French writer François Poulain de la Barre, in a series of works published in the 1670s, used the new science to assert the equality of women's minds, most men resisted the idea. Clergy, lawyers, scholars, and playwrights attacked women's growing public influence. Women, they complained, were corrupting forces and needed restraint. Only marriage, "this salutary yoke," could control their passions and weaknesses. Women were accused of raising "the banner of prostitution in the salons, in the promenades, and in the streets." Molière wrote plays denouncing women's pretension to judge literary merit. English playwrights derided learned women by creating characters with names such as Lady Knowall, Lady Meanwell, and Mrs. Lovewit.

A real-life target of the English playwrights was Aphra Behn (1640–1689), one of the first professional woman authors, who supported herself by journalism, wrote plays and poetry, and translated scientific works. Her short novel *Oroonoko* (1688) told the story of an African prince mistakenly sold into slavery. The story was so successful that it was adapted by playwrights and performed repeatedly in England and France for the next hundred years.

Women also played important roles in the new colonies. In order to establish more permanent

---

salon: An informal gathering held regularly in private homes and presided over by a socially eminent woman; salons spread from France in the seventeenth century to other countries in the eighteenth century.

and settled colonies, governments promoted the emigration of women so that male colonists would set up orderly Christian white households rather than pursuing sexual relations with native or slave women.

Reforming Popular Culture

Controversies over female influence had little effect on the unschooled peasants who made up most of Europe's population. Their culture had three main elements: their religion, which shaped every aspect of life and death; the knowledge needed to work at farming or in a trade; and popular forms of entertainment such as village fairs and dances. What changed most noticeably in the seventeenth century was the social elites' attitude toward lower-class culture. The division between elite and popular culture widened as elites insisted on their difference from the lower orders and tried to instill new forms of discipline in their social inferiors. These efforts did not always succeed, however, as villagers tenaciously clung to their own traditions.

Popular Religion. In the seventeenth century, Protestant and Catholic churches alike pushed hard to change popular religious practices. Their campaigns against popular "paganism" began during the sixteenth-century Protestant Reformation and Catholic Counter-Reformation but reached much of rural Europe only in the seventeenth century. Puritans in England tried to root out maypole dances, Sunday village fairs, gambling, taverns, and bawdy ballads because they interfered with sober observance of the Sabbath. In Lutheran Norway, pastors denounced a widespread belief in the miracle-working powers of St. Olaf. The word *superstition* previously meant "false religion" (Protestantism was a superstition for Catholics, Catholicism for Protestants); in the seventeenth century, it took on its modern meaning of irrational fears, beliefs, and practices, which anyone educated or refined would avoid.

The Catholic campaign against superstitious practices found a ready ally in Louis XIV. While the Sun King reformed the nobles at court through etiquette and manners, Catholic bishops in the French provinces trained parish priests to reform their flocks by using catechisms in local dialects and insisting that parishioners attend Mass. The church faced a formidable challenge. One bishop in France complained in 1671, "Can you believe that there are in this diocese entire villages where no one has even heard of Jesus Christ?" In some places, believers sacrificed animals to the Virgin, prayed to

the new moon, and worshipped at the sources of streams as in pre-Christian times.

Like its Protestant counterpart, the Catholic campaign against ignorance and superstition helped extend state power. Clergy, officials, and local police worked together to limit carnival celebrations, to regulate pilgrimages to shrines, and to replace "indecent" images of saints with more restrained and decorous ones. In Catholicism, the cult of the Virgin Mary and devotions closely connected with Jesus, such as the Holy Sacrament and the Sacred Heart, took precedence over the celebration of popular saints who seemed to have pagan origins or were credited with unverified miracles. Reformers everywhere tried to limit the number of feast days on the grounds that they encouraged lewd behavior.

New Attitudes toward Poverty. The campaign for more disciplined religious practices helped generate a new attitude toward the poor. Poverty previously had been closely linked with charity and virtue in Christianity; it was a Christian duty to give alms to the poor, and Jesus and many of the saints had purposely chosen lives of poverty. In the sixteenth and seventeenth centuries, the upper classes, the church, and the state increasingly regarded the poor as dangerous, deceitful, and lacking in character. "Criminal laziness is the source of all their vices," wrote a Jesuit expert on the poor. The courts had previously expelled beggars from cities; now local leaders, both Catholic and Protestant, tried to reform their character. Municipal magistrates collected taxes for poor relief, and local notables organized charities; together they transformed hospitals into houses of confinement for beggars. In Catholic France, upper-class women's religious associations, known as confraternities, set up asylums that confined prostitutes (by arrest if necessary) and rehabilitated them. Confraternities also founded hospices where orphans learned proper behavior and respect for their betters. Such groups advocated harsh discipline as the cure for poverty.

As hard times increased the numbers of the poor and the rates of violent crime as well, attitudes toward the poor hardened. The elites tried to separate the very poor from society either to change them or to keep them from contaminating others. Hospitals became holding pens for society's unwanted members; in them, the poor joined the disabled, the incurably diseased, and the insane. The founding of hospitals demonstrates the connection between elites' attitudes and state building. In 1676, Louis XIV ordered every French city to establish a hospital, and his government took charge of the finances. Other rulers soon followed the same path.

Popular Resistance to Reform.   Even as elites set themselves apart and reformers from church and state tried to regulate popular activities, villagers and townspeople pushed back with reassertions of their own values. For hundreds of years, peasants had maintained their own forms of village justice — called variously "rough music," "ride on a donkey," "skimmington," "charivari," or in North America, "shivaree." If a young man married a much older woman for her money, for example, villagers would serenade the couple by ringing bells, playing crude flutes, banging pots and pans, and shooting muskets. If a man was rumored to have been physically assaulted by his wife, a reversal of the usual sex roles, he (or effigies of him and his wife) might be ridden on a donkey facing backward (to signify the role reversal) and pelted with dung before being ducked in a nearby pond or river. Anyone who transgressed the local customs governing family life — adulterers, for example — might suffer a similar fate. Processions sometimes included the display of horned animal heads (a symbol of adultery) or obscene drawings, and people made up mocking ryhmes and songs for various occasions. Some villagers singled out rebellious women, wife beaters, and fathers deemed excessively cruel to their children. Others directed their mockery at tax officials, gamekeepers on big estates who tried to keep villagers from hunting, or unpopular preachers.

No matter how much care went into controlling religious festivals, such events almost invariably opened the door to popular reinterpretation and sometimes drunken celebration. When the Spanish introduced Corpus Christi processions to their colony in Peru in the seventeenth century, elite Incas dressed in royal costumes to carry the banners of their parishes. Their clothing and ornaments combined Christian symbols with their own indigenous ones. They thus signaled their conversion to Catholicism but also reasserted their own prior identities. The Corpus Christi festival, held in late May or early June, conveniently took place about the same time as Inca festivals from the pre-Spanish era. Carnival, the days preceding Lent on the Christian calendar (Mardi Gras, or Fat Tuesday, is the last of them), offered the occasion for public revelry of all sorts. Although Catholic clergy worked hard to clamp down on the more riotous aspects of Carnival, many towns and villages still held parades, like those of modern New

Corpus Christi Procession in Peru
This painting shows a Catholic procession by Incas that took place in the late 1670s in Cuzco, Peru. The Inca in front is wearing his native dress and he is followed by a float and religious figures carrying traditional Catholic imagery. *(Museo del Arzobispo, Cuzco, Peru.)*

Orleans or Rio de Janeiro, that included companies of local men dressed in special costumes and gigantic stuffed figures, sometimes with animal skins or heads, or elaborate masks.

> **REVIEW:** How did elite and popular culture become more separate in the seventeenth century?

Conclusion

The search for order took place on various levels, from the reform of the disorderly poor to the establishment of bureaucratic routines in government. The absolutist government of Louis XIV served as a model for all those who aimed to increase the power of the central state. Even Louis's rivals — such as the Holy Roman Emperor Leopold I and Frederick William, the Great Elector of Brandenburg-Prussia — followed his lead in centralizing authority and building up their armies. Whether absolutist or constitutionalist in form, seventeenth-century states aimed to penetrate more deeply into the lives of their subjects. They wanted more men for their armed forces; higher taxes to support their projects; and more control over foreign trade, religious dissent, and society's unwanted.

Some tears had begun to appear, however, in the seamless fabric of state power. The civil war

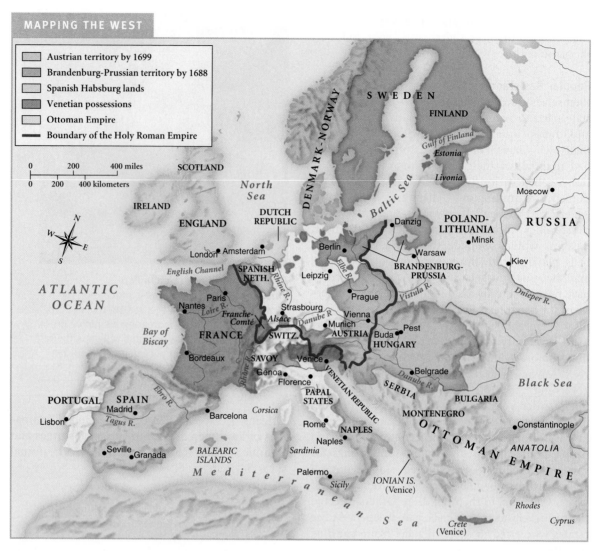

MAPPING THE WEST

Austrian territory by 1699
Brandenburg-Prussian territory by 1688
Spanish Habsburg lands
Venetian possessions
Ottoman Empire
Boundary of the Holy Roman Empire

Europe at the End of the Seventeenth Century
Size was not necessarily an advantage in the late 1600s. Poland-Lithuania, a large country on the map, had been fatally weakened by internal conflicts. In the next century it would disappear entirely. While the Ottoman Empire still controlled an extensive territory, outside of Anatolia its rule depended on intermediaries. The Austrian Habsburgs had pushed the Turks out of Hungary and back into the Balkans. The tiny Dutch Republic, meanwhile, had become very rich through international commerce and was the envy of far larger nations.

between Charles I and Parliament in England in the 1640s opened the way to new demands for political participation. When Parliament overthrew James II in 1688, it also insisted that the new king and queen, William and Mary, agree to a Bill of Rights. Left on their own during the turmoil in England, the English North American colonies developed distinctive forms of representative government. In the eighteenth century, new levels of economic growth and the appearance of new social groups would exert pressures on the European state system. The success of seventeenth-century rulers created the political and economic conditions in which their critics would flourish.

For Further Exploration

■ **For suggested references, including Web sites, for topics in this chapter,** see page SR-1 at the end of the book.

■ **For additional primary-source material from this period,** see Chapter 16 in *Sources of The Making of the West,* Third Edition.

■ **For Web sites and documents related to topics in this chapter,** see *Make History* at bedfordstmartins.com/hunt.

CHAPTER REVIEW

KEY TERMS AND PEOPLE

constitutionalism (484)

absolutism (484)

Louis XIV (484)

revocation of the Edict
of Nantes (489)

bureaucracy (489)

mercantilism (490)

Frederick William
of Hohenzollern (493)

Stenka Razin (496)

Levellers (499)

William, prince
of Orange (504)

Glorious Revolution
(504)

social contract (504)

classicism (510)

salon (513)

REVIEW QUESTIONS

1. How "absolute" was the power of Louis XIV?

2. Why did absolutism flourish everywhere in eastern Europe except Poland-Lithuania?

3. What differences over religion and politics caused the conflict between king and Parliament in England?

4. Why did constitutionalism thrive in the Dutch Republic and the British North American colonies, even as their participation in the slave trade grew?

5. How did elite and popular culture become more separate in the seventeenth century?

MAKING CONNECTIONS

1. What accounts for the success of absolutism in some parts of Europe and its failure in others?

2. How did religious differences in the late seventeenth century still cause political conflict?

3. Why was the search for order a major theme in science, politics, and the arts during this period?

> **For practice quizzes, a customized study plan, and other study tools,** see the Online Study Guide at bedfordstmartins.com/hunt.

IMPORTANT EVENTS

1642–1646	Civil war between King Charles I and Parliament in England
1648	Peace of Westphalia ends Thirty Years' War; the Fronde revolt challenges royal authority in France; Ukrainian Cossack warriors rebel against the king of Poland-Lithuania; Spain formally recognizes independence of the Dutch Republic
1649	Execution of Charles I of England; new Russian legal code assigns all to hereditary class
1651	Thomas Hobbes publishes *Leviathan*
1660	Monarchy restored in England
1661	Slave code set up in Barbados
1667	Louis XIV begins first of many wars that continue throughout his reign
1678	Madame de Lafayette anonymously publishes her novel *The Princess of Clèves*
1683	Austrian Habsburgs break the Turkish siege of Vienna
1685	Louis XIV revokes toleration for French Protestants granted by the Edict of Nantes
1688	Parliament deposes James II and invites his daughter, Mary, and her husband, William of Orange, to take the throne
1690	John Locke publishes *Two Treatises of Government* and *Essay Concerning Human Understanding*

The Atlantic System and Its Consequences
1690–1740

Johann Sebastian Bach (1685–1750), composer of mighty organ fugues and church cantatas, was not above amusing his Leipzig audiences, many of them university students. In 1732, he produced a cantata about a young woman in love — with coffee. Her old-fashioned father rages that he won't find her a husband unless she gives up the fad. She agrees, secretly vowing to admit no suitor who will not promise in the marriage contract to let her brew coffee whenever she wants. Bach offers this conclusion:

> The cat won't give up its mouse,
> Girls stay faithful coffee-sisters
> Mother loves her coffee habit,
> Grandma sips it gladly too —
> Why then shout at the daughters?

Bach's era might well be called the age of coffee. European travelers at the end of the sixteenth century had noticed Middle Eastern people drinking a "black drink," *kavah*, and the Turks took coffee beans with them on their military campaigns in eastern Europe. Few Europeans sampled the drink at first, and the Arab monopoly on its production kept prices high. This changed around 1700 when the Dutch East India Company introduced coffee plants to Java and other Indonesian islands. Coffee production then spread to the French Caribbean, where African slaves provided the plantation labor. In Europe, imported coffee spurred the development of a new kind of meeting place: the first coffeehouse opened in London in 1652, and the idea spread quickly to other European cities. Men gathered in coffeehouses to drink, read newspapers, and talk politics. As a London newspaper commented in 1737, "There's scarce an Alley in City and Suburbs but has a Coffeehouse in it, which may be called the School of Public Spirit, where every Man over Daily and Weekly Journals, a Mug, or a Dram . . . devotes himself to that glorious one, his Country."

London Coffeehouse
This gouache (a variant on watercolor painting) from about 1725 depicts a scene from a London coffeehouse located in the courtyard of the Royal Exchange (merchants' bank). Middle-class men (wearing wigs) read newspapers, drink coffee, smoke pipes, and discuss the news of the day. The coffeehouse draws them out of their homes into a new public space. *(© British Museum, London/The Bridgeman Art Library.)*

European consumption of coffee, tea, chocolate, and other novelties increased dramatically as European nations forged worldwide economic links. At the center of this new global economy was the **Atlantic system**, the web of trade routes that bound together western Europe, Africa, and the Americas. Europeans bought slaves in western Africa, transported them to be sold in the colonies in North and South America and the Caribbean, bought raw commodities such as coffee and sugar that were produced by the new colonial plantations, and then sold those commodities in European ports for refining and reshipment. This Atlantic system, which first took clear shape in the early eighteenth century, became the hub of European expansion throughout the world.

Coffee drinking is just one example of the many new social and cultural patterns that took root between 1690 and 1740. Improvements in agricultural production at home reinforced the effects of trade overseas; Europeans now had more disposable income for extras, and they spent their money not only in the new coffeehouses and cafés that sprang up all over Europe but also on newspapers, musical concerts, paintings, and novels. A new middle-class public began to make its presence felt in every domain of culture and social life.

Although the rise of the Atlantic system gave Europe new prominence in the global context, European rulers still focused most of their political, diplomatic, and military energies on their rivalries within Europe. A coalition of countries succeeded in containing French aggression, and a more balanced diplomatic system emerged. In eastern Europe, Prussia and Austria had to contend with the

rising power of Russia under Peter the Great. In western Europe, both Spain and the Dutch Republic declined in influence but continued to vie with Britain and France for colonial spoils in the Atlantic. The more evenly matched competition among the great powers encouraged the development of diplomatic skills and drew attention to public health as a way of encouraging population growth.

In the aftermath of Louis XIV's revocation of the Edict of Nantes in 1685, a new intellectual movement known as the Enlightenment began to germinate. An initial impetus came from French Protestant refugees who published works critical of absolutism in politics and religion. Increased prosperity, the growth of a middle-class public, and the decline in warfare after Louis XIV's death in 1715 helped fuel this new critical spirit. Fed by the popularization of science and the growing interest in travel literature, the Enlightenment encouraged greater skepticism about religious and state authority. Eventually, the movement would question almost every aspect of social and political life in Europe. The Enlightenment began in western Europe in those countries — Britain, France, and the Dutch Republic — most affected by the new Atlantic system. It too was a product of the age of coffee.

> **FOCUS QUESTION:** What were the most important consequences of the growth of the Atlantic system?

The Atlantic System and the World Economy

Although their ships had been circling the globe since the early 1500s, Europeans did not draw most of the world into their economic orbit until the 1700s. Western European trading nations sent

---

Atlantic system: The network of trade established in the 1700s that bound together western Europe, Africa, and the Americas. Europeans sold slaves from western Africa and bought commodities that were produced by the new colonial plantations in North and South America and the Caribbean.

■ **1690s** Development of Caribbean plantations

■ **1694** Bank of England established; Astell, *A Serious Proposal to the Ladies*

■ **1697** Bayle, *Historical and Critical Dictionary*

■ **1699** Turks forced to recognize Austrian rule over Hungary, Transylvania

■ **1703** Building of St. Petersburg begins; first Russian newspaper

■ **1713–1714** Peace of Utrecht

■ **1714–1727** King George I of England

■ **1715** Death of Louis XIV

| 1690 | 1700 | 1710 |

ships loaded with goods to buy slaves from local rulers on the western coast of Africa; the slaves were then transported to the colonies in North and South America and the Caribbean and sold to the owners of plantations producing coffee, sugar, cotton, and tobacco. Money from the slave trade was used to buy the raw commodities produced in the colonies and ship them back to Europe, where they were refined or processed and then sold within Europe and around the world. The Atlantic system and the growth of international trade thus helped create a new consumer society.

Slavery and the Atlantic System

Spain and Portugal dominated Atlantic trade in the sixteenth and seventeenth centuries, but in the eighteenth century European trade in the Atlantic rapidly expanded and became more systematically interconnected (Map 17.1). By 1630, Portugal had already sent sixty thousand African slaves to Brazil to work on the new **plantations** (large tracts of lands that produced staple crops, were farmed by slave labor, and were owned by colonial settlers from western Europe), which were producing some fifteen thousand tons of sugar a year. Realizing that plantations producing staples for Europeans could bring fabulous wealth, the European powers grew less interested in the dwindling trade in precious metals and more eager to colonize. In the 1690s, large-scale planters of sugar, tobacco, and coffee began displacing small farmers who relied on one or two servants. Planters and their plantations won out because cheap slave labor allowed them to produce mass quantities of commodities at low prices.

plantation: A large tract of land that produced staple crops such as sugar, coffee, and tobacco; was farmed by slave labor; and was owned by a colonial settler.

State-chartered private companies from Portugal, France, Britain, the Dutch Republic, Prussia, and even Denmark exploited the 3,500-mile coastline of West Africa for slaves. Before 1675, most blacks taken from Africa had been sent to Brazil, but by 1700 half of the African slaves were landing in the Caribbean (Figure 17.1). Thereafter, the plantation economy began to expand on the North American mainland. The numbers stagger the imagination. Before 1650, slave traders transported about seven thousand Africans each year

---

FIGURE 17.1 African Slaves Imported into American Territories, 1701–1810
During the eighteenth century, planters in the newly established Caribbean colonies imported millions of African slaves to work the new plantations that produced sugar, coffee, indigo, and cotton for the European market. The vast majority of African slaves transported to the Americas ended up in either the Caribbean or Brazil. Why were so many slaves transported to the Caribbean islands, which are relatively small compared to Spanish or British North America? *(Adapted from Philip D. Curtin, The Atlantic Slave Trade: A Census [Madison: University of Wisconsin Press, 1969].)*

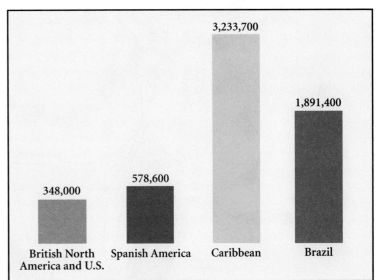

British North America and U.S. — 348,000
Spanish America — 578,600
Caribbean — 3,233,700
Brazil — 1,891,400

■ 1720 Last plague outbreak in western Europe

■ 1721 Treaty of Nystad; Montesquieu, *Persian Letters*

■ 1733 War of the Polish Succession; Voltaire, *Letters Concerning the English Nation*

1720   1730   1740

■ 1719 Defoe, *Robinson Crusoe*

■ 1741 Handel, *Messiah*

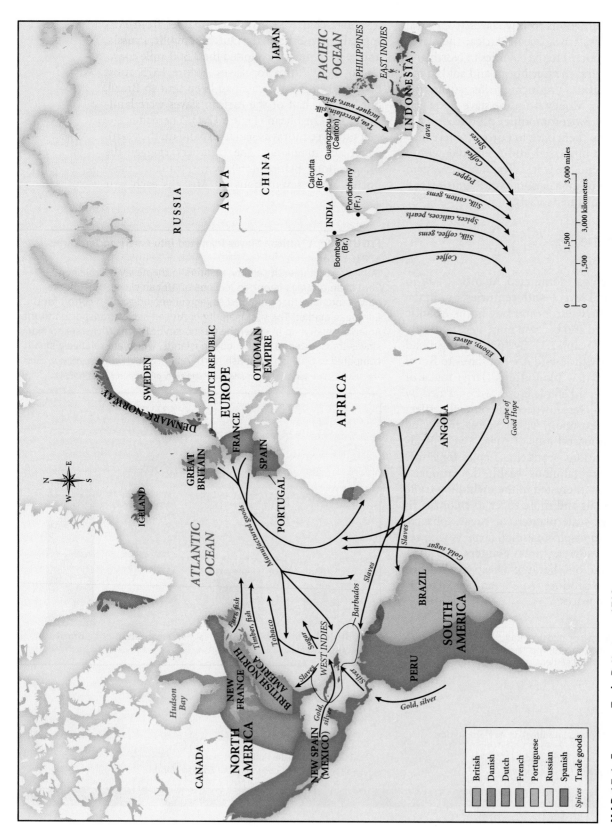

MAP 17.1 European Trade Patterns, c. 1740

By 1740, the European powers had colonized much of North and South America and incorporated their colonies there into a worldwide system of commerce centered on the slave trade and plantation production of staple crops. Europeans still sought spices and luxury goods in China and the East Indies, but outside of Java, few Europeans had settled permanently in these areas.

■ How did control over colonies determine dominance in international trade in this period?

across the Atlantic; this rate doubled between 1650 and 1675, nearly doubled again in the next twenty-five years, and kept increasing until the 1780s (Figure 17.2, below). In all, more than eleven million Africans, not counting those who were captured but died before or during the sea voyage, were transported to the Americas before the slave trade began to wind down after 1850. Many individual traders gained spectacular wealth, but companies did not always make profits. The English Royal African Company, for example, delivered 100,000 slaves to the Caribbean and imported thirty thousand tons of sugar to Britain yet lost money after the few profitable years following its founding in 1672.

The Life of the Slaves.   The balance of white and black populations in the New World colonies was determined by the staples produced. Because they did not own plantations, New England merchants and farmers bought few slaves. Blacks—both slave and free—made up only 3 percent of the population in eighteenth-century New England, compared with 60 percent in South Carolina. On the whole, the British North American colonies contained a higher proportion of African Americans

from 1730 to 1765 than at any other time in American history. The imbalance of whites and blacks was even more extreme in the Caribbean, where most indigenous people had already died fighting Europeans or the diseases brought by them. By 1713, the French Caribbean colony of St. Domingue (on the western part of Hispaniola, present-day Haiti) had four times as many black slaves as whites; by 1754, slaves there outnumbered whites more than ten to one.

Enslaved women and men suffered terribly. Most had been sold to European traders by Africans from the west coast who acquired them through warfare or kidnapping. The vast majority were between fourteen and thirty-five years old. Before they were crammed onto the ships for the three-month trip, their heads were shaved, they were stripped naked, and some were branded with red-hot irons. Men and women were separated. Men were shackled with leg irons. Sailors and officers raped the women whenever they wished and beat those who refused their advances. In the cramped and appalling conditions of the voyage, as many as one-fourth of the slaves died.

Those who survived the transit were forced into degrading and oppressive conditions. Upon

---

FIGURE 17.2 Annual Imports in the Atlantic Slave Trade, 1450–1870
The importation of slaves to the American territories reached its height in the second half of the eighteenth century and began to decline around 1800. Yet despite the abolition of the slave trade by the British in 1807, commerce in slaves did not seriously diminish until after the revolutions of 1848.
(Adapted from Philip D. Curtin, The Atlantic Slave Trade: A Census *(Madison: University of Wisconsin Press, 1969). Reprinted by permission of the University of Wisconsin Press.)*

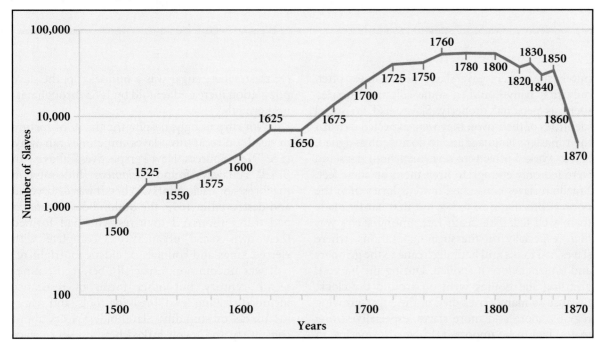

Oral History and the Life of Slaves

Historians have found it difficult to reconstruct slave life from the point of view of the slaves themselves, in part because slaves newly imported from Africa to the New World did not speak the language of their captors. Scholars have attempted to fill in this blank by using a variety of overlapping sources. The most interesting and controversial of these sources are oral histories taken from descendants of slaves. In some former slave societies, these descendants still tell stories about their ancestors' first days under slavery. The controversy comes from using present-day memories to shed light on eighteenth-century lives.

One of the regions most intensively studied in this fashion is Suriname (formerly Dutch Guiana), on the northeast coast of South America between present-day Guyana and French Guiana. This region is a good source of oral histories because 10 percent of the African slaves transported there between the 1680s and the 1750s escaped from the plantations and fled into the nearby rain forests. There they set up their own societies and developed their own language, in which they carried on the oral traditions of the first runaway slaves. The descendants of the runaway slaves recounted the following details:

> In slavery, there was hardly anything to eat. It was at the place called Providence Plantation. They whipped you there till your ass was burning. Then they would give you a bit of plain rice in a calabash [a bowl made from a hard-shelled tropical American fruit]. . . . And the gods told them that this is no way for human beings to live. They would help them. Let each person go where he could. So they ran.

From other sources, historians have learned that there was a major slave rebellion at Providence Plantation in Suriname in 1693.

By comparing such oral histories to written accounts of plantation owners, missionaries, and Dutch colonial officials, historians have been able to paint a richly detailed picture not only of slavery but also of runaway slave societies, which were especially numerous in South America. At the end of the eighteenth century, a Portuguese-speaking Jew named David de Ishak Cohen Nassy wrote his own history of plantation life based on records from the local Jewish community that are now lost. Because the Dutch, unlike most other Europeans, allowed Jews to own slaves, Portuguese-speaking Jews from Brazil owned about one-third of the plantations and slaves in Suriname. Nassy gave the following account of Suriname's first slave revolt:

> There was in the year 1690 a revolt on a plantation situated on the Cassewinica Creek, behind Jews Savannah, belonging to a Jew named Imanuël Machado, where, having killed their master, [the slaves] fled, carrying away with them everything that was there. . . . The Jews . . . in an expedition which they undertook against the rebels, killed many of them and brought back several who were punished by death on the very spot.

The oral histories told about the revolt from the runaway slaves' perspective:

> There had been a great council meeting [of runaway slaves] in the forest. . . . They decided to burn a different one of [Machado's] plantations from the place where he had whipped Lanu [one of the runaway slaves] because they would find more tools there. This was the Cassewinica Plantation, which had many slaves. They knew all about this plantation from slavery times. So, they at-

purchase, masters gave slaves new names, often only first names, and in some colonies branded them as personal property. Slaves had no social identities of their own; they were expected to learn their master's language and to do any job assigned. Slaves worked fifteen- to seventeen-hour days and were fed only enough to keep them on their feet. Brazilian slaves consumed more calories than the poorest Brazilians do today, but that hardly made them well fed. The death rate among slaves was high, especially on the sugar plantations, where slaves had to cut and haul sugarcane to the grinders and boilers before it spoiled. During the harvest, grinding and boiling went on around the clock. Because so many slaves died in the sugar-growing regions, more and more slaves, especially strong males, had to be imported. In North America, in contrast, where sugar was a minor crop, the slave population increased tenfold by 1863 through natural growth.

Not surprisingly, despite the threat of torture or death on recapture, slaves sometimes ran away. (See "New Sources, New Perspectives," above.) In Brazil, runaways found *quilombos* (hideouts) in the forests or backcountry. When it was discovered and destroyed in 1695, the quilombo of Palmares had thirty thousand fugitives who had formed their own social organization, complete with elected kings and councils of elders. Outright revolt was uncommon, especially before the nineteenth century, but other forms of resistance included stealing food, breaking tools, and feigning illness or stupidity. Slaveholders' fears about conspiracy and revolt lurked beneath the surface

Slaves of Suriname in the 1770s

John Gabriel Stedman published an account of his participation in a five-year expedition against the runaway slaves of Suriname that took place in the 1770s. He provided drawings such as the one reproduced here, which shows Africans who have just come off a slave ship. *(The New York Public Library/Art Resource, NY.)*

the main town of the colony in exchange for agreeing to return all future runaways. The runaways had not destroyed the slave system, but they had gained their own independence alongside it. From their oral histories it is possible to retrace their efforts to build new lives in a strange place, in which they combined African practices with New World experiences.

Source: Richard Price, *Alabi's World* (Baltimore: Johns Hopkins University Press, 1990), 17, 9.

QUESTIONS TO CONSIDER

1. What did the runaway slaves mentioned in these accounts aim to accomplish when they attacked plantations?
2. Why would runaway slaves make an agreement with the Dutch colonial officials to return future runaways?
3. Can oral histories recorded in the twentieth century be considered accurate versions of events that took place in the eighteenth century? How can they be tested?

FURTHER READING

Price, Richard. *Alabi's World.* 1990.
Stedman, John Gabriel. *Narrative of a Five Years' Expedition Against the Revolted Negroes of Surinam.* Edited, and with an introduction and notes, by Richard Price and Sally Price. 1988.

tacked. It was at night. They killed the head of the plantation, a white man. They took all the things, everything they needed.

The runaway slaves saw the attack as part of their ongoing effort to build a life in the rain forest, away from the whites.

Over the next decades, the runaway slaves fought a constant series of battles with plantation owners and Dutch officials. Finally, in 1762, the Dutch granted the runaway slaves their freedom in a peace agreement and allowed them to trade in

---

of every slave-based society. In 1710, the royal governor of Virginia reminded the colonial legislature of the need for unceasing vigilance: "We are not to Depend on Either Their Stupidity, or that Babel of Languages among 'em; freedom Wears a Cap which Can Without a Tongue, Call Togather all Those who Long to Shake off the fetters of Slavery." Masters defended whipping and other forms of physical punishment as essential to maintaining discipline. Laws called for the castration of a slave who struck a white person.

Effects of the Slave Trade on Europe.　Plantation owners often left their colonial possessions in the care of agents and merely collected the revenue so that they could live as wealthy landowners back home, where they built opulent mansions and

gained influence in local and national politics. William Beckford, for example, had been sent from Jamaica to school in England as a young boy. When he inherited sugar plantations and shipping companies from his father and older brother, he moved the headquarters of the family business to London in the 1730s to be close to the government and financial markets. His holdings formed the single most powerful economic interest in Jamaica, but he preferred to live in England, where he could buy works of art for his many luxurious homes, hold political office (he was lord mayor of London and a member of Parliament), and even lend money to the government.

The slave trade permanently altered consumption patterns for ordinary people. Sugar had been prescribed as a medicine before the end of the

Caribbean Sugar Mill
This seventeenth-century engraving of a sugar mill or grinder makes the work seem much less difficult than it was in practice. Slaves cut the sugarcane and then hauled it from the fields to the mill, where it was crushed. Many slaves lost fingers or hands in the process. The slaves then collected the juice (bottom center) and carried it to the boilers, shown at the bottom left and right. The sap was poured into molds and dried. Then the bricks of raw sugar were exported to Europe for refining.
(The Granger Collection, New York.)

sixteenth century, but the development of plantations in Brazil and the Caribbean made it a standard food item. By 1700, the British were sending home fifty million pounds of sugar a year, a figure that doubled by 1730. During the French Revolution of the 1790s, sugar shortages would become a cause for rioting in Paris. Equally pervasive was the spread of tobacco; by the 1720s, Britain was importing two hundred shiploads of tobacco from Virginia and Maryland annually, and men of every country and class smoked pipes or took snuff.

The Origins of Modern Racism.   The traffic in slaves disturbed many Europeans. As a government memorandum to the Spanish king explained in 1610: "Modern theologians in published books commonly report on, and condemn as unjust, the acts of enslavement which take place in provinces of this Royal Empire." Between 1667 and 1671, the French Dominican monk Father Du Tertre published three volumes in which he denounced the mistreatment of slaves in the French colonies.

In the 1700s, however, slaveholders began to justify their actions by demeaning the mental and spiritual qualities of the enslaved Africans. White Europeans and colonists sometimes described black slaves as animal-like, akin to apes. A leading New England Puritan asserted about the slaves: "Indeed their *Stupidity* is a *Discouragement*. It may seem, unto as little purpose, to *Teach*, as to *wash an Aethiopian* [Ethiopian]." One of the great para-

doxes of this time was that talk of liberty and self-evident rights, especially prevalent in Britain and its North American colonies, coexisted with the belief that some people were meant to be slaves. Although Christians believed in principle in a kind of spiritual equality between blacks and whites, the churches often defended or at least did not oppose the inequities of slavery.

World Trade and Settlement

The Atlantic system helped extend European trade relations across the globe. The textiles that Atlantic shippers exchanged for slaves on the west coast of Africa, for example, were manufactured in India and exported by the British and French East India Companies. As much as one-quarter of the British exports to Africa in the eighteenth century were actually re-exports from India. To expand its trade in the rest of the world, Europeans seized territories and tried to establish permanent settlements. The eighteenth-century extension of European power prepared the way for western global domination in the nineteenth and twentieth centuries.

The Americas.   In contrast to the sparsely inhabited trading outposts in Asia and Africa, the colonies in the Americas bulged with settlers. The British North American colonies, for example, contained about 1.5 million nonnative (that is, white settler and black slave) residents by 1750.

While the Spanish competed with the Portuguese for control of South America, the French competed with the British for control of North America. Spanish and British settlers came to blows over the boundary between the British colonies and Florida, which was held by Spain.

Local economies shaped colonial social relations; men in French trapper communities in Canada, for example, had little in common with the men and women of the plantation societies in Barbados or Brazil. Racial attitudes also differed from place to place. The Spanish and Portuguese tolerated intermarriage with the native populations in both America and Asia. Sexual contact, both inside and outside marriage, fostered greater racial variety in the Spanish and Portuguese colonies than in the French or the English territories (though mixed-race people could be found everywhere). By 1800, **mestizos**, children of Spanish men and Indian women, accounted for more than a quarter of the population in the Spanish colonies, and many of them aspired to join the local elite. However, greater racial diversity seems not to have improved the treatment of slaves.

Where intermarriage between colonizers and natives was common, conversion to Christianity proved most successful. Even while maintaining their native religious beliefs, many Indians in the Spanish colonies had come to consider themselves devout Catholics by 1700. Indian carpenters and artisans in the villages produced innumerable altars, retables (painted panels), and sculpted images to adorn their local churches, and individual families put up domestic shrines. Yet the clergy remained overwhelmingly Spanish: the church hierarchy concluded that the Indians' humility and innocence made them unsuitable for the priesthood.

In the early years of American colonization, many more men than women emigrated from Europe. Although the sex imbalance began to decline at the end of the seventeenth century, it remained substantial; two and a half times more men than women were among the immigrants leaving Liverpool, England, between 1697 and 1707, for example. Women who emigrated as indentured servants ran great risks: if they did not die of disease during the voyage, they were likely to give birth to illegitimate children (the fate of at least one in five servant women) or be virtually sold into marriage. Upper-class women were often kept in seclusion, especially in the Spanish and Portuguese colonies.

The uncertainties of life in the American colonies provided new opportunities for European women and men willing to live outside the law, however. In the 1500s and 1600s, the English and Dutch governments had routinely authorized pirates to prey on the ships of their rivals, the Spanish and Portuguese. Then, in the late 1600s, English, French, and Dutch bands made up of deserters and crews from wrecked vessels began to form their own associations of pirates, especially in the Caribbean. Called **buccaneers** from their custom of curing strips of beef, called *boucan* by the native Caribs of the islands, the pirates governed themselves and preyed on everyone's shipping without regard to national origin. After 1700, the colonial governments tried to stamp out piracy. As one British judge argued in 1705, "A pirate is in perpetual war with every individual and every state. . . . They are worse than ravenous beasts."

Africa and Asia.   White settlements in Africa and Asia remained small and almost insignificant, except for their long-term potential. Europeans had little contact with East Africa and almost none with Africa's vast interior. A handful of Portuguese trading posts in Angola and a few Dutch farms on the Cape of Good Hope provided the only toeholds for future expansion. In China, the emperors had welcomed Catholic missionaries at court in the seventeenth century, but the priests' credibility diminished as they squabbled among themselves and associated with European merchants, whom the Chinese considered pirates. "The barbarians [Europeans] are like wild beasts," one Chinese official concluded. In 1720, only one thousand Europeans resided in Guangzhou (Canton), the sole place where foreigners could legally trade for spices, tea, and silk (see Map 17.1, page 522).

Europeans exercised more influence in Java (in what was then called the East Indies) and in India. Dutch coffee production in Java and nearby islands increased phenomenally in the early 1700s, and many Dutch settled there to oversee production and trade. Dutch, English, French, Portuguese, and Danish companies competed in India for spices, cotton, and silk; by the 1740s, the English and French had become the leading rivals in India, just as they were in North America. Both countries extended their power as India's Muslim rulers lost control to local Hindu princes, rebellious Sikhs, invading Persians, and their own

---

mestizo: A person born to a Spanish father and a native American mother.

buccaneers: Pirates of the Caribbean who governed themselves and preyed on international shipping.

India Cottons and Trade with the East
This colored cotton cloth (now faded with age) was painted and embroidered in Madras in southern India sometime in the late 1600s. The male figure with a mustache may be a European, but the female figures are clearly Asian. Europeans—especially the British—discovered that they could make big profits on the export of Indian cotton cloth to Europe. They also traded Indian cottons in Africa for slaves and sold large quantities in the colonies. *(V & A Images/Victoria and Albert Museum, London.)*

provincial governors. A few thousand Europeans lived in India, though many thousand more soldiers were stationed there to protect them. The staple of trade with India in the early 1700s was calico—lightweight, brightly colored cotton cloth that caught on as a fashion in Europe (see the image above).

Europeans who visited India were especially struck by what they viewed as exotic religious practices. In a book published in 1696 of his travels to western India, an Anglican minister described the fakirs (religious mendicants, or beggars of alms), "some of whom show their devotion by a shameless appearance, walking naked, without the least rag of clothes to cover them." Such writings increased European interest in the outside world but also fed a European sense of superiority that helped excuse the more violent forms of colonial domination (see The Exotic as Consumer Item, page 529).

The Birth of Consumer Society

As worldwide colonization produced new supplies of goods, from coffee to calico, population growth in Europe fueled demand for them. Beginning first in Britain, then in France and the Italian states, and finally in eastern Europe, population surged, growing by about 20 percent between 1700 and 1750. The gap between a fast-growing northwest and a more stagnant south and central Europe now diminished as regions that had lost population during the seventeenth-century downturn recovered. Cities, in particular, grew. Between 1600 and 1750,

London's population more than tripled and Paris's more than doubled.

Although contemporaries could not have realized it then, this was the start of the modern population explosion. It appears that a decline in the death rate, rather than a rise in the birthrate, explains the turnaround. Three main factors contributed to increased longevity: better weather and hence more bountiful harvests, improved agricultural techniques, and the plague's disappearance after 1720.

By the early eighteenth century, the effects of economic expansion and population growth brought about a **consumer revolution**. For example, the British East India Company began to import into Britain huge quantities of calico; British imports of tobacco doubled between 1672 and 1700; and at Nantes, the center of the French sugar trade, imports quadrupled between 1698 and 1733. Tea, chocolate, and coffee became virtual necessities. In the 1670s, only a trickle of tea reached London, but by 1720 the East India Company had sent nine million pounds to England—a figure that rose to thirty-seven million pounds by 1750. In 1700, England had two thousand coffeehouses; by 1740, every English country town had at least two. Paris got its first cafés at the end of the seventeenth century; Berlin opened its first coffeehouse in 1714; and Bach's Leipzig boasted eight by 1725.

---

consumer revolution: The rapid increase in consumption of new staples produced in the Atlantic system as well as of other items of daily life that were previously unavailable or beyond the reach of ordinary people.

The Exotic as Consumer Item

This painting by the Venetian artist Rosalba Carriera (1675–1757) is titled *Africa*. The young black girl wearing a turban represents the African continent. Carriera was known for her use of pastels. In 1720, she journeyed to Paris, where she became an associate of Antoine Watteau and helped inaugurate the rococo style in painting. Why might the artist have chosen to paint an African girl? *(Staatliche Kunstsammlungen Dresden, Gemaldegalerie Alte Meister.)*

■ **For more help analyzing this image,** see the visual activity for this chapter in the Online Study Guide at **bedfordstmartins.com/hunt**.

A new economic dynamic steadily took shape that would influence all of subsequent history. More and more people escaped the confines of a subsistence economy, in which peasants produced barely enough to support themselves from year to year. As ordinary people gained more disposable income, demand for nonessential consumer goods rose (see Document, "The Social Effects of Growing Consumption," page 530). These included not only the new colonial products such as coffee and tea but also tables, chairs, sheets, chamber pots, lamps, mirrors, and for the better off still, coffee- and teapots, china, cutlery, chests of drawers, desks, clocks, and pictures for the walls. Rising demand created more jobs and more income and yet more purchasing power in a mutually reinforcing cycle. In the English economic literature of the 1690s, writers reacted to these developments by expressing a new view of humans as consuming animals with boundless appetites. Many authors

attacked the new doctrine of consumerism, but they could not hold back the fast-growing market for consumption. Change did not occur all at once, however. The consumer revolution spread from the cities to the countryside, from England to the continent, and from western Europe to eastern Europe only over the long run.

> **REVIEW:** How was consumerism related to slavery in the early eighteenth century?

New Social and Cultural Patterns

The rise of consumption was fueled in part by a revolution in agricultural techniques that made it possible to produce larger quantities of food with a smaller agricultural workforce. As population increased, more people moved to the cities, where they found themselves caught up in innovative urban customs such as attending musical concerts and reading novels. Along with a general increase in literacy, these activities helped create a public that responded to new writers and artists. As always, people's experiences varied depending on whether they lived in wealth or poverty, in urban or rural areas, or in eastern or western Europe.

Agricultural Revolution

Although Britain, France, and the Dutch Republic shared the enthusiasm for consumer goods, Britain's domestic market grew most quickly. In Britain, as agricultural output increased 43 percent over the course of the 1700s, the population increased by 70 percent. The British imported grain to feed the growing population, but they also benefited from the development of techniques that together constituted an **agricultural revolution**. No new machinery propelled this revolution — just increasingly aggressive attitudes toward investment and management. The Dutch and the Flemish had pioneered many of these techniques in the 1600s, but the British took them further.

Four major changes occurred in British agriculture that eventually spread to other countries. First, farmers increased the amount of land under cultivation by draining wetlands and by growing crops on previously uncultivated common lands

---

agricultural revolution: Increasingly aggressive attitudes toward investment in and management of land that increased production of food in the 1700s.

DOCUMENT

The Social Effects of Growing Consumption

Daniel Defoe's adventures in real life are matched only by those of his famous fictional characters Robinson Crusoe and Moll Flanders. Though never shipwrecked like Crusoe, Defoe spent time in bankruptcy, in exile, and in prison (for writing a pamphlet satirizing Anglican treatment of dissenters). He turned his hand to various forms of commerce, in hosiery, woolens, wine, and political secrets, but most of all to mad scribbling on almost any topic imaginable. He published hundreds of books and pamphlets. In the 395-page book from which this excerpt is taken, he describes the recent fabulous growth in the import and export trade of Great Britain and contrasts the wealth gained by the "industrious" classes to the contempt shown them by the aristocracy [Gentry or Gentlemen].

Our People in general being in good Circumstances, I mean the middling, trading, and industrious People, living tolerably well, their well-faring gives Occasion to the vast Consumption of the foreign, as well as home Produce, the like of which is not to be equalled by any Nation in the World; the Particulars we shall enquire into in their Order.

How far the Multitudes of our People are encreased by these very Articles, and that to such a Degree as is scarce conceivable, is worth our Enquiry, were it not too tedious for this Place. What populous Towns are rais'd by our Manufactures, from with few Years! How are our Towns built into Cities, and small Villages (hardly known in ancient Times) grown up into populous Towns! . . .

Well might I say, as in the foregoing Chapter, That it is a Scandal upon the Understanding of the Gentry, to think contemptibly of the trading part of the Nation; seeing however the Gentlemen may value themselves upon their Birth and Blood, the Case begins to turn against them so evidently, as to Fortune and Estate, that tho' they say, the Tradesmen cannot be made Gentlemen; yet the Tradesmen are, at this Time, able to buy the Gentlemen almost in every part of the Kingdom. . . .

The ancient Families, who having wasted and exhausted their Estates, and being declin'd and decay'd in Fortune by Luxury and high Living, have restor'd and rais'd themselves again, by mixing Blood with the despis'd Tradesmen, marrying the Daughters of such Tradesmen. . . .

I might add here, that it would be worth the while for those Gentlemen, who talk so much of their antient Family Merit, and look so little at preserving the Stock, by encreasing their own: I say, it would be worth their while to look into the Roll of our Gentry, and enquire what is become of the Estates and those prodigious Numbers of lost and extinct Families, which now even the Heralds themselves can hardly find; let them tell us if those Estates are not now purchased by Tradesmen and Citizens, or the Posterity of such; and whether those Tradesmens Posterity do not now fill up the Vacancies, the Gaps, and Chasms in the great Roll or Lift of Families, as well of the Gentry, as of the Nobility themselves; and whether there are many Families left, who have not been either restored *as in our first Head*, or supply'd, *as in the second*, by the Succession of Wealth, and new Branches from the growing Greatness of Trade.

Trade, in a word, raises antient Families when sunk and decay'd: And plants new Families, where the old ones are lost and extinct.

Source: Daniel Defoe, *A Plan of the English Commerce. Being a complete prospect of the trade of this nation, as well home as foreign. In three parts,* 2nd ed. (London, 1737), 79–83.

(acreage maintained by the community for grazing). Second, those farmers who could afford it consolidated small, scattered plots into larger, more efficient units. Third, livestock raising became more closely linked to crop growing, and the yields of each increased. (See "Taking Measure," page 531.) For centuries, most farmers had rotated their fields in and out of production to replenish the soil. Now farmers planted carefully chosen fodder crops such as clover and turnips that added nutrients to the soil, thereby eliminating the need to leave a field fallow (unplanted) every two or three years. With more fodder available, farmers could raise more livestock, which in turn produced more manure to fertilize grain fields. Fourth, selective breeding of animals combined with the in-

crease in fodder to improve the quality and size of herds. New crops had only a slight impact; potatoes, for example, were introduced to Europe from South America in the 1500s, but because people feared they might cause leprosy, tuberculosis, or fevers, they were not grown in quantity until the late 1700s. By the 1730s and 1740s, agricultural output had increased dramatically, and prices for food had fallen because of these interconnected innovations.

Changes in agricultural practices did not benefit all landowners equally. The biggest British landowners consolidated their holdings in the "enclosure movement." They put pressure on small farmers and villagers to sell their land or give up their common lands. The big landlords then fenced off (enclosed) their property. Because enclosure eliminated community grazing rights, it frequently sparked a struggle between the big landlords and villagers, and in Britain it normally required an act of Parliament. Such acts became increasingly common in the second half of the eighteenth century, and by the century's end six million acres of common lands had been enclosed and developed. "Improvers" produced more food more efficiently than small farmers could and thus supported a growing population.

Contrary to the fears of contemporaries, small farmers and cottagers (those with little or no property) were not forced off the land all at once. But most villagers could not afford the litigation involved in resisting enclosure, and small landholders consequently had to sell out to landlords or farmers with larger plots. Landlords with large holdings leased their estates to tenant farmers at constantly increasing rents, and the tenant farmers in turn employed the cottagers as salaried agricultural workers. In this way the English peasantry largely disappeared, replaced by a more hierarchical society of big landlords, enterprising tenant farmers, and poor agricultural laborers.

The new agricultural techniques spread slowly from Britain and the Low Countries (the Dutch Republic and the Austrian Netherlands) to the rest of western Europe. Outside a few pockets in northern France and the western German states, however, subsistence agriculture (producing just enough to get by rather than surpluses for the market) continued to dominate farming in western Europe and Scandinavia. In southwestern Germany, for example, 80 percent of the peasants produced no surplus because their plots were too small. Unlike the populations of the highly urbanized Low Countries (where half the people lived in towns and cities), most Europeans, western and eastern, eked out their existence in the countryside and could barely participate in the new markets for consumer goods.

In eastern Europe, the condition of peasants worsened in the areas where landlords tried hardest to improve crop yields. To produce more for the Baltic grain market, aristocratic landholders in Prussia, Poland, and parts of Russia drained wetlands, cultivated moors, and built dikes. They also forced peasants off lands that the peasants had worked for themselves, increased compulsory labor services (the critical element in serfdom), and began to manage their estates directly. Some eastern landowners grew fabulously wealthy. The Potocki family in the Polish Ukraine, for example, owned three million acres of land and had 130,000

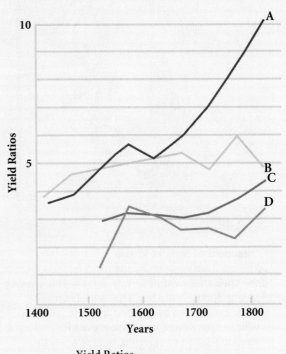

Yield Ratios
A = Britain and the Low Countries
B = France, Spain, and Italy
C = Central Europe and Scandinavia
D = Eastern Europe

Relationship of Crop Harvested to Seed Used, 1400–1800
The impact and even the timing of the agricultural revolution can be determined by this figure, based on yield ratios (the number of grains produced for each seed planted). Britain, the Dutch Republic, and the Austrian Netherlands all experienced huge increases in crop yields after 1700. Other European regions lagged behind right into the 1800s. Why is crop yield such an important measure? *(From Peter J. Hugill, World Trade since 1431: Geography, Technology, and Capitalism (Johns Hopkins University Press, 1995), 56.)*

serfs. In parts of Poland and Russia, the serfs hardly differed from slaves in status, and their "masters" ran their huge estates much like American plantations (see the image on page 532).

Social Life in the Cities

Because of emigration from the countryside, cities grew in population and consequently exercised more influence on culture and social life. Between

Treatment of Serfs in Russia
Visitors from western Europe often remarked on the cruel treatment of serfs in Russia. This drawing by one such visitor shows the punishment that could be inflicted by landowners. Serfs could be whipped for almost any reason, even for making a soup too salty or neglecting to bow when the lord's family passed by. Their condition worsened in the 1700s, as landowners began to sell serfs much like slaves. Although life for Russian serfs was more brutal than for peasants elsewhere, upper classes in every country regarded the serfs as dirty, deceitful, and brutish. *(New York Public Library/Art Resource, NY.)*

1650 and 1750, cities with at least ten thousand inhabitants increased in population by 44 percent. From the eighteenth century onward, urban growth would be continuous. Along with the general growth of cities, an important south-to-north shift occurred in the pattern of urbanization. Around 1500, half of the people in cities of at least ten thousand residents could be found in the Italian states, Spain, or Portugal; by 1700, the urbanization of northwestern and southern Europe was roughly equal. Eastern Europe, despite the huge cities of Istanbul and Moscow, was still less urban than western Europe. London was by far the most populous European city, with 675,000 inhabitants in 1750; Berlin had 90,000 people, Warsaw only 23,000.

Urban Social Classes. Many landowners kept a residence in town, so the separation between rural and city life was not as extreme as might be imagined, at least not for the very rich. At the top of the ladder in the big cities were the landed nobles. Some of them filled their lives only with conspicuous consumption of fine food, extravagant clothing, coaches, books, and opera; others held key political, administrative, or judicial offices. However they spent their time, these rich families employed thousands of artisans, shopkeepers, and domestic servants. Many English peers (highest-ranking nobles) had thirty or forty servants at each of their homes.

The middle classes of officials, merchants, professionals, and landowners occupied the next rung down on the social ladder. London's population, for example, included about twenty thousand middle-class families (constituting, at most, one-sixth of the city's population). In this period the middle classes began to develop distinctive ways of life that set them apart from both the rich noble landowners and the lower classes. Unlike the rich nobles, the middle classes lived primarily in the cities and towns, even if they owned small country estates. They ate more moderately than nobles but much better than peasants or laborers. For breakfast the British middle classes ate toast and rolls and, after 1700, drank tea. Dinner, served midday, consisted of roasted or boiled beef or mutton, poultry or pork, and vegetables. Supper was a light meal of bread and cheese with cake or pie. Beer was the main drink in London, and many families brewed their own. Even children drank beer because of the lack of fresh water.

Below the middle classes came the artisans and shopkeepers (most of whom were organized in professional guilds), then the journeymen, apprentices, servants, and laborers. At the bottom of the social scale were the unemployed poor, who survived by intermittent work and charity. Women married to artisans and shopkeepers often kept the accounts, supervised employees, and ran the household as well. Every middle-class and upper-class family employed servants; artisans and shopkeepers frequently hired them too. Women from poorer families usually worked as domestic servants until they married. Four out of five domestic servants in the city were female. In large cities such as London, the servant population grew faster than the population of the city as a whole.

Signs of Social Distinction. Social status in the cities was readily visible. Wide, spacious streets graced rich districts; the houses had gardens, and the air was relatively fresh. In poor districts, the streets were narrow, dirty, dark, humid, and smelly, and the houses were damp and crowded. The poorest people were homeless, sleeping under

Vauxhall Gardens, London
This hand-colored print from the mid-eighteenth century shows the newly refurbished gardens near the Thames River. Prosperous families show off their brightly-colored clothes and listen to a public concert by the orchestra seated just above them. These activities helped form a more self-conscious public.
(© Bibliothèque des Arts Décoratifs, Paris, France/The Bridgeman Art Library.)

bridges or in abandoned buildings. A Neapolitan prince described his homeless neighbors as "lying like filthy animals, with no distinction of age or sex." In some districts, rich and poor lived in the same buildings; the poor clambered up to shabby, cramped apartments on the top floors.

Like shelter, clothing was a reliable social indicator. The poorest workingwomen in Paris wore woolen skirts and blouses of dark colors over petticoats, a bodice, and a corset. They also donned caps of various sorts, cotton stockings, and shoes (probably their only pair). Workingmen dressed even more drably. Many occupations could be recognized by their dress: no one could confuse lawyers in their dark robes with masons or butchers in their special aprons, for example. People higher on the social ladder were more likely to sport a variety of fabrics, colors, and unusual designs in their clothing and to own many different outfits. Social status was not an abstract idea; it permeated every detail of daily life.

The Growth of a Literate Public. The ability to read and write also reflected social differences. People in the upper classes were more literate than those in the lower classes; city people were more literate than peasants. Protestant countries appear to have been more successful at promoting education and literacy than Catholic countries, perhaps because of the Protestant emphasis on Bible reading. Widespread literacy among the lower classes was first achieved in the Protestant areas of Switzerland and in Presbyterian Scotland, and rates were also very high in the New England colonies and the Scandinavian countries. In France, literacy doubled in the eighteenth century thanks to the spread of parish schools, but still only one in two men and one in four women could read and write. Most peasants remained illiterate. Although some Protestant German states encouraged primary education, schooling remained woefully inadequate almost everywhere in Europe: few schools existed, teachers received low wages, and no country had yet established a national system of control or supervision.

Despite the deficiencies of primary education, a new literate public arose especially among the middle classes of the cities. More books and periodicals were published than ever before, another aspect of the consumer revolution. The trend began in the 1690s in Britain and the Dutch Republic and gradually accelerated. In 1695, the British government allowed the licensing system, through which it controlled publications, to lapse, and new newspapers and magazines appeared almost immediately. The first London daily newspaper came out in 1702, and in 1709 Joseph Addison and Richard Steele published the first literary magazine, *The Spectator*. They devoted their magazine to the cultural improvement of the increasingly influential middle class. By the 1720s, twenty-four provincial newspapers were published in England. In the London coffeehouses, an edition of a single newspaper might reach ten thousand male readers. Women did their reading at home. Except in the Dutch Republic, newspapers on the continent lagged behind and often consisted mainly of advertising with little critical commentary. France, for example, had no daily paper until 1777.

New Tastes in the Arts

The new literate public did not just read newspapers; its members now pursued an interest in painting, attended concerts, and besieged booksellers in search of popular novels. Because increased trade and prosperity put money into the hands of the growing middle classes, a new urban audience began to compete with the churches, rulers, and courtiers as chief patrons for new work. As the public for the arts expanded, printed commentary on them emerged, setting the stage for the appearance of political and social criticism. New artistic tastes thus had effects far beyond the realm of the arts.

Rococo Painting. Developments in painting reflected the tastes of the new public, as the **rococo** style challenged the hold of the baroque and classical schools, especially in France. Like the baroque, the rococo emphasized irregularity and asymmetry, movement and curvature, but it did so on a much smaller, subtler scale. Many rococo paintings depicted scenes of intimate sensuality rather than the monumental, emotional grandeur favored by classical and baroque painters. Personal portraits and pastoral paintings took the place of heroic landscapes and grand, ceremonial canvases. Rococo paintings adorned homes as well as palaces and served as a form of interior decoration rather than as a statement of piety. Its decorative quality made rococo art an ideal complement to newly discovered materials such as stucco and porcelain, especially the porcelain vases now imported from China.

Rococo, like *baroque*, was an invented word (from the French word *rocaille*, meaning "shellwork") and originally a derogatory label, meaning "frivolous decoration." But the great French rococo painters, such as Antoine Watteau (1684–1721) and François Boucher (1703–1770), were much more than mere decorators. Although both em-

Rococo Painting
The rococo emphasis on interiors, on decoration, and on intimacy rather than monumental grandeur are evident in François Boucher's painting *The Luncheon* (1739). The painting also draws attention to new consumer items, from the mirror and the clock to chocolate, children's toys, a small Buddha statue, and the intricately designed furniture. (*The Art Archive/Galleria Degli Uffizi/Dagli Orti (A).*)

rococo: A style of painting that emphasized irregularity and asymmetry, movement and curvature, but on a smaller, more intimate scale than the baroque.

phasized the erotic in their depictions, Watteau captured the melancholy side of a passing aristocratic style of life, and Boucher painted middle-class people at home during their daily activities. Both painters thereby contributed to the emergence of new sensibilities in art that increasingly attracted a middle-class public.

Music for the Public.　The first public music concerts were performed in England in the 1670s, becoming much more regular and frequent in the 1690s. City concert halls typically seated about two hundred, but the relatively high price of tickets limited attendance to the better-off. Music clubs provided entertainment in smaller towns and villages. On the continent, Frankfurt organized the first regular public concerts in 1712; Hamburg and Paris began holding them within a few years. Opera continued to spread in the eighteenth century; Venice had sixteen public opera houses by 1700, and the Covent Garden opera house opened in London in 1732.

The growth of a public that appreciated and supported music had much the same effect as the extension of the reading public: like authors, composers could now begin to liberate themselves from court patronage and work for a paying audience. This development took time to solidify, however, and court or church patrons still commissioned much eighteenth-century music. Bach, a German Lutheran, wrote his *St. Matthew Passion* for Good Friday services in 1729 while he was organist and choirmaster for the leading church in Leipzig. He composed secular works (like the "Coffee Cantata") for the public and a variety of private patrons.

The composer George Frideric Handel (1685–1759) was among the first to grasp the new directions in music. A German by birth, he wrote operas in Italy and then moved in 1710 to Britain, where he wrote music for the court and began composing oratorios. The oratorio, a form Handel introduced in Britain, combined the drama of opera with the majesty of religious and ceremonial music and featured the chorus over the soloists. The "Hallelujah Chorus" from Handel's oratorio *Messiah* (1741) is perhaps the single best-known piece of Western classical music. It reflected the composer's personal, deeply felt piety but also his willingness to combine musical materials into a dramatic form that captured the enthusiasm of the new public. In 1740, a poem about Handel published in the *Gentleman's Magazine* exulted: "His art so modulates the sounds in all, / Our passions, as he pleases, rise and fall." Music had become an integral part of the new middle-class public's culture.

Novels.　Nothing captured the imagination of the new public more than the novel, the literary genre whose very name underscored the eighteenth-century taste for novelty. More than three hundred French novels appeared between 1700 and 1730. During this unprecedented explosion, the novel took on its modern form and became more concerned with individual psychology and social description than with the adventure tales popular earlier (such as Miguel de Cervantes's *Don Quixote*). The novel's popularity was closely tied to the expansion of the reading public, and novels were available in serial form in periodicals or from the many booksellers who served the new market.

Women figured prominently in novels as characters, and women writers abounded. The English novel *Love in Excess* (1719) quickly reached a sixth printing, and its author, Eliza Haywood (1693?–1756), earned her living turning out a stream of novels with titles such as *Persecuted Virtue*, *Constancy Rewarded*, and *The History of Betsy Thoughtless*—all showing a concern for the proper place of women as models of virtue in a changing world. When her husband deserted her and her two children, Haywood first worked as an actress but soon turned to writing plays and novels. In the 1740s, she began publishing a magazine, *The Female Spectator*, which argued in favor of higher education for women.

Haywood's male counterpart was Daniel Defoe (1660–1731), a merchant's son who had a diverse and colorful career as a manufacturer, political spy, novelist, and social commentator (see Document, "The Social Effects of Growing Consumption," page 530). Defoe wrote about schemes for national improvement, the state of English trade, the economic condition of the countryside, the effects of the plague, and the history of pirates; he is most well known, however, for his novels *Robinson Crusoe* (1719) and *Moll Flanders* (1722). The story of the adventures of a shipwrecked sailor, *Robinson Crusoe* portrayed the new values of the time: to survive, Crusoe had to employ fearless entrepreneurial ingenuity. He had to be ready for the unexpected and be able to improvise in every situation. He was, in short, the model for the new man in an expanding economy. Crusoe's patronizing attitude toward the black man Friday now draws much critical attention, but his discovery of Friday shows how the fate of blacks and whites had become intertwined in the new colonial environment.

Religious Revivals

Despite the novel's growing popularity, religious books and pamphlets still sold in huge numbers, and most Europeans remained devout, even as their religions were changing. In this period, a Protestant revivalist movement known as **Pietism** rocked the complacency of the established churches in the German Lutheran states, the Dutch Republic, and Scandinavia. Pietists believed in a mystical religion of the heart; they wanted a deeply emotional, even ecstatic religion. They urged intense Bible study, which in turn promoted popular education and contributed to the increase in literacy. Many Pietists attended catechism instruction every day and also went to morning and evening prayer meetings in addition to regular Sunday services. Although Pietism appealed to both Lutherans and Calvinists, it had the greatest impact in Lutheran Prussia, where it taught the virtues of hard work, obedience, and devotion to duty.

Catholicism also had its versions of religious revival, especially in France. A Frenchwoman, Jeanne Marie Guyon (1648–1717), attracted many noblewomen and a few leading clergymen to her own Catholic brand of Pietism, known as Quietism. Claiming miraculous visions and astounding prophecies, she urged a mystical union with God through prayer and simple devotion. Despite papal condemnation and intense controversy within Catholic circles in France, Guyon had followers all over Europe.

Even more influential were the Jansenists, who gained many new adherents to their austere form of Catholicism despite Louis XIV's harassment and repeated condemnation by the papacy. Under the pressure of religious and political persecution, Jansenism took a revivalist turn in the 1720s. At the funeral of a Jansenist priest in Paris in 1727, the crowd who flocked to the grave claimed to witness a series of miraculous healings. Within a few years, a cult formed around the priest's tomb and clandestine Jansenist presses were reporting new miracles to the reading public. When the French government tried to suppress the cult, one enraged wit placed a sign at the tomb that read, "By order of the king, God is forbidden to work miracles here." Some believers fell into frenzied convulsions, claiming to be inspired by the Holy Spirit through the intercession of the dead priest. After

midcentury, Jansenism became even more politically active as its adherents joined in opposition to the crown's policies on religion.

> **REVIEW:** How were new social trends reflected in cultural life in the late 1600s and early 1700s?

Consolidation of the European State System

The spread of Pietism and Jansenism reflected the emergence of a middle-class public that now participated in every new development, including religion. The middle classes could pursue these interests because the European state system gradually stabilized despite the increasing competition for wealth in the Atlantic system. Warfare settled three main issues between 1690 and 1740: a coalition of powers held Louis XIV's France in check on the continent, Great Britain emerged from the wars against Louis as the preeminent maritime power, and Russia defeated Sweden in the contest for supremacy in the Baltic. After Louis XIV's death in 1715, Europe enjoyed the fruits of a more balanced diplomatic system, in which warfare became less frequent and less widespread. States could then spend their resources establishing and expanding control over their own populations, both at home and in their colonies.

French Ambitions Thwarted

Lying on his deathbed in 1715, the seventy-six-year-old Louis XIV watched helplessly as his accomplishments began to unravel. Not only had his plans for territorial expansion been frustrated, but his incessant wars had exhausted the treasury, despite new taxes. In 1689, Louis's rival, William III, prince of Orange and king of England and Scotland (r. 1689–1702), had set out to forge a European alliance that eventually included Britain, the Dutch Republic, Sweden, Austria, and Spain. The allies fought Louis to a stalemate in the War of the League of Augsburg, sometimes called the Nine Years' War (1689–1697), and when hostilities resumed four years later, they finally put an end to Louis's expansionist ambitions.

The War of the Spanish Succession, 1701–1713.
When the mentally and physically feeble Charles II (r. 1665–1700) of Spain died without a direct heir, all of Europe poised for a fight over the spoils.

Pietism: A Protestant revivalist movement of the early eighteenth century that emphasized deeply emotional individual religious experience.

English and French Claims after the Peace of Utrecht, 1714

Hudson Bay

Newfoundland

English claim

French claim

Nova Scotia

English claim

0   500   1000 miles
0   500   1000 kilometers

0   200   400 miles
0   200   400 kilometers

SWEDEN

St. Petersburg

DENMARK-NORWAY

North Sea

Baltic Sea

Moscow

SCOTLAND
Edinburgh

IRELAND
Dublin

RUSSIA

GREAT BRITAIN

ENGLAND
London

DUTCH REPUBLIC

Utrecht

Hanover

BRANDENBURG-PRUSSIA
Berlin

Elbe R.

POLAND-LITHUANIA

Warsaw

Kiev

English Channel

Cologne

Rhine R.

HOLY ROMAN EMPIRE

Vistula R.

ATLANTIC OCEAN

Paris

Loire R.

FRANCE

Austrian Neth.

AUSTRIA

Vienna

HUNGARY

Buda   Pest

SWISS CONFED.

Danube R.

SAVOY

MILAN VENICE

GENOA

Black Sea

PORTUGAL

Madrid

SPAIN

Lisbon

Corsica

TUSCANY PAPAL STATES

Marseille

Minorca (Gr. Br.)

Rome

Sardinia

BALEARIC IS.

KINGDOM OF NAPLES

OTTOMAN EMPIRE

Constantinople

Gibraltar (Gr. Br.)

Sicily

Mediterranean Sea

Territories gained after the Peace of Utrecht, 1714

- French Bourbon lands
- Spanish Bourbon lands
- Austrian Habsburg lands
- Prussian lands
- Great Britain
- To Great Britain
- To the Austrian Empire
- The Jacobite rising of 1715
- Main areas of fighting during the War of the Spanish Succession, 1701–1713
- Boundary of the Holy Roman Empire

MAP 17.2 Europe, c. 1715

Although Louis XIV succeeded in putting his grandson Philip on the Spanish throne, France emerged considerably weakened from the War of Spanish Succession. France ceded large territories in Canada to Britain, which also gained key Mediterranean outposts from Spain as well as a monopoly on providing slaves to the Spanish colonies. Spanish losses were catastrophic. Philip had to renounce any future claim to the French crown and give up considerable territories in the Netherlands and Italy to the Austrians.

■ How did the competing English and French claims in North America around 1715 create potential conflicts for the future?

The Spanish succession could not help but be a burning issue. Even though Spanish power had declined since Spain's golden age in the sixteenth century, Spain still had extensive territories in Italy and the Netherlands as well as colonies overseas. Before Charles died, he named Louis XIV's second grandson, Philip, duke of Anjou, as his heir, but the Austrian emperor Leopold I refused to accept Charles's deathbed will.

In the ensuing war, the French lost several major battles and had to accept disadvantageous terms in the **Peace of Utrecht** of 1713–1714 (Map 17.2). Although Philip was recognized as king of Spain, he had to renounce any future claim to the French crown, thus barring unification of the two kingdoms. Spain surrendered its territories in Italy and the Netherlands to the Austrians and Gibraltar to the British; France ceded possessions in North America (Newfoundland, the Hudson Bay area, and most of Nova Scotia) to Britain. France no longer threatened to dominate European power politics.

The Death of Louis XIV and the Regency. At home, Louis's policy of absolutism had fomented bitter hostility. Nobles fiercely resented his promotions of commoners to high office. The duke of Saint-Simon complained that "falseness, servility, admiring glances, combined with a dependent and cringing attitude, above all, an appearance of being nothing without him, were the only ways of pleasing him." Archbishop Fénelon, who tutored the king's grandson, called for reform. An admirer of Guyon's Quietism, Fénelon severely criticized the "steady stream of extravagant adulation, which reaches the point of idolatry"; the constant, bloody wars; and the misery of the people.

On his deathbed, Louis XIV offered sound advice to his five-year-old great-grandson and successor, Louis XV (r. 1715–1774): "Do not imitate my love of building nor my liking for war." After being named regent, the duke of Orléans (1674–1723), nephew of the dead king, revived some of the parlements' powers and tried to give leading nobles a greater say in political affairs. To raise much-needed funds, in 1719 the regent encouraged the Scottish financier John Law to set up an official trading company for North America and a state bank that issued paper money and stock (without them, trade depended on the available supply of gold and silver). The bank was supposed to offer lower interest rates to the state, thus cut-

ting the cost of financing the government's debts. The value of the stock rose rapidly in a frenzy of speculation, only to crash a few months later. With it vanished any hope of establishing a state bank or issuing paper money for nearly a century.

France finally achieved a measure of financial stability under the leadership of Cardinal Hercule de Fleury (1653–1743), the most powerful member of the government after the death of the regent. Fleury aimed to avoid adventure abroad and keep social peace at home; he balanced the budget and carried out a large project for road and canal construction. Colonial trade boomed. Peace and the acceptance of limits on territorial expansion inaugurated a century of French prosperity.

British Rise and Dutch Decline

The British and the Dutch had formed a coalition against Louis XIV under their joint ruler William III, who was simultaneously stadholder (elected head) of the Dutch Republic and, with his English wife, Mary (d. 1694), ruler of England, Wales, and Scotland. After William's death in 1702, the British and Dutch went their separate ways. Over the next decades, England incorporated Scotland and subjugated Ireland, becoming "Great Britain." At the same time, Dutch imperial power declined; by 1700, Great Britain dominated the seas and the Dutch, with their small population of less than two million, came to depend on alliances with bigger powers.

From England to Great Britain. English relations with Scotland and Ireland were complicated by the problem of succession: William and Mary had no children. To ensure a Protestant succession, Parliament ruled that Mary's sister, Anne, would succeed William and Mary and that the Protestant House of Hanover in Germany would succeed Anne if she had no surviving heirs. Catholics were excluded. When Queen Anne (r. 1702–1714) died leaving no children, the elector of Hanover, a Protestant great-grandson of James I, consequently became King George I (r. 1714–1727). The House of Hanover—renamed the House of Windsor during World War I—still occupies the British throne.

Support from the Scots and Irish for this solution did not come easily, because many in Scotland and Ireland supported the claims to the throne of the deposed Catholic king, James II, and, after his death in 1701, his son James Edward. Out of fear of this Jacobitism (from the Latin *Jacobus* for "James"), Scottish Protestant leaders agreed to the Act of Union of 1707, which abolished the

---

Peace of Utrecht: Treaties drawn up in 1713–1714 that ended the War of the Spanish Succession.

Scottish Parliament and affirmed the Scots' recognition of the Protestant Hanoverian succession. The Scots agreed to obey the Parliament of Great Britain, which would include Scottish members in the House of Commons and the House of Lords. A Jacobite rebellion in Scotland in 1715, aiming to restore the Stuart line, was suppressed. The threat of Jacobitism nonetheless continued into the 1740s (see Map 17.2, page 537).

The Irish — 90 percent of whom were Catholic — proved even more difficult to subdue. When James II had gone to Ireland in 1689 to raise a Catholic rebellion against the new monarchs of England, William III responded by taking command of the joint English and Dutch forces and defeating James's Irish supporters. James fled to France, and the Catholics in Ireland faced yet more confiscation and legal restrictions. By 1700, Irish Catholics, who in 1640 had owned 60 percent of the land in Ireland, owned just 14 percent. The Protestant-controlled Irish Parliament passed a series of laws limiting the rights of the Catholic majority: Catholics could not bear arms, send their children abroad for education, establish Catholic schools at home, or marry Protestants. Catholics could not sit in Parliament, nor could they vote for its members unless they took an oath renouncing

Catholic doctrine. These and a host of other laws reduced Catholic Ireland to the status of a colony; one English official commented in 1745, "The poor people of Ireland are used worse than negroes." Most of the Irish were peasants who lived in primitive housing and subsisted on a meager diet that included no meat.

The Parliament of Great Britain was soon dominated by the Whigs. In Britain's constitutional system, the monarch ruled with Parliament. The crown chose the ministers, directed policy, and supervised administration, while Parliament raised revenue, passed laws, and represented the interests of the people to the crown. The powers of Parliament were reaffirmed by the Triennial Act in 1694, which provided that Parliaments meet at least once every three years (this was extended to seven years in 1716, after the Whigs had established their ascendancy). Only 200,000 propertied men could vote, out of a population of more than five million, and, not surprisingly, most members of Parliament came from the landed gentry. In fact, a few hundred families controlled all the important political offices.

George I and George II (r. 1727–1760) relied on one man, Sir **Robert Walpole** (1676–1745), to help them manage their relations with Parliament.

Sir Robert Walpole at a Cabinet Meeting
Sir Robert Walpole and George II developed the institution of a cabinet, which brought together the important heads of departments. Their cabinet was the ancestor of modern cabinets in both Great Britain and the United States. Because of its modest size, its similarities to modern forms should not be overstated, however. How would discussions in the new coffeehouses (shown in the opening illustration to this chapter) influence the kinds of decisions made by Walpole and his cabinet? (© *The Fotomas Index, U.K./The Bridgeman Art Library.*)

Robert Walpole: The first, or "prime," minister of the House of Commons of Great Britain's Parliament. Although appointed initially by the king, through his long period of leadership (1721–1742) he effectively established the modern pattern of parliamentary government.

From his position as First Lord of the Treasury, Walpole made himself into the first, or "prime," minister, leading the House of Commons from 1721 to 1742 (see illustration, page 539). Although appointed initially by the king, Walpole established an enduring pattern of parliamentary government in which a prime minister from the leading party guided legislation through the House of Commons. Walpole also built a vast patronage machine that dispensed government jobs to win support for the crown's policies. Walpole's successors relied more and more on the patronage system and eventually alienated not only the Tories but also the middle classes in London and even the North American colonies.

The partisan division between the Whigs, who supported the Hanoverian succession and the rights of dissenting Protestants, and the Tories, who had backed the Stuart line and the Anglican church, did not hamper Great Britain's pursuit of economic, military, and colonial power. In this period, Great Britain became a great power on the world stage by virtue of its navy and its ability to finance major military involvement in the wars against Louis XIV. The founding in 1694 of the Bank of England — which, unlike the French bank, endured — enabled the government to raise money at low interest for foreign wars. By the 1740s, the government could borrow more than four times what it could in the 1690s.

The Dutch Eclipse. When William of Orange (William III of England) died in 1702, he left no heirs, and for forty-five years the Dutch lived without a stadholder. The merchant ruling class of some two thousand families dominated the Dutch Republic more than ever, but they presided over a country that counted for less in international power politics. In some areas, Dutch decline was only relative: the Dutch population was not growing as fast as others, for example, and the Dutch share of the Baltic trade decreased from 50 percent in 1720 to less than 30 percent by the 1770s. After 1720, the Baltic countries — Prussia, Russia, Denmark, and Sweden — began to ban imports of manufactured goods to protect their own industries, and Dutch trade in particular suffered. The output of Leiden textiles dropped to one-third of its 1700 level by 1740. Shipbuilding, paper manufacturing, tobacco processing, salt refining, and pottery production all dwindled as well. The Dutch East India Company saw its political and military grip loosened in India, Ceylon, and Java.

The biggest exception to the downward trend was trade with the New World, which increased with escalating demands for sugar and tobacco. The Dutch shifted their interest away from great power rivalries toward those areas of international trade and finance where they could establish an enduring presence.

Russia's Emergence as a European Power

The commerce and shipbuilding of the Dutch and British so impressed Russian tsar Peter I (r. 1689–1725) that he traveled incognito to their shipyards in 1697 to learn their methods firsthand. Known to history as **Peter the Great**, he dragged Russia kicking and screaming all the way to great-power status. Although he came to the throne while still a minor (on the eve of his tenth birthday), grew up under the threat of a palace coup, and enjoyed little formal education, his accomplishments soon matched his seven-foot-tall stature. Peter transformed public life in Russia and established an absolutist state on the Western model. His attempts to create a society patterned after western Europe, known as **Westernization**, ignited an enduring controversy: Did Peter set Russia on a course of inevitable Westernization required to compete with the West? Or did he forever and fatally disrupt Russia's natural evolution into a distinctive Slavic society?

Westernization. To pursue his goal of Westernizing Russian culture, Peter set up the first greenhouses, laboratories, and technical schools and founded the Russian Academy of Sciences. He ordered translations of Western classics and hired a German theater company to perform the French plays of Molière. He replaced the traditional Russian calendar with the Western one,[1] introduced Arabic numerals, and brought out the first public newspaper. He ordered his officials and the nobles to shave their beards (see the illustration on page 541) and dress in Western fashion, and he even

---

[1] Peter introduced the Julian calendar, then still used in Protestant but not Catholic countries. Later in the eighteenth century, Protestant Europe abandoned the Julian for the Gregorian calendar. Not until 1918 was the Gregorian calendar adopted in Russia, at which point Russia's calendar had fallen thirteen days behind Europe's.

Peter the Great: Russian tsar Peter I (r. 1689–1725), who undertook the Westernization of Russia and built a new capital city named after himself, St. Petersburg.

Westernization: The effort, especially in Peter the Great's Russia, to make society and social customs resemble counterparts in western Europe, especially France, Britain, and the Dutch Republic.

Peter the Great Modernizes Russia

In this popular print, a barber forces a protesting noble to conform to western fashions. Peter the Great ordered all nobles, merchants, and middle-class professionals to cut off their beards or pay a huge tax to keep them. An early biographer of Peter claimed that those who lost their beards saved them to put in their coffins, in fear that they would not enter heaven without them. Most western Europeans applauded these attempts to modernize Russia, but many Russians deeply resented the attack on traditional ways. Why was everyday appearance such a contested issue in Russia? *(The Visual Connection.)*

issued precise regulations about the suitable style of jacket, boots, and cap (generally French or German).

Peter encouraged foreigners to move to Russia to offer their advice and skills, especially for building the capital city. Named St. Petersburg after the tsar, the new capital symbolized Russia's opening to the West. Construction began in 1703 in a Baltic province that had been recently conquered from Sweden. By the end of 1709, forty thousand recruits a year found themselves assigned to the work. Peter ordered skilled workers to move to the new city and commanded all landowners possessing more than forty serf households to build houses there. In the 1720s, a German minister described St. Petersburg "as a wonder of the world, considering its magnificent palaces, . . . and the short time that was employed in the building of it." By 1710, the permanent population of the capital reached eight thousand. At Peter's death in 1725, it had forty thousand residents.

As a new city far from the Russian heartland around Moscow, St. Petersburg represented a decisive break with Russia's past. Peter widened that gap by every means possible. At his new capital he tried to improve the traditionally denigrated, secluded status of women by ordering them to dress in European styles and appear publicly at his dinners for diplomatic representatives. Imitating French manners, he decreed that women attend his new social salons of officials, officers, and merchants for conversation and dancing. A foreigner headed every one of Peter's new technical and vocational schools, and for its first eight years the new Academy of Sciences included no Russians. Every ministry was assigned a foreign adviser. Upper-class Russians learned French or German, which they spoke even at home. Such changes affected only the very top of Russian society, however; the mass of the population had no contact with the new ideas and ended up paying for the innovations either in ruinous new taxation or by building St. Petersburg, a project that cost the lives of thousands of workers. Serfs remained tied to the land, completely dominated by their noble lords.

Peter the Great's Brand of Absolutism. Peter also reorganized government and finance on Western models and, like other absolute rulers, strengthened his army. With ruthless recruiting methods, which included branding a cross on every recruit's left hand to prevent desertion, he forged an army of 200,000 men and equipped it with modern weapons. He created schools for artillery, engineering, and military medicine and built the first navy in Russian history. Not surprisingly, taxes tripled.

The tsar allowed nothing to stand in his way. He did not hesitate to use torture, and he executed thousands. He allowed a special guard regiment

Peter the Great
In this painting by Gottfried Danhauer (1680–1733/7), the Russian tsar appears against the background of his most famous battle, Poltava. The angel holds a laurel wreath, symbol of victory, over his head. (© Tretyakov Gallery, Moscow, Russia/The Bridgeman Art Library.)

unprecedented power to expedite cases against those suspected of rebellion, espionage, pretensions to the throne, or just "unseemly utterances" against him. Opposition to his policies reached into his own family: because his only son, Alexei, had allied himself with Peter's critics, the tsar threw him into prison, where the young man mysteriously died.

To control the often restive nobility, Peter insisted that all noblemen engage in state service. A Table of Ranks (1722) classified them into military, administrative, and court categories, a codification of social and legal relationships in Russia that would last for nearly two centuries. All social and material advantages now depended on serving the crown. Because the nobles lacked a secure independent status, Peter could command them to a degree that was unimaginable in western Europe. State service was not only compulsory but also permanent. Moreover, the male children of those in service had to be registered by the age of ten and begin serving at fifteen. To increase his authority over the Russian Orthodox church, Peter allowed the office of patriarch (supreme head) to remain vacant, and in 1721 he replaced it with the

Holy Synod, a bureaucracy of laymen under his supervision. To many Russians, Peter was the devil incarnate.

Changes in the Balance of Power in the East.
Peter the Great's success in building up state power changed the balance of power in eastern Europe. Overcoming initial military setbacks, Russia eventually defeated Sweden and took its place as the leading power in the Baltic region. Russia could then compete with Prussia, Austria, and France in the rivalries between great powers.

Sweden had dominated the Baltic region since the Thirty Years' War (1618–1648), and though the monarchy lost some of its power under Queen Christina (r. 1632–1654), the daughter of Gustavus Adolphus, the Swedish kings quickly recovered their position. When Peter the Great joined an anti-Swedish coalition in 1700 with Denmark, Saxony, and Poland, Sweden's Charles XII (r. 1697–1718) stood up to the test. Still in his teens at the beginning of the Great Northern War, Charles first defeated Denmark, then destroyed the new Russian army, and quickly marched into Poland and Saxony. After defeating the Poles and occupying Saxony, Charles invaded Russia. Here Peter's rebuilt army finally defeated the Swedish king at the battle of Poltava (1709).

The Russian victory resounded everywhere. The Russian ambassador to Vienna reported, "It is commonly said that the tsar will be formidable to all Europe, that he will be a kind of northern Turk." Prussia and other German states joined the anti-Swedish alliance, and when Charles XII died in battle in 1718, negotiations finally ended the Great Northern War. By the terms of the Treaty of Nystad (1721), Sweden ceded its eastern Baltic provinces — Livonia, Estonia, Ingria, and southern Karelia — to Russia. Sweden also lost territories on the north German coast to Prussia and the other allied German states (Map 17.3). An aristocratic reaction against Charles XII's incessant demands for war supplies swept away Sweden's absolutist regime, essentially removing Sweden from great power competition.

Prussia had to make the most of every military opportunity, as it did in the Great Northern War, because it was much smaller in size and population than Russia, Austria, or France. King Frederick William I (r. 1713–1740) doubled the size of the Prussian army; though still smaller than those of his rivals, it was the best-trained and most up-to-date force in Europe. By 1740, Prussia had Europe's highest proportion of men at arms (1 of every 28 people, versus 1 in 157 in France and 1 in 64 in Russia) and the highest proportion of nobles in the military (1 in 7 noblemen, as compared with 1 in 33 in France and 1 in 50 in Russia).

The army so dominated life in Prussia that the country earned the label "a large army with a small state attached." Frederick William, known as the "Sergeant King," was one of the first rulers to wear a military uniform as his everyday dress. He subordinated the entire domestic administration to the army's needs. He also installed a system for recruiting soldiers by local district quotas. He financed the army's growth by subjecting all the provinces to an excise tax on food, drink, and manufactured goods and by increasing rents on crown lands. Prussia was now poised to become one of the major players on the continent, but it could not enter into military engagements foolishly given the size of its forces and chose to sit on the sidelines during the next conflict.

War broke out in 1733 when the king of Poland-Lithuania died. France, Spain, and Sardinia joined in the War of Polish Succession (1733–1735) against Austria and Russia, each side supporting rival claimants to the Polish throne. Although Peter the Great had been followed by a series of weak rulers, Russian forces were still strong enough to drive the French candidate out of Poland-Lithuania, prompting France to accept the Austrian candidate. In exchange, Austria gave the province of Lorraine to the French candidate, the father-in-law of Louis XV, with the promise that the province would pass to France on his death.

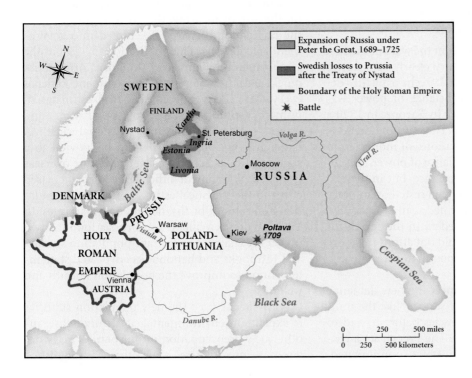

MAP 17.3 Russia and Sweden after the Great Northern War, 1721
After the Great Northern War, Russia supplanted Sweden as the major power in the north. Although Russia had a much larger population from which to draw its armies, Sweden made the most of its advantages and gave way only after a great military struggle.

France and Britain went back to pursuing their colonial rivalries. Prussia and Russia concentrated on shoring up their influence within Poland-Lithuania.

Austria did not want to become mired in a long struggle in Poland-Lithuania because its armies still faced the Turks on its southeastern border. Even though the Austrians had forced the Turks to recognize their rule over all of Hungary and Transylvania in 1699 and occupied Belgrade in 1717, the Turks did not stop fighting. In the 1730s, the Turks retook Belgrade, and Russia now claimed a role in the struggle against the Turks. Moreover, Hungary, though "liberated" from Turkish rule, proved less than enthusiastic about submitting to Austria. In 1703, the wealthiest Hungarian noble landlord, Ferenc Rákóczi (1676–1735), raised an army of seventy thousand men who fought for "God, Fatherland, and Liberty" until 1711. They forced the Austrians to recognize local Hungarian institutions, grant amnesty, and restore confiscated estates in exchange for confirming hereditary Austrian rule.

Austrian Conquest of Hungary, 1657–1730

The Power of Diplomacy and the Importance of Population

No single power emerged from the wars of the first half of the eighteenth century clearly superior to the others, and the Peace of Utrecht explicitly declared that maintaining a balance of power was crucial to maintaining peace in Europe. In 1720 a British pamphleteer wrote, "There is not, I believe, any doctrine in the law of nations, of more certain truth . . . than this of the balance of power." Diplomacy helped maintain the balance, but in the end this system of equilibrium often rested on military force, such as the leagues formed against Louis XIV or the coalition against Sweden. In the search for ever larger armies, states could not afford to ignore the general health of their populations.

Diplomatic Services. To meet the new demands placed on it, the diplomatic service, like the military and financial bureaucracies before it, had to develop regular procedures. The French set a pattern that the other European states soon imitated.

By 1685, France had embassies in all the important capitals. Nobles of ancient families served as ambassadors to Rome, Madrid, Vienna, and London, whereas royal officials were chosen for Switzerland, the Dutch Republic, and Venice. The ambassador selected and paid for his own staff. This practice could make the journey to a new post cumbersome, because the staff might be as large as eighty people, and they brought along all their own furniture, pictures, silverware, and tapestries. It took one French ambassador ten weeks to get from Paris to Stockholm.

Despite a new emphasis on honest and informed negotiation, rulers still employed secret agents and often sent covert instructions that negated the official ones sent by their own foreign offices. This behind-the-scenes diplomacy had some advantages because it allowed rulers to break with past alliances, but it also led to confusion and sometimes scandal, for the rulers often engaged unreliable adventurers as their confidential agents. Still, the diplomatic system in the early eighteenth century proved successful enough to ensure a continuation of the principles of the Peace of Westphalia (1648); in the midst of every crisis and war, the great powers would convene and hammer out a written agreement detailing the requirements for peace.

Public Health. Adroit diplomacy could smooth the road toward peace, but success in war still depended on sheer numbers—of men and of muskets. Because each state's strength depended largely on the size of its army, the growth and health of the population increasingly entered into government calculations. The publication in 1690 of the Englishman William Petty's *Political Arithmetick* quickened the interest of government officials everywhere. Petty offered statistical estimates of human capital—that is, of population and wages—to determine Britain's national wealth. A large, growing population could be as vital to a state's future as access to silver mines or overseas trade, so government officials devoted increased effort to the statistical estimation of total population and rates of births, deaths, and marriages. In 1727, Frederick William I of Prussia founded two university chairs to encourage population studies, and textbooks and handbooks advocated state intervention to improve the population's health and welfare.

Physicians used the new population statistics to explain the environmental causes of disease, another new preoccupation in this period. Petty devised a quantitative scale that distinguished healthy from unhealthy places largely on the basis of air quality, an early precursor of modern environmental studies. Cities were the unhealthiest places because excrement (animal and human) and garbage accumulated where people lived densely packed together. Medical geographers gathered and analyzed data on climate, disease, and population, searching for correlations to help direct policy. As a result of these efforts, local governments undertook such measures as draining low-lying areas, burying refuse, and cleaning wells, all of which eventually helped lower the death rates from epidemic diseases.

Not all changes came from direct government intervention. Hospitals, founded originally as charities concerned foremost with the moral worthiness of the poor, gradually evolved into medical institutions that defined patients by their diseases. The process of diagnosis changed as physicians began to use specialized Latin terms for illnesses. The gap between medical experts and their patients increased, as physicians now also relied on postmortem dissections in the hospital to gain better knowledge, a practice most patients' families resented. Press reports of body snatching and grave robbing by surgeons and their apprentices outraged the public well into the 1800s.

Despite the change in hospitals, individual health care remained something of a free-for-all in which physicians competed with bloodletters, itinerant venereal-disease doctors, bonesetters, druggists, midwives, and "cunning women," who specialized in home remedies. The medical profession, with nationwide organizations and licensing, had not yet emerged, and no clear line separated trained physicians from quacks. In any case, trained physicians were few in number and almost nonexistent outside cities. Patients were as likely to catch a deadly disease in the hospital as to be cured there. Antiseptics were virtually unknown. Because doctors believed most insanity was caused by disorders in the system of bodily "humors," their prescribed treatments included blood transfusions; ingestion of bitter substances such as coffee, quinine, and even soap; immersion in water; various forms of exercise; and burning or cauterizing the body to allow black vapors to escape.

Hardly any infectious diseases could be cured, though inoculation against smallpox spread from the Middle East to Europe in the early eighteenth century, thanks largely to the efforts of Lady Mary Wortley Montagu (1689–1762). In 1716, Montagu accompanied her husband to Constantinople, where he took up a post as British ambassador to the Ottoman Empire. She returned in 1718, after witnessing firsthand the Turkish use of inoculation. When a new smallpox epidemic threatened England in 1721, she called on her physician to inoculate her daughter. Two patients died after inoculation in the following months, prompting clergymen and physicians to attack the practice, which remained in dispute for decades. Inoculation against smallpox began to spread more widely after 1796, when the English physician Edward Jenner developed a serum based on cowpox, a milder disease. Many other diseases spread quickly in the unsanitary conditions of urban life. Ordinary people washed or changed clothes rarely, lived in overcrowded housing with poor ventilation, and got their water from contaminated sources such as refuse-filled rivers.

Public bathhouses had disappeared from cities in the sixteenth and seventeenth centuries because they seemed a source of disorderly behavior and epidemic illness. In the eighteenth century, even private bathing came into disfavor because people feared the effects of contact with water. Fewer than one in ten newly built private mansions in Paris had baths. Bathing was hazardous, physicians insisted, because it opened the body to disease. One manners manual of 1736 admonished, "It is correct to clean the face every morning by using a white cloth to cleanse it. It is less good to wash with water, because it renders the face susceptible to cold in winter and sun in summer." The upper classes associated cleanliness not with baths but with frequently changed linens, powdered hair, and perfume, which was thought to strengthen the body and refresh the brain by counteracting corrupt and foul air.

> **REVIEW:** What events and developments led to greater stability and less warfare in the European state system?

The Birth of the Enlightenment

Economic expansion, the emergence of a new consumer society, and the stabilization of the European state system all generated optimism about the future. The intellectual corollary was the **Enlightenment**, a term used later in the eighteenth century to describe the loosely knit group of writers

---

Enlightenment: The eighteenth-century intellectual movement whose proponents believed that human beings could apply a critical, reasoning spirit to every problem.

and scholars who believed that human beings could apply a critical, reasoning spirit to every problem they encountered in this world. The new secular, scientific, and critical attitude first emerged in the 1690s, scrutinizing everything from the absolutism of Louis XIV to the traditional role of women in society. After 1740, criticism took a more systematic turn as writers provided new theories for the organization of society and politics; but as early as the 1720s, established authorities realized they faced a new set of challenges. Even while slavery expanded in the Atlantic system, Enlightenment writers began to insist on the need for new freedoms in Europe.

Popularization of Science and Challenges to Religion

The writers of the Enlightenment glorified the geniuses of the new science and championed the scientific method as the solution for all social problems. (See "Terms of History," page 547.) One of the most influential popularizations was the French writer Bernard de Fontenelle's *Conversations on the Plurality of Worlds* (1686). Presented as a dialogue between an aristocratic woman and a man of the world, the book made the Coperni-

can, heliocentric view of the universe available to the literate public. By 1700, mathematics and science had become fashionable pastimes in high society, and the public flocked to lectures explaining scientific discoveries. Journals complained that scientific learning had become the passport to female affection: "There were two young ladies in Paris whose heads had been so turned by this branch of learning that one of them declined to listen to a proposal of marriage unless the candidate for her hand undertook to learn how to make telescopes." Such writings poked fun at women with intellectual interests, but they also demonstrated that women now participated in discussions of science.

The New Skepticism. Interest in science spread in literate circles because it offered a model for all forms of knowledge. As the prestige of science increased, some developed a skeptical attitude toward attempts to enforce religious conformity. A French Huguenot refugee from Louis XIV's persecutions, Pierre Bayle (1647–1706), launched an internationally influential campaign against religious intolerance from his safe haven in the Dutch Republic. His *News from the Republic of Letters* (first published in 1684) bitterly criticized the poli-

A Budding Scientist
In this engraving, *Astrologia*, by the Dutch artist Jacob Gole (c. 1660–1723), an upper-class woman looks through a telescope to do her own astronomical investigations. Women with intellectual interests were often disparaged by men, and women were not allowed to attend university classes in any European country. Yet because many astronomical observatories were set up in private homes rather than public buildings or universities, wives and daughters of scientists could make observations and even publish their own findings. *(Bibliothèque nationale de France.)*

cies of Louis XIV and was quickly banned in Paris and condemned in Rome. After attacking Louis XIV's anti-Protestant policies, Bayle took a more general stand in favor of religious toleration. No state in Europe officially offered complete tolerance, though the Dutch Republic came closest with its tacit acceptance of Catholics, dissident Protestant groups, and open Jewish communities. In 1697, Bayle published the *Historical and Critical Dictionary*, which cited all the errors and delusions that he could find in past and present writers of all religions. Even religion must meet the test of reasonableness: "Any particular dogma, whatever it may be, whether it is advanced on the authority of the Scriptures, or whatever else may be its origins, is to be regarded as false if it clashes with the clear and definite conclusions of the natural understanding [reason]."

Although Bayle claimed to be a believer himself, his insistence on rational investigation seemed to challenge the authority of faith. As one critic complained, "It is notorious that the works of M. Bayle have unsettled a large number of readers, and cast doubt on some of the most widely accepted principles of morality and religion." Bayle asserted, for example, that atheists might possess moral codes as effective as those of the devout. Bayle's *Dictionary* became a model of critical thought in the West.

Other scholars challenged the authority of the Bible by subjecting it to historical criticism. Discoveries in geology in the early eighteenth century showed that marine fossils dated immensely further back than the biblical flood. Investigations of miracles, comets, and oracles, like the growing literature against belief in witchcraft, urged the use of reason to combat superstition and prejudice. Comets, for example, should not be considered evil omens just because earlier generations had passed down such a belief. Defenders of church and state published books warning of the new skepticism's dangers. The spokesman for Louis XIV's absolutism, Bishop Bossuet, warned that "reason is the guide of their choice, but reason only brings them face to face with vague conjectures and baffling perplexities." Human beings, the traditionalists held, were simply incapable of subjecting everything to reason, especially in the realm of religion.

State authorities found religious skepticism particularly unsettling because it threatened to undermine state power too. The extensive literature of criticism was not limited to France, but much of it was published in French, and the French government took the lead in suppressing the more outspoken works. Forbidden books were then

TERMS OF HISTORY

Progress

Believing as they did in the possibilities of improvement, many Enlightenment writers preached a new doctrine about the meaning of human history. They challenged the traditional Christian belief that the original sin of Adam and Eve condemned human beings to unhappiness in this world and offered instead an optimistic vision: human nature, they claimed, was inherently good, and progress would be continuous if education developed human capacities to the utmost. Science and reason could bring happiness in this world. The idea of novelty or newness itself now seemed positive rather than threatening. Europeans began to imagine that they could surpass all those who preceded them in history, and they began to think of themselves as more "advanced" than the "backward" cultures they encountered in other parts of the world.

More than an intellectual concept, the idea of progress included a new conception of historical time and of Europeans' place within world history. Europeans stopped looking back, whether to a lost Garden of Eden or to the writings of Greek and Roman antiquity. Growing prosperity, European dominance overseas, and the scientific revolution oriented them toward the future. Europeans began to apply the word *modern* to their epoch, to distinguish it from the Middle Ages (a new term), and they considered their modern period superior in achievement. Consequently, Europeans took it as their mission to bring their modern, enlightened ways of progress to the areas they colonized.

The economic and ecological catastrophes, destructive wars, and genocides of the twentieth century cast much doubt on this rosy vision of continuing progress. As the philosopher George Santayana (1863–1952) complained, "The cry was for vacant freedom and indeterminate progress: *Vorwarts! Avanti! Onward! Full Speed Ahead!*, without asking whether directly before you was a bottomless pit." Historians are now chastened in their claims about progress. They would no longer side with the German philosopher Georg W. F. Hegel, who proclaimed in 1832, "The history of the world is none other than the progress of the consciousness of freedom." They worry about the nationalistic claims inherent, for example, in the English historian Thomas Babington Macaulay's insistence that "the history of England is emphatically the history of progress" (1843). As with many other historical questions, the final word is not yet in: Is there a direction in human history that can correctly be called progress? Or is history, as many in ancient times thought, a set of repeating cycles?

Voltaire, *Letters Concerning the English Nation* (1733)

In the 1720s, Voltaire (1694–1778) visited both the Dutch Republic and England. He learned English and came to admire English political institutions and customs, using comparison with them to criticize religious intolerance and Catholic censorship in France. In this selection from a letter on Locke, Voltaire develops the argument that religion should be considered a matter of faith and conscience and be separated from arguments concerning philosophy. He also shows his disdain for the common people.

We must not be apprehensive that any philosophical opinion will ever prejudice the religion of a country. Though our demonstrations clash directly with our mysteries, that's nothing to the purpose, for the latter are not less revered upon that account by our Christian philosophers, who know very well that objects of reason and those of faith are of a very different nature. Philosophers will never form a religious sect, the reason of which is, their writings are not calculated for the vulgar, and they themselves are free from enthusiasm. If we divide mankind into twenty parts, it will be found that nineteen of these consist of persons employed in manual labour, who will never know that such a man as Mr. Locke existed. In the remaining twentieth part how few are readers? And among such as are so, twenty amuse themselves with romances to one who studies philosophy. The thinking part of mankind are confined to a very small number, and these will never disturb the peace and tranquillity of the world.

Neither Montaigne, Locke, Bayle, Spinoza, Hobbes, Lord Shaftesbury, Collins nor Toland lightened up the firebrand of discord in their countries; this has generally been the work of divines, who, being at first puffed up with the ambition of becoming chiefs of a sect, soon grew very desirous of being at the head of a party. But what do I say? All the works of the modern philosophers put together will never make so much noise as even the dispute which arose among the Franciscans [a Catholic religious order] merely about the fashion of their sleeves and of their cowls.

Source: Peter Gay, ed., *The Enlightenment: A Comprehensive Anthology* (New York: Simon & Schuster, 1973), 166.

often published in the Dutch Republic, Britain, or Switzerland and smuggled back across the border to a public whose appetite was only whetted by censorship.

The Young Voltaire.   The most influential writer of the early Enlightenment was a Frenchman born into the upper middle class, François-Marie Arouet, known by his pen name, **Voltaire** (1694–1778). Voltaire took inspiration from Bayle, noting: "He gives facts with such odious fidelity, he exposes the arguments for and against with such dastardly impartiality, he is so intolerably intelligible, that he leads people of only ordinary common sense to judge and even to doubt." In his early years, Voltaire suffered arrest, imprisonment, and exile, but he eventually achieved wealth and acclaim. His tangles with church and state began in the early 1730s, when he published his *Letters Concerning the English Nation* (the English version appeared in 1733), in which he devoted several

chapters to Newton and Locke and used the virtues of the British as a way to attack Catholic bigotry and government rigidity in France (see Document, "Letters Concerning the English Nation," on this page). Impressed by British toleration of religious dissent (at least among Protestants), Voltaire spent two years in exile in Britain when the French state responded to his book with yet another order for his arrest.

Voltaire also popularized Newton's scientific discoveries in his *Elements of the Philosophy of Newton* (1738). The French state and many European theologians considered Newtonianism threatening because it glorified the human mind and seemed to reduce God to an abstract, external, rationalistic force. So sensational was the success of Voltaire's book on Newton that a hostile Jesuit reported, "The great Newton, was, it is said, buried in the abyss, in the shop of the first publisher who dared to print him. . . . M. de Voltaire finally appeared, and at once Newton is understood or is in the process of being understood; all Paris resounds with Newton, all Paris stammers Newton, all Paris studies and learns Newton." The

Voltaire: The pen name of François-Marie Arouet (1694–1778), who was the most influential writer of the early Enlightenment.

success was international, too. Before long, Voltaire was elected a fellow of the Royal Society in London and in Edinburgh, as well as to twenty other scientific academies. Voltaire's fame continued to grow, reaching truly astounding proportions in the 1750s and 1760s (see Chapter 18).

Travel Literature and the Challenge to Custom and Tradition

Just as scientific method could be used to question religious and even state authority, a more general skepticism also emerged from the expanding knowledge about the world outside of Europe. During the seventeenth and eighteenth centuries, the number of travel accounts dramatically increased as travel writers used the contrast between their home societies and other cultures to criticize the customs of European society.

Visitors to the new colonies sought something resembling "the state of nature," that is, ways of life that preceded sophisticated social and political organization—although they often misinterpreted different forms of society and politics as having no organization at all. Travelers to the Americas found "noble savages" (native peoples) who appeared to live in conditions of great freedom and equality; they were "naturally good" and "happy" without taxes, lawsuits, or much organized government. In China, in contrast, travelers found a people who enjoyed prosperity and an ancient civilization. Christian missionaries made little headway in China, and visitors had to admit that China's religious systems had flourished for four or five thousand years with no input from Europe or from Christianity. The basic lesson of travel literature in the 1700s, then, was that customs varied: justice, freedom, property, good government, religion, and morality all were relative to the place. One critic complained that travel encouraged free thinking and the destruction of religion: "Some complete their demoralization by extensive travel, and lose whatever shreds of religion remained to them. Every day they see a new religion, new customs, new rites."

Travel literature turned explicitly political in Montesquieu's *Persian Letters* (1721). Charles-Louis de Secondat, baron of Montesquieu (1689–1755), the son of an eminent judicial family, was a high-ranking judge in a French court. He published *Persian Letters* anonymously in the Dutch Republic, and the book went into ten printings in just one year—a best seller for the times. Montesquieu tells the story of two Persians, Rica and Usbek, who leave their country "for love of knowledge" and travel to Europe. They visit France in the last years of Louis XIV's reign, writing of the king: "He has a minister who is only eighteen years old, and a mistress of eighty. . . . Although he avoids the bustle of towns, and is rarely seen in company, his one concern, from morning till night, is to get himself talked about." Other passages ridicule the pope. Beneath the satire, however, was a serious investigation into the foundation of good government and morality. Montesquieu chose Persians for his travelers because they came from what was widely considered the most despotic of all governments, in which rulers had life-and-death powers over their subjects. In the book, the Persians constantly compare France to Persia, suggesting that the French monarchy might verge on despotism.

The paradox of a judge publishing an anonymous work attacking the regime that employed him demonstrates the complications of the intellectual scene in this period. Montesquieu's anonymity did not last long, and soon Parisian society lionized him. In the late 1720s, he sold his judgeship and traveled extensively in Europe, staying eighteen months in Britain. In 1748, he published a widely influential work on comparative government, *The Spirit of Laws*. The Vatican soon listed both *Persian Letters* and *The Spirit of Laws* on its Index of forbidden books.

Raising the Woman Question

Many of the letters exchanged in *Persian Letters* focused on women, marriage, and the family because Montesquieu considered the position of women a sure indicator of the nature of government and morality. Although Montesquieu was not a feminist, his depiction of Roxana, the favorite wife in Usbek's harem, struck a chord with many women. Roxana revolts against the authority of Usbek's eunuchs and writes a final letter to her husband announcing her impending suicide: "I may have lived in servitude, but I have always been free, I have amended your laws according to the laws of nature, and my mind has always remained independent." Women writers used the same language of tyranny and freedom to argue for concrete changes in their status. Feminist ideas were not entirely new, but they were presented systematically for the first time during the Enlightenment and represented a fundamental challenge to the ways of traditional societies.

The most systematic of these women writers was the English author Mary Astell (1666–1731), the daughter of a businessman and herself a supporter of the Tory party and the Anglican religious establishment. In 1694, she published *A Serious Proposal to the Ladies*, in which she advocated founding a private women's college to remedy women's lack of education. Addressing women, she asked, "How can you be content to be in the World like Tulips in a Garden, to make a fine *shew* [show] and be good for nothing?" Astell argued for intellectual training based on Descartes's principles, in which reason, debate, and careful consideration of the issues took priority over custom or tradition. Her book was an immediate success: five printings appeared by 1701. In later works such as *Reflections upon Marriage* (1706), Astell criticized the relationship between the sexes within marriage: "If absolute sovereignty be not necessary in a state, how comes it to be so in a family? . . . *If all men are born free*, how is it that all women are born slaves?" Her critics accused her of promoting subversive ideas and of contradicting the Bible.

Astell's work inspired other women to write in a similar vein. The anonymous *Essay in Defence of the Female Sex* (1696) attacked "the Usurpation of Men; and the Tyranny of Custom," which prevented women from getting an education. In the introduction to the work of one of the best-known female poets, Elizabeth Singer Rowe, a friend of the author complained of the "notorious Violations on the Liberties of Freeborn English Women" that came from "a plain and an open design to render us meer [mere] Slaves, perfect Turkish Wives."

Most male writers unequivocally stuck to the traditional view of women, which held that women were less capable of reasoning than men and therefore did not need systematic education. Such opinions often rested on biological suppositions. The long-dominant Aristotelian view of reproduction held that only the male seed carried spirit and individuality. At the beginning of the eighteenth century, however, scientists began to undermine this belief. Physicians and surgeons began to champion the doctrine of *ovism* — that the female egg was essential in making new humans. During the decades that followed, male Enlightenment writers would continue to debate women's nature and appropriate social roles.

> **REVIEW:** What were the major issues in the early decades of the Enlightenment?

Conclusion

Europeans crossed a major threshold in the first half of the eighteenth century. They moved silently but nonetheless momentously from an economy governed by scarcity and the threat of famine to one of ever-increasing growth and the prospect of continuing improvement. Expansion of colonies overseas and economic development at home created greater wealth, longer life spans, and higher expectations for the future. In these better times for many, a spirit of optimism prevailed. People could now spend money on newspapers, novels, and travel literature as well as on coffee, tea, and cotton cloth. The growing literate public avidly followed the latest trends in religious debates, art, and music. Not everyone shared equally in the benefits, however: slaves toiled in misery for their masters in the Americas, eastern European serfs found themselves ever more closely bound to their noble lords, and rural folk almost everywhere tasted few fruits of consumer society.

Politics changed too as population and production increased and cities grew. Experts urged government intervention to improve public health, and states found it in their interest to settle many international disputes by diplomacy, which itself became more regular and routine. The consolidation of the European state system allowed a tide of criticism and new thinking about society to swell in Great Britain and France and begin to spill throughout Europe. Ultimately, the combination of the Atlantic system and the Enlightenment would give rise to a series of Atlantic revolutions.

FOR FURTHER EXPLORATION

■ **For suggested references, including Web sites, for topics in this chapter,** see page SR-1 at the end of the book.

■ **For additional primary-source material from this period,** see Chapter 17 in *Sources of THE MAKING OF THE WEST,* Third Edition.

■ **For Web sites and documents related to topics in this chapter,** see *Make History* at bedfordstmartins.com/hunt.

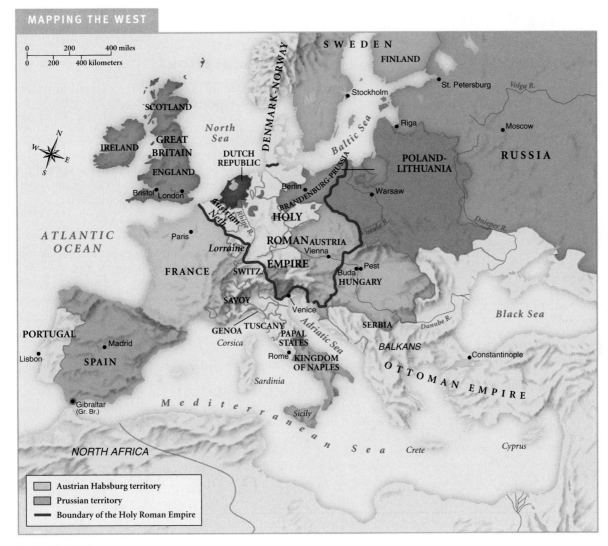

Europe in 1740

By 1740, Europe had achieved a kind of diplomatic equilibrium in which no one power predominated. But the relative balance should not deflect attention from important underlying changes: Spain, the Dutch Republic, Poland-Lithuania, and Sweden had all declined in power and influence while Great Britain, Russia, Prussia, and Austria had solidified their positions, each in a different way. France's ambitions had been thwarted, but its combination of a big army and rich overseas possessions made it a major player for a long time to come.

CHAPTER REVIEW

KEY TERMS AND PEOPLE

Atlantic system (520)
plantation (521)
mestizo (527)
buccaneers (527)
consumer revolution (528)
agricultural revolution (529)
rococo (534)

Pietism (536)
Peace of Utrecht (538)
Robert Walpole (539)
Peter the Great (540)
Westernization (540)
Enlightenment (545)
Voltaire (548)

MAKING CONNECTIONS

1. How did the rise of slavery and the plantation system change European politics and society?

2. Why was the Enlightenment born just at the moment that the Atlantic system took shape?

3. What were the major differences between the wars of the first half of the eighteenth century and those of the seventeenth century? (Refer to Chapters 15 and 16.)

> **For practice quizzes, a customized study plan, and other study tools,** see the Online Study Guide at bedfordstmartins.com/hunt.

REVIEW QUESTIONS

1. How was consumerism related to slavery in the early eighteenth century?

2. How were new social trends reflected in cultural life in the late 1600s and early 1700s?

3. What events and developments led to greater stability and less warfare in the European state system?

4. What were the major issues in the early decades of the Enlightenment?

IMPORTANT EVENTS

1690s	Beginning of rapid development of plantations in Caribbean
1694	Bank of England established; Mary Astell's *A Serious Proposal to the Ladies* argues for the founding of a private women's college
1697	Pierre Bayle publishes *Historical and Critical Dictionary*, detailing errors of religious writers
1699	Turks forced to recognize Habsburg rule over Hungary and Transylvania
1703	Peter the Great begins construction of St. Petersburg, founds first Russian newspaper
1713–1714	Peace of Utrecht
1714	Elector of Hanover becomes King George I of England
1715	Death of Louis XIV
1719	Daniel Defoe publishes *Robinson Crusoe*
1720	Last outbreak of bubonic plague in western Europe
1721	Treaty of Nystad; Montesquieu publishes *Persian Letters* anonymously in the Dutch Republic
1733	War of the Polish Succession; Voltaire's *Letters Concerning the English Nation* attacks French intolerance and narrow-mindedness
1741	George Frideric Handel composes *Messiah*

Appendix
USEFUL FACTS AND FIGURES

PROMINENT ROMAN EMPERORS

Julio-Claudians

27 B.C.E.–14 C.E.	Augustus
14–37	Tiberius
37–41	Gaius (Caligula)
41–54	Claudius
54–68	Nero

Flavian Dynasty

69–79	Vespasian
79–81	Titus
81–96	Domitian

Golden Age Emperors

96–98	Nerva
98–117	Trajan
117–138	Hadrian
138–161	Antoninus Pius
161–180	Marcus Aurelius

Severan Emperors

193–211	Septimius Severus
211–217	Antoninus (Caracalla)
217–218	Macrinus
222–235	Severus Alexander

Period of Instability

235–238	Maximinus Thrax
238–244	Gordian III
244–249	Philip the Arab
249–251	Decius
251–253	Trebonianus Gallus
253–260	Valerian
270–275	Aurelian
275–276	Tacitus
276–282	Probus
283–285	Carinus

Dominate

284–305	Diocletian
306	Constantius
306–337	Constantine I
337–340	Constantine II
337–350	Constans I
337–361	Constantius II
361–363	Julian
363–364	Jovian
364–375	Valentinian I
364–378	Valens
367–383	Gratian
375–392	Valentinian II
378–395	Theodosius I (the Great)

The Western Empire

395–423	Honorius
406–407	Marcus
407–411	Constantine III
409–411	Maximus
411–413	Jovinus
412–413	Sebastianus
423–425	Johannes
425–455	Valentinian III
455–456	Avitus
457–461	Majorian
461–465	Libius Severus
467–472	Anthemius
473–474	Glycerius
474–475	Julius Nepos
475–476	Romulus Augustulus

PROMINENT BYZANTINE EMPERORS

Dynasty of Theodosius

395–408	Arcadius
408–450	Theodosius II
450–457	Marcian

Dynasty of Leo

457–474	Leo I
474	Leo II
474–491	Zeno
475–476	Basiliscus
484–488	Leontius
491–518	Anastasius

Dynasty of Justinian

518–527	Justin
527–565	Justinian I
565–578	Justin II
578–582	Tiberius II
578–582	Tiberius II (I) Constantine
582–602	Maurice
602–610	Phocas

Dynasty of Heraclius

610–641	Heraclius
641	Heraclonas
641	Constantine III
641–668	Constans II
646–647	Gregory
649–653	Olympius
669	Mezezius
668–685	Constantine IV
685–695	Justinian II (banished)
695–698	Leontius
698–705	Tiberius III (II)
705–711	Justinian II (restored)
711–713	Bardanes
713–716	Anastasius II
716–717	Theodosius III

Isaurian Dynasty

717–741	Leo III
741–775	Constantine V Copronymus
775–780	Leo IV

780–797	Constantine VI
797–802	Irene
802–811	Nicephorus I
811	Strauracius
811–813	Michael I
813–820	Leo V

Phrygian Dynasty

820–829	Michael II
821–823	Thomas
829–842	Theophilus
842–867	Michael III

Macedonian Dynasty

867–886	Basil I
869–879	Constantine
887–912	Leo VI
912–913	Alexander
913–959	Constantine VII Porphrogenitos
920–944	Romanus I Lecapenus
921–931	Christopher
924–945	Stephen
959–963	Romanus II
963–969	Nicephorus II Phocas
976–1025	Basil II
1025–1028	Constantine VIII (IX) alone
1028–1034	Romanus III Argyrus
1034–1041	Michael IV the Paphlagonian
1041–1042	Michael V Calaphates
1042	Zoe and Theodora
1042–1055	Constantine IX Monomachus
1055–1056	Theodora alone
1056–1057	Michael VI Stratioticus

Prelude to the Comnenian Dynasty

1057–1059	Isaac I Comnenos
1059–1067	Constantine X (IX) Ducas
1068–1071	Romanus IV Diogenes

1071–1078	Michael VII Ducas
1078–1081	Nicephorus III Botaniates
1080–1081	Nicephorus Melissenus

Comnenian Dynasty

1081–1118	Alexius I
1118–1143	John II
1143–1180	Manuel I
1180–1183	Alexius II
1183–1185	Andronieus I
1183–1191	Isaac, Emperor of Cyprus

Dynasty of the Angeli

1185–1195	Isaac II
1195–1203	Alexius III
1203–1204	Isaac II (restored) with Alexius IV
1204	Alexius V Ducas Murtzuphlus

Lascarid Dynasty in Nicaea

1204–1222	Theodore I Lascaris
1222–1254	John III Ducas Vatatzes
1254–1258	Theodore II Lascaris
1258–1261	John IV Lascaris

Dynasty of the Paleologi

1259–1289	Michael VIII Paleologus
1282–1328	Andronicus II
1328–1341	Andronicus III
1341–1391	John V
1347–1354	John VI Cantancuzenus
1376–1379	Andronicus IV
1379–1391	John V (restored)
1390	John VII
1391–1425	Manuel II
1425–1448	John VIII
1449–1453	Constantine XI (XIII) Dragases

PROMINENT POPES

314–335	Sylvester	1227–1241	Gregory IX	1831–1846	Gregory XVI
440–461	Leo I	1243–1254	Innocent IV	1846–1878	Pius IX
590–604	Gregory I (the Great)	1294–1303	Boniface VIII	1878–1903	Leo XIII
687–701	Sergius I	1316–1334	John XXII	1903–1914	Pius X
741–752	Zachary	1447–1455	Nicholas V	1914–1922	Benedict XV
858–867	Nicholas I	1458–1464	Pius II	1922–1939	Pius XI
1049–1054	Leo IX	1492–1503	Alexander VI	1939–1958	Pius XII
1059–1061	Nicholas II	1503–1513	Julius II	1958–1963	John XXIII
1073–1085	Gregory VII	1513–1521	Leo X	1963–1978	Paul VI
1088–1099	Urban II	1534–1549	Paul III	1978	John Paul I
1099–1118	Paschal II	1555–1559	Paul IV	1978–2005	John Paul II
1159–1181	Alexander III	1585–1590	Sixtus V	2005–	Benedict XVI
1198–1216	Innocent III	1623–1644	Urban VIII		

THE CAROLINGIAN DYNASTY

687–714	Pepin of Heristal, Mayor of the Palace
715–741	Charles Martel, Mayor of the Palace
741–751	Pepin III, Mayor of the Palace
751–768	Pepin III, King
768–814	Charlemagne, King
800–814	Charlemagne, Emperor
814–840	Louis the Pious

West Francia

840–877	Charles the Bald, King
875–877	Charles the Bald, Emperor

877–879	Louis II, King
879–882	Louis III, King
879–884	Carloman, King

Middle Kingdoms

840–855	Lothair, Emperor
855–875	Louis (Italy), Emperor
855–863	Charles (Provence), King
855–869	Lothair II (Lorraine), King

East Francia

840–876	Ludwig, King
876–880	Carloman, King
876–882	Ludwig, King
876–887	Charles the Fat, Emperor

GERMAN KINGS CROWNED EMPEROR

Saxon Dynasty

962–973	Otto I
973–983	Otto II
983–1002	Otto III
1002–1024	Henry II

Franconian Dynasty

1024–1039	Conrad II
1039–1056	Henry III
1056–1106	Henry IV
1106–1125	Henry V
1125–1137	Lothair II (Saxony)

Hohenstaufen Dynasty

1138–1152	Conrad III
1152–1190	Frederick I (Barbarossa)
1190–1197	Henry VI
1198–1208	Philip of Swabia

1198–1215	Otto IV (Welf)
1220–1250	Frederick II
1250–1254	Conrad IV

Interregnum, 1254–1273:
Emperors from Various Dynasties

1273–1291	Rudolf I (Habsburg)
1292–1298	Adolf (Nassau)
1298–1308	Albert I (Habsburg)
1308–1313	Henry VII (Luxemburg)
1314–1347	Ludwig IV (Wittelsbach)
1347–1378	Charles IV (Luxemburg)
1378–1400	Wenceslas (Luxemburg)
1400–1410	Rupert (Wittelsbach)
1410–1437	Sigismund (Luxemburg)

Habsburg Dynasty

1438–1439	Albert II
1440–1493	Frederick III

1493–1519	Maximilian I
1519–1556	Charles V
1556–1564	Ferdinand I
1564–1576	Maximilian II
1576–1612	Rudolf II
1612–1619	Matthias
1619–1637	Ferdinand II
1637–1657	Ferdinand III
1658–1705	Leopold I
1705–1711	Joseph I
1711–1740	Charles VI
1742–1745	Charles VII (not a Habsburg)
1745–1765	Francis I
1765–1790	Joseph II
1790–1792	Leopold II
1792–1806	Francis II

RULERS OF FRANCE

Capetian Dynasty

987–996	Hugh Capet
996–1031	Robert II
1031–1060	Henry I
1060–1108	Philip I
1108–1137	Louis VI
1137–1180	Louis VII
1180–1223	Philip II (Augustus)
1223–1226	Louis VIII
1226–1270	Louis IX (St. Louis)
1270–1285	Philip III
1285–1314	Philip IV
1314–1316	Louis X
1316–1322	Philip V
1322–1328	Charles IV

Valois Dynasty

1328–1350	Philip VI
1350–1364	John
1364–1380	Charles V
1380–1422	Charles VI
1422–1461	Charles VII
1461–1483	Louis XI
1483–1498	Charles VIII
1498–1515	Louis XII
1515–1547	Francis I
1547–1559	Henry II
1559–1560	Francis II
1560–1574	Charles IX
1574–1589	Henry III

Bourbon Dynasty

1589–1610	Henry IV
1610–1643	Louis XIII
1643–1715	Louis XIV
1715–1774	Louis XV
1774–1792	Louis XVI

After 1792

1792–1799	First Republic
1799–1804	Napoleon Bonaparte, First Consul
1804–1814	Napoleon I, Emperor
1814–1824	Louis XVIII (Bourbon Dynasty)
1824–1830	Charles X (Bourbon Dynasty)
1830–1848	Louis Philippe
1848–1852	Second Republic
1852–1870	Napoleon III, Emperor
1870–1940	Third Republic
1940–1944	Vichy government, Pétain regime
1944–1946	Provisional government
1946–1958	Fourth Republic
1958–	Fifth Republic

MONARCHS OF ENGLAND AND GREAT BRITAIN

Anglo-Saxon Monarchs

829–839	Egbert
839–858	Ethelwulf
858–860	Ethelbald
860–866	Ethelbert
866–871	Ethelred I
871–899	Alfred the Great
899–924	Edward the Elder
924–939	Ethelstan
939–946	Edmund I
946–955	Edred
955–959	Edwy
959–975	Edgar
975–978	Edward the Martyr
978–1016	Ethelred the Unready
1016–1035	Canute (Danish nationality)
1035–1040	Harold I
1040–1042	Hardicanute
1042–1066	Edward the Confessor
1066	Harold II

Norman Monarchs

1066–1087	William I (the Conqueror)
1087–1100	William II
1100–1135	Henry I

House of Blois

1135–1154	Stephen

House of Plantagenet

1154–1189	Henry II
1189–1199	Richard I
1199–1216	John
1216–1272	Henry III
1272–1307	Edward I
1307–1327	Edward II
1327–1377	Edward III
1377–1399	Richard II

House of Lancaster

1399–1413	Henry IV
1413–1422	Henry V
1422–1461	Henry VI

House of York

1461–1483	Edward IV
1483	Edward V
1483–1485	Richard III

House of Tudor

1485–1509	Henry VII
1509–1547	Henry VIII
1547–1553	Edward VI
1553–1558	Mary
1558–1603	Elizabeth I

House of Stuart

1603–1625	James I
1625–1649	Charles I

Commonwealth and Protectorate (1649–1660)

1653–1658	Oliver Cromwell
1658–1659	Richard Cromwell

House of Stuart (Restored)

1660–1685	Charles II
1685–1688	James II
1689–1694	William III and Mary II
1694–1702	William III (alone)
1702–1714	Anne

House of Hanover

1714–1727	George I
1727–1760	George II
1760–1820	George III
1820–1830	George IV
1830–1837	William IV
1837–1901	Victoria

House of Saxe-Coburg-Gotha

1901–1910	Edward VII

House of Windsor

1910–1936	George V
1936	Edward VIII
1936–1952	George VI
1952–	Elizabeth II

PRIME MINISTERS OF GREAT BRITAIN

Term	Prime Minister	Government
1721–1742	Sir Robert Walpole	Whig
1742–1743	Spencer Compton, Earl of Wilmington	Whig
1743–1754	Henry Pelham	Whig
1754–1756	Thomas Pelham-Holles, Duke of Newcastle	Whig
1756–1757	William Cavendish, Duke of Devonshire	Whig
1757–1761	William Pitt (the Elder), Earl of Chatham	Whig
1761–1762	Thomas Pelham-Holles, Duke of Newcastle	Whig
1762–1763	John Stuart, Earl of Bute	Tory
1763–1765	George Grenville	Whig
1765–1766	Charles Watson-Wentworth, Marquess of Rockingham	Whig
1766–1768	William Pitt, Earl of Chatham (the Elder)	Whig
1768–1770	Augustus Henry Fitzroy, Duke of Grafton	Whig
1770–1782	Frederick North (Lord North)	Tory
1782	Charles Watson-Wentworth, Marquess of Rockingham	Whig
1782–1783	William Petty FitzMaurice, Earl of Shelburn	Whig
1783	William Henry Cavendish Bentinck, Duke of Portland	Whig
1783–1801	William Pitt (the Younger)	Tory
1801–1804	Henry Addington	Tory
1804–1806	William Pitt (the Younger)	Tory
1806–1807	William Wyndham Grenville (Baron Grenville)	Whig
1807–1809	William Henry Cavendish Bentinck, Duke of Portland	Tory
1809–1812	Spencer Perceval	Tory
1812–1827	Robert Banks Jenkinson, Earl of Liverpool	Tory
1827	George Canning	Tory
1827–1828	Frederick John Robinson (Viscount Goderich)	Tory
1828–1830	Arthur Wellesley, Duke of Wellington	Tory
1830–1834	Charles Grey (Earl Grey)	Whig
1834	William Lamb, Viscount Melbourne	Whig
1834–1835	Sir Robert Peel	Tory
1835–1841	William Lamb, Viscount Melbourne	Whig
1841–1846	Sir Robert Peel	Tory
1846–1852	John Russell (Lord)	Whig
1852	Edward Geoffrey–Smith Stanley Derby, Earl of Derby	Whig
1852–1855	George Hamilton Gordon Aberdeen, Earl of Aberdeen	Peelite
1855–1858	Henry John Temple Palmerston, Viscount Palmerston	Tory
1858–1859	Edward Geoffrey–Smith Stanley Derby, Earl of Derby	Whig
1859–1865	Henry John Temple Palmerston, Viscount Palmerston	Tory
1865–1866	John Russell (Earl)	Liberal
1866–1868	Edward Geoffrey–Smith Stanley Derby, Earl of Derby	Tory
1868	Benjamin Disraeli, Earl of Beaconfield	Conservative
1868–1874	William Ewart Gladstone	Liberal
1874–1880	Benjamin Disraeli, Earl of Beaconfield	Conservative
1880–1885	William Ewart Gladstone	Liberal
1885–1886	Robert Arthur Talbot, Marquess of Salisbury	Conservative
1886	William Ewart Gladstone	Liberal
1886–1892	Robert Arthur Talbot, Marquess of Salisbury	Conservative
1892–1894	William Ewart Gladstone	Liberal
1894–1895	Archibald Philip–Primrose Rosebery, Earl of Rosebery	Liberal
1895–1902	Robert Arthur Talbot, Marquess of Salisbury	Conservative
1902–1905	Arthur James Balfour, Earl of Balfour	Conservative
1905–1908	Sir Henry Campbell-Bannerman	Liberal
1908–1915	Herbert Henry Asquith	Liberal
1915–1916	Herbert Henry Asquith	Coalition
1916–1922	David Lloyd George, Earl Lloyd-George of Dwyfor	Coalition
1922–1923	Andrew Bonar Law	Conservative
1923–1924	Stanley Baldwin, Earl Baldwin of Bewdley	Conservative
1924	James Ramsay MacDonald	Labour
1924–1929	Stanley Baldwin, Earl Baldwin of Bewdley	Conservative
1929–1931	James Ramsay MacDonald	Labour
1931–1935	James Ramsay MacDonald	Coalition
1935–1937	Stanley Baldwin, Earl Baldwin of Bewdley	Coalition
1937–1940	Neville Chamberlain	Coalition
1940–1945	Winston Churchill	Coalition
1945	Winston Churchill	Conservative
1945–1951	Clement Attlee, Earl Attlee	Labour
1951–1955	Sir Winston Churchill	Conservative
1955–1957	Sir Anthony Eden, Earl of Avon	Conservative
1957–1963	Harold Macmillan, Earl of Stockton	Conservative

(Continued)

PRIME MINISTERS OF GREAT BRITAIN (CONTINUED)

Term	Prime Minister	Government	Term	Prime Minister	Government
1963–1964	Sir Alec Frederick Douglas-Home, Lord Home of the Hirsel	Conservative	1976–1979	James Callaghan, Lord Callaghan of Cardiff	Labour
1964–1970	Harold Wilson, Lord Wilson of Rievaulx	Labour	1979–1990	Margaret Thatcher (Baroness)	Conservative
			1990–1997	John Major	Conservative
1970–1974	Edward Heath	Conservative	1997–2007	Tony Blair	Labour
1974–1976	Harold Wilson, Lord Wilson of Rievaulx	Labour	2007–	Gordon Brown	Labour

RULERS OF PRUSSIA AND GERMANY

1701–1713	*Frederick I
1713–1740	*Frederick William I
1740–1786	*Frederick II (the Great)
1786–1797	*Frederick William II
1797–1840	*Frederick William III
1840–1861	*Frederick William IV
1861–1888	*William I (German emperor after 1871)
1888	Frederick III
1888–1918	*William II
1918–1933	Weimar Republic
1933–1945	Third Reich (Nazi dictatorship under Adolf Hitler)
1945–1952	Allied occupation
1949–1990	Division of Federal Republic of Germany in west and German Democratic Republic in east
1990–	Federal Republic of Germany (reunited)

*King of Prussia

RULERS OF AUSTRIA AND AUSTRIA-HUNGARY

1493–1519	*Maximilian I (Archduke)
1519–1556	*Charles V
1556–1564	*Ferdinand I
1564–1576	*Maximilian II
1576–1612	*Rudolf II
1612–1619	*Matthias
1619–1637	*Ferdinand II
1637–1657	*Ferdinand III
1658–1705	*Leopold I
1705–1711	*Joseph I
1711–1740	*Charles VI
1740–1780	Maria Theresa
1780–1790	*Joseph II
1790–1792	*Leopold II
1792–1835	*Francis II (emperor of Austria as Francis I after 1804)
1835–1848	Ferdinand I
1848–1916	Francis Joseph (after 1867 emperor of Austria and king of Hungary)
1916–1918	Charles I (emperor of Austria and king of Hungary)
1918–1938	Republic of Austria (dictatorship after 1934)
1945–1956	Republic restored, under Allied occupation
1956–	Free Republic

*Also bore title of Holy Roman Emperor

LEADERS OF POST–WORLD WAR II GERMANY

West Germany (Federal Republic of Germany), 1949–1990

Years	Chancellor	Party
1949–1963	Konrad Adenauer	Christian Democratic Union (CDU)
1963–1966	Ludwig Erhard	Christian Democratic Union (CDU)
1966–1969	Kurt Georg Kiesinger	Christian Democratic Union (CDU)
1969–1974	Willy Brandt	Social Democratic Party (SPD)
1974–1982	Helmut Schmidt	Social Democratic Party (SPD)
1982–1990	Helmut Kohl	Christian Democratic Union (CDU)

LEADERS OF POST–WORLD WAR II GERMANY (CONTINUED)

East Germany (German Democratic Republic), 1949–1990

Years	Communist Party Leader
1946–1971	Walter Ulbricht
1971–1989	Erich Honecker
1989–1990	Egon Krenz

Federal Republic of Germany (reunited), 1990–

Years	Chancellor	Party
1990–1998	Helmut Kohl	Christian Democratic Union (CDU)
1998–2005	Gerhard Schroeder	Social Democratic Party (SPD)
2005–	Angela Merkel	Christian Democratic Union (CDU)

RULERS OF RUSSIA, THE USSR, AND THE RUSSIAN FEDERATION

c. 980–1015	Vladimir	1689–1725	Peter I (the Great)
1019–1054	Yaroslav the Wise	1725–1727	Catherine I
1176–1212	Vsevolod III	1727–1730	Peter II
1462–1505	Ivan III	1730–1740	Anna
1505–1553	Vasily III	1740–1741	Ivan VI
1553–1584	Ivan IV	1741–1762	Elizabeth
1584–1598	Theodore I	1762	Peter III
1598–1605	Boris Godunov	1762–1796	Catherine II (the Great)
1605	Theodore II	1796–1801	Paul
1606–1610	Vasily IV	1801–1825	Alexander I
1613–1645	Michael	1825–1855	Nicholas I
1645–1676	Alexius	1855–1881	Alexander II
1676–1682	Theodore III	1881–1894	Alexander III
1682–1689	Ivan V and Peter I	1894–1917	Nicholas II

Union of Soviet Socialist Republics (USSR)*

1917–1924	Vladimir Ilyich Lenin
1924–1953	Joseph Stalin
1953–1964	Nikita Khrushchev
1964–1982	Leonid Brezhnev
1982–1984	Yuri Andropov
1984–1985	Konstantin Chernenko
1985–1991	Mikhail Gorbachev

Russian Federation

1991–1999	Boris Yeltsin
1999–	Vladimir Putin

*USSR established in 1922

RULERS OF SPAIN

1479–1504	Ferdinand and Isabella	1746–1759	Ferdinand VI	1873–1874	Republic
1504–1506	Ferdinand and Philip I	1759–1788	Charles III	1874–1885	Alfonso XII
1506–1516	Ferdinand and Charles I	1788–1808	Charles IV	1886–1931	Alfonso XIII
1516–1556	Charles I (Holy Roman Emperor Charles V)	1808	Ferdinand VII	1931–1939	Republic
		1808–1813	Joseph Bonaparte	1939–1975	Fascist dictatorship under Francisco Franco
1556–1598	Philip II	1814–1833	Ferdinand VII (restored)		
1598–1621	Philip III				
1621–1665	Philip IV	1833–1868	Isabella II	1975–	Juan Carlos I
1665–1700	Charles II	1868–1870	Republic		
1700–1746	Philip V	1870–1873	Amadeo		

RULERS OF ITALY

1861–1878	Victor Emmanuel II
1878–1900	Humbert I
1900–1946	Victor Emmanuel III
1922–1943	Fascist dictatorship under Benito Mussolini (maintained in northern Italy until 1945)
1946 (May 9–June 13)	Humbert II
1946–	Republic

SECRETARIES-GENERAL OF THE UNITED NATIONS

		Nationality
1946–1952	Trygve Lie	Norway
1953–1961	Dag Hammarskjöld	Sweden
1961–1971	U Thant	Myanmar
1972–1981	Kurt Waldheim	Austria
1982–1991	Javier Pérez de Cuéllar	Peru
1992–1996	Boutros Boutros-Ghali	Egypt
1997–2006	Kofi A. Annan	Ghana
2007–	Ban Kimoon	South Korea

UNITED STATES PRESIDENTIAL ADMINISTRATIONS

Term(s)	President	Political Party	Term(s)	President	Political Party
1789–1797	George Washington	No party designation	1889–1893	Benjamin Harrison	Republican
1797–1801	John Adams	Federalist	1893–1897	Grover Cleveland	Democratic
1801–1809	Thomas Jefferson	Democratic-Republican	1897–1901	William McKinley	Republican
1809–1817	James Madison	Democratic-Republican	1901–1909	Theodore Roosevelt	Republican
1817–1825	James Monroe	Democratic-Republican	1909–1913	William H. Taft	Republican
1825–1829	John Quincy Adams	Democratic-Republican	1913–1921	Woodrow Wilson	Democratic
1829–1837	Andrew Jackson	Democratic	1921–1923	Warren G. Harding	Republican
1837–1841	Martin Van Buren	Democratic	1923–1929	Calvin Coolidge	Republican
1841	William H. Harrison	Whig	1929–1933	Herbert C. Hoover	Republican
1841–1845	John Tyler	Whig	1933–1945	Franklin D. Roosevelt	Democratic
1845–1849	James K. Polk	Democratic	1945–1953	Harry S. Truman	Democratic
1849–1850	Zachary Taylor	Whig	1953–1961	Dwight D. Eisenhower	Republican
1850–1853	Millard Filmore	Whig	1961–1963	John F. Kennedy	Democratic
1853–1857	Franklin Pierce	Democratic	1963–1969	Lyndon B. Johnson	Democratic
1857–1861	James Buchanan	Democratic	1969–1974	Richard M. Nixon	Republican
1861–1865	Abraham Lincoln	Republican	1974–1977	Gerald R. Ford	Republican
1865–1869	Andrew Johnson	Republican	1977–1981	Jimmy Carter	Democratic
1869–1877	Ulysses S. Grant	Republican	1981–1989	Ronald W. Reagan	Republican
1877–1881	Rutherford B. Hayes	Republican	1989–1993	George H. W. Bush	Republican
1881	James A. Garfield	Republican	1993–2001	William J. Clinton	Democratic
1881–1885	Chester A. Arthur	Republican	2001–	George W. Bush	Republican
1885–1889	Grover Cleveland	Democratic			

MAJOR WARS OF THE MODERN ERA

1546–1555	German Wars of Religion	1796–1815	Napoleonic wars
1526–1571	Ottoman wars	1846–1848	Mexican-American War
1562–1598	French Wars of Religion	1853–1856	Crimean War
1566–1609, 1621–1648	Revolt of the Netherlands	1861–1865	United States Civil War
1618–1648	Thirty Years' War	1870–1871	Franco-Prussian War
1642–1648	English Civil War	1894–1895	Sino-Japanese War
1652–1678	Anglo-Dutch Wars	1898	Spanish-American War
1667–1697	Wars of Louis XIV	1904–1905	Russo-Japanese War
1683–1697	Ottoman wars	1914–1918	World War I
1689–1697	War of the League of Augsburg	1939–1945	World War II
1702–1714	War of Spanish Succession	1946–1975	Vietnam wars
1702–1721	Great Northern War	1950–1953	Korean War
1714–1718	Ottoman wars	1990–1991	Persian Gulf War
1740–1748	War of Austrian Succession	1991–1997	Civil War in the former Yugoslavia
1756–1763	Seven Years' War	2003–	Iraq War
1775–1781	American Revolution		

Glossary of Key Terms and People

This glossary contains definitions of terms and people that are central to your understanding of the material covered in this textbook. Each term or person in the glossary is in boldface in the text when it is first defined, then listed again in the corresponding Chapter Review section to signal its importance. We have also included the page number on which the full discussion of the term or person appears so that you can easily locate the complete explanation to strengthen your historical vocabulary.

For words or names not defined here, two additional resources may be useful: the index, which will direct you to many more topics discussed in the text, and a good dictionary.

Abbasids (268): The dynasty of caliphs that, in 750, took over from the Umayyads in all of the Islamic realm except for Spain (al-Andalus). From their new capital at Baghdad, they presided over a wealthy realm until the late ninth century.

absolutism (484): A system of government in which the ruler claims sole and uncontestable power.

agora (78): The central market square of a Greek city-state, a popular gathering place for conversation.

agricultural revolution (529): Increasingly aggressive attitudes toward investment in and management of land that increased production of food in the 1700s.

Alexander the Great (110): The fourth-century B.C.E. Macedonian king whose conquest of the Persian Empire led to the greatly increased cultural interactions of Greece and the Near East in the Hellenistic Age.

Alexius I (Alexius Comnenus) (312): The Byzantine emperor (r. 1081–1118) whose leadership marked a new triumph of the *dynatoi*. His request to Pope Urban II for troops to fight the Turks turned into the First Crusade.

Alfred the Great (287): King of Wessex (r. 871–899) and the first king to rule over most of England. He organized a successful defense against Viking invaders, had key Latin works translated into the vernacular, and wrote a law code for the whole of England.

Anabaptists (436): Sixteenth-century Protestants who believed that only adults could truly have faith and accept baptism.

apostolic succession (184): The principle by which Christian bishops traced their authority back to the apostles of Jesus.

aretê (44): The Greek value of competitive individual excellence.

Arianism (210): The Christian doctrine named after Arius, who argued that Jesus was "begotten" by God and did not have an identical nature with God the Father.

Aristotle (108): Greek philosopher famous for his scientific investigations, development of logical argument, and practical ethics.

asceticism (212): The practice of self-denial, especially through spiritual discipline; a doctrine for Christians emphasized by Augustine.

Atlantic system (520): The network of trade established in the 1700s that bound together western Europe, Africa, and the Americas. Europeans sold slaves from western Africa and bought commodities that were produced by the new colonial plantations in North and South America and the Caribbean.

Augustine (208): Bishop in North Africa whose writings defining religious orthodoxy made him the most influential theologian in Western civilization.

Augustus (165): The honorary name meaning "divinely favored" that the Roman Senate bestowed on Octavian; it became shorthand for "Roman imperial ruler."

Avignon papacy (379): The period (1309–1378) during which the popes ruled from Avignon rather than from Rome.

baroque (472): An artistic style of the seventeenth century that featured curves, exaggerated lighting, intense emotions, release from restraint, and even a kind of artistic sensationalism.

Basil II (267): The Byzantine emperor (r. 976–1025) who presided over the end of the Bulgar threat (earning the name Bulgar-Slayer) and the conversion of Kievan Russia to Christianity.

battle of Hastings (320): The battle of 1066 that replaced the Anglo-Saxon king with a Norman one and thus tied England to the rest of Europe as never before.

Black Death (388): The term historians give to the plague that swept through Europe in 1346–1353.

Boniface VIII (377): The pope (r. 1294–1303) who unsuccessfully asserted the special place of the pope in the church and the spiritual subordination of the king.

buccaneers (527): Pirates of the Caribbean who governed themselves and preyed on international shipping.

bureaucracy (489): A network of state officials carrying out orders according to a regular and routine line of authority.

Calvin, John (432): French-born Christian humanist (1509–1564) and founder of Calvinism, one of the major branches of the Protestant Reformation; he led the reform movement in Geneva, Switzerland, from 1541 to 1564.

Capetian dynasty (288): A long-lasting dynasty of French kings, taking their name from Hugh Capet (r. 987–996).

Carolingian (273): The Frankish dynasty that ruled a western European empire from 751 to the late 800s; its greatest vigor was in the time of Charlemagne (r. 768–814) and Louis the Pious (r. 814–840).

castellan (285): The holder of a castle. In the tenth and eleventh centuries, castellans became important local lords, taking over the rights of the ban (to call up men to military service, to collect taxes, or to administer justice).

Catherine de Médicis (453): Italian-born mother of French king Charles X; she served as regent and tried but failed to prevent religious warfare between Calvinists and Catholics.

chansons de geste (348): Epic poems of the twelfth century about knightly and heroic deeds.

Charlemagne (273): The Carolingian king (r. 768–814) whose conquests greatly expanded the Frankish kingdom. He was crowned emperor on December 25, 800.

Charles V (430): Holy Roman Emperor (r. 1519–1556) and the most powerful ruler in sixteenth-century Europe; he reigned over the Low Countries, Spain, Spain's Italian and New World dominions, and the Austrian Habsburg lands.

Christ (181): Greek for "anointed one," in Hebrew *Mashiach* or in English *Messiah*; in apocalyptic thought, God's agent sent to conquer the forces of evil.

Christian humanism (427): A general intellectual trend in the sixteenth century that coupled love of classical learning, as in Renaissance humanism, with an emphasis on Christian piety.

Cicero (150): Rome's most famous orator and author of the doctrine of *humanitas*.

city-state (7): An urban center exercising political and economic control over the surrounding countryside.

civilization (4): A way of life that includes political states based on cities with dense populations, large buildings constructed for communal activities, diverse economies, a sense of local identity, and some knowledge of writing.

classicism (510): A style of painting and architecture that reflected the ideals of the art of antiquity; in classicism, geometric shapes, order, and harmony of lines take precedence over the sensuous, exuberant, and emotional forms of the baroque.

coloni (200): Literally, "cultivators"; tenant farmers in the Roman Empire who became bound by law to the land they worked and whose children were legally required to continue to farm the same land.

Colosseum (175): Rome's fifty-thousand-seat amphitheater built by the Flavian dynasty for gladiatorial combats and other spectacles.

Columbus, Christopher (421): An Italian sailor (1451–1506) who opened up the New World by sailing west across the Atlantic in search of a route to Asia.

common law (338): Begun by Henry II (r. 1154–1189), the English royal law carried out by the king's justices in eyre (traveling justices). It applied to the entire kingdom and thus was "common" to all.

commune (301): In a medieval town, a sworn association of citizens who formed a legal corporate body. The commune appointed or elected officials, made laws, kept the peace, and administered justice.

Concordat of Worms (307): The agreement between pope and emperor in 1122 that ended the Investiture Conflict.

constitutionalism (484): A system of government in which rulers share power with parliaments made up of elected representatives.

consumer revolution (528): The rapid increase in consumption of new staples produced in the Atlantic system as well as of other items of daily life that were previously unavailable or beyond the reach of ordinary people.

cortes (377): The earliest European representative institution, called initially to consent to royal wishes; first convoked in 1188 by the king of Castile-León.

Cortés, Hernán (425): A Spanish explorer (1485–1547) who captured the Aztec capital, Tenochtitlán (present-day Mexico City), in 1519.

Council of Trent (439): A general council of the Catholic church that met at Trent between 1545 and 1563 to set Catholic doctrine, reform church practices, and defend the church against the Protestant challenge.

cult (53): In ancient Greece, a set of official, publicly funded religious activities for a deity overseen by priests and priestesses.

cuneiform (10): The earliest form of writing, invented in Mesopotamia and done with wedge-shaped characters.

curials (200): The social elite in Roman empires' cities and towns, most of whom were obliged to serve on municipal senates and collect taxes for the imperial government, paying any shortfalls themselves.

Cyrus (37): Founder of the Persian Empire.

debasement of coinage (189): Putting less silver in a coin without changing its face value; practiced during the third-century C.E. crisis in Rome.

decurions (177): Municipal senate members in the Roman Empire responsible for collecting local taxes.

Delian League (74): The naval alliance led by Athens in the Golden Age that became the basis for the Athenian Empire.

demes (63): The villages and city neighborhoods that formed the constituent political units of Athenian democracy in the late Archaic Age.

demography (P-10): The study of the size, growth, density, distribution, and vital statistics of the human population.

Diaspora (42): The dispersal of the Jewish population from their homeland.

dominate (197): The blatantly authoritarian style of Roman rule from Diocletian (r. 284–305) onward; the word was derived from *dominus* ("master" or "lord") and contrasted with *principate*.

dualism (107): The philosophical idea that the human soul (or mind) and body are separate.

dynatoi (266): The "powerful men" who dominated the countryside of the Byzantine Empire in the tenth and eleventh centuries and to some degree challenged the authority of the emperor.

Edict of Milan (203): The proclamation of Roman co-emperors Constantine and Licinius decreeing free choice of religion in the empire.

Edict of Nantes (455): The decree issued by French king Henry IV in 1598 that granted the Huguenots a large measure of religious toleration.

Elizabeth I (458): English queen (r. 1558–1603) who oversaw the return of the Protestant Anglican church and, in 1588, the successful defense of the realm against the Spanish Armada.

empire (12): A political state in which one or more formerly independent territories or peoples are ruled by a single sovereign power.

Enlightenment (545): The eighteenth-century intellectual movement whose proponents believed that human beings could apply a critical, reasoning spirit to every problem.

Epicureanism (123): The philosophy founded by Epicurus of Athens to help people achieve a life of true pleasure, by which he meant "absence of disturbance."

epigrams (121): Short poems written by women in the Hellenistic Age; many were about other women and the writer's personal feelings.

equites (152): Wealthy Roman businessmen who chose not to pursue a government career.

Fatimids (270): Members of the tenth-century Shi'ite dynasty who derived their name from Fatimah, the daughter of Muhammad and wife of Ali; they dominated in parts of North Africa, Egypt, and even Syria.

fiefs (282): Grants of land, theoretically temporary, from lords to their noble dependents (*fideles* or, later, vassals) given in recognition of services, usually military, done or expected in the future; also called *benefices*.

First Crusade (313): The massive armed pilgrimage to Jerusalem that lasted from 1096 to 1099. It resulted in the massacre of Jews in the Rhineland (1095), the sack of Jerusalem (1099), and the setting up of the crusader states.

First Triumvirate (158): The coalition formed in 60 B.C.E. by Pompey, Crassus, and Caesar. (The word *triumvirate* means "group of three.")

Five Pillars of Islam (235): The five essential practices of Islam, namely, the *zakat* (alms); the fast of Ramadan; the *hajj* (pilgrimage to Mecca); the *salat* (formal worship); and the *shahadah* (profession of faith).

Fourth Crusade (351): The crusade that lasted from 1202 to 1204; its original goal was to recapture Jerusalem, but the crusaders ended up conquering Constantinople instead.

Fourth Lateran Council (360): The council that met in 1215 and covered the important topics of Christianity, among them the nature of the sacraments, the obligations of the laity, and policies toward heretics and Jews.

Franciscans (349): A religious order, founded by St. Francis (c. 1182–1226), dedicated to poverty and preaching, particularly in towns and cities.

Frederick I (Barbarossa) (342): King of Germany (r. 1152–1190) and emperor (crowned 1155) who tried to cement the power of the German king through conquest (for example, of northern Italy) and the bonds of vassalage.

Frederick II (373): The king of Sicily and Germany, as well as emperor (r. 1212–1250), who allowed the German princes a free hand as he battled the pope for control of Italy.

Frederick William of Hohenzollern (493): The Great Elector of Brandenburg-Prussia (r. 1640–1688) who brought his nation through the end of the Thirty Years' War and then succeeded in welding his scattered lands into an absolutist state.

Glorious Revolution (504): The events of 1688 when Tories and Whigs replaced England's monarch James II with his Protestant daughter, Mary, and her husband, Dutch ruler William of Orange; William and Mary agreed to a Bill of Rights that guaranteed rights to Parliament.

Golden Horde (380): The political institution set up by the Mongol Empire in Russia, lasting from the thirteenth to the fifteenth century.

Gothic architecture (333): The style of architecture that started in the Île-de-France in the twelfth century and eventually became the quintessential cathedral style of the Middle Ages, characterized by pointed arches, ribbed vaults, and stained-glass windows.

Great Famine (381): The shortage of food and accompanying social ills that besieged northern Europe between 1315 and 1322.

Great Persecution (202): The violent program initiated by Diocletian in 303 to make Christians convert to traditional religion or risk confiscation of their property and even death.

Great Schism (398): The papal dispute of 1378–1417 when the church had two or even three popes. The Great Schism was ended by the Council of Constance.

Gregorian reform (305): The papal movement for church reform associated with Gregory VII (r. 1073–1085); its ideal included ending the purchase of church offices, clerical marriage, and lay investiture.

Gregory of Tours (247): Bishop of Tours (in Gaul) from 573 to 594, the chief source for the history and culture of the Merovingian kingdoms.

Gregory the Great (256): The pope (r. 590–604) who sent missionaries to Anglo-Saxon England, wrote influential books, tried to reform the church, and had contact with the major ruling families of Europe and Byzantium.

guild (300): A trade organization within a city or town that controlled product quality and cost and outlined members' responsibilities. Guilds were also social or religious associations.

Hammurabi (14): King of Babylonia in the eighteenth century B.C.E., famous for his law code.

Hanseatic League (409): A league of northern European cities formed in the fourteenth century to protect their mutual interests in trade and defense.

heliocentrism (475): The view articulated by Polish clergyman Nicolaus Copernicus that the earth and planets revolve around the sun.

Hellenistic (115): An adjective meaning "Greek-like" that is today used as a chronological term for the period 323–30 B.C.E.

helot (59): A slave owned by the Spartan city-state; such slaves came from parts of Greece conquered by the Spartans.

Henry II (336): King of England (r. 1154–1189) who ended the period of civil war there and affirmed and expanded royal powers. He is associated with the creation of common law in England.

Henry IV (305): King of Germany (r. 1056–1106), crowned emperor in 1084. From 1073 until his death, he was embroiled in the Investiture Conflict with Pope Gregory VII.

Henry VIII (433): The English king (r. 1509–1547) who first opposed the Protestant Reformation and then broke with the Catholic church, naming himself head of the Anglican church in the Act of Supremacy of 1534.

Heraclius (240): The Byzantine emperor who reversed the fortunes of war with the Persians in the first quarter of the seventh century.

heresy (184): False doctrine; specifically, the beliefs banned for Christians by councils of bishops.

hetaira (83): A witty and attractive woman who charged fees to entertain at a symposium.

hierarchy (P-7): The system of ranking people in society according to their importance and dominance.

hieroglyphs (17): The ancient Egyptian pictographic script for writing official texts.

Hijra (235): The emigration of Muhammad from Mecca to Medina. Its date, 622, marks the year 1 of the Islamic calendar.

Homer (44): Greece's first and most famous author, who composed *The Iliad* and *The Odyssey*.

Homo sapiens sapiens (P-5): The scientific name (in Latin) of the type of early human being identical to people today; it means "wise, wise human being."

hoplite (53): A heavily armed Greek infantryman. Hoplites constituted the main strike force of a city-state's militia.

hubris (95): The Greek term for violent arrogance.

humanism (402): A literary and linguistic movement cultivated in particular in the fourteenth through the sixteenth centuries and founded on reviving classical Latin and Greek texts, styles, and values.

humanitas (150): The Roman orator Cicero's ideal of "humaneness," meaning generous and honest treatment of others based on natural law.

Hundred Years' War (392): The long war between England and France, 1337–1453; it produced numerous social upheavals yet left both states more powerful than before.

hunter-gatherers (P-5): Human beings who roam to hunt and gather food in the wild and do not live in permanent, settled communities.

iconoclasm (245): Literally, "icon breaking"; referring to the destruction of icons, or images of holy people. Byzantine emperors banned icons from 726 to 787; a modified ban was revived in 815 and lasted until 843.

Innocent III (360): The pope (r. 1198–1216) who called the Fourth Lateran Council; he was arguably the most powerful, respected, and prestigious of medieval popes.

Investiture Conflict (306): The confrontation between Gregory VII and Henry IV that began in 1073 over lay investiture and the nature of church leadership. It was resolved in 1122 by the Concordat of Worms.

Jacquerie (396): The 1358 uprising of French peasants against the nobles amid the Hundred Years' War; it was brutally put down.

Jesuits (439): Members of the Society of Jesus, a Catholic religious order founded by Ignatius of Loyola (1491–1556) and approved by the pope in 1540. Jesuits served as missionaries and educators all over the world.

Joan of Arc (392): A peasant girl (1412–1431) whose conviction that God had sent her to save France in fact helped France win the Hundred Years' War.

Julian the Apostate (205): The Roman emperor (r. 361–363), who rejected Christianity and tried to restore traditional religion as the state religion. *Apostate* means "renegade from the faith."

Julio-Claudians (173): The ruling family of the early principate from Augustus through Nero, descended from the aristocratic families of the Julians and the Claudians.

Justinian and Theodora (221): Sixth-century emperor and empress of the eastern Roman Empire, famous for waging costly wars to reunite the empire.

Koine (127): The "common" or "shared" form of the Greek language that became the international language in the Hellenistic period.

ladder of offices (142): The series of Roman elective government offices from quaestor to aedile to praetor to consul.

lay investiture (303): The installation of clerics into their offices by lay people, normally rulers or lords.

Lepanto (455): A site off the Greek coast where, in 1571, the allied Catholic forces of Spain's king Philip II, Venice, and the papacy defeated the Ottoman Turks in a great sea battle; the victory gave the Christian powers control of the Mediterranean.

Levellers (499): Disgruntled soldiers in Cromwell's New Model Army who wanted to "level" social differences and extend political participation to all male property owners.

Linear B (28): The Mycenaeans' pictographic script for writing Greek.

Lombards (240): The people who settled in Italy during the sixth century, following Justinian's reconquest. A king ruled the north of Italy, while dukes ruled the south. In between was the papacy, which felt threatened both by Lombard Arianism and by the Lombards' geographical proximity to Rome.

Louis IX (375): A French king (r. 1226–1270) revered as a military leader and a judge; he was declared a saint after his death.

Louis XIV (484): French king (r. 1643–1715) who personified the absolutist ruler; in theory he shared his power with no one, but in practice he had to gain the cooperation of nobles, local officials, and even the ordinary subjects who manned his armies and paid his taxes.

Luther, Martin (429): A German monk (1483–1546) who started the Protestant Reformation in 1517 by challenging the practices and doctrines of the Catholic church and advocating salvation through faith alone.

Maat (17): The Egyptian goddess ("What Is Right") embodying truth, justice, and cosmic order.

Magna Carta (340): The charter of baronial liberties that King John was forced to agree to in 1215. It implied that royal power was subject to custom and law.

martyr (183): Greek for "witness," the term for someone who dies for his or her religious beliefs.

materialism (123): A philosophical doctrine of the Hellenistic Age that denied metaphysics and claimed instead that only things consisting of matter truly exist.

Medici (412): The ruling family of Florence during much of the fifteenth to the seventeenth centuries.

Mediterranean polyculture (26): The cultivation of olives, grapes, and grains in a single, interrelated agricultural system.

Mehmed II (396): The sultan under whom the Ottoman Turks conquered Constantinople in 1453.

mercantilism (490): The doctrine that governments must intervene to increase national wealth by whatever means possible.

Merovingian dynasty (252): The royal dynasty that ruled Gaul from about 486 to 751.

mestizo (527): A person born to a Spanish father and a native American mother.

metaphysics (107): Philosophical ideas about the ultimate nature of reality beyond the reach of human senses.

metic (82): A foreigner granted permanent residence status in Athens in return for paying taxes and serving in the military.

monotheism (5): The belief in only one god, as in Judaism, Christianity, and Islam.

moral dualism (39): The belief that the world is the arena for an ongoing battle for control between divine forces of good and evil.

mos maiorum (134): Literally, "the way of the elders"; the set of Roman values handed down from the ancestors.

mystery cults (81): Religious worship that provided initiation into secret knowledge and divine protection, including hope for a better afterlife.

Neolithic Age (P-4): The "New Stone" Age, dating from about 10,000 to 4000 B.C.E.

Neolithic Revolution (P-8): The invention of agriculture, the domestication of animals, and the consequent changes in human society that occurred about 10,000–8000 B.C.E. in the Near East.

Neoplatonism (188): Plotinus's spiritual philosophy, based mainly on Plato's ideas, which was very influential for Christian intellectuals.

Nicene Creed (210): The doctrine agreed on by the council of bishops convened by Constantine at Nicaea in 325 to defend orthodoxy against Arianism; it declared that God the Father and Jesus were "of one substance" (*homoousion*).

optimates (153): The Roman political faction supporting the "best," or highest, social class; established during the late republic.

orders (142): The two groups of people in the Roman republic — patricians (aristocratic families) and plebeians (all other citizens).

orthodoxy (184): True doctrine; specifically, the beliefs defined for Christians by councils of bishops.

ostracism (76): An annual procedure in Athenian radical democracy by which a man could be voted out of the city-state for ten years; its purpose was to prevent tyranny.

Ottonian kings (289): The tenth- and early-eleventh-century kings of Germany; beginning with Otto I (r. 936–973), they claimed the imperial crown and worked closely with their bishops to rule a vast territory.

palace society (25): Minoan and Mycenaean social and political organization centered on multichambered buildings housing the rulers and the administration of the state.

Paleolithic Age (P-4): The "Old Stone" Age, dating from about 200,000 to 10,000 B.C.E.

Parthenon (78): The massive temple to Athena as a warrior goddess built atop the Athenian acropolis in the Golden Age of Greece.

patria potestas (136): Literally, "father's power"; the legal power a Roman father possessed over the children and slaves in his family, including owning all their property and having the right to punish them, even with death.

patriarchy (P-15): Dominance by men in society and politics.

patron-client system (136): The interlocking network of mutual obligations between Roman patrons (social superiors) and clients (social inferiors).

Pax Romana (164): The two centuries of relative peace and prosperity in the Roman Empire under the early principate begun by Augustus.

Peace of Augsburg (446): The treaty of 1555 that settled disputes between Holy Roman Emperor Charles V and his Protestant princes. It recognized the Lutheran church and established the principle that all Catholic or Lutheran princes enjoyed the sole right to determine the religion of their lands and subjects.

Peace of God (287): A movement begun by bishops in the south of France around 990, first to limit the violence done to property and to the unarmed, and later, with the Truce of God, to limit fighting between warriors.

Peace of Utrecht (538): Treaties drawn up in 1713–1714 that ended the War of the Spanish Succession.

Peace of Westphalia (463): The settlement (1648) of the Thirty Years' War; it established enduring religious divisions in the Holy Roman Empire by which Lutheranism would dominate in the north, Calvinism in the area of the Rhine River, and Catholicism in the south.

Pericles (75): Athens's political leader during the Golden Age.

Peter the Great (540): Russian tsar Peter I (r. 1689–1725), who undertook the Westernization of Russia and built a new capital city named after himself, St. Petersburg.

Petrarch, Francis (402): An Italian poet (1304–1374) who revived the styles of classical authors; he is considered the first Renaissance humanist.

Philip II (455): King of Spain (r. 1556–1598) and the most powerful ruler in Europe; he reigned over the western Habsburg lands and all the Spanish colonies recently settled in the New World.

Philip II (Philip Augustus) (340): King of France (r. 1180–1223) who bested the English king John and won most of John's continental territories, thus immeasurably strengthening the power of the Capetian dynasty.

Pietism (536): A Protestant revivalist movement of the early eighteenth century that emphasized deeply emotional individual religious experience.

plantation (521): A large tract of land that produced staple crops such as sugar, coffee, and tobacco; was farmed by slave labor; and was owned by a colonial settler.

Plato (107): A follower of Socrates who became Greece's most famous philosopher.

plebiscites (143): Resolutions passed by the Plebeian Assembly; such resolutions gained the force of law in 287 B.C.E.

polis (47): The Greek city-state, an independent community of citizens.

political states (P-4): People living in a defined territory with boundaries and organized under a system of government with powerful officials, leaders, and judges.

politiques (455): Political advisers during the sixteenth-century French Wars of Religion who argued that compromise in matters of religion would strengthen the monarchy.

polytheism (5): The worship of multiple gods.

populares (153): The Roman political faction supporting the common people; established during the late republic.

praetorian guard (166): The group of soldiers stationed in Rome under the emperor's control; first formed by Augustus.

predestination (432): John Calvin's doctrine that God preordained salvation or damnation for each person before creation; those chosen for salvation were considered the "elect."

principate (164): The Roman political system invented by Augustus as a disguised monarchy with the *princeps* ("first man") as emperor.

proletarians (153): In the Roman republic, the mass of people so poor they owned no property.

Puritans (458): Strict Calvinists who opposed all vestiges of Catholic ritual in the Church of England.

Qur'an (234): The holy book of Islam, considered the word of God (Allah) as revealed to the Prophet Muhammad.

radical democracy (76): The Athenian system of democracy established in the 460s and 450s B.C.E. that extended direct political power and participation in the court system to all adult male citizens.

raison d'état (464): French for "reason of state," the political doctrine, first proposed by Cardinal Richelieu of France, which held that the state's interests should prevail over those of religion.

rationalism (65): The philosophic idea that people must justify their claims by logic and reason, not myth.

Razin, Stenka (496): The head of a powerful band of pirates and outlaws in southern Russia, who in 1667 led a rebellion that promised peasants liberation from noble landowners and officials; Razin was captured by the tsar's army in 1671 and publicly executed in Moscow.

reconquista (305): The collective name for the wars waged by the Christian princes of Spain against the Muslim-ruled regions to their south. These wars were considered holy, akin to the crusades.

redistributive economy (14): A system in which state officials control the production and distribution of goods.

res publica (140): Literally, "the people's matter" or "the public business"; the Romans' name for their republic and the source of our word *republic*.

revocation of the Edict of Nantes (489): French king Louis XIV's decision to eliminate the rights of Calvinists granted in the edict of 1598; Louis banned all Calvinist public activities and forced those who refused to embrace the state religion to flee.

rococo (534): A style of painting that emphasized irregularity and asymmetry, movement and curvature, but on a smaller, more intimate scale than the baroque.

Romanization (177): The spread of Roman law and culture in the provinces of the Roman Empire.

ruler cults (128): Cults that involved worship of a Hellenistic ruler as a savior god.

salon (513): An informal gathering held regularly in private homes and presided over by a socially eminent woman; salons spread from France in the seventeenth century to other countries in the eighteenth century.

Sappho (64): The most famous woman lyric poet of ancient Greece, a native of Lesbos.

scholasticism (367): The method of logical inquiry used by the scholastics, the scholars of the medieval universities; it applied Aristotelian logic to biblical and other authoritative texts in an attempt to summarize and reconcile all knowledge.

scientific method (475): The combination of experimental observation and mathematical deduction that was used to determine the laws of nature and became the secular standard of truth.

Sea Peoples (29): The diverse groups of raiders who devastated the eastern Mediterranean region in the period of calamities around 1200–1000 B.C.E.

secularization (471): The trend toward making religious faith a private domain rather than one directly connected to state power and science; it prompted a search for nonreligious explanations for political authority and natural phenomena.

simony (303): The sin of giving gifts or paying money to get a church office.

social contract (504): The doctrine that all political authority derives not from divine right but from an implicit contract between citizens and their rulers.

Socratic method (90): The Athenian philosopher Socrates' method of teaching through conversation, in which he asked probing questions to make his listeners examine their most cherished assumptions.

Solon (62): Athenian political reformer whose changes promoted early democracy.

Sophists (88): Competitive intellectuals and teachers in ancient Greece who offered expensive courses in persuasive public speaking and new ways of philosophic and religious thinking beginning around 450 B.C.E.

Statute in Favor of the Princes (374): A statute finalized by Frederick II in 1232 that gave the German princes sovereign power within their own principalities.

St. Bernard (309): The most important Cistercian abbot (early twelfth century) and the chief preacher of the Second Crusade.

Stoicism (123): The Hellenistic philosophy whose followers believed in fate but also in pursuing virtue by cultivating good sense, justice, courage, and temperance.

Suleiman the Magnificent (443): Sultan of the Ottoman Empire (r. 1520–1566) at the time of its greatest power.

Synod of Whitby (253): The meeting of churchmen and King Oswy of Northumbria in 664 that led to the adoption of the Roman brand of Christianity in England.

tetrarchy (198): The "rule by four," consisting of two co-emperors and two assistant emperors/designated successors, initiated by Diocletian to subdivide the ruling of the Roman Empire into four regions.

Themistocles (71): Athens's leader during the great Persian invasion of Greece.

Theodosius I (205): The Roman emperor (r. 379–395) who made Christianity the state religion by ending public sacrifices in the traditional cults and closing their temples; in 395 he also divided the empire into western and eastern halves to be ruled by his sons.

Torah (40): The first five books of the Hebrew Bible, also referred to as the Pentateuch. It contains early Jewish law.

Treaty of Verdun (278): The treaty that, in 843, split the Carolingian Empire into three parts; its borders roughly outline modern western European states.

triremes (74): Greek wooden warships rowed by 170 oarsmen sitting on three levels and equipped with a battering ram at the bow.

troubadours (347): Vernacular poets in southern France in the twelfth and early thirteenth centuries who sang of love, longing, and courtesy.

Twelve Tables (142): The first written Roman law code, enacted between 451 and 449 B.C.E.

Umayyad caliphate (237): The caliphs (successors of Muhammad) who traced their ancestry to Umayyah, a member of Muhammad's tribe. The dynasty lasted from 661 to 750.

Urban II (312): The pope (r. 1088–1099) responsible for calling the First Crusade in 1095.

Visigoths (216): The name given to the barbarians whom Alaric united and led on a military campaign into the western Roman Empire to establish a new kingdom; they sacked Rome in 410.

Voltaire (548): The pen name of François-Marie Arouet (1694–1778), who was the most influential writer of the early Enlightenment.

Walpole, Robert (539): The first, or "prime," minister of the House of Commons of Great Britain's Parliament. Although appointed initially by the king, through his long period of leadership (1721–1742) he effectively established the modern pattern of parliamentary government.

wergild (219): Under Frankish law, the payment that a murderer had to make as compensation for the crime, to prevent feuds of revenge.

Westernization (540): The effort, especially in Peter the Great's Russia, to make society and social customs resemble counterparts in western Europe, especially France, Britain, and the Dutch Republic.

William, prince of Orange (504): Dutch ruler who, with his Protestant wife, Mary (daughter of James II), ruled England after the Glorious Revolution of 1688.

wisdom literature (20): Texts giving instructions for proper behavior by officials.

ziggurats (8): Mesopotamian temples of massive size built on a stair-step design.

Suggested References

PROLOGUE

Çatalhöyük: Excavations of a Neolithic Anatolian Höyük: **http://www.catalhoyuk.com**

Clark, J. Desmond, et al. "Stratigraphic, Chronological and Behavioural Contexts of Pleistocene *Homo Sapiens* from Middle Awash, Ethiopia." *Nature* 423 (June 12, 2003): 747–52.

Diamond, Jared. *Guns, Germs, and Steel: The Fates of Human Societies.* 1999.

Fagan, Brian M. *People of the Earth: An Introduction to World Prehistory.* 11th ed. 2003.

Klein, Richard G. *The Dawn of Human Culture.* 2002.

Lewis-Williams, David, and David Pearce. *Inside the Neolithic Mind: Consciousness, Cosmos and the Realm of the Gods.* 2005.

Mithen, Steven. *After the Ice: A Global Human History 20,000–5000 BC.* 2004.

Sahara Desert: **http://news.bbc.co.uk/2/hi/science/nature/5192410.stm**

Wenke, Robert J. *Patterns in Prehistory: Humankind's First Three Million Years.* 4th ed. 1999. White, Tim D., et al. "Pleistocene *Homo Sapiens* from Middle Awash, Ethiopia." *Nature* 423 (June 12, 2003): 742–47.

CHAPTER 1

Mesopotamia, Home of the First Civilization, 4000–1000 B.C.E.

Archaeological exploration in Mesopotamia (present-day Iraq) has been almost completely halted for more than a decade. Scholars have therefore been limited to studying already excavated material and texts. Modern translations have made Mesopotamian myths more accessible to today's readers.

Alcock, Susan, et al., eds. *Empires.* 2001.

Ancient Near East: **http://www.etana.org/abzu**

Aruz, Joan, ed. *Art of the First Cities: The Third Millennium B.C. from the Mediterranean to the Indus.* 2003.

Bertman, Stephen. *Handbook to Life in Ancient Mesopotamia.* 2003.

Bienkowski, Piotr, and Alan Millard, eds. *Dictionary of the Ancient Near East.* 2000.

Bottéro, Jean. *Everyday Life in Mesopotamia.* Trans. Antonia Nevill. 2001.

*Chavalas, Mark W., ed. *The Ancient Near East. Historical Sources in Translation.* 2006.

Crawford, Harriet. *Sumer and the Sumerians.* 1991.

*Dalley, Stephanie, trans. *Myths from Mesopotamia: Creation, The Flood, Gilgamesh, and Others.* 1991.

Mieroop, Marc van de. *A History of the Ancient Near East. c. 3000–323 BC.* 2003.

*Richardson, M. E. J. *Hammurabi's Laws: Text, Translation and Glossary.* 2000.

Snell, Daniel C. *A Companion to the Ancient Near East.* 2004.

Sumerian literature: **http://www-etcsl.orient.ox.ac.uk**

Egypt, Home of the First Unified Country, 3050–1000 B.C.E.

Research and writing on ancient Egypt continue at a furious pace, while scholars studying the eastern Mediterranean region increasingly emphasize the interaction of its various cultures in trade and in war.

Assmann, Jan. *The Search for God in Ancient Egypt.* Trans. David Lorton. 2001.

Baines, John. *Religion and Society in Ancient Egypt.* 2003.

Hawass, Zahi. *Silent Images: Women in Pharaonic Egypt.* 2000.

*Lichtheim, Miriam. *Ancient Egyptian Literature.* 3 vols. 1973.

Meskell, Lynn. *Private Life in New Kingdom Egypt.* 2002.

Morkot, Robert G. *The Black Pharaohs: Egypt's Nubian Rulers.* 2000.

Partridge, Robert B. *Fighting Pharaohs: Weapons and Warfare in Ancient Egypt.* 2002.

Redford, Donald B., ed. *The Oxford Encyclopedia of Ancient Egypt.* 2000.

Roehrig, Catherine H., ed. *Hatshepsut: From Queen to Pharaoh.* 2005.

Sahara Desert: **http://www.sciencemag.org/cgi/content/abstract/1130989v1**, **http://news.nationalgeographic.com/news/2006/07/060720-sahara.html**

*Simpson, William Kelly, ed. *The Literature of Ancient Egypt. An Anthology of Stories, Instructions, and Poetry.* 3rd ed. 2003.

Spalinger, Anthony J. *War in Ancient Egypt.* 2004.

Thebes in ancient Egypt: **http://www.thebanmappingproject.com**

Virtual Museum of Nautical Archaeology (including the Uluburun shipwreck): **http://ina.tamu.edu/vm.htm**

The Hittites, Minoans, and Mycenaeans, 2200–1000 B.C.E.

Archaeology provides the securest evidence for the emergence of Greek and Anatolian civilizations. It has not yet, however, revealed what initiated the period of calamities around 1200–1000 B.C.E.

Bryce, Trevor. *Life and Society in the Hittite World.* 2002.

Crete and the Aegean Islands: **http://harpy.uccs.edu/greek/crete.html**

Dickinson, Oliver. *The Aegean Bronze Age.* 1994.

Fagan, Brian. *The Long Summer: How Climate Changed Civilization.* 2003.

Farnoux, Alexandre. *Knossos: Searching for the Legendary Palace of King Minos.* Trans. David J. Baker. 1996.

Minoan civilization: **http://www.culture.gr/2/21/211/21123m/e211wm01.html**

Mycenaean civilization: **http://harpy.uccs.edu/greek/mycenae.html**

Sanders, N. K. *The Sea Peoples: Warriors of the Ancient Mediterranean, 1250–1150 B.C.* Rev. ed. 1985.

*Singer, Itamar. *Hittite Prayers: Writings from the Ancient World.* 2002.

*Primary source.

CHAPTER 2

From Dark Age to Empire in the Near East, 1000–500 B.C.E.

Recent surveys of ancient Near Eastern history take an integrative approach to the subject, treating its various empires comparatively. The significance of Persian religion for later faiths has also been an active field of study.

Brosius, Maria. *Women in Ancient Persia, 559–331 B.C.* 1996.
Kugel, James. *The God of Old: Inside the Lost World of the Bible.* 2003.
*Lieber, David L., ed. *Etz Hayim: Torah and Commentary.* 2001.
*Malandra, William W. *An Introduction to Ancient Iranian Religion: Readings from the Avesta and the Achaemenid Inscriptions.* 1983.
Persepolis and Ancient Iran: **http://www.oi.uchicago.edu/OI/ MUS/PA/IRAN/PAAI/PAAI_Persepolis.html**
Silberman, Neil, and Israel Finkelstein. *The Bible Unearthed: Archaeology's New Vision of Ancient Israel and the Origin of Its Sacred Texts.* 2002.
Stiebing, William H., Jr. *Ancient Near Eastern History and Culture.* 2003.

Remaking Greek Civilization, 1000–750 B.C.E.

Scholarship on the Dark Age, such as by Sarah Morris, emphasizes that it was not as dark as sometimes asserted in the past because Greece was never completely cut off from contact with the Near East.

Hanson, Victor Davis. *The Other Greeks: The Family Farm and the Agrarian Roots of Western Civilization.* 1995.
*Hesiod. *Theogony; Works and Days.* Trans. M. L. West. 1999.
Lavelle, B. M. *Fame, Money, and Power: The Rise of Peisistratos and "Democratic" Tyranny at Athens.* 2005.
Miller, Stephen G. *Ancient Greek Athletics.* 2004.
Morris, Ian, ed. *The Dark Ages of Greece.* 2006.
Morris, Sarah P. *Daidalos and the Origins of Greek Art.* 1992.
Olympia: **http://harpy.uccs.edu/greek/olympia.html**
Social justice in Homer's *Odyssey:* **http://www.chs.harvard.edu/ discussion_series.sec/the_homeric_odyssey.ssp**

The Creation of the Greek Polis, 750–500 B.C.E.

The Greek city-state did not spring up in a cultural vacuum, but the scarcity of sources for this period makes it difficult to evaluate the importance of various influences on it.

Burkert, Walter. *The Orientalizing Revolution: The Near Eastern Influence on Greek Culture in the Early Archaic Age.* Trans. Margaret E. Pinder and Walter Burkert. 1992.
Fisher, Nick, and Hans van Wees, eds. *Archaic Greece: New Approaches and Evidence.* 1998.
Garlan, Yvon. *Slavery in Ancient Greece.* Rev. ed. Trans. Janet Lloyd. 1988.
Garland, Robert. *Religion and the Greeks.* 1994.
Tsetskhladze, Gocha R., ed. *Greek Colonisation: An Account of Greek Colonies and Other Settlements Overseas.* Volume 1. 2006.
Wees, Hans van, ed. *War and Violence in Ancient Greece.* 2000.

New Directions for the Polis, 750–500 B.C.E.

Contemporary scholarship stresses the diversity of city-state governance and customs, but, as always in ancient history, the scarcity of hard evidence hinders our gaining a clear picture.

Anhalt, Emily Katz. *Solon the Singer: Politics and Poetics.* 1993.

Archaic Greek sculpture: **http://harpy.uccs.edu/greek/archaicsculpt .html**
Balot, Ryan K. *Greek Political Thought.* 2005.
*Barnes, Jonathan. *Early Greek Philosophy.* 1987.
*Campbell, David A. *Greek Lyric.* Five volumes. 1982–1993.
Cartledge, Paul. *Spartan Reflections.* 2001.
Halperin, David M. *One Hundred Years of Homosexuality and Other Essays on Greek Love.* 1990.
Hurwitt, Jeffrey M. *The Art and Culture of Early Greece, 1100–480 B.C.* 1985.
McGlew, James F. *Tyranny and Political Culture in Ancient Greece.* 1993.
*Robinson, Eric W. *Ancient Greek Democracy: Readings and Sources.* 2003.

CHAPTER 3

Wars between Persia and Greece

Like many groups in history, the ancient Greeks defined their own identity by contrasting themselves with others, especially non-Greek-speaking peoples ("barbarians"). The Persian Wars strengthened their sense of difference from other peoples ruled by kings.

Georges, Pericles. *Barbarian Asia and the Greek Experience: From the Archaic Period to the Age of Xenophon.* 1994.
Hall, Jonathan M. *Ethnic Identity in Greek Antiquity.* 1997.
Hanson, Victor Davis. *The Wars of the Ancient Greeks.* 1999.
*Herodotus. *The Histories.* Translated Aubrey de Sélincourt. Revised by John Marincola. New edition, 1996.
Persian art: **http://www.oi.uchicago.edu/OI/MUS/GALLERY/ PERSIAN/New_Persian_Gallery.html**
Strauss, Barry. *The Battle of Salamis: The Naval Encounter That Saved Greece — and Western Civilization.* 2005.
Wees, Hans van, ed. *War and Violence in Ancient Greece.* 2000.

Athenian Confidence in the Golden Age

Athenian government remains significant for modern scholars in debates over direct versus representative democracy and the nature of citizenship. Online resources are also now available and important for studying the full context of Golden Age Athens.

Athenian democracy: **http://www.stoa.org/projects/demos/home**
Cahill, Nicholas. *Household and City Organization at Olynthus.* 2001.
Camp, John M. *The Archaeology of Athens.* 2001.
Cohen, Edward E. *The Athenian Nation.* 2000.
Ober, Josiah, and Charles W. Hedrick, eds. *Demokratia: A Conversation on Democracies, Ancient and Modern.* 1996.
Parthenon: **http://www.perseus.tufts.edu/cgi-bin/vor?x=16&y= 13&lookup=parthenon**

Tradition and Innovation in Athens's Golden Age

Lively debates continue about how to measure and evaluate the difference between ancient Greek and modern Western customs. Davidson, for example, has rebutted the recent idea that Greeks considered sex a game of aggressive domination.

Blundell, Sue. *Women in Ancient Greece.* 1995.
Brunschwig, Jacques, and Geoffrey E. R. Lloyd, eds. *Greek Thought: A Guide to Classical Knowledge.* 2000.
Davidson, James. *Courtesans and Fishcakes: The Consuming Passions of Classical Athens.* 1998.

Fisher, N. R. E. *Slavery in Classical Greece.* 1995.
Greek gods: **http://www.getty.edu/art/gettyguide/display ObjectList? sub=2031503**
Herman, Gabriel. *Morality and Behavior in Democratic Athens.* 2006.
Parker, Robert. *Athenian Religion: A History.* 1996.
Patterson, Cynthia B. *The Family in Greek History.* 1998.

The End of the Golden Age

Controversy still exists over whether to explain the Athenian defeat in the Peloponnesian War as caused by political disunity and failure of leadership at Athens, or by Persia's financial support of Sparta; Strassler's edition of Thucydides is the best resource for assessing the evidence of the most important ancient source.

Hanson, Victor Davis. *A War Like No Other. How the Athenians and Spartans Fought the Peloponnesian War.* 2005.
Kagan, Donald. *The Peloponnesian War.* 2003.
Lazenby, J. F. *The Spartan Army.* 1985.
The Peloponnesian War and Athenian Life: **http://www.perseus.tufts .edu/cgi-bin/ptext?doc=Perseus%3Atext%3A1999.04.0009& query=head%3D%23212**
*Pseudo-Xenophon, *Constitution of the Athenians.* Trans. G. W. Bowersock, in *Xenophon VII. Scripta Minora.* 1971.
*Strassler, Robert B., ed. *The Landmark Thucydides: A Comprehensive Guide to the Peloponnesian War.* 1996.

CHAPTER 4

Classical Greece after the Peloponnesian War, 400–350 B.C.E.

The works of Plato and Aristotle, unlike those of many ancient authors, have survived in quantity. Xenophon's *Hellenica* and *Anabasis* offer action-packed accounts of the wars of the early fourth century B.C.E.

*Aristotle. *Complete Works.* Ed. Jonathan Barnes. 1985.
Barnes, Jonathan. *Aristotle.* 1982.
Fortenbaugh, William W. *Aristotle's Practical Side: On His Psychology, Ethics, Politics and Rhetoric.* 2006.
Garnsey, Peter. *Ideas of Slavery from Aristotle to Augustine.* 1996.
*Plato. *The Collected Dialogues* (including *Apology*, *Crito*, and *Republic*). Eds. Edith Hamilton and Huntington Cairns. 1963.
Tritle, Lawrence A., ed. *The Greek World in the Fourth Century: From the Fall of the Athenian Empire to the Successors of Alexander.* 1997.
*Xenophon. *A History of My Times (Hellenica).* Trans. Rex Warner. 1979.
———. *The Persian Expedition (Anabasis).* Trans. Rex Warner. 1972.

The Rise of Macedonia, 359–323 B.C.E.

Modern scholars energetically debate Alexander's character; Bosworth, for example, brands him a natural-born killer, while O'Brien sees him as overcome by alcoholism.

*Arrian. *The Campaigns of Alexander (Anabasis).* Trans. Aubrey de Sélincourt. 1971.
Borza, Eugene N. *In the Shadow of Olympus: The Emergence of Macedon.* 1990.
Bosworth, A. B. *Alexander and the East: The Tragedy of Triumph.* 1996.
———. *Conquest and Empire: The Reign of Alexander the Great.* 1988.
Carney, Elizabeth Donnelly. *Women and Monarchy in Macedonia.* 2000.
Heckel, Waldemar. *Who's Who in the Age of Alexander the Great.* 2006.
Macedonian royal tombs at Aigai: **http://alexander.macedonia .culture.gr/2/21/211/21117a/e211qa07.html**
O'Brien, John Maxwell. *Alexander the Great, the Invisible Enemy: A Biography.* 1992.
*Plutarch. *The Age of Alexander.* Trans. Ian Scott-Kilvert. 1973.
Stoneman, Richard. *Alexander the Great.* 2nd ed. 2004.

The Hellenistic Kingdoms, 323–30 B.C.E.

Recent research stresses the innovative responses of Hellenistic kings to the challenges of ruling multicultural empires. Underwater archaeology has begun to reveal ancient Alexandria in Egypt, whose harbor district has sunk below the level of today's Mediterranean Sea.

*Austin, M. M. *The Hellenistic World from Alexander to the Roman Conquest: A Selection of Ancient Sources in Translation.* 1981.
*Burstein, Stanley M. *The Hellenistic Age from the Battle of Ipsos to the Death of Kleopatra VII.* 1985.
Chaniotis, Angelos. *War in the Hellenistic World.* 2005.
Ellis, Walter M. *Ptolemy of Egypt.* 1994.
Empereur, Jean-Yves. *Alexandria: Jewel of Egypt.* 2002.
Erskine, Andrew. *A Companion to the Hellenistic World.* 2003.
Lewis, Naphtali. *Greeks in Ptolemaic Egypt.* 1986.
Ptolemaic Egypt: **http://www.houseofptolemy.org**
Sherwin-White, Susan, and Amélie Kuhrt. *From Samarkhand to Sardis: A New Approach to the Seleucid Empire.* 1993.
Shipley, Graham. *The Greek World After Alexander 323–30 B.C.* 2000.

Hellenistic Culture

Old scholarship viewed Hellenistic culture as "impure" and less valuable than Classical Age culture because it mixed traditions. Scholars today identify the imaginative ways in which Hellenistic thinkers and artists combined the old and the new. Hellenistic philosophy has become important in the study of ethics.

Ancient Alexandria in Egypt: **http://ce.eng.usf.edu/pharos/alexandria**
Archimedes: **http://www.mcs.drexel.edu/~crorres/Archimedes/ contents.html**
*Bartlett, John R. *Jews in the Hellenistic World: Josephus, Aristeas, The Sibylline Oracles, Eupolemus.* 1985.
Chamoux, François. *Hellenistic Civilization.* Trans. Michel Roussel. 2003.
Inwood, Brad, ed. *The Cambridge Companion to the Stoics.* 2003.
Long, A. A. *Hellenistic Philosophy: Stoics, Epicureans, Sceptics.* 2nd ed. 1986.
*Menander. *The Plays and Fragments.* Trans. Maurice Balme. 2002.
Mikalson, Jon D. *Religion in Hellenistic Athens.* 1998.
Pollard, Justin, and Howard Reid. *The Rise and Fall of Alexandria: The Birthplace of the Modern Mind.* 2006.
Pollitt, J. J. *Art in the Hellenistic Age.* 1986.
Pomeroy, Sarah B. *Women in Hellenistic Egypt: From Alexander to Cleopatra.* Rev. ed. 1990.
Schäfer, Peter. *Judeophobia: Attitudes toward the Jews in the Ancient World.* 1997.
Sharples, R. W. *Stoics, Epicureans, and Sceptics: An Introduction to Hellenistic Philosophy.* 1996.
Snyder, Jane M. *The Woman and the Lyre: Women Writers in Classical Greece and Rome.* 1989.
Walker, Susan, and Peter Higgs, eds. *Cleopatra of Egypt: From History to Myth.* 2001.

*Primary source.

CHAPTER 5

Roman Social and Religious Traditions

Scholarship on Roman culture emphasizes how Roman values were grounded in religious belief. Study of stories about Rome's foundation shows how Romans in the late republic relied on those tales to define their national identity.

Ancient Rome: **http://www.vroma.org**

Bradley, Keith. *Slavery and Society at Rome.* 1994.

*Cicero. *On Duties.* Eds. M. T. Griffin and E. M. Atkins. 1991.

Gardner, Jane. *Women in Roman Law and Society.* 1986.

Harvey, Paul, and Celia Schultz, eds. *Religion in Republican Rome.* 2006.

Pallottino, Massimo. *A History of Earliest Italy.* Trans. M. Ryle and K. Soper. 1991.

Rawson, Beryl, ed. *The Family in Ancient Rome: New Perspectives.* 1986.

Wiseman, T. P. *Remus: A Roman Myth.* 1995.

From Monarchy to Republic

Scholars now stress the Romans' own shaping of their state and culture. Interpretation of the struggle of the orders concentrates on the effects of the overlapping interests of patricians and plebeians.

Cornell, T. J. *The Beginnings of Rome: Italy and Rome from the Bronze Age to the Punic Wars (c. 1000–264 B.C.).* 1995.

Flower, Harriet, ed. *The Cambridge Companion to the Roman Republic.* 2004.

Ladder of offices: **http://www.vroma.org/~bmcmanus/romangvt.html**

*Livy. *From the Founding of the City*, Books 1–5. From *The Early History of Rome.* Trans. Aubrey de Sélincourt. 2002.

MacNamara, Ellen. *The Etruscans.* 1991.

Miles, Gary B. *Livy: Reconstructing Early Rome.* 1992.

Stewart, Roberta. *Public Office in Early Rome: Ritual Procedure and Political Practice.* 1998.

Roman Imperialism and Its Consequences

Controversy over Roman imperialism remains a major topic. Works on Roman warfare now offer a vivid sense of what life on the ground was like during Rome's wars of expansion.

Conte, Gian Biagio. *Latin Literature: A History.* Trans. Joseph B. Solodow; rev. Don Fowler and Glenn W. Most. 1994.

Daly, Gregory. *Cannae. The Experience of Battle in the Second Punic War.* 2002.

Etruscan art and objects: **http://mv.vatican.va/3_EN/pages/MGE/MGE_Main.html**

Harris, William V. *War and Imperialism in Republican Rome, 327–70 B.C.* 1985.

Lancel, Serge. *Carthage: A History.* Trans. Antonia Nevill. 1995.

*Livy. *From the Founding of the City*, Books 6–10, 21–45. From *Rome and Italy.* Trans. Betty Radice. 1986.

Roman slavery: **www.chs.harvard.edu/publications.sec/online_print_books.ssp/frank_m._snowden_jr./snowden_bradley_tei.xml_7**

Scheidel, Walter. "Human Mobility in Roman Italy, I: The Free Population." *Journal of Roman Studies* 94 (2004): 1–26.

———. "Human Mobility in Roman Italy, II: The Slave Population." *Journal of Roman Studies* 95 (2005): 64–79.

Toynbee, J. M. C. *Roman Historical Portraits.* 1978.

Upheaval in the Late Republic

Cicero's many letters and speeches and Caesar's memoirs give vivid personal views of the late republic. New arguments about the failure of the republic now stress political issues and not just personal connections as significant sources of discord.

Beard, Mary, and Michael Crawford. *Rome in the Late Republic.* 1985.

*Caesar. *The Civil War.* Trans. John Carter. 1997.

*———. *The Gallic War.* Trans. Carolyn Hammond. 1998.

*Catullus. *The Poems.* Trans. Guy Lee. 1998.

*Cicero. *Philippic Orations.* From *Philippics.* Trans. Walter C. Ker. 1969.

Gruen, Erich. *The Last Generation of the Roman Republic.* 1995.

Jiménez, Ramon L. *Caesar Against Rome: The Great Roman Civil War.* 2000.

Julius Caesar: **http://www.vroma.org/~bmcmanus/caesar.html**

Keaveney, Arthur. *Sulla: The Last Republican.* 1982.

Shaw, Brent D. *Spartacus and the Slave Wars: A Brief History with Documents.* 2001.

Southern, Pat. *Cleopatra.* 1999.

Stockton, David. *The Gracchi.* 1979.

CHAPTER 6

Creating the Roman Peace

Whether scholars label Augustus tyrant or reformer, they agree that he was a brilliant visionary. Recent research on the ways Augustus and his successors communicated the meaning of empire to the public stresses the role of grandiose and often violent spectacles.

Barrett, Anthony A. *Livia: First Lady of Imperial Rome.* 2002.

Futrell, Alison. *Blood in the Arena: The Spectacle of Roman Power.* 1997.

Galinsky, Karl. *Augustan Culture.* 1996.

Horace's poetry and country house: **http://www.humnet.ucla.edu/horaces-villa**

Potter, David. *A Companion to the Roman Empire.* 2006.

Roman emperors: **http://www.roman-emperors.org**

Roman technology: **http://www.unc.edu/courses/rometech/public/frames/art_set.html**

Southern, Pat. *Augustus.* 1998.

*Suetonius. *The Twelve Caesars.* Trans. Robert Graves. 1979.

*Virgil. *Aeneid.* Trans. Robert Fagles. 2006.

Maintaining the Roman Peace

Research shows that the Roman Peace was made possible both by the devotion to duty of emperors such as Marcus Aurelius and by the general prosperity that emerged during the absence of civil war.

*Apuleius, *The Golden Ass.* Trans. P. G. Walsh. 1995.

Atkins, Margaret, and Robin Osborne. *Poverty in the Roman World.* 2006.

Ball, Warwick. *Rome in the East: The Transformation of an Empire.* 2001.

Champlin, Edward. *Nero.* 2003.

Garnsey, Peter, and Richard Saller. *The Roman Empire: Economy, Society, and Culture.* 1987.

*Marcus Aurelius. *Meditations.* Trans. A. L. Farguharson. 1998.

Mattern, Susan. *Rome and the Enemy: Imperial Strategy in the Principate.* 1999.

Treggiari, Susan. *Roman Marriage: Iusti Coniuges from the Time of Cicero to the Time of Ulpian.* 1991.

Wiedemann, Thomas. *The Julio-Claudian Emperors, A.D. 14–70.* 1989.

The Emergence of Christianity

Scholarly debate concerning early Christianity remains energetic. The sources' meanings are hotly contested because both the ancient authors and their modern interpreters usually have particular points of view.

Crossan, John Dominic, and Jonathan L. Reed. *Excavating Jesus: Beneath the Stones, Behind the Texts.* 2001.

Early Christianity: **http://www.wabashcenter.wabash.edu/internet/ early.htm**

*Ehrman, Bart D., ed. *The New Testament and Other Early Christian Writings: A Reader.* 1998.

Kraemer, Ross Shephard. *Her Share of the Blessings: Women's Religion among Pagans, Jews, and Christians in the Greco-Roman World.* 1992.

MacMullen, Ramsay. *Voting About God in Early Church Councils.* 2006.

Mitchell, Margaret M., and Frances M. Young. *Cambridge History of Christianity.* 2006.

Nickelsburg, George W. E. *Ancient Judaism and Christian Origins. Diversity, Continuity, and Transformation.* 2003.

Schürer, Emil. *The History of the Jewish People in the Age of Jesus Christ (175 B.C.–A.D. 135).* Rev. ed. 4 vols. 1973–1987.

Torjesen, Karen Jo. *When Women Were Priests: Women's Leadership in the Early Church and the Scandal of Their Subordination in the Rise of Christianity.* 1993.

Turcan, Robert. *The Cults of the Roman Empire.* Trans. Antonia Nevill. 1996.

The Third-Century Crisis

The fundamental problem in the third century remained the same: the Roman monarchy's propensity to generate civil war and the inevitably disastrous effects on the economy. Hence, scholarly study of the crisis emphasizes military and political history.

Bowman, Alan, et al. *The Cambridge Ancient History.* Vol. 12, *The Crisis of Empire, AD 193–337.* 2005.

Campbell, Brian. *Warfare and Society in Imperial Rome, 31 B.C.–A.D. 284.* 2002.

Decius, the persecutor of Christians: **http://www.roman-emperors.org/ decius.htm**

*Dodgeon, Michael H., and Samuel N. C. Lieu. *The Roman Eastern Frontier and the Persian Wars A.D. 226–363: A Documentary History.* 1994.

Elton, Hugh. *Frontiers of the Roman Empire.* 1996.

Grant, Michael. *The Collapse and Recovery of the Roman Empire.* 1999.

*Herodian. *The History (180 to 238 C.E.).* Trans. C. R. Whittaker. 1969.

Southern, Pat. *The Roman Empire from Severus to Constantine.* 2001.

CHAPTER 7

Reorganizing the Empire, 284–395

Scholars continue to debate the religious motives of Diocletian and Constantine. Understanding them is challenging because their religious sensibilities, markedly different from those of most modern believers, so deeply influenced their political actions.

Bowersock, G. W., Peter Brown, and Oleg Grabar, eds. *Late Antiquity: A Guide to the Postclassical World.* 1999.

Elsner, Jaś. *Imperial Rome and Christian Triumph: The Art of the Roman Empire A.D. 100–450.* 1998.

*Grubbs, Judith Evans. *Women and Law in the Roman Empire: A Sourcebook on Marriage, Divorce, and Widowhood.* 2002.

Mitchell, Stephen. *A History of the Later Roman Empire, AD 284–641.* 2006.

Southern, Pat, and Karen R. Dixon. *The Late Roman Army.* 1996.

Christianizing the Empire, 312–c. 540

Recent research has deepened our appreciation of the emotional depths that the Christianization of the empire stirred for both polytheists and Christians. People's ideas about themselves changed as their ideas about divinity changed.

Brown, Peter. *Augustine of Hippo: A Biography.* Rev. ed. 2000.

Caner, Daniel. *Wandering, Begging Monks: Spiritual Authority and the Promotion of Monasticism in Late Antiquity.* 2002.

Curran, John. *Pagan City and Christian Capital: Rome in the Fourth Century.* 2000.

Drake, H. A. *Constantine and the Bishops: The Politics of Intolerance.* 2000.

*Early Christian literature: **http://www.voskrese.info/spl/index.html**

Glancy, Jennifer A. *Slavery in Early Christianity.* 2002.

*Lee, A. D. *Pagans and Christians in Late Antiquity: A Sourcebook.* 2000.

*Maas, Michael. *Readings in Late Antiquity: A Sourcebook.* 2000.

MacMullen, Ramsay. *Christianity and Paganism in the Fourth to Eighth Centuries.* 1997.

Odahl, Charles. *Constantine and the Christian Empire.* 2nd ed. 2006.

Rives, James B. *Religion in the Roman Empire.* 2006.

Trombley, Frank R. *Hellenic Religion and Christianization c. 370–529.* Vol. 2. 2001.

Non-Roman Kingdoms in the West, c. 370–550s

Debate continues over how to categorize the social and cultural transformation of the Roman world in the fourth and fifth centuries and the development of separate ethnic identities by the non-Roman peoples who created new kingdoms inside the empire's borders.

Burns, Thomas. *Rome and the Barbarians.* 2003.

Carr, Karen Eva. *Vandals to Visigoths: Rural Settlement Patterns in Early Medieval Spain.* 2002.

*Drew, Katherine Fischer, trans. *The Laws of the Salian Franks.* 1991.

Geary, Patrick J. *The Myth of Nations: The Medieval Origins of Europe.* 2001.

Goffart, Walter. *Barbarians and Romans, A.D. 418–584.* 1987.

Halsall, Guy. *Barbarian Migrations and the Roman West.* 2007.

Heather, Peter. *The Goths.* 1996.

Lançon, Bertrand. *Rome in Late Antiquity: Everyday Life and Urban Change, A.D. 312–609.* Trans. Antonia Nevill. 2001.

MacGeorge, Penny. *Late Roman Warlords.* 2002.

*Mathisen, Ralph W. *People, Personal Expression, and Social Relations in Late Antiquity.* 2 vols. 2002.

The Roman Empire in the East, c. 500–565

Scholars of the eastern Roman Empire (also called the Byzantine empire after about 500 C.E.) emphasize the challenge posed to its rulers in trying to maintain order and prosperity for their multicultural and multilingual population.

Eastern Roman (Byzantine) civilization: **http://www.fordham.edu/ halsall/byzantium**

*Geanakoplos, Deno J. *Byzantium: Church, Society, and Civilization Seen Through Contemporary Eyes.* 1986.

Haldon, John. *The Byzantine Wars.* 2001.

Kalavrezou, Ioli. *Byzantine Women and Their World.* 2003.

Matthews, John. *The Journey of Theophanes. Travel, Business, and Daily Life in the Roman East.* 2006.

Moorhead, John. *The Roman Empire Divided, 400–700.* 2001.

Women in Byzantine history, bibliography: **http://www.doaks.org/ WomeninByzantium.html**

CHAPTER 8

Islam: A New Religion and a New Empire

The classic discussion is in Hodgson. Crone's book is considered highly controversial. Berkey's book is balanced and up-to-date.

Ahmed, Leila. *Women and Gender in Islam: Historical Roots of a Modern Debate.* 1992.

Berkey, Jonathan P. *The Formation of Islam: Religion and Society in the Near East, 600–1800.* 2003.

Crone, Patricia. *Meccan Trade and the Rise of Islam.* 1987.

Donner, Fred McGraw. *The Early Islamic Conquests.* 1981.

Hodgson, Marshall G. S. *The Venture of Islam: Conscience and History in a World Civilization.* Vol. 1, *The Classical Age of Islam.* 1974.

*Islamic Sourcebook: **http://www.fordham.edu/halsall/islam/ islamsbook.html**

Kennedy, Hugh. *The Prophet and the Age of the Caliphates: The Islamic Near East from the Sixth to the Eleventh Century.* 1986.

Byzantium: A Christian Empire under Siege

While some scholars (Ousterhout and Brubaker) concentrate on religion, culture, and the role of icons, others (Treadgold, Whittow) tend to stress politics and war.

Connor, Carolyn L. *Women of Byzantium.* 2004.

*Geanakoplos, Deno John, ed. and trans. *Byzantium: Church, Society, and Civilization Seen through Contemporary Eyes.* 1986.

Haldon, J. F. *Byzantium in the Seventh Century: The Transformation of a Culture.* 1990.

Norwich, John Julius. *Byzantium: The Early Centuries.* 1989.

Ousterhout, Robert, and Leslie Brubaker. *The Sacred Image East and West.* 1995.

*Selected sources: Byzantium: **http://www.fordham.edu/halsall/ sbook1c.html**

Treadgold, Warren. *A History of the Byzantine State and Society.* 1997.

Whittow, Mark. *The Making of Byzantium, 600–1025.* 1996.

Western Europe: A Medley of Kingdoms

Smith and Wickham provide new and complementary overviews. Keen interest in the role of the cults of the saints in early medieval society is reflected in Van Dam. While interest in Anglo-Saxon England has not diminished, other parts of the British Isles are receiving new attention, as Smyth demonstrates.

*Bede. *A History of the English Church and People.* Trans. Leo Sherley-Price. 1991.

Collins, Roger. *Early Medieval Spain: Unity in Diversity, 400–1000.* 1983.

*Fouracre, Paul, and Richard A. Gerberding. *Late Merovingian France: History and Hagiography, 640–720.* 1996.

Geary, Patrick. *Before France and Germany: The Creation and Transformation of the Merovingian World.* 1988.

*Gregory of Tours. *The History of the Franks.* Trans. Lewis Thorpe. 1976.

Heinzelmann, Martin. *Gregory of Tours: History and Society in the Sixth Century.* 2001.

Smith, Julia M. H. *Europe after Rome: A New Cultural History 500–1000.* 2005.

Smyth, A. P. *Warlords and Holy Men: Scotland, AD 80–1000.* 1984.

Van Dam, Raymond. *Saints and Their Miracles in Late Antique Gaul.* 1993.

Wickham, Chris. *Framing the Early Middle Ages: Europe and the Mediterranean, 400–800.* 2005.

*The World of Gregory of Tours: **http://www.nipissingu.ca/ department/history/MUHLBERGER/4505/GREGORY.HTM**

CHAPTER 9

Byzantium: Renewed Strength and Influence

Recent studies of Byzantium stress the revival in the arts and literature, but Whittow is excellent on political, social, and religious issues. Almost nothing was available in English on eastern Europe and Russia until the 1980s.

Brubaker, Leslie, and Julia M. H. Smith. *Gender in the Early Medieval World: East and West, 300–900.* 2004.

Fine, Jon V. A., Jr. *The Early Medieval Balkans: A Critical Survey from the Sixth to the Late Twelfth Century.* 1983.

Franklin, Simon, and Jonathan Shepard. *The Emergence of Rus, 750–1200.* 1996.

Garland, Lynda. *Byzantine Empresses: Women and Power in Byzantium, AD 527–1204.* 1999.

Maguire, Henry, ed. *Byzantine Court Culture from 829 to 1204.* 1997.

*Psellus, Michael. *Fourteen Byzantine Rulers: The Chronographia.* Trans. E. R. A. Sewter. 1966.

Whittow, Mark. *The Making of Byzantium, 600–1025.* 1996.

The Islamic World: From Unity to Fragmentation

The traditional approach to the Islamic world is political (Kennedy). Glick is unusual in taking a comparative approach. The newest issue for scholars is the role of women in medieval Islamic society (Spellberg). Cobb illustrates the forces that later tore the Abbasid caliphate apart.

Cobb, Paul M. *White Banners: Contention in Abbasid Syria, 750–880.* 2001.

Glick, Thomas. *Islamic and Christian Spain in the Early Middle Ages: Comparative Perspectives on Social and Cultural Formation.* 1979.

Islamic sources: **http://www.fordham.edu/halsall/sbook1d.html**

Kennedy, Hugh. *The Prophet and the Age of the Caliphates: The Islamic Near East from the Sixth to the Eleventh Century.* 1986.

Makdisi, George. *The Rise of Colleges.* 1981.

Spellberg, Denise. *Politics, Gender, and the Islamic Past.* 1994.

The Creation and Division of a New European Empire

Many of the primary sources for the Carolingian world are now available in English translation, thanks in large part to the work of Dutton. Hodges and Whitehouse provide the perspective of archaeologists. The

*Primary source.

Carolingian renaissance is increasingly recognized as a long-term development rather than simply the achievement of Charlemagne.

Becher, Matthias. *Charlemagne*. 2003.
*Dutton, Paul Edward, ed. *Carolingian Civilization: A Reader*. 1993.
*———, ed. and trans. *Charlemagne's Courtier: The Complete Einhard*. 1998.
*Einhard and Notker the Stammerer. *Two Lives of Charlemagne*. Trans. Lewis Thorpe. 1969.
Hodges, Richard, and David Whitehouse. *Mohammed, Charlemagne, and the Origins of Europe*. 1983.
McKitterick, Rosamond. *Carolingian Culture: Emulation and Innovation*. 1994.
Nelson, Janet. *Charles the Bald*. 1987.
Riche, Pierre. *Daily Life in the World of Charlemagne*. Trans. J. A. McNamara. 1978.

After the Carolingians: The Emergence of Local Rule

Historians used to lament the passing of the Carolingian Empire. More recently, however, they have come to appreciate the strengths and adaptive strategies of the post-Carolingian world. Duby speaks of the agricultural "takeoff" of the period, whereas Head and Landes explore new institutions of peace.

Duby, Georges. *The Early Growth of the European Economy: Warriors and Peasants from the Seventh to the Twelfth Century*. Trans. H. B. Clark. 1974.
Engel, Pál. *The Realm of St. Stephen: A History of Medieval Hungary, 895–1526*. Trans. Tamás Pálosfalvi. 2001.
Forte, Angelo, Richard Oram, and Frederick Pederson. *Viking Empires*. 2005.
Frantzen, Allen. *King Alfred*. 1986.
Goldberg, Eric J. *Struggle for Empire: Kingship and Conflict under Louis the German, 817–876*. 2006.
Head, Thomas, and Richard Landes, eds. *The Peace of God: Social Violence and Religious Response in France around the Year 1000*. 1992.
Jones, Gwyn. *A History of the Vikings*. Rev. ed. 1984.
*Medieval and Renaissance manuscripts: **http://www.columbia.edu/cu/libraries/indiv/rare/images/date.html**
Sweeney, Del, ed. *Agriculture in the Middle Ages: Technology, Practice, and Representation*. 1995.
*Whitelock, Dorothy, ed. *English Historical Documents*. Vol. 1. 2nd ed. 1979.

CHAPTER 10

The Commercial Revolution

The idea of a commercial revolution in the Middle Ages originated with Lopez. Hyde explores the society and government of the Italian communes.

Constable, Olivia Remie. *Trade and Traders in Muslim Spain: The Commercial Realignment of the Iberian Peninsula, 900–1500*. 1994.
Hyde, J. K. *Society and Politics in Medieval Italy: The Evolution of Civil Life, 1000–1350*. 1973.
Lopez, Robert S. *The Commercial Revolution of the Middle Ages, 950–1350*. 1976.
*———, and Irving W. Raymond. *Medieval Trade in the Mediterranean World*. 1955.

Church Reform and Its Aftermath

The Investiture Conflict, which pitted the pope against the emperor, has been particularly important to German historians. Blumenthal gives a useful overview, while Miller gives the key primary sources. The consequences of church reform and the new papal monarchy included the growth of canon law (see Brundage). Little provides the now-classic discussion of the new monastic orders of poverty.

Berman, Constance Hoffman. *The Cistercian Evolution: The Invention of a Religious Order in Twelfth-Century Europe*. 2000.
Blumenthal, Uta-Renate. *The Investiture Controversy: Church & Monarchy from the 9th to the 12th Century*. 1991.
Brundage, James A. *Medieval Canon Law*. 1995.
Little, Lester K. *Religious Poverty and the Profit Economy in Medieval Europe*. 1978.
*Miller, Maureen C. *Power and the Holy in the Age of the Investiture Conflict*. 2005.
Robinson, Ian S. *Henry IV of Germany*. 2000.

The Crusades

A perennially popular topic, the crusade movement as a whole is given balanced treatment by Tyerman, while Asbridge covers the First Crusade in lively detail.

Asbridge, Thomas. *The First Crusade: A New History*. 2004.
Crusades: **http://www.medievalcrusades.com**
*Kerak castle: **http://www.vkrp.org/studies/historical/town-castle**
*Peters, Edward, ed. *The First Crusade: The Chronicle of Fulcher of Chartres and Other Source Materials*. 1971.
Tyerman, Christopher. *God's War: A New History of the Crusades*. 2006.

The Revival of Monarchies

The growth of monarchical power and the development of state institutions are topics of keen interest to historians. Clanchy points to the use of writing and recordkeeping in government. Suger shows the importance of the royal image. Douglas and Hallam each discuss different aspects of the Norman conquest of England.

Bayeux Tapestry: **http://www.bayeuxtapestry.org.uk/Index.htm**
Chibnall, Marjorie. *Anglo-Norman England, 1066–1166*. 1986.
Clanchy, Michael. *From Memory to Written Record: England 1066–1307*. 2nd ed. 1993.
Douglas, David C. *William the Conqueror: The Norman Impact upon England*. 1967.
Dunbabin, Jean. *France in the Making, 843–1180*. 1985.
Grant, Lindy. *Abbot Suger of St-Denis: Church and State in Early Twelfth-Century France*. 1998.
Hallam, Elizabeth M. *Domesday Book through Nine Centuries*. 1986.
*Suger. *The Deeds of Louis the Fat*. Trans. Richard C. Cusimano and John Moorhead. 1992.

CHAPTER 11

New Schools and Churches

Abelard's story is both entertaining and revealing. The life and works of Peter the Chanter are masterfully presented in Baldwin's study. Coldstream looks at Gothic architecture in its full European context.

*Abelard's *The Story of My Misfortunes*: **http://www.fordham.edu/halsall/source/abelard-sel.html**

Baldwin, John. *Masters, Princes and Merchants: The Social Views of Peter the Chanter and His Circle*. 1970.

Bouchard, Constance Brittain. *"Every Valley Shall Be Exalted": The Discourse of Opposites in Twelfth-Century Thought*. 2003.

Clanchy, Michael. *Abelard: A Medieval Life*. 1997.

Coldstream, Nicola. *Medieval Architecture*. 2002.

Gothic architecture: **http://www.bc.edu/bc_org/avp/cas/fnart/arch/gothic_arch.html**

The Letters of Abelard and Heloise. Trans. Betty Radice. 1974.

Governments as Institutions

The medieval origins of modern state institutions is a traditional interest of historians studying the medieval period. Hudson explores the growth of royal institutions of justice. Baldwin gives a carefully focused account of the French experience. Bartlett insists on the differences between medieval and modern political institutions.

Baldwin, John W. *The Government of Philip Augustus: Foundations of French Royal Power in the Middle Ages*. 1986.

Bartlett, Robert. *England under the Norman and Angevin Kings, 1075–1225*. 2000.

Evergates, Theodore, ed. *Aristocratic Women in Medieval France*. 1999.

Fuhrmann, Horst. *Germany in the High Middle Ages, c. 1050–1200*. Trans. T. Reuter. 1986.

Hudson, John. *The Formation of the English Common Law: Law and Society in England from the Norman Conquest to Magna Carta*. 1996.

Jordan, Karl. *Henry the Lion: A Biography*. Trans. P. S. Falla. 1986.

*Otto of Freising. *The Deeds of Frederick Barbarossa*. Trans. C. C. Mierow. 1953.

The Growth of a Vernacular High Culture

Chrétien de Troyes's *Yvain* is a good example of a twelfth-century romance, while troubadour poetry is collected in Goldin's anthology. Cheyette gives an illuminating account of one southern French ruler and her world, and Wheeler and Parsons's collection sheds light on another.

Bouchard, Constance B. *"Strong of Body, Brave and Noble": Chivalry and Society in Medieval France*. 1998.

Cheyette, Fredric L. *Ermengard of Narbonne and the World of the Troubadours*. 2001.

*Chrétien de Troyes. *Yvain: The Knight of the Lion*. Trans. Burton Raffel. 1987.

Crouch, David. *William Marshal: Court, Career, and Chivalry in the Angevin Empire, 1147–1219*. 1990.

*Goldin, Frederick. *Lyrics of the Troubadors and Trouvères: Original Texts, with Translations*. 1973.

The Song of Roland. Trans. P. Terry. 1965.

Troubadour poetry: **http://globegate.utm.edu/french/globegate_mirror/occit.html**

Wheeler, Bonnie, and John Carmi Parsons, ed. *Eleanor of Aquitaine: Lord and Lady*. 2003.

Religious Fervor and Crusade

The Little Flowers of Saint Francis gives a good idea of Franciscan spirituality, while the Franciscans are explored as part of wider religious, social, and economic movements in Little's study. Audisio looks sympathetically at one heretical group. Tyerman intelligently sums up the crusading movement as a whole.

Audisio, Gabriel. *The Waldensian Dissent: Persecution and Survival, c. 1170–c. 1570*. Trans. Claire Davison. 1999.

Bartlett, Robert. *The Making of Europe: Conquest, Colonization, and Cultural Change, 950–1350*. 1993.

Christiansen, Eric. *The Northern Crusades*. 2nd ed. 1998.

The Little Flowers of Saint Francis. Trans. L. Sherley-Price. 1959.

Little, Lester K. *Religious Poverty and the Profit Economy in Medieval Europe*. 1978.

Robson, Michael. *The Franciscans in the Middle Ages*. 2006.

Tyerman, Christopher. *Fighting for Christendom: Holy War and the Crusades*. 2004.

Wakefield, Walter L. *Heresy, Crusade, and Inquisition in Southern France, 1100–1250*. 1974.

CHAPTER 12

The Church's Mission

Historians (e.g., Sayers) remain interested in the important religious figures behind the thirteenth-century church. Bynum looks at the impact of new church doctrine on the laity and the way the laity actively interpreted it. There is considerable interest in the persecution of minorities — see Jordan, Moore, and Nirenberg.

Bynum, Caroline Walker. *Holy Feast and Holy Fast: The Religious Significance of Food to Medieval Women*. 1987.

*Fourth Lateran Council: **http://www.fordham.edu/halsall/source/lat4-select.html**

Jordan, William Chester. *The French Monarchy and the Jews: From Philip Augustus to the Last Capetians*. 1989.

Moore, R. I. *The Formation of a Persecuting Society: Power and Deviance in Western Europe, 950–1250*. 1987.

Nirenberg, David. *Communities of Violence: Persecution of Minorities in the Middle Ages*. 1996.

Sayers, Jane. *Innocent III: Leader of Europe, 1198–1216*. 1994.

The Medieval Synthesis

There is always lively interest in Thomas Aquinas (see, e.g., McInerny and Nichols). For literature, Dante is key. Gothic art and architecture is well covered in Duby's work.

*Dante. *The Divine Comedy*. Many editions; recommended are translations by Mark Musa and John Ciardi. The *Inferno* has been particularly well translated by Robert Pinsky and, most recently, by Robert Hollander and Jean Hollander.

Duby, Georges. *The Age of the Cathedrals: Art and Society, 980–1420*. Trans. Eleanor Levieux and Barbara Thompson. 1981.

McInerny, Ralph M. *Aquinas*. 2004

Nichols, Aidan. *Discovering Aquinas: An Introduction to His Life, Work and Influence*. 2003.

Panofsky, Erwin. *Gothic Architecture and Scholasticism*. 1951.

Smart, Alastair. *The Dawn of Italian Painting, 1250–1400*. 1978.

*Thomas Aquinas: **http://www.newadvent.org/summa**

The Politics of Control

Thirteenth-century states used to be seen as harbingers of modern ones, but the newest history suggests that this is anachronistic. Thus, Abulafia argues that Frederick II followed models of medieval rulership, and O'Callaghan shows how far different medieval representative institutions were from their modern counterparts. Only in the last ten or so years have historians studied the prelude to Columbus's voyages by looking at medieval precedents.

Abulafia, David. *Frederick II: A Medieval Emperor*. 1988.

Campbell, Mary B. *The Witness and the Other World: Exotic European Travel Writing, 400–1600*. 1989.

Farmer, Sharon. *Surviving Poverty in Medieval Paris: Gender, Ideology, and the Daily Lives of the Poor*. 2002.

Fernández-Armesto, Felipe. *Before Columbus: Exploration and Colonization from the Mediterranean to the Atlantic, 1229–1492*. 1987.

*Joinville, Jean de, and Geoffroy de Villehardouin. *Chronicles of the Crusades*. Trans. M. R. B. Shaw. 1963.

Jordan, William Chester. *The Great Famine: Northern Europe in the Early Fourteenth Century*. 1996.

Morgan, David. *The Mongols*. 1986.

O'Callaghan, Joseph F. *The Cortes of Castille-León, 1188–1350*. 1989.

Richard, Jean. *Saint Louis: Crusader King of France*. Trans. Jean Birrell. 1992.

Strayer, Joseph R. *The Reign of Philip the Fair*. 1980.

CHAPTER 13

Crisis: Disease, War, and Schism

Aberth provides a good overview, while Blumenfeld-Kosinski and Bynum explore various aspects of late medieval piety.

Aberth, John. *From the Brink of the Apocalypse: Confronting Famine, War, Plague, and Death in the Later Middle Ages*. 2001.

Babinger, Franz. *Mehmed the Conqueror and His Time*. 1978.

Benedictow, Ole J. *The Black Death, 1346–1353: The Complete History*. 2004.

The Black Death. Ed. and trans. Rosemary Horrox. 1994.

Blumenfeld-Kosinski, Renate. *Poets, Saints, and Visionaries of the Great Schism, 1378–1417*. 2006.

*Books of Hours: **http://www.wellesley.edu/Library/SpecColl/BookOfHours/bookhome.html**

Bynum, Caroline. *Wonderful Blood. Theology and Practice in Late Medieval Northern Germany and Beyond*. 2006.

*Joan of Arc. *La Pucelle*. Trans. Craig Taylor. 2006.

The Renaissance: New Forms of Thought and Expression

Once considered a purely Italian phenomenon, the Renaissance is now understood to have penetrated all of Europe and the court of the Ottoman sultan as well.

Bisaha, Nancy. *Creating East and West: Renaissance Humanists and the Ottoman Turks*. 2004.

Boehm, Barbara Drake, and Jiří Fajt, eds. *Prague: The Crown of Bohemia, 1347–1437*. 2005.

*Elmer, Peter, Nick Webb, and Roberta Wood, eds. *The Renaissance in Europe: An Anthology*. 2000.

Grendler, Paul F. *The Universities of the Italian Renaissance*. 2002.

Jardine, Lisa, and Jerry Brotton. *Global Interests: Renaissance Art between East and West*. 2000.

Kent, F. W. *Lorenzo de' Medici and the Art of Magnificence*. 2004.

Kirkpatrick, Robin. *The European Renaissance: 1400–1600*. 2002.

Consolidating Power

Cohn and Hay both provide overviews, but most recent books on the period specialize in one country or another.

Cohn, Samuel K., Jr. *Lust for Liberty: The Politics of Social Revolt in Medieval Europe, 1200–1425*. 2006.

Hay, Denys. *Europe in the Fourteenth and Fifteenth Centuries*. 2nd ed. 1989.

Herlihy, David, and Christiane Klapisch-Zuber. *Tuscans and Their Families: A Study of the Florentine Catasto of 1427*. 1985.

Imber, Colin. *The Ottoman Empire, 1300–1650: The Structure of Power*. 2002.

The Letters of the Rožmberk Sisters: Noblewomen in Fifteenth-Century Bohemia. Ed and trans. John M. Klassen. 2001.

O'Callaghan, Joseph F. *A History of Medieval Spain*. 1975.

CHAPTER 14

Widening Horizons

The study of European voyages of exploration and conquest has been reshaped by a more global historical perspective, which pays as much attention to indigenous peoples' reactions to the newcomers as it does to the conditions experienced by the Europeans.

Buisseret, David. *The Mapmakers' Quest: Depicting New Worlds in Renaissance Europe*. 2003.

Christopher Columbus: **http://www.ibiblio.org/expo/1492.exhibit/Intro.html**

Crosby, Alfred. *The Colombian Exchange: Biological and Cultural Consequences of 1492*. 1972.

Fritze, Ronald. *New Worlds: The Great Voyages of Discovery, 1400–1600*. 2005.

Subrahmanyam, Sanjay. *The Career and Legend of Vasco da Gama*. 1997.

*Symcox, Geoffrey, and Blair Sullivan. *Christopher Columbus and the Enterprise of the Indies: A Brief History with Documents*. 2005.

The Protestant Reformation

While continuing to refine our understanding of the leading Protestant reformers, recent scholars have also offered new interpretations that take into consideration the popular impact of the reformers' teachings.

Bernard, G. W. *The King's Reformation: Henry VIII and the Remaking of the English Church*. 2005.

Eisenstein, Elizabeth. *The Printing Revolution in Early Modern Europe*. 2005.

Essential Works of Erasmus. Ed. W. T. H. Jackson. 1965.

*Hillerbrand, Hans J., ed. *The Protestant Reformation*. 1969.

Hsia, R. Po-chia, ed. *Cambridge History of Christianity*. Vol. 6, *Reform and Expansion 1500–1660*. 2006.

Jardine, Lisa. *Erasmus: Man of Letters*. 1993.

Martin Luther's writings: **http://www.ctsfw.edu/etext/luther**

Rublack, Ulinka. *Reformation Europe*. 2005.

Reshaping Society through Religion

The most important trend in recent scholarship has been the consideration of the impact of the Reformation on society and culture. Many studies have shown the limited influence of the ideas

*Primary source.

of reformers; others document the persistence of traditional religious habits and practices well past the sixteenth century.

Bagchi, David, and David Steinmetz. *The Cambridge Companion to Reformation Theology.* 2004.

Collinson, Patrick. *The Reformation: A History.* 2004.

Koenigsberger, H. B. *Early Modern Europe 1500–1789.* 1999.

Marshall, Sherrin, ed. *Women in Reformation and Counter-Reformation Europe: Public and Private Worlds.* 1989.

*Müntzer, Thomas. *Revelation and Revolution: Basic Writings of Thomas Müntzer.* 1993.

O'Malley, John W. *Trent and All That.* 2000.

Wiesner, Merry. *Christianity and the Regulation of Sexuality in the Early Modern World.* 2000.

A Struggle for Mastery

Still focused on the struggle between the Habsburg and Valois dynasties, historical scholarship has also moved out in the direction of cultural and military history.

*Guicciardini, Francesco. *The History of Italy.* Trans. Sidney Alexander. 1969.

Kleinschmidt, Harald. *Charles V: The World Emperor.* 2004.

Levin, Carole, Debra Barrett-Graves, and Jo Eldridge Carney, eds. *"High and Mighty Queens" of Early Modern England: Realities and Representations.* 2003.

MacHardy, Karin. *War, Religion, and Court Patronage in Habsburg Austria, 1521–1622.* 2003.

Shaw, Christine, ed. *Italy and the European Powers: The Impact of War, 1500–1530.* 2006.

Tanner, Marie. *The Last Descendant of Aeneas: The Hapsburgs and the Mythic Image of the Emperor.* 1993.

CHAPTER 15

Religious Conflicts and State Power, 1560–1618

The personalities of rulers such as Elizabeth I of England and Philip II of Spain remain central to the religious and political conflicts of this period.

Benedict, Philip. *Christ's Churches Purely Reformed: A Social History of Calvinism.* 2002.

Elizabeth I: **http://englishhistory.net/tudor/monarchs/eliz1.html**

Holt, Mack P. *The French Wars of Religion, 1562–1629.* 1995.

Kamen, Henry. *Spain, 1469–1714: A Society of Conflict.* 2005.

Mattingly, Garrett. *The Defeat of the Spanish Armada.* 2nd ed. 1988.

Philip II: **http://www.historylearningsite.co.uk/Phillip.htm**

*Pryor, Felix. *Elizabeth I: Her Life in Letters.* 2003.

The Thirty Years' War, 1618–1648

As ethnic conflicts erupt again in eastern Europe, historians have traced their roots back to the intertwined religious, ethnic, and dynastic struggles of the Thirty Years' War.

Bonney, Richard. *The Thirty Years' War 1618–1648.* 2002.

Parker, Geoffrey. *The Military Revolution: Military Innovation and the Rise of the West, 1500–1800.* 1996.

Parrott, David. *Richelieu's Army: War, Government and Society in France, 1624–1642.* 2001.

Pursell, Brennan C. *The Winter King: Frederick V of the Palatinate and the Coming of the Thirty Years' War.* 2003.

Economic Crisis and Realignment

Painstaking archival research has enabled historians to reconstruct the demographic, economic, and social history of the period discussed in this chapter. Recently, attention has shifted to the competition for empire in the New World.

Ashton, Trevor H., ed. *Crisis in Europe.* 1965.

Braudel, Fernand. *The Mediterranean and the Mediterranean World in the Age of Philip the Second.* 2 vols. Trans. Siân Reynolds. 1972–1973.

*Greer, Allan, ed. *Jesuit Relations: Natives and Missionaries in Seventeenth-Century North America.* 2000.

Seymour, M. J. *The Transformation of the North Atlantic World, 1492–1763: An Introduction.* 2004.

Wiesner, Merry E. *Women and Gender in Early Modern Europe.* 2nd ed. 2000.

The Rise of Secular and Scientific Worldviews

The transformation of intellectual and cultural life has long fascinated scholars. Recent works have developed a new kind of study called microhistory, which focuses on one person (like Ginzburg's Italian miller).

Briggs, Robin. *Witches & Neighbors: The Social and Cultural Context of European Witchcraft.* 1996.

The Galileo Project: **http://riceinfo.rice.edu/ Galileo**

Ginzburg, Carlo. *The Cheese and the Worms: The Cosmos of a Sixteenth-Century Miller.* Trans. John Tedeschi and Anne Tedeschi. 1992.

Isaac Newton: **http://www.newtonproject.ic.ac.uk/prism.php?id'1**

Thomas, Keith. *Religion and the Decline of Magic.* 1971.

CHAPTER 16

Louis XIV: Absolutism and Its Limits

Recent studies have insisted that absolutism could never be entirely absolute because the king depended on collaboration and cooperation to enforce his policies. Some of the best sources for Louis XIV's reign are the letters written by important noblewomen.

*Beik, William. *Louis XIV and Absolutism: A Brief Study with Documents.* 2000.

*Forster, Elborg, trans. *A Woman's Life in the Court of the Sun King: Elisabeth Charlotte, Duchesse d'Orléans.* 1984.

Rowlands, Guy. *The Dynastic State and the Army under Louis XIV: Royal Service and Private Interest, 1661 to 1701.* 2002.

*Sévigné, Madame de. *Selected Letters.* Trans. Leonard Tancock. 1982.

Treasure, G. R. R. *Louis XIV.* 2001.

Versailles: **http://www.chateauversailles.fr**

Absolutism in Central and Eastern Europe

Too often central and eastern European forms of state development have been characterized as backward in comparison with those of western Europe. Now historians emphasize the patterns of ruler-elite cooperation shared with western Europe, but they also underscore the weight of serfdom in eastern economies and political systems.

Barkey, Karen. *The Ottoman Route to State Centralization*. 1994.

Çiçek, Kemal, ed. *The Great Ottoman-Turkish Civilisation*. 4 vols. 2000.

Kotilaine, Jarmo, and Marshall Poe, eds. *Modernizing Muscovy: Reform and Social Change in Seventeenth-Century Russia*. 2004.

Vierhaus, Rudolf. *Germany in the Age of Absolutism*. Trans. Jonathan B. Knudsen. 1988.

Wilson, Peter H. *German Armies: War and German Politics, 1648–1806*. 1998.

Constitutionalism in England

Though recent interpretations of the English revolutions emphasize the limits on radical change, Hill's portrayal of the radical ferment of ideas remains fundamental.

Cromwell: **http://www.olivercromwell.org**

*Graham, Elspeth, et al., eds. *Her Own Life: Autobiographical Writings by Seventeenth-Century English Women*. 1989.

*Haller, William, and Godfrey Davies, eds. *The Leveller Tracts, 1647–1653*. 1944.

Hill, Christopher. *The World Turned Upside Down: Radical Ideas during the English Revolution*. 1972.

*Pincus, Steven C. A. *England's Glorious Revolution, 1688–1689*. 2006.

Outposts of Constitutionalism

Studies of the Dutch Republic emphasize the importance of trade and consumerism. Recent work on the colonies has begun to explore the intersecting experiences of settlers, native Americans, and African slaves.

France in America: **http://international.loc.gov/intldl/fiahtml/ fiatheme.html#track1**

Gragg, Larry. *Englishmen Transplanted: The English Colonization of Barbados, 1627–1660*. 2003.

Price, J. L. *The Dutch Republic in the Seventeenth Century*. 1998.

Schama, Simon. *The Embarrassment of Riches: An Interpretation of Dutch Culture in the Golden Age*. 1988.

Thornton, John. *Africa and Africans in the Making of the Atlantic World, 1400–1800*. 1992.

The Search for Order in Elite and Popular Culture

Historians do not always agree about the meaning of popular culture: Was it something widely shared by all social classes or a set of activities increasingly identified with the lower classes, as Burke argues? Was discipline of the lower classes increasing as members of the court learned the new emphasis on manners, as Elias argues?

Burke, Peter. *Popular Culture in Early Modern Europe*. 1978.

Davis, Natalie Zemon. *Women on the Margins: Three Seventeenth-Century Lives*. 1995.

Elias, Norbert. *The Civilizing Process*. Trans. Edmund Jephcott. 2000.

*Fitzmaurice, James, ed. *Margaret Cavendish: Sociable Letters*. 1997.

*Molière (Jean-Baptiste Poquelin). *The Bourgeois [Middle-Class] Gentleman*. Trans. Bernard Sahlins. 2000.

CHAPTER 17

The Atlantic System and the World Economy

It is easier to find sources on individual parts of the system than on the workings of the interlocking trade as a whole, but work has been rapidly increasing in this area. The Dunn book remains one of the classic studies of how the plantation system took root.

Blackburn, Robin. *The Making of New World Slavery: From the Baroque to the Modern, 1492–1800*. 1997.

Dunn, Richard S. *Sugar and Slaves: The Rise of the Planter Class in the English West Indies, 1624–1713*. 1972.

Harms, Robert. *The Diligent: A Voyage Through the Worlds of the Slave Trade*. 2003.

McKendrick, Neil, John Brewer, and J. H. Plumb. *The Birth of a Consumer Society: The Commercialization of Eighteenth-Century England*. 1982.

Slave movement during the eighteenth and nineteenth centuries: **http://dpls.dacc.wisc.edu/slavedata**

New Social and Cultural Patterns

Many of the novels of the early eighteenth century provide fascinating insights into the development of new social attitudes and customs. In particular, see Daniel Defoe's *Robinson Crusoe* (1719) and *Moll Flanders* (1722); the many novels of Eliza Haywood; and Antoine François Prévost's *Manon Lescaut* (1731), a French psychological novel about a nobleman's fatal love for an unfaithful woman, which became the basis for an opera in the nineteenth century.

Earle, Peter. *The Making of the English Middle Class: Business, Society, and Family Life in London, 1660–1730*. 1989.

Eighteenth-Century Resources: **http://andromeda.rutgers.edu/ ~jlynch/18th/index.html**

Handel's Messiah: The New Interactive Edition. CD-ROM. 1997.

Roche, Daniel. *The People of Paris: An Essay in Popular Culture in the Eighteenth Century*. Trans. Marie Evans. 1987.

Consolidation of the European State System

Studies of rulers and states can be supplemented by works on public health.

Black, Jeremy, ed. *The Origins of War in Early Modern Europe*. 1987.

Brewer, John. *The Sinews of Power: War, Money, and the English State, 1688–1783*. 1990.

Brockliss, Laurence, and Colin Jones. *The Medical World of Early Modern France*. 1997.

Cracraft, James. *The Petrine Revolution in Russian Culture*. 2004.

Hughes, Lindsey. *Peter the Great: A Biography*. 2002.

Porter, Roy. *Madness: A Brief History*. 2002.

War of the Spanish Succession: **http://www.historyworld.net/wrldhis/ PlainTextHistories.asp?historyid=ad06**

The Birth of the Enlightenment

The definitive study of the early Enlightenment is the book by Hazard, but many others have contributed biographies of individual figures or, more recently, studies of women writers.

*Primary source.

Besterman, Theodore. *Voltaire.* 1969.

Grendy, Isobel. *Lady Mary Wortley Montagu.* 1999.

Hazard, Paul. *The European Mind: The Critical Years, 1680–1715.* 1990.

*Hill, Bridget, ed. *The First English Feminist: Reflections upon Marriage and Other Writings by Mary Astell.* 1986.

*Jacob, Margaret C. *The Enlightenment: A Brief History with Selected Readings.* 2000.

Women Writers Online: **http://www.wwp.brown.edu/texts/wwoentry.html**

*Primary source.

Additional Credits

Chapter 1, page 15: "Hammurabi's Laws for Physicians." Source: translation adapted from *Ancient Near Eastern Texts Relating to the Old Testament*, 3rd ed. with supplement, by James B. Pritchard. Copyright © 1950, 1955, 1969, renewed 1978 by Princeton University Press. Reprinted by permission of Princeton University Press. **Page 22:** "Declaring Innocence on Judgment Day in Ancient Egypt." Source: *The Book of the Dead*. Reprinted in *Ancient Egyptian Literature: A Book of Readings*, translated by Miriam Lichtheim, Vol II: *The New Kingdom*. Published by the University of California Press (1976). Copyright © 1973–1980 by the Regents of the University of California. Reprinted courtesy of the University of California Press via Copyright Clearance Center in the format Textbook.

Chapter 3, page 90: "Sophists Argue Both Sides of a Case." Source: *Dissoi Logio 1.1–6*. Translation adapted from *The Older Sophists* by Rosamund Kent Sprague, editor. Copyright © 1972 by Rosamund Kent Sprague. Reprinted by permission of the University of South Carolina Press.

Chapter 6, page 186: "Tertullian's Defense of His Fellow Christians, 197 C.E." Source: *Apology*, Tertullian, LCL 250, 10.1, 23.2–3, 35.1, 40.1–2. Translation by T. R. Glover. Copyright © 1931 by the President and Fellows of Harvard College. The Loeb Classical Library ® is a registered trademark of the President and Fellows of Harvard College. Reprinted by permission of the publishers and Trustees of the Loeb Classical Library. **Page 186:** "Pliny on Early Imperial Policy toward Christians, 112 C.E." Source: *The Letters of the Younger Pliny*, Book 10, Nos. 96 and 97, translated with an introduction by Betty Radice. Penguin Classics 1963, reprinted 1969. Copyright © by Betty Radice, 1963, 1969. Reprinted by permission of Penguin Books Ltd.

Chapter 8, page 234: The Fatihah of the Qur'an: "The Opening." Source: *Approaching the Qur'an: The Early Revelations*, introduced and translated by Michael Sells. Copyright © 1999 by White Cloud Press. Reprinted by permission of White Cloud Press via Copyright Clearance Center in the format Textbook. **Page 238:** Excerpt from "Is What You Knew Kept Secret." Source: *Desert Tracings: Six Classic Arabian Odes*, introduced and translated by Michael Sells. Copyright © 1989 by Michael Sells and reprinted with permission by Wesleyan University Press.

Chapter 9, page 272: "When She Approached." Source: Salma Khadra Jayyusi "Andalusi Poetry: The Golden Period," in *The Legacy of Muslim Spain*, edited by Salma Khadra Jayyusi, 2 vols. Copyright © 1994 by Leiden Brill. Reprinted by permission of Koninklijke Brill NV. **Page 276:** "Charles as Emperor." Source: *Charlemagne's Courier: The Complete Einhard*, edited and translated by Paul Edward Dutton. Copyright © 1998 by Paul Edward Dutton. Reprinted by permission of Broadview Press. **Page 276:** "The Father of Europe." Source: *Carolingian Civilization: A Reader*, edited by Paul Edward Dutton, 2d ed. Copyright © 2004 by Broadview Press. Reprinted by permission of Broadview Press. **Page 277:** "The Chief Bishop." Source: *Einhard and Notker the Stammerer: Two Lives of Charlemagne*, translated by Lewis Thorpe. Copyright © 1969 by Lewis Thorpe. Reprinted by permission of Penguin Group Ltd.

Chapter 10, page 305: "A Byzantine View of Papal Primacy." Source: *Byzantium: Church, Society, and Civilization Seen through Contemporary Eyes* by Deno John Geanakoplos. Published by the University of Chicago Press, 1984. Originally quoting from *Byzantium and the Roman Primacy*, translated by Edwin A. Quain, S. J. Copyright © 1966–1979 by Fordham University Press. Reprinted by permission of the publisher. **Page 314:** "The Chronicle of Fulcher of Chartres." Source: *The First Crusade: The Chronicle of Fulcher of Chartres and Other Source Materials* by Edward Peters, editor. Copyright © 1971 by Edward Peters. Reprinted with permission of the University of Pennsylvania Press. **Page 314:** "The Jewish Experience as Told by Solomon Bar Simson (mid-twelfth century)." Source: *The Jews and the Crusaders: The Hebrew Chronicles of the First and Second Crusaders*, translated and edited by Shlomo Eidelberg. Copyright © 1977. Reprinted by permission of The University of Wisconsin Press. Reprinted in *Readings in Medieval History* (Peterborough, Ontario, Canada: Broadview Press, 1989), 433–34, ed. by Patrick J. Geary. **Page 315:** "The Seizure of Jerusalem as Told by Ibn Al-Athir (early thirteenth century)." Source: *Readings in Medieval History* by Patrick J. Geary,

editor. Copyright © 1989 by Patrick J. Geary. Reprinted by permission of Broadview Press. **Page 318:** "The Cairo Geniza." Source: Mark Cohen. Quote from pp. 22–23 in *The Voice of the Poor in the Middle Ages: An Anthology of Documents from the Cairo Geniza*. Copyright © 2005. Published by Princeton University Press. **Page 322:** "Penances for the Invaders (1070)." Source: *English Historical Documents*, volume 2: 1041–1189, edited by David C. Douglas and George W. Greenaway, 2nd edition. Copyright © 1981, 649. Reprinted with permission.

Chapter 11, page 342: "Magna Carta, 1215." Source: *English Historical Documents*, volume 3, edited by Harry Rothwell. Copyright © 1975 by Harry Rothwell. Published by Eyre & Spottiswoode. Reprinted by permission of Taylor & Francis Books Ltd. **Page 343:** "The Barons at Parliament Refuse to Give the King an Aid, 1242." Source: *English History Documents*, 3:355–56. Copyright © 1975 by Harry Rothwell. Published by Eyre & Spottiswoode. Reprinted by permission of Taylor & Francis Books Ltd. **Page 344:** "Frederick I's Reply to the Romans." Source: *The Crisis of Church and State, 1050–1300: With Selected Documents* by Brian Tierney. Copyright © 1964 by Prentice-Hall, Inc. Copyright © 1992 by Brian Tierney. Reprinted with permission of Simon & Schuster Adult Publishing Group. 103–104. All rights reserved. **Page 348:** "Troubadour Song: 'I Never Died for Love.'" Source: *Songs of the Troubadours and Trouvères* by Samuel N. Rosenberg, Margaret Switten, and Gerard Le Vot. Reproduced by permission of Taylor & Francis/Garland Publishing, 110. www.taylorandfrancis.com. **Page 355:** "The Children's Crusade (1212)." Source: *Medieval Popular Religion 1000–1500: A Reader*, edited by John Shinners. Copyright © 1997 by John Shinners. Reprinted by permission of Broadview Press.

Chapter 12, page 365: "Raimond de l'Aire's Testimony." Source: *Heresy and Authority in Medieval Europe: Documents in Translation* by Edward Peters. Copyright © 1980 by Edward Peters. Reprinted with permission of the University of Pennsylvania Press. **Page 369:** "The Debate between Reason and the Lover." Source: *The Romance of the Rose* by Guillaume de Lorris and Jean de Meun, edited by Charles W. Dunn. Translated by Harry W. Robbins. Copyright © 1962 by Florence L. Robbins. Used by permission of Dutton, a division of Penguin Group (USA) Inc. **Page 379:** "*Ausculta Fili* (Listen, Beloved Son)." Source: *The Crisis of Church and State, 1050–1300*, edited by Brian Tierney (Medieval Academy Reprints for Teaching, No. 21, published by University of Toronto Press (1964).

Chapter 13, page 394: "Joan the Visionary." Source: *Joan of Arc: La Pucelle*, translated and annotated by Craig Taylor. Copyright © 2006 by Manchester University Press. **Page 398:** "Wat Tyler's Rebellion (1381)." Source: *The Great Revolt of 1381* by Charles Oman. Originally published in 1906 in Oxford at the Clarendon Press. Copyright © 1969 by Greenwood Press, Publishers. **Page 404:** "Giovanni Pico della Mirandola, *Oration on the Dignity of Man*." Source: *Oration on the Dignity of Man* in *The Renaissance Philosophy of Man* by Ernst Cassirer, Paul Oskar Kristeller, and John Herman Randall Jr. Translated by Elizabeth Livermore Forbes. Copyright © 1948 by The University of Chicago Press, reprinted by permission.

Chapter 15, page 462: "The Horrors of the Thirty Years' War." Source: *The Adventures of Simplicius Simpliccissimus*, translated by George Schulz-Behrend, 2nd ed. (Rochester, NY: Camden House, 1993). Reprinted by permission of Camden House, an imprint of Boydell & Brewer, Inc. **Page 477:** "Sentence Pronounced against Galileo (1663)." Source: *The Galileo Affairs: A Documentary History*, edited by Maurice A. Finocchiaro. Copyright © 1989 by Maurice A. Finocchiaro. Reprinted by permission of the University of California Press, 291, via Copyright Clearance Center in the format Textbook.

Chapter 16, page 487: "Marie de Sévigné, Letter Describing the French Court (1675)." Source: *Madame de Sévigné: Selected Letters*. Translated with an Introduction by Leonard Tancock. Copyright © by Leonard Tancock, 1982. All rights reserved. Reprinted by permission of Penguin Books Ltd. **Page 500:** "Lucy Hutchinson, Memoirs of the Life of Colonel Hutchinson (1664–1671)." Source: *The Good Old Cause: The English Revolution of 1640–1660, Its Causes, Course and Consequences*, by Christopher Hill and Edmund Dell, eds. Copyright © 1949 by Christopher Hill and Edmund Dell. Reprinted by permission

Index